Collins
French
Dictionary

Published by Collins
An imprint of HarperCollins
Publishers
Westerhill Road
Bishopbriggs
Glasgow G64 2QT
www.harpercollins.co.uk

This Edition 2014

10 9 8 7 6 5 4 3 2 1

© HarperCollins Publishers 2014

ISBN 978-0-00-794285-5
ISBN 978-0-00-794281-7
ISBN 978-0-00-758333-1
ISBN 978-0-00-794236-7

Collins® is a registered trademark of
HarperCollins Publishers Limited

www.collins.co.uk
www.collinsdictionary.com

Printed in Great Britain by Clays Ltd,
St Ives plc

A catalogue record for this book is
available from the British Library.

If you would like to comment on any
aspect of this book, please contact us
at the above address or online.
E-mail: dictionaries@harpercollins.
co.uk

Acknowledgements
We would like to thank those authors
and publishers who kindly gave
permission for copyright material
to be used in the Collins Corpus.
We would also like to thank Times
Newspapers Ltd for providing
valuable data.

TABLE DES MATIÈRES CONTENTS

INTRODUCTION

Nous sommes très heureux que vous ayez choisi ce dictionnaire et espérons que vous aimerez l'utiliser et que vous en tirerez profit au lycée, à la maison, en vacances ou au travail.

INTRODUCTION

We are delighted that you have decided to buy this dictionary and hope you will enjoy and benefit from using it at school, at home, on holiday or at work.

abréviation	*ab(b)r*	abbreviation
adjectif, locution adjectivale	*adj*	adjective, adjectival phrase
administration	*Admin*	administration
adverbe, locution adverbiale	*adv*	adverb, adverbial phrase
agriculture	*Agr*	agriculture
anatomie	*Anat*	anatomy
architecture	*Archit*	architecture
article défini	*art déf*	definite article
article indéfini	*art indéf*	indefinite article
automobile	*Aut(o)*	the motor car and motoring
aviation, voyages aériens	*Aviat*	flying, air travel
biologie	*Bio(l)*	biology
botanique	*Bot*	botany
anglais britannique	*BRIT*	British English
chimie	*Chem*	chemistry
commerce, finance, banque	*Comm*	commerce, finance, banking
informatique	*Comput*	computing
conjonction	*conj*	conjunction
construction	*Constr*	building
nom utilisé comme adjectif	*cpd*	compound element
cuisine	*Culin*	cookery
article défini	*def art*	definite article
déterminant: article; adjectif démonstratif ou indéfini *etc*	*dét*	determiner: article, demonstrative *etc*
économie	*Écon, Econ*	economics
électricité, électronique	*Élec, Elec*	electricity, electronics
en particulier	*esp*	especially
exclamation, interjection	*excl*	exclamation, interjection
féminin	*f*	feminine
langue familière (! emploi vulgaire)	*fam(!)*	colloquial usage (! particularly offensive)
emploi figuré	*fig*	figurative use
(verbe anglais) dont la particule est inséparable	*fus*	(phrasal verb) where the particle is inseparable
généralement	*gén, gen*	generally
géographie, géologie	*Géo, Geo*	geography, geology
géométrie	*Géom, Geom*	geometry
langue familière (! emploi vulgaire)	*inf(!)*	colloquial usage (! particularly offensive)
infinitif	*infin*	infinitive
informatique	*Inform*	computing
invariable	*inv*	invariable
irrégulier	*irreg*	irregular
domaine juridique	*Jur*	law

ABRÉVIATIONS

grammaire, linguistique	*Ling*	grammar, linguistics
masculin	*m*	masculine
mathématiques, algèbre	*Math*	mathematics, calculus
médecine	*Méd, Med*	medical term, medicine
masculin ou féminin	*m/f*	masculine or feminine
domaine militaire, armée	*Mil*	military matters
musique	*Mus*	music
nom	*n*	noun
navigation, nautisme	*Navig, Naut*	sailing, navigation
nom ou adjectif numéral	*num*	numeral noun or adjective
	o.s.	oneself
péjoratif	*péj, pej*	derogatory, pejorative
photographie	*Phot(o)*	photography
physiologie	*Physiol*	physiology
pluriel	*pl*	plural
politique	*Pol*	politics
participe passé	*pp*	past participle
préposition	*prép, prep*	preposition
pronom	*pron*	pronoun
psychologie, psychiatrie	*Psych*	psychology, psychiatry
temps du passé	*pt*	past tense
quelque chose	*qch*	
quelqu'un	*qn*	
religion, domaine ecclésiastique	*Rel*	religion
	sb	somebody
enseignement, système scolaire et universitaire	*Scol*	schooling, schools and universities
singulier	*sg*	singular
	sth	something
subjonctif	*sub*	subjunctive
sujet (grammatical)	*su(b)j*	(grammatical) subject
superlatif	*superl*	superlative
techniques, technologie	*Tech*	technical term, technology
télécommunications	*Tél, Tel*	telecommunications
télévision	*TV*	television
typographie	*Typ(o)*	typography, printing
anglais des USA	*US*	American English
verbe (auxiliaire)	*vb (aux)*	(auxiliary) verb
verbe intransitif	*vi*	intransitive verb
verbe transitif	*vt*	transitive verb
zoologie	*Zool*	zoology
marque déposée	®	registered trademark
indique une équivalence culturelle	≈	introduces a cultural equivalent

ABBREVIATIONS

TRANCRIPTION PHONÉTIQUE

CONSONNES		CONSONANTS
NB. **p, b, t, d, k, g** sont suivis d'une aspiration en anglais.		NB. **p, b, t, d, k, g** are not aspirated in French.
pou**p**ée	p	**p**u**pp**y
bom**b**e	b	**b**a**b**y
ten**t**e **th**ermal	t	**t**en**t**
din**d**e	d	**d**a**dd**y
co**q** **qu**i **k**épi	k	**c**or**k** **k**iss **ch**ord
ga**g**e ba**gu**e	g	**g**a**g** **gu**ess
sale **c**e na**t**ion	s	**s**o ri**c**e ki**ss**
zéro ro**s**e	z	cou**s**in bu**zz**
ta**ch**e **ch**at	ʃ	**sh**eep **s**ugar
gilet **j**uge	ʒ	plea**s**ure bei**g**e
	tʃ	**ch**ur**ch**
	dʒ	**j**u**dg**e **g**eneral
fer **ph**are	f	**f**arm ra**ff**le
ver**v**eine	v	**v**ery re**v**el
	θ	**th**in ma**th**s
	ð	**th**at o**th**er
lent sa**ll**e	l	**l**ittle ba**ll**
ra**r**e **r**ent**r**er	ʀ	
	r	**r**at **r**a**r**e
ma**m**an fe**mm**e	m	**m**u**mm**y co**m**b
non bo**nn**e	n	**n**o ra**n**
a**gn**eau vi**gn**e	ɲ	
	ŋ	si**ng**ing ba**n**k
	h	**h**at re**h**earse
yeux pa**ill**e pied	j	**y**et
n**ou**er **ou**i	w	**w**all **w**ail
h**u**ile l**u**i	ɥ	
	x	lo**ch**
DIVERS		**MISCELLANEOUS**
pour l'anglais: le r final se prononce en liaison devant une voyelle	r	in English transcription: final r can be pronounced before a vowel
pour l'anglais: précède la syllabe accentuée	'	in French wordlist: no liaison before aspirate h

En règle générale, la prononciation est donnée entre crochets après chaque entrée. Toutefois, du côté anglais-français et dans le cas des expressions composées de deux ou plusieurs mots non réunis par un trait d'union et faisant l'objet d'une entrée séparée, la prononciation doit être cherchée sous chacun des mots constitutifs de l'expression en question.

PHONETIC TRANCRIPTION

VOYELLES			**VOWELS**

NB. La mise en équivalence de certains sons n'indique qu'une ressemblance approximative.

NB. The pairing of some vowel sounds only indicates approximate equivalence.

ici vie lyrique	i i:	heel bead
	ɪ	hit pity
jouer été	e	
lait jouet merci	ɛ	set tent
plat amour	a æ	bat apple
bas pâte	ɑ ɑ:	after car calm
	ʌ	fun cousin
le premier	ə	over above
beurre peur	œ	
peu deux	ø ə:	urgent fern work
or homme	ɔ	wash pot
mot eau gauche	o ɔ:	born cork
genou roue	u	full hook
	u:	boom shoe
rue urne	y	

DIPHTONGUES		**DIPHTHONGS**
	ɪə	beer tier
	ɛə	tear fair there
	eɪ	date plaice day
	aɪ	life buy cry
	au	owl foul now
	əu	low no
	ɔɪ	boil boy oily
	uə	poor tour

NASALES		**NASAL VOWELS**
matin plein	ɛ̃	
brun	œ̃	
sang an dans	ɑ̃	
non pont	ɔ̃	

In general, we give the pronunciation of each entry in square brackets after the word in question. However, on the English-French side, where the entry is composed of two or more unhyphenated words, each of which is given elsewhere in this dictionary, you will find the pronunciation of each word in its alphabetical position.

FRENCH VERB TABLES

1 Present participle **2** Past participle **3** Present **4** Imperfect **5** Future
6 Conditional **7** Present subjunctive

acquérir 1 acquérant **2** acquis
3 acquiers, acquérons,
acquièrent **4** acquérais
5 acquerrai **7** acquière

ALLER 1 allant **2** allé **3** vais, vas, va,
allons, allez, vont **4** allais **5** irai
6 irais **7** aille

asseoir 1 asseyant **2** assis **3** assieds,
asseyons, asseyez, asseyent
4 asseyais **5** assiérai **7** asseye

atteindre 1 atteignant **2** atteint
3 atteins, atteignons
4 atteignais **7** atteigne

AVOIR 1 ayant **2** eu **3** ai, as, a,
avons, avez, ont **4** avais **5** aurai
6 aurais **7** aie, aies, ait, ayons,
ayez, aient

battre 1 battant **2** battu **3** bats, bat,
battons **4** battais **7** batte

boire 1 buvant **2** bu **3** bois, buvons,
boivent **4** buvais **7** boive

bouillir 1 bouillant **2** bouilli **3** bous,
bouillons **4** bouillais **7** bouille

conclure 1 concluant **2** conclu
3 conclus, concluons
4 concluais **7** conclue

conduire 1 conduisant **2** conduit
3 conduis, conduisons
4 conduisais **7** conduise

connaître 1 connaissant **2** connu
3 connais, connaît, connaissons
4 connaissais **7** connaisse

coudre 1 cousant **2** cousu **3** couds,
cousons, cousez, cousent
4 cousais **7** couse

courir 1 courant **2** couru **3** cours,
courons **4** courais **5** courrai
7 coure

couvrir 1 couvrant **2** couvert
3 couvre, couvrons **4** couvrais
7 couvre

craindre 1 craignant **2** craint
3 crains, craignons **4** craignais
7 craigne

croire 1 croyant **2** cru **3** crois,
croyons, croient **4** croyais
7 croie

croître 1 croissant **2** crû, crue, crus,
crues **3** croîs, croissons
4 croissais **7** croisse

cueillir 1 cueillant **2** cueilli
3 cueille, cueillons **4** cueillais
5 cueillerai **7** cueille

devoir 1 devant **2** dû, due, dus,
dues **3** dois, devons, doivent
4 devais **5** devrai **7** doive

dire 1 disant **2** dit **3** dis, disons,
dites, disent **4** disais **7** dise

dormir 1 dormant **2** dormi **3** dors,
dormons **4** dormais **7** dorme

écrire 1 écrivant **2** écrit **3** écris,
écrivons **4** écrivais **7** écrive

ÊTRE 1 étant **2** été **3** suis, es, est,
sommes, êtes, sont **4** étais
5 serai **6** serais **7** sois, sois, soit,
soyons, soyez, soient

FAIRE 1 faisant **2** fait **3** fais, fais,
fait, faisons, faites, font
4 faisais **5** ferai **6** ferais **7** fasse

falloir 2 fallu **3** faut **4** fallait
5 faudra **7** faille

FINIR 1 finissant **2** fini **3** finis,
finis, finit, finissons, finissez,
finissent **4** finissais **5** finirai
6 finirais **7** finisse

fuir 1 fuyant **2** fui **3** fuis, fuyons,
fuient **4** fuyais **7** fuie

joindre 1 joignant **2** joint **3** joins,
joignons **4** joignais **7** joigne

lire 1 lisant **2** lu **3** lis, lisons **4** lisais
7 lise

luire 1 luisant **2** lui **3** luis, luisons**

4 luisais **7** luise

maudire 1 maudissant **2** maudit **3** maudis, maudissons **4** maudissait **7** maudisse

mentir 1 mentant **2** menti **3** mens, mentons **4** mentais **7** mente

mettre 1 mettant **2** mis **3** mets, mettons **4** mettais **7** mette

mourir 1 mourant **2** mort **3** meurs, mourons, meurent **4** mourais **5** mourrai **7** meure

naître 1 naissant **2** né **3** nais, naît, naissons **4** naissais **7** naisse

offrir 1 offrant **2** offert **3** offre, offrons **4** offrais **7** offre

PARLER 1 parlant **2** parlé **3** parle, parles, parle, parlons, parlez, parlent **4** parlais, parlais, parlait, parlions, parliez, parlaient **5** parlerai, parleras, parlera, parlerons, parlerez, parleront **6** parlerais, parlerais, parlerait, parlerions, parleriez, parleraient **7** parle, parles, parle, parlions, parliez, parlent *impératif* parle! parlons! parlez!

partir 1 partant **2** parti **3** pars, partons **4** partais **7** parte

plaire 1 plaisant **2** plu **3** plais, plaît, plaisons **4** plaisais **7** plaise

pleuvoir 1 pleuvant **2** plu **3** pleut, pleuvent **4** pleuvait **5** pleuvra **7** pleuve

pourvoir 1 pourvoyant **2** pourvu **3** pourvois, pourvoyons, pourvoyez **4** pourvoyais **7** pourvoie

pouvoir 1 pouvant **2** pu **3** peux, peut, pouvons, peuvent **4** pouvais **5** pourrai **7** puisse

prendre 1 prenant **2** pris **3** prends, prenons, prennent **4** prenais **7** prenne

prévoir like voir **5** prévoirai

RECEVOIR 1 recevant **2** reçu **3** reçois, reçois, reçoit, recevons, recevez, reçoivent **4** recevais **5** recevrai **6** recevrais **7** reçoive

RENDRE 1 rendant **2** rendu **3** rends, rends, rend, rendons, rendez, rendent **4** rendais **5** rendrai **6** rendrais **7** rende

résoudre 1 résolvant **2** résolu **3** résous, résout, résolvons **4** résolvais **7** résolve

rire 1 riant **2** ri **3** ris, rions **4** riais **7** rie

savoir 1 sachant **2** su **3** sais, savons, savent **4** savais **5** saurai **7** sache *impératif* sache! sachons! sachez!

servir 1 servant **2** servi **3** sers, servons **4** servais **7** serve

sortir 1 sortant **2** sorti **3** sors, sortons **4** sortais **7** sorte

souffrir 1 souffrant **2** souffert **3** souffre, souffrons **4** souffrais **7** souffre

suffire 1 suffisant **2** suffi **3** suffis, suffisons **4** suffisais **7** suffise

suivre 1 suivant **2** suivi **3** suis, suivons **4** suivais **7** suive

taire 1 taisant **2** tu **3** tais, taisons **4** taisais **7** taise

tenir 1 tenant **2** tenu **3** tiens, tenons, tiennent **4** tenais **5** tiendrai **7** tienne

vaincre 1 vainquant **2** vaincu **3** vaincs, vainc, vainquons **4** vainquais **7** vainque

valoir 1 valant **2** valu **3** vaux, vaut, valons **4** valais **5** vaudrai **7** vaille

venir 1 venant **2** venu **3** viens, venons, viennent **4** venais **5** viendrai **7** vienne

vivre 1 vivant **2** vécu **3** vis, vivons **4** vivais **7** vive

voir 1 voyant **2** vu **3** vois, voyons, voient **4** voyais **5** verrai **7** voie

vouloir 1 voulant **2** voulu **3** veux, veut, voulons, veulent **4** voulais **5** voudrai **7** veuille; *impératif* veuillez!

VERBES IRRÉGULIERS ANGLAIS

PRÉSENT	PASSÉ	PARTICIPE	PRÉSENT	PASSÉ	PARTICIPE
arise	arose	arisen	**fight**	fought	fought
awake	awoke	awoken	**find**	found	found
be	was, were	been	**flee**	fled	fled
(am, is,			**fling**	flung	flung
are; being)			**fly**	flew	flown
bear	bore	born(e)	**forbid**	forbad(e)	forbidden
beat	beat	beaten	**forecast**	forecast	forecast
become	became	become	**forget**	forgot	forgotten
begin	began	begun	**forgive**	forgave	forgiven
bend	bent	bent	**forsake**	forsook	forsaken
bet	bet,	bet,	**freeze**	froze	frozen
	betted	betted	**get**	got	got,
bid (*at auction,*	bid	bid			(us) gotten
cards)			**give**	gave	given
bid (*say*)	bade	bidden	**go** (goes)	went	gone
bind	bound	bound	**grind**	ground	ground
bite	bit	bitten	**grow**	grew	grown
bleed	bled	bled	**hang**	hung	hung
blow	blew	blown	**hang** (*execute*)	hanged	hanged
break	broke	broken	**have**	had	had
breed	bred	bred	**hear**	heard	heard
bring	brought	brought	**hide**	hid	hidden
build	built	built	**hit**	hit	hit
burn	burnt,	burnt,	**hold**	held	held
	burned	burned	**hurt**	hurt	hurt
burst	burst	burst	**keep**	kept	kept
buy	bought	bought	**kneel**	knelt,	knelt,
can	could	(*been able*)		kneeled	kneeled
cast	cast	cast	**know**	knew	known
catch	caught	caught	**lay**	laid	laid
choose	chose	chosen	**lead**	led	led
cling	clung	clung	**lean**	leant,	leant,
come	came	come		leaned	leaned
cost	cost	cost	**leap**	leapt,	leapt,
cost (*work*	costed	costed		leaped	leaped
out price of)			**learn**	learnt,	learnt,
creep	crept	crept		learned	learned
cut	cut	cut	**leave**	left	left
deal	dealt	dealt	**lend**	lent	lent
dig	dug	dug	**let**	let	let
do (*does*)	did	done	**lie** (lying)	lay	lain
draw	drew	drawn	**light**	lit,	lit,
dream	dreamed,	dreamed,		lighted	lighted
	dreamt	dreamt	**lose**	lost	lost
drink	drank	drunk	**make**	made	made
drive	drove	driven	**may**	might	–
dwell	dwelt	dwelt	**mean**	meant	meant
eat	ate	eaten	**meet**	met	met
fall	fell	fallen	**mistake**	mistook	mistaken
feed	fed	fed	**mow**	mowed	mown,
feel	felt	felt			mowed

xii

PRÉSENT	PASSÉ	PARTICIPE	PRÉSENT	PASSÉ	PARTICIPE
must	(had to)	(had to)	spend	spent	spent
pay	paid	paid	spill	spilt,	spilt,
put	put	put		spilled	spilled
quit	quit,	quit,	spin	spun	spun
	quitted	quitted	spit	spat	spat
read	read	read	spoil	spoiled,	spoiled,
rid	rid	rid		spoilt	spoilt
ride	rode	ridden	spread	spread	spread
ring	rang	rung	spring	sprang	sprung
rise	rose	risen	stand	stood	stood
run	ran	run	steal	stole	stolen
saw	sawed	sawed,	stick	stuck	stuck
		sawn	sting	stung	stung
say	said	said	stink	stank	stunk
see	saw	seen	stride	strode	stridden
seek	sought	sought	strike	struck	struck
sell	sold	sold	strive	strove	striven
send	sent	sent	swear	swore	sworn
set	set	set	sweep	swept	swept
sew	sewed	sewn	swell	swelled	swollen,
shake	shook	shaken			swelled
shear	sheared	shorn,	swim	swam	swum
		sheared	swing	swung	swung
shed	shed	shed	take	took	taken
shine	shone	shone	teach	taught	taught
shoot	shot	shot	tear	tore	torn
show	showed	shown	tell	told	told
shrink	shrank	shrunk	think	thought	thought
shut	shut	shut	throw	threw	thrown
sing	sang	sung	thrust	thrust	thrust
sink	sank	sunk	tread	trod	trodden
sit	sat	sat	wake	woke,	woken,
slay	slew	slain		waked	waked
sleep	slept	slept	wear	wore	worn
slide	slid	slid	weave	wove	woven
sling	slung	slung	weave (wind)	weaved	weaved
slit	slit	slit	wed	wedded,	wedded,
smell	smelt,	smelt,		wed	wed
	smelled	smelled	weep	wept	wept
sow	sowed	sown,	win	won	won
		sowed	wind	wound	wound
speak	spoke	spoken	wring	wrung	wrung
speed	sped,	sped,	write	wrote	written
	speeded	speeded			
spell	spelt,	spelt,			
	spelled	spelled			

LES NOMBRES		NUMBERS
un (une)	1	one
deux	2	two
trois	3	three
quatre	4	four
cinq	5	five
six	6	six
sept	7	seven
huit	8	eight
neuf	9	nine
dix	10	ten
onze	11	eleven
douze	12	twelve
treize	13	thirteen
quatorze	14	fourteen
quinze	15	fifteen
seize	16	sixteen
dix-sept	17	seventeen
dix-huit	18	eighteen
dix-neuf	19	nineteen
vingt	20	twenty
vingt et un (une)	21	twenty-one
vingt-deux	22	twenty-two
trente	30	thirty
quarante	40	forty
cinquante	50	fifty
soixante	60	sixty
soixante-dix	70	seventy
soixante-et-onze	71	seventy-one
soixante-douze	72	seventy
quatre-vingts	80	eighty
quatre-vingt-un (-une)	81	eighty-one
quatre-vingt-dix	90	ninety
cent	100	a hundred, one hundred
cent un (une)	101	a hundred and one
deux cents	200	two hundred
deux cent un (une)	201	two hundred and one
quatre cents	400	four hundred
mille	1000	a thousand
cinq mille	5000	five thousand
un million	1000000	a million

LES NOMBRES

premier (première), 1er (1ère)
deuxième, 2e or 2ème
troisième, 3e or 3ème
quatrième, 4e or 4ème
cinquième, 5e or 5ème
sixième, 6e or 6ème
septième
huitième
neuvième
dixième
onzième
douzième
treizième
quartorzième
quinzième
seizième
dix-septième
dix-huitième
dix-neuvième
vingtième
vingt-et-unième
vingt-deuxième
trentième
centième
cent-unième
millième

NUMBERS

first, 1st
second, 2nd
third, 3rd
fourth, 4th
fifth, 5th
sixth, 6th
seventh
eighth
ninth
tenth
eleventh
twelfth
thirteenth
fourteenth
fifteenth
sixteenth
seventeenth
eighteenth
nineteenth
twentieth
twenty-first
twenty-second
thirtieth
hundredth
hundred-and-first
thousandth

LES FRACTIONS ETC

un demi
un tiers
un quart
un cinquième
zéro virgule cinq, 0,5
trois virgule quatre, 3,4
dix pour cent
cent pour cent

FRACTIONS ETC

a half
a third
a quarter
a fifth
(nought) point five, 0.5
three point four, 3.4
ten per cent
a hundred per cent

EXEMPLES

elle habite au septième (étage)
il habite au sept
au chapître/à la page sept
il est arrivé (le) septième

EXAMPLES

she lives on the 7th floor
he lives at number 7
chapter/page 7
he came in 7th

L'HEURE

THE TIME

quelle heure est-il?

what time is it?

il est ...

it's ou *it is ...*

minuit
une heure (du matin)

midnight, twelve p.m.
one o'clock (in the
   morning), one (a.m.)

une heure cinq
une heure dix
une heure et quart

five past one
ten past one
a quarter past one,
   one fifteen

une heure vingt-cinq

twenty-five past one,
   one twenty-five

une heure et demie, une heure trente
deux heures moins vingt-cinq, une
   heure trente-cinq
deux heures moins vingt, une heure
   quarante
deux heures moins le quart, une heure
   quarante-cinq
deux heures moins dix, une heure
   cinquante
midi

half-past one, one thirty
twenty-five to two,
   one thirty-five
twenty to two, one forty

a quarter to two,
   one forty-five
ten to two, one fifty

twelve o'clock, midday,
   noon

deux heures (de l'après-midi),
   quatorze heures
sept heures (du soir), dix-sept heures

two o'clock (in the
   afternoon), two (p.m.)
seven o'clock (in the
   evening), seven (p.m.)

à quelle heure?

(at) what time?

à minuit
à sept heures

at midnight
at seven o'clock

dans vingt minutes
il y a un quart d'heure

in twenty minutes
fifteen minutes ago

FRANÇAIS | ANGLAIS
FRENCH | ENGLISH

7 (*caractérisation, manière*): **l'homme aux yeux bleus** the man with the blue eyes; **à leur grande surprise** much to their surprise; **à ce qu'il prétend** according to him, from what he says; **à la russe** the Russian way; **à nous deux nous n'avons pas su le faire** we couldn't do it, even between the two of us
8 (*but, destination*): **tasse à café** coffee cup; **maison à vendre** house for sale; **je n'ai rien à lire** I don't have anything to read; **à bien réfléchir ...** thinking about it ..., on reflection ...
9 (*rapport, évaluation, distribution*): **100 km/unités à l'heure** 100 km/units per *ou* an hour; **payé au mois/à l'heure** paid monthly/by the hour; **cinq à six** five to six; **ils sont arrivés à quatre** four of them arrived

a [a] *vb voir* **avoir**

 MOT-CLÉ

à [a] (*à + le* = **au**, *à + les* = **aux**) *prép* **1** (*endroit, situation*) at, in; **être à Paris/au Portugal** to be in Paris/Portugal; **être à la maison/à l'école** to be at home/at school; **à la campagne** in the country; **c'est à 10 km/à 20 minutes (d'ici)** it's 10 km/20 minutes away
2 (*direction*) to; **aller à Paris/au Portugal** to go to Paris/Portugal; **aller à la maison/à l'école** to go home/to school; **à la campagne** to the country
3 (*temps*): **à 3 heures/minuit** at 3 o'clock/midnight; **au printemps/mois de juin** in the spring/the month of June; **à Noël/Pâques** at Christmas/Easter; **à demain/lundi!** see you tomorrow/on Monday!
4 (*attribution, appartenance*) to; **le livre est à Paul/à lui/à nous** this book is Paul's/his/ours; **un ami à moi** a friend of mine; **donner qch à qn** to give sth to sb
5 (*moyen*) with; **se chauffer au gaz** to have gas heating; **à bicyclette** on a *ou* by bicycle; **à pied** on foot; **à la main/machine** by hand/machine
6 (*provenance*) from; **boire à la bouteille** to drink from the bottle

abaisser [abese] *vt* to lower, bring down; (*manette*) to pull down; **s'abaisser** *vi* to go down; (*fig*) to demean o.s.
abandon [abɑ̃dɔ̃] *nm* abandoning; giving up; withdrawal; **être à l'~** to be in a state of neglect; **laisser à l'~** to abandon
abandonner [abɑ̃dɔne] *vt* (*personne*) to abandon; (*projet, activité*) to abandon, give up; (*Sport*) to retire *ou* withdraw from; (*céder*) to surrender; **s'~ à** (*paresse, plaisirs*) to give o.s. up to
abat-jour [abaʒuʀ] *nm inv* lampshade
abats [aba] *nmpl* (*de bœuf, porc*) offal *sg*; (*de volaille*) giblets
abattement [abatmɑ̃] *nm*: **abattement fiscal** ≈ tax allowance
abattoir [abatwaʀ] *nm* slaughterhouse
abattre [abatʀ] *vt* (*arbre*) to cut down, fell; (*mur, maison*) to pull down; (*avion, personne*) to shoot down; (*animal*) to shoot, kill; (*fig*) to wear out, tire out; to demoralize; **s'abattre** *vi* to crash down; **ne pas se laisser ~** to keep one's spirits up, not to let things get one down; **s'~ sur** to beat down on; (*fig*) to rain down on; **~ du travail** *ou* **de la besogne** to get through a lot of work
abbaye [abei] *nf* abbey
abbé [abe] *nm* priest; (*d'une abbaye*) abbot
abcès [apsɛ] *nm* abscess
abdiquer [abdike] *vi* to abdicate
abdominaux [abdɔmino] *nmpl*: **faire des ~** to do sit-ups
abeille [abɛj] *nf* bee
aberrant, e [abeʀɑ̃, ɑ̃t] *adj* absurd
aberration [abeʀasjɔ̃] *nf* aberration
abîme [abim] *nm* abyss, gulf
abîmer [abime] *vt* to spoil, damage; **s'abîmer** *vi* to get spoilt *ou* damaged
aboiement [abwamɑ̃] *nm* bark, barking
abolir [abɔliʀ] *vt* to abolish
abominable [abɔminabl] *adj* abominable

abondance [abɔ̃dɑ̃s] nf abundance

abondant, e [abɔ̃dɑ̃, ɑ̃t] adj plentiful, abundant, copious; **abonder** vi to abound, be plentiful; **abonder dans le sens de qn** to concur with sb

abonné, e [abɔne] nm/f subscriber; season ticket holder

abonnement [abɔnmɑ̃] nm subscription; (transports, concerts) season ticket

abonner [abɔne] vt: **s'~ à** to subscribe to, take out a subscription to

abord [abɔʀ] nm: **au premier ~** at first sight, initially; **abords** nmpl (environs) surroundings; **d'~** first

abordable [abɔʀdabl] adj (prix) reasonable; (personne) approachable

aborder [abɔʀde] vi to land ▷ vt (sujet, difficulté) to tackle; (personne) to approach; (rivage etc) to reach

aboutir [abutiʀ] vi (négociations etc) to succeed; **~ à** to end up at; **n'~ à rien** to come to nothing

aboyer [abwaje] vi to bark

abréger [abʀeʒe] vt to shorten

abreuver [abʀœve]: **s'abreuver** vi to drink; **abreuvoir** nm watering place

abréviation [abʀevjasjɔ̃] nf abbreviation

abri [abʀi] nm shelter; **être à l'~** to be under cover; **se mettre à l'~** to shelter; **à l'~ de** (vent, soleil) sheltered from; (danger) safe from

abricot [abʀiko] nm apricot

abriter [abʀite] vt to shelter; **s'abriter** vt to shelter, take cover

abrupt, e [abʀypt] adj sheer, steep; (ton) abrupt

abruti, e [abʀyti] adj stunned, dazed ▷ nm/f (fam) idiot, moron; **~ de travail** overworked

absence [apsɑ̃s] nf absence; (Méd) blackout; **avoir des ~s** to have mental blanks

absent, e [apsɑ̃, ɑ̃t] adj absent ▷ nm/f absentee; **absenter**: **s'absenter** vi to take time off work; (sortir) to leave, go out

absolu, e [apsɔly] adj absolute; **absolument** adv absolutely

absorbant, e [apsɔʀbɑ̃, ɑ̃t] adj absorbent

absorber [apsɔʀbe] vt to absorb; (gén Méd: manger, boire) to take

abstenir [apstəniʀ] vb: **s'~ de qch/de faire** to refrain from sth/from doing

abstrait, e [apstʀɛ, ɛt] adj abstract

absurde [apsyʀd] adj absurd

abus [aby] nm abuse; **~ de confiance** breach of trust; **il y a de l'~!** (fam) that's a bit much!; **abuser** vi to go too far, overstep the mark; **abuser de** (duper) to take advantage of; **s'abuser** vi (se méprendre) to be mistaken; **abusif, -ive** adj exorbitant; (punition) excessive

académie [akademi] nf academy; (Scol: circonscription) ≈ regional education authority

● **ACADÉMIE FRANÇAISE**
●
● The **Académie française** was founded by
● Cardinal Richelieu in 1635, during the reign
● of Louis XIII. It is made up of forty elected
● scholars and writers who are known as 'les
● Quarante' or 'les Immortels'. One of the
● **Académie**'s functions is to keep an eye on
● the development of the French language,
● and its recommendations are frequently
● the subject of lively public debate. It has
● produced several editions of its famous
● dictionary and also awards various literary
● prizes.

acajou [akaʒu] nm mahogany

acariâtre [akaʀjɑtʀ] adj cantankerous

accablant, e [akablɑ̃, ɑ̃t] adj (chaleur) oppressive; (témoignage, preuve) overwhelming

accabler [akable] vt to overwhelm, overcome; **~ qn d'injures** to heap ou shower abuse on sb; **~ qn de travail** to overwork sb

acclamie [akalmi] nf lull

accaparer [akapaʀe] vt to monopolize; (suj: travail etc) to take up (all) the time ou attention of

accéder [aksede]: **~ à** vt (lieu) to reach; (accorder: requête) to grant, accede to

accélérateur [akseleʀatœʀ] nm accelerator

accélérer [akseleʀe] vt to speed up ▷ vi to accelerate

accent [aksɑ̃] nm accent; (Phonétique, fig) stress; **mettre l'~ sur** (fig) to stress; **~ aigu/grave/circonflexe** acute/grave/circumflex accent; **accentuer** (Ling) to accent; (fig) to accentuate, emphasize; **s'accentuer** vi to become more marked ou pronounced

acceptation [aksɛptasjɔ̃] nf acceptance

accepter [aksɛpte] vt to accept; **~ de faire** to agree to do; **acceptez-vous les cartes de crédit?** do you take credit cards?

accès [aksɛ] nm (à un lieu) access; (Méd: de toux) fit; (: de fièvre) bout; **d'~ facile** easily accessible; **facile d'~** easy to get to; **accès de colère** fit of anger; **accessible** adj accessible; (livre, sujet): **accessible à qn** within the reach of sb

accessoire [akseswaʀ] adj secondary; incidental ▷ nm accessory; (Théâtre) prop

accident [aksidɑ̃] nm accident; **par ~** by chance; **j'ai eu un ~** I've had an accident; **accident de la route** road accident; **accidenté, e** adj damaged; injured; (relief, terrain) uneven; hilly; **accidentel, le** adj accidental

acclamer [aklame] vt to cheer, acclaim

acclimater [aklimate]: **s'acclimater** vi (personne) to adapt (o.s.)

accolade [akɔlad] nf (amicale) embrace; (signe) brace

accommoder [akɔmɔde] vt (Culin) to prepare; **s'accommoder de** vt to put up with; (se contenter de) to make do with

accompagnateur, -trice [akɔ̃paɲatœr, tris] nm/f (Mus) accompanist; (de voyage: guide) guide; (de voyage organisé) courier

accompagner [akɔ̃paɲe] vt to accompany, be ou go ou come with; (Mus) to accompany

accompli, e [akɔ̃pli] adj accomplished; voir aussi **fait**

accomplir [akɔ̃plir] vt (tâche, projet) to carry out; (souhait) to fulfil; **s'accomplir** vi to be fulfilled

accord [akɔr] nm agreement; (entre des styles, tons etc) harmony; (Mus) chord; **d'~!** OK!; **se mettre d'~** to come to an agreement; **être d'~ (pour faire qch)** to agree (to do sth)

accordéon [akɔrdeɔ̃] nm (Mus) accordion

accorder [akɔrde] vt (faveur, délai) to grant; (harmoniser) to match; (Mus) to tune; (valeur, importance) to attach

accoster [akɔste] vt (Navig) to draw alongside ▷ vi to berth

accouchement [akuʃmɑ̃] nm delivery, (child)birth; labour

accoucher [akuʃe] vi to give birth, have a baby; **~ d'un garçon** to give birth to a boy

accouder [akude]: **s'accouder** vi: **s'~ à/ contre/sur** to rest one's elbows on/against/ on; **accoudoir** nm armrest

accoupler [akuple] vt to couple; (pour la reproduction) to mate; **s'accoupler** vt to mate

accourir [akurir] vi to rush ou run up

accoutumance [akutymɑ̃s] nf (gén) adaptation; (Méd) addiction

accoutumé, e [akutyme] adj (habituel) customary, usual

accoutumer [akutyme] vt: **s'~ à** to get accustomed ou used to

accroc [akro] nm (déchirure) tear; (fig) hitch, snag

accrochage [akrɔʃaʒ] nm (Auto) collision; (dispute) clash, brush

accrocher [akrɔʃe] vt (fig) to catch, attract; **s'accrocher** (se disputer) to have a clash ou brush; **~ qch à** (suspendre) to hang sth (up) on; (attacher: remorque) to hitch sth (up) to; **~ qch (à)** (déchirer) to catch sth (on); **il a accroché ma voiture** he bumped into my car; **s'~ à** (rester pris à) to catch on; (agripper, fig) to hang on ou cling to

accroissement [akrwasmɑ̃] nm increase

accroître [akrwatr]: **s'accroître** vi to increase

accroupir [akrupir]: **s'accroupir** vi to squat, crouch (down)

accru, e [akry] pp de **accroître**

accueil [akœj] nm welcome; **comité d'~** reception committee; **accueillir** vt to welcome; (aller chercher) to meet, collect

accumuler [akymyle] vt to accumulate, amass; **s'accumuler** vi to accumulate; to pile up

accusation [akyzasjɔ̃] nf (gén) accusation; (Jur) charge; (partie): **l'~** the prosecution

accusé, e [akyze] nm/f accused; defendant; **accusé de réception** acknowledgement of receipt

accuser [akyze] vt to accuse; (fig) to emphasize, bring out; to show; **~ qn de** to accuse sb of; (Jur) to charge sb with; **~ réception de** to acknowledge receipt of

acéré, e [asere] adj sharp

acharné, e [aʃarne] adj (efforts) relentless; (lutte, adversaire) fierce, bitter

acharner [aʃarne] vb: **s'~ contre** to set o.s. against; (suj: malchance) to dog; **s'~ à faire** to try doggedly to do; (persister) to persist in doing; **s'~ sur qn** to hound sb

achat [aʃa] nm purchase; **faire des ~s** to do some shopping; **faire l'~ de qch** to purchase sth

acheter [aʃ(ə)te] vt to buy, purchase; (soudoyer) to buy; **~ qch à** (marchand) to buy ou purchase sth from; (ami etc: offrir) to buy sth for; **où est-ce que je peux ~ des cartes postales?** where can I buy (some) postcards?; **acheteur, -euse** nm/f buyer; shopper; (Comm) buyer

achever [aʃ(ə)ve] vt to complete, finish; (blessé) to finish off; **s'achever** vi to end

acide [asid] adj sour, sharp; (Chimie) acid(ic) ▷ nm (Chimie) acid; **acidulé, e** adj slightly acid; **bonbons acidulés** acid drops

acier [asje] nm steel; **aciérie** nf steelworks sg

acné [akne] nf acne

acompte [akɔ̃t] nm deposit

à-côté [akote] nm side-issue; (argent) extra

à-coup [aku] nm: **par ~s** by fits and starts

acoustique [akustik] nf (d'une salle) acoustics pl

acquéreur [akerœr] nm buyer, purchaser

acquérir [akerir] vt to acquire

acquis, e [aki, iz] pp de **acquérir** ▷ nm (accumulated) experience; **son aide nous est ~e** we can count on her help

acquitter [akite] vt (Jur) to acquit; (facture) to pay, settle; **s'acquitter de** vt (devoir) to discharge; (promesse) to fulfil

âcre [ɑkr] adj acrid, pungent

acrobate [akrɔbat] nm/f acrobat; **acrobatie** nf acrobatics sg

acte [akt] nm act, action; (Théâtre) act; **prendre ~ de** to note, take note of; **faire ~ de candidature** to apply; **faire ~ de présence** to put in an appearance; **acte de naissance**

birth certificate

acteur [aktœʀ] nm actor

actif, -ive [aktif, iv] adj active ▷ nm (Comm) assets pl; (fig): **avoir à son ~** to have to one's credit; **population active** working population

action [aksjɔ̃] nf (gén) action; (Comm) share; **une bonne ~** a good deed; **actionnaire** nm/f shareholder; **actionner** vt (mécanisme) to activate; (machine) to operate

activer [aktive] vt to speed up; **s'activer** vi to bustle about; to hurry up

activité [aktivite] nf activity; **en ~** (volcan) active; (fonctionnaire) in active life

actrice [aktʀis] nf actress

actualité [aktɥalite] nf (d'un problème) topicality; (événements): **l'~** current events; **actualités** nfpl (Cinéma, TV) the news; **d'~** topical

actuel, le [aktɥɛl] adj (présent) present; (d'actualité) topical; **à l'heure ~le** at the present time; **actuellement** adv at present, at the present time

   Attention à ne pas traduire **actuellement** par **actually**.

acupuncture [akypɔ̃ktyʀ] nf acupuncture

adaptateur [adaptatœʀ] nm (Élec) adapter

adapter [adapte] vt to adapt; **s'adapter (à)** (suj: personne) to adapt (to); **~ qch à** (approprier) to adapt sth to (fit); **~ qch sur/dans/à** (fixer) to fit sth on/into/to

addition [adisjɔ̃] nf addition; (au café) bill; **l'~, s'il vous plaît** could I have the bill, please?; **additionner** vt to add (up)

adepte [adɛpt] nm/f follower

adéquat, e [adekwa(t), at] adj appropriate, suitable

adhérent, e [adeʀɑ̃, ɑ̃t] nm/f member

adhérer [adeʀe]: **~ à** vt (coller) to adhere ou stick to; (se rallier à) to join; **adhésif, -ive** adj adhesive, sticky; **ruban adhésif** sticky ou adhesive tape

adieu, x [adjø] excl goodbye ▷ nm farewell

adjectif [adʒɛktif] nm adjective

adjoint, e [adʒwɛ̃, wɛ̃t] nm/f assistant; **adjoint au maire** deputy mayor; **directeur adjoint** assistant manager

admettre [admɛtʀ] vt (laisser entrer) to admit; (candidat: Scol) to pass; (tolérer) to allow, accept; (reconnaître) to admit, acknowledge

administrateur, -trice [administʀatœʀ, tʀis] nm/f (Comm) director; (Admin) administrator

administration [administʀasjɔ̃] nf administration; **l'A~** ≈ the Civil Service

administrer [administʀe] vt (firme) to manage, run; (biens, remède, sacrement etc) to administer

admirable [admiʀabl] adj admirable, wonderful

admirateur, -trice [admiʀatœʀ, tʀis] nm/f admirer

admiration [admiʀasjɔ̃] nf admiration

admirer [admiʀe] vt to admire

admis, e [admi, iz] pp de **admettre**

admissible [admisibl] adj (candidat) eligible; (comportement) admissible, acceptable

ADN sigle m (= acide désoxyribonucléique) DNA

adolescence [adɔlesɑ̃s] nf adolescence

adolescent, e [adɔlesɑ̃, ɑ̃t] nm/f adolescent, teenager

adopter [adɔpte] vt to adopt; **adoptif, -ive** adj (parents) adoptive; (fils, pays) adopted

adorable [adɔʀabl] adj delightful, adorable

adorer [adɔʀe] vt to adore; (Rel) to worship

adosser [adose] vt: **~ qch à ou contre** to stand sth against; **s'adosser à/contre** to lean with one's back against

adoucir [adusiʀ] vt (goût, température) to make milder; (avec du sucre) to sweeten; (peau, voix) to soften; (caractère) to mellow

adresse [adʀɛs] nf (domicile) address; (dextérité) skill, dexterity; **~ électronique** email address

adresser [adʀese] vt (lettre: expédier) to send; (: écrire l'adresse sur) to address; (injure, compliments) to address; **s'adresser à** (parler à) to speak to, address; (s'informer auprès de) to go and see; (: bureau) to inquire at; (suj: livre, conseil) to be aimed at; **~ la parole à** to speak to, address

adroit, e [adʀwa, wat] adj skilful, skilled

ADSL sigle m (= asymmetrical digital subscriber line) ADSL, broadband

adulte [adylt] nm/f adult, grown-up ▷ adj (chien, arbre) fully-grown, mature; (attitude) adult, grown-up

adverbe [advɛʀb] nm adverb

adversaire [advɛʀsɛʀ] nm/f (Sport, gén) opponent, adversary

aération [aeʀasjɔ̃] nf airing; (circulation de l'air) ventilation

aérer [aeʀe] vt to air; (fig) to lighten

aérien, ne [aeʀjɛ̃, jɛn] adj (Aviat) air cpd, aerial; (câble, métro) overhead; (fig) light; **compagnie ~ne** airline

aéro... [aeʀo] préfixe: **aérobic** nm aerobics sg; **aérogare** nf airport (buildings); (en ville) air terminal; **aéroglisseur** nm hovercraft; **aérophagie** nf (Méd) wind, aerophagia (Méd); **aéroport** nm airport; **aérosol** nm aerosol

affaiblir [afebliʀ] vi to weaken; **s'affaiblir** to weaken

affaire [afɛʀ] nf (problème, question) matter; (criminelle, judiciaire) case; (scandaleuse etc) affair; (entreprise) business; (marché, transaction) deal; business no pl; (occasion intéressante) bargain; **affaires** nfpl (intérêts publics et privés) affairs; (activité commerciale) business *sg*; (*effets personnels*) things, belongings; **ce sont mes ~s** (*cela me concerne*) that's my business; **occupe-toi de tes ~s!** mind your own business!; **ça fera l'~** that will do (nicely); **se tirer d'~** to sort it *ou* things out for o.s.; **avoir ~ à** (*être en contact*) to be dealing with; **les A~s étrangères** Foreign Affairs; **affairer: s'affairer** *vi* to busy o.s., bustle about

affamé, e [afame] *adj* starving

affecter [afɛkte] *vt* to affect; **~ qch à** to allocate *ou* allot sth to; **~ qn à** to appoint sb to; (*diplomate*) to post sb to

affectif, -ive [afɛktif, iv] *adj* emotional

affection [afɛksjɔ̃] *nf* affection; (*mal*) ailment; **affectionner** *vt* to be fond of; **affectueux, -euse** *adj* affectionate

affichage [afiʃaʒ] *nm* billposting; (*électronique*) display; **"~ interdit"** "stick no bills"; **affichage à cristaux liquides** liquid crystal display, LCD

affiche [afiʃ] *nf* poster; (*officielle*) notice; (*Théâtre*) bill; **être à l'~** to be on

afficher [afiʃe] *vt* (*affiche*) to put up; (*réunion*) to put up a notice about; (*électroniquement*) to display; (*fig*) to exhibit, display; **"défense d'~"** "no bill posters"; **s'afficher** *vr* (*péj*) to flaunt o.s.; (*électroniquement*) to be displayed

affilée [afile]: **d'~** *adv* at a stretch

affirmatif, -ive [afiʀmatif, iv] *adj* affirmative

affirmer [afiʀme] *vt* to assert

affligé, e [afliʒe] *adj* distressed, grieved; **~ de** (*maladie, tare*) afflicted with

affliger [afliʒe] *vt* (*peiner*) to distress, grieve

affluence [aflyɑ̃s] *nf* crowds *pl*; **heures d'~** rush hours; **jours d'~** busiest days

affluent [aflyɑ̃] *nm* tributary

affolement [afɔlmɑ̃] *nm* panic

affoler [afɔle] *vt* to throw into a panic; **s'affoler** *vi* to panic

affranchir [afʀɑ̃ʃiʀ] *vt* to put a stamp *ou* stamps on; (*à la machine*) to frank (BRIT), meter (US); (*fig*) to free, liberate; **affranchissement** *nm* postage

affreux, -euse [afʀø, øz] *adj* dreadful, awful

affront [afʀɔ̃] *nm* affront; **affrontement** *nm* clash, confrontation

affronter [afʀɔ̃te] *vt* to confront, face

affût [afy] *nm*: **à l'~ (de)** (*gibier*) lying in wait (for); (*fig*) on the look-out (for)

Afghanistan [afganistɑ̃] *nm*: **l'~** Afghanistan

afin [afɛ̃]: **~ que** *conj* so that, in order that; **~ de faire** in order to do, so as to do

africain, e [afʀikɛ̃, ɛn] *adj* African ▷ *nm/f*: **A~, e** African

Afrique [afʀik] *nf*: **l'~** Africa; **l'Afrique du Nord/Sud** North/South Africa

agacer [agase] *vt* to irritate

âge [ɑʒ] *nm* age; **quel ~ as-tu?** how old are you?; **prendre de l'~** to be getting on (in years); **le troisième ~** (*période*) retirement; (*personnes âgées*) senior citizens; **âgé, e** *adj* old, elderly; **âgé de 10 ans** 10 years old

agence [aʒɑ̃s] *nf* agency, office; (*succursale*) branch; **agence de voyages** travel agency; **agence immobilière** estate (BRIT) *ou* real estate (US) agent's (office)

agenda [aʒɛ̃da] *nm* diary; **~ électronique** PDA

> Attention à ne pas traduire *agenda* par le mot anglais *agenda*.

agenouiller [aʒ(ə)nuje]: **s'agenouiller** *vi* to kneel (down)

agent, e [aʒɑ̃, ɑ̃t] *nm/f* (*aussi*: **~(e) de police**) policeman(policewoman); (*Admin*) official, officer; **agent immobilier** estate agent (BRIT), realtor (US)

agglomération [aglɔmeʀasjɔ̃] *nf* town; built-up area; **l'~ parisienne** the urban area of Paris

aggraver [agʀave]: **s'aggraver** *vi* to worsen

agile [aʒil] *adj* agile, nimble

agir [aʒiʀ] *vi* to act; **il s'agit de** (*ça traite de*) it is about; (*il est important de*) it's a matter *ou* question of; **il s'agit de faire** we (*ou* you *etc*) must do; **de quoi s'agit-il?** what is it about?

agitation [aʒitasjɔ̃] *nf* (hustle and) bustle; (*trouble*) agitation, excitement; (*politique*) unrest, agitation

agité, e [aʒite] *adj* fidgety, restless; (*troublé*) agitated, perturbed; (*mer*) rough

agiter [aʒite] *vt* (*bouteille, chiffon*) to shake; (*bras, mains*) to wave; (*préoccuper, exciter*) to perturb

agneau, x [aɲo] *nm* lamb

agonie [agɔni] *nf* mortal agony, death pangs *pl*; (*fig*) death throes *pl*

agrafe [agʀaf] *nf* (*de vêtement*) hook, fastener; (*de bureau*) staple; **agrafer** *vt* to fasten; to staple; **agrafeuse** *nf* stapler

agrandir [agʀɑ̃diʀ] *vt* to enlarge; **s'agrandir** *vi* (*ville, famille*) to grow, expand; (*trou, écart*) to get bigger; **agrandissement** *nm* (*Photo*) enlargement

agréable [agʀeabl] *adj* pleasant, nice

agréé, e [agʀee] *adj*: **concessionnaire ~** registered dealer

agréer [agʀee] *vt* (*requête*) to accept; **~ à** to please, suit; **veuillez ~, Monsieur/Madame, mes salutations distinguées** (*personne nommée*) yours sincerely; (*personne non nommée*) yours faithfully

agrégation [agʀegasjɔ̃] *nf* highest teaching diploma in France; **agrégé, e** *nm/f* holder of the *agrégation*

agrément [agʀemɑ̃] *nm* (*accord*) consent, approval; (*attraits*) charm, attractiveness; (*plaisir*) pleasure

agresser [agʀese] vt to attack; **agresseur** nm aggressor, attacker; (Pol, Mil) aggressor; **agressif, -ive** adj aggressive

agricole [agʀikɔl] adj agricultural; **agriculteur** nm farmer; **agriculture** nf agriculture, farming

agripper [agʀipe] vt to grab, clutch; **s'agripper à** to cling (on) to, clutch, grip

agro-alimentaire [agʀoalimɑ̃tɛʀ] nm farm-produce industry

agrumes [agʀym] nmpl citrus fruit(s)

aguets [age] nmpl: **être aux ~** to be on the look out

ai [e] vb voir **avoir**

aide [ɛd] nm/f assistant; carer ▷ nf assistance, help; (secours financier) aid; **à l'~ de** (avec) with the help ou aid of; **appeler (qn) à l'~** to call for help (from sb); **à l'~!** help!; **aide judiciaire** legal aid; **aide ménagère** ≈ home help (BRIT) ou helper (US); **aide-mémoire** nm inv memoranda pages pl; (key facts) handbook; **aide-soignant, e** nm/f auxiliary nurse

aider [ede] vt to help; **~ à qch** to help (towards) sth; **~ qn à faire qch** to help sb to do sth; **pouvez-vous m'~?** can you help me?; **s'aider de** (se servir de) to use, make use of

aïe [aj] excl ouch!

aie etc [ɛ] vb voir **avoir**

aigle [ɛgl] nm eagle

aigre [ɛgʀ] adj sour, sharp; (fig) sharp, cutting; **aigre-doux, -ce** adj (sauce) sweet and sour; **aigreur** nf sourness; sharpness; **aigreurs d'estomac** heartburn sg

aigu, ë [egy] adj (objet, douleur) sharp; (son, voix) high-pitched, shrill; (note) high(-pitched)

aiguille [eguij] nf needle; (de montre) hand; **aiguille à tricoter** knitting needle

aiguiser [egize] vt to sharpen; (fig) to stimulate; (: sens) to excite

ail [aj] nm garlic

aile [ɛl] nf wing; **aileron** nm (de requin) fin; **ailier** nm winger

aille etc [aj] vb voir **aller**

ailleurs [ajœʀ] adv elsewhere, somewhere else; **partout/nulle part ~** everywhere/ nowhere else; **d'~** (du reste) moreover, besides; **par ~** (d'autre part) moreover, furthermore

aimable [ɛmabl] adj kind, nice

aimant [ɛmɑ̃] nm magnet

aimer [eme] vt to love; (d'amitié, affection, par goût) to like; (souhait): **j'aimerais ...** I would like ...; **j'aime faire du ski** I like skiing; **je t'aime** I love you; **bien ~ qn/qch** to like sb/sth; **j'aime mieux Paul (que Pierre)** I prefer Paul (to Pierre); **j'aimerais mieux faire** I'd much rather do

aine [ɛn] nf groin

aîné, e [ene] adj elder, older; (le plus âgé) eldest, oldest ▷ nm/f oldest child ou one, oldest boy ou son/girl ou daughter

ainsi [ɛ̃si] adv (de cette façon) like this, in this way, thus; (ce faisant) thus ▷ conj thus, so; **~ que** (comme) (just) as; (et aussi) as well as; **pour ~ dire** so to speak; **et ~ de suite** and so on

air [ɛʀ] nm air; (mélodie) tune; (expression) look, air; **prendre l'~** to get some (fresh) air; **avoir l'~** (sembler) to look, appear; **il a l'~ triste/malade** he looks sad/ill; **avoir l'~ de** to look like; **il a l'~ de dormir** he looks as if he's sleeping; **en l'~** (promesses) empty

airbag [ɛʀbag] nm airbag

aisance [ɛzɑ̃s] nf ease; (richesse) affluence

aise [ɛz] nf comfort; **être à l'~** ou **à son ~** to be comfortable; (pas embarrassé) to be at ease; (financièrement) to be comfortably off; **se mettre à l'~** to make o.s. comfortable; **être mal à l'~** to be uncomfortable; (gêné) to be ill at ease; **en faire à son ~** to do as one likes; **aisé, e** adj easy; (assez riche) well-to-do, well-off

aisselle [ɛsɛl] nf armpit

ait [ɛ] vb voir **avoir**

ajonc [aʒɔ̃] nm gorse no pl

ajourner [aʒuʀne] vt (réunion) to adjourn; (décision) to defer, postpone

ajouter [aʒute] vt to add

alarme [alaʀm] nf alarm; **donner l'~** to give ou raise the alarm; **alarmer** vt to alarm; **s'alarmer** vi to become alarmed

Albanie [albani] nf: **l'~** Albania

album [albɔm] nm album

alcool [alkɔl] nm: **l'~** alcohol; **un ~** a spirit, a brandy; **bière sans ~** non-alcoholic ou alcohol-free beer; **alcool à brûler** methylated spirits (BRIT), wood alcohol (US); **alcool à 90°** surgical spirit; **alcoolique** adj, nm/f alcoholic; **alcoolisé, e** adj alcoholic; **une boisson non alcoolisée** a soft drink; **alcoolisme** nm alcoholism; **alco(o)test®** nm Breathalyser®; (test) breath-test

aléatoire [aleatwaʀ] adj uncertain; (Inform) random

alentour [alɑ̃tuʀ] adv around, round about; **alentours** nmpl (environs) surroundings; **aux ~s de** in the vicinity ou neighbourhood of, round about; (temps) round about

alerte [alɛʀt] adj agile, nimble; brisk, lively ▷ nf alert; warning; **alerte à la bombe** bomb scare; **alerter** vt to alert

algèbre [alʒɛbʀ] nf algebra

Alger [alʒe] n Algiers

Algérie [alʒeʀi] nf: **l'~** Algeria; **algérien, ne** adj Algerian ▷ nm/f: **Algérien, ne** Algerian

algue [alg] nf (gén) seaweed no pl; (Bot) alga

alibi [alibi] nm alibi

aligner [aliɲe] vt to align, line up; (idées, chiffres) to string together; (adapter): **~ qch sur** to bring sth into alignment with; **s'aligner**

(soldats etc) to line up; **s'~ sur** (Pol) to align o.s. on

aliment [alimɑ̃] nm food; **alimentation** nf (commerce) food trade; (magasin) grocery store; (régime) diet; (en eau etc, de moteur) supplying; (Inform) feed; **alimenter** vt to feed; (Tech): **alimenter (en)** to supply (with); to feed (with); (fig) to sustain, keep going

allaiter [alete] vt to (breast-)feed, nurse; (suj: animal) to suckle

allécher [aleʃe] vt: **~ qn** to make sb's mouth water; to tempt ou entice sb

allée [ale] nf (de jardin) path; (en ville) avenue, drive; **~s et venues** comings and goings

allégé, e [aleʒe] adj (yaourt etc) low-fat

alléger [aleʒe] vt (voiture) to make lighter; (chargement) to lighten; (souffrance) to alleviate, soothe

Allemagne [almaɲ] nf: **l'~** Germany; **allemand, e** adj German ▷ nm/f: **Allemand, e** German ▷ nm (Ling) German

aller [ale] nm (trajet) outward journey; (billet: aussi: **~ simple**) single (BRIT) ou one-way (US) ticket; **~ (et) retour** return (ticket) (BRIT), round-trip ticket (US) ▷ vi (gén) to go; **~ à** (convenir) to suit; (suj: forme, pointure etc) to fit; **~ (bien) avec** (couleurs, style etc) to go (well) with; **je vais y ~/me fâcher** I'm going to go/to get angry; **~ chercher qn** to go and get ou fetch (BRIT) sb; **~ voir** to go and see, go to see; **allez!** come on!; **allons!** come now!; **comment allez-vous?** how are you?; **comment ça va?** how are you?; (affaires etc) how are things?; **il va bien/mal** he's well/not well, he's fine/ill; **ça va bien/mal** (affaires etc) it's going well/not going well; **~ mieux** to be better; **s'en ~** (partir) to be off, go, leave; (disparaître) to go away

allergie [alɛrʒi] nf allergy

allergique [alɛrʒik] adj: **~ à** allergic to; **je suis ~ à la pénicilline** I'm allergic to penicillin

alliance [aljɑ̃s] nf (Mil, Pol) alliance; (bague) wedding ring

allier [alje] vt (Pol, gén) to ally; (fig) to combine; **s'allier** to become allies; to combine

allô [alo] excl hullo, hallo

allocation [alɔkasjɔ̃] nf allowance; **allocation (de) chômage** unemployment benefit; **allocations familiales** ≈ child benefit

allonger [alɔ̃ʒe] vt to lengthen, make longer; (étendre: bras, jambe) to stretch (out); **s'allonger** vi to get longer; (se coucher) to lie down, stretch out; **~ le pas** to hasten one's step(s)

allumage [alymaʒ] nm (Auto) ignition

allume-cigare [alymsigar] nm inv cigar lighter

allumer [alyme] vt (lampe, phare, radio) to put ou switch on; (pièce) to put ou switch

the light(s) on in; (feu) to light; **s'allumer** vi (lumière, lampe) to come ou go on; **je n'arrive pas à ~ le chauffage** I can't turn the heating on

allumette [alymɛt] nf match

allure [alyr] nf (vitesse) speed, pace; (démarche) walk; (aspect, air) look; **avoir de l'~** to have style; **à toute ~** at top speed

allusion [a(l)lyzjɔ̃] nf allusion; (sous-entendu) hint; **faire ~ à** to allude ou refer to; to hint at

 MOT-CLÉ

alors [alɔr] adv **1** (à ce moment-là) then, at that time; **il habitait alors à Paris** he lived in Paris at that time

2 (par conséquent) then; **tu as fini? alors je m'en vais** have you finished? I'm going then; **et alors?** so what?

▷ conj: **alors que 1** (au moment où) when, as; **il est arrivé alors que je partais** he arrived as I was leaving

2 (tandis que) whereas, while; **alors que son frère travaillait dur, lui se reposait** while his brother was working hard, HE would rest

3 (bien que) even though; **il a été puni alors qu'il n'a rien fait** he was punished, even though he had done nothing

alourdir [alurdir] vt to weigh down, make heavy

Alpes [alp] nfpl: **les ~** the Alps

alphabet [alfabɛ] nm alphabet; (livre) ABC (book)

alpinisme [alpinism] nm mountaineering, climbing

Alsace [alzas] nf Alsace; **alsacien, ne** adj Alsatian ▷ nm/f: **Alsacien, ne** Alsatian

altermondialisme [altɛrmɔ̃djalism] nm anti-globalism; **altermondialiste** adj, nm/f anti-globalist

alternatif, -ive [altɛrnatif, iv] adj alternating; **alternative** nf (choix) alternative; **alterner** vi to alternate

altitude [altityd] nf altitude, height

alto [alto] nm (instrument) viola

aluminium [alyminjɔm] nm aluminium (BRIT), aluminum (US)

amabilité [amabilite] nf kindness

amaigrissant, e [amegrisɑ̃, ɑ̃t] adj (régime) slimming

amande [amɑ̃d] nf (de l'amandier) almond; **amandier** nm almond (tree)

amant [amɑ̃] nm lover

amas [ama] nm heap, pile; **amasser** vt to amass

amateur [amatœr] nm amateur; **en ~** (péj) amateurishly; **amateur de musique/sport** music/sport lover

ambassade [ãbasad] nf embassy; **l'~ de France** the French Embassy; **ambassadeur, -drice** nm/f ambassador(-dress)

ambiance [ãbjãs] nf atmosphere; **il y a de l'~** there's a great atmosphere

ambigu, ë [ãbigy] adj ambiguous

ambitieux, -euse [ãbisjø, jøz] adj ambitious

ambition [ãbisjɔ̃] nf ambition

ambulance [ãbylãs] nf ambulance; **appelez une ~!** call an ambulance!; **ambulancier, -ière** nm/f ambulance man(-woman) (BRIT), paramedic (US)

âme [am] nf soul; **âme sœur** kindred spirit

amélioration [ameljɔrasjɔ̃] nf improvement

améliorer [ameljɔre] vt to improve; **s'améliorer** vi to improve, get better

aménager [amenaʒe] vt (agencer, transformer) to fit out; to lay out; (: quartier, territoire) to develop; (installer) to fix up, put in; **ferme aménagée** converted farmhouse

amende [amãd] nf fine; **faire ~ honorable** to make amends

amener [am(ə)ne] vt to bring; (causer) to bring about; **s'amener** vi to show up (fam), turn up; **~ qn à faire qch** to lead sb to do sth

amer, amère [amɛr] adj bitter

américain, e [amerikɛ̃, ɛn] adj American ▷ nm/f: **A~, e** American

Amérique [amerik] nf: **l'~** America; **Amérique centrale/latine** Central/Latin America; **l'Amérique du Nord/Sud** North/South America

amertume [amɛrtym] nf bitterness

ameublement [amœbləmã] nm furnishing; (meubles) furniture

ami, e [ami] nm/f friend; (amant/maîtresse) boyfriend/girlfriend ▷ adj: **pays/groupe ~** friendly country/group; **petit ~/petite ~e** boyfriend/girlfriend

amiable [amjabl]: **à l'~** adv (Jur) out of court; (gén) amicably

amiante [amjãt] nm asbestos

amical, e, -aux [amikal, o] adj friendly; **amicalement** adv in a friendly way; (dans une lettre) (with) best wishes

amincir [amɛ̃sir] vt: **~ qn** to make sb thinner ou slimmer; (suj: vêtement) to make sb look slimmer

amincissant, e [amɛ̃sisã, ãt] adj: **régime ~** (slimming) diet; **crème ~e** slimming cream

amiral, -aux [amiral, o] nm admiral

amitié [amitje] nf friendship; **prendre en ~** to befriend; **faire** ou **présenter ses ~s à qn** to send sb one's best wishes; **"~s"** (dans une lettre) "(with) best wishes"

amonceler [amɔ̃s(ə)le] vt to pile ou heap up; **s'amonceler** vi to pile ou heap up; (fig) to accumulate

amont [amɔ̃]: **en ~** adv upstream

amorce [amɔrs] nf (sur un hameçon) bait; (explosif) cap; primer; priming; (fig: début) beginning(s), start

amortir [amɔrtir] vt (atténuer: choc) to absorb, cushion; (bruit, douleur) to deaden; (Comm: dette) to pay off; **~ un achat** to make a purchase pay for itself; **amortisseur** nm shock absorber

amour [amur] nm love; **faire l'~** to make love; **amoureux, -euse** adj (regard, tempérament) amorous; (vie, problèmes) love cpd; (personne): **être amoureux (de qn)** to be in love (with sb); **tomber amoureux (de qn)** to fall in love (with sb) ▷ nmpl courting couple(s); **amour-propre** nm self-esteem, pride

ampère [ãpɛr] nm amp(ere)

amphithéâtre [ãfiteatr] nm amphitheatre; (d'université) lecture hall ou theatre

ample [ãpl] adj (vêtement) roomy, ample; (gestes, mouvement) broad; (ressources) ample; **amplement** adv: **c'est amplement suffisant** that's more than enough; **ampleur** nf (de dégâts, problème) extent

amplificateur [ãplifikatœr] nm amplifier

amplifier [ãplifje] vt (fig) to expand, increase

ampoule [ãpul] nf (électrique) bulb; (de médicament) phial; (aux mains, pieds) blister

amusant, e [amyzã, ãt] adj (divertissant, spirituel) entertaining, amusing; (comique) funny, amusing

amuse-gueule [amyzgœl] nm inv appetizer, snack

amusement [amyzmã] nm (divertissement) amusement; (jeu etc) pastime, diversion

amuser [amyze] vt (divertir) to entertain, amuse; (égayer, faire rire) to amuse; **s'amuser** vi (jouer) to play; (se divertir) to enjoy o.s., have fun; (fig) to mess around

amygdale [amidal] nf tonsil

an [ã] nm year; **avoir quinze ans** to be fifteen (years old); **le jour de l'an, le premier de l'an, le nouvel an** New Year's Day

analphabète [analfabɛt] nm/f illiterate

analyse [analiz] nf analysis; (Méd) test; **analyser** vt to analyse; to test

ananas [anana(s)] nm pineapple

anatomie [anatɔmi] nf anatomy

ancêtre [ãsɛtr] nm/f ancestor

anchois [ãʃwa] nm anchovy

ancien, ne [ãsjɛ̃, jɛn] adj old; (de jadis, de l'antiquité) ancient; (précédent, ex-) former, old; (par l'expérience) senior ▷ nm/f (dans une tribu) elder; **ancienneté** nf (Admin) (length of) service; (privilèges obtenus) seniority

ancre [ãkr] nf anchor; **jeter/lever l'~** to cast/weigh anchor; **ancrer** vt (Constr: câble etc) to anchor; (fig) to fix firmly

Andorre [ãdɔr] nf Andorra

andouille [ãduj] nf (Culin) sausage made of

chitterlings; (fam) clot, nit

âne [ɑn] nm donkey, ass; (péj) dunce

anéantir [aneɑ̃tiʀ] vt to annihilate, wipe out; (fig) to obliterate, destroy

anémie [anemi] nf anaemia; **anémique** adj anaemic

anesthésie [anestezi] nf anaesthesia; **faire une ~ locale/générale à qn** to give sb a local/general anaesthetic

ange [ɑ̃ʒ] nm angel; **être aux ~s** to be over the moon

angine [ɑ̃ʒin] nf throat infection; **angine de poitrine** angina

anglais, e [ɑ̃glɛ, ɛz] adj English ▷ nm/f: **A~, e** Englishman(-woman) ▷ nm (Ling) English; **les A~** the English; **filer à l'~e** to take French leave

angle [ɑ̃gl] nm angle; (coin) corner; **angle droit** right angle

Angleterre [ɑ̃glətɛʀ] nf: **l'~** England

anglo... [ɑ̃glɔ] préfixe Anglo-, anglo(-); **anglophone** adj English-speaking

angoisse [ɑ̃gwas] nf anguish, distress; **angoissé, e** adj (personne) distressed

anguille [ɑ̃gij] nf eel

animal, e, -aux [animal, o] adj, nm animal

animateur, -trice [animatœʀ, tʀis] nm/f (de télévision) host; (de groupe) leader, organizer

animation [animasjɔ̃] nf (voir animé) busyness; liveliness; (Cinéma: technique) animation

animé, e [anime] adj (lieu) busy, lively; (conversation, réunion) lively, animated

animer [anime] vt (ville, soirée) to liven up; (mener) to lead

anis [ani(s)] nm (Culin) aniseed; (Bot) anise

ankyloser [ɑ̃kiloze]: **s'ankyloser** vi to get stiff

anneau, x [ano] nm (de rideau, bague) ring; (de chaîne) link

année [ane] nf year

annexe [anɛks] adj (problème) related; (document) appended; (salle) adjoining ▷ nf (bâtiment) annex(e); (jointe à une lettre) enclosure

anniversaire [anivɛʀsɛʀ] nm birthday; (d'un événement, bâtiment) anniversary

annonce [anɔ̃s] nf announcement; (signe, indice) sign; (aussi: **~ publicitaire**) advertisement; **les petites ~s** the classified advertisements, the small ads

annoncer [anɔ̃se] vt to announce; (être le signe de) to herald; **s'~ bien/difficile** to look promising/difficult

annuaire [anɥɛʀ] nm yearbook, annual; **annuaire téléphonique** (telephone) directory, phone book

annuel, le [anɥɛl] adj annual, yearly

annulation [anylasjɔ̃] nf cancellation

annuler [anyle] vt (rendez-vous, voyage) to cancel, call off; (jugement) to quash (BRIT), repeal (US); (Math, Physique) to cancel out; **je voudrais ~ ma réservation** I'd like to cancel my reservation

anonymat [anɔnima] nm anonymity; **garder l'~** to remain anonymous

anonyme [anɔnim] adj anonymous; (fig) impersonal

anorak [anɔʀak] nm anorak

anorexie [anɔʀɛksi] nf anorexia

anormal, e, -aux [anɔʀmal, o] adj abnormal

ANPE sigle f (= Agence nationale pour l'emploi) national employment agency

antarctique [ɑ̃taʀktik] adj Antarctic ▷ nm: **l'A~** the Antarctic

antenne [ɑ̃tɛn] nf (de radio) aerial; (d'insecte) antenna, feeler; (poste avancé) outpost; (petite succursale) sub-branch; **passer à l'~** to go on the air; **antenne parabolique** satellite dish

antérieur, e [ɑ̃teʀjœʀ] adj (d'avant) previous, earlier; (de devant) front

anti... [ɑ̃ti] préfixe anti...; **antialcoolique** adj anti-alcohol; **antibiotique** nm antibiotic; **antibrouillard** adj: **phare antibrouillard** fog lamp (BRIT) ou light (US)

anticipation [ɑ̃tisipasjɔ̃] nf: **livre/film d'~** science fiction book/film

anticipé, e [ɑ̃tisipe] adj: **avec mes remerciements ~s** thanking you in advance ou anticipation

anticiper [ɑ̃tisipe] vt (événement, coup) to anticipate, foresee

anti...: **anticorps** nm antibody; **antidote** nm antidote; **antigel** nm antifreeze; **antihistaminique** nm antihistamine

antillais, e [ɑ̃tijɛ, ɛz] adj West Indian, Caribbean ▷ nm/f: **A~, e** West Indian, Caribbean

Antilles [ɑ̃tij] nfpl: **les ~** the West Indies; **les Grandes/Petites ~** the Greater/Lesser Antilles

antilope [ɑ̃tilɔp] nf antelope

anti...: **antimite(s)** adj, nm: **(produit) antimite(s)** mothproofer; moth repellent; **antimondialisation** nf anti-globalization; **antipathique** adj unpleasant, disagreeable; **antipelliculaire** adj anti-dandruff

antiquaire [ɑ̃tikɛʀ] nm/f antique dealer

antique [ɑ̃tik] adj antique; (très vieux) ancient, antiquated; **antiquité** nf (objet) antique; **l'Antiquité** Antiquity; **magasin d'antiquités** antique shop

anti...: **antirabique** adj rabies cpd; **antirouille** adj inv anti-rust cpd; **antisémite** adj anti-Semitic; **antiseptique** adj, nm antiseptic

antivirus [ɑ̃ti'viʀys] nm (Inform) antivirus; **antivol** adj, nm: **(dispositif) antivol** anti-theft device

anxieux, -euse [ɑ̃ksjø, jøz] adj anxious,

worried

AOC sigle f (= appellation d'origine contrôlée) label guaranteeing the quality of wine

août [u(t)] nm August

apaiser [apeze] vt (colère, douleur) to soothe; (personne) to calm (down), pacify; **s'apaiser** vi (tempête, bruit) to die down, subside; (personne) to calm down

apercevoir [apɛʀsəvwaʀ] vt to see; **s'apercevoir de** vt to notice; **s'~ que** to notice that

aperçu [apɛʀsy] nm (vue d'ensemble) general survey

apéritif [apeʀitif] nm (boisson) aperitif; (réunion) drinks pl

à-peu-près [apøpʀɛ] (péj) nm inv vague approximation

apeuré, e [apœʀe] adj frightened, scared

aphte [aft] nm mouth ulcer

apitoyer [apitwaje] vt to move to pity; **s'apitoyer (sur)** to feel pity (for)

aplatir [aplatiʀ] vt to flatten; **s'aplatir** vi to become flatter; (écrasé) to be flattened

aplomb [aplɔ̃] nm (équilibre) balance, equilibrium; (fig) self-assurance; nerve; **d'~** steady

apostrophe [apɔstʀɔf] nf (signe) apostrophe

apparaître [apaʀɛtʀ] vi to appear

appareil [apaʀɛj] nm (outil, machine) piece of apparatus, device; (électrique, ménager) appliance; (avion) (aero)plane, aircraft inv; (téléphonique) phone; (dentier) brace (BRIT), braces (US); **"qui est à l'~?"** "who's speaking?"; **dans le plus simple ~** in one's birthday suit; **appareil(-photo)** camera; **appareiller** vi (Navig) to cast off, get under way ▷ vt (assortir) to match up

apparemment [apaʀamɑ̃] adv apparently

apparence [apaʀɑ̃s] nf appearance; **en ~** apparently

apparent, e [apaʀɑ̃, ɑ̃t] adj visible; (évident) obvious; (superficiel) apparent

apparenté, e [apaʀɑ̃te] adj: **~ à** related to; (fig) similar to

apparition [apaʀisjɔ̃] nf appearance; (surnaturelle) apparition

appartement [apaʀtəmɑ̃] nm flat (BRIT), apartment (US)

appartenir [apaʀtəniʀ]: **~ à** vt to belong to; **il lui appartient de** it is his duty to

apparu, e [apaʀy] pp de **apparaître**

appât [apɑ] nm (Pêche) bait; (fig) lure, bait

appel [apɛl] nm call; (nominal) roll call; (: Scol) register; (Mil: recrutement) call-up; **faire ~ à** (invoquer) to appeal to; (avoir recours à) to call on; (nécessiter) to call for, require; **faire ou interjeter ~** (Jur) to appeal; **faire l'~** to call the roll; (Scol) to call the register; **sans ~** (fig) final, irrevocable; **faire un ~ de phares** to

flash one's headlights; **appel d'offres** (Comm) invitation to tender; **appel (téléphonique)** (tele)phone call

appelé [ap(ə)le] nm (Mil) conscript

appeler [ap(ə)le] vt to call; (faire venir: médecin etc) to call, send for; **s'appeler** vi: **elle s'appelle Gabrielle** her name is Gabrielle, she's called Gabrielle; **comment vous appelez-vous?** what's your name?; **comment ça s'appelle?** what is it called?; **être appelé à** (fig) to be destined to

appendicite [apɑ̃disit] nf appendicitis

appesantir [apəzɑ̃tiʀ]: **s'appesantir** vi to grow heavier; **s'~ sur** (fig) to dwell on

appétissant, e [apetisɑ̃, ɑ̃t] adj appetizing, mouth-watering

appétit [apeti] nm appetite; **bon ~!** enjoy your meal!

applaudir [aplodiʀ] vt to applaud ▷ vi to applaud, clap; **applaudissements** nmpl applause sg, clapping sg

application [aplikasjɔ̃] nf application

appliquer [aplike] vt to apply; (loi) to enforce; **s'appliquer** vi (élève etc) to apply o.s.; **s'~ à** to apply to

appoint [apwɛ̃] nm (extra) contribution ou help; **avoir/faire l'~** to have/give the right change ou money; **chauffage d'~** extra heating

apporter [apɔʀte] vt to bring

appréciable [apʀesjabl] adj appreciable

apprécier [apʀesje] vt to appreciate; (évaluer) to estimate, assess

appréhender [apʀeɑ̃de] vt (craindre) to dread; (arrêter) to apprehend

apprendre [apʀɑ̃dʀ] vt to learn; (événement, résultats) to learn of, hear of; **~ qch à qn** (informer) to tell sb (of) sth; (enseigner) to teach sb sth; **~ à faire qch** to learn to do sth; **~ à qn à faire qch** to teach sb to do sth; **apprenti, e** nm/f apprentice; **apprentissage** nm learning; (Comm, Scol: période) apprenticeship

apprêter [apʀete] vt: **s'~ à faire qch** to get ready to do sth

appris, e [apʀi, iz] pp de **apprendre**

apprivoiser [apʀivwaze] vt to tame

approbation [apʀɔbasjɔ̃] nf approval

approcher [apʀɔʃe] vi to approach, come near ▷ vt to approach; (rapprocher): **~ qch (de qch)** to bring ou put sth near (to sth); **s'approcher de** to approach, go ou come near to; **~ de** (lieu, but) to draw near to; (quantité, moment) to approach

approfondir [apʀɔfɔ̃diʀ] vt to deepen; (question) to go further into

approprié, e [apʀɔpʀije] adj: **~ (à)** appropriate (to), suited to

approprier [apʀɔpʀije]: **s'approprier** vt to appropriate, take over; **s'~ en** to stock up with

approuver [apʁuve] vt to agree with; (*trouver louable*) to approve of

approvisionner [apʁɔvizjɔne] vt to supply; (*compte bancaire*) to pay funds into; **s'approvisionner en** to stock up with

approximatif, -ive [apʁɔksimatif, iv] adj approximate, rough; (*termes*) vague

appt abr = **appartement**

appui [apɥi] nm support; **prendre ~ sur** to lean on; (*objet*) to rest on; **l'~ de la fenêtre** the windowsill, the window ledge

appuyer [apɥije] vt (*poser*): **~ qch sur/contre** to lean ou rest sth on/against; (*soutenir: personne, demande*) to support, back (up) ▷ vi: **~ sur** (*bouton*) to press, push; (*mot, détail*) to stress, emphasize; **~ sur le frein** to brake, to apply the brakes; **s'appuyer sur** to lean on; (*fig: compter sur*) to rely on

après [apʁe] prép after ▷ adv afterwards; **2 heures ~** 2 hours later; **~ qu'il est** ou **soit parti** after he left; **~ avoir fait** after having done; **d'~** (*selon*) according to; **~ coup** after the event, afterwards; **~ tout** (*au fond*) after all; **et (puis) ~?** so what?; **après-demain** adv the day after tomorrow; **après-midi** nm ou nf inv afternoon; **après-rasage** nm inv aftershave; **après-shampooing** nm inv conditioner; **après-ski** nm inv snow boot

après-soleil [apʁesɔlej] adj inv after-sun cpd ▷ nm after-sun cream ou lotion

apte [apt] adj capable; **~ à qch/faire qch** capable of sth/doing sth; **~ (au service)** (*Mil*) fit (for service)

aquarelle [akwaʁɛl] nf watercolour

aquarium [akwaʁjɔm] nm aquarium

arabe [aʁab] adj Arabic; (*désert, cheval*) Arabian; (*nation, peuple*) Arab ▷ nm/f: **A~** Arab ▷ nm (*Ling*) Arabic

Arabie [aʁabi] nf: **l'~ (Saoudite)** Saudi Arabia

arachide [aʁaʃid] nf (*plante*) groundnut (plant); (*graine*) peanut, groundnut

araignée [aʁeɲe] nf spider

arbitraire [aʁbitʁɛʁ] adj arbitrary

arbitre [aʁbitʁ] nm (*Sport*) referee; (: *Tennis, Cricket*) umpire; (*fig*) arbiter, judge; (*Jur*) arbitrator; **arbitrer** vt to referee; to umpire; to arbitrate

arbre [aʁbʁ] nm tree; (*Tech*) shaft

arbuste [aʁbyst] nm small shrub

arc [aʁk] nm (*arme*) bow; (*Géom*) arc; (*Archit*) arch; **en ~ de cercle** semi-circular

arcade [aʁkad] nf arch(way); **arcades** nfpl (*série*) arcade sg, arches

arc-en-ciel [aʁkɑ̃sjɛl] nm rainbow

arche [aʁʃ] nf arch; **arche de Noé** Noah's Ark

archéologie [aʁkeɔlɔʒi] nf arch(a)eology; **archéologue** nm/f arch(a)eologist

archet [aʁʃe] nm bow

archipel [aʁʃipɛl] nm archipelago

architecte [aʁʃitɛkt] nm architect

architecture [aʁʃitɛktyʁ] nf architecture

archives [aʁʃiv] nfpl (*collection*) archives

arctique [aʁktik] adj Arctic ▷ nm: **l'A~** the Arctic

ardent, e [aʁdɑ̃, ɑ̃t] adj (*soleil*) blazing; (*amour*) ardent, passionate; (*prière*) fervent

ardoise [aʁdwaz] nf slate

ardu, e [aʁdy] adj (*travail*) arduous; (*problème*) difficult

arène [aʁɛn] nf arena; **arènes** nfpl (*amphithéâtre*) bull-ring sg

arête [aʁɛt] nf (*de poisson*) bone; (*d'une montagne*) ridge

argent [aʁʒɑ̃] nm (*métal*) silver; (*monnaie*) money; **argent de poche** pocket money; **argent liquide** ready money, (ready) cash; **argenterie** nf silverware

argentin, e [aʁʒɑ̃tɛ̃, in] adj Argentinian ▷ nm/f: **A~, e** Argentinian

Argentine [aʁʒɑ̃tin] nf: **l'~** Argentina

argentique [aʁʒɑ̃tik] adj (*appareil-photo*) film cpd

argile [aʁʒil] nf clay

argot [aʁgo] nm slang; **argotique** adj slang cpd; (*très familier*) slangy

argument [aʁgymɑ̃] nm argument

argumenter [aʁgymɑ̃te] vi to argue

aride [aʁid] adj arid

aristocratie [aʁistɔkʁasi] nf aristocracy; **aristocratique** adj aristocratic

arithmétique [aʁitmetik] adj arithmetic(al) ▷ nf arithmetic

arme [aʁm] nf weapon; **armes** nfpl (*armement*) weapons, arms; (*blason*) (coat of) arms; **~s de destruction massive** weapons of mass destruction; **arme à feu** firearm

armée [aʁme] nf army; **armée de l'air** Air Force; **armée de terre** Army

armer [aʁme] vt to arm; (*arme à feu*) to cock; (*appareil-photo*) to wind on; **~ qch de** to reinforce sth with; **s'armer de** to arm o.s. with

armistice [aʁmistis] nm armistice; **l'A~** ≈ Remembrance (*BRIT*) ou Veterans (*US*) Day

armoire [aʁmwaʁ] nf (tall) cupboard; (*penderie*) wardrobe (*BRIT*), closet (*US*)

armure [aʁmyʁ] nf armour no pl, suit of armour; **armurier** nm gunsmith

arnaque [aʁnak] (*fam*) f swindling; **c'est de l'~** it's a rip-off; **arnaquer** (*fam*) vt to swindle

arobase [aʁɔbaz] nf (*symbole*) at symbol; **"paul ~ société point fr"** "paul at société dot fr"

aromates [aʁɔmat] nmpl seasoning sg, herbs (and spices)

aromathérapie [aʁɔmateʁapi] nf aromatherapy

aromatisé, e [aʁɔmatize] adj flavoured

arôme [aʁom] nm aroma

arracher [aʀaʃe] vt to pull out; (page etc) to tear off, tear out; (légumes, herbe) to pull up; (bras etc) to tear off; **s'arracher** vt (article recherché) to fight over; **~ qch à qn** to snatch sth from sb; (fig) to wring sth out of sb

arrangement [aʀɑ̃ʒmɑ̃] nm agreement, arrangement

arranger [aʀɑ̃ʒe] vt (gén) to arrange; (réparer) to fix, put right; (régler: différend) to settle, sort out; (convenir à) to suit, be convenient for; **cela m'arrange** that suits me (fine); **s'arranger** vi (se mettre d'accord) to come to an agreement; **je vais m'~** I'll manage; **ça va s'~** it'll sort itself out

arrestation [aʀɛstasjɔ̃] nf arrest

arrêt [aʀɛ] nm stopping; (de bus etc) stop; (Jur) judgment, decision; **à l'~** stationary; **tomber en ~ devant** to stop short in front of; **sans ~** (sans interruption) non-stop; (très fréquemment) continually; **arrêt de travail** stoppage (of work)

arrêter [aʀete] vt to stop; (chauffage etc) to turn off, switch off; (fixer: date etc) to appoint, decide on; (criminel, suspect) to arrest; **s'arrêter** vi to stop; **~ de faire** to stop doing; **arrêtez-vous ici/au coin, s'il vous plaît** could you stop here/at the corner, please?

arrhes [aʀ] nfpl deposit sg

arrière [aʀjɛʀ] nm back; (Sport) fullback ▷ adj inv: **siège/roue ~** back ou rear seat/wheel; **à l'~** behind, at the back; **en ~** behind; (regarder) back, behind; (tomber, aller) backwards; **arrière-goût** nm aftertaste; **arrière-grand-mère** nf great-grandmother; **arrière-grand-père** nm great-grandfather; **arrière-pays** nm inv hinterland; **arrière-pensée** nf ulterior motive; mental reservation; **arrière-plan** nm background; **à l'arrière-plan** in the background; **arrière-saison** nf late autumn

arrimer [aʀime] vt to secure; (cargaison) to stow

arrivage [aʀivaʒ] nm consignment

arrivée [aʀive] nf arrival; (ligne d'arrivée) finish

arriver [aʀive] vi to arrive; (survenir) to happen, occur; **il arrive à Paris à 8h** he gets to ou arrives in Paris at 8; **à quelle heure arrive le train de Lyon?** what time does the train from Lyons get in?; **~ à** (atteindre) to reach; **~ à faire qch** to succeed in doing sth; **en ~ à** (finir par) to come to; **il arrive que** it happens that; **il lui arrive de faire** he sometimes does

arrobase [aʀɔbaz] nf (Inform) @, 'at' sign

arrogance [aʀɔgɑ̃s] nf arrogance

arrogant, e [aʀɔgɑ̃, ɑ̃t] adj arrogant

arrondissement [aʀɔ̃dismɑ̃] nm (Admin) ≈ district

arroser [aʀoze] vt to water; (victoire) to celebrate (over a drink); (Culin) to baste; **arrosoir** nm watering can

arsenal, -aux [aʀsənal, o] nm (Navig) naval dockyard; (Mil) arsenal; (fig) gear, paraphernalia

art [aʀ] nm art

artère [aʀtɛʀ] nf (Anat) artery; (rue) main road

arthrite [aʀtʀit] nf arthritis

artichaut [aʀtiʃo] nm artichoke

article [aʀtikl] nm article; (Comm) item, article; **à l'~ de la mort** at the point of death

articulation [aʀtikylasjɔ̃] nf articulation; (Anat) joint

articuler [aʀtikyle] vt to articulate

artificiel, le [aʀtifisjɛl] adj artificial

artisan [aʀtizɑ̃] nm artisan, (self-employed) craftsman; **artisanal, e, -aux** adj of ou made by craftsmen; (péj) cottage industry cpd; **de fabrication artisanale** home-made; **artisanat** nm arts and crafts pl

artiste [aʀtist] nm/f artist; (de variétés) entertainer; (musicien etc) performer; **artistique** adj artistic

as¹ [a] vb voir **avoir**

as² [ɑs] nm ace

ascenseur [asɑ̃sœʀ] nm lift (BRIT), elevator (US)

ascension [asɑ̃sjɔ̃] nf ascent; (de montagne) climb; **l'A~** (Rel) the Ascension

● **ASCENSION**

● The **fête de l'Ascension** is a public holiday
● in France. It always falls on a Thursday,
● usually in May. Many French people take
● the following Friday off work too and enjoy
● a long weekend.

asiatique [azjatik] adj Asiatic, Asian ▷ nm/f: **A~** Asian

Asie [azi] nf: **l'~** Asia

asile [azil] nm (refuge) refuge, sanctuary; (Pol): **droit d'~** (political) asylum

aspect [aspɛ] nm appearance, look; (fig) aspect, side; **à l'~ de** at the sight of

asperge [aspɛʀʒ] nf asparagus no pl

asperger [aspɛʀʒe] vt to spray, sprinkle

asphalte [asfalt] nm asphalt

asphyxier [asfiksje] vt to suffocate, asphyxiate; (fig) to stifle

aspirateur [aspiʀatœʀ] nm vacuum cleaner; **passer l'~** to vacuum

aspirer [aspiʀe] vt (air) to inhale; (liquide) to suck (up); (suj: appareil) to suck up; **~ à** to aspire to

aspirine [aspiʀin] nf aspirin

assagir [asaʒiʀ]: **s'assagir** vi to quieten down, settle down

assaisonnement [asɛzɔnmɑ̃] nm seasoning

assaisonner [asɛzɔne] vt to season

assassin [asasɛ̃] nm murderer; assassin;

assassiner vt to murder; (*esp Pol*) to assassinate

assaut [aso] nm assault, attack; **prendre d'~** to storm, assault; **donner l'~ à** to attack

assécher [asefe] vt to drain

assemblage [asɑ̃blaʒ] nm (*action*) assembling; (*de couleurs, choses*) collection

assemblée [asɑ̃ble] nf (*réunion*) meeting; (*assistance*) gathering; (*Pol*) assembly; **l'A~ nationale** the National Assembly (*the lower house of the French Parliament*)

assembler [asɑ̃ble] vt (*joindre, monter*) to assemble, put together; (*amasser*) to gather (together), collect (together); **s'assembler** vi to gather

asseoir [aswaʀ] vt (*malade, bébé*) to sit up; (*personne debout*) to sit down; (*autorité, réputation*) to establish; **s'asseoir** vi to sit (o.s.) down

assez [ase] adv (*suffisamment*) enough, sufficiently; (*passablement*) rather, quite, fairly; **~ de pain/livres** enough ou sufficient bread/ books; **vous en avez ~?** have you got enough?; **j'en ai ~!** I've had enough!

assidu, e [asidy] adj (*appliqué*) assiduous, painstaking; (*ponctuel*) regular

assied etc [asje] vb voir **asseoir**

assiérai etc [asjeʀe] vb voir **asseoir**

assiette [asjɛt] nf plate; (*contenu*) plate(ful); **il n'est pas dans son ~** he's not feeling quite himself; **assiette à dessert** dessert plate; **assiette anglaise** assorted cold meats; **assiette creuse** (soup) dish, soup plate; **assiette plate** (dinner) plate

assimiler [asimile] vt to assimilate, absorb; (*comparer*): **~ qch/qn à** to liken ou compare sth/sb to; **s'assimiler** vr (*s'intégrer*) to be assimilated, assimilate

assis, e [asi, iz] pp de **asseoir** ▷ adj sitting (down), seated

assistance [asistɑ̃s] nf (*public*) audience; (*aide*) assistance; **enfant de l'A~ publique** child in care

assistant, e [asistɑ̃, ɑ̃t] nm/f assistant; (*d'université*) probationary lecturer; **assistant(e) social(e)** social worker

assisté, e [asiste] adj (*Auto*) power assisted; **~ par ordinateur** computer-assisted; **direction ~e** power steering

assister [asiste] vt (*aider*) to assist; **~ à** (*scène, événement*) to witness; (*conférence, séminaire*) to attend, be at; (*spectacle, match*) to be at, see

association [asɔsjasjɔ̃] nf association

associé, e [asɔsje] nm/f associate; (*Comm*) partner

associer [asɔsje] vt to associate; **s'associer** vi to join together; **s'~ à qn pour faire** to join (forces) with sb to do; **s'~ à** (*couleurs, qualités*) to be combined with; (*opinions, joie de qn*) to share in; **~ qn à** (*profits*) to give sb a share of; (*affaire*) to make sb a partner in; (*joie, triomphe*) to include sb in; **~ qch à** (*allier à*) to combine sth with

assoiffé, e [aswafe] adj thirsty

assommer [asɔme] vt (*étourdir, abrutir*) to knock out, stun

Assomption [asɔ̃psjɔ̃] nf: **l'~** the Assumption

● **ASSOMPTION**
●
● The **fête de l'Assomption**, more
● commonly known as **'le 15 août'** is a national
● holiday in France. Traditionally, large
● numbers of holidaymakers leave home
● on 15 August, frequently causing chaos on
● the roads.

assorti, e [asɔʀti] adj matched, matching; (*varié*) assorted; **~ à** matching; **assortiment** nm assortment, selection

assortir [asɔʀtiʀ] vt to match; **~ qch à** to match sth with; **~ qch de** to accompany sth with

assouplir [asupliʀ] vt to make supple; (*fig*) to relax; **assouplissant** nm (*fabric*) softener

assumer [asyme] vt (*fonction, emploi*) to assume, take on

assurance [asyʀɑ̃s] nf (*certitude*) assurance; (*confiance en soi*) (self-)confidence; (*contrat*) insurance (policy); (*secteur commercial*) insurance; **assurance au tiers** third-party insurance; **assurance maladie** health insurance; **assurance tous risques** (*Auto*) comprehensive insurance; **assurances sociales** ≈ National Insurance (BRIT), ≈ Social Security (US); **assurance-vie** nf life assurance ou insurance

assuré, e [asyʀe] adj (*certain: réussite, échec*) certain, sure; (*air*) assured; (*pas*) steady ▷ nm/f insured (person); **assurément** adv assuredly, most certainly

assurer [asyʀe] vt (*Finance*) to insure; (*victoire etc*) to ensure; (*frontières, pouvoir*) to make secure; (*service*) to provide, operate; **s'assurer (contre)** (*Comm*) to insure o.s. (against); **s'~ de/que** (*vérifier*) to make sure of/that; **s'~ (de)** (*aide de qn*) to secure; **~ à qn que** to assure sb that; **~ qn de** to assure sb of

asthmatique [asmatik] adj, nm/f asthmatic

asthme [asm] nm asthma

asticot [astiko] nm maggot

astre [astʀ] nm star

astrologie [astʀɔlɔʒi] nf astrology

astronaute [astʀonot] nm/f astronaut

astronomie [astʀɔnɔmi] nf astronomy

astuce [astys] nf shrewdness, astuteness; (*truc*) trick, clever way; **astucieux, -euse** adj clever

atelier [atəlje] *nm* workshop; (*de peintre*) studio

athée [ate] *adj* atheistic ▷ *nm/f* atheist

Athènes [atɛn] *n* Athens

athlète [atlɛt] *nm/f* (*Sport*) athlete; **athlétisme** *nm* athletics *sg*

atlantique [atlɑ̃tik] *adj* Atlantic ▷ *nm*: **l'(océan) A~** the Atlantic (Ocean)

atlas [atlas] *nm* atlas

atmosphère [atmɔsfɛʀ] *nf* atmosphere

atome [atom] *nm* atom; **atomique** *adj* atomic, nuclear

atomiseur [atɔmizœʀ] *nm* atomizer

atout [atu] *nm* trump; (*fig*) asset

atroce [atʀɔs] *adj* atrocious

attachant, e [ataʃɑ̃, ɑ̃t] *adj* engaging, lovable, likeable

attache [ataʃ] *nf* clip, fastener; (*fig*) tie

attacher [ataʃe] *vt* to tie up; (*étiquette*) to attach, tie on; (*ceinture*) to fasten ▷ *vi* (*poêle, riz*) to stick; **s'attacher à** (*par affection*) to become attached to; **~ qch à** to tie *ou* attach sth to

attaque [atak] *nf* attack; (*cérébrale*) stroke; (*d'épilepsie*) fit

attaquer [atake] *vt* to attack ▷ *vi* to attack; **s'attaquer à** *vt* (*personne*) to attack; (*problème*) to tackle; **~ qn en justice** to bring an action against sb, sue sb

attarder [ataʀde]: **s'attarder** *vi* to linger

atteindre [atɛ̃dʀ] *vt* (*gén*) to reach; (*blesser*) to hit; (*émouvoir*) to affect; **atteint, e** *adj* (*Méd*): **être atteint de** to be suffering from; **atteinte** *nf*: **hors d'atteinte** out of reach; **porter atteinte à** to strike a blow at

attendant [atɑ̃dɑ̃] *adv*: **en ~** meanwhile, in the meantime

attendre [atɑ̃dʀ] *vt* (*gén*) to wait for; (*être destiné ou réservé à*) to await, be in store for ▷ *vi* to wait; **s'attendre à (ce que)** to expect (that); **attendez-moi, s'il vous plaît** wait for me, please; **~ un enfant** to be expecting a baby; **~ de faire/d'être** to wait until one does/is; **attendez qu'il vienne** wait until he comes; **~ qch de** to expect sth of

Attention à ne pas traduire *attendre* par *to attend*.

attendrir [atɑ̃dʀiʀ] *vt* to move (to pity); (*viande*) to tenderize

attendu, e [atɑ̃dy] *adj* (*visiteur*) expected; (*événement*) long-awaited; **~ que** considering that, since

attentat [atɑ̃ta] *nm* assassination attempt; **attentat à la pudeur** indecent assault *no pl*; **attentat suicide** suicide bombing

attente [atɑ̃t] *nf* wait; (*espérance*) expectation

attenter [atɑ̃te]: **~ à** *vt* (*liberté*) to violate; **~ à la vie de qn** to make an attempt on sb's life

attentif, -ive [atɑ̃tif, iv] *adj* (*auditeur*) attentive; (*examen*) careful; **~ à** careful to

attention [atɑ̃sjɔ̃] *nf* attention; (*prévenance*) attention, thoughtfulness *no pl*; **à l'~ de** for the attention of; **faire ~ (à)** to be careful (of); **faire ~ (à ce) que** to be *ou* make sure that; **~!** careful!, watch out!; **~ à la voiture!** watch out for that car!; **attentionné, e** *adj* thoughtful, considerate

atténuer [atenɥe] *vt* (*douleur*) to alleviate, ease; (*couleurs*) to soften; **s'atténuer** *vi* to ease; (*violence etc*) to abate

atterrir [ateʀiʀ] *vi* to land; **atterrissage** *nm* landing

attestation [atɛstasjɔ̃] *nf* certificate

attirant, e [atiʀɑ̃, ɑ̃t] *adj* attractive, appealing

attirer [atiʀe] *vt* to attract; (*appâter*) to lure, entice; **~ qn dans un coin/vers soi** to draw sb into a corner/towards one; **~ l'attention de qn** to attract sb's attention; **~ l'attention de qn sur** to draw sb's attention to; **s'~ des ennuis** to bring trouble upon o.s., get into trouble

attitude [atityd] *nf* attitude; (*position du corps*) bearing

attraction [atʀaksjɔ̃] *nf* (*gén*) attraction; (*de cabaret, cirque*) number

attrait [atʀɛ] *nm* appeal, attraction

attraper [atʀape] *vt* (*gén*) to catch; (*habitude, amende*) to get, pick up; (*fam: duper*) to con; **se faire ~** (*fam*) to be told off

attrayant, e [atʀɛjɑ̃, ɑ̃t] *adj* attractive

attribuer [atʀibɥe] *vt* (*prix*) to award; (*rôle, tâche*) to allocate, assign; (*imputer*): **~ qch à** to attribute sth to; **s'attribuer** *vt* (*s'approprier*) to claim for o.s.

attrister [atʀiste] *vt* to sadden

attroupement [atʀupmɑ̃] *nm* crowd

attrouper [atʀupe]: **s'attrouper** *vi* to gather

au [o] *prép* +*dét* = **à** + **le**

aubaine [obɛn] *nf* godsend

aube [ob] *nf* dawn, daybreak; **à l'~** at dawn *ou* daybreak

aubépine [obepin] *nf* hawthorn

auberge [obɛʀʒ] *nf* inn; **auberge de jeunesse** youth hostel

aubergine [obɛʀʒin] *nf* aubergine

aucun, e [okœ̃, yn] *dét* no, *tournure négative* +*any*; (*positif*) any ▷ *pron* none, *tournure négative* +*any*; any(one); **sans ~ doute** without any doubt; **plus qu'~ autre** more than any other; **il le fera mieux qu'~ de nous** he'll do it better than any of us; **~ des deux** neither of the two; **~ d'entre eux** none of them

audace [odas] *nf* daring, boldness; (*péj*) audacity; **audacieux, -euse** *adj* daring, bold

au-delà [od(ə)la] *adv* beyond ▷ *nm*: **l'~** the hereafter; **~ de** beyond

au-dessous [odsu] *adv* underneath; below;

~ de under(neath), below; (*limite, somme etc*) below, under; (*dignité, condition*) below

au-dessus [odsy] *adv* above; **~ de** above

au-devant [od(ə)vɑ̃]: **~ de** *prép*: **aller ~ de** (*personne, danger*) to go (out) and meet; (*souhaits de qn*) to anticipate

audience [odjɑ̃s] *nf* audience; (*Jur: séance*) hearing

audiovisuel, le [odjovizɥɛl] *adj* audiovisual

audition [odisjɔ̃] *nf* (*ouïe, écoute*) hearing; (*Jur: de témoins*) examination; (*Mus, Théâtre: épreuve*) audition

auditoire [oditwaʀ] *nm* audience

augmentation [ɔgmɑ̃tasjɔ̃] *nf* increase; **augmentation (de salaire)** rise (in salary) (*BRIT*), (pay) raise (*US*)

augmenter [ɔgmɑ̃te] *vt* (*gén*) to increase; (*salaire, prix*) to increase, raise, put up; (*employé*) to increase the salary of ▷ *vi* to increase

augure [ogyʀ] *nm*: **de bon/mauvais ~** of good/ill omen

aujourd'hui [oʒuʀdɥi] *adv* today

aumône [omon] *nf inv* alms *sg*; **aumônier** *nm* chaplain

auparavant [oparavɑ̃] *adv* before(hand)

auprès [opʀɛ]: **~ de** *prép* next to, close to; (*recourir, s'adresser*) to; (*en comparaison de*) compared with

auquel [okɛl] *prép +pron* = **à +lequel**

aurai *etc* [ɔʀe] *vb voir* **avoir**

aurons *etc* [oʀɔ̃] *vb voir* **avoir**

aurore [ɔʀɔʀ] *nf* dawn, daybreak

ausculter [ɔskylte] *vt* to sound (the chest of)

aussi [osi] *adv* (*également*) also, too; (*de comparaison*) as ▷ *conj* therefore, consequently; **~ fort que** as strong as; **moi ~** me too

aussitôt [osito] *adv* straight away, immediately; **~ que** as soon as

austère [osteʀ] *adj* austere

austral, e [ɔstral] *adj* southern

Australie [ostrali] *nf*: **l'~** Australia; **australien, ne** *adj* Australian ▷ *nm/f*: **Australien, ne** Australian

autant [otɑ̃] *adv* (*intensité*) so much; **je ne savais pas que tu la détestais ~** I didn't know you hated her so much; (*comparatif*): **~ (que)** as much (as); (*nombre*) as many (as); **~ (de)** so much (*ou* many); as much (*ou* many); **~ partir** we (*ou you etc*) may as well leave; **~ dire que ...** one might as well say that ...; **pour ~ for all that; **d'~ plus/mieux (que)** all the more/the better (since)

autel [otɛl] *nm* altar

auteur [otœʀ] *nm* author

authentique [otɑ̃tik] *adj* authentic, genuine

auto [oto] *nf* car

auto...: **autobiographie** *nf* autobiography;

autobronzant *nm* self-tanning cream (*or* lotion *etc*); **autobus** *nm* bus; **autocar** *nm* coach

autochtone [otɔktɔn] *nm/f* native

auto...: **autocollant, e** *adj* self-adhesive; (*enveloppe*) self-seal ▷ *nm* sticker; **autocuiseur** *nm* pressure cooker; **autodéfense** *nf* self-defence; **autodidacte** *nm/f* self-taught person; **auto-école** *nf* driving school; **autographe** *nm* autograph

automate [ɔtɔmat] *nm* (*machine*) (automatic) machine

automatique [ɔtɔmatik] *adj* automatic ▷ *nm*: **l'~** direct dialling

automne [ɔtɔn] *nm* autumn (*BRIT*), fall (*US*)

automobile [ɔtɔmɔbil] *adj* motor *cpd*, car *cpd* ▷ *nf* (motor) car; **automobiliste** *nm/f* motorist

autonome [ɔtɔnɔm] *adj* autonomous; **autonomie** *nf* autonomy; (*Pol*) self-government, autonomy

autopsie [ɔtɔpsi] *nf* post-mortem (examination), autopsy

autoradio [otoʀadjo] *nm* car radio

autorisation [ɔtɔʀizasjɔ̃] *nf* permission, authorization; (*papiers*) permit

autorisé, e [ɔtɔʀize] *adj* (*opinion, sources*) authoritative

autoriser [ɔtɔʀize] *vt* to give permission for, authorize; (*fig*) to allow (of)

autoritaire [ɔtɔʀiteʀ] *adj* authoritarian

autorité [ɔtɔʀite] *nf* authority; **faire ~** to be authoritative; **les ~s** the authorities

autoroute [otoʀut] *nf* motorway (*BRIT*), highway (*US*); **~ l'information** (*Inform*) information superhighway

⬤ **AUTOROUTE**

⬤
⬤ Motorways in France, indicated by blue
⬤ road signs with the letter A followed by a
⬤ number, are toll roads. The speed limit is
⬤ 130 km/h (110 km/h when it is raining). At
⬤ the tollgate, the lanes marked 'réservé' and
⬤ with an orange 't' are reserved for people
⬤ who subscribe to 'télépéage', an electronic
⬤ payment system.

auto-stop [otostɔp] *nm*: **faire de l'~** to hitch-hike; **prendre qn en ~** to give sb a lift; **auto-stoppeur, -euse** *nm/f* hitch-hiker

autour [otuʀ] *adv* around; **~ de** around; **tout ~** all around

 MOT-CLÉ

autre [otʀ] *adj* **1** (*différent*) other, different; **je préférerais un autre verre** I'd prefer another *ou* a different glass

2 (*supplémentaire*) other; **je voudrais un autre verre d'eau** I'd like another glass of water
3: **autre chose** something else; **autre part** somewhere else; **d'autre part** on the other hand
▷ *pron*: **un autre** another (one); **nous/vous autres** us/you; **d'autres** others; **l'autre** the other (one); **les autres** the others; (*autrui*) others; **l'un et l'autre** both of them; **se détester l'un l'autre/les uns les autres** to hate each other *ou* one another; **d'une semaine à l'autre** from one week to the next; (*incessamment*) any week now; **entre autres** (*personnes*) among others; (*choses*) among other things

autrefois [otʀəfwa] *adv* in the past
autrement [otʀəmɑ̃] *adv* differently; (*d'une manière différente*) in another way; (*sinon*) otherwise; **~ dit** in other words
Autriche [otʀiʃ] *nf*: **l'~** Austria; **autrichien, ne** *adj* Austrian ▷ *nm/f*: **Autrichien, ne** Austrian
autruche [otʀyʃ] *nf* ostrich
aux [o] *prép +dét* = **à +les**
auxiliaire [ɔksiljɛʀ] *adj, nm/f* auxiliary
auxquelles [okɛl] *prép +pron* = **à +lesquelles**
auxquels [okɛl] *prép +pron* = **à +lesquels**
avalanche [avalɑ̃ʃ] *nf* avalanche
avaler [avale] *vt* to swallow
avance [avɑ̃s] *nf* (*de troupes etc*) advance; progress; (*d'argent*) advance; (*sur un concurrent*) lead; (*amoureuses*) advances; **(être) en ~** (to be) early; (*sur un programme*) (to be) ahead of schedule; **à l'~, d'~** in advance
avancé, e [avɑ̃se] *adj* advanced; (*travail*) well on, well under way
avancement [avɑ̃smɑ̃] *nm* (*professionnel*) promotion
avancer [avɑ̃se] *vi* to move forward, advance; (*projet, travail*) to make progress; (*montre, réveil*) to be fast; to gain ▷ *vt* to move forward, advance; (*argent*) to advance; (*montre, pendule*) to put forward; **s'avancer** *vi* to move forward, advance; (*fig*) to commit o.s.
avant [avɑ̃] *prép, adv* before ▷ *adj inv*: **siège/roue ~** front seat/wheel ▷ *nm* (*d'un véhicule, bâtiment*) front; (*Sport: joueur*) forward; **~ qu'il (ne) parte** before he goes *ou* leaves; **~ de partir** before leaving; **~ tout** (*surtout*) above all; **à l'~** (*dans un véhicule*) in (the) front; **en ~** (*se pencher, tomber*) forward(s); **partir en ~** to go on ahead; **en ~ de** in front of
avantage [avɑ̃taʒ] *nm* advantage; **avantages sociaux** fringe benefits; **avantager** *vt* (*favoriser*) to favour; (*embellir*) to flatter; **avantageux, -euse** *adj* (*prix*) attractive
avant...: **avant-bras** *nm inv* forearm; **avant-coureur** *adj inv*: **signe avant-coureur** advance indication *ou* sign; **avant-dernier, -ière** *adj, nm/f* next to last, last but one; **avant-goût** *nm* foretaste; **avant-hier** *adv* the day before yesterday; **avant-première** *nf* (*de film*) preview; **avant-veille** *nf*: **l'avant-veille** two days before

avare [avaʀ] *adj* miserly, avaricious ▷ *nm/f* miser; **~ de** (*compliments etc*) sparing of
avec [avɛk] *prép* with; (*à l'égard de*) to(wards), with; **et ~ ça?** (*dans magasin*) anything else?
avenir [avniʀ] *nm* future; **à l'~** in future; **politicien/métier d'~** politician/job with prospects *ou* a future
aventure [avɑ̃tyʀ] *nf* adventure; (*amoureuse*) affair; **aventureux, -euse** *adj* adventurous, venturesome; (*projet*) risky, chancy
avenue [avny] *nf* avenue
avérer [aveʀe]: **s'avérer** *vb +attrib* to prove (to be)
averse [avɛʀs] *nf* shower
averti, e [avɛʀti] *adj* (well-)informed
avertir [avɛʀtiʀ] *vt*: **~ qn (de qch/que)** to warn sb (of sth/that); (*renseigner*) to inform sb (of sth/that); **avertissement** *nm* warning; **avertisseur** *nm* horn, siren
aveu, x [avø] *nm* confession
aveugle [avœgl] *adj* blind ▷ *nm/f* blind man/woman
aviation [avjasjɔ̃] *nf* aviation; (*sport*) flying; (*Mil*) air force
avide [avid] *adj* eager; (*péj*) greedy, grasping
avion [avjɔ̃] *nm* (aero)plane (BRIT), (air)plane (US); **aller (quelque part) en ~** to go (somewhere) by plane, fly (somewhere); **par ~** by airmail; **avion à réaction** jet (plane)
aviron [aviʀɔ̃] *nm* oar; (*sport*): **l'~** rowing
avis [avi] *nm* opinion; (*notification*) notice; **à mon ~** in my opinion; **changer d'~** to change one's mind; **jusqu'à nouvel ~** until further notice
aviser [avize] *vt* (*informer*): **~ qn de/que** to advise *ou* inform sb of/that ▷ *vi* to think about things, assess the situation; **nous ~ons sur place** we'll work something out once we're there; **s'~ de qch/que** to become suddenly aware of sth/that; **s'~ de faire** to take it into one's head to do
avocat, e [avɔka, at] *nm/f* (*Jur*) barrister (BRIT), lawyer ▷ *nm* (*Culin*) avocado (pear); **~ de la défense** counsel for the defence; **avocat général** assistant public prosecutor
avoine [avwan] *nf* oats *pl*

 MOT-CLÉ

avoir [avwaʀ] *nm* assets *pl*, resources *pl*; (*Comm*) credit
▷ *vt* **1** (*posséder*) to have; **elle a 2 enfants/une belle maison** she has (got) 2 children/a lovely

house; **il a les yeux bleus** he has (got) blue eyes; **vous avez du sel?** do you have any salt?; **avoir du courage/de la patience** to be brave/patient

2 (âge, dimensions) to be; **il a 3 ans** he is 3 (years old); **le mur a 3 mètres de haut** the wall is 3 metres high; voir aussi **faim**; **peur** etc

3 (fam: duper) to do, have; **on vous a eu!** (dupé) you've been done ou had!; (fait une plaisanterie) we ou they had you there

4: **en avoir après** ou **contre qn** to have a grudge against sb; **en avoir assez** to be fed up; **j'en ai pour une demi-heure** it'll take me half an hour

5 (obtenir, attraper) to get; **j'ai réussi à avoir mon train** I managed to get ou catch my train; **j'ai réussi à avoir le renseignement qu'il me fallait** I managed to get (hold of) the information I needed

6 (éprouver): **avoir de la peine** to be ou feel sad

▷ vb aux **1** to have; **avoir mangé/dormi** to have eaten/slept

2 (avoir + à + infinitif): **avoir à faire qch** to have to do sth; **vous n'avez qu'à lui demander** you only have to ask him

▷ vb impers **1**: **il y a** (+ singulier) there is; (+ pluriel) there are; **il y avait du café/des gâteaux** there was coffee/there were cakes; **qu'y-a-t-il?, qu'est-ce qu'il y a?** what's the matter?, what is it?; **il doit y avoir une explication** there must be an explanation; **il n'y a qu'à ...** we (ou you etc) will just have to ...; **il ne peut y en avoir qu'un** there can only be one

2 (temporel): **il y a 10 ans** 10 years ago; **il y a 10 ans/longtemps que je le sais** I've known it for 10 years/a long time; **il y a 10 ans qu'il est arrivé** it's 10 years since he arrived

avortement [avɔʀtəmã] nm abortion
avouer [avwe] vt (crime, défaut) to confess (to); **~ avoir fait/que** to admit ou confess to having done/that
avril [avʀil] nm April
axe [aks] nm axis; (de roue etc) axle; (fig) main line; **axe routier** main road, trunk road (BRIT), highway (US)
ayons etc [ejɔ̃] vb voir **avoir**

bâbord [babɔʀ] nm: **à ~** to port, on the port side
baby-foot [babifut] nm table football
bac [bak] abr m = **baccalauréat** ▷ nm (récipient) tub
baccalauréat [bakalɔʀea] nm high school diploma
bâcler [bakle] vt to botch (up)
baffe [baf] (fam) nf slap, clout
bafouiller [bafuje] vi, vt to stammer
bagage [bagaʒ] nm piece of luggage; (connaissances) background, knowledge; **nos ~s ne sont pas arrivés** our luggage hasn't arrived; **bagage à main** piece of hand-luggage
bagarre [bagaʀ] nf fight, brawl; **bagarrer: se bagarrer** vi to have a fight ou scuffle, fight
bagnole [baɲɔl] (fam) nf car
bague [bag] nf ring; **bague de fiançailles** engagement ring
baguette [baget] nf stick; (cuisine chinoise) chopstick; (de chef d'orchestre) baton; (pain) stick of (French) bread; **baguette magique** magic wand
baie [bɛ] nf (Géo) bay; (fruit) berry; **baie (vitrée)** picture window
baignade [bɛɲad] nf bathing; **"~ interdite"** "no bathing"
baigner [bɛɲe] vt (bébé) to bath; **se baigner** vi to have a swim, go swimming ou bathing;

baignoire nf bath(tub)

bail [baj, bo] (pl **baux**) nm lease

bâiller [baje] vi to yawn; (être ouvert) to gape

bain [bɛ̃] nm bath; **prendre un ~** to have a bath; **se mettre dans le ~** (fig) to get into it ou things; **bain de bouche** mouthwash; **bain moussant** bubble bath; **bain de soleil**: **prendre un bain de soleil** to sunbathe; **bain-marie** nm: **faire chauffer au bain-marie** (boîte etc) to immerse in boiling water

baiser [beze] nm kiss ▷ vt (main, front) to kiss; (fam!) to screw (!)

baisse [bɛs] nf fall, drop; **être en ~** to be falling, be declining

baisser [bese] vt to lower; (radio, chauffage) to turn down ▷ vi to fall, drop, go down; (vue, santé) to fail, dwindle; **se baisser** vi to bend down

bal [bal] nm dance; (grande soirée) ball; **bal costumé** fancy-dress ball

balade [balad] (fam) nf (à pied) walk, stroll; (en voiture) drive; **balader** (fam): **se balader** vi to go for a walk ou stroll; to go for a drive; **baladeur** nm personal stereo, Walkman®

balai [balɛ] nm broom, brush

balance [balɑ̃s] nf scales pl; (signe): **la B~** Libra; **balance commerciale** balance of trade

balancer [balɑ̃se] vt to swing; (fam: lancer) to fling, chuck; (: jeter) to chuck out; **se balancer** vi to swing, rock; **se ~ de** (fam) not to care about; **balançoire** nf swing; (sur pivot) seesaw

balayer [baleje] vt (feuilles etc) to sweep up, brush up; (pièce) to sweep; (objections) to sweep aside; (suj: radar) to scan; **balayeur, -euse** nm/f roadsweeper

balbutier [balbysje] vi, vt to stammer

balcon [balkɔ̃] nm balcony; (Théâtre) dress circle; **avez-vous une chambre avec ~?** do you have a room with a balcony?

Bâle [bɑl] n Basle, Basel

Baléares [baleaʁ] nfpl: **les ~** the Balearic Islands, the Balearics

baleine [balɛn] nf whale

balise [baliz] nf (Navig) beacon; (marker) buoy; (Aviat) runway light, beacon; (Auto, Ski) sign, marker; **baliser** vt to mark out (with lights etc)

balle [bal] nf (de fusil) bullet; (de sport) ball; (fam: franc) franc

ballerine [balʁin] nf (danseuse) ballet dancer; (chaussure) ballet shoe

ballet [balɛ] nm ballet

ballon [balɔ̃] nm (de sport) ball; (jouet, Aviat) balloon; **ballon de football** football

balnéaire [balneɛʁ] adj seaside cpd; **station ~** seaside resort

balustrade [balystʁad] nf railings pl, handrail

bambin [bɑ̃bɛ̃] nm little child

bambou [bɑ̃bu] nm bamboo

banal, e [banal] adj banal, commonplace; (péj) trite; **banalité** nf banality

banane [banan] nf banana; (sac) waist-bag, bum-bag

banc [bɑ̃] nm seat, bench; (de poissons) shoal; **banc d'essai** (fig) testing ground

bancaire [bɑ̃kɛʁ] adj banking; (chèque, carte) bank cpd

bancal, e [bɑ̃kal] adj wobbly

bandage [bɑ̃daʒ] nm bandage

bande [bɑ̃d] nf (de tissu etc) strip; (Méd) bandage; (motif) stripe; (magnétique etc) tape; (groupe) band; (: péj) bunch; **faire ~ à part** to keep to o.s.; **bande dessinée** comic strip; **bande sonore** sound track

bande-annonce [bɑ̃danɔ̃s] nf trailer

bandeau, x [bɑ̃do] nm headband; (sur les yeux) blindfold

bander [bɑ̃de] vt (blessure) to bandage; **~ les yeux à qn** to blindfold sb

bandit [bɑ̃di] nm bandit

bandoulière [bɑ̃duljɛʁ] nf: **en ~** (slung ou worn) across the shoulder

Bangladesh [bɑ̃gladɛʃ] nm: **le ~** Bangladesh

banlieue [bɑ̃ljø] nf suburbs pl; **lignes/ quartiers de ~** suburban lines/areas; **trains de ~** commuter trains

bannir [baniʁ] vt to banish

banque [bɑ̃k] nf bank; (activités) banking; **banque de données** data bank

banquet [bɑ̃kɛ] nm dinner; (d'apparat) banquet

banquette [bɑ̃kɛt] nf seat

banquier [bɑ̃kje] nm banker

banquise [bɑ̃kiz] nf ice field

baptême [batɛm] nm christening; baptism; **baptême de l'air** first flight

baptiser [batize] vt to baptize, christen

bar [baʁ] nm bar

baraque [baʁak] nf shed; (fam) house; (dans une fête foraine) stall, booth; **baraqué, e** (fam) adj well-built, hefty

barbare [baʁbaʁ] adj barbaric

barbe [baʁb] nf beard; **la ~!** (fam) damn it!; **quelle ~!** (fam) what a drag ou bore!; **à la ~ de qn** under sb's nose; **barbe à papa** candy-floss (BRIT), cotton candy (US)

barbelé [baʁbəle] adj, nm: **(fil de fer) ~** barbed wire no pl

barbiturique [baʁbityʁik] nm barbiturate

barbouiller [baʁbuje] vt to daub; **avoir l'estomac barbouillé** to feel queasy

barbu, e [baʁby] adj bearded

barder [baʁde] (fam) vi: **ça va ~** sparks will fly, things are going to get hot

barème [baʁɛm] nm (Scol) scale; (table de référence) table

baril [baʁi(l)] nm barrel; (poudre) keg

bariolé, e [baʁjɔle] adj gaudily-coloured

baromètre [baʀɔmɛtʀ] *nm* barometer

baron, ne [baʀɔ̃] *nm/f* baron(ess)

baroque [baʀɔk] *adj* (Art) baroque; (fig) weird

barque [baʀk] *nf* small boat

barquette [baʀkɛt] *nf* (pour repas) tray; (pour fruits) punnet

barrage [baʀaʒ] *nm* dam; (sur route) roadblock, barricade

barre [baʀ] *nf* bar; (Navig) helm; (écrite) line, stroke

barreau, x [baʀo] *nm* bar; (Jur): **le ~** the Bar

barrer [baʀe] *vt* (route etc) to block; (mot) to cross out; (chèque) to cross (BRIT); (Navig) to steer; **se barrer** (fam) *vi* to clear off

barrette [baʀɛt] *nf* (pour cheveux) (hair) slide (BRIT) ou clip (US)

barricader [baʀikade]: **se barricader** *vi* to barricade o.s.

barrière [baʀjɛʀ] *nf* fence; (obstacle) barrier; (porte) gate

barrique [baʀik] *nf* barrel, cask

bar-tabac [baʀtaba] *nm* bar (which sells tobacco and stamps)

bas, basse [ba, bas] *adj* low ▷ *nm* bottom, lower part; (chaussette) stocking ▷ *adv* low; (parler) softly; **au ~ mot** at the lowest estimate; **en ~** down below; (d'une liste, d'un mur etc) at/to the bottom; (dans une maison) downstairs; **en ~ de** at the bottom of; **un enfant en ~ âge** a young child; **à ~ ...!** down with ...!

bas-côté [bakote] *nm* (de route) verge (BRIT), shoulder (US)

basculer [baskyle] *vi* to fall over, topple (over); (benne) to tip up ▷ *vt* (contenu) to tip out; (benne) to tip up

base [baz] *nf* base; (Pol) rank and file; (fondement, principe) basis; **de ~** basic; **à ~ de café** etc coffee etc -based; **base de données** database; **baser** *vt* to base; **se baser sur** *vt* (preuves) to base one's argument on

bas-fond [bafɔ̃] *nm* (Navig) shallow; **bas-fonds** *nmpl* (fig) dregs

basilic [bazilik] *nm* (Culin) basil

basket [baskɛt] *nm* trainer (BRIT), sneaker (US); (aussi: **~-ball**) basketball

basque [bask] *adj* Basque ▷ *nm/f*: **B~** Basque; **le Pays Basque** the Basque Country

basse [bas] *adj voir* **bas** ▷ *nf* (Mus) bass; **basse-cour** *nf* farmyard

bassin [basɛ̃] *nm* (pièce d'eau) pond, pool; (de fontaine;: Géo) basin; (Anat) pelvis; (portuaire) dock

bassine [basin] *nf* (ustensile) basin; (contenu) bowl(ful)

basson [basɔ̃] *nm* bassoon

bat [ba] *vb voir* **battre**

bataille [bataj] *nf* (Mil) battle; (rixe) fight; **elle avait les cheveux en ~** her hair was a mess

bateau, x [bato] *nm* boat, ship; **bateau-mouche** *nm* passenger pleasure boat (on the Seine)

bâti, e [bati] *adj*: **bien ~** well-built; **terrain ~** piece of land that has been built on

bâtiment [batimɑ̃] *nm* building; (Navig) ship, vessel; (industrie) building trade

bâtir [batiʀ] *vt* to build

bâtisse [batis] *nf* building

bâton [batɔ̃] *nm* stick; **parler à ~s rompus** to chat about this and that

bats [ba] *vb voir* **battre**

battement [batmɑ̃] *nm* (de cœur) beat; (intervalle) interval; **10 minutes de ~** 10 minutes to spare

batterie [batʀi] *nf* (Mil, Élec) battery; (Mus) drums *pl*, drum kit; **batterie de cuisine** pots and pans *pl*, kitchen utensils *pl*

batteur [batœʀ] *nm* (Mus) drummer; (appareil) whisk

battre [batʀ] *vt* to beat; (blé) to thresh; (passer au peigne fin) to scour; (cartes) to shuffle ▷ *vi* (cœur) to beat; (volets etc) to bang, rattle; **se battre** *vi* to fight; **~ la mesure** to beat time; **~ son plein** to be at its height, be going full swing; **~ des mains** to clap one's hands

baume [bom] *nm* balm

bavard, e [bavaʀ, aʀd] *adj* (very) talkative; gossipy; **bavarder** *vi* to chatter; (commérer) to gossip; (divulguer un secret) to blab

baver [bave] *vi* to dribble; (chien) to slobber; **en ~** (fam) to have a hard time (of it)

bavoir [bavwaʀ] *nm* bib

bavure [bavyʀ] *nf* smudge; (fig) hitch; (policière etc) blunder

bazar [bazaʀ] *nm* general store; (fam) jumble; **bazarder** (fam) *vt* to chuck out

BCBG *sigle adj* (= bon chic bon genre) preppy, smart and trendy

BD *sigle f* = **bande dessinée**

bd *abr* = **boulevard**

béant, e [beɑ̃, ɑ̃t] *adj* gaping

beau, bel, belle [bo, bɛl] (*mpl* **~x**) *adj* beautiful, lovely; (homme) handsome; (femme) beautiful ▷ *adv*: **il fait ~** the weather's fine ▷ *nm*: **faire le ~** (chien) to sit up and beg; **un ~ jour** one (fine) day; **de plus belle** more than ever, even more; **on a ~ essayer** however hard we try; **bel et bien** well and truly; **le plus ~ c'est que ...** the best of it is that ...

 MOT-CLÉ

beaucoup [boku] *adv* **1** a lot; **il boit beaucoup** he drinks a lot; **il ne boit pas beaucoup** he doesn't drink much *ou* a lot **2** (suivi de plus, trop etc) much, a lot; **il est beaucoup plus grand** he is much *ou* a lot taller; **c'est beaucoup plus cher** it's a lot *ou* much more expensive; **il a beaucoup plus de temps que moi** he has much ou a lot more time than me; **il y a beaucoup plus de touristes ici** there are a lot ou many more tourists here; **beaucoup trop vite** much too fast; **il fume beaucoup trop** he smokes far too much

3: **beaucoup de** (*nombre*) many, a lot of; (*quantité*) a lot of; **beaucoup d'étudiants/de touristes** a lot of ou many students/tourists; **beaucoup de courage** a lot of courage; **il n'a pas beaucoup d'argent** he hasn't got much ou at lot of money

4: **de beaucoup** by far

beau...: **beau-fils** nm son-in-law; (*remariage*) stepson; **beau-frère** nm brother-in-law; **beau-père** nm father-in-law; (*remariage*) stepfather

beauté [bote] nf beauty; **de toute ~** beautiful; **finir qch en ~** to complete sth brilliantly

beaux-arts [bozaʀ] nmpl fine arts

beaux-parents [bopaʀɑ̃] nmpl wife's/husband's family, in-laws

bébé [bebe] nm baby

bec [bɛk] nm beak, bill; (*de théière*) spout; (*de casserole*) lip; (*fam*) mouth; **bec de gaz** (street) gaslamp

bêche [bɛʃ] nf spade; **bêcher** vt to dig

bedaine [bədɛn] nf paunch

bedonnant, e [bədɔnɑ̃, ɑ̃t] adj potbellied

bée [be] adj: **bouche ~** gaping

bégayer [begeje] vt, vi to stammer

beige [bɛʒ] adj beige

beignet [bɛɲɛ] nm fritter

bel [bɛl] adj voir **beau**

bêler [bele] vi to bleat

belette [bəlɛt] nf weasel

belge [bɛlʒ] adj Belgian ▷ nm/f: **B~** Belgian

Belgique [bɛlʒik] nf: **la ~** Belgium

bélier [belje] nm ram; (*signe*): **le B~** Aries

belle [bɛl] adj voir **beau** ▷ nf (*Sport*): **la ~** the decider; **belle-fille** nf daughter-in-law; (*remariage*) stepdaughter; **belle-mère** nf mother-in-law; stepmother; **belle-sœur** nf sister-in-law

belvédère [bɛlvedɛʀ] nm panoramic viewpoint (*or small building there*)

bémol [bemɔl] nm (*Mus*) flat

bénédiction [benediksjɔ̃] nf blessing

bénéfice [benefis] nm (*Comm*) profit; (*avantage*) benefit; **bénéficier**: **bénéficier de** vt to enjoy; (*situation*) to benefit by ou from; **bénéfique** adj beneficial

Benelux [benelyks] nm: **le ~** Benelux, the Benelux countries

bénévole [benevɔl] adj voluntary, unpaid

bénin, -igne [benɛ̃, iɲ] adj minor, mild; (*tumeur*) benign

bénir [beniʀ] vt to bless; **bénit, e** adj

consecrated; **eau bénite** holy water

benne [bɛn] nf skip; (*de téléphérique*) (cable) car; **benne à ordures** (*amovible*) skip

béquille [bekij] nf crutch; (*de bicyclette*) stand

berceau, x [bɛʀso] nm cradle, crib

bercer [bɛʀse] vt to rock, cradle; (*suj: musique etc*) to lull; **~ qn de** (*promesses etc*) to delude sb with; **berceuse** nf lullaby

béret [beʀɛ] nm (*aussi*: **~ basque**) beret

berge [bɛʀʒ] nf bank

berger, -ère [bɛʀʒe, ɛʀ] nm/f shepherd(-ess); **berger allemand** alsatian (*BRIT*), German shepherd

Berlin [bɛʀlɛ̃] n Berlin

Bermudes [bɛʀmyd] nfpl: **les (îles) ~** Bermuda

Berne [bɛʀn(ə)] n Bern

berner [bɛʀne] vt to fool

besogne [bəzɔɲ] nf work no pl, job

besoin [bəzwɛ̃] nm need; **avoir ~ de qch/faire qch** to need sth/to do sth; **au ~** if need be; **le ~** (*pauvreté*) need, want; **être dans le ~** to be in need ou want; **faire ses ~s** to relieve o.s.

bestiole [bɛstjɔl] nf (tiny) creature

bétail [betaj] nm livestock, cattle pl

bête [bɛt] nf animal; (*bestiole*) insect, creature ▷ adj stupid, silly; **il cherche la petite ~** he's being pernickety ou over fussy; **bête noire** pet hate; **bête sauvage** wild beast ou animal

bêtise [betiz] nf stupidity; (*action*) stupid thing (to say ou do)

béton [betɔ̃] nm concrete; **(en) ~** (*alibi, argument*) cast iron; **béton armé** reinforced concrete

betterave [bɛtʀav] nf beetroot (*BRIT*), beet (*US*); **betterave sucrière** sugar beet

Beur [bœʀ] nm/f person of North African origin living in France

beurre [bœʀ] nm butter; **beurrer** vt to butter; **beurrier** nm butter dish

biais [bjɛ] nm (*moyen*) device, expedient; (*aspect*) angle; **en ~, de ~** (*obliquement*) at an angle; **par le ~ de** by means of

bibelot [biblo] nm trinket, curio

biberon [bibʀɔ̃] nm (feeding) bottle; **nourrir au ~** to bottle-feed

bible [bibl] nf bible

biblio... [bibl] préfixe: **bibliobus** nm mobile library van; **bibliothécaire** nm/f librarian; **bibliothèque** nf library; (*meuble*) bookcase

bic® [bik] nm Biro®

bicarbonate [bikaʀbɔnat] nm: **~ (de soude)** bicarbonate of soda

biceps [bisɛps] nm biceps

biche [biʃ] nf doe

bicolore [bikɔlɔʀ] adj two-coloured

bicoque [bikɔk] (*péj*) nf shack

bicyclette [bisiklɛt] nf bicycle

bidet [bidɛ] nm bidet
bidon [bidɔ̃] nm can ▷ adj inv (fam) phoney
bidonville [bidɔ̃vil] nm shanty town
bidule [bidyl] (fam) nm thingumajig

○ **MOT-CLÉ**

bien [bjɛ̃] nm 1 (avantage, profit): **faire du bien à qn** to do sb good; **dire du bien de** to speak well of; **c'est pour son bien** it's for his own good
2 (possession, patrimoine) possession, property; **son bien le plus précieux** his most treasured possession; **avoir du bien** to have property; **biens (de consommation** etc) (consumer etc) goods
3 (moral): **le bien** good; **distinguer le bien du mal** to tell good from evil
▷ adv 1 (de façon satisfaisante) well; **elle travaille/mange bien** she works/eats well; **croyant bien faire, je/il ...** thinking I/he was doing the right thing, I/he ...; **tiens-toi bien!** (assieds-toi correctement) sit up straight!; (debout) stand up straight!; (sois sage) behave yourself!; (prépare-toi) wait for it!; **c'est bien fait!** it serves him (ou her etc) right!
2 (valeur intensive) quite; **bien jeune** quite young; **bien assez** quite enough; **bien mieux** (very) much better; **j'espère bien y aller** I do hope to go; **je veux bien le faire** (concession) I'm quite willing to do it; **il faut bien le faire** it has to be done; **Paul est bien venu, n'est-ce pas?** Paul did come, didn't he?; **où peut-il bien être passé?** where can he have got to?
3 (beaucoup): **bien du temps/des gens** quite a time/a number of people
4 (au moins) at least; **cela fait bien deux ans que je ne l'ai pas vu** I haven't seen him for at least ou a good two years
▷ adj inv 1 (en bonne forme, à l'aise): **je me sens bien** I feel fine; **je ne me sens pas bien** I don't feel well; **on est bien dans ce fauteuil** this chair is very comfortable
2 (joli, beau) good-looking; **tu es bien dans cette robe** you look good in that dress
3 (satisfaisant) good; **elle est bien, cette maison/secrétaire** it's a good house/she's a good secretary; **c'est bien?** is that ou is it O.K.?; **c'est très bien (comme ça)** it's fine (like that)
4 (moralement) right; (: personne) good, nice; (respectable) respectable; **ce n'est pas bien de ...** it's not right to ...; **elle est bien, cette femme** she's a nice woman, she's a good sort; **des gens bien** respectable people
5 (en bons termes): **être bien avec qn** to be on good terms with sb
▷ préfixe: **bien-aimé, e** adj, nm/f beloved; **bien-être** nm well-being; **bienfaisance** nf charity; **bienfait** nm act of generosity, benefaction;

(de la science etc) benefit; **bienfaiteur, -trice** nm/f benefactor/benefactress; **bien-fondé** nm soundness; **bien que** conj (al)though; **bien sûr** adv certainly

bientôt [bjɛ̃to] adv soon; **à ~** see you soon
bienveillant, e [bjɛ̃vɛjɑ̃, ɑ̃t] adj kindly
bienvenu, e [bjɛ̃vny] adj welcome; **bienvenue** nf: **souhaiter la bienvenue à** to welcome; **bienvenue à** welcome to
bière [bjɛʀ] nf (boisson) beer; (cercueil) bier; **bière blonde** lager; **bière brune** brown ale (BRIT), dark beer (US); **bière (à la) pression** draught beer
bifteck [biftɛk] nm steak
bigorneau, x [bigɔʀno] nm winkle
bigoudi [bigudi] nm curler
bijou, x [biʒu] nm jewel; **bijouterie** nf jeweller's (shop); **bijoutier, -ière** nm/f jeweller
bikini [bikini] nm bikini
bilan [bilɑ̃] nm (fig) (net) outcome; (: de victimes) toll; (Comm) balance sheet(s); **un ~ de santé** a (medical) checkup; **faire le ~ de** to assess, review; **déposer son ~** to file a bankruptcy statement
bile [bil] nf bile; **se faire de la ~** (fam) to worry o.s. sick
bilieux, -euse [biljø, øz] adj bilious; (fig: colérique) testy
bilingue [bilɛ̃g] adj bilingual
billard [bijaʀ] nm (jeu) billiards sg; (table) billiard table
bille [bij] nf (gén) ball; (du jeu de billes) marble
billet [bijɛ] nm (aussi: ~ de banque) (bank)note; (de cinéma, de bus etc) ticket; (courte lettre) note; **billet électronique** e-ticket; **billetterie** nf ticket office; (distributeur) ticket machine; (Banque) cash dispenser
billion [biljɔ̃] nm billion (BRIT), trillion (US)
bimensuel, le [bimɑ̃sɥɛl] adj bimonthly
bio [bjɔ] adj inv organic
bio... [bjɔ] préfixe bio...; **biochimie** nf biochemistry; **biographie** nf biography; **biologie** nf biology; **biologique** adj biological; (produits, aliments) organic; **biométrie** nf biometrics; **biotechnologie** nf biotechnology; **bioterrorisme** nm bioterrorism
Birmanie [biʀmani] nf Burma
bis [bis] adv: **12 ~** 12a ou A ▷ excl, nm encore
biscotte [biskɔt] nf toasted bread (sold in packets)
biscuit [biskɥi] nm biscuit (BRIT), cookie (US)
bise [biz] nf (fam: baiser) kiss; (vent) North wind; **grosses ~s (de)** (sur lettre) love and kisses (from)
bisexuel, le [bisɛksɥɛl] adj bisexual
bisou [bizu] (fam) nm kiss
bissextile [bisɛkstil] adj: **année ~** leap year

bistro(t) [bistʀo] *nm* bistro, café
bitume [bitym] *nm* asphalt
bizarre [bizaʀ] *adj* strange, odd
blague [blag] *nf* (*propos*) joke; (*farce*) trick; **sans ~!** no kidding!; **blaguer** *vi* to joke
blaireau, x [blɛʀo] *nm* (*Zool*) badger; (*brosse*) shaving brush
blâme [blɑm] *nm* blame; (*sanction*) reprimand; **blâmer** *vt* to blame
blanc, blanche [blɑ̃, blɑ̃ʃ] *adj* white; (*non imprimé*) blank ▷ *nm/f* white, white man(-woman) ▷ *nm* (*couleur*) white; (*espace non écrit*) blank; (*aussi:* **~ d'œuf**) (egg-)white; (*aussi:* **~ de poulet**) breast, white meat; (*aussi:* **vin ~**) white wine; (*chèque* **en ~**) blank cheque; **à ~** (*chauffer*) white-hot; (*tirer, charger*) with blanks; **blanche** *nf* (*Mus*) minim (BRIT), half-note (US); **blancheur** *nf* whiteness
blanchir [blɑ̃ʃiʀ] *vt* (*gén*) to whiten; (*linge*) to launder; (*Culin*) to blanch; (*fig: disculper*) to clear ▷ *vi* (*cheveux*) to go white; **blanchisserie** *nf* laundry
blason [blazɔ̃] *nm* coat of arms
blasphème [blasfɛm] *nm* blasphemy
blazer [blazɛʀ] *nm* blazer
blé [ble] *nm* wheat; **blé noir** buckwheat
bled [blɛd] *nm* (*péj*) hole
blême [blɛm] *adj* pale
blessé, e [blese] *adj* injured ▷ *nm/f* injured person, casualty
blesser [blese] *vt* to injure; (*délibérément*) to wound; (*offenser*) to hurt; **se blesser** to injure o.s.; **se ~ au pied** to injure one's foot; **blessure** *nf* (*accidentelle*) injury; (*intentionnelle*) wound
bleu, e [blø] *adj* blue; (*bifteck*) very rare ▷ *nm* (*couleur*) blue; (*contusion*) bruise; (*vêtement: aussi:* **~s**) overalls *pl*; (*fromage*) blue cheese; **bleu marine** navy blue; **bleuet** *nm* cornflower
bloc [blɔk] *nm* (*de pierre etc*) block; (*de papier à lettres*) pad; (*ensemble*) group, block; **serré à ~** tightened right down; **en ~** as a whole; **bloc opératoire** operating ou theatre block; **blocage** *nm* (*des prix*) freezing; (*Psych*) hang-up; **bloc-notes** *nm* note pad
blog, blogue [blɔg] *nm* blog; **bloguer** *vi* to blog
blond, e [blɔ̃, blɔ̃d] *adj* fair, blond; (*sable, blés*) golden
bloquer [blɔke] *vt* (*passage*) to block; (*pièce mobile*) to jam; (*crédits, compte*) to freeze
blottir [blɔtiʀ]: **se blottir** *vi* to huddle up
blouse [bluz] *nf* overall
blouson [bluzɔ̃] *nm* blouson jacket; **blouson noir** (*fig*) ≈ rocker
bluff [blœf] *nm* bluff
bobine [bɔbin] *nf* reel; (*Élec*) coil
bobo [bobo] *abr m/f* = *bourgeois bohème* (*fam*) boho

bocal, -aux [bɔkal, o] *nm* jar
bock [bɔk] *nm* glass of beer
bœuf [bœf] *nm* ox; (*Culin*) beef
bof [bɔf] (*fam*) *excl* don't care!; (*pas terrible*) nothing special
bohémien, ne [bɔemjɛ̃, -ɛn] *nm/f* gipsy
boire [bwaʀ] *vt* to drink; (*s'imprégner de*) to soak up; **~ un coup** (*fam*) to have a drink
bois [bwa] *nm* wood; **de ~, en ~** wooden; **boisé, e** *adj* woody, wooded
boisson [bwasɔ̃] *nf* drink
boîte [bwat] *nf* box; (*fam: entreprise*) firm; **aliments en ~** canned ou tinned (BRIT) foods; **boîte à gants** glove compartment; **boîte à ordures** dustbin (BRIT), trashcan (US); **boîte aux lettres** letter box; **boîte d'allumettes** box of matches; (*vide*) matchbox; **boîte de conserves** can ou tin (BRIT) of food; **boîte (de nuit)** night club; **boîte de vitesses** gear box; **boîte postale** PO Box; **boîte vocale** (*Tél*) voice mail
boiter [bwate] *vi* to limp; (*fig: raisonnement*) to be shaky
boîtier [bwatje] *nm* case
boive *etc* [bwav] *vb voir* **boire**
bol [bɔl] *nm* bowl; **un ~ d'air** a breath of fresh air; **j'en ai ras le ~** (*fam*) I'm fed up with this; **avoir du ~** (*fam*) to be lucky
bombarder [bɔ̃baʀde] *vt* to bomb; **~ qn de** (*cailloux, lettres*) to bombard sb with
bombe [bɔ̃b] *nf* bomb; (*atomiseur*) (aerosol) spray

 MOT-CLÉ

bon, bonne [bɔ̃, bɔn] *adj* **1** (*agréable, satisfaisant*) good; **un bon repas/restaurant** a good meal/restaurant; **être bon en maths** to be good at maths (BRIT) ou math (US)
2 (*charitable*): **être bon (envers)** to be good (to)
3 (*correct*) right; **le bon numéro/moment** the right number/moment
4 (*souhaits*): **bon anniversaire!** happy birthday!; **bon voyage!** have a good trip!; **bonne chance!** good luck!; **bonne année!** happy New Year!; **bonne nuit!** good night!
5 (*approprié, apte*): **bon à/pour** fit to/for; **à quoi bon?** what's the use?
6: **bon enfant** *adj inv* accommodating, easygoing; **bonne femme** (*péj*) woman; **de bonne heure** early; **bon marché** *adj inv, adv* cheap; **bon mot** witticism; **bon sens** common sense; **bon vivant** jovial chap; **bonnes œuvres** charitable works, charities
▷ *nm* **1** (*billet*) voucher; (*aussi:* **bon cadeau**) gift voucher; **bon d'essence** petrol coupon; **bon du Trésor** Treasury bond
2: **avoir du bon** to have its good points; **pour**

de bon for good
▷ *adv*: **il fait bon** it's *ou* the weather is fine;
sentir bon to smell good; **tenir bon** to stand
firm
▷ *excl* good!; **ah bon?** really?; **bon, je reste**
right then, I'll stay; *voir aussi* **bonne**

bonbon [bɔ̃bɔ̃] *nm* (boiled) sweet
bond [bɔ̃] *nm* leap; **faire un ~** to leap in the air
bondé, e [bɔ̃de] *adj* packed (full)
bondir [bɔ̃diʀ] *vi* to leap
bonheur [bɔnœʀ] *nm* happiness; **porter ~ (à
qn)** to bring (sb) luck; **au petit ~** haphazardly;
par ~ fortunately
bonhomme [bɔnɔm] (*pl* **bonshommes**) *nm*
fellow; **bonhomme de neige** snowman
bonjour [bɔ̃ʒuʀ] *excl*, *nm* hello; (*selon l'heure*)
good morning/afternoon; **c'est simple
comme ~!** it's easy as pie!
bonne [bɔn] *adj voir* **bon** ▷ *nf* (*domestique*)
maid
bonnet [bɔnɛ] *nm* hat; (*de soutien-gorge*) cup;
bonnet de bain bathing cap
bonsoir [bɔ̃swaʀ] *excl* good evening
bonté [bɔ̃te] *nf* kindness *no pl*
bonus [bɔnys] *nm* no-claims bonus; (*de DVD*)
extras *pl*
bord [bɔʀ] *nm* (*de table, verre, falaise*) edge;
(*de rivière, lac*) bank; (*de route*) side; (**monter**)
à ~ (to go) on board; **jeter par-dessus ~** to
throw overboard; **le commandant de/les
hommes du ~** the ship's master/crew; **au ~ de
la mer** at the seaside; **au ~ de la route** at the
roadside; **être au ~ des larmes** to be on the
verge of tears
bordeaux [bɔʀdo] *nm* Bordeaux (wine) ▷ *adj
inv* maroon
bordel [bɔʀdɛl] *nm* brothel; (*fam!*) bloody
mess (!)
border [bɔʀde] *vt* (*être le long de*) to line; (*qn
dans son lit*) to tuck up; (*garnir*): **~ qch de** to
edge sth with
bordure [bɔʀdyʀ] *nf* border; **en ~ de** on the
edge of
borne [bɔʀn] *nf* boundary stone; (*aussi:
~ kilométrique*) kilometre-marker,
≈ milestone; **bornes** *nfpl* (*fig*) limits; **dépasser
les ~s** to go too far
borné, e [bɔʀne] *adj* (*personne*) narrow-
minded
borner [bɔʀne] *vt*: **se ~ à faire** (*se contenter de*)
to content o.s. with doing; (*se limiter à*) to limit
o.s. to doing
bosniaque [bɔsnjak] *adj* Bosnian ▷ *nm/f*:
B~ Bosnian
Bosnie-Herzégovine [bɔsniɛʀzegɔvin] *nf*
Bosnia-Herzegovina
bosquet [bɔskɛ] *nm* grove
bosse [bɔs] *nf* (*de terrain etc*) bump; (*enflure*)

lump; (*du bossu, du chameau*) hump; **avoir la
~ des maths** *etc* (*fam*) to have a gift for maths
etc; **il a roulé sa ~** (*fam*) he's been around
bosser [bɔse] (*fam*) *vi* (*travailler*) to work;
(*travailler dur*) to slave (away)
bossu, e [bɔsy] *nm/f* hunchback
botanique [bɔtanik] *nf* botany ▷ *adj*
botanic(al)
botte [bɔt] *nf* (*soulier*) (high) boot; (*gerbe*): **~ de
paille** bundle of straw; **botte de radis/
d'asperges** bunch of radishes/asparagus;
bottes de caoutchouc wellington boots
bottin [bɔtɛ̃] *nm* directory
bottine [bɔtin] *nf* ankle boot
bouc [buk] *nm* goat; (*barbe*) goatee; **bouc
émissaire** scapegoat
boucan [bukɑ̃] (*fam*) *nm* din, racket
bouche [buʃ] *nf* mouth; **faire du ~ à ~ à qn**
to give sb the kiss of life *ou* mouth-to-mouth
resuscitation (*BRIT*); **rester ~ bée** to stand
open-mouthed; **bouche d'égout** manhole;
bouche d'incendie fire hydrant; **bouche de
métro** métro entrance
bouché, e [buʃe] *adj* (*flacon etc*) stoppered;
(*temps, ciel*) overcast; (*péj fam: personne*) thick
(*fam*); **c'est un secteur ~** there's no future in
that area; **avoir le nez ~** to have a blocked(-
up) nose; **l'évier est ~** the sink's blocked
bouchée [buʃe] *nf* mouthful; **bouchées à la
reine** chicken vol-au-vents
boucher, -ère [buʃe] *nm/f* butcher ▷ *vt* (*trou*)
to fill up; (*obstruer*) to block (up); **se boucher**
vi (*tuyau etc*) to block up, get blocked up; **j'ai
le nez bouché** my nose is blocked; **se ~ le nez**
to hold one's nose; **boucherie** *nf* butcher's
(shop); (*fig*) slaughter
bouchon [buʃɔ̃] *nm* stopper; (*de tube*) top; (*en
liège*) cork; (*fig: embouteillage*) holdup; (*Pêche*)
float
boucle [bukl] *nf* (*forme, figure*) loop; (*objet*)
buckle; **boucle (de cheveux)** curl; **boucle
d'oreille** earring
bouclé, e [bukle] *adj* (*cheveux*) curly
boucler [bukle] *vt* (*fermer: ceinture etc*) to
fasten; (*terminer*) to finish off; (*fam: enfermer*) to
shut away; (*quartier*) to seal off ▷ *vi* to curl
bouder [bude] *vi* to sulk ▷ *vt* to stay away
from
boudin [budɛ̃] *nm*: **~ (noir)** black pudding;
boudin blanc white pudding
boue [bu] *nf* mud
bouée [bwe] *nf* buoy; **bouée (de sauvetage)**
lifebuoy
boueux, -euse [bwø, øz] *adj* muddy
bouffe [buf] (*fam*) *nf* grub (*fam*), food
bouffée [bufe] *nf* (*de cigarette*) puff; **une ~
d'air pur** a breath of fresh air; **bouffée de
chaleur** hot flush (*BRIT*) *ou* flash (*US*)
bouffer [bufe] (*fam*) *vi* to eat

bouffi, e [bufi] *adj* swollen

bouger [buʒe] *vi* to move; (*dent etc*) to be loose; (*s'activer*) to get moving ▷ *vt* to move; **les prix/les couleurs n'ont pas bougé** prices/colours haven't changed

bougie [buʒi] *nf* candle; (*Auto*) spark(ing) plug

bouillabaisse [bujabɛs] *nf* type of fish soup

bouillant, e [bujɑ̃, ɑ̃t] *adj* (*qui bout*) boiling; (*très chaud*) boiling (hot)

bouillie [buji] *nf* (*de bébé*) cereal; **en ~** (*fig*) crushed

bouillir [bujiʀ] *vi, vt* to boil; **~ d'impatience** to seethe with impatience

bouilloire [bujwaʀ] *nf* kettle

bouillon [bujɔ̃] *nm* (*Culin*) stock *no pl*; **bouillonner** *vi* to bubble; (*fig: idées*) to bubble up

bouillotte [bujɔt] *nf* hot-water bottle

boulanger, -ère [bulɑ̃ʒe, ɛʀ] *nm/f* baker; **boulangerie** *nf* bakery

boule [bul] *nf* (*gén*) ball; (*de pétanque*) bowl; **boule de neige** snowball

boulette [bulɛt] *nf* (*de viande*) meatball

boulevard [bulvaʀ] *nm* boulevard

bouleversement [bulvɛʀsəmɑ̃] *nm* upheaval

bouleverser [bulvɛʀse] *vt* (*émouvoir*) to overwhelm; (*causer du chagrin*) to distress; (*pays, vie*) to disrupt; (*papiers, objets*) to turn upside down

boulimie [bulimi] *nf* bulimia

boulimique [bulimik] *adj* bulimic

boulon [bulɔ̃] *nm* bolt

boulot, te [bulo, ɔt] *adj* plump, tubby ▷ *nm* (*fam: travail*) work

boum [bum] *nm* bang ▷ *nf* (*fam*) party

bouquet [bukɛ] *nm* (*de fleurs*) bunch (of flowers), bouquet; (*de persil etc*) bunch; **c'est le ~!** (*fam*) that takes the biscuit!

bouquin [bukɛ̃] (*fam*) *nm* book; **bouquiner** (*fam*) *vi* to read

bourdon [buʀdɔ̃] *nm* bumblebee

bourg [buʀ] *nm* small market town

bourgeois, e [buʀʒwa, waz] (*péj*) *adj* ≈ (upper) middle class; **bourgeoisie** *nf* ≈ upper middle classes *pl*

bourgeon [buʀʒɔ̃] *nm* bud

Bourgogne [buʀgɔɲ] *nf*: **la ~** Burgundy ▷ *nm*: **bourgogne** burgundy (wine)

bourguignon, ne [buʀgiɲɔ̃, ɔn] *adj* of *ou* from Burgundy, Burgundian

bourrasque [buʀask] *nf* squall

bourratif, -ive [buʀatif, iv] (*fam*) *adj* filling, stodgy (*pej*)

bourré, e [buʀe] *adj* (*fam: ivre*) plastered, tanked up (*BRIT*); (*rempli*): **~ de** crammed full of

bourrer [buʀe] *vt* (*pipe*) to fill; (*poêle*) to pack; (*valise*) to cram (full)

bourru, e [buʀy] *adj* surly, gruff

bourse [buʀs] *nf* (*subvention*) grant; (*porte-monnaie*) purse; **la B~** the Stock Exchange

bous [bu] *vb voir* **bouillir**

bousculade [buskylad] *nf* (*hâte*) rush; (*cohue*) crush; **bousculer** *vt* (*heurter*) to knock into; (*fig*) to push, rush

boussole [busɔl] *nf* compass

bout [bu] *vb voir* **bouillir** ▷ *nm* bit; (*d'un bâton etc*) tip; (*d'une ficelle, table, rue, période*) end; **au ~ de** at the end of, after; **pousser qn à ~** to push sb to the limit; **venir à ~ de** to manage to finish; **à ~ portant** (at) point-blank (range)

bouteille [butɛj] *nf* bottle; (*de gaz butane*) cylinder

boutique [butik] *nf* shop

bouton [butɔ̃] *nm* button; (*sur la peau*) spot; (*Bot*) bud; **boutonner** *vt* to button up; **boutonnière** *nf* buttonhole; **bouton-pression** *nm* press stud

bovin, e [bɔvɛ̃, in] *adj* bovine; **bovins** *nmpl* cattle *pl*

bowling [buliŋ] *nm* (tenpin) bowling; (*salle*) bowling alley

boxe [bɔks] *nf* boxing

BP *abr* = **boîte postale**

bracelet [bʀaslɛ] *nm* bracelet

braconnier [bʀakɔnje] *nm* poacher

brader [bʀade] *vt* to sell off; **braderie** *nf* cut-price shop/stall

braguette [bʀagɛt] *nf* fly *ou* flies *pl* (*BRIT*), zipper (*US*)

braise [bʀɛz] *nf* embers *pl*

brancard [bʀɑ̃kaʀ] *nm* (*civière*) stretcher; **brancardier** *nm* stretcher-bearer

branche [bʀɑ̃ʃ] *nf* branch

branché, e [bʀɑ̃ʃe] (*fam*) *adj* trendy

brancher [bʀɑ̃ʃe] *vt* to connect (up); (*en mettant la prise*) to plug in

brandir [bʀɑ̃diʀ] *vt* to brandish

braquer [bʀake] *vi* (*Auto*) to turn (the wheel) ▷ *vt* (*revolver etc*): **~ qch sur** to aim sth at, point sth at; (*mettre en colère*): **~ qn** to put sb's back up

bras [bʀɑ] *nm* arm; **~ dessus, ~ dessous** arm in arm; **se retrouver avec qch sur les ~** (*fam*) to be landed with sth; **bras droit** (*fig*) right hand man

brassard [bʀasaʀ] *nm* armband

brasse [bʀas] *nf* (*nage*) breast-stroke; **brasse papillon** butterfly (stroke)

brassée [bʀase] *nf* armful

brasser [bʀase] *vt* to mix; **~ l'argent/les affaires** to handle a lot of money/business

brasserie [bʀasʀi] *nf* (*restaurant*) café-restaurant; (*usine*) brewery

brave [bʀav] *adj* (*courageux*) brave; (*bon, gentil*) good, kind

braver [bʀave] *vt* to defy

bravo [bʀavo] *excl* bravo ▷ *nm* cheer

bravoure [bravur] nf bravery

break [brɛk] nm (Auto) estate car

brebis [brəbi] nf ewe; **brebis galeuse** black sheep

bredouiller [brəduje] vi, vt to mumble, stammer

bref, brève [brɛf, ɛv] adj short, brief ▷ adv in short; **d'un ton ~** sharply, curtly; **en ~** in short, in brief

Brésil [brezil] nm Brazil

Bretagne [brətaɲ] nf Brittany

bretelle [brətɛl] nf (de vêtement, de sac) strap; (d'autoroute) slip road (BRIT), entrance/exit ramp (US); **bretelles** nfpl (pour pantalon) braces (BRIT), suspenders (US)

breton, ne [brətɔ̃, ɔn] adj Breton ▷ nm/f: **B~, ne** Breton

brève [brɛv] adj voir **bref**

brevet [brəvɛ] nm diploma, certificate; **brevet des collèges** exam taken at the age of 15; **brevet (d'invention)** patent; **breveté, e** adj patented

bricolage [brikɔlaʒ] nm: **le ~** do-it-yourself

bricoler [brikɔle] vi (petits travaux) to do DIY jobs; (passe-temps) to potter about ▷ vt (réparer) to fix up; **bricoleur, -euse** nm/f handyman(-woman), DIY enthusiast

bridge [bridʒ] nm (Cartes) bridge

brièvement [brijɛvmɑ̃] adv briefly

brigade [brigad] nf (Police) squad; (Mil) brigade; **brigadier** nm sergeant

brillamment [brijamɑ̃] adv brilliantly

brillant, e [brijɑ̃, ɑ̃t] adj (remarquable) bright; (luisant) shiny, shining

briller [brije] vi to shine

brin [brɛ̃] nm (de laine, ficelle etc) strand; (fig): **un ~ de** a bit of

brindille [brɛ̃dij] nf twig

brioche [brijɔʃ] nf brioche (bun); (fam: ventre) paunch

brique [brik] nf brick; (de lait) carton

briquet [brikɛ] nm (cigarette) lighter

brise [briz] nf breeze

briser [brize] vt to break; **se briser** vi to break

britannique [britanik] adj British ▷ nm/f: **B~** British person, Briton; **les B~s** the British

brocante [brɔkɑ̃t] nf junk, second-hand goods pl; **brocanteur, -euse** nm/f junkshop owner; junk dealer

broche [brɔʃ] nf brooch; (Culin) spit; (Méd) pin; **à la ~** spit-roasted

broché, e [brɔʃe] adj (livre) paper-backed

brochet [brɔʃɛ] nm pike inv

brochette [brɔʃɛt] nf (ustensile) skewer; (plat) kebab

brochure [brɔʃyr] nf pamphlet, brochure, booklet

broder [brɔde] vt to embroider ▷ vi: **~ (sur les faits ou une histoire)** to embroider the facts;

broderie nf embroidery

bronches [brɔ̃ʃ] nfpl bronchial tubes; **bronchite** nf bronchitis

bronze [brɔ̃z] nm bronze

bronzer [brɔ̃ze] vi to get a tan; **se bronzer** to sunbathe

brosse [brɔs] nf brush; **coiffé en ~** with a crewcut; **brosse à cheveux** hairbrush; **brosse à dents** toothbrush; **brosse à habits** clothesbrush; **brosser** vt (nettoyer) to brush; (fig: tableau etc) to paint; **se brosser les dents** to brush one's teeth

brouette [bruɛt] nf wheelbarrow

brouillard [brujar] nm fog

brouiller [bruje] vt (œufs, message) to scramble; (idées) to mix up; (rendre trouble) to cloud; (désunir: amis) to set at odds; **se brouiller** vi (vue) to cloud over; (gens): **se ~ (avec)** to fall out (with)

brouillon, ne [brujɔ̃, ɔn] adj (sans soin) untidy; (qui manque d'organisation) disorganized ▷ nm draft; **(papier) ~** rough paper

broussailles [brusaj] nfpl undergrowth sg; **broussailleux, -euse** adj bushy

brousse [brus] nf: **la ~** the bush

brouter [brute] vi to graze

brugnon [bryɲɔ̃] nm (Bot) nectarine

bruiner [bruine] vb impers: **il bruine** it's drizzling, there's a drizzle

bruit [brui] nm: **un ~** a noise, a sound; (fig: rumeur) a rumour; **le ~** noise; **sans ~** without a sound, noiselessly; **bruit de fond** background noise

brûlant, e [brylɑ̃, ɑ̃t] adj burning; (liquide) boiling (hot)

brûlé, e [bryle] adj (fig: démasqué) blown ▷ nm: **odeur de ~** smell of burning

brûler [bryle] vt to burn; (suj: eau bouillante) to scald; (consommer: électricité, essence) to use; (feu rouge, signal) to go through ▷ vi to burn; (jeu): **tu brûles!** you're getting hot!; **se brûler** to burn o.s.; (s'ébouillanter) to scald o.s.

brûlure [brylyr] nf (lésion) burn; **brûlures d'estomac** heartburn sg

brume [brym] nf mist

brun, e [brœ̃, bryn] adj (gén, bière) brown; (cheveux, tabac) dark; **elle est ~e** she's got dark hair

brunch [brœntʃ] nm brunch

brushing [brœʃiŋ] nm blow-dry

brusque [brysk] adj abrupt

brut, e [bryt] adj (minerai, soie) raw; (diamant) rough; (Comm) gross; **(pétrole) ~** crude (oil)

brutal, e, -aux [brytal, o] adj brutal

Bruxelles [brysɛl] n Brussels

bruyamment [bruijamɑ̃] adv noisily

bruyant, e [bruijɑ̃, ɑ̃t] adj noisy

bruyère [bryjɛr] nf heather

BTS sigle m (= brevet de technicien supérieur) vocational training certificate taken at the end of a higher education course

bu, e [by] pp de **boire**

buccal, e, -aux [bykal, o] adj: **par voie ~e** orally

bûche [byʃ] nf log; **prendre une ~** (fig) to come a cropper; **bûche de Noël** Yule log

bûcher [byʃe] nm (funéraire) pyre; (supplice) stake ▷ vi (fam) to swot (BRIT), slave (away) ▷ vt (fam) to swot up (BRIT), slave away at

budget [bydʒɛ] nm budget

buée [bye] nf (sur une vitre) mist

buffet [byfɛ] nm (meuble) sideboard; (de réception) buffet; **buffet (de gare)** (station) buffet, snack bar

buis [bɥi] nm box tree; (bois) box(wood)

buisson [bɥisɔ̃] nm bush

bulbe [bylb] nm (Bot, Anat) bulb

Bulgarie [bylgaʀi] nf Bulgaria

bulle [byl] nf bubble

bulletin [byltɛ̃] nm (communiqué, journal) bulletin; (Scol) report; **bulletin d'informations** news bulletin; **bulletin (de vote)** ballot paper; **bulletin météorologique** weather report

bureau, x [byʀo] nm (meuble) desk; (pièce, service) office; **bureau de change** (foreign) exchange office ou bureau; **bureau de poste** post office; **bureau de tabac** tobacconist's (shop); **bureaucratie** [byʀokʀasi] nf bureaucracy

bus¹ [by] vb voir **boire**

bus² [bys] nm bus; **à quelle heure part le ~?** what time does the bus leave?

buste [byst] nm (torse) chest; (seins) bust

but¹ [by] vb voir **boire**

but² [by(t)] nm (cible) target; (fig) goal, aim; (Football etc) goal; **de ~ en blanc** point-blank; **avoir pour ~ de faire** to aim to do; **dans le ~ de** with the intention of

butane [bytan] nm (camping) butane; (usage domestique) Calor gas®

butiner [bytine] vi (abeilles) to gather nectar

buvais etc [byvɛ] vb voir **boire**

buvard [byvaʀ] nm blotter

buvette [byvɛt] nf bar

c' [s] dét voir **ce**

ça [sa] pron (pour désigner) this; (: plus loin) that; (comme sujet indéfini) it; **ça m'étonne que ...** it surprises me that ...; **comment ça va?** how are you?; **ça va?** (d'accord?) O.K.?, all right?; **où ça?** where's that?; **pourquoi ça?** why's that?; **qui ça?** who's that?; **ça alors!** well really!; **ça fait 10 ans (que)** it's 10 years (since); **c'est ça** that's right; **ça y est** that's it

cabane [kaban] nf hut, cabin

cabaret [kabaʀɛ] nm night club

cabillaud [kabijo] nm cod inv

cabine [kabin] nf (de bateau) cabin; (de piscine etc) cubicle; (de camion, train) cab; (d'avion) cockpit; **cabine d'essayage** fitting room; **cabine (téléphonique)** call ou (tele)phone box

cabinet [kabinɛ] nm (petite pièce) closet; (de médecin) surgery (BRIT), office (US); (de notaire etc) office; (: clientèle) practice; (Pol) Cabinet; **cabinets** nmpl (w.-c.) toilet sg; **cabinet de toilette** toilet

câble [kabl] nm cable; **le ~** (TV) cable television, cablevision (US)

cacahuète [kakaɥɛt] nf peanut

cacao [kakao] nm cocoa

cache [kaʃ] nm mask, card (for masking)

cache-cache [kaʃkaʃ] nm: **jouer à ~** to play hide-and-seek

cachemire [kaʃmiʀ] nm cashmere

cacher [kaʃe] vt to hide, conceal; **se cacher** vi (volontairement) to hide; (être caché) to be hidden ou concealed; **~ qch à qn** to hide ou conceal sth from sb

cachet [kaʃɛ] nm (comprimé) tablet; (de la poste) postmark; (rétribution) fee; (fig) style, character

cachette [kaʃɛt] nf hiding place; **en ~** on the sly, secretly

cactus [kaktys] nm cactus

cadavre [kadɑvʀ] nm corpse, (dead) body

caddie® [kadi] nm (supermarché) trolley (BRIT), (grocery) cart (US)

cadeau, x [kado] nm present, gift; **faire un ~ à qn** to give sb a present ou gift; **faire ~ de qch à qn** to make a present of sth to sb, give sb sth as a present

cadenas [kadna] nm padlock

cadet, te [kadɛ, ɛt] adj younger; (le plus jeune) youngest ▷ nm/f youngest child ou one

cadran [kadʀɑ̃] nm dial; **cadran solaire** sundial

cadre [kadʀ] nm frame; (environnement) surroundings pl ▷ nm/f (Admin) managerial employee, executive; **dans le ~ de** (fig) within the framework ou context of

cafard [kafaʀ] nm cockroach; **avoir le ~** (fam) to be down in the dumps

café [kafe] nm coffee; (bistro) café ▷ adj inv coffee(-coloured); **café au lait** white coffee; **café noir** black coffee; **café tabac** tobacconist's or newsagent's serving coffee and spirits; **cafetière** nf (pot) coffee-pot

cage [kaʒ] nf cage; **cage (d'escalier)** stairwell; **cage thoracique** rib cage

cageot [kaʒo] nm crate

cagoule [kagul] nf (passe-montagne) balaclava

cahier [kaje] nm notebook; **cahier de brouillon** jotter (BRIT), rough notebook; **cahier d'exercices** exercise book

caille [kaj] nf quail

caillou, x [kaju] nm (little) stone; **caillouteux, -euse** adj (route) stony

Caire [kɛʀ] nm: **le ~** Cairo

caisse [kɛs] nf box; (tiroir où l'on met la recette) till; (où l'on paye) cash desk (BRIT), check-out; (de banque) cashier's desk; **caisse d'épargne** savings bank; **caisse de retraite** pension fund; **caisse enregistreuse** cash register; **caissier, -ière** nm/f cashier

cake [kɛk] nm fruit cake

calandre [kalɑ̃dʀ] nf radiator grill

calcaire [kalkɛʀ] nm limestone ▷ adj (eau) hard; (Géo) limestone cpd

calcul [kalkyl] nm calculation; **le ~** (Scol) arithmetic; **calcul (biliaire)** (gall)stone; **calculatrice** nf calculator; **calculer** vt to calculate, work out; **calculette** nf pocket calculator

cale [kal] nf (de bateau) hold; (en bois) wedge

calé, e [kale] (fam) adj clever, bright

caleçon [kalsɔ̃] nm (d'homme) boxer shorts; (de femme) leggings

calendrier [kalɑ̃dʀije] nm calendar; (fig) timetable

calepin [kalpɛ̃] nm notebook

caler [kale] vt to wedge ▷ vi (moteur, véhicule) to stall

calibre [kalibʀ] nm calibre

câlin, e [kɑlɛ̃, in] adj cuddly, cuddlesome; (regard, voix) tender

calmant [kalmɑ̃] nm tranquillizer, sedative; (pour la douleur) painkiller

calme [kalm] adj calm, quiet ▷ nm calm(ness), quietness; **sans perdre son ~** without losing one's cool (inf) ou composure; **calmer** vt to calm (down); (douleur, inquiétude) to ease, soothe; **se calmer** vi to calm down

calorie [kalɔʀi] nf calorie

camarade [kamaʀad] nm/f friend, pal; (Pol) comrade

Cambodge [kɑ̃bɔdʒ] nm: **le ~** Cambodia

cambriolage [kɑ̃bʀijolaʒ] nm burglary; **cambrioler** vt to burgle (BRIT), burglarize (US); **cambrioleur, -euse** nm/f burglar

camelote [kamlɔt] (fam) nf rubbish, trash, junk

caméra [kameʀa] nf (Cinéma, TV) camera; (d'amateur) cine-camera

Cameroun [kamʀun] nm: **le ~** Cameroon

caméscope® [kameskɔp] nm camcorder®

camion [kamjɔ̃] nm lorry (BRIT), truck; **camion de dépannage** breakdown (BRIT) ou tow (US) truck; **camionnette** nf (small) van; **camionneur** nm (chauffeur) lorry (BRIT) ou truck driver; (entrepreneur) haulage contractor (BRIT), trucker (US)

camomille [kamɔmij] nf camomile; (boisson) camomile tea

camp [kɑ̃] nm camp; (fig) side

campagnard, e [kɑ̃paɲaʀ, aʀd] adj country cpd

campagne [kɑ̃paɲ] nf country, countryside; (Mil, Pol, Comm) campaign; **à la ~** in the country

camper [kɑ̃pe] vi to camp ▷ vt to sketch; **se ~ devant** to plant o.s. in front of; **campeur, -euse** nm/f camper

camping [kɑ̃piŋ] nm camping; **faire du ~** to go camping; **(terrain de) camping** campsite, camping site; **camping-car** nm camper, motorhome (US); **camping-gaz®** nm inv camp(ing) stove

Canada [kanada] nm: **le ~** Canada; **canadien, ne** adj Canadian ▷ nm/f: **Canadien, ne** Canadian; **canadienne** nf (veste) fur-lined jacket

canal, -aux [kanal, o] nm canal; (naturel, TV) channel; **canalisation** nf (tuyau) pipe

canapé [kanape] nm settee, sofa
canard [kanaʀ] nm duck; (fam: journal) rag
cancer [kɑ̃sɛʀ] nm cancer; (signe): **le C~** Cancer
cancre [kɑ̃kʀ] nm dunce
candidat, e [kɑ̃dida, at] nm/f candidate; (à un poste) applicant, candidate; **candidature** nf (Pol) candidacy; (à poste) application; **poser sa candidature à un poste** to apply for a job
cane [kan] nf (female) duck
canette [kanɛt] nf (de bière) (flip-top) bottle
canevas [kanva] nm (Couture) canvas
caniche [kaniʃ] nm poodle
canicule [kanikyl] nf scorching heat
canif [kanif] nm penknife, pocket knife
canne [kan] nf (walking) stick; **canne à pêche** fishing rod; **canne à sucre** sugar cane
cannelle [kanɛl] nf cinnamon
canoë [kanoe] nm canoe; (sport) canoeing; **canoë (kayak)** kayak
canot [kano] nm ding(h)y; **canot de sauvetage** lifeboat; **canot pneumatique** inflatable ding(h)y
cantatrice [kɑ̃tatʀis] nf (opera) singer
cantine [kɑ̃tin] nf canteen
canton [kɑ̃tɔ̃] nm district consisting of several communes; (en Suisse) canton
caoutchouc [kautʃu] nm rubber; **caoutchouc mousse** foam rubber
cap [kap] nm (Géo) cape; (promontoire) headland; (fig: tournant) watershed; (Navig): **changer de ~** to change course; **mettre le ~ sur** to head ou steer for
CAP sigle m (= Certificat d'aptitude professionnelle) vocational training certificate taken at secondary school
capable [kapabl] adj able, capable; **~ de qch/faire** capable of sth/doing
capacité [kapasite] nf (compétence) ability; (Jur, contenance) capacity
cape [kap] nf cape, cloak; **rire sous ~** to laugh up one's sleeve
CAPES [kapɛs] sigle m (= Certificat d'aptitude pédagogique à l'enseignement secondaire) teaching diploma
capitaine [kapitɛn] nm captain
capital, e, -aux [kapital, o] adj (œuvre) major; (question, rôle) fundamental ▷ nm capital; (fig) stock; **d'une importance ~e** of capital importance; **capitaux** nmpl (fonds) capital sg; **capital (social)** authorized capital; **capitale** nf (ville) capital; (lettre) capital (letter); **capitalisme** nm capitalism; **capitaliste** adj, nm/f capitalist
caporal, -aux [kapɔʀal, o] nm lance corporal
capot [kapo] nm (Auto) bonnet (BRIT), hood (US)
câpre [kɑpʀ] nf caper
caprice [kapʀis] nm whim, caprice; **faire**

des ~s to make a fuss; **capricieux, -euse** adj (fantasque) capricious, whimsical; (enfant) awkward
Capricorne [kapʀikɔʀn] nm: **le ~** Capricorn
capsule [kapsyl] nf (de bouteille) cap; (Bot etc, spatiale) capsule
capter [kapte] vt (ondes radio) to pick up; (fig) to win, capture
captivant, e [kaptivɑ̃, ɑ̃t] adj captivating
capturer [kaptyʀe] vt to capture
capuche [kapyʃ] nf hood
capuchon [kapyʃɔ̃] nm hood; (de stylo) cap, top
car [kaʀ] nm coach ▷ conj because, for
carabine [kaʀabin] nf rifle
caractère [kaʀaktɛʀ] nm (gén) character; **avoir bon/mauvais ~** to be good-/ill-natured; **en ~s gras** in bold type; **en petits ~s** in small print; **~s d'imprimerie** (block) capitals
caractériser [kaʀakteʀize] vt to be characteristic of; **se ~ par** to be characterized ou distinguished by
caractéristique [kaʀakteʀistik] adj, nf characteristic
carafe [kaʀaf] nf (pour eau, vin ordinaire) carafe
caraïbe [kaʀaib] adj Caribbean ▷ n: **les C~s** the Caribbean (Islands)
carambolage [kaʀɑ̃bɔlaʒ] nm multiple crash, pileup
caramel [kaʀamɛl] nm (bonbon) caramel, toffee; (substance) caramel
caravane [kaʀavan] nf caravan; **caravaning** nm caravanning
carbone [kaʀbɔn] nm carbon; (double) carbon (copy)
carbonique [kaʀbɔnik] adj: **gaz ~** carbon dioxide; **neige ~** dry ice
carbonisé, e [kaʀbɔnize] adj charred
carburant [kaʀbyʀɑ̃] nm (motor) fuel
carburateur [kaʀbyʀatœʀ] nm carburettor
cardiaque [kaʀdjak] adj cardiac, heart cpd ▷ nm/f heart patient; **être ~** to have heart trouble
cardigan [kaʀdigɑ̃] nm cardigan
cardiologue [kaʀdjɔlɔg] nm/f cardiologist, heart specialist
carême [kaʀɛm] nm: **le C~** Lent
carence [kaʀɑ̃s] nf (manque) deficiency
caresse [kaʀɛs] nf caress
caresser [kaʀese] vt to caress; (animal) to stroke
cargaison [kaʀgɛzɔ̃] nf cargo, freight
cargo [kaʀgo] nm cargo boat, freighter
caricature [kaʀikatyʀ] nf caricature
carie [kaʀi] nf: **la ~ (dentaire)** tooth decay; **une ~** a bad tooth
carnaval [kaʀnaval] nm carnival
carnet [kaʀnɛ] nm (calepin) notebook; (de

tickets, timbres etc) book; **carnet de chèques** cheque book

carotte [kaʀɔt] *nf* carrot

carré, e [kaʀe] *adj* square; (*fig: franc*) straightforward ▷ *nm* (*Math*) square; **mètre/kilomètre ~** square metre/kilometre

carreau, x [kaʀo] *nm* (*par terre*) (floor) tile; (*au mur*) (wall) tile; (*de fenêtre*) (window) pane; (*motif*) check, square; (*Cartes: couleur*) diamonds *pl*; **tissu à ~x** checked fabric

carrefour [kaʀfuʀ] *nm* crossroads *sg*

carrelage [kaʀlaʒ] *nm* (*sol*) (tiled) floor

carrelet [kaʀlɛ] *nm* (*poisson*) plaice

carrément [kaʀemɑ̃] *adv* (*franchement*) straight out, bluntly; (*sans hésiter*) straight; (*intensif*) completely; **c'est ~ impossible** it's completely impossible

carrière [kaʀjɛʀ] *nf* (*métier*) career; (*de roches*) quarry; **militaire de ~** professional soldier

carrosserie [kaʀɔsʀi] *nf* body, coachwork *no pl*

carrure [kaʀyʀ] *nf* build; (*fig*) stature, calibre

cartable [kaʀtabl] *nm* satchel, (school)bag

carte [kaʀt] *nf* (*de géographie*) map; (*marine, du ciel*) chart; (*d'abonnement, à jouer*) card; (*au restaurant*) menu; (*aussi:* **~ de visite**) (visiting) card; **pouvez-vous me l'indiquer sur la ~?** can you show me (it) on the map?; **à la ~** (*au restaurant*) à la carte; **est-ce qu'on peut voir la ~?** can we see the menu?; **donner ~ blanche à qn** to give sb a free rein; **carte bancaire** cash card; **Carte Bleue®** debit card; **carte à puce** smart card; **carte de crédit** credit card; **carte de fidélité** loyalty card; **carte d'identité** identity card; **carte de séjour** residence permit; **carte grise** (*Auto*) ≈ (car) registration book, logbook; **carte memoire** (*d'appareil-photo numérique*) memory card; **carte postale** postcard; **carte routière** road map

carter [kaʀtɛʀ] *nm* sump

carton [kaʀtɔ̃] *nm* (*matériau*) cardboard; (*boîte*) (cardboard) box; **faire un ~** (*fam*) to score a hit; **carton (à dessin)** portfolio

cartouche [kaʀtuʃ] *nf* cartridge; (*de cigarettes*) carton

cas [kɑ] *nm* case; **ne faire aucun ~ de** to take no notice of; **en aucun ~** on no account; **au ~ où** in case; **en ~ de** in case of, in the event of; **en ~ de besoin** if need be; **en tout ~** in any case, at any rate

cascade [kaskad] *nf* waterfall, cascade

case [kɑz] *nf* (*hutte*) hut; (*compartiment*) compartment; (*sur un formulaire, de mots croisés etc*) box

caser [kɑze] (*fam*) *vt* (*placer*) to put (away); (*loger*) to put up; **se caser** *vi* (*se marier*) to settle down; (*trouver un emploi*) to find a (steady) job

caserne [kazɛʀn] *nf* barracks *pl*

casier [kɑzje] *nm* (*pour courrier*) pigeonhole; (*compartiment*) compartment; (*à clef*) locker; **casier judiciaire** police record

casino [kazino] *nm* casino

casque [kask] *nm* helmet; (*chez le coiffeur*) (hair-)drier; (*pour audition*) (head-)phones *pl*, headset

casquette [kaskɛt] *nf* cap

casse...: **casse-croûte** *nm inv* snack; **casse-noix** *nm inv* nutcrackers *pl*; **casse-pieds** (*fam*) *adj inv*: **il est casse-pieds** he's a pain in the neck

casser [kɑse] *vt* to break; (*Jur*) to quash; **se casser** *vi* to break; **~ les pieds à qn** (*fam: irriter*) to get on sb's nerves; **se ~ la tête** (*fam*) to go to a lot of trouble

casserole [kasʀɔl] *nf* saucepan

casse-tête [kastɛt] *nm inv* (*difficultés*) headache (*fig*)

cassette [kasɛt] *nf* (*bande magnétique*) cassette; (*coffret*) casket

cassis [kasis] *nm* blackcurrant

cassoulet [kasulɛ] *nm* bean and sausage hot-pot

catalogue [katalɔg] *nm* catalogue

catalytique [katalitik] *adj*: **pot ~** catalytic convertor

catastrophe [katastʀɔf] *nf* catastrophe, disaster

catéchisme [kateʃism] *nm* catechism

catégorie [kategɔʀi] *nf* category; **catégorique** *adj* categorical

cathédrale [katedʀal] *nf* cathedral

catholique [katɔlik] *adj, nm/f* (Roman) Catholic; **pas très ~** a bit shady *ou* fishy

cauchemar [koʃmaʀ] *nm* nightmare

cause [koz] *nf* cause; (*Jur*) lawsuit, case; **à ~ de** because of, owing to; **pour ~ de** on account of; **(et) pour ~** and for (a very) good reason; **être en ~** (*intérêts*) to be at stake; **remettre en ~** to challenge; **causer** *vt* to cause ▷ *vi* to chat, talk

caution [kosjɔ̃] *nf* guarantee, security; (*Jur*) bail (bond); (*fig*) backing, support; **libéré sous ~** released on bail

cavalier, -ière [kavalje, jɛʀ] *adj* (*désinvolte*) offhand ▷ *nm/f* rider; (*au bal*) partner ▷ *nm* (*Échecs*) knight

cave [kav] *nf* cellar

CD *sigle m* (= *compact disc*) CD

CD-ROM [sedeʀɔm] *sigle m* CD-ROM

MOT-CLÉ

ce, cette [sə, sɛt] (*devant nm* **cet** + *voyelle ou h aspiré*; *pl* **ces**) *dét* (*proximité*) this; these *pl*; (*non-proximité*) that; those *pl*; **cette maison(-ci/là)** this/that house; **cette nuit** (*qui vient*) tonight; (*passée*) last night

▷ **pron 1**: **c'est** it's ou it is; **c'est un peintre** he's ou he is a painter; **c'est un peintre** they're ou they are painters; **c'est le facteur** etc (à la porte) it's the postman; **c'est toi qui lui a parlé** it was you who spoke to him; **qui est-ce?** who is it?; (en désignant) who is he/she?; **qu'est-ce?** what is it?

2: **ce qui, ce que**: **ce qui me plaît, c'est sa franchise** what I like about him ou her is his ou her frankness; **il est bête, ce qui me chagrine** he's stupid, which saddens me; **tout ce qui bouge** everything that ou which moves; **tout ce que je sais** all I know; **ce dont j'ai parlé** what I talked about; **ce que c'est grand!** it's so big!; voir aussi **-ci**; **est-ce que**; **n'est-ce pas**; **c'est-à-dire**

ceci [səsi] pron this
céder [sede] vt (donner) to give up ▷ vi (chaise, barrage) to give way; (personne) to give in; **~ à** to yield to, give in to
CEDEX [sedɛks] sigle m (= courrier d'entreprise à distribution exceptionnelle) postal service for bulk users
cédille [sedij] nf cedilla
ceinture [sɛ̃tyʀ] nf belt; (taille) waist; **ceinture de sécurité** safety ou seat belt
cela [s(ə)la] pron that; (comme sujet indéfini) it; **~ m'étonne que ...** it surprises me that ...; **quand/où ~?** when/where (was that)?
célèbre [selɛbʀ] adj famous; **célébrer** vt to celebrate
céleri [sɛlʀi] nm: **~(-rave)** celeriac; **céleri en branche** celery
célibataire [selibatɛʀ] adj single, unmarried ▷ nm bachelor ▷ nf unmarried woman
celle, celles [sɛl] pron voir **celui**
cellule [selyl] nf (gén) cell; **~ souche** stem cell
cellulite [selylit] nf cellulite

 MOT-CLÉ

celui, celle [səlɥi, sɛl] (mpl **ceux**, fpl **celles**) pron **1**: **celui-ci/là, celle-ci/là** this one/that one; **ceux-ci, celles-ci** these (ones); **ceux-là, celles-là** those (ones)

2: **celui qui bouge** the one which ou that moves; (personne) the one who moves; **celui que je vois** the one (which ou that) I see; (personne) the one (whom) I see; **celui dont je parle** the one I'm talking about; **celui de mon frère** my brother's; **celui du salon/du dessous** the one in (ou from) the lounge/below

3 (valeur indéfinie): **celui qui veut** whoever wants

cendre [sɑ̃dʀ] nf ash; **cendres** nfpl (d'un défunt) ashes; **sous la ~** (Culin) in (the) embers;

cendrier nm ashtray
censé, e [sɑ̃se] adj: **être ~ faire** to be supposed to do
censeur [sɑ̃sœʀ] nm (Scol) deputy-head (BRIT), vice-principal (US)
censure [sɑ̃syʀ] nf censorship; **censurer** vt (Cinéma, Presse) to censor; (Pol) to censure
cent [sɑ̃] num a hundred, one hundred ▷ nm (US, Canada etc) cent; (partie de l'euro) cent; **centaine** nf: **une centaine (de)** about a hundred, a hundred or so; **des centaines (de)** hundreds (of); **centenaire** adj hundred-year-old ▷ nm (anniversaire) centenary; (monnaie) cent; **centième** num hundredth; **centigrade** nm centigrade; **centilitre** nm centilitre; **centime** nm centime; **centime d'euro** nm euro cent; **centimètre** nm centimetre; (ruban) tape measure, measuring tape
central, e, -aux [sɑ̃tʀal, o] adj central ▷ nm: **~ (téléphonique)** (telephone) exchange; **centrale** nf power station; **centrale électrique/nucléaire** power/nuclear power station
centre [sɑ̃tʀ] nm centre; **centre commercial/sportif/culturel** shopping/sports/arts centre; **centre d'appels** call centre; **centre-ville** nm town centre, downtown (area) (US)
cèpe [sɛp] nm (edible) boletus
cependant [s(ə)pɑ̃dɑ̃] adv however
céramique [seʀamik] nf ceramics sg
cercle [sɛʀkl] nm circle; **cercle vicieux** vicious circle
cercueil [sɛʀkœj] nm coffin
céréale [seʀeal] nf cereal
cérémonie [seʀemoni] nf ceremony; **sans ~** (inviter, manger) informally
cerf [sɛʀ] nm stag
cerf-volant [sɛʀvɔlɑ̃] nm kite
cerise [s(ə)ʀiz] nf cherry; **cerisier** nm cherry (tree)
cerner [sɛʀne] vt (Mil etc) to surround; (fig: problème) to delimit, define
certain, e [sɛʀtɛ̃, ɛn] adj certain ▷ dét certain; **d'un ~ âge** past one's prime, not so young; **un ~ temps** (quite) some time; **un ~ Georges** someone called Georges; **~s** pron some; **certainement** adv (probablement) most probably ou likely; (bien sûr) certainly, of course
certes [sɛʀt] adv (sans doute) admittedly; (bien sûr) of course
certificat [sɛʀtifika] nm certificate
certifier [sɛʀtifje] vt: **~ qch à qn** to assure sb of sth; **copie certifiée conforme** certified copy of the original
certitude [sɛʀtityd] nf certainty
cerveau, x [sɛʀvo] nm brain
cervelas [sɛʀvəla] nm saveloy
cervelle [sɛʀvɛl] nf (Anat) brain; (Culin) brains

ces [se] *dét voir* **ce**

CES *sigle m* (= *collège d'enseignement secondaire*) ≈ (junior) secondary school (BRIT)

cesse [sɛs]: **sans ~** *adv* (*tout le temps*) continually, constantly; (*sans interruption*) continuously; **il n'a eu de ~ que** he did not rest until; **cesser** *vt* to stop ▷ *vi* to stop, cease; **cesser de faire** to stop doing; **cessez-le-feu** *nm inv* ceasefire

c'est-à-dire [sɛtadiʀ] *adv* that is (to say)

cet, cette [sɛt] *dét voir* **ce**

ceux [sø] *pron voir* **celui**

chacun, e [ʃakœ̃, yn] *pron* each; (*indéfini*) everyone, everybody

chagrin [ʃagʀɛ̃] *nm* grief, sorrow; **avoir du ~** to be grieved

chahut [ʃay] *nm* uproar; **chahuter** *vt* to rag, bait ▷ *vi* to make an uproar

chaîne [ʃɛn] *nf* chain; (*Radio, TV: stations*) channel; **travail à la ~** production line work; **réactions en ~** chain reaction *sg*; **chaîne de montagnes** mountain range; **chaîne (hi-fi)** hi-fi system

chair [ʃɛʀ] *nf* flesh; **avoir la ~ de poule** to have goosepimples *ou* gooseflesh; **bien en ~** plump, well-padded; **en ~ et en os** in the flesh; **~ à saucisse** sausage meat

chaise [ʃɛz] *nf* chair; **chaise longue** deckchair

châle [ʃɑl] *nm* shawl

chaleur [ʃalœʀ] *nf* heat; (*fig: accueil*) warmth; **chaleureux, -euse** *adj* warm

chamailler [ʃamaje]: **se chamailler** *vi* to squabble, bicker

chambre [ʃɑ̃bʀ] *nf* bedroom; (*Pol, Comm*) chamber; **faire ~ à part** to sleep in separate rooms; **je voudrais une ~ pour deux personnes** I'd like a double room; **chambre à air** (*de pneu*) (inner) tube; **chambre à coucher** bedroom; **chambre à un lit/à deux lits** (*à l'hôtel*) single-/twin-bedded room; **chambre d'amis** spare *ou* guest room; **chambre d'hôte** ≈ bed and breakfast; **chambre meublée** bedsit(ter) (BRIT), furnished room; **chambre noire** (*Photo*) darkroom

chameau, x [ʃamo] *nm* camel

chamois [ʃamwa] *nm* chamois

champ [ʃɑ̃] *nm* field; **champ de bataille** battlefield; **champ de courses** racecourse

champagne [ʃɑ̃paɲ] *nm* champagne

champignon [ʃɑ̃piɲɔ̃] *nm* mushroom; (*terme générique*) fungus; **champignon de Paris** *ou* **de couche** button mushroom

champion, ne [ʃɑ̃pjɔ̃, jɔn] *adj, nm/f* champion; **championnat** *nm* championship

chance [ʃɑ̃s] *nf*: **la ~** luck; **chances** *nfpl* (*probabilités*) chances; **avoir de la ~** to be lucky; **il a des ~s de réussir** he's got a good chance of passing; **bonne ~!** good luck!

change [ʃɑ̃ʒ] *nm* (*devises*) exchange

changement [ʃɑ̃ʒmɑ̃] *nm* change; **changement de vitesses** gears *pl*

changer [ʃɑ̃ʒe] *vt* (*modifier*) to change, alter; (*remplacer, Comm*) to change ▷ *vi* to change, alter; **se changer** *vi* to change (o.s.); **~ de** (*remplacer: adresse, nom, voiture etc*) to change one's; (*échanger: place, train etc*) to change; **~ d'avis** to change one's mind; **~ de vitesse** to change gear; **il faut ~ à Lyon** you *ou* we *etc* have to change in Lyons; **où est-ce que je peux ~ de l'argent?** where can I change some money?

chanson [ʃɑ̃sɔ̃] *nf* song

chant [ʃɑ̃] *nm* song; (*art vocal*) singing; (*d'église*) hymn

chantage [ʃɑ̃taʒ] *nm* blackmail; **faire du ~** to use blackmail

chanter [ʃɑ̃te] *vt, vi* to sing; **si cela lui chante** (*fam*) if he feels like it; **chanteur, -euse** *nm/f* singer

chantier [ʃɑ̃tje] *nm* (building) site; (*sur une route*) roadworks *pl*; **mettre en ~** to put in hand; **chantier naval** shipyard

chantilly [ʃɑ̃tiji] *nf voir* **crème**

chantonner [ʃɑ̃tɔne] *vi, vt* to sing to oneself, hum

chapeau, x [ʃapo] *nm* hat; **~!** well done!

chapelle [ʃapɛl] *nf* chapel

chapitre [ʃapitʀ] *nm* chapter

chaque [ʃak] *dét* each, every; (*indéfini*) every

char [ʃaʀ] *nm* (*Mil*): **~ (d'assaut)** tank; **~ à voile** sand yacht

charbon [ʃaʀbɔ̃] *nm* coal; **charbon de bois** charcoal

charcuterie [ʃaʀkytʀi] *nf* (*magasin*) pork butcher's shop and delicatessen; (*produits*) cooked pork meats *pl*; **charcutier, -ière** *nm/f* pork butcher

chardon [ʃaʀdɔ̃] *nm* thistle

charge [ʃaʀʒ] *nf* (*fardeau*) load, burden; (*Élec, Mil, Jur*) charge; (*rôle, mission*) responsibility; **charges** *nfpl* (*du loyer*) service charges; **à la ~ de** (*dépendant de*) dependent upon; (*aux frais de*) chargeable to; **prendre en ~** to take charge of; (*suj: véhicule*) to take on; (*dépenses*) to take care of; **charges sociales** social security contributions

chargement [ʃaʀʒəmɑ̃] *nm* (*objets*) load

charger [ʃaʀʒe] *vt* (*voiture, fusil, caméra*) to load; (*batterie*) to charge ▷ *vi* (*Mil etc*) to charge; **se ~ de** to see to, take care of

chariot [ʃaʀjo] *nm* trolley; (*charrette*) waggon

charité [ʃaʀite] *nf* charity; **faire la ~ à** to give (something) to

charmant, e [ʃaʀmɑ̃, ɑ̃t] *adj* charming

charme [ʃaʀm] *nm* charm; **charmer** *vt* to charm

charpente [ʃaʀpɑ̃t] *nf* frame(work); **charpentier** *nm* carpenter

charrette [ʃaʀɛt] nf cart

charter [ʃaʀtɛʀ] nm (vol) charter flight

chasse [ʃas] nf hunting; (au fusil) shooting; (poursuite) chase; (aussi: ~ **d'eau**) flush; **prendre en ~** to give chase to; **tirer la ~ (d'eau)** to flush the toilet, pull the chain; **~ à courre** hunting; **chasse-neige** nm inv snowplough (BRIT), snowplow (US); **chasser** vt to hunt; (expulser) to chase away ou out, drive away ou out; **chasseur, -euse** nm/f hunter ▷ nm (avion) fighter

chat¹ [ʃa] nm cat

chat² [tʃat] nm (Internet) chat room

châtaigne [ʃatɛɲ] nf chestnut

châtain [ʃatɛ̃] adj inv (cheveux) chestnut (brown); (personne) chestnut-haired

château, x [ʃato] nm (forteresse) castle; (résidence royale) palace; (manoir) mansion; **château d'eau** water tower; **château fort** stronghold, fortified castle

châtiment [ʃatimɑ̃] nm punishment

chaton [ʃatɔ̃] nm (Zool) kitten

chatouiller [ʃatuje] vt to tickle; **chatouilleux, -euse** adj ticklish

chatte [ʃat] nf (she-)cat

chatter [tʃate] vi (Internet) to chat

chaud, e [ʃo, ʃod] adj (gén) warm; (très chaud) hot; **il fait ~** it's warm; it's hot; **avoir ~** to be warm; to be hot; **ça me tient ~** it keeps me warm; **rester au ~** to stay in the warm

chaudière [ʃodjɛʀ] nf boiler

chauffage [ʃofaʒ] nm heating; **chauffage central** central heating

chauffe-eau [ʃofo] nm inv water-heater

chauffer [ʃofe] vt to heat ▷ vi to heat up, warm up; (trop chauffer: moteur) to overheat; **se chauffer** vi (au soleil) to warm o.s.

chauffeur [ʃofœʀ] nm driver; (privé) chauffeur

chaumière [ʃomjɛʀ] nf (thatched) cottage

chaussée [ʃose] nf road(way)

chausser [ʃose] vt (bottes, skis) to put on; (enfant) to put shoes on; **~ du 38/42** to take size 38/42

chaussette [ʃosɛt] nf sock

chausson [ʃosɔ̃] nm slipper; (de bébé) bootee; **chausson (aux pommes)** (apple) turnover

chaussure [ʃosyʀ] nf shoe; **chaussures basses** flat shoes; **chaussures montantes** ankle boots; **chaussures de ski** ski boots

chauve [ʃov] adj bald; **chauve-souris** nf bat

chauvin, e [ʃovɛ̃, in] adj chauvinistic

chaux [ʃo] nf lime; **blanchi à la ~** whitewashed

chef [ʃɛf] nm head, leader; (de cuisine) chef; **commandant en ~** commander-in-chief; **chef d'accusation** charge; **chef d'entreprise** company head; **chef d'État** head of state; **chef de famille** head of the family; **chef de file** (de parti etc) leader; **chef de gare** station master; **chef d'orchestre** conductor; **chef-d'œuvre** nm masterpiece; **chef-lieu** nm county town

chemin [ʃ(ə)mɛ̃] nm path; (itinéraire, direction, trajet) way; **en ~** on the way; **chemin de fer** railway (BRIT), railroad (US)

cheminée [ʃ(ə)mine] nf chimney; (à l'intérieur) chimney piece, fireplace; (de bateau) funnel

chemise [ʃ(ə)miz] nf shirt; (dossier) folder; **chemise de nuit** nightdress

chemisier [ʃ(ə)mizje] nm blouse

chêne [ʃɛn] nm oak (tree); (bois) oak

chenil [ʃ(ə)nil] nm kennels pl

chenille [ʃ(ə)nij] nf (Zool) caterpillar

chèque [ʃɛk] nm cheque (BRIT), check (US); **est-ce que je peux payer par ~?** can I pay by cheque?; **chèque sans provision** bad cheque; **chèque de voyage** traveller's cheque; **chéquier** [ʃekje] nm cheque book

cher, -ère [ʃɛʀ] adj (aimé) dear; (coûteux) expensive, dear ▷ adv: **ça coûte ~** it's expensive

chercher [ʃɛʀʃe] vt to look for; (gloire etc) to seek; **aller ~** to go for, go and fetch; **~ à faire** to try to do; **chercheur, -euse** nm/f researcher, research worker

chéri, e [ʃeʀi] adj beloved, dear; **(mon) ~** darling

cheval, -aux [ʃ(ə)val, o] nm horse; (Auto): **~ (vapeur)** horsepower no pl; **faire du ~** to ride; **à ~** on horseback; **à ~ sur** astride; (fig) overlapping; **cheval de course** racehorse

chevalier [ʃ(ə)valje] nm knight

chevalière [ʃ(ə)valjɛʀ] nf signet ring

chevaux [ʃavo] nmpl de **cheval**

chevet [ʃ(ə)ve] nm: **au ~ de qn** at sb's bedside; **lampe de chevet** bedside lamp

cheveu, x [ʃ(ə)vø] nm hair; **cheveux** nmpl (chevelure) hair sg; **avoir les ~x courts** to have short hair

cheville [ʃ(ə)vij] nf (Anat) ankle; (de bois) peg; (pour une vis) plug

chèvre [ʃɛvʀ] nf (she-)goat

chèvrefeuille [ʃɛvʀəfœj] nm honeysuckle

chevreuil [ʃəvʀœj] nm roe deer inv; (Culin) venison

 MOT-CLÉ

chez [ʃe] prép 1 (à la demeure de) at; (: direction) to; **chez qn** at/to sb's house ou place; **je suis chez moi** I'm at home; **je rentre chez moi** I'm going home; **allons chez Nathalie** let's go to Nathalie's
2 (+profession) at; (: direction) to; **chez le boulanger/dentiste** at ou to the baker's/dentist's

3 (*dans le caractère, l'œuvre de*) in; **chez ce poète** in this poet's work; **c'est ce que je préfère chez lui** that's what I like best about him

chic [ʃik] *adj inv* chic, smart; (*fam: généreux*) nice, decent ▷ *nm* stylishness; **~ (alors)!** (*fam*) great!; **avoir le ~ de** to have the knack of
chicorée [ʃikɔʀe] *nf* (*café*) chicory; (*salade*) endive
chien [ʃjɛ̃] *nm* dog; **chien d'aveugle** guide dog; **chien de garde** guard dog
chienne [ʃjɛn] *nf* dog, bitch
chiffon [ʃifɔ̃] *nm* (piece of) rag; **chiffonner** *vt* to crumple; (*fam: tracasser*) to concern
chiffre [ʃifʀ] *nm* (*représentant un nombre*) figure, numeral; (*montant, total*) total, sum; **en ~s ronds** in round figures; **chiffre d'affaires** turnover; **chiffrer** *vt* (*dépense*) to put a figure to, assess; (*message*) to (en)code, cipher; **se chiffrer à** to add up to, amount to
chignon [ʃiɲɔ̃] *nm* chignon, bun
Chili [ʃili] *nm*: **le ~** Chile; **chilien, ne** *adj* Chilean ▷ *nm/f*: **Chilien, ne** Chilean
chimie [ʃimi] *nf* chemistry; **chimiothérapie** [ʃimjɔteʀapi] *nf* chemotherapy; **chimique** *adj* chemical; **produits chimiques** chemicals
chimpanzé [ʃɛ̃pãze] *nm* chimpanzee
Chine [ʃin] *nf*: **la ~** China; **chinois, e** *adj* Chinese ▷ *nm/f*: **Chinois, e** Chinese ▷ *nm* (*Ling*) Chinese
chiot [ʃjo] *nm* pup(py)
chips [ʃips] *nfpl* crisps (BRIT), (potato) chips (US)
chirurgie [ʃiʀyʀʒi] *nf* surgery; **chirurgie esthétique** plastic surgery; **chirurgien, ne** *nm/f* surgeon
chlore [klɔʀ] *nm* chlorine
choc [ʃɔk] *nm* (*heurt*) impact, shock; (*collision*) crash; (*moral*) shock; (*affrontement*) clash
chocolat [ʃɔkɔla] *nm* chocolate; **chocolat au lait** milk chocolate
chœur [kœʀ] *nm* (*chorale*) choir; (*Opéra, Théâtre*) chorus; **en ~** in chorus
choisir [ʃwaziʀ] *vt* to choose, select
choix [ʃwa] *nm* choice, selection; **avoir le ~** to have the choice; **premier ~** (*Comm*) class one; **de ~** choice, selected; **au ~** as you wish
chômage [ʃomaʒ] *nm* unemployment; **mettre au ~** to make redundant, put out of work; **être au ~** to be unemployed *ou* out of work; **chômeur, -euse** *nm/f* unemployed person
choquer [ʃɔke] *vt* (*offenser*) to shock; (*deuil*) to shake
chorale [kɔʀal] *nf* choir
chose [ʃoz] *nf* thing; **c'est peu de ~** it's nothing (really)
chou, x [ʃu] *nm* cabbage; **mon petit ~** (my) sweetheart; **chou à la crème** choux

bun; **chou de Bruxelles** Brussels sprout; **choucroute** *nf* sauerkraut
chouette [ʃwɛt] *nf* owl ▷ *adj* (*fam*) great, smashing
chou-fleur [ʃuflœʀ] *nm* cauliflower
chrétien, ne [kʀetjɛ̃, jɛn] *adj, nm/f* Christian
Christ [kʀist] *nm*: **le ~** Christ; **christianisme** *nm* Christianity
chronique [kʀɔnik] *adj* chronic ▷ *nf* (*de journal*) column, page; (*historique*) chronicle; (*Radio, TV*): **la ~ sportive** the sports review
chronologique [kʀɔnɔlɔʒik] *adj* chronological
chronomètre [kʀɔnɔmɛtʀ] *nm* stopwatch; **chronométrer** *vt* to time
chrysanthème [kʀizãtɛm] *nm* chrysanthemum

> ● **CHRYSANTHÈME**
> ●
> ● Chrysanthemums are strongly associated
> ● with funerals in France, and therefore
> ● should not be given as gifts.

chuchotement [ʃyʃɔtmã] *nm* whisper
chuchoter [ʃyʃɔte] *vt, vi* to whisper
chut [ʃyt] *excl* sh!
chute [ʃyt] *nf* fall; (*déchet*) scrap; **faire une ~ (de 10 m)** to fall (10 m); **chute (d'eau)** waterfall; **chute libre** free fall; **chutes de pluie/neige** rainfall/snowfall
Chypre [ʃipʀ] *nf* Cyprus
-ci [si] *adv voir* **par** ▷ *dét*: **ce garçon~** this boy; **ces femmes~** these women
cible [sibl] *nf* target
ciboulette [sibulɛt] *nf* (small) chive
cicatrice [sikatʀis] *nf* scar; **cicatriser** *vt* to heal
ci-contre [sikɔ̃tʀ] *adv* opposite
ci-dessous [sidəsu] *adv* below
ci-dessus [sidəsy] *adv* above
cidre [sidʀ] *nm* cider
Cie *abr* (= *compagnie*) Co.
ciel [sjɛl] *nm* sky; (*Rel*) heaven
cieux [sjø] *nmpl de* **ciel**
cigale [sigal] *nf* cicada
cigare [sigaʀ] *nm* cigar
cigarette [sigaʀɛt] *nf* cigarette
ci-inclus, e [siɛ̃kly, yz] *adj, adv* enclosed
ci-joint, e [siʒwɛ̃, ɛ̃t] *adj, adv* enclosed
cil [sil] *nm* (eye)lash
cime [sim] *nf* top; (*montagne*) peak
ciment [simã] *nm* cement
cimetière [simtjɛʀ] *nm* cemetery; (*d'église*) churchyard
cinéaste [sineast] *nm/f* film-maker
cinéma [sinema] *nm* cinema
cinq [sɛ̃k] *num* five; **cinquantaine** *nf*: **une cinquantaine (de)** about fifty; **avoir la**

cinquantaine (*âge*) to be around fifty;
cinquante num fifty; **cinquantenaire** adj,
nm/f fifty-year-old; **cinquième** num fifth ▷ nf
(*Scol*) year 8 (BRIT), seventh grade (US)
cintre [sɛ̃tʀ] nm: **~ coat-hanger**
cintré, e [sɛ̃tʀe] adj (*chemise*) fitted
cirage [siʀaʒ] nm (shoe) polish
circonflexe [siʀkɔ̃flɛks] adj: **accent ~**
circumflex accent
circonstance [siʀkɔ̃stɑ̃s] nf circumstance;
(*occasion*) occasion; **circonstances**
atténuantes mitigating circumstances
circuit [siʀkɥi] nm (*Élec, Tech*) circuit; (*trajet*)
tour, (round) trip
circulaire [siʀkylɛʀ] adj, nf circular
circulation [siʀkylasjɔ̃] nf circulation; (*Auto*):
la ~ (the) traffic
circuler [siʀkyle] vi (*sang, devises*) to circulate;
(*véhicules*) to drive (along); (*passants*) to walk
along; (*train, bus*) to run; **faire ~** (*nouvelle*) to
spread (about), circulate; (*badauds*) to move on
cire [siʀ] nf wax; **ciré** nm oilskin; **cirer** vt to
wax, polish
cirque [siʀk] nm circus; (*fig*) chaos, bedlam;
quel ~! what a carry-on!
ciseau, x [sizo] nm: **~ (à bois)** chisel; **ciseaux**
nmpl (*paire de ciseaux*) (pair of) scissors
citadin, e [sitadɛ̃, in] nm/f city dweller
citation [sitasjɔ̃] nf (*d'auteur*) quotation; (*Jur*)
summons sg
cité [site] nf town; (*plus grande*) city; **cité**
universitaire students' residences pl
citer [site] vt (*un auteur*) to quote (from);
(*nommer*) to name; (*Jur*) to summon
citoyen, ne [sitwajɛ̃, jɛn] nm/f citizen
citron [sitʀɔ̃] nm lemon; **citron pressé** (fresh)
lemon juice; **citron vert** lime; **citronnade** nf
still lemonade
citrouille [sitʀuj] nf pumpkin
civet [sivɛ] nm: **~ de lapin** rabbit stew
civière [sivjɛʀ] nf stretcher
civil, e [sivil] adj (*mariage, poli*) civil; (*non
militaire*) civilian; **en ~** in civilian clothes; **dans
le ~** in civilian life
civilisation [sivilizasjɔ̃] nf civilization
clair, e [klɛʀ] adj light; (*pièce*) light, bright; (*eau,
son, fig*) clear ▷ adv: **voir ~** to see clearly; **tirer
qch au ~** to clear sth up, clarify sth; **mettre
au ~** (*notes etc*) to tidy up ▷ nm: **~ de lune**
moonlight; **clairement** adv clearly
clairière [klɛʀjɛʀ] nf clearing
clandestin, e [klɑ̃dɛstɛ̃, in] adj clandestine,
secret; (*mouvement*) underground; (*travailleur,
immigration*) illegal; **passager ~** stowaway
claque [klak] nf (*gifle*) slap; **claquer** vi (*porte*)
to bang, slam; (*fam: mourir*) to snuff it ▷ vt
(*porte*) to slam, bang; (*doigts*) to snap; (*fam:
dépenser*) to blow; **il claquait des dents** his
teeth were chattering; **être claqué** (*fam*) to

be dead tired; **se claquer un muscle** to pull ou
strain a muscle; **claquettes** nfpl tap-dancing
sg; (*chaussures*) flip-flops
clarinette [klaʀinɛt] nf clarinet
classe [klɑs] nf class; (*Scol: local*) class(room);
(: *leçon, élèves*) class; **aller en ~** to go to school;
classement nm (*rang: Scol*) place; (: *Sport*)
placing; (*liste: Scol*) class list (in order of merit);
(: *Sport*) placings pl
classer [klɑse] vt (*idées, livres*) to classify;
(*papiers*) to file; (*candidat, concurrent*) to grade;
(*Jur: affaire*) to close; **se ~ premier/dernier**
to come first/last; (*Sport*) to finish first/last;
classeur nm (*cahier*) file
classique [klɑsik] adj classical; (*sobre: coupe
etc*) classic(al); (*habituel*) standard, classic
clavecin [klav(ə)sɛ̃] nm harpsichord
clavicule [klavikyl] nf collarbone
clavier [klavje] nm keyboard
clé [kle] nf key; (*Mus*) clef; (*de mécanicien*)
spanner (BRIT), wrench (US); **prix ~s en
main** (*d'une voiture*) on-the-road price; **clé de
contact** ignition key; **clé USB** USB key
clef [kle] nf = **clé**
clergé [klɛʀʒe] nm clergy
cliché [klife] nm (*fig*) cliché; (*négatif*) negative;
(*photo*) print
client, e [klijɑ̃, klijɑ̃t] nm/f (*acheteur*)
customer, client; (*d'hôtel*) guest, patron; (*du
docteur*) patient; (*de l'avocat*) client; **clientèle**
nf (*du magasin*) customers pl, clientèle; (*du
docteur, de l'avocat*) practice
cligner [kliɲe] vi: **~ des yeux** to blink (one's
eyes); **~ de l'œil** to wink; **clignotant** nm
(*Auto*) indicator; **clignoter** vi (*étoiles etc*) to
twinkle; (*lumière*) to flicker
climat [klima] nm climate
climatisation [klimatizasjɔ̃] nf air
conditioning; **climatisé, e** adj air-conditioned
clin d'œil [klɛ̃dœj] nm wink; **en un clin d'œil**
in a flash
clinique [klinik] nf private hospital
clip [klip] nm (*boucle d'oreille*) clip-on; **(vidéo)
~** (pop) video
cliquer [klike] vt to click; **~ sur** to click on
clochard, e [klɔʃaʀ, aʀd] nm/f tramp
cloche [klɔʃ] nf (*d'église*) bell; (*fam*) clot;
clocher nm church tower; (*en pointe*) steeple
▷ vi (*fam*) to be ou go wrong; **de clocher** (*péj*)
parochial
cloison [klwazɔ̃] nf partition (wall)
clonage [klɔnaʒ] nm cloning
cloner [klɔne] vt to clone
cloque [klɔk] nf blister
clore [klɔʀ] vt to close
clôture [klotyʀ] nf closure; (*barrière*) enclosure
clou [klu] nm nail; **clous** nmpl (*passage clouté*)
pedestrian crossing; **pneus à ~s** studded
tyres; **le ~ du spectacle** the highlight of the

show; **clou de girofle** clove

clown [klun] *nm* clown

club [klœb] *nm* club

CNRS *sigle m* (= *Centre nationale de la recherche scientifique*) ≈ SERC (BRIT), ≈ NSF (US)

coaguler [kɔagyle] *vt, vi* (*aussi*: **se ~**: *sang*) to coagulate

cobaye [kɔbaj] *nm* guinea-pig

coca [kɔka] *nm* Coke®

cocaïne [kɔkain] *nf* cocaine

coccinelle [kɔksinɛl] *nf* ladybird (BRIT), ladybug (US)

cocher [kɔʃe] *vt* to tick off

cochon, ne [kɔʃɔ̃, ɔn] *nm* pig ▷ *adj* (*fam*) dirty, smutty; **cochon d'Inde** guinea pig; **cochonnerie** (*fam*) *nf* (*saleté*) filth; (*marchandise*) rubbish, trash

cocktail [kɔktɛl] *nm* cocktail; (*réception*) cocktail party

cocorico [kɔkɔriko] *excl, nm* cock-a-doodle-do

cocotte [kɔkɔt] *nf* (*en fonte*) casserole; **ma ~** (*fam*) sweetie (pie); **cocotte (minute)**® pressure cooker

code [kɔd] *nm* code ▷ *adj*: **phares ~s** dipped lights; **se mettre en ~(s)** to dip one's (head)lights; **code à barres** bar code; **code civil** Common Law; **code de la route** highway code; **code pénal** penal code; **code postal** (*numéro*) post (BRIT) ou zip (US) code

cœur [kœr] *nm* heart; (*Cartes: couleur*) hearts *pl*; (: *carte*) heart; **avoir bon ~** to be kind-hearted; **avoir mal au ~** to feel sick; **par ~** by heart; **de bon ~** willingly; **cela lui tient à ~** that's (very) close to his heart

coffre [kɔfr] *nm* (*meuble*) chest; (*d'auto*) boot (BRIT), trunk (US); **coffre-fort** *nm* safe; **coffret** *nm* casket

cognac [kɔɲak] *nm* brandy, cognac

cogner [kɔɲe] *vi* to knock; **se ~ contre** to knock ou bump into; **se ~ la tête** to bang one's head

cohérent, e [kɔerɑ̃, ɑ̃t] *adj* coherent, consistent

coiffé, e [kwafe] *adj*: **bien/mal ~** with tidy/untidy hair; **~ d'un chapeau** wearing a hat

coiffer [kwafe] *vt* (*fig: surmonter*) to cover, top; **se coiffer** *vi* to do one's hair; **~ qn** to do sb's hair; **coiffeur, -euse** *nm/f* hairdresser; **coiffeuse** *nf* (*table*) dressing table; **coiffure** *nf* (*cheveux*) hairstyle, hairdo; (*art*): **la coiffure** hairdressing

coin [kwɛ̃] *nm* corner; (*pour coincer*) wedge; **l'épicerie du ~** the local grocer; **dans le ~** (*aux alentours*) in the area, around about; (*habiter*) locally; **je ne suis pas du ~** I'm not from here; **au ~ du feu** by the fireside; **regard en ~** sideways glance

coincé, e [kwɛ̃se] *adj* stuck, jammed; (*fig:*

inhibé) inhibited, hung up (*fam*)

coïncidence [kɔɛ̃sidɑ̃s] *nf* coincidence

coing [kwɛ̃] *nm* quince

col [kɔl] *nm* (*de chemise*) collar; (*encolure, cou*) neck; (*de montagne*) pass; **col de l'utérus** cervix; **col roulé** polo-neck

colère [kɔlɛr] *nf* anger; **une ~** a fit of anger; **(se mettre) en ~ (contre qn)** (to get) angry (with sb); **coléreux, -euse, colérique** *adj* quick-tempered, irascible

colin [kɔlɛ̃] *nm* hake

colique [kɔlik] *nf* diarrhoea

colis [kɔli] *nm* parcel

collaborer [kɔ(l)labɔre] *vi* to collaborate; **~ à** to collaborate on; (*revue*) to contribute to

collant, e [kɔlɑ̃, ɑ̃t] *adj* sticky; (*robe etc*) clinging, skintight; (*péj*) clinging ▷ *nm* (*bas*) tights *pl*; (*de danseur*) leotard

colle [kɔl] *nf* glue; (*à papiers peints*) (wallpaper) paste; (*fam: devinette*) teaser, riddle; (*Scol: fam*) detention

collecte [kɔlɛkt] *nf* collection; **collectif, -ive** *adj* collective; (*visite, billet*) group *cpd*

collection [kɔlɛksjɔ̃] *nf* collection; (*Édition*) series; **collectionner** *vt* to collect; **collectionneur, -euse** *nm/f* collector

collectivité [kɔlɛktivite] *nf* group; **collectivités locales** (*Admin*) local authorities

collège [kɔlɛʒ] *nm* (*école*) (secondary) school; (*assemblée*) body; **collégien** *nm* schoolboy

collègue [kɔ(l)lɛg] *nm/f* colleague

coller [kɔle] *vt* (*papier, timbre*) to stick (on); (*affiche*) to stick up; (*enveloppe*) to stick down; (*morceaux*) to stick ou glue together; (*Comput*) to paste; (*fam: mettre, fourrer*) to stick, shove; (*Scol: fam*) to keep in ▷ *vi* (*être collant*) to be sticky; (*adhérer*) to stick; **~ à** to stick to; **être collé à un examen** (*fam*) to fail an exam

collier [kɔlje] *nm* (*bijou*) necklace; (*de chien, Tech*) collar

colline [kɔlin] *nf* hill

collision [kɔlizjɔ̃] *nf* collision, crash; **entrer en ~ (avec)** to collide (with)

collyre [kɔlir] *nm* eye drops

colombe [kɔlɔ̃b] *nf* dove

Colombie [kɔlɔ̃bi] *nf*: **la ~** Colombia

colonie [kɔlɔni] *nf* colony; **colonie (de vacances)** holiday camp (*for children*)

colonne [kɔlɔn] *nf* column; **se mettre en ~ par deux** to get into twos; **colonne (vertébrale)** spine, spinal column

colorant [kɔlɔrɑ̃] *nm* colouring

colorer [kɔlɔre] *vt* to colour

colorier [kɔlɔrje] *vt* to colour (in)

coloris [kɔlɔri] *nm* colour, shade

colza [kɔlza] *nm* rape(seed)

coma [kɔma] *nm* coma; **être dans le ~** to be in a coma

combat [kɔ̃ba] *nm* fight, fighting *no pl*;

combat de boxe boxing match; **combattant** *nm*: **ancien combattant** war veteran; **combattre** *vt* to fight; (*épidémie, ignorance*) to combat, fight against

combien [kɔ̃bjɛ̃] *adv* (*quantité*) how much; (*nombre*) how many; **~ de** (*quantité*) how much; (*nombre*) how many; **~ de temps** how long; **~ ça coûte/pèse?** how much does it cost/weigh?; **on est le ~ aujourd'hui?** (*fam*) what's the date today?

combinaison [kɔ̃binɛzɔ̃] *nf* combination; (*astuce*) scheme; (*de femme*) slip; (*de plongée*) wetsuit; (*bleu de travail*) boiler suit (BRIT), coveralls *pl* (US)

combiné [kɔ̃bine] *nm* (*aussi:* **~ téléphonique**) receiver

comble [kɔ̃bl] *adj* (*salle*) packed (full) ▷ *nm* (*du bonheur, plaisir*) height; **combles** *nmpl* (*Constr*) attic *sg*, loft *sg*; **c'est le ~!** that beats everything!

combler [kɔ̃ble] *vt* (*trou*) to fill in; (*besoin, lacune*) to fill; (*déficit*) to make good; (*satisfaire*) to fulfil

comédie [kɔmedi] *nf* comedy; (*fig*) playacting *no pl*; **faire la ~** (*fam*) to make a fuss; **comédie musicale** musical; **comédien, ne** *nm/f* actor(-tress)

comestible [kɔmɛstibl] *adj* edible

comique [kɔmik] *adj* (*drôle*) comical; (*Théâtre*) comic ▷ *nm* (*artiste*) comic, comedian

commandant [kɔmɑ̃dɑ̃] *nm* (*gén*) commander, commandant; (*Navig, Aviat*) captain

commande [kɔmɑ̃d] *nf* (*Comm*) order; **commandes** *nfpl* (*Aviat etc*) controls; **sur ~** to order; **commander** *vt* (*Comm*) to order; (*diriger, ordonner*) to command; **commander à qn de faire** to command *ou* order sb to do; **je peux commander, s'il vous plaît?** can I order, please?

 MOT-CLÉ

comme [kɔm] *prép* **1** (*comparaison*) like; **tout comme son père** just like his father; **fort comme un bœuf** as strong as an ox; **joli comme tout** ever so pretty

2 (*manière*) like; **faites-le comme ça** do it like this, do it this way; **comme ci, comme ça** so-so, middling; **comme il faut** (*correctement*) properly

3 (*en tant que*) as a; **donner comme prix** to give as a prize; **travailler comme secrétaire** to work as a secretary

▷ *conj* **1** (*ainsi que*) as; **elle écrit comme elle parle** she writes as she talks; **comme si** as if

2 (*au moment où, alors que*) as; **il est parti comme j'arrivais** he left as I arrived

3 (*parce que, puisque*) as; **comme il était en**

retard, il ... as he was late, he ...

▷ *adv*: **comme il est fort/c'est bon!** he's so strong/it's so good!

commencement [kɔmɑ̃smɑ̃] *nm* beginning, start

commencer [kɔmɑ̃se] *vt, vi* to begin, start; **~ à ou de faire** to begin *ou* start doing

comment [kɔmɑ̃] *adv* how; **~?** (*que dites-vous*) pardon?; **et ~!** and how!

commentaire [kɔmɑ̃tɛʁ] *nm* (*remarque*) comment, remark; (*exposé*) commentary

commerçant, e [kɔmɛʁsɑ̃, ɑ̃t] *nm/f* shopkeeper, trader

commerce [kɔmɛʁs] *nm* (*activité*) trade, commerce; (*boutique*) business; **~ électronique** e-commerce; **~ équitable** fair trade; **commercial, e, -aux** *adj* commercial, trading; (*péj*) commercial; **les commerciaux** the sales people; **commercialiser** *vt* to market

commissaire [kɔmisɛʁ] *nm* (*de police*) ≈ (police) superintendent; **commissaire aux comptes** (*Admin*) auditor; **commissariat** *nm* police station

commission [kɔmisjɔ̃] *nf* (*comité, pourcentage*) commission; (*message*) message; (*course*) errand; **commissions** *nfpl* (*achats*) shopping *sg*

commode [kɔmɔd] *adj* (*pratique*) convenient, handy; (*facile*) easy; (*personne*): **pas ~** awkward (to deal with) ▷ *nf* chest of drawers

commun, e [kɔmœ̃, yn] *adj* common; (*pièce*) communal, shared; (*effort*) joint; **ça sort du ~** it's out of the ordinary; **le ~ des mortels** the common run of people; **en ~** (*faire*) jointly; **mettre en ~** to pool, share; **communs** *nmpl* (*bâtiments*) outbuildings; **d'un ~ accord** by mutual agreement

communauté [kɔmynote] *nf* community

commune [kɔmyn] *nf* (*Admin*) commune, ≈ district; (: *urbaine*) ≈ borough

communication [kɔmynikasjɔ̃] *nf* communication

communier [kɔmynje] *vi* (*Rel*) to receive communion

communion [kɔmynjɔ̃] *nf* communion

communiquer [kɔmynike] *vt* (*nouvelle, dossier*) to pass on, convey; (*peur etc*) to communicate ▷ *vi* to communicate; **se communiquer à** (*se propager*) to spread to

communisme [kɔmynism] *nm* communism; **communiste** *adj, nm/f* communist

commutateur [kɔmytatœʁ] *nm* (*Élec*) (change-over) switch, commutator

compact, e [kɔ̃pakt] *adj* (*dense*) dense; (*appareil*) compact

compagne [kɔ̃paɲ] *nf* companion

compagnie [kɔ̃paɲi] *nf* (*firme, Mil*) company;

tenir ~ à qn to keep sb company; **fausser ~ à qn** to give sb the slip, slip ou sneak away from sb; **compagnie aérienne** airline (company)

compagnon [kɔ̃paɲɔ̃] nm companion

comparable [kɔ̃paʀabl] adj: **~ (à)** comparable (to)

comparaison [kɔ̃paʀɛzɔ̃] nf comparison

comparer [kɔ̃paʀe] vt to compare; **~ qch/qn à** ou **et** (pour choisir) to compare sth/sb with ou and; (pour établir une similitude) to compare sth/sb to

compartiment [kɔ̃paʀtimɑ̃] nm compartment; **un ~ non-fumeurs** a non-smoking compartment (BRIT) ou car (US)

compas [kɔ̃pɑ] nm (Géom) (pair of) compasses pl; (Navig) compass

compatible [kɔ̃patibl] adj compatible

compatriote [kɔ̃patʀijɔt] nm/f compatriot

compensation [kɔ̃pɑ̃sasjɔ̃] nf compensation

compenser [kɔ̃pɑ̃se] vt to compensate for, make up for

compétence [kɔ̃petɑ̃s] nf competence

compétent, e [kɔ̃petɑ̃, ɑ̃t] adj (apte) competent, capable

compétition [kɔ̃petisjɔ̃] nf (gén) competition; (Sport: épreuve) event; **la ~ automobile** motor racing

complément [kɔ̃plemɑ̃] nm complement; (reste) remainder; **complément d'information** (Admin) supplementary ou further information; **complémentaire** adj complementary; (additionnel) supplementary

complet, -ète [kɔ̃plɛ, ɛt] adj complete; (plein: hôtel etc) full ▷ nm (aussi: **~-veston**) suit; **pain complet** wholemeal bread; **complètement** adv completely; **compléter** vt (porter à la quantité voulue) to complete; (augmenter: connaissances, études) to complement, supplement; (: garde-robe) to add to

complexe [kɔ̃plɛks] adj, nm complex; **complexe hospitalier/industriel** hospital/industrial complex; **complexé, e** adj mixed-up, hung-up

complication [kɔ̃plikasjɔ̃] nf complexity, intricacy; (difficulté, ennui) complication; **complications** nfpl (Méd) complications

complice [kɔ̃plis] nm accomplice

compliment [kɔ̃plimɑ̃] nm (louange) compliment; **compliments** nmpl (félicitations) congratulations

compliqué, e [kɔ̃plike] adj complicated, complex; (personne) complicated

comportement [kɔ̃pɔʀtəmɑ̃] nm behaviour

comporter [kɔ̃pɔʀte] vt (consister en) to consist of, comprise; (inclure) to have; **se comporter** vi to behave

composer [kɔ̃poze] vt (musique, texte) to compose; (mélange, équipe) to make up; (numéro) to dial; (constituer) to make up, form ▷ vi (transiger) to come to terms; **se composer de** to be composed of, be made up of;

compositeur, -trice nm/f (Mus) composer;

composition nf composition; (Scol) test

composter [kɔ̃pɔste] vt (billet) to punch

- **COMPOSTER**
-
- In France you have to punch your ticket on
- the platform to validate it before getting
- onto the train.

compote [kɔ̃pɔt] nf stewed fruit no pl; **compote de pommes** stewed apples

compréhensible [kɔ̃pʀeɑ̃sibl] adj comprehensible; (attitude) understandable

compréhensif, -ive [kɔ̃pʀeɑ̃sif, iv] adj understanding

> Attention à ne pas traduire **compréhensif** par **comprehensive**.

comprendre [kɔ̃pʀɑ̃dʀ] vt to understand; (se composer de) to comprise, consist of

compresse [kɔ̃pʀɛs] nf compress

comprimé [kɔ̃pʀime] nm tablet

compris, e [kɔ̃pʀi, iz] pp de **comprendre** ▷ adj (inclus) included; **~ entre** (situé) contained between; **l'électricité ~e/non ~e, y/non ~ l'électricité** including/excluding electricity; **100 euros tout ~** 100 euros all inclusive ou all-in

comptabilité [kɔ̃tabilite] nf (activité) accounting, accountancy; (comptes) accounts pl, books pl; (service) accounts office

comptable [kɔ̃tabl] nm/f accountant

comptant [kɔ̃tɑ̃] adv: **payer ~** to pay cash; **acheter ~** to buy for cash

compte [kɔ̃t] nm count, (total, montant) count, (right) number; (bancaire, facture) account; **comptes** nmpl (Finance) accounts, books; (fig) explanation sg; **en fin de ~** all things considered; **s'en tirer à bon ~** to get off lightly; **pour le ~ de** on behalf of; **pour son propre ~** for one's own benefit; **régler un ~** (s'acquitter de qch) to settle an account; (se venger) to get one's own back; **rendre des ~s à qn** (fig) to be answerable to sb; **tenir ~ de** to take account of; **travailler à son ~** to work for oneself; **rendre ~ (à qn) de qch** to give (sb) an account of sth; voir aussi **rendre**; **compte à rebours** countdown; **compte courant** current account; **compte rendu** account, report; (de film, livre) review; **compte-gouttes** nm inv dropper

compter [kɔ̃te] vt to count; (facturer) to charge for; (avoir à son actif, comporter) to have; (prévoir) to allow, reckon; (penser, espérer): **~ réussir** to expect to succeed ▷ vi to count; (être économe) to economize; (figurer): **~ parmi** to be ou rank among; **~ sur** to count (up)on; **~**

avec qch/qn to reckon with ou take account of sth/sb; **sans ~ que** besides which
compteur [kɔ̃tœʀ] nm meter; **compteur de vitesse** speedometer
comptine [kɔ̃tin] nf nursery rhyme
comptoir [kɔ̃twaʀ] nm (de magasin) counter; (bar) bar
con, ne [kɔ̃, kɔn] (fam!) adj damned ou bloody (BRIT) stupid (!)
concentrer [kɔ̃sɑ̃tʀe] vt to concentrate; **se concentrer** vi to concentrate
concerner [kɔ̃sɛʀne] vt to concern; **en ce qui me concerne** as far as I am concerned
concert [kɔ̃sɛʀ] nm concert; **de ~** (décider) unanimously
concessionnaire [kɔ̃sesjɔnɛʀ] nm/f agent, dealer
concevoir [kɔ̃s(ə)vwaʀ] vt (idée, projet) to conceive (of); (comprendre) to understand; (enfant) to conceive; **bien/mal conçu** well-/badly-designed
concierge [kɔ̃sjɛʀʒ] nm/f caretaker
concis, e [kɔ̃si, iz] adj concise
conclure [kɔ̃klyʀ] vt to conclude; **conclusion** nf conclusion
conçois etc [kɔ̃swa] vb voir **concevoir**
concombre [kɔ̃kɔ̃bʀ] nm cucumber
concours [kɔ̃kuʀ] nm competition; (Scol) competitive examination; (assistance) aid, help; **concours de circonstances** combination of circumstances; **concours hippique** horse show
concret, -ète [kɔ̃kʀɛ, ɛt] adj concrete
conçu, e [kɔ̃sy] pp de **concevoir**
concubinage [kɔ̃kybinaʒ] nm (Jur) cohabitation
concurrence [kɔ̃kyʀɑ̃s] nf competition; **faire ~ à** to be in competition with; **jusqu'à ~ de** up to
concurrent, e [kɔ̃kyʀɑ̃, ɑ̃t] nm/f (Sport, Écon etc) competitor; (Scol) candidate
condamner [kɔ̃dane] vt (blâmer) to condemn; (Jur) to sentence; (porte, ouverture) to fill in, block up; **~ qn à 2 ans de prison** to sentence sb to 2 years' imprisonment
condensation [kɔ̃dɑ̃sasjɔ̃] nf condensation
condition [kɔ̃disjɔ̃] nf condition; **conditions** nfpl (tarif, prix) terms; (circonstances) conditions; **sans ~s** unconditionally; **à ~ de** ou **que** provided that; **conditionnel, le** nm conditional (tense)
conditionnement [kɔ̃disjɔnmɑ̃] nm (emballage) packaging
condoléances [kɔ̃dɔleɑ̃s] nfpl condolences
conducteur, -trice [kɔ̃dyktœʀ, tʀis] nm/f driver ▷ nm (Élec etc) conductor
conduire [kɔ̃dʒᴜiʀ] vt to drive; (délégation, troupeau) to lead; **se conduire** vi to behave; **~ à** to lead to; **~ qn quelque part** to take sb

somewhere; to drive sb somewhere
conduite [kɔ̃dʒᴜit] nf (comportement) behaviour; (d'eau, de gaz) pipe; **sous la ~ de** led by
confection [kɔ̃fɛksjɔ̃] nf (fabrication) making; (Couture): **la ~** the clothing industry
conférence [kɔ̃feʀɑ̃s] nf conference; (exposé) lecture; **conférence de presse** press conference
confesser [kɔ̃fese] vt to confess; **confession** nf confession; (culte: catholique etc) denomination
confetti [kɔ̃feti] nm confetti no pl
confiance [kɔ̃fjɑ̃s] nf (en l'honnêteté de qn) confidence, trust; (en la valeur de qch) faith; **avoir ~ en** to have confidence ou faith in, trust; **faire ~ à qn** to trust sb; **mettre qn en ~** to win sb's trust; **confiance en soi** self-confidence
confiant, e [kɔ̃fjɑ̃, jɑ̃t] adj confident; trusting
confidence [kɔ̃fidɑ̃s] nf confidence; **confidentiel, le** adj confidential
confier [kɔ̃fje] vt: **~ à qn** (objet, travail) to entrust to sb; (secret, pensée) to confide to sb; **se ~ à qn** to confide in sb
confirmation [kɔ̃fiʀmasjɔ̃] nf confirmation
confirmer [kɔ̃fiʀme] vt to confirm
confiserie [kɔ̃fizʀi] nf (magasin) confectioner's ou sweet shop; **confiseries** nfpl (bonbons) confectionery sg
confisquer [kɔ̃fiske] vt to confiscate
confit, e [kɔ̃fi, it] adj: **fruits ~s** crystallized fruits; **confit d'oie** nm conserve of goose
confiture [kɔ̃fityʀ] nf jam
conflit [kɔ̃fli] nm conflict
confondre [kɔ̃fɔ̃dʀ] vt (jumeaux, faits) to confuse, mix up; (témoin, menteur) to confound; **se confondre** vi to merge; **se ~ en excuses** to apologize profusely
conforme [kɔ̃fɔʀm] adj: **~ à** (loi, règle) in accordance with; **conformément** adv: **conformément à** in accordance with; **conformer** vt: **se conformer à** to conform to
confort [kɔ̃fɔʀ] nm comfort; **tout ~** (Comm) with all modern conveniences; **confortable** adj comfortable
confronter [kɔ̃fʀɔ̃te] vt to confront
confus, e [kɔ̃fy, yz] adj (vague) confused; (embarrassé) embarrassed; **confusion** nf (voir confus) confusion; embarrassment; (voir confondre) confusion, mixing up
congé [kɔ̃ʒe] nm (vacances) holiday; **en ~** on holiday; **semaine/jour de ~** week/day off; **prendre ~ de qn** to take one's leave of sb; **donner son ~ à** to give in one's notice to; **congé de maladie** sick leave; **congé de maternité** maternity leave; **congés payés** paid holiday
congédier [kɔ̃ʒedje] vt to dismiss
congélateur [kɔ̃ʒelatœʀ] nm freezer

congeler [kɔ̃ʒ(ə)le] vt to freeze; **les produits congelés** frozen foods

congestion [kɔ̃ʒɛstjɔ̃] nf congestion

Congo [kɔ̃go] nm: **le ~** Congo, the Democratic Republic of the Congo

congrès [kɔ̃gʀɛ] nm congress

conifère [kɔnifɛʀ] nm conifer

conjoint, e [kɔ̃ʒwɛ̃, wɛ̃t] adj joint ▷ nm/f spouse

conjonctivite [kɔ̃ʒɔ̃ktivit] nf conjunctivitis

conjoncture [kɔ̃ʒɔ̃ktyʀ] nf circumstances pl; **la ~ actuelle** the present (economic) situation

conjugaison [kɔ̃ʒygɛzɔ̃] nf (Ling) conjugation

connaissance [kɔnɛsɑ̃s] nf (savoir) knowledge no pl; (personne connue) acquaintance; **être sans ~** to be unconscious; **perdre/reprendre ~** to lose/regain consciousness; **à ma/sa ~** to (the best of) my/his knowledge; **faire la ~ de qn** to meet sb

connaisseur, -euse [kɔnɛsœʀ, øz] nm/f connoisseur

connaître [kɔnɛtʀ] vt to know; (éprouver) to experience; (avoir: succès) to have, enjoy; **~ de nom/vue** to know by name/sight; **ils se sont connus à Genève** they (first) met in Geneva; **s'y ~ en qch** to know a lot about sth

connecter [kɔnɛkte] vt to connect; **se ~ à Internet** to log onto the Internet

connerie [kɔnʀi] (fam!) nf stupid thing (to do/say)

connexion [kɔnɛksjɔ̃] nf connection

connu, e [kɔny] adj (célèbre) well-known

conquérir [kɔ̃keʀiʀ] vt to conquer; **conquête** nf conquest

consacrer [kɔ̃sakʀe] vt (employer) to devote, dedicate; (Rel) to consecrate; **se ~ à qch** to dedicate ou devote o.s. to sth

conscience [kɔ̃sjɑ̃s] nf conscience; **avoir/ prendre ~ de** to be/become aware of; **perdre ~** to lose consciousness; **avoir bonne/ mauvaise ~** to have a clear/guilty conscience; **consciencieux, -euse** adj conscientious; **conscient, e** adj conscious

consécutif, -ive [kɔ̃sekytif, iv] adj consecutive; **~ à** following upon

conseil [kɔ̃sɛj] nm (avis) piece of advice; (assemblée) council; **des ~s** advice; **prendre ~ (auprès de qn)** to take advice (from sb); **conseil d'administration** board (of directors); **conseil des ministres** ≈ the Cabinet; **conseil municipal** town council

conseiller, -ère [kɔ̃seje, ɛʀ] nm/f adviser ▷ vt (personne) to advise; (méthode, action) to recommend, advise; **~ à qn de** to advise sb to; **pouvez-vous me ~ un bon restaurant?** can you suggest a good restaurant?

consentement [kɔ̃sɑ̃tmɑ̃] nm consent

consentir [kɔ̃sɑ̃tiʀ] vt to agree, consent

conséquence [kɔ̃sekɑ̃s] nf consequence;

en ~ (donc) consequently; (de façon appropriée) accordingly; **conséquent, e** adj logical, rational; (fam: important) substantial; **par conséquent** consequently

conservateur, -trice [kɔ̃sɛʀvatœʀ, tʀis] nm/f (Pol) conservative; (de musée) curator ▷ nm (pour aliments) preservative

conservatoire [kɔ̃sɛʀvatwaʀ] nm academy

conserve [kɔ̃sɛʀv] nf (gén pl) canned ou tinned (BRIT) food; **en ~** canned, tinned (BRIT)

conserver [kɔ̃sɛʀve] vt (faculté) to retain, keep; (amis, livres) to keep; (préserver, Culin) to preserve

considérable [kɔ̃sideʀabl] adj considerable, significant, extensive

considération [kɔ̃sideʀasjɔ̃] nf consideration; (estime) esteem

considérer [kɔ̃sideʀe] vt to consider; **~ qch comme** to regard sth as

consigne [kɔ̃siɲ] nf (de gare) left luggage (office) (BRIT), checkroom (US); (ordre, instruction) instructions pl; **consigne automatique** left-luggage locker

consister [kɔ̃siste] vi: **~ en/à faire** to consist of/in doing

consoler [kɔ̃sɔle] vt to console

consommateur, -trice [kɔ̃sɔmatœʀ, tʀis] nm/f (Écon) consumer; (dans un café) customer

consommation [kɔ̃sɔmasjɔ̃] nf (boisson) drink; (Écon) consumption; **de ~** (biens, sociétés) consumer cpd

consommer [kɔ̃sɔme] vt (suj: personne) to eat ou drink, consume; (: voiture, machine) to use, consume; (mariage) to consummate ▷ vi (dans un café) to (have a) drink

consonne [kɔ̃sɔn] nf consonant

constamment [kɔ̃stamɑ̃] adv constantly

constant, e [kɔ̃stɑ̃, ɑ̃t] adj constant; (personne) steadfast

constat [kɔ̃sta] nm (de police, d'accident) report; **~ (à l')amiable** jointly-agreed statement for insurance purposes; **~ d'échec** acknowledgement of failure

constatation [kɔ̃statasjɔ̃] nf (observation) (observed) fact, observation

constater [kɔ̃state] vt (remarquer) to note; (Admin, Jur: attester) to certify

consterner [kɔ̃stɛʀne] vt to dismay

constipé, e [kɔ̃stipe] adj constipated

constitué, e [kɔ̃stitɥe] adj: **~ de** made up ou composed of

constituer [kɔ̃stitɥe] vt (équipe) to set up; (dossier, collection) to put together; (suj: éléments: composer) to make up, constitute; (représenter, être) to constitute; **se ~ prisonnier** to give o.s. up

constructeur, -trice [kɔ̃stʀyktœʀ, tʀis] nm/f manufacturer, builder

constructif, -ive [kɔ̃stʀyktif, iv] adj

constructive

construction [kɔ̃stʀyksjɔ̃] nf construction, building

construire [kɔ̃stʀyiʀ] vt to build, construct

consul [kɔ̃syl] nm consul; **consulat** nm consulate

consultant [kɔ̃syltɑ̃] adj, nm consultant

consultation [kɔ̃syltasjɔ̃] nf consultation; **heures de ~** (Méd) surgery (BRIT) ou office (US) hours

consulter [kɔ̃sylte] vt to consult ▷ vi (médecin) to hold surgery (BRIT), be in (the office) (US)

contact [kɔ̃takt] nm contact; **au ~ de** (air, peau) on contact with; (gens) through contact with; **mettre/couper le ~** (Auto) to switch on/off the ignition; **entrer en** ou **prendre ~ avec** to get in touch ou contact with; **contacter** vt to contact, get in touch with

contagieux, -euse [kɔ̃taʒjø, jøz] adj infectious; (par le contact) contagious

contaminer [kɔ̃tamine] vt to contaminate

conte [kɔ̃t] nm tale; **conte de fées** fairy tale

contempler [kɔ̃tɑ̃ple] vt to contemplate, gaze at

contemporain, e [kɔ̃tɑ̃pɔʀɛ̃, ɛn] adj, nm/f contemporary

contenir [kɔ̃t(ə)niʀ] vt to contain; (avoir une capacité de) to hold

content, e [kɔ̃tɑ̃, ɑ̃t] adj pleased, glad; **~ de** pleased with; **contenter** vt to satisfy, please; **se contenter de** to content o.s. with

contenu [kɔ̃t(ə)ny] nm (d'un récipient) contents pl; (d'un texte) content

conter [kɔ̃te] vt to recount, relate

conteste [kɔ̃tɛst]: **sans ~** adv unquestionably, indisputably; **contester** vt to question ▷ vi (Pol, gén) rebel (against established authority)

contexte [kɔ̃tɛkst] nm context

continent [kɔ̃tinɑ̃] nm continent

continu, e [kɔ̃tiny] adj continuous; **faire la journée ~e** to work without taking a full lunch break; **(courant) continu** direct current, DC

continuel, le [kɔ̃tinɥɛl] adj (qui se répète) constant, continual; (continu) continuous

continuer [kɔ̃tinɥe] vt (travail, voyage etc) to continue (with), carry on (with), go on (with); (prolonger: alignement, rue) to continue ▷ vi (vie, bruit) to continue, go on; **~ à** ou **de faire** to go on ou continue doing

contourner [kɔ̃tuʀne] vt to go round; (difficulté) to get round

contraceptif, -ive [kɔ̃tʀasɛptif, iv] adj, nm contraceptive; **contraception** nf contraception

contracté, e [kɔ̃tʀakte] adj tense

contracter [kɔ̃tʀakte] vt (muscle etc) to tense, contract; (maladie, dette) to contract; (assurance) to take out; **se contracter** vi

(muscles) to contract

contractuel, le [kɔ̃tʀaktɥɛl] nm/f (agent) traffic warden

contradiction [kɔ̃tʀadiksjɔ̃] nf contradiction; **contradictoire** adj contradictory, conflicting

contraignant, e [kɔ̃tʀeɲɑ̃, ɑ̃t] adj restricting

contraindre [kɔ̃tʀɛ̃dʀ] vt: **~ qn à faire** to compel sb to do; **contrainte** nf constraint

contraire [kɔ̃tʀɛʀ] adj, nm opposite; **~ à** contrary to; **au ~** on the contrary

contrarier [kɔ̃tʀaʀje] vt (personne: irriter) to annoy; (fig: projets) to thwart, frustrate; **contrariété** nf annoyance

contraste [kɔ̃tʀast] nm contrast

contrat [kɔ̃tʀa] nm contract

contravention [kɔ̃tʀavɑ̃sjɔ̃] nf parking ticket

contre [kɔ̃tʀ] prép against; (en échange) (in exchange) for; **par ~** on the other hand

contrebande [kɔ̃tʀəbɑ̃d] nf (trafic) contraband, smuggling; (marchandise) contraband, smuggled goods pl; **faire la ~ de** to smuggle

contrebas [kɔ̃tʀəba]: **en ~** adv (down) below

contrebasse [kɔ̃tʀəbas] nf (double) bass

contre...: **contrecoup** nm repercussions pl; **contredire** vt (personne) to contradict; (faits) to refute

contrefaçon [kɔ̃tʀəfasɔ̃] nf forgery

contre...: **contre-indication** (pl contre-indications) nf (Méd) contra-indication; **"contre-indication en cas d'eczéma"** "should not be used by people with eczema"; **contre-indiqué, e** adj (Méd) contraindicated; (déconseillé) unadvisable, ill-advised

contremaître [kɔ̃tʀəmɛtʀ] nm foreman

contre-plaqué [kɔ̃tʀəplake] nm plywood

contresens [kɔ̃tʀəsɑ̃s] nm (erreur) misinterpretation; (de traduction) mistranslation; **à ~** the wrong way

contretemps [kɔ̃tʀətɑ̃] nm hitch; **à ~** (fig) at an inopportune moment

contribuer [kɔ̃tʀibɥe]: **~ à** vt to contribute towards; **contribution** nf contribution; **mettre à contribution** to call upon; **contributions directes/indirectes** direct/indirect taxation

contrôle [kɔ̃tʀol] nm checking no pl, check; (des prix) monitoring, control; (test) test, examination; **perdre le ~ de** (véhicule) to lose control of; **contrôle continu** (Scol) continuous assessment; **contrôle d'identité** identity check

contrôler [kɔ̃tʀole] vt (vérifier) to check; (surveiller: opérations) to supervise; (: prix) to monitor, control; (maîtriser, Comm: firme) to control; **contrôleur, -euse** nm/f (de train) (ticket) inspector; (de bus) (bus) conductor(-tress)

controversé, e [kɔ̃tʀɔvɛʀse] adj (personnage, question) controversial

contusion [kɔ̃tyzjɔ̃] nf bruise, contusion

convaincre [kɔ̃vɛ̃kʀ] vt: ~ **qn (de qch)** to convince sb (of sth); ~ **qn (de faire)** to persuade sb (to do)

convalescence [kɔ̃valesɑ̃s] nf convalescence

convenable [kɔ̃vnabl] adj suitable; (assez bon, respectable) decent

convenir [kɔ̃vniʀ] vi to be suitable; ~ **à** to suit; ~ **de** (bien-fondé de qch) to admit (to), acknowledge; (date, somme etc) to agree upon; ~ **que** (admettre) to admit that; ~ **de faire** to agree to do

convention [kɔ̃vɑ̃sjɔ̃] nf convention; **conventions** nfpl (convenances) convention sg; **convention collective** (Écon) collective agreement; **conventionné, e** adj (Admin) applying charges laid down by the state

convenu, e [kɔ̃vny] pp de **convenir** ▷ adj agreed

conversation [kɔ̃vɛʀsasjɔ̃] nf conversation

convertir [kɔ̃vɛʀtiʀ] vt: ~ **qn (à)** to convert sb (to); **se convertir (à)** to be converted (to); ~ **qch en** to convert sth into

conviction [kɔ̃viksjɔ̃] nf conviction

convienne etc [kɔ̃vjɛn] vb voir **convenir**

convivial, e, -aux [kɔ̃vivjal, jo] adj (Inform) user-friendly

convocation [kɔ̃vɔkasjɔ̃] nf (document) notification to attend; (: Jur) summons sg

convoquer [kɔ̃vɔke] vt (assemblée) to convene; (subordonné) to summon; (candidat) to ask to attend

coopération [kɔɔpeʀasjɔ̃] nf co-operation; (Admin): **la C~** ≈ Voluntary Service Overseas (BRIT), ≈ Peace Corps (US)

coopérer [kɔɔpeʀe] vi: ~ **(à)** to co-operate (in)

coordonné, e [kɔɔʀdɔne] adj coordinated; **coordonnées** nfpl (adresse etc) address and telephone number

coordonner [kɔɔʀdɔne] vt to coordinate

copain [kɔpɛ̃] (fam) nm mate, pal; (petit ami) boyfriend

copie [kɔpi] nf copy; (Scol) script, paper; **copier** vt, vi to copy; **copier coller** (Comput) copy and paste; **copier sur** to copy from; **copieur** nm (photo)copier

copieux, -euse [kɔpjø, jøz] adj copious

copine [kɔpin] (fam) nf mate, pal; (petite amie) girlfriend

coq [kɔk] nm cock, rooster

coque [kɔk] nf (de noix, mollusque) shell; (de bateau) hull; **à la ~** (Culin) (soft-)boiled

coquelicot [kɔkliko] nm poppy

coqueluche [kɔklyʃ] nf whooping-cough

coquet, te [kɔkɛ, ɛt] adj appearance-

conscious; (logement) smart, charming

coquetier [kɔk(ə)tje] nm egg-cup

coquillage [kɔkijaʒ] nm (mollusque) shellfish inv; (coquille) shell

coquille [kɔkij] nf shell; (Typo) misprint; **coquille St Jacques** scallop

coquin, e [kɔkɛ̃, in] adj mischievous, roguish; (polisson) naughty

cor [kɔʀ] nm (Mus) horn; (Méd): ~ **(au pied)** corn

corail, -aux [kɔʀaj, o] nm coral no pl

Coran [kɔʀɑ̃] nm: **le ~** the Koran

corbeau, x [kɔʀbo] nm crow

corbeille [kɔʀbɛj] nf basket; **corbeille à papier** waste paper basket ou bin

corde [kɔʀd] nf rope; (de violon, raquette) string; **usé jusqu'à la ~** threadbare; **corde à linge** washing ou clothes line; **corde à sauter** skipping rope; **cordes vocales** vocal cords; **cordée** nf (d'alpinistes) rope, roped party

cordialement [kɔʀdjalmɑ̃] adv (formule épistolaire) (kind) regards

cordon [kɔʀdɔ̃] nm cord, string; **cordon de police** police cordon; **cordon ombilical** umbilical cord

cordonnerie [kɔʀdɔnʀi] nf shoe repairer's (shop); **cordonnier** nm shoe repairer

Corée [kɔʀe] nf: **la ~ du Sud/du Nord** South/North Korea

coriace [kɔʀjas] adj tough

corne [kɔʀn] nf horn; (de cerf) antler

cornée [kɔʀne] nf cornea

corneille [kɔʀnɛj] nf crow

cornemuse [kɔʀnəmyz] nf bagpipes pl

cornet [kɔʀnɛ] nm (paper) cone; (de glace) cornet, cone

corniche [kɔʀniʃ] nf (route) coast road

cornichon [kɔʀniʃɔ̃] nm gherkin

Cornouailles [kɔʀnwaj] nf Cornwall

corporel, le [kɔʀpɔʀɛl] adj bodily; (punition) corporal

corps [kɔʀ] nm body; **à ~ perdu** headlong; **prendre ~** to take shape; **corps électoral** the electorate; **corps enseignant** the teaching profession

correct, e [kɔʀɛkt] adj correct; (fam: acceptable: salaire, hôtel) reasonable, decent; **correcteur, -trice** nm/f (Scol) examiner; **correction** nf (voir corriger) correction; (voir correct) correctness; (coups) thrashing

correspondance [kɔʀɛspɔ̃dɑ̃s] nf correspondence; (de train, d'avion) connection; **cours par ~** correspondence course; **vente par ~** mail-order business

correspondant, e [kɔʀɛspɔ̃dɑ̃, ɑ̃t] nm/f correspondent; (Tél) person phoning (ou being phoned)

correspondre [kɔʀɛspɔ̃dʀ] vi to correspond, tally; ~ **à** to correspond to; ~ **avec qn** to correspond with sb

corrida [kɔrida] nf bullfight

corridor [kɔridɔr] nm corridor

corrigé [kɔriʒe] nm (Scol: d'exercice) correct version

corriger [kɔriʒe] vt (devoir) to correct; (punir) to thrash; ~ qn de (défaut) to cure sb of

corrompre [kɔrɔ̃pr] vt to corrupt; (acheter: témoin etc) to bribe

corruption [kɔrypsjɔ̃] nf corruption; (de témoins) bribery

corse [kɔrs] adj, nm/f Corsican ▷ nf: **la C~** Corsica

corsé, e [kɔrse] adj (café) full-flavoured; (sauce) spicy; (problème) tough

cortège [kɔrtɛʒ] nm procession

cortisone [kɔrtizɔn] nf cortisone

corvée [kɔrve] nf chore, drudgery no pl

cosmétique [kɔsmetik] nm beauty care product

cosmopolite [kɔsmɔpɔlit] adj cosmopolitan

costaud, e [kɔsto, od] (fam) adj strong, sturdy

costume [kɔstym] nm (d'homme) suit; (de théâtre) costume; **costumé, e** adj dressed up; **bal costumé** fancy dress ball

cote [kɔt] nf (en Bourse) quotation; **cote d'alerte** danger ou flood level; **cote de popularité** (popularity) rating

côte [kot] nf (rivage) coast(line); (pente) hill; (Anat) rib; (d'un tricot, tissu) rib, ribbing no pl; **à ~** side by side; **la Côte (d'Azur)** the (French) Riviera

côté [kote] nm (gén) side; (direction) way, direction; **de chaque ~ (de)** on each side (of); **de tous les ~s** from all directions; **de quel ~ est-il parti?** which way did he go?; **de ce/de l'autre ~** this/the other way; **du ~ de** (provenance) from; (direction) towards; (proximité) near; **de ~** (regarder) sideways; **mettre qch de ~** to put sth aside; **mettre de l'argent de ~** to save some money; **à ~** (right) nearby; (voisins) next door; **à ~ de** beside, next to; (en comparaison) compared to; **être aux ~s de** to be by the side of

Côte d'Ivoire [kotdivwar] nf: **la Côte d'Ivoire** Côte d'Ivoire, the Ivory Coast

côtelette [kotlɛt] nf chop

côtier, -ière [kotje, jɛr] adj coastal

cotisation [kɔtizasjɔ̃] nf subscription, dues pl; (pour une pension) contributions pl

cotiser [kɔtize] vi: ~ (à) to pay contributions (to); **se cotiser** vi to club together

coton [kɔtɔ̃] nm cotton; **coton hydrophile** cotton wool (brit), absorbent cotton (us); **Coton-tige®** nm cotton bud

cou [ku] nm neck

couchant [kuʃɑ̃] adj: **soleil ~** setting sun

couche [kuʃ] nf layer; (de peinture, vernis) coat; (de bébé) nappy (brit), diaper (us); **couches**

sociales social levels ou strata

couché, e [kuʃe] adj lying down; (au lit) in bed

coucher [kuʃe] vt (personne) to put to bed; (: loger) to put up; (objet) to lay on its side ▷ vi to sleep; ~ **avec qn** to sleep with sb; **se coucher** vi (pour dormir) to go to bed; (pour se reposer) to lie down; (soleil) to set; **coucher de soleil** sunset

couchette [kuʃɛt] nf couchette; (pour voyageur, sur bateau) berth

coucou [kuku] nm cuckoo

coude [kud] nm (Anat) elbow; (de tuyau, de la route) bend; ~ **à ~** shoulder to shoulder, side by side

coudre [kudr] vt (bouton) to sew on ▷ vi to sew

couette [kwɛt] nf duvet, quilt; **couettes** nfpl (cheveux) bunches

couffin [kufɛ̃] nm Moses basket

couler [kule] vi to flow, run; (fuir: stylo, récipient) to leak; (nez) to run; (sombrer: bateau) to sink ▷ vt (cloche, sculpture) to cast; (bateau) to sink; (faire échouer: personne) to bring down

couleur [kulœr] nf colour (brit), color (us); (Cartes) suit; **film/télévision en ~s** colo(u)r film/television; **de ~** (homme, femme: vieilli) colo(u)red

couleuvre [kulœvr] nf grass snake

coulisses [kulis] nfpl (Théâtre) wings; (fig): **dans les ~** behind the scenes

couloir [kulwar] nm corridor, passage; (d'avion) aisle; (de bus) gangway; ~ **aérien/de navigation** air/shipping lane

coup [ku] nm (heurt, choc) knock; (affectif) blow, shock; (agressif) blow; (avec arme à feu) shot; (de l'horloge) stroke; (tennis, golf) stroke; (boxe) blow; (fam: fois) time; **donner un ~ de balai** to give the floor a sweep; **boire un ~** (fam) to have a drink; **être dans le ~** (impliqué) to be in on it; (à la page) to be hip ou trendy; **du ~ ...** as a result; **d'un seul ~** (subitement) suddenly; (à la fois) at one go; **du premier ~** first time; **du même ~** at the same time; **à tous les ~s** (fam) every time; **tenir le ~** to hold out; **après ~** afterwards; **à ~ sûr** definitely, without fail; ~ **sur ~** in quick succession; **sur le ~** outright; **sous le ~ de** (surprise etc) under the influence of; **coup de chance** stroke of luck; **coup de coude** nudge (with the elbow); **coup de couteau** stab (of a knife); **coup d'envoi** kick-off; **coup d'essai** first attempt; **coup d'État** coup; **coup de feu** shot; **coup de filet** (Police) haul; **coup de foudre** (fig) love at first sight; **coup de frein** (sharp) braking no pl; **coup de grâce** coup de grâce, death blow; **coup de main**: **donner un coup de main à qn** to give sb a (helping) hand; **coup d'œil** glance; **coup de pied** kick; **coup de poing** punch; **coup de soleil** sunburn no pl; **coup de sonnette** ring of the bell; **coup de téléphone** phone call; **coup de tête** (*fig*) (sudden) impulse; **coup de théâtre** (*fig*) dramatic turn of events; **coup de tonnerre** clap of thunder; **coup de vent** gust of wind; **en coup de vent** (*rapidement*) in a tearing hurry; **coup franc** free kick

coupable [kupabl] *adj* guilty ▷ *nm/f* (*gén*) culprit; (*Jur*) guilty party

coupe [kup] *nf* (*verre*) goblet; (*à fruits*) dish; (*Sport*) cup; (*de cheveux, de vêtement*) cut; (*graphique, plan*) (cross) section

couper [kupe] *vt* to cut; (*retrancher*) to cut (out); (*route, courant*) to cut off; (*appétit*) to take away; (*vin à table*) to dilute ▷ *vi* to cut; (*prendre un raccourci*) to take a short-cut; **se couper** *vi* (*se blesser*) to cut o.s.; **~ la parole à qn** to cut sb short; **nous avons été coupés** we've been cut off

couple [kupl] *nm* couple

couplet [kuplɛ] *nm* verse

coupole [kupɔl] *nf* dome

coupon [kupɔ̃] *nm* (*ticket*) coupon; (*reste de tissu*) remnant

coupure [kupyr] *nf* cut; (*billet de banque*) note; (*de journal*) cutting; **coupure de courant** power cut

cour [kur] *nf* (*de ferme, jardin*) (court)yard; (*d'immeuble*) back yard; (*Jur, royale*) court; **faire la ~ à qn** to court sb; **cour d'assises** court of assizes; **cour de récréation** playground

courage [kuraʒ] *nm* courage, bravery; **courageux, -euse** *adj* brave, courageous

couramment [kuramɑ̃] *adv* commonly; (*parler*) fluently

courant, e [kurɑ̃, ɑ̃t] *adj* (*fréquent*) common; (*Comm, gén: normal*) standard; (*en cours*) current ▷ *nm* current; (*fig*) movement; (*: d'opinion*) trend; **être au ~ (de)** (*fait, nouvelle*) to know (about); **mettre qn au ~ (de)** to tell sb (about); (*nouveau travail etc*) to teach sb the basics (of); **se tenir au ~ (de)** (*techniques etc*) to keep o.s. up-to-date (on); **dans le ~ de** (*pendant*) in the course of; **le 10 ~** (*Comm*) the 10th inst.; **courant d'air** draught; **courant électrique** (electric) current, power

courbature [kurbatyr] *nf* ache

courbe [kurb] *adj* curved ▷ *nf* curve

coureur, -euse [kurœr, øz] *nm/f* (*Sport*) runner (*ou* driver); (*péj*) womanizer; manhunter

courge [kurʒ] *nf* (*Culin*) marrow; **courgette** *nf* courgette (brit), zucchini (us)

courir [kurir] *vi* to run ▷ *vt* (*Sport: épreuve*) to compete in; (*risque*) to run; (*danger*) to face; **~ les magasins** to go round the shops; **le bruit court que** the rumour is going round that

couronne [kurɔn] *nf* crown; (*de fleurs*) wreath, circlet

courons *etc* [kurɔ̃] *vb voir* **courir**

courriel [kurjɛl] *nm* e-mail

courrier [kurje] *nm* mail, post; (*lettres à écrire*) letters *pl*; **est-ce que j'ai du ~?** are there any letters for me?; **courrier électronique** e-mail

▪ Attention à ne pas traduire **courrier** par le mot anglais *courier*.

courroie [kurwa] *nf* strap; (*Tech*) belt

courrons *etc* [kurɔ̃] *vb voir* **courir**

cours [kur] *nm* (*leçon*) class; (*: particulier*) lesson; (*série de leçons, cheminement*) course; (*écoulement*) flow; (*Comm: de devises*) rate; (*: de denrées*) price; **donner libre ~ à** to give free expression to; **avoir ~** (*Scol*) to have a class *ou* lecture; **en ~** (*année*) current; (*travaux*) in progress; **en ~ de route** on the way; **au ~ de** in the course of, during; **le ~ de change** the exchange rate; **cours d'eau** waterway; **cours du soir** night school

course [kurs] *nf* running; (*Sport: épreuve*) race; (*d'un taxi*) journey, trip; (*commission*) errand; **courses** *nfpl* (*achats*) shopping *sg*; **faire des ~s** to do some shopping

court, e [kur, kurt(ə)] *adj* short ▷ *adv* short ▷ *nm*: **~ (de tennis)** (tennis) court; **à ~ de** short of; **prendre qn de ~** to catch sb unawares; **court-circuit** *nm* short-circuit

courtoisie [kurtwazi] *nf* courtesy

couru, e [kury] *pp de* **courir**

cousais *etc* [kuze] *vb voir* **coudre**

couscous [kuskus] *nm* couscous

cousin, e [kuzɛ̃, in] *nm/f* cousin

coussin [kusɛ̃] *nm* cushion

cousu, e [kuzy] *pp de* **coudre**

coût [ku] *nm* cost; **le ~ de la vie** the cost of living

couteau, x [kuto] *nm* knife

coûter [kute] *vt, vi* to cost; **combien ça coûte?** how much is it?, what does it cost?; **ça coûte trop cher** it's too expensive; **coûte que coûte** at all costs; **coûteux, -euse** *adj* costly, expensive

coutume [kutym] *nf* custom

couture [kutyr] *nf* sewing; (*profession*) dressmaking; (*points*) seam; **couturier** *nm* fashion designer; **couturière** *nf* dressmaker

couvent [kuvɑ̃] *nm* (*de sœurs*) convent; (*de frères*) monastery

couver [kuve] *vt* to hatch; (*maladie*) to be coming down with ▷ *vi* (*feu*) to smoulder; (*révolte*) to be brewing

couvercle [kuvɛrkl] *nm* lid; (*de bombe aérosol etc, qui se visse*) cap, top

couvert, e [kuvɛr, ɛrt] *pp de* **couvrir** ▷ *adj* (*ciel*) overcast ▷ *nm* place setting; (*place à table*) place; **couverts** *nmpl* (*ustensiles*) cutlery *sg*; **~ de** covered with *ou* in; **mettre le ~** to lay the table

couverture [kuvɛrtyr] *nf* blanket; (*de livre, assurance, fig*) cover; (*presse*) coverage

couvre-lit [kuvʀəli] nm bedspread

couvrir [kuvʀiʀ] vt to cover; **se couvrir** vi (s'habiller) to cover up; (se coiffer) to put on one's hat; (ciel) to cloud over

cow-boy [koboj] nm cowboy

crabe [kʀab] nm crab

cracher [kʀaʃe] vi, vt to spit

crachin [kʀaʃɛ̃] nm drizzle

craie [kʀɛ] nf chalk

craindre [kʀɛ̃dʀ] vt to fear, be afraid of; (être sensible à: chaleur, froid) to be easily damaged by

crainte [kʀɛ̃t] nf fear; **de ~ de/que** for fear of/that; **craintif, -ive** adj timid

crampe [kʀɑ̃p] nf cramp; **j'ai une ~ à la jambe** I've got cramp in my leg

cramponner [kʀɑ̃pɔne] vb: **se ~ (à)** to hang ou cling on (to)

cran [kʀɑ̃] nm (entaille) notch; (de courroie) hole; (fam: courage) guts pl

crâne [kʀɑn] nm skull

crapaud [kʀapo] nm toad

craquement [kʀakmɑ̃] nm crack, snap; (du plancher) creak, creaking no pl

craquer [kʀake] vi (bois, plancher) to creak; (fil, branche) to snap; (couture) to come apart; (fig: accusé) to break down; (: fam) to crack up ▷ vt (allumette) to strike; **j'ai craqué** (fam) I couldn't resist it

crasse [kʀas] nf grime, filth; **crasseux, -euse** adj grimy, filthy

cravache [kʀavaʃ] nf (riding) crop

cravate [kʀavat] nf tie

crawl [kʀol] nm crawl; **dos ~é** backstroke

crayon [kʀɛjɔ̃] nm pencil; **crayon à bille** ball-point pen; **crayon de couleur** crayon, colouring pencil; **crayon-feutre** (pl **crayons-feutres**) nm felt(-tip) pen

création [kʀeasjɔ̃] nf creation

crèche [kʀɛʃ] nf (de Noël) crib; (garderie) crèche, day nursery

crédit [kʀedi] nm (gén) credit; **crédits** nmpl (fonds) funds; **payer/acheter à ~** to pay/buy on credit ou on easy terms; **faire ~ à qn** to give sb credit; **créditer** vt: **créditer un compte (de)** to credit an account (with)

créer [kʀee] vt to create

crémaillère [kʀemajɛʀ] nf: **pendre la ~** to have a house-warming party

crème [kʀɛm] nf cream; (entremets) cream dessert ▷ adj inv cream(-coloured); **un (café) ~** ≈ a white coffee; **crème anglaise** (egg) custard; **crème Chantilly** whipped cream; **crème à raser** shaving cream; **crème solaire** suntan lotion

créneau, x [kʀeno] nm (de fortification) crenel(le); (dans marché) gap, niche; (Auto): **faire un ~** to reverse into a parking space (between two cars alongside the kerb)

crêpe [kʀɛp] nf (galette) pancake ▷ nm (tissu) crêpe; **crêperie** nf pancake shop ou restaurant

crépuscule [kʀepyskyl] nm twilight, dusk

cresson [kʀesɔ̃] nm watercress

creuser [kʀøze] vt (trou, tunnel) to dig; (sol) to dig a hole in; (fig) to go (deeply) into; **ça creuse** that gives you a real appetite; **se ~ la cervelle** (fam) to rack one's brains

creux, -euse [kʀø, kʀøz] adj hollow ▷ nm hollow; **heures creuses** slack periods; (électricité, téléphone) off-peak periods; **avoir un ~** (fam) to be hungry

crevaison [kʀəvɛzɔ̃] nf puncture

crevé, e [kʀəve] (fam) adj (fatigué) shattered (BRIT), exhausted

crever [kʀəve] vt (ballon) to burst ▷ vi (pneu) to burst; (automobiliste) to have a puncture (BRIT) ou a flat (tire) (US); (fam) to die

crevette [kʀəvɛt] nf: **~ (rose)** prawn; **crevette grise** shrimp

cri [kʀi] nm cry, shout; (d'animal: spécifique) cry, call; **c'est le dernier ~** (fig) it's the latest fashion

criard, e [kʀijaʀ, kʀijaʀd] adj (couleur) garish, loud; (voix) yelling

cric [kʀik] nm (Auto) jack

crier [kʀije] vi (pour appeler) to shout, cry (out); (de douleur etc) to scream, yell ▷ vt (injure) to shout (out), yell (out)

crime [kʀim] nm crime; (meurtre) murder; **criminel, le** nm/f criminal; (assassin) murderer

crin [kʀɛ̃] nm (de cheval) hair no pl

crinière [kʀinjɛʀ] nf mane

crique [kʀik] nf creek, inlet

criquet [kʀikɛ] nm grasshopper

crise [kʀiz] nf crisis; (Méd) attack; (: d'épilepsie) fit; **piquer une ~ de nerfs** to go hysterical; **crise cardiaque** heart attack; **crise de foie: avoir une crise de foie** to have really bad indigestion

cristal, -aux [kʀistal, o] nm crystal

critère [kʀitɛʀ] nm criterion

critiquable [kʀitikabl] adj open to criticism

critique [kʀitik] adj critical ▷ nm/f (de théâtre, musique) critic ▷ nf criticism; (Théâtre etc: article) review

critiquer [kʀitike] vt (dénigrer) to criticize; (évaluer) to assess, examine (critically)

croate [kʀɔat] adj Croatian ▷ nm/f: **C~** Croat, Croatian

Croatie [kʀɔasi] nf: **la ~** Croatia

crochet [kʀɔʃɛ] nm hook; (détour) detour; (Tricot: aiguille) crochet hook; (: technique) crochet; **vivre aux ~s de qn** to live ou sponge off sb

crocodile [kʀɔkɔdil] nm crocodile

croire [kʀwaʀ] vt to believe; **se ~ fort** to think one is strong; **~ que** to believe ou think that; **~ à, ~ en** to believe in

croisade [kʀwazad] nf crusade

croisement [kʀwazmɑ̃] nm (carrefour) crossroads sg; (Bio) crossing; (: résultat) crossbreed

croiser [kʀwaze] vt (personne, voiture) to pass; (route) to cross, cut across; (Bio) to cross; **se croiser** vi (personnes, véhicules) to pass each other; (routes, lettres) to cross; (regards) to meet; **~ les jambes/bras** to cross one's legs/fold one's arms

croisière [kʀwazjɛʀ] nf cruise

croissance [kʀwasɑ̃s] nf growth

croissant [kʀwasɑ̃] nm (à manger) croissant; (motif) crescent

croître [kʀwatʀ] vi to grow

croix [kʀwa] nf cross; **la Croix Rouge** the Red Cross

croque-monsieur [kʀɔkməsjø] nm inv toasted ham and cheese sandwich

croquer [kʀɔke] vt (manger) to crunch; (: fruit) to munch; (dessiner) to sketch; **chocolat à croquer** plain dessert chocolate

croquis [kʀɔki] nm sketch

crotte [kʀɔt] nf droppings pl; **crottin** nm dung, manure; (fromage) (small round) cheese (made of goat's milk)

croustillant, e [kʀustijɑ̃, ɑ̃t] adj crisp

croûte [kʀut] nf crust; (du fromage) rind; (Méd) scab; **en ~** (Culin) in pastry

croûton [kʀutɔ̃] nm (Culin) crouton; (bout du pain) crust, heel

croyant, e [kʀwajɑ̃, ɑ̃t] nm/f believer

CRS sigle fpl (= Compagnies républicaines de sécurité) state security police force ⊳ sigle m member of the CRS

cru, e [kʀy] pp de **croire** ⊳ adj (non cuit) raw; (lumière, couleur) harsh; (paroles) crude ⊳ nm (vignoble) vineyard; (vin) wine; **un grand ~** a great vintage; **jambon ~** Parma ham

crû [kʀy] pp de **croître**

cruauté [kʀyote] nf cruelty

cruche [kʀyʃ] nf pitcher, jug

crucifix [kʀysifi] nm crucifix

crudités [kʀydite] nfpl (Culin) selection of raw vegetables

crue [kʀy] nf (inondation) flood

cruel, le [kʀyɛl] adj cruel

crus etc [kʀy] vb voir **croire**; **croître**

crûs etc [kʀy] vb voir **croître**

crustacés [kʀystase] nmpl shellfish

Cuba [kyba] nf Cuba; **cubain, e** adj Cuban ⊳ nm/f: **Cubain, e** Cuban

cube [kyb] nm cube; (jouet) brick; **mètre ~** cubic metre; **2 au ~** = 2 cubed

cueillette [kœjɛt] nf picking; (quantité) crop, harvest

cueillir [kœjiʀ] vt (fruits, fleurs) to pick, gather; (fig) to catch

cuiller [kɥijɛʀ], **cuillère** [kɥijɛʀ] nf spoon; **cuiller à café** coffee spoon; (Culin) ≈ teaspoonful; **cuiller à soupe** soup-spoon; (Culin) ≈ tablespoonful; **cuillerée** nf spoonful

cuir [kɥiʀ] nm leather; **cuir chevelu** scalp

cuire [kɥiʀ] vt (aliments) to cook; (au four) to bake ⊳ vi to cook; **bien cuit** (viande) well done; **trop cuit** overdone

cuisine [kɥizin] nf (pièce) kitchen; (art culinaire) cookery, cooking; (nourriture) cooking, food; **faire la ~** to cook; **cuisiné, e** adj: **plat cuisiné** ready-made meal ou dish; **cuisiner** vt to cook; (fam) to grill ⊳ vi to cook; **cuisinier, -ière** nm/f cook; **cuisinière** nf (poêle) cooker

cuisse [kɥis] nf thigh; (Culin) leg

cuisson [kɥisɔ̃] nf cooking

cuit, e [kɥi, kɥit] pp de **cuire**

cuivre [kɥivʀ] nm copper; **les cuivres** (Mus) the brass

cul [ky] (fam!) nm arse (!)

culminant, e [kylminɑ̃, ɑ̃t] adj: **point ~** highest point

culot [kylo] (fam) nm (effronterie) cheek

culotte [kylɔt] nf (de femme) knickers pl (BRIT), panties pl

culte [kylt] nm (religion) religion; (hommage, vénération) worship; (protestant) service

cultivateur, -trice [kyltivatœʀ, tʀis] nm/f farmer

cultivé, e [kyltive] adj (personne) cultured, cultivated

cultiver [kyltive] vt to cultivate; (légumes) to grow, cultivate

culture [kyltyʀ] nf cultivation; (connaissances etc) culture; **les ~s intensives** intensive farming; **culture physique** physical training; **culturel, le** adj cultural

cumin [kymɛ̃] nm cumin

cure [kyʀ] nf (Méd) course of treatment; **cure d'amaigrissement** slimming (BRIT) ou weight-loss (US) course; **cure de repos** rest cure

curé [kyʀe] nm parish priest

cure-dent [kyʀdɑ̃] nm toothpick

curieux, -euse [kyʀjø, jøz] adj (indiscret) curious, inquisitive; (étrange) strange, curious ⊳ nmpl (badauds) onlookers; **curiosité** nf curiosity; (site) unusual feature

curriculum vitae [kyʀikylɔmvite] nm inv curriculum vitae

cutané, e [kytane] adj skin

cuve [kyv] nf (à mazout etc) tank

cuvée [kyve] nf vintage

cuvette [kyvɛt] nf (récipient) bowl, basin; (Géo) basin

CV sigle m (Auto) = **cheval vapeur**; (Comm) = **curriculum vitae**

cybercafé [sibɛʀkafe] nm Internet café

cyberespace [sibɛʀɛspas] nm cyberspace

cybernaute [sibɛʀnot] nm/f Internet user

cyclable [siklabl] adj: **piste ~** cycle track

cycle [sikl] *nm* cycle; **cyclisme** *nm* cycling;
  cycliste *nm/f* cyclist ▷ *adj* cycle *cpd*; **coureur**
  cycliste racing cyclist
cyclomoteur [siklomotœʀ] *nm* moped
cyclone [siklon] *nm* hurricane
cygne [siɲ] *nm* swan
cylindre [silɛ̃dʀ] *nm* cylinder; **cylindrée**
  nf (*Auto*) (cubic) capacity; **une (voiture de)**
  grosse cylindrée a big-engined car
cymbale [sɛ̃bal] *nf* cymbal
cynique [sinik] *adj* cynical
cystite [sistit] *nf* cystitis

d' [d] *prép voir* **de**
dactylo [daktilo] *nf* (*aussi:* **~graphe**) typist;
  (*aussi:* **~graphie**) typing
dada [dada] *nm* hobby-horse
daim [dɛ̃] *nm* (fallow) deer *inv*; (*cuir suédé*)
  suede
daltonien, ne [daltɔnjɛ̃, jɛn] *adj* colour-blind
dame [dam] *nf* lady; (*Cartes, Échecs*) queen;
  dames *nfpl* (*jeu*) draughts *sg* (*BRIT*), checkers
  sg (*US*)
Danemark [danmaʀk] *nm* Denmark
danger [dɑ̃ʒe] *nm* danger; **être en ~** (*personne*)
  to be in danger; **mettre en ~** (*personne*) to
  put in danger; (*projet, carrière*) to jeopardize;
  dangereux, -euse *adj* dangerous
danois, e [danwa, waz] *adj* Danish ▷ *nm/f*:
  D~, e Dane ▷ *nm* (*Ling*) Danish

 MOT-CLÉ

dans [dɑ̃] *prép* **1** (*position*) in; (*à l'intérieur de*)
  inside; **c'est dans le tiroir/le salon** it's in the
  drawer/lounge; **dans la boîte** in *ou* inside the
  box; **je l'ai lu dans le journal** I read it in the
  newspaper; **marcher dans la ville** to walk
  about the town
  2 (*direction*) into; **elle a couru dans le salon**
  she ran into the lounge; **monter dans une**
  voiture/le bus to get into a car/on to the bus
  3 (*provenance*) out of, from; **je l'ai pris dans**

le tiroir/salon I took it out of *ou* from the drawer/lounge; **boire dans un verre** to drink out of *ou* from a glass

4 (*temps*) in; **dans 2 mois** in 2 months, in 2 months' time

5 (*approximation*) about; **dans les 20 euros** about 20 euros

danse [dɑ̃s] *nf*: **la ~** dancing; **une ~** a dance; **la ~ classique** ballet; **danser** *vi, vt* to dance; **danseur, -euse** *nm/f* ballet dancer; (*au bal etc*) dancer; (: *cavalier*) partner

date [dat] *nf* date; **de longue ~** longstanding; **date de naissance** date of birth; **date limite** deadline; **dater** *vt, vi* to date; **dater de** to date from; **à dater de** (as) from

datte [dat] *nf* date

dauphin [dofɛ̃] *nm* (*Zool*) dolphin

davantage [davɑ̃taʒ] *adv* more; (*plus longtemps*) longer; **~ de** more

 MOT-CLÉ

de, d' [də] (*de +le =* **du**, *de +les =* **des**) *prép*
1 (*appartenance*) of; **le toit de la maison** the roof of the house; **la voiture d'Ann/de mes parents** Ann's/my parents' car
2 (*provenance*) from; **il vient de Londres** he comes from London; **elle est sortie du cinéma** she came out of the cinema
3 (*caractérisation, mesure*): **un mur de brique/bureau d'acajou** a brick wall/mahogany desk; **un billet de 50 euros** a 50 euro note; **une pièce de 2 m de large** *ou* **large de 2 m** a room 2m wide, a 2m-wide room; **un bébé de 10 mois** a 10-month-old baby; **12 mois de crédit/travail** 12 months' credit/work; **être payé 20 euros de l'heure** to be paid 20 euros an *ou* per hour; **augmenter de 10 euros** to increase by 10 euros; **de 14 à 18** from 14 to 18
4 (*moyen*) with; **je l'ai fait de mes propres mains** I did it with my own two hands
5 (*cause*): **mourir de faim** to die of hunger; **rouge de colère** red with fury
6 (*devant infinitif*) to; **il m'a dit de rester** he told me to stay
▷ *dét* **1** (*phrases affirmatives*) some (*souvent omis*); **du vin, de l'eau, des pommes** (some) wine, (some) water, (some) apples; **des enfants sont venus** some children came; **pendant des mois** for months
2 (*phrases interrogatives et négatives*) any; **a-t-il du vin?** has he got any wine?; **il n'a pas de pommes/d'enfants** he hasn't (got) any apples/children, he has no apples/children

dé [de] *nm* (*à jouer*) die *ou* dice; (*aussi*: **dé à coudre**) thimble

déballer [debale] *vt* to unpack

débarcadère [debarkadɛr] *nm* wharf

débardeur [debardœr] *nm* (*maillot*) tank top

débarquer [debarke] *vt* to unload, land ▷ *vi* to disembark; (*fig: fam*) to turn up

débarras [debara] *nm* (*pièce*) lumber room; (*placard*) junk cupboard; **bon ~!** good riddance!; **débarrasser** *vt* to clear; **se débarrasser de** *vt* to get rid of; **débarrasser qn de** (*vêtements, paquets*) to relieve sb of; **débarrasser (la table)** to clear the table

débat [deba] *nm* discussion, debate; **débattre** *vt* to discuss, debate; **se débattre** *vi* to struggle

débit [debi] *nm* (*d'un liquide, fleuve*) flow; (*d'un magasin*) turnover (of goods); (*élocution*) delivery; (*bancaire*) debit; **débit de boissons** drinking establishment; **débit de tabac** tobacconist's

déblayer [debleje] *vt* to clear

débloquer [debloke] *vt* (*prix, crédits*) to free

déboîter [debwate] *vt* (*Auto*) to pull out; **se ~ le genou** *etc* to dislocate one's knee *etc*

débordé, e [deborde] *adj*: **être ~ (de)** (*travail, demandes*) to be snowed under (with)

déborder [deborde] *vi* to overflow; (*lait etc*) to boil over; **~ (de) qch** (*dépasser*) to extend beyond sth; **~ de** (*joie, zèle*) to be brimming over with *ou* bursting with

débouché [debuʃe] *nm* (*pour vendre*) outlet; (*perspective d'emploi*) opening

déboucher [debuʃe] *vt* (*évier, tuyau etc*) to unblock; (*bouteille*) to uncork ▷ *vi*: **~ de** to emerge from; **~ sur** (*études*) to lead on to

debout [d(ə)bu] *adv*: **être ~** (*personne*) to be standing, stand; (: *levé, éveillé*) to be up; **se mettre ~** to stand up; **se tenir ~** to stand; **~!** stand up!; (*du lit*) get up!; **cette histoire ne tient pas ~** this story doesn't hold water

déboutonner [debutone] *vt* to undo, unbutton

débraillé, e [debraje] *adj* slovenly, untidy

débrancher [debrɑ̃ʃe] *vt* to disconnect; (*appareil électrique*) to unplug

débrayage [debrejaʒ] *nm* (*Auto*) clutch; **débrayer** *vi* (*Auto*) to declutch; (*cesser le travail*) to stop work

débris [debri] *nmpl* fragments; **des ~ de verre** bits of glass

débrouillard, e [debrujar, ard] (*fam*) *adj* smart, resourceful

débrouiller [debruje] *vt* to disentangle, untangle; **se débrouiller** *vi* to manage; **débrouillez-vous** you'll have to sort things out yourself

début [deby] *nm* beginning, start; **débuts** *nmpl* (*de carrière*) début *sg*; **~ juin** in early June; **débutant, e** *nm/f* beginner, novice; **débuter** *vi* to begin, start; (*faire ses débuts*) to start out

décaféiné, e [dekafeine] *adj* decaffeinated

décalage [dekalaʒ] nm gap; **décalage horaire** time difference

décaler [dekale] vt to shift

décapotable [dekapɔtabl] adj convertible

décapsuleur [dekapsylœr] nm bottle-opener

décédé, e [desede] adj deceased

décéder [desede] vi to die

décembre [desãbr] nm December

décennie [deseni] nf decade

décent, e [desã, ãt] adj decent

déception [desɛpsjɔ̃] nf disappointment

décès [desɛ] nm death

décevoir [des(ə)vwar] vt to disappoint

décharge [deʃarʒ] nf (dépôt d'ordures) rubbish tip ou dump; (électrique) electrical discharge; **décharger** vt (marchandise, véhicule) to unload; (tirer) to discharge; **décharger qn de** (responsabilité) to relieve sb of, release sb from

déchausser [deʃose] vt (skis) to take off; **se déchausser** vi to take off one's shoes; (dent) to come ou work loose

déchet [deʃɛ] nm (reste) scrap; **déchets** nmpl (ordures) refuse sg, rubbish sg; **~s nucléaires** nuclear waste

déchiffrer [deʃifre] vt to decipher

déchirant, e [deʃirã, ãt] adj heart-rending

déchirement [deʃirmã] nm (chagrin) wrench, heartbreak; (gén pl: conflit) rift, split

déchirer [deʃire] vt to tear; (en morceaux) to tear up; (arracher) to tear out; (fig: conflit) to tear (apart); **se déchirer** vi to tear, rip; **se ~ un muscle** to tear a muscle

déchirure [deʃiryr] nf (accroc) tear, rip; **déchirure musculaire** torn muscle

décidé, e [deside] adj (personne, air) determined; **c'est ~** it's decided; **décidément** adv really

décider [deside] vt: **~ qch** to decide on sth; **~ de faire/que** to decide to do/that; **~ qn (à faire qch)** to persuade sb (to do sth); **se décider (à faire)** to decide (to do), make up one's mind (to do); **se ~ pour** to decide on ou in favour of

décimal, e, -aux [desimal, o] adj decimal

décimètre [desimetr] nm decimetre

décisif, -ive [desizif, iv] adj decisive

décision [desizjɔ̃] nf decision

déclaration [deklarasjɔ̃] nf declaration; (discours: Pol etc) statement; **déclaration d'impôts** ou **de revenus** ≈ tax return; **déclaration de vol: faire une déclaration de vol** to report a theft

déclarer [deklare] vt to declare; (décès, naissance) to register; **se déclarer** vi (feu) to break out

déclencher [deklãʃe] vt (mécanisme etc) to release; (sonnerie) to set off; (attaque, grève) to launch; (provoquer) to trigger off; **se**

déclencher vi (sonnerie) to go off

décliner [dekline] vi to decline ▷ vt (invitation) to decline; (nom, adresse) to state

décoiffer [dekwafe] vt: **~ qn** to mess up sb's hair; **je suis toute décoiffée** my hair is in a real mess

déçois etc [deswa] vb voir **décevoir**

décollage [dekɔlaʒ] nm (Aviat) takeoff

décoller [dekɔle] vt to unstick ▷ vi (avion) to take off; **se décoller** vi to come unstuck

décolleté, e [dekɔlte] adj low-cut ▷ nm low neck(line); (plongeant) cleavage

décolorer [dekɔlɔre]: **se décolorer** vi to fade; **se faire ~ les cheveux** to have one's hair bleached

décommander [dekɔmãde] vt to cancel; **se décommander** vi to cry off

déconcerter [dekɔ̃sɛrte] vt to disconcert, confound

décongeler [dekɔ̃ʒ(ə)le] vt to thaw

déconner [dekɔne] (fam) vi to talk rubbish

déconseiller [dekɔ̃seje] vt: **~ qch (à qn)** to advise (sb) against sth; **c'est déconseillé** it's not recommended

décontracté, e [dekɔ̃trakte] adj relaxed, laid-back (fam)

décontracter [dekɔ̃trakte]: **se décontracter** vi to relax

décor [dekɔr] nm décor; (paysage) scenery; **décorateur** nm (interior) decorator; **décoration** nf decoration; **décorer** vt to decorate

décortiquer [dekɔrtike] vt to shell; (fig: texte) to dissect

découdre [dekudr]: **se découdre** vi to come unstitched

découper [dekupe] vt (papier, tissu etc) to cut up; (viande) to carve; (article) to cut out

décourager [dekuraʒe] vt to discourage; **se décourager** vi to lose heart, become discouraged

décousu, e [dekuzy] adj unstitched; (fig) disjointed, disconnected

découvert, e [dekuvɛr, ɛrt] adj (tête) bare, uncovered; (lieu) open, exposed ▷ nm (bancaire) overdraft; **découverte** nf discovery; **faire la découverte de** to discover

découvrir [dekuvrir] vt to discover; (enlever ce qui couvre) to uncover; (dévoiler) to reveal; **se découvrir** vi (chapeau) to take off one's hat; (vêtement) to take something off; (ciel) to clear

décrire [dekrir] vt to describe

décrocher [dekrɔʃe] vt (détacher) to take down; (téléphone) to take off the hook; (: pour répondre) to lift the receiver; (fam: contrat etc) to get, land ▷ vi (fam: abandonner) to drop out; (: cesser d'écouter) to switch off

déçu, e [desy] pp de **décevoir**

dédaigner [dedɛɲe] vt to despise, scorn;

(*négliger*) to disregard, spurn; **dédaigneux, -euse** *adj* scornful, disdainful; **dédain** *nm* scorn, disdain

dedans [dədɑ̃] *adv* inside; (*pas en plein air*) indoors, inside ▷ *nm* inside; **au ~** inside

dédicacer [dedikase] *vt*: **~ (à qn)** to sign (for sb), autograph (for sb)

dédier [dedje] *vt*: **~ à** to dedicate to

dédommagement [dedɔmaʒmɑ̃] *nm* compensation

dédommager [dedɔmaʒe] *vt*: **~ qn (de)** to compensate sb (for)

dédouaner [dedwane] *vt* to clear through customs

déduire [deduiʀ] *vt*: **~ qch (de)** (*ôter*) to deduct sth (from); (*conclure*) to deduce *ou* infer sth (from)

défaillance [defajɑ̃s] *nf* (*syncope*) blackout; (*fatigue*) (sudden) weakness *no pl*; (*technique*) fault, failure; **défaillance cardiaque** heart failure

défaire [defɛʀ] *vt* to undo; (*installation*) to take down, dismantle; **se défaire** *vi* to come undone; **se ~ de** to get rid of

défait, e [defɛ, ɛt] *adj* (*visage*) haggard, ravaged; **défaite** *nf* defeat

défaut [defo] *nm* (*moral*) fault, failing, defect; (*tissus*) fault, flaw; (*manque, carence*): **~ de** shortage of; **prendre qn en ~** to catch sb out; **faire ~** (*manquer*) to be lacking; **à ~ de** for lack *ou* want of

défavorable [defavɔʀabl] *adj* unfavourable (BRIT), unfavorable (US)

défavoriser [defavɔʀize] *vt* to put at a disadvantage

défectueux, -euse [defɛktɥø, øz] *adj* faulty, defective

défendre [defɑ̃dʀ] *vt* to defend; (*interdire*) to forbid; **se défendre** *vi* to defend o.s.; **~ à qn qch/de faire** to forbid sb sth/to do; **il se défend** (*fam*: se débrouille) he can hold his own; **se ~ de/contre** (*se protéger*) to protect o.s. from/against; **se ~ de** (*se garder de*) to refrain from

défense [defɑ̃s] *nf* defence; (*d'éléphant etc*) tusk; **ministre de la ~** Minister of Defence (BRIT), Defence Secretary (US); **"~ de fumer"** "no smoking"

défi [defi] *nm* challenge; **lancer un ~ à qn** to challenge sb; **sur un ton de ~** defiantly

déficit [defisit] *nm* (*Comm*) deficit

défier [defje] *vt* (*provoquer*) to challenge; (*mort, autorité*) to defy; **~ qn de faire qch** to challenge *ou* defy sb to do sth

défigurer [defigyʀe] *vt* to disfigure

défilé [defile] *nm* (*Géo*) (narrow) gorge *ou* pass; (*soldats*) parade; (*manifestants*) procession, march

défiler [defile] *vi* (*troupes*) to march past;

(*sportifs*) to parade; (*manifestants*) to march; (*visiteurs*) to pour, stream; **faire ~ un document** (*Comput*) to scroll a document; **se défiler** *vi*: **il s'est défilé** (*fam*) he wriggled out of it

définir [definiʀ] *vt* to define

définitif, -ive [definitif, iv] *adj* (*final*) final, definitive; (*pour longtemps*) permanent, definitive; (*refus*) definite; **définitive** *nf*: **en définitive** eventually; (*somme toute*) in fact; **définitivement** *adv* (*partir, s'installer*) for good

déformer [defɔʀme] *vt* to put out of shape; (*pensée, fait*) to distort; **se déformer** *vi* to lose its shape

défouler [defule]: **se défouler** *vi* to unwind, let off steam

défunt, e [defœ̃, œ̃t] *adj* (*mort*) late *before n* ▷ *nm/f* deceased

dégagé, e [degaʒe] *adj* (*route, ciel*) clear; **sur un ton ~** casually

dégager [degaʒe] *vt* (*exhaler*) to give off; (*délivrer*) to free, extricate; (*désencombrer*) to clear; (*isoler: idée, aspect*) to bring out; **~ qn de** (*engagement, parole etc*) to release *ou* free sb from; **se dégager** *vi* (*passage, ciel*) to clear

dégâts [dega] *nmpl* damage *sg*; **faire des ~** to cause damage

dégel [deʒɛl] *nm* thaw; **dégeler** *vt* to thaw (out)

dégivrer [deʒivʀe] *vt* (*frigo*) to defrost; (*vitres*) to de-ice

dégonflé, e [degɔ̃fle] *adj* (*pneu*) flat

dégonfler [degɔ̃fle] *vt* (*pneu, ballon*) to let down, deflate; **se dégonfler** *vi* (*fam*) to chicken out

dégouliner [deguline] *vi* to trickle, drip

dégourdi, e [deguʀdi] *adj* smart, resourceful

dégourdir [deguʀdiʀ] *vt*: **se ~ les jambes** to stretch one's legs (*fig*)

dégoût [degu] *nm* disgust, distaste; **dégoûtant, e** *adj* disgusting; **dégoûté, e** *adj* disgusted; **dégoûté de** sick of; **dégoûter** *vt* to disgust; **dégoûter qn de qch** to put sb off sth

dégrader [degrade] *vt* (*Mil: officier*) to degrade; (*abîmer*) to damage, deface; **se dégrader** *vi* (*relations, situation*) to deteriorate

degré [dəgʀe] *nm* degree

dégressif, -ive [degresif, iv] *adj* on a decreasing scale

dégringoler [degrɛ̃gɔle] *vi* to tumble (down)

déguisement [degizmɑ̃] *nm* (*pour s'amuser*) fancy dress

déguiser [degize]: **se déguiser (en)** *vi* (*se costumer*) to dress up (as); (*pour tromper*) to disguise o.s. (as)

dégustation [degystasjɔ̃] *nf* (*de fromages etc*) sampling; **~ de vins** wine-tasting session

déguster [degyste] vt (vins) to taste; (fromages etc) to sample; (savourer) to enjoy, savour

dehors [dəɔʀ] adv outside; (en plein air) outdoors ▷ nm outside ▷ nmpl (apparences) appearances; **mettre** ou **jeter ~** (expulser) to throw out; **au ~** outside; **au ~ de** outside; **en ~ de** (hormis) apart from

déjà [deʒa] adv already; (auparavant) before, already

déjeuner [deʒœne] vi to (have) lunch; (le matin) to have breakfast ▷ nm lunch

delà [dəla] adv: **en ~ (de), au ~ (de)** beyond

délacer [delase] vt (chaussures) to undo

délai [delɛ] nm (attente) waiting period; (sursis) extension of time; (temps accordé) time limit; **sans ~** without delay; **dans les ~s** within the time limit

délaisser [delese] vt to abandon, desert

délasser [delɑse] vt to relax; **se délasser** vi to relax

délavé, e [delave] adj faded

délayer [deleje] vt (Culin) to mix (with water etc); (peinture) to thin down

delco(r) [dɛlko] nm (Auto) distributor

délégué, e [delege] nm/f representative

déléguer [delege] vt to delegate

délibéré, e [delibeʀe] adj (conscient) deliberate

délicat, e [delika, at] adj delicate; (plein de tact) tactful; (attention) thoughtful; **délicatement** adv delicately; (avec douceur) gently

délice [delis] nm delight

délicieux, -euse [delisjø, jøz] adj (au goût) delicious; (sensation) delightful

délimiter [delimite] vt (terrain) to delimit, demarcate

délinquant, e [delɛ̃kɑ̃, -ɑ̃t] adj, nm/f delinquent

délirer [deliʀe] vi to be delirious; **tu délires!** (fam) you're crazy!

délit [deli] nm (criminal) offence

délivrer [delivʀe] vt (prisonnier) to (set) free, release; (passeport) to issue

deltaplane(r) [dɛltaplan] nm hang-glider

déluge [delyʒ] nm (pluie) downpour; (biblique) Flood

demain [d(ə)mɛ̃] adv tomorrow; **~ matin/ soir** tomorrow morning/evening

demande [d(ə)mɑ̃d] nf (requête) request; (revendication) demand; (d'emploi) application; (Écon): **la ~** demand; **"~s d'emploi"** (annonces) "situations wanted"

demandé, e [d(ə)mɑ̃de] adj (article etc): **très ~** (very) much in demand

demander [d(ə)mɑ̃de] vt to ask for; (chemin, heure etc) to ask; (nécessiter) to require, demand; **~ qch à qn** to ask sb for sth; **~ un service à qn** to ask sb a favour; **~ à qn de faire**

qch to ask sb to do sth; **je ne demande pas mieux que de ...** I'll be only too pleased to ...; **se ~ si/pourquoi** etc to wonder whether/why etc; **demandeur, -euse** nm/f: **demandeur d'emploi** job-seeker; **demandeur d'asile** asylum-seeker

démangeaison [demɑ̃ʒɛzɔ̃] nf itching; **avoir des ~s** to be itching

démanger [demɑ̃ʒe] vi to itch

démaquillant [demakijɑ̃] nm make-up remover

démaquiller [demakije] vt: **se démaquiller** to remove one's make-up

démarche [demaʀʃ] nf (allure) gait, walk; (intervention) step; (fig: intellectuelle) thought processes pl; **faire les ~s nécessaires (pour obtenir qch)** to take the necessary steps (to obtain sth)

démarrage [demaʀaʒ] nm start

démarrer [demaʀe] vi (conducteur) to start (up); (véhicule) to move off; (travaux) to get moving; **démarreur** nm (Auto) starter

démêlant [demɛlɑ̃] nm conditioner

démêler [demele] vt to untangle; **démêlés** nmpl problems

déménagement [demenaʒmɑ̃] nm move; **camion de déménagement** removal van

déménager [demenaʒe] vt (meubles) to (re)move ▷ vi to move (house); **déménageur** nm removal man

démerder [demɛʀde] (fam): **se démerder** vi to sort things out for o.s.

démettre [demɛtʀ] vt: **~ qn de** (fonction, poste) to dismiss sb from; **se ~ l'épaule** etc to dislocate one's shoulder etc

demeurer [d(ə)mœʀe] vi (habiter) to live; (rester) to remain

demi, e [d(ə)mi] adj half ▷ nm (bière) ≈ half-pint (0,25 litres) ▷ préfixe: **~...** half-, semi..., demi-; **trois heures/bouteilles et ~es** three and a half hours/bottles, three hours/bottles and a half; **il est 2 heures et ~e/midi et ~** it's half past 2/half past 12; **à ~** half-; **à la ~e** (heure) on the half-hour; **demi-douzaine** nf half-dozen, half a dozen; **demi-finale** nf semifinal; **demi-frère** nm half-brother; **demi-heure** nf half-hour, half an hour; **demi-journée** nf half-day, half a day; **demi-litre** nm half-litre, half a litre; **demi-livre** nf half-pound, half a pound; **demi-pension** (à l'hôtel) half-board; **demi-pensionnaire** nm/f: **être demi-pensionnaire** to take school lunches

démis, e [demi, iz] adj (épaule etc) dislocated

demi-sœur [dəmisœʀ] nf half-sister

démission [demisjɔ̃] nf resignation; **donner sa ~** to give ou hand in one's notice; **démissionner** vi to resign

demi-tarif [dəmitaʀif] nm half-price;

voyager à ~ to travel half-fare
demi-tour [dəmituʀ] *nm* about-turn; **faire ~** to turn (and go) back
démocratie [demɔkʀasi] *nf* democracy; **démocratique** *adj* democratic
démodé, e [demode] *adj* old-fashioned
demoiselle [d(ə)mwazɛl] *nf* (*jeune fille*) young lady; (*célibataire*) single lady, maiden lady; **demoiselle d'honneur** bridesmaid
démolir [demɔliʀ] *vt* to demolish
démon [demɔ̃] *nm* (*enfant turbulent*) devil, demon; **le D~** the Devil
démonstration [demɔ̃stʀasjɔ̃] *nf* demonstration
démonter [demɔ̃te] *vt* (*machine etc*) to take down, dismantle; **se démonter** (*meuble*) to be dismantled, be taken to pieces; (*personne*) to lose countenance
démontrer [demɔ̃tʀe] *vt* to demonstrate
démouler [demule] *vt* to turn out
démuni, e [demyni] *adj* (*sans argent*) impoverished; **~ de** without
dénicher [deniʃe] (*fam*) *vt* (*objet*) to unearth; (*restaurant etc*) to discover
dénier [denje] *vt* to deny
dénivellation [denivelasjɔ̃] *nf* (*pente*) slope
dénombrer [denɔ̃bʀe] *vt* to count
dénomination [denɔminasjɔ̃] *nf* designation, appellation
dénoncer [denɔ̃se] *vt* to denounce; **se dénoncer** to give o.s. up, come forward
dénouement [denumɑ̃] *nm* outcome
dénouer [denwe] *vt* to unknot, undo
denrée [dɑ̃ʀe] *nf*: **denrées alimentaires** foodstuffs
dense [dɑ̃s] *adj* dense; **densité** *nf* density
dent [dɑ̃] *nf* tooth; **dent de lait/de sagesse** milk/wisdom tooth; **dentaire** *adj* dental; **cabinet dentaire** dental surgery (BRIT), dentist's office (US)
dentelle [dɑ̃tɛl] *nf* lace *no pl*
dentier [dɑ̃tje] *nm* denture
dentifrice [dɑ̃tifʀis] *nm* toothpaste
dentiste [dɑ̃tist] *nm/f* dentist
dentition [dɑ̃tisjɔ̃] *nf* teeth
dénué, e [denɥe] *adj*: **~ de** devoid of
déodorant [deɔdɔʀɑ̃] *nm* deodorant
déontologie [deɔ̃tɔlɔʒi] *nf* code of practice
dépannage [depanaʒ] *nm*: **service de ~** (Auto) breakdown service
dépanner [depane] *vt* (*voiture, télévision*) to fix, repair; (*fig*) to bail out, help out; **dépanneuse** *nf* breakdown lorry (BRIT), tow truck (US)
dépareillé, e [depaʀeje] *adj* (*collection, service*) incomplete; (*objet*) odd
départ [depaʀ] *nm* departure; (*Sport*) start; **au ~** at the start; **la veille de son ~** the day before he leaves/left

département [depaʀtəmɑ̃] *nm* department

dépassé, e [depase] *adj* superseded, outmoded; **il est complètement ~** he's completely out of his depth, he can't cope
dépasser [depase] *vt* (*véhicule, concurrent*) to overtake; (*endroit*) to pass, go past; (*somme, limite*) to exceed; (*fig: en beauté etc*) to surpass, outshine ▷ *vi* (*jupon etc*) to show; **se dépasser** to excel o.s.
dépaysé, e [depeize] *adj* disoriented
dépaysement [depeizmɑ̃] *nm* (*changement*) change of scenery
dépêcher [depeʃe]: **se dépêcher** *vi* to hurry
dépendance [depɑ̃dɑ̃s] *nf* dependence; (*bâtiment*) outbuilding
dépendre [depɑ̃dʀ]: **~ de** *vt* to depend on; (*financièrement etc*) to be dependent on; **ça dépend** it depends
dépens [depɑ̃] *nmpl*: **aux ~ de** at the expense of
dépense [depɑ̃s] *nf* spending *no pl*, expense, expenditure *no pl*; **dépenser** *vt* to spend; (*énergie*) to expend, use up; **se dépenser** *vi* to exert o.s.
dépeupler [depœple]: **se dépeupler** *vi* to become depopulated
dépilatoire [depilatwaʀ] *adj*: **crème ~** hair-removing *ou* depilatory cream
dépister [depiste] *vt* to detect; (*voleur*) to track down
dépit [depi] *nm* vexation, frustration; **en ~ de** in spite of; **en ~ du bon sens** contrary to all good sense; **dépité, e** *adj* vexed, frustrated
déplacé, e [deplase] *adj* (*propos*) out of place, uncalled-for
déplacement [deplasmɑ̃] *nm* (*voyage*) trip, travelling *no pl*; **en ~** away
déplacer [deplase] *vt* (*table, voiture*) to move, shift; **se déplacer** *vi* to move; (*voyager*) to travel; **se ~ une vertèbre** to slip a disc
déplaire [deplɛʀ] *vt*: **ça me déplaît** I don't like this, I dislike this; **se déplaire** *vi* to be unhappy; **déplaisant, e** *adj* disagreeable
dépliant [deplijɑ̃] *nm* leaflet
déplier [deplije] *vt* to unfold
déposer [depoze] *vt* (*gén: mettre, poser*) to lay *ou* put down; (*à la banque, à la consigne*) to

deposit; (*passager*) to drop (off), set down; (*roi*) to depose; (*plainte*) to lodge; (*marque*) to register; **se déposer** *vi* to settle; **dépositaire** *nm/f* (*Comm*) agent; **déposition** *nf* statement

dépôt [depo] *nm* (*à la banque, sédiment*) deposit; (*entrepôt*) warehouse, store

dépourvu, e [depurvy] *adj*: ~ **de** lacking in, without; **prendre qn au** ~ to catch sb unprepared

dépression [depresjɔ̃] *nf* depression; **dépression (nerveuse)** (nervous) breakdown

déprimant, e [deprimɑ̃, ɑ̃t] *adj* depressing

déprimer [deprime] *vi* to be/get depressed

 MOT-CLÉ

depuis [dəpɥi] *prép* **1** (*point de départ dans le temps*) since; **il habite Paris depuis 1983/l'an dernier** he has been living in Paris since 1983/last year; **depuis quand?** since when?; **depuis quand le connaissez-vous?** how long have you known him?

2 (*temps écoulé*) for; **il habite Paris depuis 5 ans** he has been living in Paris for 5 years; **je le connais depuis 3 ans** I've known him for 3 years

3 (*lieu*): **il a plu depuis Metz** it's been raining since Metz; **elle a téléphoné depuis Valence** she rang from Valence

4 (*quantité, rang*) from; **depuis les plus petits jusqu'aux plus grands** from the youngest to the oldest

▷ *adv* (*temps*) since (then); **je ne lui ai pas parlé depuis** I haven't spoken to him since (then); **depuis que** *conj* (ever) since; **depuis qu'il m'a dit ça** (ever) since he said that to me

député, e [depyte] *nm/f* (*Pol*) ≈ Member of Parliament (BRIT), ≈ Member of Congress (US)

dérangement [derɑ̃ʒmɑ̃] *nm* (*gêne*) trouble; (*gastrique etc*) disorder; **en** ~ (*téléphone, machine*) out of order

déranger [derɑ̃ʒe] *vt* (*personne*) to trouble, bother; (*projets*) to disrupt, upset; (*objets, vêtements*) to disarrange; **se déranger** *vi*: **surtout ne vous dérangez pas pour moi** please don't put yourself out on my account; **est-ce que cela vous dérange si ...?** do you mind if ...?

déraper [derape] *vi* (*voiture*) to skid; (*personne, semelles*) to slip

dérégler [deregle] *vt* (*mécanisme*) to put out of order; (*estomac*) to upset

dérisoire [derizwar] *adj* derisory

dérive [deriv] *nf*: **aller à la** ~ (*Navig, fig*) to drift

dérivé, e [derive] *nm* (*Tech*) by-product

dermatologue [dermatɔlɔg] *nm/f* dermatologist

dernier, -ière [dernje, jer] *adj* last; (*le plus récent*) latest, last; **lundi/le mois** ~ last Monday/month; **c'est le** ~ **cri** it's the very latest thing; **en** ~ last; **ce** ~ the latter; **dernièrement** *adv* recently

dérogation [derɔgasjɔ̃] *nf* (special) dispensation

dérouiller [deruje] *vt*: **se** ~ **les jambes** to stretch one's legs (*fig*)

déroulement [derulmɑ̃] *nm* (*d'une opération etc*) progress

dérouler [derule] *vt* (*ficelle*) to unwind; **se dérouler** *vi* (*avoir lieu*) to take place; (*se passer*) to go (off); **tout s'est déroulé comme prévu** everything went as planned

dérouter [derute] *vt* (*avion, train*) to reroute, divert; (*étonner*) to disconcert, throw (out)

derrière [derjer] *adv, prép* behind ▷ *nm* (*d'une maison*) back; (*postérieur*) behind, bottom; **les pattes de** ~ the back *ou* hind legs; **par** ~ from behind; (*fig*) behind one's back

des [de] *dét voir* **de** ▷ *prép* +*dét* = **de** +**les**

dès [dɛ] *prép* from; ~ **que** as soon as; ~ **son retour** as soon as he was (*ou* is) back

désaccord [dezakɔr] *nm* disagreement

désagréable [dezagreabl] *adj* unpleasant

désagrément [dezagremɑ̃] *nm* annoyance, trouble *no pl*

désaltérer [dezaltere] *vt*: **se désaltérer** to quench one's thirst

désapprobateur, -trice [dezaprɔbatœr, tris] *adj* disapproving

désapprouver [dezapruve] *vt* to disapprove of

désarmant, e [dezarmɑ̃, ɑ̃t] *adj* disarming

désastre [dezastr] *nm* disaster; **désastreux, -euse** *adj* disastrous

désavantage [dezavɑ̃taʒ] *nm* disadvantage; **désavantager** *vt* to put at a disadvantage

descendre [desɑ̃dr] *vt* (*escalier, montagne*) to go (*ou* come) down; (*valise, paquet*) to take *ou* get down; (*étagère etc*) to lower; (*fam: abattre*) to shoot down ▷ *vi* to go (*ou* come) down; (*passager: s'arrêter*) to get out, alight; ~ **à pied/en voiture** to walk/drive down; ~ **de** (*famille*) to be descended from; ~ **du train** to get out of *ou* get off the train; ~ **de cheval** to dismount; ~ **d'un arbre** to climb down from a tree; ~ **à l'hôtel** to stay at a hotel

descente [desɑ̃t] *nf* descent, going down; (*chemin*) way down; (*Ski*) downhill (race); **au milieu de la** ~ halfway down; **descente de lit** bedside rug; **descente (de police)** (police) raid

description [deskripsjɔ̃] *nf* description

déséquilibre [dezekilibr] *nm* (*position*): **en** ~ unsteady; (*fig: des forces, du budget*) imbalance

désert, e [dezer, ert] *adj* deserted ▷ *nm* desert; **désertique** *adj* desert *cpd*

désespéré, e [dezespere] *adj* desperate

désespérer [dezɛspeʀe] vi: **~ (de)** to despair (of); **désespoir** nm despair; **en désespoir de cause** in desperation

déshabiller [dezabije] vt to undress; **se déshabiller** vi to undress (o.s.)

déshydraté, e [dezidʀate] adj dehydrated

désigner [deziɲe] vt (montrer) to point out, indicate; (dénommer) to denote; (candidat etc) to name

désinfectant, e [dezɛ̃fɛktɑ̃, ɑ̃t] adj, nm disinfectant

désinfecter [dezɛ̃fɛkte] vt to disinfect

désintéressé, e [dezɛ̃teʀese] adj disinterested, unselfish

désintéresser [dezɛ̃teʀese] vt: **se ~ (de)** to lose interest (in)

désintoxication [dezɛ̃tɔksikasjɔ̃] nf: **faire une cure de ~** to undergo treatment for alcoholism (ou drug addiction)

désinvolte [dezɛ̃vɔlt] adj casual, off-hand

désir [deziʀ] nm wish; (sensuel) desire; **désirer** vt to want, wish for; (sexuellement) to desire; **je désire ...** (formule de politesse) I would like ...

désister [deziste]: **se désister** vi to stand down, withdraw

désobéir [dezɔbeiʀ] vi: **~ (à qn/qch)** to disobey (sb/sth); **désobéissant, e** adj disobedient

désodorisant [dezɔdɔʀizɑ̃] nm air freshener, deodorizer

désolé, e [dezɔle] adj (paysage) desolate; **je suis ~** I'm sorry

désordonné, e [dezɔʀdɔne] adj untidy

désordre [dezɔʀdʀ] nm disorder(liness), untidiness; (anarchie) disorder; **en ~** in a mess, untidy

désormais [dezɔʀmɛ] adv from now on

desquelles [dekɛl] prép +pron = **de +lesquelles**

desquels [dekɛl] prép +pron = **de +lesquels**

dessécher [deseʃe]: **se dessécher** vi to dry out

desserrer [deseʀe] vt to loosen; (frein) to release

dessert [desɛʀ] nm dessert, pudding

desservir [desɛʀviʀ] vt (ville, quartier) to serve; (débarrasser): **~ (la table)** to clear the table

dessin [desɛ̃] nm (œuvre, art) drawing; (motif) pattern, design; **dessin animé** cartoon (film); **dessin humoristique** cartoon; **dessinateur, -trice** nm/f drawer; (de bandes dessinées) cartoonist; (industriel) draughtsman(-woman) (BRIT), draftsman(-woman) (US); **dessiner** vt to draw; (concevoir) to design; **se dessiner** vi (forme) to be outlined; (fig: solution) to emerge

dessous [d(ə)su] adv underneath, beneath ▷ nm underside ▷ nmpl (sous-vêtements) underwear sg; **en ~, par ~** underneath; **au-~**

(de) below; (peu digne de) beneath; **avoir le ~** to get the worst of it; **les voisins du ~** the downstairs neighbours; **dessous-de-plat** nm inv tablemat

dessus [d(ə)sy] adv on top; (collé, écrit) on it ▷ nm top; **en ~** above; **par ~** adv over it ▷ prép over; **au-~ (de)** above; **les voisins de ~** the upstairs neighbours; **avoir le ~** to get the upper hand; **sens ~ dessous** upside down; **dessus-de-lit** nm inv bedspread

destin [dɛstɛ̃] nm fate; (avenir) destiny

destinataire [dɛstinatɛʀ] nm/f (Postes) addressee; (d'un colis) consignee

destination [dɛstinasjɔ̃] nf (lieu) destination; (usage) purpose; **à ~ de** bound for, travelling to

destiner [dɛstine] vt: **~ qch à qn** (envisager de donner) to intend sb to have sth; (adresser) to intend sth for sb; **être destiné à** (usage) to be meant for; **se ~ à l'enseignement** to intend to become a teacher

détachant [detaʃɑ̃] nm stain remover

détacher [detaʃe] vt (enlever) to detach, remove; (délier) to untie; (Admin): **~ qn (auprès de** ou **à)** to post sb (to); **se détacher** vi (se séparer) to come off; (: page) to come out; (se défaire) to come undone; **se ~ sur** to stand out against; **se ~ de** (se désintéresser) to grow away from

détail [detaj] nm detail; (Comm): **le ~** retail; **en ~** in detail; **au ~** (Comm) retail; **détaillant** nm retailer; **détaillé, e** adj (plan, explications) detailed; (facture) itemized; **détailler** vt (expliquer) to explain in detail

détecter [detɛkte] vt to detect

détective [detɛktiv] nm: **détective (privé)** private detective

déteindre [detɛ̃dʀ] vi (au lavage) to run, lose its colour; **~ sur** (vêtement) to run into; (fig) to rub off on

détendre [detɑ̃dʀ] vt (corps, esprit) to relax; **se détendre** vi (ressort) to lose its tension; (personne) to relax

détenir [det(ə)niʀ] vt (record, pouvoir, secret) to hold; (prisonnier) to detain, hold

détente [detɑ̃t] nf relaxation

détention [detɑ̃sjɔ̃] nf (d'armes) possession; (captivité) detention; **détention préventive** custody

détenu, e [det(ə)ny] nm/f prisoner

détergent [detɛʀʒɑ̃] nm detergent

détériorer [deteʀjɔʀe] vt to damage; **se détériorer** vi to deteriorate

déterminé, e [detɛʀmine] adj (résolu) determined; (précis) specific, definite

déterminer [detɛʀmine] vt (fixer) to determine; **~ qn à faire qch** to decide sb to do sth; **se ~ à faire qch** to make up one's mind to do sth

détester [detɛste] vt to hate, detest

détour [detuʀ] nm detour; (tournant) bend,
curve; **ça vaut le ~** it's worth the trip; **sans ~**
(fig) plainly

détourné, e [detuʀne] adj (moyen)
roundabout

détourner [detuʀne] vt to divert; (par la force)
to hijack; (yeux, tête) to turn away; (de l'argent)
to embezzle; **se détourner** vi to turn away

détraquer [detʀake] vt to put out of order;
(estomac) to upset; **se détraquer** vi (machine)
to go wrong

détriment [detʀimɑ̃] nm: **au ~ de** to the
detriment of

détroit [detʀwa] nm strait

détruire [detʀɥiʀ] vt to destroy

dette [dɛt] nf debt

DEUG sigle m (= diplôme d'études universitaires
générales) diploma taken after 2 years at university

deuil [dœj] nm (perte) bereavement; (période)
mourning; **être en ~** to be in mourning

deux [dø] num two; **tous les ~** both; **ses
~ mains** both his hands, his two hands;
~ fois twice; **deuxième** num second;
deuxièmement adv secondly; **deux-pièces**
nm inv (tailleur) two-piece suit; (de bain) two-
piece (swimsuit); (appartement) two-roomed
flat (BRIT) ou apartment (US); **deux-points**
nm inv colon sg; **deux-roues** nm inv two-wheeled
vehicle

devais [dəvɛ] vb voir **devoir**

dévaluation [devalɥasjɔ̃] nf devaluation

devancer [d(ə)vɑ̃se] vt (coureur, rival) to get
ahead of; (arriver) to arrive before; (prévenir:
questions, désirs) to anticipate

devant [d(ə)vɑ̃] adv in front; (à distance: en
avant) ahead ▷ prép in front of; (en avant)
ahead of; (avec mouvement: passer) past; (en
présence de) before, in front of; (étant donné) in
view of ▷ nm front; **prendre les ~s** to make
the first move; **les pattes de ~** the front legs,
the forelegs; **par ~** (boutonner) at the front;
(entrer) the front way; **aller au-~ de qn** to go
out to meet sb; **aller au-~ de** (désirs de qn) to
anticipate

devanture [d(ə)vɑ̃tyʀ] nf (étalage) display;
(vitrine) (shop) window

développement [dev(ə)lɔpmɑ̃] nm
development; **pays en voie de ~** developing
countries

développer [dev(ə)lɔpe] vt to develop; **se
développer** vi to develop

devenir [dəv(ə)niʀ] vb +attrib to become; **que
sont-ils devenus?** what has become of them?

devez [dəve] vb voir **devoir**

déviation [devjasjɔ̃] nf (Auto) diversion (BRIT),
detour (US)

devienne etc [dəvjɛn] vb voir **devenir**

deviner [d(ə)vine] vt to guess; (apercevoir) to
distinguish; **devinette** nf riddle

devis [d(ə)vi] nm estimate, quotation

devise [dəviz] nf (formule) motto, watchword;
devises nfpl (argent) currency sg

dévisser [devise] vt to unscrew, undo; **se
dévisser** vi to come unscrewed

devoir [d(ə)vwaʀ] nm duty; (Scol) homework
no pl; (: en classe) exercise ▷ vt (argent, respect):
~ qch (à qn) to owe (sb) sth; (+infin: obligation):
il doit le faire he has to do it, he must do it; (:
intention): **le nouveau centre commercial
doit ouvrir en mai** the new shopping centre
is due to open in May; (: probabilité): **il doit
être tard** it must be late; (: fatalité): **cela
devait arriver** it was bound to happen;
combien est-ce que je vous dois? how much
do I owe you?

dévorer [devɔʀe] vt to devour

dévoué, e [devwe] adj devoted

dévouer [devwe]: **se dévouer** vi (se sacrifier):
se ~ (pour) to sacrifice o.s. (for); (se consacrer):
se ~ à to devote ou dedicate o.s. to

devrai [dəvʀe] vb voir **devoir**

dézipper [dezipe] vt to unzip

diabète [djabɛt] nm diabetes sg; **diabétique**
nm/f diabetic

diable [djabl] nm devil

diabolo [djabɔlo] nm (boisson) lemonade with
fruit cordial

diagnostic [djagnɔstik] nm diagnosis sg;
diagnostiquer vt to diagnose

diagonal, e, -aux [djagɔnal, o] adj diagonal;
diagonale nf diagonal; **en diagonale**
diagonally

diagramme [djagʀam] nm chart, graph

dialecte [djalɛkt] nm dialect

dialogue [djalɔg] nm dialogue

diamant [djamɑ̃] nm diamond

diamètre [djamɛtʀ] nm diameter

diapositive [djapozitiv] nf transparency,
slide

diarrhée [djaʀe] nf diarrhoea

dictateur [diktatœʀ] nm dictator; **dictature**
nf dictatorship

dictée [dikte] nf dictation

dicter [dikte] vt to dictate

dictionnaire [diksjɔnɛʀ] nm dictionary

dièse [djɛz] nm sharp

diesel [djezɛl] nm diesel ▷ adj inv diesel

diète [djɛt] nf (jeûne) starvation diet; (régime)
diet; **diététique** adj: **magasin diététique**
health food shop (BRIT) ou store (US)

dieu, x [djø] nm god; **D~** God; **mon D~!** good
heavens!

différemment [difeʀamɑ̃] adv differently

différence [difeʀɑ̃s] nf difference; **à la ~ de**
unlike; **différencier** vt to differentiate

différent, e [difeʀɑ̃, ɑ̃t] adj (dissemblable)
different; **~ de** different from; (divers) different,
various

différer [difere] vt to postpone, put off ▷ vi: ~ **(de)** to differ (from)

difficile [difisil] adj difficult; (exigeant) hard to please; **difficilement** adv with difficulty

difficulté [difikylte] nf difficulty; **en ~** (bateau, alpiniste) in difficulties

diffuser [difyze] vt (chaleur) to diffuse; (émission, musique) to broadcast; (nouvelle) to circulate; (Comm) to distribute

digérer [diʒeRe] vt to digest; (fam: accepter) to stomach, put up with; **digestif** nm (after-dinner) liqueur; **digestion** nf digestion

digne [diɲ] adj dignified; **~ de** worthy of; **~ de foi** trustworthy; **dignité** nf dignity

digue [dig] nf dike, dyke

dilemme [dilɛm] nm dilemma

diligence [diliʒɑ̃s] nf stagecoach

diluer [dilɥe] vt to dilute

dimanche [dimɑ̃ʃ] nm Sunday

dimension [dimɑ̃sjɔ̃] nf (grandeur) size; (dimensions) dimensions

diminuer [diminɥe] vt to reduce, decrease; (ardeur etc) to lessen; (dénigrer) to belittle ▷ vi to decrease, diminish; **diminutif** nm (surnom) pet name

dinde [dɛ̃d] nf turkey

dindon [dɛ̃dɔ̃] nm turkey

dîner [dine] nm dinner ▷ vi to have dinner

dingue [dɛ̃g] (fam) adj crazy

dinosaure [dinɔzɔR] nm dinosaur

diplomate [diplɔmat] adj diplomatic ▷ nm diplomat; (fig) diplomatist; **diplomatie** nf diplomacy

diplôme [diplom] nm diploma; **avoir des ~s** to have qualifications; **diplômé, e** adj qualified

dire [diR] nm: **au ~ de** according to ▷ vt to say; (secret, mensonge, heure) to tell; **~ qch à qn** to tell sb sth; **~ à qn qu'il fasse** ou **de faire** to tell sb to do; **on dit que** they say that; **ceci ou cela dit** that being said; **si cela lui dit** (plaire) if he fancies it; **que dites-vous de** (penser) what do you think of; **on dirait que** it looks (ou sounds etc) as if; **dis/dites (donc)!** I say!; **se ~ (à soi-même)** to say to o.s.; **se ~ malade** (se prétendre) to claim one is ill; **ça ne se dit pas** (impoli) you shouldn't say that; (pas en usage) you don't say that

direct, e [diRɛkt] adj direct ▷ nm (TV): **en ~** live; **directement** adv directly

directeur, -trice [diRɛktœR, tRis] nm/f (d'entreprise) director; (de service) manager(-eress); (d'école) head(teacher) (BRIT), principal (US)

direction [diRɛksjɔ̃] nf (sens) direction; (d'entreprise) management; (Auto) steering; **"toutes ~s"** "all routes"

dirent [diR] vb voir **dire**

dirigeant, e [diRiʒɑ̃, ɑ̃t] adj (classe) ruling ▷ nm/f (d'un parti etc) leader

diriger [diRiʒe] vt (entreprise) to manage, run; (véhicule) to steer; (orchestre) to conduct; (recherches, travaux) to supervise; **~ sur** (arme) to point ou level ou aim at; **~ son regard sur** to look in the direction of; **se diriger** vi (s'orienter) to find one's way; **se ~ vers** ou **sur** to make ou head for

dis [di] vb voir **dire**

discerner [disɛRne] vt to discern, make out

discipline [disiplin] nf discipline; **discipliner** vt to discipline

discontinu, e [diskɔ̃tiny] adj intermittent

discontinuer [diskɔ̃tinɥe] vi: **sans ~** without stopping, without a break

discothèque [diskɔtɛk] nf (boîte de nuit) disco(thèque)

discours [diskuR] nm speech

discret, -ète [diskRɛ, ɛt] adj discreet; (parfum, maquillage) unobtrusive; **discrétion** nf discretion; **à discrétion** as much as one wants

discrimination [diskRiminasjɔ̃] nf discrimination; **sans ~** indiscriminately

discussion [diskysjɔ̃] nf discussion

discutable [diskytabl] adj debatable

discuter [diskyte] vt (débattre) to discuss; (contester) to question, dispute ▷ vi to talk; (protester) to argue; **~ de** to discuss

dise [diz] vb voir **dire**

disjoncteur [disʒɔ̃ktœR] nm (Élec) circuit breaker

disloquer [dislɔke]: **se disloquer** vi (parti, empire) to break up; (meuble) to come apart; (épaule) to be dislocated

disons [dizɔ̃] vb voir **dire**

disparaître [dispaRɛtR] vi to disappear; (se perdre: traditions etc) to die out; **faire ~** (tache) to remove; (douleur) to get rid of

disparition [dispaRisjɔ̃] nf disappearance; **espèce en voie de ~** endangered species

disparu, e [dispaRy] nm/f missing person ▷ adj: **être porté ~** to be reported missing

dispensaire [dispɑ̃sɛR] nm community clinic

dispenser [dispɑ̃se] vt: **~ qn de** to exempt sb from

disperser [dispɛRse] vt to scatter; **se disperser** vi to break up

disponible [disponibl(ə)] adj available

disposé, e [dispoze] adj: **bien/mal ~** (humeur) in a good/bad mood; **~ à** (prêt à) willing ou prepared to

disposer [dispoze] vt to arrange ▷ vi: **vous pouvez ~** you may leave; **~ de** to have (at one's disposal); **se ~ à faire** to prepare to do, be about to do

dispositif [dispozitif] nm device; (fig) system, plan of action

disposition [dispozisjɔ̃] nf (arrangement) arrangement, layout; (humeur) mood;

prendre ses ~s to make arrangements; **avoir des ~s pour la musique** etc to have a special aptitude for music etc; **à la ~ de qn** at sb's disposal; **je suis à votre ~** I am at your service

disproportionné, e [dispʀɔpɔʀsjɔne] adj disproportionate, out of all proportion

dispute [dispyt] nf quarrel, argument; **disputer** vt (match) to play; (combat) to fight; **se disputer** vi to quarrel

disqualifier [diskalifje] vt to disqualify

disque [disk] nm (Mus) record; (forme, pièce) disc; (Sport) discus; **disque compact** compact disc; **disque dur** hard disk; **disquette** nf floppy disk, diskette

dissertation [disɛʀtasjɔ̃] nf (Scol) essay

dissimuler [disimyle] vt to conceal

dissipé, e [disipe] adj (élève) undisciplined, unruly

dissolvant [disɔlvɑ̃] nm nail polish remover

dissuader [disɥade] vt: **~ qn de faire** to dissuade sb from doing

distance [distɑ̃s] nf distance; (fig: écart) gap; **à ~** at ou from a distance; **distancer** vt to outdistance

distant, e [distɑ̃, ɑ̃t] adj (réservé) distant; **~ de** (lieu) far away from

distillerie [distilʀi] nf distillery

distinct, e [distɛ̃(kt), ɛ̃kt] adj distinct; **distinctement** adv distinctly, clearly; **distinctif, -ive** adj distinctive

distingué, e [distɛ̃ge] adj distinguished

distinguer [distɛ̃ge] vt to distinguish; **se ~ de** to be distinguished by

distraction [distʀaksjɔ̃] nf (inattention) absent-mindedness; (passe-temps) distraction, entertainment

distraire [distʀɛʀ] vt (divertir) to entertain, divert; (déranger) to distract; **se distraire** vi to amuse ou enjoy o.s.; **distrait, e** adj absent-minded

distrayant, e [distʀɛjɑ̃, ɑ̃t] adj entertaining

distribuer [distʀibɥe] vt to distribute, hand out; (Cartes) to deal (out); (courrier) to deliver; **distributeur** nm (Comm) distributor; **distributeur (automatique)** (vending) machine; **distributeur de billets** (cash) dispenser

dit, e [di, dit] pp de **dire** ▷ adj (fixé): **le jour ~** the arranged day; (surnommé): **X, ~ Pierrot** X, known as Pierrot

dites [dit] vb voir **dire**

divan [divɑ̃] nm divan

divers, e [divɛʀ, ɛʀs] adj (varié) diverse, varied; (différent) different, various; **~es personnes** various ou several people

diversité [divɛʀsite] nf (variété) diversity

divertir [divɛʀtiʀ]: **se divertir** vi to amuse ou enjoy o.s.; **divertissement** nm distraction, entertainment

diviser [divize] vt to divide; **division** nf division

divorce [divɔʀs] nm divorce; **divorcé, e** nm/f divorcee; **divorcer** vi to get a divorce, get divorced; **divorcer de** ou **d'avec qn** to divorce sb

divulguer [divylge] vt to disclose

dix [dis] num ten; **dix-huit** num eighteen; **dix-huitième** num eighteenth; **dixième** num tenth; **dix-neuf** num nineteen; **dix-neuvième** num nineteenth; **dix-sept** num seventeen; **dix-septième** num seventeenth

dizaine [dizɛn] nf: **une ~ (de)** about ten, ten or so

do [do] nm (note) C; (en chantant la gamme) do(h)

docile [dɔsil] adj docile

dock [dɔk] nm dock; **docker** nm docker

docteur [dɔktœʀ] nm doctor; **doctorat** nm doctorate

doctrine [dɔktʀin] nf doctrine

document [dɔkymɑ̃] nm document; **documentaire** adj, nm documentary; **documentation** nf documentation, literature; **documenter** vt: **se documenter (sur)** to gather information (on)

dodo [dodo] nm (langage enfantin): **aller faire ~** to go to beddy-byes

dogue [dɔg] nm mastiff

doigt [dwa] nm finger; **à deux ~s de** within an inch of; **un ~ de lait/whiskey** a drop of milk/whisky; **doigt de pied** toe

doit etc [dwa] vb voir **devoir**

dollar [dɔlaʀ] nm dollar

domaine [dɔmɛn] nm estate, property; (fig) domain, field

domestique [dɔmɛstik] adj domestic ▷ nm/f servant, domestic

domicile [dɔmisil] nm home, place of residence; **à ~** at home; **livrer à ~** to deliver; **domicilié, e** adj: **"domicilié à ..."** "address ..."

dominant, e [dɔminɑ̃, ɑ̃t] adj (opinion) predominant

dominer [dɔmine] vt to dominate; (sujet) to master; (surpasser) to outclass, surpass; (surplomber) to tower above, dominate ▷ vi to be in the dominant position; **se dominer** vi to control o.s.

domino [dɔmino] nm domino; **dominos** nmpl (jeu) dominoes sg

dommage [dɔmaʒ] nm: **~s** (dégâts) damage no pl; **c'est ~!** what a shame!; **c'est ~ que** it's a shame ou pity that

dompter [dɔ̃(p)te] vt to tame; **dompteur, -euse** nm/f trainer

DOM-ROM [dɔmʀɔm] sigle m (= départements et régions d'outre-mer) French overseas departments and regions

don [dɔ̃] nm gift; (charité) donation; **avoir des ~s pour** to have a gift ou talent for; **elle a le ~**

de m'énerver she's got a knack of getting on my nerves

donc [dɔ̃k] conj therefore, so; (après une digression) so, then

donné, e [dɔne] adj (convenu: lieu, heure) given; (pas cher: fam): **c'est ~** it's a gift; **étant ~ que ...** given that ...; **données** nfpl data

donner [dɔne] vt to give; (vieux habits etc) to give away; (spectacle) to put on; **~ qch à qn** to give sb sth, give sth to sb; **~ sur** (suj: fenêtre, chambre) to look (out) onto; **ça donne soif/faim** it makes you (feel) thirsty/hungry; **se ~ à fond** to give one's all; **se ~ du mal** to take (great) trouble; **s'en ~ à cœur joie** (fam) to have a great time

 MOT-CLÉ

dont [dɔ̃] pron relatif 1 (appartenance: objets) whose, of which; (appartenance: êtres animés) whose; **la maison dont le toit est rouge** the house the roof of which is red, the house whose roof is red; **l'homme dont je connais la sœur** the man whose sister I know
2 (parmi lesquel(le)s): **2 livres, dont l'un est ...** 2 books, one of which is ...; **il y avait plusieurs personnes, dont Gabrielle** there were several people, among them Gabrielle; **10 blessés, dont 2 grièvement** 10 injured, 2 of them seriously
3 (complément d'adjectif, de verbe): **le fils dont il est si fier** the son he's so proud of; **le pays dont il est originaire** the country he's from; **la façon dont il l'a fait** the way he did it; **ce dont je parle** what I'm talking about

dopage [dɔpaʒ] nm (Sport) drug use; (de cheval) doping

doré, e [dɔre] adj golden; (avec dorure) gilt, gilded

dorénavant [dɔrenavɑ̃] adv henceforth

dorer [dɔre] vt to gild; **(faire) ~** (Culin) to brown

dorloter [dɔrlɔte] vt to pamper

dormir [dɔrmir] vi to sleep; (être endormi) to be asleep

dortoir [dɔrtwar] nm dormitory

dos [do] nm back; (de livre) spine; **"voir au ~"** "see over"; **de ~** from the back

dosage [dozaʒ] nm mixture

dose [doz] nf dose; **doser** vt to measure out; **il faut savoir doser ses efforts** you have to be able to pace yourself

dossier [dosje] nm (documents) file; (de chaise) back; (Presse) feature; (Comput) folder; **un ~ scolaire** a school report

douane [dwan] nf customs pl; **douanier, -ière** adj customs cpd ▷ nm customs officer

double [dubl] adj, adv double ▷ nm (2 fois plus): **le ~ (de)** twice as much (ou many) (as); (autre exemplaire) duplicate, copy; (sosie) double; (Tennis) doubles sg; **en ~ (exemplaire)** in duplicate; **faire ~ emploi** to be redundant; **double-cliquer** vi (Inform) to double-click

doubler [duble] vt (multiplier par 2) to double; (vêtement) to line; (dépasser) to overtake, pass; (film) to dub; (acteur) to stand in for ▷ vi to double

doublure [dublyr] nf lining; (Cinéma) stand-in

douce [dus] adj voir **doux**; **douceâtre** adj sickly sweet; **doucement** adv gently; (lentement) slowly; **douceur** nf softness; (de quelqu'un) gentleness; (de climat) mildness

douche [duʃ] nf shower; **prendre une ~** to have ou take a shower; **doucher: se doucher** vi to have ou take a shower

doué, e [dwe] adj gifted, talented; **être ~ pour** to have a gift for

douille [duj] nf (Élec) socket

douillet, te [dujɛ, ɛt] adj cosy; (péj: à la douleur) soft

douleur [dulœr] nf pain; (chagrin) grief, distress; **douloureux, -euse** adj painful

doute [dut] nm doubt; **sans ~** no doubt; (probablement) probably; **sans aucun ~** without a doubt; **douter** vt to doubt; **douter de** (sincérité de qn) to have (one's) doubts about; (réussite) to be doubtful of; **douter que** to doubt if ou whether; **se douter de qch/que** to suspect sth/that; **je m'en doutais** I suspected as much; **douteux, -euse** adj (incertain) doubtful; (péj) dubious-looking

Douvres [duvr] n Dover

doux, douce [du, dus] adj soft; (sucré) sweet; (peu fort: moutarde, clément: climat) mild; (pas brusque) gentle

douzaine [duzɛn] nf (12) dozen; (environ 12): **une ~ (de)** a dozen or so

douze [duz] num twelve; **douzième** num twelfth

dragée [draʒe] nf sugared almond

draguer [drage] vt (rivière) to dredge; (fam) to try to pick up

dramatique [dramatik] adj dramatic; (tragique) tragic ▷ nf (TV) (television) drama

drame [dram] nm drama

drap [dra] nm (de lit) sheet; (tissu) woollen fabric

drapeau, x [drapo] nm flag

drap-housse [draus] nm fitted sheet

dresser [drese] vt (mettre vertical, monter) to put up, erect; (liste) to draw up; (animal) to train; **se dresser** vi (obstacle) to stand; (personne) to draw o.s. up; **~ qn contre qn** to set sb against sb; **~ l'oreille** to prick up one's ears

drogue [drɔg] nf drug; **la ~** drugs pl; **drogué, e** nm/f drug addict; **droguer** vt (victime) to drug; **se droguer** vi (aux stupéfiants) to take drugs; (péj: de médicaments) to dose o.s. up; **droguerie** nf hardware shop; **droguiste** nm keeper/owner of a hardware shop

droit, e [dʀwa, dʀwat] adj (non courbe) straight; (vertical) upright, straight; (fig: loyal) upright, straight(forward); (opposé à gauche) right, right-hand ▷ adv straight ▷ nm (prérogative) right; (taxe) duty, tax; (: d'inscription) fee; (Jur): **le ~** law; **avoir le ~ de** to be allowed to; **avoir ~ à** to be entitled to; **être dans son ~** to be within one's rights; **à ~e** on the right; (direction) (to the) right; **droits d'auteur** royalties; **droits d'inscription** enrolment fee; **droite** nf (Pol): **la droite** the right (wing); **droitier, -ière** adj right-handed

drôle [dʀol] adj funny; **une ~ d'idée** a funny idea

dromadaire [dʀɔmadɛʀ] nm dromedary

du [dy] dét voir **de** ▷ prép +dét = **de + le**

dû, due [dy] vb voir **devoir** ▷ adj (somme) owing, owed; (causé par): **dû à** due to ▷ nm due

dune [dyn] nf dune

duplex [dyplɛks] nm (appartement) split-level apartment, duplex

duquel [dykɛl] prép +pron = **de +lequel**

dur, e [dyʀ] adj (pierre, siège, travail, problème) hard; (voix, climat) harsh; (sévère) hard, harsh; (cruel) hard(-hearted); (porte, col) stiff; (viande) tough ▷ adv hard ▷ nm (fam: meneur) tough nut; **~ d'oreille** hard of hearing

durant [dyʀɑ̃] prép (au cours de) during; (pendant) for; **des mois ~** for months

durcir [dyʀsiʀ] vt, vi to harden; **se durcir** vi to harden

durée [dyʀe] nf length; (d'une pile etc) life; **de courte ~** (séjour) short

durement [dyʀmɑ̃] adv harshly

durer [dyʀe] vi to last

dureté [dyʀte] nf hardness; harshness; stiffness; toughness

durit(r) [dyʀit] nf (car radiator) hose

duvet [dyvɛ] nm down; (sac de couchage) down-filled sleeping bag

DVD sigle m (= digital versatile disc) DVD

dynamique [dinamik] adj dynamic; **dynamisme** nm dynamism

dynamo [dinamo] nf dynamo

dyslexie [dislɛksi] nf dyslexia, word-blindness

eau, x [o] nf water; **eaux** nfpl (Méd) waters; **prendre l'~** to leak, let in water; **tomber à l'~** (fig) to fall through; **eau de Cologne** eau de Cologne; **eau courante** running water; **eau de javel** bleach; **eau de toilette** toilet water; **eau douce** fresh water; **eau gazeuse** sparkling (mineral) water; **eau minérale** mineral water; **eau plate** still water; **eau salée** salt water; **eau-de-vie** nf brandy

ébène [ebɛn] nf ebony; **ébéniste** nm cabinetmaker

éblouir [ebluiʀ] vt to dazzle

éboueur [ebwœʀ] nm dustman (BRIT), garbageman (US)

ébouillanter [ebujɑ̃te] vt to scald; (Culin) to blanch

éboulement [ebulmɑ̃] nm rock fall

ébranler [ebʀɑ̃le] vt to shake; (affaiblir) to weaken; **s'ébranler** vi (partir) to move off

ébullition [ebylisjɔ̃] nf boiling point; **en ~** boiling

écaille [ekaj] nf (de poisson) scale; (matière) tortoiseshell; **écailler** vt (poisson) to scale; **s'écailler** vi to flake ou peel (off)

écart [ekaʀ] nm gap; **à l'~** out of the way; **à l'~ de** away from; **faire un ~** (voiture) to swerve

écarté, e [ekaʀte] adj (lieu) out-of-the-way, remote; (ouvert): **les jambes ~es** legs apart; **les bras ~s** arms outstretched

écarter [ekaʀte] vt (séparer) to move apart,

separate; (éloigner) to push back, move away; (ouvrir: bras, jambes) to spread, open; (: rideau) to draw (back); (éliminer: candidat, possibilité) to dismiss; **s'écarter** vi to part; (s'éloigner) to move away; **s'~ de** to wander from

échafaudage [eʃafodaʒ] nm scaffolding

échalote [eʃalɔt] nf shallot

échange [eʃɑ̃ʒ] nm exchange; **en ~ de** in exchange ou return for; **échanger** vt: **échanger qch (contre)** to exchange sth (for)

échantillon [eʃɑ̃tijɔ̃] nm sample

échapper [eʃape]: **~ à** vt (gardien) to escape (from); (punition, péril) to escape; **s'échapper** vi to escape; **~ à qn** (détail, sens) to escape sb; (objet qu'on tient) to slip out of sb's hands; **laisser ~** (cri etc) to let out; **l'~ belle** to have a narrow escape

écharde [eʃaʀd] nf splinter (of wood)

écharpe [eʃaʀp] nf scarf; **avoir le bras en ~** to have one's arm in a sling

échauffer [eʃofe] vt (moteur) to overheat; **s'échauffer** vi (Sport) to warm up; (dans la discussion) to become heated

échéance [eʃeɑ̃s] nf (d'un paiement: date) settlement date; (fig) deadline; **à brève ~** in the short term; **à longue ~** in the long run

échéant [eʃeɑ̃]: **le cas ~** adv if the case arises

échec [eʃɛk] nm failure; (Échecs): **~ et mat/au roi** checkmate/check; **échecs** nmpl (jeu) chess sg; **tenir en ~** to hold in check

échelle [eʃɛl] nf ladder; (fig, d'une carte) scale

échelon [eʃ(ə)lɔ̃] nm (d'échelle) rung; (Admin) grade; **échelonner** vt to space out

échiquier [eʃikje] nm chessboard

écho [eko] nm echo; **échographie** nf: **passer une échographie** to have a scan

échouer [eʃwe] vi to fail; **s'échouer** vi to run aground

éclabousser [eklabuse] vt to splash

éclair [eklɛʀ] nm (d'orage) flash of lightning, lightning no pl; (gâteau) éclair

éclairage [eklɛʀaʒ] nm lighting

éclaircie [eklɛʀsi] nf bright interval

éclaircir [eklɛʀsiʀ] vt to lighten; (fig: mystère) to clear up; (: point) to clarify; **s'éclaircir** vi (ciel) to clear; **s'~ la voix** to clear one's throat; **éclaircissement** nm (sur un point) clarification

éclairer [eklɛʀe] vt (lieu) to light (up); (personne: avec une lampe etc) to light the way for; (fig: problème) to shed light on ▷ vi: **~ mal/ bien** to give a poor/good light; **s'~ à la bougie** to use candlelight

éclat [ekla] nm (de bombe, de verre) fragment; (du soleil, d'une couleur etc) brightness, brilliance; (d'une cérémonie) splendour; (scandale): **faire un ~** to cause a commotion; **éclats de voix** shouts; **éclat de rire** roar of laughter

éclatant, e [eklatɑ̃, ɑ̃t] adj brilliant

éclater [eklate] vi (pneu) to burst; (bombe) to explode; (guerre) to break out; (groupe, parti) to break up; **~ en sanglots/de rire** to burst out sobbing/laughing

écluse [eklyz] nf lock

écœurant, e [ekœʀɑ̃, ɑ̃t] adj (gâteau etc) sickly; (fig) sickening

écœurer [ekœʀe] vt: **~ qn** (nourriture) to make sb feel sick; (conduite, personne) to disgust sb

école [ekɔl] nf school; **aller à l'~** to go to school; **école maternelle** nursery school; **école primaire** primary (BRIT) ou grade (US) school; **école secondaire** secondary (BRIT) ou high (US) school; **écolier, -ière** nm/f schoolboy(-girl)

écologie [ekɔlɔʒi] nf ecology; **écologique** adj environment-friendly; **écologiste** nm/f ecologist

économe [ekɔnɔm] adj thrifty ▷ nm/f (de lycée etc) bursar (BRIT), treasurer (US)

économie [ekɔnɔmi] nf economy; (gain: d'argent, de temps etc) saving; (science) economics sg; **économies** nfpl (pécule) savings; **économique** adj (avantageux) economical; (Écon) economic; **économiser** vt, vi to save

écorce [ekɔʀs] nf bark; (de fruit) peel

écorcher [ekɔʀʃe] vt: **s'~ le genou/la main** to graze one's knee/one's hand; **écorchure** nf graze

écossais, e [ekɔsɛ, ɛz] adj Scottish ▷ nm/f: **É~, e** Scot

Écosse [ekɔs] nf: **l'~** Scotland

écouter [ekute] vt to listen to; **s'écouter** (malade) to be a bit of a hypochondriac; **si je m'écoutais** if I followed my instincts; **écouteur** nm (Tél) receiver; **écouteurs** nmpl (casque) headphones pl, headset

écran [ekʀɑ̃] nm screen; **petit ~** television; **~ total** sunblock

écrasant, e [ekʀazɑ̃, ɑ̃t] adj overwhelming

écraser [ekʀaze] vt to crush; (piéton) to run over; **s'écraser** vi to crash; **s'~ contre** to crash into

écrémé, e [ekʀeme] adj (lait) skimmed

écrevisse [ekʀəvis] nf crayfish inv

écrire [ekʀiʀ] vt to write; **s'écrire** to write to each other; **ça s'écrit comment?** how is it spelt?; **écrit** nm (examen) written paper; **par écrit** in writing

écriteau, x [ekʀito] nm notice, sign

écriture [ekʀityʀ] nf writing; **écritures** nfpl (Comm) accounts, books; **l'É~ (sainte), les É~s** the Scriptures

écrivain [ekʀivɛ̃] nm writer

écrou [ekʀu] nm nut

écrouler [ekʀule]: **s'écrouler** vi to collapse

écru, e [ekʀy] adj (couleur) off-white, écru

écume [ekym] nf foam

écureuil [ekyrœj] nm squirrel

écurie [ekyri] nf stable

eczéma [ɛgzema] nm eczema

EDF sigle f (= Électricité de France) national electricity company

Édimbourg [edɛ̃bur] n Edinburgh

éditer [edite] vt (publier) to publish; (annoter) to edit; **éditeur, -trice** nm/f publisher; **édition** nf edition; (industrie du livre) publishing

édredon [edrədɔ̃] nm eiderdown

éducateur, -trice [edykatœr, tris] nm/f teacher; (en école spécialisée) instructor

éducatif, -ive [edykatif, iv] adj educational

éducation [edykasjɔ̃] nf education; (familiale) upbringing; (manières) (good) manners pl; **éducation physique** physical education

éduquer [edyke] vt to educate; (élever) to bring up

effacer [efase] vt to erase, rub out; **s'effacer** vi (inscription etc) to wear off; (pour laisser passer) to step aside

effarant, e [efarɑ̃, ɑ̃t] adj alarming

effectif, -ive [efɛktif, iv] adj real ⊳ nm (Scol) (pupil) numbers pl; (entreprise) staff, workforce; **effectivement** adv (réellement) actually, really; (en effet) indeed

effectuer [efɛktɥe] vt (opération) to carry out; (trajet) to make

effervescent, e [efɛrvesɑ̃, ɑ̃t] adj effervescent

effet [efɛ] nm effect; (impression) impression; **effets** nmpl (vêtements etc) things; **faire ~** (médicament) to take effect; **faire de l'~** (impressionner) to make an impression; **faire bon/mauvais ~ sur qn** to make a good/bad impression on sb; **en ~** indeed; **effet de serre** greenhouse effect

efficace [efikas] adj (personne) efficient; (action, médicament) effective; **efficacité** nf efficiency; effectiveness

effondrer [efɔ̃dre]: **s'effondrer** vi to collapse

efforcer [efɔrse]: **s'efforcer de** vt: **s'~ de faire** to try hard to do

effort [efɔr] nm effort

effrayant, e [efrejɑ̃, ɑ̃t] adj frightening

effrayer [efreje] vt to frighten, scare; **s'~ (de)** to be frightened ou scared (by)

effréné, e [efrene] adj wild

effronté, e [efrɔ̃te] adj cheeky

effroyable [efrwajabl] adj horrifying, appalling

égal, e, -aux [egal, o] adj equal; (constant: vitesse) steady ⊳ nm/f equal; **être ~ à** (prix, nombre) to be equal to; **ça lui est ~** it's all the same to him, he doesn't mind; **sans ~** matchless, unequalled; **d'~ à ~** as equals; **également** adv equally; (aussi) too, as well;

égaler vt to equal; **égaliser** vt (sol, salaires) to level (out); (chances) to equalize ⊳ vi (Sport) to equalize; **égalité** nf equality; **être à égalité** to be level

égard [egar] nm: **~s** mpl consideration sg; **à cet ~** in this respect; **par ~ pour** out of consideration for; **à l'~ de** towards

égarer [egare] vt to mislay; **s'égarer** vi to get lost, lose one's way; (objet) to go astray

églefin [egləfɛ̃] nm haddock

église [egliz] nf church; **aller à l'~** to go to church

égoïsme [egɔism] nm selfishness; **égoïste** adj selfish

égout [egu] nm sewer

égoutter [egute] vi to drip; **s'égoutter** vi to drip; **égouttoir** nm draining board; (mobile) draining rack

égratignure [egratiɲyr] nf scratch

Égypte [eʒipt] nf: **l'~** Egypt; **égyptien, ne** adj Egyptian ⊳ nm/f: **Égyptien, ne** Egyptian

eh [e] excl hey!; **eh bien!** well!

élaborer [elabɔre] vt to elaborate; (projet, stratégie) to work out; (rapport) to draft

élan [elɑ̃] nm (Zool) elk, moose; (Sport) run up; (fig: de tendresse etc) surge; **prendre de l'~** to gather speed

élancer [elɑ̃se]: **s'élancer** vi to dash, hurl o.s.

élargir [elarʒir] vt to widen; **s'élargir** vi to widen; (vêtement) to stretch

élastique [elastik] adj elastic ⊳ nm (de bureau) rubber band; (pour la couture) elastic no pl

élection [elɛksjɔ̃] nf election

électricien, ne [elɛktrisjɛ̃, jɛn] nm/f electrician

électricité [elɛktrisite] nf electricity; **allumer/éteindre l'~** to put on/off the light

électrique [elɛktrik] adj electric(al)

électrocuter [elɛktrɔkyte] vt to electrocute

électroménager [elɛktromenaʒe] adj, nm: **appareils ~s, l'~** domestic (electrical) appliances

électronique [elɛktrɔnik] adj electronic ⊳ nf electronics sg

élégance [elegɑ̃s] nf elegance

élégant, e [elegɑ̃, ɑ̃t] adj elegant

élément [elemɑ̃] nm element; (pièce) component, part; **élémentaire** adj elementary

éléphant [elefɑ̃] nm elephant

élevage [el(ə)vaʒ] nm breeding; (de bovins) cattle rearing; **truite d'~** farmed trout

élevé, e [el(ə)ve] adj high; **bien/mal ~** well-/ill-mannered

élève [elɛv] nm/f pupil

élever [el(ə)ve] vt (enfant) to bring up, raise; (animaux) to breed; (hausser: taux, niveau) to raise; (édifier: monument) to put up, erect; **s'élever** vi (avion) to go up; (niveau,

température) to rise; **s'~ à** (*suj: frais, dégâts*) to
amount to, add up to; **s'~ contre qch** to rise
up against sth; **~ la voix** to raise one's voice;
éleveur, -euse *nm/f* breeder

éliminatoire [eliminatwaʀ] *nf* (*Sport*) heat

éliminer [elimine] *vt* to eliminate

élire [eliʀ] *vt* to elect

elle [ɛl] *pron* (*sujet*) she; (: *chose*) it; (*complément*)
her; it; **~s** (*sujet*) they; (*complément*) them;
~-même herself; itself; **~s-mêmes** themselves;
voir aussi **il**

éloigné, e [elwaɲe] *adj* distant, far-off;
(*parent*) distant

éloigner [elwaɲe] *vt* (*échéance*) to put off,
postpone; (*soupçons, danger*) to ward off;
(*objet*): **~ qch (de)** to move ou take sth away
(from); (*personne*): **~ qn (de)** to take sb away ou
remove sb (from); **s'éloigner (de)** (*personne*)
to go away (from); (*véhicule*) to move away
(from); (*affectivement*) to grow away (from)

élu, e [ely] *pp de* **élire** ▷ *nm/f* (*Pol*) elected
representative

Élysée [elize] *nm*: **(le palais de) l'~** the Élysée
Palace (*the French president's residence*)

émail, -aux [emaj, o] *nm* enamel

e-mail [imel] *nm* e-mail; **envoyer qch par ~**
to e-mail sth

émanciper [emɑ̃sipe]: **s'émanciper** *vi* (*fig*) to
become emancipated *ou* liberated

emballage [ɑ̃balaʒ] *nm* (*papier*) wrapping;
(*boîte*) packaging

emballer [ɑ̃bale] *vt* to wrap (up); (*dans un
carton*) to pack (up); (*fig: fam*) to thrill (to bits);
s'emballer *vi* (*moteur*) to race; (*cheval*) to bolt;
(*fig: personne*) to get carried away

embarcadère [ɑ̃baʀkadɛʀ] *nm* wharf, pier

embarquement [ɑ̃baʀkəmɑ̃] *nm* (*de
passagers*) boarding; (*de marchandises*) loading

embarquer [ɑ̃baʀke] *vt* (*personne*) to embark;
(*marchandise*) to load; (*fam*) to cart off ▷ *vi*
(*passager*) to board; **s'embarquer** *vi* to board;
s'~ dans (*affaire, aventure*) to embark upon

embarras [ɑ̃baʀa] *nm* (*gêne*) embarrassment;
mettre qn dans l'~ to put sb in an awkward
position; **vous n'avez que l'~ du choix** the
only problem is choosing

embarrassant, e [ɑ̃baʀasɑ̃, ɑ̃t] *adj*
embarrassing

embarrasser [ɑ̃baʀase] *vt* (*encombrer*) to
clutter (up); (*gêner*) to hinder, hamper; **~ qn**
to put sb in an awkward position; **s'~ de** to
burden o.s. with

embaucher [ɑ̃boʃe] *vt* to take on, hire

embêter [ɑ̃bete] *vt* to bother; **s'embêter** *vi*
(*s'ennuyer*) to be bored

emblée [ɑ̃ble]: **d'~** *adv* straightaway

embouchure [ɑ̃buʃyʀ] *nf* (*Géo*) mouth

embourber [ɑ̃buʀbe]: **s'embourber** *vi* to get
stuck in the mud

embouteillage [ɑ̃butɛjaʒ] *nm* traffic jam

embranchement [ɑ̃bʀɑ̃ʃmɑ̃] *nm* (*routier*)
junction

embrasser [ɑ̃bʀase] *vt* to kiss; (*sujet, période*)
to embrace, encompass

embrayage [ɑ̃bʀɛjaʒ] *nm* clutch

embrouiller [ɑ̃bʀuje] *vt* to muddle up; (*fils*)
to tangle (up); **s'embrouiller** *vi* (*personne*) to
get in a muddle

embruns [ɑ̃bʀœ̃] *nmpl* sea spray *sg*

embué, e [ɑ̃bɥe] *adj* misted up

émeraude [em(ə)ʀod] *nf* emerald

émerger [emɛʀʒe] *vi* to emerge; (*faire saillie,
aussi fig*) to stand out

émeri [em(ə)ʀi] *nm*: **toile** *ou* **papier ~** emery
paper

émerveiller [emɛʀveje] *vt* to fill with
wonder; **s'émerveiller de** to marvel at

émettre [emɛtʀ] *vt* (*son, lumière*) to give out,
emit; (*message etc: Radio*) to transmit; (*billet,
timbre, emprunt*) to issue; (*hypothèse, avis*) to
voice, put forward ▷ *vi* to broadcast

émeus *etc* [emø] *vb voir* **émouvoir**

émeute [emøt] *nf* riot

émigrer [emigʀe] *vi* to emigrate

émincer [emɛ̃se] *vt* to cut into thin slices

émission [emisjɔ̃] *nf* (*Radio, TV*) programme,
broadcast; (*d'un message*) transmission; (*de
timbre*) issue

emmêler [ɑ̃mele] *vt* to tangle (up); (*fig*) to
muddle up; **s'emmêler** *vi* to get in a tangle

emménager [ɑ̃menaʒe] *vi* to move in; **~
dans** to move into

emmener [ɑ̃m(ə)ne] *vt* to take (with one);
(*comme otage, capture*) to take away; **~ qn au
cinéma** to take sb to the cinema

emmerder [ɑ̃mɛʀde] (*fam!*) *vt* to bug, bother;
s'emmerder *vi* to be bored stiff

émoticone [emɔticɔn] *nm* smiley

émotif, -ive [emɔtif, iv] *adj* emotional

émotion [emosjɔ̃] *nf* emotion

émouvoir [emuvwaʀ] *vt* to move;
s'émouvoir *vi* to be moved; (*s'indigner*) to
be roused

empaqueter [ɑ̃pakte] *vt* to parcel up

emparer [ɑ̃paʀe]: **s'emparer de** *vt* (*objet*) to
seize, grab; (*comme otage, MIL*) to seize; (*suj:
peur etc*) to take hold of

empêchement [ɑ̃pɛʃmɑ̃] *nm* (*unexpected*)
obstacle, hitch

empêcher [ɑ̃peʃe] *vt* to prevent; **~ qn de
faire** to prevent *ou* stop sb (from) doing; **il
n'empêche que** nevertheless; **il n'a pas pu s'~
de rire** he couldn't help laughing

empereur [ɑ̃pʀœʀ] *nm* emperor

empiffrer [ɑ̃pifʀe]: **s'~** (*fam*) *vi* to stuff o.s.

empiler [ɑ̃pile] *vt* to pile (up)

empire [ɑ̃piʀ] *nm* empire; (*fig*) influence

empirer [ɑ̃piʀe] *vi* to worsen, deteriorate

emplacement [ɑ̃plasmɑ̃] nm site
emploi [ɑ̃plwa] nm (utilisation) use; (Comm, Écon) employment; (poste) job, situation; **mode d'~** directions for use; **emploi du temps** timetable, schedule
employé, e [ɑ̃plwaje] nm/f employee; **employé de bureau** office employee ou clerk
employer [ɑ̃plwaje] vt to use; (ouvrier, main-d'œuvre) to employ; **s'~ à faire** to apply o.s. to doing; **employeur, -euse** nm/f employer
empoigner [ɑ̃pwaɲe] vt to grab
empoisonner [ɑ̃pwazɔne] vt to poison; (empester: air, pièce) to stink out; (fam) **~ qn** to drive sb mad
emporter [ɑ̃pɔrte] vt to take (with one); (en dérobant ou enlevant, emmener: blessés, voyageurs) to take away; (entraîner) to carry away; **s'emporter** vi (de colère) to lose one's temper; **l'~ (sur)** to get the upper hand (of); **plats à ~** take-away meals
empreinte [ɑ̃prɛ̃t] nf: **~ (de pas)** footprint; **empreintes (digitales)** fingerprints
empressé, e [ɑ̃prese] adj attentive
empresser [ɑ̃prese]: **s'empresser** vi: **s'~ auprès de qn** to surround sb with attentions; **s'~ de faire** (se hâter) to hasten to do
emprisonner [ɑ̃prizɔne] vt to imprison
emprunt [ɑ̃prœ̃] nm loan
emprunter [ɑ̃prœ̃te] vt to borrow; (itinéraire) to take, follow
ému, e [emy] pp de **émouvoir** ▷ adj (gratitude) touched; (compassion) moved

MOT-CLÉ

en [ɑ̃] prép 1 (endroit, pays) in; (direction) to; **habiter en France/ville** to live in France/town; **aller en France/ville** to go to France/town
2 (moment, temps) in; **en été/juin** in summer/June; **en 3 jours** in 3 days
3 (moyen) by; **en avion/taxi** by plane/taxi
4 (composition) made of; **c'est en verre** it's (made of) glass; **un collier en argent** a silver necklace
5 (description, état): **une femme (habillée) en rouge** a woman (dressed) in red; **peindre qch en rouge** to paint sth red; **en T/étoile** T/star-shaped; **en chemise/chaussettes** in one's shirt-sleeves/socks; **en soldat** as a soldier; **cassé en plusieurs morceaux** broken into several pieces; **en réparation** being repaired, under repair; **en vacances** on holiday; **en deuil** in mourning; **le même en plus grand** the same but ou only bigger
6 (avec gérondif) while, on, by; **en dormant** while sleeping, as one sleeps; **en sortant** on going out, as he etc went out; **sortir en**

courant to run out
7 (comme) as; **je te parle en ami** I'm talking to you as a friend
▷ pron 1 (indéfini): **j'en ai/veux** I have/want some; **en as-tu?** have you got any?; **je n'en veux pas** I don't want any; **j'en ai 2** I've got 2; **combien y en a-t-il?** how many (of them) are there?; **j'en ai assez** I've got enough (of it ou them); (j'en ai marre) I've had enough
2 (provenance) from there; **j'en viens** I've come from there
3 (cause): **il en est malade/perd le sommeil** he is ill/can't sleep because of it
4 (complément de nom, d'adjectif, de verbe): **j'en connais les dangers** I know its ou the dangers; **j'en suis fier** I am proud of it ou him ou her ou them; **j'en ai besoin** I need it ou them

encadrer [ɑ̃kadre] vt (tableau, image) to frame; (fig: entourer) to surround; (personnel, soldats etc) to train
encaisser [ɑ̃kese] vt (chèque) to cash; (argent) to collect; (fam: coup, défaite) to take
en-cas [ɑ̃kɑ] nm snack
enceinte [ɑ̃sɛ̃t] adj f: **~ (de 6 mois)** (6 months) pregnant ▷ nf (mur) wall; (espace) enclosure; **enceinte (acoustique)** (loud)speaker
encens [ɑ̃sɑ̃] nm incense
enchaîner [ɑ̃ʃene] vt to chain up; (mouvements, séquences) to link (together) ▷ vi to carry on
enchanté, e [ɑ̃ʃɑ̃te] adj (ravi) delighted; (magique) enchanted; **~ (de faire votre connaissance)** pleased to meet you
enchère [ɑ̃ʃɛr] nf bid; **mettre/vendre aux ~s** to put up for (sale by)/sell by auction
enclencher [ɑ̃klɑ̃ʃe] vt (mécanisme) to engage; **s'enclencher** vi to engage
encombrant, e [ɑ̃kɔ̃brɑ̃, ɑ̃t] adj cumbersome, bulky
encombrement [ɑ̃kɔ̃brəmɑ̃] nm: **être pris dans un ~** to be stuck in a traffic jam
encombrer [ɑ̃kɔ̃bre] vt to clutter (up); (gêner) to hamper; **s'~ de** (bagages etc) to load ou burden o.s. with

MOT-CLÉ

encore [ɑ̃kɔr] adv 1 (continuation) still; **il y travaille encore** he's still working on it; **pas encore** not yet
2 (de nouveau) again; **j'irai encore demain** I'll go again tomorrow; **encore une fois** (once) again; **(et puis) quoi encore?** what next?
3 (en plus): **encore un peu de viande?** a little more meat?; **encore deux jours** two more days
4 (intensif) even, still; **encore plus fort/mieux** even louder/better, louder/better still

5 (restriction) even so ou then, only; **encore pourrais-je le faire si ...** even so, I might be able to do it if ...; **si encore** if only

encourager [ãkuraʒe] vt to encourage; **~ qn à faire qch** to encourage sb to do sth

encourir [ãkuRiR] vt to incur

encre [ãkR] nf ink; **encre de Chine** Indian ink

encyclopédie [ãsiklɔpedi] nf encyclopaedia

endetter [ãdete]: **s'endetter** vi to get into debt

endive [ãdiv] nf chicory no pl

endormi, e [ãdɔRmi] adj asleep

endormir [ãdɔRmiR] vt to put to sleep; (suj: chaleur etc) to send to sleep; (Méd: dent, nerf) to anaesthetize; (fig: soupçons) to allay; **s'endormir** vi to fall asleep, go to sleep

endroit [ãdRwa] nm place; (opposé à l'envers) right side; **à l'~** (vêtement) the right way out; (objet posé) the right way round

endurance [ãdyRãs] nf endurance

endurant, e [ãdyRã, ãt] adj tough, hardy

endurcir [ãdyRsiR]: **s'endurcir** vi (physiquement) to become tougher; (moralement) to become hardened

endurer [ãdyRe] vt to endure, bear

énergétique [enεRʒetik] adj (aliment) energy-giving

énergie [enεRʒi] nf (Physique) energy; (Tech) power; (morale) vigour, spirit; **énergique** adj energetic, vigorous; (mesures) drastic, stringent

énervant, e [enεRvã, ãt] adj irritating, annoying

énerver [enεRve] vt to irritate, annoy; **s'énerver** vi to get excited, get worked up

enfance [ãfãs] nf childhood

enfant [ãfã] nm/f child; **enfantin, e** adj (puéril) childlike; (langage, jeu etc) children's cpd

enfer [ãfεR] nm hell

enfermer [ãfεRme] vt to shut up; (à clef, interner) to lock up; **s'enfermer** to shut o.s. away

enfiler [ãfile] vt (vêtement) to slip on, slip into; (perles) to string; (aiguille) to thread

enfin [ãfε̃] adv at last; (en énumérant) lastly; (toutefois) still; (pour conclure) in a word; (somme toute) after all

enflammer [ãflame]: **s'enflammer** vi to catch fire; (Méd) to become inflamed

enflé, e [ãfle] adj swollen

enfler [ãfle] vi to swell (up)

enfoncer [ãfɔ̃se] vt (clou) to drive in; (faire pénétrer): **~ qch dans** to push (ou drive) sth into; (forcer: porte) to break open; **s'enfoncer** vi to sink; **s'~ dans** to sink into; (forêt, ville) to disappear into

enfouir [ãfwiR] vt (dans le sol) to bury; (dans un tiroir etc) to tuck away

enfuir [ãfɥiR]: **s'enfuir** vi to run away ou off

engagement [ãgaʒmã] nm commitment; **sans ~** without obligation

engager [ãgaʒe] vt (embaucher) to take on; (: artiste) to engage; (commencer) to start; (lier) to bind, commit; (impliquer) to involve; (investir) to invest, lay out; (inciter) to urge; (introduire: clé) to insert; **s'engager** vi (promettre) to commit o.s.; (Mil) to enlist; (débuter: conversation etc) to start (up); **s'~ à faire** to undertake to do; **s'~ dans** (rue, passage) to turn into; (fig: affaire, discussion) to enter into, embark on

engelures [ãʒlyR] nfpl chilblains

engin [ãʒε̃] nm machine; (outil) instrument; (Auto) vehicle; (Aviat) aircraft inv

> Attention à ne pas traduire **engin** par le mot anglais **engine**.

engloutir [ãglutiR] vt to swallow up

engouement [ãgumã] nm (sudden) passion

engouffrer [ãgufRe] vt to swallow up, devour; **s'engouffrer dans** to rush into

engourdir [ãguRdiR] vt to numb; (fig) to dull, blunt; **s'engourdir** vi to go numb

engrais [ãgRε] nm manure; **engrais chimique** chemical fertilizer

engraisser [ãgRese] vt to fatten (up)

engrenage [ãgRənaʒ] nm gears pl, gearing; (fig) chain

engueuler [ãgœle] (fam) vt to bawl at

enhardir [ãaRdiR]: **s'enhardir** vi to grow bolder

énigme [enigm] nf riddle

enivrer [ãnivRe] vt: **s'~** to get drunk

enjamber [ãʒãbe] vt to stride over

enjeu, x [ãʒø] nm stakes pl

enjoué, e [ãʒwe] adj playful

enlaidir [ãlediR] vt to make ugly ▷ vi to become ugly

enlèvement [ãlεvmã] nm (rapt) abduction, kidnapping

enlever [ãl(ə)ve] vt (ôter: gén) to remove; (: vêtement, lunettes) to take off; (emporter: ordures etc) to take away; (kidnapper) to abduct, kidnap; (obtenir: prix, contrat) to win; (prendre): **~ qch à qn** to take sth (away) from sb

enliser [ãlize]: **s'enliser** vi to sink, get stuck

enneigé, e [ãneʒe] adj (route, maison) snowed-up; (paysage) snowy

ennemi, e [εnmi] adj hostile; (Mil) enemy cpd ▷ nm/f enemy

ennui [ãnɥi] nm (lassitude) boredom; (difficulté) trouble no pl; **avoir des ~s** to have problems; **ennuyer** vt to bother; (lasser) to bore; **s'ennuyer** vi to be bored; **si cela ne vous ennuie pas** if it's no trouble (to you); **ennuyeux, -euse** adj boring, tedious; (embêtant) annoying

énorme [enɔRm] adj enormous, huge;

énormément adv enormously; **énormément de neige/gens** an enormous amount of snow/number of people

enquête [ɑ̃kɛt] nf (de journaliste, de police) investigation; (judiciaire, administrative) inquiry; (sondage d'opinion) survey; **enquêter** vi: **enquêter (sur)** to investigate

enragé, e [ɑ̃raʒe] adj (Méd) rabid, with rabies; (fig) fanatical

enrageant, e [ɑ̃raʒɑ̃, ɑ̃t] adj infuriating

enrager [ɑ̃raʒe] vi to be in a rage

enregistrement [ɑ̃r(ə)ʒistrəmɑ̃] nm recording; **enregistrement des bagages** baggage check-in

enregistrer [ɑ̃r(ə)ʒistre] vt (Mus etc) to record; (fig: mémoriser) to make a mental note of; (bagages: à l'aéroport) to check in

enrhumer [ɑ̃ryme] vt: **s'~, être enrhumé** to catch a cold

enrichir [ɑ̃riʃir] vt to make rich(er); (fig) to enrich; **s'enrichir** vi to get rich(er)

enrouer [ɑ̃rwe]: **s'enrouer** vi to go hoarse

enrouler [ɑ̃rule] vt (fil, corde) to wind (up); **s'~ (autour de qch)** to wind (around sth)

enseignant, e [ɑ̃sɛɲɑ̃, ɑ̃t] nm/f teacher

enseignement [ɑ̃sɛɲ(ə)mɑ̃] nm teaching; (Admin) education

enseigner [ɑ̃sɛɲe] vt, vi to teach; **~ qch à qn** to teach sb sth

ensemble [ɑ̃sɑ̃bl] adv together ▷ nm (groupement) set; (vêtements) outfit; (totalité): **l'~ du/de la** the whole ou entire; (unité, harmonie) unity; **impression/idée d'~** overall ou general impression/idea; **dans l'~** (en gros) on the whole

ensoleillé, e [ɑ̃sɔleje] adj sunny

ensuite [ɑ̃sɥit] adv then, next; (plus tard) afterwards, later

entamer [ɑ̃tame] vt (pain, bouteille) to start; (hostilités, pourparlers) to open

entasser [ɑ̃tase] vt (empiler) to pile up, heap up; **s'entasser** vi (s'amonceler) to pile up; **s'~ dans** (personnes) to cram into

entendre [ɑ̃tɑ̃dr] vt to hear; (comprendre) to understand; (vouloir dire) to mean; **s'entendre** vi (sympathiser) to get on; (se mettre d'accord) to agree; **j'ai entendu dire que** I've heard (it said) that; **~ parler de** to hear of

entendu, e [ɑ̃tɑ̃dy] adj (réglé) agreed; (au courant: air) knowing; **(c'est) ~** all right, agreed; **bien ~** of course

entente [ɑ̃tɑ̃t] nf understanding; (accord, traité) agreement; **à double ~** (sens) with a double meaning

enterrement [ɑ̃tɛrmɑ̃] nm (cérémonie) funeral, burial

enterrer [ɑ̃tere] vt to bury

entêtant, e [ɑ̃tɛtɑ̃, ɑ̃t] adj heady

en-tête [ɑ̃tɛt] nm heading; **papier à ~** headed notepaper

entêté, e [ɑ̃tete] adj stubborn

entêter [ɑ̃tete]: **s'entêter** vi: **s'~ (à faire)** to persist (in doing)

enthousiasme [ɑ̃tuzjasm] nm enthusiasm; **enthousiasmer** vt to fill with enthusiasm; **s'enthousiasmer (pour qch)** to get enthusiastic (about sth); **enthousiaste** adj enthusiastic

entier, -ère [ɑ̃tje, jɛr] adj whole; (total: satisfaction etc) complete; (fig: caractère) unbending ▷ nm (Math) whole; **en ~** totally; **lait ~** full-cream milk; **entièrement** adv entirely, wholly

entonnoir [ɑ̃tɔnwar] nm funnel

entorse [ɑ̃tɔrs] nf (Méd) sprain; (fig): **~ au règlement** infringement of the rule

entourage [ɑ̃turaʒ] nm circle; (famille) circle of family/friends; (ce qui enclôt) surround

entourer [ɑ̃ture] vt to surround; (apporter son soutien à) to rally round; **~ de** to surround with; **s'~ de** to surround o.s. with

entracte [ɑ̃trakt] nm interval

entraide [ɑ̃trɛd] nf mutual aid

entrain [ɑ̃trɛ̃] nm spirit; **avec/sans ~** spiritedly/half-heartedly

entraînement [ɑ̃trɛnmɑ̃] nm training

entraîner [ɑ̃trɛne] vt (charrier) to carry ou drag along; (Tech) to drive; (emmener: personne) to take (off); (influencer) to lead; (Sport) to train; (impliquer) to entail; **s'entraîner** vi (Sport) to train; **s'~ à qch/à faire** to train o.s. for sth/to do; **~ qn à faire** (inciter) to lead sb to do; **entraîneur, -euse** nm/f (Sport) coach, trainer ▷ nm (Hippisme) trainer

entre [ɑ̃tr] prép between; (parmi) among(st); **l'un d'~ eux/nous** one of them/us; **ils se battent ~ eux** they are fighting among(st) themselves; **~ autres (choses)** among other things; **entrecôte** nf entrecôte ou rib steak

entrée [ɑ̃tre] nf entrance; (accès: au cinéma etc) admission; (billet) (admission) ticket; (Culin) first course

entre...: **entrefilet** nm paragraph (short article); **entremets** nm (cream) dessert

entrepôt [ɑ̃trəpo] nm warehouse

entreprendre [ɑ̃trəprɑ̃dr] vt (se lancer dans) to undertake; (commencer) to begin ou start (upon)

entrepreneur, -euse [ɑ̃trəprənœr, øz] nm/f: **entrepreneur (en bâtiment)** (building) contractor

entreprise [ɑ̃trəpriz] nf (société) firm, concern; (action) undertaking, venture

entrer [ɑ̃tre] vi to go (ou come) in, enter ▷ vt (Inform) to enter, input; **(faire) ~ qch dans** to get sth into; **~ dans** (gén) to enter; (pièce) to go (ou come) into, enter; (club) to join; (heurter) to run into; **~ à l'hôpital** to go into hospital;

faire ~ (*visiteur*) to show in

entre-temps [ãtrətã] *adv* meanwhile

entretenir [ãtrət(ə)niʀ] *vt* to maintain; (*famille, maîtresse*) to support, keep; **~ qn (de)** to speak to sb (about)

entretien [ãtrətjɛ̃] *nm* maintenance; (*discussion*) discussion, talk; (*pour un emploi*) interview

entrevoir [ãtrəvwaʀ] *vt* (*à peine*) to make out; (*brièvement*) to catch a glimpse of

entrevue [ãtrəvy] *nf* (*audience*) interview

entrouvert, e [ãtruvɛʀ, ɛʀt] *adj* half-open

énumérer [enymeʀe] *vt* to list

envahir [ãvaiʀ] *vt* to invade; (*suj: inquiétude, peur*) to come over; **envahissant, e** (*péj*) *adj* (*personne*) intrusive

enveloppe [ãv(ə)lɔp] *nf* (*de lettre*) envelope; (*crédits*) budget; **envelopper** *vt* to wrap; (*fig*) to envelop, shroud

enverrai *etc* [ãveʀe] *vb voir* **envoyer**

envers [ãvɛʀ] *prép* towards, to ▷ *nm* other side; (*d'une étoffe*) wrong side; **à l'~** (*verticalement*) upside down; (*pull*) back to front; (*chaussettes*) inside out

envie [ãvi] *nf* (*sentiment*) envy; (*souhait*) desire, wish; **avoir ~ de (faire)** to feel like (doing); (*plus fort*) to want (to do); **avoir ~ que** to wish that; **cette glace me fait ~** I fancy some of that ice cream; **envier** *vt* to envy; **envieux, -euse** *adj* envious

environ [ãviʀɔ̃] *adv*: **~ 3 h/2 km** (around) about 3 o'clock/2 km; *voir aussi* **environs**

environnant, e [ãviʀɔnã, ãt] *adj* surrounding

environnement [ãviʀɔnmã] *nm* environment

environs [ãviʀɔ̃] *nmpl* surroundings; **aux ~ de** (round) about

envisager [ãvizaʒe] *vt* to contemplate, envisage; **~ de faire** to consider doing

envoler [ãvɔle]: **s'envoler** *vi* (*oiseau*) to fly away *ou* off; (*avion*) to take off; (*papier, feuille*) to blow away; (*fig*) to vanish (into thin air)

envoyé, e [ãvwaje] *nm/f* (*Pol*) envoy; (*Presse*) correspondent; **envoyé spécial** special correspondent

envoyer [ãvwaje] *vt* to send; (*lancer*) to hurl, throw; **~ chercher** to send for; **~ promener qn** (*fam*) to send sb packing

épagneul, e [epaɲœl] *nm/f* spaniel

épais, se [epɛ, ɛs] *adj* thick; **épaisseur** *nf* thickness

épanouir [epanwiʀ]: **s'épanouir** *vi* (*fleur*) to bloom, come out; (*visage*) to light up; (*personne*) to blossom

épargne [eparɲ] *nf* saving

épargner [eparɲe] *vt* to save; (*ne pas tuer ou endommager*) to spare ▷ *vi* to save; **~ qch à qn** to spare sb sth

éparpiller [eparpije] *vt* to scatter; **s'éparpiller** *vi* to scatter; (*fig*) to dissipate one's efforts

épatant, e [epatã, ãt] (*fam*) *adj* super

épater [epate] (*fam*) *vt* (*étonner*) to amaze; (*impressionner*) to impress

épaule [epol] *nf* shoulder

épave [epav] *nf* wreck

épée [epe] *nf* sword

épeler [ep(ə)le] *vt* to spell

éperon [epʀɔ̃] *nm* spur

épervier [epɛʀvje] *nm* sparrowhawk

épi [epi] *nm* (*de blé, d'orge*) ear; (*de maïs*) cob

épice [epis] *nf* spice

épicé, e [epise] *adj* spicy

épicer [epise] *vt* to spice

épicerie [episʀi] *nf* grocer's shop; (*denrées*) groceries *pl*; **épicerie fine** delicatessen; **épicier, -ière** *nm/f* grocer

épidémie [epidemi] *nf* epidemic

épiderme [epidɛʀm] *nm* skin

épier [epje] *vt* to spy on, watch closely

épilepsie [epilɛpsi] *nf* epilepsy

épiler [epile] *vt* (*jambes*) to remove the hair from; (*sourcils*) to pluck

épinards [epinaʀ] *nmpl* spinach *sg*

épine [epin] *nf* thorn, prickle; (*d'oursin etc*) spine

épingle [epɛ̃gl] *nf* pin; **épingle de nourrice** *ou* **de sûreté** safety pin

épisode [epizɔd] *nm* episode; **film/roman à ~s** serial; **épisodique** *adj* occasional

épluche-légumes [eplyʃlegym] *nm inv* (potato) peeler

éplucher [eplyʃe] *vt* (*fruit, légumes*) to peel; (*fig*) to go over with a fine-tooth comb; **épluchures** *nfpl* peelings

éponge [epɔ̃ʒ] *nf* sponge; **éponger** *vt* (*liquide*) to mop up; (*surface*) to sponge; (*fig: déficit*) to soak up

époque [epɔk] *nf* (*de l'histoire*) age, era; (*de l'année, la vie*) time; **d'~** (*meuble*) period *cpd*

épouse [epuz] *nf* wife; **épouser** *vt* to marry

épousseter [epuste] *vt* to dust

épouvantable [epuvãtabl] *adj* appalling, dreadful

épouvantail [epuvãtaj] *nm* scarecrow

épouvante [epuvãt] *nf* terror; **film d'~** horror film; **épouvanter** *vt* to terrify

époux [epu] *nm* husband ▷ *nmpl* (married) couple

épreuve [epʀœv] *nf* (*d'examen*) test; (*malheur, difficulté*) trial, ordeal; (*Photo*) print; (*Typo*) proof; (*Sport*) event; **à toute ~** unfailing; **mettre à l'~** to put to the test

éprouver [epʀuve] *vt* (*tester*) to test; (*marquer, faire souffrir*) to afflict, distress; (*ressentir*) to experience

épuisé, e [epɥize] *adj* exhausted; (*livre*) out of

print; **épuisement** nm exhaustion

épuiser [epɥize] vt (fatiguer) to exhaust, wear ou tire out; (stock, sujet) to exhaust; **s'épuiser** vi to wear out o.s. out, exhaust o.s.

épuisette [epɥizɛt] nf shrimping net

équateur [ekwatœʀ] nm equator; **(la république de) l'É~** Ecuador

équation [ekwasjɔ̃] nf equation

équerre [ekɛʀ] nf (à dessin) (set) square

équilibre [ekilibʀ] nm balance; **garder/perdre l'~** to keep/lose one's balance; **être en ~** to be balanced; **équilibré, e** adj well-balanced; **équilibrer** vt to balance

équipage [ekipaʒ] nm crew

équipe [ekip] nf team; **travailler en ~** to work as a team

équipé, e [ekipe] adj: **bien/mal ~** well-/poorly-equipped

équipement [ekipmɑ̃] nm equipment

équiper [ekipe] vt to equip; **~ qn/qch de** to equip sb/sth with

équipier, -ière [ekipje, jɛʀ] nm/f team member

équitation [ekitasjɔ̃] nf (horse-)riding; **faire de l'~** to go riding

équivalent, e [ekivalɑ̃, ɑ̃t] adj, nm equivalent

équivaloir [ekivalwaʀ]: **~ à** vt to be equivalent to

érable [eʀabl] nm maple

érafler [eʀafle] vt to scratch; **éraflure** nf scratch

ère [ɛʀ] nf era; **en l'an 1050 de notre ~** in the year 1050 A.D.

érection [eʀɛksjɔ̃] nf erection

éroder [eʀɔde] vt to erode

érotique [eʀɔtik] adj erotic

errer [eʀe] vi to wander

erreur [eʀœʀ] nf mistake, error; **faire ~** to be mistaken; **par ~** by mistake

éruption [eʀypsjɔ̃] nf eruption; (Méd) rash

es [ɛ] vb voir **être**

ès [ɛs] prép: **licencié ès lettres/sciences** ≈ Bachelor of Arts/Science

ESB sigle f (= encéphalopathie spongiforme bovine) BSE

escabeau, x [ɛskabo] nm (tabouret) stool; (échelle) stepladder

escalade [ɛskalad] nf climbing no pl; (Pol etc) escalation; **escalader** vt to climb

escale [ɛskal] nf (Navig: durée) call; (endroit) port of call; (Aviat) stop(over); **faire ~ à** (Navig) to put in at; (Aviat) to stop over at; **vol sans ~** nonstop flight

escalier [ɛskalje] nm stairs pl; **dans l'~** ou **les ~s** on the stairs; **escalier mécanique** ou **roulant** escalator

escapade [ɛskapad] nf: **faire une ~** to go on a jaunt; (s'enfuir) to run away ou off

escargot [ɛskaʀgo] nm snail

escarpé, e [ɛskaʀpe] adj steep

esclavage [ɛsklavaʒ] nm slavery

esclave [ɛsklav] nm/f slave

escompte [ɛskɔ̃t] nm discount

escrime [ɛskʀim] nf fencing

escroc [ɛskʀo] nm swindler, conman; **escroquer** vt: **escroquer qch (à qn)** to swindle sth (out of sb); **escroquerie** nf swindle

espace [ɛspas] nm space; **espacer** vt to space out; **s'espacer** vi (visites etc) to become less frequent

espadon [ɛspadɔ̃] nm swordfish inv

espadrille [ɛspadʀij] nf rope-soled sandal

Espagne [ɛspaɲ] nf: **l'~** Spain; **espagnol, e** adj Spanish ▷ nm/f: **Espagnol, e** Spaniard ▷ nm (Ling) Spanish

espèce [ɛspɛs] nf (Bio, Bot, Zool) species inv; (gén: sorte) sort, kind, type; (péj): **~ maladroit/de brute!** you clumsy oaf/you brute!; **espèces** nfpl (Comm) cash sg; **payer en ~** to pay (in) cash

espérance [ɛspeʀɑ̃s] nf hope; **espérance de vie** life expectancy

espérer [ɛspeʀe] vt to hope for; **j'espère (bien)** I hope so; **~ que/faire** to hope that/to do

espiègle [ɛspjɛgl] adj mischievous

espion, ne [ɛspjɔ̃, jɔn] nm/f spy; **espionnage** nm espionage, spying; **espionner** vt to spy (up)on

espoir [ɛspwaʀ] nm hope; **dans l'~ de/que** in the hope of/that; **reprendre ~** not to lose hope

esprit [ɛspʀi] nm (intellect) mind; (humour) wit; (mentalité, d'une loi etc, fantôme etc) spirit; **faire de l'~** to try to be witty; **reprendre ses ~s** to come to; **perdre l'~** to lose one's mind

esquimau, de, -x [ɛskimo, od] adj Eskimo ▷ nm/f: **E~, de** Eskimo ▷ nm: **E~®** ice lolly (BRIT), popsicle (US)

essai [esɛ] nm (tentative) attempt, try; (de produit) testing; (Rugby) try; (Littérature) essay; **à l'~** on a trial basis; **mettre à l'~** to put to the test

essaim [esɛ̃] nm swarm

essayer [eseje] vt to try; (vêtement, chaussures) to try (on); (méthode, voiture) to try (out) ▷ vi to try; **~ de faire** to try ou attempt to do

essence [esɑ̃s] nf (de voiture) petrol (BRIT), gas(oline) (US); (extrait de plante) essence; (espèce: d'arbre) species inv

essentiel, le [esɑ̃sjɛl] adj essential; **c'est l'~** (ce qui importe) that's the main thing; **l'~ de** the main part of

essieu, x [esjø] nm axle

essor [esɔʀ] nm (de l'économie etc) rapid expansion

essorer [esɔʀe] vt (en tordant) to wring (out);

(*par la force centrifuge*) to spin-dry; **essoreuse** *nf* spin-dryer

essouffler [esufle]: **s'essouffler** *vi* to get out of breath

essuie-glace [esɥiglas] *nm inv* windscreen (*BRIT*) *ou* windshield (*US*) wiper

essuyer [esɥije] *vt* to wipe; (*fig: échec*) to suffer; **s'essuyer** *vi* (*après le bain*) to dry o.s.; **~ la vaisselle** to dry up

est¹ [ɛ] *vb voir* **être**

est² [ɛst] *nm* east ▷ *adj inv* east; (*région*) east(ern); **à l'~** in the east; (*direction*) to the east, east(wards); **à l'~ de** (to the) east of

est-ce que [ɛskə] *adv*: **~ c'est cher/c'était bon?** is it expensive/was it good?; **quand est-ce qu'il part?** when does he leave?, when is he leaving?; *voir aussi* **que**

esthéticienne [ɛstetisjɛn] *nf* beautician

esthétique [ɛstetik] *adj* attractive

estimation [ɛstimasjɔ̃] *nf* valuation; (*chiffre*) estimate

estime [ɛstim] *nf* esteem, regard; **estimer** *vt* (*respecter*) to esteem; (*expertiser: bijou etc*) to value; (*évaluer: coût etc*) to assess, estimate; (*penser*): **estimer que/être** to consider that/o.s. to be

estival, e, -aux [ɛstival, o] *adj* summer *cpd*

estivant, e [ɛstivɑ̃, ɑ̃t] *nm/f* (summer) holiday-maker

estomac [ɛstɔma] *nm* stomach

estragon [ɛstʀagɔ̃] *nm* tarragon

estuaire [ɛstɥɛʀ] *nm* estuary

et [e] *conj* and; **et lui?** what about him?; **et alors!** so what!

étable [etabl] *nf* cowshed

établi [etabli] *nm* (work)bench

établir [etablir] *vt* (*papiers d'identité, facture*) to make out; (*liste, programme*) to draw up; (*entreprise*) to set up; (*réputation, usage, fait, culpabilité*) to establish; **s'établir** *vi* to be established; **s'~ (à son compte)** to set up in business; **s'~ à/près de** to settle in/near

établissement [etablismɑ̃] *nm* (*entreprise, institution*) establishment; **établissement scolaire** school, educational establishment

étage [etaʒ] *nm* (*d'immeuble*) storey, floor; **à l'~** upstairs; **au 2ème ~** on the 2nd (*BRIT*) *ou* 3rd (*US*) floor; **c'est à quel ~?** what floor is it on?

étagère [etaʒɛʀ] *nf* (*rayon*) shelf; (*meuble*) shelves *pl*

étai [etɛ] *nm* stay, prop

étain [etɛ̃] *nm* pewter *no pl*

étais *etc* [etɛ] *vb voir* **être**

étaler [etale] *vt* (*carte, nappe*) to spread (out); (*peinture*) to spread; (*échelonner: paiements, vacances*) to spread, stagger; (*marchandises*) to display; (*connaissances*) to parade; **s'étaler** *vi* (*liquide*) to spread out; (*fam*) to fall flat on one's face; **s'~ sur** (*suj: paiements etc*) to be spread out over

étalon [etalɔ̃] *nm* (*cheval*) stallion

étanche [etɑ̃ʃ] *adj* (*récipient*) watertight; (*montre, vêtement*) waterproof

étang [etɑ̃] *nm* pond

étant [etɑ̃] *vb voir* **être**; **donné**

étape [etap] *nf* stage; (*lieu d'arrivée*) stopping place; (*: Cyclisme*) staging point

état [eta] *nm* (*Pol, condition*) state; **en mauvais ~** in poor condition; **en ~ (de marche)** in (working) order; **remettre en ~** to repair; **hors d'~** out of order; **être en ~/hors d'~ de faire** to be in a/in no fit state to do; **être dans tous ses ~s** to be in a state; **faire ~ de** (*alléguer*) to put forward; **l'É~** the State; **état civil** civil status; **état des lieux** inventory of fixtures; **États-Unis** *nmpl*: **les États-Unis** the United States

etc. [ɛtsetera] *adv* etc

et c(a)etera [ɛtsetera] *adv* et cetera, and so on

été [ete] *pp de* **être** ▷ *nm* summer

éteindre [etɛ̃dʀ] *vt* (*lampe, lumière, radio*) to turn *ou* switch off; (*cigarette, feu*) to put out, extinguish; **s'éteindre** *vi* (*feu, lumière*) to go out; (*mourir*) to pass away; **éteint, e** *adj* (*fig*) lacklustre, dull; (*volcan*) extinct

étendre [etɑ̃dʀ] *vt* (*pâte, liquide*) to spread; (*carte etc*) to spread out; (*linge*) to hang up; (*bras, jambes*) to stretch out; (*fig: agrandir*) to extend; **s'étendre** *vi* (*augmenter, se propager*) to spread; (*terrain, forêt etc*) to stretch; (*s'allonger*) to stretch out; (*se coucher*) to lie down; (*fig: expliquer*) to elaborate

étendu, e [etɑ̃dy] *adj* extensive

éternel, le [etɛʀnɛl] *adj* eternal

éternité [etɛʀnite] *nf* eternity; **ça a duré une ~** it lasted for ages

éternuement [etɛʀnymɑ̃] *nm* sneeze

éternuer [etɛʀnɥe] *vi* to sneeze

êtes [ɛt(z)] *vb voir* **être**

Éthiopie [etjɔpi] *nf*: **l'~** Ethiopia

étiez [etje] *vb voir* **être**

étinceler [etɛ̃s(ə)le] *vi* to sparkle

étincelle [etɛ̃sɛl] *nf* spark

étiquette [etiket] *nf* label; (*protocole*): **l'~** etiquette

étirer [etire]: **s'étirer** *vi* (*personne*) to stretch; (*convoi, route*): **s'~ sur** to stretch over

étoile [etwal] *nf* star; **à la belle ~** in the open; **étoile de mer** starfish; **étoile filante** shooting star; **étoilé, e** *adj* starry

étonnant, e [etɔnɑ̃, ɑ̃t] *adj* amazing

étonnement [etɔnmɑ̃] *nm* surprise, amazement

étonner [etɔne] *vt* to surprise, amaze; **s'étonner que/de** to be amazed that/at; **cela m'~ait (que)** (*j'en doute*) I'd be very surprised (if)

étouffer [etufe] vt to suffocate; (bruit) to muffle; (scandale) to hush up ▷ vi to suffocate; **s'étouffer** vi (en mangeant etc) to choke; **on étouffe** it's stifling

étourderie [eturdəri] nf (caractère) absent-mindedness no pl; (faute) thoughtless blunder

étourdi, e [eturdi] adj (distrait) scatterbrained, heedless

étourdir [eturdir] vt (assommer) to stun, daze; (griser) to make dizzy ou giddy; **étourdissement** nm dizzy spell

étrange [etrãʒ] adj strange

étranger, -ère [etrãʒe, ɛr] adj foreign; (pas de la famille, non familier) strange ▷ nm/f foreigner; stranger ▷ nm: **à l'~** abroad

étrangler [etrãgle] vt to strangle; **s'étrangler** vi (en mangeant etc) to choke

 MOT-CLÉ

être [ɛtr] nm being; **être humain** human being
▷ vb +attrib **1** (état, description) to be; **il est instituteur** he is ou he's a teacher; **vous êtes grand/intelligent/fatigué** you are ou you're tall/clever/tired
2 (+à: appartenir) to be; **le livre est à Paul** the book is Paul's ou belongs to Paul; **c'est à moi/eux** it is ou it's mine/theirs
3 (+de: provenance): **il est de Paris** he is from Paris; (: appartenance): **il est des nôtres** he is one of us
4 (date): **nous sommes le 10 janvier** it's the 10th of January (today)
▷ vi to be; **je ne serai pas ici demain** I won't be here tomorrow
▷ vb aux **1** to have; to be; **être arrivé/allé** to have arrived/gone; **il est parti** he has left, he has gone
2 (forme passive) to be; **être fait par** to be made by; **il a été promu** he has been promoted
3 (+à: obligation): **c'est à réparer** it needs repairing; **c'est à essayer** it should be tried; **il est à espérer que ...** it is ou it's to be hoped that ...
▷ vb impers **1**: **il est** +adjectif it is +adjective; **il est impossible de le faire** it's impossible to do it
2 (heure, date): **il est 10 heures** it is ou it's 10 o'clock
3 (emphatique): **c'est moi** it's me; **c'est à lui de le faire** it's up to him to do it

étrennes [etrɛn] nfpl Christmas box sg
étrier [etrije] nm stirrup
étroit, e [etrwa, wat] adj narrow; (vêtement) tight; (fig: liens, collaboration) close; **à l'~** cramped; **~ d'esprit** narrow-minded

étude [etyd] nf studying; (ouvrage, rapport) study; (Scol: salle de travail) study room; **études** nfpl (Scol) studies; **être à l'~** (projet etc) to be under consideration; **faire des ~s (de droit/médecine)** to study (law/medicine)

étudiant, e [etydjã, jãt] nm/f student

étudier [etydje] vt, vi to study

étui [etyi] nm case

eu, eue [y] pp de **avoir**

euh [ø] excl er

euro [øro] nm euro

Europe [ørɔp] nf: **l'~** Europe; **européen, ne** adj European ▷ nm/f: **Européen, ne** European

eus etc [y] vb voir **avoir**

eux [ø] pron (sujet) they; (objet) them

évacuer [evakɥe] vt to evacuate

évader [evade]: **s'évader** vi to escape

évaluer [evalɥe] vt (expertiser) to appraise, evaluate; (juger approximativement) to estimate

évangile [evãʒil] nm gospel; **É-** Gospel

évanouir [evanwir]: **s'évanouir** vi to faint; (disparaître) to vanish, disappear; **évanouissement** nm (syncope) fainting fit

évaporer [evapɔre]: **s'évaporer** vi to evaporate

évasion [evazjɔ̃] nf escape

éveillé, e [eveje] adj awake; (vif) alert, sharp; **éveiller** vt to (a)waken; (soupçons etc) to arouse; **s'éveiller** vi to (a)waken; (fig) to be aroused

événement [evenmã] nm event

éventail [evãtaj] nm fan; (choix) range

éventualité [evãtɥalite] nf eventuality; possibility; **dans l'~ de** in the event of

éventuel, le [evãtɥɛl] adj possible

> Attention à ne pas traduire **éventuel** par **eventual**.

éventuellement adv possibly

> Attention à ne pas traduire **éventuellement** par **eventually**.

évêque [evɛk] nm bishop

évidemment [evidamã] adv (bien sûr) of course; (certainement) obviously

évidence [evidãs] nf obvious fact; (fait) obvious fact; **de toute ~** quite obviously ou evidently; **être en ~** to be clearly visible; **mettre en ~** (fait) to highlight; **évident, e** adj obvious, evident; **ce n'est pas évident!** (fam) it's not that easy!

évier [evje] nm (kitchen) sink

éviter [evite] vt to avoid; **~ de faire** to avoid doing; **~ qch à qn** to spare sb sth

évoluer [evɔlɥe] vi (enfant, maladie) to develop; (situation, moralement) to evolve, develop; (aller et venir) to move about; **évolution** nf development, evolution

évoquer [evɔke] vt to call to mind, evoke; (mentionner) to mention

ex- [ɛks] préfixe ex-; **son ~mari** her ex-husband;

son **~femme** his ex-wife

exact, e [εgza(kt), εgzakt] adj exact; (correct) correct; (ponctuel) punctual; **l'heure ~e** the right ou exact time; **exactement** adv exactly

ex aequo [εgzeko] adj equally placed; **arriver ~** to finish neck and neck

exagéré, e [εgzaʒere] adj (prix etc) excessive

exagérer [εgzaʒere] vt to exaggerate ▷ vi to exaggerate; (abuser) to go too far

examen [εgzamɛ̃] nm examination; (Scol) exam, examination; **à l'~** under consideration; **examen médical** (medical) examination; (analyse) test

examinateur, -trice [εgzaminatœr, tris] nm/f examiner

examiner [εgzamine] vt to examine

exaspérant, e [εgzasperã, ãt] adj exasperating

exaspérer [εgzaspere] vt to exasperate

exaucer [εgzose] vt (vœu) to grant

excéder [εksede] vt (dépasser) to exceed; (agacer) to exasperate

excellent, e [εkselã, ãt] adj excellent

excentrique [εksãtrik] adj eccentric

excepté, e [εksεpte] adj, prép: **les élèves ~s, ~ les élèves** except for the pupils

exception [εksεpsjɔ̃] nf exception; **à l'~ de** except for, with the exception of; **d'~** (mesure, loi) special, exceptional; **exceptionnel, le** adj exceptional; **exceptionnellement** adv exceptionally

excès [εksε] nm surplus ▷ nmpl excesses; **faire des ~** to overindulge; **excès de vitesse** speeding no pl; **excessif, -ive** adj excessive

excitant, e [εksitã, ãt] adj exciting ▷ nm stimulant; **excitation** nf (état) excitement

exciter [εksite] vt to excite; (suj: café etc) to stimulate; **s'exciter** vi to get excited

exclamer [εksklame]: **s'exclamer** vi to exclaim

exclure [εksklyr] vt (faire sortir) to expel; (ne pas compter) to exclude, leave out; (rendre impossible) to exclude, rule out; **il est exclu que** it's out of the question that …; **il n'est pas exclu que …** it's not impossible that …; **exclusif, -ive** adj exclusive; **exclusion** nf exclusion; **à l'exclusion de** with the exclusion ou exception of; **exclusivité** nf (Comm) exclusive rights pl; **film passant en exclusivité à** film showing only at

excursion [εkskyrsjɔ̃] nf (en autocar) excursion, trip; (à pied) walk, hike

excuse [εkskyz] nf excuse; **excuses** nfpl (regret) apology sg, apologies; **excuser** vt to excuse; **s'excuser (de)** to apologize (for); **excusez-moi** I'm sorry; (pour attirer l'attention) excuse me

exécuter [εgzekyte] vt (tuer) to execute; (tâche etc) to execute, carry out; (Mus: jouer) to perform, execute; **s'exécuter** vi to comply

exemplaire [εgzãplεr] nm copy

exemple [εgzãpl] nm example; **par ~** for instance, for example; **donner l'~** to set an example

exercer [εgzεrse] vt (pratiquer) to exercise, practise; (influence, contrôle) to exert; (former) to exercise, train; **s'exercer** vi (sportif, musicien) to practise

exercice [εgzεrsis] nm exercise

exhiber [εgzibe] vt (montrer: papiers, certificat) to present, produce; (péj) to display, flaunt; **s'exhiber** vi to parade; (suj: exhibitionniste) to expose o.s.; **exhibitionniste** nm/f flasher

exigeant, e [εgziʒã, ãt] adj demanding; (péj) hard to please

exiger [εgziʒe] vt to demand, require

exil [εgzil] nm exile; **exiler** vt to exile; **s'exiler** vi to go into exile

existence [εgzistãs] nf existence

exister [εgziste] vi to exist; **il existe un/des** there is a/are (some)

exorbitant, e [εgzɔrbitã, ãt] adj exorbitant

exotique [εgzɔtik] adj exotic; **yaourt aux fruits ~s** tropical fruit yoghurt

expédier [εkspedje] vt (lettre, paquet) to send; (troupes) to dispatch; (fam: travail etc) to dispose of, dispatch; **expéditeur, -trice** nm/f sender; **expédition** nf sending; (scientifique, sportive, Mil) expedition

expérience [εkspεrjãs] nf (de la vie) experience; (scientifique) experiment

expérimenté, e [εkspεrimãte] adj experienced

expérimenter [εkspεrimãte] vt to test out, experiment with

expert, e [εkspεr, εrt] adj, nm expert; **~ en objets d'art** art appraiser; **expert-comptable** nm ≈ chartered accountant (BRIT), ≈ certified public accountant (US)

expirer [εkspire] vi (prendre fin, mourir) to expire; (respirer) to breathe out

explication [εksplikasjɔ̃] nf explanation; (discussion) discussion; (dispute) argument

explicite [εksplisit] adj explicit

expliquer [εksplike] vt to explain; **s'expliquer** to explain (o.s.); **s'~ avec qn** (discuter) to explain o.s. to sb; **son erreur s'explique** one can understand his mistake

exploit [εksplwa] nm exploit, feat; **exploitant, e** nm/f: **exploitant (agricole)** farmer; **exploitation** nf exploitation; (d'une entreprise) running; **exploitation agricole** farming concern; **exploiter** vt (personne, don) to exploit; (entreprise, ferme) to run, operate; (mine) to exploit, work

explorer [εksplɔre] vt to explore

exploser [εksploze] vi to explode, blow up; (engin explosif) to go off; (personne: de colère) to flare up; **explosif, -ive** adj, nm explosive; **explosion** nf explosion; (de joie, colère) outburst

exportateur, -trice [εkspɔʀtatœʀ, tʀis] adj export cpd, exporting ▷ nm exporter

exportation [εkspɔʀtasjɔ̃] nf (action) exportation; (produit) export

exporter [εkspɔʀte] vt to export

exposant [εkspozɑ̃] nm exhibitor

exposé, e [εkspoze] nm talk ▷ adj: ~ **au sud** facing south

exposer [εkspoze] vt (marchandise) to display; (peinture) to exhibit, show; (parler de) to explain, set out; (mettre en danger, orienter, Photo) to expose; **s'~ à** (soleil, danger) to expose o.s. to; **exposition** nf (manifestation) exhibition; (Photo) exposure

exprès¹ [εkspʀε] adv (délibérément) on purpose; (spécialement) specially; **faire ~ de faire qch** to do sth on purpose

exprès², -esse [εkspʀεs] adj inv (lettre, colis) express

express [εkspʀεs] adj, nm: **(café) ~** espresso (coffee); **(train) ~** fast train

expressif, -ive [εkspʀεsif, iv] adj expressive

expression [εkspʀεsjɔ̃] nf expression

exprimer [εkspʀime] vt (sentiment, idée) to express; (jus, liquide) to press out; **s'exprimer** vi (personne) to express o.s

expulser [εkspylse] vt to expel; (locataire) to evict; (Sport) to send off

exquis, e [εkski, iz] adj exquisite

extasier [εkstazje]: **s'extasier sur** vt to go into raptures over

exténuer [εkstenɥe] vt to exhaust

extérieur, e [εksteʀjœʀ] adj (porte, mur etc) outer, outside; (au dehors: escalier, w.-c.) outside; (commerce) foreign; (influences) external; (apparent: calme, gaieté etc) surface cpd ▷ nm (d'une maison, d'un récipient etc) outside, exterior; (apparence) exterior; **à l'~** outside; (à l'étranger) abroad

externat [εksteʀna] nm day school

externe [εksteʀn] adj external, outer ▷ nm/f (Méd) non-resident medical student (BRIT), extern (US); (Scol) day pupil

extincteur [εkstɛ̃ktœʀ] nm (fire) extinguisher

extinction [εkstɛ̃ksjɔ̃] nf: **extinction de voix** loss of voice

extra [εkstʀa] adj inv first-rate; (fam) fantastic ▷ nm inv extra help

extraire [εkstʀεʀ] vt to extract; **~ qch de** to extract sth from; **extrait** nm extract; **extrait de naissance** birth certificate

extraordinaire [εkstʀaɔʀdineʀ] adj extraordinary; (Pol: mesures etc) special

extravagant, e [εkstʀavagɑ̃, ɑ̃t] adj extravagant

extraverti, e [εkstʀaveʀti] adj extrovert

extrême [εkstʀεm] adj, nm extreme; **d'un ~ à l'autre** from one extreme to another; **extrêmement** adv extremely; **Extrême-Orient** nm Far East

extrémité [εkstʀemite] nf end; (situation) straits pl, plight; (geste désespéré) extreme action; **extrémités** nfpl (pieds et mains) extremities

exubérant, e [εgzybeʀɑ̃, ɑ̃t] adj exuberant

f

F abr = **franc**; (*appartement*): **un F2/F3** a one-
/two-bedroom flat (BRIT) ou apartment (US)
fa [fa] nm inv (Mus) F; (*en chantant la gamme*) fa
fabricant, e [fabʀikɑ̃, ɑ̃t] nm/f manufacturer
fabrication [fabʀikasjɔ̃] nf manufacture
fabrique [fabʀik] nf factory; **fabriquer** vt
to make; (*industriellement*) to manufacture;
(*fig*): **qu'est-ce qu'il fabrique?** (*fam*) what is
he doing?
fac [fak] (*fam*) abr f (Scol) = **faculté**
façade [fasad] nf front, façade
face [fas] nf face; (*fig: aspect*) side ▷ adj: **le côté
~** heads; **en ~ de** opposite; (*fig*) in front of; **de ~**
(*voir*) face on; **~ à** facing; (*fig*) faced with, in the
face of; **faire ~ à** to face; **~ à ~** adv facing each
other ▷ nm inv encounter
fâché, e [fɑʃe] adj angry; (*désolé*) sorry
fâcher [fɑʃe] vt to anger; **se fâcher (contre
qn)** vi to get angry (with sb); **se ~ avec** (*se
brouiller*) to fall out with
facile [fasil] adj easy; (*caractère*) easy-
going; **facilement** adv easily; **facilité** nf
easiness; (*disposition, don*) aptitude; **facilités**
(*possibilités*) facilities; (Comm) terms; **faciliter**
vt to make easier
façon [fasɔ̃] nf (*manière*) way; (*d'une robe etc*)
making-up, cut; **façons** nfpl (*péj*) fuss sg; **de ~
à/à ce que** so as to/that; **de toute ~** anyway,
in any case; **sans ~** (*accepter*) without fuss;
non merci, sans ~ no thanks, honestly

facteur, -trice [faktœʀ] nm/f
postman(-woman) (BRIT), mailman(-woman)
(US) ▷ nm (Math, fig: *élément*) factor
facture [faktyʀ] nf (*à payer: gén*) bill; (Comm)
invoice
facultatif, -ive [fakyltatif, iv] adj optional
faculté [fakylte] nf (*intellectuelle, d'université*)
faculty; (*pouvoir, possibilité*) power
fade [fad] adj insipid
faible [fɛbl] adj weak; (*voix, lumière, vent*) faint;
(*rendement, revenu*) low ▷ nm (*pour quelqu'un*)
weakness, soft spot; **faiblesse** nf weakness;
faiblir vi to weaken; (*lumière*) to dim; (*vent*)
to drop
faïence [fajɑ̃s] nf earthenware no pl
faillir [fajiʀ] vi: **j'ai failli tomber** I almost ou
very nearly fell
faillite [fajit] nf bankruptcy; **faire ~** to go
bankrupt
faim [fɛ̃] nf hunger; **avoir ~** to be hungry;
rester sur sa ~ (*aussi fig*) to be left wanting
more
fainéant, e [fɛneɑ̃, ɑ̃t] nm/f idler, loafer

 MOT-CLÉ

faire [fɛʀ] vt **1** (*fabriquer, être l'auteur de*) to
make; **faire du vin/une offre/un film** to
make wine/an offer/a film; **faire du bruit** to
make a noise
2 (*effectuer: travail, opération*) to do; **que faites-
vous?** (*quel métier etc*) what do you do?; (*quelle
activité: au moment de la question*) what are you
doing?; **faire la lessive** to do the washing
3 (*études*) to do; (*sport, musique*) to play; **faire
du droit/du français** to do law/French; **faire
du rugby/piano** to play rugby/the piano
4 (*simuler*): **faire le malade/l'innocent** to act
the invalid/the innocent
5 (*transformer, avoir un effet sur*): **faire de qn
un frustré/avocat** to make sb frustrated/a
lawyer; **ça ne me fait rien** (*m'est égal*) I don't
care ou mind; (*me laisse froid*) it has no effect
on me; **ça ne fait rien** it doesn't matter; **faire
que** (*impliquer*) to mean that
6 (*calculs, prix, mesures*): **2 et 2 font 4** 2 and 2
are ou make 4; **ça fait 10 m/15 euros** it's 10
m/15 euros; **je vous le fais 10 euros** I'll let
you have it for 10 euros; **je fais du 40** I take
a size 40
7 (*distance*): **faire du 50 (à l'heure)** to do 50
(km an hour); **nous avons fait 1000 km en
2 jours** we did ou covered 1000 km in 2 days;
faire l'Europe to tour ou do Europe; **faire les
magasins** to go shopping
8: **qu'a-t-il fait de sa valise?** what has he
done with his case?
9: **ne faire que**: **il ne fait que critiquer** (*sans
cesse*) all he (ever) does is criticize; (*seulement*)

he's only criticizing

10 (*dire*) to say; **"vraiment?" fit-il** "really?" he said

11 (*maladie*) to have; **faire du diabète** to have diabetes *sg*

▷ *vi* **1** (*agir, s'y prendre*) to act, do; **il faut faire vite** we (*ou* you *etc*) must act quickly; **comment a-t-il fait pour?** how did he manage to?; **faites comme chez vous** make yourself at home

2 (*paraître*) to look; **faire vieux/démodé** to look old/old-fashioned; **ça fait bien** it looks good

▷ *vb substitut* to do; **ne le casse pas comme je l'ai fait** don't break it as I did; **je peux le voir? — faites!** can I see it? — please do!

▷ *vb impers* **1**: **il fait beau** *etc* the weather is fine *etc*; *voir aussi* **jour**; **froid** *etc*

2 (*temps écoulé, durée*): **ça fait 2 ans qu'il est parti** it's 2 years since he left; **ça fait 2 ans qu'il y est** he's been there for 2 years

▷ *vb semi-aux* **1**: **faire** (+*infinitif: action directe*) to make; **faire tomber/bouger qch** to make sth fall/move; **faire démarrer un moteur/chauffer de l'eau** to start up an engine/heat some water; **cela fait dormir** it makes you sleep; **faire travailler les enfants** to make the children work *ou* get the children to work; **il m'a fait traverser la rue** he helped me to cross the street

2 (*indirectement, par un intermédiaire*): **faire réparer qch** to get *ou* have sth repaired; **faire punir les enfants** to have the children punished

se faire *vi* **1** (*être convenable*): **cela se fait beaucoup/ne se fait pas** it's done a lot/not done

2: **se faire** +*nom ou pron*: **se faire une jupe** to make o.s. a skirt; **se faire des amis** to make friends; **se faire du souci** to worry; **il ne s'en fait pas** he doesn't worry

3: **se faire** +*adj* (*devenir*): **se faire vieux** to get old; **se faire beau** to do o.s. up

4: **se faire à** (*s'habituer*) to get used to; **je n'arrive pas à me faire à la nourriture/au climat** I can't get used to the food/climate

5: **se faire** +*infinitif*: **se faire examiner la vue/opérer** to have one's eyes tested/have an operation; **se faire couper les cheveux** to get one's hair cut; **il va se faire tuer/punir** he's going to get himself killed/get punished; **il s'est fait aider** he got somebody to help him; **il s'est fait aider par Simon** he got Simon to help him; **se faire faire un vêtement** to get a garment made for o.s.

6 (*impersonnel*): **comment se fait-il/faisait-il que?** how is it/was it that?

faire-part [fɛʀpaʀ] *nm inv* announcement (*of birth, marriage etc*)

faisan, e [fəzɑ̃, an] *nm/f* pheasant

faisons [fəzɔ̃] *vb voir* **faire**

fait, e [fɛ, fɛt] *adj* (*mûr: fromage, melon*) ripe

▷ *nm* (*événement*) event, occurrence; (*réalité, donnée*) fact; **être au ~ (de)** to be informed (of); **au ~** (*à propos*) by the way; **en venir au ~** to get to the point; **du ~ de ceci/qu'il a menti** because of *ou* on account of this/his having lied; **de ce ~** for this reason; **en ~** in fact; **prendre qn sur le ~** to catch sb in the act; **c'est bien ~ pour lui** (*ou* **eux** *etc*) it serves him (*ou* them *etc*) right; **fait divers** news item

faites [fɛt] *vb voir* **faire**

falaise [falɛz] *nf* cliff

falloir [falwaʀ] *vb impers*: **il faut qu'il parte/a fallu qu'il parte** (*obligation*) he has to *ou* must leave/had to leave; **il a fallu le faire** it had to be done; **il faudrait qu'elle rentre** she should come *ou* go back, she ought to come *ou* go back; **il faut faire attention** you have to be careful; **il me faudrait 100 euros** I would need 100 euros; **il vous faut tourner à gauche après l'église** you have to turn left past the church; **nous avons ce qu'il (nous) faut** we have what we need; **il ne fallait pas** you shouldn't have (done); **comme il faut** (*personne*) proper; (*agir*) properly; **s'en falloir** *vr*: **il s'en est fallu de 100 euros/5 minutes** we/they *etc* were 100 euros short/5 minutes late (*ou* early); **il s'en faut de beaucoup qu'il soit** he is far from being; **il s'en est fallu de peu que cela n'arrive** it very nearly happened

famé, e [fame] *adj*: **mal ~** disreputable, of ill repute

fameux, -euse [famø, øz] *adj* (*illustre*) famous; (*bon: repas, plat etc*) first-rate, first-class; (*valeur intensive*) real, downright

familial, e, -aux [familjal, jo] *adj* family *cpd*

familiarité [familjaʀite] *nf* familiarity

familier, -ère [familje, jɛʀ] *adj* (*connu*) familiar; (*atmosphère*) informal, friendly; (*Ling*) informal, colloquial ▷ *nm* regular (visitor)

famille [famij] *nf* family; **il a de la ~ à Paris** he has relatives in Paris

famine [famin] *nf* famine

fanatique [fanatik] *adj* fanatical ▷ *nm/f* fanatic

faner [fane]: **se faner** *vi* to fade

fanfare [fɑ̃faʀ] *nf* (*orchestre*) brass band; (*musique*) fanfare

fantaisie [fɑ̃tezi] *nf* (*spontanéité*) fancy, imagination; (*caprice*) whim ▷ *adj*: **bijou ~** costume jewellery

fantasme [fɑ̃tasm] *nm* fantasy

fantastique [fɑ̃tastik] *adj* fantastic

fantôme [fɑ̃tom] *nm* ghost, phantom

faon [fɑ̃] *nm* fawn

FAQ *sigle f* (= *foire aux questions*) FAQ

farce [faʀs] *nf* (*viande*) stuffing; (*blague*) (practical) joke; (*Théâtre*) farce; **farcir** *vt* (*viande*) to stuff

farder [faʀde]: **se farder** *vi* to make (o.s.) up

farine [faʀin] *nf* flour

farouche [faʀuʃ] *adj* (*timide*) shy, timid

fart [faʀt] *nm* (ski) wax

fascination [fasinasjɔ̃] *nf* fascination

fasciner [fasine] *vt* to fascinate

fascisme [faʃism] *nm* fascism

fasse *etc* [fas] *vb voir* **faire**

fastidieux, -euse [fastidjø, jøz] *adj* tedious, tiresome

fatal, e [fatal] *adj* fatal; (*inévitable*) inevitable; **fatalité** *nf* (*destin*) fate; (*coïncidence*) fateful coincidence

fatidique [fatidik] *adj* fateful

fatigant, e [fatigã, ãt] *adj* tiring; (*agaçant*) tiresome

fatigue [fatig] *nf* tiredness, fatigue; **fatigué, e** *adj* tired; **fatiguer** *vt* to tire, make tired; (*fig: agacer*) to annoy ▷ *vi* (*moteur*) to labour, strain; **se fatiguer** to get tired

fauché, e [foʃe] (*fam*) *adj* broke

faucher [foʃe] *vt* (*herbe*) to cut; (*champs, blés*) to reap; (*fig: véhicule*) to mow down; (*fam: voler*) to pinch

faucon [fokɔ̃] *nm* falcon, hawk

faudra [fodʀa] *vb voir* **falloir**

faufiler [fofile]: **se faufiler** *vi*: **se ~ dans** to edge one's way into; **se ~ parmi/entre** to thread one's way among/between

faune [fon] *nf* (*Zool*) wildlife, fauna

fausse [fos] *adj voir* **faux**; **faussement** *adv* (*accuser*) wrongly, wrongfully; (*croire*) falsely

fausser [fose] *vt* (*objet*) to bend, buckle; (*fig*) to distort; **~ compagnie à qn** to give sb the slip

faut [fo] *vb voir* **falloir**

faute [fot] *nf* (*erreur*) mistake, error; (*mauvaise action*) misdemeanour; (*Football etc*) offence; (*Tennis*) fault; **c'est de sa/ma ~** it's his *ou* her/my fault; **être en ~** to be in the wrong; **~ de** (*temps, argent*) for *ou* through lack of; **sans ~** without fail; **faute de frappe** typing error; **faute professionnelle** professional misconduct *no pl*

fauteuil [fotœj] *nm* armchair; (*au théâtre*) seat; **fauteuil roulant** wheelchair

fautif, -ive [fotif, iv] *adj* (*responsable*) at fault, in the wrong; (*incorrect*) incorrect, inaccurate; **il se sentait ~** he felt guilty

fauve [fov] *nm* wildcat ▷ *adj* (*couleur*) fawn

faux¹ [fo] *nf* scythe

faux², fausse [fo, fos] *adj* (*inexact*) wrong; (*voix*) out of tune; (*billet*) fake, forged; (*sournois, postiche*) false ▷ *adv* (*Mus*) out of tune ▷ *nm* (*copie*) fake, forgery; **faire ~ bond à qn** to let sb down; **faire un ~ pas** to trip; (*fig*) to make a faux pas; **fausse alerte** false alarm; **fausse**

couche miscarriage; **faux frais** *nmpl* extras, incidental expenses; **faux mouvement** awkward movement; **fausse note** wrong note; **faux témoignage** (*délit*) perjury; **faux-filet** *nm* sirloin

faveur [favœʀ] *nf* favour; **traitement de ~** preferential treatment; **en ~ de** in favour of

favorable [favoʀabl] *adj* favourable

favori, te [favoʀi, it] *adj, nm/f* favourite

favoriser [favoʀize] *vt* to favour

fax [faks] *nm* fax

fécond, e [fekɔ̃, ɔ̃d] *adj* fertile; **féconder** *vt* to fertilize

féculent [fekylã] *nm* starchy food

fédéral, e, -aux [fedeʀal, o] *adj* federal

fée [fe] *nf* fairy

feignant, e [fɛɲã, ãt] *nm/f* = **fainéant, e**

feindre [fɛ̃dʀ] *vt* to feign; **~ de faire** to pretend to do

fêler [fele] *vt* to crack; **se fêler** to crack

félicitations [felisitasjɔ̃] *nfpl* congratulations

féliciter [felisite] *vt*: **~ qn (de)** to congratulate sb (on)

félin, e [felɛ̃, in] *nm* (big) cat

femelle [fəmɛl] *adj, nf* female

féminin, e [feminɛ̃, in] *adj* feminine; (*sexe*) female; (*équipe, vêtements etc*) women's ▷ *nm* (*Ling*) feminine; **féministe** *adj* feminist

femme [fam] *nf* woman; (*épouse*) wife; **femme au foyer** housewife; **femme de chambre** chambermaid; **femme de ménage** cleaning lady

fémur [femyʀ] *nm* femur, thighbone

fendre [fãdʀ] *vt* (*couper en deux*) to split; (*fissurer*) to crack; (*traverser: foule, air*) to cleave through; **se fendre** *vi* to crack

fenêtre [f(ə)nɛtʀ] *nf* window

fenouil [fənuj] *nm* fennel

fente [fãt] *nf* (*fissure*) crack; (*de boîte à lettres etc*) slit

fer [fɛʀ] *nm* iron; **fer à cheval** horseshoe; **fer à friser** curling tongs *pl*; **fer (à repasser)** iron; **fer forgé** wrought iron

ferai *etc* [fəʀe] *vb voir* **faire**

fer-blanc [fɛʀblã] *nm* tin(plate)

férié, e [feʀje] *adj*: **jour ~** public holiday

ferions *etc* [fəʀjɔ̃] *vb voir* **faire**

ferme [fɛʀm] *adj* firm ▷ *adv* (*travailler etc*) hard ▷ *nf* (*exploitation*) farm; (*maison*) farmhouse

fermé, e [fɛʀme] *adj* closed, shut; (*gaz, eau etc*) off; (*fig: milieu*) exclusive

fermenter [fɛʀmãte] *vi* to ferment

fermer [fɛʀme] *vt* to close, shut; (*cesser l'exploitation de*) to close down, shut down; (*eau, électricité, robinet*) to turn off; (*aéroport, route*) to close ▷ *vi* to close, shut; (*magasin: définitivement*) to close down, shut down; **~ à clef** to lock; **se fermer** *vi* to close, shut

fermeté [fɛʀməte] nf firmness

fermeture [fɛʀmətyʀ] nf closing; (dispositif) catch; **heures de ~** closing times; **fermeture éclair®** ou **à glissière** zip (fastener) (BRIT), zipper (US)

fermier [fɛʀmje] nm farmer

féroce [feʀɔs] adj ferocious, fierce

ferons [fəʀɔ̃] vb voir **faire**

ferrer [feʀe] vt (cheval) to shoe

ferroviaire [feʀɔvjɛʀ] adj rail(way) cpd (BRIT), rail(road) cpd (US)

ferry(-boat) [feʀe(-bot)] nm ferry

fertile [fɛʀtil] adj fertile; **~ en incidents** eventful, packed with incidents

fervent, e [fɛʀvɑ̃, ɑ̃t] adj fervent

fesse [fɛs] nf buttock; **fessée** nf spanking

festin [fɛstɛ̃] nm feast

festival [fɛstival] nm festival

festivités [fɛstivite] nfpl festivities

fêtard, e [fɛtaʀ, aʀd] (fam) nm/f high liver, merry-maker

fête [fɛt] nf (religieuse) feast; (publique) holiday; (réception) party; (kermesse) fête, fair; (du nom) feast day, name day; **faire la ~** to live it up; **faire ~ à qn** to give sb a warm welcome; **les ~s (de fin d'année)** the festive season; **la salle des ~s** the village hall; **la ~ des Mères/Pères** Mother's/Father's Day; **fête foraine** (fun) fair; **fêter** vt to celebrate; (personne) to have a celebration for

feu, x [fø] nm (gén) fire; (signal lumineux) light; (de cuisinière) ring; **feux** nmpl (Auto) (traffic) lights; **au ~!** (incendie) fire!; **à ~ doux/vif** over a slow/brisk heat; **à petit ~** (Culin) over a gentle heat; (fig) slowly; **faire ~** to fire; **ne pas faire long ~** not to last long; **prendre ~** to catch fire; **mettre le ~ à** to set fire to; **faire du ~** to make a fire; **avez-vous du ~?** (pour cigarette) have you (got) a light?; **feu arrière** rear light; **feu d'artifice** (spectacle) fireworks pl; **feu de joie** bonfire; **feu orange/rouge/vert** amber (BRIT) ou yellow (US)/red/green light; **feux de brouillard** fog lights ou lamps; **feux de croisement** dipped (BRIT) ou dimmed (US) headlights; **feux de position** sidelights; **feux de route** headlights

feuillage [fœjaʒ] nm foliage, leaves pl

feuille [fœj] nf (d'arbre) leaf; (de papier) sheet; **feuille de calcul** spreadsheet; **feuille d'impôts** tax form; **feuille de maladie** medical expenses claim form; **feuille de paie** pay slip

feuillet [fœjɛ] nm leaf

feuilleté, e [fœjte] adj: **pâte ~** flaky pastry

feuilleter [fœjte] vt (livre) to leaf through

feuilleton [fœjtɔ̃] nm serial

feutre [føtʀ] nm felt; (chapeau) felt hat; (aussi: **stylo-~**) felt-tip pen; **feutré, e** adj (atmosphère) muffled

fève [fɛv] nf broad bean

février [fevʀije] nm February

fiable [fjabl] adj reliable

fiançailles [fjɑ̃saj] nfpl engagement sg

fiancé, e [fjɑ̃se] nm/f fiancé(e) ▷ adj: **être ~ (à)** to be engaged (to)

fiancer [fjɑ̃se]: **se fiancer (avec)** vi to become engaged (to)

fibre [fibʀ] nf fibre; **fibre de verre** fibreglass, glass fibre

ficeler [fis(ə)le] vt to tie up

ficelle [fisɛl] nf string no pl; (morceau) piece ou length of string

fiche [fiʃ] nf (pour fichier) (index) card; (formulaire) form; (Élec) plug; **fiche de paye** pay slip

ficher [fiʃe] vt (dans un fichier) to file; (Police) to put on file; (fam: faire) to do; (: donner) to give; (: mettre) to stick ou shove; **fiche-(moi) le camp!** (fam) clear off!; **fiche-moi la paix!** (fam) leave me alone!; **se ficher de** (fam: rire de) to make fun of; (être indifférent à) not to care about

fichier [fiʃje] nm file; **~ joint** (Comput) attachment

fichu, e [fiʃy] pp de **ficher** (fam) ▷ adj (fam: fini, inutilisable) bust, done for; (: intensif) wretched, darned ▷ nm (foulard) (head)scarf; **mal ~** (fam) feeling lousy

fictif, -ive [fiktif, iv] adj fictitious

fiction [fiksjɔ̃] nf fiction; (fait imaginé) invention

fidèle [fidɛl] adj faithful ▷ nm/f (Rel): **les ~s** (à l'église) the congregation sg; **fidélité** nf (d'un conjoint) fidelity, faithfulness; (d'un ami, client) loyalty

fier¹ [fje]: **se fier à** vt to trust

fier², fière [fjɛʀ] adj proud; **~ de** proud of; **fierté** nf pride

fièvre [fjɛvʀ] nf fever; **avoir de la ~/39 de ~** to have a high temperature/a temperature of 39°C; **fiévreux, -euse** adj feverish

figer [fiʒe]: **se figer** vi (huile) to congeal; (personne) to freeze

fignoler [fiɲɔle] (fam) vt to polish up

figue [fig] nf fig; **figuier** nm fig tree

figurant, e [figyʀɑ̃, ɑ̃t] nm/f (Théâtre) walk-on; (Cinéma) extra

figure [figyʀ] nf (visage) face; (forme, personnage) figure; (illustration) picture, diagram

figuré, e [figyʀe] adj (sens) figurative

figurer [figyʀe] vi to appear ▷ vt to represent; **se figurer que** to imagine that

fil [fil] nm (brin, fig: d'une histoire) thread; (électrique) wire; (d'un couteau) edge; **au ~ des années** with the passing of the years; **au ~ de l'eau** with the stream ou current; **coup de ~** (fam) phone call; **donner/recevoir un coup de ~** to make/get ou receive a phone call; **fil de fer** wire; **fil de fer barbelé** barbed wire

file [fil] *nf* line; (*Auto*) lane; **en ~ indienne** in single file; **à la ~** (*d'affilée*) in succession; **file (d'attente)** queue (BRIT), line (US)

filer [file] *vt* (*tissu, toile*) to spin; (*prendre en filature*) to shadow, tail; (*fam: donner*): **~ qch à qn** to slip sb sth ▷ *vi* (*bas*) to run; (*aller vite*) to fly past; (*fam: partir*) to make *ou* be off; **~ doux** to toe the line

filet [filɛ] *nm* net; (*Culin*) fillet; (*d'eau, de sang*) trickle; **filet (à provisions)** string bag

filiale [filjal] *nf* (*Comm*) subsidiary

filière [filjɛʀ] *nf* (*carrière*) path; **suivre la ~** (*dans sa carrière*) to work one's way up (through the hierarchy)

fille [fij] *nf* girl; (*opposé à fils*) daughter; **vieille ~** old maid; **fillette** *nf* (little) girl

filleul, e [fijœl] *nm/f* godchild, godson/ daughter

film [film] *nm* (*pour photo*) (roll of) film; (*œuvre*) film, picture, movie

fils [fis] *nm* son; **fils à papa** daddy's boy

filtre [filtʀ] *nm* filter; **filtrer** *vt* to filter; (*fig: candidats, visiteurs*) to screen

fin[1] [fɛ̃] *nf* end; **fins** *nfpl* (*but*) ends; **prendre ~** to come to an end; **mettre ~ à** to put an end to; **à la ~** in the end, eventually; **en ~ de compte** in the end; **sans ~** endless; **~ juin** at the end of June; **fin prêt** quite ready

fin[2], **e** [fɛ̃, fin] *adj* (*papier, couche, fil*) thin; (*cheveux, visage*) fine; (*taille*) neat, slim; (*esprit, remarque*) subtle ▷ *adv* (*couper*) finely; **fines herbes** mixed herbs; **avoir la vue/l'ouïe fine** to have keen eyesight/hearing; **repas/vin fin** gourmet meal/fine wine

final, e [final, o] *adj* final ▷ *nm* (*Mus*) finale; **finale** *nf* final; **quarts de finale** quarter finals; **finalement** *adv* finally, in the end; (*après tout*) after all

finance [finɑ̃s] *nf* **finances** *nfpl* (*situation*) finances; (*activités*) finance *sg*; **moyennant ~** for a fee; **financer** *vt* to finance; **financier, -ière** *adj* financial

finesse [finɛs] *nf* thinness; (*raffinement*) fineness; (*subtilité*) subtlety

fini, e [fini] *adj* finished; (*Math*) finite ▷ *nm* (*d'un objet manufacturé*) finish

finir [finiʀ] *vt* to finish ▷ *vi* to finish, end; **~ par faire** to end up *ou* finish up doing; **~ de faire** to finish doing; (*cesser*) to stop doing; **il finit par m'agacer** he's beginning to get on my nerves; **en ~ avec** to be *ou* have done with; **il va mal ~** he will come to a bad end

finition [finisjɔ̃] *nf* (*résultat*) finish

finlandais, e [fɛ̃lɑ̃dɛ, ɛz] *adj* Finnish ▷ *nm/f*: **F~, e** Finn

Finlande [fɛ̃lɑ̃d] *nf*: **la ~** Finland

finnois, e [finwa, waz] *adj* Finnish ▷ *nm* (*Ling*) Finnish

fioul [fjul] *nm* fuel oil

firme [firm] *nf* firm

fis [fi] *vb voir* **faire**

fisc [fisk] *nm* tax authorities *pl*; **fiscal, e, -aux** *adj* tax *cpd*, fiscal; **fiscalité** *nf* tax system

fissure [fisyʀ] *nf* crack; **fissurer** *vt* to crack; **se fissurer** *vi* to crack

fit [fi] *vb voir* **faire**

fixation [fiksasjɔ̃] *nf* (*attache*) fastening; (*Psych*) fixation

fixe [fiks] *adj* fixed; (*emploi*) steady, regular ▷ *nm* (*salaire*) basic salary; (*téléphone*) landline; **à heure ~** at a set time; **menu à prix ~** set menu

fixé, e [fikse] *adj*: **être ~ (sur)** (*savoir à quoi s'en tenir*) to have made up one's mind (about)

fixer [fikse] *vt* (*attacher*): **~ qch (à/sur)** to fix *ou* fasten sth (to/onto); (*déterminer*) to fix, set; (*regarder*) to stare at; **se fixer** *vi* (*s'établir*) to settle down; **se ~ sur** (*suj: attention*) to focus on

flacon [flakɔ̃] *nm* bottle

flageolet [flaʒɔlɛ] *nm* (*Culin*) dwarf kidney bean

flagrant, e [flagʀɑ̃, ɑ̃t] *adj* flagrant, blatant; **en ~ délit** in the act

flair [flɛʀ] *nm* sense of smell; (*fig*) intuition; **flairer** *vt* (*humer*) to sniff (at); (*détecter*) to scent

flamand, e [flamɑ̃, ɑ̃d] *adj* Flemish ▷ *nm* (*Ling*) Flemish ▷ *nm/f*: **F~, e** Fleming

flamant [flamɑ̃] *nm* flamingo

flambant, e [flɑ̃bɑ̃, ɑ̃t] *adj*: **~ neuf** brand new

flambé, e [flɑ̃be] *adj* (*Culin*) flambé

flambée [flɑ̃be] *nf* blaze; (*fig: des prix*) explosion

flamber [flɑ̃be] *vi* to blaze (up)

flamboyer [flɑ̃bwaje] *vi* to blaze (up)

flamme [flam] *nf* flame; (*fig*) fire, fervour; **en ~s** on fire, ablaze

flan [flɑ̃] *nm* (*Culin*) custard tart *ou* pie

flanc [flɑ̃] *nm* side; (*Mil*) flank

flancher [flɑ̃ʃe] (*fam*) *vi* to fail, pack up

flanelle [flanɛl] *nf* flannel

flâner [flɑne] *vi* to stroll

flanquer [flɑ̃ke] *vt* to flank; (*fam: mettre*) to chuck, shove; (: *jeter*): **~ par terre/à la porte** to fling to the ground/chuck out

flaque [flak] *nf* (*d'eau*) puddle; (*d'huile, de sang etc*) pool

flash [flaʃ] (*pl* **~es**) *nm* (*Photo*) flash; **flash d'information** newsflash

flatter [flate] *vt* to flatter; **se ~ de qch** to pride o.s. on sth; **flatteur, -euse** *adj* flattering

flèche [flɛʃ] *nf* arrow; (*de clocher*) spire; **monter en ~** (*fig*) to soar, rocket; **partir en ~** to be off like a shot; **fléchette** *nf* dart

flétrir [fletʀiʀ] *vi* to wither; **se flétrir** *vi* to wither

fleur [flœʀ] *nf* flower; (*d'un arbre*) blossom; **en ~** (*arbre*) in blossom; **à ~s** flowery

fleuri, e [flœʀi] adj (jardin) in flower ou bloom; (tissu, papier) flowery

fleurir [flœʀiʀ] vi (rose) to flower; (arbre) to blossom; (fig) to flourish ▷ vt (tombe) to put flowers on; (chambre) to decorate with flowers

fleuriste [flœʀist] nm/f florist

fleuve [flœv] nm river

flexible [flɛksibl] adj flexible

flic [flik] (fam: péj) nm cop

flipper [flipœʀ] nm pinball (machine)

flirter [flœʀte] vi to flirt

flocon [flɔkɔ̃] nm flake

flore [flɔʀ] nf flora

florissant, e [flɔʀisɑ̃, ɑ̃t] adj (économie) flourishing

flot [flo] nm flood, stream; **flots** nmpl (de la mer) waves; **être à ~** (Navig) to be afloat; **entrer à ~s** to stream ou pour in

flottant, e [flɔtɑ̃, ɑ̃t] adj (vêtement) loose

flotte [flɔt] nf (Navig) fleet; (fam: eau) water; (: pluie) rain

flotter [flɔte] vi to float; (nuage, odeur) to drift; (drapeau) to fly; (vêtements) to hang loose; (fam: pleuvoir) to rain; **faire ~** to float; **flotteur** nm float

flou, e [flu] adj fuzzy, blurred; (fig) woolly, vague

fluide [flɥid] adj fluid; (circulation etc) flowing freely ▷ nm fluid

fluor [flyɔʀ] nm: **dentifrice au ~** fluoride toothpaste

fluorescent, e [flyɔʀesɑ̃, ɑ̃t] adj fluorescent

flûte [flyt] nf flute; (verre) flute (glass); (pain) (thin) French stick; **~! drat it!; flûte traversière/à bec** flute/recorder

flux [fly] nm incoming tide; (écoulement) flow; **le ~ et le reflux** the ebb and flow

foc [fɔk] nm jib

foi [fwa] nf faith; **digne de ~** reliable; **être de bonne/mauvaise ~** to be sincere/insincere; **ma ~ ...** well ...

foie [fwa] nm liver; **crise de ~** stomach upset

foin [fwɛ̃] nm hay; **faire du ~** (fig: fam) to kick up a row

foire [fwaʀ] nf fair; (fête foraine) (fun) fair; **faire la ~** (fig: fam) to whoop it up; **~ aux questions** (Internet) FAQs; **foire (exposition)** trade fair

fois [fwa] nf time; **une/deux ~** once/twice; **2 ~ 2** 2 times 2; **une ~** (passé) once; (futur) sometime; **une ~ pour toutes** once and for all; **une ~ que** once; **des ~** (parfois) sometimes; **à la ~** (ensemble) at once

fol [fɔl] adj voir **fou**

folie [fɔli] nf (d'une décision, d'un acte) madness, folly; (état) madness, insanity; **la ~ des grandeurs** delusions of grandeur; **faire des ~s** (en dépenses) to be extravagant

folklorique [fɔlklɔʀik] adj folk cpd; (fam) weird

folle [fɔl] adj, nf voir **fou**; **follement** adv (très) madly, wildly

foncé, e [fɔ̃se] adj dark

foncer [fɔ̃se] vi to go darker; (fam: aller vite) to tear ou belt along; **~ sur** to charge at

fonction [fɔ̃ksjɔ̃] nf function; (emploi, poste) post, position; **fonctions** nfpl (professionnelles) duties; **voiture de ~** company car; **en ~ de** (par rapport à) according to; **faire ~ de** to serve as; **la ~ publique** the state ou civil (BRIT) service; **fonctionnaire** nm/f state employee, local authority employee; (dans l'administration) ≈ civil servant; **fonctionner** vi to work, function

fond [fɔ̃] nm (d'un récipient, trou) bottom; (d'une salle, scène) back; (d'un tableau, décor) background; (opposé à la forme) content; (Sport): **le ~** long distance (running); **au ~ de** at the bottom of; at the back of; **à ~** (connaître, soutenir) thoroughly; (appuyer, visser) right down ou home; **à ~ (de train)** (fam) full tilt; **dans le ~, au ~** (en somme) basically, really; **de ~ en comble** from top to bottom; **fond de teint** foundation (cream); voir aussi **fonds**

fondamental, e, -aux [fɔ̃damɑ̃tal, o] adj fundamental

fondant, e [fɔ̃dɑ̃, ɑ̃t] adj (neige) melting; (poire) that melts in the mouth

fondation [fɔ̃dasjɔ̃] nf founding; (établissement) foundation; **fondations** nfpl (d'une maison) foundations

fondé, e [fɔ̃de] adj (accusation etc) well-founded; **être ~ à** to have grounds for ou good reason to

fondement [fɔ̃dmɑ̃] nm: **sans ~** (rumeur etc) groundless, unfounded

fonder [fɔ̃de] vt to found; (fig) to base; **se fonder sur** (suj: personne) to base o.s. on

fonderie [fɔ̃dʀi] nf smelting works sg

fondre [fɔ̃dʀ] vt (aussi: **faire ~**) to melt; (dans l'eau) to dissolve; (fig: mélanger) to merge, blend ▷ vi (à la chaleur) to melt; (dans l'eau) to dissolve; (fig) to melt away; (se précipiter): **~ sur** to swoop down on; **~ en larmes** to burst into tears

fonds [fɔ̃] nm (Comm): **~ (de commerce)** business ▷ nmpl (argent) funds

fondu, e [fɔ̃dy] adj (beurre, neige) melted; (métal) molten; **fondue** nf (Culin) fondue

font [fɔ̃] vb voir **faire**

fontaine [fɔ̃tɛn] nf fountain; (source) spring

fonte [fɔ̃t] nf melting; (métal) cast iron; **la ~ des neiges** the (spring) thaw

foot [fut] (fam) nm football

football [futbol] nm football, soccer; **footballeur** nm footballer

footing [futiŋ] nm jogging; **faire du ~** to go jogging

forain, e [fɔʀɛ̃, ɛn] adj fairground cpd ▷ nm

(*marchand*) stallholder; (*acteur*) fairground entertainer

forçat [fɔʀsa] nm convict

force [fɔʀs] nf strength; (*Physique, Mécanique*) force; **forces** nfpl (*physiques*) strength sg; (*Mil*) forces; **à ~ d'insister** by dint of insisting; **as he** (*ou* I *etc*) kept on insisting; **de ~** forcibly, by force; **dans la ~ de l'âge** in the prime of life; **les forces de l'ordre** the police no pl

forcé, e [fɔʀse] adj forced; **c'est ~** (*fam*) it's inevitable; **forcément** adv inevitably; **pas forcément** not necessarily

forcer [fɔʀse] vt to force; (*voix*) to strain ▷ vi (*Sport*) to overtax o.s.; **~ la dose** (*fam*) to overdo it; **se ~ (à faire)** to force o.s. (to do)

forestier, -ère [fɔʀɛstje, jɛʀ] adj forest cpd

forêt [fɔʀɛ] nf forest

forfait [fɔʀfɛ] nm (*Comm*) all-in deal ou price; **déclarer ~** to withdraw; **forfaitaire** adj inclusive

forge [fɔʀʒ] nf forge, smithy; **forgeron** nm (black)smith

formaliser [fɔʀmalize]: **se formaliser** vi: **se ~ (de)** to take offence (at)

formalité [fɔʀmalite] nf formality; **simple ~** mere formality

format [fɔʀma] nm size; **formater** vt (*disque*) to format

formation [fɔʀmasjɔ̃] nf (*développement*) forming; (*apprentissage*) training; **formation permanente** ou **continue** continuing education

forme [fɔʀm] nf (*gén*) form; (*d'un objet*) shape, form; **formes** nfpl (*bonnes manières*) proprieties; (*d'une femme*) figure sg; **en ~ de poire** pear-shaped, in the shape of a pear; **être en ~** (*Sport etc*) to be on form; **en bonne et due ~** in due form

formel, le [fɔʀmɛl] adj (*catégorique*) definite, positive; **formellement** adv (*absolument*) positively; **formellement interdit** strictly forbidden

former [fɔʀme] vt to form; (*éduquer*) to train; **se former** vi to form

formidable [fɔʀmidabl] adj tremendous

formulaire [fɔʀmylɛʀ] nm form

formule [fɔʀmyl] nf (*gén*) formula; (*expression*) phrase; **formule de politesse** polite phrase; (*en fin de lettre*) letter ending

fort, e [fɔʀ, fɔʀt] adj strong; (*intensité, rendement*) high, great; (*corpulent*) stout; (*doué*) good, able ▷ adv (*serrer, frapper*) hard; (*parler*) loud(ly); (*beaucoup*) greatly, very much; (*très*) very ▷ nm (*édifice*) fort; (*point fort*) strong point, forte; **forte tête** rebel; **forteresse** nf stronghold

fortifiant [fɔʀtifjɑ̃] nm tonic

fortune [fɔʀtyn] nf fortune; **faire ~** to make one's fortune; **de ~** makeshift; **fortuné, e** adj wealthy

forum [fɔʀɔm] nm forum; **~ de discussion** (*Internet*) message board

fosse [fos] nf (*grand trou*) pit; (*tombe*) grave

fossé [fose] nm ditch; (*fig*) gulf, gap

fossette [fosɛt] nf dimple

fossile [fosil] nm fossil

fou (fol), folle [fu, fɔl] adj mad; (*déréglé etc*) wild, erratic; (*fam: extrême, très grand*) terrific, tremendous ▷ nm/f madman(-woman) ▷ nm (*du roi*) jester; **être fou de** to be mad ou crazy about; **avoir le fou rire** to have the giggles

foudre [fudʀ] nf: **la ~** lightning

foudroyant, e [fudʀwajɑ̃, ɑ̃t] adj (*progrès*) lightning cpd; (*succès*) stunning; (*maladie, poison*) violent

fouet [fwɛ] nm whip; (*Culin*) whisk; **de plein ~** (*se heurter*) head on; **fouetter** vt to whip; (*crème*) to whisk

fougère [fuʒɛʀ] nf fern

fougue [fug] nf ardour, spirit; **fougueux, -euse** adj fiery

fouille [fuj] nf search; **fouilles** nfpl (*archéologiques*) excavations; **fouiller** vt to search; (*creuser*) to dig ▷ vi to rummage; **fouillis** nm jumble, muddle

foulard [fulaʀ] nm scarf

foule [ful] nf crowd; **la ~** crowds pl; **une ~ de** masses of

foulée [fule] nf stride

fouler [fule] vt to press; (*sol*) to tread upon; **se ~ la cheville** to sprain one's ankle; **ne pas se ~** not to overexert o.s.; **il ne se foule pas** he doesn't put himself out; **foulure** nf sprain

four [fuʀ] nm oven; (*de potier*) kiln; (*Théâtre: échec*) flop

fourche [fuʀʃ] nf pitchfork

fourchette [fuʀʃɛt] nf fork; (*Statistique*) bracket, margin

fourgon [fuʀgɔ̃] nm van; (*Rail*) wag(g)on; **fourgonnette** nf (small) van

fourmi [fuʀmi] nf ant; **avoir des ~s dans les jambes/mains** to have pins and needles in one's legs/hands; **fourmilière** nf ant-hill; **fourmiller** vi to swarm

fourneau, x [fuʀno] nm stove

fourni, e [fuʀni] adj (*barbe, cheveux*) thick; (*magasin*): **bien ~ (en)** well stocked (with)

fournir [fuʀniʀ] vt to supply; (*preuve, exemple*) to provide, supply; (*effort*) to put in; **~ qch à qn** to supply sth to sb, supply ou provide sb with sth; **fournisseur, -euse** nm/f supplier; **fournisseur d'accès à Internet** (*Internet*) service provider, ISP; **fourniture** nf supply(ing); **fournitures scolaires** school stationery

fourrage [fuʀaʒ] nm fodder

fourré, e [fuʀe] adj (*bonbon etc*) filled; (*manteau etc*) fur-lined ▷ nm thicket

fourrer [fuʀe] (fam) vt to stick, shove; **se fourrer dans/sous** to get into/under

fourrière [fuʀjɛʀ] nf pound

fourrure [fuʀyʀ] nf fur; (sur l'animal) coat

foutre [futʀ] (fam!) vt = **ficher; foutu, e** (fam!) adj = **fichu, e**

foyer [fwaje] nm (maison) home; (famille) family; (de cheminée) hearth; (de jeunes etc) (social) club; (résidence) hostel; (salon) foyer; **lunettes à double ~** bi-focals

fracassant, e [fʀakasɑ̃, ɑ̃t] adj (succès) thundering

fraction [fʀaksjɔ̃] nf fraction

fracture [fʀaktyʀ] nf fracture; **fracture du crâne** fractured skull; **fracturer** vt (coffre, serrure) to break open; (os, membre) to fracture; **se fracturer le crâne** to fracture one's skull

fragile [fʀaʒil] adj fragile, delicate; (fig) frail; **fragilité** nf fragility

fragment [fʀagmɑ̃] nm (d'un objet) fragment, piece

fraîche [fʀɛʃ] adj voir **frais; fraîcheur** nf coolness; (d'un aliment) freshness; **fraîchir** vi to get cooler; (vent) to freshen

frais, fraîche [fʀɛ, fʀɛʃ] adj fresh; (froid) cool ▷ adv (récemment) newly, fresh(ly) ▷ nm: **mettre au ~** to put in a cool place ▷ nmpl (gén) expenses; (Comm) costs; **il fait ~** it's cool; **servir ~** serve chilled; **prendre le ~** to take a breath of cool air; **faire des ~** to go to a lot of expense; **frais de scolarité** school fees (BRIT), tuition (US); **frais généraux** overheads

fraise [fʀɛz] nf strawberry; **fraise des bois** wild strawberry

framboise [fʀɑ̃bwaz] nf raspberry

franc, franche [fʀɑ̃, fʀɑ̃ʃ] adj (personne) frank, straightforward; (visage) open; (net: refus) clear; (: coupure) clean; (intensif) downright ▷ nm franc

français, e [fʀɑ̃sɛ, ɛz] adj French ▷ nm/f: **F~, e** Frenchman(-woman) ▷ nm (Ling) French

France [fʀɑ̃s] nf: **la ~** France; **~ 2, ~ 3** public-sector television channels

● **FRANCE TÉLÉVISION**
●
● **France 2** and **France 3** are public-sector
● television channels. France 2 is a national
● general interest and entertainment
● channel; France 3 provides regional news
● and information as well as programmes for
● the national network.

franche [fʀɑ̃ʃ] adj voir **franc; franchement** adv frankly; (nettement) definitely; (tout à fait: mauvais etc) downright

franchir [fʀɑ̃ʃiʀ] vt (obstacle) to clear, get over; (seuil, ligne, rivière) to cross; (distance) to cover

franchise [fʀɑ̃ʃiz] nf frankness; (douanière)

exemption; (Assurances) excess

franc-maçon [fʀɑ̃masɔ̃] nm freemason

franco [fʀɑ̃ko] adv (Comm): **~ (de port)** postage paid

francophone [fʀɑ̃kɔfɔn] adj French-speaking

franc-parler [fʀɑ̃paʀle] nm inv outspokenness; **avoir son ~** to speak one's mind

frange [fʀɑ̃ʒ] nf fringe

frangipane [fʀɑ̃ʒipan] nf almond paste

frappant, e [fʀapɑ̃, ɑ̃t] adj striking

frappé, e [fʀape] adj iced

frapper [fʀape] vt to hit, strike; (étonner) to strike; **~ dans ses mains** to clap one's hands; **frappé de stupeur** dumbfounded

fraternel, le [fʀatɛʀnɛl] adj brotherly, fraternal; **fraternité** nf brotherhood

fraude [fʀod] nf fraud; (Scol) cheating; **passer qch en ~** to smuggle sth in (ou out); **fraude fiscale** tax evasion

frayeur [fʀɛjœʀ] nf fright

fredonner [fʀədɔne] vt to hum

freezer [fʀizœʀ] nm freezing compartment

frein [fʀɛ̃] nm brake; **mettre un ~ à** (fig) to curb, check; **frein à main** handbrake; **freiner** vi to brake ▷ vt (progrès etc) to check

frêle [fʀɛl] adj frail, fragile

frelon [fʀəlɔ̃] nm hornet

frémir [fʀemiʀ] vi (de peur, d'horreur) to shudder; (de colère) to shake; (feuillage) to quiver

frêne [fʀɛn] nm ash

fréquemment [fʀekamɑ̃] adv frequently

fréquent, e [fʀekɑ̃, ɑ̃t] adj frequent

fréquentation [fʀekɑ̃tasjɔ̃] nf frequenting; **fréquentations** nfpl (relations) company sg; **avoir de mauvaises ~s** to be in with the wrong crowd, keep bad company

fréquenté, e [fʀekɑ̃te] adj: **très ~** (very) busy; **mal ~** patronized by disreputable elements

fréquenter [fʀekɑ̃te] vt (lieu) to frequent; (personne) to see; **se fréquenter** to see each other

frère [fʀɛʀ] nm brother

fresque [fʀɛsk] nf (Art) fresco

fret [fʀɛ(t)] nm freight

friand, e [fʀijɑ̃, fʀijɑ̃d] adj: **~ de** very fond of ▷ nm: **~ au fromage** cheese puff

friandise [fʀijɑ̃diz] nf sweet

fric [fʀik] (fam) nm cash, dough

friche [fʀiʃ]: **en ~** adj, adv (lying) fallow

friction [fʀiksjɔ̃] nf (massage) rub, rub-down; (Tech, fig) friction

frigidaire® [fʀiʒidɛʀ] nm refrigerator

frigo [fʀigo] (fam) nm fridge

frigorifique [fʀigɔʀifik] adj refrigerating

frileux, -euse [fʀilø, øz] adj sensitive to (the) cold

frimer [fʀime] (fam) vi to show off

fringale [fʀɛ̃gal] (fam) nf: **avoir la ~** to be ravenous

fringues [fʀɛ̃g] (fam) nfpl clothes

fripé, e [fʀipe] adj crumpled

frire [fʀiʀ] vt, vi: **faire ~** to fry

frisé, e [fʀize] adj (cheveux) curly; (personne) curly-haired

frisson [fʀisɔ̃] nm (de froid) shiver; (de peur) shudder; **frissonner** vi (de fièvre, froid) to shiver; (d'horreur) to shudder

frit, e [fʀi, fʀit] pp de **frire**; **frite** nf: **(pommes) frites** chips (BRIT), French fries; **friteuse** nf chip pan; **friteuse électrique** deep fat fryer; **friture** nf (huile) (deep) fat; (plat): **friture (de poissons)** fried fish

froid, e [fʀwa, fʀwad] adj, nm cold; **il fait ~** it's cold; **avoir/prendre ~** to be/catch cold; **être en ~ avec** to be on bad terms with; **froidement** adv (accueillir) coldly; (décider) coolly

froisser [fʀwase] vt to crumple (up), crease; (fig) to hurt, offend; **se froisser** vi to crumple, crease; (personne) to take offence; **se ~ un muscle** to strain a muscle

frôler [fʀole] vt to brush against; (suj: projectile) to skim past; (fig) to come very close to

fromage [fʀɔmaʒ] nm cheese; **fromage blanc** soft white cheese

froment [fʀɔmɑ̃] nm wheat

froncer [fʀɔ̃se] vt to gather; **~ les sourcils** to frown

front [fʀɔ̃] nm forehead, brow; (Mil) front; **de ~** (se heurter) head-on; (rouler) together (i.e. 2 or 3 abreast); (simultanément) at once; **faire ~ à** to face up to

frontalier, -ère [fʀɔ̃talje, jɛʀ] adj border cpd, frontier cpd; **(travailleurs) ~s** people who commute across the border

frontière [fʀɔ̃tjɛʀ] nf frontier, border

frotter [fʀote] vi to rub, scrape ▷ vt to rub; (pommes de terre, plancher) to scrub; **~ une allumette** to strike a match

fruit [fʀɥi] nm fruit gen no pl; **fruits de mer** seafood(s); **fruits secs** dried fruit sg; **fruité, e** adj fruity; **fruitier, -ère** adj: **arbre fruitier** fruit tree

frustrer [fʀystʀe] vt to frustrate

fuel(-oil) [fjul(ɔjl)] nm fuel oil; (domestique) heating oil

fugace [fygas] adj fleeting

fugitif, -ive [fyʒitif, iv] adj (fugace) fleeting ▷ nm/f fugitive

fugue [fyg] nf: **faire une ~** to run away, abscond

fuir [fɥiʀ] vt to flee from; (éviter) to shun ▷ vi to run away; (gaz, robinet) to leak

fuite [fɥit] nf flight; (écoulement, divulgation)

leak; **être en ~** to be on the run; **mettre en ~** to put to flight

fulgurant, e [fylgyʀɑ̃, ɑ̃t] adj lightning cpd, dazzling

fumé, e [fyme] adj (Culin) smoked; (verre) tinted; **fumée** nf smoke

fumer [fyme] vi to smoke; (soupe) to steam ▷ vt to smoke

fûmes [fym] vb voir **être**

fumeur, -euse [fymœʀ, øz] nm/f smoker

fumier [fymje] nm manure

funérailles [fyneʀaj] nfpl funeral sg

fur [fyʀ]: **au ~ et à mesure** adv as one goes along; **au ~ et à mesure que** as

furet [fyʀɛ] nm ferret

fureter [fyʀ(ə)te] (péj) vi to nose about

fureur [fyʀœʀ] nf fury; **être en ~** to be infuriated; **faire ~** to be all the rage

furie [fyʀi] nf fury; (femme) shrew, vixen; **en ~** (mer) raging; **furieux, -euse** adj furious

furoncle [fyʀɔ̃kl] nm boil

furtif, -ive [fyʀtif, iv] adj furtive

fus [fy] vb voir **être**

fusain [fyzɛ̃] nm (Art) charcoal

fuseau, x [fyzo] nm (pour filer) spindle; (pantalon) (ski) pants; **fuseau horaire** time zone

fusée [fyze] nf rocket

fusible [fyzibl] nm (Élec: fil) fuse wire; (: fiche) fuse

fusil [fyzi] nm (de guerre, à canon rayé) rifle, gun; (de chasse, à canon lisse) shotgun, gun; **fusillade** nf gunfire no pl, shooting no pl; **fusiller** vt to shoot; **fusiller qn du regard** to look daggers at sb

fusionner [fyzjɔne] vi to merge

fût [fy] vb voir **être** ▷ nm (tonneau) barrel, cask

futé, e [fyte] adj crafty; **Bison ~®** TV and radio traffic monitoring service

futile [fytil] adj futile; frivolous

futur, e [fytyʀ] adj, nm future

fuyard, e [fɥijaʀ, aʀd] nm/f runaway

galerie de peinture (private) art gallery; **galerie marchande** shopping arcade

galet [galɛ] nm pebble

galette [galɛt] nf flat cake; **galette des Rois** cake eaten on Twelfth Night

galipette [galipɛt] nf somersault

Galles [gal] nfpl: **le pays de ~** Wales; **gallois, e** adj Welsh ▷ nm/f: **Gallois, e** Welshman(-woman) ▷ nm (Ling) Welsh

galon [galɔ̃] nm (Mil) stripe; (décoratif) piece of braid

galop [galo] nm gallop; **galoper** vi to gallop

gambader [gɑ̃bade] vi (animal, enfant) to leap about

gamin, e [gamɛ̃, in] nm/f kid ▷ adj childish

gamme [gam] nf (Mus) scale; (fig) range

gang [gɑ̃g] nm (de criminels) gang

gant [gɑ̃] nm glove; **gant de toilette** face flannel (BRIT), face cloth

garage [gaʀaʒ] nm garage; **garagiste** nm/f garage owner; (employé) garage mechanic

garantie [gaʀɑ̃ti] nf guarantee; **(bon de) ~** guarantee ou warranty slip

garantir [gaʀɑ̃tiʀ] vt to guarantee; **~ à qn que** to assure sb that

garçon [gaʀsɔ̃] nm boy; (célibataire): **vieux ~** bachelor; **garçon (de café)** (serveur) waiter; **garçon de courses** messenger

garde [gaʀd(ə)] nm (de prisonnier) guard; (de domaine etc) warden; (soldat, sentinelle) guardsman ▷ nf (soldats) guard; **de ~** on duty; **monter la ~** to stand guard; **mettre en ~** to warn; **prendre ~ (à)** to be careful (of); **garde champêtre** nm rural policeman; **garde du corps** nm bodyguard; **garde à vue** nf (Jur) = police custody; **garde-boue** nm inv mudguard; **garde-chasse** nm gamekeeper

garder [gaʀde] vt (conserver) to keep; (surveiller: enfants) to look after; (: immeuble, lieu, prisonnier) to guard; **se garder** vi (aliment: se conserver) to keep; **se ~ de faire** to be careful not to do; **~ le lit/la chambre** to stay in bed/indoors; **pêche/chasse gardée** private fishing/hunting (ground)

garderie [gaʀdəʀi] nf day nursery, crèche

garde-robe [gaʀdəʀɔb] nf wardrobe

gardien, ne [gaʀdjɛ̃, jɛn] nm/f (garde) guard; (de prison) warder; (de domaine, réserve) warden; (de musée etc) attendant; (de phare, cimetière) keeper; (d'immeuble) caretaker; (fig) guardian;

Gabon [gabɔ̃] nm: **le ~** Gabon

gâcher [gɑʃe] vt (gâter) to spoil; (gaspiller) to waste; **gâchis** nm waste no pl

gaffe [gaf] nf blunder; **faire ~ (fam)** to be careful

gage [gaʒ] nm (dans un jeu) forfeit; (fig: de fidélité, d'amour) token; **gages** nmpl (salaire) wages; **mettre en ~** to pawn

gagnant, e [gaɲɑ̃, ɑ̃t] adj: **billet/numéro ~** winning ticket/number ▷ nm/f winner

gagne-pain [gaɲpɛ̃] nm inv job

gagner [gaɲe] vt to win; (somme d'argent, revenu) to earn; (aller vers, atteindre) to reach; (envahir: sommeil, peur) to overcome; (: mal) to spread to ▷ vi to win; (fig) to gain; **~ du temps/de la place** to gain time/save space; **~ sa vie** to earn one's living

gai, e [ge] adj cheerful; (un peu ivre) merry; **gaiement** adv cheerfully; **gaieté** nf cheerfulness; **de gaieté de cœur** with a light heart

gain [gɛ̃] nm (revenu) earnings pl; (bénéfice: gén pl) profits pl

gala [gala] nm official reception; **de ~** (soirée etc) gala

galant, e [galɑ̃, ɑ̃t] adj (courtois) courteous, gentlemanly; (entreprenant) flirtatious, gallant; (scène, rendez-vous) romantic

galerie [galʀi] nf gallery; (Théâtre) circle; (de voiture) roof rack; (fig: spectateurs) audience;

gardien de but goalkeeper; **gardien de la paix** policeman; **gardien de nuit** night watchman

gare¹ [gaʀ] *nf* station; **gare routière** bus station

gare² [gaʀ] *excl*: **~ à ...!** mind ...!; **~ à toi!** watch out!

garer [gaʀe] *vt* to park; **se garer** *vi* to park

garni, e [gaʀni] *adj (plat)* served with vegetables *(and chips or rice etc)*

garniture [gaʀnityʀ] *nf (Culin)* vegetables *pl*; **garniture de frein** brake lining

gars [ga] *(fam) nm* guy

Gascogne [gaskɔɲ] *nf* Gascony; **le golfe de ~** the Bay of Biscay

gas-oil [gazɔjl] *nm* diesel (oil)

gaspiller [gaspije] *vt* to waste

gastronome [gastʀɔnɔm] *nm/f* gourmet; **gastronomique** *adj* gastronomic

gâteau, x [gato] *nm* cake; **gâteau sec** biscuit

gâter [gate] *vt* to spoil; **se gâter** *vi (dent, fruit)* to go bad; *(temps, situation)* to change for the worse

gâteux, -euse [gatø, øz] *adj* senile

gauche [goʃ] *adj* left, left-hand; *(maladroit)* awkward, clumsy ▷ *nf (Pol)* left (wing); **le bras ~** the left arm; **le côté ~** the left-hand side; **à ~** on the left; *(direction)* (to the) left; **gaucher, -ère** *adj* left-handed; **gauchiste** *nm/f* leftist

gaufre [gofʀ] *nf* waffle

gaufrette [gofʀɛt] *nf* wafer

gaulois, e [golwa, waz] *adj* Gallic ▷ *nm/f*: **G~, e** Gaul

gaz [gaz] *nm inv* gas; **ça sent le ~** I can smell gas, there's a smell of gas

gaze [gaz] *nf* gauze

gazette [gazɛt] *nf* news sheet

gazeux, -euse [gazø, øz] *adj (boisson)* fizzy; *(eau)* sparkling

gazoduc [gazodyk] *nm* gas pipeline

gazon [gazɔ̃] *nm (herbe)* grass; *(pelouse)* lawn

geai [ʒɛ] *nm* jay

géant, e [ʒeɑ̃, ɑ̃t] *adj* gigantic; *(Comm)* giant-size ▷ *nm/f* giant

geindre [ʒɛ̃dʀ] *vi* to groan, moan

gel [ʒɛl] *nm* frost

gélatine [ʒelatin] *nf* gelatine

gelée [ʒ(ə)le] *nf* jelly; *(gel)* frost

geler [ʒ(ə)le] *vt, vi* to freeze; **il gèle** it's freezing

gélule [ʒelyl] *nf (Méd)* capsule

Gémeaux [ʒemo] *nmpl*: **les ~** Gemini

gémir [ʒemiʀ] *vi* to groan, moan

gênant, e [ʒɛnɑ̃, ɑ̃t] *adj (irritant)* annoying; *(embarrassant)* embarrassing

gencive [ʒɑ̃siv] *nf* gum

gendarme [ʒɑ̃daʀm] *nm* gendarme; **gendarmerie** *nf* military police force in countryside and small towns; their police station or barracks

gendre [ʒɑ̃dʀ] *nm* son-in-law

gêné, e [ʒene] *adj* embarrassed

gêner [ʒene] *vt (incommoder)* to bother; *(encombrer)* to be in the way; *(embarrasser)*: **~ qn** to make sb feel ill-at-ease; **se gêner** to put o.s. out; **ne vous gênez pas!** don't mind me!

général, e, -aux [ʒeneʀal, o] *adj, nm* general; **en ~** usually, in general; **généralement** *adv* generally; **généraliser** *vt, vi* to generalize; **se généraliser** *vi* to become widespread; **généraliste** *nm/f* general practitioner, G.P.

génération [ʒeneʀasjɔ̃] *nf* generation

généreux, -euse [ʒeneʀø, øz] *adj* generous

générique [ʒeneʀik] *nm (Cinéma)* credits *pl*

générosité [ʒeneʀozite] *nf* generosity

genêt [ʒ(ə)nɛ] *nm* broom *no pl (shrub)*

génétique [ʒenetik] *adj* genetic

Genève [ʒ(ə)nɛv] *n* Geneva

génial, e, -aux [ʒenjal, jo] *adj* of genius; *(fam: formidable)* fantastic, brilliant

génie [ʒeni] *nm* genius; *(Mil)*: **le ~** the Engineers *pl*; **génie civil** civil engineering

genièvre [ʒənjɛvʀ] *nm* juniper

génisse [ʒenis] *nf* heifer

génital, e, -aux [ʒenital, o] *adj* genital; **les parties ~es** the genitals

génoise [ʒenwaz] *nf* sponge cake

genou, x [ʒ(ə)nu] *nm* knee; **à ~x** on one's knees; **se mettre à ~x** to kneel down

genre [ʒɑ̃ʀ] *nm* kind, type, sort; *(Ling)* gender; **avoir bon ~** to look a nice sort; **avoir mauvais ~** to be coarse-looking; **ce n'est pas son ~** it's not like him

gens [ʒɑ̃] *nmpl (in some phrases)* people *pl*

gentil, le [ʒɑ̃ti, ij] *adj* kind; *(enfant: sage)* good; *(endroit etc)* nice; **gentillesse** *nf* kindness; **gentiment** *adv* kindly

géographie [ʒeɔgʀafi] *nf* geography

géologie [ʒeɔlɔʒi] *nf* geology

géomètre [ʒeɔmɛtʀ] *nm/f (arpenteur)* (land) surveyor

géométrie [ʒeɔmetʀi] *nf* geometry; **géométrique** *adj* geometric

géranium [ʒeʀanjɔm] *nm* geranium

gérant, e [ʒeʀɑ̃, ɑ̃t] *nm/f* manager(-eress); **gérant d'immeuble** (managing) agent

gerbe [ʒɛʀb] *nf (de fleurs)* spray; *(de blé)* sheaf

gercé, e [ʒɛʀse] *adj* chapped

gerçure [ʒɛʀsyʀ] *nf* crack

gérer [ʒeʀe] *vt* to manage

germain, e [ʒɛʀmɛ̃, ɛn] *adj*: **cousin ~** first cousin

germe [ʒɛʀm] *nm* germ; **germer** *vi* to sprout; *(semence)* to germinate

geste [ʒɛst] *nm* gesture

gestion [ʒɛstjɔ̃] *nf* management

Ghana [gana] *nm*: **le ~** Ghana

gibier [ʒibje] *nm (animaux)* game

gicler [ʒikle] *vi* to spurt, squirt

gifle [ʒifl] nf slap (in the face); **gifler** vt to slap (in the face)

gigantesque [ʒigɑ̃tɛsk] adj gigantic

gigot [ʒigo] nm leg (of mutton ou lamb)

gigoter [ʒigɔte] vi to wriggle (about)

gilet [ʒile] nm waistcoat; (pull) cardigan; **gilet de sauvetage** life jacket

gin [dʒin] nm gin; **~-tonic** gin and tonic

gingembre [ʒɛ̃ʒɑ̃bʀ] nm ginger

girafe [ʒiʀaf] nf giraffe

giratoire [ʒiʀatwaʀ] adj: **sens ~** roundabout

girofle [ʒiʀɔfl] nf: **clou de ~** clove

girouette [ʒiʀwɛt] nf weather vane ou cock

gitan, e [ʒitɑ̃, an] nm/f gipsy

gîte [ʒit] nm (maison) home; (abri) shelter; **gîte (rural)** (country) holiday cottage (BRIT), gîte (self-catering accommodation in the country)

givre [ʒivʀ] nm (hoar) frost; **givré, e** adj covered in frost; (fam: fou) nuts; **orange givrée** orange sorbet (served in peel)

glace [glas] nf ice; (crème glacée) ice cream; (miroir) mirror; (de voiture) window

glacé, e [glase] adj (mains, vent, pluie) freezing; (lac) frozen; (boisson) iced

glacer [glase] vt to freeze; (gâteau) to ice; (fig): **~ qn** (intimider) to chill sb; (paralyser) to make sb's blood run cold

glacial, e, -aux [glasjal, jo] adj icy

glacier [glasje] nm (Géo) glacier; (marchand) ice-cream maker

glacière [glasjɛʀ] nf icebox

glaçon [glasɔ̃] nm icicle; (pour boisson) ice cube

glaïeul [glajœl] nm gladiolus

glaise [glɛz] nf clay

gland [glɑ̃] nm acorn; (décoration) tassel

glande [glɑ̃d] nf gland

glissade [glisad] nf (par jeu) slide; (chute) slip; **faire des ~s sur la glace** to slide on the ice

glissant, e [glisɑ̃, ɑ̃t] adj slippery

glissement [glismɑ̃] nm: **glissement de terrain** landslide

glisser [glise] vi (avancer) to glide ou slide along; (coulisser, tomber) to slide; (déraper) to slip; (être glissant) to be slippery ▷ vt to slip; **se glisser dans/entre** to slip into/between

global, e, -aux [glɔbal, o] adj overall

globe [glɔb] nm globe

globule [glɔbyl] nm (du sang): **~ blanc/rouge** white/red corpuscle

gloire [glwaʀ] nf glory

glousser [gluse] vi to cluck; (rire) to chuckle

glouton, ne [glutɔ̃, ɔn] adj gluttonous

gluant, e [glyɑ̃, ɑ̃t] adj sticky, gummy

glucose [glykoz] nm glucose

glycine [glisin] nf wisteria

GO sigle (= grandes ondes) LW

goal [gol] nm goalkeeper

gobelet [gɔblɛ] nm (en étain, verre, argent) tumbler; (d'enfant, de pique-nique) beaker; (à dés) cup

goéland [gɔelɑ̃] nm (sea)gull

goélette [gɔelɛt] nf schooner

goinfre [gwɛ̃fʀ] nm glutton

golf [gɔlf] nm golf; (terrain) golf course; **golf miniature** crazy (BRIT) ou miniature golf

golfe [gɔlf] nm gulf; (petit) bay

gomme [gɔm] nf (à effacer) rubber (BRIT), eraser; **gommer** vt to rub out (BRIT), erase

gonflé, e [gɔ̃fle] adj swollen; **il est ~** (fam: courageux) he's got some nerve; (impertinent) he's got a nerve

gonfler [gɔ̃fle] vt (pneu, ballon: en soufflant) to blow up; (: avec une pompe) to pump up; (nombre, importance) to inflate ▷ vi to swell (up); (Culin: pâte) to rise

gonzesse [gɔ̃zɛs] (fam) nf chick, bird (BRIT)

gorge [gɔʀʒ] nf (Anat) throat; (vallée) gorge; **gorgée** nf (petite) sip; (grande) gulp

gorille [gɔʀij] nm gorilla; (fam) bodyguard

gosse [gɔs] (fam) nm/f kid

goudron [gudʀɔ̃] nm tar; **goudronner** vt to tar(mac) (BRIT), asphalt (US)

gouffre [gufʀ] nm abyss, gulf

goulot [gulo] nm neck; **boire au ~** to drink from the bottle

goulu, e [guly] adj greedy

gourde [guʀd] nf (récipient) flask; (fam) (clumsy) clot ou oaf ▷ adj oafish

gourdin [guʀdɛ̃] nm club, bludgeon

gourmand, e [guʀmɑ̃, ɑ̃d] adj greedy; **gourmandise** nf greed; (bonbon) sweet

gousse [gus] nf: **gousse d'ail** clove of garlic

goût [gu] nm taste; **avoir bon ~** to taste good; **de bon ~** tasteful; **de mauvais ~** tasteless; **prendre ~ à** to develop a taste ou a liking for

goûter [gute] vt (essayer) to taste; (apprécier) to enjoy ▷ vi to have (afternoon) tea ▷ nm (afternoon) tea; **je peux ~?** can I have a taste?

goutte [gut] nf drop; (Méd) gout; (alcool) brandy; **tomber ~ à ~** to drip; **une ~ de whisky** a drop of whisky; **goutte-à-goutte** nm (Méd) drip

gouttière [gutjɛʀ] nf gutter

gouvernail [guvɛʀnaj] nm rudder; (barre) helm, tiller

gouvernement [guvɛʀnəmɑ̃] nm government

gouverner [guvɛʀne] vt to govern

grâce [gʀas] nf (charme, Rel) grace; (faveur) favour; (Jur) pardon; **faire ~ à qn de qch** to spare sb sth; **dèmander ~** to beg for mercy; **~ à** thanks to; **gracieux, -euse** adj graceful

grade [gʀad] nm rank; **monter en ~** to be promoted

gradin [gʀadɛ̃] nm tier; step; **gradins** nmpl (de stade) terracing sg

gradué, e [gʀadɥe] adj: **verre ~** measuring jug

graduel, le [gʀadɥɛl] adj gradual

graduer [gradɥe] vt (effort etc) to increase gradually; (règle, verre) to graduate
graffiti [grafiti] nmpl graffiti
grain [grɛ̃] nm (gén) grain; (Navig) squall; **grain de beauté** beauty spot; **grain de café** coffee bean; **grain de poivre** peppercorn
graine [grɛn] nf seed
graissage [grɛsaʒ] nm lubrication, greasing
graisse [grɛs] nf fat; (lubrifiant) grease; **graisser** vt to lubricate, grease; (tacher) to make greasy; **graisseux, -euse** adj greasy
grammaire [gra(m)mɛr] nf grammar
gramme [gram] nm gramme
grand, e [grɑ̃, grɑ̃d] adj (haut) tall; (gros, vaste, large) big, large; (plus âgé) big; (adulte) grown-up; (important, brillant) great ▷ adv: **~ ouvert** wide open; **au ~ air** in the open (air); **les grands blessés** the severely injured; **grand ensemble** housing scheme; **grand magasin** department store; **grande personne** grown-up; **grande surface** hypermarket; **grandes écoles** prestigious schools at university level; **grandes lignes** (Rail) main lines; **grandes vacances** summer holidays (BRIT) ou vacation (US); **grand-chose** nm/f inv: **pas grand-chose** not much; **Grande-Bretagne** nf (Great) Britain; **grandeur** nf (dimension) size; **grandeur nature** life-size; **grandiose** adj imposing; **grandir** vi to grow ▷ vt: **grandir qn** (suj: vêtement, chaussure) to make sb look taller; **grand-mère** nf grandmother; **grand-peine**: **à grand-peine** adv with difficulty; **grand-père** nm grandfather; **grands-parents** nmpl grandparents
grange [grɑ̃ʒ] nf barn
granit [granit] nm granite
graphique [grafik] adj graphic ▷ nm graph
grappe [grap] nf cluster; **grappe de raisin** bunch of grapes
gras, se [grɑ, grɑs] adj (viande, soupe) fatty; (personne) fat; (surface, main) greasy; (plaisanterie) coarse; (Typo) bold ▷ nm (Culin) fat; **faire la ~se matinée** to have a lie-in (BRIT), sleep late (US); **grassement** adv: **grassement payé** handsomely paid
gratifiant, e [gratifjɑ̃, jɑ̃t] adj gratifying, rewarding
gratin [gratɛ̃] nm (plat) cheese-topped dish; (croûte) cheese topping; (fam: élite) upper crust; **gratiné, e** adj (Culin) au gratin
gratis [gratis] adv free
gratitude [gratityd] nf gratitude
gratte-ciel [gratsjɛl] nm inv skyscraper
gratter [grate] vt (avec un outil) to scrape; (enlever: avec un outil) to scrape off; (: avec un ongle) to scratch; (enlever avec un ongle) to scratch off ▷ vi (irriter) to be scratchy; (démanger) to itch; **se gratter** to scratch (o.s.)

gratuit, e [gratɥi, ɥit] adj (entrée, billet) free; (fig) gratuitous
grave [grav] adj (maladie, accident) serious, bad; (sujet, problème) serious, grave; (air) grave, solemn; (voix, son) deep, low-pitched; **gravement** adv seriously; (parler, regarder) gravely
graver [grave] vt (plaque, nom) to engrave; (CD, DVD) to burn
graveur [gravœr] nm engraver; **graveur de CD/DVD** CD/DVD writer
gravier [gravje] nm gravel no pl; **gravillons** nmpl loose chippings ou gravel sg
gravir [gravir] vt to climb (up)
gravité [gravite] nf (de maladie, d'accident) seriousness; (de sujet, problème) gravity
graviter [gravite] vi to revolve
gravure [gravyr] nf engraving; (reproduction) print
gré [gre] nm: **à son ~** to one's liking; **de bon ~** willingly; **contre le ~ de qn** against sb's will; **de son (plein) ~** of one's own free will; **bon ~ mal ~** like it or not; **de ~ ou de force** whether one likes it or not; **savoir ~ à qn de qch** to be grateful to sb for sth
grec, grecque [grɛk] adj Greek; (classique: vase etc) Grecian ▷ nm/f: **G~, Grecque** Greek ▷ nm (Ling) Greek
Grèce [grɛs] nf: **la ~** Greece
greffe [grɛf] nf (Bot, Méd: de tissu) graft; (Méd: d'organe) transplant; **greffer** vt (Bot, Méd: tissu) to graft; (Méd: organe) to transplant
grêle [grɛl] adj (very) thin ▷ nf hail; **grêler** vb impers: **il grêle** it's hailing; **grêlon** nm hailstone
grelot [grəlo] nm little bell
grelotter [grələte] vi to shiver
grenade [grənad] nf (explosive) grenade; (Bot) pomegranate; **grenadine** nf grenadine
grenier [grənje] nm attic; (de ferme) loft
grenouille [grənuj] nf frog
grès [grɛ] nm sandstone; (poterie) stoneware
grève [grɛv] nf (d'ouvriers) strike; (plage) shore; **se mettre en/faire ~** to go on/be on strike; **grève de la faim** hunger strike; **grève sauvage** wildcat strike
gréviste [grevist] nm/f striker
grièvement [grijɛvmɑ̃] adv seriously
griffe [grif] nf claw; (de couturier) label; **griffer** vt to scratch
grignoter [griɲote] vt (personne) to nibble at; (souris) to gnaw at ▷ vi to nibble
gril [gril] nm steak ou grill pan; **faire cuire au ~** to grill; **grillade** nf (viande etc) grill
grillage [grijaʒ] nm (treillis) wire netting; (clôture) wire fencing
grille [grij] nf (clôture) wire fence; (portail) (metal) gate; (d'égout) (metal) grate; (fig) grid
grille-pain [grijpɛ̃] nm inv toaster

griller [gʀije] vt (pain) to toast; (viande) to grill; (fig: ampoule etc) to blow; **faire ~** to toast; to grill; (châtaignes) to roast; **~ un feu rouge** to jump the lights

grillon [gʀijɔ̃] nm cricket

grimace [gʀimas] nf grimace; (pour faire rire): **faire des ~s** to pull ou make faces

grimper [gʀɛ̃pe] vi, vt to climb

grincer [gʀɛ̃se] vi (objet métallique) to grate; (plancher, porte) to creak; **~ des dents** to grind one's teeth

grincheux, -euse [gʀɛ̃ʃø, øz] adj grumpy

grippe [gʀip] nf flu, influenza; **grippe aviaire** bird flu; **grippé, e** adj: **être grippé** to have flu

gris, e [gʀi, gʀiz] adj grey; (ivre) tipsy

grisaille [gʀizaj] nf greyness, dullness

griser [gʀize] vt to intoxicate

grive [gʀiv] nf thrush

Groenland [gʀɔenlãd] nm Greenland

grogner [gʀɔɲe] vi to growl; (fig) to grumble; **grognon, ne** adj grumpy

grommeler [gʀɔm(ə)le] vi to mutter to o.s.

gronder [gʀɔ̃de] vi to rumble; (fig: révolte) to be brewing ▷ vt to scold; **se faire ~** to get a telling-off

gros, se [gʀo, gʀos] adj big, large; (obèse) fat; (travaux, dégâts) extensive; (épais) thick; (rhume, averse) heavy ▷ adv: **risquer/gagner ~** to risk/win a lot ▷ nm/f fat man/woman ▷ nm (Comm): **le ~** the wholesale business; **le ~ de** the bulk of; **prix de gros** wholesale price; **par ~ temps/grosse mer** in rough weather/heavy seas; **en ~** roughly; (Comm) wholesale; **gros lot** jackpot; **gros mot** swearword; **gros plan** (Photo) close-up; **gros sel** cooking salt; **gros titre** headline; **grosse caisse** big drum

groseille [gʀozɛj] nf: **~ (rouge/blanche)** red/white currant; **groseille à maquereau** gooseberry

grosse [gʀos] adj voir **gros**; **grossesse** nf pregnancy; **grosseur** nf size; (tumeur) lump

grossier, -ière [gʀosje, jɛʀ] adj coarse; (insolent) rude; (dessin) rough; (travail) roughly done; (imitation, instrument) crude; (évident: erreur) gross; **grossièrement** adv (sommairement) roughly; (vulgairement) coarsely; **grossièreté** nf rudeness; (mot): **dire des grossièretés** to use coarse language

grossir [gʀosiʀ] vi (personne) to put on weight ▷ vt (exagérer) to exaggerate; (au microscope) to magnify; (suj: vêtement): **~ qn** to make sb look fatter

grossiste [gʀosist] nm/f wholesaler

grotesque [gʀotɛsk] adj (extravagant) grotesque; (ridicule) ludicrous

grotte [gʀɔt] nf cave

groupe [gʀup] nm group; **groupe de parole** support group; **groupe sanguin** blood group; **groupe scolaire** school complex; **grouper** vt

to group; **se grouper** vi to gather

grue [gʀy] nf crane

GSM [ʒeɛsɛm] nm, adj GSM

guenon [gənɔ̃] nf female monkey

guépard [gepaʀ] nm cheetah

guêpe [gɛp] nf wasp

guère [gɛʀ] adv (avec adjectif, adverbe): **ne ... ~** hardly; (avec verbe: pas beaucoup): **ne ... ~** tournure négative +much; (pas souvent) hardly ever; (pas longtemps) tournure négative +(very) long; **il n'y a ~ que/de** there's hardly anybody (ou anything) but/hardly any; **ce n'est ~ difficile** it's hardly difficult; **nous n'avons ~ de temps** we have hardly any time

guérilla [geʀija] nf guerrilla warfare

guérillero [geʀijeʀo] nm guerrilla

guérir [geʀiʀ] vt (personne, maladie) to cure; (membre, plaie) to heal ▷ vi (malade, maladie) to be cured; (blessure) to heal; **guérison** nf (de maladie) curing; (de membre, plaie) healing; (de malade) recovery; **guérisseur, -euse** nm/f healer

guerre [gɛʀ] nf war; **en ~** at war; **faire la ~ à** to wage war against; **guerre civile/mondiale** civil/world war; **guerrier, -ière** adj warlike ▷ nm/f warrior

guet [gɛ] nm: **faire le ~** to be on the watch ou look-out; **guet-apens** [gɛtapã] nm ambush; **guetter** vt (épier) to watch (intently); (attendre) to watch (out) for; (hostilement) to be lying in wait for

gueule [gœl] nf (d'animal) mouth; (fam: figure) face; (: bouche) mouth; **ta ~!** (fam) shut up!; **avoir la ~ de bois** (fam) to have a hangover; be hung over; **gueuler** (fam) vi to bawl

gui [gi] nm mistletoe

guichet [giʃɛ] nm (de bureau, banque) counter; **les ~s** (à la gare, au théâtre) the ticket office sg

guide [gid] nm (personne) guide; (livre) guide (book) ▷ nf (éclaireuse) girl guide; **guider** vt to guide

guidon [gidɔ̃] nm handlebars pl

guignol [giɲɔl] nm ≈ Punch and Judy show; (fig) clown

guillemets [gijmɛ] nmpl: **entre ~** in inverted commas

guindé, e [gɛ̃de] adj (personne, air) stiff, starchy; (style) stilted

Guinée [gine] nf Guinea

guirlande [giʀlãd] nf (fleurs) garland; **guirlande de Noël** tinsel garland

guise [giz] nf: **à votre ~** as you wish ou please; **en ~ de** by way of

guitare [gitaʀ] nf guitar

Guyane [gɥijan] nf: **la ~ (française)** French Guiana

gym [ʒim] nf (exercices) gym; **gymnase** nm gym(nasium); **gymnaste** nm/f gymnast; **gymnastique** nf gymnastics sg; (au réveil etc)

keep-fit exercises *pl*
gynécologie [ʒinekɔlɔʒi] *nf* gynaecology;
  gynécologique *adj* gynaecological;
  gynécologue *nm/f* gynaecologist

habile [abil] *adj* skilful; (*malin*) clever; **habileté**
  [abilte] *nf* skill, skilfulness; cleverness
habillé, e [abije] *adj* dressed; (*chic*) dressy
habiller [abije] *vt* to dress; (*fournir en
  vêtements*) to clothe; (*couvrir*) to cover;
  s'habiller *vi* to dress (o.s.); (*se déguiser, mettre
  des vêtements chic*) to dress up
habit [abi] *nm* outfit; **habits** *nmpl* (*vêtements*)
  clothes; **habit (de soirée)** evening dress; (*pour
  homme*) tails *pl*
habitant, e [abitɑ̃, ɑ̃t] *nm/f* inhabitant; (*d'une
  maison*) occupant; **loger chez l'~** to stay with
  the locals
habitation [abitasjɔ̃] *nf* house; **habitations
  à loyer modéré** (block of) council flats
habiter [abite] *vt* to live in ▷ *vi*: **~ à/dans** to
  live in; **où habitez-vous?** where do you live?
habitude [abityd] *nf* habit; **avoir l'~ de qch**
  to be used to sth; **avoir l'~ de faire** to be in the
  habit of doing; (*expérience*) to be used to doing;
  d'~ usually; **comme d'~** as usual
habitué, e [abitɥe] *nm/f* (*de maison*) regular
  visitor; (*de café*) regular (customer)
habituel, le [abitɥɛl] *adj* usual
habituer [abitɥe] *vt*: **~ qn à** to get sb used to;
  s'habituer à to get used to
'hache ['aʃ] *nf* axe
'hacher ['aʃe] *vt* (*viande*) to mince; (*persil*)
  to chop; **'hachis** *nm* mince *no pl*; **hachis
  Parmentier** ≈ shepherd's pie

'haie ['ɛ] nf hedge; (Sport) hurdle

'haillons ['ɑjõ] nmpl rags

'haine ['ɛn] nf hatred

'haïr ['aiʀ] vt to detest, hate

'hâlé, e ['ɑle] adj (sun)tanned, sunburnt

haleine [alɛn] nf breath; hors d'~ out of breath; tenir en ~ (attention) to hold spellbound; (incertitude) to keep in suspense; de longue ~ long-term

'haleter ['alte] vt to pant

'hall ['ol] nm hall

'halle ['al] nf (covered) market; halles nfpl (d'une grande ville) central food market sg

hallucination [alysinasjõ] nf hallucination

'halte ['alt] nf stop, break; (endroit) stopping place ▷ excl stop!; faire halte to stop

haltère [altɛʀ] nm dumbbell, barbell; haltères nmpl: (poids et) ~s (activité) weightlifting sg; haltérophilie nf weightlifting

'hamac ['amak] nm hammock

'hameau, x ['amo] nm hamlet

hameçon [amsõ] nm (fish) hook

'hanche ['ɑ̃ʃ] nf hip

'handball ['ɑ̃dbal] nm handball

'handicapé, e ['ɑ̃dikape] adj disabled, handicapped ▷ nm/f handicapped person; handicapé mental/physique mentally/ physically handicapped person; 'handicapé moteur person with a movement disorder

'hangar ['ɑ̃gaʀ] nm shed; (Aviat) hangar

'hanneton ['antõ] nm cockchafer

'hanter ['ɑ̃te] vt to haunt

'hantise ['ɑ̃tiz] nf obsessive fear

'harceler ['aʀsəle] vt to harass; harceler qn de questions to plague sb with questions

'hardi, e ['aʀdi] adj bold, daring

'hareng ['aʀɑ̃] nm herring; hareng saur kipper, smoked herring

'hargne ['aʀɲ] nf aggressiveness; 'hargneux, -euse adj aggressive

'haricot ['aʀiko] nm bean; 'haricot blanc haricot bean; 'haricot vert green bean; 'haricot rouge kidney bean

harmonica [aʀmɔnika] nm mouth organ

harmonie [aʀmɔni] nf harmony; harmonieux, -euse adj harmonious; (couleurs, couple) well-matched

'harpe ['aʀp] nf harp

'hasard ['azaʀ] nm: le hasard chance, fate; un hasard a coincidence; au hasard (aller) aimlessly; (choisir) at random; par hasard by chance; à tout hasard (en cas de besoin) just in case; (en espérant trouver ce qu'on cherche) on the off chance (BRIT)

'hâte ['ɑt] nf haste; à la hâte hurriedly, hastily; en hâte posthaste, with all possible speed; avoir hâte de to be eager ou anxious to; 'hâter vt to hasten; se hâter vi to hurry;

'hâtif, -ive adj (travail) hurried; (décision, jugement) hasty

'hausse ['os] nf rise, increase; être en hausse to be going up; 'hausser vt to raise; hausser les épaules to shrug (one's shoulders)

'haut, e ['o, 'ot] adj high; (grand) tall ▷ adv high ▷ nm top (part); de 3 m de haut 3 m high, 3 m in height; des hauts et des bas ups and downs; en haut lieu in high places; à haute voix, (tout) haut aloud, out loud; du haut de from the top of; de haut en bas from top to bottom; plus haut higher up, further up; (dans un texte) above; (parler) louder; en haut (être/aller) at/to the top; (dans une maison) upstairs; en haut de at the top of; 'haut débit broadband

'hautain, e ['otɛ̃, ɛn] adj haughty

'hautbois ['obwa] nm oboe

'hauteur ['otœʀ] nf height; à la hauteur de (accident) near; (fig: tâche, situation) equal to; à la hauteur (fig) up to it

'haut-parleur ['opaʀlœʀ] nm (loud)speaker

Hawaï [awai] n: les îles ~ Hawaii

'Haye ['ɛ] n: la Haye the Hague

hebdomadaire [ɛbdomadɛʀ] adj, nm weekly

hébergement [ebɛʀʒəmɑ̃] nm accommodation

héberger [ebɛʀʒe] vt (touristes) to accommodate, lodge; (amis) to put up; (réfugiés) to take in

hébergeur [ebɛʀʒœʀ] nm (Internet) host

hébreu, x [ebʀø] adj m, nm Hebrew

Hébrides [ebʀid] nf: les ~ the Hebrides

hectare [ɛktaʀ] nm hectare

'hein ['ɛ̃] excl eh?

'hélas ['elas] excl alas! ▷ adv unfortunately

'héler ['ele] vt to hail

hélice [elis] nf propeller

hélicoptère [elikɔptɛʀ] nm helicopter

helvétique [ɛlvetik] adj Swiss

hématome [ematom] nm nasty bruise

hémisphère [emisfɛʀ] nm: l'~ nord/sud the northern/southern hemisphere

hémorragie [emɔʀaʒi] nf bleeding no pl, haemorrhage

hémorroïdes [emɔʀɔid] nfpl piles, haemorrhoids

'hennir ['eniʀ] vi to neigh, whinny

hépatite [epatit] nf hepatitis

herbe [ɛʀb] nf grass; (Culin, Méd) herb; ~s de Provence mixed herbs; en ~ unripe; (fig) budding; herbicide nm weed-killer; herboriste nm/f herbalist

héréditaire [eʀeditɛʀ] adj hereditary

'hérisson ['eʀisõ] nm hedgehog

héritage [eʀitaʒ] nm inheritance; (coutumes, système) heritage, legacy

hériter [eʀite] vi: ~ de qch (de qn) to inherit sth (from sb); héritier, -ière nm/f heir(-ess)

hermétique [ɛʀmetik] adj airtight; watertight; (fig: obscur) abstruse; (: impénétrable) impenetrable

hermine [ɛʀmin] nf ermine

'hernie ['ɛʀni] nf hernia

héroïne [eʀɔin] nf heroine; (drogue) heroin

héroïque [eʀɔik] adj heroic

'héron ['eʀɔ̃] nm heron

'héros ['eʀo] nm hero

hésitant, e [ezitɑ̃, ɑ̃t] adj hesitant

hésitation [ezitasjɔ̃] nf hesitation

hésiter [ezite] vi: **~ (à faire)** to hesitate (to do)

hétérosexuel, le [eteʀɔsɛksɥɛl] adj heterosexual

'hêtre ['ɛtʀ] nm beech

heure [œʀ] nf hour; (Scol) period; (moment) time; **c'est l'~** it's time; **quelle ~ est-il?** what time is it?; **2 ~s (du matin)** 2 o'clock (in the morning); **être à l'~** to be on time; (montre) to be right; **mettre à l'~** to set right; **à une ~ avancée (de la nuit)** at a late hour (of the night); **de bonne ~** early; **à toute ~** at any time; **24 ~s sur 24** round the clock, 24 hours a day; **à l'~ qu'il est** at this time (of day); by now; **sur l'~** at once; **à quelle ~ ouvre le musée/ magasin?** what time does the museum/shop open?; **heures de bureau** office hours; **heure de pointe** rush hour; (téléphone) peak period; **heures supplémentaires** overtime sg

heureusement [œʀøzmɑ̃] adv (par bonheur) fortunately, luckily

heureux, -euse [œʀø, øz] adj happy; (chanceux) lucky, fortunate

'heurt ['œʀ] nm (choc) collision; (conflit) clash

'heurter ['œʀte] vt (mur) to strike, hit; (personne) to collide with

hexagone [ɛgzagɔn] nm hexagon; **l'H~** (la France) France (because of its shape)

hiberner [ibɛʀne] vi to hibernate

'hibou, x ['ibu] nm owl

'hideux, -euse ['idø, øz] adj hideous

hier [jɛʀ] adv yesterday; **~ matin/midi** yesterday morning/lunchtime; **~ soir** last night, yesterday evening; **toute la journée d'~** all day yesterday; **toute la matinée d'~** all yesterday morning

'hiérarchie ['jeʀaʀʃi] nf hierarchy

hindou, e [ɛ̃du] adj Hindu ▷ nm/f: **H~, e** Hindu

hippique [ipik] adj equestrian, horse cpd; **un club ~** a riding centre; **un concours ~** a horse show; **hippisme** nm (horse)riding

hippodrome [ipodʀom] nm racecourse

hippopotame [ipopotam] nm hippopotamus

hirondelle [iʀɔ̃dɛl] nf swallow

'hisser ['ise] vt to hoist, haul up

histoire [istwaʀ] nf (science, événements) history; (anecdote, récit, mensonge) story; (affaire) business no pl; **histoires** nfpl (chichis) fuss no pl; (ennuis) trouble sg; **historique** adj historical; (important) historic ▷ nm: **faire l'historique de** to give the background to

'hit-parade ['itpaʀad] nm: **le hit-parade** the charts

hiver [ivɛʀ] nm winter; **hivernal, e, -aux** adj winter cpd; (glacial) wintry; **hiverner** vi to winter

HLM nm ou f (= habitation à loyer modéré) council flat; **des ~** council housing

'hobby ['ɔbi] nm hobby

'hocher ['ɔʃe] vt: **hocher la tête** to nod; (signe négatif ou dubitatif) to shake one's head

'hockey ['ɔkɛ] nm: **hockey (sur glace/gazon)** (ice/field) hockey

'hold-up ['ɔldœp] nm inv hold-up

'hollandais, e ['ɔlɑ̃dɛ, ɛz] adj Dutch ▷ nm (Ling) Dutch ▷ nm/f: **Hollandais, e** Dutchman(-woman)

'Hollande ['ɔlɑ̃d] nf: **la Hollande** Holland

'homard ['ɔmaʀ] nm lobster

homéopathique [ɔmeopatik] adj homoeopathic

homicide [ɔmisid] nm murder; **homicide involontaire** manslaughter

hommage [ɔmaʒ] nm tribute; **rendre ~ à** to pay tribute to

homme [ɔm] nm man; **homme d'affaires** businessman; **homme d'État** statesman; **homme de main** hired man; **homme de paille** stooge; **l'homme de la rue** the man on the street

homo...: homogène adj homogeneous; **homologue** nm/f counterpart; **homologué, e** adj (Sport) ratified; (tarif) authorized; **homonyme** nm (Ling) homonym; (d'une personne) namesake; **homosexuel, le** adj homosexual

'Hong Kong ['ɔ̃gkɔ̃g] n Hong Kong

'Hongrie ['ɔ̃gʀi] nf: **la Hongrie** Hungary; **'hongrois, e** adj Hungarian ▷ nm/f: **Hongrois, e** Hungarian ▷ nm (Ling) Hungarian

honnête [ɔnɛt] adj (intègre) honest; (juste, satisfaisant) fair; **honnêtement** adv honestly; **honnêteté** nf honesty

honneur [ɔnœʀ] nm honour; (mérite) credit; **en l'~ de** in honour of; (événement) on the occasion of; **faire ~ à** (engagements) to honour; (famille) to be a credit to; (fig: repas etc) to do justice to

honorable [ɔnɔʀabl] adj worthy, honourable; (suffisant) decent

honoraire [ɔnɔʀɛʀ] adj honorary; **professeur ~** professor emeritus; **honoraires** nmpl fees

honorer [ɔnɔʀe] vt to honour; (estimer) to hold in high regard; (faire honneur à) to do credit to

'honte ['ɔ̃t] nf shame; **avoir honte de** to be ashamed of; **faire honte à qn** to make sb (feel)

ashamed; **'honteux, -euse** adj ashamed;
(conduite, acte) shameful, disgraceful

hôpital, -aux [ɔpital, o] nm hospital; **où
est l'~ le plus proche?** where is the nearest
hospital?

'hoquet [ɔkɛ] nm: **avoir le hoquet** to have
(the) hiccoughs

horaire [ɔRɛR] adj hourly ▷ nm timetable,
schedule; **horaires** nmpl (d'employé) hours;
horaire souple flexitime

horizon [ɔRizɔ̃] nm horizon

horizontal, e, -aux [ɔRizɔ̃tal, o] adj
horizontal

horloge [ɔRlɔʒ] nf clock; **l'~ parlante**
the speaking clock; **horloger, -ère** nm/f
watchmaker; clockmaker

'hormis ['ɔRmi] prép save

horoscope [ɔRɔskɔp] nm horoscope

horreur [ɔRœR] nf horror; **quelle ~!** how
awful!; **avoir ~ de** to loathe ou detest;
horrible adj horrible; **horrifier** vt to horrify

'hors ['ɔR] prép: **hors de** out of; **hors pair**
outstanding; **hors de propos** inopportune;
être hors de soi to be beside o.s.; **'hors
d'usage** out of service; **'hors-bord** nm inv
speedboat (with outboard motor); **'hors-
d'œuvre** nm inv hors d'œuvre; **'hors-la-loi**
nm inv outlaw; **'hors-service** adj inv out of order;
'hors-taxe adj (boutique, articles) duty-free

hortensia [ɔRtɑ̃sja] nm hydrangea

hospice [ɔspis] nm (de vieillards) home

hospitalier, -ière [ɔspitalje, jɛR] adj
(accueillant) hospitable; (Méd: service, centre)
hospital cpd

hospitaliser [ɔspitalize] vt to take/send to
hospital, hospitalize

hospitalité [ɔspitalite] nf hospitality

hostie [ɔsti] nf host (Rel)

hostile [ɔstil] adj hostile; **hostilité** nf hostility

hôte [ot] nm (maître de maison) host; (invité)
guest

hôtel [otɛl] nm hotel; **aller à l'~** to stay in
a hotel; **hôtel de ville** town hall; **hôtel
(particulier)** (private) mansion; **hôtellerie** nf
hotel business

● **HÔTELS**

● There are six categories of hotel in France,
from zero ('non classé') to four stars and
luxury four stars ('quatre étoiles luxe').
Prices include VAT but not breakfast. In
some towns, guests pay a small additional
tourist tax, the 'taxe de séjour'.

hôtesse [otɛs] nf hostess; **hôtesse (de l'air)**
stewardess, air hostess (BRIT)

'houblon ['ublɔ̃] nm (Bot) hop; (pour la bière)
hops pl

houille ['uj] nf coal; **'houille blanche**
hydroelectric power

'houle ['ul] nf swell; **'houleux, -euse** adj
stormy

'hourra ['uRa] excl hurrah!

'housse ['us] nf cover

'houx ['u] nm holly

hublot ['yblo] nm porthole

'huche ['yʃ] nf: **huche à pain** bread bin

'huer ['ɥe] vt to boo

huile [ɥil] nf oil

huissier [ɥisje] nm usher; (Jur) ≈ bailiff

'huit ['ɥi(t)] num eight; **samedi en huit** a
week on Saturday; **dans huit jours** in a week;
'huitaine nf: **une huitaine (de jours)** a week
or so; **'huitième** num eighth

huître [ɥitR] nf oyster

humain, e [ymɛ̃, ɛn] adj human;
(compatissant) humane ▷ nm human (being);
humanitaire adj humanitarian; **humanité**
nf humanity

humble [œ̃bl] adj humble

'humer ['yme] vt (plat) to smell; (parfum) to
inhale

humeur [ymœR] nf mood; **de bonne/
mauvaise ~** in a good/bad mood

humide [ymid] adj damp; (main, yeux) moist;
(climat, chaleur) humid; (saison, route) wet

humilier [ymilje] vt to humiliate

humilité [ymilite] nf humility, humbleness

humoristique [ymɔRistik] adj humorous

humour [ymuR] nm humour; **avoir de l'~** to
have a sense of humour; **humour noir** black
humour

'huppé, e ['ype] (fam) adj posh

'hurlement ['yRləmɑ̃] nm howling no pl, howl,
yelling no pl, yell

'hurler ['yRle] vi to howl, yell

'hutte ['yt] nf hut

hydratant, e [idRatɑ̃, ɑ̃t] adj (crème)
moisturizing

hydraulique [idRolik] adj hydraulic

hydravion [idRavjɔ̃] nm seaplane

hydrogène [idRɔʒɛn] nm hydrogen

hydroglisseur [idRɔglisœR] nm hydroplane

hyène [jɛn] nf hyena

hygiène [iʒjɛn] nf hygiene

hygiénique [iʒenik] adj hygienic

hymne [imn] nm hymn

hyperlien [ipɛRljɛ̃] nm hyperlink

hypermarché [ipɛRmaRʃe] nm hypermarket

hypermétrope [ipɛRmetRɔp] adj long-
sighted

hypertension [ipɛRtɑ̃sjɔ̃] nf high blood
pressure

hypnose [ipnoz] nf hypnosis; **hypnotiser** vt
to hypnotize

hypocrisie [ipɔkRizi] nf hypocrisy; **hypocrite**
adj hypocritical

hypothèque [ipɔtɛk] *nf* mortgage
hypothèse [ipɔtɛz] *nf* hypothesis
hystérique [isteʀik] *adj* hysterical

iceberg [ajsbɛʀg] *nm* iceberg
ici [isi] *adv* here; **jusqu'~** as far as this; (*temps*) so far; **d'~ demain** by tomorrow; **d'~ là** by then, in the meantime; **d'~ peu** before long
icône [ikon] *nf* icon
idéal, e, -aux [ideal, o] *adj* ideal ▷ *nm* ideal; **idéaliste** *adj* idealistic ▷ *nm/f* idealist
idée [ide] *nf* idea; **avoir dans l'~ que** to have an idea that; **se faire des ~s** to imagine things, get ideas into one's head; **avoir des ~s noires** to have black *ou* dark thoughts; **idées reçues** received wisdom *sg*
identifier [idãtifje] *vt* to identify; **s'identifier** *vi*: **s'~ avec** *ou* **à qn/qch** (*héros etc*) to identify with sb/sth
identique [idãtik] *adj*: **~ (à)** identical (to)
identité [idãtite] *nf* identity
idiot, e [idjo, idjɔt] *adj* idiotic ▷ *nm/f* idiot
idole [idɔl] *nf* idol
if [if] *nm* yew
ignoble [iɲɔbl] *adj* vile
ignorant, e [iɲɔʀã, ãt] *adj* ignorant; **~ de** ignorant of, not aware of
ignorer [iɲɔʀe] *vt* not to know; (*personne*) to ignore
il [il] *pron* he; (*animal, chose, en tournure impersonnelle*) it; **il fait froid** it's cold; **Pierre est-il arrivé?** has Pierre arrived?; **il a gagné** he won; *voir* **avoir**
île [il] *nf* island; **l'île Maurice** Mauritius; **les**

îles anglo-normandes the Channel Islands;
les îles britanniques the British Isles
illégal, e, -aux [i(l)legal, o] adj illegal
illimité, e [i(l)limite] adj unlimited
illisible [i(l)lizibl] adj illegible; (roman)
unreadable
illogique [i(l)lɔʒik] adj illogical
illuminer [i(l)lymine] vt to light up;
(monument, rue: pour une fête) to illuminate; (:
au moyen de projecteurs) to floodlight
illusion [i(l)lyzjɔ̃] nf illusion; **se faire des ~s** to
delude o.s.; **faire ~** to delude ou fool people
illustration [i(l)lystʀasjɔ̃] nf illustration
illustré, e [i(l)lystʀe] adj illustrated ▷ nm
comic
illustrer [i(l)lystʀe] vt to illustrate; **s'illustrer**
to become famous, win fame
ils [il] pron they
image [imaʒ] nf (gén) picture; (métaphore)
image; **image de marque** brand image;
(fig) public image; **imagé, e** adj (texte) full of
imagery; (langage) colourful
imaginaire [imaʒinɛʀ] adj imaginary
imagination [imaʒinasjɔ̃] nf imagination;
avoir de l'~ to be imaginative
imaginer [imaʒine] vt to imagine; (inventer:
expédient) to devise, think up; **s'imaginer** vt
(se figurer: scène etc) to imagine, picture; **s'~
que** to imagine that
imbécile [ɛ̃besil] adj idiotic ▷ nm/f idiot
imbu, e [ɛ̃by] adj: **~ de** full of
imitateur, -trice [imitatœʀ, tʀis] nm/f (gén)
imitator; (Music-Hall) impersonator
imitation [imitasjɔ̃] nf imitation; (de
personnalité) impersonation
imiter [imite] vt to imitate; (contrefaire) to
forge; (ressembler à) to look like
immangeable [ɛ̃mɑ̃ʒabl] adj inedible
immatriculation [imatʀikylasjɔ̃] nf
registration

● **IMMATRICULATION**
●
● The last two numbers on vehicle licence
● plates show which 'département' of France
● the vehicle is registered in. For example, a
● car registered in Paris has the number 75 on
● its licence plates.

immatriculer [imatʀikyle] vt to register;
faire/se faire ~ to register
immédiat, e [imedja, jat] adj immediate
▷ nm: **dans l'~** for the time being;
immédiatement adv immediately
immense [i(m)mɑ̃s] adj immense
immerger [imɛʀʒe] vt to immerse, submerge
immeuble [imœbl] nm building; (à usage
d'habitation) block of flats
immigration [imigʀasjɔ̃] nf immigration

immigré, e [imigʀe] nm/f immigrant
imminent, e [iminɑ̃, ɑ̃t] adj imminent
immobile [i(m)mɔbil] adj still, motionless
immobilier, -ière [imɔbilje, jɛʀ] adj
property cpd ▷ nm: **l'~** the property business
immobiliser [imɔbilize] vt (gén) to
immobilize; (circulation, véhicule, affaires) to
bring to a standstill; **s'immobiliser** (personne)
to stand still; (machine, véhicule) to come to
a halt
immoral, e, -aux [i(m)mɔʀal, o] adj
immoral
immortel, le [imɔʀtɛl] adj immortal
immunisé, e [im(m)ynize] adj: **~ contre**
immune to
immunité [imynite] nf immunity
impact [ɛ̃pakt] nm impact
impair, e [ɛ̃pɛʀ] adj odd ▷ nm faux pas,
blunder
impardonnable [ɛ̃paʀdɔnabl] adj
unpardonable, unforgivable
imparfait, e [ɛ̃paʀfɛ, ɛt] adj imperfect
impartial, e, -aux [ɛ̃paʀsjal, jo] adj
impartial, unbiased
impasse [ɛ̃pɑs] nf dead end, cul-de-sac; (fig)
deadlock
impassible [ɛ̃pasibl] adj impassive
impatience [ɛ̃pasjɑ̃s] nf impatience
impatient, e [ɛ̃pasjɑ̃, jɑ̃t] adj impatient;
impatienter: s'impatienter vi to get
impatient
impeccable [ɛ̃pekabl] adj (parfait) perfect;
(propre) impeccable; (fam) smashing
impensable [ɛ̃pɑ̃sabl] adj (événement
hypothétique) unthinkable; (événement qui a eu
lieu) unbelievable
impératif, -ive [ɛ̃peʀatif, iv] adj imperative
▷ nm (Ling) imperative; **impératifs** nmpl
(exigences: d'une fonction, d'une charge)
requirements; (: de la mode) demands
impératrice [ɛ̃peʀatʀis] nf empress
imperceptible [ɛ̃pɛʀsɛptibl] adj
imperceptible
impérial, e, -aux [ɛ̃peʀjal, jo] adj imperial
impérieux, -euse [ɛ̃peʀjø, jøz] adj (caractère,
ton) imperious; (obligation, besoin) pressing,
urgent
impérissable [ɛ̃peʀisabl] adj undying
imperméable [ɛ̃pɛʀmeabl] adj waterproof;
(fig): **~ à** impervious to ▷ nm raincoat
impertinent, e [ɛ̃pɛʀtinɑ̃, ɑ̃t] adj
impertinent
impitoyable [ɛ̃pitwajabl] adj pitiless,
merciless
implanter [ɛ̃plɑ̃te]: **s'implanter** vi to be
set up
impliquer [ɛ̃plike] vt to imply; **~ qn (dans)** to
implicate sb (in)
impoli, e [ɛ̃pɔli] adj impolite, rude

impopulaire [ɛ̃pɔpylɛʀ] adj unpopular

importance [ɛ̃pɔʀtɑ̃s] nf importance; (de somme) size; (de retard, dégâts) extent; **sans ~** unimportant

important, e [ɛ̃pɔʀtɑ̃, ɑ̃t] adj important; (en quantité: somme, retard) considerable, sizeable; (: dégâts) extensive; (péj: airs, ton) self-important ▷ nm: **l'~** the important thing

importateur, -trice [ɛ̃pɔʀtatœʀ, tʀis] nm/f importer

importation [ɛ̃pɔʀtasjɔ̃] nf importation; (produit) import

importer [ɛ̃pɔʀte] vt (Comm) to import; (maladies, plantes) to introduce ▷ vi (être important) to matter; **il importe qu'il fasse** it is important that he should do; **peu m'importe** (je n'ai pas de préférence) I don't mind; (je m'en moque) I don't care; **peu importe (que)** it doesn't matter (if); voir aussi **n'importe**

importun, e [ɛ̃pɔʀtœ̃, yn] adj irksome, importunate; (arrivée, visite) inopportune, ill-timed ▷ nm intruder; **importuner** vt to bother

imposant, e [ɛ̃pozɑ̃, ɑ̃t] adj imposing

imposer [ɛ̃poze] vt (taxer) to tax; **s'imposer** (être nécessaire) to be imperative; **~ qch à qn** to impose sth on sb; **en ~ à** to impress; **s'~ comme** to emerge as; **s'~ par** to win recognition through

impossible [ɛ̃posibl] adj impossible; **il m'est ~ de le faire** it is impossible for me to do it, I can't possibly do it; **faire l'~** to do one's utmost

imposteur [ɛ̃pɔstœʀ] nm impostor

impôt [ɛ̃po] nm tax; **impôt foncier** land tax; **impôt sur le chiffre d'affaires** corporation (BRIT) ou corporate (US) tax; **impôt sur le revenu** income tax; **impôts locaux** rates, local taxes (US), ≈ council tax (BRIT)

impotent, e [ɛ̃pɔtɑ̃, ɑ̃t] adj disabled

impraticable [ɛ̃pʀatikabl] adj (projet) impracticable, unworkable; (piste) impassable

imprécis, e [ɛ̃pʀesi, iz] adj imprecise

imprégner [ɛ̃pʀeɲe] vt (tissu) to impregnate; (lieu, air) to fill; **s'imprégner de** (fig) to absorb

imprenable [ɛ̃pʀənabl] adj (forteresse) impregnable; **vue ~** unimpeded outlook

impression [ɛ̃pʀesjɔ̃] nf impression; (d'un ouvrage, tissu) printing; **faire bonne/ mauvaise ~** to make a good/bad impression; **impressionnant, e** adj (imposant) impressive; (bouleversant) upsetting; **impressionner** vt (frapper) to impress; (bouleverser) to upset

imprévisible [ɛ̃pʀevizibl] adj unforeseeable

imprévu, e [ɛ̃pʀevy] adj unforeseen, unexpected ▷ nm (incident) unexpected incident; **des vacances pleines d'~** holidays full of surprises; **en cas d'~** if anything unexpected happens; **sauf ~** unless anything unexpected crops up

imprimante [ɛ̃pʀimɑ̃t] nf printer; **imprimante (à) laser** laser printer

imprimé [ɛ̃pʀime] nm (formulaire) printed form; (Postes) printed matter no pl; (tissu) printed fabric; **~ à fleur** floral print

imprimer [ɛ̃pʀime] vt to print; (publier) to publish; **imprimerie** nf printing; (établissement) printing works sg; **imprimeur** nm printer

impropre [ɛ̃pʀɔpʀ] adj inappropriate; **~ à** unfit for

improviser [ɛ̃pʀɔvize] vt, vi to improvise

improviste [ɛ̃pʀɔvist]: **à l'~** adv unexpectedly, without warning

imprudence [ɛ̃pʀydɑ̃s] nf (d'une personne, d'une action) carelessness no pl; (d'une remarque) imprudence no pl; **commettre une ~** to do something foolish

imprudent, e [ɛ̃pʀydɑ̃, ɑ̃t] adj (conducteur, geste, action) careless; (remarque) unwise, imprudent; (projet) foolhardy

impuissant, e [ɛ̃pɥisɑ̃, ɑ̃t] adj helpless; (sans effet) ineffectual; (sexuellement) impotent

impulsif, -ive [ɛ̃pylsif, iv] adj impulsive

impulsion [ɛ̃pylsjɔ̃] nf (Élec, instinct) impulse; (élan, influence) impetus

inabordable [inabɔʀdabl] adj (cher) prohibitive

inacceptable [inaksɛptabl] adj unacceptable

inaccessible [inaksesibl] adj inaccessible; **~ à** impervious to

inachevé, e [inaʃ(ə)ve] adj unfinished

inactif, -ive [inaktif, iv] adj inactive; (remède) ineffective; (Bourse: marché) slack

inadapté, e [inadapte] adj (gén): **~ à** not adapted to, unsuited to; (Psych) maladjusted

inadéquat, e [inadekwa(t), kwat] adj inadequate

inadmissible [inadmisibl] adj inadmissible

inadvertance [inadvɛʀtɑ̃s]: **par ~** adv inadvertently

inanimé, e [inanime] adj (matière) inanimate; (évanoui) unconscious; (sans vie) lifeless

inanition [inanisjɔ̃] nf: **tomber d'~** to faint with hunger (and exhaustion)

inaperçu, e [inapɛʀsy] adj: **passer ~** to go unnoticed

inapte [inapt] adj: **~ à** incapable of; (Mil) unfit for

inattendu, e [inatɑ̃dy] adj unexpected

inattentif, -ive [inatɑ̃tif, iv] adj inattentive; **~ à** (dangers, détails) heedless of; **inattention** nf lack of attention; **une faute** ou **une erreur d'inattention** a careless mistake

inaugurer [inogyʀe] vt (monument) to unveil; (exposition, usine) to open; (fig) to inaugurate

inavouable [inavwabl] adj shameful;

(bénéfices) undisclosable

incalculable [ɛ̃kalkylabl] *adj* incalculable

incapable [ɛ̃kapabl] *adj* incapable; **~ de faire** incapable of doing; *(empêché)* unable to do

incapacité [ɛ̃kapasite] *nf (incompétence)* incapability; *(impossibilité)* incapacity; **dans l'~ de faire** unable to do

incarcérer [ɛ̃kaʀseʀe] *vt* to incarcerate, imprison

incassable [ɛ̃kɑsabl] *adj* unbreakable

incendie [ɛ̃sɑ̃di] *nm* fire; **incendie criminel** arson *no pl*; **incendie de forêt** forest fire; **incendier** *vt (mettre le feu à)* to set fire to, set alight; *(brûler complètement)* to burn down

incertain, e [ɛ̃sɛʀtɛ̃, ɛn] *adj* uncertain; *(temps)* unsettled; *(imprécis: contours)* indistinct, blurred; **incertitude** *nf* uncertainty

incessamment [ɛ̃sesamɑ̃] *adv* very shortly

incident [ɛ̃sidɑ̃] *nm* incident; **incident de parcours** minor hitch *ou* setback; **incident technique** technical difficulties *pl*

incinérer [ɛ̃sineʀe] *vt (ordures)* to incinerate; *(mort)* to cremate

incisive [ɛ̃siziv] *nf* incisor

inciter [ɛ̃site] *vt:* **~ qn à (faire) qch** to encourage sb to do sth; *(à la révolte etc)* to incite sb to do sth

incivilité [ɛ̃sivilite] *nf (grossièreté)* incivility; **incivilités** *nfpl* antisocial behaviour *sg*

inclinable [ɛ̃klinabl] *adj:* **siège à dossier ~** reclining seat

inclination [ɛ̃klinasjɔ̃] *nf (penchant)* inclination

incliner [ɛ̃kline] *vt (pencher)* to tilt ▷ *vi:* **~ à qch/à faire** to incline towards sth/doing; **s'incliner** *vr (se pencher)* to bow; **s'~ devant** *(par respect)* to pay one's respects

inclure [ɛ̃klyʀ] *vt* to include; *(joindre à un envoi)* to enclose

inclus, e [ɛ̃kly, -yz] *pp de* **inclure** ▷ *adj* included; *(joint à un envoi)* enclosed ▷ *adv:* **est-ce que le service est ~?** is service included?; **jusqu'au 10 mars ~** until 10th March inclusive

incognito [ɛ̃kɔɲito] *adv* incognito ▷ *nm:* **garder l'~** to remain incognito

incohérent, e [ɛ̃kɔeʀɑ̃, ɑ̃t] *adj (comportement)* inconsistent; *(geste, langage, texte)* incoherent

incollable [ɛ̃kɔlabl] *adj (riz)* non-stick; **il est ~** *(fam)* he's got all the answers

incolore [ɛ̃kɔlɔʀ] *adj* colourless

incommoder [ɛ̃kɔmɔde] *vt (chaleur, odeur):* **~ qn** to bother sb

incomparable [ɛ̃kɔ̃paʀabl] *adj* incomparable

incompatible [ɛ̃kɔ̃patibl] *adj* incompatible

incompétent, e [ɛ̃kɔ̃petɑ̃, ɑ̃t] *adj* incompetent

incomplet, -ète [ɛ̃kɔ̃plɛ, ɛt] *adj* incomplete

incompréhensible [ɛ̃kɔ̃pʀeɑ̃sibl] *adj* incomprehensible

incompris, e [ɛ̃kɔ̃pʀi, iz] *adj* misunderstood

inconcevable [ɛ̃kɔ̃s(ə)vabl] *adj* inconceivable

inconfortable [ɛ̃kɔ̃fɔʀtabl(ə)] *adj* uncomfortable

incongru, e [ɛ̃kɔ̃gʀy] *adj* unseemly

inconnu, e [ɛ̃kɔny] *adj* unknown ▷ *nm/f* stranger ▷ *nm:* **l'~** the unknown; **inconnue** *nf* unknown factor

inconsciemment [ɛ̃kɔ̃sjamɑ̃] *adv* unconsciously

inconscient, e [ɛ̃kɔ̃sjɑ̃, jɑ̃t] *adj* unconscious; *(irréfléchi)* thoughtless, reckless; *(sentiment)* subconscious ▷ *nm (Psych):* **l'~** the unconscious; **~ de** unaware of

inconsidéré, e [ɛ̃kɔ̃sideʀe] *adj* ill-considered

inconsistant, e [ɛ̃kɔ̃sistɑ̃, ɑ̃t] *adj (fig)* flimsy, weak

inconsolable [ɛ̃kɔ̃sɔlabl] *adj* inconsolable

incontestable [ɛ̃kɔ̃tɛstabl] *adj* indisputable

incontinent, e [ɛ̃kɔ̃tinɑ̃, ɑ̃t] *adj* incontinent

incontournable [ɛ̃kɔ̃tuʀnabl] *adj* unavoidable

incontrôlable [ɛ̃kɔ̃tʀolabl] *adj* unverifiable; *(irrépressible)* uncontrollable

inconvénient [ɛ̃kɔ̃venjɑ̃] *nm* disadvantage, drawback; **si vous n'y voyez pas d'~** if you have no objections

incorporer [ɛ̃kɔʀpɔʀe] *vt:* **~ (à)** to mix in (with); **~ (dans)** *(paragraphe etc)* to incorporate (in); *(Mil: appeler)* to recruit (into); **il a très bien su s'~ à notre groupe** he was very easily incorporated into our group

incorrect, e [ɛ̃kɔʀɛkt] *adj (impropre, inconvenant)* improper; *(défectueux)* faulty; *(inexact)* incorrect; *(impoli)* impolite; *(déloyal)* underhand

incorrigible [ɛ̃kɔʀiʒibl] *adj* incorrigible

incrédule [ɛ̃kʀedyl] *adj* incredulous; *(Rel)* unbelieving

incroyable [ɛ̃kʀwajabl] *adj* incredible

incruster [ɛ̃kʀyste] *vt (Art)* to inlay; **s'incruster** *vi (invité)* to take root

inculpé, e [ɛ̃kylpe] *nm/f* accused

inculper [ɛ̃kylpe] *vt:* **~ (de)** to charge (with)

inculquer [ɛ̃kylke] *vt:* **~ qch à** to inculcate sth in *ou* instil sth into

Inde [ɛ̃d] *nf:* **l'~** India

indécent, e [ɛ̃desɑ̃, ɑ̃t] *adj* indecent

indécis, e [ɛ̃desi, iz] *adj (par nature)* indecisive; *(temporairement)* undecided

indéfendable [ɛ̃defɑ̃dabl] *adj* indefensible

indéfini, e [ɛ̃defini] *adj (imprécis, incertain)* undefined; *(illimité, Ling)* indefinite; **indéfiniment** *adv* indefinitely; **indéfinissable** *adj* indefinable

indélébile [ɛ̃delebil] *adj* indelible

indélicat, e [ēdelika, at] *adj* tactless

indemne [ēdɛmn] *adj* unharmed;
indemniser *vt*: **indemniser qn (de)** to
compensate sb (for)

indemnité [ēdɛmnite] *nf* (*dédommagement*)
compensation *no pl*; (*allocation*) allowance;
indemnité de licenciement redundancy
payment

indépendamment [ēdepãdamã] *adv*
independently; **~ de** (*abstraction faite de*)
irrespective of; (*en plus de*) over and above

indépendance [ēdepãdãs] *nf* independence

indépendant, e [ēdepãdã, ãt] *adj*
independent; **~ de** independent of;
travailleur ~ self-employed worker

indescriptible [ēdɛskriptibl] *adj*
indescribable

indésirable [ēdezirabl] *adj* undesirable

indestructible [ēdɛstryktibl] *adj*
indestructible

indéterminé, e [ēdetɛrmine] *adj* (*date, cause,
nature*) unspecified; (*forme, longueur, quantité*)
indeterminate

index [ēdɛks] *nm* (*doigt*) index finger; (*d'un livre
etc*) index; **mettre à l'~** to blacklist

indicateur [ēdikatœr] *nm* (*Police*) informer;
(*Tech*) gauge, indicator ▷ *adj*: **panneau ~**
signpost; **indicateur des chemins de fer**
railway timetable; **indicateur de rues** street
directory

indicatif, -ive [ēdikatif, iv] *adj*: **à titre ~** for
(your) information ▷ *nm* (*Ling*) indicative;
(*Radio*) theme *ou* signature tune; (*Tél*) dialling
code (*BRIT*), area code (*US*); **quel est l'~ de ...**
what's the code for ...?

indication [ēdikasjõ] *nf* indication;
(*renseignement*) information *no pl*; **indications**
nfpl (*directives*) instructions

indice [ēdis] *nm* (*marque, signe*) indication,
sign; (*Police: lors d'une enquête*) clue; (*Jur:
présomption*) piece of evidence; (*Science, Écon,
Tech*) index; **~ de protection** (sun protection)
factor

indicible [ēdisibl] *adj* inexpressible

indien, ne [ēdjē, jɛn] *adj* Indian ▷ *nm/f*: **I~,
ne** Indian

indifféremment [ēdiferamã] *adv* (*sans
distinction*) equally (well)

indifférence [ēdiferãs] *nf* indifference

indifférent, e [ēdiferã, ãt] *adj* (*peu intéressé*)
indifferent; **ça m'est ~** it doesn't matter to me;
elle m'est ~e I am indifferent to her

indigène [ēdiʒɛn] *adj* native, indigenous; (*des
gens du pays*) local ▷ *nm/f* native

indigeste [ēdiʒɛst] *adj* indigestible

indigestion [ēdiʒɛstjõ] *nf* indigestion *no pl*;
avoir une ~ to have indigestion

indigne [ēdiɲ] *adj* unworthy

indigner [ēdiɲe] *vt*: **s'~ de qch** to get annoyed

about sth; **s'~ contre qn** to get annoyed
with sb

indiqué, e [ēdike] *adj* (*date, lieu*) agreed;
(*traitement*) appropriate; (*conseillé*) advisable

indiquer [ēdike] *vt* (*suj: pendule, aiguille*) to
show; (: *étiquette, panneau*) to show, indicate;
(*renseigner sur*) to point out, tell; (*déterminer:
date, lieu*) to give, state; (*signaler, dénoter*) to
indicate, point to; **~ qch/qn à qn** (*montrer du
doigt*) to point sth/sb out to sb; (*faire connaître:
médecin, restaurant*) to tell sb of sth/sb;
pourriez-vous m'~ les toilettes/l'heure?
could you direct me to the toilets/tell me the
time?

indiscipliné, e [ēdisipline] *adj* undisciplined

indiscret, -ète [ēdiskrɛ, ɛt] *adj* indiscreet

indiscutable [ēdiskytabl] *adj* indisputable

indispensable [ēdispãsabl] *adj*
indispensable, essential

indisposé, e [ēdispoze] *adj* indisposed

indistinct, e [ēdistē(kt), ēkt] *adj* indistinct;
indistinctement *adv* (*voir, prononcer*)
indistinctly; (*sans distinction*) indiscriminately

individu [ēdividy] *nm* individual; **individuel,
le** *adj* (*gén*) individual; (*responsabilité, propriété,
liberté*) personal; **chambre individuelle** single
room; **maison individuelle** detached house

indolore [ēdɔlɔr] *adj* painless

Indonésie [ēdɔnezi] *nf* Indonesia

indu, e [ēdy] *adj*: **à une heure ~e** at some
ungodly hour

indulgent, e [ēdylʒã, ãt] *adj* (*parent, regard*)
indulgent; (*juge, examinateur*) lenient

industrialisé, e [ēdystrijalize] *adj*
industrialized

industrie [ēdystri] *nf* industry; **industriel, le**
adj industrial ▷ *nm* industrialist

inébranlable [inebrãlabl] *adj* (*masse,
colonne*) solid; (*personne, certitude, foi*)
unshakeable

inédit, e [inedi, it] *adj* (*correspondance, livre*)
hitherto unpublished; (*spectacle, moyen*) novel,
original; (*film*) unreleased

inefficace [inefikas] *adj* (*remède, moyen*)
ineffective; (*machine, employé*) inefficient

inégal, e, -aux [inegal, o] *adj* unequal;
(*irrégulier*) uneven; **inégalable** *adj* matchless;
inégalé, e *adj* (*record*) unequalled; (*beauté*)
unrivalled; **inégalité** *nf* inequality

inépuisable [inepɥizabl] *adj* inexhaustible

inerte [inɛrt] *adj* (*immobile*) lifeless; (*sans
réaction*) passive

inespéré, e [inɛspere] *adj* unexpected,
unhoped-for

inestimable [inɛstimabl] *adj* priceless; (*fig:
bienfait*) invaluable

inévitable [inevitabl] *adj* unavoidable; (*fatal,
habituel*) inevitable

inexact, e [inɛgza(kt), akt] *adj* inaccurate

inexcusable [inɛkskyzabl] adj unforgivable

inexplicable [inɛksplikabl] adj inexplicable

in extremis [inɛkstremis] adv at the last minute ▷ adj last-minute

infaillible [ɛ̃fajibl] adj infallible

infarctus [ɛ̃faʀktys] nm: **~ (du myocarde)** coronary (thrombosis)

infatigable [ɛ̃fatigabl] adj tireless

infect, e [ɛ̃fɛkt] adj revolting; (personne) obnoxious; (temps) foul

infecter [ɛ̃fɛkte] vt (atmosphère, eau) to contaminate; (Méd) to infect; **s'infecter** to become infected ou septic; **infection** nf infection; (puanteur) stench

inférieur, e [ɛ̃feʀjœʀ] adj lower; (en qualité, intelligence) inferior; **~ à** (somme, quantité) less ou smaller than; (moins bon que) inferior to

infernal, e, -aux [ɛ̃fɛʀnal, o] adj (insupportable: chaleur, rythme) infernal; (: enfant) horrid; (satanique, effrayant) diabolical

infidèle [ɛ̃fidɛl] adj unfaithful

infiltrer [ɛ̃filtre]: **s'infiltrer** vr: **s'~ dans** to get into; (liquide) to seep through; (fig: groupe, ennemi) to infiltrate

infime [ɛ̃fim] adj minute, tiny

infini, e [ɛ̃fini] adj infinite ▷ nm infinity; **à l'~** endlessly; **infiniment** adv infinitely; **infinité** nf: **une infinité de** an infinite number of

infinitif [ɛ̃finitif] nm infinitive

infirme [ɛ̃fiʀm] adj disabled ▷ nm/f disabled person

infirmerie [ɛ̃fiʀməʀi] nf medical room

infirmier, -ière [ɛ̃fiʀmje] nm/f nurse; **infirmière chef** sister

infirmité [ɛ̃fiʀmite] nf disability

inflammable [ɛ̃flamabl] adj (in)flammable

inflation [ɛ̃flasjɔ̃] nf inflation

influençable [ɛ̃flyɑ̃sabl] adj easily influenced

influence [ɛ̃flyɑ̃s] nf influence; **influencer** vt to influence; **influent, e** adj influential

informaticien, ne [ɛ̃fɔʀmatisjɛ̃, jɛn] nm/f computer scientist

information [ɛ̃fɔʀmasjɔ̃] nf (renseignement) piece of information; (Presse, TV: nouvelle) item of news; (diffusion de renseignements, Inform) information; (Jur) inquiry, investigation; **informations** nfpl (TV) news sg

informatique [ɛ̃fɔʀmatik] nf (technique) data processing; (science) computer science ▷ adj computer cpd; **informatiser** vt to computerize

informer [ɛ̃fɔʀme] vt: **~ qn (de)** to inform sb (of); **s'informer** vr: **s'~ (de/si)** to inquire ou find out (about/whether); **s'~ sur** to inform o.s. about

infos [ɛ̃fo] nfpl: **les ~** the news sg

infraction [ɛ̃fʀaksjɔ̃] nf offence; **~ à** violation ou breach of; **être en ~** to be in breach of the law

infranchissable [ɛ̃fʀɑ̃ʃisabl] adj impassable; (fig) insuperable

infrarouge [ɛ̃fʀaʀuʒ] adj infrared

infrastructure [ɛ̃fʀastʀyktyʀ] nf (Aviat, Mil) ground installations pl; (Écon: touristique etc) infrastructure

infuser [ɛ̃fyze] vt, vi (thé) to brew; (tisane) to infuse; **infusion** nf (tisane) herb tea

ingénier [ɛ̃ʒenje]: **s'ingénier** vi: **s'~ à faire** to strive to do

ingénierie [ɛ̃ʒeniʀi] nf engineering

ingénieur [ɛ̃ʒenjœʀ] nm engineer; **ingénieur du son** sound engineer

ingénieux, -euse [ɛ̃ʒenjø, jøz] adj ingenious, clever

ingrat, e [ɛ̃gʀa, at] adj (personne) ungrateful; (travail, sujet) thankless; (visage) unprepossessing

ingrédient [ɛ̃gʀedjɑ̃] nm ingredient

inhabité, e [inabite] adj uninhabited

inhabituel, le [inabituɛl] adj unusual

inhibition [inibisjɔ̃] nf inhibition

inhumain, e [inymɛ̃, ɛn] adj inhuman

inimaginable [inimaʒinabl] adj unimaginable

ininterrompu, e [inɛ̃teʀɔ̃py] adj (file, série) unbroken; (flot, vacarme) uninterrupted, non-stop; (effort) unremitting, continuous; (suite, ligne) unbroken

initial, e, -aux [inisjal, jo] adj initial; **initiales** nfpl (d'un nom, sigle etc) initials

initiation [inisjasjɔ̃] nf: **~ à** introduction to

initiative [inisjativ] nf initiative

initier [inisje] vt: **~ qn à** to initiate sb into; (faire découvrir: art, jeu) to introduce sb to

injecter [ɛ̃ʒekte] vt to inject; **injection** nf injection; **à injection** (Auto) fuel injection cpd

injure [ɛ̃ʒyʀ] nf insult, abuse no pl; **injurier** vt to insult, abuse; **injurieux, -euse** adj abusive, insulting

injuste [ɛ̃ʒyst] adj unjust, unfair; **injustice** nf injustice

inlassable [ɛ̃lasabl] adj tireless

inné, e [i(n)ne] adj innate, inborn

innocent, e [inɔsɑ̃, ɑ̃t] adj innocent; **innocenter** vt to clear, prove innocent

innombrable [i(n)nɔ̃bʀabl] adj innumerable

innover [inɔve] vi to break new ground

inoccupé, e [inɔkype] adj unoccupied

inodore [inɔdɔʀ] adj (gaz) odourless; (fleur) scentless

inoffensif, -ive [inɔfɑ̃sif, iv] adj harmless, innocuous

inondation [inɔ̃dasjɔ̃] nf flood

inonder [inɔ̃de] vt to flood; **~ de** to flood with

inopportun, e [inɔpɔʀtœ̃, yn] adj ill-timed, untimely

inoubliable [inublijabl] adj unforgettable

inouï, e [inwi] adj unheard-of, extraordinary

inox [inɔks] nm stainless steel

inquiet, -ète [ɛ̃kjɛ, ɛ̃kjɛt] adj anxious; **inquiétant, e** adj worrying, disturbing; **inquiéter** vt to worry; **s'inquiéter** to worry; **s'inquiéter de** to worry about; (s'enquérir de) to inquire about; **inquiétude** nf anxiety

insaisissable [ɛ̃sezisabl] adj (fugitif, ennemi) elusive; (différence, nuance) imperceptible

insalubre [ɛ̃salybr] adj insalubrious

insatisfait, e [ɛ̃satisfɛ, ɛt] adj (non comblé) unsatisfied; (mécontent) dissatisfied

inscription [ɛ̃skripsjɔ̃] nf inscription; (immatriculation) enrolment

inscrire [ɛ̃skrir] vt (marquer: sur son calepin etc) to note ou write down; (: sur un mur, une affiche etc) to write; (: dans la pierre, le métal) to inscribe; (mettre: sur une liste, un budget etc) to put down; **s'inscrire** (pour une excursion etc) to put one's name down; **s'~ (à)** (club, parti) to join; (université) to register ou enrol (at); (examen, concours) to register (for); **~ qn à** (club, parti) to enrol sb at

insecte [ɛ̃sɛkt] nm insect; **insecticide** nm insecticide

insensé, e [ɛ̃sɑ̃se] adj mad

insensible [ɛ̃sɑ̃sibl] adj (nerf, membre) numb; (dur, indifférent) insensitive

inséparable [ɛ̃separabl] adj inseparable ▷ nm: **~s** (oiseaux) lovebirds

insigne [ɛ̃siɲ] nm (d'un parti, club) badge; (d'une fonction) insignia ▷ adj distinguished

insignifiant, e [ɛ̃siɲifjɑ̃, jɑ̃t] adj insignificant; trivial

insinuer [ɛ̃sinɥe] vt to insinuate; **s'insinuer dans** (fig) to worm one's way into

insipide [ɛ̃sipid] adj insipid

insister [ɛ̃siste] vi to insist; (continuer à sonner) to keep on trying; **~ sur** (détail, sujet) to lay stress on

insolation [ɛ̃sɔlasjɔ̃] nf (Méd) sunstroke no pl

insolent, e [ɛ̃sɔlɑ̃, ɑ̃t] adj insolent

insolite [ɛ̃sɔlit] adj strange, unusual

insomnie [ɛ̃sɔmni] nf insomnia no pl; **avoir des ~s** to sleep badly, not be able to sleep

insouciant, e [ɛ̃susjɑ̃, jɑ̃t] adj carefree; **~ du danger** heedless of (the) danger

insoupçonnable [ɛ̃supsɔnabl] adj unsuspected; (personne) above suspicion

insoupçonné, e [ɛ̃supsɔne] adj unsuspected

insoutenable [ɛ̃sut(ə)nabl] adj (argument) untenable; (chaleur) unbearable

inspecter [ɛ̃spɛkte] vt to inspect; **inspecteur, -trice** nm/f inspector; **inspecteur d'Académie** (regional) director of education; **inspecteur des finances** ≈ tax inspector (BRIT), ≈ Internal Revenue Service agent (US); **inspecteur (de police)** (police) inspector; **inspection** nf inspection

inspirer [ɛ̃spire] vt (gén) to inspire ▷ vi (aspirer) to breathe in; **s'inspirer** vr: **s'~ de** to be inspired by

instable [ɛ̃stabl] adj unstable; (meuble, équilibre) unsteady; (temps) unsettled

installation [ɛ̃stalasjɔ̃] nf (mise en place) installation; **installations** nfpl (de sport, dans un camping) facilities; **l'installation électrique** wiring

installer [ɛ̃stale] vt (loger, placer) to put; (meuble, gaz, électricité) to put in; (rideau, étagère, tente) to put up; (appartement) to fit out; **s'installer** (s'établir: artisan, dentiste etc) to set o.s. up; (se loger) to settle; (emménager) to settle in; (sur un siège, à un emplacement) to settle (down); (fig: maladie, grève) to take a firm hold

instance [ɛ̃stɑ̃s] nf (Admin: autorité) authority; **affaire en ~** matter pending; **être en ~ de divorce** to be awaiting a divorce

instant [ɛ̃stɑ̃] nm moment, instant; **dans un ~** in a moment; **à l'~** this instant; **je l'ai vu à l'~** I've just this minute seen him, I saw him a moment ago; **pour l'~** for the moment, for the time being

instantané, e [ɛ̃stɑ̃tane] adj (lait, café) instant; (explosion, mort) instantaneous ▷ nm snapshot

instar [ɛ̃star]: **à l'~ de** prép following the example of, like

instaurer [ɛ̃stɔre] vt to institute; (couvre-feu) to impose; **s'instaurer** vr (paix) to be established; (doute) to set in

instinct [ɛ̃stɛ̃] nm instinct; **instinctivement** adv instinctively

instituer [ɛ̃stitɥe] vt to establish

institut [ɛ̃stity] nm institute; **institut de beauté** beauty salon; **Institut universitaire de technologie** ≈ polytechnic

instituteur, -trice [ɛ̃stitytœr, tris] nm/f (primary school) teacher

institution [ɛ̃stitysjɔ̃] nf institution; (collège) private school; **institutions** nfpl (structures politiques et sociales) institutions

instructif, -ive [ɛ̃stryktif, iv] adj instructive

instruction [ɛ̃stryksjɔ̃] nf (enseignement, savoir) education; (Jur: preliminary) investigation and hearing; **instructions** nfpl (ordres, mode d'emploi) instructions; **instruction civique** civics sg

instruire [ɛ̃strɥir] vt (élèves) to teach; (recrues) to train; (Jur: affaire) to conduct the investigation for; **s'instruire** to educate o.s.; **instruit, e** adj educated

instrument [ɛ̃strymɑ̃] nm instrument; **instrument à cordes/à vent** stringed/wind instrument; **instrument de mesure** measuring instrument; **instrument de musique** musical instrument; **instrument de travail** (working) tool

insu [ɛ̃sy] nm: **à l'~ de qn** without sb knowing (it)

insuffisant, e [ɛ̃syfizɑ̃, ɑ̃t] adj (en quantité) insufficient; (en qualité) inadequate; (sur une copie) poor

insulaire [ɛ̃sylɛʀ] adj island cpd; (attitude) insular

insuline [ɛ̃sylin] nf insulin

insulte [ɛ̃sylt] nf insult; **insulter** vt to insult

insupportable [ɛ̃sypɔʀtabl] adj unbearable

insurmontable [ɛ̃syʀmɔ̃tabl] adj (difficulté) insuperable; (aversion) unconquerable

intact, e [ɛ̃takt] adj intact

intarissable [ɛ̃taʀisabl] adj inexhaustible

intégral, e, -aux [ɛ̃tegʀal, o] adj complete; **texte ~** unabridged version; **bronzage ~** all-over suntan; **intégralement** adv in full; **intégralité** nf whole; **dans son intégralité** in full; **intégrant, e** adj: **faire partie intégrante de** to be an integral part of

intègre [ɛ̃tɛgʀ] adj upright

intégrer [ɛ̃tegʀe]: **s'intégrer** vr: **s'~ à** ou **dans qch** to become integrated into sth; **bien s'~** to fit in

intégrisme [ɛ̃tegʀism] nm fundamentalism

intellectuel, le [ɛ̃telɛktɥel] adj intellectual ▷ nm/f intellectual; (péj) highbrow

intelligence [ɛ̃teliʒɑ̃s] nf intelligence; (compréhension): **l'~ de** the understanding of; (complicité): **regard d'~** glance of complicity; (accord): **vivre en bonne ~ avec qn** to be on good terms with sb

intelligent, e [ɛ̃teliʒɑ̃, ɑ̃t] adj intelligent

intelligible [ɛ̃teliʒibl] adj intelligible

intempéries [ɛ̃tɑ̃peʀi] nfpl bad weather sg

intenable [ɛ̃t(ə)nabl] adj (chaleur) unbearable

intendant, e [ɛ̃tɑ̃dɑ̃] nm/f (Mil) quartermaster; (Scol) bursar

intense [ɛ̃tɑ̃s] adj intense; **intensif, -ive** adj intensive; **un cours intensif** a crash course

intenter [ɛ̃tɑ̃te] vt: **~ un procès contre** ou **à** to start proceedings against

intention [ɛ̃tɑ̃sjɔ̃] nf intention; (Jur) intent; **avoir l'~ de faire** to intend to do; **à l'~ de** for; (renseignement) for the benefit of; (film, ouvrage) aimed at; **à cette ~** with this aim in view; **intentionné, e** adj: **bien intentionné** well-meaning ou **-intentioned**; **mal intentionné** ill-intentioned

interactif, -ive [ɛ̃teʀaktif, iv] adj (Comput) interactive

intercepter [ɛ̃teʀsepte] vt to intercept; (lumière, chaleur) to cut off

interchangeable [ɛ̃teʀʃɑ̃ʒabl] adj interchangeable

interdiction [ɛ̃teʀdiksjɔ̃] nf ban; **interdiction de fumer** no smoking

interdire [ɛ̃teʀdiʀ] vt to forbid; (Admin) to ban, prohibit; (: journal, livre) to ban; **~ à qn de faire** to forbid sb to do; (suj: empêchement) to prevent sb from doing

interdit, e [ɛ̃teʀdi, it] pp de **interdire** ▷ adj (stupéfait) taken aback; **film ~ aux moins de 18/12 ans** ≈ 18-/12A-rated film; **"stationnement ~"** "no parking"

intéressant, e [ɛ̃teʀesɑ̃, ɑ̃t] adj interesting; (avantageux) attractive

intéressé, e [ɛ̃teʀese] adj (parties) involved, concerned; (amitié, motifs) self-interested

intéresser [ɛ̃teʀese] vt (captiver) to interest; (toucher) to be of interest to; (Admin: concerner) to affect, concern; **s'intéresser** vr: **s'~ à** to be interested in

intérêt [ɛ̃teʀɛ] nm interest; (égoïsme) self-interest; **tu as ~ à accepter** it's in your interest to accept; **tu as ~ à te dépêcher** you'd better hurry

intérieur, e [ɛ̃teʀjœʀ] adj (mur, escalier, poche) inside; (commerce, politique) domestic; (cour, calme, vie) inner; (navigation) inland ▷ nm: **l'~** (d'une maison, d'un récipient etc) the inside; (d'un pays, aussi: décor, mobilier) the interior; **à l'~ (de)** inside; **ministère de l'I~e** ≈ Home Office (BRIT), ≈ Department of the Interior (US); **intérieurement** adv inwardly

intérim [ɛ̃teʀim] nm interim period; **faire de l'~** to temp; **assurer l'~ (de)** to deputize (for); **par ~** interim

intérimaire [ɛ̃teʀimɛʀ] adj (directeur, ministre) acting; (secrétaire, personnel) temporary ▷ nm/f (secrétaire) temporary secretary, temp (BRIT)

interlocuteur, -trice [ɛ̃teʀlɔkytœʀ, tʀis] nm/f speaker; **son ~** the person he was speaking to

intermédiaire [ɛ̃teʀmedjɛʀ] adj intermediate; (solution) temporary ▷ nm/f intermediary; (Comm) middleman; **sans ~** directly; **par l'~ de** through

interminable [ɛ̃teʀminabl] adj endless

intermittence [ɛ̃teʀmitɑ̃s] nf: **par ~** sporadically, intermittently

internat [ɛ̃teʀna] nm boarding school

international, e, -aux [ɛ̃teʀnasjɔnal, o] adj, nm/f international

internaute [ɛ̃teʀnot] nm/f Internet user

interne [ɛ̃teʀn] adj internal ▷ nm/f (Scol) boarder; (Méd) houseman

Internet [ɛ̃teʀnɛt] nm: **l'~** the Internet

interpeller [ɛ̃teʀpəle] vt (appeler) to call out to; (apostropher) to shout at; (Police, Pol) to question; (concerner) to concern

interphone [ɛ̃teʀfɔn] nm intercom; (d'immeuble) entry phone

interposer [ɛ̃teʀpoze] vt: **s'interposer** to intervene; **par personnes interposées** through a third party

interprète [ɛ̃teʀpʀɛt] nm/f interpreter; (porte-

parole) spokesperson; **pourriez-vous nous servir d' ~?** could you act as our interpreter?
interpréter [ɛ̃tɛʀpʀete] *vt* to interpret; (*jouer*) to play; (*chanter*) to sing
interrogatif, -ive [ɛ̃tɛʀɔgatif, iv] *adj* (*Ling*) interrogative
interrogation [ɛ̃tɛʀɔgasjɔ̃] *nf* question; (*action*) questioning; **~ écrite/orale** (*Scol*) written/oral test
interrogatoire [ɛ̃tɛʀɔgatwaʀ] *nm* (*Police*) questioning *no pl*; (*Jur, aussi fig*) cross-examination
interroger [ɛ̃tɛʀɔʒe] *vt* to question; (*Inform*) to consult; (*Scol*) to test
interrompre [ɛ̃tɛʀɔ̃pʀ] *vt* (*gén*) to interrupt; (*négociations*) to break off; (*match*) to stop; **s'interrompre** to break off; **interrupteur** *nm* switch; **interruption** *nf* interruption; (*pause*) break; **sans interruption** without stopping; **interruption (volontaire) de grossesse** termination (of pregnancy)
intersection [ɛ̃tɛʀsɛksjɔ̃] *nf* intersection
intervalle [ɛ̃tɛʀval] *nm* (*espace*) space; (*de temps*) interval; **dans l'~** in the meantime; **à deux jours d'~** two days apart
intervenir [ɛ̃tɛʀvəniʀ] *vi* (*gén*) to intervene; **~ auprès de qn** to intervene with sb; **intervention** *nf* intervention; (*discours*) speech; **intervention chirurgicale** (*Méd*) (surgical) operation
interview [ɛ̃tɛʀvju] *nf* interview
intestin [ɛ̃tɛstɛ̃] *nm* intestine
intime [ɛ̃tim] *adj* intimate; (*vie*) private; (*conviction*) inmost; (*dîner, cérémonie*) quiet ▷ *nm/f* close friend; **un journal ~** a diary
intimider [ɛ̃timide] *vt* to intimidate
intimité [ɛ̃timite] *nf*: **dans l'~** in private; (*sans formalités*) with only a few friends, quietly
intolérable [ɛ̃tɔleʀabl] *adj* intolerable
intox [ɛ̃tɔks] (*fam*) *nf* brainwashing
intoxication [ɛ̃tɔksikasjɔ̃] *nf*: **intoxication alimentaire** food poisoning
intoxiquer [ɛ̃tɔksike] *vt* to poison; (*fig*) to brainwash
intraitable [ɛ̃tʀɛtabl] *adj* inflexible, uncompromising
intransigeant, e [ɛ̃tʀɑ̃ziʒɑ̃, ɑ̃t] *adj* intransigent
intrépide [ɛ̃tʀepid] *adj* dauntless
intrigue [ɛ̃tʀig] *nf* (*scénario*) plot; **intriguer** *vt* to puzzle, intrigue
introduction [ɛ̃tʀɔdyksjɔ̃] *nf* introduction
introduire [ɛ̃tʀɔdɥiʀ] *vt* to introduce; (*visiteur*) to show in; (*aiguille, clef*) to insert *ou* introduce sth into; **s'introduire** *vr* (*techniques, usages*) to be introduced; **s'~ (dans)** to get in(to); (*dans un groupe*) to get o.s. accepted (into)
introuvable [ɛ̃tʀuvabl] *adj* which cannot be

found; (*Comm*) unobtainable
intrus, e [ɛ̃tʀy, yz] *nm/f* intruder
intuition [ɛ̃tɥisjɔ̃] *nf* intuition
inusable [inyzabl] *adj* hard-wearing
inutile [inytil] *adj* useless; (*superflu*) unnecessary; **inutilement** *adv* unnecessarily; **inutilisable** *adj* unusable
invalide [ɛ̃valid] *adj* disabled ▷ *nm*: **~ de guerre** disabled ex-serviceman
invariable [ɛ̃vaʀjabl] *adj* invariable
invasion [ɛ̃vazjɔ̃] *nf* invasion
inventaire [ɛ̃vɑ̃tɛʀ] *nm* inventory; (*Comm: liste*) stocklist; (: *opération*) stocktaking *no pl*
inventer [ɛ̃vɑ̃te] *vt* to invent; (*subterfuge*) to devise, invent; (*histoire, excuse*) to make up, invent; **inventeur** *nm* inventor; **inventif, -ive** *adj* inventive; **invention** *nf* invention
inverse [ɛ̃vɛʀs] *adj* opposite ▷ *nm*: **l'~** the opposite; **dans l'ordre ~** in the reverse order; **en sens ~** in (*ou* from) the opposite direction; **dans le sens ~ des aiguilles d'une montre** anticlockwise; **tu t'es trompé, c'est l'~** you've got it wrong, it's the other way round; **inversement** *adv* conversely; **inverser** *vt* to invert, reverse; (*Élec*) to reverse
investir [ɛ̃vɛstiʀ] *vt* to invest; **~ qn de** (*d'une fonction, d'un pouvoir*) to vest *ou* invest sb with; **s'investir** *vr*: **s'~ dans** (*Psych*) to put a lot into; **investissement** *nm* investment
invisible [ɛ̃vizibl] *adj* invisible
invitation [ɛ̃vitasjɔ̃] *nf* invitation
invité, e [ɛ̃vite] *nm/f* guest
inviter [ɛ̃vite] *vt* to invite; **~ qn à faire qch** to invite sb to do sth
invivable [ɛ̃vivabl] *adj* unbearable
involontaire [ɛ̃vɔlɔ̃tɛʀ] *adj* (*mouvement*) involuntary; (*insulte*) unintentional; (*complice*) unwitting
invoquer [ɛ̃vɔke] *vt* (*Dieu, muse*) to call upon, invoke; (*prétexte*) to put forward (as an excuse); (*loi, texte*) to refer to
invraisemblable [ɛ̃vʀesɑ̃blabl] *adj* (*fait, nouvelle*) unlikely, improbable; (*insolence, habit*) incredible
iode [jɔd] *nm* iodine
irai *etc* [iʀe] *vb voir* **aller**
Irak [iʀak] *nm* Iraq; **irakien, ne** *adj* Iraqi ▷ *nm/f*: **Irakien, ne** Iraqi
Iran [iʀɑ̃] *nm* Iran; **iranien, ne** *adj* Iranian ▷ *nm/f*: **Iranien, ne** Iranian
irions *etc* [iʀjɔ̃] *vb voir* **aller**
iris [iʀis] *nm* iris
irlandais, e [iʀlɑ̃dɛ, ɛz] *adj* Irish ▷ *nm/f*: **I~, e** Irishman(-woman)
Irlande [iʀlɑ̃d] *nf* Ireland; **la République d'~** the Irish Republic; **la mer d'~** the Irish Sea; **Irlande du Nord** Northern Ireland
ironie [iʀɔni] *nf* irony; **ironique** *adj* ironical; **ironiser** *vi* to be ironical

irons *etc* [iʀɔ̃] *vb voir* **aller**

irradier [iʀadje] *vt* to irradiate

irraisonné, e [iʀezɔne] *adj* irrational

irrationnel, le [iʀasjɔnɛl] *adj* irrational

irréalisable [iʀealizabl] *adj* unrealizable; *(projet)* impracticable

irrécupérable [iʀekypeʀabl] *adj* beyond repair; *(personne)* beyond redemption

irréel, le [iʀeɛl] *adj* unreal

irréfléchi, e [iʀefleʃi] *adj* thoughtless

irrégularité [iʀegylaʀite] *nf* irregularity; *(de travail, d'effort, de qualité)* unevenness *no pl*

irrégulier, -ière [iʀegylje, jɛʀ] *adj* irregular; *(travail, effort, qualité)* uneven; *(élève, athlète)* erratic

irrémédiable [iʀemedjabl] *adj* irreparable

irremplaçable [iʀɑ̃plasabl] *adj* irreplaceable

irréparable [iʀepaʀabl] *adj (objet)* beyond repair; *(dommage etc)* irreparable

irréprochable [iʀepʀɔʃabl] *adj* irreproachable, beyond reproach; *(tenue)* impeccable

irrésistible [iʀezistibl] *adj* irresistible; *(besoin, désir, preuve, logique)* compelling; *(amusant)* hilarious

irrésolu, e [iʀezɔly] *adj (personne)* irresolute; *(problème)* unresolved

irrespectueux, -euse [iʀɛspɛktɥø, øz] *adj* disrespectful

irresponsable [iʀɛspɔ̃sabl] *adj* irresponsible

irriguer [iʀige] *vt* to irrigate

irritable [iʀitabl] *adj* irritable

irriter [iʀite] *vt* to irritate

irruption [iʀypsjɔ̃] *nf*: **faire ~ (chez qn)** to burst in (on sb)

Islam [islam] *nm*: **l'~** Islam; **islamique** *adj* Islamic; **islamophobie** *nf* Islamophobia

Islande [islɑ̃d] *nf* Iceland

isolant, e [izɔlɑ̃, ɑ̃t] *adj* insulating; *(insonorisant)* soundproofing

isolation [izɔlasjɔ̃] *nf* insulation; **~ acoustique** soundproofing

isolé, e [izɔle] *adj* isolated; *(contre le froid)* insulated

isoler [izɔle] *vt* to isolate; *(prisonnier)* to put in solitary confinement; *(ville)* to cut off, isolate; *(contre le froid)* to insulate; **s'isoler** *vi* to isolate o.s.

Israël [isʀaɛl] *nm* Israel; **israélien, ne** *adj* Israeli ▷ *nm/f*: **Israélien, ne** Israeli; **israélite** *adj* Jewish ▷ *nm/f*: **Israélite** Jew (Jewess)

issu, e [isy] *adj*: **~ de** *(né de)* descended from; *(résultant de)* stemming from; **issue** *nf (ouverture, sortie)* exit; *(solution)* way out, solution; *(dénouement)* outcome; **à l'issue de** at the conclusion *ou* close of; **voie sans issue** dead end; **issue de secours** emergency exit

Italie [itali] *nf* Italy; **italien, ne** *adj* Italian ▷ *nm/f*: **Italien, ne** Italian ▷ *nm (Ling)* Italian

italique [italik] *nm*: **en ~** in italics

itinéraire [itineʀɛʀ] *nm* itinerary, route; **itinéraire bis** alternative route

IUT *sigle m* = **Institut universitaire de technologie**

IVG *sigle f* (= *interruption volontaire de grossesse*) abortion

ivoire [ivwaʀ] *nm* ivory

ivre [ivʀ] *adj* drunk; **~ de** *(colère, bonheur)* wild with; **ivrogne** *nm/f* drunkard

j' [ʒ] pron voir **je**

jacinthe [ʒasɛ̃t] nf hyacinth

jadis [ʒadis] adv long ago

jaillir [ʒajiʀ] vi (liquide) to spurt out; (cris, réponses) to burst forth

jais [ʒɛ] nm jet; **(d'un noir) de ~** jet-black

jalousie [ʒaluzi] nf jealousy; (store) slatted blind

jaloux, -ouse [ʒalu, uz] adj jealous; **être ~ de** to be jealous of

jamaïquain, e [ʒamaikɛ̃, -ɛn] adj Jamaican ▷ nm/f: **J~, e** Jamaican

Jamaïque [ʒamaik] nf: **la ~** Jamaica

jamais [ʒamɛ] adv never; (sans négation) ever; **ne ... ~** never; **je ne suis ~ allé en Espagne** I've never been to Spain; **si ~ vous passez dans la région, venez nous voir** if you happen to be/if you're ever in this area, come and see us; **à ~** for ever

jambe [ʒɑ̃b] nf leg

jambon [ʒɑ̃bɔ̃] nm ham

jante [ʒɑ̃t] nf (wheel) rim

janvier [ʒɑ̃vje] nm January

Japon [ʒapɔ̃] nm Japan; **japonais, e** adj Japanese ▷ nm/f: **Japonais, e** Japanese ▷ nm (Ling) Japanese

jardin [ʒaʀdɛ̃] nm garden; **jardin d'enfants** nursery school; **jardinage** nm gardening; **jardiner** vi to do some gardening; **jardinier, -ière** nm/f gardener; **jardinière** nf planter; (de fenêtre) window box; **jardinière de légumes** (Culin) mixed vegetables

jargon [ʒaʀgɔ̃] nm (baragouin) gibberish; (langue professionnelle) jargon

jarret [ʒaʀɛ] nm back of knee; (Culin) knuckle, shin

jauge [ʒoʒ] nf (instrument) gauge; **jauge (de niveau) d'huile** (Auto) dipstick

jaune [ʒon] adj, nm yellow ▷ adv (fam): **rire ~** to laugh on the other side of one's face; **jaune d'œuf** (egg) yolk; **jaunir** vi, vt to turn yellow; **jaunisse** nf jaundice

Javel [ʒavɛl] nf voir **eau**

javelot [ʒavlo] nm javelin

je, j' [ʒə] pron I

jean [dʒin] nm jeans pl

Jésus-Christ [ʒezykʀi(st)] n Jesus Christ; **600 avant/après ~ ou J.-C.** 600 B.C./A.D.

jet [ʒɛ] nm (lancer: action) throwing no pl; (: résultat) throw; (jaillissement: d'eaux) jet; (: de sang) spurt; **jet d'eau** spray

jetable [ʒ(ə)tabl] adj disposable

jetée [ʒəte] nf jetty; (grande) pier

jeter [ʒ(ə)te] vt (gén) to throw; (se défaire de) to throw away ou out; **~ qch à qn** to throw sth to sb; (de façon agressive) to throw sth at sb; **~ un coup d'œil (à)** to take a look (at); **~ un sort à qn** to cast a spell on sb; **se ~ sur qn** to rush at sb; **se ~ dans** (suj: fleuve) to flow into

jeton [ʒ(ə)tɔ̃] nm (au jeu) counter

jette etc [ʒɛt] vb voir **jeter**

jeu, x [ʒø] nm (divertissement, Tech: d'une pièce) play; (Tennis: partie, Football etc: façon de jouer) game; (Théâtre etc) acting; (série d'objets, jouet) set; (Cartes) hand; (au casino): **le ~** gambling; **remettre en ~** (Football) to throw in; **être en ~** (fig) to be at stake; **entrer/mettre en ~** (fig) to come/bring into play; **jeu de cartes** pack of cards; **jeu d'échecs** chess set; **jeu de hasard** game of chance; **jeu de mots** pun; **jeu de société** board game; **jeu télévisé** television quiz; **jeu vidéo** video game

jeudi [ʒødi] nm Thursday

jeun [ʒœ̃]: **à ~** adv on an empty stomach; **être à ~** to have eaten nothing; **rester à ~** not to eat anything

jeune [ʒœn] adj young; **jeunes** nmpl: **les ~s** young people; **jeune fille** girl; **jeune homme** young man; **jeunes gens** young people

jeûne [ʒøn] nm fast

jeunesse [ʒœnɛs] nf youth; (aspect) youthfulness

joaillier, -ière [ʒoaje, -jɛʀ] nm/f jeweller

jogging [dʒɔgiŋ] nm jogging; (survêtement) tracksuit; **faire du ~** to go jogging

joie [ʒwa] nf joy

joindre [ʒwɛ̃dʀ] vt to join; (à une lettre): **~ qch à** to enclose sth with; (contacter) to contact, get in touch with; **se ~ à qn** to join sb; **se ~ à**

qch to join in sth

joint, e [ʒwɛ̃, ɛt] adj: **pièce ~** (de lettre) enclosure; (de mail) attachment ▷ nm joint; (ligne) join; **joint de culasse** cylinder head gasket

joli, e [ʒɔli] adj pretty, attractive; **une ~e somme/situation** a tidy sum/a nice little job; **c'est du ~!** (ironique) that's very nice!; **c'est bien ~, mais ...** that's all very well but ...

jonc [ʒɔ̃] nm (bul)rush

jonction [ʒɔ̃ksjɔ̃] nf junction

jongleur, -euse [ʒɔ̃glœr, øz] nm/f juggler

jonquille [ʒɔ̃kij] nf daffodil

Jordanie [ʒɔrdani] nf: **la ~** Jordan

joue [ʒu] nf cheek

jouer [ʒwe] vt to play; (somme d'argent, réputation) to stake, wager; (simuler: sentiment) to affect, feign ▷ vi to play; (Théâtre, Cinéma) to act; (au casino) to gamble; (bois, porte: se voiler) to warp; (clef, pièce: avoir du jeu) to be loose; **~ sur** (miser) to gamble on; **~ de** (Mus) to play; **~ à** (jeu, sport, roulette) to play; **~ un tour à qn** to play a trick on sb; **~ serré** to play a close game; **~ la comédie** to put on an act; **à toi/nous de ~** it's your/our go ou turn; **bien joué!** well done!; **on joue Hamlet au théâtre X** Hamlet is on at the X theatre

jouet [ʒwɛ] nm toy; **être le ~ de** (illusion etc) to be the victim of

joueur, -euse [ʒwœr, øz] nm/f player; **être beau/mauvais ~** to be a good/bad loser

jouir [ʒwir] vi (sexe: fam) to come ▷ vt: **~ de** to enjoy

jour [ʒur] nm day; (opposé à la nuit) day, daytime; (clarté) daylight; (fig: aspect) light; (ouverture) gap; **de ~** (crème, service) day cpd; **travailler de ~** to work during the day; **voyager de ~** to travel by day; **au ~ le ~** from day to day; **de nos ~s** these days; **du ~ au lendemain** overnight; **il fait ~** it's daylight; **au grand ~** (fig) in the open; **mettre au ~** to disclose; **mettre à ~** to update; **donner le ~ à** to give birth to; **voir le ~** to be born; **le ~ J** D-day; **jour férié** public holiday; **jour ouvrable** working day

journal, -aux [ʒurnal, o] nm (news)paper; (spécialisé) journal; (intime) diary; **journal de bord** log; **journal parlé/télévisé** radio/television news sg

journalier, -ière [ʒurnalje, jɛr] adj daily; (banal) everyday

journalisme [ʒurnalism] nm journalism; **journaliste** nm/f journalist

journée [ʒurne] nf day; **faire la ~ continue** to work over lunch

joyau, x [ʒwajo] nm gem, jewel

joyeux, -euse [ʒwajø, øz] adj joyful, merry; **~ Noël!** merry Christmas!; **~ anniversaire!** happy birthday!

jubiler [ʒybile] vi to be jubilant, exult

judas [ʒyda] nm (trou) spy-hole

judiciaire [ʒydisjɛr] adj judicial

judicieux, -euse [ʒydisjø, jøz] adj judicious

judo [ʒydo] nm judo

juge [ʒyʒ] nm judge; **juge d'instruction** examining (brit) ou committing (us) magistrate; **juge de paix** justice of the peace

jugé [ʒyʒe] nm: **au ~** adv by guesswork

jugement [ʒyʒmɑ̃] nm judgment; (Jur: au pénal) sentence; (: au civil) decision

juger [ʒyʒe] vt to judge; (estimer) to consider; **~ qn/qch satisfaisant** to consider sb/sth (to be) satisfactory; **~ bon de faire** to see fit to do

juif, -ive [ʒɥif, ʒɥiv] adj Jewish ▷ nm/f: **J~, ive** Jew (Jewess)

juillet [ʒɥijɛ] nm July

● **14 JUILLET**
●
● **Le 14 juillet** is a national holiday in France
● and commemorates the storming of the
● Bastille during the French Revolution.
● Throughout the country there are
● celebrations, which feature parades, music,
● dancing and firework displays. In Paris a
● military parade along the Champs-Élysées
● is attended by the President.

juin [ʒɥɛ̃] nm June

jumeau, -elle, x [ʒymo, ɛl] adj, nm/f twin

jumeler [ʒym(ə)le] vt to twin

jumelle [ʒymɛl] adj, nf voir **jumeau**; **jumelles** nfpl (appareil) binoculars

jument [ʒymɑ̃] nf mare

jungle [ʒɶ̃gl] nf jungle

jupe [ʒyp] nf skirt

jupon [ʒypɔ̃] nm waist slip

juré, e [ʒyre] nm/f juror ▷ adj: **ennemi ~** sworn enemy

jurer [ʒyre] vt (obéissance etc) to swear, vow ▷ vi (dire des jurons) to swear, curse; (dissoner): **~ (avec)** to clash (with); **~ de faire/que** to swear to do/that; **~ de qch** (s'en porter garant) to swear to sth

juridique [ʒyridik] adj legal

juron [ʒyrɔ̃] nm curse, swearword

jury [ʒyri] nm jury; (Art, Sport) panel of judges; (Scol) board of examiners

jus [ʒy] nm juice; (de viande) gravy, (meat) juice; **jus de fruit** fruit juice

jusque [ʒysk]: **jusqu'à** prép (endroit) as far as, (up) to; (moment) until, till; (limite) up to; **~ sur/dans** up to; (y compris) even on/in; **jusqu'à ce que** until; **jusqu'à présent** ou **maintenant** so far; **jusqu'où?** how far?

justaucorps [ʒystokɔr] nm leotard

juste [ʒyst] adj (équitable) just, fair; (légitime) just; (exact) right; (pertinent) apt; (étroit) tight;

(*insuffisant*) on the short side ▷ *adv* rightly, correctly; (*chanter*) in tune; (*exactement, seulement*) just; **~ assez/au-dessus** just enough/above; **au ~** exactly; **le ~ milieu** the happy medium; **c'était ~** it was a close thing; **pouvoir tout ~ faire** to be only just able to do; **justement** *adv* justly; (*précisément*) just, precisely; **justesse** *nf* (*précision*) accuracy; (*d'une remarque*) aptness; (*d'une opinion*) soundness; **de justesse** only just

justice [ʒystis] *nf* (*équité*) fairness, justice; (*Admin*) justice; **rendre ~ à qn** to do sb justice

justificatif, -ive [ʒystifikatif, iv] *adj* (*document*) supporting; **pièce justificative** written proof

justifier [ʒystifje] *vt* to justify; **~ de** to prove

juteux, -euse [ʒytø, øz] *adj* juicy

juvénile [ʒyvenil] *adj* youthful

K [ka] *nm* (*Inform*) K

kaki [kaki] *adj inv* khaki

kangourou [kãguʁu] *nm* kangaroo

karaté [kaʁate] *nm* karate

kascher [kaʃɛʁ] *adj* kosher

kayak [kajak] *nm* canoe, kayak; **faire du ~** to go canoeing

képi [kepi] *nm* kepi

kermesse [kɛʁmɛs] *nf* fair; (*fête de charité*) bazaar, (charity) fête

kidnapper [kidnape] *vt* to kidnap

kilo [kilo] *nm* = **kilogramme**

kilo...: **kilogramme** *nm* kilogramme; **kilométrage** *nm* number of kilometres travelled, ≈ mileage; **kilomètre** *nm* kilometre; **kilométrique** *adj* (*distance*) in kilometres

kinésithérapeute [kineziteʁapøt] *nm/f* physiotherapist

kiosque [kjɔsk] *nm* kiosk, stall

kir [kiʁ] *nm* kir (*white wine with blackcurrant liqueur*)

kit [kit] *nm* kit; **~ piéton** *ou* **mains libres** hands-free kit; **en ~** in kit form

kiwi [kiwi] *nm* kiwi

klaxon [klaksɔn] *nm* horn; **klaxonner** *vi, vt* to hoot (*BRIT*), honk (*US*)

km *abr* = **kilomètre**

km/h *abr* (= *kilomètres/heure*) ≈ mph

K.-O. (*fam*) *adj inv* shattered, knackered

Kosovo [kɔsɔvo] *nm* Kosovo

Koweit, Kuweit [kɔwɛt] *nm*: **le ~** Kuwait
k-way® [kawɛ] *nm* (lightweight nylon)
  cagoule
kyste [kist] *nm* cyst

l' [l] *art déf voir* **le**
la [la] *art déf voir* **le** ▷ *nm* (*Mus*) A; (*en chantant
  la gamme*) la
là [la] *adv* there; (*ici*) here; (*dans le temps*) then;
  elle n'est pas là she isn't here; **c'est là que**
  this is where; **là où** where; **de là** (*fig*) hence;
  par là (*fig*) by that; *voir aussi* **-ci**; **ce**; **celui**;
  là-bas *adv* there
laboratoire [labɔʀatwaʀ] *nm* laboratory;
  laboratoire de langues language laboratory
laborieux, -euse [labɔʀjø, jøz] *adj* (*tâche*)
  laborious
labourer *vt* to plough
labyrinthe [labiʀɛ̃t] *nm* labyrinth, maze
lac [lak] *nm* lake
lacet [lasɛ] *nm* (*de chaussure*) lace; (*de route*)
  sharp bend; (*piège*) snare
lâche [lɑʃ] *adj* (*poltron*) cowardly; (*desserré*)
  loose, slack ▷ *nm/f* coward
lâcher [lɑʃe] *vt* to let go of; (*ce qui tombe,
  abandonner*) to drop; (*oiseau, animal: libérer*)
  to release, set free; (*fig: mot, remarque*) to let
  slip, come out with ▷ *vi* (*freins*) to fail; **~ les
  amarres** (*Navig*) to cast off (the moorings); **~
  prise** to let go
lacrymogène [lakʀimɔʒɛn] *adj*: **gaz ~**
  teargas
lacune [lakyn] *nf* gap
là-dedans [ladədɑ̃] *adv* inside (there), in it;
  (*fig*) in that

là-dessous [ladsu] adv underneath, under there; (fig) behind that

là-dessus [ladsy] adv on there; (fig: sur ces mots) at that point; (: à ce sujet) about that

lagune [lagyn] nf lagoon

là-haut [lao] adv up there

laid, e [lɛ, lɛd] adj ugly; **laideur** nf ugliness no pl

lainage [lɛnaʒ] nm (vêtement) woollen garment; (étoffe) woollen material

laine [lɛn] nf wool

laïque [laik] adj lay, civil; (Scol) state cpd ▷ nm/ f layman(-woman)

laisse [lɛs] nf (de chien) lead, leash; **tenir en ~** to keep on a lead ou leash

laisser [lese] vt to leave ▷ vb aux: **~ qn faire** to let sb do; **se ~ aller** to let o.s. go; **laisse-toi faire** let me (ou him etc) do it; **laisser-aller** nm carelessness, slovenliness; **laissez-passer** nm inv pass

lait [lɛ] nm milk; **frère/sœur de ~** foster brother/sister; **lait concentré/condensé** condensed/evaporated milk; **lait écrémé/ entier** skimmed/full-cream (BRIT) ou whole milk; **laitage** nm dairy product; **laiterie** nf dairy; **laitier, -ière** adj dairy cpd ▷ nm/f milkman (dairywoman)

laiton [lɛtɔ̃] nm brass

laitue [lety] nf lettuce

lambeau, x [lɑ̃bo] nm scrap; **en ~x** in tatters, tattered

lame [lam] nf blade; (vague) wave; (lamelle) strip; **lame de fond** ground swell no pl; **lame de rasoir** razor blade; **lamelle** nf thin strip ou blade

lamentable [lamɑ̃tabl] adj appalling

lamenter [lamɑ̃te] vb: **se ~ (sur)** to moan (over)

lampadaire [lɑ̃padɛʀ] nm (de salon) standard lamp; (dans la rue) street lamp

lampe [lɑ̃p] nf lamp; (Tech) valve; **lampe à bronzer** sun lamp; **lampe à pétrole** oil lamp; **lampe de poche** torch (BRIT), flashlight (US); **lampe halogène** halogen lamp

lance [lɑ̃s] nf spear; **lance d'incendie** fire hose

lancée [lɑ̃se] nf: **être/continuer sur sa ~** to be under way/keep going

lancement [lɑ̃smɑ̃] nm launching

lance-pierres [lɑ̃spjɛʀ] nm inv catapult

lancer [lɑ̃se] nm (Sport) throwing no pl, throw ▷ vt to throw; (émettre; projeter) to throw out, send out; (produit, fusée, bateau, artiste) to launch; (injure) to hurl, fling; **se lancer** vi (prendre de l'élan) to build up speed; (se précipiter): **se ~ sur** ou **contre** to rush at; **se ~ dans** (discussion) to launch into; (aventure) to embark on; **~ qch à qn** to throw sth to sb; (de façon agressive) to throw sth at sb; **~ un cri** ou **un appel** to shout ou call out; **lancer du poids** putting the shot

landau [lɑ̃do] nm pram (BRIT), baby carriage (US)

lande [lɑ̃d] nf moor

langage [lɑ̃gaʒ] nm language

langouste [lɑ̃gust] nf crayfish inv; **langoustine** nf Dublin Bay prawn

langue [lɑ̃g] nf (Anat, Culin) tongue; (Ling) language; **tirer la ~ (à)** to stick one's tongue (at); **de ~ française** French-speaking; **quelles ~s parlez-vous?** what languages do you speak?; **langue maternelle** native language, mother tongue; **langues vivantes** modern languages

langueur [lɑ̃gœʀ] nf languidness

languir [lɑ̃giʀ] vi to languish; (conversation) to flag; **faire ~ qn** to keep sb waiting

lanière [lanjɛʀ] nf (de fouet) lash; (de sac, bretelle) strap

lanterne [lɑ̃tɛʀn] nf (portable) lantern; (électrique) light, lamp; (de voiture) (side)light

laper [lape] vt to lap up

lapidaire [lapidɛʀ] adj (fig) terse

lapin [lapɛ̃] nm rabbit; (peau) rabbitskin; (fourrure) cony; **poser un ~ à qn** (fam) to stand sb up

Laponie [laponi] nf Lapland

laps [laps] nm: **~ de temps** space of time, time no pl

laque [lak] nf (vernis) lacquer; (pour cheveux) hair spray

laquelle [lakɛl] pron voir **lequel**

larcin [laʀsɛ̃] nm theft

lard [laʀ] nm (bacon) (streaky) bacon; (graisse) fat

lardon [laʀdɔ̃] nm: **~s** chopped bacon

large [laʀʒ] adj wide, broad; (fig) generous ▷ adv: **calculer/voir ~** to allow extra/think big ▷ nm (largeur): **5 m de ~** 5 m wide ou in width; (mer): **le ~** the open sea; **au ~ de** off; **large d'esprit** broad-minded; **largement** adv widely; (de loin) greatly; (au moins) easily; (généreusement) generously; **c'est largement suffisant** that's ample; **largesse** nf generosity; **largesses** nfpl (dons) liberalities; **largeur** nf (qu'on mesure) width; (impression visuelle) wideness, width; (d'esprit) broadness

larguer [laʀge] vt to drop; **~ les amarres** to cast off (the moorings)

larme [laʀm] nf tear; (fam: goutte) drop; **en ~s** in tears; **larmoyer** vi (yeux) to water; (se plaindre) to whimper

larvé, e [laʀve] adj (fig) latent

laryngite [laʀɛ̃ʒit] nf laryngitis

las, lasse [lɑ, lɑs] adj weary

laser [lazɛʀ] nm: (rayon) **~** laser (beam); **chaîne** ou **platine ~** laser disc (player); **disque ~** laser disc

lasse [lɑs] adj voir **las**

lasser [lɑse] vt to weary, tire; **se lasser de** vt

to grow weary *ou* tired of

latéral, e, -aux [lateʀal, o] *adj* side *cpd*, lateral

latin, e [latɛ̃, in] *adj* Latin ▷ *nm/f*: **L~, e** Latin ▷ *nm* (*Ling*) Latin

latitude [latityd] *nf* latitude

lauréat, e [lɔʀea, at] *nm/f* winner

laurier [lɔʀje] *nm* (*Bot*) laurel; **feuille de ~** (*Culin*) bay leaf

lavable [lavabl] *adj* washable

lavabo [lavabo] *nm* washbasin; **lavabos** *nmpl* (*toilettes*) toilet *sg*

lavage [lavaʒ] *nm* washing *no pl*, wash; **lavage de cerveau** brainwashing *no pl*

lavande [lavɑ̃d] *nf* lavender

lave [lav] *nf* lava *no pl*

lave-linge [lavlɛ̃ʒ] *nm inv* washing machine

laver [lave] *vt* to wash; (*tache*) to wash off; **se laver** *vi* to have a wash, wash; **se ~ les mains/dents** to wash one's hands/clean one's teeth; **~ la vaisselle/le linge** to wash the dishes/clothes; **~ qn de** (*accusation*) to clear sb of; **laverie** *nf*: **laverie (automatique)** launderette; **lavette** *nf* dish cloth; (*fam*) drip; **laveur, -euse** *nm/f* cleaner; **lave-vaisselle** *nm inv* dishwasher; **lavoir** *nm* wash house; (*évier*) sink

laxatif, -ive [laksatif, iv] *adj, nm* laxative

layette [lɛjɛt] *nf* baby clothes

MOT-CLÉ

le [lə], **la**, **l'** (*pl* **les**) *art déf* **1** the; **le livre/la pomme/l'arbre** the book/the apple/the tree; **les étudiants** the students

2 (*noms abstraits*): **le courage/l'amour/la jeunesse** courage/love/youth

3 (*indiquant la possession*): **se casser la jambe** *etc* to break one's leg *etc*; **levez la main** put your hand up; **avoir les yeux gris/le nez rouge** to have grey eyes/a red nose

4 (*temps*): **le matin/soir** in the morning/evening; mornings/evenings; **le jeudi** *etc* (*d'habitude*) on Thursdays *etc*; (*ce jeudi-là etc*) on (the) Thursday

5 (*distribution, évaluation*) a, an; **10 euros le mètre/kilo** 10 euros a *ou* per metre/kilo; **le tiers/quart de** a third/quarter of

▷ *pron* **1** (*personne: mâle*) him; (*: femelle*) her; (*: pluriel*) them; **je le/la/les vois** I can see him/her/them

2 (*animal, chose: singulier*) it; (*: pluriel*) them; **je le** (*ou* **la**) **vois** I can see it; **je les vois** I can see them

3 (*remplaçant une phrase*): **je ne le savais pas** I didn't know (about it); **il était riche et ne l'est plus** he was once rich but no longer is

lécher [leʃe] *vt* to lick; (*laper: lait, eau*) to lick

ou lap up; **se ~ les doigts/lèvres** to lick one's fingers/lips; **lèche-vitrines** *nm*: **faire du lèche-vitrines** to go window-shopping

leçon [l(ə)sɔ̃] *nf* lesson; **faire la ~ à** (*fig*) to give a lecture to; **leçons de conduite** driving lessons; **leçons particulières** private lessons *ou* tuition *sg* (BRIT)

lecteur, -trice [lɛktœʀ, tʀis] *nm/f* reader; (*d'université*) foreign language assistant ▷ *nm* (*Tech*): **~ de cassettes/CD/DVD** cassette/CD/DVD player; **lecteur de disquette(s)** disk drive; **lecteur MP3** MP3 player

lecture [lɛktyʀ] *nf* reading

> Attention à ne pas traduire *lecture* par le mot anglais *lecture*.

ledit [lədi], **ladite** (*mpl* **lesdits**, *fpl* **lesdites**) *dét* the aforesaid

légal, e, -aux [legal, o] *adj* legal; **légaliser** *vt* to legalize; **légalité** *nf* law

légendaire [leʒɑ̃dɛʀ] *adj* legendary

légende [leʒɑ̃d] *nf* (*mythe*) legend; (*de carte, plan*) key; (*de dessin*) caption

léger, -ère [leʒe, ɛʀ] *adj* light; (*bruit, retard*) slight; (*personne: superficiel*) thoughtless; (*: volage*) free and easy; **à la légère** (*parler, agir*) rashly, thoughtlessly; **légèrement** *adv* (*s'habiller, bouger*) lightly; (*un peu*) slightly; **manger légèrement** to eat a light meal; **légèreté** *nf* lightness; (*d'une remarque*) flippancy

législatif, -ive [leʒislatif, iv] *adj* legislative; **législatives** *nfpl* general election *sg*

légitime [leʒitim] *adj* (*Jur*) lawful, legitimate; (*fig*) rightful, legitimate; **en état de ~ défense** in self-defence

legs [lɛg] *nm* legacy

léguer [lege] *vt*: **~ qch à qn** (*Jur*) to bequeath sth to sb

légume [legym] *nm* vegetable; **légumes secs** pulses; **légumes verts** green vegetables, greens

lendemain [lɑ̃dmɛ̃] *nm*: **le ~** the next *ou* following day; **le ~ matin/soir** the next *ou* following morning/evening; **le ~ de** the day after

lent, e [lɑ̃, lɑ̃t] *adj* slow; **lentement** *adv* slowly; **lenteur** *nf* slowness *no pl*

lentille [lɑ̃tij] *nf* (*Optique*) lens *sg*; (*Culin*) lentil; **lentilles de contact** contact lenses

léopard [leɔpaʀ] *nm* leopard

lèpre [lɛpʀ] *nf* leprosy

MOT-CLÉ

lequel, laquelle [ləkɛl, lakɛl] (*mpl* **lesquels**, *fpl* **lesquelles**) (*à + lequel = auquel, de + lequel = duquel etc*) *pron* **1** (*interrogatif*) which, which one; **lequel des deux?** which one?

2 (relatif: personne: sujet) who; (: objet, après préposition) whom; (: chose) which
▷ adj: **auquel cas** in which case

les [le] dét voir **le**

lesbienne [lɛsbjɛn] nf lesbian

léser [leze] vt to wrong

lésiner [lezine] vi: **ne pas ~ sur les moyens** (pour mariage etc) to push the boat out

lésion [lezjɔ̃] nf lesion, damage no pl

lessive [lesiv] nf (poudre) washing powder; (linge) washing no pl, wash; **lessiver** vt to wash; (fam: fatiguer) to tire out, exhaust

lest [lɛst] nm ballast

leste [lɛst] adj sprightly, nimble

lettre [lɛtʀ] nf letter; **lettres** nfpl (littérature) literature sg; (Scol) arts (subjects); **à la ~** literally; **en toutes ~s** in full; **lettre piégée** letter bomb

leucémie [løsemi] nf leukaemia

 MOT-CLÉ

leur [lœʀ] adj possessif their; **leur maison** their house; **leurs amis** their friends
▷ pron **1** (objet indirect) (to) them; **je leur ai dit la vérité** I told them the truth; **je le leur ai donné** I gave it to them, I gave them it
2 (possessif): **le(la) leur, les leurs** theirs

levain [ləvɛ̃] nm leaven

levé, e [ləve] adj: **être ~** to be up; **levée** nf (Postes) collection

lever [l(ə)ve] vt (vitre, bras etc) to raise; (soulever de terre, supprimer: interdiction, siège) to lift; (impôts, armée) to levy ▷ vi to rise ▷ nm: **au ~** on getting up; **se lever** vi to get up; (soleil) to rise; (jour) to break; (brouillard) to lift; **ça va se ~** (temps) it's going to clear up; **lever de soleil** sunrise; **lever du jour** daybreak

levier [ləvje] nm lever

lèvre [lɛvʀ] nf lip

lévrier [levʀije] nm greyhound

levure [l(ə)vyʀ] nf yeast; **levure chimique** baking powder

lexique [lɛksik] nm vocabulary; (glossaire) lexicon

lézard [lezaʀ] nm lizard

lézarde [lezaʀd] nf crack

liaison [ljɛzɔ̃] nf (rapport) connection; (transport) link; (amoureuse) affair; (Phonétique) liaison; **entrer/être en ~ avec** to get/be in contact with

liane [ljan] nf creeper

liasse [ljas] nf wad, bundle

Liban [libɑ̃] nm: **le ~** (the) Lebanon

libeller [libele] vt (chèque, mandat): **~ (au nom de)** to make out (to); (lettre) to word

libellule [libelyl] nf dragonfly

libéral, e, -aux [liberal, o] adj, nm/f liberal; **profession ~e** (liberal) profession

libérer [libeʀe] vt (délivrer) to free, liberate; (relâcher: prisonnier) to discharge, release; (: d'inhibitions) to liberate; (gaz) to release; **se libérer** vi (de rendez-vous) to get out of previous engagements

liberté [libɛʀte] nf freedom; (loisir) free time; **libertés** nfpl (privautés) liberties; **mettre/être en ~** to set/be free; **en ~ provisoire/surveillée/conditionnelle** on bail/probation/parole

libraire [libʀɛʀ] nm/f bookseller

librairie [libʀɛʀi] nf bookshop

> Attention à ne pas traduire **librairie** par **library**.

libre [libʀ] adj free; (route, voie) clear; (place, salle) free; (ligne) not engaged; (Scol) non-state; **~ de qch/de faire** free from sth/to do; **la place est ~?** is this seat free?; **libre arbitre** free will; **libre-échange** nm free trade; **libre-service** nm self-service store

Libye [libi] nf: **la ~** Libya

licence [lisɑ̃s] nf (permis) permit; (diplôme) degree; (liberté) liberty; **licencié, e** nm/f (Scol): **licencié ès lettres/en droit** ≈ Bachelor of Arts/Law

licenciement [lisɑ̃simɑ̃] nm redundancy

licencier [lisɑ̃sje] vt (débaucher) to make redundant, lay off; (renvoyer) to dismiss

licite [lisit] adj lawful

lie [li] nf dregs pl, sediment

lié, e [lje] adj: **très ~ avec** very friendly with ou close to

Liechtenstein [liʃtɛnʃtain] nm: **le ~** Liechtenstein

liège [ljɛʒ] nm cork

lien [ljɛ̃] nm (corde, fig: affectif) bond; (rapport) link, connection; **lien de parenté** family tie; **lien hypertexte** hyperlink

lier [lje] vt (attacher) to tie up; (joindre) to link up; (fig: unir, engager) to bind; **~ conversation (avec)** to strike up a conversation (with); **~ connaissance avec** to get to know

lierre [ljɛʀ] nm ivy

lieu, x [ljø] nm place; **lieux** nmpl (locaux) premises; (endroit: d'un accident etc) scene sg; **en ~ sûr** in a safe place; **en premier ~** in the first place; **en dernier ~** lastly; **avoir ~** to take place; **tenir ~ de** to serve as; **donner ~ à** to give rise to; **au ~ de** instead of; **arriver/être sur les ~x** to arrive at/be on the scene; **lieu commun** cliché; **lieu-dit** (pl **lieux-dits**) nm locality

lieutenant [ljøt(ə)nɑ̃] nm lieutenant

lièvre [ljɛvʀ] nm hare

ligament [ligamɑ̃] nm ligament

ligne [liɲ] nf (gén) line; (Transports: liaison) service; (: trajet) route; (silhouette) figure;

garder la ~ to keep one's figure; **entrer en ~ de compte** to come into it; **en ~** (*Inform*) online; **~ fixe** (*Tél*) land line (phone)

lignée [liɲe] *nf* line, lineage

ligoter [ligɔte] *vt* to tie up

ligue [lig] *nf* league

lilas [lila] *nm* lilac

limace [limas] *nf* slug

limande [limɑ̃d] *nf* dab

lime [lim] *nf* file; **lime à ongles** nail file; **limer** *vt* to file

limitation [limitasjɔ̃] *nf*: **limitation de vitesse** speed limit

limite [limit] *nf* (*de terrain*) boundary; (*partie ou point extrême*) limit; **à la ~** (*au pire*) if the worst comes (*ou* came) to the worst; **vitesse/charge ~** maximum speed/load; **cas ~** borderline case; **date ~** deadline; **date ~ de vente/consommation** sell-by/best-before date; **limiter** *vt* (*restreindre*) to limit, restrict; (*délimiter*) to border; **limitrophe** *adj* border *cpd*

limoger [limɔʒe] *vt* to dismiss

limon [limɔ̃] *nm* silt

limonade [limɔnad] *nf* lemonade

lin [lɛ̃] *nm* (*tissu*) linen

linceul [lɛ̃sœl] *nm* shroud

linge [lɛ̃ʒ] *nm* (*serviettes etc*) linen; (*lessive*) washing; (*aussi*: **~ de corps**) underwear; **lingerie** *nf* lingerie, underwear

lingot [lɛ̃go] *nm* ingot

linguistique [lɛ̃gɥistik] *adj* linguistic ▷ *nf* linguistics *sg*

lion, ne [ljɔ̃, ljɔn] *nm/f* lion (lioness); (*signe*): **le L~** Leo; **lionceau, x** *nm* lion cub

liqueur [likœr] *nf* liqueur

liquidation [likidasjɔ̃] *nf* (*vente*) sale

liquide [likid] *adj* liquid ▷ *nm* liquid; (*Comm*): **en ~** in ready money *ou* cash; **je n'ai pas de ~** I haven't got any cash; **liquider** *vt* to liquidate; (*Comm: articles*) to clear, sell off

lire [lir] *nf* (*monnaie*) lira ▷ *vt*, *vi* to read

lis [lis] *nm* = **lys**

Lisbonne [lizbɔn] *n* Lisbon

lisible [lizibl] *adj* legible

lisière [lizjɛr] *nf* (*de forêt*) edge

lisons [lizɔ̃] *vb voir* **lire**

lisse [lis] *adj* smooth

liste [list] *nf* list; **faire la ~ de** to list; **liste de mariage** wedding (present) list; **liste électorale** electoral roll; **listing** *nm* (*Inform*) printout

lit [li] *nm* bed; **petit ~, ~ à une place** single bed; **grand ~, ~ à deux places** double bed; **faire son ~** to make one's bed; **aller/se mettre au ~** to go to/get into bed; **lit de camp** campbed; **lit d'enfant** cot (*BRIT*), crib (*US*)

literie [litri] *nf* bedding, bedclothes *pl*

litige [litiʒ] *nm* dispute

litre [litr] *nm* litre

littéraire [literɛr] *adj* literary ▷ *nm/f* arts student; **elle est très ~** she's very literary

littéral, e, -aux [literal, o] *adj* literal

littérature [literatyr] *nf* literature

littoral, -aux [litɔral, o] *nm* coast

livide [livid] *adj* livid, pallid

livraison [livrɛzɔ̃] *nf* delivery

livre [livr] *nm* book ▷ *nf* (*monnaie*) pound; (*poids*) half a kilo, ≈ pound; **livre de poche** paperback

livré, e [livre] *adj*: **~ à soi-même** left to o.s. *ou* one's own devices

livrer [livre] *vt* (*Comm*) to deliver; (*otage, coupable*) to hand over; (*secret, information*) to give away; **se livrer à** (*se confier*) to confide in; (*se rendre, s'abandonner*) to give o.s. up to; (*faire: pratiques, actes*) to indulge in; (*enquête*) to carry out

livret [livrɛ] *nm* booklet; (*d'opéra*) libretto; **livret de caisse d'épargne** (savings) bankbook; **livret de famille** (official) family record book; **livret scolaire** (school) report book

livreur, -euse [livrœr, øz] *nm/f* delivery boy *ou* man/girl *ou* woman

local, e, -aux [lɔkal, o] *adj* local ▷ *nm* (*salle*) premises *pl*; *voir aussi* **locaux**; **localité** *nf* locality

locataire [lɔkatɛr] *nm/f* tenant; (*de chambre*) lodger

location [lɔkasjɔ̃] *nf* (*par le locataire, le loueur*) renting; (*par le propriétaire*) renting out, letting; (*Théâtre*) booking office; **"~ de voitures"** "car rental"; **habiter en ~** to live in rented accommodation; **prendre une ~ (pour les vacances)** to rent a house *etc* (for the holidays)

> Attention à ne pas traduire *location* par le mot anglais *location*.

locomotive [lɔkɔmɔtiv] *nf* locomotive, engine

locution [lɔkysjɔ̃] *nf* phrase

loge [lɔʒ] *nf* (*Théâtre: d'artiste*) dressing room; (: *de spectateurs*) box; (*de concierge, francmaçon*) lodge

logement [lɔʒmɑ̃] *nm* accommodation *no pl* (*BRIT*), accommodations *pl* (*US*); (*appartement*) flat (*BRIT*), apartment (*US*); (*Pol, Admin*): **le ~** housing *no pl*

loger [lɔʒe] *vt* to accommodate ▷ *vi* to live; **être logé, nourri** to have board and lodging; **se loger** *vr*: **trouver à se ~** to find somewhere to live; **se ~ dans** (*suj: balle, flèche*) to lodge itself in; **logeur, -euse** *nm/f* landlord(-lady)

logiciel [lɔʒisjɛl] *nm* software

logique [lɔʒik] *adj* logical ▷ *nf* logic

logo [lɔgo] *nm* logo

loi [lwa] *nf* law; **faire la ~** to lay down the law

loin [lwɛ̃] adv far; (dans le temps: futur) a long way off; (: passé) a long time ago; **plus ~** further; **~ de** far from; **c'est ~ d'ici?** is it far from here?; **au ~** far off; **de ~** from a distance; (fig: de beaucoup) by far

lointain, e [lwɛ̃tɛ̃, ɛn] adj faraway, distant; (dans le futur, passé) distant; (cause, parent) remote, distant ▷ nm: **dans le ~** in the distance

loir [lwaʀ] nm dormouse

Loire [lwaʀ] nf: **la ~** the (River) Loire

loisir [lwaziʀ] nm: **heures de ~** spare time; **loisirs** nmpl (temps libre) leisure sg; (activités) leisure activities; **avoir le ~ de faire** to have the time ou opportunity to do; **à ~** at leisure

londonien, ne [lɔ̃dɔnjɛ̃, jɛn] adj London cpd, of London ▷ nm/f: **L~, ne** Londoner

Londres [lɔ̃dʀ] n London

long, longue [lɔ̃, lɔ̃g] adj long ▷ adv: **en savoir ~** to know a great deal ▷ nm: **de 3 m de ~** 3 m long, 3 m in length; **ne pas faire ~ feu** not to last long; **(tout) le ~ de** (all) along; **tout au ~ de** (année, vie) throughout; **de ~ en large** (marcher) to and fro, up and down; voir aussi **longue**

longer [lɔ̃ʒe] vt to go (ou walk ou drive) along(side); (suj: mur, route) to border

longiligne [lɔ̃ʒiliɲ] adj long-limbed

longitude [lɔ̃ʒityd] nf longitude

longtemps [lɔ̃tɑ̃] adv (for) a long time, (for) long; **avant ~** before long; **pour** ou **pendant ~** for a long time; **mettre ~ à faire** to take a long time to do; **il en a pour ~?** will he be long?

longue [lɔ̃g] adj voir **long** ▷ nf: **à la ~** in the end; **longuement** adv (longtemps) for a long time; (en détail) at length

longueur [lɔ̃gœʀ] nf length; **longueurs** nfpl (fig: d'un film etc) tedious parts; **en ~** lengthwise; **tirer en ~** to drag on; **à ~ de journée** all day long

loquet [lɔkɛ] nm latch

lorgner [lɔʀɲe] vt to eye; (fig) to have one's eye on

lors [lɔʀ]: **~ de** prép at the time of; during

lorsque [lɔʀsk] conj when, as

losange [lɔzɑ̃ʒ] nm diamond

lot [lo] nm (part) share; (de loterie) prize; (fig: destin) fate, lot; (Comm, Inform) batch; **le gros ~** the jackpot

loterie [lɔtʀi] nf lottery

lotion [losjɔ̃] nf lotion; **lotion après rasage** aftershave (lotion)

lotissement [lɔtismɑ̃] nm housing development; (parcelle) plot, lot

loto [lɔto] nm lotto

lotte [lɔt] nf monkfish

louanges [lwɑ̃ʒ] nfpl praise sg

loubard [lubaʀ] (fam) nm lout

louche [luʃ] adj shady, fishy, dubious ▷ nf ladle; **loucher** vi to squint

louer [lwe] vt (maison: suj: propriétaire) to let, rent (out); (: locataire) to rent; (voiture etc: entreprise) to hire out (BRIT), rent (out); (: locataire) to hire, rent; (réserver) to book; (faire l'éloge de) to praise; **"à ~"** "to let" (BRIT), "for rent" (US); **je voudrais ~ une voiture** I'd like to hire (BRIT) ou rent (US) a car

loup [lu] nm wolf; **jeune ~** young go-getter

loupe [lup] nf magnifying glass; **à la ~** in minute detail

louper [lupe] (fam) vt (manquer) to miss; (examen) to flunk

lourd, e [luʀ, luʀd] adj, adv heavy; **c'est trop ~** it's too heavy; **~ de** (conséquences, menaces) charged with; **il fait ~** the weather is close, it's sultry; **lourdaud, e** (péj) adj clumsy; **lourdement** adv heavily

loutre [lutʀ] nf otter

louveteau, x [luv(ə)to] nm wolf-cub; (scout) cub (scout)

louvoyer [luvwaje] vi (fig) to hedge, evade the issue

loyal, e, -aux [lwajal, o] adj (fidèle) loyal, faithful; (fair-play) fair; **loyauté** nf loyalty, faithfulness; fairness

loyer [lwaje] nm rent

lu, e [ly] pp de **lire**

lubie [lybi] nf whim, craze

lubrifiant [lybʀifjɑ̃] nm lubricant

lubrifier [lybʀifje] vt to lubricate

lubrique [lybʀik] adj lecherous

lucarne [lykaʀn] nf skylight

lucide [lysid] adj lucid; (accidenté) conscious

lucratif, -ive [lykʀatif, iv] adj lucrative, profitable; **à but non ~** non profit-making

lueur [lɥœʀ] nf (pâle) (faint) light; (chatoyante) glimmer no pl; (fig) glimmer; gleam

luge [lyʒ] nf sledge (BRIT), sled (US)

lugubre [lygybʀ] adj gloomy, dismal

MOT-CLÉ

lui [lɥi] pron **1** (objet indirect: mâle) (to) him; (: femelle) (to) her; (: chose, animal) (to) it; **je lui ai parlé** I have spoken to him (ou to her); **il lui a offert un cadeau** he gave him (ou her) a present

2 (après préposition, comparatif: personne) him; (: chose, animal) it; **elle est contente de lui** she is pleased with him; **je la connais mieux que lui** I know her better than he does; I know her better than him; **ce livre est à lui** this book is his, this is his book; **c'est à lui de jouer** it's his turn ou go

3 (sujet, forme emphatique) he; **lui, il est à Paris** HE is in Paris; **c'est lui qui l'a fait** HE did it

4 (*objet, forme emphatique*) him; **c'est lui que j'attends** I'm waiting for HIM
5: **lui-même** himself; itself

luire [lɥiʀ] *vi* to shine; (*en rougeoyant*) to glow
lumière [lymjɛʀ] *nf* light; **mettre en ~** (*fig*) to highlight; **lumière du jour** daylight
luminaire [lyminɛʀ] *nm* lamp, light
lumineux, -euse [lyminø, øz] *adj* luminous; (*éclairé*) illuminated; (*ciel, couleur*) bright; (*rayon*) of light, light *cpd*; (*fig: regard*) radiant
lunatique [lynatik] *adj* whimsical, temperamental
lundi [lœdi] *nm* Monday; **on est ~** it's Monday; **le(s) ~(s)** on Mondays; "**à ~**" "see you on Monday"; **lundi de Pâques** Easter Monday
lune [lyn] *nf* moon; **lune de miel** honeymoon
lunette [lynɛt] *nf*: **~s** *nfpl* glasses, spectacles; (*protectrices*) goggles; **lunette arrière** (*Auto*) rear window; **lunettes de soleil** sunglasses; **lunettes noires** dark glasses
lustre [lystʀ] *nm* (*de plafond*) chandelier; (*fig: éclat*) lustre; **lustrer** *vt* to shine
luth [lyt] *nm* lute
lutin [lytɛ̃] *nm* imp, goblin
lutte [lyt] *nf* (*conflit*) struggle; (*sport*) wrestling; **lutter** *vi* to fight, struggle
luxe [lyks] *nm* luxury; **de ~** luxury *cpd*
Luxembourg [lyksɑ̃buʀ] *nm*: **le ~** Luxembourg
luxer [lykse] *vt*: **se ~ l'épaule** to dislocate one's shoulder
luxueux, -euse [lyksɥø, øz] *adj* luxurious
lycée [lise] *nm* ≈ secondary school; **lycéen, ne** *nm/f* secondary school pupil
Lyon [ljɔ̃] *n* Lyons
lyophilisé, e [ljɔfilize] *adj* (*café*) freeze-dried
lyrique [liʀik] *adj* lyrical; (*Opéra*) lyric; **artiste ~** opera singer
lys [lis] *nm* lily

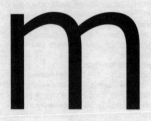

M *abr* = **Monsieur**
m' [m] *pron voir* **me**
ma [ma] *adj voir* **mon**
macaron [makaʀɔ̃] *nm* (*gâteau*) macaroon; (*insigne*) (round) badge
macaronis [makaʀɔni] *nmpl* macaroni *sg*; **~ au fromage** *ou* **en gratin** macaroni cheese (*BRIT*), macaroni and cheese (*US*)
macédoine [masedwan] *nf*: **~ de fruits** fruit salad; **~ de légumes** mixed vegetables; **la M~** Macedonia
macérer [masere] *vi, vt* to macerate; (*dans du vinaigre*) to pickle
mâcher [maʃe] *vt* to chew; **ne pas ~ ses mots** not to mince one's words
machin [maʃɛ̃] (*fam*) *nm* thing(umajig); (*personne*): **M~(e)** *nm(f)* what's-his-(*ou* her)-name
machinal, e, -aux [maʃinal, o] *adj* mechanical, automatic
machination [maʃinasjɔ̃] *nf* frame-up
machine [maʃin] *nf* machine; (*locomotive*) engine; **machine à laver/coudre** washing/sewing machine; **machine à sous** fruit machine
mâchoire [maʃwaʀ] *nf* jaw
mâchonner [maʃɔne] *vt* to chew (at)
maçon [masɔ̃] *nm* builder; (*poseur de briques*) bricklayer; **maçonnerie** *nf* (*murs*) brickwork; (*pierres*) masonry, stonework

Madagascar [madagaskaʀ] nf
Madagascar

Madame [madam] (pl **Mesdames**) nf:
~ **Dupont** Mrs Dupont; **occupez-vous
de ~/Monsieur/Mademoiselle** please
serve this lady/gentleman/(young) lady;
bonjour ~/Monsieur/Mademoiselle
good morning; (ton déférent) good morning
Madam/Sir/Madam; (le nom est connu) good
morning Mrs/Mr/Miss X; **~/Monsieur/
Mademoiselle!** (pour appeler) Madam/Sir/
Miss!; **~/Monsieur/Mademoiselle** (sur lettre)
Dear Madam/Sir/Madam; **chère ~/cher
Monsieur/chère Mademoiselle** Dear Mrs/
Mr/Miss X; **Mesdames** Ladies; **mesdames,
mesdemoiselles, messieurs** ladies and
gentlemen

madeleine [madlɛn] nf madeleine, small
sponge cake

Mademoiselle [madmwazɛl] (pl
Mesdemoiselles) nf Miss; voir aussi
Madame

madère [madɛʀ] nm Madeira (wine)

Madrid [madʀid] n Madrid

magasin [magazɛ̃] nm (boutique) shop;
(entrepôt) warehouse; **en ~** (Comm) in
stock

magazine [magazin] nm magazine

Maghreb [magʀɛb] nm: **le ~** North Africa;
maghrébin, e adj North African ▷ nm/f:
Maghrébin, e North African

magicien, ne [maʒisjɛ̃, jɛn] nm/f
magician

magie [maʒi] nf magic; **magique** adj magic;
(enchanteur) magical

magistral, e, -aux [maʒistʀal, o] adj (œuvre,
adresse) masterly; (ton) authoritative; **cours
~** lecture

magistrat [maʒistʀa] nm magistrate

magnétique [maɲetik] adj magnetic

magnétophone [maɲetɔfɔn] nm tape
recorder; **magnétophone à cassettes**
cassette recorder

magnétoscope [maɲetɔskɔp] nm video-
tape recorder

magnifique [maɲifik] adj
magnificent

magret [magʀɛ] nm: **~ de canard** duck
steaklet

mai [mɛ] nm May

maigre [mɛgʀ] adj (very) thin, skinny; (viande)
lean; (fromage) low-fat; (végétation) thin,
sparse; (fig) poor, meagre, skimpy; **jours ~s**
days of abstinence, fish days; **maigreur** nf
thinness; **maigrir** vi to get thinner, lose
weight; **maigrir de 2 kilos** to lose 2 kilos

mail [mɛl] nm e-mail

maille [maj] nf stitch; **maille à l'endroit/
l'envers** plain/purl stitch

maillet [majɛ] nm mallet

maillon [majɔ̃] nm link

maillot [majo] nm (aussi: **~ de corps**) vest; (de
sportif) jersey; **maillot de bain** swimming ou
bathing (BRIT) costume, swimsuit; (d'homme)
(swimming ou bathing (BRIT)) trunks pl

main [mɛ̃] nf hand; **à la ~** (tenir, avoir) in one's
hand; (faire, tricoter etc) by hand; **se donner la
~** to hold hands; **donner** ou **tendre la ~ à qn**
to hold out one's hand to sb; **se serrer la ~** to
shake hands; **serrer la ~ à qn** to shake hands
with sb; **sous la ~** to ou at hand; **haut les ~s!**
hands up!; **attaque à ~ armée** armed attack;
à remettre en ~s propres to be delivered
personally; **mettre la dernière ~ à** to put the
finishing touches to; **se faire/perdre la ~** to
get one's hand in/lose one's touch; **avoir qch
bien en ~** to have (got) the hang of sth; **main-
d'œuvre** nf manpower, labour; **mainmise** nf
(fig): **mainmise sur** complete hold on; **mains
libres** adj inv (téléphone, kit) hands-free

maint, e [mɛ̃, mɛ̃t] adj many a; **~s** many; **à
~es reprises** time and (time) again

maintenant [mɛ̃t(ə)nɑ̃] adv now;
(actuellement) nowadays

maintenir [mɛ̃t(ə)niʀ] vt (retenir, soutenir)
to support; (contenir: foule etc) to hold back;
(conserver, affirmer) to maintain; **se maintenir**
vi (prix) to keep steady; (amélioration) to persist

maintien [mɛ̃tjɛ̃] nm (sauvegarde)
maintenance; (attitude) bearing

maire [mɛʀ] nm mayor; **mairie** nf (bâtiment)
town hall; (administration) town council

mais [mɛ] conj but; **~ non!** of course not!; **~**

m

enfin but after all; (*indignation*) look here!
maïs [mais] *nm* maize (BRIT), corn (US)
maison [mɛzɔ̃] *nf* house; (*chez-soi*) home;
(*Comm*) firm ▷ *adj inv* (*Culin*) home-made;
(*fig*) in-house, own; **à la ~** at home; (*direction*)
home; **maison de repos** convalescent home;
maison de retraite old people's home;
maison close *ou* **de passe** brothel; **maison
de santé** mental home; **maison des jeunes**
≈ youth club; **maison mère** parent company
maître, -esse [mɛtʀ, mɛtʀɛs] *nm/f*
master (mistress); (*Scol*) teacher,
schoolmaster(-mistress) ▷ *nm* (*peintre etc*)
master; (*titre*): **M~** Maître, *term of address gen
for a barrister* ▷ *adj* (*principal, essentiel*) main;
être ~ de (*soi, situation*) to be in control of; **une
~sse femme** a managing woman; **maître
chanteur** blackmailer; **maître d'école**
schoolmaster; **maître d'hôtel** (*domestique*)
butler; (*d'hôtel*) head waiter; **maître
nageur** lifeguard; **maîtresse** *nf* (*amante*)
mistress; **maîtresse (d'école)** teacher,
(school)mistress; **maîtresse de maison**
hostess; (*ménagère*) housewife
maîtrise [metʀiz] *nf* (*aussi*: **~ de soi**)
self-control, self-possession; (*habileté*) skill,
mastery; (*suprématie*) mastery, command;
(*diplôme*) ≈ master's degree; **maîtriser** *vt*
(*cheval, incendie*) to (bring under) control;
(*sujet*) to master; (*émotion*) to control, master;
se maîtriser to control o.s.
majestueux, -euse [maʒɛstɥø, øz] *adj*
majestic
majeur, e [maʒœʀ] *adj* (*important*) major; (*Jur*)
of age ▷ *nm* (*doigt*) middle finger; **en ~e partie**
for the most part; **la ~e partie de** most of
majorer [maʒɔʀe] *vt* to increase
majoritaire [maʒɔʀitɛʀ] *adj* majority *cpd*
majorité [maʒɔʀite] *nf* (*gén*) majority; (*parti*)
party in power; **en ~** mainly; **avoir la ~** to have
the majority
majuscule [maʒyskyl] *adj, nf*: **(lettre) ~**
capital (letter)
mal [mal, mo] (*pl* **maux**) *nm* (*opposé au bien*)
evil; (*tort, dommage*) harm; (*douleur physique*)
pain, ache; (*maladie*) illness, sickness *no pl*
▷ *adv* badly ▷ *adj* bad, wrong; **être ~ à l'aise**
to be uncomfortable; **être ~ avec qn** to
be on bad terms with sb; **il a ~ compris** he
misunderstood; **se sentir** *ou* **se trouver ~**
to feel ill *ou* unwell; **dire/penser du ~ de** to
speak/think ill of; **ne voir aucun ~ à** to see
no harm in, see nothing wrong in; **faire ~ à
qn** to hurt sb; **se faire ~** to hurt o.s.; **avoir
du ~ à faire qch** to have trouble doing sth; **se
donner du ~ pour faire qch** to go to a lot of
trouble to do sth; **ça fait ~** it hurts; **j'ai ~ au
dos** my back hurts; **avoir ~ à la tête/à la
gorge/aux dents** to have a headache/a sore

throat/toothache; **avoir le ~ du pays** to be
homesick; *voir aussi* **cœur**; **maux**; **mal de mer**
seasickness; **mal en point** in a bad state
malade [malad] *adj* ill, sick; (*poitrine, jambe*)
bad; (*plante*) diseased ▷ *nm/f* invalid, sick
person; (*à l'hôpital etc*) patient; **tomber ~** to
fall ill; **être ~ du cœur** to have heart trouble
ou a bad heart; **malade mental** mentally ill
person; **maladie** *nf* (*spécifique*) disease, illness;
(*mauvaise santé*) illness, sickness; **maladif, -ive**
adj sickly; (*curiosité, besoin*) pathological
maladresse [maladʀɛs] *nf* clumsiness *no pl*;
(*gaffe*) blunder
maladroit, e [maladʀwa, wat] *adj* clumsy
malaise [malɛz] *nm* (*Méd*) feeling of faintness;
(*fig*) uneasiness, malaise; **avoir un ~** to feel
faint
Malaisie [malɛzi] *nf*: **la ~** Malaysia
malaria [malaʀja] *nf* malaria
malaxer [malakse] *vt* (*pétrir*) to knead;
(*mélanger*) to mix
malbouffe [malbuf] (*fam*) *nf*: **la ~** junk food
malchance [malʃɑ̃s] *nf* misfortune, ill luck *no
pl*; **par ~** unfortunately; **malchanceux, -euse**
adj unlucky
mâle [mɑl] *adj* (*aussi Élec, Tech*) male; (*viril: voix,
traits*) manly ▷ *nm* male
malédiction [malediksjɔ̃] *nf* curse
mal...: **malentendant, e** *nm/f*: **les
malentendants** the hard of hearing;
malentendu *nm* misunderstanding; **il
y a eu un malentendu** there's been a
misunderstanding; **malfaçon** *nf* fault;
malfaisant, e *adj* evil, harmful; **malfaiteur**
nm lawbreaker, criminal; (*voleur*) burglar, thief;
malfamé, e *adj* disreputable
malgache [malgaʃ] *adj* Madagascan,
Malagasy ▷ *nm/f*: **M~** Madagascan, Malagasy
▷ *nm* (*Ling*) Malagasy
malgré [malgʀe] *prép* in spite of, despite; **~
tout** all the same
malheur [malœʀ] *nm* (*situation*) adversity,
misfortune; (*événement*) misfortune; (*:
très grave*) disaster, tragedy; **faire un ~** to
be a smash hit; **malheureusement** *adv*
unfortunately; **malheureux, -euse** *adj* (*triste*)
unhappy, miserable; (*infortuné, regrettable*)
unfortunate; (*malchanceux*) unlucky;
(*insignifiant*) wretched ▷ *nm/f* poor soul
malhonnête [malɔnɛt] *adj* dishonest;
malhonnêteté *nf* dishonesty
malice [malis] *nf* mischievousness;
(*méchanceté*): **par ~** out of malice *ou* spite; **sans
~** guileless; **malicieux, -euse** *adj* mischievous
  Attention à ne pas traduire *malicieux*
  par *malicious*.
malin, -igne [malɛ̃, maliɲ] *adj* (*futé: f gén:
aussi*: **maline**) smart, shrewd; (*Méd*) malignant
malingre [malɛ̃gʀ] *adj* puny

malle [mal] nf trunk; **mallette** nf (small) suitcase; (porte-documents) attaché case

malmener [malməne] vt to manhandle; (fig) to give a rough handling to

malodorant, e [malɔdɔrɑ̃, ɑ̃t] adj foul- ou ill-smelling

malpoli, e [malpɔli] adj impolite

malsain, e [malsɛ̃, ɛn] adj unhealthy

malt [malt] nm malt

Malte [malt] nf Malta

maltraiter [maltrete] vt to manhandle, ill-treat

malveillance [malvejɑ̃s] nf (animosité) ill will; (intention de nuire) malevolence

malversation [malvɛrsasjɔ̃] nf embezzlement

maman [mamɑ̃] nf mum(my), mother

mamelle [mamɛl] nf teat

mamelon [mam(ə)lɔ̃] nm (Anat) nipple

mamie [mami] (fam) nf granny

mammifère [mamifɛr] nm mammal

mammouth [mamut] nm mammoth

manche [mɑ̃ʃ] nf (de vêtement) sleeve; (d'un jeu, tournoi) round; (Géo): **la M~** the Channel ▷ nm (d'outil, casserole) handle; (de pelle, pioche etc) shaft; **à ~s courtes/longues** short-/long-sleeved; **manche à balai** broomstick; (Inform, Aviat) joystick m inv

manchette [mɑ̃ʃɛt] nf (de chemise) cuff; (coup) forearm blow; (titre) headline

manchot [mɑ̃ʃo] nm one-armed man; armless man; (Zool) penguin

mandarine [mɑ̃darin] nf mandarin (orange), tangerine

mandat [mɑ̃da] nm (postal) postal ou money order; (d'un député etc) mandate; (procuration) power of attorney, proxy; (Police) warrant; **mandat d'arrêt** warrant for arrest; **mandat de perquisition** search warrant; **mandataire** nm/f (représentant) representative; (Jur) proxy

manège [manɛʒ] nm riding school; (à la foire) roundabout, merry-go-round; (fig) game, ploy

manette [manɛt] nf lever, tap; **manette de jeu** joystick

mangeable [mɑ̃ʒabl] adj edible, eatable

mangeoire [mɑ̃ʒwar] nf trough, manger

manger [mɑ̃ʒe] vt to eat; (ronger: suj: rouille etc) to eat into ou away ▷ vi to eat; **donner à ~ à** (enfant) to feed; **est-ce qu'on peut ~ quelque chose?** can we have something to eat?

mangue [mɑ̃g] nf mango

maniable [manjabl] adj (outil) handy; (voiture, voilier) easy to handle

maniaque [manjak] adj finicky, fussy ▷ nm/f (méticuleux) fusspot; (fou) maniac

manie [mani] nf (tic) odd habit; (obsession) mania; **avoir la ~ de** to be obsessive about

manier [manje] vt to handle

manière [manjɛr] nf (façon) way, manner; **manières** nfpl (attitude) manners; (chichis) fuss sg; **de ~ à** so as to; **de cette ~** in this way ou manner; **d'une certaine ~** in a way; **de toute ~** in any case; **d'une ~ générale** generally speaking, as a general rule

maniéré, e [manjere] adj affected

manifestant, e [manifɛstɑ̃, ɑ̃t] nm/f demonstrator

manifestation [manifɛstasjɔ̃] nf (de joie, mécontentement) expression, demonstration; (symptôme) outward sign; (culturelle etc) event; (Pol) demonstration

manifeste [manifɛst] adj obvious, evident ▷ nm manifesto; **manifester** vt (volonté, intentions) to show, indicate; (joie, peur) to express, show ▷ vi to demonstrate; **se manifester** vi (émotion) to show ou express itself; (difficultés) to arise; (symptômes) to appear

manigancer [manigɑ̃se] vt to plot

manipulation [manipylasjɔ̃] nf handling; (Pol, génétique) manipulation

manipuler [manipyle] vt to handle; (fig) to manipulate

manivelle [manivɛl] nf crank

mannequin [mankɛ̃] nm (Couture) dummy; (Mode) model

manœuvre [manœvr] nf (gén) manoeuvre (BRIT), maneuver (US) ▷ nm labourer; **manœuvrer** vt to manoeuvre (BRIT), maneuver (US); (levier, machine) to operate ▷ vi to manoeuvre

manoir [manwar] nm manor ou country house

manque [mɑ̃k] nm (insuffisance): **~ de** lack of; (vide) emptiness, gap; (Méd) withdrawal; **être en état de ~** to suffer withdrawal symptoms

manqué, e [mɑ̃ke] adj failed; **garçon ~** tomboy

manquer [mɑ̃ke] vi (faire défaut) to be lacking; (être absent) to be missing; (échouer) to fail ▷ vt to miss ▷ vb impers: **il (nous) manque encore 10 euros** we are still 10 euros short; **il manque des pages (au livre)** there are some pages missing (from the book); **il/cela me manque** I miss him/this; **~ à** (règles etc) to be in breach of, fail to observe; **~ de** to lack; **je ne ~ai pas de le lui dire** I'll be sure to tell him; **il a manqué (de) se tuer** he very nearly got killed

mansarde [mɑ̃sard] nf attic; **mansardé, e** adj: **chambre mansardée** attic room

manteau, x [mɑ̃to] nm coat

manucure [manykyr] nf manicurist

manuel, le [manɥɛl] adj manual ▷ nm (ouvrage) manual, handbook

manufacture [manyfaktyr] nf factory; **manufacturé, e** adj manufactured

manuscrit, e [manyskri, it] adj handwritten

▷ *nm* manuscript

manutention [manytɑ̃sjɔ̃] *nf* (*Comm*) handling

mappemonde [mapmɔ̃d] *nf* (*plane*) map of the world; (*sphère*) globe

maquereau, x [makʀo] *nm* (*Zool*) mackerel *inv*; (*fam*) pimp

maquette [maket] *nf* (*à échelle réduite*) (scale) model; (*d'une page illustrée*) paste-up

maquillage [makijaʒ] *nm* making up; (*crème etc*) make-up

maquiller [makije] *vt* (*personne, visage*) to make up; (*truquer: passeport, statistique*) to fake; (: *voiture volée*) to do over (*respray etc*); **se maquiller** *vi* to make up (one's face)

maquis [maki] *nm* (*Géo*) scrub; (*Mil*) maquis, underground fighting *no pl*

maraîcher, -ère [maʀeʃe, ɛʀ] *adj*: **cultures maraîchères** market gardening *sg* ▷ *nm/f* market gardener

marais [maʀɛ] *nm* marsh, swamp

marasme [maʀasm] *nm* stagnation, slump

marathon [maʀatɔ̃] *nm* marathon

marbre [maʀbʀ] *nm* marble

marc [maʀ] *nm* (*de raisin, pommes*) marc

marchand, e [maʀʃɑ̃, ɑ̃d] *nm/f* shopkeeper, tradesman(-woman); (*au marché*) stallholder; (*de vins, charbon*) merchant ▷ *adj*: **prix/valeur ~(e)** market price/value; **marchand de fruits** fruiterer (BRIT), fruit seller (US); **marchand de journaux** newsagent; **marchand de légumes** greengrocer (BRIT), produce dealer (US); **marchand de poissons** fishmonger (BRIT), fish seller (US); **marchander** *vi* to bargain, haggle; **marchandise** *nf* goods *pl*, merchandise *no pl*

marche [maʀʃ] *nf* (*d'escalier*) step; (*activité*) walking; (*promenade, trajet, allure*) walk; (*démarche*) walk, gait; (*Mil etc, Mus*) march; (*fonctionnement*) running; (*des événements*) course; **dans le sens de la ~** (*Rail*) facing the engine; **en ~** (*monter etc*) while the vehicle is moving *ou* in motion; **mettre en ~** to start; **se mettre en ~** (*personne*) to get moving; (*machine*) to start; **être en état de ~** to be in working order; **marche à suivre** (*correct*) procedure; **marche arrière** reverse (gear); **faire marche arrière** to reverse; (*fig*) to backtrack, back-pedal

marché [maʀʃe] *nm* market; (*transaction*) bargain, deal; **faire du ~ noir** to buy and sell on the black market; **marché aux puces** flea market

marcher [maʀʃe] *vi* to walk; (*Mil*) to march; (*aller: voiture, train, affaires*) to go; (*prospérer*) to go well; (*fonctionner*) to work, run; (*fam: consentir*) to go along, agree; (: *croire naïvement*) to be taken in; **faire ~ qn** (*taquiner*) to pull sb's leg; (*tromper*) to lead sb up the garden path;

comment est-ce que ça marche? how does this work?; **marcheur, -euse** *nm/f* walker

mardi [maʀdi] *nm* Tuesday; **Mardi gras** Shrove Tuesday

mare [maʀ] *nf* pond; (*flaque*) pool

marécage [maʀekaʒ] *nm* marsh, swamp; **marécageux, -euse** *adj* marshy

maréchal, -aux [maʀeʃal, o] *nm* marshal

marée [maʀe] *nf* tide; (*poissons*) fresh (sea) fish; **marée haute/basse** high/low tide; **marée noire** oil slick

marelle [maʀɛl] *nf*: (**jouer à**) **la ~** (to play) hopscotch

margarine [maʀgaʀin] *nf* margarine

marge [maʀʒ] *nf* margin; **en ~ de** (*fig*) on the fringe of; **marge bénéficiaire** profit margin

marginal, e, -aux [maʀʒinal, o] *nm/f* (*original*) eccentric; (*déshérité*) dropout

marguerite [maʀgəʀit] *nf* marguerite, (oxeye) daisy; (*d'imprimante*) daisy-wheel

mari [maʀi] *nm* husband

mariage [maʀjaʒ] *nm* marriage; (*noce*) wedding; **mariage civil/religieux** registry office (BRIT) *ou* civil wedding/church wedding

marié, e [maʀje] *adj* married ▷ *nm* (bride)groom; **les ~s** the bride and groom; **les (jeunes) ~s** the newly-weds

marier [maʀje] *vt* to marry; (*fig*) to blend; **se ~ (avec)** to marry, get married (to)

marin, e [maʀɛ̃, in] *adj* sea *cpd*, marine ▷ *nm* sailor

marine [maʀin] *adj* voir **marin** ▷ *adj inv* navy (blue) ▷ *nm* (*Mil*) marine ▷ *nf* navy; **marine marchande** merchant navy

mariner [maʀine] *vt*: **faire ~** to marinade

marionnette [maʀjɔnɛt] *nf* puppet

maritalement [maʀitalmɑ̃] *adv*: **vivre ~** to live as husband and wife

maritime [maʀitim] *adj* sea *cpd*, maritime

mark [maʀk] *nm* mark

marmelade [maʀmələd] *nf* stewed fruit, compote; **marmelade d'oranges** marmalade

marmite [maʀmit] *nf* (*cooking-)pot

marmonner [maʀmɔne] *vt, vi* to mumble, mutter

marmotter [maʀmɔte] *vt* to mumble

Maroc [maʀɔk] *nm*: **le ~** Morocco; **marocain, e** [maʀɔkɛ̃, ɛn] *adj* Moroccan ▷ *nm/f*: **Marocain, e** Moroccan

maroquinerie [maʀɔkinʀi] *nf* (*articles*) fine leather goods *pl*; (*boutique*) shop selling fine leather goods

marquant, e [maʀkɑ̃, ɑ̃t] *adj* outstanding

marque [maʀk] *nf* mark; (*Comm: de nourriture*) brand; (: *de voiture, produits manufacturés*) make; (*de disques*) label; **de ~** (*produits*) high-class; (*visiteur etc*) distinguished, well-known; **une grande ~ de vin** a well-known brand of wine; **marque de fabrique** trademark;

marque déposée registered trademark

marquer [maʀke] vt to mark; (inscrire) to write down; (bétail) to brand; (Sport: but etc) to score; (: joueur) to mark; (accentuer: taille etc) to emphasize; (manifester: refus, intérêt) to show ▷ vi (événement) to stand out, be outstanding; (Sport) to score; **~ les points** to keep the score

marqueterie [maʀkɛtʀi] nf inlaid work, marquetry

marquis [maʀki] nm marquis, marquess

marraine [maʀɛn] nf godmother

marrant, e [maʀɑ̃, ɑ̃t] (fam) adj funny

marre [maʀ] (fam) adv: **en avoir ~ de** to be fed up with

marrer [maʀe]: **se ~** (fam) vi to have a (good) laugh

marron [maʀɔ̃] nm (fruit) chestnut ▷ adj inv brown; **marrons glacés** candied chestnuts; **marronnier** nm chestnut (tree)

mars [maʀs] nm March

Marseille [maʀsɛj] n Marseilles

marteau, x [maʀto] nm hammer; **être ~** (fam) to be nuts; **marteau-piqueur** nm pneumatic drill

marteler [maʀtəle] vt to hammer

martien, ne [maʀsjɛ̃, jɛn] adj Martian, of ou from Mars

martyr, e [maʀtiʀ] nm/f martyr ▷ adj: **enfants ~s** battered children; **martyre** nm martyrdom; (fig: sens affaibli) agony, torture; **martyriser** vt (Rel) to martyr; (fig) to bully; (enfant) to batter, beat

marxiste [maʀksist] adj, nm/f Marxist

mascara [maskaʀa] nm mascara

masculin, e [maskylɛ̃, in] adj masculine; (sexe, population) male; (équipe, vêtements) men's; (viril) manly ▷ nm masculine

masochiste [mazɔʃist] adj masochistic

masque [mask] nm mask; **masque de beauté** face pack ou mask; **masque de plongée** diving mask; **masquer** vt (cacher: paysage, porte) to hide, conceal; (dissimuler: vérité, projet) to mask, obscure

massacre [masakʀ] nm massacre, slaughter; **massacrer** vt to massacre, slaughter; (fam: texte etc) to murder

massage [masaʒ] nm massage

masse [mas] nf mass; (Élec) earth; (maillet) sledgehammer; (péj): **la ~** the masses pl; **une ~ de** (fam) masses ou loads of; **en ~** adv (acheter) in bulk; (en foule) en masse ▷ adj (exécutions, production) mass cpd

masser [mase] vt (assembler: gens) to gather; (pétrir) to massage; **se masser** vi (foule) to gather; **masseur, -euse** nm/f masseur(-euse)

massif, -ive [masif, iv] adj (porte) solid, massive; (visage) heavy, large; (bois, or) solid; (dose) massive; (déportations etc) mass cpd ▷ nm (montagneux) massif; (de fleurs) clump, bank; **le M~ Central** the Massif Central

massue [masy] nf club, bludgeon

mastic [mastik] nm (pour vitres) putty; (pour fentes) filler

mastiquer [mastike] vt (aliment) to chew, masticate

mat, e [mat] adj (couleur, métal) mat(t); (bruit, son) dull ▷ adj inv (Échecs): **être ~** to be checkmate

mât [mɑ] nm (Navig) mast; (poteau) pole, post

match [matʃ] nm match; **faire ~ nul** to draw; **match aller** first leg; **match retour** second leg, return match

matelas [mat(ə)lɑ] nm mattress; **matelas pneumatique** air bed ou mattress

matelot [mat(ə)lo] nm sailor, seaman

mater [mate] vt (personne) to bring to heel, subdue; (révolte) to put down

matérialiser [mateʀjalize]: **se matérialiser** vi to materialize

matérialiste [mateʀjalist] adj materialistic

matériau [mateʀjo] nm material; **matériaux** nmpl material(s)

matériel, le [mateʀjɛl] adj material ▷ nm equipment no pl; (de camping etc) gear no pl; (Inform) hardware

maternel, le [mateʀnɛl] adj (amour, geste) motherly, maternal; (grand-père, oncle) maternal; **maternelle** nf (aussi: **école maternelle**) (state) nursery school

maternité [mateʀnite] nf (établissement) maternity hospital; (état de mère) motherhood, maternity; (grossesse) pregnancy; **congé de ~** maternity leave

mathématique [matematik] adj mathematical; **mathématiques** nfpl (science) mathematics sg

maths [mat] (fam) nfpl maths

matière [matjeʀ] nf matter; (Comm, Tech) material, matter no pl; (fig: d'un livre etc) subject matter, material; (Scol) subject; **en ~ de** as regards; **matières grasses** fat content sg; **matières premières** raw materials

Matignon [matiɲɔ̃] nm: **(l'hôtel) ~** the French Prime Minister's residence

matin [matɛ̃] nm, adv morning; **le ~** (pendant le matin) in the morning; **demain/hier/ dimanche ~** tomorrow/yesterday/Sunday morning; **tous les ~s** every morning; **une heure du ~** one o'clock in the morning; **du ~ au soir** from morning till night; **de bon** ou **grand ~** early in the morning; **matinal, e, -aux** adj (toilette, gymnastique) morning cpd; **être matinal** (personne) to be up early; to be an early riser; **matinée** nf morning; (spectacle) matinée

matou [matu] nm tom(cat)

matraque [matʀak] nf (de policier) truncheon (BRIT), billy (US)

m

matricule [matʀikyl] *nm* (*Mil*) regimental number; (*Admin*) reference number

matrimonial, e, -aux [matʀimɔnjal, jo] *adj* marital, marriage *cpd*

maudit, e [modi, -it] (*fam*) *adj* (*satané*) blasted, confounded

maugréer [mogʀee] *vi* to grumble

maussade [mosad] *adj* sullen; (*temps*) gloomy

mauvais, e [mɔvɛ, ɛz] *adj* bad; (*faux*): **le ~ numéro/moment** the wrong number/ moment; (*méchant, malveillant*) malicious, spiteful ▷ *adv*: **il fait ~** the weather is bad; **sentir ~** to have a nasty smell, smell nasty; **la mer est ~e** the sea is rough; **mauvais joueur** bad loser; **mauvaise herbe** weed; **mauvaise langue** gossip, scandalmonger (BRIT); **mauvaise plaisanterie** nasty trick

mauve [mov] *adj* mauve

maux [mo] *nmpl de* **mal**

maximum [maksimɔm] *adj, nm* maximum; **au ~** (*le plus possible*) as much as one can; (*tout au plus*) at the (very) most *ou* maximum; **faire le ~** to do one's level best

mayonnaise [majɔnɛz] *nf* mayonnaise

mazout [mazut] *nm* (fuel) oil

me, m' [m(ə)] *pron* (*direct: téléphoner, attendre etc*) me; (*indirect: parler, donner etc*) (to) me; (*réfléchi*) myself

mec [mɛk] (*fam*) *nm* bloke, guy

mécanicien, ne [mekanisjɛ̃, jɛn] *nm/f* mechanic; (*Rail*) (train *ou* engine) driver; **pouvez-vous nous envoyer un ~?** can you send a mechanic?

mécanique [mekanik] *adj* mechanical ▷ *nf* (*science*) mechanics *sg*; (*mécanisme*) mechanism; **ennui ~** engine trouble *no pl*

mécanisme [mekanism] *nm* mechanism

méchamment [meʃamɑ̃] *adv* nastily, maliciously, spitefully

méchanceté [meʃɑ̃ste] *nf* nastiness, maliciousness; **dire des ~s à qn** to say spiteful things to sb

méchant, e [meʃɑ̃, ɑ̃t] *adj* nasty, malicious, spiteful; (*enfant: pas sage*) naughty; (*animal*) vicious

mèche [mɛʃ] *nf* (*de cheveux*) lock; (*de lampe, bougie*) wick; (*d'un explosif*) fuse; **se faire faire des ~s** to have highlights put in one's hair; **de ~ avec** in league with

méchoui [meʃwi] *nm* barbecue of a whole roast sheep

méconnaissable [mekɔnɛsabl] *adj* unrecognizable

méconnaître [mekɔnɛtʀ] *vt* (*ignorer*) to be unaware of; (*mésestimer*) to misjudge

mécontent, e [mekɔ̃tɑ̃, ɑ̃t] *adj*: **~ (de)** discontented *ou* dissatisfied *ou* displeased (with); (*contrarié*) annoyed (at);

mécontentement *nm* dissatisfaction, discontent, displeasure; (*irritation*) annoyance

Mecque [mɛk] *nf*: **la ~** Mecca

médaille [medaj] *nf* medal

médaillon [medajɔ̃] *nm* (*bijou*) locket

médecin [med(ə)sɛ̃] *nm* doctor

médecine [med(ə)sin] *nf* medicine

média [medja] *nmpl*: **les ~** the media; **médiatique** *adj* media *cpd*

médical, e, -aux [medikal, o] *adj* medical; **passer une visite ~e** to have a medical

médicament [medikamɑ̃] *nm* medicine, drug

médiéval, e, -aux [medjeval, o] *adj* medieval

médiocre [medjɔkʀ] *adj* mediocre, poor

méditer [medite] *vi* to meditate

Méditerranée [mediteʀane] *nf*: **la (mer) ~** the Mediterranean (Sea); **méditerranéen, ne** *adj* Mediterranean ▷ *nm/f*: **Méditerranéen, ne** native *ou* inhabitant of a Mediterranean country

méduse [medyz] *nf* jellyfish

méfait [mefɛ] *nm* (*faute*) misdemeanour, wrongdoing; **méfaits** *nmpl* (*ravages*) ravages, damage *sg*

méfiance [mefjɑ̃s] *nf* mistrust, distrust

méfiant, e [mefjɑ̃, jɑ̃t] *adj* mistrustful, distrustful

méfier [mefje]: **se méfier** *vi* to be wary; to be careful; **se ~ de** to mistrust, distrust, be wary of

mégaoctet [megaɔkte] *nm* megabyte

mégarde [megaʀd] *nf*: **par ~** (*accidentellement*) accidentally; (*par erreur*) by mistake

mégère [meʒɛʀ] *nf* shrew

mégot [mego] (*fam*) *nm* cigarette end

meilleur, e [mejœʀ] *adj, adv* better ▷ *nm*: **le ~** the best; **le ~ des deux** the better of the two; **il fait ~ qu'hier** it's better weather than yesterday; **meilleur marché** (*inv*) cheaper

mél [mɛl] *nm* e-mail

mélancolie [melɑ̃kɔli] *nf* melancholy, gloom; **mélancolique** *adj* melancholic, melancholy

mélange [melɑ̃ʒ] *nm* mixture; **mélanger** *vt* to mix; (*vins, couleurs*) to blend; (*mettre en désordre*) to mix up, muddle (up)

mêlée [mele] *nf* mêlée, scramble; (*Rugby*) scrum(mage)

mêler [mele] *vt* (*unir*) to mix; (*embrouiller*) to muddle (up), mix up; **se mêler** *vi* to mix, mingle; **se ~ à** (*personne: se joindre*) to join; (: *s'associer à*) to mix with; **se ~ de** (*suj: personne*) to meddle with, interfere in; **mêle-toi de ce qui te regarde** *ou* **de tes affaires!** mind your own business!

mélodie [melɔdi] *nf* melody; **mélodieux, -euse** *adj* melodious

melon [m(ə)lɔ̃] *nm* (*Bot*) (honeydew) melon;

(aussi: **chapeau ~**) bowler (hat)
membre [mɑ̃bʀ] nm (Anat) limb; (personne, pays, élément) member ▷ adj member cpd
mémé [meme] (fam) nf granny

 MOT-CLÉ

même [mɛm] adj **1** (avant le nom) same; **en même temps** at the same time; **ils ont les mêmes goûts** they have the same ou similar tastes
2 (après le nom: renforcement): **il est la loyauté même** he is loyalty itself; **ce sont ses paroles mêmes** they are his very words
▷ pron: **le(la) même** the same one
▷ adv **1** (renforcement): **il n'a même pas pleuré** he didn't even cry; **même lui l'a dit** even HE said it; **ici même** at this very place; **même si** even if
2: **à même**: **à même la bouteille** straight from the bottle; **à même la peau** next to the skin; **être à même de faire** to be in a position to do, be able to do
3: **de même**: **faire de même** to do likewise; **lui de même** so does (ou did ou is) he; **de même que** just as; **il en va de même pour** the same goes for

mémoire [memwaʀ] nf memory ▷ nm (Scol) dissertation, paper; **mémoires** nmpl (souvenirs) memoirs; **à la ~ de** to the ou in memory of; **de ~** from memory; **mémoire morte** read-only memory, ROM; **mémoire vive** random access memory, RAM
mémorable [memɔʀabl] adj memorable, unforgettable
menace [mənas] nf threat; **menacer** vt to threaten
ménage [menaʒ] nm (travail) housework; (couple) (married) couple; (famille, Admin) household; **faire le ~** to do the housework; **ménagement** nm care and attention; **ménager, -ère** adj household cpd, domestic ▷ vt (traiter: personne) to handle with tact; (utiliser) to use sparingly; (prendre soin de) to take (great) care of, look after; (organiser) to arrange; **ménagère** nf housewife
mendiant, e [mɑ̃djɑ̃, jɑ̃t] nm/f beggar
mendier [mɑ̃dje] vi to beg ▷ vt to beg (for)
mener [m(ə)ne] vt to lead; (enquête) to conduct; (affaires) to manage ▷ vi: **~ à/dans** (emmener) to take to/into; **~ qch à bien** to see sth through (to a successful conclusion), complete sth successfully
meneur, -euse [mənœʀ, øz] nm/f leader; (péj) agitator
méningite [menɛ̃ʒit] nf meningitis no pl
ménopause [menopoz] nf menopause
menottes [mənɔt] nfpl handcuffs

mensonge [mɑ̃sɔ̃ʒ] nm lie; (action) lying no pl; **mensonger, -ère** adj false
mensualité [mɑ̃sɥalite] nf (traite) monthly payment
mensuel, le [mɑ̃sɥel] adj monthly
mensurations [mɑ̃syʀasjɔ̃] nfpl measurements
mental, e, -aux [mɑ̃tal, o] adj mental; **mentalité** nf mentality
menteur, -euse [mɑ̃tœʀ, øz] nm/f liar
menthe [mɑ̃t] nf mint
mention [mɑ̃sjɔ̃] nf (annotation) note, comment; (Scol) grade; **~ bien** ≈ grade B, ≈ good pass; (Université) ≈ upper 2nd class pass (BRIT); ≈ pass with (high) honors (US); (Admin): **"rayer les ~s inutiles"** "delete as appropriate"; **mentionner** vt to mention
mentir [mɑ̃tiʀ] vi to lie
menton [mɑ̃tɔ̃] nm chin
menu, e [məny] adj (personne) slim, slight; (frais, difficulté) minor ▷ adv (couper, hacher) very fine ▷ nm menu; **~ touristique/gastronomique** economy/gourmet's menu
menuiserie [mənɥizʀi] nf (métier) joinery, carpentry; (passe-temps) woodwork; **menuisier** nm joiner, carpenter
méprendre [mepʀɑ̃dʀ]: **se méprendre** vi: **se ~ sur** to be mistaken (about)
mépris [mepʀi] nm (dédain) contempt, scorn; **au ~ de** regardless of, in defiance of; **méprisable** adj contemptible, despicable; **méprisant, e** adj scornful; **méprise** nf mistake, error; **mépriser** vt to scorn, despise; (gloire, danger) to scorn, spurn
mer [mɛʀ] nf sea; (marée) tide; **en ~** at sea; **en haute** ou **pleine ~** off shore, on the open sea; **la ~ du Nord/Rouge/Noire/Morte** the North/Red/Black/Dead Sea
mercenaire [mɛʀsənɛʀ] nm mercenary, hired soldier
mercerie [mɛʀsəʀi] nf (boutique) haberdasher's shop (BRIT), notions store (US)
merci [mɛʀsi] excl thank you ▷ nf: **à la ~ de qn/qch** at sb's mercy/the mercy of sth; **~ beaucoup** thank you very much; **~ de** thank you for; **sans ~** merciless(ly)
mercredi [mɛʀkʀədi] nm Wednesday; **~ des Cendres** Ash Wednesday; voir aussi **lundi**
mercure [mɛʀkyʀ] nm mercury
merde [mɛʀd] (fam!) nf shit (!) ▷ excl (bloody) hell (!)
mère [mɛʀ] nf mother; **mère célibataire** single parent, unmarried mother; **mère de famille** housewife, mother
merguez [mɛʀgez] nf merguez sausage (type of spicy sausage from N Africa)
méridional, e, -aux [meʀidjɔnal, o] adj southern ▷ nm/f Southerner
meringue [məʀɛ̃g] nf meringue

m

mérite [merit] nm merit; **avoir du ~ (à faire qch)** to deserve credit (for doing sth); **mériter** vt to deserve

merle [mɛrl] nm blackbird

merveille [mɛrvɛj] nf marvel, wonder; **faire ~** to work wonders; **à ~** perfectly, wonderfully; **merveilleux, -euse** adj marvellous, wonderful

mes [me] adj voir **mon**

mésange [mezɑ̃ʒ] nf tit(mouse)

mésaventure [mezavɑ̃tyr] nf misadventure, misfortune

Mesdames [medam] nfpl de **Madame**

Mesdemoiselles [medmwazɛl] nfpl de **Mademoiselle**

mesquin, e [mɛskɛ̃, in] adj mean, petty; **mesquinerie** nf meanness; (procédé) mean trick

message [mesaʒ] nm message; **est-ce que je peux laisser un ~?** can I leave a message?; **~ SMS** text message; **messager, -ère** nm/f messenger; **messagerie** nf (Internet): **messagerie électronique** e-mail; **messagerie vocale** (service) voice mail; **messagerie instantanée** instant messenger

messe [mɛs] nf mass; **aller à la ~** to go to mass

Messieurs [mesjø] nmpl de **Monsieur**

mesure [m(ə)zyr] nf (évaluation, dimension) measurement; (récipient) measure; (Mus: cadence) time, tempo; (: division) bar; (retenue) moderation; (disposition) measure, step; **sur ~** (costume) made-to-measure; **dans la ~ où** insofar as, inasmuch as; **à ~ que** as; **être en ~ de** to be in a position to; **dans une certaine ~** to a certain extent

mesurer [məzyre] vt to measure; (juger) to weigh up, assess; (modérer: ses paroles etc) to moderate

métal, -aux [metal, o] nm metal; **métallique** adj metallic

météo [meteo] nf (bulletin) weather report

météorologie [meteɔrɔlɔʒi] nf meteorology

méthode [metɔd] nf method; (livre, ouvrage) manual, tutor

méticuleux, -euse [metikylø, øz] adj meticulous

métier [metje] nm (profession: gén) job; (: manuel) trade; (artisanal) craft; (technique, expérience) (acquired) skill ou technique; (aussi: **~ à tisser**) (weaving) loom

métis, se [metis] adj, nm/f half-caste, half-breed

métrage [metraʒ] nm: **long/moyen/court ~** full-length/medium-length/short film

mètre [mɛtr] nm metre; (règle) (metre) rule; (ruban) tape measure; **métrique** adj metric

métro [metro] nm underground (BRIT), subway

métropole [metrɔpɔl] nf (capitale) metropolis; (pays) home country

mets [me] nm dish

metteur [metœr] nm: **~ en scène** (Théâtre) producer; (Cinéma) director

 MOT-CLÉ

mettre [mɛtr] vt **1** (placer) to put; **mettre en bouteille/en sac** to bottle/put in bags ou sacks

2 (vêtements: revêtir) to put on; (: porter) to wear; **mets ton gilet** put your cardigan on; **je ne mets plus mon manteau** I no longer wear my coat

3 (faire fonctionner: chauffage, électricité) to put on; (: réveil, minuteur) to set; (installer: gaz, eau) to put in, lay on; **mettre en marche** to start up

4 (consacrer): **mettre du temps à faire qch** to take time to do sth ou over sth

5 (noter, écrire) to say, put (down); **qu'est-ce qu'il a mis sur la carte?** what did he say ou write on the card?; **mettez au pluriel ...** put ... into the plural

6 (supposer): **mettons que ...** let's suppose ou say that ...

7: y mettre du sien to pull one's weight

se mettre vi **1** (se placer): **vous pouvez vous mettre là** you can sit (ou stand) there; **où ça se met?** where does it go?; **se mettre au lit** to get into bed; **se mettre au piano** to sit down at the piano; **se mettre de l'encre sur les doigts** to get ink on one's fingers

2 (s'habiller): **se mettre en maillot de bain** to get into ou put on a swimsuit; **n'avoir rien à se mettre** to have nothing to wear

3: se mettre à to begin, start; **se mettre à faire** to begin ou start doing ou to do; **se mettre au piano** to start learning the piano; **se mettre au régime** to go on a diet; **se mettre au travail/à l'étude** to get down to work/one's studies

meuble [mœbl] nm piece of furniture; **des ~s** furniture; **meublé** nm furnished flatlet (BRIT) ou room; **meubler** vt to furnish

meuf [mœf] nf (fam) woman

meugler [møgle] vi to low, moo

meule [møl] nf (de foin, blé) stack; (de fromage) round; (à broyer) millstone

meunier [mønje] nm miller

meurs etc [mœr] vb voir **mourir**

meurtre [mœrtr] nm murder; **meurtrier, -ière** adj (arme etc) deadly; (fureur, instincts) murderous ▷ nm/f murderer(-eress)

meurtrir [mœrtrir] vt to bruise; (fig) to wound

meus etc [mœ] vb voir **mouvoir**

meute [møt] *nf* pack

mexicain, e [mɛksikɛ̃, ɛn] *adj* Mexican
▷ *nm/f*: **M-, e** Mexican

Mexico [mɛksiko] *n* Mexico City

Mexique [mɛksik] *nm*: **le ~** Mexico

mi [mi] *nm* (*Mus*) E; (*en chantant la gamme*) mi
▷ *préfixe*: **mi...** half(-); mid-; **à la mi-janvier**
in mid-January; **à mi-jambes/corps** (up *ou*
down) to the knees/waist; **à mi-hauteur**
halfway up

miauler [mjole] *vi* to mew

miche [miʃ] *nf* round *ou* cob loaf

mi-chemin [miʃmɛ̃]: **à ~** *adv* halfway, midway

mi-clos, e [miklo, kloz] *adj* half-closed

micro [mikʀo] *nm* mike, microphone; (*Inform*)
micro

microbe [mikʀɔb] *nm* germ, microbe

micro...: **micro-onde** *nf*: **four à micro-ondes**
microwave oven; **micro-ordinateur** *nm*
microcomputer; **microscope** *nm* microscope;
microscopique *adj* microscopic

midi [midi] *nm* midday, noon; (*moment du
déjeuner*) lunchtime; (*sud*) south; **à ~** at 12
(o'clock) *ou* midday *ou* noon; **le M~** the South
(of France), the Midi

mie [mi] *nf* crumb (of the loaf)

miel [mjɛl] *nm* honey; **mielleux, -euse** *adj*
(*personne*) unctuous, syrupy

mien, ne [mjɛ̃, mjɛn] *pron*: **le(la) ~(ne), les
~(ne)s** mine; **les ~s** my family

miette [mjɛt] *nf* (*de pain, gâteau*) crumb; (*fig:
de la conversation etc*) scrap; **en ~s** in pieces
ou bits

MOT-CLÉ

mieux [mjø] *adv* **1** (*d'une meilleure façon*):
mieux (que) better (than); **elle travaille/
mange mieux** she works/eats better; **aimer
mieux** to prefer; **elle va mieux** she is better;
de mieux en mieux better and better
2 (*de la meilleure façon*) best; **ce que je
connais le mieux** what I know best; **les
livres les mieux faits** the best-made books
▷ *adj* **1** (*plus à l'aise, en meilleure forme*) better;
se sentir mieux to feel better
2 (*plus satisfaisant*) better; **c'est mieux ainsi**
it's better like this; **c'est le mieux des deux**
it's the better of the two; **le(la) mieux, les
mieux** the best; **demandez-lui, c'est le
mieux** ask him, it's the best thing
3 (*plus joli*) better-looking; **il est mieux que
son frère** (*plus beau*) he's better-looking than
his brother; (*plus gentil*) he's nicer than his
brother; **il est mieux sans moustache** he
looks better without a moustache
4: **au mieux** at best; **au mieux avec** on the
best of terms with; **pour le mieux** for the
best

▷ *nm* **1** (*progrès*) improvement
2: **de mon/ton mieux** as best I/you can (*ou*
could); **faire de son mieux** to do one's best

mignon, ne [miɲɔ̃, ɔn] *adj* sweet, cute

migraine [migʀɛn] *nf* headache; (*Méd*)
migraine

mijoter [miʒɔte] *vt* to simmer; (*préparer avec
soin*) to cook lovingly; (*fam: tramer*) to plot,
cook up ▷ *vi* to simmer

milieu, x [miljø] *nm* (*centre*) middle; (*Bio,
Géo*) environment; (*entourage social*) milieu;
(*provenance*) background; (*pègre*): **le ~** the
underworld; **au ~ de** in the middle of; **au beau
ou en plein ~ (de)** right in the middle (of); **un
juste ~** a happy medium

militaire [militɛʀ] *adj* military, army *cpd* ▷ *nm*
serviceman

militant, e [militɑ̃, ɑ̃t] *adj*, *nm/f* militant

militer [milite] *vi* to be a militant

mille [mil] *num* a *ou* one thousand ▷ *nm*
(*mesure*): **~ (marin)** nautical mile; **mettre
dans le ~** (*fig*) to be bang on target;
millefeuille *nm* cream *ou* vanilla slice;
millénaire *nm* millennium ▷ *adj* thousand-
year-old; (*fig*) ancient; **mille-pattes** *nm inv*
centipede

millet [mijɛ] *nm* millet

milliard [miljaʀ] *nm* milliard, thousand
million (*BRIT*), billion (*US*); **milliardaire** *nm/f*
multimillionaire (*BRIT*), billionaire (*US*)

millier [milje] *nm* thousand; **un ~ (de)** a
thousand *ou* so, about a thousand; **par ~s** in
(their) thousands, by the thousand

milligramme [miligram] *nm* milligramme

millimètre [milimɛtʀ] *nm* millimetre

million [miljɔ̃] *nm* million; **deux ~s de** two
million; **millionnaire** *nm/f* millionaire

mime [mim] *nm/f* (*acteur*) mime(r) ▷ *nm* (*art*)
mime, miming; **mimer** *vt* to mime; (*singer*) to
mimic, take off

minable [minabl] *adj* (*décrépit*) shabby(-
looking); (*médiocre*) pathetic

mince [mɛ̃s] *adj* thin; (*personne, taille*) slim,
slender; (*fig: profit, connaissances*) slight, small,
weak ▷ *excl*: **~ alors!** drat it!, darn it! (*US*);
minceur *nf* thinness; (*d'une personne*) slimness,
slenderness; **mincir** *vi* to get slimmer

mine [min] *nf* (*physionomie*) expression, look;
(*allure*) exterior, appearance; (*de crayon*) lead;
(*gisement, explosif, fig: source*) mine; **avoir
bonne ~** (*personne*) to look well; (*ironique*) to
look an utter idiot; **avoir mauvaise ~** to look
unwell *ou* poorly; **faire ~ de faire** to make a
pretence of doing; **~ de rien** although you
wouldn't think so

miner [mine] *vt* (*saper*) to undermine, erode;
(*Mil*) to mine

minerai [minʀɛ] *nm* ore

m

minéral, e, -aux [mineʀal, o] *adj, nm*
mineral

minéralogique [mineʀalɔʒik] *adj*: **plaque ~**
number (BRIT) *ou* license (US) plate; **numéro ~**
registration (BRIT) *ou* license (US) number

minet, te [mine, ɛt] *nm/f* (*chat*) pussy-cat;
(*péj*) young trendy

mineur, e [minœʀ] *adj* minor ▷ *nm/f* (*Jur*)
minor, person under age ▷ *nm* (*travailleur*)
miner

miniature [minjatyʀ] *adj, nf* miniature

minibus [minibys] *nm* minibus

minier, -ière [minje, jɛʀ] *adj* mining

mini-jupe [miniʒyp] *nf* mini-skirt

minime [minim] *adj* minor, minimal

minimessage [minimesaʒ] *nm* text message

minimiser [minimize] *vt* to minimize; (*fig*)
to play down

minimum [minimɔm] *adj, nm* minimum; **au
~** (*au moins*) at the very least

ministère [ministɛʀ] *nm* (*aussi Rel*) ministry;
(*cabinet*) government

ministre [ministʀ] *nm* (*aussi Rel*) minister;
ministre d'État senior minister *ou* secretary

Minitel® [minitɛl] *nm* videotext terminal and
service

minoritaire [minɔʀitɛʀ] *adj* minority

minorité [minɔʀite] *nf* minority; **être en ~** to
be in the *ou* a minority

minuit [minɥi] *nm* midnight

minuscule [minyskyl] *adj* minute, tiny ▷ *nf*:
(**lettre**) **~** small letter

minute [minyt] *nf* minute; **à la ~** (just) this
instant; (*faire*) there and then; **minuter** *vt* to
time; **minuterie** *nf* time switch

minutieux, -euse [minysjø, jøz] *adj*
(*personne*) meticulous; (*travail*) minutely
detailed

mirabelle [miʀabɛl] *nf* (cherry) plum

miracle [miʀakl] *nm* miracle

mirage [miʀaʒ] *nm* mirage

mire [miʀ] *nf*: **point de ~** (*fig*) focal point

miroir [miʀwaʀ] *nm* mirror

miroiter [miʀwate] *vi* to sparkle, shimmer;
faire ~ qch à qn to paint sth in glowing
colours for sb, dangle sth in front of sb's eyes

mis, e [mi, miz] *pp de* **mettre** ▷ *adj*: **bien ~**
well-dressed

mise [miz] *nf* (*argent: au jeu*) stake; (*tenue*)
clothing, attire; **être de ~** to be acceptable
ou in season; **mise à jour** updating; **mise au
point** (*fig*) clarification; **mise de fonds** capital
outlay; **mise en plis** set; **mise en scène**
production

miser [mize] *vt* (*enjeu*) to stake, bet; **~ sur**
(*cheval, numéro*) to bet on; (*fig*) to bank *ou*
count on

misérable [mizeʀabl] *adj* (*lamentable,
malheureux*) pitiful, wretched; (*pauvre*) poverty-
stricken; (*insignifiant, mesquin*) miserable
▷ *nm/f* wretch

misère [mizɛʀ] *nf* (extreme) poverty,
destitution; **misères** *nfpl* (*malheurs*) woes,
miseries; (*ennuis*) little troubles; **salaire de ~**
starvation wage

missile [misil] *nm* missile

mission [misjɔ̃] *nf* mission; **partir en
~** (*Admin, Pol*) to go on an assignment;
missionnaire *nm/f* missionary

mité, e [mite] *adj* moth-eaten

mi-temps [mitɑ̃] *nf inv* (*Sport: période*) half; (:
pause) half-time; **à ~** part-time

miteux, -euse [mitø, øz] *adj* (*lieu*) seedy

mitigé, e [mitiʒe] *adj*: **sentiments ~s** mixed
feelings

mitoyen, ne [mitwajɛ̃, jɛn] *adj* (*mur*)
common, party *cpd*; **maisons ~nes** semidetached houses; (*plus de deux*) terraced (BRIT)
ou row (US) houses

mitrailler [mitʀaje] *vt* to machine-gun; (*fig*)
to pelt, bombard; (: *photographier*) to take shot
after shot of; **mitraillette** *nf* submachine
gun; **mitrailleuse** *nf* machine gun

mi-voix [mivwa]: **à ~** *adv* in a low *ou* hushed
voice

mixage [miksaʒ] *nm* (*Cinéma*) (sound) mixing

mixer [miksœʀ] *nm* (food) mixer

mixte [mikst] *adj* (*gén*) mixed; (*Scol*) mixed,
coeducational; **cuisinière ~** combined gas and
electric cooker (BRIT) *ou* stove (US)

mixture [mikstyʀ] *nf* mixture; (*fig*)
concoction

Mlle (*pl* **~s**) *abr* = **Mademoiselle**

MM *abr* = **Messieurs**

Mme (*pl* **~s**) *abr* = **Madame**

mobile [mɔbil] *adj* mobile; (*pièce de machine*)
moving ▷ *nm* (*motif*) motive; (*œuvre d'art*)
mobile; (**téléphone**) **~** mobile (phone)

mobilier, -ière [mɔbilje, jɛʀ] *nm* furniture

mobiliser [mɔbilize] *vt* to mobilize

mocassin [mɔkasɛ̃] *nm* moccasin

moche [mɔʃ] (*fam*) *adj* (*laid*) ugly; (*mauvais*)

rotten

modalité [mɔdalite] *nf* form, mode

mode [mɔd] *nf* fashion ▷ *nm* (*manière*) form, mode; (*Ling*) mood; (*Mus, Inform*) mode; **à la ~** fashionable, in fashion; **mode d'emploi** directions *pl* (for use); **mode de paiement** method of payment; **mode de vie** lifestyle

modèle [mɔdɛl] *adj, nm* model; (*qui pose: de peintre*) sitter; **modèle déposé** registered design; **modèle réduit** small-scale model; **modeler** *vt* to model

modem [mɔdɛm] *nm* modem

modéré, e [mɔdeʀe] *adj, nm/f* moderate

modérer [mɔdeʀe] *vt* to moderate; **se modérer** *vi* to restrain o.s.

moderne [mɔdɛʀn] *adj* modern ▷ *nm* (*style*) modern style; (*meubles*) modern furniture; **moderniser** *vt* to modernize

modeste [mɔdɛst] *adj* modest; **modestie** *nf* modesty

modifier [mɔdifje] *vt* to modify, alter; **se modifier** *vi* to alter

modique [mɔdik] *adj* modest

module [mɔdyl] *nm* module

moelle [mwal] *nf* marrow

moelleux, -euse [mwalø, øz] *adj* soft; (*gâteau*) light and moist

mœurs [mœʀ] *nfpl* (*conduite*) morals; (*manières*) manners; (*pratiques sociales, mode de vie*) habits

moi [mwa] *pron* me; (*emphatique*): **~, je ...** for my part, I ..., I myself ...; **c'est ~ qui l'ai fait** I did it, it was me who did it; **apporte-le-~** bring it to me; **à ~** mine; (*dans un jeu*) my turn; **moi-même** *pron* myself; (*emphatique*) I myself

moindre [mwɛdʀ] *adj* lesser; lower; **le(la) ~, les ~s** the least, the slightest; **merci — c'est la ~ des choses!** thank you — it's a pleasure!

moine [mwan] *nm* monk, friar

moineau, x [mwano] *nm* sparrow

 MOT-CLÉ

moins [mwɛ] *adv* **1** (*comparatif*): **moins (que)** less (than); **moins grand que** less tall than, not as tall as; **il a 3 ans de moins que moi** he's 3 years younger than me; **moins je travaille, mieux je me porte** the less I work, the better I feel

2 (*superlatif*): **le moins** (the) least; **c'est ce que j'aime le moins** it's what I like (the) least; **le(la) moins doué(e)** the least gifted; **au moins, du moins** at least; **pour le moins** at the very least

3: **moins de** (*quantité*) less (than); (*nombre*) fewer (than); **moins de sable/d'eau** less sand/water; **moins de livres/gens** fewer books/people; **moins de 2 ans** less than 2 years; **moins de midi** not yet midday

4: **de moins, en moins**: **100 euros/3 jours de moins** 100 euros/3 days less; **3 livres en moins** 3 books fewer; **3 books too few**; **de l'argent en moins** less money; **le soleil en moins** but for the sun, minus the sun; **de moins en moins** less and less

5: **à moins de, à moins que** unless; **à moins de faire** unless we do (he does *etc*); **à moins que tu ne fasses** unless you do; **à moins d'un accident** barring any accident

▷ *prép*: **4 moins 2** 4 minus 2; **il est moins 5** it's 5 to; **il fait moins 5** it's 5 (degrees) below (freezing), it's minus 5

mois [mwa] *nm* month

moisi [mwazi] *nm* mould, mildew; **odeur de ~** musty smell; **moisir** *vi* to go mouldy; **moisissure** *nf* mould *no pl*

moisson [mwasɔ̃] *nf* harvest; **moissonner** *vt* to harvest, reap; **moissonneuse** *nf* (*machine*) harvester

moite [mwat] *adj* sweaty, sticky

moitié [mwatje] *nf* half; **la ~** half; **la ~ de** half (of); **la ~ du temps** half the time; **à la ~ de** halfway through; **à ~** (*avant le verbe*) half; (*avant l'adjectif*) half-; **à ~ prix** (at) half-price

molaire [mɔlɛʀ] *nf* molar

molester [mɔlɛste] *vt* to manhandle, maul (about)

molle [mɔl] *adj voir* **mou**; **mollement** *adv* (*péj: travailler*) sluggishly; (*protester*) feebly

mollet [mɔlɛ] *nm* calf ▷ *adj m*: **œuf ~** soft-boiled egg

molletonné, e [mɔltɔne] *adj* fleece-lined

mollir [mɔliʀ] *vi* (*fléchir*) to relent; (*substance*) to go soft

mollusque [mɔlysk] *nm* mollusc

môme [mom] (*fam*) *nm/f* (*enfant*) brat

moment [mɔmɑ̃] *nm* moment; **ce n'est pas le ~** this is not the (right) time; **au même ~** at the same time; (*instant*) at the same moment; **pour un bon ~** for a good while; **pour le ~** for the moment, for the time being; **au ~ de** at the time of; **au ~ où** just as; **à tout ~** (*peut arriver etc*) at any time *ou* moment; (*constamment*) constantly, continually; **en ce ~** at the moment; at present; **sur le ~** at the time; **par ~s** now and then, at times; **d'un ~ à l'autre** any time (now); **du ~ où** *ou* **que** seeing that, since; **momentané, e** *adj* temporary, momentary; **momentanément** *adv* (*court instant*) for a short while

momie [mɔmi] *nf* mummy

mon, ma [mɔ̃, ma] (*pl* **mes**) *adj* my

Monaco [mɔnako] *nm* Monaco

monarchie [mɔnaʀʃi] *nf* monarchy

monastère [mɔnastɛʀ] *nm* monastery

mondain, e [mɔ̃dɛ̃, ɛn] *adj* (*vie*) society *cpd*

monde [mɔ̃d] *nm* world; (*haute société*): **le ~**

m

(high) society; **il y a du ~** (beaucoup de gens) there are a lot of people; (quelques personnes) there are some people; **beaucoup/peu de ~** many/few people; **mettre au ~** to bring into the world; **pas le moins du ~** not in the least; **mondial, e, -aux** adj (population) world cpd; (influence) world-wide; **mondialement** adv throughout the world; **mondialisation** nf globalization

monégasque [mɔnegask] adj Monegasque, of ou from Monaco ▷ nm/f: **M~** Monegasque, person ou inhabitant of Monaco

monétaire [mɔnetɛʀ] adj monetary

moniteur, -trice [mɔnitœʀ, tʀis] nm/f (Sport) instructor(-tress); (de colonie de vacances) supervisor ▷ nm (écran) monitor

monnaie [mɔnɛ] nf (Écon, gén: moyen d'échange) currency; (petites pièces): **avoir de la ~** to have (some) change; **une pièce de ~** a coin; **faire de la ~** to get (some) change; **avoir/faire la ~ de 20 euros** to have change of/get change for 20 euros; **rendre à qn la ~ (sur 20 euros)** to give sb the change (out of ou from 20 euros); **gardez la ~** keep the change; **désolé, je n'ai pas de ~** sorry, I don't have any change; **avez-vous de la ~?** do you have any change?

monologue [mɔnɔlɔg] nm monologue, soliloquy; **monologuer** vi to soliloquize

monopole [mɔnɔpɔl] nm monopoly

monotone [mɔnɔtɔn] adj monotonous

Monsieur [məsjø] (pl **Messieurs**) titre Mr ▷ nm (homme quelconque): **un/le monsieur** a/the gentleman; **~, ...** (en tête de lettre) Dear Sir, ...; voir aussi **Madame**

monstre [mɔ̃stʀ] nm monster ▷ adj (fam: colossal) monstrous; **un travail ~** a fantastic amount of work; **monstrueux, -euse** adj monstrous

mont [mɔ̃] nm: **par ~s et par vaux** up hill and down dale; **le Mont Blanc** Mont Blanc

montage [mɔ̃taʒ] nm (assemblage: d'appareil) assembly; (Photo) photomontage; (Cinéma) editing

montagnard, e [mɔ̃taɲaʀ, aʀd] adj mountain cpd ▷ nm/f mountain-dweller

montagne [mɔ̃taɲ] nf (cime) mountain; (région): **la ~** the mountains pl; **montagnes russes** big dipper sg, switchback sg; **montagneux, -euse** adj mountainous; (basse montagne) hilly

montant, e [mɔ̃tɑ̃, ɑ̃t] adj rising; **pull à col ~** high-necked jumper ▷ nm (somme, total) (sum) total, (total) amount; (de fenêtre) upright; (de lit) post

monte-charge [mɔ̃tʃaʀʒ] nm inv goods lift, hoist

montée [mɔ̃te] nf (des prix, hostilités) rise; (escalade) climb; (côte) hill; **au milieu de la ~** halfway up

monter [mɔ̃te] vt (escalier, côte) to go (ou come) up; (valise, paquet) to take (ou bring) up; (étagère) to raise; (tente, échafaudage) to put up; (machine) to assemble; (Cinéma) to edit; (Théâtre) to put on, stage; (société etc) to set up ▷ vi to go (ou come) up; (prix, niveau, température) to go up, rise; (passager) to get on; **~ à cheval** (faire du cheval) to ride (a horse); **~ sur** to climb up onto; **~ sur** ou **à un arbre/une échelle** to climb (up) a tree/ladder; **se monter à** (frais etc) to add up to, come to

montgolfière [mɔ̃gɔlfjɛʀ] nf hot-air balloon

montre [mɔ̃tʀ] nf watch; **contre la ~** (Sport) against the clock

Montréal [mɔ̃real] n Montreal

montrer [mɔ̃tʀe] vt to show; **~ qch à qn** to show sb sth; **pouvez-vous me ~ où c'est?** can you show me where it is?

monture [mɔ̃tyʀ] nf (cheval) mount; (de lunettes) frame; (d'une bague) setting

monument [mɔnymɑ̃] nm monument; **monument aux morts** war memorial

moquer [mɔke]: **se moquer de** vt to make fun of, laugh at; (fam: se désintéresser de) not to care about; (tromper): **se ~ de qn** to take sb for a ride

moquette [mɔkɛt] nf fitted carpet

moqueur, -euse [mɔkœʀ, øz] adj mocking

moral, e, -aux [mɔʀal, o] adj moral ▷ nm morale; **avoir le ~** (fam) to be in good spirits; **avoir le ~ à zéro** (fam) to be really down; **morale** nf (mœurs) morals pl; (valeurs) moral standards pl, morality; (d'une fable etc) moral; **faire la morale à** to lecture, preach at; **moralité** nf morality; (de fable) moral

morceau, x [mɔʀso] nm piece, bit; (d'une œuvre) passage, extract; (Mus) piece; (Culin: de viande) cut; (de sucre) lump; **mettre en ~x** to pull to pieces ou bits; **manger un ~** to have a bite (to eat)

morceler [mɔʀsəle] vt to break up, divide up

mordant, e [mɔʀdɑ̃, ɑ̃t] adj (ton, remarque) scathing, cutting; (ironie, froid) biting ▷ nm (style) bite, punch

mordiller [mɔʀdije] vt to nibble at, chew at

mordre [mɔʀdʀ] vt to bite ▷ vi (poisson) to bite; **~ sur** (fig) to go over into, overlap into; **~ à l'hameçon** to bite, rise to the bait

mordu, e [mɔʀdy] (fam) nm/f enthusiast; **un ~ de jazz** a jazz fanatic

morfondre [mɔʀfɔ̃dʀ]: **se morfondre** vi to mope

morgue [mɔʀg] nf (arrogance) haughtiness; (lieu: de la police) morgue; (: à l'hôpital) mortuary

morne [mɔʀn] adj dismal, dreary

morose [mɔʀoz] adj sullen, morose

mors [mɔʀ] nm bit

morse [mɔʀs] nm (Zool) walrus; (Tél) Morse (code)

morsure [mɔʀsyʀ] nf bite

mort¹ [mɔʀ] nf death

mort², e [mɔʀ, mɔʀt] pp de **mourir** ▷ adj dead ▷ nm/f (défunt) dead man ou woman; (victime): **il y a eu plusieurs ~s** several people were killed, there were several killed; **~ de peur/fatigue** frightened to death/dead tired

mortalité [mɔʀtalite] nf mortality, death rate

mortel, le [mɔʀtɛl] adj (poison etc) deadly, lethal; (accident, blessure) fatal; (silence, ennemi) deadly; (péché) mortal; (fam: ennuyeux) deadly boring

mort-né, e [mɔʀne] adj (enfant) stillborn

mortuaire [mɔʀtɥɛʀ] adj: **avis ~** death announcement

morue [mɔʀy] nf (Zool) cod inv

mosaïque [mɔzaik] nf mosaic

Moscou [mɔsku] n Moscow

mosquée [mɔske] nf mosque

mot [mo] nm word; (message) line, note; **~ à ~** word for word; **mot de passe** password; **mots croisés** crossword (puzzle) sg

motard [mɔtaʀ] nm biker; (policier) motorcycle cop

motel [mɔtɛl] nm motel

moteur, -trice [mɔtœʀ, tʀis] adj (Anat, Physiol) motor; (Tech) driving; (Auto): **à 4 roues motrices** 4-wheel drive ▷ nm engine, motor; **à ~** power-driven, motor cpd; **moteur de recherche** search engine

motif [mɔtif] nm (cause) motive; (décoratif) design, pattern, motif; **sans ~** groundless

motivation [mɔtivasjɔ̃] nf motivation

motiver [mɔtive] vt to motivate; (justifier) to justify, account for

moto [mɔto] nf (motor)bike; **motocycliste** nm/f motorcyclist

motorisé, e [mɔtɔʀize] adj (personne) having transport ou a car

motrice [mɔtʀis] adj voir **moteur**

motte [mɔt] nf: **~ de terre** lump of earth, clod (of earth); **motte de beurre** lump of butter

mou (mol), molle [mu, mɔl] adj soft; (personne) lethargic; (protestations) weak ▷ nm: **avoir du mou** to be slack

mouche [muʃ] nf fly

moucher [muʃe]: **se moucher** vi to blow one's nose

moucheron [muʃʀɔ̃] nm midge

mouchoir [muʃwaʀ] nm handkerchief, hanky; **mouchoir en papier** tissue, paper hanky

moudre [mudʀ] vt to grind

moue [mu] nf pout; **faire la ~** to pout; (fig) to pull a face

mouette [mwɛt] nf (sea)gull

moufle [mufl] nf (gant) mitt(en)

mouillé, e [muje] adj wet

mouiller [muje] vt (humecter) to wet, moisten; (tremper): **~ qn/qch** to make sb/sth wet ▷ vi (Navig) to lie ou be at anchor; **se mouiller** to get wet; (fam: prendre des risques) to commit o.s.

moulant, e [mulɑ̃, ɑ̃t] adj figure-hugging

moule [mul] nf mussel ▷ nm (Culin) mould; **moule à gâteaux** nm cake tin (BRIT) ou pan (US)

mouler [mule] vt (suj: vêtement) to hug, fit closely round

moulin [mulɛ̃] nm mill; **moulin à café** coffee mill; **moulin à eau** watermill; **moulin à légumes** (vegetable) shredder; **moulin à paroles** (fig) chatterbox; **moulin à poivre** pepper mill; **moulin à vent** windmill

moulinet [mulinɛ] nm (de canne à pêche) reel; (mouvement): **faire des ~s avec qch** to whirl sth around

moulinette® [mulinɛt] nf (vegetable) shredder

moulu, e [muly] pp de **moudre**

mourant, e [muʀɑ̃, ɑ̃t] adj dying

mourir [muʀiʀ] vi to die; (civilisation) to die out; **~ de froid/faim** to die of exposure/hunger; **~ de faim/d'ennui** (fig) to be starving/be bored to death; **~ d'envie de faire** to be dying to do

mousse [mus] nf (Bot) moss; (de savon) lather; (écume: sur eau, bière) froth, foam; (Culin) mousse ▷ nm (Navig) ship's boy; **mousse à raser** shaving foam

mousseline [muslin] nf muslin; **pommes ~** mashed potatoes

mousser [muse] vi (bière, détergent) to foam; (savon) to lather; **mousseux, -euse** adj frothy ▷ nm: **(vin) mousseux** sparkling wine

mousson [musɔ̃] nf monsoon

moustache [mustaʃ] nf moustache; **moustaches** nfpl (du chat) whiskers pl; **moustachu, e** adj with a moustache

moustiquaire [mustikɛʀ] nf mosquito net

moustique [mustik] nm mosquito

moutarde [mutaʀd] nf mustard

mouton [mutɔ̃] nm sheep inv; (peau) sheepskin; (Culin) mutton

mouvement [muvmɑ̃] nm movement; (fig: impulsion) gesture; **avoir un bon ~** to make a nice gesture; **en ~** in motion; on the move; **mouvementé, e** adj (vie, poursuite) eventful; (réunion) turbulent

mouvoir [muvwaʀ]: **se mouvoir** vi to move

moyen, ne [mwajɛ̃, jɛn] adj average; (tailles, prix) medium; (de grandeur moyenne) medium-sized ▷ nm (façon) means sg, way; **moyens** nmpl (capacités) means; **très ~** (résultats) pretty poor; **je n'en ai pas les ~s** I can't afford it; **au ~ de** by means of; **par tous les ~s** by every possible means, every possible way; **par**

ses propres ~s all by oneself; **moyen âge** Middle Ages *pl*; **moyen de transport** means of transport

moyennant [mwajɛnɑ̃] *prép* (*somme*) for; (*service, conditions*) in return for; (*travail, effort*) with

moyenne [mwajɛn] *nf* average; (*Math*) mean; (*Scol*) pass mark; **en ~** on (an) average; **moyenne d'âge** average age

Moyen-Orient [mwajɛnɔʀjɑ̃] *nm*: **le ~** the Middle East

moyeu, x [mwajø] *nm* hub

MST *sigle f* (= *maladie sexuellement transmissible*) STD

mû, mue [my] *pp de* **mouvoir**

muer [mɥe] *vi* (*oiseau, mammifère*) to moult; (*serpent*) to slough; (*jeune garçon*): **il mue** his voice is breaking

muet, te [mɥe, mɥɛt] *adj* dumb; (*fig*): **~ d'admiration** *etc* speechless with admiration *etc*; (*Cinéma*) silent ▷ *nm/f* mute

mufle [myfl] *nm* muzzle; (*fam: goujat*) boor

mugir [myʒiʀ] *vi* (*taureau*) to bellow; (*vache*) to low; (*fig*) to howl

muguet [mygɛ] *nm* lily of the valley

mule [myl] *nf* (*Zool*) (she-)mule

mulet [mylɛ] *nm* (*Zool*) (he-)mule

multinationale [myltinasjɔnal] *nf* multinational

multiple [myltipl] *adj* multiple, numerous; (*varié*) many, manifold; **multiplication** *nf* multiplication; **multiplier** *vt* to multiply; **se multiplier** *vi* to multiply

municipal, e, -aux [mynisipal, o] *adj* (*élections, stade*) municipal; (*conseil*) town *cpd*; **piscine/bibliothèque ~e** public swimming pool/library; **municipalité** *nf* (*ville*) municipality; (*conseil*) town council

munir [myniʀ] *vt*: **~ qch de** to equip sth with; **se ~ de** to arm o.s. with

munitions [mynisjɔ̃] *nfpl* ammunition *sg*

mur [myʀ] *nm* wall; **mur du son** sound barrier

mûr, e [myʀ] *adj* ripe; (*personne*) mature

muraille [myʀaj] *nf* (high) wall

mural, e, -aux [myʀal, o] *adj* wall *cpd*; (*art*) mural

mûre [myʀ] *nf* blackberry

muret [myʀɛ] *nm* low wall

mûrir [myʀiʀ] *vi* (*fruit, blé*) to ripen; (*abcès*) to come to a head; (*fig: idée, personne*) to mature ▷ *vt* (*projet*) to nurture; (*personne*) to (make) mature

murmure [myʀmyʀ] *nm* murmur; **murmurer** *vi* to murmur

muscade [myskad] *nf* (*aussi:* **noix (de) ~**) nutmeg

muscat [myska] *nm* (*raisins*) muscat grape; (*vin*) muscatel (wine)

muscle [myskl] *nm* muscle; **musclé, e** *adj*

muscular; (*fig*) strong-arm

museau, x [myzo] *nm* muzzle; (*Culin*) brawn

musée [myze] *nm* museum; (*de peinture*) art gallery

museler [myz(ə)le] *vt* to muzzle; **muselière** *nf* muzzle

musette [myzɛt] *nf* (*sac*) lunchbag

musical, e, -aux [myzikal, o] *adj* musical

music-hall [myzikol] *nm* (*salle*) variety theatre; (*genre*) variety

musicien, ne [myzisjɛ̃, jɛn] *adj* musical ▷ *nm/f* musician

musique [myzik] *nf* music

● **FÊTE DE LA MUSIQUE**

● The **Fête de la Musique** is a music festival
● which takes place every year on 21 June.
● Throughout France, local musicians
● perform free of charge in parks, streets and
● squares.

musulman, e [myzylmɑ̃, an] *adj, nm/f* Moslem, Muslim

mutation [mytasjɔ̃] *nf* (*Admin*) transfer

muter [myte] *vt* to transfer, move

mutilé, e [mytile] *nm/f* disabled person (*through loss of limbs*)

mutiler [mytile] *vt* to mutilate, maim

mutin, e [mytɛ̃, in] *adj* (*air, ton*) mischievous, impish ▷ *nm/f* (*Mil, Navig*) mutineer; **mutinerie** *nf* mutiny

mutisme [mytism] *nm* silence

mutuel, le [mytɥɛl] *adj* mutual; **mutuelle** *nf* voluntary insurance premiums for back-up health cover

myope [mjɔp] *adj* short-sighted

myosotis [mjɔzɔtis] *nm* forget-me-not

myrtille [miʀtij] *nf* bilberry

mystère [mistɛʀ] *nm* mystery; **mystérieux, -euse** *adj* mysterious

mystifier [mistifje] *vt* to fool

mythe [mit] *nm* myth

mythologie [mitɔlɔʒi] *nf* mythology

n

n' [n] *adv voir* **ne**

nacre [nakʀ] *nf* mother of pearl

nage [naʒ] *nf* swimming; (*manière*) style of swimming, stroke; **traverser/s'éloigner à la ~** to swim across/away; **en ~** bathed in sweat; **nageoire** *nf* fin; **nager** *vi* to swim; **nageur, -euse** *nm/f* swimmer

naïf, -ïve [naif, naiv] *adj* naïve

nain, e [nɛ̃, nɛn] *nm/f* dwarf

naissance [nɛsɑ̃s] *nf* birth; **donner ~ à** to give birth to; (*fig*) to give rise to; **lieu de ~** place of birth

naître [nɛtʀ] *vi* to be born; (*fig*): **~ de** to arise from, be born out of; **il est né en 1960** he was born in 1960; **faire ~** (*fig*) to give rise to, arouse

naïveté [naivte] *nf* naïvety

nana [nana] (*fam*) *nf* (*fille*) chick, bird (BRIT)

nappe [nap] *nf* tablecloth; (*de pétrole, gaz*) layer; **napperon** *nm* table-mat

naquit *etc* [naki] *vb voir* **naître**

narguer [naʀge] *vt* to taunt

narine [naʀin] *nf* nostril

natal, e [natal] *adj* native; **natalité** *nf* birth rate

natation [natasjɔ̃] *nf* swimming

natif, -ive [natif, iv] *adj* native

nation [nasjɔ̃] *nf* nation; **national, e, -aux** *adj* national; **nationale** *nf*: **(route) nationale** ≈ A road (BRIT), ≈ state highway (US);

nationaliser *vt* to nationalize; **nationalisme** *nm* nationalism; **nationalité** *nf* nationality

natte [nat] *nf* (*cheveux*) plait; (*tapis*) mat

naturaliser [natyʀalize] *vt* to naturalize

nature [natyʀ] *nf* nature ▷ *adj, adv* (*Culin*) plain, without seasoning or sweetening; (*café, thé*) black, without sugar; (*yaourt*) natural; **payer en ~** to pay in kind; **nature morte** still life; **naturel, le** *adj* (*gén, aussi enfant*) natural ▷ *nm* (*absence d'affectation*) naturalness; (*caractère*) disposition, nature; **naturellement** *adv* naturally; (*bien sûr*) of course

naufrage [nofʀaʒ] *nm* (ship)wreck; **faire ~** to be shipwrecked

nausée [noze] *nf* nausea; **avoir la ~** to feel sick

nautique [notik] *adj* nautical, water *cpd*; **sports ~s** water sports

naval, e [naval] *adj* naval; (*industrie*) shipbuilding

navet [navɛ] *nm* turnip; (*péj: film*) rubbishy film

navette [navɛt] *nf* shuttle; **faire la ~ (entre)** to go to and fro ou shuttle (between)

navigateur [navigatœʀ] *nm* (*Navig*) seafarer; (*Inform*) browser

navigation [navigasjɔ̃] *nf* navigation, sailing

naviguer [navige] *vi* to navigate, sail; **~ sur Internet** to browse the Internet

navire [naviʀ] *nm* ship

navrer [navʀe] *vt* to upset, distress; **je suis navré** I'm so sorry

ne, n' [n(ə)] *adv voir* **pas**; **plus**; **jamais** *etc*; (*sans valeur négative: non traduit*): **c'est plus loin que je ne le croyais** it's further than I thought

né, e [ne] *pp* (*voir naître*): **né en 1960** born in 1960; **née Scott** née Scott

néanmoins [neɑ̃mwɛ̃] *adv* nevertheless

néant [neɑ̃] *nm* nothingness; **réduire à ~** to bring to nought; (*espoir*) to dash

nécessaire [neseseʀ] *adj* necessary ▷ *nm* necessary; (*sac*) kit; **je vais faire le ~** I'll see to it; **nécessaire de couture** sewing kit; **nécessaire de toilette** toilet bag; **nécessité** *nf* necessity; **nécessiter** *vt* to require

nectar [nɛktaʀ] *nm* nectar

néerlandais, e [neeʀlɑ̃dɛ, ɛz] *adj* Dutch

nef [nɛf] *nf* (*d'église*) nave

néfaste [nefast] *adj* (*nuisible*) harmful; (*funeste*) ill-fated

négatif, -ive [negatif, iv] *adj* negative ▷ *nm* (*Photo*) negative

négligé, e [negliʒe] *adj* (*en désordre*) slovenly ▷ *nm* (*tenue*) negligee

négligeable [negliʒabl] *adj* negligible

négligent, e [negliʒɑ̃, ɑ̃t] *adj* careless, negligent

négliger [negliʒe] *vt* (*tenue*) to be careless

about; (*avis, précautions*) to disregard; (*épouse, jardin*) to neglect; **~ de faire** to fail to do, not bother to do

négociant, e [negɔsjɑ̃, jɑ̃t] *nm/f* merchant

négociation [negɔsjasjɔ̃] *nf* negotiation

négocier [negɔsje] *vi, vt* to negotiate

nègre [nɛgʀ] (*péj*) *nm* (*écrivain*) ghost (writer)

neige [nɛʒ] *nf* snow; **neiger** *vi* to snow

nénuphar [nenyfaʀ] *nm* water-lily

néon [neɔ̃] *nm* neon

néo-zélandais, e [neozelɑ̃dɛ, ɛz] *adj* New Zealand *cpd* ▷ *nm/f*: **Néo-Zélandais, e** New Zealander

Népal [nepal] *nm*: **le ~** Nepal

nerf [nɛʀ] *nm* nerve; **être sur les ~s** to be all keyed up; **nerveux, -euse** *adj* nervous; (*irritable*) touchy, nervy; (*voiture*) nippy, responsive; **nervosité** *nf* excitability, tenseness; (*irritabilité passagère*) irritability, nerviness

n'est-ce pas? [nɛspa] *adv* isn't it?, won't you? *etc, selon le verbe qui précède*

Net [nɛt] *nm* (*Internet*): **le ~** the Net

net, nette [nɛt] *adj* (*sans équivoque, distinct*) clear; (*évident: amélioration, différence*) marked, distinct; (*propre*) neat, clean; (*Comm: prix, salaire*) net ▷ *adv* (*refuser*) flatly ▷ *nm*: **mettre au ~** to copy out; **s'arrêter ~** to stop dead; **nettement** *adv* clearly, distinctly; (*incontestablement*) decidedly; **netteté** *nf* clearness

nettoyage [netwajaʒ] *nm* cleaning; **nettoyage à sec** dry cleaning

nettoyer [netwaje] *vt* to clean

neuf¹ [nœf] *num* nine

neuf², neuve [nœf, nœv] *adj* new; **remettre à ~** to do up (as good as new), refurbish; **quoi de ~?** what's new?

neutre [nøtʀ] *adj* neutral; (*Ling*) neuter

neuve [nœv] *adj voir* **neuf²**

neuvième [nœvjɛm] *num* ninth

neveu, x [n(ə)vø] *nm* nephew

New York [njujɔʀk] *n* New York

nez [ne] *nm* nose; **~ à ~ avec** face to face with; **avoir du ~** to have flair

ni [ni] *conj*: **ni ... ni** neither ... nor; **je n'aime ni les lentilles ni les épinards** I like neither lentils nor spinach; **il n'a dit ni oui ni non** he didn't say either yes or no; **elles ne sont venues ni l'une ni l'autre** neither of them came; **il n'a rien vu ni entendu** he didn't see or hear anything

niche [niʃ] *nf* (*du chien*) kennel; (*de mur*) recess, niche; **nicher** *vi* to nest

nid [ni] *nm* nest; **nid de poule** pothole

nièce [njɛs] *nf* niece

nier [nje] *vt* to deny

Nil [nil] *nm*: **le ~** the Nile

n'importe [nɛ̃pɔʀt] *adv*: **n'importe qui/quoi/où** anybody/anything/anywhere; **n'importe quand** any time; **n'importe quel/quelle** any; **n'importe lequel/laquelle** any (one); **n'importe comment** (*sans soin*) carelessly

niveau, x [nivo] *nm* level; (*des élèves, études*) standard; **niveau de vie** standard of living

niveler [niv(ə)le] *vt* to level

noble [nɔbl] *adj* noble; **noblesse** *nf* nobility; (*d'une action etc*) nobleness

noce [nɔs] *nf* wedding; (*gens*) wedding party (*ou* guests *pl*); **faire la ~** (*fam*) to go on a binge; **noces d'argent/d'or/de diamant** silver/golden/diamond wedding (anniversary)

nocif, -ive [nɔsif, iv] *adj* harmful

nocturne [nɔktyʀn] *adj* nocturnal ▷ *nf* late-night opening

Noël [nɔɛl] *nm* Christmas

nœud [nø] *nm* knot; (*ruban*) bow; **nœud papillon** bow tie

noir, e [nwaʀ] *adj* black; (*obscur, sombre*) dark ▷ *nm/f* black man/woman ▷ *nm*: **dans le ~** in the dark; **travail au ~** moonlighting; **travailler au ~** to work on the side; **noircir** *vt, vi* to blacken; **noire** *nf* (*Mus*) crotchet (BRIT), quarter note (US)

noisette [nwazɛt] *nf* hazelnut

noix [nwa] *nf* walnut; (*Culin*): **une ~ de beurre** a knob of butter; **à la ~** (*fam*) worthless; **noix de cajou** cashew nut; **noix de coco** coconut; **noix muscade** nutmeg

nom [nɔ̃] *nm* name; (*Ling*) noun; **nom de famille** surname; **nom de jeune fille** maiden name

nomade [nɔmad] *nm/f* nomad

nombre [nɔ̃bʀ] *nm* number; **venir en ~** to come in large numbers; **depuis ~ d'années** for many years; **au ~ de mes amis** among my friends; **nombreux, -euse** *adj* many, numerous; (*avec nom sg: foule etc*) large; **peu nombreux** few; **de nombreux cas** many cases

nombril [nɔ̃bʀi(l)] *nm* navel

nommer [nɔme] *vt* to name; (*élire*) to appoint, nominate; **se nommer**; **il se nomme Pascal** his name's Pascal, he's called Pascal

non [nɔ̃] *adv* (*réponse*) no; (*avec loin, sans, seulement*) not; **~ (pas) que** not that; **moi ~ plus** neither do I, I don't either; **c'est bon ~?** (*exprimant le doute*) it's good, isn't it?; **je pense que ~** I don't think so

non alcoolisé, e [nɔ̃alkɔlize] *adj* non alcoholic

nonchalant, e [nɔ̃ʃalɑ̃, ɑ̃t] *adj* nonchalant

non-fumeur, -euse [nɔ̃fymœʀ, øz] *nm/f* non-smoker

non-sens [nɔ̃sɑ̃s] *nm* absurdity

nord [nɔʀ] nm North ▷ adj northern; north; **au ~** (situation) in the north; (direction) to the north; **au ~ de** (to the) north of; **nord-africain, e** adj North-African ▷ nm/f: **Nord-Africain, e** North African; **nord-est** nm North-East; **nord-ouest** nm North-West

normal, e, -aux [nɔʀmal, o] adj normal; **c'est tout à fait ~** it's perfectly natural; **vous trouvez ça ~?** does it seem right to you?; **normale** nf: **la normale** the norm, the average; **normalement** adv (en général) normally

normand, e [nɔʀmɑ̃, ɑ̃d] adj of Normandy ▷ nm/f: **N~, e** (de Normandie) Norman

Normandie [nɔʀmɑ̃di] nf Normandy

norme [nɔʀm] nf norm; (Tech) standard

Norvège [nɔʀvɛʒ] nf Norway; **norvégien, ne** adj Norwegian ▷ nm/f: **Norvégien, ne** Norwegian ▷ nm (Ling) Norwegian

nos [no] adj voir **notre**

nostalgie [nɔstalʒi] nf nostalgia; **nostalgique** adj nostalgic

notable [nɔtabl] adj (fait) notable, noteworthy; (marqué) noticeable, marked ▷ nm prominent citizen

notaire [nɔtɛʀ] nm solicitor

notamment [nɔtamɑ̃] adv in particular, among others

note [nɔt] nf (écrite, Mus) note; (Scol) mark (BRIT), grade; (facture) bill; **note de service** memorandum

noter [nɔte] vt (écrire) to write down; (remarquer) to note, notice; (devoir) to mark, grade

notice [nɔtis] nf summary, short article; (brochure) leaflet, instruction book

notifier [nɔtifje] vt: **~ qch à qn** to notify sb of sth, notify sth to sb

notion [nɔsjɔ̃] nf notion, idea

notoire [nɔtwaʀ] adj widely known; (en mal) notorious

notre [nɔtʀ] (pl nos) adj our

nôtre [notʀ] pron: **le ~, la ~, les ~s** ours ▷ adj ours; **les ~s** ours; (alliés etc) our own people; **soyez des ~s** join us

nouer [nwe] vt to tie, knot; (fig: alliance etc) to strike up

noueux, -euse [nwø, øz] adj gnarled

nourrice [nuʀis] nf (gardienne) child-minder

nourrir [nuʀiʀ] vt to feed; (fig: espoir) to harbour, nurse; **nourrissant, e** adj nourishing, nutritious; **nourrisson** nm (unweaned) infant; **nourriture** nf food

nous [nu] pron (sujet) we; (objet) us; **nous-mêmes** pron ourselves

nouveau (nouvel), -elle, x [nuvo, nuvɛl] adj new ▷ nm: **y a-t-il du nouveau?** is there anything new on this? ▷ nm/f new pupil (ou employee); **de nouveau, à nouveau** again;

nouveau venu, nouvelle venue newcomer; **nouveaux mariés** newly-weds; **nouveau-né, e** nm/f newborn baby; **nouveauté** nf novelty; (objet) new thing ou article

nouvel [nuvɛl] adj voir **nouveau**; **Nouvel An** New Year

nouvelle [nuvɛl] adj voir **nouveau** ▷ nf (piece of) news sg; (Littérature) short story; **je suis sans ~s de lui** I haven't heard from him; **Nouvelle-Calédonie** nf New Caledonia; **Nouvelle-Zélande** nf New Zealand

novembre [nɔvɑ̃bʀ] nm November

○ **NOVEMBRE**
○
○ **Le 11 novembre** is a public holiday in
○ France commemorating the signing of the
○ armistice, near Compiègne, at the end of
○ World War I.

noyade [nwajad] nf drowning no pl

noyau, x [nwajo] nm (de fruit) stone; (Bio, Physique) nucleus; (fig: centre) core

noyer [nwaje] nm walnut (tree); (bois) walnut ▷ vt to drown; (moteur) to flood; **se noyer** vi to be drowned, drown; (suicide) to drown o.s.

nu, e [ny] adj naked; (membres) naked, bare; (pieds, mains, chambre, fil électrique) bare ▷ nm (Art) nude; **tout nu** stark naked; **se mettre nu** to strip

nuage [nɥaʒ] nm cloud; **nuageux, -euse** adj cloudy

nuance [nɥɑ̃s] nf (de couleur, sens) shade; **il y a une ~ (entre)** there's a slight difference (between); **nuancer** vt (opinion) to bring some reservations ou qualifications to

nucléaire [nykleɛʀ] adj nuclear ▷ nm: **le ~** nuclear energy

nudiste [nydist] nm/f nudist

nuée [nɥe] nf: **une ~ de** a cloud ou host ou swarm of

nuire [nɥiʀ] vi to be harmful; **~ à** to harm, do damage to; **nuisible** adj harmful; **animal nuisible** pest

nuit [nɥi] nf night; **il fait ~** it's dark; **cette ~** (hier) last night; (aujourd'hui) tonight; **de ~** (vol, service) night cpd; **nuit blanche** sleepless night

nul, nulle [nyl] adj (aucun) no; (minime) nil, non-existent; (non valable) null; (péj): **être ~ (en)** to be useless ou hopeless (at) ▷ pron none, no one; **match ou résultat ~** draw; **~le part** nowhere; **nullement** adv by no means

numérique [nymeʀik] adj numerical; (affichage, son, télévision) digital

numéro [nymeʀo] nm number; (spectacle) act, turn; (Presse) issue, number; **numéro de téléphone** (tele)phone number; **numéro**

n

vert ≈ freefone® number (BRIT), ≈ toll-free number (US); **numéroter** vt to number
nuque [nyk] nf nape of the neck
nu-tête [nytɛt] adj inv, adv bareheaded
nutritif, -ive [nytʀitif, iv] adj (besoins, valeur) nutritional; (nourrissant) nutritious
nylon [nilɔ̃] nm nylon

oasis [ɔazis] nf oasis
obéir [ɔbeiʀ] vi to obey; **~ à** to obey; **obéissance** nf obedience; **obéissant, e** adj obedient
obèse [ɔbez] adj obese; **obésité** nf obesity
objecter [ɔbʒɛkte] vt: **~ que** to object that; **objecteur** nm: **objecteur de conscience** conscientious objector
objectif, -ive [ɔbʒɛktif, iv] adj objective ▷ nm objective; (Photo) lens sg, objective
objection [ɔbʒɛksjɔ̃] nf objection
objectivité [ɔbʒɛktivite] nf objectivity
objet [ɔbʒɛ] nm object; (d'une discussion, recherche) subject; **être** ou **faire l'~ de** (discussion) to be the subject of; (soins) to be given ou shown; **sans ~** purposeless; (craintes) groundless; **(bureau des) ~s trouvés** lost property sg (BRIT), lost-and-found sg (US); **objet d'art** objet d'art; **objets de valeur** valuables; **objets personnels** personal items
obligation [ɔbligasjɔ̃] nf obligation; (Comm) bond, debenture; **obligatoire** adj compulsory, obligatory; **obligatoirement** adv necessarily; (fam: sans aucun doute) inevitably
obliger [ɔbliʒe] vt (contraindre): **~ qn à faire** to force ou oblige sb to do; **je suis bien obligé (de le faire)** I have to (do it)
oblique [ɔblik] adj oblique; **en ~** diagonally
oblitérer [ɔblitere] vt (timbre-poste) to cancel
obnubiler [ɔbnybile] vt to obsess

obscène [ɔpsɛn] *adj* obscene

obscur, e [ɔpskyʀ] *adj* dark; *(méconnu)* obscure; **obscurcir** *vt* to darken; *(fig)* to obscure; **s'obscurcir** *vi* to grow dark; **obscurité** *nf* darkness; **dans l'obscurité** in the dark, in darkness

obsédé, e [ɔpsede] *nm/f*: **un ~ de jazz** a jazz fanatic; **obsédé sexuel** sex maniac

obséder [ɔpsede] *vt* to obsess, haunt

obsèques [ɔpsɛk] *nfpl* funeral *sg*

observateur, -trice [ɔpsɛʀvatœʀ, tʀis] *adj* observant, perceptive ▷ *nm/f* observer

observation [ɔpsɛʀvasjɔ̃] *nf* observation; *(d'un règlement etc)* observance; *(reproche)* reproof; **être en ~** *(Méd)* to be under observation

observatoire [ɔpsɛʀvatwaʀ] *nm* observatory

observer [ɔpsɛʀve] *vt* (regarder) to observe, watch; *(scientifiquement; aussi règlement etc)* to observe; *(surveiller)* to watch; *(remarquer)* to observe, notice; **faire ~ qch à qn** *(dire)* to point out sth to sb

obsession [ɔpsesjɔ̃] *nf* obsession

obstacle [ɔpstakl] *nm* obstacle; *(Équitation)* jump, hurdle; **faire ~ à** *(projet)* to hinder, put obstacles in the path of

obstiné, e [ɔpstine] *adj* obstinate

obstiner [ɔpstine]: **s'obstiner** *vi* to insist, dig one's heels in; **s'~ à faire** to persist (obstinately) in doing

obstruer [ɔpstʀye] *vt* to block, obstruct

obtenir [ɔptəniʀ] *vt* to obtain, get; *(résultat)* to achieve, obtain; **~ de pouvoir faire** to obtain permission to do

obturateur [ɔptyʀatœʀ] *nm* (Photo) shutter

obus [ɔby] *nm* shell

occasion [ɔkazjɔ̃] *nf* (aubaine, possibilité) opportunity; *(circonstance)* occasion; *(Comm: article non neuf)* secondhand buy; *(: acquisition avantageuse)* bargain; **à plusieurs ~s** on several occasions; **à l'~** sometimes, on occasions; **d'~** secondhand; **occasionnel, le** *adj* (non régulier) occasional

occasionner [ɔkazjɔne] *vt* to cause

occident [ɔksidã] *nm*: **l'O~** the West; **occidental, e, -aux** *adj* western; *(Pol)* Western ▷ *nm/f* Westerner

occupation [ɔkypasjɔ̃] *nf* occupation

occupé, e [ɔkype] *adj* (personne) busy; *(place, sièges)* taken; *(toilettes)* engaged; *(Mil, Pol)* occupied; **la ligne est ~e** the line's engaged (BRIT) ou busy (US)

occuper [ɔkype] *vt* to occupy; *(poste)* to hold; **s'occuper de** *(être responsable de)* to be in charge of; *(se charger de: affaire)* to take charge of, deal with; *(: clients etc)* to attend to; **s'~ (à qch)** to occupy o.s. ou keep o.s. busy (with sth)

occurrence [ɔkyʀɑ̃s] *nf*: **en l'~** in this case

océan [ɔseã] *nm* ocean

octet [ɔktɛ] *nm* byte

octobre [ɔktɔbʀ] *nm* October

oculiste [ɔkylist] *nm/f* eye specialist

odeur [ɔdœʀ] *nf* smell

odieux, -euse [ɔdjø, jøz] *adj* hateful

odorant, e [ɔdɔʀã, ãt] *adj* sweet-smelling, fragrant

odorat [ɔdɔʀa] *nm* (sense of) smell

œil [œj] *(pl* **yeux**) *nm* eye; **avoir un ~ au beurre noir** ou **poché** to have a black eye; **à l'~** *(fam)* for free; **à l'~ nu** with the naked eye; **ouvrir l'~** *(fig)* to keep one's eyes open ou an eye out; **fermer les yeux (sur)** *(fig)* to turn a blind eye (to); **les yeux fermés** *(aussi fig)* with one's eyes shut

œillères [œjɛʀ] *nfpl* blinkers (BRIT), blinders (US)

œillet [œjɛ] *nm* (Bot) carnation

œuf [œf, *pl* ø] *nm* egg; **œuf à la coque** boiled egg; **œuf au plat** fried egg; **œuf dur** hard-boiled egg; **œuf de Pâques** Easter egg; **œufs brouillés** scrambled eggs

œuvre [œvʀ] *nf* (tâche) task, undertaking; *(livre, tableau etc)* work; *(ensemble de la production artistique)* works *pl* ▷ *nm* (Constr): **le gros ~** the shell; **mettre en ~** *(moyens)* to make use of; **œuvre de bienfaisance** charity; **œuvre d'art** work of art

offense [ɔfɑ̃s] *nf* insult; **offenser** *vt* to offend, hurt; **s'offenser de qch** to take offence (BRIT) ou offense (US) at sth

offert, e [ɔfɛʀ, ɛʀt] *pp de* **offrir**

office [ɔfis] *nm* (agence) bureau, agency; *(Rel)* service ▷ *nm ou nf* (pièce) pantry; **faire ~ de** to act as; **d'~** automatically; **office du tourisme** tourist bureau

officiel, le [ɔfisjɛl] *adj, nm/f* official

officier [ɔfisje] *nm* officer

officieux, -euse [ɔfisjø, jøz] *adj* unofficial

offrande [ɔfʀɑ̃d] *nf* offering

offre [ɔfʀ] *nf* offer; *(aux enchères)* bid; *(Admin: soumission)* tender; *(Écon)*: **l'~ et la demande** supply and demand; **"~s d'emploi"** "situations vacant"; **offre d'emploi** job advertised; **offre publique d'achat** takeover bid

offrir [ɔfʀiʀ] *vt*: **~ (à qn)** to offer (to sb); *(faire cadeau de)* to give (to sb); **s'offrir** *vt* (vacances, voiture) to treat o.s. to; **~ (à qn) de faire qch** to offer to do sth (for sb); **s'~ à boire à qn** (chez soi) to offer sb a drink; **je vous offre un verre** I'll buy you a drink

OGM *sigle m* (= organisme génétiquement modifié) GMO

oie [wa] *nf* (Zool) goose

oignon [ɔɲɔ̃] *nm* onion; *(de tulipe etc)* bulb

oiseau, x [wazo] *nm* bird; **oiseau de proie** bird of prey

oisif, -ive [wazif, iv] *adj* idle

o

oléoduc [ɔleɔdyk] *nm* (oil) pipeline
olive [ɔliv] *nf* (*Bot*) olive; **olivier** *nm* olive (tree)
OLP *sigle f* (= *Organisation de libération de la Palestine*) PLO
olympique [ɔlɛ̃pik] *adj* Olympic
ombragé, e [ɔ̃braʒe] *adj* shaded, shady
ombre [ɔ̃bʀ] *nf* (*espace non ensoleillé*) shade; (*ombre portée, tache*) shadow; **à l'~** in the shade; **dans l'~** (*fig*) in the dark; **ombre à paupières** eyeshadow
omelette [ɔmlɛt] *nf* omelette; **omelette norvégienne** baked Alaska
omettre [ɔmɛtʀ] *vt* to omit, leave out
omoplate [ɔmɔplat] *nf* shoulder blade

 MOT-CLÉ

on [ɔ̃] *pron* **1** (*indéterminé*) you, one; **on peut le faire ainsi** you ou one can do it like this, it can be done like this
2 (*quelqu'un*): **on les a attaqués** they were attacked; **on vous demande au téléphone** there's a phone call for you, you're wanted on the phone
3 (*nous*) we; **on va y aller demain** we're going tomorrow
4 (*les gens*) they; **autrefois, on croyait ...** they used to believe ...
5: **on ne peut plus** *adv*: **on ne peut plus stupide** as stupid as can be

oncle [ɔ̃kl] *nm* uncle
onctueux, -euse [ɔ̃ktɥø, øz] *adj* creamy, smooth
onde [ɔ̃d] *nf* wave; **~s courtes/moyennes** short/medium wave *sg*; **grandes ~s** long wave *sg*
ondée [ɔ̃de] *nf* shower
on-dit [ɔ̃di] *nm inv* rumour
onduler [ɔ̃dyle] *vi* to undulate; (*cheveux*) to wave
onéreux, -euse [ɔnerø, øz] *adj* costly
ongle [ɔ̃gl] *nm* nail
ont [ɔ̃] *vb voir* **avoir**
ONU *sigle f* (= *Organisation des Nations Unies*) UN
onze [ɔ̃z] *num* eleven; **onzième** *num* eleventh
OPA *sigle f* = **offre publique d'achat**
opaque [ɔpak] *adj* opaque
opéra [ɔpera] *nm* opera; (*édifice*) opera house
opérateur, -trice [ɔperatœr, tris] *nm/f* operator; **opérateur (de prise de vues)** cameraman
opération [ɔperasjɔ̃] *nf* operation; (*Comm*) dealing
opératoire [ɔperatwar] *adj* (*choc etc*) post-operative
opérer [ɔpere] *vt* (*personne*) to operate on; (*faire, exécuter*) to carry out, make ▷ *vi* (*remède*:

faire effet) to act, work; (*Méd*) to operate; **s'opérer** *vi* (*avoir lieu*) to occur, take place; **se faire ~** to have an operation
opérette [ɔperɛt] *nf* operetta, light opera
opinion [ɔpinjɔ̃] *nf* opinion; **l'opinion (publique)** public opinion
opportun, e [ɔpɔrtœ̃ yn] *adj* timely, opportune; **opportuniste** *nm/f* opportunist
opposant, e [ɔpozɑ̃, ɑ̃t] *nm/f* opponent
opposé, e [ɔpoze] *adj* (*direction*) opposite; (*faction*) opposing; (*opinions, intérêts*) conflicting; (*contre*): **~ à** opposed to, against ▷ *nm*: **l'~** the other ou opposite side (ou direction); (*contraire*) the opposite; **à l'~** (*fig*) on the other hand; **à l'~ de** (*fig*) contrary to, unlike
opposer [ɔpoze] *vt* (*personnes, équipes*) to oppose; (*couleurs*) to contrast; **s'opposer** *vi* (*équipes*) to confront each other; (*opinions*) to conflict; (*couleurs, styles*) to contrast; **s'~ à** (*interdire*) to oppose; **~ qch à** (*comme obstacle, défense*) to set sth against; (*comme objection*) to put sth forward against
opposition [ɔpozisjɔ̃] *nf* opposition; **par ~ à** as opposed to; **entrer en ~ avec** to come into conflict with; **faire ~ à un chèque** to stop a cheque
oppressant, e [ɔpresɑ̃, ɑ̃t] *adj* oppressive
oppresser [ɔprese] *vt* to oppress; **oppression** *nf* oppression
opprimer [ɔprime] *vt* to oppress
opter [ɔpte] *vi*: **~ pour** to opt for
opticien, ne [ɔptisjɛ̃, jɛn] *nm/f* optician
optimisme [ɔptimism] *nm* optimism; **optimiste** *nm/f* optimist ▷ *adj* optimistic
option [ɔpsjɔ̃] *nf* option; **matière à ~** (*Scol*) optional subject
optique [ɔptik] *adj* (*nerf*) optic; (*verres*) optical ▷ *nf* (*fig: manière de voir*) perspective
or [ɔr] *nm* gold ▷ *conj* now, but; **en or** (*objet*) gold *cpd*; **une affaire en or** a real bargain; **il croyait gagner or il a perdu** he was sure he would win and yet he lost
orage [ɔraʒ] *nm* (thunder)storm; **orageux, -euse** *adj* stormy
oral, e, -aux [ɔral, o] *adj, nm* oral; **par voie ~e** (*Méd*) orally
orange [ɔrɑ̃ʒ] *nf* orange ▷ *adj inv* orange; **orangé, e** *adj* orangey, orange-coloured; **orangeade** *nf* orangeade; **oranger** *nm* orange tree
orateur [ɔratœr] *nm* speaker
orbite [ɔrbit] *nf* (*Anat*) (eye-)socket; (*Physique*) orbit
Orcades [ɔrkad] *nfpl*: **les ~** the Orkneys, the Orkney Islands
orchestre [ɔrkɛstr] *nm* orchestra; (*de jazz*) band; (*places*) stalls *pl* (BRIT), orchestra (US)
orchidée [ɔrkide] *nf* orchid

ordinaire [ɔrdinɛr] *adj* ordinary; (*qualité*) standard; (*péj: commun*) common ▷ *nm* ordinary; (*menus*) everyday fare ▷ *nf* (*essence*) ≈ two-star (petrol) (BRIT), ≈ regular gas (US); **d'~** usually, normally; **comme à l'~** as usual

ordinateur [ɔrdinatœr] *nm* computer; **ordinateur individuel** *ou* **personnel** personal computer; **ordinateur portable** laptop (computer)

ordonnance [ɔrdɔnɑ̃s] *nf* (*Méd*) prescription; (*Mil*) orderly, batman (BRIT); **pouvez-vous me faire une ~?** can you write me a prescription?

ordonné, e [ɔrdɔne] *adj* tidy, orderly

ordonner [ɔrdɔne] *vt* (*agencer*) to organize, arrange; (*donner un ordre*): **~ à qn de faire** to order sb to do; (*Rel*) to ordain; (*Méd*) to prescribe

ordre [ɔrdr] *nm* order; (*propreté et soin*) orderliness, tidiness; (*nature*): **d'~ pratique** of a practical nature; **ordres** *nmpl* (*Rel*) holy orders; **mettre en ~** to tidy (up), put in order; **par ~ alphabétique/d'importance** in alphabetical order/in order of importance; **à l'~ de qn** payable to sb; **être aux ~s de qn/sous les ~s de qn** to be at sb's disposal/under sb's command; **jusqu'à nouvel ~** until further notice; **de premier ~** first-rate; **ordre du jour** (*d'une réunion*) agenda; **à l'ordre du jour** (*fig*) topical; **ordre publique** law and order

ordure [ɔrdyr] *nf* filth *no pl*; **ordures** *nfpl* (*balayures, déchets*) rubbish *sg*, refuse *sg*; **ordures ménagères** household refuse

oreille [ɔrɛj] *nf* ear; **avoir de l'~** to have a good ear (for music)

oreiller [ɔreje] *nm* pillow

oreillons [ɔrejɔ̃] *nmpl* mumps *sg*

ores [ɔr]: **d'~ et déjà** *adv* already

orfèvrerie [ɔrfɛvrəri] *nf* goldsmith's (*ou* silversmith's) trade; (*ouvrage*) gold (*ou* silver) plate

organe [ɔrgan] *nm* organ; (*porte-parole*) representative, mouthpiece

organigramme [ɔrganigram] *nm* (*tableau hiérarchique*) organization chart; (*schéma*) flow chart

organique [ɔrganik] *adj* organic

organisateur, -trice [ɔrganizatœr, tris] *nm/f* organizer

organisation [ɔrganizasjɔ̃] *nf* organization; **Organisation des Nations Unies** United Nations (Organization)

organiser [ɔrganize] *vt* to organize; (*mettre sur pied: service etc*) to set up; **s'organiser** to get organized

organisme [ɔrganism] *nm* (*Bio*) organism; (*corps, Admin*) body

organiste [ɔrganist] *nm/f* organist

orgasme [ɔrgasm] *nm* orgasm, climax

orge [ɔrʒ] *nf* barley

orgue [ɔrg] *nm* organ

orgueil [ɔrgœj] *nm* pride; **orgueilleux, -euse** *adj* proud

oriental, e, -aux [ɔrjɑ̃tal, -o] *adj* (*langue, produit*) oriental; (*frontière*) eastern

orientation [ɔrjɑ̃tasjɔ̃] *nf* (*de recherches*) orientation; (*d'une maison etc*) aspect; (*d'un journal*) leanings *pl*; **avoir le sens de l'~** to have a (good) sense of direction; **orientation professionnelle** careers advisory service

orienté, e [ɔrjɑ̃te] *adj* (*fig: article, journal*) slanted; **bien/mal ~** (*appartement*) well/badly positioned; **~ au sud** facing south, with a southern aspect

orienter [ɔrjɑ̃te] *vt* (*tourner: antenne*) to direct, turn; (*personne, recherches*) to direct; (*fig: élève*) to orientate; **s'orienter** (*se repérer*) to find one's bearings; **s'~ vers** (*fig*) to turn towards

origan [ɔrigɑ̃] *nm* oregano

originaire [ɔriʒinɛr] *adj*: **être ~ de** to be a native of

original, e, -aux [ɔriʒinal, o] *adj* original; (*bizarre*) eccentric ▷ *nm/f* eccentric ▷ *nm* (*document etc, Art*) original

origine [ɔriʒin] *nf* origin; **origines** *nfpl* (*d'une personne*) origins; **d'~** (*pays*) of origin; **d'~ suédoise** of Swedish origin; (*pneus etc*) original; **à l'~** originally; **originel, le** *adj* original

orme [ɔrm] *nm* elm

ornement [ɔrnəmɑ̃] *nm* ornament

orner [ɔrne] *vt* to decorate, adorn

ornière [ɔrnjɛr] *nf* rut

orphelin, e [ɔrfəlɛ̃, in] *adj* orphan(ed) ▷ *nm/f* orphan; **orphelin de mère/de père** motherless/fatherless; **orphelinat** *nm* orphanage

orteil [ɔrtɛj] *nm* toe; **gros ~** big toe

orthographe [ɔrtɔgraf] *nf* spelling

ortie [ɔrti] *nf* (stinging) nettle

os [ɔs] *nm* bone; **os à moelle** marrowbone

osciller [ɔsile] *vi* (*au vent etc*) to rock; (*fig*): **~ entre** to waver *ou* fluctuate between

osé, e [oze] *adj* daring, bold

oseille [ozɛj] *nf* sorrel

oser [oze] *vi, vt* to dare; **~ faire** to dare (to) do

osier [ozje] *nm* willow; **d'~, en ~** wicker(work)

osseux, -euse [ɔsø, øz] *adj* bony; (*tissu, maladie, greffe*) bone *cpd*

otage [ɔtaʒ] *nm* hostage; **prendre qn comme ~** to take sb hostage

OTAN *sigle f* (= *Organisation du traité de l'Atlantique Nord*) NATO

otarie [ɔtari] *nf* sea-lion

ôter [ote] *vt* to remove; (*soustraire*) to take away; **~ qch à qn** to take sth (away) from sb; **~ qch de** to remove sth from

otite [ɔtit] *nf* ear infection

ou [u] *conj* or; **ou ... ou** either ... or; **ou bien** or (else)

 MOT-CLÉ

où [u] *pron relatif* **1** (*position, situation*) where, that (*souvent omis*); **la chambre où il était** the room (that) he was in, the room where he was; **la ville où je l'ai rencontré** the town where I met him; **la pièce d'où il est sorti** the room he came out of; **le village d'où je viens** the village I come from; **les villes par où il est passé** the towns he went through **2** (*temps, état*) that (*souvent omis*); **le jour où il est parti** the day (that) he left; **au prix où c'est** at the price it is
▷ *adv* **1** (*interrogation*) where; **où est-il/va-t-il?** where is he/is he going?; **par où?** which way?; **d'où vient que ...?** how come ...?
2 (*position*) where; **je sais où il est** I know where he is; **où que l'on aille** wherever you go

ouate ['wat] *nf* cotton wool (*BRIT*), cotton (*US*)

oubli [ubli] *nm* (*acte*): **l'~** forgetting; (*trou de mémoire*) lapse of memory; (*négligence*) omission, oversight; **tomber dans l'~** to sink into oblivion

oublier [ublije] *vt* to forget; (*laisser quelque part: chapeau etc*) to leave behind; (*ne pas voir: erreurs etc*) to miss; **j'ai oublié ma clé/mon passeport** I've forgotten my key/passport

ouest [west] *nm* west ▷ *adj inv* west; (*région*) western; **à l'~** in the west; (*direction*) (to the) west, westwards; **à l'~ de** (to the) west of

ouf ['uf] *excl* phew!

oui ['wi] *adv* yes

ouï-dire ['widir]: **par ~** *adv* by hearsay

ouïe [wi] *nf* hearing; **ouïes** *nfpl* (*de poisson*) gills

ouragan [uragɑ̃] *nm* hurricane

ourlet [urlɛ] *nm* hem

ours [urs] *nm* bear; **ours blanc/brun** polar/ brown bear; **ours (en peluche)** teddy (bear)

oursin [ursɛ̃] *nm* sea urchin

ourson [ursɔ̃] *nm* (bear-)cub

ouste [ust] *excl* hop it!

outil [uti] *nm* tool; **outiller** *vt* to equip

outrage [utraʒ] *nm* insult; **outrage à la pudeur** indecent conduct *no pl*

outrance [utrɑ̃s]: **à ~** *adv* excessively, to excess

outre [utr] *prép* besides ▷ *adv*: **passer ~ à** to disregard, take no notice of; **en ~** besides, moreover; **~ mesure** to excess; (*manger, boire*) immoderately; **outre-Atlantique** *adv* across the Atlantic; **outre-mer** *adv* overseas

ouvert, e [uver, ert] *pp de* **ouvrir** ▷ *adj* open; (*robinet, gaz etc*) on; **ouvertement** *adv* openly;

ouverture *nf* opening; (*Mus*) overture; **heures d'ouverture** (*Comm*) opening hours; **ouverture d'esprit** open-mindedness

ouvrable [uvrabl] *adj*: **jour ~** working day, weekday

ouvrage [uvraʒ] *nm* (*tâche, de tricot etc*) work *no pl*; (*texte, livre*) work

ouvre-boîte(s) [uvrəbwat] *nm inv* tin (*BRIT*) *ou* can opener

ouvre-bouteille(s) [uvrəbutɛj] *nm inv* bottle-opener

ouvreuse [uvrøz] *nf* usherette

ouvrier, -ière [uvrije, ijer] *nm/f* worker ▷ *adj* working-class; (*conflit*) industrial; (*mouvement*) labour *cpd*; **classe ouvrière** working class

ouvrir [uvrir] *vt* (*gén*) to open; (*brèche, passage, Méd: abcès*) to open up; (*commencer l'exploitation de, créer*) to open (up); (*eau, électricité, chauffage, robinet*) to turn on ▷ *vi* to open; to open up; **s'ouvrir** *vi* to open; **s'~ à qn** to open one's heart to sb; **est-ce ouvert au public?** is it open to the public?; **quand est-ce que le musée est ouvert?** when is the museum open?; **à quelle heure ouvrez-vous?** what time do you open?; **~ l'appétit à qn** to whet sb's appetite

ovaire [over] *nm* ovary

ovale [oval] *adj* oval

OVNI [ovni] *sigle m* (= *objet volant non identifié*) UFO

oxyder [okside]: **s'oxyder** *vi* to become oxidized

oxygène [oksiʒɛn] *nm* oxygen

oxygéné, e [oksiʒene] *adj*: **eau ~e** hydrogen peroxide

ozone [ozon] *nf* ozone; **la couche d'~** the ozone layer

P

pacifique [pasifik] *adj* peaceful ▷ *nm*: **le P~, l'océan P~** the Pacific (Ocean)

pack [pak] *nm* pack

pacotille [pakɔtij] *nf* cheap junk

PACS *sigle m* (= *pacte civil de solidarité*) contract of civil partnership; **pacser: se pacser** *vi* to sign a contract of civil partnership

pacte [pakt] *nm* pact, treaty

pagaille [pagaj] *nf* mess, shambles *sg*

page [paʒ] *nf* page ▷ *nm* page (boy); **à la ~** (*fig*) up-to-date; **page d'accueil** (*Inform*) home page; **page Web** (*Inform*) web page

paiement [pɛmɑ̃] *nm* payment

païen, ne [pajɛ̃, pajɛn] *adj*, *nm/f* pagan, heathen

paillasson [pajasɔ̃] *nm* doormat

paille [paj] *nf* straw

pain [pɛ̃] *nm* (*substance*) bread; (*unité*) loaf (of bread); (*morceau*): **~ de savon** *etc* bar of soap *etc*; **pain au chocolat** chocolate-filled pastry; **pain aux raisins** currant bun; **pain bis/complet** brown/wholemeal (BRIT) *ou* wholewheat (US) bread; **pain d'épice** ≈ gingerbread; **pain de mie** sandwich loaf; **pain grillé** toast

pair, e [pɛʀ] *adj* (*nombre*) even ▷ *nm* peer; **aller de ~** to go hand in hand *ou* together; **jeune fille au ~** au pair; **paire** *nf* pair

paisible [pezibl] *adj* peaceful, quiet

paix [pɛ] *nf* peace; **faire/avoir la ~** to make/have peace; **fiche-lui la ~!** (*fam*) leave him alone!

Pakistan [pakistɑ̃] *nm*: **le ~** Pakistan

palais [palɛ] *nm* palace; (*Anat*) palate

pâle [pɑl] *adj* pale; **bleu ~** pale blue

Palestine [palɛstin] *nf*: **la ~** Palestine

palette [palɛt] *nf* (*de peintre*) palette; (*produits*) range

pâleur [pɑlœʀ] *nf* paleness

palier [palje] *nm* (*d'escalier*) landing; (*fig*) level, plateau; **par ~s** in stages

pâlir [pɑliʀ] *vi* to turn *ou* go pale; (*couleur*) to fade

pallier [palje] *vt* to offset, make up for

palme [palm] *nf* (*de plongeur*) flipper; **palmé, e** *adj* (*pattes*) webbed

palmier [palmje] *nm* palm tree; (*gâteau*) heart-shaped biscuit made of flaky pastry

pâlot, te [pɑlo, ɔt] *adj* pale, peaky

palourde [paluʀd] *nf* clam

palper [palpe] *vt* to feel, finger

palpitant, e [palpitɑ̃, ɑ̃t] *adj* thrilling

palpiter [palpite] *vi* (*cœur, pouls*) to beat; (: *plus fort*) to pound, throb

paludisme [palydism] *nm* malaria

pamphlet [pɑ̃flɛ] *nm* lampoon, satirical tract

pamplemousse [pɑ̃pləmus] *nm* grapefruit

pan [pɑ̃] *nm* section, piece ▷ *excl* bang!

panache [panaʃ] *nm* plume; (*fig*) spirit, panache

panaché, e [panaʃe] *adj*: **glace ~e** mixed-flavour ice cream ▷ *nm* (*bière*) shandy

pancarte [pɑ̃kaʀt] *nf* sign, notice

pancréas [pɑ̃kʀeas] *nm* pancreas

pané, e [pane] *adj* fried in breadcrumbs

panier [panje] *nm* basket; **mettre au ~** to chuck away; **panier à provisions** shopping basket; **panier-repas** *nm* packed lunch

panique [panik] *nf, adj* panic; **paniquer** *vi* to panic

panne [pan] *nf* breakdown; **être/tomber en ~** to have broken down/break down; **être en ~ d'essence** *ou* **sèche** to have run out of petrol (BRIT) *ou* gas (US); **ma voiture est en ~** my car has broken down; **panne d'électricité** *ou* **de courant** power cut *ou* failure

panneau, x [pano] *nm* (*écriteau*) sign, notice; **panneau d'affichage** notice board; **panneau de signalisation** roadsign; **panneau indicateur** signpost

panoplie [panɔpli] *nf* (*jouet*) outfit; (*fig*) array

panorama [panɔʀama] *nm* panorama

panse [pɑ̃s] *nf* paunch

pansement [pɑ̃smɑ̃] *nm* dressing, bandage; **pansement adhésif** sticking plaster

pantacourt [pɑ̃takuʀ] *nm* three-quarter length trousers *pl*

pantalon [pɑ̃talɔ̃] *nm* trousers *pl*, pair of trousers; **pantalon de ski** ski pants *pl*

panthère [pɑ̃tɛʀ] nf panther
pantin [pɑ̃tɛ̃] nm puppet
pantoufle [pɑ̃tufl] nf slipper
paon [pɑ̃] nm peacock
papa [papa] nm dad(dy)
pape [pap] nm pope
paperasse [papʀas] (péj) nf bumf no pl,
papers pl; **paperasserie** (péj) nf paperwork no
pl; (tracasserie) red tape no pl
papeterie [papetʀi] nf (magasin) stationer's
(shop)
papi nm (fam) granddad
papier [papje] nm paper; (article) article;
papiers nmpl (aussi: **~s d'identité**)
(identity) papers; **papier à lettres** writing
paper, notepaper; **papier (d')aluminium**
aluminium (BRIT) ou aluminum (US) foil,
tinfoil; **papier calque** tracing paper; **papier
de verre** sandpaper; **papier hygiénique** ou
(de) toilette toilet paper; **papier journal**
newspaper; **papier peint** wallpaper
papillon [papijɔ̃] nm butterfly; (fam:
contravention) (parking) ticket; **papillon de
nuit** moth
papillote [papijɔt] nf: **en ~** cooked in tinfoil
papoter [papɔte] vi to chatter
paquebot [pak(ə)bo] nm liner
pâquerette [pakʀɛt] nf daisy
Pâques [pɑk] nm, nfpl Easter

PÂQUES

In France, Easter eggs are said to be brought
by the Easter bells or **cloches de Pâques**
which fly from Rome and drop them in
people's gardens.

paquet [pakɛ] nm packet; (colis) parcel; (fig:
tas): **~ de** pile ou heap of; **un ~ de cigarettes,
s'il vous plaît** a packet of cigarettes, please;
paquet-cadeau nm: **pouvez-vous me faire
un paquet-cadeau, s'il vous plaît?** can you
gift-wrap it for me, please?
par [paʀ] prép by; **finir etc ~** to end etc with; **~
amour** out of love; **passer ~** Lyon/la côte to
go via ou through Lyons/along the coast; **~ la
fenêtre** (jeter, regarder) out of the window; **3 ~
jour/personne** 3 a ou per day/person; **2 ~ 2** in
twos; **~ ici** this way; (dans le coin) round here;
~-ci, ~-là here and there; **~ temps de pluie** in
wet weather
parabolique [paʀabɔlik] adj: **antenne ~**
parabolic ou dish aerial
parachute [paʀaʃyt] nm parachute;
parachutiste nm/f parachutist; (Mil)
paratrooper
parade [paʀad] nf (spectacle, défilé) parade;
(Escrime, Boxe) parry
paradis [paʀadi] nm heaven, paradise

paradoxe [paʀadɔks] nm paradox
paraffine [paʀafin] nf paraffin
parages [paʀaʒ] nmpl: **dans les ~ (de)** in the
area ou vicinity (of)
paragraphe [paʀagʀaf] nm paragraph
paraître [paʀɛtʀ] vb +attrib to seem, look,
appear ▷ vi to appear; (être visible) to show;
(Presse, Édition) to be published, come out,
appear ▷ vb impers: **il paraît que** it seems ou
appears that, they say that
parallèle [paʀalɛl] adj parallel; (non officiel)
unofficial ▷ nm (comparaison): **faire un ~
entre** to draw a parallel between ▷ nf parallel
(line)
paralyser [paʀalize] vt to paralyse
paramédical, e, -aux [paʀamedikal, o]
adj: **personnel ~** paramedics pl, paramedical
workers pl
paraphrase [paʀafʀɑz] nf paraphrase
parapluie [paʀaplɥi] nm umbrella
parasite [paʀazit] nm parasite; **parasites**
nmpl (Tél) interference sg
parasol [paʀasɔl] nm parasol, sunshade
paratonnerre [paʀatɔnɛʀ] nm lightning
conductor
parc [paʀk] nm (public) park, gardens pl; (de
château etc) grounds pl; (d'enfant) playpen; **parc
à thème** theme park; **parc d'attractions**
amusement park; **parc de stationnement**
car park
parcelle [paʀsɛl] nf fragment, scrap; (de
terrain) plot, parcel
parce que [paʀsk(ə)] conj because
parchemin [paʀʃəmɛ̃] nm parchment
parc(o)mètre [paʀkmɛtʀ] nm parking
meter
parcourir [paʀkuʀiʀ] vt (trajet, distance) to
cover; (article, livre) to skim ou glance through;
(lieu) to go all over, travel up and down; (suj:
frisson) to run through
parcours [paʀkuʀ] nm (trajet) journey;
(itinéraire) route
par-dessous [paʀd(ə)su] prép, adv
under(neath)
pardessus [paʀdəsy] nm overcoat
par-dessus [paʀd(ə)sy] prép over (the top of)
▷ adv over (the top); **~ le marché** on top of all
that; **~ tout** above all; **en avoir ~ la tête** to
have had enough
par-devant [paʀd(ə)vɑ̃] adv (passer) round
the front
pardon [paʀdɔ̃] nm forgiveness no pl ▷ excl
sorry!; (pour interpeller etc) excuse me!;
demander ~ à qn (de) to apologize to sb (for);
je vous demande ~ I'm sorry; (pour interpeller)
excuse me; **pardonner** vt to forgive;
pardonner qch à qn to forgive sb for sth
pare...: **pare-brise** nm inv windscreen (BRIT),
windshield (US); **pare-chocs** nm inv bumper;

pare-feu [paʀfø] nm inv (de foyer) fireguard; (Inform) firewall

pareil, le [paʀɛj] adj (identique) the same, alike; (similaire) similar; (tel): **un courage/ livre ~** such courage/a book, courage/a book like this; **de ~s livres** such books; **faire ~** to do the same (thing); **~ à** the same as; (similaire) similar to; **sans ~** unparalleled, unequalled

parent, e [paʀɑ̃, ɑ̃t] nm/f: **un(e) ~(e)** a relative ou relation; **parents** nmpl (père et mère) parents; **parenté** nf (lien) relationship

parenthèse [paʀɑ̃tɛz] nf (ponctuation) bracket, parenthesis; (digression) parenthesis, digression; **entre ~s** in brackets; (fig) incidentally

paresse [paʀɛs] nf laziness; **paresseux, -euse** adj lazy

parfait, e [paʀfɛ, ɛt] adj perfect ▷ nm (Ling) perfect (tense); **parfaitement** adv perfectly ▷ excl (most) certainly

parfois [paʀfwa] adv sometimes

parfum [paʀfœ̃] nm (produit) perfume, scent; (odeur: de fleur) scent, fragrance; (goût) flavour; **quels ~s avez-vous?** what flavours do you have?; **parfumé, e** adj (fleur, fruit) fragrant; (femme) perfumed; **parfumé au café** coffee-flavoured; **parfumer** vt (suj: odeur, bouquet) to perfume; (crème, gâteau) to flavour; **parfumerie** nf (produits) perfumes pl; (boutique) perfume shop

pari [paʀi] nm bet; **parier** vt to bet

Paris [paʀi] n Paris; **parisien, ne** adj Parisian; (Géo, Admin) Paris cpd ▷ nm/f: **Parisien, ne** Parisian

parité [paʀite] nf (Pol): **~ hommes-femmes** balanced representation of men and women

parjure [paʀʒyʀ] nm perjury

parking [paʀkiŋ] nm (lieu) car park

Attention à ne pas traduire **parking** par le mot anglais **parking**.

parlant, e [paʀlɑ̃, ɑ̃t] adj (regard) eloquent; (Cinéma) talking

parlement [paʀləmɑ̃] nm parliament; **parlementaire** adj parliamentary ▷ nm/f member of parliament

parler [paʀle] vi to speak, talk; (avouer) to talk; **~ (à qn) de** to talk ou speak (to sb) about; **~ en français** to speak French/in French; **~ affaires** to talk business; **sans ~ de** (fig) not to mention, to say nothing of; **tu parles!** (fam: bien sûr) you bet!; **parlez-vous français?** do you speak French?; **je ne parle pas anglais** I don't speak English; **est-ce que je peux ~ à ...?** can I speak to ...?

parloir [paʀlwaʀ] nm (de prison, d'hôpital) visiting room

parmi [paʀmi] prép among(st)

paroi [paʀwa] nf wall; (cloison) partition

paroisse [paʀwas] nf parish

parole [paʀɔl] nf (faculté): **la ~** speech; (mot, promesse) word; **paroles** nfpl (Mus) words, lyrics; **tenir ~** to keep one's word; **prendre la ~** to speak; **demander la ~** to ask for permission to speak; **je te crois sur ~** I'll take your word for it

parquet [paʀkɛ] nm (parquet) floor; (Jur): **le ~** the Public Prosecutor's department

parrain [paʀɛ̃] nm godfather; **parrainer** vt (suj: entreprise) to sponsor

pars [paʀ] vb voir **partir**

parsemer [paʀsəme] vt (suj: feuilles, papiers) to be scattered over; **~ qch de** to scatter sth with

part [paʀ] nf (qui revient à qn) share; (fraction, partie) part; **à ~** ▷ adv (séparément) separately; (de côté) aside ▷ prép apart from, except for; **prendre ~ à** (débat etc) to take part in; (soucis, douleur de qn) to share in; **faire ~ de qch à qn** to announce sth to sb, inform sb of sth; **pour ma ~** as for me, as far as I'm concerned; **à ~ entière** full; **de la ~ de** (au nom de) on behalf of; (donné par) from; **de toute(s) ~(s)** from all sides ou quarters; **de ~ et d'autre** on both sides, on either side; **d'une ~ ... d'autre ~** on the one hand ... on the other hand; **d'autre ~** (de plus) moreover; **faire la ~ des choses** to make allowances

partage [paʀtaʒ] nm (fractionnement) dividing up; (répartition) sharing (out) no pl, share-out

partager [paʀtaʒe] vt to share; (distribuer, répartir) to share (out); (morceler, diviser) to divide (up); **se partager** vt (héritage etc) to share between themselves (ou ourselves)

partenaire [paʀtənɛʀ] nm/f partner

parterre [paʀtɛʀ] nm (de fleurs) (flower) bed; (Théâtre) stalls pl

parti [paʀti] nm (Pol) party; (décision) course of action; (personne à marier) match; **tirer ~ de** to take advantage of, turn to good account; **prendre ~ (pour/contre)** to take sides ou a stand (for/against); **parti pris** bias

partial, e, -aux [paʀsjal, jo] adj biased, partial

participant, e [paʀtisipɑ̃, ɑ̃t] nm/f participant; (à un concours) entrant

participation [paʀtisipasjɔ̃] nf participation; (financière) contribution

participer [paʀtisipe]: **~ à** vt (course, réunion) to take part in; (frais etc) to contribute to; (chagrin, succès de qn) to share (in)

particularité [paʀtikylaʀite] nf (distinctive) characteristic

particulier, -ière [paʀtikylje, jɛʀ] adj (spécifique) particular; (spécial) special, particular; (personnel, privé) private; (étrange) peculiar, odd ▷ *nm* (*individu: Admin*) private individual; **~ à** peculiar to; **en ~** (*surtout*) in particular, particularly; (*en privé*) in private; **particulièrement** *adv* particularly

partie [paʀti] *nf* (*gén*) part; (*Jur etc: protagonistes*) party; (*de cartes, tennis etc*) game; **une ~ de pêche** a fishing party *ou* trip; **en ~** partly, in part; **faire ~ de** (*suj: chose*) to be part of; **prendre qn à ~** to take sb to task; **en grande ~** largely, in the main; **partie civile** (*Jur*) party claiming damages in a criminal case

partiel, le [paʀsjɛl] *adj* partial ▷ *nm* (*Scol*) class exam

partir [paʀtiʀ] *vi* (*gén*) to go; (*quitter*) to go, leave; (*tache*) to go, come out; **~ de** (*lieu: quitter*) to leave; (*: commencer à*) to start from; **~ pour/à** (*lieu, pays etc*) to leave for/go off to; **à ~ de** from; **le train/le bus part à quelle heure?** what time does the train/bus leave?

partisan, e [paʀtizɑ̃, an] *nm/f* partisan ▷ *adj*: **être ~ de qch/de faire** to be in favour of sth/doing

partition [paʀtisjɔ̃] *nf* (*Mus*) score

partout [paʀtu] *adv* everywhere; **~ où il allait** everywhere *ou* wherever he went

paru [paʀy] *pp de* **paraître**

parution [paʀysjɔ̃] *nf* publication

parvenir [paʀvəniʀ] : **~ à** *vt* (*atteindre*) to reach; (*réussir*): **~ à faire** to manage to do, succeed in doing; **faire ~ qch à qn** to have sth sent to sb

pas¹ [pɑ] *nm* (*enjambée, Danse*) step; (*allure, mesure*) pace; (*bruit*) (foot)step; (*trace*) footprint; **~ à ~** step by step; **au ~** at walking pace; **marcher à grands ~** to stride along; **à ~ de loup** stealthily; **faire les cent ~** to pace up and down; **faire le premier ~** to make the first move; **sur le ~ de la porte** on the doorstep

 MOT-CLÉ

pas² [pɑ] *adv* **1** (*en corrélation avec ne, non etc*) not; **il ne pleure pas** (*habituellement*) he does not *ou* doesn't cry; (*maintenant*) he's not *ou* isn't crying; **il n'a pas pleuré/ne pleurera pas** he did not *ou* didn't/will not *ou* won't cry; **ils n'ont pas de voiture/ d'enfants** they don't have *ou* haven't got a car/any children; **il m'a dit de ne pas le faire** he told me not to do it; **non pas que ...** not that ...

2 (*employé sans ne etc*): **pas moi** not me, I don't (*ou* can't *etc*); **elle travaille, (mais) lui pas** *ou* **pas lui** she works but he doesn't *ou* does not; **une pomme pas mûre** an unripe apple; **pas du tout** not at all; **pas de sucre, merci** no sugar, thanks; **ceci est à vous ou pas?** is this yours or not?, is this yours or isn't it?

3: **pas mal** (*joli: personne, maison*) not bad; **pas mal fait** not badly done *ou* made; **comment ça va? — pas mal** how are things? — not bad; **pas mal de** quite a lot of

passage [pasaʒ] *nm* (*fait de passer*) *voir* **passer**; (*lieu, prix de la traversée, extrait*) passage; (*chemin*) way; **de ~** (*touristes*) passing through; **passage à niveau** level crossing; **passage clouté** pedestrian crossing; **passage interdit** no entry; **passage souterrain** subway (BRIT), underpass

passager, -ère [pasaʒe, ɛʀ] *adj* passing ▷ *nm/f* passenger

passant, e [pasɑ̃, ɑ̃t] *adj* (*rue, endroit*) busy ▷ *nm/f* passer-by; **en ~** in passing

passe [pɑs] *nf* (*Sport, Navig*) pass; **être en ~ de faire** to be on the way to doing; **être dans une mauvaise ~** to be going through a rough patch

passé, e [pɑse] *adj* (*révolu*) past; (*dernier: semaine etc*) last; (*couleur*) faded ▷ *prép* after ▷ *nm* past; (*Ling*) past (tense); **~ de mode** out of fashion; **passé composé** perfect (tense); **passé simple** past historic (tense)

passe-partout [pɑspaʀtu] *nm inv* master *ou* skeleton key ▷ *adj inv* all-purpose

passeport [pɑspɔʀ] *nm* passport

passer [pɑse] *vi* (*aller*) to go; (*voiture, piétons: défiler*) to pass (by), go by; (*facteur, laitier etc*) to come, call; (*pour rendre visite*) to call *ou* drop in; (*film, émission*) to be on; (*temps, jours*) to pass, go by; (*couleur*) to fade; (*mode*) to die out; (*douleur*) to pass, go away; (*Scol*): **~ dans la classe supérieure** to go up to the next class ▷ *vt* (*frontière, rivière etc*) to cross; (*douane*) to go through; (*examen*) to sit, take; (*visite médicale etc*) to have; (*journée, temps*) to spend; (*enfiler: vêtement*) to slip on; (*film, pièce*) to show, put on; (*disque*) to play, put on; (*commande*) to place; (*marché, accord*) to agree on; **se passer** *vi* (*avoir lieu: scène, action*) to take place; (*se dérouler: entretien etc*) to go; (*s'écouler: semaine etc*) to pass, go by; (*arriver*): **que s'est-il passé?** what happened?; **~ qch à qn** (*sel etc*) to pass sth to sb; (*prêter*) to lend sb sth; (*lettre, message*) to pass sth on to sb; (*tolérer*) to let sb get away with sth; **~ par** to go through; **~ avant qch/qn** (*fig*) to come before sth/sb; **~ un coup de fil à qn** (*fam*) to give sb a ring; **laisser ~** (*air, lumière, personne*) to let through; (*occasion*) to let slip, miss; (*erreur*) to overlook; **~ à la radio/télévision** to be on the radio/on television; **~ à table** to sit down to eat; **~ au salon** to go into the sitting-room; **~ son tour** to miss one's turn; **~ la seconde** (*Auto*) to change into second; **~**

le balai/l'aspirateur to sweep up/hoover; **je vous passe M. Dupont** (*je vous mets en communication avec lui*) I'm putting you through to Mr Dupont; (*je lui passe l'appareil*) here is Mr Dupont, I'll hand you over to Mr Dupont; **se ~ de** to go ou do without

passerelle [pasʀɛl] *nf* footbridge; (*de navire, avion*) gangway

passe-temps [pastɑ̃] *nm inv* pastime

passif, -ive [pasif, iv] *adj* passive

passion [pasjɔ̃] *nf* passion; **passionnant, e** *adj* fascinating; **passionné, e** *adj* (*personne*) passionate; (*récit*) impassioned; **être passionné de** to have a passion for; **passionner** *vt* (*personne*) to fascinate, grip

passoire [paswaʀ] *nf* sieve; (*à légumes*) colander; (*à thé*) strainer

pastèque [pastɛk] *nf* watermelon

pasteur [pastœʀ] *nm* (*protestant*) minister, pastor

pastille [pastij] *nf* (*à sucer*) lozenge, pastille

patate [patat] *nf* (*fam: pomme de terre*) spud; **patate douce** sweet potato

patauger [patoʒe] *vi* to splash about

pâte [pat] *nf* (*à tarte*) pastry; (*à pain*) dough; (*à frire*) batter; **pâtes** *nfpl* (*macaroni etc*) pasta *sg*; **pâte à modeler** modelling clay, Plasticine® (BRIT); **pâte brisée** shortcrust pastry; **pâte d'amandes** almond paste, marzipan; **pâte de fruits** crystallized fruit *no pl*; **pâte feuilletée** puff ou flaky pastry

pâté [pate] *nm* (*charcuterie*) pâté; (*tache*) ink blot; **pâté de maisons** block (of houses); **pâté (de sable)** sandpie; **pâté en croûte** ≈ pork pie

pâtée [pate] *nf* mash, feed

patente [patɑ̃t] *nf* (*Comm*) trading licence

paternel, le [patɛʀnɛl] *adj* (*amour, soins*) fatherly; (*ligne, autorité*) paternal

pâteux, -euse [patø, øz] *adj* pasty; (*langue*) coated

pathétique [patetik] *adj* moving

patience [pasjɑ̃s] *nf* patience

patient, e [pasjɑ̃, jɑ̃t] *adj, nm/f* patient; **patienter** *vi* to wait

patin [patɛ̃] *nm* skate; (*sport*) skating; **patins (à glace)** (ice) skates; **patins à roulettes** roller skates

patinage [patinaʒ] *nm* skating

patiner [patine] *vi* to skate; (*roue, voiture*) to spin; **se patiner** *vi* (*meuble, cuir*) to acquire a sheen; **patineur, -euse** *nm/f* skater; **patinoire** *nf* skating rink, (ice) rink

pâtir [patiʀ]: **~ de** *vt* to suffer because of

pâtisserie [patisʀi] *nf* (*boutique*) cake shop; (*gâteau*) cake, pastry; (*à la maison*) pastry- ou cake-making, baking; **pâtissier, -ière** *nm/f* pastrycook

patois [patwa] *nm* dialect, patois

patrie [patʀi] *nf* homeland

patrimoine [patʀimwan] *nm* (*culture*) heritage

● **JOURNÉES DU PATRIMOINE**
●
● Once a year, important public buildings are
● open to the public for a weekend. During
● these **Journées du Patrimoine**, there are
● guided visits and talks based on a particular
● theme.

patriotique [patʀijɔtik] *adj* patriotic

patron, ne [patʀɔ̃, ɔn] *nm/f* boss; (*Rel*) patron saint ▷ *nm* (*Couture*) pattern; **patronat** *nm* employers *pl*; **patronner** *vt* to sponsor, support

patrouille [patʀuj] *nf* patrol

patte [pat] *nf* (*jambe*) leg; (*pied: de chien, chat*) paw; (*: d'oiseau*) foot

pâturage [pɑtyʀaʒ] *nm* pasture

paume [pom] *nf* palm

paumé, e [pome] (*fam*) *nm/f* drop-out

paupière [popjɛʀ] *nf* eyelid

pause [poz] *nf* (*arrêt*) break; (*en parlant, Mus*) pause

pauvre [povʀ] *adj* poor; **les pauvres** *nmpl* the poor; **pauvreté** *nf* (*état*) poverty

pavé, e [pave] *adj* (*cour*) paved; (*chaussée*) cobbled ▷ *nm* (*bloc*) paving stone; cobblestone

pavillon [pavijɔ̃] *nm* (*de banlieue*) small (detached) house; pavilion; (*drapeau*) flag

payant, e [pɛjɑ̃, ɑ̃t] *adj* (*spectateurs etc*) paying; (*fig: entreprise*) profitable; (*effort*) which pays off; **c'est ~** you have to pay, there is a charge

paye [pɛj] *nf* pay, wages *pl*

payer [peje] *vt* (*créancier, employé, loyer*) to pay; (*achat, réparations, fig: faute*) to pay for ▷ *vi* to pay; (*métier*) to be well-paid; (*tactique etc*) to pay off; **il me l'a fait ~ 10 euros** he charged me 10 euros for it; **~ qch à qn** to buy sth for sb, buy sb sth; **se ~ la tête de qn** (*fam*) to take the mickey out of sb; **est-ce que je peux ~ par carte de crédit?** can I pay by credit card?

pays [pei] *nm* country; (*région*) region; **du ~** local

paysage [peizaʒ] *nm* landscape

paysan, ne [peizɑ̃, an] *nm/f* farmer; (*péj*) peasant ▷ *adj* (*agricole*) farming; (*rural*) country

Pays-Bas [peiba] *nmpl*: **les ~** the Netherlands

PC *nm* (*Inform*) PC

PDA *sigle m* (= *personal digital assistant*) PDA

PDG *sigle m* = **président directeur général**

péage [peaʒ] *nm* toll; (*endroit*) tollgate

peau, x [po] *nf* skin; **gants de ~** fine leather gloves; **être bien/mal dans sa ~** to be quite at ease/ill-at-ease; **peau de chamois** (*chiffon*) chamois leather, shammy

P

pêche [pɛʃ] nf (fruit) peach; (sport, activité) fishing; (poissons pêchés) catch; **pêche à la ligne** (en rivière) angling

péché [peʃe] nm sin

pécher [peʃe] vi (Rel) to sin

pêcher [peʃe] nm peach tree ▷ vi to go fishing ▷ vt (attraper) to catch; (être pêcheur de) to fish for

pécheur, -eresse [peʃœʀ, peʃʀɛs] nm/f sinner

pêcheur [pɛʃœʀ] nm fisherman; (à la ligne) angler

pédagogie [pedagɔʒi] nf educational methods pl, pedagogy; **pédagogique** adj educational

pédale [pedal] nf pedal

pédalo [pedalo] nm pedal-boat

pédant, e [pedɑ̃, ɑ̃t] (péj) adj pedantic

pédestre [pedɛstʀ] adj: **randonnée ~** ramble; **sentier ~** pedestrian footpath

pédiatre [pedjatʀ] nm/f paediatrician, child specialist

pédicure [pedikyʀ] nm/f chiropodist

pègre [pɛgʀ] nf underworld

peigne [pɛɲ] nm comb; **peigner** vt to comb (the hair of); **se peigner** vi to comb one's hair; **peignoir** nm dressing gown; **peignoir de bain** bathrobe

peindre [pɛ̃dʀ] vt to paint; (fig) to portray, depict

peine [pɛn] nf (affliction) sorrow, sadness no pl; (mal, effort) trouble no pl, effort; (difficulté) difficulty; (Jur) sentence; **avoir de la ~** to be sad; **faire de la ~ à qn** to distress ou upset sb; **prendre la ~ de faire** to go to the trouble of doing; **se donner de la ~** to make an effort; **ce n'est pas la ~ de faire** there's no point in doing, it's not worth doing; **à ~** scarcely, barely; **à ~ ... que** hardly ... than, no sooner ... than; **peine capitale** capital punishment; **peine de mort** death sentence ou penalty; **peiner** vi (personne) to work hard; (moteur, voiture) to labour ▷ vt to grieve, sadden

peintre [pɛ̃tʀ] nm painter; **peintre en bâtiment** painter (and decorator)

peinture [pɛ̃tyʀ] nf painting; (matière) paint; (surfaces peintes: aussi: **~s**) paintwork; **"~ fraîche"** "wet paint"

péjoratif, -ive [peʒɔʀatif, iv] adj pejorative, derogatory

Pékin [pekɛ̃] n Beijing

pêle-mêle [pɛlmɛl] adv higgledy-piggledy

peler [pəle] vt, vi to peel

pèlerin [pɛlʀɛ̃] nm pilgrim

pèlerinage [pɛlʀinaʒ] nm pilgrimage

pelle [pɛl] nf shovel; (d'enfant, de terrassier) spade

pellicule [pelikyl] nf film; **pellicules** nfpl (Méd) dandruff sg; **je voudrais une ~ de 36 poses** I'd like a 36-exposure film

pelote [p(ə)lɔt] nf (de fil, laine) ball; **pelote basque** pelota

peloton [p(ə)lɔtɔ̃] nm group, squad; (Cyclisme) pack

pelotonner [p(ə)lɔtɔne]: **se pelotonner** vi to curl (o.s.) up

pelouse [p(ə)luz] nf lawn

peluche [p(ə)lyʃ] nf: **(animal en) ~** fluffy animal, soft toy; **chien/lapin en ~** fluffy dog/rabbit

pelure [p(ə)lyʀ] nf peeling, peel no pl

pénal, e, -aux [penal, o] adj penal; **pénalité** nf penalty

penchant [pɑ̃ʃɑ̃] nm (tendance) tendency, propensity; (faible) liking, fondness

pencher [pɑ̃ʃe] vi to tilt, lean over ▷ vt to tilt; **se pencher** vi to lean over; (se baisser) to bend down; **se ~ sur** (fig: problème) to look into; **~ pour** to be inclined to favour

pendant [pɑ̃dɑ̃] prép (au cours de) during; (indique la durée) for; **~ que** while

pendentif [pɑ̃dɑ̃tif] nm pendant

penderie [pɑ̃dʀi] nf wardrobe

pendre [pɑ̃dʀ] vt, vi to hang; **se ~** (se suicider) to hang o.s.; **~ qch à** (mur) to hang sth (up) on; (plafond) to hang sth (up) from

pendule [pɑ̃dyl] nf clock ▷ nm pendulum

pénétrer [penetʀe] vi, vt to penetrate; **~ dans** to enter

pénible [penibl] adj (travail) hard; (sujet) painful; (personne) tiresome; **péniblement** adv with difficulty

péniche [peniʃ] nf barge

pénicilline [penisilin] nf penicillin

péninsule [penɛ̃syl] nf peninsula

pénis [penis] nm penis

pénitence [penitɑ̃s] nf (peine) penance; (repentir) penitence; **pénitencier** nm penitentiary

pénombre [penɔ̃bʀ] nf (faible clarté) half-light; (obscurité) darkness

pensée [pɑ̃se] nf thought; (démarche, doctrine) thinking no pl; (fleur) pansy; **en ~** in one's mind

penser [pɑ̃se] vi, vt to think; **~ à** (ami, vacances) to think of ou about; (réfléchir à: problème, offre) to think about ou over; (prévoir) to think of; **faire ~ à** to remind one of; **~ faire qch** to be thinking of doing sth, intend to do sth; **pensif, -ive** adj pensive, thoughtful

pension [pɑ̃sjɔ̃] nf (allocation) pension; (prix du logement) board and lodgings, bed and board; (école) boarding school; **pension alimentaire** (de divorcée) maintenance allowance, alimony; **pension complète** full board; **pension de famille** boarding house, guesthouse; **pensionnaire** nm/f (Scol) boarder; **pensionnat** nm boarding school

pente [pɑ̃t] nf slope; **en ~** sloping

Pentecôte [pɑ̃tkot] nf: **la ~** Whitsun (BRIT), Pentecost

pénurie [penyʀi] nf shortage

pépé [pepe] (fam) nm grandad

pépin [pepɛ̃] nm (Bot: graine) pip; (ennui) snag, hitch

pépinière [pepinjɛʀ] nf nursery

perçant, e [pɛʀsɑ̃, ɑ̃t] adj (cri) piercing, shrill; (regard) piercing

percepteur, -trice [pɛʀsɛptœʀ, tʀis] nm/f tax collector

perception [pɛʀsɛpsjɔ̃] nf perception; (bureau) tax office

percer [pɛʀse] vt to pierce; (ouverture etc) to make; (mystère, énigme) to penetrate ▷ vi to break through; **perceuse** nf drill

percevoir [pɛʀsəvwaʀ] vt (distinguer) to perceive, detect; (taxe, impôt) to collect; (revenu, indemnité) to receive

perche [pɛʀʃ] nf (bâton) pole

percher [pɛʀʃe] vt, vi to perch; **se percher** vi to perch; **perchoir** nm perch

perçois etc [pɛʀswa] vb voir **percevoir**

perçu, e [pɛʀsy] pp de **percevoir**

percussion [pɛʀkysjɔ̃] nf percussion

percuter [pɛʀkyte] vt to strike; (suj: véhicule) to crash into

perdant, e [pɛʀdɑ̃, ɑ̃t] nm/f loser

perdre [pɛʀdʀ] vt to lose; (gaspiller: temps, argent) to waste; (personne: moralement etc) to ruin ▷ vi to lose; (sur une vente etc) to lose out; **se perdre** vi (s'égarer) to get lost, lose one's way; (denrées) to go to waste; **j'ai perdu mon portefeuille/passeport** I've lost my wallet/ passport; **je me suis perdu** (et je le suis encore) I'm lost; (et je ne le suis plus) I got lost

perdrix [pɛʀdʀi] nf partridge

perdu, e [pɛʀdy] pp de **perdre** ▷ adj (isolé) out-of-the-way; (Comm: emballage) non-returnable; (malade): **il est ~** there's no hope left for him; **à vos moments ~s** in your spare time

père [pɛʀ] nm father; **père de famille** father; **le père Noël** Father Christmas

perfection [pɛʀfɛksjɔ̃] nf perfection; **à la ~** to perfection; **perfectionné, e** adj sophisticated; **perfectionner** vt to improve, perfect; **se perfectionner en anglais** to improve one's English

perforer [pɛʀfɔʀe] vt (poinçonner) to punch

performant, e [pɛʀfɔʀmɑ̃, ɑ̃t] adj: **très ~** high-performance cpd

perfusion [pɛʀfyzjɔ̃] nf: **faire une ~ à qn** to put sb on a drip

péril [peʀil] nm peril

périmé, e [peʀime] adj (Admin) out-of-date, expired

périmètre [peʀimɛtʀ] nm perimeter

période [peʀjɔd] nf period; **périodique** adj periodic ▷ nm periodical; **garniture ou serviette périodique** sanitary towel (BRIT) ou napkin (US)

périphérique [peʀifeʀik] adj (quartiers) outlying ▷ nm (Auto): **boulevard ~** ring road (BRIT), beltway (US)

périr [peʀiʀ] vi to die, perish

périssable [peʀisabl] adj perishable

perle [pɛʀl] nf pearl; (de plastique, métal, sueur) bead

permanence [pɛʀmanɑ̃s] nf permanence; (local) (duty) office; **assurer une ~** (service public, bureaux) to operate ou maintain a basic service; **être de ~** to be on call ou duty; **en ~** continuously

permanent, e [pɛʀmanɑ̃, ɑ̃t] adj permanent; (spectacle) continuous; **permanente** nf perm

perméable [pɛʀmeabl] adj (terrain) permeable; **~ à** (fig) receptive ou open to

permettre [pɛʀmɛtʀ] vt to allow, permit; **~ à qn de faire/qch** to allow sb to do/sth; **se ~ de faire** to take the liberty of doing

permis [pɛʀmi] nm permit, licence; **permis de conduire** driving licence (BRIT), driver's license (US); **permis de construire** planning permission (BRIT), building permit (US); **permis de séjour** residence permit; **permis de travail** work permit

permission [pɛʀmisjɔ̃] nf permission; (Mil) leave; **avoir la ~ de faire** to have permission to do; **en ~** on leave

Pérou [peʀu] nm Peru

perpétuel, le [pɛʀpetɥɛl] adj perpetual; **perpétuité** nf: **à perpétuité** for life; **être condamné à perpétuité** to receive a life sentence

perplexe [pɛʀplɛks] adj perplexed, puzzled

perquisitionner [pɛʀkizisjɔne] vi to carry out a search

perron [pɛʀɔ̃] nm steps pl (leading to entrance)

perroquet [pɛʀɔkɛ] nm parrot

perruche [peʀyʃ] nf budgerigar (BRIT), budgie (BRIT), parakeet (US)

perruque [peʀyk] nf wig

persécuter [pɛʀsekyte] vt to persecute

persévérer [pɛʀseveʀe] vi to persevere

persil [pɛʀsi] nm parsley

Persique [pɛʀsik] adj: **le golfe ~** the (Persian) Gulf

persistant, e [pɛʀsistɑ̃, ɑ̃t] adj persistent

persister [pɛʀsiste] vi to persist; **~ à faire qch** to persist in doing sth

personnage [pɛʀsɔnaʒ] nm (individu) character, individual; (célébrité) important person; (de roman, film) character; (Peinture) figure

personnalité [pɛʀsɔnalite] nf personality; (personnage) prominent figure

personne [pɛʀsɔn] nf person ▷ pron nobody,

P

no one; *(avec négation en anglais)* anybody, anyone; **personne âgée** elderly person; **personnel, le** *adj* personal; *(égoïste)* selfish ▷ *nm* staff, personnel; **personnellement** *adv* personally

perspective [pɛʀspɛktiv] *nf* (*Art*) perspective; *(vue)* view; *(point de vue)* viewpoint, angle; *(chose envisagée)* prospect; **en ~** in prospect

perspicace [pɛʀspikas] *adj* clear-sighted, gifted with *(ou* showing) insight; **perspicacité** *nf* clear-sightedness

persuader [pɛʀsɥade] *vt*: **~ qn (de faire)** to persuade sb (to do); **persuasif, -ive** *adj* persuasive

perte [pɛʀt] *nf* loss; *(de temps)* waste; *(fig: morale)* ruin; **à ~ de vue** as far as the eye can *(ou* could) see; **pertes blanches** (vaginal) discharge *sg*

pertinent, e [pɛʀtinɑ̃, ɑ̃t] *adj* apt, relevant

perturbation [pɛʀtyʀbasjɔ̃] *nf*: **perturbation (atmosphérique)** atmospheric disturbance

perturber [pɛʀtyʀbe] *vt* to disrupt; (*Psych*) to perturb, disturb

pervers, e [pɛʀvɛʀ, ɛʀs] *adj* perverted

pervertir [pɛʀvɛʀtiʀ] *vt* to pervert

pesant, e [pəzɑ̃, ɑ̃t] *adj* heavy; *(fig: présence)* burdensome

pèse-personne [pɛzpɛʀsɔn] *nm* (bathroom) scales *pl*

peser [pəze] *vt* to weigh ▷ *vi* to weigh; *(fig: avoir de l'importance)* to carry weight; **~ lourd** to be heavy

pessimiste [pesimist] *adj* pessimistic ▷ *nm/f* pessimist

peste [pɛst] *nf* plague

pétale [petal] *nm* petal

pétanque [petɑ̃k] *nf* type of bowls

pétard [petaʀ] *nm* banger (BRIT), firecracker

péter [pete] *vi* (*fam: casser*) to bust; *(fam!)* to fart (!)

pétillant, e [petijɑ̃, ɑ̃t] *adj* (*eau etc*) sparkling

pétiller [petije] *vi* (*feu*) to crackle; *(champagne)* to bubble; *(yeux)* to sparkle

petit, e [p(ə)ti, it] *adj* small; *(avec nuance affective)* little; *(voyage)* short, little; *(bruit etc)* faint, slight ▷ *nm/f* (*petit enfant*) little boy/girl;

child; **petits** *nmpl* (*d'un animal*) young *no pl*; **faire des ~s** to have kittens *(ou* puppies *etc)*; **la classe des ~s** the infant class; **les tout-~s** the little ones, the tiny tots *(fam)*; **~ à ~** bit by bit, gradually; **petit(e) ami(e)** boyfriend/girlfriend; **petit déjeuner** breakfast; **le petit déjeuner est à quelle heure?** what time is breakfast?; **petit four** petit four; **petit pain** (bread) roll; **les petites annonces** the small ads; **petits pois** (garden) peas; **petite-fille** *nf* granddaughter; **petit-fils** *nm* grandson

pétition [petisjɔ̃] *nf* petition

petits-enfants [pətizɑ̃fɑ̃] *nmpl* grandchildren

pétrin [petʀɛ̃] *nm* (*fig*): **dans le ~** *(fam)* in a jam *ou* fix

pétrir [petʀiʀ] *vt* to knead

pétrole [petʀɔl] *nm* oil; *(pour lampe, réchaud etc)* paraffin (oil); **pétrolier, -ière** *nm* oil tanker

 Attention à ne pas traduire *pétrole* par le mot anglais *petrol*.

○ **MOT-CLÉ**

peu [pø] *adv* **1** *(modifiant verbe, adjectif, adverbe)*: **il boit peu** he doesn't drink (very) much; **il est peu bavard** he's not very talkative; **peu avant/après** shortly before/afterwards
2 *(modifiant nom)*: **peu de**: **peu de gens/d'arbres** few *ou* not (very) many people/trees; **il a peu d'espoir** he hasn't (got) much hope, he has little hope; **pour peu de temps** for (only) a short while
3: **peu à peu** little by little; **à peu près** just about, more or less; **à peu près 10 kg/10 euros** approximately 10 kg/10 euros
▷ *nm* **1**: **le peu de gens qui** the few people who; **le peu de sable qui** what little sand, the little sand which
2: **un peu** a little; **un petit peu** a little bit; **un peu d'espoir** a little hope; **elle est un peu bavarde** she's quite *ou* rather talkative; **un peu plus de** slightly more than; **un peu moins de** slightly less than; *(avec pluriel)* slightly fewer than
▷ *pron*: **peu le savent** few know (it); **de peu** (only) just

peuple [pœpl] *nm* people; **peupler** *vt* (*pays, région*) to populate; *(étang)* to stock; *(suj: hommes, poissons)* to inhabit

peuplier [pøplije] *nm* poplar (tree)

peur [pœʀ] *nf* fear; **avoir ~ (de/de faire/que)** to be frightened *ou* afraid (of/of doing/that); **faire ~ à** to frighten; **de ~ de/que** for fear of/that; **peureux, -euse** *adj* fearful, timorous

peut [pø] *vb voir* **pouvoir**

peut-être [pøtɛtʀ] *adv* perhaps, maybe; **~ que** perhaps, maybe; **~ bien qu'il fera/est** he may well do/be

phare [faʀ] nm (en mer) lighthouse; (de véhicule) headlight

pharmacie [faʀmasi] nf (magasin) chemist's (BRIT), pharmacy; (de salle de bain) medicine cabinet; **pharmacien, ne** nm/f pharmacist, chemist (BRIT)

phénomène [fenɔmɛn] nm phenomenon

philosophe [filɔzɔf] nm/f philosopher ▷ adj philosophical

philosophie [filɔzɔfi] nf philosophy

phobie [fɔbi] nf phobia

phoque [fɔk] nm seal

phosphorescent, e [fɔsfɔresɑ̃, ɑ̃t] adj luminous

photo [fɔto] nf photo(graph); **prendre en ~** to take a photo of; **pourriez-vous nous prendre en ~, s'il vous plaît?** would you take a picture of us, please?; **faire de la ~** to take photos; **photo d'identité** passport photograph; **photocopie** nf photocopy; **photocopier** vt to photocopy; **photocopieuse** nf photocopier; **photographe** nm/f photographer; **photographie** nf (technique) photography; (cliché) photograph; **photographier** vt to photograph

phrase [fʀɑz] nf sentence

physicien, ne [fizisjɛ̃, jɛn] nm/f physicist

physique [fizik] adj physical ▷ nm physique ▷ nf physics sg; **au ~** physically; **physiquement** adv physically

pianiste [pjanist] nm/f pianist

piano [pjano] nm piano; **pianoter** vi to tinkle away (at the piano)

pic [pik] nm (instrument) pick(axe); (montagne) peak; (Zool) woodpecker; **à ~** vertically; (fig: tomber, arriver) just at the right time

pichet [piʃɛ] nm jug

picorer [pikɔʀe] vt to peck

pie [pi] nf magpie

pièce [pjɛs] nf (d'un logement) room; (Théâtre) play; (de machine) part; (de monnaie) coin; (document) document; (fragment, de collection) piece; **dix euros ~** ten euros each; **vendre à la ~** to sell separately; **travailler à la ~** to do piecework; **un maillot une ~** a one-piece swimsuit; **un deux-~s cuisine** a two-room(ed) flat (BRIT) ou apartment (US) with kitchen; **pièce à conviction** exhibit; **pièce d'eau** ornamental lake ou pond; **pièce de rechange** spare (part); **pièce d'identité: avez-vous une pièce d'identité?** have you got any (means of) identification?; **pièce jointe** (Comput) attachment; **pièce montée** tiered cake; **pièces détachées** spares, (spare) parts; **pièces justificatives** supporting documents

pied [pje] nm foot; (de table) leg; (de lampe) base; **~s nus** ou **nus-~s** barefoot; **à ~** on foot;

au **~ de la lettre** literally; **avoir ~** to be able to touch the bottom, not to be out of one's depth; **avoir le ~ marin** to be a good sailor; **sur ~** (debout, rétabli) up and about; **mettre sur ~** (entreprise) to set up; **c'est le ~** (fam) it's brilliant; **mettre les ~s dans le plat** (fam) to put one's foot in it; **il se débrouille comme un ~** (fam) he's completely useless; **pied-noir** nm Algerian-born Frenchman

piège [pjɛʒ] nm trap; **prendre au ~** to trap; **piéger** vt (avec une bombe) to booby-trap; **lettre/voiture piégée** letter-/car-bomb

piercing [pjɛʀsiŋ] nm body piercing

pierre [pjɛʀ] nf stone; **pierre tombale** tombstone; **pierreries** nfpl gems, precious stones

piétiner [pjetine] vi (trépigner) to stamp (one's foot); (fig) to be at a standstill ▷ vt to trample on

piéton, ne [pjetɔ̃, ɔn] nm/f pedestrian; **piétonnier, -ière** adj: **rue** ou **zone piétonnière** pedestrian precinct

pieu, x [pjø] nm post; (pointu) stake

pieuvre [pjœvʀ] nf octopus

pieux, -euse [pjø, pjøz] adj pious

pigeon [piʒɔ̃] nm pigeon

piger [piʒe] (fam) vi, vt to understand

pigiste [piʒist] nm/f freelance(r)

pignon [piɲɔ̃] nm (de mur) gable

pile [pil] nf (tas) pile; (Élec) battery ▷ adv (fam: s'arrêter etc) dead; **à deux heures ~** at two on the dot; **jouer à ~ ou face** to toss up (for it); **~ ou face?** heads or tails?

piler [pile] vt to crush, pound

pilier [pilje] nm pillar

piller [pije] vt to pillage, plunder, loot

pilote [pilɔt] nm pilot; (de voiture) driver ▷ adj pilot cpd; **pilote de course** racing driver; **pilote de ligne** airline pilot; **piloter** vt (avion) to pilot, fly; (voiture) to drive

pilule [pilyl] nf pill; **prendre la ~** to be on the pill

piment [pimɑ̃] nm (aussi: **~ rouge**) chilli; (fig) spice, piquancy; **~ doux** pepper, capsicum; **pimenté, e** adj (plat) hot, spicy

pin [pɛ̃] nm pine

pinard [pinaʀ] (fam) nm (cheap) wine, plonk (BRIT)

pince [pɛ̃s] nf (outil) pliers pl; (de homard, crabe) pincer, claw; (Couture: pli) dart; **pince à épiler** tweezers pl; **pince à linge** clothes peg (BRIT) ou pin (US)

pincé, e [pɛ̃se] adj (air) stiff

pinceau, x [pɛ̃so] nm (paint)brush

pincer [pɛ̃se] vt to pinch; (fam) to nab

pinède [pinɛd] nf pinewood, pine forest

pingouin [pɛ̃gwɛ̃] nm penguin

ping-pong® [piŋpɔ̃g] nm table tennis

pinson [pɛ̃sɔ̃] nm chaffinch

pintade [pɛ̃tad] nf guinea-fowl

pion [pjɔ̃] nm (Échecs) pawn; (Dames) piece; (Scol) supervisor

pionnier [pjɔnje] nm pioneer

pipe [pip] nf pipe; **fumer la ~** to smoke a pipe

piquant, e [pikɑ̃, ɑ̃t] adj (barbe, rosier etc) prickly; (saveur, sauce) hot, pungent; (détail) titillating; (froid) biting ▷ nm (épine) thorn, prickle; (fig) spiciness, spice

pique [pik] nf pike; (fig) cutting remark ▷ nm (Cartes) spades pl

pique-nique [piknik] nm picnic; **pique-niquer** vi to have a picnic

piquer [pike] vt (suj: guêpe, fumée, orties) to sting; (: moustique) to bite; (: barbe) to prick; (: froid) to bite; (Méd) to give a jab to; (: chien, chat) to put to sleep; (intérêt) to arouse; (fam: voler) to pinch ▷ vi (avion) to go into a dive

piquet [pike] nm (pieu) post, stake; (de tente) peg

piqûre [pikyʀ] nf (d'épingle) prick; (d'ortie) sting; (de moustique) bite; (Méd) injection, shot (US); **faire une ~ à qn** to give sb an injection

pirate [piʀat] nm, adj pirate; **pirate de l'air** hijacker

pire [piʀ] adj worse; (superlatif): **le(la) ~ ...** the worst ... ▷ nm: **le ~ (de)** the worst (of); **au ~** at (the very) worst

pis [pi] nm (de vache) udder ▷ adj, adv worse; **de mal en ~** from bad to worse

piscine [pisin] nf (swimming) pool; **piscine couverte** indoor (swimming) pool

pissenlit [pisɑ̃li] nm dandelion

pistache [pistaʃ] nf pistachio (nut)

piste [pist] nf (d'un animal, sentier) track, trail; (indice) lead; (de stade) track; (de cirque) ring; (de danse) floor; (de patinage) rink; (de ski) run; (Aviat) runway; **piste cyclable** cycle track

pistolet [pistɔlɛ] nm (arme) pistol, gun; (à peinture) spray gun; **pistolet-mitrailleur** nm submachine gun

piston [pistɔ̃] nm (Tech) piston; **avoir du ~** (fam) to have friends in the right places; **pistonner** vt (candidat) to pull strings for

piteux, -euse [pitø, øz] adj pitiful, sorry (avant le nom); **en ~ état** in a sorry state

pitié [pitje] nf pity; **il me fait ~** I feel sorry for him; **avoir ~ de** (compassion) to pity, feel sorry for; (merci) to have pity ou mercy on

pitoyable [pitwajabl] adj pitiful

pittoresque [pitɔʀɛsk] adj picturesque

PJ sigle f (= police judiciaire) ≈ CID (BRIT), ≈ FBI (US)

placard [plakaʀ] nm (armoire) cupboard; (affiche) poster, notice

place [plas] nf (emplacement, classement) place; (de ville, stade) square; (espace libre) room, space; (de parking) space; (siège: de train, cinéma, voiture) seat; (emploi) job; **en ~** (mettre) in its place; **sur ~** on the spot; **faire ~ à** to give way to; **ça prend de la ~** it takes up a lot of room ou space; **à la ~ de** in place of, instead of; **à votre ~ ...** if I were you ...; **je voudrais réserver deux ~s** I'd like to book two seats; **la ~ est prise?** is this seat taken?; **se mettre à la ~ de qn** to put o.s. in sb's place ou in sb's shoes

placé, e [plase] adj: **haut ~** (fig) high-ranking; **être bien/mal ~** (spectateur) to have a good/a poor seat; (concurrent) to be in a good/bad position; **il est bien ~ pour le savoir** he is in a position to know

placement [plasmɑ̃] nm (Finance) investment; **agence ou bureau de ~** employment agency

placer [plase] vt to place; (convive, spectateur) to seat; (argent) to place, invest; **se ~ au premier rang** to go and stand (ou sit) in the first row

plafond [plafɔ̃] nm ceiling

plage [plaʒ] nf beach; **plage arrière** (Auto) parcel ou back shelf

plaider [plede] vi (avocat) to plead ▷ vt to plead; **~ pour** (fig) to speak for; **plaidoyer** nm (Jur) speech for the defence; (fig) plea

plaie [plɛ] nf wound

plaignant, e [plɛɲɑ̃, ɑ̃t] nm/f plaintiff

plaindre [plɛ̃dʀ] vt to pity, feel sorry for; **se plaindre** vi (gémir) to moan; (protester): **se ~ (à qn) (de)** to complain (to sb) (about); (souffrir): **se ~ de** to complain of

plaine [plɛn] nf plain

plain-pied [plɛ̃pje] adv: **de ~ (avec)** on the same level (as)

plainte [plɛ̃t] nf (gémissement) moan, groan; (doléance) complaint; **porter ~** to lodge a complaint

plaire [plɛʀ] vi to be a success, be successful; **ça plaît beaucoup aux jeunes** it's very popular with young people; **~ à: cela me plaît** I like it; **se ~ quelque part** to like being somewhere ou like it somewhere; **s'il vous plaît** please

plaisance [plɛzɑ̃s] nf (aussi: **navigation de ~**) (pleasure) sailing, yachting

plaisant, e [plɛzɑ̃, ɑ̃t] adj pleasant; (histoire, anecdote) amusing

plaisanter [plɛzɑ̃te] vi to joke; **plaisanterie** nf joke

plaisir [pleziʀ] nm pleasure; **faire ~ à qn** (délibérément) to be nice to sb, please sb; **ça me fait ~** I like (doing); **j'espère que ça te fera ~** I hope you'll like it; **pour le ~** for pleasure

plaît [plɛ] vb voir **plaire**

plan, e [plɑ̃, an] adj flat ▷ nm plan; (fig) level, plane; (Cinéma) shot; **au premier/second ~** in the foreground/middle distance; **à l'arrière ~** in the background; **plan d'eau** lake

planche [plɑ̃ʃ] nf (pièce de bois) plank,

(wooden) board; (*illustration*) plate; **planche à repasser** ironing board; **planche (à roulettes)** skateboard; **planche (à voile)** (*sport*) windsurfing

plancher [plɑ̃ʃe] *nm* floor; floorboards *pl* ▷ *vi* (*fam*) to work hard

planer [plane] *vi* to glide; (*fam: rêveur*) to have one's head in the clouds; **~ sur** (*fig: danger*) to hang over

planète [planɛt] *nf* planet

planeur [planœʀ] *nm* glider

planifier [planifje] *vt* to plan

planning [planiŋ] *nm* programme, schedule; **planning familial** family planning

plant [plɑ̃] *nm* seedling, young plant

plante [plɑ̃t] *nf* plant; **la plante du pied** the sole (of the foot); **plante verte** *ou* **d'appartement** house plant

planter [plɑ̃te] *vt* (*plante*) to plant; (*enfoncer*) to hammer *ou* drive in; (*tente*) to put up, pitch; (*fam: personne*) to dump; **se planter** (*fam: se tromper*) to get it wrong

plaque [plak] *nf* plate; (*de verglas, d'eczéma*) patch; (*avec inscription*) plaque; **plaque chauffante** hotplate; **plaque de chocolat** bar of chocolate; **plaque tournante** (*fig*) centre

plaqué, e [plake] *adj*: **~ or/argent** gold-/silver-plated

plaquer [plake] *vt* (*Rugby*) to bring down; (*fam: laisser tomber*) to drop

plaquette [plakɛt] *nf* (*de chocolat*) bar; (*beurre*) pack(et); **plaquette de frein** brake pad

plastique [plastik] *adj, nm* plastic; **plastiquer** *vt* to blow up (*with a plastic bomb*)

plat, e [pla, -at] *adj* flat; (*cheveux*) straight; (*style*) flat, dull ▷ *nm* (*récipient, Culin*) dish; (*d'un repas*) course; **à ~ ventre** face down; **à ~** (*pneu, batterie*) flat; (*fam: personne*) dead beat; **plat cuisiné** pre-cooked meal; **plat de résistance** main course; **plat du jour** dish of the day

platane [platan] *nm* plane tree

plateau, x [plato] *nm* (*support*) tray; (*Géo*) plateau; (*Cinéma*) set; **plateau à fromages** cheese board

plate-bande [platbɑ̃d] *nf* flower bed

plate-forme [platfɔʀm] *nf* platform; **plate-forme de forage/pétrolière** drilling/oil rig

platine [platin] *nm* platinum ▷ *nf* (*d'un tourne-disque*) turntable; **platine laser** compact disc *ou* CD player

plâtre [plɑtʀ] *nm* (*matériau*) plaster; (*statue*) plaster statue; (*Méd*) (plaster) cast; **avoir un bras dans le ~** to have an arm in plaster

plein, e [plɛ̃, plɛn] *adj* full ▷ *nm*: **faire le ~ (d'essence)** to fill up (with petrol); **à ~es mains** (*ramasser*) in handfuls; **à ~ temps** full-time; **en ~ air** in the open air; **en ~ soleil** in direct sunlight; **en ~e nuit/rue** in the

middle of the night/street; **en ~ jour** in broad daylight; **le ~, s'il vous plaît** fill it up, please

pleurer [plœʀe] *vi* to cry; (*yeux*) to water ▷ *vt* to mourn (for); **~ sur** to lament (over), to bemoan

pleurnicher [plœʀniʃe] *vi* to snivel, whine

pleurs [plœʀ] *nmpl*: **en ~** in tears

pleut [plø] *vb voir* **pleuvoir**

pleuvoir [pløvwaʀ] *vb impers* to rain ▷ *vi* (*coups*) to rain down; (*critiques, invitations*) to shower down; **il pleut** it's raining; **il pleut des cordes** it's pouring (down), it's raining cats and dogs

pli [pli] *nm* fold; (*de jupe*) pleat; (*de pantalon*) crease

pliant, e [plijɑ̃, plijɑ̃t] *adj* folding

plier [plije] *vt* to fold; (*pour ranger*) to fold up; (*genou, bras*) to bend ▷ *vi* to bend; (*fig*) to yield; **se ~ à** to submit to

plisser [plise] *vt* (*jupe*) to put pleats in; (*yeux*) to screw up; (*front*) to crease

plomb [plɔ̃] *nm* (*métal*) lead; (*d'une cartouche*) (lead) shot; (*Pêche*) sinker; (*Élec*) fuse; **sans ~** (*essence etc*) unleaded

plomberie [plɔ̃bʀi] *nf* plumbing

plombier [plɔ̃bje] *nm* plumber

plonge [plɔ̃ʒ] *nf* washing-up

plongeant, e [plɔ̃ʒɑ̃, ɑ̃t] *adj* (*vue*) from above; (*décolleté*) plunging

plongée [plɔ̃ʒe] *nf* (*Sport*) diving *no pl*; (*sans scaphandre*) skin diving; **~ sous-marine** diving

plongeoir [plɔ̃ʒwaʀ] *nm* diving board

plongeon [plɔ̃ʒɔ̃] *nm* dive

plonger [plɔ̃ʒe] *vi* to dive ▷ *vt*: **~ qch dans** to plunge sth into; **se ~ dans** (*études, lecture*) to bury *ou* immerse o.s. in; **plongeur** *nm* diver

plu [ply] *pp de* **plaire**; *de* **pleuvoir**

pluie [plɥi] *nf* rain

plume [plym] *nf* feather; (*pour écrire*) (pen) nib; (*fig*) pen

plupart [plypaʀ]: **la ~** *pron* the majority, most (of them); **la ~ des** most, the majority of; **la ~ du temps/d'entre nous** most of the time/of us; **pour la ~** for the most part, mostly

pluriel [plyʀjɛl] *nm* plural

plus¹ [ply] *vb voir* **plaire**

 MOT-CLÉ

plus² [ply] *adv* **1** (*forme négative*): **ne ... plus** no more, no longer; **je n'ai plus d'argent** I've got no more money *ou* no money left; **il ne travaille plus** he's no longer working, he doesn't work any more

2 [ply, plyz + *voyelle*] (*comparatif*) more, ...+er; (*superlatif*): **le plus** the most, the ...+est; **plus grand/intelligent (que)** bigger/more intelligent (than); **le plus grand/intelligent** the biggest/most intelligent; **tout au plus** at

the very most
3 [plys, plyz + *voyelle*] (*davantage*) more; **il travaille plus (que)** he works more (than); **plus il travaille, plus il est heureux** the more he works, the happier he is; **plus de 10 personnes/3 heures** more than ou over 10 people/3 hours; **3 heures de plus que** 3 hours more than; **de plus** what's more, moreover; **il a 3 ans de plus que moi** he's 3 years older than me; **3 kilos en plus** 3 kilos more; **en plus de** in addition to; **de plus en plus** more and more; **plus ou moins** more or less; **ni plus ni moins** no more, no less
▷ *prép* [plys]: **4 plus 2** 4 plus 2

plusieurs [plyziœʀ] *dét, pron* several; **ils sont ~** there are several of them
plus-value [plyvaly] *nf* (*bénéfice*) surplus
plutôt [plyto] *adv* rather; **je préfère ~ celui-ci** I'd rather have this one; **~ que (de) faire** rather than ou instead of doing
pluvieux, -euse [plyvjø, jøz] *adj* rainy, wet
PME *sigle f* (= *petite(s) et moyenne(s) entreprise(s)*) small business(es)
PMU *sigle m* (= *Pari mutuel urbain*) system of betting on horses; (*café*) betting agency
PNB *sigle m* (= *produit national brut*) GNP
pneu [pnø] *nm* tyre (BRIT), tire (US); **j'ai un ~ crevé** I've got a flat tyre
pneumonie [pnømɔni] *nf* pneumonia
poche [pɔʃ] *nf* pocket; (*sous les yeux*) bag, pouch; **argent de ~** pocket money
pochette [pɔʃɛt] *nf* (*d'aiguilles etc*) case; (*mouchoir*) breast pocket handkerchief; (*sac à main*) clutch bag; **pochette de disque** record sleeve
poêle [pwal] *nm* stove ▷ *nf*: **~ (à frire)** frying pan
poème [pɔɛm] *nm* poem
poésie [pɔezi] *nf* (*poème*) poem; (*art*): **la ~** poetry
poète [pɔɛt] *nm* poet
poids [pwa] *nm* weight; (*Sport*) shot; **vendre au ~** to sell by weight; **perdre/prendre du ~** to lose/put on weight; **poids lourd** (*camion*) lorry (BRIT), truck (US)
poignant, e [pwaɲɑ̃, ɑ̃t] *adj* poignant
poignard [pwaɲaʀ] *nm* dagger; **poignarder** *vt* to stab, knife
poigne [pwaɲ] *nf* grip; **avoir de la ~** (*fig*) to rule with a firm hand
poignée [pwaɲe] *nf* (*de sel etc, fig*) handful; (*de couvercle, porte*) handle; **poignée de main** handshake
poignet [pwaɲɛ] *nm* (*Anat*) wrist; (*de chemise*) cuff
poil [pwal] *nm* (*Anat*) hair; (*de pinceau, brosse*) bristle; (*de tapis*) strand; (*pelage*) coat; **à ~** (*fam*) starkers; **au ~** (*fam*) hunky-

dory; **poilu, e** *adj* hairy
poinçonner [pwɛ̃sɔne] *vt* (*bijou*) to hallmark; (*billet*) to punch
poing [pwɛ̃] *nm* fist; **coup de ~** punch
point [pwɛ̃] *nm* point; (*endroit*) place; (*marque, signe*) dot; (: *de ponctuation*) full stop, period (US); (*Couture, Tricot*) stitch ▷ *adv* = **pas²**; **faire le ~** (*fig*) to take stock (of the situation); **sur le ~ de faire** (just) about to do; **à tel ~ que** so much so that; **mettre au ~** (*procédé*) to develop; (*affaire*) to settle; **à ~** (*Culin: viande*) medium; **à ~ (nommé)** just at the right time; **deux ~s** colon; **point de côté** stitch (*pain*); **point d'exclamation/d'interrogation** exclamation/question mark; **point de repère** landmark; (*dans le temps*) point of reference; **point de vente** retail outlet; **point de vue** viewpoint; (*fig: opinion*) point of view; **point faible** weak spot; **point final** full stop, period (US); **point mort**: **au point mort** (*Auto*) in neutral; **points de suspension** suspension points
pointe [pwɛ̃t] *nf* point; (*clou*) tack; (*fig*): **une ~ de** a hint of; **être à la ~ de** (*fig*) to be in the forefront of; **sur la ~ des pieds** on tiptoe; **en ~** pointed, tapered; **de ~** (*technique etc*) leading; **heures de ~** peak hours
pointer [pwɛ̃te] *vt* (*diriger: canon, doigt*): **~ sur qch** to point at sth ▷ *vi* (*employé*) to clock in
pointillé [pwɛ̃tije] *nm* (*trait*) dotted line
pointilleux, -euse [pwɛ̃tijø, øz] *adj* particular, pernickety
pointu, e [pwɛ̃ty] *adj* pointed; (*voix*) shrill; (*analyse*) precise
pointure [pwɛ̃tyʀ] *nf* size
point-virgule [pwɛ̃viʀgyl] *nm* semi-colon
poire [pwaʀ] *nf* pear; (*fam: péj*) mug
poireau, x [pwaʀo] *nm* leek
poirier [pwaʀje] *nm* pear tree
pois [pwa] *nm* (*Bot*) pea; (*sur une étoffe*) dot, spot; **~ chiche** chickpea; **à ~** (*cravate etc*) spotted, polka-dot *cpd*
poison [pwazɔ̃] *nm* poison
poisseux, -euse [pwasø, øz] *adj* sticky
poisson [pwasɔ̃] *nm* fish *gén inv*; (*Astrol*): **P~s** Pisces; **~ d'avril** April fool; (*blague*) April Fool's Day trick; *see note*; **poisson rouge** goldfish; **poissonnerie** *nf* fish-shop; **poissonnier, -ière** *nm/f* fishmonger (BRIT), fish merchant (US)

● **POISSON D'AVRIL**
●
●
● The traditional April Fools' Day prank in
● France involves attaching a cut-out paper
● fish, known as a 'poisson d'avril', to the back
● of one's victim, without being caught.

poitrine [pwatʀin] *nf* chest; (*seins*) bust,

bosom; (Culin) breast
poivre [pwavʀ] nm pepper
poivron [pwavʀɔ̃] nm pepper, capsicum
polaire [pɔlɛʀ] adj polar
pôle [pol] nm (Géo, Élec) pole; **le ~ Nord/Sud**
the North/South Pole
poli, e [pɔli] adj polite; (lisse) smooth
police [pɔlis] nf police; **police judiciaire**
≈ Criminal Investigation Department (BRIT),
≈ Federal Bureau of Investigation (US); **police
secours** ≈ emergency services pl (BRIT),
≈ paramedics pl (US); **policier, -ière** adj police
cpd ⊳ nm policeman; (aussi: **roman policier**)
detective novel
polir [pɔliʀ] vt to polish
politesse [pɔlitɛs] nf politeness
politicien, ne [pɔlitisjɛ̃, jɛn] (péj) nm/f
politician
politique [pɔlitik] adj political ⊳ nf politics sg;
(mesures, méthode) policies pl
politiquement [pɔlitikmɑ̃] adv politically; **~
correct** politically correct
pollen [pɔlɛn] nm pollen
polluant, e [pɔlɥɑ̃, ɑ̃t] adj polluting ⊳ nm
(produit): **~** pollutant; **non ~** non-polluting
polluer [pɔlɥe] vt to pollute; **pollution** nf
pollution
polo [pɔlo] nm (chemise) polo shirt
Pologne [pɔlɔɲ] nf: **la ~** Poland; **polonais,
e** adj Polish ⊳ nm/f: **Polonais, e** Pole ⊳ nm
(Ling) Polish
poltron, ne [pɔltʀɔ̃, ɔn] adj cowardly
polycopier [pɔlikɔpje] vt to duplicate
Polynésie [pɔlinezi] nf: **la ~** Polynesia; **la ~
française** French Polynesia
polyvalent, e [pɔlivalɑ̃, ɑ̃t] adj (rôle) varied;
(salle) multi-purpose
pommade [pɔmad] nf ointment, cream
pomme [pɔm] nf apple; **tomber dans
les ~s** (fam) to pass out; **pomme d'Adam**
Adam's apple; **pomme de pin** pine ou fir cone;
pomme de terre potato
pommette [pɔmɛt] nf cheekbone
pommier [pɔmje] nm apple tree
pompe [pɔ̃p] nf pump; (faste) pomp (and
ceremony); **pompe (à essence)** petrol
pump; **pompes funèbres** funeral parlour sg,
undertaker's sg; **pomper** vt to pump; (aspirer)
to pump up; (absorber) to soak up
pompeux, -euse [pɔ̃pø, øz] adj pompous
pompier [pɔ̃pje] nm fireman
pompiste [pɔ̃pist] nm/f petrol (BRIT) ou gas
(US) pump attendant
poncer [pɔ̃se] vt to sand (down)
ponctuation [pɔ̃ktɥasjɔ̃] nf punctuation
ponctuel, le [pɔ̃ktɥɛl] adj punctual
pondéré, e [pɔ̃deʀe] adj level-headed,
composed
pondre [pɔ̃dʀ] vt to lay

poney [pɔnɛ] nm pony
pont [pɔ̃] nm bridge; (Navig) deck; **faire
le ~** to take the extra day off; see note; **pont
suspendu** suspension bridge; **pont-levis** nm
drawbridge

● **PONT**
●
● The expression 'faire le pont' refers to the
● practice of taking a Monday or Friday off
● to make a long weekend if a public holiday
● falls on a Tuesday or Thursday. The French
● commonly take an extra day off work to
● give four consecutive days' holiday at
● 'l'Ascension', 'le 14 juillet' and 'le 15 août'.

pop [pɔp] adj inv pop
populaire [pɔpylɛʀ] adj popular;
(manifestation) mass cpd; (milieux, quartier)
working-class; (expression) vernacular
popularité [pɔpylaʀite] nf popularity
population [pɔpylasjɔ̃] nf population
populeux, -euse [pɔpylø, øz] adj densely
populated
porc [pɔʀ] nm pig; (Culin) pork
porcelaine [pɔʀsəlɛn] nf porcelain, china;
piece of china(ware)
porc-épic [pɔʀkepik] nm porcupine
porche [pɔʀʃ] nm porch
porcherie [pɔʀʃəʀi] nf pigsty
pore [pɔʀ] nm pore
porno [pɔʀno] adj porno ⊳ nm porn
port [pɔʀ] nm harbour, port; (ville) port; (de
l'uniforme etc) wearing; (pour lettre) postage;
(pour colis, aussi: posture) carriage; **port
d'arme** (Jur) carrying of a firearm; **port payé**
postage paid
portable [pɔʀtabl] adj (portatif) portable;
(téléphone) mobile ⊳ nm (Comput) laptop
(computer); (téléphone) mobile (phone)
portail [pɔʀtaj] nm gate
portant, e [pɔʀtɑ̃, ɑ̃t] adj: **bien/mal ~** in
good/poor health
portatif, -ive [pɔʀtatif, iv] adj portable
porte [pɔʀt] nf door; (de ville, jardin) gate;
mettre à la ~ to throw out; **porte-avions**
nm inv aircraft carrier; **porte-bagages**
nm inv luggage rack; **porte-bonheur** nm
inv lucky charm; **porte-clefs** nm inv key
ring; **porte-documents** nm inv attaché ou
document case
porté, e [pɔʀte] adj: **être ~ à faire** to be
inclined to do; **être ~ sur qch** to be keen on
sth; **portée** nf (d'une arme) range; (fig: effet)
impact, import; (: capacité) scope, capability;
(de chatte etc) litter; (Mus) stave, staff; **à/hors
de portée de** within/out of reach (of); **à
portée de (la) main** within (arm's) reach; **à
la portée de qn** (fig) at sb's level, within sb's

p

capabilities

porte...: portefeuille nm wallet;
portemanteau, x nm (cintre) coat hanger; (au
mur) coat rack; **porte-monnaie** nm inv purse;
porte-parole nm inv spokesman

porter [pɔʀte] vt to carry; (sur soi: vêtement,
barbe, bague) to wear; (fig: responsabilité etc)
to bear, carry; (inscription, nom, fruits) to bear;
(coup) to deal; (attention) to turn; (apporter): ~
qch à qn to take sth to sb ▷ vi (voix) to carry;
(coup, argument) to hit home; **se porter** vi (se
sentir): **se ~ bien/mal** to be well/unwell; **~ sur**
(recherches) to be concerned with; **se faire ~
malade** to report sick

porteur, -euse [pɔʀtœʀ, øz] nm/f (de
bagages) porter; (de chèque) bearer

porte-voix [pɔʀtəvwa] nm inv megaphone

portier [pɔʀtje] nm doorman

portière [pɔʀtjɛʀ] nf door

portion [pɔʀsjɔ̃] nf (part) portion, share;
(partie) portion, section

porto [pɔʀto] nm port (wine)

portrait [pɔʀtʀɛ] nm (peinture) portrait;
(photo) photograph; **portrait-robot** nm
Identikit® ou photo-fit® picture

portuaire [pɔʀtɥɛʀ] adj port cpd,
harbour cpd

portugais, e [pɔʀtygɛ, ɛz] adj Portuguese
▷ nm/f: **P~, e** Portuguese ▷ nm (Ling)
Portuguese

Portugal [pɔʀtygal] nm: **le ~** Portugal

pose [poz] nf (de moquette) laying; (attitude, d'un
modèle) pose; (Photo) exposure

posé, e [poze] adj serious

poser [poze] vt to put; (installer: moquette,
carrelage) to lay; (rideaux, papier peint) to hang;
(question) to ask; (principe, conditions) to lay
ou set down; (difficulté) to pose; (formuler:
problème) to formulate ▷ vi (modèle) to pose;
se poser vi (oiseau, avion) to land; (question)
to arise; **~ qch (sur)** (déposer) to put sth down
(on); **~ qch sur/quelque part** (placer) to put
sth on/somewhere; **~ sa candidature à un
poste** to apply for a post

positif, -ive [pozitif, iv] adj positive

position [pozisjɔ̃] nf position; **prendre ~** (fig)
to take a stand

posologie [pozɔlɔʒi] nf dosage

posséder [posede] vt to own, possess;
(qualité, talent) to have, possess; (sexuellement)
to possess; **possession** nf ownership no pl,
possession; **prendre possession de qch** to
take possession of sth

possibilité [posibilite] nf possibility;
possibilités nfpl (potentiel) potential sg

possible [posibl] adj possible; (projet,
entreprise) feasible ▷ nm: **faire son ~** to do all
one can, do one's utmost; **le plus/moins de
livres ~** as many/few books as possible; **le**
plus vite ~ as quickly as possible; **aussitôt/
dès que ~** as soon as possible

postal, e, -aux [pɔstal, o] adj postal

poste¹ [pɔst] nf (service) post, postal service;
(administration, bureau) post office; **mettre à
la ~** to post; **poste restante** poste restante
(BRIT), general delivery (US)

poste² [pɔst] nm (fonction, Mil) post; (Tél)
extension; (de radio etc) set; **poste (de police)**
police station; **poste de secours** first-aid
post; **poste d'essence** filling station; **poste
d'incendie** fire point; **poste de pilotage**
cockpit, flight deck

poster [pɔste] vt to post; **où est-ce que je
peux ~ ces cartes postales?** where can I post
these cards?

postérieur, e [pɔsteʀjœʀ] adj (date) later;
(partie) back ▷ nm (fam) behind

postuler [pɔstyle] vi: **~ à** ou **pour un emploi**
to apply for a job

pot [po] nm (en verre) jar; (en terre) pot; (en
plastique, carton) carton; (en métal) tin;
(fam: chance) luck; **avoir du ~** (fam) to be
lucky; **boire** ou **prendre un ~** (fam) to have
a drink; **petit ~ (pour bébé)** (jar of) baby
food; **~ catalytique** catalytic converter; **pot
d'échappement** exhaust pipe

potable [pɔtabl] adj: **eau (non) ~**
(non-)drinking water

potage [pɔtaʒ] nm soup; **potager, -ère**
adj: **(jardin) potager** kitchen ou vegetable
garden

pot-au-feu [pɔtofø] nm inv (beef) stew

pot-de-vin [pɔdvɛ̃] nm bribe

pote [pɔt] (fam) nm pal

poteau, x [pɔto] nm post; **poteau indicateur**
signpost

potelé, e [pɔt(ə)le] adj plump, chubby

potentiel, le [pɔtɑ̃sjɛl] adj, nm potential

poterie [pɔtʀi] nf pottery; (objet) piece of
pottery

potier, -ière [pɔtje, jɛʀ] nm/f potter

potiron [pɔtiʀɔ̃] nm pumpkin

pou, x [pu] nm louse

poubelle [pubɛl] nf (dust)bin

pouce [pus] nm thumb

poudre [pudʀ] nf powder; (fard) (face)
powder; (explosif) gunpowder; **en ~: café en
~** instant coffee; **lait en ~** dried ou powdered
milk; **poudreuse** nf powder snow; **poudrier**
nm (powder) compact

pouffer [pufe] vi: **~ (de rire)** to burst out
laughing

poulailler [pulaje] nm henhouse

poulain [pulɛ̃] nm foal; (fig) protégé

poule [pul] nf hen; (Culin) (boiling) fowl; **poule
mouillée** coward

poulet [pulɛ] nm chicken; (fam) cop

poulie [puli] nf pulley

pouls [pu] nm pulse; **prendre le ~ de qn** to feel sb's pulse

poumon [pumɔ̃] nm lung

poupée [pupe] nf doll

pour [puʀ] prép for ▷ nm: **le ~ et le contre** the pros and cons; **~ faire** (so as) to do, in order to do; **~ avoir fait** for having done; **~ que** so that, in order that; **fermé ~ (cause de) travaux** closed for refurbishment ou alterations; **c'est ~ ça que ...** that's why ...; **quoi faire?** what for?; **~ 20 euros d'essence** 20 euros' worth of petrol; **~ cent** per cent; **~ ce qui est de** as for

pourboire [puʀbwaʀ] nm tip; **combien de ~ est-ce qu'il faut laisser?** how much should I tip?

pourcentage [puʀsɑ̃taʒ] nm percentage

pourchasser [puʀʃase] vt to pursue

pourparlers [puʀpaʀle] nmpl talks, negotiations

pourpre [puʀpʀ] adj crimson

pourquoi [puʀkwa] adv, conj why ▷ nm inv: **le ~ (de)** the reason (for)

pourrai etc [puʀe] vb voir **pouvoir**

pourri, e [puʀi] adj rotten

pourrir [puʀiʀ] vi to rot; (fruit) to go rotten ou bad ▷ vt to rot; (fig) to spoil thoroughly; **pourriture** nf rot

poursuite [puʀsɥit] nf pursuit, chase; **poursuites** nfpl (Jur) legal proceedings

poursuivre [puʀsɥivʀ] vt to pursue, chase (after); (obséder) to haunt; (Jur) to bring proceedings against, prosecute; (: au civil) to sue; (but) to strive towards; (continuer: études etc) to carry on with, continue; **se poursuivre** vi to go on, continue

pourtant [puʀtɑ̃] adv yet; **c'est ~ facile** (and) yet it's easy

pourtour [puʀtuʀ] nm perimeter

pourvoir [puʀvwaʀ] vt: **~ qch/qn de** to equip sth/sb with ▷ vi: **~ à** to provide for; **pourvu, e** adj: **pourvu de** equipped with; **pourvu que** (si) provided that, so long as; (espérons que) let's hope (that)

pousse [pus] nf growth; (bourgeon) shoot

poussée [puse] nf thrust; (d'acné) eruption; (fig: prix) upsurge

pousser [puse] vt to push; (émettre: cri, soupir) to give; (stimuler: élève) to urge on; (poursuivre: études, discussion) to carry on (further) ▷ vi to push; (croître) to grow; **se pousser** vi to move over; **~ qn à** (inciter) to urge ou press sb to; (acculer) to drive sb to; **faire ~** (plante) to grow

poussette [puset] nf push chair (BRIT), stroller (US)

poussière [pusjɛʀ] nf dust; **poussiéreux, -euse** adj dusty

poussin [pusɛ̃] nm chick

poutre [putʀ] nf beam

 MOT-CLÉ

pouvoir [puvwaʀ] nm power; (Pol: dirigeants): **le pouvoir** those in power; **les pouvoirs publics** the authorities; **pouvoir d'achat** purchasing power
▷ vb semi-aux **1** (être en état de) can, be able to; **je ne peux pas le réparer** I can't ou I am not able to repair it; **déçu de ne pas pouvoir le faire** disappointed not to be able to do it
2 (avoir la permission) can, may, be allowed to; **vous pouvez aller au cinéma** you can ou may go to the pictures
3 (probabilité, hypothèse) may, might, could; **il a pu avoir un accident** he may ou might ou could have had an accident; **il aurait pu le dire!** he might ou could have said (so)!
▷ vb impers may, might, could; **il peut arriver que** it may ou might ou could happen that; **il pourrait pleuvoir** it might rain
▷ vt can, be able to; **j'ai fait tout ce que j'ai pu** I did all I could; **je n'en peux plus** (épuisé) I'm exhausted; (à bout) I can't take any more
▷ vi: **se pouvoir: il se peut que** it may ou might be that; **cela se pourrait** that's quite possible

prairie [pʀeʀi] nf meadow

praline [pʀalin] nf sugared almond

praticable [pʀatikabl] adj passable, practicable

pratiquant, e [pʀatikɑ̃, ɑ̃t] nm/f (regular) churchgoer

pratique [pʀatik] nf practice ▷ adj practical; **pratiquement** adv (pour ainsi dire) practically, virtually; **pratiquer** vt to practise; (l'équitation, la pêche) to go in for; (le golf, football) to play; (intervention, opération) to carry out

pré [pʀe] nm meadow

préalable [pʀealabl] adj preliminary; **au ~** beforehand

préambule [pʀeɑ̃byl] nm preamble; (fig) prelude; **sans ~** straight away

préau [pʀeo] nm (Scol) covered playground

préavis [pʀeavi] nm notice

précaution [pʀekosjɔ̃] nf precaution; **avec ~** cautiously; **par ~** as a precaution

précédemment [pʀesedamɑ̃] adv before, previously

précédent, e [pʀesedɑ̃, ɑ̃t] adj previous ▷ nm precedent; **sans ~** unprecedented; **le jour ~** the day before, the previous day

précéder [pʀesede] vt to precede

prêcher [pʀeʃe] vt to preach

précieux, -euse [pʀesjø, jøz] adj precious; (aide, conseil) invaluable

précipice [pʀesipis] nm drop, chasm

précipitamment [pʀesipitamɑ̃] *adv*
hurriedly, hastily
précipitation [pʀesipitasjɔ̃] *nf (hâte)* haste
précipité, e [pʀesipite] *adj* hurried, hasty
précipiter [pʀesipite] *vt (hâter: départ)* to
hasten; *(faire tomber):* **~ qn/qch du haut
de** to throw *ou* hurl sb/sth off *ou* from; **se
précipiter** *vi* to speed up; **se ~ sur/vers** to
rush at/towards
précis, e [pʀesi, iz] *adj* precise; *(mesures)*
accurate, precise; **à 4 heures ~es** at 4 o'clock
sharp; **précisément** *adv* precisely; **préciser**
vt (expliquer) to be more specific about, clarify;
(spécifier) to state, specify; **se préciser** *vi* to
become clear(er); **précision** *nf* precision;
(détail) point *ou* detail; **demander des
précisions** to ask for further explanation
précoce [pʀekɔs] *adj* early; *(enfant)* precocious
préconçu, e [pʀekɔ̃sy] *adj* preconceived
préconiser [pʀekɔnize] *vt* to advocate
prédécesseur [pʀedesesœʀ] *nm* predecessor
prédilection [pʀedileksjɔ̃] *nf:* **avoir une ~
pour** to be partial to
prédire [pʀediʀ] *vt* to predict
prédominer [pʀedɔmine] *vi* to predominate
préface [pʀefas] *nf* preface
préfecture [pʀefektyʀ] *nf* prefecture;
préfecture de police police headquarters *pl*
préférable [pʀefeʀabl] *adj* preferable
préféré, e [pʀefeʀe] *adj, nm/f* favourite
préférence [pʀefeʀɑ̃s] *nf* preference; **de ~**
preferably
préférer [pʀefeʀe] *vt:* **~ qn/qch (à)** to prefer
sb/sth (to), like sb/sth better (than); **~ faire**
to prefer to do; **je préférerais du thé** I would
rather have tea, I'd prefer tea
préfet [pʀefɛ] *nm* prefect
préhistorique [pʀeistɔʀik] *adj* prehistoric
préjudice [pʀeʒydis] *nm (matériel)* loss;
(moral) harm *no pl;* **porter ~ à** to harm, be
detrimental to; **au ~ de** at the expense of
préjugé [pʀeʒyʒe] *nm* prejudice; **avoir un ~
contre** to be prejudiced *ou* biased against
prélasser [pʀelase] *vi:* **se prélasser** *vi* to lounge
prélèvement [pʀelɛvmɑ̃] *nm (montant)*
deduction; **faire un ~ de sang** to take a blood
sample
prélever [pʀel(ə)ve] *vt (échantillon)* to take; **~
(sur)** *(montant)* to deduct (from); *(argent: sur
son compte)* to withdraw (from)
prématuré, e [pʀematyʀe] *adj* premature
▷ *nm* premature baby
premier, -ière [pʀəmje, jɛʀ] *adj* first; *(rang)*
front; *(fig: objectif)* basic; **le ~ venu** the first
person to come along; **de ~ ordre** first-rate;
Premier ministre Prime Minister; **première**
nf (Scol) year 12 (BRIT), eleventh grade (US);
(Aviat, Rail etc) first class; **premièrement** *adv*
firstly

prémonition [pʀemɔnisjɔ̃] *nf* premonition
prenant, e [pʀənɑ̃, ɑ̃t] *adj* absorbing,
engrossing
prénatal, e [pʀenatal] *adj (Méd)* antenatal
prendre [pʀɑ̃dʀ] *vt* to take; *(repas)* to have; *(se
procurer)* to get; *(malfaiteur, poisson)* to catch;
(passager) to pick up; *(personnel)* to take on;
(traiter: personne) to handle; *(voix, ton)* to put
on; *(ôter):* **~ qch à** to take sth from; *(coincer):* **se
~ les doigts dans** to get one's fingers caught
in ▷ *vi (liquide, ciment)* to set; *(greffe, vaccin)* to
take; *(feu: foyer)* to go; *(se diriger):* **~ à gauche**
to turn (to the) left; **~ froid** to catch cold; **se
~ pour** to think one is; **s'en ~ à** to attack; **se ~
d'amitié pour** to befriend; **s'y ~** *(procéder)* to
set about it
preneur [pʀənœʀ] *nm:* **être/trouver ~** to be
willing to buy/find a buyer
prénom [pʀenɔ̃] *nm* first *ou* Christian name
préoccupation [pʀeɔkypasjɔ̃] *nf (souci)*
concern; *(idée fixe)* preoccupation
préoccuper [pʀeɔkype] *vt (inquiéter)* to
worry; *(absorber)* to preoccupy; **se ~ de** to be
concerned with
préparatifs [pʀepaʀatif] *nmpl* preparations
préparation [pʀepaʀasjɔ̃] *nf* preparation
préparer [pʀepaʀe] *vt* to prepare; *(café, thé)*
to make; *(examen)* to prepare for; *(voyage,
entreprise)* to plan; **se préparer** *vi (orage,
tragédie)* to brew, be in the air; **~ qch à qn**
(surprise etc) to have sth in store for sb; **se ~ (à
qch/faire)** to prepare (o.s.) *ou* get ready (for
sth/to do)
prépondérant, e [pʀepɔ̃deʀɑ̃, ɑ̃t] *adj* major,
dominating
préposé, e [pʀepoze] *nm/f* employee;
(facteur) postman
préposition [pʀepozisjɔ̃] *nf* preposition
près [pʀɛ] *adv* near, close; **~ de** near (to), close
to; *(environ)* nearly, almost; **de ~** closely; **à 5
kg ~** to within 5 kg; **il n'est pas à 10
minutes ~** he can spare 10 minutes; **est-ce
qu'il y a une banque ~ d'ici?** is there a bank
nearby?
présage [pʀezaʒ] *nm* omen
presbyte [pʀesbit] *adj* long-sighted
presbytère [pʀesbitɛʀ] *nm* presbytery
prescription [pʀeskʀipsjɔ̃] *nf* prescription
prescrire [pʀeskʀiʀ] *vt* to prescribe
présence [pʀezɑ̃s] *nf* presence; *(au bureau, à
l'école)* attendance
présent, e [pʀezɑ̃, ɑ̃t] *adj, nm* present; **à ~
(que)** now (that)
présentation [pʀezɑ̃tasjɔ̃] *nf* presentation;
(de nouveau venu) introduction; *(allure)*
appearance; **faire les ~s** to do the
introductions
présenter [pʀezɑ̃te] *vt* to present; *(excuses,
condoléances)* to offer; *(invité, conférencier):*

~ **qn (à)** to introduce sb (to) ▷ vi: ~ **bien** to have a pleasing appearance; **se présenter** vi (occasion) to arise; **se ~ à** (examen) to sit; (élection) to stand at, run for; **je vous présente Nadine** this is Nadine, could I introduce you to Nadine?

préservatif [pʀezɛʀvatif] nm condom, sheath

préserver [pʀezɛʀve] vt: ~ **de** (protéger) to protect from

président [pʀezidɑ̃] nm (Pol) president; (d'une assemblée, Comm) chairman; **président directeur général** chairman and managing director; **présidentielles** nfpl presidential elections

présider [pʀezide] vt to preside over; (dîner) to be the guest of honour at

presque [pʀɛsk] adv almost, nearly; ~ **personne** hardly anyone; ~ **rien** hardly anything; ~ **pas** hardly (at all); ~ **pas (de)** hardly any

presqu'île [pʀɛskil] nf peninsula

pressant, e [pʀesɑ̃, ɑ̃t] adj urgent

presse [pʀɛs] nf press; (affluence): **heures de ~** busy times

pressé, e [pʀese] adj in a hurry; (travail) urgent; **orange ~e** freshly-squeezed orange juice

pressentiment [pʀesɑ̃timɑ̃] nm foreboding, premonition

pressentir [pʀesɑ̃tiʀ] vt to sense

presse-papiers [pʀɛspapje] nm inv paperweight

presser [pʀese] vt (fruit, éponge) to squeeze; (bouton) to press; (allure) to speed up; (inciter): ~ **qn de faire** to urge ou press sb to do ▷ vi to be urgent; **se presser** vi (se hâter) to hurry (up); **se ~ contre qn** to squeeze up against sb; **le temps presse** there's not much time; **rien ne presse** there's no hurry

pressing [pʀesiŋ] nm (magasin) dry-cleaner's

pression [pʀesjɔ̃] nf pressure; (bouton) press stud; (fam: bière) draught beer; **faire ~ sur** to put pressure on; **sous ~** pressurized, under pressure; (fig) under pressure; **pression artérielle** blood pressure

prestataire [pʀɛstatɛʀ] nm/f supplier

prestation [pʀɛstasjɔ̃] nf (allocation) benefit; (d'une entreprise) service provided; (d'un artiste) performance

prestidigitateur, -trice [pʀɛstidiʒitatœʀ, tʀis] nm/f conjurer

prestige [pʀɛstiʒ] nm prestige; **prestigieux, -euse** adj prestigious

présumer [pʀezyme] vt: ~ **que** to presume ou assume that

prêt, e [pʀɛ, pʀɛt] adj ready ▷ nm (somme) loan; **quand est-ce que mes photos seront ~es?** when will my photos be ready?; **prêt-à-**

porter nm ready-to-wear ou off-the-peg (BRIT) clothes pl

prétendre [pʀetɑ̃dʀ] vt (affirmer): ~ **que** to claim that; (avoir l'intention de): ~ **faire qch** to mean ou intend to do sth; **prétendu, e** adj (supposé) so-called

> Attention à ne pas traduire **prétendre** par to pretend.

prétentieux, -euse [pʀetɑ̃sjø, jøz] adj pretentious

prétention [pʀetɑ̃sjɔ̃] nf claim; (vanité) pretentiousness

prêter [pʀete] vt (livres, argent): ~ **qch (à)** to lend sth (to); (supposer): ~ **à qn** (caractère, propos) to attribute to sb; **pouvez-vous me ~ de l'argent?** can you lend me some money?

prétexte [pʀetɛkst] nm pretext, excuse; **sous aucun ~** on no account; **prétexter** vt to give as a pretext ou an excuse

prêtre [pʀɛtʀ] nm priest

preuve [pʀœv] nf proof; (indice) proof, evidence no pl; **faire ~ de** to show; **faire ses ~s** to prove o.s. (ou itself)

prévaloir [pʀevalwaʀ] vi to prevail

prévenant, e [pʀev(ə)nɑ̃, ɑ̃t] adj thoughtful, kind

prévenir [pʀev(ə)niʀ] vt (éviter: catastrophe etc) to avoid, prevent; (anticiper: désirs, besoins) to anticipate; ~ **qn (de)** (avertir) to warn sb (about); (informer) to tell ou inform sb (about)

préventif, -ive [pʀevɑ̃tif, iv] adj preventive

prévention [pʀevɑ̃sjɔ̃] nf prevention; **prévention routière** road safety

prévenu, e [pʀev(ə)ny] nm/f (Jur) defendant, accused

prévision [pʀevizjɔ̃] nf: ~**s** predictions; (Écon) forecast sg; **en ~ de** in anticipation of; **prévisions météorologiques** weather forecast sg

prévoir [pʀevwaʀ] vt (anticiper) to foresee; (s'attendre à) to expect, reckon on; (organiser: voyage etc) to plan; (envisager) to allow; **comme prévu** as planned; **prévoyant, e** adj gifted with (ou showing) foresight; **prévu, e** pp de **prévoir**

prier [pʀije] vi to pray ▷ vt (Dieu) to pray to; (implorer) to beg; (demander): ~ **qn de faire** to ask sb to do; **se faire ~** to need coaxing ou persuading; **je vous en prie** (allez-y) please do; (de rien) don't mention it; **prière** nf prayer; **"prière de ..."** "please ..."

primaire [pʀimɛʀ] adj primary ▷ nm (Scol) primary education

prime [pʀim] nf (bonus) bonus; (subvention) premium; (Comm: cadeau) free gift; (Assurances, Bourse) premium ▷ adj: **de ~ abord** at first glance; **primer** vt (récompenser) to award a prize to ▷ vi to dominate; to be most important

primevère [pʀimvɛʀ] nf primrose
primitif, -ive [pʀimitif, iv] adj primitive;
(originel) original
prince [pʀɛ̃s] nm prince; **princesse** nf
princess
principal, e, -aux [pʀɛ̃sipal, o] adj principal,
main ▷ nm (Scol) principal, head(master);
(essentiel) main thing
principe [pʀɛ̃sip] nm principle; **par ~** on
principle; **en ~** (habituellement) as a rule;
(théoriquement) in principle
printemps [pʀɛ̃tɑ̃] nm spring
priorité [pʀijɔʀite] nf priority; (Auto) right of
way; **priorité à droite** right of way to vehicles
coming from the right
pris, e [pʀi, pʀiz] pp de **prendre** ▷ adj (place)
taken; (mains) full; (personne) busy; **avoir le
nez/la gorge ~(e)** to have a stuffy nose/a
hoarse throat; **être ~ de panique** to be panic-
stricken
prise [pʀiz] nf (d'une ville) capture; (Pêche,
Chasse) catch; (point d'appui ou pour empoigner)
hold; (Élec: fiche) plug; (: femelle) socket; **être
aux ~s avec** to be grappling with; **prise de
courant** power point; **prise de sang** blood
test; **prise multiple** adaptor
priser [pʀize] vt (estimer) to prize, value
prison [pʀizɔ̃] nf prison; **aller/être en ~** to go
to/be in prison ou jail; **prisonnier, -ière** nm/f
prisoner ▷ adj captive
privé, e [pʀive] adj private; (en punition): **tu es
~ de télé!** no TV for you! ▷ nm (Comm) private
sector; **en ~** in private
priver [pʀive] vt: **~ qn de** to deprive sb of; **se
priver de** to go ou do without
privilège [pʀivilɛʒ] nm privilege
prix [pʀi] nm price; (récompense, Scol) prize;
hors de ~ exorbitantly priced; **à aucun ~** not
at any price; **à tout ~** at all costs
probable [pʀɔbabl] adj likely, probable;
probablement adv probably
problème [pʀɔblɛm] nm problem
procédé [pʀɔsede] nm (méthode) process;
(comportement) behaviour no pl
procéder [pʀɔsede] vi to proceed;
(moralement) to behave; **~ à** to carry out
procès [pʀɔsɛ] nm trial; (poursuites)
proceedings pl; **être en ~ avec** to be involved
in a lawsuit with
processus [pʀɔsesys] nm process
procès-verbal, -aux [pʀɔsɛvɛʀbal, o] nm
(de réunion) minutes pl; (aussi: **P.-V.**) parking
ticket
prochain, e [pʀɔʃɛ̃, ɛn] adj next; (proche:
départ, arrivée) impending ▷ nm fellow man;
la ~e fois/semaine ~e next time/week;
prochainement adv soon, shortly
proche [pʀɔʃ] adj nearby; (dans le temps)
imminent; (parent, ami) close; **proches** nmpl

(parents) close relatives; **être ~ (de)** to be near,
be close (to)
proclamer [pʀɔklame] vt to proclaim
procuration [pʀɔkyʀasjɔ̃] nf proxy
procurer [pʀɔkyʀe] vt: **~ qch à qn** (fournir) to
obtain sth for sb; (causer: plaisir etc) to bring
sb sth; **se procurer** vt to get; **procureur** nm
public prosecutor
prodige [pʀɔdiʒ] nm marvel, wonder;
(personne) prodigy; **prodiguer** vt (soins,
attentions): **prodiguer qch à qn** to give sb sth
producteur, -trice [pʀɔdyktœʀ, tʀis] nm/f
producer
productif, -ive [pʀɔdyktif, iv] adj productive
production [pʀɔdyksjɔ̃] nf production;
(rendement) output
productivité [pʀɔdyktivite] nf productivity
produire [pʀɔdɥiʀ] vt to produce; **se
produire** vi (événement) to happen, occur;
(acteur) to perform, appear
produit [pʀɔdɥi] nm product; **produit
chimique** chemical; **produits agricoles**
farm produce sg; **produits de beauté** beauty
products, cosmetics; **produits d'entretien**
cleaning products
prof [pʀɔf] (fam) nm teacher
proférer [pʀɔfeʀe] vt to utter
professeur, e [pʀɔfesœʀ] nm/f teacher; (de
faculté) (university) lecturer; (: titulaire d'une
chaire) professor
profession [pʀɔfesjɔ̃] nf occupation;
~ libérale (liberal) profession; **sans ~**
unemployed; **professionnel, le** adj, nm/f
professional
profil [pʀɔfil] nm profile; **de ~** in profile
profit [pʀɔfi] nm (avantage) benefit,
advantage; (Comm, Finance) profit; **au ~ de** in
aid of; **tirer ~ de** to profit from; **profitable** adj
(utile) beneficial; (lucratif) profitable; **profiter**
vi: **profiter de** (situation, occasion) to take
advantage of; (vacances, jeunesse etc) to make
the most of
profond, e [pʀɔfɔ̃, ɔ̃d] adj deep; (sentiment,
intérêt) profound; **profondément** adv
deeply; **il dort profondément** he is sound
asleep; **profondeur** nf depth; **l'eau a quelle
profondeur?** how deep is the water?
programme [pʀɔgʀam] nm programme;
(Scol) syllabus, curriculum; (Inform) program;
programmer vt (émission) to schedule;
(Inform) to program; **programmeur, -euse**
nm/f programmer
progrès [pʀɔgʀɛ] nm progress no pl; **faire des
~** to make progress; **progresser** vi to progress;
progressif, -ive adj progressive
proie [pʀwa] nf prey no pl
projecteur [pʀɔʒɛktœʀ] nm (pour film)
projector; (de théâtre, cirque) spotlight
projectile [pʀɔʒɛktil] nm missile

projection [prɔʒɛksjɔ̃] nf projection; (séance) showing

projet [prɔʒɛ] nm plan; (ébauche) draft; **projet de loi** bill; **projeter** vt (envisager) to plan; (film, photos) to project; (ombre, lueur) to throw, cast; (jeter) to throw up (ou off ou out)

prolétaire [prɔletɛr] adj, nmf proletarian

prolongement [prɔlɔ̃ʒmɑ̃] nm extension; **dans le ~ de** running on from

prolonger [prɔlɔ̃ʒe] vt (débat, séjour) to prolong; (délai, billet, rue) to extend; **se prolonger** vi to go on

promenade [prɔm(ə)nad] nf walk (ou drive ou ride); **faire une ~** to go for a walk; **une ~ en voiture/à vélo** a drive/(bicycle) ride

promener [prɔm(ə)ne] vt (chien) to take out for a walk; (doigts, regard): **~ qch sur** to run sth over; **se promener** vi to go for (ou be out for) a walk

promesse [prɔmɛs] nf promise

promettre [prɔmɛtr] vt to promise ▷ vi to be ou look promising; **~ à qn de faire** to promise sb that one will do

promiscuité [prɔmiskɥite] nf (chambre) lack of privacy

promontoire [prɔmɔ̃twar] nm headland

promoteur, -trice [prɔmɔtœr, tris] nm/f: **promoteur (immobilier)** property developer (BRIT), real estate developer (US)

promotion [prɔmosjɔ̃] nf promotion; **en ~** on special offer

promouvoir [prɔmuvwar] vt to promote

prompt, e [prɔ̃(pt), prɔ̃(p)t] adj swift, rapid

prôner [prone] vt (préconiser) to advocate

pronom [prɔnɔ̃] nm pronoun

prononcer [prɔnɔ̃se] vt to pronounce; (dire) to utter; (discours) to deliver; **se prononcer** vi to be pronounced; **comment est-ce que ça se prononce?** how do you pronounce ou say it?; **se ~ (sur)** (se décider) to reach a decision (on ou about), give a verdict (on); **prononciation** nf pronunciation

pronostic [prɔnɔstik] nm (Méd) prognosis; (fig: aussi: **~s**) forecast

propagande [prɔpagɑ̃d] nf propaganda

propager [prɔpaʒe] vt to spread; **se propager** vi to spread

prophète [prɔfɛt] nm prophet

prophétie [prɔfesi] nf prophecy

propice [prɔpis] adj favourable

proportion [prɔpɔrsjɔ̃] nf proportion; **toute(s) ~(s) gardée(s)** making due allowance(s)

propos [prɔpo] nm (intention) intention, aim; (sujet): **à quel ~?** what about? ▷ nmpl (paroles) talk no pl, remarks; **à ~ de** about, regarding; **à tout ~** for the slightest thing ou reason; **à ~** by the way; (opportunément) at the right moment

proposer [prɔpoze] vt to propose; **~ qch**

(à qn) (suggérer) to suggest sth (to sb), propose sth (to sb); (offrir) to offer (sb) sth; **se ~ (pour faire)** to offer one's services (to do); **proposition** (suggestion) nf proposal, suggestion; (Ling) clause

propre [prɔpr] adj clean; (net) neat, tidy; (possessif) own; (sens) literal; (particulier): **~ à** peculiar to; (approprié): **~ à** suitable for ▷ nm: **recopier au ~** to make a fair copy of; **proprement** adv (avec propreté) cleanly; **le village proprement dit** the village itself; **à proprement parler** strictly speaking; **propreté** nf cleanliness

propriétaire [prɔprijetɛr] nm/f owner; (pour le locataire) landlord(-lady)

propriété [prɔprijete] nf property; (droit) ownership

propulser [prɔpylse] vt to propel

prose [proz] nf (style) prose

prospecter [prɔspɛkte] vt to prospect; (Comm) to canvass

prospectus [prɔspɛktys] nm leaflet

prospère [prɔspɛr] adj prosperous; **prospérer** vi to prosper

prosterner [prɔstɛrne]: **se prosterner** vi to bow low, prostrate o.s.

prostituée [prɔstitɥe] nf prostitute

prostitution [prɔstitysjɔ̃] nf prostitution

protecteur, -trice [prɔtɛktœr, tris] adj protective; (air, ton: péj) patronizing ▷ nm/f protector

protection [prɔtɛksjɔ̃] nf protection; (d'un personnage influent: aide) patronage

protéger [prɔteʒe] vt to protect; **se ~ de/ contre** to protect o.s. from

protège-slip [prɔtɛʒslip] nm panty liner

protéine [prɔtein] nf protein

protestant, e [prɔtɛstɑ̃, ɑ̃t] adj, nm/f Protestant

protestation [prɔtɛstasjɔ̃] nf (plainte) protest

protester [prɔtɛste] vi: **~ (contre)** to protest (against ou about); **~ de** (son innocence) to protest

prothèse [prɔtɛz] nf: **prothèse dentaire** denture

protocole [prɔtɔkɔl] nm (fig) etiquette

proue [pru] nf bow(s pl), prow

prouesse [prues] nf feat

prouver [pruve] vt to prove

provenance [prɔv(ə)nɑ̃s] nf origin; **avion en ~ de** plane (arriving) from

provenir [prɔv(ə)nir]: **~ de** vt to come from

proverbe [prɔvɛrb] nm proverb

province [prɔvɛ̃s] nf province

proviseur [prɔvizœr] nm ≈ head(teacher) (BRIT), ≈ principal (US)

provision [prɔvizjɔ̃] nf (réserve) stock, supply;

provisions *nfpl* (*vivres*) provisions, food *no pl*

provisoire [pʀɔvizwaʀ] *adj* temporary;
provisoirement *adv* temporarily

provocant, e [pʀɔvɔkɑ̃, ɑ̃t] *adj* provocative

provoquer [pʀɔvɔke] *vt* (*défier*) to provoke;
(*causer*) to cause, bring about; (*inciter*): ~ **qn à**
to incite sb to

proxénète [pʀɔksenɛt] *nm* procurer

proximité [pʀɔksimite] *nf* nearness,
closeness; (*dans le temps*) imminence,
closeness; **à ~** near ou close by; **à ~ de** near
(to), close to

prudemment [pʀydamɑ̃] *adv* carefully;
wisely, sensibly

prudence [pʀydɑ̃s] *nf* carefulness; **avec ~**
carefully; **par ~** as a precaution

prudent, e [pʀydɑ̃, ɑ̃t] *adj* (*pas téméraire*)
careful; (: *en général*) safety-conscious; (*sage,
conseillé*) wise, sensible; **c'est plus ~** it's wiser

prune [pʀyn] *nf* plum

pruneau, x [pʀyno] *nm* prune

prunier [pʀynje] *nm* plum tree

PS *sigle m* = **parti socialiste**

pseudonyme [psødɔnim] *nm* (*gén*) fictitious
name; (*d'écrivain*) pseudonym, pen name

psychanalyse [psikanaliz] *nf*
psychoanalysis

psychiatre [psikjatʀ] *nm/f* psychiatrist;
psychiatrique *adj* psychiatric

psychique [psiʃik] *adj* psychological

psychologie [psikɔlɔʒi] *nf* psychology;
psychologique *adj* psychological;
psychologue *nm/f* psychologist

pu [py] *pp de* **pouvoir**

puanteur [pɥɑ̃tœʀ] *nf* stink, stench

pub [pyb] *nf* (*fam: annonce*) ad, advert;
(*pratique*) advertising

public, -ique [pyblik] *adj* public; (*école,
instruction*) state *cpd* ▷ *nm* public; (*assistance*)
audience; **en ~** in public

publicitaire [pyblisitɛʀ] *adj* advertising *cpd*;
(*film*) publicity *cpd*

publicité [pyblisite] *nf* (*méthode, profession*)
advertising; (*annonce*) advertisement;
(*révélations*) publicity

publier [pyblije] *vt* to publish

publipostage [pyblipɔstaʒ] *nm* mailing *m*

publique [pyblik] *adj voir* **public**

puce [pys] *nf* flea; (*Inform*) chip; **carte à ~**
smart card; (**marché aux**) **~s** flea market *sg*

pudeur [pydœʀ] *nf* modesty; **pudique** *adj*
(*chaste*) modest; (*discret*) discreet

puer [pɥe] (*péj*) *vi* to stink

puéricultrice [pɥeʀikyltʀis] *nf* p(a)ediatric
nurse

puéril, e [pɥeʀil] *adj* childish

puis [pɥi] *vb voir* **pouvoir** ▷ *adv* then

puiser [pɥize] *vt*: ~ (**dans**) to draw (from)

puisque [pɥisk] *conj* since

puissance [pɥisɑ̃s] *nf* power; **en ~** *adj*
potential

puissant, e [pɥisɑ̃, ɑ̃t] *adj* powerful

puits [pɥi] *nm* well

pull(-over) [pyl(ɔvɛʀ)] *nm* sweater

pulluler [pylyle] *vi* to swarm

pulpe [pylp] *nf* pulp

pulvériser [pylveʀize] *vt* to pulverize;
(*liquide*) to spray

punaise [pynɛz] *nf* (*Zool*) bug; (*clou*) drawing
pin (BRIT), thumbtack (US)

punch [pɔ̃ʃ] *nm* (*boisson*) punch

punir [pyniʀ] *vt* to punish; **punition** *nf*
punishment

pupille [pypij] *nf* (*Anat*) pupil ▷ *nm/f* (*enfant*)
ward

pupitre [pypitʀ] *nm* (*Scol*) desk

pur, e [pyʀ] *adj* pure; (*vin*) undiluted; (*whisky*)
neat; **en ~e perte** to no avail; **c'est de la folie
~e** it's sheer madness

purée [pyʀe] *nf*: ~ (**de pommes de terre**)
mashed potatoes *pl*; **purée de marrons**
chestnut purée

purement [pyʀmɑ̃] *adv* purely

purgatoire [pyʀgatwaʀ] *nm* purgatory

purger [pyʀʒe] *vt* (*Méd, Pol*) to purge; (*Jur:
peine*) to serve

pur-sang [pyʀsɑ̃] *nm inv* thoroughbred

pus [py] *nm* pus

putain [pytɛ̃] (*fam!*) *nf* whore (!)

puzzle [pœzl] *nm* jigsaw (puzzle)

P.-V. [peve] *sigle m* = **procès-verbal**

pyjama [piʒama] *nm* pyjamas *pl* (BRIT),
pajamas *pl* (US)

pyramide [piʀamid] *nf* pyramid

Pyrénées [piʀene] *nfpl*: **les ~** the Pyrenees

QI sigle m (= quotient intellectuel) IQ

quadragénaire [k(w)adraʒenɛr] nm/f man/woman in his/her forties

quadruple [k(w)adrypl] nm: **le ~ de** four times as much as

quai [ke] nm (de port) quay; (de gare) platform; **être à ~** (navire) to be alongside; **de quel ~ part le train pour Paris?** which platform does the Paris train go from?

qualification [kalifikasjɔ̃] nf (aptitude) qualification

qualifier [kalifje] vt to qualify; **se qualifier** vi to qualify; **~ qch/qn de** to describe sth/sb as

qualité [kalite] nf quality

quand [kɑ̃] conj, adv when; **~ je serai riche** when I'm rich; **~ même** all the same; **~ même, il exagère!** really, he overdoes it!; **~ bien même** even though

quant [kɑ̃]: **~ à** prép (pour ce qui est de) as for, as to; (au sujet de) regarding

quantité [kɑ̃tite] nf quantity, amount; (grand nombre): **une** ou **des ~(s) de** a great deal of

quarantaine [karɑ̃tɛn] nf (Méd) quarantine; **avoir la ~** (âge) to be around forty; **une ~ (de)** forty or so, about forty

quarante [karɑ̃t] num forty

quart [kar] nm (fraction) quarter; (surveillance) watch; **un ~ de vin** a quarter

litre of wine; **le ~ de** a quarter of; **quart d'heure** quarter of an hour; **quarts de finale** quarter finals

quartier [kartje] nm (de ville) district, area; (de bœuf) quarter; (de fruit) piece; **cinéma de ~** local cinema; **avoir ~ libre** (fig) to be free; **quartier général** headquarters pl

quartz [kwarts] nm quartz

quasi [kazi] adv almost, nearly; **quasiment** adv almost, nearly; **quasiment jamais** hardly ever

quatorze [katɔrz] num fourteen

quatorzième [katɔrzjɛm] num fourteenth

quatre [katr] num four; **à ~ pattes** on all fours; **se mettre en ~ pour qn** to go out of one's way for sb; **~ à ~** (monter, descendre) four at a time; **quatre-vingt-dix** num ninety; **quatre-vingts** num eighty; **quatrième** num fourth ▷ nf (Scol) year 9 (BRIT), eighth grade (US)

quatuor [kwatɥɔr] nm quartet(te)

 MOT-CLÉ

que [kə] conj **1** (introduisant complétive) that; **il sait que tu es là** he knows (that) you're here; **je veux que tu acceptes** I want you to accept; **il a dit que oui** he said he would (ou it was etc)

2 (reprise d'autres conjonctions): **quand il rentrera et qu'il aura mangé** when he gets back and (when) he has eaten; **si vous y allez et que vous ...** if you go there and if you ...

3 (en tête de phrase: hypothèse, souhait etc): **qu'il le veuille ou non** whether he likes it or not; **qu'il fasse ce qu'il voudra!** let him do as he pleases!

4 (après comparatif) than, as; voir aussi **plus; aussi; autant** etc

5 (seulement): **ne ... que** only; **il ne boit que de l'eau** he only drinks water

6 (temps): **il y a 4 ans qu'il est parti** it is 4 years since he left, he left 4 years ago ▷ adv (exclamation): **qu'il** ou **qu'est-ce qu'il est bête/court vite!** he's so silly!/he runs so fast!; **que de livres!** what a lot of books! ▷ pron **1** (relatif: personne) whom; (: chose) that, which; **l'homme que je vois** the man (whom) I see; **le livre que tu vois** the book (that ou which) you see; **un jour que j'étais ...** a day when I was ...

2 (interrogatif) what; **que fais-tu?, qu'est-ce que tu fais?** what are you doing?; **qu'est-ce que c'est?** what is it?, what's that?; **que faire?** what can one do?

Québec [kebɛk] n: **le ~** Quebec; **québecois, e** adj Quebec ▷ nm/f: **Québecois, e** Quebecker

▷ nm (Ling) Quebec French

○ **MOT-CLÉ**

quel, quelle [kɛl] adj **1** (interrogatif: personne)
who; (: chose) what; **quel est cet homme?**
who is this man?; **quel est ce livre?** what
is this book?; **quel livre/homme?** what
book/man?; (parmi un certain choix) which
book/man?; **quels acteurs préférez-vous?**
which actors do you prefer?; **dans quels pays
êtes-vous allé?** which ou what countries did
you go to?
2 (exclamatif): **quelle surprise!** what a
surprise!
3: **quel que soit le coupable** whoever is
guilty; **quel que soit votre avis** whatever
your opinion

quelconque [kɛlkɔ̃k] adj (indéfini): **un
ami/prétexte ~** some friend/pretext or
other; (médiocre: repas) indifferent, poor; (laid:
personne) plain-looking

○ **MOT-CLÉ**

quelque [kɛlk] adj **1** (au singulier) some; (au
pluriel) a few, some; (tournure interrogative) any;
quelque espoir some hope; **il a quelques
amis** he has a few ou some friends; **a-t-il
quelques amis?** does he have any friends?; **les
quelques livres qui** the few books which; **20
kg et quelque(s)** a bit over 20 kg
2: **quelque ... que**: **quelque livre qu'il
choisisse** whatever (ou whichever) book he
chooses
3: **quelque chose** something; (tournure
interrogative) anything; **quelque chose
d'autre** something else; anything else;
quelque part somewhere; anywhere; **en
quelque sorte** as it were
▷ adv **1** (environ): **quelque 100 mètres** some
100 metres
2: **quelque peu** rather, somewhat

quelquefois [kɛlkəfwa] adv sometimes
quelques-uns, -unes [kɛlkəzœ̃, yn] pron a
few, some
quelqu'un [kɛlkœ̃] pron someone, somebody;
(+ tournure interrogative) anyone, anybody;
quelqu'un d'autre someone ou somebody
else; (+ tournure interrogative) anybody else
qu'en dira-t-on [kɑ̃diʁatɔ̃] nm inv: **le qu'en
dira-t-on** gossip, what people say
querelle [kəʁɛl] nf quarrel; **quereller: se
quereller** vi to quarrel
qu'est-ce que [kɛskə] vb + conj voir **que**
qu'est-ce qui [kɛski] vb + conj voir **qui**
question [kɛstjɔ̃] nf question; (fig) matter,

issue; **il a été ~ de** we (ou they) spoke about;
de quoi est-il ~? what is it about?; **il n'en
est pas ~** there's no question of it; **en ~** in
question; **hors de ~** out of the question;
remettre en ~ to question; **questionnaire**
nm questionnaire; **questionner** vt to
question
quête [kɛt] nf collection; (recherche) quest,
search; **faire la ~** (à l'église) to take the
collection; (artiste) to pass the hat round
quetsche [kwɛtʃ] nf kind of dark-red plum
queue [kø] nf tail; (fig: du classement) bottom;
(: de poêle) handle; (: de fruit, feuille) stalk; (: de
train, colonne, file) rear; **faire la ~** to queue (up)
(BRIT), line up (US); **queue de cheval** ponytail;
queue de poisson (Auto): **faire une queue de
poisson à qn** to cut in front of sb

○ **MOT-CLÉ**

qui [ki] pron **1** (interrogatif: personne) who; (:
chose): **qu'est-ce qui est sur la table?** what
is on the table?; **qui est-ce qui?** who?; **qui est-
ce que?** who?; **à qui est ce sac?** whose bag is
this?; **à qui parlais-tu?** who were you talking
to?, to whom were you talking?; **chez qui
allez-vous?** whose house are you going to?
2 (relatif: personne) who; (+ prép) whom; **l'ami
de qui je vous ai parlé** the friend I told you
about; **la dame chez qui je suis allé** the lady
whose house I went to
3 (sans antécédent): **amenez qui vous voulez**
bring who you like; **qui que ce soit** whoever
it may be

quiconque [kikɔ̃k] pron (celui qui) whoever,
anyone who; (n'importe qui) anyone, anybody
quille [kij] nf: (jeu de) **~s** skittles sg (BRIT),
bowling (US)
quincaillerie [kɛ̃kajʁi] nf (ustensiles)
hardware; (magasin) hardware shop
quinquagénaire [kɛ̃kaʒenɛʁ] nm/f man/
woman in his/her fifties
quinquennat [kɛ̃kena] nm five year term of
office (of French President)
quinte [kɛ̃t] nf: **~ (de toux)** coughing fit
quintuple [kɛ̃typl] nm: **le ~ de** five times as
much as
quinzaine [kɛ̃zɛn] nf: **une ~ (de)** about
fifteen, fifteen or so; **une ~ (de jours)** a
fortnight (BRIT), two weeks
quinze [kɛ̃z] num fifteen; **dans ~ jours** in a
fortnight('s time), in two weeks(' time)
quinzième [kɛ̃zjɛm] num fifteenth
quiproquo [kipʁɔko] nm misunderstanding
quittance [kitɑ̃s] nf (reçu) receipt
quitte [kit] adj: **être ~ envers qn** to be no
longer in sb's debt; (fig) to be quits with sb; **~ à
faire** even if it means doing

quitter [kite] *vt* to leave; (*vêtement*) to take off; **se quitter** *vi* (*couples, interlocuteurs*) to part; **ne quittez pas** (*au téléphone*) hold the line

qui-vive [kiviv] *nm*: **être sur le ~** to be on the alert

O MOT-CLÉ

quoi [kwa] *pron interrog* **1** what; **quoi de neuf?** what's new?; **quoi?** (*qu'est-ce que tu dis?*) what? **2** (*avec prép*): **à quoi tu penses?** what are you thinking about?; **de quoi parlez-vous?** what are you talking about?; **à quoi bon?** what's the use?
▷ *pron rel*: **as-tu de quoi écrire?** do you have anything to write with?; **il n'y a pas de quoi** (please) don't mention it; **il n'y a pas de quoi rire** there's nothing to laugh about
▷ *pron* (*locutions*): **quoi qu'il arrive** whatever happens; **quoi qu'il en soit** be that as it may; **quoi que ce soit** anything at all
▷ *excl* what!

quoique [kwak] *conj* (al)though
quotidien, ne [kɔtidjɛ̃, jɛn] *adj* daily; (*banal*) everyday ▷ *nm* (*journal*) daily (paper); **quotidiennement** *adv* daily

r. *abr* = **route**; **rue**
rab [ʀab] (*fam*) *nm* (*nourriture*) extra; **est-ce qu'il y a du ~?** are there any seconds?
rabâcher [ʀabɑʃe] *vt* to keep on repeating
rabais [ʀabɛ] *nm* reduction, discount; **rabaisser** *vt* (*dénigrer*) to belittle; (*rabattre: prix*) to reduce
Rabat [ʀaba(t)] *n* Rabat
rabattre [ʀabatʀ] *vt* (*couvercle, siège*) to pull down; (*déduire*) to reduce; **se rabattre** *vi* (*se refermer: couvercle*) to fall shut; (*véhicule, coureur*) to cut in; **se ~ sur** to fall back on
rabbin [ʀabɛ̃] *nm* rabbi
rabougri, e [ʀabugʀi] *adj* stunted
raccommoder [ʀakɔmɔde] *vt* to mend, repair
raccompagner [ʀakɔ̃paɲe] *vt* to take *ou* see back
raccord [ʀakɔʀ] *nm* link; (*retouche*) touch up; **raccorder** *vt* to join (up), link up; (*suj: pont etc*) to connect, link
raccourci [ʀakuʀsi] *nm* short cut
raccourcir [ʀakuʀsiʀ] *vt* to shorten ▷ *vi* (*jours*) to grow shorter, draw in
raccrocher [ʀakʀɔʃe] *vt* (*tableau*) to hang back up; (*récepteur*) to put down ▷ *vi* (*Tél*) to hang up, ring off
race [ʀas] *nf* race; (*d'animaux, fig*) breed; **de ~** purebred, pedigree
rachat [ʀaʃa] *nm* buying; (*du même objet*)

buying back

racheter [Raʃ(ə)te] vt (article perdu) to buy another; (après avoir vendu) to buy back; (d'occasion) to buy; (Comm: part, firme) to buy up; (davantage): **~ du lait/3 œufs** to buy more milk/another 3 eggs ou 3 more eggs; **se racheter** vi (fig) to make amends

racial, e, -aux [Rasjal, jo] adj racial

racine [Rasin] nf root; **racine carrée/ cubique** square/cube root

racisme [Rasism] nm racism

raciste [Rasist] adj, nm/f racist

racket [Raket] nm racketeering no pl

raclée [Rakle] (fam) nf hiding, thrashing

racler [Rakle] vt (surface) to scrape; **se ~ la gorge** to clear one's throat

racontars [Rakɔ̃taR] nmpl story, lie

raconter [Rakɔ̃te] vt: **~ (à qn)** (décrire) to relate (to sb), tell (sb) about; (dire de mauvaise foi) to tell (sb); **~ une histoire** to tell a story

radar [RadaR] nm radar

rade [Rad] nf (natural) harbour; **rester en ~** (fig) to be left stranded

radeau, x [Rado] nm raft

radiateur [RadjatœR] nm radiator, heater; (Auto) radiator; **radiateur électrique** electric heater ou fire

radiation [Radjasjɔ̃] nf (Physique) radiation

radical, e, -aux [Radikal, o] adj radical

radieux, -euse [Radjø, jøz] adj radiant

radin, e [Radɛ̃, in] (fam) adj stingy

radio [Radjo] nf radio; (Méd) X-ray ▷ nm radio operator; **à la ~** on the radio; **radioactif, -ive** adj radioactive; **radiocassette** nm cassette radio, radio cassette player; **radiographie** nf radiography; (photo) X-ray photograph; **radiophonique** adj radio cpd; **radio-réveil** (pl **radios-réveils**) nm radio alarm clock

radis [Radi] nm radish

radoter [Radɔte] vi to ramble on

radoucir [RadusiR]: **se radoucir** vi (temps) to become milder; (se calmer) to calm down

rafale [Rafal] nf (vent) gust (of wind); (tir) burst of gunfire

raffermir [RafɛRmiR] vt to firm up

raffiner [Rafine] vt to refine; **raffinerie** nf refinery

raffoler [Rafɔle]: **~ de** vt to be very keen on

rafle [Rafl] nf (de police) raid; **rafler** (fam) vt to swipe, nick

rafraîchir [RafReʃiR] vt (atmosphère, température) to cool (down); (aussi: **mettre à ~**) to chill; (fig: rénover) to brighten up; **se rafraîchir** vi (temps) to grow cooler; (en se lavant) to freshen up; (en buvant) to refresh o.s.; **rafraîchissant, e** adj refreshing; **rafraîchissement** nm (boisson) cool drink; **rafraîchissements** nmpl (boissons, fruits etc) refreshments

rage [Raʒ] nf (Méd): **la ~** rabies; (fureur) rage, fury; **faire ~** to rage; **rage de dents** (raging) toothache

ragot [Rago] (fam) nm malicious gossip no pl

ragoût [Ragu] nm stew

raide [Rɛd] adj stiff; (câble) taut, tight; (escarpé) steep; (droit: cheveux) straight; (fam: sans argent) flat broke; (osé) daring, bold ▷ adv (en pente) steeply; **~ mort** stone dead; **raideur** nf (rigidité) stiffness; **avec raideur** (répondre) stiffly, abruptly; **raidir** vt (muscles) to stiffen; **se raidir** vi (tissu) to stiffen; (personne) to tense up; (: se préparer moralement) to brace o.s.; (fig: position) to harden

raie [Rɛ] nf (Zool) skate, ray; (rayure) stripe; (des cheveux) parting

raifort [RɛfɔR] nm horseradish

rail [Raj] nm rail; (chemins de fer) railways pl; **par ~** by rail

railler [Raje] vt to scoff at, jeer at

rainure [RɛnyR] nf groove

raisin [Rɛzɛ̃] nm (aussi: **~s**) grapes pl; **raisins secs** raisins

raison [Rɛzɔ̃] nf reason; **avoir ~** to be right; **donner ~ à qn** to agree with sb; (événement) to prove sb right; **perdre la ~** to become insane; **se faire une ~** to learn to live with it; **~ de plus** all the more reason; **à plus forte ~** all the more so; **en ~ de** because of; **à ~ de** at the rate of; **sans ~** for no reason; **raison sociale** corporate name; **raisonnable** adj reasonable, sensible

raisonnement [Rɛzɔnmɑ̃] nm (façon de réfléchir) reasoning; (argumentation) argument

raisonner [Rɛzɔne] vi (penser) to reason; (argumenter, discuter) to argue ▷ vt (personne) to reason with

rajeunir [RaʒœniR] vt (suj: coiffure, robe): **~ qn** to make sb look younger; (fig: personnel) to inject new blood into ▷ vi to become (ou look) younger

rajouter [Raʒute] vt to add

rajuster [Raʒyste] vt (vêtement) to straighten, tidy; (salaires) to adjust

ralenti [Ralɑ̃ti] nm: **au ~** (fig) at a slower pace; **tourner au ~** (Auto) to tick over, idle

ralentir [Ralɑ̃tiR] vt to slow down

râler [Rɑle] vi to groan; (fam) to grouse, moan (and groan)

rallier [Ralje] vt (rejoindre) to rejoin; (gagner à sa cause) to win over

rallonge [Ralɔ̃ʒ] nf (de table) (extra) leaf

rallonger [Ralɔ̃ʒe] vt to lengthen

rallye [Rali] nm rally; (Pol) march

ramassage [Ramasaʒ] nm: **ramassage scolaire** school bus service

ramasser [Ramase] vt (objet tombé ou par terre, fam) to pick up; (recueillir: copies, ordures) to collect; (récolter) to gather; **ramassis** (péj) nm (de voyous) bunch; (d'objets) jumble

rambarde [ʀɑ̃baʀd] nf guardrail

rame [ʀam] nf (aviron) oar; (de métro) train; (de papier) ream

rameau, x [ʀamo] nm (small) branch; **les Rameaux** (Rel) Palm Sunday sg

ramener [ʀam(ə)ne] vt to bring back; (reconduire) to take back; **~ qch à** (réduire à) to reduce sth to

ramer [ʀame] vi to row

ramollir [ʀamɔliʀ] vt to soften; **se ramollir** vi to go soft

rampe [ʀɑ̃p] nf (d'escalier) banister(s pl); (dans un garage) ramp; (Théâtre): **la ~** the footlights pl; **rampe de lancement** launching pad

ramper [ʀɑ̃pe] vi to crawl

rancard [ʀɑ̃kaʀ] (fam) nm (rendez-vous) date

rancart [ʀɑ̃kaʀ] nm: **mettre au ~** (fam) to scrap

rance [ʀɑ̃s] adj rancid

rancœur [ʀɑ̃kœʀ] nf rancour

rançon [ʀɑ̃sɔ̃] nf ransom

rancune [ʀɑ̃kyn] nf grudge, rancour; **garder ~ à qn (de qch)** to bear sb a grudge (for sth); **sans ~!** no hard feelings!; **rancunier, -ière** adj vindictive, spiteful

randonnée [ʀɑ̃dɔne] nf (pédestre) walk, ramble; (: en montagne) hike, hiking no pl; **la ~** (activité) hiking, walking; **une ~ à cheval** a pony trek

rang [ʀɑ̃] nm (rangée) row; (grade, classement) rank; **rangs** nmpl (Mil) ranks; **se mettre en ~s** to get into ou form rows; **au premier ~** in the first row; (fig) ranking first

rangé, e [ʀɑ̃ʒe] adj (vie) well-ordered; (personne) steady

rangée [ʀɑ̃ʒe] nf row

ranger [ʀɑ̃ʒe] vt (mettre de l'ordre dans) to tidy up; (classer, grouper) to order, arrange; (mettre à sa place) to put away; (fig: classer): **~ qn/qch parmi** to rank sb/sth among; **se ranger** vi (véhicule, conducteur) to pull over ou in; (piéton) to step aside; (s'assagir) to settle down; **se ~ à** (avis) to come round to

ranimer [ʀanime] vt (personne) to bring round; (douleur, souvenir) to revive; (feu) to rekindle

rapace [ʀapas] nm bird of prey

râpe [ʀɑp] nf (Culin) grater; **râper** vt (Culin) to grate

rapide [ʀapid] adj fast; (prompt: coup d'œil, mouvement) quick ▷ nm express (train); (de cours d'eau) rapid; **rapidement** adv fast; quickly

rapiécer [ʀapjese] vt to patch

rappel [ʀapɛl] nm (Théâtre) curtain call; (Méd: vaccination) booster; (deuxième avis) reminder; **rappeler** vt to call back; (ambassadeur, Mil) to recall; (faire se souvenir): **rappeler qch à qn** to

remind sb of sth; **se rappeler** vt (se souvenir de) to remember, recall; **pouvez-vous rappeler plus tard?** can you call back later?

rapport [ʀapɔʀ] nm (lien, analogie) connection; (compte rendu) report; (profit) yield, return; **rapports** nmpl (entre personnes, pays) relations; **avoir ~ à** to have something to do with; **être/se mettre en ~ avec qn** to be/get in touch with sb; **par ~ à** in relation to; **rapports (sexuels)** (sexual) intercourse sg; **rapport qualité-prix** value (for money)

rapporter [ʀapɔʀte] vt (rendre, ramener) to bring back; (bénéfice) to yield, bring in; (mentionner, répéter) to report ▷ vi (investissement) to give a good return ou yield; (activité) to be very profitable; **se ~ à** to relate to

rapprochement [ʀapʀɔʃmɑ̃] nm (de nations) reconciliation; (rapport) parallel

rapprocher [ʀapʀɔʃe] vt (deux objets) to bring closer together; (fig: ennemis, partis etc) to bring together; (comparer) to establish a parallel between; (chaise d'une table): **~ qch (de)** to bring sth closer (to); **se rapprocher** vi to draw closer ou nearer; **se ~ de** to come closer to; (présenter une analogie avec) to be close to

raquette [ʀakɛt] nf (de tennis) racket; (de ping-pong) bat

rare [ʀɑʀ] adj rare; **se faire ~** to become scarce; **rarement** adv rarely, seldom

ras, e [ʀɑ, ʀɑz] adj (poil, herbe) short; (tête) close-cropped ▷ adv short; **en ~e campagne** in open country; **à ~ bords** to the brim; **en avoir ~ le bol** (fam) to be fed up

raser [ʀɑze] vt (barbe, cheveux) to shave off; (menton, personne) to shave; (fam: ennuyer) to bore; (démolir) to raze (to the ground); (frôler) to graze, skim; **se raser** vi to shave; (fam) to be bored (to tears); **rasoir** nm razor

rassasier [ʀasazje] vt: **être rassasié** to have eaten one's fill

rassemblement [ʀasɑ̃bləmɑ̃] nm (groupe) gathering; (Pol) union

rassembler [ʀasɑ̃ble] vt (réunir) to assemble, gather; (documents, notes) to gather together, collect; **se rassembler** vi to gather

rassurer [ʀasyʀe] vt to reassure; **se rassurer** vi to reassure o.s.; **rassure-toi** don't worry

rat [ʀa] nm rat

rate [ʀat] nf spleen

raté, e [ʀate] adj (tentative) unsuccessful, failed ▷ nm/f (fam: personne) failure

râteau, x [ʀɑto] nm rake

rater [ʀate] vi (affaire, projet etc) to go wrong, fail ▷ vt (fam: cible, train, occasion) to miss; (plat) to spoil; (examen) to fail; **nous avons raté notre train** we missed our train

ration [ʀasjɔ̃] nf ration

RATP sigle f (= Régie autonome des transports parisiens) Paris transport authority

rattacher [Rataʃe] vt (animal, cheveux) to tie up again; (fig: relier): **~ qch à** to link sth with

rattraper [RatRape] vt (fugitif) to recapture; (empêcher de tomber) to catch (hold of); (atteindre, rejoindre) to catch up with; (réparer: erreur) to make up for; **se rattraper** vi to make up for it; **se ~ (à)** (se raccrocher) to stop o.s. falling (by catching hold of)

rature [RatyR] nf deletion, erasure

rauque [Rok] adj (voix) hoarse

ravages [Ravaʒ] nmpl: **faire des ~** to wreak havoc

ravi, e [Ravi] adj: **être ~ de/que** to be delighted with/that

ravin [Ravɛ̃] nm gully, ravine

ravir [RaviR] vt (enchanter) to delight; **à ~** adv beautifully

raviser [Ravize]: **se raviser** vi to change one's mind

ravissant, e [Ravisɑ̃, ɑ̃t] adj delightful

ravisseur, -euse [RavisœR, øz] nm/f abductor, kidnapper

ravitailler [Ravitaje] vt (en vivres, munitions) to provide with fresh supplies; (avion) to refuel; **se ~ (en)** to get fresh supplies (of)

raviver [Ravive] vt (feu, douleur) to revive; (couleurs) to brighten up

rayé, e [Reje] adj (à rayures) striped

rayer [Reje] vt (érafler) to scratch; (barrer) to cross out; (d'une liste) to cross off

rayon [Rejɔ̃] nm (de soleil etc) ray; (Géom) radius; (de roue) spoke; (étagère) shelf; (de grand magasin) department; **dans un ~ de** within a radius of; **rayon de soleil** sunbeam; **rayons X** X-rays

rayonnement [Rejɔnmɑ̃] nm (fig: d'une culture) influence

rayonner [Rejɔne] vi (fig) to shine forth; (personne: de joie, de beauté) to be radiant; (touriste) to go touring (from one base)

rayure [RejyR] nf (motif) stripe; (éraflure) scratch; **à ~s** striped

raz-de-marée [Radmare] nm inv tidal wave

ré [Re] nm (Mus) D; (en chantant la gamme) re

réaction [Reaksjɔ̃] nf reaction

réadapter [Readapte]: **se réadapter (à)** vi to readjust (to)

réagir [ReaʒiR] vi to react

réalisateur, -trice [RealizatœR, tRis] nm/f (TV, Cinéma) director

réalisation [Realizasjɔ̃] nf realization; (cinéma) production; **en cours de ~** under way

réaliser [Realize] vt (projet, opération) to carry out, realize; (rêve, souhait) to realize, fulfil; (exploit) to achieve; (film) to produce; (se rendre compte de) to realize; **se réaliser** vi to be realized

réaliste [Realist] adj realistic

réalité [Realite] nf reality; **en ~** in (actual) fact; **dans la ~** in reality

réanimation [Reanimasjɔ̃] nf resuscitation; **service de ~** intensive care unit

rébarbatif, -ive [RebaRbatif, iv] adj forbidding

rebattu, e [R(ə)baty] adj hackneyed

rebelle [Rəbɛl] nm/f rebel ▷ adj (troupes) rebel; (enfant) rebellious; (mèche etc) unruly

rebeller [R(ə)bele]: **se rebeller** vi to rebel

rebondir [R(ə)bɔ̃diR] vi (ballon: au sol) to bounce; (: contre un mur) to rebound; (fig) to get moving again

rebord [R(ə)bɔR] nm edge; **le ~ de la fenêtre** the windowsill

rebours [R(ə)buR]: **à ~** adv the wrong way

rebrousser [R(ə)bRuse] vt: **~ chemin** to turn back

rebuter [Rəbyte] vt to put off

récalcitrant, e [RekalsitRɑ̃, ɑ̃t] adj refractory

récapituler [Rekapityle] vt to recapitulate, sum up

receler [R(ə)səle] vt (produit d'un vol) to receive; (fig) to conceal; **receleur, -euse** nm/f receiver

récemment [Resamɑ̃] adv recently

recensement [R(ə)sɑ̃smɑ̃] nm (population) census

recenser [R(ə)sɑ̃se] vt (population) to take a census of; (inventorier) to list

récent, e [Resɑ̃, ɑ̃t] adj recent

récépissé [Resepise] nm receipt

récepteur [ReseptœR] nm receiver

réception [Resepsjɔ̃] nf receiving no pl; (accueil) reception, welcome; (bureau) reception desk; (réunion mondaine) reception, party; **réceptionniste** nm/f receptionist

recette [R(ə)sɛt] nf recipe; (Comm) takings pl; **recettes** nfpl (Comm: rentrées) receipts; **faire ~** (spectacle, exposition) to be a winner

recevoir [R(ə)səvwaR] vt to receive; (client, patient) to see; **être reçu** (à un examen) to pass

rechange [R(ə)ʃɑ̃ʒ]: **de ~** adj (pièces, roue) spare; (fig: solution) alternative; **des vêtements de ~** a change of clothes

recharge [R(ə)ʃaRʒ] nf refill; **rechargeable** adj (stylo etc) refillable; **recharger** vt (stylo) to refill; (batterie) to recharge

réchaud [Reʃo] nm (portable) stove

réchauffer [Reʃofe] vt (plat) to reheat; (mains, personne) to warm; **se réchauffer** vi (température) to get warmer; (personne) to warm o.s. (up)

rêche [Rɛʃ] adj rough

recherche [R(ə)ʃɛRʃ] nf (action) search; (raffinement) studied elegance; (scientifique etc): **la ~** research; **recherches** nfpl (de la police) investigations; (scientifiques) research sg; **la ~ de** the search for; **être à la ~ de qch** to be looking for sth

recherché, e [ʀ(ə)ʃɛʀʃe] adj (rare, demandé) much sought-after; (raffiné: style) mannered; (: tenue) elegant

rechercher [ʀ(ə)ʃɛʀʃe] vt (objet égaré, personne) to look for; (causes, nouveau procédé) to try to find; (bonheur, compliments) to seek

rechute [ʀ(ə)ʃyt] nf (Méd) relapse

récidiver [ʀesidive] vi to commit a subsequent offence; (fig) to do it again

récif [ʀesif] nm reef

récipient [ʀesipjã] nm container

réciproque [ʀesipʀɔk] adj reciprocal

récit [ʀesi] nm story; **récital** nm recital; **réciter** vt to recite

réclamation [ʀeklɑmasjõ] nf complaint; **(service des) ~s** complaints department

réclame [ʀeklɑm] nf ad, advert(isement); **en ~** on special offer; **réclamer** vt to ask for; (revendiquer) to claim, demand ▷ vi to complain

réclusion [ʀeklyzjõ] nf imprisonment

recoin [ʀəkwɛ̃] nm nook, corner

reçois etc [ʀəswa] vb voir **recevoir**

récolte [ʀekɔlt] nf harvesting, gathering; (produits) harvest, crop; **récolter** vt to harvest, gather (in); (fig) to collect

recommandé [ʀ(ə)kɔmɑ̃de] nm (Postes): **en ~** by registered mail

recommander [ʀ(ə)kɔmɑ̃de] vt to recommend; (Postes) to register

recommencer [ʀ(ə)kɔmɑ̃se] vt (reprendre: lutte, séance) to resume, start again; (refaire: travail, explications) to start afresh, start (over) again ▷ vi to start again; (récidiver) to do it again

récompense [ʀekõpɑ̃s] nf reward; (prix) award; **récompenser** vt: **récompenser qn (de** ou **pour)** to reward sb (for)

réconcilier [ʀekõsilje] vt to reconcile; **se réconcilier (avec)** to make up (with)

reconduire [ʀ(ə)kõdɥiʀ] vt (raccompagner) to take ou see back; (renouveler) to renew

réconfort [ʀekõfɔʀ] nm comfort; **réconforter** vt (consoler) to comfort

reconnaissance [ʀ(ə)kɔnɛsɑ̃s] nf (gratitude) gratitude, gratefulness; (action de reconnaître) recognition; (Mil) reconnaissance, recce; **reconnaissant, e** adj grateful; **je vous serais reconnaissant de bien vouloir ...** I would be most grateful if you would (kindly) ...

reconnaître [ʀ(ə)kɔnɛtʀ] vt to recognize; (Mil: lieu) to reconnoitre; (Jur: enfant, torts) to acknowledge; **~ que** to admit ou acknowledge that; **~ qn/qch à** (l'identifier grâce à) to recognize sb/sth by; **reconnu, e** adj (indiscuté, connu) recognized

reconstituer [ʀ(ə)kõstitɥe] vt (événement, accident) to reconstruct; (fresque, vase brisé) to piece together, reconstitute

reconstruire [ʀ(ə)kõstʀɥiʀ] vt to rebuild

reconvertir [ʀ(ə)kõvɛʀtiʀ]: **se reconvertir dans** vr (un métier, une branche) to go into

record [ʀ(ə)kɔʀ] nm, adj record

recoupement [ʀ(ə)kupmã] nm: **par ~** by cross-checking

recouper [ʀ(ə)kupe]: **se recouper** vi (témoignages) to tie ou match up

recourber [ʀ(ə)kuʀbe]: **se recourber** vi to curve (up), bend (up)

recourir [ʀ(ə)kuʀiʀ]: **~ à** vt (ami, agence) to turn ou appeal to; (force, ruse, emprunt) to resort to

recours [ʀ(ə)kuʀ] nm: **avoir ~ à = recourir à**; **en dernier ~** as a last resort

recouvrer [ʀ(ə)kuvʀe] vt (vue, santé etc) to recover, regain

recouvrir [ʀ(ə)kuvʀiʀ] vt (couvrir à nouveau) to re-cover; (couvrir entièrement, aussi fig) to cover

récréation [ʀekʀeasjõ] nf (Scol) break

recroqueviller [ʀ(ə)kʀɔk(ə)vije]: **se recroqueviller** vi (personne) to huddle up

recrudescence [ʀ(ə)kʀydesɑ̃s] nf fresh outbreak

recruter [ʀ(ə)kʀyte] vt to recruit

rectangle [ʀɛktɑ̃gl] nm rectangle; **rectangulaire** adj rectangular

rectificatif [ʀɛktifikatif] nm correction

rectifier [ʀɛktifje] vt (calcul, adresse, paroles) to correct; (erreur) to rectify

rectiligne [ʀɛktilin] adj straight

recto [ʀɛkto] nm front (of a page); **~ verso** on both sides (of the page)

reçu, e [ʀ(ə)sy] pp de **recevoir** ▷ adj (candidat) successful; (admis, consacré) accepted ▷ nm (Comm) receipt; **je peux avoir un ~, s'il vous plaît?** can I have a receipt, please?

recueil [ʀəkœj] nm collection; **recueillir** vt to collect; (voix, suffrages) to win; (accueillir: réfugiés, chat) to take in; **se recueillir** vi to gather one's thoughts, meditate

recul [ʀ(ə)kyl] nm (éloignement) distance; (déclin) decline; **être en ~** to be on the decline; **avec du ~** with hindsight; **avoir un mouvement de ~** to recoil; **prendre du ~** to stand back; **reculé, e** adj remote; **reculer** vi to move back, back away; (Auto) to reverse, back (up); (fig) to (be on the) decline ▷ vt to move back; (véhicule) to reverse, back (up); (date, décision) to postpone; **reculer devant** (danger, difficulté) to shrink from; **reculons: à reculons** adv backwards

récupérer [ʀekypeʀe] vt to recover, get back; (heures de travail) to make up; (déchets) to salvage ▷ vi to recover

récurer [ʀekyʀe] vt to scour; **poudre à ~** scouring powder

reçut [Rəsy] vb voir **recevoir**

recycler [R(ə)sikle] vt (Tech) to recycle; **se recycler** vi to retrain

rédacteur, -trice [Redaktœr, tris] nm/f (journaliste) writer; subeditor; (d'ouvrage de référence) editor, compiler

rédaction [Redaksjɔ̃] nf writing; (rédacteurs) editorial staff; (Scol: devoir) essay, composition

redescendre [R(ə)desɑ̃dR] vi to go back down ▷ vt (pente etc) to go down

rédiger [Rediʒe] vt to write; (contrat) to draw up

redire [R(ə)diR] vt to repeat; **trouver à ~ à** to find fault with

redoubler [R(ə)duble] vi (tempête, violence) to intensify; (Scol) to repeat a year; **~ de patience/prudence** to be doubly patient/careful

redoutable [R(ə)dutabl] adj formidable, fearsome

redouter [R(ə)dute] vt to dread

redressement [R(ə)drɛsmɑ̃] nm (économique) recovery

redresser [R(ə)drɛse] vt (relever) to set upright; (pièce tordue) to straighten out; (situation, économie) to put right; **se redresser** vi (personne) to sit (ou stand) up (straight); (économie) to recover

réduction [Redyksjɔ̃] nf reduction; **y a-t-il une ~ pour les étudiants?** is there a reduction for students?

réduire [RedɥiR] vt to reduce; (prix, dépenses) to cut, reduce; **réduit** nm (pièce) tiny room

rééducation [Reedykasjɔ̃] nf (d'un membre) re-education; (de délinquants, d'un blessé) rehabilitation

réel, le [Reɛl] adj real; **réellement** adv really

réexpédier [Reɛkspedje] vt (à l'envoyeur) to return, send back; (au destinataire) to send on, forward

refaire [R(ə)fɛR] vt to do again; (faire de nouveau: sport) to take up again; (réparer, restaurer) to do up

réfectoire [RefɛktwaR] nm refectory

référence [Referɑ̃s] nf reference; **références** nfpl (recommandations) reference sg

référer [Refere]: **se référer à** vt to refer to

refermer [R(ə)fɛRme] vt to close ou shut again; **se refermer** vi (porte) to close ou shut (again)

refiler [R(ə)file] vi (fam) to palm off

réfléchi, e [Refleʃi] adj (caractère) thoughtful; (action) well-thought-out; (Ling) reflexive; **c'est tout ~** my mind's made up

réfléchir [RefleʃiR] vt to reflect ▷ vi to think; **~ à** to think about

reflet [R(ə)flɛ] nm reflection; (sur l'eau etc) sheen no pl, glint; **refléter** vt to reflect; **se refléter** vi to be reflected

réflexe [Reflɛks] nm, adj reflex

réflexion [Reflɛksjɔ̃] nf (de la lumière etc) reflection; (fait de penser) thought; (remarque) remark; **~ faite, à la ~** on reflection

réflexologie [Reflɛksɔlɔʒi] nf reflexology

réforme [RefɔRm] nf reform; (Rel): **la R~** the Reformation; **réformer** vt to reform; (Mil) to declare unfit for service

refouler [R(ə)fule] vt (envahisseurs) to drive back; (larmes) to force back; (désir, colère) to repress

refrain [R(ə)frɛ̃] nm refrain, chorus

refréner [Rəfrene], **réfréner** [Refrene] vt to curb, check

réfrigérateur [RefRiʒeRatœR] nm refrigerator, fridge

refroidir [R(ə)frwadiR] vt to cool; (fig: personne) to put off ▷ vi to cool (down); **se refroidir** vi (temps) to get cooler ou colder; (fig: ardeur) to cool (off); **refroidissement** nm (grippe etc) chill

refuge [R(ə)fyʒ] nm refuge; **réfugié, e** adj, nm/f refugee; **réfugier: se réfugier** vi to take refuge

refus [R(ə)fy] nm refusal; **ce n'est pas de ~!** I won't say no, it's welcome; **refuser** vt to refuse; (Scol: candidat) to fail; **refuser qch à qn** to refuse sb sth; **refuser du monde** to have to turn people away; **se refuser à faire** to refuse to do

regagner [R(ə)gaɲe] vt (faveur) to win back; (lieu) to get back to

régal [Regal] nm treat; **régaler: se régaler** vi to have a delicious meal; (fig) to enjoy o.s.

regard [R(ə)gaR] nm (coup d'œil) look, glance; (expression) look (in one's eye); **au ~ de** (loi, morale) from the point of view of; **en ~ de** in comparison with

regardant, e [R(ə)gaRdɑ̃, ɑ̃t] adj (économe) tight-fisted; **peu ~ (sur)** very free (about)

regarder [R(ə)gaRde] vt to look at; (film, télévision, match) to watch; (concerner) to concern ▷ vi to look; **ne pas ~ à la dépense** to spare no expense; **~ qn/qch comme** to regard sb/sth as

régie [Reʒi] nf (Comm, Industrie) state-owned company; (Théâtre, Cinéma) production; (Radio, TV) control room

régime [Reʒim] nm (Pol) régime; (Méd) diet; (Admin: carcéral, fiscal etc) system; (de bananes, dattes) bunch; **se mettre au/suivre un ~** to go on/be on a diet

régiment [Reʒimɑ̃] nm regiment

région [Reʒjɔ̃] nf region; **régional, e, -aux** adj regional

régir [ReʒiR] vt to govern

régisseur [ReʒisœR] nm (d'un domaine) steward; (Cinéma, TV) assistant director; (Théâtre) stage manager

registre [ʀəʒistʀ] nm register

réglage [ʀeglaʒ] nm adjustment

règle [ʀɛgl] nf (instrument) ruler; (loi) rule; **règles** nfpl (menstruation) period sg; **en ~** (papiers d'identité) in order; **en ~ générale** as a (general) rule

réglé, e [ʀegle] adj (vie) well-ordered; (arrangé) settled

règlement [ʀɛgləmɑ̃] nm (paiement) settlement; (arrêté) regulation; (règles, statuts) regulations pl, rules pl; **réglementaire** adj conforming to the regulations; (tenue) regulation cpd; **réglementation** nf (règles) regulations; **réglementer** vt to regulate

régler [ʀegle] vt (conflit, facture) to settle; (personne) to settle up with; (mécanisme, machine) to regulate, adjust; (thermostat etc) to set, adjust

réglisse [ʀeglis] nf liquorice

règne [ʀɛɲ] nm (d'un roi etc, fig) reign; **le ~ végétal/animal** the vegetable/animal kingdom; **régner** vi (roi) to rule, reign; (fig) to reign

regorger [ʀ(ə)gɔʀʒe] vi: **~ de** to overflow with, be bursting with

regret [ʀ(ə)gʀɛ] nm regret; **à ~** with regret; **sans ~** with no regrets; **regrettable** adj regrettable; **regretter** vt to regret; (personne) to miss; **je regrette mais ...** I'm sorry but ...

regrouper [ʀ(ə)gʀupe] vt (grouper) to group together; (contenir) to include, comprise; **se regrouper** vi to gather (together)

régulier, -ière [ʀegylje, jɛʀ] adj (gén) regular; (vitesse, qualité) steady; (égal: couche, ligne) even; (Transports: ligne, service) scheduled, regular; (légal) lawful, in order; (honnête) straight, on the level; **régulièrement** adv regularly; (uniformément) evenly

rehausser [ʀaose] vt (relever) to heighten, raise; (fig: souligner) to set off, enhance

rein [ʀɛ̃] nm kidney; **reins** nmpl (dos) back sg

reine [ʀɛn] nf queen

reine-claude [ʀɛnklod] nf greengage

réinscriptible [ʀeɛ̃skʀiptibl] adj (CD, DVD) rewritable

réinsertion [ʀeɛ̃sɛʀsjɔ̃] nf (de délinquant) reintegration, rehabilitation

réintégrer [ʀeɛ̃tegʀe] vt (lieu) to return to; (fonctionnaire) to reinstate

rejaillir [ʀ(ə)ʒajiʀ] vi to splash up; **~ sur** (fig: scandale) to rebound on; (: gloire) to be reflected on

rejet [ʀəʒɛ] nm rejection; **rejeter** vt (relancer) to throw back; (écarter) to reject; (déverser) to throw out, discharge; (vomir) to bring ou throw up; **rejeter la responsabilité de qch sur qn** to lay the responsibility for sth at sb's door

rejoindre [ʀ(ə)ʒwɛ̃dʀ] vt (famille, régiment) to rejoin, return to; (lieu) to get (back) to; (suj: route etc) to meet, join; (rattraper) to catch up (with); **se rejoindre** vi to meet; **je te rejoins à la gare** I'll see ou meet you at the station

réjouir [ʀeʒwiʀ] vt to delight; **se ~ (de qch/de faire)** to be delighted (about sth/to do); **réjouissances** nfpl (fête) festivities

relâche [ʀəlaʃ] nm ou nf: **sans ~** without respite ou a break; **relâché, e** adj loose, lax; **relâcher** vt (libérer) to release; (desserrer) to loosen; **se relâcher** vi (discipline) to become slack ou lax; (élève etc) to slacken off

relais [ʀ(ə)lɛ] nm (Sport): **(course de) ~** relay (race); **prendre le ~ (de)** to take over (from); **relais routier** ≈ transport café (BRIT), ≈ truck stop (US)

relancer [ʀ(ə)lɑ̃se] vt (balle) to throw back; (moteur) to restart; (fig) to boost, revive; (harceler): **~ qn** to pester sb

relatif, -ive [ʀ(ə)latif, iv] adj relative

relation [ʀ(ə)lasjɔ̃] nf (rapport) relation(ship); (connaissance) acquaintance; **relations** nfpl (rapports) relations; (connaissances) connections; **être/entrer en ~(s) avec** to be/get in contact with

relaxer [ʀəlakse]: **se relaxer** vi to relax

relayer [ʀ(ə)leje] vt (collaborateur, coureur etc) to relieve; **se relayer** vi (dans une activité) to take it in turns

reléguer [ʀ(ə)lege] vt to relegate

relevé, e [ʀəl(ə)ve] adj (manches) rolled-up; (sauce) highly-seasoned ▷ nm (de compteur) reading; **relevé bancaire** ou **de compte** bank statement

relève [ʀəlɛv] nf (personne) relief; **prendre la ~** to take over

relever [ʀəl(ə)ve] vt (meuble) to stand up again; (personne tombée) to help up; (vitre, niveau de vie) to raise; (inf) to turn up; (style) to elevate; (plat, sauce) to season; (sentinelle, équipe) to relieve; (fautes) to pick out; (défi) to accept, take up; (noter: adresse etc) to take down, note; (: plan) to sketch; (compteur) to read; (ramasser: cahiers) to collect, take in; **se relever** vi (se remettre debout) to get up; **~ de** (maladie) to be recovering from; (être du ressort de) to be a matter for; (fig) to pertain to; **~ qn de** (fonctions) to relieve sb of; **~ la tête** to look up

relief [ʀəljɛf] nm relief; **mettre en ~** (fig) to bring out, highlight

relier [ʀəlje] vt to link up; (livre) to bind; **~ qch à** to link sth to

religieux, -euse [ʀ(ə)liʒjø, jøz] adj religious ▷ nm monk

religion [ʀ(ə)liʒjɔ̃] nf religion

relire [ʀ(ə)liʀ] vt (à nouveau) to reread, read again; (vérifier) to read over

reluire [ʀ(ə)lɥiʀ] vi to gleam

remanier [ʀ(ə)manje] vt to reshape, recast;

(Pol) to reshuffle

remarquable [R(ə)maʀkabl] adj remarkable

remarque [R(ə)maʀk] nf remark; (écrite) note

remarquer [R(ə)maʀke] vt (voir) to notice; **se remarquer** vi to be noticeable; **faire ~ (à qn) que** to point out (to sb) that; **faire ~ qch (à qn)** to point sth out (to sb); **remarquez, ...** mind you ...; **se faire ~** to draw attention to o.s.

rembourrer [Rãbure] vt to stuff

remboursement [Rãbuʀsəmã] nm (de dette, d'emprunt) repayment; (de frais) refund; **rembourser** vt to pay back, repay; (frais, billet etc) to refund; **se faire rembourser** to get a refund

remède [R(ə)mɛd] nm (médicament) medicine; (traitement, fig) remedy, cure

remémorer [R(ə)memɔre]: **se remémorer** vt to recall, recollect

remerciements [Rəmɛʀsimã] nmpl thanks; **(avec) tous mes ~** (with) grateful ou many thanks

remercier [R(ə)mɛʀsje] vt to thank; (congédier) to dismiss; **~ qn de/d'avoir fait** to thank sb for/for having done

remettre [R(ə)mɛtʀ] vt (replacer) to put back; (vêtement) to put back on; (ajouter) to add; (ajourner): **~ qch (à)** to postpone sth (until); **se remettre** vi: **se ~ (de)** to recover (from); **~ qch à qn** (donner: lettre, clé etc) to hand over sth to sb; (: prix, décoration) to present sb with sth; **se ~ à faire qch** to start doing sth again; **s'en ~ à** to leave it (up) to

remise [R(ə)miz] nf (rabais) discount; (local) shed; **remise de peine** reduction of sentence; **remise des prix** prize-giving; **remise en cause** ou **question** calling into question, challenging; **remise en jeu** (Football) throw-in

remontant [R(ə)mɔ̃tã] nm tonic, pick-me-up

remonte-pente [R(ə)mɔ̃tpãt] nm ski-lift

remonter [R(ə)mɔ̃te] vi to go back up; (prix, température) to go up again ▷ vt (pente) to go up; (fleuve) to sail (ou swim etc) up; (manches, pantalon) to roll up; (col) to turn up; (niveau, limite) to raise; (fig: personne) to buck up; (qch de démonté) to put back together, reassemble; (montre) to wind up; **~ le moral à qn** to raise sb's spirits; **~ à** (dater de) to date ou go back to

remords [R(ə)mɔʀ] nm remorse no pl; **avoir des ~** to feel remorse

remorque [R(ə)mɔʀk] nf trailer; **remorquer** vt to tow; **remorqueur** nm tug(boat)

remous [Rəmu] nm (d'un navire) (back)wash no pl; (de rivière) swirl, eddy ▷ nmpl (fig) stir sg

remparts [Rãpaʀ] nmpl walls, ramparts

remplaçant, e [Rãplasã, ãt] nm/f replacement, stand-in; (Scol) supply teacher

remplacement [Rãplasmã] nm replacement; **faire des ~s** (professeur) to do supply teaching; (secrétaire) to temp

remplacer [Rãplase] vt to replace; **~ qch/qn par** to replace sth/sb with

rempli, e [Rãpli] adj (emploi du temps) full, busy; **~ de** full of, filled with

remplir [Rãpliʀ] vt to fill (up); (questionnaire) to fill out ou up; (obligations, fonction, condition) to fulfil; **se remplir** vi to fill up

remporter [Rãpɔʀte] vt (marchandise) to take away; (fig) to win, achieve

remuant, e [Rəmɥã, ãt] adj restless

remue-ménage [R(ə)mymenaʒ] nm inv commotion

remuer [Rəmɥe] vt to move; (café, sauce) to stir ▷ vi to move; **se remuer** vi to move; (fam: s'activer) to get a move on

rémunérer [Remyneʀe] vt to remunerate

renard [R(ə)naʀ] nm fox

renchérir [Rãʃeʀiʀ] vi (fig): **~ (sur)** (en paroles) to add something (to)

rencontre [Rãkɔ̃tʀ] nf meeting; (imprévue) encounter; **aller à la ~ de qn** to go and meet sb; **rencontrer** vt to meet; (mot, expression) to come across; (difficultés) to meet with; **se rencontrer** vi to meet

rendement [Rãdmã] nm (d'un travailleur, d'une machine) output; (d'un champ) yield

rendez-vous [Rãdevu] nm appointment; (d'amoureux) date; (lieu) meeting place; **donner ~ à qn** to arrange to meet sb; **avoir/prendre ~ (avec)** to have/make an appointment (with); **j'ai ~ avec ...** I have an appointment with ...; **je voudrais prendre ~** I'd like to make an appointment

rendre [Rãdʀ] vt (restituer) to give back, return; (invitation) to return, repay; (vomir) to bring up; (exprimer, traduire) to render; (faire devenir): **~ qn célèbre/qch possible** to make sb famous/sth possible; **se rendre** vi (capituler) to surrender, give o.s. up; (aller): **se ~ quelque part** to go somewhere; **~ la monnaie à qn** to give sb his change; **se ~ compte de qch** to realize sth

rênes [Rɛn] nfpl reins

renfermé, e [Rãfɛʀme] adj (fig) withdrawn ▷ nm: **sentir le ~** to smell stuffy

renfermer [Rãfɛʀme] vt to contain

renforcer [Rãfɔʀse] vt to reinforce; **renfort: renforts** nmpl reinforcements; **à grand renfort de** with a great deal of

renfrogné, e [Rãfʀɔɲe] adj sullen

renier [Rənje] vt (personne) to disown, repudiate; (foi) to renounce

renifler [R(ə)nifle] vi, vt to sniff

renne [Rɛn] nm reindeer inv

renom [Rənɔ̃] nm reputation; (célébrité) renown; **renommé, e** adj celebrated, renowned; **renommée** nf fame

renoncer [R(ə)nɔ̃se]: **~ à** vt to give up; **~ à faire** to give up the idea of doing

renouer [Rənwe] vt: **~ avec** (habitude) to take

up again

renouveler [R(ə)nuv(ə)le] vt to renew; (exploit, méfait) to repeat; **se renouveler** vi (incident) to recur, happen again; **renouvellement** nm (remplacement) renewal

rénover [Renɔve] vt (immeuble) to renovate, do up; (quartier) to redevelop

renseignement [Rɑ̃sɛɲmɑ̃] nm information no pl, piece of information; **(guichet des) ~s** information office; **(service des) ~s** (Tél) directory enquiries (BRIT), information (US)

renseigner [Rɑ̃seɲe] vt: **~ qn (sur)** to give information to sb (about); **se renseigner** vi to ask for information, make inquiries

rentabilité [Rɑ̃tabilite] nf profitability

rentable [Rɑ̃tabl] adj profitable

rente [Rɑ̃t] nf private income; (pension) pension

rentrée [Rɑ̃tre] nf: **~ (d'argent)** cash no pl coming in; **la ~ (des classes)** the start of the new school year

rentrer [Rɑ̃tre] vi (revenir chez soi) to go (ou come) (back) home; (entrer de nouveau) to go (ou come) back in; (entrer) to go (ou come) in; (air, clou: pénétrer) to go in; (revenu) to come in ▷ vt to bring in; (véhicule) to put away; (chemise dans pantalon etc) to tuck in; (griffes) to draw in; **~ le ventre** to pull in one's stomach; **~ dans** (heurter) to crash into; **~ dans l'ordre** to be back to normal; **~ dans ses frais** to recover one's expenses; **je rentre mardi** I'm going ou coming home on Tuesday

renverse [Rɑ̃vɛRs]: **à la ~** adv backwards

renverser [Rɑ̃vɛRse] vt (faire tomber: chaise, verre) to knock over, overturn; (liquide, contenu) to spill, upset; (piéton) to knock down; (retourner) to turn upside down; (: ordre des mots etc) to reverse; (fig: gouvernement etc) to overthrow; (fam: stupéfier) to bowl over; **se renverser** vi (verre, vase) to fall over; (contenu) to spill

renvoi [Rɑ̃vwa] nm (d'employé) dismissal; (d'élève) expulsion; (référence) cross-reference; (éructation) belch; **renvoyer** vt to send back; (congédier) to dismiss; (élève: définitivement) to expel; (lumière) to reflect; (ajourner): **renvoyer qch (à)** to put sth off ou postpone sth (until)

repaire [R(ə)pɛR] nm den

répandre [RepɑdR] vt (renverser) to spill; (étaler, diffuser) to spread; (odeur) to give off; **se répandre** vi to spill; (se propager) to spread; **répandu, e** adj (opinion, usage) widespread

réparation [RepaRasjɔ̃] nf repair

réparer [RepaRe] vt to repair; (fig: offense) to make up for, atone for; (: oubli, erreur) to put right; **où est-ce que je peux le faire ~?** where can I get it fixed?

repartie [RepaRti] nf retort; **avoir de la ~** to be quick at repartee

repartir [R(ə)paRtiR] vi to leave again; (voyageur) to set off again; (fig) to get going again; **~ à zéro** to start from scratch (again)

répartir [RepaRtiR] vt (pour attribuer) to share out; (pour disperser, disposer) to divide up; (poids) to distribute; **se répartir** vt (travail, rôles) to share out between themselves; **répartition** nf (des richesses etc) distribution

repas [R(ə)pɑ] nm meal

repassage [R(ə)pɑsaʒ] nm ironing

repasser [R(ə)pɑse] vi to come (ou go) back ▷ vt (vêtement, tissu) to iron; (examen) to retake, resit; (film) to show again; (leçon: revoir) to go over (again)

repentir [RəpɑtiR] nm repentance; **se repentir** vi to repent; **se ~ d'avoir fait qch** (regretter) to regret having done sth

répercussions [RepɛRkysjɔ̃] nfpl (fig) repercussions

répercuter [RepɛRkyte]: **se répercuter** vi (bruit) to reverberate; (fig): **se ~ sur** to have repercussions on

repère [R(ə)pɛR] nm mark; (monument, événement) landmark

repérer [R(ə)peRe] vt (fam: erreur, personne) to spot; (: endroit) to locate; **se repérer** vi to find one's way about

répertoire [RepɛRtwaR] nm (liste) (alphabetical) list; (carnet) index notebook; (Inform) folder, directory; (d'un artiste) repertoire

répéter [Repete] vt to repeat; (préparer: leçon) to learn, go over; (Théâtre) to rehearse; **se répéter** vi (redire) to repeat o.s.; (se reproduire) to be repeated, recur; **pouvez-vous ~, s'il vous plaît?** can you repeat that, please?

répétition [Repetisjɔ̃] nf repetition; (Théâtre) rehearsal; **~ générale** (final) dress rehearsal

répit [Repi] nm respite; **sans ~** without letting up

replier [R(ə)plije] vt (rabattre) to fold down ou over; **se replier** vi (troupes, armée) to withdraw, fall back; (sur soi-même) to withdraw into o.s.

réplique [Replik] nf (repartie, fig) reply; (Théâtre) line; (copie) replica; **répliquer** vi to reply; (riposter) to retaliate

répondeur [RepɔdœR] nm: **~ (automatique)** (Tél) answering machine

répondre [RepɔdR] vi to answer, reply; (freins) to respond; **~ à** to reply to, answer; (affection, salut) to return; (provocation) to respond to; (correspondre à: besoin) to answer; (: conditions) to meet; (: description) to match; (avec impertinence): **~ à qn** to answer sb back; **~ de** to answer for

réponse [Repɔs] nf answer, reply; **en ~ à** in reply to

reportage [R(ə)pɔRtaʒ] nm report

reporter¹ [RəpɔRtɛR] nm reporter

reporter² [ʀəpɔʀte] vt (ajourner): **~ qch (à)** to postpone sth (until); (transférer): **~ qch sur** to transfer sth to; **se reporter à** (époque) to think back to; (document) to refer to

repos [ʀ(ə)po] nm rest; (tranquillité) peace (and quiet); (Mil): **~!** stand at easel; **ce n'est pas de tout ~!** it's no picnic!

reposant, e [ʀ(ə)pozɑ̃, ɑ̃t] adj restful

reposer [ʀ(ə)poze] vt (verre, livre) to put down; (délasser) to rest ▷ vi: **laisser ~** (pâte) to leave to stand; **se reposer** vi to rest; **se ~ sur qn** to rely on sb; **~ sur** (fig) to rest on

repoussant, e [ʀ(ə)pusɑ̃, ɑ̃t] adj repulsive

repousser [ʀ(ə)puse] vi to grow again ▷ vt to repel, repulse; (offre) to turn down, reject; (personne) to push back; (différer) to put back

reprendre [ʀ(ə)pʀɑ̃dʀ] vt (objet prêté, donné) to take back; (prisonnier, ville) to recapture; (firme, entreprise) to take over; (le travail) to resume; (emprunter: argument, idée) to take up, use; (refaire: article etc) to go over again; (vêtement) to alter; (réprimander) to tell off; (corriger) to correct; (chercher): **je viendrai te ~ à 4 h** I'll come and fetch you at 4; (se resservir de): **~ du pain/un œuf** to take (ou eat) more bread/another egg ▷ vi (classes, pluie) to start (up) again; (activités, travaux, combats) to resume, start (up) again; (affaires) to pick up; (dire): **reprit-il** he went on; **~ des forces** to recover one's strength; **~ courage** to take new heart; **~ la route** to resume one's journey, set off again; **~ haleine** ou **son souffle** to get one's breath back

représentant, e [ʀ(ə)pʀezɑ̃tɑ̃, ɑ̃t] nm/f representative

représentation [ʀ(ə)pʀezɑ̃tasjɔ̃] nf (symbole, image) representation; (spectacle) performance

représenter [ʀ(ə)pʀezɑ̃te] vt to represent; (donner: pièce, opéra) to perform; **se représenter** vt (se figurer) to imagine

répression [ʀepʀesjɔ̃] nf repression

réprimer [ʀepʀime] vt (émotions) to suppress; (peuple etc) to repress

repris [ʀ(ə)pʀi] nm: **~ de justice** ex-prisoner, ex-convict

reprise [ʀ(ə)pʀiz] nf (recommencement) resumption; (économique) recovery; (TV) repeat; (Comm) trade-in, part exchange; (raccommodage) mend; **à plusieurs ~s** on several occasions

repriser [ʀ(ə)pʀize] vt (chaussette, lainage) to darn; (tissu) to mend

reproche [ʀ(ə)pʀɔʃ] nm (remontrance) reproach; **faire des ~s à qn** to reproach sb; **sans ~(s)** beyond reproach; **reprocher** vt: **reprocher qch à qn** to reproach ou blame sb for sth; **reprocher qch à** (critiquer) to have sth against

reproduction [ʀ(ə)pʀɔdyksjɔ̃] nf reproduction

reproduire [ʀ(ə)pʀɔdɥiʀ] vt to reproduce; **se reproduire** vi (Bio) to reproduce; (recommencer) to recur, re-occur

reptile [ʀɛptil] nm reptile

république [ʀepyblik] nf republic

répugnant, e [ʀepyɲɑ̃, ɑ̃t] adj disgusting

répugner [ʀepyɲe]: **~ à** vt: **~ à qn** to repel ou disgust sb; **~ à faire** to be loath ou reluctant to do

réputation [ʀepytasjɔ̃] nf reputation; **réputé, e** adj renowned

requérir [ʀəkeʀiʀ] vt (nécessiter) to require, call for

requête [ʀəkɛt] nf request

requin [ʀəkɛ̃] nm shark

requis, e [ʀəki, iz] adj required

RER sigle m (= réseau express régional) Greater Paris high-speed train service

rescapé, e [ʀɛskape] nm/f survivor

rescousse [ʀɛskus] nf: **aller à la ~ de qn** to go to sb's aid ou rescue

réseau, x [ʀezo] nm network

réservation [ʀezɛʀvasjɔ̃] nf booking, reservation; **j'ai confirmé ma ~ par fax/e-mail** I confirmed my booking by fax/e-mail

réserve [ʀezɛʀv] nf (retenue) reserve; (entrepôt) storeroom; (restriction, d'Indiens) reservation; (de pêche, chasse) preserve; **de ~** (provisions etc) in reserve

réservé, e [ʀezɛʀve] adj reserved; **chasse/pêche ~e** private hunting/fishing

réserver [ʀezɛʀve] vt to reserve; (chambre, billet etc) to book, reserve; (fig: destiner) to have in store; (garder): **~ qch pour/à** to keep ou save sth for; **je voudrais ~ une chambre pour deux personnes** I'd like to book a double room; **j'ai réservé une table au nom de ...** I booked a table in the name of ...

réservoir [ʀezɛʀvwaʀ] nm tank

résidence [ʀezidɑ̃s] nf residence; **résidence secondaire** second home; **résidence universitaire** hall of residence (BRIT), dormitory (US); **résidentiel, le** adj residential; **résider** vi: **résider à/dans/en** to reside in; **résider dans** (fig) to lie in

résidu [ʀezidy] nm residue no pl

résigner [ʀeziɲe]: **se résigner** vi: **se ~ (à qch/à faire)** to resign o.s. (to sth/to doing)

résilier [ʀezilje] vt to terminate

résistance [ʀezistɑ̃s] nf resistance; (de réchaud, bouilloire: fil) element

résistant, e [ʀezistɑ̃, ɑ̃t] adj (personne) robust, tough; (matériau) strong, hard-wearing

résister [ʀeziste] vi to resist; **~ à** (assaut, tentation) to resist; (supporter: gel etc) to withstand; (désobéir à) to stand up to, oppose

résolu, e [ʀezɔly] pp de **résoudre** ▷ adj: **être ~ à qch/faire** to be set upon sth/doing

résolution [Rezɔlysjɔ̃] *nf (fermeté, décision)* resolution; *(d'un problème)* solution

résolve *etc* [Rezɔlv] *vb voir* **résoudre**

résonner [Rezɔne] *vi (cloche, pas)* to reverberate, resound; *(salle)* to be resonant

résorber [Rezɔrbe]: **se résorber** *vi (fig: chômage)* to be reduced; *(: déficit)* to be absorbed

résoudre [Rezudr] *vt* to solve; **se ~ à faire** to bring o.s. to do

respect [Rɛspɛ] *nm* respect; **tenir en ~** to keep at bay; **présenter ses ~s à qn** to pay one's respects to sb; **respecter** *vt* to respect; **respectueux, -euse** *adj* respectful

respiration [RɛspiRasjɔ̃] *nf* breathing *no pl*

respirer [RɛspiRe] *vi* to breathe; *(fig: se détendre)* to get one's breath; *(: se rassurer)* to breathe again ▷ *vt* to breathe (in), inhale; *(manifester: santé, calme etc)* to exude

resplendir [Rɛsplãdir] *vi* to shine; *(fig):* **~ (de)** to be radiant (with)

responsabilité [Rɛspɔ̃sabilite] *nf* responsibility; *(légale)* liability

responsable [Rɛspɔ̃sabl] *adj* responsible ▷ *nm/f (coupable)* person responsible; *(personne compétente)* person in charge; *(de parti, syndicat)* official; **~ de** responsible for

ressaisir [R(ə)sezir]: **se ressaisir** *vi* to regain one's self-control

ressasser [R(ə)sase] *vt* to keep going over

ressemblance [R(ə)sãblãs] *nf* resemblance, similarity, likeness

ressemblant, e [R(ə)sãblã, ãt] *adj (portrait)* lifelike, true to life

ressembler [R(ə)sãble]: **~ à** *vt* to be like, resemble; *(visuellement)* to look like; **se ressembler** *vi* to be *(ou* look) alike

ressentiment [R(ə)sãtimã] *nm* resentment

ressentir [R(ə)sãtir] *vt* to feel; **se ~ de** to feel *(ou* show) the effects of

resserrer [R(ə)sere] *vt (nœud, boulon)* to tighten (up); *(fig: liens)* to strengthen

resservir [R(ə)sɛrvir] *vi* to do *ou* serve again; **~ qn (d'un plat)** to give sb a second helping (of a dish); **se ~ de** *(plat)* to take a second helping of; *(outil etc)* to use again

ressort [R(ə)sɔr] *nm (pièce)* spring; *(énergie)* spirit; *(recours):* **en dernier ~** as a last resort; *(compétence):* **être du ~ de** to fall within the competence of

ressortir [RəsɔRtir] *vi* to go *(ou* come) out (again); *(contraster)* to stand out; **~ de** to emerge from; **faire ~** *(fig: souligner)* to bring out

ressortissant, e [R(ə)sɔrtisã, ãt] *nm/f* national

ressources [R(ə)surs] *nfpl (moyens)* resources

ressusciter [Resysite] *vt (fig)* to revive, bring back ▷ *vi* to rise (from the dead)

restant, e [Rɛstã, ãt] *adj* remaining ▷ *nm:*

le ~ (de) the remainder (of); **un ~ de** *(de trop)* some left-over

restaurant [Rɛstɔrã] *nm* restaurant; **pouvez-vous m'indiquer un bon ~?** can you recommend a good restaurant?

restauration [Rɛstɔrasjɔ̃] *nf* restoration; *(hôtellerie)* catering; **restauration rapide** fast food

restaurer [Rɛstɔre] *vt* to restore; **se restaurer** *vi* to have something to eat

reste [Rɛst] *nm (restant):* **le ~ (de)** the rest (of); *(de trop):* **un ~ (de)** some left-over; **restes** *nmpl (nourriture)* left-overs; *(d'une cité etc, dépouille mortelle)* remains; **du ~, au ~** besides, moreover

rester [Rɛste] *vi* to stay, remain; *(subsister)* to remain, be left; *(durer)* to last, live on ▷ *vb impers:* **il reste du pain/2 œufs** there's some bread/there are 2 eggs left (over); **restons-en là** let's leave it at that; **il me reste assez de temps** I have enough time left; **il ne me reste plus qu'à ...** I've just got to ...

restituer [Rɛstitɥe] *vt (objet, somme):* **~ qch (à qn)** to return sth (to sb)

restreindre [Rɛstrɛ̃dr] *vt* to restrict, limit

restriction [Rɛstriksjɔ̃] *nf* restriction

résultat [Rezylta] *nm* result; **résultats** *nmpl (d'examen, d'élection)* results *pl*

résulter [Rezylte]: **~ de** *vt* to result from, be the result of

résumé [Rezyme] *nm* summary, résumé; **en ~** in brief; *(pour conclure)* to sum up

résumer [Rezyme] *vt (texte)* to summarize; *(récapituler)* to sum up

> Attention à ne pas traduire *résumer* par *to resume*.

résurrection [Rezyrɛksjɔ̃] *nf* resurrection

rétablir [Retablir] *vt* to restore, re-establish; **se rétablir** *vi (guérir)* to recover; *(silence, calme)* to return, be restored; **rétablissement** *nm* restoring; *(guérison)* recovery

retaper [R(ə)tape] *(fam) vt (maison, voiture etc)* to do up; *(revigorer)* to buck up

retard [R(ə)tar] *nm (d'une personne attendue)* lateness *no pl*; *(sur l'horaire, un programme)* delay; *(fig: scolaire, mental etc)* backwardness; **en ~ (de 2 heures)** (2 hours) late; **avoir du ~** to be late; *(sur un programme)* to be behind (schedule); **prendre du ~** *(train, avion)* to be delayed; **sans ~** without delay; **désolé d'être en ~** sorry I'm late; **le vol a deux heures de ~** the flight is two hours late

retardataire [R(ə)tardatɛr] *nm/f* latecomer

retardement [R(ə)tardəmã]: **à ~** *adj* delayed action *cpd*; **bombe à ~** time bomb

retarder [R(ə)tarde] *vt* to delay; *(montre)* to put back ▷ *vi (montre)* to be slow; **~ qn (d'une heure)** *(sur un horaire)* to delay sb (an hour); **~ qch (de 2 jours)** *(départ, date)* to put sth back

(2 days)

retenir [Rət(ə)niR] vt (garder, retarder) to keep, detain; (maintenir: objet qui glisse, fig: colère, larmes) to hold back; (se rappeler) to retain; (réserver) to reserve; (accepter: proposition etc) to accept; (fig: empêcher d'agir): **~ qn (de faire)** to hold sb back (from doing); (prélever): **~ qch (sur)** to deduct sth (from); **se retenir** vi (se raccrocher): **se ~ à** to hold onto; (se contenir) **se ~ de faire** to restrain o.s. from doing; **~ son souffle** to hold one's breath

retentir [R(ə)tãtiR] vi to ring out; **retentissant, e** adj resounding

retenue [Rət(ə)ny] nf (prélèvement) deduction; (Scol) detention; (modération) (self-)restraint

réticence [Retisãs] nf hesitation, reluctance no pl; **réticent, e** adj hesitant, reluctant

rétine [Retin] nf retina

retiré, e [R(ə)tiRe] adj (vie) secluded; (lieu) remote

retirer [R(ə)tiRe] vt (vêtement, lunettes) to take off, remove; (argent, plainte) to withdraw; (reprendre: bagages, billets) to collect, pick up; (extraire): **~ qch de** to take sth out of, remove sth from

retomber [R(ə)tõbe] vi (à nouveau) to fall again; (atterrir: après un saut etc) to land; (échoir): **~ sur qn** to fall on sb

rétorquer [RetɔRke] vt: **~ (à qn) que** to retort (to sb) that

retouche [R(ə)tuʃ] nf (sur vêtement) alteration; **retoucher** vt (photographie) to touch up; (texte, vêtement) to alter

retour [R(ə)tuR] nm return; **au ~** (en route) on the way back; **à mon ~** when I get/got back; **être de ~ (de)** to be back (from); **par ~ du courrier** by return of post; **quand serons-nous de ~?** when do we get back?

retourner [R(ə)tuRne] vt (dans l'autre sens: matelas, crêpe etc) to turn (over); (: sac, vêtement) to turn inside out; (fam: bouleverser) to shake; (renvoyer, restituer): **~ qch à qn** to return sth to sb ▷ vi (aller, revenir): **~ quelque part/à** to go back ou return somewhere/to; **se retourner** vi (tourner la tête) to turn round; **~ à** (état, activité) to return to, go back to; **se ~ contre** (fig) to turn against

retrait [R(ə)tRE] nm (d'argent) withdrawal; **en ~** set back; **retrait du permis (de conduire)** disqualification from driving (BRIT), revocation of driver's license (US)

retraite [R(ə)tRET] nf (d'un employé) retirement; (revenu) pension; (d'une armée, Rel) retreat; **prendre sa ~** to retire; **retraite anticipée** early retirement; **retraité, e** adj retired ▷ nm/f pensioner

retrancher [R(ə)tRãʃe] vt (nombre, somme):

~ qch de to take ou deduct sth from; **se ~ derrière/dans** to take refuge behind/in

rétrécir [RetResiR] vt (vêtement) to take in ▷ vi to shrink; **se rétrécir** (route, vallée) to narrow

rétro [RetRo] adj inv: **la mode ~** the nostalgia vogue

rétroprojecteur [RetRopRɔʒɛktœR] nm overhead projector

rétrospective [RetRɔspɛktiv] nf (Art) retrospective; (Cinéma) season, retrospective; **rétrospectivement** adv in retrospect

retrousser [R(ə)tRuse] vt to roll up

retrouvailles [R(ə)tRuvaj] nfpl reunion sg

retrouver [R(ə)tRuve] vt (fugitif, objet perdu) to find; (calme, santé) to regain; (revoir) to see again; (rejoindre) to meet (again), join; **se retrouver** vi to meet; (s'orienter) to find one's way; **se ~ quelque part** to find o.s. somewhere; **s'y ~** (y voir clair) to make sense of it; (rentrer dans ses frais) to break even; **je ne retrouve plus mon portefeuille** I can't find my wallet (BRIT) ou billfold (US)

rétroviseur [RetRɔvizœR] nm (rear-view) mirror

réunion [Reynjõ] nf (séance) meeting

réunir [ReyniR] vt (rassembler) to gather together; (inviter: amis, famille) to have round, have in; (cumuler: qualités etc) to combine; (rapprocher: ennemis) to bring together (again), reunite; (rattacher: parties) to join (together); **se réunir** vi (se rencontrer) to meet

réussi, e [Reysi] adj successful

réussir [ReysiR] vi to succeed, be successful; (à un examen) to pass ▷ vt to make a success of; **~ à faire** to succeed in doing; **~ à qn** (être bénéfique à) to agree with sb; **réussite** nf success; (Cartes) patience

revaloir [R(ə)valwaR] vt: **je vous revaudrai cela** I'll repay you some day; (en mal) I'll pay you back for this

revanche [R(ə)vãʃ] nf revenge; (sport) revenge match; **en ~** on the other hand

rêve [REv] nm dream; **de ~** dream cpd; **faire un ~** to have a dream

réveil [REvɛj] nm waking up no pl; (fig) awakening; (pendule) alarm (clock); **au ~** on waking (up); **réveiller** vt (personne) to wake up; (fig) to awaken, revive; **se réveiller** vi to wake up; **pouvez-vous me réveiller à 7 heures, s'il vous plaît?** could I have an alarm call at 7am, please?

réveillon [REvɛjõ] nm Christmas Eve; (de la Saint-Sylvestre) New Year's Eve; **réveillonner** vi to celebrate Christmas Eve (ou New Year's Eve)

révélateur, -trice [RevelatœR, tRis] adj: **~ (de qch)** revealing (sth)

révéler [Revele] vt to reveal; **se révéler** vi to be revealed, reveal itself ▷ vb +attrib: **se ~**

difficile/aisé to prove difficult/easy
revenant, e [ʀ(ə)vənɑ̃, ɑ̃t] nm/f ghost
revendeur, -euse [ʀ(ə)vɑ̃dœʀ, øz] nm/f
(*détaillant*) retailer; (*de drogue*) (drug-)dealer
revendication [ʀ(ə)vɑ̃dikasjɔ̃] nf claim,
demand
revendiquer [ʀ(ə)vɑ̃dike] vt to claim,
demand; (*responsabilité*) to claim
revendre [ʀ(ə)vɑ̃dʀ] vt (*d'occasion*) to resell;
(*détailler*) to sell; **à ~** (*en abondance*) to spare
revenir [ʀəv(ə)niʀ] vi to come back; (*coûter*):
~ cher/à 100 euros (à qn) to cost (sb) a
lot/100 euros; **~ à** (*reprendre: études, projet*) to
return to, go back to; (*équivaloir à*) to amount
to; **~ à qn** (*part, honneur*) to go to sb, be sb's;
(*souvenir, nom*) to come back to sb; **~ sur**
(*question, sujet*) to go back over; (*engagement*)
to go back on; **~ à soi** to come round; **n'en
pas ~ : je n'en reviens pas** I can't get over
it; **~ sur ses pas** to retrace one's steps; **cela
revient à dire que/au même** it amounts to
saying that/the same thing; **faire ~** (*Culin*)
to brown
revenu [ʀəv(ə)ny] nm income; **revenus** nmpl
income *sg*
rêver [ʀeve] vi, vt to dream; **~ de/à** to dream of
réverbère [ʀeveʀbɛʀ] nm street lamp *ou* light;
réverbérer vt to reflect
revers [ʀ(ə)vɛʀ] nm (*de feuille, main*) back;
(*d'étoffe*) wrong side; (*de pièce, médaille*) back,
reverse; (*Tennis, Ping-Pong*) backhand; (*de veste*)
lapel; (*fig: échec*) setback
revêtement [ʀ(ə)vɛtmɑ̃] nm (*des sols*)
flooring; (*de chaussée*) surface
revêtir [ʀ(ə)vetiʀ] vt (*habit*) to don, put on;
(*prendre: importance, apparence*) to take on; **~
qch de** to cover sth with
rêveur, -euse [ʀɛvœʀ, øz] adj dreamy ▷ nm/f
dreamer
revient [ʀəvjɛ̃] vb voir **revenir**
revigorer [ʀ(ə)vigɔʀe] vt (*air frais*) to
invigorate, brace up; (*repas, boisson*) to revive,
buck up
revirement [ʀ(ə)viʀmɑ̃] nm change of mind;
(*d'une situation*) reversal
réviser [ʀevize] vt to revise; (*machine*) to
overhaul, service
révision [ʀevizjɔ̃] nf revision; (*de voiture*)
servicing *no pl*
revivre [ʀ(ə)vivʀ] vi (*reprendre des forces*) to
come alive again ▷ vt (*épreuve, moment*) to
relive
revoir [ʀəvwaʀ] vt to see again; (*réviser*) to
revise ▷ nm: **au ~** goodbye
révoltant, e [ʀevɔltɑ̃, ɑ̃t] adj revolting,
appalling
révolte [ʀevɔlt] nf rebellion, revolt
révolter [ʀevɔlte] vt to revolt; **se révolter
(contre)** to rebel (against)

révolu, e [ʀevɔly] adj past; (*Admin*): **âgé de 18
ans ~s** over 18 years of age
révolution [ʀevɔlysjɔ̃] nf revolution;
révolutionnaire adj, nm/f revolutionary
revolver [ʀevɔlvɛʀ] nm gun; (*à barillet*)
revolver
révoquer [ʀevɔke] vt (*fonctionnaire*) to
dismiss; (*arrêt, contrat*) to revoke
revue [ʀ(ə)vy] nf review; (*périodique*) review,
magazine; (*de music-hall*) variety show; **passer
en ~** (*mentalement*) to go through
rez-de-chaussée [ʀed(ə)ʃose] nm inv ground
floor
RF sigle f = **République française**
Rhin [ʀɛ̃] nm Rhine
rhinocéros [ʀinɔseʀɔs] nm rhinoceros
Rhône [ʀon] nm Rhone
rhubarbe [ʀybaʀb] nf rhubarb
rhum [ʀɔm] nm rum
rhumatisme [ʀymatism] nm
rheumatism *no pl*
rhume [ʀym] nm cold; **rhume de cerveau**
head cold; **le rhume des foins** hay fever
ricaner [ʀikane] vi (*avec méchanceté*) to
snigger; (*bêtement*) to giggle
riche [ʀiʃ] adj rich; (*personne, pays*) rich,
wealthy; **~ en** rich in; **richesse** nf wealth;
(*fig: de sol, musée etc*) richness; **richesses** nfpl
(*ressources, argent*) wealth *sg*; (*fig: trésors*)
treasures
ricochet [ʀikɔʃɛ] nm: **faire des ~s** to skip
stones
ride [ʀid] nf wrinkle
rideau, x [ʀido] nm curtain; **rideau de fer**
(*boutique*) metal shutter(s)
rider [ʀide] vt to wrinkle; **se rider** vi to
become wrinkled
ridicule [ʀidikyl] adj ridiculous ▷ nm:
le ~ ridicule; **ridiculiser** vt to ridicule; **se
ridiculiser** vi to make a fool of o.s.

 MOT-CLÉ

rien [ʀjɛ̃] pron 1: **(ne) ... rien** nothing, *tournure
négative + anything*; **qu'est-ce que vous avez?
— rien** what have you got? — nothing; **il n'a
rien dit/fait** he said/did nothing; he hasn't
said/done anything; **n'avoir peur de rien** to
be afraid *ou* frightened of nothing, not to be
afraid *ou* frightened of anything; **il n'a rien**
(*n'est pas blessé*) he's all right; **ça ne fait rien** it
doesn't matter; **de rien!** not at all!
2: **rien de: rien d'intéressant** nothing
interesting; **rien d'autre** nothing else; **rien du
tout** nothing at all
3: **rien que** just, only; nothing but; **rien que
pour lui faire plaisir** only *ou* just to please
him; **rien que la vérité** nothing but the truth;
rien que cela that alone

▷ *nm*: **un petit rien** (*cadeau*) a little something; **des riens** trivia *pl*; **un rien de** a hint of; **en un rien de temps** in no time at all

rieur, -euse [R(i)jœR, R(i)jøz] *adj* cheerful

rigide [Riʒid] *adj* stiff; (*fig*) rigid; strict

rigoler [Rigɔle] *vi* (*fam: rire*) to laugh; (*s'amuser*) to have (some) fun; (*plaisanter*) to be joking *ou* kidding; **rigolo, -ote** (*fam*) *adj* funny ▷ *nm/f* comic; (*péj*) fraud, phoney

rigoureusement [RiguRøzmɑ̃] *adv* (*vrai*) absolutely; (*interdit*) strictly

rigoureux, -euse [RiguRø, øz] *adj* rigorous; (*hiver*) hard, harsh

rigueur [RigœR] *nf* rigour; **"tenue de soirée de ~"** "formal dress only"; **à la ~** at a pinch; **tenir ~ à qn de qch** to hold sth against sb

rillettes [Rijɛt] *nfpl* potted meat (*made from pork or goose*)

rime [Rim] *nf* rhyme

rinçage [Rɛ̃saʒ] *nm* rinsing (out); (*opération*) rinse

rincer [Rɛ̃se] *vt* to rinse; (*récipient*) to rinse out

ringard, e [Rɛ̃gaR, aRd] (*fam*) *adj* old-fashioned

riposter [Ripɔste] *vi* to retaliate ▷ *vt*: **~ que** to retort that

rire [RiR] *vi* to laugh; (*se divertir*) to have fun ▷ *nm* laugh; **le ~** laughter; **~ de** to laugh at; **pour ~** (*pas sérieusement*) for a joke *ou* a laugh

risible [Rizibl] *adj* laughable

risque [Risk] *nm* risk; **le ~** danger; **à ses ~s et périls** at his own risk; **risqué, e** *adj* risky; (*plaisanterie*) risqué, daring; **risquer** *vt* to risk; (*allusion, question*) to venture, hazard; **ça ne risque rien** it's quite safe; **risquer de: il risque de se tuer** he could get himself killed; **ce qui risque de se produire** what might *ou* could well happen; **il ne risque pas de recommencer** there's no chance of him doing that again; **se risquer à faire** (*tenter*) to venture *ou* dare to do

rissoler [Risɔle] *vi, vt*: **(faire) ~** to brown

ristourne [RistuRn] *nf* discount

rite [Rit] *nm* rite; (*fig*) ritual

rivage [Rivaʒ] *nm* shore

rival, e, -aux [Rival, o] *adj, nm/f* rival; **rivaliser** *vi*: **rivaliser avec** (*personne*) to rival, vie with; **rivalité** *nf* rivalry

rive [Riv] *nf* shore; (*de fleuve*) bank; **riverain, e** *nm/f* riverside (*ou* lakeside) resident; (*d'une route*) local resident

rivière [RivjɛR] *nf* river

riz [Ri] *nm* rice; **rizière** *nf* paddy-field, ricefield

RMI *sigle m* (= *revenu minimum d'insertion*) ≈ income support (BRIT), ≈ welfare (US)

RN *sigle f* = **route nationale**

robe [Rɔb] *nf* dress; (*de juge*) robe; (*pelage*) coat; **robe de chambre** dressing gown; **robe**

de mariée wedding dress; **robe de soirée** evening dress

robinet [Rɔbinɛ] *nm* tap (BRIT), faucet (US)

robot [Rɔbo] *nm* robot; **robot de cuisine** food processor

robuste [Rɔbyst] *adj* robust, sturdy; **robustesse** *nf* robustness, sturdiness

roc [Rɔk] *nm* rock

rocade [Rɔkad] *nf* bypass

rocaille [Rɔkaj] *nf* loose stones *pl*; (*jardin*) rockery, rock garden

roche [Rɔʃ] *nf* rock

rocher [Rɔʃe] *nm* rock

rocheux, -euse [Rɔʃø, øz] *adj* rocky

rodage [Rɔdaʒ] *nm*: **en ~** = running in

rôder [Rode] *vi* to roam about; (*de façon suspecte*) to lurk (about *ou* around); **rôdeur, -euse** *nm/f* prowler

rogne [Rɔɲ] (*fam*) *nf*: **être en ~** to be in a temper

rogner [Rɔɲe] *vt* to clip; **~ sur** (*fig*) to cut down *ou* back on

rognons [Rɔɲɔ̃] *nmpl* (*Culin*) kidneys

roi [Rwa] *nm* king; **la fête des Rois, les Rois** Twelfth Night

rôle [Rol] *nm* role, part

rollers [RɔlœR] *nmpl* Rollerblades®

romain, e [Rɔmɛ̃, ɛn] *adj* Roman ▷ *nm/f*: **R~, e** Roman

roman, e [Rɔmɑ̃, an] *adj* (*Archit*) Romanesque ▷ *nm* novel; **roman policier** detective story

romancer [Rɔmɑ̃se] *vt* (*agrémenter*) to romanticize; **romancier, -ière** *nm/f* novelist; **romanesque** *adj* (*amours, aventures*) storybook *cpd*; (*sentimental: personne*) romantic

roman-feuilleton [Rɔmɑ̃fœjtɔ̃] *nm* serialized novel

romanichel, le [Rɔmaniʃɛl] (*péj*) *nm/f* gipsy

romantique [Rɔmɑ̃tik] *adj* romantic

romarin [RɔmaRɛ̃] *nm* rosemary

Rome [Rɔm] *n* Rome

rompre [RɔpR] *vt* to break; (*entretien, fiançailles*) to break off ▷ *vi* (*fiancés*) to break it off; **se rompre** *vi* to break; **rompu, e** *adj* (*fourbu*) exhausted

ronces [Rɔ̃s] *nfpl* brambles

ronchonner [Rɔ̃ʃɔne] (*fam*) *vi* to grouse, grouch

rond, e [Rɔ̃, Rɔ̃d] *adj* round; (*joues, mollets*) well-rounded; (*fam: ivre*) tight ▷ *nm* (*cercle*) ring; (*fam: sou*): **je n'ai plus un ~** I haven't a penny left; **en ~** (*s'asseoir, danser*) in a ring; **ronde** *nf* (*gén: de surveillance*) rounds *pl*, patrol; (*danse*) round (dance); (*Mus*) semibreve (BRIT), whole note (US); **à la ronde** (*alentour*): **à 10 km à la ronde** for 10 km round; **rondelet, te** *adj* plump

rondelle [Rɔ̃dɛl] *nf* (*tranche*) slice, round; (*Tech*) washer

rond-point [Rɔ̃pwɛ̃] nm roundabout
ronflement [Rɔ̃fləmɑ̃] nm snore, snoring
ronfler [Rɔ̃fle] vi to snore; (moteur, poêle) to hum
ronger [Rɔ̃ʒe] vt to gnaw (at); (suj: vers, rouille) to eat into; **se ~ les ongles** to bite one's nails; **se ~ les sangs** to worry o.s. sick; **rongeur** nm rodent
ronronner [Rɔ̃Rɔne] vi to purr
rosbif [Rɔsbif] nm: **du ~** roasting beef; (cuit) roast beef
rose [Roz] nf rose ▷ adj pink; **rose bonbon** adj inv candy pink
rosé, e [Roze] adj pinkish; **(vin) ~** rosé
roseau, x [Rozo] nm reed
rosée [Roze] nf dew
rosier [Rozje] nm rosebush, rose tree
rossignol [Rɔsiɲɔl] nm (Zool) nightingale
rotation [Rɔtasjɔ̃] nf rotation
roter [Rɔte] (fam) vi to burp, belch
rôti [Roti] nm: **du ~** roasting meat; (cuit) roast meat; **un ~ de bœuf/porc** a joint of beef/pork
rotin [Rɔtɛ̃] nm rattan (cane); **fauteuil en ~** cane (arm)chair
rôtir [Rotir] vi, vt (aussi: **faire ~**) to roast; **rôtisserie** nf (restaurant) steakhouse; (traiteur) roast meat shop; **rôtissoire** nf (roasting) spit
rotule [Rɔtyl] nf kneecap
rouage [Rwaʒ] nm cog (wheel), gearwheel; **les ~s de l'État** the wheels of State
roue [Ru] nf wheel; **roue de secours** spare wheel
rouer [Rwe] vt: **~ qn de coups** to give sb a thrashing
rouge [Ruʒ] adj, nm/f red ▷ nm red; **(vin) ~** red wine; **sur la liste ~** ex-directory (BRIT), unlisted (US); **passer au ~** (signal) to go red; (automobiliste) to go through a red light; **rouge à joue** blusher; **rouge (à lèvres)** lipstick; **rouge-gorge** nm robin (redbreast)
rougeole [Ruʒɔl] nf measles sg
rougeoyer [Ruʒwaje] vi to glow red
rouget [Ruʒe] nm mullet
rougeur [Ruʒœr] nf redness; (Méd: tache) red blotch
rougir [Ruʒir] vi to turn red; (de honte, timidité) to blush, flush; (de plaisir, colère) to flush
rouille [Ruj] nf rust; **rouillé, e** adj rusty; **rouiller** vt to rust ▷ vi to rust, go rusty
roulant, e [Rulɑ̃, ɑ̃t] adj (meuble) on wheels; (tapis etc) moving; **escalier ~** escalator
rouleau, x [Rulo] nm roll; (à mise en plis, à peinture, vague) roller; **rouleau à pâtisserie** rolling pin
roulement [Rulmɑ̃] nm (rotation) rotation; (bruit) rumbling no pl, rumble; **travailler par ~** to work on a rota (BRIT) ou rotation (US) basis; **roulement (à billes)** ball bearings pl;

roulement de tambour drum roll
rouler [Rule] vt to roll; (papier, tapis) to roll up; (Culin: pâte) to roll out; (fam: duper) to do, con ▷ vi (bille, boule) to roll; (voiture, train) to go, run; (automobiliste) to drive; (bateau) to roll; **se ~ dans** (boue) to roll in; (couverture) to roll o.s. (up) in
roulette [Rulɛt] nf (de table, fauteuil) castor; (de dentiste) drill; (jeu) roulette; **à ~s** on castors; **ça a marché comme sur des ~s** (fam) it went off very smoothly
roulis [Ruli] nm roll(ing)
roulotte [Rulɔt] nf caravan
roumain, e [Rumɛ̃, ɛn] adj Rumanian ▷ nm/f: **R~, e** Rumanian
Roumanie [Rumani] nf Rumania
rouquin, e [Rukɛ̃, in] (péj) nm/f redhead
rouspéter [Ruspete] (fam) vi to moan
rousse [Rus] adj voir **roux**
roussir [Rusir] vt to scorch ▷ vi (Culin): **faire ~** to brown
route [Rut] nf road; (fig: chemin) way; (itinéraire, parcours) route; (fig: voie) road, path; **il y a 3h de ~** it's a 3-hour ride ou journey; **en ~** on the way; **en ~!** let's go!; **mettre en ~** to start up; **se mettre en ~** to set off; **quelle ~ dois-je prendre pour aller à ...?** which road do I take for ...?; **route nationale** ≈ A road (BRIT), ≈ state highway (US); **routier, -ière** adj road cpd ▷ nm (camionneur) (long-distance) lorry (BRIT) ou truck (US) driver; (restaurant) ≈ transport café (BRIT), ≈ truck stop (US)
routine [Rutin] nf routine; **routinier, -ière** (péj) adj (activité) humdrum; (personne) addicted to routine
rouvrir [Ruvrir] vt, vi to reopen, open again; **se rouvrir** vi to reopen, open again
roux, rousse [Ru, Rus] adj red; (personne) red-haired ▷ nm/f redhead
royal, e, -aux [Rwajal, o] adj royal; (cadeau etc) fit for a king
royaume [Rwajom] nm kingdom; (fig) realm; **le Royaume-Uni** the United Kingdom
royauté [Rwajote] nf (régime) monarchy
ruban [Rybɑ̃] nm ribbon; **ruban adhésif** adhesive tape
rubéole [Rybeɔl] nf German measles sg, rubella
rubis [Rybi] nm ruby
rubrique [Rybrik] nf (titre, catégorie) heading; (Presse: article) column
ruche [Ryʃ] nf hive
rude [Ryd] adj (au toucher) rough; (métier, tâche) hard; (climat) severe, harsh; (bourru) harsh, rough; (fruste: manières) rugged, tough; (fam: fameux) jolly good; **rudement** (fam) adv (très) terribly
rudimentaire [Rydimɑ̃ter] adj rudimentary, basic

rudiments [ʀydimɑ̃] *nmpl*: **avoir des ~ d'anglais** to have a smattering of English

rue [ʀy] *nf* street

ruée [ʀɥe] *nf* rush

ruelle [ʀɥɛl] *nf* alley(-way)

ruer [ʀɥe] *vi* (*cheval*) to kick out; **se ruer** *vi*: **se ~ sur** to pounce on; **se ~ vers/dans/hors de** to rush *ou* dash towards/into/out of

rugby [ʀygbi] *nm* rugby (football)

rugir [ʀyʒiʀ] *vi* to roar

rugueux, -euse [ʀygø, øz] *adj* rough

ruine [ʀɥin] *nf* ruin; **ruiner** *vt* to ruin; **ruineux, -euse** *adj* ruinous

ruisseau, x [ʀɥiso] *nm* stream, brook

ruisseler [ʀɥis(ə)le] *vi* to stream

rumeur [ʀymœʀ] *nf* (*nouvelle*) rumour; (*bruit confus*) rumbling

ruminer [ʀymine] *vt* (*herbe*) to ruminate; (*fig*) to ruminate on *ou* over, chew over

rupture [ʀyptyʀ] *nf* (*séparation, désunion*) break-up, split; (*de négociations etc*) breakdown; (*de contrat*) breach; (*dans continuité*) break

rural, e, -aux [ʀyʀal, o] *adj* rural, country *cpd*

ruse [ʀyz] *nf*: **la ~** cunning, craftiness; (*pour tromper*) trickery; **une ~** a trick, a ruse; **rusé, e** *adj* cunning, crafty

russe [ʀys] *adj* Russian ▷ *nm/f*: **R~** Russian ▷ *nm* (*Ling*) Russian

Russie [ʀysi] *nf*: **la ~** Russia

rustine® [ʀystin] *nf* rubber repair patch (*for bicycle tyre*)

rustique [ʀystik] *adj* rustic

rythme [ʀitm] *nm* rhythm; (*vitesse*) rate; (: *de la vie*) pace, tempo; **rythmé, e** *adj* rhythmic(al)

s' [s] *pron voir* **se**

sa [sa] *adj voir* **son¹**

sable [sabl] *nm* sand

sablé [sable] *nm* shortbread biscuit

sabler [sable] *vt* (*contre le verglas*) to grit; **~ le champagne** to drink champagne

sabot [sabo] *nm* clog; (*de cheval*) hoof; **sabot de frein** brake shoe

saboter [sabote] *vt* to sabotage; (*bâcler*) to make a mess of, botch

sac [sak] *nm* bag; (*à charbon etc*) sack; **mettre à ~** to sack; **sac à dos** rucksack; **sac à main** handbag; **sac de couchage** sleeping bag; **sac de voyage** travelling bag

saccadé, e [sakade] *adj* jerky; (*respiration*) spasmodic

saccager [sakaʒe] *vt* (*piller*) to sack; (*dévaster*) to create havoc in

saccharine [sakaʀin] *nf* saccharin

sachet [saʃɛ] *nm* (small) bag; (*de sucre, café*) sachet; **du potage en ~** packet soup; **sachet de thé** tea bag

sacoche [sakɔʃ] *nf* (*gén*) bag; (*de bicyclette*) saddlebag

sacré, e [sakʀe] *adj* sacred; (*fam: satané*) blasted; (: *fameux*): **un ~ toupet** a heck of a cheek

sacrement [sakʀəmɑ̃] *nm* sacrament

sacrifice [sakʀifis] *nm* sacrifice; **sacrifier** *vt* to sacrifice

sacristie [sakʀisti] nf (catholique) sacristy; (protestante) vestry

sadique [sadik] adj sadistic

safran [safʀɑ̃] nm saffron

sage [saʒ] adj wise; (enfant) good

sage-femme [saʒfam] nf midwife

sagesse [saʒɛs] nf wisdom

Sagittaire [saʒitɛʀ] nm: **le ~** Sagittarius

Sahara [saaʀa] nm: **le ~** the Sahara (desert)

saignant, e [sɛɲɑ̃, ɑ̃t] adj (viande) rare

saigner [seɲe] vi to bleed ▷ vt to bleed; (animal) to kill (by bleeding); **~ du nez** to have a nosebleed

saillir [sajiʀ] vi to project, stick out; (veine, muscle) to bulge

sain, e [sɛ̃, sɛn] adj healthy; **~ et sauf** safe and sound, unharmed; **~ d'esprit** sound in mind, sane

saindoux [sɛ̃du] nm lard

saint, e [sɛ̃, sɛ̃t] adj holy ▷ nm/f saint; **le Saint Esprit** the Holy Spirit ou Ghost; **la Sainte Vierge** the Blessed Virgin; **la Saint-Sylvestre** New Year's Eve; **sainteté** nf holiness

sais etc [sɛ] vb voir **savoir**

saisie [sezi] nf seizure; **saisie (de données)** (data) capture

saisir [seziʀ] vt to take hold of, grab; (fig: occasion) to seize; (comprendre) to grasp; (entendre) to get, catch; (données) to capture; (Culin) to fry quickly; (Jur: biens, publication) to seize; **saisissant, e** adj startling, striking

saison [sɛzɔ̃] nf season; **haute/basse/morte ~** high/low/slack season; **saisonnier, -ière** adj seasonal

salade [salad] nf (Bot) lettuce etc; (Culin) (green) salad; (fam: confusion) tangle, muddle; **salade composée** mixed salad; **salade de fruits** fruit salad; **saladier** nm (salad) bowl

salaire [salɛʀ] nm (annuel, mensuel) salary; (hebdomadaire, journalier) pay, wages pl; **salaire minimum interprofessionnel de croissance** index-linked guaranteed minimum wage

salarié, e [salaʀje] nm/f salaried employee; wage-earner

salaud [salo] (fam!) nm sod (!), bastard (!)

sale [sal] adj dirty, filthy; (fam: mauvais) nasty

salé, e [sale] adj (mer, goût) salty; (Culin: amandes, beurre etc) salted; (: gâteaux) savoury; (fam: grivois) spicy; (: facture) steep

saler [sale] vt to salt

saleté [salte] nf (état) dirtiness; (crasse) dirt, filth; (tache) dirt no pl; (fam: méchanceté) dirty trick; (camelote) rubbish no pl; (: obscénité) filthy thing to say)

salière [saljɛʀ] nf saltcellar

salir [saliʀ] vt to (make) dirty; (fig: quelqu'un) to soil the reputation of; **se salir** vi to get dirty; **salissant, e** adj (tissu) which shows the dirt;

(travail) dirty, messy

salle [sal] nf room; (d'hôpital) ward; (de restaurant) dining room; (d'un cinéma) auditorium; (: public) audience; **salle à manger** dining room; **salle d'attente** waiting room; **salle de bain(s)** bathroom; **salle de classe** classroom; **salle de concert** concert hall; **salle d'eau** shower-room; **salle d'embarquement** (à l'aéroport) departure lounge; **salle de jeux** (pour enfants) playroom; **salle de séjour** living room; **salle des ventes** saleroom

salon [salɔ̃] nm lounge, sitting room; (mobilier) lounge suite; (exposition) exhibition, show; **salon de coiffure** hairdressing salon; **salon de thé** tearoom

salope [salɔp] (fam!) nf bitch (!); **saloperie** (fam!) nf (action) dirty trick; (chose sans valeur) rubbish no pl

salopette [salɔpɛt] nf dungarees pl; (d'ouvrier) overall(s)

salsifis [salsifi] nm salsify

salubre [salybʀ] adj healthy, salubrious

saluer [salɥe] vt (pour dire bonjour, fig) to greet; (pour dire au revoir) to take one's leave; (Mil) to salute

salut [saly] nm (geste) wave; (parole) greeting; (Mil) salute; (sauvegarde) safety; (Rel) salvation ▷ excl (fam: bonjour) hi (there); (: au revoir) see you, bye

salutations [salytasjɔ̃] nfpl greetings; **Veuillez agréer, Monsieur, mes ~ distinguées** yours faithfully

samedi [samdi] nm Saturday

SAMU [samy] sigle m (= service d'assistance médicale d'urgence) ≈ ambulance (service) (BRIT), ≈ paramedics pl (US)

sanction [sɑ̃ksjɔ̃] nf sanction; **sanctionner** vt (loi, usage) to sanction; (punir) to punish

sandale [sɑ̃dal] nf sandal

sandwich [sɑ̃dwi(t)ʃ] nm sandwich; **je voudrais un ~ au jambon/fromage** I'd like a ham/cheese sandwich

sang [sɑ̃] nm blood; **en ~** covered in blood; **se faire du mauvais ~** to fret, get in a state; **sang-froid** nm calm, sangfroid; **de sang-froid** in cold blood; **sanglant, e** adj bloody

sangle [sɑ̃gl] nf strap

sanglier [sɑ̃glije] nm (wild) boar

sanglot [sɑ̃glo] nm sob; **sangloter** vi to sob

sangsue [sɑ̃sy] nf leech

sanguin, e [sɑ̃gɛ̃, in] adj blood cpd

sanitaire [sanitɛʀ] adj health cpd; **sanitaires** nmpl (lieu) bathroom sg

sans [sɑ̃] prép without; **un pull ~ manches** a sleeveless jumper; **~ faute** without fail; **~ arrêt** without a break; **~ ça** (fam) otherwise; **~ qu'il s'en aperçoive** without him ou his noticing; **sans-abri** nmpl homeless; **sans-**

emploi nm/f inv unemployed person; **les sans-emploi** the unemployed; **sans-gêne** adj inv inconsiderate

santé [sɑ̃te] nf health; **en bonne ~** in good health; **boire à la ~ de qn** to drink (to) sb's health; **à ta/votre ~!** cheers!

saoudien, ne [saudjɛ̃, jɛn] adj Saudi Arabian ▷ nm/f: **S~, ne** Saudi Arabian

saoul, e [su, sul] adj = **soûl**

saper [sape] vt to undermine, sap

sapeur-pompier [sapœʀpɔ̃pje] nm fireman

saphir [safiʀ] nm sapphire

sapin [sapɛ̃] nm fir (tree); (bois) fir; **sapin de Noël** Christmas tree

sarcastique [saʀkastik] adj sarcastic

Sardaigne [saʀdɛɲ] nf: **la ~** Sardinia

sardine [saʀdin] nf sardine

SARL sigle f (= société à responsabilité limitée) ≈ plc (BRIT), ≈ Inc. (US)

sarrasin [saʀazɛ̃] nm buckwheat

satané, e [satane] (fam) adj confounded

satellite [satelit] nm satellite

satin [satɛ̃] nm satin

satire [satiʀ] nf satire; **satirique** adj satirical

satisfaction [satisfaksjɔ̃] nf satisfaction

satisfaire [satisfɛʀ] vt to satisfy; **~ à** (conditions) to meet; **satisfaisant, e** adj (acceptable) satisfactory; **satisfait, e** adj satisfied; **satisfait de** satisfied ou satisfied with

saturer [satyʀe] vt to saturate

sauce [sos] nf sauce; (avec un rôti) gravy; **sauce tomate** tomato sauce; **saucière** nf sauceboat

saucisse [sosis] nf sausage

saucisson [sosisɔ̃] nm (slicing) sausage

sauf, sauve [sof, sov] adj unharmed, unhurt; (fig: honneur) intact, saved ▷ prép except; **laisser la vie sauve à qn** to spare sb's life; **~ si** (à moins que) unless; **~ erreur** if I'm not mistaken; **~ avis contraire** unless you hear to the contrary

sauge [soʒ] nf sage

saugrenu, e [sogʀəny] adj preposterous

saule [sol] nm willow (tree)

saumon [somɔ̃] nm salmon inv

saupoudrer [supudʀe] vt: **~ qch de** to sprinkle sth with

saur [sɔʀ] adj m: **hareng ~** smoked herring, kipper

saut [so] nm jump; (discipline sportive) jumping; **faire un ~ chez qn** to pop over to sb's (place); **saut à l'élastique** bungee jumping; **saut à la perche** pole vaulting; **saut en hauteur/longueur** high/long jump; **saut périlleux** somersault

sauter [sote] vi to jump, leap; (exploser) to blow up, explode; (: fusibles) to blow; (se détacher) to pop out (ou off) ▷ vt to jump (over), leap (over); (fig: omettre) to skip, miss

(out); **faire ~** to blow up; (Culin) to sauté; **~ à la corde** to skip; **~ au cou de qn** to fly into sb's arms; **~ sur une occasion** to jump at an opportunity; **~ aux yeux** to be (quite) obvious

sauterelle [sotʀɛl] nf grasshopper

sautiller [sotije] vi (oiseau) to hop; (enfant) to skip

sauvage [sovaʒ] adj (gén) wild; (peuplade) savage; (farouche: personne) unsociable; (barbare) wild, savage; (non officiel) unauthorized, unofficial; **faire du camping ~** to camp in the wild ▷ nm/f savage; (timide) unsociable type

sauve [sov] adj f voir **sauf**

sauvegarde [sovgaʀd] nf safeguard; (Inform) backup; **sauvegarder** vt to safeguard; (Inform: enregistrer) to save; (: copier) to back up

sauve-qui-peut [sovkipø] excl run for your life!

sauver [sove] vt to save; (porter secours à) to rescue; (récupérer) to salvage, rescue; **se sauver** vi (s'enfuir) to run away; (fam: partir) to be off; **sauvetage** nm rescue; **sauveteur** nm rescuer; **sauvette: à la sauvette** adv (se marier etc) hastily, hurriedly; **sauveur** nm saviour (BRIT), savior (US)

savant, e [savɑ̃, ɑ̃t] adj scholarly, learned ▷ nm scientist

saveur [savœʀ] nf flavour; (fig) savour

savoir [savwaʀ] vt to know; (être capable de): **il sait nager** he can swim ▷ nm knowledge; **se savoir** vi (être connu) to be known; **je ne sais pas** I don't know; **je ne sais pas parler français** I don't speak French; **savez-vous où je peux ...?** do you know where I can ...?; **je n'en sais rien** I (really) don't know; **à ~ that** is, namely; **faire ~ qch à qn** to let sb know sth; **pas que je sache** not as far as I know

savon [savɔ̃] nm (produit) soap; (morceau) bar of soap; (fam): **passer un ~ à qn** to give sb a good dressing-down; **savonner** vt to soap; **savonnette** nf bar of soap

savourer [savuʀe] vt to savour; **savoureux, -euse** adj tasty; (fig: anecdote) spicy, juicy

saxo(phone) [saksɔ(fɔn)] nm sax(ophone)

scabreux, -euse [skabʀø, øz] adj risky; (indécent) improper, shocking

scandale [skɑ̃dal] nm scandal; **faire un ~** (scène) to make a scene; (Jur) to create a disturbance; **faire ~** to scandalize people; **scandaleux, -euse** adj scandalous, outrageous

scandinave [skɑ̃dinav] adj Scandinavian ▷ nm/f: **S~** Scandinavian

Scandinavie [skɑ̃dinavi] nf Scandinavia

scarabée [skaʀabe] nm beetle

scarlatine [skaʀlatin] nf scarlet fever

scarole [skaʀɔl] nf endive

sceau, x [so] nm seal

sceller [sele] vt to seal

scénario [senaʀjo] nm scenario

scène [sɛn] nf (gén) scene; (estrade, fig: théâtre) stage; **entrer en ~** to come on stage; **mettre en ~** (Théâtre) to stage; (Cinéma) to direct; **faire une ~ (à qn)** to make a scene (with sb); **scène de ménage** domestic scene

sceptique [sɛptik] adj sceptical

schéma [ʃema] nm (diagramme) diagram, sketch; **schématique** adj diagrammatic(al), schematic; (fig) oversimplified

sciatique [sjatik] nf sciatica

scie [si] nf saw

sciemment [sjamɑ̃] adv knowingly

science [sjɑ̃s] nf science; (savoir) knowledge; **sciences humaines/sociales** social sciences; **sciences naturelles** (Scol) natural science sg, biology sg; **sciences po** political science ou studies pl; **science-fiction** nf science fiction; **scientifique** adj scientific ▷ nm/f scientist; (étudiant) science student

scier [sje] vt to saw; (retrancher) to saw off; **scierie** nf sawmill

scintiller [sɛ̃tije] vi to sparkle; (étoile) to twinkle

sciure [sjyʀ] nf: **~ (de bois)** sawdust

sclérose [skleʀoz] nf: **sclérose en plaques** multiple sclerosis

scolaire [skɔlɛʀ] adj school cpd; **scolariser** vt to provide with schooling/schools; **scolarité** nf schooling

scooter [skutœʀ] nm (motor) scooter

score [skɔʀ] nm score

scorpion [skɔʀpjɔ̃] nm (signe): **le S~** Scorpio

scotch [skɔtʃ] nm (whisky) scotch, whisky; **S~®** (adhésif) Sellotape® (BRIT), Scotch® tape (US)

scout, e [skut] adj, nm scout

script [skʀipt] nm (écriture) printing; (Cinéma) (shooting) script

scrupule [skʀypyl] nm scruple

scruter [skʀyte] vt to scrutinize; (l'obscurité) to peer into

scrutin [skʀytɛ̃] nm (vote) ballot; (ensemble des opérations) poll

sculpter [skylte] vt to sculpt; (bois) to carve; **sculpteur** nm sculptor; **sculpture** nf sculpture

SDF sigle m: **sans domicile fixe** homeless person; **les ~** the homeless

MOT-CLÉ

se [sə], **s'** pron **1** (emploi réfléchi) oneself; (: masc) himself; (: fém) herself; (: sujet non humain) itself; (: pl) themselves; **se savonner** to soap o.s.

2 (réciproque) one another, each other; **ils s'aiment** they love one another ou each other

3 (passif): **cela se répare facilement** it is

easily repaired

4 (possessif): **se casser la jambe/se laver les mains** to break one's leg/wash one's hands

séance [seɑ̃s] nf (d'assemblée) meeting, session; (de tribunal) sitting, session; (musicale, Cinéma, Théâtre) performance

seau, x [so] nm bucket, pail

sec, sèche [sɛk, sɛʃ] adj dry; (raisins, figues) dried; (cœur: insensible) hard, cold ▷ nm: **tenir au ~** to keep in a dry place ▷ adv hard; **je le bois ~** I drink it straight ou neat; **à ~** (puits) dried up

sécateur [sekatœʀ] nm secateurs pl (BRIT), shears pl

sèche [sɛʃ] adj f voir **sec**; **sèche-cheveux** nm inv hair-drier; **sèche-linge** nm inv tumble dryer; **sèchement** adv (répondre) drily

sécher [seʃe] vt to dry; (dessécher: peau, blé) to dry (out); (: étang) to dry up; (fam: cours) to skip ▷ vi to dry; to dry out; to dry up; (fam: candidat) to be stumped; **se sécher** (après le bain) to dry o.s.; **sécheresse** nf dryness; (absence de pluie) drought; **séchoir** nm drier

second, e¹ [s(ə)gɔ̃, ɔ̃d] adj second ▷ nm (assistant) second in command; (Navig) first mate ▷ nf (Scol) year 11 (BRIT), tenth grade (US); (Aviat, Rail etc) second class; **voyager en ~e** to travel second-class; **secondaire** adj secondary; **seconde²** nf second; **seconder** vt to assist

secouer [s(ə)kwe] vt to shake; (passagers) to rock; (traumatiser) to shake (up)

secourir [s(ə)kuʀiʀ] vt (venir en aide à) to assist, aid; **secourisme** nm first aid; **secouriste** nm/f first-aid worker

secours [s(ə)kuʀ] nm help, aid, assistance ▷ nmpl aid sg; **au ~!** help!; **appeler au ~** to shout ou call for help; **porter ~ à qn** to give sb assistance, help sb; **les premiers ~** first aid sg

● **ÉQUIPES DE SECOURS**
●
● Emergency phone numbers can be dialled
● free from public phones. For the police
● ('la police') dial 17; for medical services ('le
● SAMU') dial 15; for the fire brigade ('les
● sapeurs pompiers'), dial 18.

secousse [s(ə)kus] nf jolt, bump; (électrique) shock; (fig: psychologique) jolt, shock

secret, -ète [səkʀɛ, ɛt] adj secret; (fig: renfermé) reticent, reserved ▷ nm secret; (discrétion absolue): **le ~** secrecy; **en ~** in secret, secretly; **secret professionel** professional secrecy

secrétaire [s(ə)kʀetɛʀ] nm/f secretary ▷ nm (meuble) writing desk; **secrétaire de direction** private ou personal secretary; **secrétaire**

d'État junior minister; **secrétariat** nm
(profession) secretarial work; (bureau) office;
(: d'organisation internationale) secretariat

secteur [sɛktœʀ] nm sector; (zone) area;
(Élec): **branché sur ~** plugged into the mains
(supply)

section [sɛksjɔ̃] nf section; (de parcours
d'autobus) fare stage; (Mil: unité) platoon;
sectionner vt to sever

sécu [seky] abrf = **sécurité sociale**

sécurité [sekyʀite] nf (absence de danger)
safety; (absence de troubles) security; **système
de ~** security system; **être en ~** to be safe; **la
sécurité routière** road safety; **la sécurité
sociale** ≈ (the) Social Security (BRIT), ≈ Welfare
(US)

sédentaire [sedɑ̃tɛʀ] adj sedentary

séduction [sedyksjɔ̃] nf seduction; (charme,
attrait) appeal, charm

séduire [seduiʀ] vt to charm; (femme: abuser
de) to seduce; **séduisant, e** adj (femme)
seductive; (homme, offre) very attractive

ségrégation [segʀegasjɔ̃] nf segregation

seigle [sɛgl] nm rye

seigneur [sɛɲœʀ] nm lord

sein [sɛ̃] nm breast; (entrailles) womb; **au ~ de**
(équipe, institution) within

séisme [seism] nm earthquake

seize [sɛz] num sixteen; **seizième** num
sixteenth

séjour [seʒuʀ] nm stay; (pièce) living room;
séjourner vi to stay

sel [sɛl] nm salt; (fig: piquant) spice

sélection [selɛksjɔ̃] nf selection;
sélectionner vt to select

self-service [sɛlfsɛʀvis] adj, nm self-service

selle [sɛl] nf saddle; **selles** nfpl (Méd) stools;
seller vt to saddle

selon [s(ə)lɔ̃] prép according to; (en se
conformant à) in accordance with; **~ que**
according to whether; **~ moi** as I see it

semaine [s(ə)mɛn] nf week; **en ~** during the
week, on weekdays

semblable [sɑ̃blabl] adj similar; (de ce genre):
de ~s mésaventures such mishaps ▷ nm
fellow creature ou man; **~ à** similar to, like

semblant [sɑ̃blɑ̃] nm: **un ~ de ...** a semblance
of ...; **faire ~ (de faire)** to pretend (to do)

sembler [sɑ̃ble] vb +attrib to seem ▷ vb impers:
il semble (bien) que/inutile de it (really)
seems ou appears that/useless to; **il me
semble que** it seems to me that; **comme bon
lui semble** as he sees fit

semelle [s(ə)mɛl] nf sole; (intérieure) insole,
inner sole

semer [s(ə)me] vt to sow; (fig: éparpiller)
to scatter; (: confusion) to spread; (fam:
poursuivants) to lose, shake off; **semé de**
(difficultés) riddled with

semestre [s(ə)mɛstʀ] nm half-year; (Scol)
semester

séminaire [seminɛʀ] nm seminar

semi-remorque [səmiʀəmɔʀk] nm
articulated lorry (BRIT), semi(trailer) (US)

semoule [s(ə)mul] nf semolina

sénat [sena] nm senate; **sénateur** nm senator

Sénégal [senegal] nm: **le ~** Senegal

sens [sɑ̃s] nm (Physiol.) sense; (signification)
meaning, sense; (direction) direction; **à mon
~** to my mind; **dans le ~ des aiguilles d'une
montre** clockwise; **dans le ~ contraire des
aiguilles d'une montre** anticlockwise; **dans
le mauvais ~** (aller) the wrong way, in the
wrong direction; **le bon ~** common sense;
sens dessus dessous upside down; **sens
interdit/unique** one-way street

sensation [sɑ̃sasjɔ̃] nf sensation; **à ~** (péj)
sensational; **faire ~** to cause ou create
a sensation; **sensationnel, le** adj (fam)
fantastic, terrific

sensé, e [sɑ̃se] adj sensible

sensibiliser [sɑ̃sibilize] vt: **~ qn à** to make sb
sensitive to

sensibilité [sɑ̃sibilite] nf sensitivity

sensible [sɑ̃sibl] adj sensitive; (aux sens)
perceptible; (appréciable: différence, progrès)
appreciable, noticeable; **~ à** sensitive to;
sensiblement adv (à peu près): **ils sont
sensiblement du même âge** they are
approximately the same age; **sensiblerie** nf
sentimentality

⚠ Attention à ne pas traduire **sensible** par
le mot anglais **sensible**.

sensuel, le [sɑ̃suɛl] adj (personne) sensual;
(musique) sensuous

sentence [sɑ̃tɑ̃s] nf (jugement) sentence

sentier [sɑ̃tje] nm path

sentiment [sɑ̃timɑ̃] nm feeling; **recevez
mes ~s respectueux** (personne nommée)
yours sincerely; (personne non nommée)
yours faithfully; **sentimental, e, -aux** adj
sentimental; (vie, aventure) love cpd

sentinelle [sɑ̃tinɛl] nf sentry

sentir [sɑ̃tiʀ] vt (par l'odorat) to smell; (par le
goût) to taste; (au toucher, fig) to feel; (répandre
une odeur de) to smell of; (: ressemblance) to
smell like ▷ vi to smell; **~ mauvais** to smell
bad; **se ~ bien** to feel good; **se ~ mal** (être
indisposé) to feel unwell ou ill; **se ~ le courage/
la force de faire** to feel brave/strong enough
to do; **il ne peut pas le ~** (fam) he can't stand
him; **je ne me sens pas bien** I don't feel well

séparation [sepaʀasjɔ̃] nf separation;
(cloison) division, partition

séparé, e [sepaʀe] adj (distinct) separate;
(époux) separated; **séparément** adv
separately

séparer [sepaʀe] vt to separate; (désunir) to

drive apart; (*détacher*): **~ qch de** to pull sth (off) from; **se séparer** vi (*époux, amis*) to separate, part; (*se diviser: route etc*) to divide; **se ~ de** (*époux*) to separate ou part from; (*employé, objet personnel*) to part with

sept [sɛt] *num* seven; **septante** (BELGIQUE, SUISSE) *adj inv* seventy

septembre [sɛptɑ̃bʀ] *nm* September

septicémie [sɛptisemi] *nf* blood poisoning, septicaemia

septième [sɛtjɛm] *num* seventh

séquelles [sekɛl] *nfpl* after-effects; (*fig*) aftermath *sg*

serbe [sɛʀb(ə)] *adj* Serbian

Serbie [sɛʀbi] *nf*: **la ~** Serbia

serein, e [səʀɛ̃, ɛn] *adj* serene

sergent [sɛʀʒɑ̃] *nm* sergeant

série [seʀi] *nf* series *inv*; (*de clés, casseroles, outils*) set; (*catégorie: Sport*) rank; **en ~** in quick succession; (*Comm*) mass *cpd*; **de ~** (*voiture*) standard; **hors ~** (*Comm*) custom-built; **série noire** (*crime*) thriller

sérieusement [seʀjøzmɑ̃] *adv* seriously

sérieux, -euse [seʀjø, jøz] *adj* serious; (*élève, employé*) reliable, responsible; (*client, maison*) reliable, dependable ▷ *nm* seriousness; (*d'une entreprise etc*) reliability; **garder son ~** to keep a straight face; **prendre qch/qn au ~** to take sth/sb seriously

serin [s(ə)ʀɛ̃] *nm* canary

seringue [s(ə)ʀɛ̃g] *nf* syringe

serment [sɛʀmɑ̃] *nm* (*juré*) oath; (*promesse*) pledge, vow

sermon [sɛʀmɔ̃] *nm* sermon

séropositif, -ive [seʀopozitif, iv] *adj* (*Méd*) HIV positive

serpent [sɛʀpɑ̃] *nm* snake; **serpenter** vi to wind

serpillière [sɛʀpijɛʀ] *nf* floorcloth

serre [sɛʀ] *nf* (*Agr*) greenhouse; **serres** *nfpl* (*griffes*) claws, talons

serré, e [seʀe] *adj* (*habits*) tight; (*fig: lutte, match*) tight, close-fought; (*passagers etc*) (tightly) packed; (*réseau*) dense; **avoir le cœur ~** to have a heavy heart

serrer [seʀe] *vt* (*tenir*) to grip ou hold tight; (*comprimer, coincer*) to squeeze; (*poings, mâchoires*) to clench; (*suj: vêtement*) to be too tight for; (*ceinture, nœud, vis*) to tighten ▷ *vi*: **~ à droite** to keep ou get over to the right

serrure [seʀyʀ] *nf* lock; **serrurier** *nm* locksmith

sert *etc* [sɛʀ] *vb voir* **servir**

servante [sɛʀvɑ̃t] *nf* (maid)servant

serveur, -euse [sɛʀvœʀ, øz] *nm/f* waiter (waitress)

serviable [sɛʀvjabl] *adj* obliging, willing to help

service [sɛʀvis] *nm* service; (*assortiment de vaisselle*) set, service; (*bureau: de la vente etc*) department, section; (*travail*) duty; **premier ~** (*série de repas*) first sitting; **être de ~** to be on duty; **faire le ~** to serve; **rendre un ~ à qn** to do sb a favour; (*objet: s'avérer utile*) to come in useful ou handy for sb; **mettre en ~** to put into service ou operation; **~ compris/non compris** service included/not included; **hors ~** out of order; **service après vente** after sales service; **service d'ordre** police (*ou* stewards) in charge of maintaining order; **service militaire** military service; *see note*; **services secrets** secret service *sg*

● **SERVICE MILITAIRE**
●
●
● Until 1997, French men over the age of 18
● who were passed as fit, and who were not
● in full-time higher education, were required
● to do ten months' "service militaire".
● Conscientious objectors were required to
● do two years' community service.
● Since 1997, military service has been
● suspended in France. However, all sixteen-
● year-olds, both male and female, are
● required to register for a compulsory one-
● day training course, the "JAPD" ("journée
● d'appel de préparation à la défense"), which
● covers basic information on the principles
● and organization of defence in France, and
● also advises on career opportunities in the
● military and in the voluntary sector. Young
● people must attend the training day before
● their eighteenth birthday.

serviette [sɛʀvjɛt] *nf* (*de table*) (table) napkin, serviette; (*de toilette*) towel; (*porte-documents*) briefcase; **serviette hygiénique** sanitary towel

servir [sɛʀviʀ] *vt* to serve; (*au restaurant*) to wait on; (*au magasin*) to serve, attend to ▷ *vi* (*Tennis*) to serve; (*Cartes*) to deal; **se servir** vi (*prendre d'un plat*) to help o.s.; **vous êtes servi?** are you being served?; **~ à qn** (*diplôme, livre*) to be of use to sb; **~ à qch/faire** (*outil etc*) to be used for sth/doing; **ça ne sert à rien** it's no use; **~ (à qn) de** to serve as (for sb); **se ~ de** (*plat*) to help o.s. to; (*voiture, outil, relations*) to use; **sers-toi!** help yourself!

serviteur [sɛʀvitœʀ] *nm* servant

ses [se] *adj voir* **son¹**

seuil [sœj] *nm* doorstep; (*fig*) threshold

seul, e [sœl] *adj* (*sans compagnie*) alone; (*unique*): **un ~ livre** only one book, a single book ▷ *adv* (*vivre*) alone, on one's own ▷ *nm, nf*: **il en reste un(e) ~(e)** there's only one left; **le ~ livre** the only book; **parler tout ~** to talk to oneself; **faire qch (tout) ~** to do sth (all) on one's own ou (all) by oneself; **à**

lui (tout) ~ single-handed, on his own; **se sentir** ~ to feel lonely; **seulement** adv only; **non seulement ... mais aussi** ou **encore** not only ... but also

sève [sɛv] nf sap

sévère [sevɛʀ] adj severe

sexe [sɛks] nm sex; (organes génitaux) genitals, sex organs; **sexuel, le** adj sexual

shampooing [ʃɑ̃pwɛ̃] nm shampoo

Shetland [ʃɛtlɑ̃d] n: **les îles** ~ the Shetland Islands, Shetland

short [ʃɔʀt] nm (pair of) shorts pl

 MOT-CLÉ

si [si] adv **1** (oui) yes; **"Paul n'est pas venu"** — **"si!"** "Paul hasn't come" — "yes, he has!"; **je vous assure que si** I assure you he did ou she is etc

2 (tellement) so; **si gentil/rapidement** so kind/fast; **(tant et) si bien que** so much so that; **si rapide qu'il soit** however fast he may be

▷ conj if; **si tu veux** if you want; **je me demande si** I wonder if ou whether; **si seulement** if only

▷ nm (Mus) B; (en chantant la gamme) ti

Sicile [sisil] nf: **la** ~ Sicily

SIDA [sida] sigle m (= syndrome immuno-déficitaire acquis) AIDS sg

sidéré, e [sideʀe] adj staggered

sidérurgie [sideʀyʀʒi] nf steel industry

siècle [sjɛkl] nm century

siège [sjɛʒ] nm seat; (d'entreprise) head office; (d'organisation) headquarters pl; (Mil) siege; **siège social** registered office; **siéger** vi to sit

sien, ne [sjɛ̃, sjɛn] pron: **le(la)** ~**(ne), les** ~**(ne)s** (homme) his; (femme) hers; (chose, animal) its

sieste [sjɛst] nf (afternoon) snooze ou nap; **faire la** ~ to have a snooze ou nap

sifflement [sifləmɑ̃] nm: **un** ~ a whistle

siffler [sifle] vi (gén) to whistle; (en respirant) to wheeze; (serpent, vapeur) to hiss ▷ vt (chanson) to whistle; (chien etc) to whistle for; (fille) to whistle at; (pièce, orateur) to hiss, boo; (fin du match, départ) to blow one's whistle for; (fam: verre) to guzzle

sifflet [sifle] nm whistle; **coup de** ~ whistle

siffloter [siflɔte] vi, vt to whistle

sigle [sigl] nm acronym

signal, -aux [siɲal, o] nm signal; (indice, écriteau) sign; **donner le** ~ **de** to give the signal for; **signal d'alarme** alarm signal; **signalement** nm description, particulars pl

signaler [siɲale] vt to indicate; (personne: faire un signe) to signal; (vol, perte) to report; (faire remarquer): ~ **qch à qn/(à qn) que** to point out

sth to sb/(to sb) that; **je voudrais** ~ **un vol** I'd like to report a theft

signature [siɲatyʀ] nf signature; (action) signing

signe [siɲ] nm sign; (Typo) mark; **faire un** ~ **de la main** to give a sign with one's hand; **faire** ~ **à qn** (fig: contacter) to get in touch with sb; **faire** ~ **à qn d'entrer** to motion (to) sb to come in; **signer** vt to sign; **se signer** vi to cross o.s.; **où dois-je signer?** where do I sign?

significatif, -ive [siɲifikatif, iv] adj significant

signification [siɲifikasjɔ̃] nf meaning

signifier [siɲifje] vt (vouloir dire) to mean; (faire connaître): ~ **qch (à qn)** to make sth known (to sb)

silence [silɑ̃s] nm silence; (Mus) rest; **garder le** ~ to keep silent, say nothing; **silencieux, -euse** adj quiet, silent ▷ nm silencer

silhouette [silwɛt] nf outline, silhouette; (allure) figure

sillage [sijaʒ] nm wake

sillon [sijɔ̃] nm furrow; (de disque) groove; **sillonner** vt to criss-cross

simagrées [simaɡʀe] nfpl fuss sg

similaire [similɛʀ] adj similar; **similicuir** nm imitation leather; **similitude** nf similarity

simple [sɛ̃pl] adj simple; (non multiple) single ▷ nm: ~ **messieurs/dames** men's/ladies' singles sg ▷ nm/f: ~ **d'esprit** simpleton

simplicité [sɛ̃plisite] nf simplicity; **en toute** ~ quite simply

simplifier [sɛ̃plifje] vt to simplify

simuler [simyle] vt to sham, simulate

simultané, e [simyltane] adj simultaneous

sincère [sɛ̃sɛʀ] adj sincere; **sincèrement** adv sincerely; (pour parler franchement) honestly, really; **sincérité** nf sincerity

Singapour [sɛ̃gapuʀ] nm Singapore

singe [sɛ̃ʒ] nm monkey; (de grande taille) ape; **singer** vt to ape, mimic; **singeries** nfpl antics

singulariser [sɛ̃gylaʀize]: **se singulariser** vi to call attention to o.s.

singularité [sɛ̃gylaʀite] nf peculiarity

singulier, -ière [sɛ̃gylje, jɛʀ] adj remarkable, singular ▷ nm singular

sinistre [sinistʀ] adj sinister ▷ nm (incendie) blaze; (catastrophe) disaster; (Assurances) damage (giving rise to a claim); **sinistré, e** adj disaster-stricken ▷ nm/f disaster victim

sinon [sinɔ̃] conj (autrement, sans quoi) otherwise, or else; (sauf) except, other than; (si ce n'est) if not

sinueux, -euse [sinɥø, øz] adj winding

sinus [sinys] nm (Anat) sinus; (Géom) sine; **sinusite** nf sinusitis

sirène [siʀɛn] nf siren; **sirène d'alarme** fire alarm; (en temps de guerre) air-raid siren

sirop [siʀo] nm (à diluer: de fruit etc) syrup;

(*pharmaceutique*) syrup, mixture; **~ pour la toux** cough mixture

siroter [sirɔte] *vt* to sip

sismique [sismik] *adj* seismic

site [sit] *nm* (*paysage, environnement*) setting; (*d'une ville etc: emplacement*) site; **site (pittoresque)** beauty spot; **sites touristiques** places of interest; **site Web** (*Inform*) website

sitôt [sito] *adv*: **~ parti** as soon as he *etc* had left; **~ que** as soon as; **pas de ~** not for a long time

situation [sitɥasjɔ̃] *nf* situation; (*d'un édifice, d'une ville*) position, location; **situation de famille** marital status

situé, e [sitɥe] *adj* situated

situer [sitɥe] *vt* to site, situate; (*en pensée*) to set, place; **se situer** *vi* to be situated

six [sis] *num* six; **sixième** *num* sixth ▷ *nf* (*Scol*) year 7 (*BRIT*), sixth grade (*US*)

skaï® [skaj] *nm* Leatherette®

ski [ski] *nm* (*objet*) ski; (*sport*) skiing; **faire du ~** to ski; **ski de fond** cross-country skiing; **ski nautique** water-skiing; **ski de piste** downhill skiing; **ski de randonnée** cross-country skiing; **skier** *vi* to ski; **skieur, -euse** *nm/f* skier

slip [slip] *nm* (*sous-vêtement*) pants *pl*, briefs *pl*; (*de bain: d'homme*) trunks *pl*; (: *du bikini*) (bikini) briefs *pl*

slogan [slɔgɑ̃] *nm* slogan

Slovaquie [slɔvaki] *nf*: **la ~** Slovakia

SMIC [smik] *sigle m* = **salaire minimum interprofessionnel de croissance**

smoking [smɔkiŋ] *nm* dinner *ou* evening suit

SMS *sigle m* (= *short message service*) (*service*) SMS; (*message*) text message

SNCF *sigle f* (= *Société nationale des chemins de fer français*) French railways

snob [snɔb] *adj* snobbish ▷ *nm/f* snob; **snobisme** *nm* snobbery, snobbishness

sobre [sɔbʀ] *adj* (*personne*) temperate, abstemious; (*élégance, style*) sober

sobriquet [sɔbʀikɛ] *nm* nickname

social, e, -aux [sɔsjal, jo] *adj* social

socialisme [sɔsjalism] *nm* socialism; **socialiste** *nm/f* socialist

société [sɔsjete] *nf* society; (*sportive*) club; (*Comm*) company; **la ~ de consommation** the consumer society; **société anonyme** ≈ limited (*BRIT*) *ou* incorporated (*US*) company

sociologie [sɔsjɔlɔʒi] *nf* sociology

socle [sɔkl] *nm* (*de colonne, statue*) plinth, pedestal; (*de lampe*) base

socquette [sɔkɛt] *nf* ankle sock

sœur [sœʀ] *nf* sister; (*religieuse*) nun, sister

soi [swa] *pron* oneself; **en ~** (*intrinsèquement*) in itself; **cela va de ~** that *ou* it goes without saying; **soi-disant** *adj inv* so-called ▷ *adv* supposedly

soie [swa] *nf* silk; **soierie** *nf* (*tissu*) silk

soif [swaf] *nf* thirst; **avoir ~** to be thirsty; **donner ~ à qn** to make sb thirsty

soigné, e [swaɲe] *adj* (*tenue*) well-groomed, neat; (*travail*) careful, meticulous

soigner [swaɲe] *vt* (*malade, maladie: suj: docteur*) to treat; (*suj: infirmière, mère*) to nurse, look after; (*travail, détails*) to take care over; (*jardin, invités*) to look after; **soigneux, -euse** *adj* (*propre*) tidy, neat; (*appliqué*) painstaking, careful

soi-même [swamɛm] *pron* oneself

soin [swɛ̃] *nm* (*application*) care; (*propreté, ordre*) tidiness, neatness; **soins** *nmpl* (*à un malade, blessé*) treatment *sg*, medical attention *sg*; (*hygiène*) care *sg*; **prendre ~ de** to take care of, look after; **prendre ~ de faire** to take care to do; **les premiers ~s** first aid *sg*

soir [swaʀ] *nm* evening; **ce ~** this evening, tonight; **à ce ~!** see you this evening (*ou* tonight)!; **sept/dix heures du ~** seven in the evening/ten at night; **demain ~** tomorrow evening, tomorrow night; **soirée** *nf* evening; (*réception*) party

soit¹ [swa] *vb voir* **être** ▷ *conj* (*à savoir*) namely; (*ou*): **~ ... ~** either ... or; **~ que ... ~ que** *ou* **ou que** whether ... or whether

soit² [swat] *adv* so be it, very well

soixantaine [swasɑ̃tɛn] *nf*: **une ~ (de)** sixty or so, about sixty; **avoir la ~** (*âge*) to be around sixty

soixante [swasɑ̃t] *num* sixty; **soixante-dix** *num* seventy

soja [sɔʒa] *nm* soya; (*graines*) soya beans *pl*; **germes de ~** beansprouts

sol [sɔl] *nm* ground; (*de logement*) floor; (*Agr*) soil; (*Mus*) G; (: *en chantant la gamme*) so(h)

solaire [sɔlɛʀ] *adj* (*énergie etc*) solar; (*crème etc*) sun *cpd*

soldat [sɔlda] *nm* soldier

solde [sɔld] *nf* pay ▷ *nm* (*Comm*) balance; **soldes** *nm ou f pl* (*articles*) sale goods; (*vente*) sales; **en ~** at sale price; **solder** *vt* (*marchandise*) to sell at sale price, sell off

sole [sɔl] *nf* sole *inv* (*fish*)

soleil [sɔlɛj] *nm* sun; (*lumière*) sun(light); (*temps ensoleillé*) sun(shine); **il fait du ~** it's sunny; **au ~** in the sun

solennel, le [sɔlanɛl] *adj* solemn

solfège [sɔlfɛʒ] *nm* musical theory

solidaire [sɔlidɛʀ] *adj*: **être ~s** to show solidarity, stand *ou* stick together; **être ~ de** (*collègues*) to stand by; **solidarité** *nf* solidarity; **par solidarité (avec)** in sympathy (with)

solide [sɔlid] *adj* solid; (*mur, maison, meuble*) solid, sturdy; (*connaissances, argument*) sound; (*personne, estomac*) robust, sturdy ▷ *nm* solid

soliste [sɔlist] *nm/f* soloist

solitaire [sɔlitɛʀ] *adj* (*sans compagnie*) solitary,

lonely; (*lieu*) lonely ▷ *nm/f* (*ermite*) recluse; (*fig: ours*) loner

solitude [sɔlityd] *nf* loneliness; (*tranquillité*) solitude

solliciter [sɔlisite] *vt* (*personne*) to appeal to; (*emploi, faveur*) to seek

sollicitude [sɔlisityd] *nf* concern

soluble [sɔlybl] *adj* soluble

solution [sɔlysjɔ̃] *nf* solution; **solution de facilité** easy way out

solvable [sɔlvabl] *adj* solvent

sombre [sɔ̃bʀ] *adj* dark; (*fig*) gloomy; **sombrer** *vi* (*bateau*) to sink; **sombrer dans** (*misère, désespoir*) to sink into

sommaire [sɔmɛʀ] *adj* (*simple*) basic; (*expéditif*) summary ▷ *nm* summary

somme [sɔm] *nf* (*Math*) sum; (*quantité*) amount; (*argent*) sum, amount ▷ *nm*: **faire un ~** to have a (short) nap; **en ~** all in all; **~ toute** all in all

sommeil [sɔmɛj] *nm* sleep; **avoir ~** to be sleepy; **sommeiller** *vi* to doze

sommet [sɔmɛ] *nm* top; (*d'une montagne*) summit, top; (*fig: de la perfection, gloire*) height

sommier [sɔmje] *nm* (bed) base

somnambule [sɔmnɑ̃byl] *nm/f* sleepwalker

somnifère [sɔmnifɛʀ] *nm* sleeping drug *no pl* (*ou* pill)

somnoler [sɔmnɔle] *vi* to doze

somptueux, -euse [sɔ̃ptɥø, øz] *adj* sumptuous

son¹, sa [sɔ̃, sa] (*pl* **ses**) *adj* (*antécédent humain: mâle*) his; (: *femelle*) her; (: *valeur indéfinie*) one's, his/her; (*antécédent non humain*) its

son² [sɔ̃] *nm* sound; (*de blé*) bran

sondage [sɔ̃daʒ] *nm*: **sondage (d'opinion)** (opinion) poll

sonde [sɔ̃d] *nf* (*Navig*) lead *ou* sounding line; (*Méd*) probe; (*Tech: de forage*) borer, driller

sonder [sɔ̃de] *vt* (*Navig*) to sound; (*Tech*) to bore, drill; (*fig: personne*) to sound out; **~ le terrain** (*fig*) to test the ground

songe [sɔ̃ʒ] *nm* dream; **songer** *vi*: **songer à** (*penser à*) to think over; (*envisager*) to consider, think of; **songer que** to think that; **songeur, -euse** *adj* pensive

sonnant, e [sɔnɑ̃, ɑ̃t] *adj*: **à 8 heures ~es** on the stroke of 8

sonné, e [sɔne] *adj* (*fam*) cracked; **il est midi ~** it's gone twelve

sonner [sɔne] *vi* to ring ▷ *vt* (*cloche*) to ring; (*glas, tocsin*) to sound; (*portier, infirmière*) to ring for; **~ faux** (*instrument*) to sound out of tune; (*rire*) to ring false

sonnerie [sɔnʀi] *nf* (*son*) ringing; (*sonnette*) bell; (*de portable*) ringtone; **sonnerie d'alarme** alarm bell

sonnette [sɔnɛt] *nf* bell; **sonnette d'alarme** alarm bell

sonore [sɔnɔʀ] *adj* (*voix*) sonorous, ringing; (*salle*) resonant; (*film, signal*) sound *cpd*; **sonorisation** *nf* (*équipement: de salle de conférences*) public address system, P.A. system; (: *de discothèque*) sound system; **sonorité** *nf* (*de piano, violon*) tone; (*d'une salle*) acoustics *pl*

sophistiqué, e [sɔfistike] *adj* sophisticated

sorbet [sɔʀbɛ] *nm* water ice, sorbet

sorcier [sɔʀsje] *nm* sorcerer

sordide [sɔʀdid] *adj* (*lieu*) squalid; (*action*) sordid

sort [sɔʀ] *nm* (*destinée*) fate; (*condition*) lot; (*magique*) curse, spell; **tirer au ~** to draw lots

sorte [sɔʀt] *nf* sort, kind; **de la ~** in that way; **de (telle) ~ que** so that; **en quelque ~** in a way; **faire en ~ que** to see to it that; **quelle ~ de ...?** what kind of ...?

sortie [sɔʀti] *nf* (*issue*) way out, exit; (*remarque drôle*) sally; (*promenade*) outing; (*le soir: au restaurant etc*) night out; (*Comm: d'un disque*) release; (: *d'un livre*) publication; (: *d'un modèle*) launching; **où est la ~?** where's the exit?; **sortie de bain** (*vêtement*) bathrobe

sortilège [sɔʀtilɛʒ] *nm* (magic) spell

sortir [sɔʀtiʀ] *vi* (*gén*) to come out; (*partir, se promener, aller au spectacle*) to go out; (*numéro gagnant*) to come up ▷ *vt* (*gén*) to take out; (*produit, modèle*) to bring out; (*fam: dire*) to come out with; **~ avec qn** to be going out with sb; **s'en ~** (*malade*) to pull through; (*d'une difficulté etc*) to get through; **~ de** (*endroit*) to go (*ou* come) out of, leave; (*provenir de*) to come from; (*compétence*) to be outside

sosie [sɔzi] *nm* double

sot, sotte [so, sɔt] *adj* silly, foolish ▷ *nm/f* fool; **sottise** *nf* (*caractère*) silliness, foolishness; (*action*) silly *ou* foolish thing

sou [su] *nm*: **près de ses ~s** tight-fisted; **sans le ~** penniless

soubresaut [subʀəso] *nm* start; (*cahot*) jolt

souche [suʃ] *nf* (*d'arbre*) stump; (*de carnet*) counterfoil (BRIT), stub

souci [susi] *nm* (*inquiétude*) worry; (*préoccupation*) concern; (*Bot*) marigold; **se faire du ~** to worry; **soucier**: **se soucier de** *vt* to care about; **soucieux, -euse** *adj* concerned, worried

soucoupe [sukup] *nf* saucer; **soucoupe volante** flying saucer

soudain, e [sudɛ̃, ɛn] *adj* (*douleur, mort*) sudden ▷ *adv* suddenly, all of a sudden

Soudan [sudɑ̃] *nm*: **le ~** Sudan

soude [sud] *nf* soda

souder [sude] *vt* (*avec fil à souder*) to solder; (*par soudure autogène*) to weld; (*fig*) to bind together

soudure [sudyʀ] *nf* soldering; welding; (*joint*) soldered joint; weld

souffle [sufl] nm (en expirant) breath; (en soufflant) puff, blow; (respiration) breathing; (d'explosion, de ventilateur) blast; (du vent) blowing; **être à bout de ~** to be out of breath; **un ~ d'air** a breath of air

soufflé, e [sufle] adj (fam: stupéfié) staggered ▷ nm (Culin) soufflé

souffler [sufle] vi (gén) to blow; (haleter) to puff (and blow) ▷ vt (feu, bougie) to blow out; (chasser: poussière etc) to blow away; (Tech: verre) to blow; (dire): **~ qch à qn** to whisper sth to sb

souffrance [sufrɑ̃s] nf suffering; **en ~** (affaire) pending

souffrant, e [sufrɑ̃, ɑ̃t] adj unwell

souffre-douleur [sufrədulœr] nm inv butt, underdog

souffrir [sufrir] vi to suffer, be in pain ▷ vt to suffer, endure; (supporter) to bear, stand; **~ de** (maladie, froid) to suffer from; **elle ne peut pas le ~** she can't stand ou bear him

soufre [sufr] nm sulphur

souhait [swɛ] nm wish; **tous nos ~s pour la nouvelle année** (our) best wishes for the New Year; **à vos ~s!** bless you!; **souhaitable** adj desirable

souhaiter [swete] vt to wish for; **~ la bonne année à qn** to wish sb a happy New Year; **~ que** to hope that

soûl, e [su, sul] adj drunk ▷ nm: **tout son ~** to one's heart's content

soulagement [sulaʒmɑ̃] nm relief

soulager [sulaʒe] vt to relieve

soûler [sule] vt: **~ qn** to get sb drunk; (suj: boisson) to make sb drunk; (fig) to make sb's head spin ou reel; **se soûler** vi to get drunk

soulever [sul(ə)ve] vt to lift; (poussière) to send up; (enthousiasme) to arouse; (question, débat) to raise; **se soulever** vi (peuple) to rise up; (personne couchée) to lift o.s. up

soulier [sulje] nm shoe

souligner [suliɲe] vt to underline; (fig) to emphasize, stress

soumettre [sumɛtr] vt (pays) to subject, subjugate; (rebelle) to put down, subdue; **~ qch à qn** (projet etc) to submit sth to sb; **se soumettre (à)** to submit (to)

soumis, e [sumi, iz] adj submissive; **soumission** nf submission

soupçon [supsɔ̃] nm suspicion; (petite quantité): **un ~ de** a hint ou touch of; **soupçonner** vt to suspect; **soupçonneux, -euse** adj suspicious

soupe [sup] nf soup

souper [supe] vi to have supper ▷ nm supper

soupeser [supəze] vt to weigh in one's hand(s); (fig) to weigh up

soupière [supjɛr] nf (soup) tureen

soupir [supir] nm sigh; **pousser un ~ de**

soulagement to heave a sigh of relief

soupirer [supire] vi to sigh

souple [supl] adj supple; (fig: règlement, caractère) flexible; (: démarche, taille) lithe, supple; **souplesse** nf suppleness; (de caractère) flexibility

source [surs] nf (point d'eau) spring; (d'un cours d'eau, fig) source; **de bonne ~** on good authority

sourcil [sursi] nm (eye)brow; **sourciller** vi: **sans sourciller** without turning a hair ou batting an eyelid

sourd, e [sur, surd] adj deaf; (bruit) muffled; (douleur) dull ▷ nm/f deaf person; **faire la ~e oreille** to turn a deaf ear; **sourdine** nf (Mus) mute; **en sourdine** softly, quietly; **sourd-muet, sourde-muette** adj deaf-and-dumb ▷ nm/f deaf-mute

souriant, e [surjɑ̃, jɑ̃t] adj cheerful

sourire [surir] nm smile ▷ vi to smile; **~ à qn** to smile at sb; (fig: plaire à) to appeal to sb; (suj: chance) to smile on sb; **garder le ~** to keep smiling

souris [suri] nf mouse

sournois, e [surnwa, waz] adj deceitful, underhand

sous [su] prép under; **~ la pluie** in the rain; **~ terre** underground; **~ peu** shortly, before long; **sous-bois** nm inv undergrowth

souscrire [suskrir]: **~ à** vt to subscribe to

sous...: **sous-directeur, -trice** nm/f assistant manager(-manageress); **sous-entendre** vt to imply, infer; **sous-entendu, e** adj implied ▷ nm innuendo, insinuation; **sous-estimer** vt to underestimate; **sous-jacent, e** adj underlying; **sous-louer** vt to sublet; **sous-marin, e** adj (flore, faune) submarine; (pêche) underwater ▷ nm submarine; **sous-pull** nm thin poloneck jersey; **soussigné, e** adj: **je soussigné** I the undersigned; **sous-sol** nm basement; **sous-titre** nm subtitle

soustraction [sustraksjɔ̃] nf subtraction

soustraire [sustrer] vt to subtract, take away; (dérober): **~ qch à qn** to remove sth from sb; **se soustraire à** (autorité etc) to elude, escape from

sous...: **sous-traitant** nm sub-contractor; **sous-traiter** vt to sub-contract; **sous-vêtements** nmpl underwear sg

soutane [sutan] nf cassock, soutane

soute [sut] nf hold

soutenir [sut(ə)nir] vt to support; (assaut, choc) to stand up to, withstand; (intérêt, effort) to keep up; (assurer): **~ que** to maintain that; **soutenu, e** adj (efforts) sustained, unflagging; (style) elevated

souterrain, e [suterɛ̃, ɛn] adj underground ▷ nm underground passage

soutien [sutjɛ̃] nm support; **soutien-gorge**

nm bra

soutirer [sutiʀe] vt: ~ **qch à qn** to squeeze ou get sth out of sb

souvenir [suv(ə)niʀ] nm (réminiscence) memory; (objet) souvenir ▷ vb: **se ~ de** to remember; **se ~ que** to remember that; **en ~ de** in memory ou remembrance of; **avec mes affectueux/meilleurs ~s, ...** with love from, .../regards, ...

souvent [suvã] adv often; **peu ~** seldom, infrequently

souverain, e [suv(ə)ʀɛ̃, ɛn] nm/f sovereign, monarch

soyeux, -euse [swajø, øz] adj silky

spacieux, -euse [spasjø, jøz] adj spacious, roomy

spaghettis [spageti] nmpl spaghetti sg

sparadrap [spaʀadʀa] nm sticking plaster (BRIT), Bandaid® (US)

spatial, e, -aux [spasjal, jo] adj (Aviat) space cpd

speaker, ine [spikœʀ, kʀin] nm/f announcer

spécial, e, -aux [spesjal, jo] adj special; (bizarre) peculiar; **spécialement** adv especially, particularly; (tout exprès) specially; **spécialiser: se spécialiser** vi to specialize; **spécialiste** nm/f specialist; **spécialité** nf speciality; (branche) special field

spécifier [spesifje] vt to specify, state

spécimen [spesimɛn] nm specimen

spectacle [spɛktakl] nm (scène) sight; (représentation) show; (industrie) show business; **spectaculaire** adj spectacular

spectateur, -trice [spɛktatœʀ, tʀis] nm/f (Cinéma etc) member of the audience; (Sport) spectator; (d'un événement) onlooker, witness

spéculer [spekyle] vi to speculate

spéléologie [speleɔlɔʒi] nf potholing

sperme [spɛʀm] nm semen, sperm

sphère [sfɛʀ] nf sphere

spirale [spiʀal] nf spiral

spirituel, le [spiʀitɥɛl] adj spiritual; (fin, piquant) witty

splendide [splãdid] adj splendid

spontané, e [spɔ̃tane] adj spontaneous; **spontanéité** nf spontaneity

sport [spɔʀ] nm sport ▷ adj inv (vêtement) casual; **faire du ~** to do sport; **sports d'hiver** winter sports; **sportif, -ive** adj (journal, association, épreuve) sports cpd; (allure, démarche) athletic; (attitude, esprit) sporting

spot [spɔt] nm (lampe) spot(light); (annonce): **spot (publicitaire)** commercial (break)

square [skwaʀ] nm public garden(s)

squelette [skəlɛt] nm skeleton; **squelettique** adj scrawny

SRAS [sʀas] sigle m (= syndrome respiratoire aigu sévère) SARS

Sri Lanka [sʀilãka] nm: **le ~** Sri Lanka

stabiliser [stabilize] vt to stabilize

stable [stabl] adj stable, steady

stade [stad] nm (Sport) stadium; (phase, niveau) stage

stage [staʒ] nm (cours) training course; **~ de formation (professionnelle)** vocational (training) course; **~ de perfectionnement** advanced training course; **stagiaire** nm/f, adj trainee

Attention à ne pas traduire *stage* par le mot anglais *stage*.

stagner [stagne] vi to stagnate

stand [stãd] nm (d'exposition) stand; (de foire) stall; **stand de tir** (à la foire, Sport) shooting range

standard [stãdaʀ] adj inv standard ▷ nm switchboard; **standardiste** nm/f switchboard operator

standing [stãdiŋ] nm standing; **de grand ~** luxury

starter [staʀtɛʀ] nm (Auto) choke

station [stasjɔ̃] nf station; (de bus) stop; (de villégiature) resort; **station de ski** ski resort; **station de taxis** taxi rank (BRIT) ou stand (US); **stationnement** nm parking; **stationner** vi to park; **station-service** nf service station

statistique [statistik] nf (science) statistics sg; (rapport, étude) statistic ▷ adj statistical

statue [staty] nf statue

statu quo [statykwo] nm status quo

statut [staty] nm status; **statuts** nmpl (Jur, Admin) statutes; **statutaire** adj statutory

Sté abr = **société**

steak [stɛk] nm steak; **~ haché** hamburger

sténo(graphie) [stenɔ(gʀafi)] nf shorthand

stérile [steʀil] adj sterile

stérilet [steʀilɛ] nm coil, loop

stériliser [steʀilize] vt to sterilize

stimulant [stimylã] nm (fig) stimulus, incentive; (physique) stimulant

stimuler [stimyle] vt to stimulate

stipuler [stipyle] vt to stipulate

stock [stɔk] nm stock; **stocker** vt to stock

stop [stɔp] nm (Auto: écriteau) stop sign; (: feu arrière) brake-light; **faire du ~** (fam) to hitch(hike); **stopper** vt, vi to stop, halt

store [stɔʀ] nm blind; (de magasin) shade, awning

strabisme [stʀabism] nm squinting

strapontin [stʀapɔ̃tɛ̃] nm jump ou foldaway seat

stratégie [stʀateʒi] nf strategy; **stratégique** adj strategic

stress [stʀɛs] nm stress; **stressant, e** adj stressful; **stresser** vt: **stresser qn** to make sb (feel) tense

strict, e [stʀikt] adj strict; (tenue, décor) severe, plain; **le ~ nécessaire/minimum** the bare essentials/minimum

strident, e [stʀidɑ̃, ɑ̃t] adj shrill, strident

strophe [stʀɔf] nf verse, stanza

structure [stʀyktyʀ] nf structure; **~s d'accueil** reception facilities

studieux, -euse [stydjø, jøz] adj studious

studio [stydjo] nm (logement) (one-roomed) flatlet (BRIT) ou apartment (US); (d'artiste, TV etc) studio

stupéfait, e [stypefɛ, ɛt] adj astonished

stupéfiant, e [stypefjɑ̃, jɑ̃t] adj (étonnant) stunning, astounding ▷ nm (Méd) drug, narcotic

stupéfier [stypefje] vt (étonner) to stun, astonish

stupeur [stypœʀ] nf astonishment

stupide [stypid] adj stupid; **stupidité** nf stupidity; (parole, acte) stupid thing (to do ou say)

style [stil] nm style

stylé, e [stile] adj well-trained

styliste [stilist] nm/f designer

stylo [stilo] nm: **~ (à encre)** (fountain) pen; **stylo (à) bille** ball-point pen

su, e [sy] pp de **savoir** ▷ nm: **au su de** with the knowledge of

suave [sɥav] adj sweet

subalterne [sybaltɛʀn] adj (employé, officier) junior; (rôle) subordinate, subsidiary ▷ nm/f subordinate

subconscient [sypkɔ̃sjɑ̃] nm subconscious

subir [sybiʀ] vt (affront, dégâts) to suffer; (opération, châtiment) to undergo

subit, e [sybi, it] adj sudden; **subitement** adv suddenly, all of a sudden

subjectif, -ive [sybʒɛktif, iv] adj subjective

subjonctif [sybʒɔ̃ktif] nm subjunctive

subjuguer [sybʒyge] vt to captivate

submerger [sybmɛʀʒe] vt to submerge; (fig) to overwhelm

subordonné, e [sybɔʀdɔne] adj, nm/f subordinate

subrepticement [sybʀɛptismɑ̃] adv surreptitiously

subside [sybzid] nm grant

subsidiaire [sybzidjɛʀ] adj: **question ~** deciding question

subsister [sybziste] vi (rester) to remain, subsist; (survivre) to live on

substance [sypstɑ̃s] nf substance

substituer [sypstitɥe] vt: **~ qn/qch à** to substitute sb/sth for; **se ~ à qn** (évincer) to substitute o.s. for sb

substitut [sypstity] nm (succédané) substitute

subterfuge [sybtɛʀfyʒ] nm subterfuge

subtil, e [syptil] adj subtle

subvenir [sybvəniʀ]: **~ à** vt to meet

subvention [sybvɑ̃sjɔ̃] nf subsidy, grant; **subventionner** vt to subsidize

suc [syk] nm (Bot) sap; (de viande, fruit) juice

succéder [syksede]: **~ à** vt to succeed; **se succéder** vi (accidents, années) to follow one another

succès [syksɛ] nm success; **avoir du ~** to be a success, be successful; **à ~** successful; **succès de librairie** bestseller

successeur [syksesœʀ] nm successor

successif, -ive [syksesif, iv] adj successive

succession [syksesjɔ̃] nf (série, Pol) succession; (Jur: patrimoine) estate, inheritance

succomber [sykɔ̃be] vi to die, succumb; (fig): **~ à** to succumb to

succulent, e [sykylɑ̃, ɑ̃t] adj (repas, mets) delicious

succursale [sykyʀsal] nf branch

sucer [syse] vt to suck; **sucette** nf (bonbon) lollipop; (de bébé) dummy (BRIT), pacifier (US)

sucre [sykʀ] nm (substance) sugar; (morceau) lump of sugar, sugar lump ou cube; **sucre d'orge** barley sugar; **sucre en morceaux/cristallisé/en poudre** lump/granulated/caster sugar; **sucre glace** icing sugar (BRIT), confectioner's sugar (US); **sucré, e** adj (produit alimentaire) sweetened; (au goût) sweet; **sucrer** vt (thé, café) to sweeten, put sugar in; **sucreries** nfpl (bonbons) sweets, sweet things; **sucrier** nm (récipient) sugar bowl

sud [syd] nm: **le ~** the south ▷ adj inv south; (côte) south, southern; **au ~** (situation) in the south; (direction) to the south; **au ~ de** (to the) south of; **sud-africain, e** adj South African ▷ nm/f: **Sud-Africain, e** South African; **sud-américain, e** adj South American ▷ nm/f: **Sud-Américain, e** South American; **sud-est** nm, adj inv south-east; **sud-ouest** nm, adj inv south-west

Suède [sɥɛd] nf: **la ~** Sweden; **suédois, e** adj Swedish ▷ nm/f: **Suédois, e** Swede ▷ nm (Ling) Swedish

suer [sɥe] vi to sweat; (suinter) to ooze; **sueur** nf sweat; **en sueur** sweating, in a sweat; **donner des sueurs froides à qn** to put sb in(to) a cold sweat

suffire [syfiʀ] vi (être assez): **~ (à qn/pour qch/pour faire)** to be enough ou sufficient (for sb/for sth/to do); **il suffit d'une négligence ...** it only takes one act of carelessness ...; **il suffit qu'on oublie pour que ...** one only needs to forget for ...; **ça suffit!** that's enough!

suffisamment [syfizamɑ̃] adv sufficiently, enough; **~ de** sufficient, enough

suffisant, e [syfizɑ̃, ɑ̃t] adj sufficient; (résultats) satisfactory; (vaniteux) self-important, bumptious

suffixe [syfiks] nm suffix

suffoquer [syfɔke] vt to choke, suffocate; (stupéfier) to stagger, astound ▷ vi to choke, suffocate

suffrage [syfʀaʒ] nm (Pol: voix) vote
suggérer [syɡʒeʀe] vt to suggest;
suggestion nf suggestion
suicide [sɥisid] nm suicide; **suicider: se
suicider** vi to commit suicide
suie [sɥi] nf soot
suisse [sɥis] adj Swiss ▷ nm: **S~** Swiss pl
inv ▷ nf: **la S~** Switzerland; **la S~ romande/
allemande** French-speaking/German-
speaking Switzerland
suite [sɥit] nf (continuation: d'énumération etc)
rest, remainder; (: de feuilleton) continuation;
(: film etc sur le même thème) sequel; (série)
series, succession; (conséquence) result; (ordre,
liaison logique) coherence; (appartement, Mus)
suite; (escorte) retinue, suite; **suites** nfpl
(d'une maladie etc) effects; **prendre la ~ de**
(directeur etc) to succeed, take over from;
donner ~ à (requête, projet) to follow up; **faire
~ à** to follow; **(faisant) ~ à votre lettre du ...**
further to your letter of the ...; **de ~** (d'affilée)
in succession; (immédiatement) at once; **par
la ~** afterwards, subsequently; **à la ~** one
after the other; **à la ~ de** (derrière) behind; (en
conséquence de) following
suivant, e [sɥivã, ãt] adj next, following
▷ prép (selon) according to; **au~!** next!
suivi, e [sɥivi] adj (effort, qualité) consistent;
(cohérent) coherent; **très/peu ~** (cours) well-
/poorly-attended
suivre [sɥivʀ] vt (gén) to follow; (Scol: cours)
to attend; (comprendre) to keep up with;
(Comm: article) to continue to stock ▷ vi to
follow; (élève: assimiler) to keep up; **se suivre**
vi (accidents etc) to follow one after the
other; **faire ~** (lettre) to forward; **"à ~"** "to be
continued"
sujet, te [syʒɛ, ɛt] adj: **être ~ à** (vertige
etc) to be liable ou subject to ▷ nm/f (d'un
souverain) subject ▷ nm subject; **au ~ de**
about; **sujet de conversation** topic ou subject
of conversation; **sujet d'examen** (Scol)
examination question
super [sypɛʀ] (fam) adj inv terrific, great,
fantastic, super
superbe [sypɛʀb] adj magnificent, superb
superficie [sypɛʀfisi] nf (surface) area
superficiel, le [sypɛʀfisjɛl] adj superficial
superflu, e [sypɛʀfly] adj superfluous
supérieur, e [sypeʀjœʀ] adj (lèvre, étages,
classes) upper; (plus élevé: température,
niveau, enseignement): **~ (à)** higher (than);
(meilleur: qualité, produit): **~ (à)** superior (to);
(excellent, hautain) superior ▷ nm, nf superior;
supériorité nf superiority
supermarché [sypɛʀmaʀʃe] nm
supermarket
superposer [sypɛʀpoze] vt (faire chevaucher)
to superimpose; **lits superposés** bunk beds

superpuissance [sypɛʀpɥisãs] nf superpower
superstitieux, -euse [sypɛʀstisjø, jøz] adj
superstitious
superviser [sypɛʀvize] vt to supervise
supplanter [syplãte] vt to supplant
suppléant, e [sypleã, -ãt] adj (professeur)
supply cpd; (juge, fonctionnaire) deputy cpd
▷ nm/f (professeur) supply teacher
suppléer [syplee] vt (ajouter: mot manquant
etc) to supply, provide; (compenser: lacune) to fill
in; **~ à** to make up for
supplément [syplemã] nm supplement;
(de frites etc) extra portion; **un ~ de travail**
extra ou additional work; **payer un ~** to pay
an additional charge; **le vin est en ~** wine
is extra; **supplémentaire** adj additional,
further; (train, bus) relief cpd, extra
supplications [syplikasjɔ̃] nfpl pleas,
entreaties
supplice [syplis] nm torture no pl
supplier [syplije] vt to implore, beseech
support [sypɔʀ] nm support; (publicitaire)
medium; (audio-visuel) aid
supportable [sypɔʀtabl] adj (douleur)
bearable
supporter¹ [sypɔʀtɛʀ] nm supporter, fan
supporter² [sypɔʀte] vt (conséquences,
épreuve) to bear, endure; (défauts, personne)
to put up with; (suj: chose: chaleur etc) to
withstand; (: personne: chaleur, vin) to be able
to take

> Attention à ne pas traduire **supporter**
> par **to support**.

supposer [sypoze] vt to suppose; (impliquer)
to presuppose; **à ~ que** supposing (that)
suppositoire [sypozitwaʀ] nm suppository
suppression [sypʀesjɔ̃] nf (voir supprimer)
cancellation; removal; deletion
supprimer [sypʀime] vt (congés, service
d'autobus etc) to cancel; (emplois, privilèges,
témoin gênant) to do away with; (cloison, cause,
anxiété) to remove; (clause, mot) to delete
suprême [sypʀɛm] adj supreme

◯ **MOT-CLÉ**

sur [syʀ] prép **1** (position) on; (par-dessus) over;
(au-dessus) above; **pose-le sur la table** put it
on the table; **je n'ai pas d'argent sur moi** I
haven't any money on me
2 (direction) towards; **en allant sur Paris**
going towards Paris; **sur votre droite** on ou
to your right
3 (à propos de) on, about; **un livre/une
conférence sur Balzac** a book/lecture on ou
about Balzac
4 (proportion) out of; **un sur 10** one in 10; (Scol)
one out of 10

5 (*mesures*) by; **4 m sur 2** 4 m by 2
6 (*succession*): **avoir accident sur accident** to have one accident after the other

sûr, e [syʁ] *adj* sure, certain; (*digne de confiance*) reliable; (*sans danger*) safe; (*diagnostic, goût*) reliable; **le plus ~ est de** the safest thing is to; **sûr de soi** self-assured, self-confident

surcharge [syʁʃaʁʒ] *nf* (*de passagers, marchandises*) excess load; **surcharger** *vt* to overload

surcroît [syʁkʁwa] *nm*: **un ~ de** additional +*nom*; **par** *ou* **de ~** moreover; **en ~** in addition

surdité [syʁdite] *nf* deafness

sûrement [syʁmɑ̃] *adv* (*certainement*) certainly; (*sans risques*) safely

surenchère [syʁɑ̃ʃɛʁ] *nf* (*aux enchères*) higher bid; **surenchérir** *vi* to bid higher; (*fig*) to try and outbid each other

surestimer [syʁɛstime] *vt* to overestimate

sûreté [syʁte] *nf* (*sécurité*) safety; (*exactitude: de renseignements etc*) reliability; (*d'un geste*) steadiness; **mettre en ~** to put in a safe place; **pour plus de ~** as an extra precaution, to be on the safe side

surf [sœʁf] *nm* surfing

surface [syʁfas] *nf* surface; (*superficie*) surface area; **une grande ~** a supermarket; **faire ~** to surface; **en ~** near the surface; (*fig*) superficially

surfait, e [syʁfɛ, ɛt] *adj* overrated

surfer [syʁfe] *vi*: **~ sur Internet** to surf *ou* browse the Internet

surgelé, e [syʁʒəle] *adj* (deep-)frozen ▷ *nm*: **les ~s** (deep-)frozen food

surgir [syʁʒiʁ] *vi* to appear suddenly; (*fig: problème, conflit*) to arise

sur...: **surhumain, e** *adj* superhuman; **sur-le-champ** *adv* immediately; **surlendemain** *nm*: **le surlendemain (soir)** two days later (in the evening); **le surlendemain de** two days after;
surmenage *nm* overwork(ing); **surmener**: **se surmener** *vi* to overwork

surmonter [syʁmɔ̃te] *vt* (*vaincre*) to overcome; (*être au-dessus de*) to top

surnaturel, le [syʁnatyʁɛl] *adj, nm* supernatural

surnom [syʁnɔ̃] *nm* nickname

surnombre [syʁnɔ̃bʁ] *nm*: **être en ~** to be too many (*ou* one too many)

surpeuplé, e [syʁpœple] *adj* overpopulated

surplace [syʁplas] *nm*: **faire du ~** to mark time

surplomber [syʁplɔ̃be] *vt, vi* to overhang

surplus [syʁply] *nm* (*Comm*) surplus; (*reste*): **~ de bois** wood left over

surprenant, e [syʁpʁənɑ̃, ɑ̃t] *adj* amazing

surprendre [syʁpʁɑ̃dʁ] *vt* (*étonner*) to surprise; (*tomber sur: intrus etc*) to catch; (*entendre*) to overhear

surpris, e [syʁpʁi, iz] *adj*: **~ (de/que)** surprised (at/that); **surprise** *nf* surprise; **faire une surprise à qn** to give sb a surprise; **surprise-partie** *nf* party

sursaut [syʁso] *nm* start, jump; **~ de** (*énergie, indignation*) sudden fit *ou* burst of; **en ~** with a start; **sursauter** *vi* to (give a) start, jump

sursis [syʁsi] *nm* (*Jur: gén*) suspended sentence; (*fig*) reprieve

surtout [syʁtu] *adv* (*avant tout, d'abord*) above all; (*spécialement, particulièrement*) especially; **~, ne dites rien!** whatever you do don't say anything!; **~ pas!** certainly *ou* definitely not!; **~ que ...** especially as ...

surveillance [syʁvɛjɑ̃s] *nf* watch; (*Police, Mil*) surveillance; **sous ~ médicale** under medical supervision

surveillant, e [syʁvɛjɑ̃, ɑ̃t] *nm/f* (*de prison*) warder; (*Scol*) monitor

surveiller [syʁveje] *vt* (*enfant, élèves, bagages*) to watch, keep an eye on; (*prisonnier, suspect*) to keep (a) watch on; (*territoire, bâtiment*) to (keep) watch over; (*travaux, cuisson*) to supervise; (*Scol: examen*) to invigilate; **~ son langage/sa ligne** to watch one's language/figure

survenir [syʁvəniʁ] *vi* (*incident, retards*) to occur, arise; (*événement*) to take place

survêtement [syʁvɛtmɑ̃] *nm* tracksuit

survie [syʁvi] *nf* survival; **survivant, e** *nm/f* survivor; **survivre** *vi* to survive; **survivre à** (*accident etc*) to survive

survoler [syʁvɔle] *vt* to fly over; (*fig: livre*) to skim through

survolté, e [syʁvɔlte] *adj* (*fig*) worked up

sus [sy(s)]: **en ~ de** *prép* in addition to, over and above; **en ~** in addition

susceptible [sysɛptibl] *adj* touchy, sensitive; **~ de faire** (*hypothèse*) liable to do

susciter [sysite] *vt* (*admiration*) to arouse; (*ennuis*): **~ (à qn)** to create (for sb)

suspect, e [syspɛ(kt), ɛkt] *adj* suspicious; (*témoignage, opinions*) suspect ▷ *nm/f* suspect; **suspecter** *vt* to suspect; (*honnêteté de qn*) to question, have one's suspicions about

suspendre [syspɑ̃dʁ] *vt* (*accrocher: vêtement*): **~ qch (à)** to hang sth up (on); (*interrompre, démettre*) to suspend

suspendu, e [syspɑ̃dy] *adj* (*accroché*): **~ à** hanging to (*ou* from); (*perché*): **~ au-dessus de** suspended over

suspens [syspɑ̃]: **en ~** *adv* (*affaire*) in abeyance; **tenir en ~** to keep in suspense

suspense [syspɛns, syspɑ̃s] *nm* suspense

suspension [syspɑ̃sjɔ̃] *nf* suspension; (*lustre*) light fitting *ou* fitment

suture [sytyʁ] *nf* (*Méd*): **point de ~** stitch

svelte [svɛlt] *adj* slender, svelte

SVP *abr* (= *s'il vous plaît*) please

sweat [swit] *nm* (*fam*) sweatshirt

sweat-shirt [switʃœrt] (*pl* **-s**) *nm* sweatshirt

syllabe [si(l)lab] *nf* syllable

symbole [sɛ̃bɔl] *nm* symbol; **symbolique**
adj symbolic(al); (*geste, offrande*) token *cpd*;
symboliser *vt* to symbolize

symétrique [simetrik] *adj* symmetrical

sympa [sɛ̃pa] (*fam*) *adj inv* nice; **sois ~, prête-
le moi** be a pal and lend it to me

sympathie [sɛ̃pati] *nf* (*inclination*) liking;
(*affinité*) friendship; (*condoléances*) sympathy;
j'ai beaucoup de ~ pour lui I like him a lot;
sympathique *adj* nice, friendly

> Attention à ne pas traduire **sympathique**
> par *sympathetic*.

sympathisant, e [sɛ̃patizɑ̃, ɑ̃t] *nm/f*
sympathizer

sympathiser [sɛ̃patize] *vi* (*voisins etc:
s'entendre*) to get on (BRIT) *ou* along (US) (well)

symphonie [sɛ̃fɔni] *nf* symphony

symptôme [sɛ̃ptom] *nm* symptom

synagogue [sinagɔg] *nf* synagogue

syncope [sɛ̃kɔp] *nf* (*Méd*) blackout; **tomber
en ~** to faint, pass out

syndic [sɛ̃dik] *nm* (*d'immeuble*) managing
agent

syndical, e, -aux [sɛ̃dikal, o] *adj* (trade)
union *cpd*; **syndicaliste** *nm/f* trade unionist

syndicat [sɛ̃dika] *nm* (*d'ouvriers, employés*)
(trade) union; **syndicat d'initiative** tourist
office; **syndiqué, e** *adj* belonging to a (trade)
union; **syndiquer: se syndiquer** *vi* to form a
trade union; (*adhérer*) to join a trade union

synonyme [sinɔnim] *adj* synonymous ▷ *nm*
synonym; **~ de** synonymous with

syntaxe [sɛ̃taks] *nf* syntax

synthèse [sɛ̃tɛz] *nf* synthesis

synthétique [sɛ̃tetik] *adj* synthetic

Syrie [siri] *nf*: **la ~** Syria

systématique [sistematik] *adj* systematic

système [sistɛm] *nm* system; **le ~ D**
resourcefulness

t' [t] *pron voir* **te**

ta [ta] *adj voir* **ton¹**

tabac [taba] *nm* tobacco; (*magasin*)
tobacconist's (shop)

tabagisme [tabaʒism] *nm*: **tabagisme
passif** passive smoking

table [tabl] *nf* table; **à ~!** dinner *etc* is ready!;
se mettre à ~ to sit down to eat; **mettre la ~**
to lay the table; **une ~ pour 4, s'il vous plaît**
a table for 4, please; **table à repasser** ironing
board; **table de cuisson** hob; **table de nuit** *ou*
de chevet bedside table; **table des matières**
(table of) contents *pl*; **table d'orientation**
viewpoint indicator; **table roulante** trolley
(BRIT), tea wagon (US)

tableau, x [tablo] *nm* (*peinture*) painting;
(*reproduction, fig*) picture; (*panneau*) board;
(*schéma*) table, chart; **tableau d'affichage**
notice board; **tableau de bord** dashboard;
(*Aviat*) instrument panel; **tableau noir**
blackboard

tablette [tablɛt] *nf* (*planche*) shelf; **tablette
de chocolat** bar of chocolate

tablier [tablije] *nm* apron

tabou [tabu] *nm* taboo

tabouret [taburɛ] *nm* stool

tac [tak] *nm*: **il m'a répondu du ~ au ~** he
answered me right back

tache [taʃ] *nf* (*saleté*) stain, mark; (*Art, de
couleur, lumière*) spot; **tache de rousseur**

freckle

tâche [taʃ] nf task

tacher [taʃe] vt to stain, mark

tâcher [taʃe] vi: **~ de faire** to try ou endeavour to do

tacheté, e [taʃte] adj spotted

tact [takt] nm tact; **avoir du ~** to be tactful

tactique [taktik] adj tactical ▷ nf (technique) tactics sg; (plan) tactic

taie [tɛ] nf: **~ (d'oreiller)** pillowslip, pillowcase

taille [taj] nf cutting; (d'arbre etc) pruning; (milieu du corps) waist; (hauteur) height; (grandeur) size; **de ~ à faire** capable of doing; **de ~** sizeable; **taille-crayon(s)** nm pencil sharpener

tailler [taje] vt (pierre, diamant) to cut; (arbre, plante) to prune; (vêtement) to cut out; (crayon) to sharpen

tailleur [tajœʀ] nm (couturier) tailor; (vêtement) suit; **en ~** (assis) cross-legged

taillis [taji] nm copse

taire [tɛʀ] vi: **faire ~ qn** to make sb be quiet; **se taire** vi to be silent ou quiet; **taisez-vous!** be quiet!

Taiwan [tajwan] nf Taiwan

talc [talk] nm talc, talcum powder

talent [talɑ̃] nm talent

talkie-walkie [tokiwoki] nm walkie-talkie

talon [talɔ̃] nm heel; (de chèque, billet) stub, counterfoil (BRIT); **talons plats/aiguilles** flat/stiletto heels

talus [taly] nm embankment

tambour [tɑ̃buʀ] nm (Mus, aussi Tech) drum; (musicien) drummer; (porte) revolving door(s pl); **tambourin** nm tambourine

Tamise [tamiz] nf: **la** ~ the Thames

tamisé, e [tamize] adj (fig) subdued, soft

tampon [tɑ̃pɔ̃] nm (de coton, d'ouate) wad, pad; (amortisseur) buffer; (bouchon) plug, stopper; (cachet, timbre) stamp; (mémoire) ~ (Inform) buffer; **tampon (hygiénique)** tampon; **tamponner** vt (timbres) to stamp; (heurter) to crash ou ram into; **tamponneuse** adj f: **autos tamponneuses** dodgems

tandem [tɑ̃dɛm] nm tandem

tandis [tɑ̃di]: **~ que** conj while

tanguer [tɑ̃ge] vi to pitch (and toss)

tant [tɑ̃] adv so much; **~ de** (sable, eau) so much; (gens, livres) so many; **~ que** as long as; (autant que) as much as; **~ mieux** that's great; (avec une certaine réserve) so much the better; **~ pis** too bad; (conciliant) never mind; **~ bien que mal** as well as can be expected

tante [tɑ̃t] nf aunt

tantôt [tɑ̃to] adv (parfois): **~ ... ~** now ... now; (cet après-midi) this afternoon

taon [tɑ̃] nm horsefly

tapage [tapaʒ] nm uproar, din

tapageur, -euse [tapaʒœʀ, øz] adj noisy; (voyant) loud, flashy

tape [tap] nf slap

tape-à-l'œil [tapalœj] adj inv flashy, showy

taper [tape] vt (porte) to bang, slam; (enfant) to slap; (dactylographier) to type (out); (fam: emprunter): **~ qn de 10 euros** to touch sb for 10 euros ▷ vi (soleil) to beat down; **se taper** vt (repas) to put away; (fam: corvée) to get landed with; **~ sur qn** to thump sb; (fig) to run sb down; **~ sur un clou** to hit a nail; **~ sur la table** to bang on the table; **~ à** (porte etc) to knock on; **~ dans** (se servir) to dig into; **~ des mains/pieds** to clap one's hands/stamp one's feet; **~ (à la machine)** to type

tapi, e [tapi] adj (blotti) crouching; (caché) hidden away

tapis [tapi] nm carpet; (petit) rug; **tapis de sol** (de tente) groundsheet; **tapis de souris** (Inform) mouse mat; **tapis roulant** (pour piétons) moving walkway; (pour bagages) carousel

tapisser [tapise] vt (avec du papier peint) to paper; (recouvrir): **~ qch (de)** to cover sth (with); **tapisserie** nf (tenture, broderie) tapestry; (papier peint) wallpaper; **tapissier-décorateur** nm interior decorator

tapoter [tapote] vt (joue, main) to pat; (objet) to tap

taquiner [takine] vt to tease

tard [taʀ] adv late; **plus ~** later (on); **au plus ~** at the latest; **sur le ~** late in life; **il est trop ~** it's too late

tarder [taʀde] vi (chose) to be a long time coming; (personne): **~ à faire** to delay doing; **il me tarde d'être** I am longing to be; **sans (plus) ~** without (further) delay

tardif, -ive [taʀdif, iv] adj late

tarif [taʀif] nm: **~ des consommations** price list; **~s postaux/douaniers** postal/customs rates; **~ des taxis** taxi fares; **~ plein/réduit** (train) full/reduced fare; (téléphone) peak/off-peak rate

tarir [taʀiʀ] vi to dry up, run dry

tarte [taʀt] nf tart; **~ aux fraises** strawberry tart; **~ Tatin** ≈ apple upside-down tart

tartine [taʀtin] nf slice of bread; **tartine de miel** slice of bread and honey; **tartiner** vt to spread; **fromage à tartiner** cheese spread

tartre [taʀtʀ] nm (des dents) tartar; (de bouilloire) fur, scale

tas [tɑ] nm heap, pile; (fig): **un ~ de** heaps of, lots of; **en ~** in a heap ou pile; **formé sur le ~** trained on the job

tasse [tɑs] nf cup; **tasse à café** coffee cup

tassé, e [tɑse] adj: **bien ~** (café etc) strong

tasser [tɑse] vt (terre, neige) to pack down; (entasser): **~ qch dans** to cram sth into; **se tasser** vi (se serrer) to squeeze up; (s'affaisser) to settle; (fig) to settle down

tâter [tɑte] vt to feel; (fig) to try out; **se tâter** (hésiter) to be in two minds; **~ de** (prison etc) to have a taste of

tatillon, ne [tatijɔ̃, ɔn] adj pernickety

tâtonnement [tɑtɔnmɑ̃] nm: **par ~s** (fig) by trial and error

tâtonner [tɑtɔne] vi to grope one's way along

tâtons [tɑtɔ̃]: **à ~** adv: **chercher/avancer à ~** to grope around for/grope one's way forward

tatouage [tatwaʒ] nm tattoo

tatouer [tatwe] vt to tattoo

taudis [todi] nm hovel, slum

taule [tol] (fam) nf nick (fam), prison

taupe [top] nf mole

taureau, x [tɔʀo] nm bull; (signe): **le T~** Taurus

taux [to] nm rate; (d'alcool) level; **taux d'intérêt** interest rate

taxe [taks] nf tax; (douanière) duty; **toutes ~s comprises** inclusive of tax; **la boutique hors ~s** the duty-free shop; **taxe à la valeur ajoutée** value-added tax; **taxe de séjour** tourist tax

taxer [takse] vt (personne) to tax; (produit) to put a tax on, tax

taxi [taksi] nm taxi; (chauffeur: fam) taxi driver; **pouvez-vous m'appeler un ~, s'il vous plaît?** can you call me a taxi, please?

Tchécoslovaquie [tʃekɔslɔvaki] nf Czechoslovakia; **tchèque** adj Czech ▷ nm/f: **Tchèque** Czech ▷ nm (Ling) Czech; **la République tchèque** the Czech Republic

Tchétchénie [tʃetʃeni] nf: **la ~** Chechnya

te, t' [tə] pron you; (réfléchi) yourself

technicien, ne [tɛknisjɛ̃, jɛn] nm/f technician

technico-commercial, e, -aux [tɛknikokɔmɛʀsjal, jo] adj: **agent ~** sales technician

technique [tɛknik] adj technical ▷ nf technique; **techniquement** adv technically

techno [tɛkno] nf (Mus) techno (music)

technologie [tɛknɔlɔʒi] nf technology; **technologique** adj technological

teck [tɛk] nm teak

tee-shirt [tiʃœʀt] nm T-shirt, tee-shirt

teindre [tɛ̃dʀ] vt to dye; **se ~ les cheveux** to dye one's hair; **teint, e** adj dyed ▷ nm (du visage) complexion; (momentané) colour ▷ nf shade; **grand teint** colourfast

teinté, e [tɛ̃te] adj: **~ de** (fig) tinged with

teinter [tɛ̃te] vt (verre, papier) to tint; (bois) to stain

teinture [tɛ̃tyʀ] nf dye; **teinture d'iode** tincture of iodine; **teinturerie** nf dry cleaner's; **teinturier** nm dry cleaner

tel, telle [tɛl] adj (pareil) such; (comme): **~ un/des ...** like a/like ...; (indéfini) such-and-such a; (intensif): **un ~/de ~s ...** such (a)/such ...; **rien de ~** nothing like it; **~ que** like, such as; **~ quel**

as it is ou stands (ou was etc); **venez ~ jour** come on such-and-such a day

télé [tele] (fam) nf TV; **à la ~** on TV ou telly

télé...: **télécabine** nf (benne) cable car; **télécarte** nf phonecard; **téléchargeable** adj downloadable; **téléchargement** nm (action) downloading; (fichier) download; **télécharger** vt to download; **télécommande** nf remote control; **télécopieur** nm fax machine; **télédistribution** nf cable TV; **télégramme** nm telegram; **télégraphier** vt to telegraph, cable; **téléguider** vt to radio-control; **télématique** nf telematics sg; **téléobjectif** nm telephoto lens sg; **télépathie** nf telepathy; **téléphérique** nm cable car

téléphone [telefɔn] nm telephone; **avoir le ~** to be on the (tele)phone; **au ~** on the phone; **téléphoner** vi to make a phone call; **téléphoner à** to phone, call up; **est-ce que je peux téléphoner d'ici?** can I make a call from here?; **téléphonique** adj (tele)phone cpd

télé...: **téléréalité** nf reality TV

télescope [telɛskɔp] nm telescope

télescoper [telɛskɔpe] vt to smash up; **se télescoper** (véhicules) to concertina

télé...: **téléscripteur** nm teleprinter; **télésiège** nm chairlift; **téléski** nm ski-tow; **téléspectateur, -trice** nm/f (television) viewer; **télétravail** nm telecommuting; **télévente** nf telesales; **téléviseur** nm television set; **télévision** nf television; **à la télévision** on television; **télévision numérique** digital TV; **télévision par câble/satellite** cable/satellite television

télex [telɛks] nm telex

telle [tɛl] adj voir **tel**; **tellement** adv (tant) so much; (si) so; **tellement de** (sable, eau) so much; (gens, livres) so many; **il s'est endormi tellement il était fatigué** he was so tired (that) he fell asleep; **pas tellement** not (all) that much; not (all) that +adjectif

téméraire [temeʀɛʀ] adj reckless, rash

témoignage [temwaɲaʒ] nm (Jur: déclaration) testimony no pl, evidence no pl; (rapport, récit) account; (fig: d'affection etc: cadeau) token, mark; (: geste) expression

témoigner [temwaɲe] vt (intérêt, gratitude) to show ▷ vi (Jur) to testify, give evidence; **~ de** to bear witness to, testify to

témoin [temwɛ̃] nm witness ▷ adj: **appartement ~** show flat (BRIT); **être ~ de** to witness; **témoin oculaire** eyewitness

tempe [tɑ̃p] nf temple

tempérament [tɑ̃peʀamɑ̃] nm temperament, disposition; **à ~** (vente) on deferred (payment) terms; (achat) by instalments, hire purchase cpd

température [tɑ̃peʀatyʀ] nf temperature; **avoir** ou **faire de la ~** to be running ou have a temperature

tempête [tɑ̃pɛt] nf storm; **tempête de
sable/neige** sand/snowstorm

temple [tɑ̃pl] nm temple; (protestant) church

temporaire [tɑ̃pɔʀɛʀ] adj temporary

temps [tɑ̃] nm (atmosphérique) weather; (durée)
time; (époque) times, time pl; (Ling) tense;
(Mus) beat; (Tech) stroke; **un ~ de chien** (fam)
rotten weather; **quel ~ fait-il?** what's the
weather like?; **il fait beau/mauvais ~** the
weather is fine/bad; **avoir le ~/tout son ~**
to have time/plenty of time; **en ~ de paix/
guerre** in peacetime/wartime; **en ~ utile
ou voulu** in due course ou time; **ces derniers
~** lately; **dans quelque ~** in a (little) while;
de ~ en ~, de ~ à autre from time to time; **à ~**
(partir, arriver) in time; **à ~ complet, à plein ~**
full-time; **à ~ partiel, à mi-~** part-time; **dans
le ~** at one time; **temps d'arrêt** pause, halt;
temps libre free ou spare time; **temps mort**
(Comm) slack period

tenable [t(ə)nabl] adj bearable

tenace [tənas] adj persistent

tenant, e [tənɑ̃, ɑ̃t] nm/f (Sport): **~ du titre**
title-holder

tendance [tɑ̃dɑ̃s] nf tendency; (opinions)
leanings pl, sympathies pl; (évolution) trend;
avoir ~ à to have a tendency to, tend to

tendeur [tɑ̃dœʀ] nm (attache) elastic strap

tendre [tɑ̃dʀ] adj tender; (bois, roche, couleur)
soft ▷ vt (élastique, peau) to stretch; (corde) to
tighten; (muscle) to tense; (fig: piège) to set,
lay; (donner): **~ qch à qn** to hold sth out to
sb; (offrir) to offer sb sth; **se tendre** vi (corde)
to tighten; (relations) to become strained; **~
à qch/à faire** to tend towards sth/to do; **~
l'oreille** to prick up one's ears; **~ la main/le
bras** to hold out one's hand/stretch out one's
arm; **tendrement** adv tenderly; **tendresse**
nf tenderness

tendu, e [tɑ̃dy] pp de **tendre** ▷ adj (corde)
tight; (muscles) tense; (relations) strained

ténèbres [tenɛbʀ] nfpl darkness sg

teneur [tənœʀ] nf content; (d'une lettre) terms
pl, content

tenir [t(ə)niʀ] vt to hold; (magasin, hôtel) to
run; (promesse) to keep ▷ vi to hold; (neige, gel)
to last; **se tenir** vi (avoir lieu) to be held, take
place; (être: personne) to stand; **~ à** (personne,
objet) to be attached to; (réputation) to care
about; **~ à faire** to be determined to do; **~ de**
(ressembler à) to take after; **ça ne tient qu'à
lui** it is entirely up to him; **~ qn pour** to regard
sb as; **~ qch de qn** (histoire) to have heard ou
learnt sth from sb; (qualité, défaut) to have
inherited ou got sth from sb; **~ dans** to fit into;
~ compte de qch to take sth into account;
~ les comptes to keep the books; **~ bon** to
stand fast; **~ le coup** to hold out; **~ au chaud**

185 | **terre**

(café, plat) to keep hot; **un manteau qui tient
chaud** a warm coat; **tiens/tenez, voilà le
stylo** there's the pen!; **tiens, voilà Alain!**
look, here's Alain!; **tiens?** (surprise) really?; **se ~
droit** to stand (ou sit) up straight; **bien se ~** to
behave well; **se ~ à qch** to hold on to sth; **s'en ~
à qch** to confine o.s. to sth

tennis [tenis] nm tennis; (court) tennis court
▷ nm ou fpl (aussi: **chaussures de ~**) tennis
ou gym shoes; **tennis de table** table tennis;
tennisman nm tennis player

tension [tɑ̃sjɔ̃] nf tension; (Méd) blood
pressure; **avoir de la ~** to have high blood
pressure

tentation [tɑ̃tasjɔ̃] nf temptation

tentative [tɑ̃tativ] nf attempt

tente [tɑ̃t] nf tent

tenter [tɑ̃te] vt (éprouver, attirer) to tempt;
(essayer): **~ qch/de faire** to attempt ou try
sth/to do; **~ sa chance** to try one's luck

tenture [tɑ̃tyʀ] nf hanging

tenu, e [t(ə)ny] pp de **tenir** ▷ adj (maison,
comptes): **bien ~** well-kept; (obligé): **~ de
faire** obliged to do ▷ nf (vêtements) clothes
pl; (comportement) (good) manners pl, good
behaviour; (d'une maison) upkeep; **en petite
~e** scantily dressed ou clad

ter [tɛʀ] adj: **16 ~** 16b ou B

terme [tɛʀm] nm term; (fin) end; **à court/
long ~** adj short-/long-term ▷ adv in the
short/long term; **avant ~** (Méd) prematurely;
mettre un ~ à to put an end ou a stop to; **en
bons ~s** on good terms

terminaison [tɛʀminɛzɔ̃] nf (Ling) ending

terminal, -aux [tɛʀminal, o] nm terminal;
terminale nf (Scol) ≈ year 13 (BRIT), ≈ twelfth
grade (US)

terminer [tɛʀmine] vt to finish; **se terminer**
vi to end; **quand est-ce que le spectacle se
termine?** when does the show finish?

terne [tɛʀn] adj dull

ternir [tɛʀniʀ] vt to dull; (fig) to sully, tarnish;
se ternir vi to become dull

terrain [tɛʀɛ̃] nm (sol, fig) ground; (Comm:
étendue de terre) land no pl; (parcelle) plot (of
land); (à bâtir) site; **sur le ~** (fig) on the field;
terrain d'aviation airfield; **terrain de
camping** campsite; **terrain de football/
rugby** football/rugby pitch (BRIT) ou field
(US); **terrain de golf** golf course; **terrain de
jeu** games field; (pour les petits) playground;
terrain de sport sports ground; **terrain
vague** waste ground no pl

terrasse [tɛʀas] nf terrace; **à la ~** (café)
outside; **terrasser** vt (adversaire) to floor; (suj:
maladie etc) to strike down

terre [tɛʀ] nf (gén, aussi Élec) earth; (substance)
soil, earth; (opposé à mer) land no pl; (contrée)
land; **terres** nfpl (terrains) lands, land sg; **en ~**

(pipe, poterie) clay cpd; **à ~ ou par ~** (mettre, être, s'asseoir) on the ground (ou floor); (jeter, tomber) to the ground, down; **terre à terre** adj inv (considération, personne) down-to-earth; **terre cuite** terracotta; **la terre ferme** dry land; **terre glaise** clay

terreau [teʀo] nm compost

terre-plein [teʀplɛ̃] nm platform; (sur chaussée) central reservation

terrestre [teʀɛstʀ] adj (surface) earth's, of the earth; (Bot, Zool, Mil) land cpd; (Rel) earthly

terreur [teʀœʀ] nf terror no pl

terrible [teʀibl] adj terrible, dreadful; (fam) terrific; **pas ~** nothing special

terrien, ne [teʀjɛ̃, jɛn] adj: **propriétaire ~** landowner ▷ nm/f (non martien etc) earthling

terrier [teʀje] nm burrow, hole; (chien) terrier

terrifier [teʀifje] vt to terrify

terrine [teʀin] nf (récipient) terrine; (Culin) pâté

territoire [teʀitwaʀ] nm territory

terroriser [teʀɔʀize] vt to terrorize

terrorisme [teʀɔʀism] nm terrorism; **terroriste** nm/f terrorist

tertiaire [teʀsjɛʀ] adj tertiary ▷ nm (Écon) service industries pl

tes [te] adj voir **ton'**

test [tɛst] nm test

testament [tɛstamɑ̃] nm (Jur) will; (Rel) Testament; (fig) legacy

tester [tɛste] vt to test

testicule [tɛstikyl] nm testicle

tétanos [tetanos] nm tetanus

têtard [tɛtaʀ] nm tadpole

tête [tɛt] nf head; (cheveux) hair no pl; (visage) face; **de ~** (comme adj: wagon etc) front cpd; (comme adv: calculer) in one's head, mentally; **perdre la ~** (fig: s'affoler) to lose one's head; (: devenir fou) to go off one's head; **tenir ~ à qn** to stand up to sb; **la ~ en bas** with one's head down; **la ~ la première** (tomber) headfirst; **faire une ~** (Football) to head the ball; **faire la ~** (fig) to sulk; **en ~** at the front; (Sport) in the lead; **à la ~ de** at the head of; **à ~ reposée** at a more leisurely moment; **n'en faire qu'à sa ~** to do as one pleases; **en avoir par-dessus la ~** to be fed up; **en ~ à ~** in private, alone together; **de la ~ aux pieds** from head to toe; **tête de lecture** (playback) head; **tête de liste** (Pol) chief candidate; **tête de mort** skull and crossbones; **tête de série** (Tennis) seeded player, seed; **tête de Turc** (fig) whipping boy (BRIT), butt; **tête-à-queue** nm inv: **faire un tête-à-queue** to spin round

téter [tete] vt: **~ (sa mère)** to suck at one's mother's breast, feed

tétine [tetin] nf teat; (sucette) dummy (BRIT), pacifier (US)

têtu, e [tety] adj stubborn, pigheaded

texte [tɛkst] nm text; (morceau choisi) passage

textile [tɛkstil] adj textile cpd ▷ nm textile; **le ~** the textile industry

Texto® [tɛksto] nm text message

texture [tɛkstyʀ] nf texture

TGV sigle m (= train à grande vitesse) high-speed train

thaïlandais, e [tajlɑ̃dɛ, ɛz] adj Thai ▷ nm/f: **T~, e** Thai

Thaïlande [tailɑ̃d] nf Thailand

thé [te] nm tea; **~ au citron** lemon tea; **~ au lait** tea with milk; **prendre le ~** to have tea; **faire le ~** to make the tea

théâtral, e, -aux [teatʀal, o] adj theatrical

théâtre [teatʀ] nm theatre; (péj: simulation) playacting; (fig: lieu): **le ~ de** the scene of; **faire du ~** to act

théière [tejɛʀ] nf teapot

thème [tɛm] nm theme; (Scol: traduction) prose (composition)

théologie [teɔlɔʒi] nf theology

théorie [teɔʀi] nf theory; **théorique** adj theoretical

thérapie [teʀapi] nf therapy

thermal, e, -aux [tɛʀmal, o] adj: **station ~e** spa; **cure ~e** water cure

thermomètre [tɛʀmɔmɛtʀ] nm thermometer

thermos® [tɛʀmos] nm ou nf: **(bouteille) thermos** vacuum ou Thermos® flask

thermostat [tɛʀmɔsta] nm thermostat

thèse [tɛz] nf thesis

thon [tɔ̃] nm tuna (fish)

thym [tɛ̃] nm thyme

Tibet [tibɛ] nm: **le ~** Tibet

tibia [tibja] nm shinbone, tibia; (partie antérieure de la jambe) shin

TIC sigle fpl (= technologies de l'information et de la communication) ICT sg

tic [tik] nm tic, (nervous) twitch; (de langage etc) mannerism

ticket [tikɛ] nm ticket; **ticket de caisse** receipt; **je peux avoir un ticket de caisse, s'il vous plaît?** can I have a receipt, please?

tiède [tjɛd] adj lukewarm; (vent, air) mild, warm; **tiédir** vi to cool; (se réchauffer) to grow warmer

tien, ne [tjɛ̃, tjɛn] pron: **le(la) ~(ne), les ~(ne)s** yours; **à la ~ne!** cheers!

tiens [tjɛ̃] vb, excl voir **tenir**

tiercé [tjɛʀse] nm system of forecast betting giving first 3 horses

tiers, tierce [tjɛʀ, tjɛʀs] adj third ▷ nm (Jur) third party; (fraction) third; **le tiers monde** the Third World

tige [tiʒ] nf stem; (baguette) rod

tignasse [tiɲas] nf (péj) mop of hair

tigre [tigʀ] nm tiger; **tigré, e** adj (rayé) striped; (tacheté) spotted; (chat) tabby; **tigresse** nf tigress

tilleul [tijœl] nm lime (tree), linden (tree); (boisson) lime(-blossom) tea

timbre [tɛ̃bʀ] nm (tampon) stamp; (aussi: ~-poste) (postage) stamp; (Mus: de voix, instrument) timbre, tone

timbré, e [tɛ̃bʀe] (fam) adj cracked

timide [timid] adj shy; (timoré) timid; **timidement** adv shyly; timidly; **timidité** nf shyness; timidity

tintamarre [tɛ̃tamaʀ] nm din, uproar

tinter [tɛ̃te] vi to ring, chime; (argent, clefs) to jingle

tique [tik] nf (parasite) tick

tir [tiʀ] nm (sport) shooting; (fait ou manière de tirer) firing no pl; (rafale) fire; (stand) shooting gallery; **tir à l'arc** archery

tirage [tiʀaʒ] nm (action) printing; (Photo) print; (de journal) circulation; (de livre: nombre d'exemplaires) (print) run; (: édition) edition; (de loterie) draw; **par ~ au sort** by drawing lots

tire [tiʀ] nf: **vol à la ~** pickpocketing

tiré, e [tiʀe] adj (traits) drawn; **~ par les cheveux** far-fetched

tire-bouchon [tiʀbuʃɔ̃] nm corkscrew

tirelire [tiʀliʀ] nf moneybox

tirer [tiʀe] vt (gén) to pull; (trait, rideau, carte, conclusion, chèque) to draw; (langue) to stick out; (en faisant feu: balle, coup) to fire; (: animal) to shoot; (journal, livre, photo) to print; (Football: corner etc) to take ▷ vi (faire feu) to fire; (faire du tir, Football) to shoot; **se tirer** vi (fam) to push off; **s'en ~** (éviter le pire) to get off; (survivre) to pull through; (se débrouiller) to manage; **~ qch de** (extraire) to take ou pull sth out of; **~ qn de** (embarras etc) to help ou get sb out of; **~ sur** (corde) to pull on ou at; (faire feu sur) to shoot ou fire at; (pipe) to draw on; (approcher de: couleur) to verge ou border on; **~ à l'arc/la carabine** to shoot with a bow and arrow/with a rifle; **~ à sa fin** to be drawing to a close; **~ qch au clair** to clear sth up; **~ au sort** to draw lots; **~ parti de** to take advantage of; **~ profit de** to profit from; **~ les cartes** to read ou tell the cards

tiret [tiʀe] nm dash

tireur [tiʀœʀ] nm gunman; **tireur d'élite** marksman

tiroir [tiʀwaʀ] nm drawer; **tiroir-caisse** nm till

tisane [tizan] nf herb tea

tisser [tise] vt to weave

tissu [tisy] nm fabric, material, cloth no pl; (Anat, Bio) tissue; **tissu-éponge** nm (terry) towelling no pl

titre [titʀ] nm (gén) title; (de journal) headline; (diplôme) qualification; (Comm) security; **en ~** (champion) official; **à juste ~** rightly; **à quel ~?** on what grounds?; **à aucun ~** on no account; **au même ~ (que)** in the same way (as); **à ~**

d'information for (your) information; **à ~ gracieux** free of charge; **à ~ d'essai** on a trial basis; **à ~ privé** in a private capacity; **titre de propriété** title deed; **titre de transport** ticket

tituber [titybe] vi to stagger (along)

titulaire [titylɛʀ] adj (Admin) with tenure ▷ nm/f (de permis) holder; **être ~ de** (diplôme, permis) to hold

toast [tost] nm slice ou piece of toast; (de bienvenue) (welcoming) toast; **porter un ~ à qn** to propose ou drink a toast to sb

toboggan [tɔbɔgɑ̃] nm slide; (Auto) flyover

toc [tɔk] excl: **~, ~** knock knock ▷ nm: **en ~** fake

tocsin [tɔksɛ̃] nm alarm (bell)

tohu-bohu [tɔybɔy] nm hubbub

toi [twa] pron you

toile [twal] nf (tableau) canvas; **de** ou **en ~** (pantalon) cotton; (sac) canvas; **la T~** (Internet) the Web; **toile cirée** oilcloth; **toile d'araignée** cobweb; **toile de fond** (fig) backdrop

toilette [twalɛt] nf (habits) outfit; **toilettes** nfpl (w.-c.) toilet sg; **faire sa ~** to have a wash, get washed; **articles de ~** toiletries; **où sont les ~s?** where's the toilet?

toi-même [twamɛm] pron yourself

toit [twa] nm roof; **toit ouvrant** sunroof

toiture [twatyʀ] nf roof

Tokyo [tɔkjo] n Tokyo

tôle [tol] nf (plaque) steel ou iron sheet; **tôle ondulée** corrugated iron

tolérable [tɔleʀabl] adj tolerable

tolérant, e [tɔleʀɑ̃, ɑ̃t] adj tolerant

tolérer [tɔleʀe] vt to tolerate; (Admin: hors taxe etc) to allow

tollé [tɔ(l)le] nm outcry

tomate [tɔmat] nf tomato; **~s farcies** stuffed tomatoes

tombe [tɔ̃b] nf (sépulture) grave; (avec monument) tomb

tombeau, x [tɔ̃bo] nm tomb

tombée [tɔ̃be] nf: **à la ~ de la nuit** at nightfall

tomber [tɔ̃be] vi to fall; (fièvre, vent) to drop; **laisser ~** (objet) to drop; (personne) to let down; (activité) to give up; **laisse ~!** forget it!; **faire ~** to knock over; **~ sur** (rencontrer) to bump into; **~ de fatigue/sommeil** to drop from exhaustion/be falling asleep on one's feet; **ça tombe bien** that's come at the right time; **il est bien tombé** he's been lucky; **~ à l'eau** (projet) to fall through; **~ en panne** to break down

tombola [tɔ̃bɔla] nf raffle

tome [tɔm] nm volume

ton¹, ta [tɔ̃, ta] (pl **tes**) adj your

ton² [tɔ̃] nm (gén) tone; (couleur) shade, tone; **de bon ~** in good taste

tonalité [tɔnalite] nf (au téléphone) dialling tone

tondeuse [tɔ̃døz] nf (à gazon) (lawn)mower;

(du coiffeur) clippers pl; (pour les moutons) shears pl

tondre [tɔ̃dʀ] vt (pelouse, herbe) to mow; (haie) to cut, clip; (mouton, toison) to shear; (cheveux) to crop

tongs [tɔ̃g] nfpl flip-flops

tonifier [tɔnifje] vt (peau, organisme) to tone up

tonique [tɔnik] adj fortifying ▷ nm tonic

tonne [tɔn] nf metric ton, tonne

tonneau, x [tɔno] nm (à vin, cidre) barrel; **faire des ~x** (voiture, avion) to roll over

tonnelle [tɔnɛl] nf bower, arbour

tonner [tɔne] vi to thunder; **il tonne** it is thundering, there's some thunder

tonnerre [tɔnɛʀ] nm thunder

tonus [tɔnys] nm energy

top [tɔp] nm: **au 3ème ~** at the 3rd stroke ▷ adj: **~ secret** top secret

topinambour [tɔpinɑ̃buʀ] nm Jerusalem artichoke

torche [tɔʀʃ] nf torch

torchon [tɔʀʃɔ̃] nm cloth; (à vaisselle) tea towel ou cloth

tordre [tɔʀdʀ] vt (chiffon) to wring; (barre, fig: visage) to twist; **se tordre** vi: **se ~ le poignet/ la cheville** to twist one's wrist/ankle; **se ~ de douleur/rire** to be doubled up with pain/ laughter; **tordu, e** adj bent; (fig) crazy

tornade [tɔʀnad] nf tornado

torrent [tɔʀɑ̃] nm mountain stream

torsade [tɔʀsad] nf: **un pull à ~s** a cable sweater

torse [tɔʀs] nm chest; (Anat, Sculpture) torso; **~ nu** stripped to the waist

tort [tɔʀ] nm (défaut) fault; **torts** nmpl (Jur) fault sg; **avoir ~** to be wrong; **être dans son ~** to be in the wrong; **donner ~ à qn** to lay the blame on sb; **causer du ~ à qn** to harm sb; **à ~** wrongly; **à ~ et à travers** wildly

torticolis [tɔʀtikɔli] nm stiff neck

tortiller [tɔʀtije] vt to twist; (moustache) to twirl; **se tortiller** vi to wriggle; (en dansant) to wiggle

tortionnaire [tɔʀsjɔnɛʀ] nm torturer

tortue [tɔʀty] nf tortoise; (d'eau douce) terrapin; (d'eau de mer) turtle

tortueux, -euse [tɔʀtɥø, øz] adj (rue) twisting; (fig) tortuous

torture [tɔʀtyʀ] nf torture; **torturer** vt to torture; (fig) to torment

tôt [to] adv early; **~ ou tard** sooner or later; **si ~** so early; (déjà) so soon; **plus ~** earlier; **au plus ~** at the earliest

total, e, -aux [tɔtal, o] adj, nm total; **au ~** in total; (fig) on the whole; **faire le ~** to work out the total; **totalement** adv totally; **totaliser** vt to total; **totalitaire** adj totalitarian; **totalité** nf: **la totalité de** all (of); the whole

+sg; **en totalité** entirely

toubib [tubib] (fam) nm doctor

touchant, e [tuʃɑ̃, ɑ̃t] adj touching

touche [tuʃ] nf (de piano, de machine à écrire) key; (de téléphone) button; (Peinture etc) stroke, touch; (fig: de nostalgie) touch; (Football: aussi: **remise en ~**) throw-in; (aussi: **ligne de ~**) touch-line; **touche dièse** (de téléphone, clavier) hash key

toucher [tuʃe] nm touch ▷ vt to touch; (palper) to feel; (atteindre: d'un coup de feu etc) to hit; (concerner) to concern, affect; (contacter) to reach, contact; (recevoir: récompense) to receive, get; (: salaire) to draw, get; (: chèque) to cash; **se toucher** (être en contact) to touch; **au ~** to the touch; **~ à** to touch; (concerner) to have to do with, concern; **je vais lui en ~ un mot** I'll have a word with him about it; **~ au but** (fig) to near one's goal; **~ à sa fin** to be drawing to a close

touffe [tuf] nf tuft

touffu, e [tufy] adj thick, dense

toujours [tuʒuʀ] adv always; (encore) still; (constamment) forever; **~ plus** more and more; **pour ~** forever; **~ est-il que** the fact remains that; **essaie ~** (you can) try anyway

toupie [tupi] nf (spinning) top

tour¹ [tuʀ] nf tower; (immeuble) high-rise block (BRIT) ou building (US); (Échecs) castle, rook; **tour de contrôle** nf control tower; **la tour Eiffel** the Eiffel Tower

tour² [tuʀ] nm (excursion) trip; (à pied) stroll, walk; (en voiture) run, ride; (Sport: aussi: **~ de piste**) lap; (d'être servi ou de jouer etc) turn; (de roue etc) revolution; (Pol: aussi: **~ de scrutin**) ballot; (ruse, de prestidigitation) trick; (de potier) wheel; (à bois, métaux) lathe; (circonférence): **de 3 m de ~** 3 m round, with a circumference ou girth of 3 m; **faire le ~ de** to go round; (à pied) to walk round; **c'est au ~ de Renée** it's Renée's turn; **à ~ de rôle, ~ à ~** in turn; **tour de chant** nm song recital; **tour de force** tour de force; **tour de garde** nm spell of duty; **tour d'horizon** nm (fig) general survey; **tour de taille/tête** nm waist/head measurement; **un 33 tours** an LP; **un 45 tours** a single

tourbe [tuʀb] nf peat

tourbillon [tuʀbijɔ̃] nm whirlwind; (d'eau) whirlpool; (fig) whirl, swirl; **tourbillonner** vi to whirl (round)

tourelle [tuʀɛl] nf turret

tourisme [tuʀism] nm tourism; **agence de ~** tourist agency; **faire du ~** to go touring; (en ville) to go sightseeing; **touriste** nm/f tourist; **touristique** adj tourist cpd; (région) touristic

tourment [tuʀmɑ̃] nm torment; **tourmenter** vt to torment; **se tourmenter** to fret, worry o.s.

tournage [tuʀnaʒ] nm (Cinéma) shooting

tournant [tuʀnɑ̃] nm (de route) bend; (fig)

turning point

tournée [turne] *nf* (*du facteur etc*) round; (*d'artiste, politicien*) tour; (*au café*) round (of drinks)

tourner [turne] *vt* to turn; (*sauce, mélange*) to stir; (*Cinéma: faire les prises de vues*) to shoot; (: *produire*) to make ▷ *vi* to turn; (*moteur*) to run; (*taximètre*) to tick away; (*lait etc*) to turn (sour); **se tourner** *vi* to turn round; **tournez à gauche/droite au prochain carrefour** turn left/right at the next junction; **mal ~** to go wrong; **~ autour de** to go round; (*péj*) to hang round; **~ à/en** to turn into; **~ qn en ridicule** to ridicule sb; **~ le dos à** (*mouvement*) to turn one's back on; (*position*) to have one's back to; **~ de l'œil** to pass out; **se ~ vers** to turn towards; (*fig*) to turn to; **se ~ les pouces** to twiddle one's thumbs

tournesol [turnəsɔl] *nm* sunflower

tournevis [turnəvis] *nm* screwdriver

tournoi [turnwa] *nm* tournament

tournure [turnyr] *nf* (*Ling*) turn of phrase; (*évolution*): **la ~ de qch** the way sth is developing; **tournure d'esprit** turn *ou* cast of mind

tourte [turt] *nf* pie

tourterelle [turtərɛl] *nf* turtledove

tous [tu] *adj, pron voir* **tout**

Toussaint [tusɛ̃] *nf*: **la ~** All Saints' Day

tousser [tuse] *vi* to cough

 MOT-CLÉ

tout, e [tu, tut] (*mpl* **tous**, *fpl* **toutes**) *adj*
1 (*avec article singulier*) all; **tout le lait** all the milk; **toute la nuit** all night, the whole night; **tout le livre** the whole book; **tout un pain** a whole loaf; **tout le temps** all the time; the whole time; **tout le monde** everybody; **c'est tout le contraire** it's quite the opposite
2 (*avec article pluriel*) every, all; **tous les livres** all the books; **toutes les nuits** every night; **toutes les fois** every time; **toutes les trois/deux semaines** every third/other *ou* second week, every three/two weeks; **tous les deux** both *ou* each of us (*ou* them *ou* you); **toutes les trois** all three of us (*ou* them *ou* you)
3 (*sans article*): **à tout âge** at any age; **pour toute nourriture, il avait ...** his only food was ...
▷ *pron* everything, all; **il a tout fait**

he's done everything; **je les vois tous** I can see them all *ou* all of them; **nous y sommes tous allés** all of us went, we all went; **c'est tout** that's all; **en tout** in all; **tout ce qu'il sait** all he knows
▷ *nm* whole; **le tout** all of it (*ou* them); **le tout est de ...** the main thing is to ...; **pas du tout** not at all
▷ *adv* **1** (*très, complètement*) very; **tout près** very near; **le tout premier** the very first; **tout seul** all alone; **le livre tout entier** the whole book; **tout en haut** right at the top; **tout droit** straight ahead
2: **tout en** while; **tout en travaillant** while working, as he *etc* works *ou* worked
3: **tout d'abord** first of all; **tout à coup** suddenly; **tout à fait** absolutely; **tout à l'heure** a short while ago; (*futur*) in a short while, shortly; **à tout à l'heure!** see you later!; **tout de même** all the same; **tout de suite** immediately, straight away; **tout simplement** quite simply

toutefois [tutfwa] *adv* however

toutes [tut] *adj, pron voir* **tout**

tout-terrain [tuterɛ̃] *adj*: **vélo ~** mountain bike; **véhicule ~** four-wheel drive

toux [tu] *nf* cough

toxicomane [tɔksikɔman] *nm/f* drug addict

toxique [tɔksik] *adj* toxic

trac [trak] *nm* (*au théâtre, en public*) stage fright; (*aux examens*) nerves *pl*; **avoir le ~** (*au théâtre, en public*) to have stage fright; (*aux examens*) to be feeling nervous

tracasser [trakase] *vt* to worry, bother; **se tracasser** to worry

trace [tras] *nf* (*empreintes*) tracks *pl*; (*marques, aussi fig*) mark; (*quantité infime, indice, vestige*) trace; **traces de pas** footprints

tracer [trase] *vt* to draw; (*piste*) to open up

tract [trakt] *nm* tract, pamphlet

tracteur [traktœr] *nm* tractor

traction [traksjɔ̃] *nf*: **~ avant/arrière** front-wheel/rear-wheel drive

tradition [tradisjɔ̃] *nf* tradition; **traditionnel, le** *adj* traditional

traducteur, -trice [tradyktœr, tris] *nm/f* translator

traduction [tradyksjɔ̃] *nf* translation

traduire [traduir] *vt* to translate; (*exprimer*) to convey; **~ qn en justice** to bring sb before the courts; **pouvez-vous me ~ ceci?** can you translate this for me?

trafic [trafik] *nm* traffic; **trafic d'armes** arms dealing; **trafiquant, e** *nm/f* trafficker; (*d'armes*) dealer; **trafiquer** (*péj*) *vt* (*vin*) to doctor; (*moteur, document*) to tamper with

tragédie [traʒedi] *nf* tragedy; **tragique** *adj* tragic

trahir [tʀaiʀ] vt to betray; **trahison** nf
betrayal; (Jur) treason

train [tʀɛ̃] nm (Rail) train; (allure) pace; **être
en ~ de faire qch** to be doing sth; **c'est bien
le ~ pour ...?** is this the train for ...?; **train
d'atterrissage** undercarriage; **train de vie**
lifestyle; **train électrique** (jouet) (electric)
train set

traîne [tʀɛn] nf (de robe) train; **être à la ~** to
lag behind

traîneau, x [tʀɛno] nm sleigh, sledge

traîner [tʀene] vt (remorque) to pull; (enfant,
chien) to drag ou trail along ▷ vi (robe, manteau)
to trail; (être en désordre) to lie around; (aller
lentement) to dawdle (along); (vagabonder, agir
lentement) to hang about; (durer) to drag on;
se traîner vi: **se ~ par terre** to crawl (on the
ground); **~ les pieds** to drag one's feet

train-train [tʀɛ̃tʀɛ̃] nm humdrum routine

traire [tʀɛʀ] vt to milk

trait [tʀɛ] nm (ligne) line; (de dessin) stroke;
(caractéristique) feature, trait; **traits** nmpl (du
visage) features; **d'un ~** (boire) in one gulp; **de
~** (animal) draught; **avoir ~ à** to concern; **trait
d'union** hyphen

traitant, e [tʀɛtɑ̃, ɑ̃t] adj (shampooing)
medicated; **votre médecin ~** your usual ou
family doctor

traite [tʀɛt] nf (Comm) draft; (Agr) milking;
d'une ~ without stopping

traité [tʀete] nm treaty

traitement [tʀɛtmɑ̃] nm treatment;
(salaire) salary; **traitement de données**
data processing; **traitement de texte** word
processing; (logiciel) word processing package

traiter [tʀete] vt to treat; (qualifier): **~ qn
d'idiot** to call sb a fool ▷ vi to deal; **~ de** to
deal with

traiteur [tʀetœʀ] nm caterer

traître, -esse [tʀetʀ, tʀetʀes] adj (dangereux)
treacherous ▷ nm traitor

trajectoire [tʀaʒektwaʀ] nf path

trajet [tʀaʒe] nm (parcours, voyage) journey;
(itinéraire) route; (distance à parcourir) distance;
il y a une heure de ~ the journey takes one
hour

trampoline [tʀɑ̃pɔlin] nm trampoline

tramway [tʀamwe] nm tram(way); (voiture)
tram(car) (BRIT), streetcar (US)

tranchant, e [tʀɑ̃ʃɑ̃, ɑ̃t] adj sharp; (fig)
peremptory ▷ nm (d'un couteau) cutting edge;
(de la main) edge; **à double ~** double-edged

tranche [tʀɑ̃ʃ] nf (morceau) slice; (arête) edge; **~
d'âge/de salaires** age/wage bracket

tranché, e [tʀɑ̃ʃe] adj (couleurs) distinct;
(opinions) clear-cut

trancher [tʀɑ̃ʃe] vt to cut, sever ▷ vi to take a
decision; **~ avec** to contrast sharply with

tranquille [tʀɑ̃kil] adj quiet; (rassuré) easy in

one's mind, with one's mind at rest; **se tenir
~** (enfant) to be quiet; **laisse-moi/laisse-ça ~**
leave me/it alone; **avoir la conscience ~** to
have a clear conscience; **tranquillisant** nm
tranquillizer; **tranquillité** nf peace (and
quiet); (d'esprit) peace of mind

transférer [tʀɑ̃sfeʀe] vt to transfer;
transfert nm transfer

transformation [tʀɑ̃sfɔʀmasjɔ̃] nf change,
alteration; (radicale) transformation; (Rugby)
conversion; **transformations** nfpl (travaux)
alterations

transformer [tʀɑ̃sfɔʀme] vt to change;
(radicalement) to transform; (vêtement) to
alter; (matière première, appartement, Rugby) to
convert; **(se) ~ en** to turn into

transfusion [tʀɑ̃sfyzjɔ̃] nf: **~ sanguine** blood
transfusion

transgénique [tʀɑ̃sʒenik] adj transgenic

transgresser [tʀɑ̃sgʀese] vt to contravene

transi, e [tʀɑ̃zi] adj numb (with cold), chilled
to the bone

transiger [tʀɑ̃ziʒe] vi to compromise

transit [tʀɑ̃zit] nm transit; **transiter** vi to
pass in transit

transition [tʀɑ̃zisjɔ̃] nf transition;
transitoire adj transitional

transmettre [tʀɑ̃smetʀ] vt (passer): **~ qch
à qn** to pass sth on to sb; (Tech, Tél, Méd)
to transmit; (TV, Radio: retransmettre) to
broadcast; **transmission** nf transmission

transparent, e [tʀɑ̃spaʀɑ̃, ɑ̃t] adj
transparent

transpercer [tʀɑ̃speʀse] vt (froid, pluie) to go
through, pierce; (balle) to go through

transpiration [tʀɑ̃spiʀasjɔ̃] nf perspiration

transpirer [tʀɑ̃spiʀe] vi to perspire

transplanter [tʀɑ̃splɑ̃te] vt (Méd, Bot) to
transplant

transport [tʀɑ̃spɔʀ] nm transport;
transports en commun public transport sg;
transporter vt to carry, move; (Comm) to
transport, convey; **transporteur** nm haulage
contractor (BRIT), trucker (US)

transvaser [tʀɑ̃svaze] vt to decant

transversal, e, -aux [tʀɑ̃sveʀsal, o] adj (rue)
which runs across; **coupe ~e** cross section

trapèze [tʀapez] nm (au cirque) trapeze

trappe [tʀap] nf trap door

trapu, e [tʀapy] adj squat, stocky

traquenard [tʀaknaʀ] nm trap

traquer [tʀake] vt to track down; (harceler)
to hound

traumatiser [tʀomatize] vt to traumatize

travail, -aux [tʀavaj] nm (gén) work; (tâche,
métier) work no pl, job; (Écon, Méd) labour; **être
sans ~** (employé) to be unemployed; voir aussi
travaux; travail (au) noir moonlighting

travailler [tʀavaje] vi to work; (bois) to warp

▷ *vt* (*bois, métal*) to work; (*objet d'art, discipline*) to work on; **cela le travaille** it is on his mind; **travailleur, -euse** *adj* hard-working ▷ *nm/f* worker; **travailleur social** social worker; **travailliste** *adj* ≈ Labour *cpd*

travaux [tʀavo] *nmpl* (*de réparation, agricoles etc*) work *sg*; (*sur route*) roadworks *pl*; (*de construction*) building (work); **travaux des champs** farmwork *sg*; **travaux dirigés** (*Scol*) tutorial *sg*; **travaux forcés** hard labour *no pl*; **travaux manuels** (*Scol*) handicrafts; **travaux ménagers** housework *no pl*; **travaux pratiques** (*Scol*) practical work; (*en laboratoire*) lab work

travers [tʀavɛʀ] *nm* fault, failing; **en ~ (de)** across; **au ~ (de)/à ~** through; **de ~** (*nez, bouche*) crooked; (*chapeau*) askew; **comprendre de ~** to misunderstand; **regarder de ~** (*fig*) to look askance at

traverse [tʀavɛʀs] *nf* (*de voie ferrée*) sleeper; **chemin de ~** shortcut

traversée [tʀavɛʀse] *nf* crossing; **combien de temps dure la ~?** how long does the crossing take?

traverser [tʀavɛʀse] *vt* (*gén*) to cross; (*ville, tunnel, aussi: percer, fig*) to go through; (*suj: ligne, trait*) to run across

traversin [tʀavɛʀsɛ̃] *nm* bolster

travesti [tʀavɛsti] *nm* transvestite

trébucher [tʀebyʃe] *vi*: **~ (sur)** to stumble (over), trip (against)

trèfle [tʀɛfl] *nm* (*Bot*) clover; (*Cartes: couleur*) clubs *pl*; (*: carte*) club; **~ à quatre feuilles** four-leaf clover

treize [tʀɛz] *num* thirteen; **treizième** *num* thirteenth

tréma [tʀema] *nm* diaeresis

tremblement [tʀɑ̃bləmɑ̃] *nm*: **tremblement de terre** earthquake

trembler [tʀɑ̃ble] *vi* to tremble, shake; **~ de** (*froid, fièvre*) to shiver *ou* tremble with; (*peur*) to shake *ou* tremble with; **~ pour qn** to fear for sb

trémousser [tʀemuse]: **se trémousser** *vi* to jig about, wriggle about

trempé, e [tʀɑ̃pe] *adj* soaking (wet), drenched; (*Tech*) tempered

tremper [tʀɑ̃pe] *vt* to soak, drench; (*aussi:* **faire ~, mettre à ~**) to soak; (*plonger*): **~ qch dans** to dip sth in(to) ▷ *vi* to soak; (*fig*): **~ dans** to be involved *ou* have a hand in; **se tremper** *vi* to have a quick dip

tremplin [tʀɑ̃plɛ̃] *nm* springboard; (*Ski*) ski-jump

trentaine [tʀɑ̃tɛn] *nf*: **une ~ (de)** thirty or so, about thirty; **avoir la ~** (*âge*) to be around thirty

trente [tʀɑ̃t] *num* thirty; **être sur son ~ et un** to be wearing one's Sunday best; **trentième** *num* thirtieth

trépidant, e [tʀepidɑ̃, ɑ̃t] *adj* (*fig: rythme*) pulsating; (*: vie*) hectic

trépigner [tʀepiɲe] *vi* to stamp (one's feet)

très [tʀɛ] *adv* very; much +*pp*, highly +*pp*

trésor [tʀezɔʀ] *nm* treasure; **Trésor (public)** public revenue; **trésorerie** *nf* (*gestion*) accounts *pl*; (*bureaux*) accounts department; **difficultés de trésorerie** cash problems, shortage of cash *ou* funds; **trésorier, -ière** *nm/f* treasurer

tressaillir [tʀesajiʀ] *vi* to shiver, shudder

tressauter [tʀesote] *vi* to start, jump

tresse [tʀɛs] *nf* braid, plait; **tresser** *vt* (*cheveux*) to braid, plait; (*fil, jonc*) to plait; (*corbeille*) to weave; (*corde*) to twist

tréteau, x [tʀeto] *nm* trestle

treuil [tʀœj] *nm* winch

trêve [tʀɛv] *nf* (*Mil, Pol*) truce; (*fig*) respite; **~ de ...** enough of this ...

tri [tʀi] *nm*: **faire le ~ (de)** to sort out; **le (bureau de) ~** (*Postes*) the sorting office

triangle [tʀijɑ̃gl] *nm* triangle; **triangulaire** *adj* triangular

tribord [tʀibɔʀ] *nm*: **à ~** starboard, on the starboard side

tribu [tʀiby] *nf* tribe

tribunal, -aux [tʀibynal, o] *nm* (*Jur*) court; (*Mil*) tribunal

tribune [tʀibyn] *nf* (*estrade*) platform, rostrum; (*débat*) forum; (*d'église, de tribunal*) gallery; (*de stade*) stand

tribut [tʀiby] *nm* tribute

tributaire [tʀibytɛʀ] *adj*: **être ~ de** to be dependent on

tricher [tʀiʃe] *vi* to cheat; **tricheur, -euse** *nm/f* cheat(er)

tricolore [tʀikɔlɔʀ] *adj* three-coloured; (*français*) red, white and blue

tricot [tʀiko] *nm* (*technique, ouvrage*) knitting *no pl*; (*vêtement*) jersey, sweater; **~ de peau** vest; **tricoter** *vt* to knit

tricycle [tʀisikl] *nm* tricycle

trier [tʀije] *vt* to sort out; (*Postes, fruits*) to sort

trimestre [tʀimɛstʀ] *nm* (*Scol*) term; (*Comm*) quarter; **trimestriel, le** *adj* quarterly; (*Scol*) end-of-term

trinquer [tʀɛ̃ke] *vi* to clink glasses

triomphe [tʀijɔ̃f] *nm* triumph; **triompher** *vi* to triumph, win; **triompher de** to triumph over, overcome

tripes [tʀip] *nfpl* (*Culin*) tripe *sg*

triple [tʀipl] *adj* triple ▷ *nm*: **le ~ (de)** (*comparaison*) three times as much (as); **en ~ exemplaire** in triplicate; **tripler** *vi, vt* to triple, treble

triplés, -ées [tʀiple] *nm/fpl* triplets

tripoter [tʀipɔte] *vt* to fiddle with

triste [tʀist] *adj* sad; (*couleur, temps, journée*) dreary; (*péj*): **~ personnage/affaire** sorry

t

individual/affair; **tristesse** nf sadness

trivial, e, -aux [tʀivjal, jo] adj coarse, crude; (commun) mundane

troc [tʀɔk] nm barter

trognon [tʀɔɲɔ̃] nm (de fruit) core; (de légume) stalk

trois [tʀwa] num three; **troisième** num third ▷ nf (Scol) year 10 (BRIT), ninth grade (US); **le troisième âge** (période de vie) one's retirement years; (personnes âgées) senior citizens pl

trombe [tʀɔ̃b] nf: **des ~s d'eau** a downpour; **en ~** like a whirlwind

trombone [tʀɔ̃bɔn] nm (Mus) trombone; (de bureau) paper clip

trompe [tʀɔ̃p] nf (d'éléphant) trunk; (Mus) trumpet, horn

tromper [tʀɔ̃pe] vt to deceive; (vigilance, poursuivants) to elude; **se tromper** vi to make a mistake, be mistaken; **se ~ de voiture/jour** to take the wrong car/get the day wrong; **se ~ de 3 cm/20 euros** to be out by 3 cm/20 euros; **je me suis trompé de route** I took the wrong road

trompette [tʀɔ̃pɛt] nf trumpet; **en ~** (nez) turned-up

trompeur, -euse [tʀɔ̃pœʀ, øz] adj deceptive

tronc [tʀɔ̃] nm (Bot, Anat) trunk; (d'église) collection box

tronçon [tʀɔ̃sɔ̃] nm section; **tronçonner** vt to saw up; **tronçonneuse** nf chainsaw

trône [tʀon] nm throne

trop [tʀo] adv (+vb) too much; (+adjectif, adverbe) too; **~ (nombreux)** too many; **~ peu (nombreux)** too few; **~ (souvent)** too often; **~ (longtemps)** (for) too long; **~ de** (nombre) too many; (quantité) too much; **de ~, en ~: des livres en ~** a few books too many; **du lait en ~** too much milk; **3 livres/3 euros de ~** 3 books too many/3 euros too much; **ça coûte ~ cher** it's too expensive

tropical, e, -aux [tʀɔpikal, o] adj tropical

tropique [tʀɔpik] nm tropic

trop-plein [tʀoplɛ̃] nm (tuyau) overflow ou outlet (pipe); (liquide) overflow

troquer [tʀɔke] vt: **~ qch contre** to barter ou trade sth for; (fig) to swap sth for

trot [tʀo] nm trot; **trotter** vi to trot

trottinette [tʀɔtinɛt] nf (child's) scooter

trottoir [tʀɔtwaʀ] nm pavement (BRIT), sidewalk (US); **faire le ~** (péj) to walk the streets; **trottoir roulant** moving walkway, travellator

trou [tʀu] nm hole; (fig) gap; (Comm) deficit; **trou d'air** air pocket; **trou de mémoire** blank, lapse of memory

troublant, e [tʀublɑ̃, ɑ̃t] adj disturbing

trouble [tʀubl] adj (liquide) cloudy; (image, photo) blurred; (affaire) shady, murky ▷ adv: **voir ~** to have blurred vision ▷ nm agitation; **troubles** nmpl (Pol) disturbances, troubles, unrest sg; (Méd) trouble sg, disorders; **trouble-fête** nm spoilsport

troubler [tʀuble] vt to disturb; (liquide) to make cloudy; (intriguer) to bother; **se troubler** vi (personne) to become flustered ou confused

trouer [tʀue] vt to make a hole (ou holes) in

trouille [tʀuj] (fam) nf: **avoir la ~** to be scared to death

troupe [tʀup] nf troop; **troupe (de théâtre)** (theatrical) company

troupeau, x [tʀupo] nm (de moutons) flock; (de vaches) herd

trousse [tʀus] nf case, kit; (d'écolier) pencil case; **aux ~s de** (fig) on the heels ou tail of; **trousse à outils** toolkit; **trousse de toilette** toilet bag

trousseau, x [tʀuso] nm (de mariée) trousseau; **trousseau de clefs** bunch of keys

trouvaille [tʀuvaj] nf find

trouver [tʀuve] vt to find; (rendre visite): **aller/venir ~ qn** to go/come and see sb; **se trouver** vi (être) to be; **je trouve que** I find ou think that; **~ à boire/critiquer** to find something to drink/criticize; **se ~ mal** to pass out

truand [tʀyɑ̃] nm gangster; **truander** vt: **se faire truander** to be swindled

truc [tʀyk] nm (astuce) way, trick; (de cinéma, prestidigitateur) trick, effect; (chose) thing, thingumajig; **avoir le ~** to have the knack; **c'est pas mon ~** (fam) it's not really my thing

truffe [tʀyf] nf truffle; (nez) nose

truffé, e [tʀyfe] adj (Culin) garnished with truffles; **~ de** (fig: citations) peppered with; (: fautes) riddled with; (: pièges) bristling with

truie [tʀyi] nf sow

truite [tʀyit] nf trout inv

truquage [tʀykaʒ] nm special effects pl

truquer [tʀyke] vt (élections, serrure, dés) to fix

TSVP sigle (= tournez svp) PTO

TTC sigle (= toutes taxes comprises) inclusive of tax

tu¹ [ty] pron you; **dire tu à qn** to use the "tu" form to sb

tu², e [ty] pp de **taire**

tuba [tyba] nm (Mus) tuba; (Sport) snorkel

tube [tyb] nm tube; (chanson) hit

tuberculose [tybɛʀkyloz] nf tuberculosis

tuer [tɥe] vt to kill; **se tuer** vi to be killed; (suicide) to kill o.s.; **se ~ au travail** (fig) to work o.s. to death; **tuerie** nf slaughter no pl

tue-tête [tytɛt]: **à ~** adv at the top of one's voice

tueur [tɥœʀ] nm killer; **tueur à gages** hired killer

tuile [tɥil] nf tile; (fam) spot of bad luck, blow

tulipe [tylip] nf tulip

tuméfié, e [tymefje] adj puffed-up, swollen

tumeur [tymœʀ] nf growth, tumour

tumulte [tymylt] *nm* commotion;
tumultueux, -euse *adj* stormy, turbulent
tunique [tynik] *nf* tunic
Tunis [tynis] *n* Tunis
Tunisie [tynizi] *nf*: **la ~** Tunisia; **tunisien, ne**
adj Tunisian ▷ *nm/f*: **Tunisien, ne** Tunisian
tunnel [tynɛl] *nm* tunnel; **le ~ sous la
Manche** the Channel Tunnel
turbulent, e [tyʀbylɑ̃, ɑ̃t] *adj* boisterous,
unruly
turc, turque [tyʀk] *adj* Turkish ▷ *nm/f*: **T~,
Turque** Turk/Turkish woman ▷ *nm* (*Ling*)
Turkish
turf [tyʀf] *nm* racing; **turfiste** *nm/f* racegoer
Turquie [tyʀki] *nf*: **la ~** Turkey
turquoise [tyʀkwaz] *nf* turquoise ▷ *adj inv*
turquoise
tutelle [tytɛl] *nf* (*Jur*) guardianship; (*Pol*)
trusteeship; **sous la ~ de** (*fig*) under the
supervision of
tuteur [tytœʀ] *nm* (*Jur*) guardian; (*de plante*)
stake, support
tutoyer [tytwaje] *vt*: **~ qn** to address sb as "tu"
tuyau, x [tɥijo] *nm* pipe; (*flexible*) tube; (*fam*)
tip; **tuyau d'arrosage** hosepipe; **tuyau
d'échappement** exhaust pipe; **tuyauterie**
nf piping *no pl*
TVA *sigle f* (= *taxe à la valeur ajoutée*) VAT
tympan [tɛ̃pɑ̃] *nm* (*Anat*) eardrum
type [tip] *nm* type; (*fam*) chap, guy ▷ *adj*
typical, classic
typé, e [tipe] *adj* ethnic
typique [tipik] *adj* typical
tyran [tiʀɑ̃] *nm* tyrant; **tyrannique** *adj*
tyrannical
tzigane [dzigan] *adj* gipsy, tzigane

ulcère [ylsɛʀ] *nm* ulcer
ultérieur, e [ylteʀjœʀ] *adj* later, subsequent;
remis à une date ~e postponed to a later
date; **ultérieurement** *adv* later, subsequently
ultime [yltim] *adj* final

 MOT-CLÉ

un, une [œ̃, yn] *art indéf* a; (*devant voyelle*) an;
un garçon/vieillard a boy/an old man; **une
fille** a girl
▷ *pron* one; **l'un des meilleurs** one of the
best; **l'un ..., l'autre** (the) one ..., the other;
les uns ..., les autres some ..., others; **l'un et
l'autre** both
(of them); **l'un ou l'autre** either (of them);
l'un l'autre each other; **les
uns les autres** one another; **pas un seul** not a
single one; **un par un** one by one
▷ *num* one; **un pamplemousse seulement**
one grapefruit only, just one grapefruit
▷ *nf*: **la une** (*Presse*) the front page

unanime [ynanim] *adj* unanimous;
unanimité *nf*: **à l'unanimité** unanimously
uni, e [yni] *adj* (*ton, tissu*) plain; (*surface*)
smooth, even; (*famille*) close(-knit); (*pays*)
united
unifier [ynifje] *vt* to unite, unify
uniforme [ynifɔʀm] *adj* uniform; (*surface,*

ton) even ▷ *nm* uniform; **uniformiser** *vt* (*systèmes*) to standardize

union [ynjɔ̃] *nf* union; **union de consommateurs** consumers' association; **union libre**: **vivre en union libre** (*en concubinage*) to cohabit; **Union européenne** European Union; **Union soviétique** Soviet Union

unique [ynik] *adj* (*seul*) only; (*exceptionnel*) unique; (*le même*): **un prix/système ~** a single price/system; **fils/fille ~** only son/daughter, only child; **sens ~** one-way street; **uniquement** *adv* only, solely; (*juste*) only, merely

unir [ynir] *vt* (*nations*) to unite; (*en mariage*) to unite, join together; **s'unir** *vi* to unite; (*en mariage*) to be joined together

unitaire [yniter] *adj*: **prix ~** unit price

unité [ynite] *nf* unit; (*harmonie, cohésion*) unity

univers [yniver] *nm* universe; **universel, le** *adj* universal

universitaire [yniversiter] *adj* university *cpd*; (*diplôme, études*) academic, university *cpd* ▷ *nm/f* academic

université [yniversite] *nf* university

urbain, e [yrbɛ̃, ɛn] *adj* urban, city *cpd*, town *cpd*; **urbanisme** *nm* town planning

urgence [yrʒɑ̃s] *nf* urgency; (*Méd etc*) emergency; **d'~** *adj* emergency *cpd* ▷ *adv* as a matter of urgency; **(service des) ~s** casualty

urgent, e [yrʒɑ̃, ɑ̃t] *adj* urgent

urine [yrin] *nf* urine; **urinoir** *nm* (public) urinal

urne [yrn] *nf* (*électorale*) ballot box; (*vase*) urn

urticaire [yrtiker] *nf* nettle rash

us [ys] *nmpl*: **us et coutumes** (habits and) customs

usage [yzaʒ] *nm* (*emploi, utilisation*) use; (*coutume*) custom; **à l'~** with use; **à l'~ de** (*pour*) for (use of); **en ~** in use; **hors d'~** out of service; **à ~ interne** (*Méd*) to be taken (internally); **à ~ externe** (*Méd*) for external use only; **usagé, e** *adj* (*usé*) worn; **usager, -ère** *nm/f* user

usé, e [yze] *adj* worn; (*banal: argument etc*) hackneyed

user [yze] *vt* (*outil*) to wear down; (*vêtement*) to wear out; (*matière*) to wear away; (*consommer: charbon etc*) to use; **s'user** *vi* (*tissu, vêtement*) to wear out; **~ de** (*moyen, procédé*) to use, employ; (*droit*) to exercise

usine [yzin] *nf* factory

usité, e [yzite] *adj* common

ustensile [ystɑ̃sil] *nm* implement; **ustensile de cuisine** kitchen utensil

usuel, le [yzɥɛl] *adj* everyday, common

usure [yzyr] *nf* wear

utérus [yterys] *nm* uterus, womb

utile [ytil] *adj* useful

utilisation [ytilizasjɔ̃] *nf* use

utiliser [ytilize] *vt* to use

utilitaire [ytiliter] *adj* utilitarian

utilité [ytilite] *nf* usefulness *no pl*; **de peu d'~** of little use *ou* help

utopie [ytɔpi] *nf* utopia

V

va [va] *vb voir* **aller**

vacance [vakɑ̃s] *nf* (Admin) vacancy; **vacances** *nfpl* holiday(s pl (BRIT)), vacation *sg* (US); **les grandes ~s** the summer holidays; **prendre des/ses ~s** to take a holiday/one's holiday(s); **aller en ~s** to go on holiday; **je suis ici en ~s** I'm here on holiday; **vacancier, -ière** *nm/f* holiday-maker

vacant, e [vakɑ̃, ɑ̃t] *adj* vacant

vacarme [vakaʀm] *nm* (bruit) racket

vaccin [vaksɛ̃] *nm* vaccine; (opération) vaccination; **vaccination** *nf* vaccination; **vacciner** *vt* to vaccinate; **être vacciné contre qch** (fam) to be cured of sth

vache [vaʃ] *nf* (Zool) cow; (cuir) cowhide ▷ *adj* (fam) rotten, mean; **vachement** (fam) *adv* (très) really; (pleuvoir, travailler) a hell of a lot; **vacherie** *nf* (action) dirty trick; (remarque) nasty remark

vaciller [vasije] *vi* to sway, wobble; (bougie, lumière) to flicker; (fig) to be failing, falter

va-et-vient [vaevjɛ̃] *nm inv* (de personnes, véhicules) comings and goings pl, to-ings and fro-ings pl

vagabond [vagabɔ̃] *nm* (rôdeur) tramp, vagrant; (voyageur) wanderer; **vagabonder** *vi* to roam, wander

vagin [vaʒɛ̃] *nm* vagina

vague [vag] *nf* wave ▷ *adj* vague; (regard) faraway; (manteau, robe) loose(-fitting); (quelconque): **un ~ bureau/cousin** some office/cousin or other; **vague de fond** ground swell; **vague de froid** cold spell

vaillant, e [vajɑ̃, ɑ̃t] *adj* (courageux) gallant; (robuste) hale and hearty

vain, e [vɛ̃, vɛn] *adj* vain; **en ~** in vain

vaincre [vɛ̃kʀ] *vt* to defeat; (fig) to conquer, overcome; **vaincu, e** *nm/f* defeated party; **vainqueur** *nm* victor; (Sport) winner

vaisseau, x [veso] *nm* (Anat) vessel; (Navig) ship, vessel; **vaisseau spatial** spaceship

vaisselier [vesəlje] *nm* dresser

vaisselle [vesɛl] *nf* (service) crockery; (plats etc à laver) (dirty) dishes pl; **faire la ~** to do the washing-up (BRIT) ou the dishes

valable [valabl] *adj* valid; (acceptable) decent, worthwhile

valet [valɛ] *nm* manservant; (Cartes) jack

valeur [valœʀ] *nf* (gén) value; (mérite) worth, merit; (Comm: titre) security; **valeurs** *nfpl* (morales) values; **mettre en ~** (détail) to highlight; (objet décoratif) to show off to advantage; **avoir de la ~** to be valuable; **sans ~** worthless; **prendre de la ~** to go up ou gain in value

valide [valid] *adj* (en bonne santé) fit; (valable) valid; **valider** *vt* to validate

valise [valiz] *nf* (suit)case; **faire ses ~s** to pack one's bags

vallée [vale] *nf* valley

vallon [valɔ̃] *nm* small valley

valoir [valwaʀ] *vi* (être valable) to hold, apply ▷ *vt* (prix, valeur, effort) to be worth; (causer): **~ qch à qn** to earn sb sth; **se valoir** *vi* to be of equal merit; (péj) to be two of a kind; **faire ~** (droits, prérogatives) to assert; **se faire ~** to make the most of o.s.; **à ~ sur** to be deducted from; **vaille que vaille** somehow or other; **cela ne me dit rien qui vaille** I don't like the look of it at all; **ce climat ne me vaut rien** this climate doesn't suit me; **~ le coup** ou **la peine** to be worth the trouble ou worth it; **~ mieux: il vaut mieux se taire** it's better to say nothing; **ça ne vaut rien** it's worthless; **que vaut ce candidat?** how good is this applicant?

valse [vals] *nf* waltz

vandalisme [vɑ̃dalism] *nm* vandalism

vanille [vanij] *nf* vanilla

vanité [vanite] *nf* vanity; **vaniteux, -euse** *adj* vain, conceited

vanne [van] *nf* gate; (fig) joke

vannerie [vanʀi] *nf* basketwork

vantard, e [vɑ̃taʀ, aʀd] *adj* boastful

vanter [vɑ̃te] *vt* to speak highly of, praise; **se vanter** *vi* to boast, brag; **se ~ de** to pride o.s. on; (péj) to boast of

vapeur [vapœʀ] *nf* steam; (émanation) vapour, fumes pl; **vapeurs** *nfpl* (bouffées) vapours; **à ~** steam-powered, steam cpd; **cuit à la ~**

steamed; **vaporeux, -euse** *adj* (*flou*) hazy,
misty; (*léger*) filmy; **vaporisateur** *nm* spray;
vaporiser *vt* (*parfum etc*) to spray

varappe [vaʀap] *nf* rock climbing

vareuse [vaʀøz] *nf* (*blouson*) pea jacket;
(*d'uniforme*) tunic

variable [vaʀjabl] *adj* variable; (*temps,
humeur*) changeable; (*divers: résultats*) varied,
various

varice [vaʀis] *nf* varicose vein

varicelle [vaʀisɛl] *nf* chickenpox

varié, e [vaʀje] *adj* varied; (*divers*) various;
hors d'œuvre ~s selection of hors d'œuvres

varier [vaʀje] *vi* to vary; (*temps, humeur*) to
change ▷ *vt* to vary; **variété** *nf* variety;
variétés *nfpl*: **spectacle/émission de
variétés** variety show

variole [vaʀjɔl] *nf* smallpox

Varsovie [vaʀsɔvi] *n* Warsaw

vas [va] *vb voir* **aller**; **~-y!** [vazi] go on!

vase [vaz] *nm* vase ▷ *nf* silt, mud; **vaseux,
-euse** *adj* silty, muddy; (*fig: confus*) woolly,
hazy; (: *fatigué*) woozy

vasistas [vazistas] *nm* fanlight

vaste [vast] *adj* vast, immense

vautour [votuʀ] *nm* vulture

vautrer [votʀe] *vb*: **se ~ dans/sur** to wallow
in/sprawl on

va-vite [vavit]: **à la ~** *adv* in a rush *ou* hurry

VDQS *sigle* (= *vin délimité de qualité supérieure*)
label guaranteeing the quality of wine

veau, x [vo] *nm* (*Zool*) calf; (*Culin*) veal; (*peau*)
calfskin

vécu, e [veky] *pp de* **vivre**

vedette [vədɛt] *nf* (*artiste etc*) star; (*canot*)
motor boat; (*police*) launch

végétal, e, -aux [veʒetal, o] *adj* vegetable
▷ *nm* vegetable, plant; **végétalien, ne** *adj,
nm/f* vegan

végétarien, ne [veʒetaʀjɛ̃, jɛn] *adj, nm/f*
vegetarian; **avez-vous des plats ~s?** do you
have any vegetarian dishes?

végétation [veʒetasjɔ̃] *nf* vegetation;
végétations *nfpl* (*Méd*) adenoids

véhicule [veikyl] *nm* vehicle; **véhicule
utilitaire** commercial vehicle

veille [vɛj] *nf* (*état*) wakefulness; (*jour*): **la ~
(de)** the day before; **la ~ au soir** the previous
evening; **à la ~ de** on the eve of; **la ~ de Noël**
Christmas Eve; **la ~ du jour de l'An** New
Year's Eve

veillée [veje] *nf* (*soirée*) evening; (*réunion*)
evening gathering; **veillée (funèbre)** wake

veiller [veje] *vi* to stay up ▷ *vt* (*malade, mort*) to
watch over, sit up with; **~ à** to attend to, see to;
~ à ce que to make sure that; **~ sur** to watch
over; **veilleur** *nm*: **veilleur de nuit** night
watchman; **veilleuse** *nf* (*lampe*) night light;
(*Auto*) sidelight; (*flamme*) pilot light

veinard, e [vɛnaʀ, aʀd] *nm/f* lucky devil

veine [vɛn] *nf* (*Anat, du bois etc*) vein; (*filon*)
vein, seam; (*fam: chance*): **avoir de la ~** to be
lucky

véliplanchiste [veliplɑ̃ʃist] *nm/f* windsurfer

vélo [velo] *nm* bike, cycle; **faire du ~** to go
cycling; **vélomoteur** *nm* moped

velours [v(ə)luʀ] *nm* velvet; **velours côtelé**
corduroy; **velouté, e** *adj* velvety ▷ *nm*:
velouté de tomates cream of tomato soup

velu, e [vəly] *adj* hairy

vendange [vɑ̃dɑ̃ʒ] *nf* (*aussi*: **~s**) grape harvest;
vendanger *vi* to harvest the grapes

vendeur, -euse [vɑ̃dœʀ, øz] *nm/f* shop
assistant ▷ *nm* (*Jur*) vendor, seller

vendre [vɑ̃dʀ] *vt* to sell; **~ qch à qn** to sell sb
sth; **"à ~"** "for sale"

vendredi [vɑ̃dʀədi] *nm* Friday; **vendredi
saint** Good Friday

vénéneux, -euse [venenø, øz] *adj* poisonous

vénérien, ne [veneʀjɛ̃, jɛn] *adj* venereal

vengeance [vɑ̃ʒɑ̃s] *nf* vengeance *no pl*,
revenge *no pl*

venger [vɑ̃ʒe] *vt* to avenge; **se venger** *vi* to
avenge o.s.; **se ~ de qch** to avenge o.s. for sth,
take one's revenge for sth; **se ~ de qn** to take
revenge on sb; **se ~ sur** to take revenge on

venimeux, -euse [vənimø, øz] *adj*
poisonous, venomous; (*fig: haineux*)
venomous, vicious

venin [vənɛ̃] *nm* venom, poison

venir [v(ə)niʀ] *vi* to come; **~ de** to come from; **~
de faire**: **je viens d'y aller/de le voir** I've just
been there/seen him; **s'il vient à pleuvoir** if
it should rain; **j'en viens à croire que** I have
come to believe that; **où veux-tu en ~?** what
are you getting at?; **faire ~** (*docteur, plombier*)
to call (out)

vent [vɑ̃] *nm* wind; **il y a du ~** it's windy; **c'est
du ~** it's all hot air; **dans le ~** (*fam*) trendy

vente [vɑ̃t] *nf* sale; **la ~** (*activité*) selling;
(*secteur*) sales *pl*; **mettre en ~** (*produit*) to put
on sale; (*maison, objet personnel*) to put up for
sale; **vente aux enchères** auction sale; **vente
de charité** jumble sale

venteux, -euse [vɑ̃tø, øz] *adj* windy

ventilateur [vɑ̃tilatœʀ] *nm* fan

ventiler [vɑ̃tile] *vt* to ventilate

ventouse [vɑ̃tuz] *nf* (*de caoutchouc*) suction
pad

ventre [vɑ̃tʀ] *nm* (*Anat*) stomach; (*légèrement
péj*) belly; (*utérus*) womb; **avoir mal au ~** to
have stomach ache (BRIT) *ou* a stomach ache
(US)

venu, e [v(ə)ny] *pp de* **venir** ▷ *adj*: **bien ~**
timely; **mal ~** out of place; **être mal ~ à** *ou* **de
faire** to have no grounds for doing, be in no
position to do

ver [vɛʀ] *nm* worm; (*des fruits etc*) maggot; (*du*

bois) woodworm *no pl; voir aussi* **vers**; **ver à soie** silkworm; **ver de terre** earthworm; **ver luisant** glow-worm; **ver solitaire** tapeworm

verbe [vɛʀb] nm verb

verdâtre [vɛʀdɑtʀ] adj greenish

verdict [vɛʀdik(t)] nm verdict

verdir [vɛʀdiʀ] vi, vt to turn green; **verdure** nf greenery

véreux, -euse [veʀø, øz] adj worm-eaten; *(malhonnête)* shady, corrupt

verge [vɛʀʒ] nf *(Anat)* penis

verger [vɛʀʒe] nm orchard

verglacé, e [vɛʀglase] adj icy, iced-over

verglas [vɛʀglɑ] nm (black) ice

véridique [veʀidik] adj truthful

vérification [veʀifikasjɔ̃] nf *(action)* checking *no pl; (contrôle)* check

vérifier [veʀifje] vt to check; *(corroborer)* to confirm, bear out

véritable [veʀitabl] adj real; *(ami, amour)* true; **un ~ désastre** an absolute disaster

vérité [veʀite] nf truth; **en ~** really, actually

verlan [vɛʀlɑ̃] nm *(fam)* (back) slang

vermeil, le [vɛʀmɛj] adj ruby red

vermine [vɛʀmin] nf vermin pl

vermoulu, e [vɛʀmuly] adj worm-eaten

verni, e [vɛʀni] adj *(fam)* lucky; **cuir ~** patent leather

vernir [vɛʀniʀ] vt *(bois, tableau, ongles)* to varnish; *(poterie)* to glaze; **vernis** nm *(enduit)* varnish; glaze; *(fig)* veneer; **vernis à ongles** nail polish *ou* varnish; **vernissage** nm *(d'une exposition)* preview

vérole [veʀɔl] nf *(variole)* smallpox

verre [vɛʀ] nm glass; *(de lunettes)* lens *sg*; **boire** *ou* **prendre un ~** to have a drink; **verres de contact** contact lenses; **verrière** nf *(paroi vitrée)* glass wall; *(toit vitré)* glass roof

verrou [veʀu] nm *(targette)* bolt; **mettre qn sous les ~s** to put sb behind bars; **verrouillage** nm locking; **verrouillage centralisé** central locking; **verrouiller** vt *(porte)* to bolt; *(ordinateur)* to lock

verrue [veʀy] nf wart

vers [vɛʀ] nm line ▷ nmpl *(poésie)* verse *sg* ▷ prép *(en direction de)* toward(s); *(près de)* around (about); *(temporel)* about, around

versant [vɛʀsɑ̃] nm slopes *pl*, side

versatile [vɛʀsatil] adj fickle, changeable

verse [vɛʀs]: **à ~** adv: **il pleut à ~** it's pouring (with rain)

Verseau [vɛʀso] nm: **le ~** Aquarius

versement [vɛʀsəmɑ̃] nm payment; **en 3 ~s** in 3 instalments

verser [vɛʀse] vt *(liquide, grains)* to pour; *(larmes, sang)* to shed; *(argent)* to pay; **~ qch sur un compte** to pay sth into an account

version [vɛʀsjɔ̃] nf version; *(Scol)* translation *(into the mother tongue)*; **film en ~ originale**

film in the original language

verso [vɛʀso] nm back; **voir au ~** see over(leaf)

vert, e [vɛʀ, vɛʀt] adj green; *(vin)* young; *(vigoureux)* sprightly ▷ nm green; **les V~s** *(Pol)* the Greens

vertèbre [vɛʀtɛbʀ] nf vertebra

vertement [vɛʀtəmɑ̃] adv *(réprimander)* sharply

vertical, e, -aux [vɛʀtikal, o] adj vertical; **verticale** nf vertical; **à la verticale** vertically; **verticalement** adv vertically

vertige [vɛʀtiʒ] nm *(peur du vide)* vertigo; *(étourdissement)* dizzy spell; *(fig)* fever; **vertigineux, -euse** adj breathtaking

vertu [vɛʀty] nf virtue; **en ~ de** in accordance with; **vertueux, -euse** adj virtuous

verve [vɛʀv] nf witty eloquence; **être en ~** to be in brilliant form

verveine [vɛʀvɛn] nf *(Bot)* verbena, vervain; *(infusion)* verbena tea

vésicule [vezikyl] nf vesicle; **vésicule biliaire** gall-bladder

vessie [vesi] nf bladder

veste [vɛst] nf jacket; **veste droite/croisée** single-/double-breasted jacket

vestiaire [vɛstjɛʀ] nm *(au théâtre etc)* cloakroom; *(de stade etc)* changing-room (BRIT), locker-room (US)

vestibule [vɛstibyl] nm hall

vestige [vɛstiʒ] nm relic; *(fig)* vestige; **vestiges** nmpl *(de ville)* remains

vestimentaire [vɛstimɑ̃tɛʀ] adj *(détail)* of dress; *(élégance)* sartorial; **dépenses ~s** clothing expenditure

veston [vɛstɔ̃] nm jacket

vêtement [vɛtmɑ̃] nm garment, item of clothing; **vêtements** nmpl clothes

vétérinaire [veteʀinɛʀ] nm/f vet, veterinary surgeon

vêtir [vetiʀ] vt to clothe, dress

vêtu, e [vety] pp de **vêtir** ▷ adj: **~ de** dressed in, wearing

vétuste [vetyst] adj ancient, timeworn

veuf, veuve [vœf, vœv] adj widowed ▷ nm widower

veuve [vœv] nf widow

vexant, e [vɛksɑ̃, ɑ̃t] adj *(contrariant)* annoying; *(blessant)* hurtful

vexation [vɛksasjɔ̃] nf humiliation

vexer [vɛkse] vt: **~ qn** to hurt sb's feelings; **se vexer** vi to be offended

viable [vjabl] adj viable; *(économie, industrie etc)* sustainable

viande [vjɑ̃d] nf meat; **je ne mange pas de ~** I don't eat meat

vibrer [vibʀe] vi to vibrate; *(son, voix)* to be vibrant; *(fig)* to be stirred; **faire ~** to (cause to) vibrate; *(fig)* to stir, thrill

V

vice [vis] nm vice; (*défaut*) fault ▷ *préfixe*: **~...** vice-; **vice de forme** legal flaw *ou* irregularity

vicié, e [visje] adj (*air*) polluted, tainted; (*Jur*) invalidated

vicieux, -euse [visjø, jøz] adj (*pervers*) lecherous; (*rétif*) unruly ▷ nm/f lecher

vicinal, e, -aux [visinal, o] adj: **chemin ~** by-road, byway

victime [viktim] nf victim; (*d'accident*) casualty

victoire [viktwar] nf victory

victuailles [viktчaj] nfpl provisions

vidange [vidāʒ] nf (*d'un fossé, réservoir*) emptying; (*Auto*) oil change; (*de lavabo: bonde*) waste outlet; **vidanges** nfpl (*matières*) sewage sg; **vidanger** vt to empty

vide [vid] adj empty ▷ nm (*Physique*) vacuum; (*espace*) (empty) space, gap; (*futilité, néant*) void; **avoir peur du ~** to be afraid of heights; **emballé sous ~** vacuum packed; **à ~** (*sans occupants*) empty; (*sans charge*) unladen

vidéo [video] nf video ▷ adj: **cassette ~** video cassette; **jeu ~** video game; **vidéoclip** nm music video; **vidéoconférence** nf videoconference

vide-ordures [vidɔrdyr] nm inv (rubbish) chute

vider [vide] vt to empty; (*Culin: volaille, poisson*) to gut, clean out; **se vider** vi to empty; **~ les lieux** to quit *ou* vacate the premises; **videur** nm (*de boîte de nuit*) bouncer, doorman

vie [vi] nf life; **être en ~** to be alive; **sans ~** lifeless; **à ~** for life; **que faites-vous dans la ~?** what do you do?

vieil [vjɛj] adj m voir **vieux**; **vieillard** nm old man; **vieille** adj, nf voir **vieux**; **vieilleries** nfpl old things; **vieillesse** nf old age; **vieillir** vi (*prendre de l'âge*) to grow old; (*population, vin*) to age; (*doctrine, auteur*) to become dated ▷ vt to age; **vieillissement** nm growing old; ageing

Vienne [vjɛn] nf Vienna

viens [vjɛ̃] vb voir **venir**

vierge [vjɛrʒ] adj virgin; (*page*) clean, blank ▷ nf virgin; (*signe*): **la V~** Virgo

Vietnam, Viet-Nam [vjɛtnam] nm Vietnam; **vietnamien, ne** adj Vietnamese ▷ nm/f: **Vietnamien, ne** Vietnamese

vieux, vieil, vieille [vjø, vjɛj] adj old ▷ nm/f old man (woman); **les vieux** nmpl old people; **un petit ~** a little old man; **mon ~/ma vieille** (*fam*) old man/girl; **prendre un coup de ~** to put years on; **vieux garçon** bachelor; **vieux jeu** adj inv old-fashioned

vif, vive [vif, viv] adj (*animé*) lively; (*alerte, brusque, aigu*) sharp; (*lumière, couleur*) bright; (*air*) crisp; (*vent, émotion*) keen; (*fort: regret, déception*) great, deep; (*vivant*): **brûlé ~** burnt alive; **de vive voix** personally; **avoir l'esprit ~** to be quick-witted; **piquer qn au ~** to cut sb to the quick; **à ~** (*plaie*) open; **avoir les nerfs à ~** to be on edge

vigne [viɲ] nf (*plante*) vine; (*plantation*) vineyard; **vigneron** nm vine grower

vignette [viɲɛt] nf (*Admin*) ≈ (road) tax disc (BRIT), ≈ license plate sticker (US); (*de médicament*) price label (*used for reimbursement*)

vignoble [viɲɔbl] nm (*plantation*) vineyard; (*vignes d'une région*) vineyards pl

vigoureux, -euse [vigurø, øz] adj vigorous, robust

vigueur [vigœr] nf vigour; **entrer en ~** to come into force; **en ~** current

vilain, e [vilɛ̃, ɛn] adj (*laid*) ugly; (*affaire, blessure*) nasty; (*pas sage: enfant*) naughty; **vilain mot** naughty *ou* bad word

villa [villa] nf (detached) house; **~ en multipropriété** time-share villa

village [vilaʒ] nm village; **villageois, e** adj village cpd ▷ nm/f villager

ville [vil] nf town; (*importante*) city; (*administration*): **la ~** the (town) council, the local authority; **ville d'eaux** spa; **ville nouvelle** new town

vin [vɛ̃] nm wine; **avoir le ~ gai** to get happy after a few drinks; **vin d'honneur** reception (with wine and snacks); **vin de pays** local wine; **vin ordinaire** *ou* **de table** table wine

vinaigre [vinɛgr] nm vinegar; **vinaigrette** nf vinaigrette, French dressing

vindicatif, -ive [vɛ̃dikatif, iv] adj vindictive

vingt [vɛ̃] num twenty; **~-quatre heures sur ~-quatre** twenty-four hours a day, round the clock; **vingtaine** nf: **une vingtaine (de)** about twenty, twenty or so; **vingtième** num twentieth

vinicole [vinikɔl] adj wine cpd, wine-growing

vinyle [vinil] nm vinyl

viol [vjɔl] nm (*d'une femme*) rape; (*d'un lieu sacré*) violation

violacé, e [vjɔlase] adj purplish, mauvish

violemment [vjɔlamā] adv violently

violence [vjɔlās] nf violence

violent, e [vjɔlā, āt] adj violent; (*remède*) drastic

violer [vjɔle] vt (*femme*) to rape; (*sépulture, loi, traité*) to violate

violet, te [vjɔlɛ, ɛt] adj, nm purple, mauve; **violette** nf (*fleur*) violet

violon [vjɔlɔ̃] nm violin; (*fam: prison*) lock-up; **violon d'Ingres** hobby; **violoncelle** nm cello; **violoniste** nm/f violinist

vipère [vipɛr] nf viper, adder

virage [viraʒ] nm (*d'un véhicule*) turn; (*d'une route, piste*) bend

virée [vire] nf trip; (*à pied*) walk; (*longue*) walking tour; (*dans les cafés*) tour

virement [viʀmɑ̃] nm (Comm) transfer

virer [viʀe] vt (Comm): **~ qch (sur)** to transfer sth (into); (fam: expulser): **~ qn** to kick sb out ▷ vi to turn; (Chimie) to change colour; **~ au bleu/rouge** to turn blue/red; **~ de bord** to tack

virevolter [viʀvɔlte] vi to twirl around

virgule [viʀgyl] nf comma; (Math) point

viril, e [viʀil] adj (propre à l'homme) masculine; (énergique, courageux) manly, virile

virtuel, le [viʀtɥɛl] adj potential; (théorique) virtual

virtuose [viʀtɥoz] nm/f (Mus) virtuoso; (gén) master

virus [viʀys] nm virus

vis¹ [vi] vb voir **voir**; **vivre**

vis² [vis] nf screw

visa [viza] nm (sceau) stamp; (validation de passeport) visa

visage [vizaʒ] nm face

vis-à-vis [vizavi] prép: **~ de qn** to(wards) sb; **en ~** facing each other

visées [vize] nfpl (intentions) designs

viser [vize] vi to aim ▷ vt to aim at; (concerner) to be aimed ou directed at; (apposer un visa sur) to stamp, visa; **~ à qch/faire** to aim at sth/at doing ou to do

visibilité [vizibilite] nf visibility

visible [vizibl] adj visible; (disponible): **est-il ~?** can he see me?, will he see visitors?

visière [vizjɛʀ] nf (de casquette) peak; (qui s'attache) eyeshade

vision [vizjɔ̃] nf vision; (sens) (eye)sight, vision; (fait de voir): **la ~ de** the sight of; **visionneuse** nf viewer

visiophone [vizjofɔn] nm videophone

visite [vizit] nf visit; **~ médicale** medical examination; **~ accompagnée** ou **guidée** guided tour; **la ~ guidée commence à quelle heure?** what time does the guided tour start?; **faire une ~ à qn** to call on sb, pay sb a visit; **rendre ~ à qn** to visit sb, pay sb a visit; **être en ~ (chez qn)** to be visiting (sb); **avoir de la ~** to have visitors; **heures de ~** (hôpital, prison) visiting hours

visiter [vizite] vt to visit; **visiteur, -euse** nm/f visitor

vison [vizɔ̃] nm mink

visser [vise] vt: **~ qch** (fixer, serrer) to screw sth on

visuel, le [vizɥɛl] adj visual

vital, e, -aux [vital, o] adj vital

vitamine [vitamin] nf vitamin

vite [vit] adv (rapidement) quickly, fast; (sans délai) quickly; (sous peu) soon; **~!** quick!; **faire ~** to be quick; **le temps passe ~** time flies

vitesse [vitɛs] nf speed; (Auto: dispositif) gear; **prendre de la ~** to pick up ou gather speed; **à toute ~** at full ou top speed; **en ~** (rapidement)

quickly; (en hâte) in a hurry

● **LIMITE DE VITESSE**
●
● The speed limit in France is 50 km/h in
● built-up areas, 90 km/h on main roads, and
● 130 km/h on motorways (110 km/h when
● it is raining).

viticulteur [vitikyltœʀ] nm wine grower

vitrage [vitʀaʒ] nm: **double ~** double glazing

vitrail, -aux [vitʀaj, o] nm stained-glass window

vitre [vitʀ] nf (window) pane; (de portière, voiture) window; **vitré, e** adj glass cpd

vitrine [vitʀin] nf (shop) window; (petite armoire) display cabinet; **en ~** in the window

vivable [vivabl] adj (personne) livable-with; (maison) fit to live in

vivace [vivas] adj (arbre, plante) hardy; (fig) indestructible, inveterate

vivacité [vivasite] nf liveliness, vivacity

vivant, e [vivɑ̃, ɑ̃t] adj (qui vit) living, alive; (animé) lively; (preuve, exemple) living ▷ nm: **du ~ de qn** in sb's lifetime; **les ~s** the living

vive [viv] adj voir **vif** ▷ vb voir **vivre** ▷ excl: **~ le roi!** long live the king!; **vivement** adv deeply ▷ excl: **vivement les vacances!** roll on the holidays!

vivier [vivje] nm (étang) fish tank; (réservoir) fishpond

vivifiant, e [vivifjɑ̃, jɑ̃t] adj invigorating

vivoter [vivɔte] vi (personne) to scrape a living, get by; (fig: affaire etc) to struggle along

vivre [vivʀ] vi, vt to live; (période) to live through; **vivres** nmpl provisions, food supplies; **~ de** to live on; **il vit encore** he is still alive; **se laisser ~** to take life as it comes; **ne plus ~** (être anxieux) to live on one's nerves; **il a vécu** (eu une vie aventureuse) he has seen life; **être facile à ~** to be easy to get on with; **faire ~ qn** (pourvoir à sa subsistance) to provide (a living) for sb

vlan [vlɑ̃] excl wham!, bang!

VO [veo] nf: **film en VO** film in the original version; **en VO sous-titrée** in the original version with subtitles

vocabulaire [vɔkabylɛʀ] nm vocabulary

vocation [vɔkasjɔ̃] nf vocation, calling

vœu, x [vø] nm (promesse) vow; (souhait) wish; **faire ~ de** to take a vow of; **tous nos ~x de bonne année, meilleurs ~x** best wishes for the New Year

vogue [vɔg] nf fashion, vogue; **en ~** in fashion, in vogue

voici [vwasi] prép (pour introduire, désigner) here is +sg, here are +pl; **et ~ que ...** and now it (ou he) ...; voir aussi **voilà**

voie [vwa] nf way; (Rail) track, line; (Auto) lane;

être en bonne ~ to be going well; **mettre qn sur la ~** to put sb on the right track; **pays en ~ de développement** developing country; **être en ~ d'achèvement/de rénovation** to be nearing completion/in the process of renovation; **par ~ buccale** ou **orale** orally; **route à ~ unique** single-track road; **route à 2/3 ~s** 2-/3-lane road; **voie de garage** (Rail) siding; **voie express** expressway; **voie ferrée** track; railway line (BRIT), railroad (US); **la voie lactée** the Milky Way; **la voie publique** the public highway

voilà [vwala] prép (en désignant) there is +sg, there are +pl; **les ~** ou **voici** here ou there they are; **en ~ voici un** here's one, there's one; **voici mon frère et ~ ma sœur** this is my brother and that's my sister; **~** ou **voici deux ans** two years ago; **~** ou **voici deux ans que** it's two years since; **~ -!** there we are!; **~ tout** that's all; **~** ou **voici** (en offrant etc) there ou here you are; **tiens! ~ Paul** look! there's Paul

voile [vwal] nm; **~** veil; (tissu léger) net ▷ nf sail; (sport) sailing; **voiler** vt to veil; (fausser: roue) to buckle; (: bois) to warp; **se voiler** vi (lune, regard) to mist over; (voix) to become husky; (roue, disque) to buckle; (planche) to warp; **voilier** nm sailing ship; (de plaisance) sailing boat; **voilure** nf (de voilier) sails pl

voir [vwaʀ] vi, vt to see; **se voir** vi (être visible) to show; (se fréquenter) to see each other; (se produire) to happen; **cela se voit** (c'est visible) that's obvious, it shows; **faire ~ qch à qn** to show sb sth; **en faire ~ à qn** (fig) to give sb a hard time; **ne pas pouvoir ~ qn** not to be able to stand sb; **voyons!** let's see now; (indignation etc) come on!; **ça n'a rien à ~ avec lui** that has nothing to do with him

voire [vwaʀ] adv even

voisin, e [vwazɛ̃, in] adj (proche) neighbouring; (contigu) next; (ressemblant) connected ▷ nm/f neighbour; **voisinage** nm (proximité) proximity; (environs) vicinity; (quartier, voisins) neighbourhood

voiture [vwatyʀ] nf car; (wagon) coach, carriage; **voiture de course** racing car; **voiture de sport** sports car

voix [vwa] nf voice; (Pol) vote; **à haute ~** aloud; **à ~ basse** in a low voice; **à 2/4 ~** (Mus) in 2/4 parts; **avoir ~ au chapitre** to have a say in the matter

vol [vɔl] nm (d'oiseau, d'avion) flight; (larcin) theft; **~ régulier** scheduled flight; **à ~ d'oiseau** as the crow flies; **au ~: attraper qch au ~** to catch sth as it flies past; **en ~** in flight; **je voudrais signaler un ~** I'd like to report a theft; **vol à main armée** armed robbery; **vol à voile** gliding; **vol libre** hang-gliding

volage [vɔlaʒ] adj fickle

volaille [vɔlaj] nf (oiseaux) poultry pl; (viande) poultry no pl; (oiseau) fowl

volant, e [vɔlɑ̃, ɑ̃t] adj voir **feuille** etc ▷ nm (d'automobile) (steering) wheel; (de commande) wheel; (objet lancé) shuttlecock; (bande de tissu) flounce

volcan [vɔlkɑ̃] nm volcano

volée [vɔle] nf (Tennis) volley; **à la ~: rattraper à la ~** to catch in mid-air; **à toute ~** (sonner les cloches) vigorously; (lancer un projectile) with full force

voler [vɔle] vi (avion, oiseau, fig) to fly; (voleur) vt (objet) to steal; (personne) to rob; **~ qch à qn** to steal sth from sb; **on m'a volé mon portefeuille** my wallet (BRIT) ou billfold (US) has been stolen; **il ne l'a pas volé!** he asked for it!

volet [vɔle] nm (de fenêtre) shutter; (de feuillet, document) section

voleur, -euse [vɔlœʀ, øz] nm/f thief ▷ adj thieving; **"au ~!"** "stop thief!"

volontaire [vɔlɔ̃tɛʀ] adj (acte, enrôlement, prisonnier) voluntary; (oubli) intentional; (caractère, personne: décidé) self-willed ▷ nm/f volunteer

volonté [vɔlɔ̃te] nf (faculté de vouloir) will; (énergie, fermeté) will(power); (souhait, désir) wish; **à ~** as much as one likes; **bonne ~** goodwill, willingness; **mauvaise ~** lack of goodwill, unwillingness

volontiers [vɔlɔ̃tje] adv (avec plaisir) willingly, gladly; (habituellement, souvent) readily, willingly; **voulez-vous boire quelque chose? — ~!** would you like something to drink? — yes, please!

volt [vɔlt] nm volt

volte-face [vɔltəfas] nf inv: **faire ~** to turn round

voltige [vɔltiʒ] nf (Équitation) trick riding; (au cirque) acrobatics sg; **voltiger** vi to flutter (about)

volubile [vɔlybil] adj voluble

volume [vɔlym] nm volume; (Géom: solide) solid; **volumineux, -euse** adj voluminous, bulky

volupté [vɔlypte] nf sensual delight ou pleasure

vomi [vɔmi] nm vomit; **vomir** vi to vomit, be sick ▷ vt to vomit, bring up; (fig) to belch out, spew out; (exécrer) to loathe, abhor

vorace [vɔʀas] adj voracious

vos [vo] adj voir **votre**

vote [vɔt] nm vote; **vote par correspondance/procuration** postal/proxy vote; **voter** vi to vote ▷ vt (projet de loi) to vote for; (loi, réforme) to pass

votre [vɔtʀ] (pl vos) adj your

vôtre [votʀ] pron: **le ~, la ~, les ~s** yours; **les ~s** (fig) your family ou folks; **à la ~** (toast) your (good) health!

vouer [vwe] vt: **~ sa vie à** (étude, cause etc) to devote one's life to; **~ une amitié éternelle à qn** to vow undying friendship to sb

 MOT-CLÉ

vouloir [vulwaʀ] nm: **le bon vouloir de qn** sb's goodwill; sb's pleasure
▷ vt **1** (exiger, désirer) to want; **vouloir faire/que qn fasse** to want to do/sb to do; **voulez-vous du thé?** would you like ou do you want some tea?; **que me veut-il?** what does he want with me?; **sans le vouloir** (involontairement) without meaning to, unintentionally; **je voudrais ceci/faire** I would ou I'd like this/to do; **le hasard a voulu que ...** as fate would have it ...; **la tradition veut que ...** it is a tradition that ...
2 (consentir): **je veux bien** (bonne volonté) I'll be happy to; (concession) fair enough, that's fine; **je peux le faire, si vous voulez** I can do it if you like; **oui, si on veut** (en quelque sorte) yes, if you like; **veuillez attendre** please wait; **veuillez agréer ...** (formule épistolaire: personne nommée) yours sincerely; (personne non nommée) yours faithfully
3: **en vouloir à qn** to bear sb a grudge; **s'en vouloir (de)** to be annoyed with o.s. (for); **il en veut à mon argent** he's after my money
4: **vouloir de: l'entreprise ne veut plus de lui** the firm doesn't want him any more; **elle ne veut pas de son aide** she doesn't want his help
5: **vouloir dire** to mean

voulu, e [vuly] adj (requis) required, requisite; (délibéré) deliberate, intentional; voir aussi **vouloir**

vous [vu] pron you; (objet indirect) (to) you; (réfléchi: sg) yourself; (: pl) yourselves; (réciproque) each other ▷ nm: **employer le ~** (vouvoyer) to use the "vous" form; **~-même** yourself; **~-mêmes** yourselves

vouvoyer [vuvwaje] vt: **~ qn** to address sb as "vous"

voyage [vwajaʒ] nm journey, trip; (fait de voyager): **le ~** travel(ling); **partir/être en ~** to go off/be away on a journey ou trip; **faire bon ~** to have a good journey; **votre ~ s'est bien passé?** how was your journey?; **voyage d'affaires/d'agrément** business/pleasure trip; **voyage de noces** honeymoon; **nous sommes en voyage de noces** we're on honeymoon; **voyage organisé** package tour

voyager [vwajaʒe] vi to travel; **voyageur, -euse** nm/f traveller; (passager) passenger; **voyageur de commerce** sales representative, commercial traveller

voyant, e [vwajɑ̃, ɑ̃t] adj (couleur) loud, gaudy

▷ nm (signal) (warning) light

voyelle [vwajɛl] nf vowel

voyou [vwaju] nm hooligan

vrac [vʀak]: **en ~** adv (au détail) loose; (en gros) in bulk; (en désordre) in a jumble

vrai, e [vʀɛ] adj (véridique: récit, faits) true; (non factice, authentique) real; **à ~ dire** to tell the truth; **vraiment** adv really; **vraisemblable** adj likely; (excuse) convincing; **vraisemblablement** adj probably; **vraisemblance** nf likelihood; (romanesque) verisimilitude

vrombir [vʀɔ̃biʀ] vi to hum

VRP sigle m (= voyageur, représentant, placier) sales rep (fam)

VTT sigle m (= vélo tout-terrain) mountain bike

vu, e [vy] pp de **voir** ▷ adj: **bien/mal vu** (fig: personne) popular/unpopular; (: chose) approved/disapproved of ▷ prép (en raison de) in view of; **vu que** in view of the fact that

vue [vy] nf (fait de voir): **la ~ de** the sight of; (sens, faculté) (eye)sight; (panorama, image, photo) view; **vues** nfpl (idées) views; (dessein) designs; **hors de ~** out of sight; **avoir en ~** to have in mind; **tirer à ~** to shoot on sight; **à ~ d'œil** visibly; **à première ~** at first sight; **de ~** by sight; **perdre de ~** to lose sight of; **en ~** (visible) in sight; (célèbre) in the public eye; **en ~ de faire** with a view to doing; **perdre la ~** to lose one's (eye)sight; **avoir ~ sur** (suj: fenêtre) to have a view of; **vue d'ensemble** overall view

vulgaire [vylgɛʀ] adj (grossier) vulgar, coarse; (ordinaire) commonplace, mundane; (péj: quelconque): **de ~s touristes** common tourists; (Bot, Zool: non latin) common; **vulgariser** vt to popularize

vulnérable [vylneʀabl] adj vulnerable

W X

wagon [vagɔ̃] *nm* (*de voyageurs*) carriage; (*de marchandises*) truck, wagon; **wagon-lit** *nm* sleeper, sleeping car; **wagon-restaurant** *nm* restaurant *ou* dining car

wallon, ne [walɔ̃, ɔn] *adj* Walloon ▷ *nm* (*Ling*) Walloon ▷ *nm/f*: **W~, ne** Walloon

watt [wat] *nm* watt

w-c *sigle mpl* (= *water-closet(s)*) toilet

Web [wɛb] *nm inv*: **le ~** the (World Wide) Web; **webmaster** [-mastœʀ], **webmestre** [-mɛstʀ] *nm/f* webmaster

week-end [wikɛnd] *nm* weekend

western [wɛstɛʀn] *nm* western

whisky [wiski] (*pl* **whiskies**) *nm* whisky

xénophobe [gzenɔfɔb] *adj* xenophobic ▷ *nm/f* xenophobe

xérès [gzeʀɛs] *nm* sherry

xylophone [gzilɔfɔn] *nm* xylophone

Y Z

y [i] *adv* (*à cet endroit*) there; (*dessus*) on it (*ou* them); (*dedans*) in it (*ou* them) ▷ *pron* (*about ou on ou of it*) (*d'après le verbe employé*); **j'y pense** I'm thinking about it; **ça y est!** that's it!; *voir aussi* **aller**; **avoir**

yacht [jɔt] *nm* yacht

yaourt [jauʀt] *nm* yoghourt; **~ nature/aux fruits** plain/fruit yogurt

yeux [jø] *nmpl de* **œil**

yoga [jɔga] *nm* yoga

yoghourt [jɔguʀt] *nm* = **yaourt**

yougoslave [jugɔslav] (*Histoire*) *adj* Yugoslav(ian) ▷ *nm/f*: **Y~** Yugoslav

Yougoslavie [jugɔslavi] *nf* (*Histoire*) Yugoslavia; **l'ex-~** the former Yugoslavia

zapper [zape] *vi* to zap

zapping [zapiŋ] *nm*: **faire du ~** to flick through the channels

zèbre [zɛbʀ(ə)] *nm* (*Zool*) zebra; **zébré, e** *adj* striped, streaked

zèle [zɛl] *nm* zeal; **faire du ~** (*péj*) to be over-zealous; **zélé, e** *adj* zealous

zéro [zeʀo] *nm* zero, nought (BRIT); **au-dessous de ~** below zero (Centigrade) *ou* freezing; **partir de ~** to start from scratch; **trois (buts) à ~** 3 (goals to) nil

zeste [zɛst] *nm* peel, zest

zézayer [zezeje] *vi* to have a lisp

zigzag [zigzag] *nm* zigzag; **zigzaguer** *vi* to zigzag

Zimbabwe [zimbabwe] *nm*: **le ~** Zimbabwe

zinc [zɛ̃g] *nm* (*Chimie*) zinc

zipper [zipe] *vt* (*Inform*) to zip

zizi [zizi] *nm* (*langage enfantin*) willy

zodiaque [zɔdjak] *nm* zodiac

zona [zona] *nm* shingles *sg*

zone [zon] *nf* zone, area; (*fam: quartiers pauvres*): **la ~** the slums; **zone bleue** ≈ restricted parking area; **zone industrielle** industrial estate

zoo [zo(o)] *nm* zoo

zoologie [zɔɔlɔʒi] *nf* zoology; **zoologique** *adj* zoological

zut [zyt] *excl* dash (it)! (BRIT), nuts! (US)

ENGLISH | FRENCH
ANGLAIS | FRANÇAIS

A [eɪ] *n* (*Mus*) la *m*

KEYWORD

a [eɪ, ə] *n* (*before vowel or silent h* **an**) *indef art*
1 un(e); **a book** un livre; **an apple** une pomme;
she's a doctor elle est médecin
2 (*instead of the number "one"*) un(e); **a year ago**
il y a un an; **a hundred/thousand** *etc* **pounds**
cent/mille *etc* livres
3 (*in expressing ratios, prices etc*): **3 a day/week**
3 par jour/semaine; **10 km an hour** 10 km à
l'heure; **£5 a person** 5£ par personne; **30p a
kilo** 30p le kilo

A2 *n* (*BRIT: Scol*) deuxième partie de l'examen
équivalent au baccalauréat
A.A. *n abbr* (*BRIT* = *Automobile Association*)
≈ ACF *m*; (= *Alcoholics Anonymous*) AA
A.A.A. *n abbr* (= *American Automobile
Association*) ≈ ACF *m*
aback [ə'bæk] *adv*: **to be taken ~** être
décontenancé(e)
abandon [ə'bændən] *vt* abandonner
abattoir ['æbətwɑː'] *n* (*BRIT*) abattoir *m*
abbey ['æbɪ] *n* abbaye *f*
abbreviation [əbriːvɪ'eɪʃən] *n* abréviation *f*
abdomen ['æbdəmən] *n* abdomen *m*
abduct [æb'dʌkt] *vt* enlever
abide [ə'baɪd] *vt* souffrir, supporter; **I can't ~**

it/him je ne le supporte pas; **abide by** *vt fus*
observer, respecter
ability [ə'bɪlɪtɪ] *n* compétence *f*; capacité *f*;
(*skill*) talent *m*
able ['eɪbl] *adj* compétent(e); **to be ~ to do sth**
pouvoir faire qch, être capable de faire qch
abnormal [æb'nɔːməl] *adj* anormal(e)
aboard [ə'bɔːd] *adv* à bord ▷ *prep* à bord de;
(*train*) dans
abolish [ə'bɒlɪʃ] *vt* abolir
abolition [æbə'lɪʃən] *n* abolition *f*
abort [ə'bɔːt] *vt* (*Med*) faire avorter; (*Comput*,
fig) abandonner; **abortion** [ə'bɔːʃən] *n*
avortement *m*; **to have an abortion** se faire
avorter

KEYWORD

about [ə'baut] *adv* **1** (*approximately*) environ,
à peu près; **about a hundred/thousand** *etc*
environ cent/mille *etc*, une centaine (de)/un
millier (de) *etc*; **it takes about 10 hours** ça
prend environ *or* à peu près 10 heures; **at
about 2 o'clock** vers 2 heures; **I've just about
finished** j'ai presque fini
2 (*referring to place*) çà et là, de-ci de-là; **to
run about** courir çà et là; **to walk about** se
promener, aller et venir; **they left all their
things lying about** ils ont laissé traîner
toutes leurs affaires
3: **to be about to do sth** être sur le point de
faire qch
▷ *prep* **1** (*relating to*) au sujet de, à propos de;
a book about London un livre sur Londres;
what is it about? de quoi s'agit-il?; **we talked
about it** nous en avons parlé; **what** *or* **how
about doing this?** et si nous faisions ceci?
2 (*referring to place*) dans; **to walk about the
town** se promener dans la ville

above [ə'bʌv] *adv* au-dessus ▷ *prep* au-
dessus de; (*more than*) plus de; **mentioned ~**
mentionné ci-dessus; **~ all** par-dessus tout,
surtout
abroad [ə'brɔːd] *adv* à l'étranger
abrupt [ə'brʌpt] *adj* (*steep, blunt*) abrupt(e);
(*sudden, gruff*) brusque
abscess ['æbsɪs] *n* abcès *m*
absence ['æbsəns] *n* absence *f*
absent ['æbsənt] *adj* absent(e); **absent-
minded** *adj* distrait(e)
absolute ['æbsəluːt] *adj* absolu(e);
absolutely [æbsə'luːtlɪ] *adv* absolument
absorb [əb'zɔːb] *vt* absorber; **to be ~ed in a
book** être plongé(e) dans un livre; **absorbent
cotton** *n* (*US*) coton *m* hydrophile; **absorbing**
adj absorbant(e); (*book, film etc*) captivant(e)
abstain [əb'steɪn] *vi*: **to ~ (from)** s'abstenir
(de)

abstract ['æbstrækt] adj abstrait(e)
absurd [əb'sə:d] adj absurde
abundance [ə'bʌndəns] n abondance f
abundant [ə'bʌndənt] adj abondant(e)
abuse n [ə'bju:s] (insults) insultes fpl, injures fpl; (ill-treatment) mauvais traitements mpl; (of power etc) abus m ▷ vt [ə'bju:z] (insult) insulter; (ill-treat) malmener; (power etc) abuser de; **abusive** adj grossier(-ière), injurieux(-euse)
abysmal [ə'bɪzməl] adj exécrable; (ignorance etc) sans bornes
academic [ækə'dɛmɪk] adj universitaire; (person: scholarly) intellectuel(-le); (pej: issue) oiseux(-euse), purement théorique ▷ n universitaire m/f; **academic year** n (University) année f universitaire; (Scol) année scolaire
academy [ə'kædəmɪ] n (learned body) académie f; (school) collège m; **~ of music** conservatoire m
accelerate [æk'sɛləreɪt] vt, vi accélérer; **acceleration** [æksɛlə'reɪʃən] n accélération f; **accelerator** n (BRIT) accélérateur m
accent ['æksɛnt] n accent m
accept [ək'sɛpt] vt accepter; **acceptable** adj acceptable; **acceptance** n acceptation f
access ['æksɛs] n accès m; **to have ~ to** (information, library etc) avoir accès à, pouvoir utiliser or consulter; (person) avoir accès auprès de; **accessible** [æk'sɛsəbl] adj accessible
accessory [æk'sɛsərɪ] n accessoire m; **~ to** (Law) accessoire à
accident ['æksɪdənt] n accident m; (chance) hasard m; **I've had an ~** j'ai eu un accident; **by ~** (by chance) par hasard; (not deliberately) accidentellement; **accidental** [æksɪ'dɛntl] adj accidentel(le); **accidentally** [æksɪ'dɛntəlɪ] adv accidentellement; **Accident and Emergency Department** n (BRIT) service m des urgences; **accident insurance** n assurance f accident
acclaim [ə'kleɪm] vt acclamer ▷ n acclamations fpl
accommodate [ə'kɔmədeɪt] vt loger, recevoir; (oblige, help) obliger; (car etc) contenir
accommodation [ə'kɔmə'deɪʃən] (us accommodations) [ə'kɔmə'deɪʃən(z)] n(pl) logement m
accompaniment [ə'kʌmpənɪmənt] n accompagnement m
accompany [ə'kʌmpənɪ] vt accompagner
accomplice [ə'kʌmplɪs] n complice m/f
accomplish [ə'kʌmplɪʃ] vt accomplir; **accomplishment** n (skill: gen pl) talent m; (completion) accomplissement m; (achievement) réussite f
accord [ə'kɔ:d] n accord m ▷ vt accorder; **of his own ~** de son plein gré; **accordance** n: **in accordance with** conformément à; **according**: **according to** prep selon;

accordingly adv (appropriately) en conséquence; (as a result) par conséquent
account [ə'kaunt] n (Comm) compte m; (report) compte rendu, récit m; **accounts** npl (Comm: records) comptabilité f, comptes; **of no ~** sans importance; **on ~** en acompte; **to buy sth on ~** acheter qch à crédit; **on no ~** en aucun cas; **on ~ of** à cause de; **to take into ~**, **take ~ of** tenir compte de; **account for** vt fus (explain) expliquer, rendre compte de; (represent) représenter; **accountable** adj: **accountable (to)** responsable (devant); **accountant** n comptable m/f; **account number** n numéro m de compte
accumulate [ə'kju:mjuleɪt] vt accumuler, amasser ▷ vi s'accumuler, s'amasser
accuracy ['ækjurəsɪ] n exactitude f, précision f
accurate ['ækjurɪt] adj exact(e), précis(e); (device) précis; **accurately** adv avec précision
accusation [ækju'zeɪʃən] n accusation f
accuse [ə'kju:z] vt: **to ~ sb (of sth)** accuser qn (de qch); **accused** n (Law) accusé(e)
accustomed [ə'kʌstəmd] adj: **~ to** habitué(e) or accoutumé(e) à
ace [eɪs] n as m
ache [eɪk] n mal m, douleur f ▷ vi (be sore) faire mal, être douloureux(-euse); **my head ~s** j'ai mal à la tête
achieve [ə'tʃi:v] vt (aim) atteindre; (victory, success) remporter, obtenir; **achievement** n exploit m, réussite f; (of aims) réalisation f
acid ['æsɪd] adj, n acide (m)
acknowledge [ək'nɔlɪdʒ] vt (also: **~ receipt of**) accuser réception de; (fact) reconnaître; **acknowledgement** n (of letter) accusé m de réception
acne ['æknɪ] n acné m
acorn ['eɪkɔ:n] n gland m
acoustic [ə'ku:stɪk] adj acoustique
acquaintance [ə'kweɪntəns] n connaissance f
acquire [ə'kwaɪər] vt acquérir; **acquisition** [ækwɪ'zɪʃən] n acquisition f
acquit [ə'kwɪt] vt acquitter; **to ~ o.s. well** s'en tirer très honorablement
acre ['eɪkər] n acre f (= 4047 m²)
acronym ['ækrənɪm] n acronyme m
across [ə'krɔs] prep (on the other side) de l'autre côté de; (crosswise) en travers de ▷ adv de l'autre côté; en travers; **to run/swim ~** traverser en courant/à la nage; **~ from** en face de
acrylic [ə'krɪlɪk] adj, n acrylique (m)
act [ækt] n acte m, action f; (Theat: part of play) acte; (: of performer) numéro m; (Law) loi f ▷ vi agir; (Theat) jouer; (pretend) jouer la comédie ▷ vt (role) jouer, tenir; **to catch sb in the ~** prendre qn sur le fait or en flagrant

délit; **to ~ as** servir de; **act up** (inf) ▷ vi (person) se conduire mal; (knee, back, injury) jouer des tours; (machine) être capricieux(-ieuse); **acting** adj suppléant(e), par intérim ▷ n (activity): **to do some acting** faire du théâtre (or du cinéma)

action ['ækʃən] n action f; (Mil) combat(s) m(pl); (Law) procès m, action en justice; **out of ~** hors de combat; (machine etc) hors d'usage; **to take ~** agir, prendre des mesures; **action replay** n (BRIT TV) ralenti m

activate ['æktɪveɪt] vt (mechanism) actionner, faire fonctionner

active ['æktɪv] adj actif(-ive); (volcano) en activité; **actively** adv activement; (discourage) vivement

activist ['æktɪvɪst] n activiste m/f

activity [æk'tɪvɪtɪ] n activité f; **activity holiday** n vacances actives

actor ['æktə'] n acteur m

actress ['æktrɪs] n actrice f

actual ['æktjuəl] adj réel(le), véritable; (emphatic use) lui-même (elle-même)

> Be careful not to translate **actual** by the French word **actuel**.

actually ['æktjuəlɪ] adv réellement, véritablement; (in fact) en fait

> Be careful not to translate **actually** by the French word **actuellement**.

acupuncture ['ækjupʌŋktʃə'] n acuponcture f

acute [ə'kjuːt] adj aigu(ë); (mind, observer) pénétrant(e)

A.D. adv abbr (= Anno Domini) ap. J.-C.

ad [æd] n abbr = **advertisement**

adamant ['ædəmənt] adj inflexible

adapt [ə'dæpt] vt adapter ▷ vi: **to ~ (to)** s'adapter (à); **adapter, adaptor** n (Elec) adaptateur m; (for several plugs) prise f multiple

add [æd] vt ajouter; (figures: also: **to ~ up**) additionner ▷ vi (fig): **it doesn't ~ up** cela ne rime à rien; **add up to** vt fus (Math) s'élever à; (fig: mean) signifier

addict ['ædɪkt] n toxicomane m/f; (fig) fanatique m/f; **addicted** [ə'dɪktɪd] adj: **to be addicted to** (drink, drugs) être adonné(e) à; (fig: football etc) être un(e) fanatique de; **addiction** [ə'dɪkʃən] n (Med) dépendance f; **addictive** [ə'dɪktɪv] adj qui crée une dépendance

addition [ə'dɪʃən] n (adding up) addition f; (thing added) ajout m; **in ~** de plus, de surcroît; **in ~ to** en plus de; **additional** adj supplémentaire

additive ['ædɪtɪv] n additif m

address [ə'drɛs] n adresse f; (talk) discours m, allocution f ▷ vt adresser; (speak to) s'adresser à; **my ~ is ...** mon adresse, c'est ...; **address book** n carnet m d'adresses

adequate ['ædɪkwɪt] adj (enough) suffisant(e); (satisfactory) satisfaisant(e)

adhere [əd'hɪə'] vi: **to ~ to** adhérer à; (fig: rule, decision) se tenir à

adhesive [əd'hiːzɪv] n adhésif m; **adhesive tape** n (BRIT) ruban m adhésif; (US Med) sparadrap m

adjacent [ə'dʒeɪsənt] adj adjacent(e), contigu(ë); **~ to** adjacent à

adjective ['ædʒɛktɪv] n adjectif m

adjoining [ə'dʒɔɪnɪŋ] adj voisin(e), adjacent(e), attenant(e)

adjourn [ə'dʒəːn] vt ajourner ▷ vi suspendre la séance; lever la séance; clore la session

adjust [ə'dʒʌst] vt (machine) ajuster, régler; (prices, wages) rajuster ▷ vi: **to ~ (to)** s'adapter (à); **adjustable** adj réglable; **adjustment** n (of machine) ajustage m, réglage m; (of prices, wages) rajustement m; (of person) adaptation f

administer [əd'mɪnɪstə'] vt administrer; **administration** [ədmɪnɪs'treɪʃən] n (management) administration f; (government) gouvernement m; **administrative** [ə d'mɪnɪstrətɪv] adj administratif(-ive)

administrator [əd'mɪnɪstreɪtə'] n administrateur(-trice)

admiral ['ædmərəl] n amiral m

admiration [ædmə'reɪʃən] n admiration f

admire [əd'maɪə'] vt admirer; **admirer** n (fan) admirateur(-trice)

admission [əd'mɪʃən] n admission f; (to exhibition, night club etc) entrée f; (confession) aveu m

admit [əd'mɪt] vt laisser entrer; admettre; (agree) reconnaître, admettre; (crime) reconnaître avoir commis; **"children not ~ted"** "entrée interdite aux enfants"; **admit to** vt fus reconnaître, avouer; **admittance** n admission f, (droit m d')entrée f; **admittedly** adv il faut en convenir

adolescent [ædəu'lɛsnt] adj, n adolescent(e)

adopt [ə'dɔpt] vt adopter; **adopted** adj adoptif(-ive), adopté(e); **adoption** [ə'dɔpʃən] n adoption f

adore [ə'dɔː'] vt adorer

adorn [ə'dɔːn] vt orner

Adriatic (Sea) [eɪdrɪ'ætɪk-] n, adj: **the Adriatic (Sea)** la mer Adriatique, l'Adriatique f

adrift [ə'drɪft] adv à la dérive

adult ['ædʌlt] n adulte m/f ▷ adj (grown-up) adulte; (for adults) pour adultes; **adult education** n éducation f des adultes

adultery [ə'dʌltərɪ] n adultère m

advance [əd'vɑːns] n avance f ▷ vt avancer ▷ vi s'avancer; **in ~** en avance, d'avance; **to make ~s to sb** (gen) faire des propositions à qn; (amorously) faire des avances à qn; **~ booking** location f; **~ notice**, **~ warning** préavis m; (verbal) avertissement m; **do I**

need to book in ~? est-ce qu'il faut réserver à l'avance?; **advanced** adj avancé(e); (Scol: studies) supérieur(e)

advantage [əd'vɑːntɪdʒ] n (also Tennis) avantage m; **to take ~ of** (person) exploiter; (opportunity) profiter de

advent ['ædvənt] n avènement m, venue f; **A~** (Rel) avent m

adventure [əd'ventʃə*] n aventure f; **adventurous** [əd'ventʃərəs] adj aventureux(-euse)

adverb ['ædvɜːb] n adverbe m

adversary ['ædvəsərɪ] n adversaire m/f

adverse ['ædvɜːs] adj adverse; (effect) négatif(-ive); (weather, publicity) mauvais(e); (wind) contraire

advert ['ædvɜːt] n abbr (BRIT) = **advertisement**

advertise ['ædvətaɪz] vi faire de la publicité or de la réclame; (in classified ads etc) mettre une annonce ▷ vt faire de la publicité or de la réclame pour; (in classified ads etc) mettre une annonce pour vendre; **to ~ for** (staff) recruter par (voie d')annonce; **advertisement** [əd'vɜːtɪsmənt] n (Comm) publicité f, réclame f; (in classified ads etc) annonce f; **advertiser** n annonceur m; **advertising** n publicité f

advice [əd'vaɪs] n conseils mpl; (notification) avis m; **a piece of ~** un conseil; **to take legal ~** consulter un avocat

advisable [əd'vaɪzəbl] adj recommandable, indiqué(e)

advise [əd'vaɪz] vt conseiller; **to ~ sb of sth** aviser or informer qn de qch; **to ~ against sth/doing sth** déconseiller qch/conseiller de ne pas faire qch; **adviser, advisor** n conseiller(-ère); **advisory** adj consultatif(-ive)

advocate n ['ædvəkɪt] (lawyer) avocat (plaidant); (upholder) défenseur m, avocat(e) ▷ vt ['ædvəkeɪt] recommander, prôner; **to be an ~ of** être partisan(e) de

Aegean [iː'dʒiːən] n, adj: **the ~ (Sea)** la mer Égée, l'Égée f

aerial ['ɛərɪəl] n antenne f ▷ adj aérien(ne)

aerobics [ɛə'rəubɪks] n aérobic m

aeroplane ['ɛərəpleɪn] n (BRIT) avion m

aerosol ['ɛərəsɒl] n aérosol m

affair [ə'fɛə*] n affaire f; (also: **love ~**) liaison f, aventure f

affect [ə'fɛkt] vt affecter; (subj: disease) atteindre; **affected** adj affecté(e); **affection** n affection f; **affectionate** adj affectueux(-euse)

afflict [ə'flɪkt] vt affliger

affluent ['æfluənt] adj (person, family, surroundings) aisé(e), riche; **the ~ society** la société d'abondance

afford [ə'fɔːd] vt (behaviour) se permettre; (provide) fournir, procurer; **can we ~ a car?** avons-nous de quoi acheter or les moyens d'acheter une voiture?; **affordable** adj abordable

Afghanistan [æf'gænɪstæn] n Afghanistan m

afraid [ə'freɪd] adj effrayé(e); **to be ~ of** or **to** avoir peur de; **I am ~ that** je crains que + sub; **I'm ~ so/not** oui/non, malheureusement

Africa ['æfrɪkə] n Afrique f; **African** adj africain(e) ▷ n Africain(e); **African-American** adj afro-américain(e) ▷ n Afro-Américain(e)

after ['ɑːftə*] prep, adv après ▷ conj après que; **it's quarter ~ two** (us) il est deux heures et quart; **~ having done/~ he left** après avoir fait/ après son départ; **to ask ~ sb** demander des nouvelles de qn; **what/who are you ~?** que/qui cherchez-vous?; **~ you!** après vous!; **~ all** après tout; **after-effects** npl (of disaster, radiation, drink etc) répercussions fpl; (of illness) séquelles fpl, suites fpl; **aftermath** n conséquences fpl; **afternoon** n après-midi m or f; **after-shave (lotion)** n lotion f après-rasage; **aftersun (lotion/cream)** n après-soleil m inv; **afterwards** (us **afterward**) adv après

again [ə'gɛn] adv de nouveau, encore (une fois); **to do sth ~** refaire qch; **~ and ~** à plusieurs reprises

against [ə'gɛnst] prep contre; (compared to) par rapport à

age [eɪdʒ] n âge m ▷ vt, vi vieillir; **he is 20 years of ~** il a 20 ans; **to come of ~** atteindre sa majorité; **it's been ~s since I saw you** ça fait une éternité que je ne t'ai pas vu; **~d 10** âgé(e) de 10 ans; **age group** n tranche f d'âge; **age limit** n limite f d'âge

agency ['eɪdʒənsɪ] n agence f

agenda [ə'dʒendə] n ordre m du jour

> Be careful not to translate **agenda** by the French word **agenda**.

agent ['eɪdʒənt] n agent m; (firm) concessionnaire m

aggravate ['ægrəveɪt] vt (situation) aggraver; (annoy) exaspérer, agacer

aggression [ə'greʃən] n agression f

aggressive [ə'gresɪv] adj agressif(-ive)

agile ['ædʒaɪl] adj agile

agitated ['ædʒɪteɪtɪd] adj inquiet(-ète)

AGM n abbr (= annual general meeting) AG f

ago [ə'gəu] adv: **2 days ~** il y a 2 jours; **not long ~** il n'y a pas longtemps; **how long ~?** il y a combien de temps (de cela)?

agony ['ægənɪ] n (pain) douleur f atroce; (distress) angoisse f; **to be in ~** souffrir le martyre

agree [ə'griː] vt (price) convenir de ▷ vi: **to ~ with** (person) être d'accord avec; (statements etc) concorder avec; (Ling) s'accorder avec; **to ~ to do** accepter de or consentir à faire;

to ~ to sth consentir à qch; **to ~ that** (*admit*) convenir *or* reconnaître que; **garlic doesn't ~ with me** je ne supporte pas l'ail; **agreeable** *adj* (*pleasant*) agréable; (*willing*) consentant(e), d'accord; **agreed** *adj* (*time, place*) convenu(e); **agreement** *n* accord *m*; **in agreement** d'accord

agricultural [ægrɪˈkʌltʃərəl] *adj* agricole

agriculture [ˈægrɪkʌltʃəʳ] *n* agriculture *f*

ahead [əˈhɛd] *adv* en avant; devant; **go right** *or* **straight ~** (*direction*) allez tout droit; **go ~!** (*permission*) allez-y!; **~ of** devant; (*fig: schedule etc*) en avance sur; **~ of time** en avance

aid [eɪd] *n* aide *f*; (*device*) appareil *m* ▷ *vt* aider; **in ~ of** en faveur de

aide [eɪd] *n* (*person*) assistant(e)

AIDS [eɪdz] *n abbr* (= *acquired immune* (*or* *immuno-*)*deficiency syndrome*) SIDA *m*

ailing [ˈeɪlɪŋ] *adj* (*person*) souffreteux(euse); (*economy*) malade

ailment [ˈeɪlmənt] *n* affection *f*

aim [eɪm] *vt*: **to ~ sth (at)** (*gun, camera*) braquer *or* pointer qch (sur); (*missile*) lancer qch (à *or* contre *or* en direction de); (*remark, blow*) destiner *or* adresser qch (à) ▷ *vi* (*also*: **to take ~**) viser ▷ *n* (*objective*) but *m*; (*skill*): **his ~ is bad** il vise mal; **to ~ at** viser; (*fig*) viser (à); **to ~ to do** avoir l'intention de faire

ain't [eɪnt] (*inf*) = **am not**; **aren't**; **isn't**

air [ɛəʳ] *n* air *m* ▷ *vt* aérer; (*idea, grievance, views*) mettre sur le tapis ▷ *cpd* (*currents, attack etc*) aérien(ne); **to throw sth into the ~** (*ball etc*) jeter qch en l'air; **by ~** par avion; **to be on the ~** (*Radio, TV: programme*) être diffusé(e); (: *station*) émettre; **airbag** *n* airbag *m*; **airbed** *n* (BRIT) matelas *m* pneumatique; **airborne** *adj* (*plane*) en vol; **as soon as the plane was airborne** dès que l'avion eut décollé; **air-conditioned** *adj* climatisé(e), à air conditionné; **air conditioning** *n* climatisation *f*; **aircraft** *n inv* avion *m*; **airfield** *n* terrain *m* d'aviation; **Air Force** *n* Armée *f* de l'air; **air hostess** *n* (BRIT) hôtesse *f* de l'air; **airing cupboard** *n* (BRIT) placard qui contient la chaudière et dans lequel on met le linge à sécher; **airlift** *n* pont aérien; **airline** *n* ligne aérienne, compagnie aérienne; **airliner** *n* avion *m* de ligne; **airmail** *n*: **by airmail** par avion; **airplane** *n* (US) avion *m*; **airport** *n* aéroport *m*; **air raid** *n* attaque aérienne; **airsick** *adj*: **to be airsick** avoir le mal de l'air; **airspace** *n* espace *m* aérien; **airstrip** *n* terrain *m* d'atterrissage; **air terminal** *n* aérogare *f*; **airtight** *adj* hermétique; **air-traffic controller** *n* aiguilleur *m* du ciel; **airy** *adj* bien aéré(e); (*manners*) dégagé(e)

aisle [aɪl] *n* (*of church: central*) allée *f* centrale; (: *side*) nef *f* latérale, bas-côté *m*; (*in theatre, supermarket*) allée; (*on plane*) couloir *m*; **aisle seat** *n* place *f* côté couloir

ajar [əˈdʒɑːʳ] *adj* entrouvert(e)

à la carte [ælæˈkɑːt] *adv* à la carte

alarm [əˈlɑːm] *n* alarme *f* ▷ *vt* alarmer; **alarm call** *n* coup *m* de fil pour réveiller; **could I have an alarm call at 7 am, please?** pouvez-vous me réveiller à 7 heures, s'il vous plaît?; **alarm clock** *n* réveille-matin *m inv*, réveil *m*; **alarmed** *adj* (*frightened*) alarmé(e); (*protected by an alarm*) protégé(e) par un système d'alarme; **alarming** *adj* alarmant(e)

Albania [ælˈbeɪnɪə] *n* Albanie *f*

albeit [ɔːlˈbiːɪt] *conj* bien que + *sub*, encore que + *sub*

album [ˈælbəm] *n* album *m*

alcohol [ˈælkəhɔl] *n* alcool *m*; **alcohol-free** *adj* sans alcool; **alcoholic** [ælkəˈhɔlɪk] *adj*, *n* alcoolique (*m/f*)

alcove [ˈælkəuv] *n* alcôve *f*

ale [eɪl] *n* bière *f*

alert [əˈləːt] *adj* alerte, vif (vive); (*watchful*) vigilant(e) ▷ *n* alerte *f* ▷ *vt* alerter; **on the ~** sur le qui-vive; (Mil) en état d'alerte

algebra [ˈældʒɪbrə] *n* algèbre *m*

Algeria [ælˈdʒɪərɪə] *n* Algérie *f*

Algerian [ælˈdʒɪərɪən] *adj* algérien(ne) ▷ *n* Algérien(ne)

Algiers [ælˈdʒɪəz] *n* Alger

alias [ˈeɪlɪəs] *adv* alias ▷ *n* faux nom, nom d'emprunt

alibi [ˈælɪbaɪ] *n* alibi *m*

alien [ˈeɪlɪən] *n* (*from abroad*) étranger(-ère); (*from outer space*) extraterrestre ▷ *adj*: **~ (to)** étranger(-ère) (à); **alienate** *vt* aliéner; (*subj: person*) s'aliéner

alight [əˈlaɪt] *adj* en feu ▷ *vi* mettre pied à terre; (*passenger*) descendre; (*bird*) se poser

align [əˈlaɪn] *vt* aligner

alike [əˈlaɪk] *adj* semblable, pareil(le) ▷ *adv* de même; **to look ~** se ressembler

alive [əˈlaɪv] *adj* vivant(e); (*active*) plein(e) de vie

 KEYWORD

all [ɔːl] *adj* (*singular*) tout(e); (*plural*) tous (toutes); **all day** toute la journée; **all night** toute la nuit; **all men** tous les hommes; **all five** tous les cinq; **all the books** tous les livres; **all his life** toute sa vie

▷ *pron* **1** tout; **I ate it all, I ate all of it** j'ai tout mangé; **all of us went** nous y sommes tous allés; **all of the boys went** tous les garçons y sont allés; **is that all?** c'est tout?; (*in shop*) ce sera tout?

2 (*in phrases*): **above all** surtout, par-dessus tout; **after all** après tout; **at all:** (*in answer to question*) pas du tout; (*in answer to thanks*) je vous en prie!; **I'm not at all tired** je ne suis pas du tout fatigué(e); **anything at all**

will do n'importe quoi fera l'affaire; **all in all** tout bien considéré, en fin de compte ▷ adv: **all alone** tout(e) seul(e); **it's not as hard as all that** ce n'est pas si difficile que ça; **all the more/the better** d'autant plus/mieux; **all but** presque, pratiquement; **the score is 2 all** le score est de 2 partout

Allah ['ælə] n Allah m

allegation [ælɪ'geɪʃən] n allégation f

alleged [ə'lɛdʒd] adj prétendu(e); **allegedly** adv à ce que l'on prétend, paraît-il

allegiance [ə'li:dʒəns] n fidélité f, obéissance f

allergic [ə'lə:dʒɪk] adj: **~ to** allergique à; **I'm ~ to penicillin** je suis allergique à la pénicilline

allergy ['ælədʒɪ] n allergie f

alleviate [ə'li:vɪeɪt] vt soulager, adoucir

alley ['ælɪ] n ruelle f

alliance [ə'laɪəns] n alliance f

allied ['ælaɪd] adj allié(e)

alligator ['ælɪgeɪtə'] n alligator m

all-in ['ɔ:lɪn] adj, adv (BRIT: charge) tout compris

allocate ['æləkeɪt] vt (share out) répartir, distribuer; **to ~ sth to** (duties) assigner or attribuer qch à; (sum, time) allouer qch à

allot [ə'lɔt] vt (share out) répartir, distribuer; **to ~ sth to** (time) allouer qch à; (duties) assigner qch à

all-out ['ɔ:laut] adj (effort etc) total(e)

allow [ə'lau] vt (practice, behaviour) permettre, autoriser; (sum to spend etc) accorder, allouer; (sum, time estimated) compter, prévoir; (claim, goal) admettre; (concede): **to ~ that** convenir que; **to ~ sb to do** permettre à qn de faire, autoriser qn à faire; **he is ~ed to ...** on lui permet de ...; **allow for** vt fus tenir compte de; **allowance** n (money received) allocation f; (: from parent etc) subside m; (: for expenses) indemnité f; (us: pocket money) argent m de poche; (Tax) somme f déductible du revenu imposable, abattement m; **to make allowances for** (person) essayer de comprendre; (thing) tenir compte de

all right adv (feel, work) bien; (as answer) d'accord

ally n ['ælaɪ] allié m ▷ vt [ə'laɪ]: **to ~ o.s. with** s'allier avec

almighty [ɔ:l'maɪtɪ] adj tout(e)-puissant(e); (tremendous) énorme

almond ['ɑ:mənd] n amande f

almost ['ɔ:lməust] adv presque

alone [ə'ləun] adj, adv seul(e); **to leave sb ~** laisser qn tranquille; **to leave sth ~** ne pas toucher à qch; **let ~ ...** sans parler de ...; encore moins ...

along [ə'lɔŋ] prep le long de ▷ adv: **is he coming ~ with us?** vient-il avec nous?; **he was hopping/limping ~** il venait or avançait

en sautillant/boitant; **~ with** avec, en plus de; (person) en compagnie de; **all ~** (all the time) depuis le début; **alongside** prep (along) le long de; (beside) à côté de ▷ adv bord à bord; côte à côte

aloof [ə'lu:f] adj distant(e) ▷ adv: **to stand ~** se tenir à l'écart or à distance

aloud [ə'laud] adv à haute voix

alphabet ['ælfəbet] n alphabet m

Alps [ælps] npl: **the ~** les Alpes fpl

already [ɔ:l'redɪ] adv déjà

alright ['ɔ:lraɪt] adv (BRIT) = **all right**

also ['ɔ:lsəu] adv aussi

altar ['ɔltə'] n autel m

alter ['ɔltə'] vt, vi changer; **alteration** [ɔltə'reɪʃən] n changement m, modification f; **alterations** npl (Sewing) retouches fpl; (Archit) modifications fpl

alternate adj [ɔl'tə:nɪt] alterné(e), alternant(e), alternatif(-ive); (us) = **alternative** ▷ vi ['ɔltə:neɪt] alterner; **to ~ with** alterner avec; **on ~ days** un jour sur deux, tous les deux jours

alternative [ɔl'tə:nətɪv] adj (solution, plan) autre, de remplacement; (lifestyle) parallèle ▷ n (choice) alternative f; (other possibility) autre possibilité f; **~ medicine** médecine alternative, médecine douce; **alternatively** adv: **alternatively one could ...** une autre or l'autre solution serait de ...

although [ɔ:l'ðəu] conj bien que + sub

altitude ['æltɪtju:d] n altitude f

altogether [ɔ:ltə'gɛðə'] adv entièrement, tout à fait; (on the whole) tout compte fait; (in all) en tout

aluminium [ælju'mɪnɪəm] (BRIT **aluminum**) [ə'lu:mɪnəm] (us) n aluminium m

always ['ɔ:lweɪz] adv toujours

Alzheimer's (disease) ['æltshaɪməz-] n maladie f d'Alzheimer

am [æm] vb see **be**

a.m. adv abbr (= ante meridiem) du matin

amalgamate [ə'mælgəmeɪt] vt, vi fusionner

amass [ə'mæs] vt amasser

amateur ['æmətə'] n amateur m

amaze [ə'meɪz] vt stupéfier; **to be ~d (at)** être stupéfait(e) (de); **amazed** adj stupéfait(e); **amazement** n surprise f, étonnement m; **amazing** adj étonnant(e), incroyable; (bargain, offer) exceptionnel(le)

Amazon ['æməzən] n (Geo) Amazone f

ambassador [æm'bæsədə'] n ambassadeur m

amber ['æmbə'] n ambre m; **at ~** (BRIT Aut) à l'orange

ambiguous [æm'bɪgjuəs] adj ambigu(ë)

ambition [æm'bɪʃən] n ambition f; **ambitious** [æm'bɪʃəs] adj ambitieux(-euse)

ambulance ['æmbjuləns] n ambulance f;

call an ~! appelez une ambulance!
ambush ['æmbʊʃ] *n* embuscade *f* ▷ *vt* tendre une embuscade à
amen ['ɑ:'mɛn] *excl* amen
amend [ə'mɛnd] *vt* (*law*) amender; (*text*) corriger; **to make ~s** réparer ses torts, faire amende honorable; **amendment** *n* (*to law*) amendement *m*; (*to text*) correction *f*
amenities [ə'mi:nɪtɪz] *npl* aménagements *mpl*, équipements *mpl*
America [ə'mɛrɪkə] *n* Amérique *f*; **American** *adj* américain(e) ▷ *n* Américain(e); **American football** *n* (BRIT) football *m* américain
amicable ['æmɪkəbl] *adj* amical(e); (*Law*) à l'amiable
amid(st) [ə'mɪd(st)] *prep* parmi, au milieu de
ammunition [æmju'nɪʃən] *n* munitions *fpl*
amnesty ['æmnɪstɪ] *n* amnistie *f*
among(st) [ə'mʌŋ(st)] *prep* parmi, entre
amount [ə'maunt] *n* (*sum of money*) somme *f*; (*total*) montant *m*; (*quantity*) quantité *f*; nombre *m* ▷ *vi*: **to ~ to** (*total*) s'élever à; (*be same as*) équivaloir à, revenir à
amp(ère) ['æmp(eər)] *n* ampère *m*
ample ['æmpl] *adj* ample, spacieux(-euse); (*enough*): **this is ~** c'est largement suffisant; **to have ~ time/room** avoir bien assez de temps/place
amplifier ['æmplɪfaɪər] *n* amplificateur *m*
amputate ['æmpjuteɪt] *vt* amputer
Amtrak ['æmtræk] (US) *n* société mixte de transports ferroviaires interurbains pour voyageurs
amuse [ə'mju:z] *vt* amuser; **amusement** *n* amusement *m*; (*pastime*) distraction *f*; **amusement arcade** *n* salle *f* de jeu; **amusement park** *n* parc *m* d'attractions
amusing [ə'mju:zɪŋ] *adj* amusant(e), divertissant(e)
an [æn, ən, n] *indef art see* **a**
anaemia [ə'ni:mɪə] (US **anemia**) *n* anémie *f*
anaemic [ə'ni:mɪk] (US **anemic**) *adj* anémique
anaesthetic [ænɪs'θɛtɪk] (US **anesthetic**) *n* anesthésique *m*
analog(ue) ['ænəlɔg] *adj* (*watch, computer*) analogique
analogy [ə'nælədʒɪ] *n* analogie *f*
analyse ['ænəlaɪz] (US **analyze**) *vt* analyser; **analysis** (*pl* **analyses**) [ə'næləsɪs, -si:z] *n* analyse *f*; **analyst** ['ænəlɪst] *n* (*political analyst etc*) analyste *m/f*; (US) psychanalyste *m/f*
analyze ['ænəlaɪz] *vt* (US) = **analyse**
anarchy ['ænəkɪ] *n* anarchie *f*
anatomy [ə'nætəmɪ] *n* anatomie *f*
ancestor ['ænsɪstər] *n* ancêtre *m*, aïeul *m*
anchor ['æŋkər] *n* ancre *f* ▷ *vi* (*also*: **to drop ~**) jeter l'ancre, mouiller ▷ *vt* mettre à l'ancre;

(*fig*): **to ~ sth to** fixer qch à
anchovy ['æntʃəvɪ] *n* anchois *m*
ancient ['eɪnʃənt] *adj* ancien(ne), antique; (*person*) d'un âge vénérable; (*car*) antédiluvien(ne)
and [ænd] *conj* et; **~ so on** et ainsi de suite; **try ~ come** tâchez de venir; **come ~ sit here** venez vous asseoir ici; **he talked ~ talked** il a parlé pendant des heures; **better ~ better** de mieux en mieux; **more ~ more** de plus en plus
Andorra [æn'dɔ:rə] *n* (principauté *f* d')Andorre *f*
anemia *etc* [ə'ni:mɪə] (US) = **anaemia** *etc*
anesthetic [ænɪs'θɛtɪk] (US) = **anaesthetic**
angel ['eɪndʒəl] *n* ange *m*
anger ['æŋgər] *n* colère *f*
angina [æn'dʒaɪnə] *n* angine *f* de poitrine
angle ['æŋgl] *n* angle *m*; **from their ~** de leur point de vue
angler ['æŋglər] *n* pêcheur(-euse) à la ligne
Anglican ['æŋglɪkən] *adj, n* anglican(e)
angling ['æŋglɪŋ] *n* pêche *f* à la ligne
angrily ['æŋgrɪlɪ] *adv* avec colère
angry ['æŋgrɪ] *adj* en colère, furieux(-euse); (*wound*) enflammé(e); **to be ~ with sb/at sth** être furieux contre qn/de qch; **to get ~** se fâcher, se mettre en colère
anguish ['æŋgwɪʃ] *n* angoisse *f*
animal ['ænɪməl] *n* animal *m* ▷ *adj* animal(e)
animated ['ænɪmeɪtɪd] *adj* animé(e)
animation [ænɪ'meɪʃən] *n* (*of person*) entrain *m*; (*of street, Cine*) animation *f*
aniseed ['ænɪsi:d] *n* anis *m*
ankle ['æŋkl] *n* cheville *f*
annex ['ænɛks] *n* (BRIT: *also*: **~e**) annexe *f* ▷ *vt* [ə'nɛks] annexer
anniversary [ænɪ'və:sərɪ] *n* anniversaire *m*
announce [ə'nauns] *vt* annoncer; (*birth, death*) faire part de; **announcement** *n* annonce *f*; (*for births etc: in newspaper*) avis *m* de faire-part; (: *letter, card*) faire-part *m*; **announcer** *n* (*Radio, TV: between programmes*) speaker(ine); (: *in a programme*) présentateur(-trice)
annoy [ə'nɔɪ] *vt* agacer, ennuyer, contrarier; **don't get ~ed!** ne vous fâchez pas!; **annoying** *adj* agaçant(e), contrariant(e)
annual ['ænjuəl] *adj* annuel(le) ▷ *n* (*Bot*) plante annuelle; (*book*) album *m*; **annually** *adv* annuellement
annum ['ænəm] *n see* **per**
anonymous [ə'nɔnɪməs] *adj* anonyme
anorak ['ænəræk] *n* anorak *m*
anorexia [ænə'rɛksɪə] *n* (*also*: **~ nervosa**) anorexie *f*
anorexic [ænə'rɛksɪk] *adj, n* anorexique (*m/f*)
another [ə'nʌðər] *adj*: **~ book** (*one more*) un

autre livre, encore un livre, un livre de plus; (*a different one*) un autre livre ▷ *pron* un(e) autre, encore un(e), un(e) de plus; *see also* **one**

answer [ˈɑːnsəʳ] *n* réponse *f*; (*to problem*) solution *f* ▷ *vi* répondre ▷ *vt* (*reply to*) répondre à; (*problem*) résoudre; (*prayer*) exaucer; **in ~ to your letter** suite à or en réponse à votre lettre; **to ~ the phone** répondre (au téléphone); **to ~ the bell** or **the door** aller or venir ouvrir (la porte); **answer back** *vi* répondre, répliquer; **answerphone** *n* (*esp* BRIT) répondeur *m* (téléphonique)

ant [ænt] *n* fourmi *f*

Antarctic [æntˈɑːktɪk] *n*: **the ~** l'Antarctique *m*

antelope [ˈæntɪləʊp] *n* antilope *f*

antenatal [ˈæntɪˈneɪtl] *adj* prénatal(e)

antenna (*pl* **-e**) [ænˈtɛnə, -niː] *n* antenne *f*

anthem [ˈænθəm] *n*: **national ~** hymne national

anthology [ænˈθɔlədʒɪ] *n* anthologie *f*

anthrax [ˈænθræks] *n* anthrax *m*

anthropology [ænθrəˈpɔlədʒɪ] *n* anthropologie *f*

anti [ˈæntɪ] *prefix* anti-; **antibiotic** [ˈæntɪbaɪˈɔtɪk] *n* antibiotique *m*; **antibody** [ˈæntɪbɔdɪ] *n* anticorps *m*

anticipate [ænˈtɪsɪpeɪt] *vt* s'attendre à, prévoir; (*wishes, request*) aller au devant de, devancer; **anticipation** [æntɪsɪˈpeɪʃən] *n* attente *f*

anticlimax [ˈæntɪˈklaɪmæks] *n* déception *f*

anticlockwise [ˈæntɪˈklɔkwaɪz] (BRIT) *adv* dans le sens inverse des aiguilles d'une montre

antics [ˈæntɪks] *npl* singeries *fpl*

anti: **antidote** [ˈæntɪdəʊt] *n* antidote *m*, contrepoison *m*; **antifreeze** [ˈæntɪfriːz] *n* antigel *m*; **anti-globalization** *n* antimondialisation *f*; **antihistamine** [æntɪˈhɪstəmɪn] *n* antihistaminique *m*; **antiperspirant** [æntɪˈpəːspɪrənt] *n* déodorant *m*

antique [ænˈtiːk] *n* (*ornament*) objet *m* d'art ancien; (*furniture*) meuble ancien ▷ *adj* ancien(ne); **antique shop** *n* magasin *m* d'antiquités

antiseptic [æntɪˈsɛptɪk] *adj*, *n* antiseptique (*m*)

antisocial [ˈæntɪˈsəʊʃəl] *adj* (*unfriendly*) peu liant(e), insociable; (*against society*) antisocial(e)

antlers [ˈæntləz] *npl* bois *mpl*, ramure *f*

anxiety [æŋˈzaɪətɪ] *n* anxiété *f*; (*keenness*): **~ to do** grand désir or impatience *f* de faire

anxious [ˈæŋkʃəs] *adj* (très) inquiet(-ète); (*always worried*) anxieux(-euse); (*worrying*) angoissant(e); (*keen*): **~ to do/that** qui tient

beaucoup à faire/à ce que + *sub*; impatient(e) de faire/que + *sub*

 KEYWORD

any [ˈɛnɪ] *adj* **1** (*in questions etc: singular*) du, de l', de la; (: *plural*) des; **do you have any butter/children/ink?** avez-vous du beurre/des enfants/de l'encre?

2 (*with negative*) de, d'; **I don't have any money/books** je n'ai pas d'argent/de livres

3 (*no matter which*) n'importe quel(le); (*each and every*) tout(e), chaque; **choose any book you like** vous pouvez choisir n'importe quel livre; **any teacher you ask will tell you** n'importe quel professeur vous le dira

4 (*in phrases*): **in any case** de toute façon; **any day now** d'un jour à l'autre; **at any moment** à tout moment, d'un instant à l'autre; **at any rate** en tout cas; **any time** n'importe quand; **he might come (at) any time** il pourrait venir n'importe quand; **come (at) any time** venez quand vous voulez

▷ *pron* **1** (*in questions etc*) en; **have you got any?** est-ce que vous en avez?; **can any of you sing?** est-ce que parmi vous il y en a qui savent chanter?

2 (*with negative*) en; **I don't have any (of them)** je n'en ai pas, je n'en ai aucun

3 (*no matter which one(s)*) n'importe lequel (or laquelle); (*anybody*) n'importe qui; **take any of those books (you like)** vous pouvez prendre n'importe lequel de ces livres

▷ *adv* **1** (*in questions etc*): **do you want any more soup/sandwiches?** voulez-vous encore de la soupe/des sandwichs?; **are you feeling any better?** est-ce que vous vous sentez mieux?

2 (*with negative*): **I can't hear him any more** je ne l'entends plus; **don't wait any longer** n'attendez pas plus longtemps; **anybody** *pron* n'importe qui; (*in interrogative sentences*) quelqu'un; (*in negative sentences*): **I don't see anybody** je ne vois personne; **if anybody should phone ...** si quelqu'un téléphone ...; **anyhow** *adv* quoi qu'il en soit; (*haphazardly*) n'importe comment; **do it anyhow you like** faites-le comme vous voulez; **she leaves things just anyhow** elle laisse tout traîner; **I shall go anyhow** j'irai de toute façon; **anyone** *pron* = **anybody**; **anything** *pron* (*no matter what*) n'importe quoi; (*in questions*) quelque chose; (*with negative*) ne ... rien; **can you see anything?** tu vois quelque chose?; **if anything happens to me ...** s'il m'arrive quoi que ce soit ...; **you can say anything you like** vous pouvez dire ce que vous voulez; **anything will do** n'importe quoi fera l'affaire; **he'll eat anything** il mange de tout; **anytime**

adv (*at any moment*) d'un moment à l'autre; (*whenever*) n'importe quand; **anyway** adv de toute façon; **anyway, I couldn't come even if I wanted to** de toute façon, je ne pouvais pas venir même si je le voulais; **I shall go anyway** j'irai quand même; **why are you phoning, anyway?** au fait, pourquoi tu me téléphones?; **anywhere** adv n'importe où; (*in interrogative sentences*) quelque part; (*in negative sentences*): **I can't see him anywhere** je ne le vois nulle part; **can you see him anywhere?** tu le vois quelque part?; **put the books down anywhere** pose les livres n'importe où; **anywhere in the world** (*no matter where*) n'importe où dans le monde

apart [əˈpɑːt] adv (*to one side*) à part; de côté; à l'écart; (*separately*) séparément; **to take/pull ~ démonter; 10 miles/a long way ~** à 10 miles/très éloignés l'un de l'autre; **~ from** prep à part, excepté

apartment [əˈpɑːtmənt] n (*us*) appartement m, logement m; (*room*) chambre f; **apartment building** n (*us*) immeuble m; maison divisée en appartements

apathy [ˈæpəθɪ] n apathie f, indifférence f

ape [eɪp] n (grand) singe ▷ vt singer

aperitif [əˈperɪtif] n apéritif m

aperture [ˈæpətʃjuəʳ] n orifice m, ouverture f; (*Phot*) ouverture (du diaphragme)

APEX [ˈeɪpɛks] n abbr (*Aviat*: = *advance purchase excursion*) APEX m

apologize [əˈpɒlədʒaɪz] vi: **to ~ (for sth to sb)** s'excuser (de qch auprès de qn), présenter des excuses (à qn pour qch)

apology [əˈpɒlədʒɪ] n excuses fpl

apostrophe [əˈpɒstrəfɪ] n apostrophe f

appal [əˈpɔːl] (*us* **appall**) vt consterner, atterrer; horrifier; **appalling** adj épouvantable; (*stupidity*) consternant(e)

apparatus [æpəˈreɪtəs] n appareil m, dispositif m; (*in gymnasium*) agrès mpl

apparent [əˈpærənt] adj apparent(e); **apparently** adv apparemment

appeal [əˈpiːl] vi (*Law*) faire or interjeter appel ▷ n (*Law*) appel m; (*request*) appel; prière f; (*charm*) attrait m, charme m; **to ~ for** demander (instamment); implorer; **to ~ to** (*beg*) faire appel à; (*be attractive*) plaire à; **it doesn't ~ to me** cela ne m'attire pas; **appealing** adj (*attractive*) attrayant(e)

appear [əˈpɪəʳ] vi apparaître, se montrer; (*Law*) comparaître; (*publication*) paraître, sortir, être publié(e); (*seem*) paraître, sembler; **it would ~ that** il semble que; **to ~ in Hamlet** jouer dans Hamlet; **to ~ on TV** passer à la télé; **appearance** n apparition f; parution f; (*look, aspect*) apparence f, aspect m

appendices [əˈpɛndɪsiːz] npl of **appendix**

appendicitis [əpɛndɪˈsaɪtɪs] n appendicite f

appendix (pl **appendices**) [əˈpɛndɪks, -siːz] n appendice m

appetite [ˈæpɪtaɪt] n appétit m

appetizer [ˈæpɪtaɪzəʳ] n (*food*) amuse-gueule m; (*drink*) apéritif m

applaud [əˈplɔːd] vt, vi applaudir

applause [əˈplɔːz] n applaudissements mpl

apple [ˈæpl] n pomme f; **apple pie** n tarte f aux pommes

appliance [əˈplaɪəns] n appareil m

applicable [əˈplɪkəbl] adj applicable; **to be ~ to** (*relevant*) valoir pour

applicant [ˈæplɪkənt] n: **~ (for)** candidat(e) (à)

application [æplɪˈkeɪʃən] n application f; (*for a job, a grant etc*) demande f; candidature f; **application form** n formulaire m de demande

apply [əˈplaɪ] vt: **to ~ (to)** (*paint, ointment*) appliquer (sur); (*law, etc*) appliquer (à) ▷ vi: **to ~ to** (*ask*) s'adresser à; (*be suitable for, relevant to*) s'appliquer à; **to ~ (for)** (*permit, grant*) faire une demande (en vue d'obtenir); (*job*) poser sa candidature (pour), faire une demande d'emploi (concernant); **to ~ o.s. to** s'appliquer à

appoint [əˈpɔɪnt] vt (*to post*) nommer, engager; (*date, place*) fixer, désigner; **appointment** n (*to post*) nomination f; (*job*) poste m; (*arrangement to meet*) rendez-vous m; **to have an appointment** avoir un rendez-vous; **to make an appointment (with)** prendre rendez-vous (avec); **I'd like to make an appointment** je voudrais prendre rendez-vous

appraisal [əˈpreɪzl] n évaluation f

appreciate [əˈpriːʃieɪt] vt (*like*) apprécier, faire cas de; (*be grateful for*) être reconnaissant(e) de; (*be aware of*) comprendre, se rendre compte de ▷ vi (*Finance*) prendre de la valeur; **appreciation** [əpriːʃɪˈeɪʃən] n appréciation f; (*gratitude*) reconnaissance f; (*Finance*) hausse f, valorisation f

apprehension [æprɪˈhɛnʃən] n appréhension f, inquiétude f

apprehensive [æprɪˈhɛnsɪv] adj inquiet(-ète), appréhensif(-ive)

apprentice [əˈprɛntɪs] n apprenti m

approach [əˈprəʊtʃ] vi approcher ▷ vt (*come near*) approcher de; (*ask, apply to*) s'adresser à; (*subject, passer-by*) aborder ▷ n approche f; accès m, abord m; démarche f (*intellectuelle*)

appropriate adj [əˈprəʊprɪət] (*tool etc*) qui convient, approprié(e); (*moment, remark*) opportun(e) ▷ vt [əˈprəʊprɪeɪt] (*take*) s'approprier

approval [əˈpruːvəl] n approbation f; **on ~** (*Comm*) à l'examen

approve [əˈpruːv] vt approuver; **approve of**

vt fus (thing) approuver; *(person)*: **they don't ~ of her** ils n'ont pas bonne opinion d'elle

approximate [ə'prɔksɪmɪt] *adj* approximatif(-ive); **approximately** *adv* approximativement

Apr. *abbr* = **April**

apricot ['eɪprɪkɔt] *n* abricot *m*

April ['eɪprəl] *n* avril *m*; **April Fools' Day** *n* le premier avril

● **APRIL FOOLS' DAY**
●
● **April Fools' Day** est le 1er avril, à l'occasion
● duquel on fait des farces de toutes sortes.
● Les victimes de ces farces sont les "April
● fools". Traditionnellement, on n'est censé
● faire des farces que jusqu'à midi.

apron ['eɪprən] *n* tablier *m*

apt [æpt] *adj (suitable)* approprié(e); *(likely)*: **~ to do** susceptible de faire; ayant tendance à faire

aquarium [ə'kwɛərɪəm] *n* aquarium *m*

Aquarius [ə'kwɛərɪəs] *n* le Verseau

Arab ['ærəb] *n* Arabe *m/f* ▷ *adj* arabe

Arabia [ə'reɪbɪə] *n* Arabie *f*; **Arabian** *adj* arabe; **Arabic** ['ærəbɪk] *adj*, *n* arabe (*m*)

arbitrary ['ɑ:bɪtrərɪ] *adj* arbitraire

arbitration [ɑ:bɪ'treɪʃən] *n* arbitrage *m*

arc [ɑ:k] *n* arc *m*

arcade [ɑ:'keɪd] *n* arcade *f*; *(passage with shops)* passage *m*, galerie *f*; *(with games)* salle *f* de jeu

arch [ɑ:tʃ] *n* arche *f*; *(of foot)* cambrure *f*, voûte *f* plantaire ▷ *vt* arquer, cambrer

archaeology [ɑ:kɪ'ɔlədʒɪ] *(us* **archeology***) n* archéologie *f*

archbishop [ɑ:tʃ'bɪʃəp] *n* archevêque *m*

archeology [ɑ:kɪ'ɔlədʒɪ] *(us)* = **archaeology**

architect ['ɑ:kɪtɛkt] *n* architecte *m*; **architectural** [ɑ:kɪ'tɛktʃərəl] *adj* architectural(e); **architecture** *n* architecture *f*

archive ['ɑ:kaɪv] *n (often pl)* archives *fpl*

Arctic ['ɑ:ktɪk] *adj* arctique ▷ *n*: **the ~** l'Arctique *m*

are [ɑ:ʳ] *vb see* **be**

area ['ɛərɪə] *n (Geom)* superficie *f*, *(zone)* région *f*; *(: smaller)* secteur *m*; *(in room)* coin *m*; *(knowledge, research)* domaine *m*; **area code** *(us) n (Tel)* indicatif *m* de zone

arena [ə'ri:nə] *n* arène *f*

aren't [ɑ:nt] = **are not**

Argentina [ɑ:dʒən'ti:nə] *n* Argentine *f*; **Argentinian** [ɑ:dʒən'tɪnɪən] *adj* argentin(e) ▷ *n* Argentin(e)

arguably ['ɑ:gjuəblɪ] *adv*: **it is ~ ...** on peut soutenir que c'est ...

argue ['ɑ:gju:] *vi (quarrel)* se disputer; *(reason)* argumenter; **to ~ that** objecter *or* alléguer que, donner comme argument que

argument ['ɑ:gjumənt] *n (quarrel)* dispute *f*, discussion *f*; *(reasons)* argument *m*

Aries ['ɛərɪz] *n* le Bélier

arise *(pt* **arose**, *pp* **~n)** [ə'raɪz, ə'rəuz, ə'rɪzn] *vi* survenir, se présenter

arithmetic [ə'rɪθmətɪk] *n* arithmétique *f*

arm [ɑ:m] *n* bras *m* ▷ *vt* armer; **arms** *npl (weapons, Heraldry)* armes *fpl*; **~ in ~** bras dessus bras dessous; **armchair** ['ɑ:mtʃɛəʳ] *n* fauteuil *m*

armed [ɑ:md] *adj* armé(e); **armed forces** *npl*: **the armed forces** les forces armées; **armed robbery** *n* vol *m* à main armée

armour *(us* **armor***)* ['ɑ:məʳ] *n* armure *f*; *(Mil: tanks)* blindés *mpl*

armpit ['ɑ:mpɪt] *n* aisselle *f*

armrest ['ɑ:mrɛst] *n* accoudoir *m*

army ['ɑ:mɪ] *n* armée *f*

A road *n (BRIT)* ≈ route nationale

aroma [ə'rəumə] *n* arôme *m*; **aromatherapy** *n* aromathérapie *f*

arose [ə'rəuz] *pt of* **arise**

around [ə'raund] *adv (tout)* autour; *(nearby)* dans les parages ▷ *prep* autour de; *(near)* près de; *(fig: about)* environ; *(: date, time)* vers; **is he ~?** est-il dans les parages or là?

arouse [ə'rauz] *vt (sleeper)* éveiller; *(curiosity, passions)* éveiller, susciter; *(anger)* exciter

arrange [ə'reɪndʒ] *vt* arranger; **to ~ to do sth** prévoir de faire qch; **arrangement** *n* arrangement *m*; **arrangements** *npl (plans etc)* arrangements *mpl*, dispositions *fpl*

array [ə'reɪ] *n (of objects)* déploiement *m*, étalage *m*

arrears [ə'rɪəz] *npl* arriéré *m*; **to be in ~ with one's rent** devoir un arriéré de loyer

arrest [ə'rɛst] *vt* arrêter; *(sb's attention)* retenir, attirer ▷ *n* arrestation *f*; **under ~** en état d'arrestation

arrival [ə'raɪvl] *n* arrivée *f*; **new ~** nouveau venu/nouvelle venue; *(baby)* nouveau-né(e)

arrive [ə'raɪv] *vi* arriver; **arrive at** *vt fus (decision, solution)* parvenir à

arrogance ['ærəgəns] *n* arrogance *f*

arrogant ['ærəgənt] *adj* arrogant(e)

arrow ['ærəu] *n* flèche *f*

arse [ɑ:s] *n (BRIT inf!)* cul *m* (!)

arson ['ɑ:sn] *n* incendie criminel

art [ɑ:t] *n* art *m*; **Arts** *npl (Scol)* les lettres *fpl*; **art college** *n* école *f* des beaux-arts

artery ['ɑ:tərɪ] *n* artère *f*

art gallery *n* musée *m* d'art; *(saleroom)* galerie *f* de peinture

arthritis [ɑ:'θraɪtɪs] *n* arthrite *f*

artichoke ['ɑ:tɪtʃəuk] *n* artichaut *m*; **Jerusalem ~** topinambour *m*

article ['ɑ:tɪkl] *n* article *m*

articulate *adj* [ɑ:'tɪkjulɪt] *(person)* qui s'exprime clairement et aisément; *(speech)*

bien articulé(e), prononcé(e) clairement
▷ *vb* [ɑːˈtɪkjuleɪt] ▷ *vi* articuler, parler
distinctement ▷ *vt* articuler
artificial [ɑːtɪˈfɪʃəl] *adj* artificiel(le)
artist [ˈɑːtɪst] *n* artiste *m/f*; **artistic** [ɑːˈtɪstɪk]
adj artistique
art school *n* ≈ école *f* des beaux-arts

 KEYWORD

as [æz] *conj* **1** (*time: moment*) comme, alors que;
à mesure que; **he came in as I was leaving**
il est arrivé comme je partais; **as the years
went by** à mesure que les années passaient;
as from tomorrow à partir de demain
2 (*since, because*) comme, puisque; **he left
early as he had to be home by 10** comme il *or*
puisqu'il devait être de retour avant 10h, il est
parti de bonne heure
3 (*referring to manner, way*) comme; **do as you
wish** faites comme vous voudrez; **as she said**
comme elle disait
▷ *adv* **1** (*in comparisons*): **as big as** aussi grand
que; **twice as big as** deux fois plus grand que;
as much *or* **many as** autant que; **as much
money/many books as** autant d'argent/de
livres que; **as soon as** dès que
2 (*concerning*): **as for** *or* **to that** quant à cela,
pour ce qui est de cela
3: **as if** *or* **though** comme si; **he looked as if
he was ill** il avait l'air d'être malade; *see also*
long; **such**; **well**
▷ *prep* (*in the capacity of*) en tant que, en qualité
de; **he works as a driver** il travaille comme
chauffeur; **as chairman of the company,
he ...** en tant que président de la société, il ...;
he gave me it as a present il me l'a offert, il
m'en a fait cadeau

a.s.a.p. *abbr* = **as soon as possible**
asbestos [æzˈbɛstəs] *n* asbeste *m*, amiante *m*
ascent [əˈsɛnt] *n* (*climb*) ascension *f*
ash [æʃ] *n* (*dust*) cendre *f*; (*also:* **~ tree**) frêne *m*
ashamed [əˈʃeɪmd] *adj* honteux(-euse),
confus(e); **to be ~ of** avoir honte de
ashore [əˈʃɔːʳ] *adv* à terre
ashtray [ˈæʃtreɪ] *n* cendrier *m*
Ash Wednesday *n* mercredi *m* des Cendres
Asia [ˈeɪʃə] *n* Asie *f*; **Asian** *n* (*from Asia*)
Asiatique *m/f*; (BRIT: *from Indian subcontinent*)
Indo-Pakistanais(-e) ▷ *adj* asiatique; indo-
pakistanais(-e)
aside [əˈsaɪd] *adv* de côté; à l'écart ▷ *n*
aparté *m*
ask [ɑːsk] *vt* demander; (*invite*) inviter; **to ~ sb
sth/to do sth** demander à qn qch/de faire
qch; **to ~ sb about sth** questionner qn au
sujet de qch; se renseigner auprès de qn au
sujet de qch; **to ~ (sb) a question** poser une

question (à qn); **to ~ sb out to dinner** inviter
qn au restaurant; **ask for** *vt fus* demander;
it's just ~ing for trouble *or* **for it** ce serait
chercher les ennuis
asleep [əˈsliːp] *adj* endormi(e); **to fall ~**
s'endormir
AS level *n abbr* (= Advanced Subsidiary level)
première partie de l'examen équivalent au
baccalauréat
asparagus [əsˈpærəgəs] *n* asperges *fpl*
aspect [ˈæspɛkt] *n* aspect *m*; (*direction in which
a building etc faces*) orientation *f*, exposition *f*
aspirations [æspəˈreɪʃənz] *npl* (*hopes,
ambition*) aspirations *fpl*
aspire [əsˈpaɪəʳ] *vi*: **to ~ to** aspirer à
aspirin [ˈæsprɪn] *n* aspirine *f*
ass [æs] *n* âne *m*; (*inf*) imbécile *m/f*; (us *inf!*)
cul *m* (!)
assassin [əˈsæsɪn] *n* assassin *m*; **assassinate**
vt assassiner
assault [əˈsɔːlt] *n* (Mil) assaut *m*; (*gen: attack*)
agression *f* ▷ *vt* attaquer; (*sexually*) violenter
assemble [əˈsɛmbl] *vt* assembler ▷ *vi*
s'assembler, se rassembler
assembly [əˈsɛmblɪ] *n* (*meeting*)
rassemblement *m*; (*parliament*) assemblée *f*;
(*construction*) assemblage *m*
assert [əˈsəːt] *vt* affirmer, déclarer; (*authority*)
faire valoir; (*innocence*) protester de; **assertion**
[əˈsəːʃən] *n* assertion *f*, affirmation *f*
assess [əˈsɛs] *vt* évaluer, estimer; (*tax,
damages*) établir *or* fixer le montant de; (*person*)
juger la valeur de; **assessment** *n* évaluation *f*,
estimation *f*; (*of tax*) fixation *f*
asset [ˈæsɛt] *n* avantage *m*, atout *m*; (*person*)
atout; **assets** *npl* (Comm) capital *m*; avoir(s)
m(pl); actif *m*
assign [əˈsaɪn] *vt* (*date*) fixer, arrêter; **to ~ sth
to** (*task*) assigner qch à; (*resources*) affecter qch
à; **assignment** *n* (*task*) mission *f*; (*homework*)
devoir *m*
assist [əˈsɪst] *vt* aider, assister; **assistance** *n*
aide *f*, assistance *f*; **assistant** *n* assistant(e),
adjoint(e); (BRIT: *also*: **shop assistant**)
vendeur(-euse)
associate *adj, n* [əˈsəʊʃɪɪt] associé(e) ▷ *vb*
[əˈsəʊʃɪeɪt] ▷ *vt* associer ▷ *vi*: **to ~ with sb**
fréquenter qn
association [əsəʊsɪˈeɪʃən] *n* association *f*
assorted [əˈsɔːtɪd] *adj* assorti(e)
assortment [əˈsɔːtmənt] *n* assortiment *m*;
(*of people*) mélange *m*
assume [əˈsjuːm] *vt* supposer; (*responsibilities
etc*) assumer; (*attitude, name*) prendre, adopter
assumption [əˈsʌmpʃən] *n* supposition *f*,
hypothèse *f*; (*of power*) assomption *f*, prise *f*
assurance [əˈʃuərəns] *n* assurance *f*
assure [əˈʃuəʳ] *vt* assurer
asterisk [ˈæstərɪsk] *n* astérisque *m*

asthma [ˈæsmə] n asthme m
astonish [əˈstɔnɪʃ] vt étonner, stupéfier;
astonished adj étonné(e); **to be astonished
at** être étonné(e) de; **astonishing** adj
étonnant(e), stupéfiant(e); **I find it
astonishing that ...** je trouve incroyable
que ... + sub; **astonishment** n (grand)
étonnement, stupéfaction f
astound [əˈstaund] vt stupéfier, sidérer
astray [əˈstreɪ] adv: **to go ~** s'égarer; (fig)
quitter le droit chemin; **to lead ~** (morally)
détourner du droit chemin
astrology [əsˈtrɔlədʒɪ] n astrologie f
astronaut [ˈæstrənɔːt] n astronaute m/f
astronomer [əsˈtrɔnəmə r] n astronome m
astronomical [æstrəˈnɔmɪkl] adj
astronomique
astronomy [əsˈtrɔnəmɪ] n astronomie f
astute [əsˈtjuːt] adj astucieux(-euse),
malin(-igne)
asylum [əˈsaɪləm] n asile m; **asylum seeker**
[-siːkə r] n demandeur(-euse) d'asile

 KEYWORD

at [æt] prep **1** (referring to position, direction) à;
at the top au sommet; **at home/school** à la
maison ou chez soi/à l'école; **at the baker's** à
la boulangerie, chez le boulanger; **to look at
sth** regarder qch
2 (referring to time): **at 4 o'clock** à 4 heures; **at
Christmas** à Noël; **at night** la nuit; **at times**
par moments, parfois
3 (referring to rates, speed etc) à; **at £1 a kilo** une
livre le kilo; **two at a time** deux à la fois; **at 50
km/h** à 50 km/h
4 (referring to manner): **at a stroke** d'un seul
coup; **at peace** en paix
5 (referring to activity): **to be at work** (in the
office etc) être au travail; (working) travailler; **to
play at cowboys** jouer aux cowboys; **to be
good at sth** être bon en qch
6 (referring to cause): **shocked/surprised/
annoyed at sth** choqué par/étonné de/agacé
par qch; **I went at his suggestion** j'y suis allé
sur son conseil
7 (symbol) arobase f

ate [eɪt] pt of **eat**
atheist [ˈeɪθɪɪst] n athée m/f
Athens [ˈæθɪnz] n Athènes
athlete [ˈæθliːt] n athlète m/f
athletic [æθˈletɪk] adj athlétique; **athletics** n
athlétisme m
Atlantic [ətˈlæntɪk] adj atlantique ▷ n: **the ~
(Ocean)** l'(océan m) Atlantique m
atlas [ˈætləs] n atlas m
A.T.M. n abbr (= Automated Telling Machine)
guichet m automatique

atmosphere [ˈætməsfɪə r] n (air) atmosphère
f; (fig: of place etc) atmosphère, ambiance f
atom [ˈætəm] n atome m; **atomic** [əˈtɔmɪk]
adj atomique; **atom(ic) bomb** n bombe f
atomique
A to Z® n (map) plan m des rues
atrocity [əˈtrɔsɪtɪ] n atrocité f
attach [əˈtætʃ] vt (gen) attacher; (document,
letter) joindre; **to be ~ed to sb/sth** (to like)
être attaché à qn/qch; **attachment** n
(tool) accessoire m; (Comput) fichier m joint;
(love): **attachment (to)** affection f (pour),
attachement m (à)
attack [əˈtæk] vt attaquer; (task etc) s'attaquer
à ▷ n attaque f; **heart ~** crise f cardiaque;
attacker n attaquant m; agresseur m
attain [əˈteɪn] vt (also: **to ~ to**) parvenir à,
atteindre; (knowledge) acquérir
attempt [əˈtempt] n tentative f ▷ vt essayer,
tenter
attend [əˈtend] vt (course) suivre; (meeting,
talk) assister à; (school, church) aller à,
fréquenter; (patient) soigner, s'occuper de;
attend to vt fus (needs, affairs etc) s'occuper de;
(customer) s'occuper de, servir; **attendance**
n (being present) présence f; (people present)
assistance f; **attendant** n employé(e);
gardien(ne) ▷ adj concomitant(e), qui
accompagne ou s'ensuit

⬛ Be careful not to translate **to attend** by
the French word **attendre**.

attention [əˈtenʃən] n attention f ▷ excl
(Mil) garde-à-vous!; **for the ~ of** (Admin) à
l'attention de
attic [ˈætɪk] n grenier m, combles mpl
attitude [ˈætɪtjuːd] n attitude f
attorney [əˈtəːnɪ] n (US: lawyer) avocat m;
Attorney General n (BRIT) ≈ procureur
général; (US) ≈ garde m des Sceaux, ministre m
de la Justice
attract [əˈtrækt] vt attirer; **attraction**
[əˈtrækʃən] n (gen pl: pleasant things)
attraction f, attrait m; (Physics) attraction;
(fig: towards sb, sth) attirance f; **attractive** adj
séduisant(e), attrayant(e)
attribute n [ˈætrɪbjuːt] attribut m ▷ vt
[əˈtrɪbjuːt]: **to ~ sth to** attribuer qch à
aubergine [ˈəubəʒiːn] n aubergine f
auburn [ˈɔːbən] adj auburn inv, châtain
roux inv
auction [ˈɔːkʃən] n (also: **sale by ~**) vente f aux
enchères ▷ vt (also: **to sell by ~**) vendre aux
enchères
audible [ˈɔːdɪbl] adj audible
audience [ˈɔːdɪəns] n (people) assistance f,
public m; (on radio) auditeurs mpl; (at theatre)
spectateurs mpl; (interview) audience f
audit [ˈɔːdɪt] vt vérifier
audition [ɔːˈdɪʃən] n audition f

auditor [ˈɔːdɪtəʳ] n vérificateur m des comptes

auditorium [ɔːdɪˈtɔːrɪəm] n auditorium m, salle f de concert or de spectacle

Aug. abbr = **August**

August [ˈɔːgəst] n août m

aunt [ɑːnt] n tante f; **auntie, aunty** n diminutive of **aunt**

au pair [ˈəʊˈpɛəʳ] n (also: ~ **girl**) jeune fille f au pair

aura [ˈɔːrə] n atmosphère f; (of person) aura f

austerity [ɔsˈtɛrɪtɪ] n austérité f

Australia [ɔsˈtreɪlɪə] n Australie f; **Australian** adj australien(ne) ▷ n Australien(ne)

Austria [ˈɔstrɪə] n Autriche f; **Austrian** adj autrichien(ne) ▷ n Autrichien(ne)

authentic [ɔːˈθɛntɪk] adj authentique

author [ˈɔːθəʳ] n auteur m

authority [ɔːˈθɔrɪtɪ] n autorité f; (permission) autorisation (formelle); **the authorities** les autorités fpl, l'administration f

authorize [ˈɔːθəraɪz] vt autoriser

auto [ˈɔːtəʊ] n (us) auto f, voiture f; **autobiography** [ɔːtəbaɪˈɒgrəfɪ] n autobiographie f; **autograph** [ˈɔːtəgrɑːf] n autographe m ▷ vt signer, dédicacer; **automatic** [ɔːtəˈmætɪk] adj automatique ▷ n (gun) automatique m; (car) voiture f à transmission automatique; **automatically** adv automatiquement; **automobile** [ˈɔːtəməbiːl] n (us) automobile f; **autonomous** [ɔːˈtɒnəməs] adj autonome; **autonomy** [ɔːˈtɒnəmɪ] n autonomie f

autumn [ˈɔːtəm] n automne m

auxiliary [ɔːgˈzɪlɪərɪ] adj, n auxiliaire (m/f)

avail [əˈveɪl] vt: **to ~ o.s. of** user de; profiter de ▷ n: **to no ~** sans résultat, en vain, en pure perte

availability [əveɪləˈbɪlɪtɪ] n disponibilité f

available [əˈveɪləbl] adj disponible

avalanche [ˈævəlɑːnʃ] n avalanche f

Ave. abbr = **avenue**

avenue [ˈævənjuː] n avenue f; (fig) moyen m

average [ˈævərɪdʒ] n moyenne f ▷ adj moyen(ne) ▷ vt (a certain figure) atteindre or faire etc en moyenne; **on ~** en moyenne

avert [əˈvɜːt] vt (danger) prévenir, écarter; (one's eyes) détourner

avid [ˈævɪd] adj avide

avocado [ævəˈkɑːdəʊ] n (BRIT: also: ~ **pear**) avocat m

avoid [əˈvɔɪd] vt éviter

await [əˈweɪt] vt attendre

awake [əˈweɪk] adj éveillé(e) ▷ vb (pt **awoke**, pp **awoken**) ▷ vt éveiller ▷ vi s'éveiller; **to be ~** être réveillé(e)

award [əˈwɔːd] n (for bravery) récompense f; (prize) prix m; (Law: damages) dommages-intérêts mpl ▷ vt (prize) décerner; (Law: damages) accorder

aware [əˈwɛəʳ] adj: ~ **of** (conscious) conscient(e) de; (informed) au courant de; **to become ~ of/that** prendre conscience de/que; se rendre compte de/que; **awareness** n conscience f, connaissance f

away [əˈweɪ] adv (au) loin; (movement): **she went ~** elle est partie ▷ adj (not in, not here) absent(e); **far ~** (au) loin; **two kilometres ~** à (une distance de) deux kilomètres, à deux kilomètres de distance; **two hours ~ by car** à deux heures de voiture or de route; **the holiday was two weeks ~** il restait deux semaines jusqu'aux vacances; **he's ~ for a week** il est parti (pour) une semaine; **to take sth ~ from sb** prendre qch à qn; **to take sth ~ from sth** (subtract) ôter qch de qch; **to work/pedal ~** travailler/pédaler à cœur joie; **to fade ~** (colour) s'estomper; (sound) s'affaiblir

awe [ɔː] n respect mêlé de crainte, effroi mêlé d'admiration; **awesome** [ˈɔːsəm] (us) adj (inf: excellent) génial(e)

awful [ˈɔːfəl] adj affreux(-euse); **an ~ lot of** énormément de; **awfully** adv (very) terriblement, vraiment

awkward [ˈɔːkwəd] adj (clumsy) gauche, maladroit(e); (inconvenient) peu pratique; (embarrassing) gênant

awoke [əˈwəʊk] pt of **awake**

awoken [əˈwəʊkən] pp of **awake**

axe [æks] (us **ax**) n hache f ▷ vt (project etc) abandonner; (jobs) supprimer

axle [ˈæksl] n essieu m

ay(e) [aɪ] excl (yes) oui

azalea [əˈzeɪlɪə] n azalée f

B [biː] n (Mus): **B** si m

B.A. abbr (Scol) = **Bachelor of Arts**

baby ['beɪbɪ] n bébé m; **baby carriage** n (US) voiture f d'enfant; **baby-sit** vi garder les enfants; **baby-sitter** n baby-sitter m/f; **baby wipe** n lingette f (pour bébé)

bachelor ['bætʃələᵊ] n célibataire m; **B~ of Arts/Science (BA/BSc)** ≈ licencié(e) ès or en lettres/sciences

back [bæk] n (of person, horse) dos m; (of hand) dos, revers m; (of house) derrière m; (of car, train) arrière m; (of chair) dossier m; (of page) verso m; (of crowd): **can the people at the ~ hear me properly?** est-ce que les gens du fond peuvent m'entendre?; (Football) arrière m; **~ to front** à l'envers ▷ vt (financially) soutenir (financièrement); (candidate: also: **~ up**) soutenir, appuyer; (horse: at races) parier or miser sur; (car) (faire) reculer ▷ vi reculer; (car etc) faire marche arrière ▷ adj (in compounds) de derrière, à l'arrière; **~ seat/wheel** (Aut) siège m/roue f arrière inv; **~ payments/rent** arriéré m de paiements/loyer; **~ garden/room** jardin/pièce sur l'arrière ▷ adv (not forward) en arrière; (returned): **he's ~** il est rentré, il est de retour; **he ran ~** il est revenu en courant; (restitution): **throw the ball ~** renvoie la balle; **can I have it ~?** puis-je le ravoir?, peux-tu me le rendre?; (again): **he called ~** il a rappelé;

back down vi rabattre de ses prétentions; **back out** vi (of promise) se dédire; **back up** vt (person) soutenir; (Comput) faire une copie de sauvegarde de; **backache** n mal m au dos; **backbencher** (BRIT) n membre du parlement sans portefeuille; **backbone** n colonne vertébrale, épine dorsale; **back door** n porte f de derrière; **backfire** vi (Aut) pétarader; (plans) mal tourner; **backgammon** n trictrac m; **background** n arrière-plan m; (of events) situation f, conjoncture f; (basic knowledge) éléments mpl de base; (experience) formation f; **family background** milieu familial; **backing** n (fig) soutien m, appui m; **backlog** n: **backlog of work** travail m en retard; **backpack** n sac m à dos; **backpacker** n randonneur(-euse); **backslash** n barre oblique inversée; **backstage** adv dans les coulisses; **backstroke** n dos crawlé; **backup** adj (train, plane) supplémentaire, de réserve; (Comput) de sauvegarde ▷ n (support) appui m, soutien m; (Comput: also: **backup file**) sauvegarde f; **backward** adj (movement) en arrière; (person, country) arriéré(e), attardé(e); **backwards** adv (move, go) en arrière; (read a list) à l'envers, à rebours; (fall) à la renverse; (walk) à reculons; **backyard** n arrière-cour f

bacon ['beɪkən] n bacon m, lard m

bacteria [bæk'tɪərɪə] npl bactéries fpl

bad [bæd] adj mauvais(e); (child) vilain(e); (mistake, accident) grave; (meat, food) gâté(e), avarié(e); **his ~ leg** sa jambe malade; **to go ~** (meat, food) se gâter; (milk) tourner

bade [bæd] pt of **bid**

badge [bædʒ] n insigne m; (of policeman) plaque f; (stick-on, sew-on) badge m

badger ['bædʒəᵊ] n blaireau m

badly ['bædlɪ] adv (work, dress etc) mal; **to reflect ~ on sb** donner une mauvaise image de qn; **~ wounded** grièvement blessé; **he needs it ~** il en a absolument besoin; **~ off** adj, adv dans la gêne

bad-mannered ['bæd'mænəd] adj mal élevé(e)

badminton ['bædmɪntən] n badminton m

bad-tempered ['bæd'tɛmpəd] adj (by nature) ayant mauvais caractère; (on one occasion) de mauvaise humeur

bag [bæg] n sac m; **~s of** (inf: lots of) des tas de; **baggage** n bagages mpl; **baggage allowance** n franchise f de bagages; **baggage reclaim** n (at airport) livraison f des bagages; **baggy** adj avachi(e), qui fait des poches; **bagpipes** npl cornemuse f

bail [beɪl] n caution f ▷ vt (prisoner: also: **grant ~ to**) mettre en liberté sous caution; (boat: also: **~ out**) écoper; **to be released on ~** être libéré(e) sous caution; **bail out** vt (prisoner) payer la caution de

bait [beɪt] n appât m ⊳ vt appâter; (fig: tease) tourmenter

bake [beɪk] vt (faire) cuire au four ⊳ vi (bread etc) cuire (au four); (make cakes etc) faire de la pâtisserie; **baked beans** npl haricots blancs à la sauce tomate; **baked potato** n pomme f de terre en robe des champs; **baker** n boulanger m; **bakery** n boulangerie f; **baking** n (process) cuisson f; **baking powder** n levure f (chimique)

balance ['bæləns] n équilibre m; (Comm: sum) solde m; (remainder) reste m; (scales) balance f ⊳ vt mettre or faire tenir en équilibre; (pros and cons) peser; (budget) équilibrer; (account) balancer; (compensate) compenser, contrebalancer; **~ of trade/payments** balance commerciale/des comptes or paiements; **balanced** adj (personality, diet) équilibré(e); (report) objectif(-ive); **balance sheet** n bilan m

balcony ['bælkənɪ] n balcon m; **do you have a room with a ~?** avez-vous une chambre avec balcon?

bald [bɔːld] adj chauve; (tyre) lisse

ball [bɔːl] n boule f; (football) ballon m; (for tennis, golf) balle f; (dance) bal m; **to play ~** jouer au ballon (or à la balle); (fig) coopérer

ballerina [bælə'riːnə] n ballerine f

ballet ['bæleɪ] n ballet m; (art) danse f (classique); **ballet dancer** n danseur(-euse) de ballet

balloon [bə'luːn] n ballon m

ballot ['bælət] n scrutin m

ballpoint (pen) ['bɔːlpɔɪnt-] n stylo m à bille

ballroom ['bɔːlrum] n salle f de bal

Baltic [bɔːltɪk] n: **the ~ (Sea)** la (mer) Baltique

bamboo [bæm'buː] n bambou m

ban [bæn] n interdiction f ⊳ vt interdire

banana [bə'nɑːnə] n banane f

band [bænd] n bande f; (at a dance) orchestre m; (Mil) musique f, fanfare f

bandage ['bændɪdʒ] n bandage m, pansement m ⊳ vt (wound, leg) mettre un pansement or un bandage sur

Band-Aid® ['bændeɪd] n (US) pansement adhésif

B. & B. n abbr = **bed and breakfast**

bandit ['bændɪt] n bandit m

bang [bæŋ] n détonation f; (of door) claquement m; (blow) coup (violent) ⊳ vt frapper (violemment); (door) claquer ⊳ vi détoner; claquer

Bangladesh [bæŋglə'dɛʃ] n Bangladesh m

Bangladeshi [bæŋglə'dɛʃɪ] adj du Bangladesh ⊳ n habitant(e) du Bangladesh

bangle ['bæŋgl] n bracelet m

bangs [bæŋz] npl (US: fringe) frange f

banish ['bænɪʃ] vt bannir

banister(s) ['bænɪstə(z)] n(pl) rampe f

(d'escalier)

banjo (pl **~es** or **~s**) ['bændʒəu] n banjo m

bank [bæŋk] n banque f; (of river, lake) bord m, rive f; (of earth) talus m, remblai m ⊳ vi (Aviat) virer sur l'aile; **bank on** vt fus miser or tabler sur; **bank account** n compte m en banque; **bank balance** n solde m bancaire; **bank card** (BRIT) n carte f d'identité bancaire; **bank charges** npl (BRIT) frais mpl de banque; **banker** n banquier m; **bank holiday** n (BRIT) jour férié (où les banques sont fermées); voir encadré; **banking** n opérations fpl bancaires; profession f de banquier; **bank manager** n directeur m d'agence (bancaire); **banknote** n billet m de banque

● **BANK HOLIDAY**
●
● Le terme **bank holiday** s'applique au
● Royaume-Uni aux jours fériés pendant
● lesquels banques et commerces sont
● fermés. Les principaux **bank holidays** à
● part Noël et Pâques se situent au mois de
● mai et fin août, et contrairement aux pays
● de tradition catholique, ne coïncident pas
● nécessairement avec une fête religieuse.

bankrupt ['bæŋkrʌpt] adj en faillite; **to go ~** faire faillite; **bankruptcy** n faillite f

bank statement n relevé m de compte

banner ['bænər] n bannière f

bannister(s) ['bænɪstə(z)] n(pl) = **banister(s)**

banquet ['bæŋkwɪt] n banquet m, festin m

baptism ['bæptɪzəm] n baptême m

baptize [bæp'taɪz] vt baptiser

bar [bɑːʳ] n (pub) bar m; (counter) comptoir m, bar; (rod: of metal etc) barre f; (of window etc) barreau m; (of chocolate) tablette f, plaque f; (fig: obstacle) obstacle m; (prohibition) mesure f d'exclusion; (Mus) mesure f ⊳ vt (road) barrer; (person) exclure; (activity) interdire; **~ of soap** savonnette f; **behind ~s** (prisoner) derrière les barreaux; **the B~** (Law) le barreau; **~ none** sans exception

barbaric [bɑː'bærɪk] adj barbare

barbecue ['bɑːbɪkjuː] n barbecue m

barbed wire ['bɑːbd-] n fil m de fer barbelé

barber ['bɑːbəʳ] n coiffeur m (pour hommes); **barber's (shop)** (US **barber (shop)**) n salon m de coiffure (pour hommes)

bar code n code m à barres, code-barre m

bare [bɛəʳ] adj nu(e) ⊳ vt mettre à nu, dénuder; (teeth) montrer; **barefoot** adj, adv nu-pieds, (les) pieds nus; **barely** adv à peine

bargain ['bɑːgɪn] n (transaction) marché m; (good buy) affaire f, occasion f ⊳ vi (haggle) marchander; (negotiate) négocier, traiter; **into the ~** par-dessus le marché; **bargain for** vt fus

(*inf*): **he got more than he ~ed for!** il en a eu
pour son argent!

barge [bɑːdʒ] *n* péniche *f*; **barge in** *vi* (*walk in*)
faire irruption; (*interrupt talk*) intervenir mal
à propos

bark [bɑːk] *n* (*of tree*) écorce *f*; (*of dog*)
aboiement *m* ▷ *vi* aboyer

barley ['bɑːlɪ] *n* orge *f*

barmaid ['bɑːmeɪd] *n* serveuse *f* (de bar),
barmaid *f*

barman ['bɑːmən] *n* serveur *m* (de bar),
barman *m*

barn [bɑːn] *n* grange *f*

barometer [bə'rɒmɪtə'] *n* baromètre *m*

baron ['bærən] *n* baron *m*; **baroness** *n*
baronne *f*

barracks ['bærəks] *npl* caserne *f*

barrage ['bærɑːʒ] *n* (*Mil*) tir *m* de barrage;
(*dam*) barrage *m*; (*of criticism*) feu *m*

barrel ['bærəl] *n* tonneau *m*; (*of gun*) canon *m*

barren ['bærən] *adj* stérile

barrette [bə'rɛt] *n* (*us*) barrette *f*

barricade [bærɪ'keɪd] *n* barricade *f*

barrier ['bærɪə'] *n* barrière *f*

barring ['bɑːrɪŋ] *prep* sauf

barrister ['bærɪstə'] *n* (*BRIT*) avocat
(plaidant)

barrow ['bærəʊ] *n* (*cart*) charrette *f* à bras

bartender ['bɑːtɛndə'] *n* (*us*) serveur *m* (de
bar), barman *m*

base [beɪs] *n* base *f* ▷ *vt* (*opinion, belief*): **to
~ sth on** baser or fonder qch sur ▷ *adj* vil(e),
bas(se)

baseball ['beɪsbɔːl] *n* base-ball *m*; **baseball
cap** *n* casquette *f* de base-ball

Basel [bɑːl] *n* = **Basle**

basement ['beɪsmənt] *n* sous-sol *m*

bases ['beɪsiːz] *npl of* **basis**

bash [bæʃ] *vt* (*inf*) frapper, cogner

basic ['beɪsɪk] *adj* (*precautions, rules*)
élémentaire; (*principles, research*)
fondamental(e); (*vocabulary, salary*) de base;
(*minimal*) réduit(e) au minimum, rudimentaire;
basically *adv* (*in fact*) en fait; (*essentially*)
fondamentalement; **basics** *npl*: **the basics**
l'essentiel *m*

basil ['bæzl] *n* basilic *m*

basin ['beɪsn] *n* (*vessel, also Geo*) cuvette *f*,
bassin *m*; (*BRIT: for food*) bol *m*; (*also:* **wash~**)
lavabo *m*

basis (*pl* **bases**) ['beɪsɪs, -siːz] *n* base *f*; **on a
part-time/trial ~** à temps partiel/à l'essai

basket ['bɑːskɪt] *n* corbeille *f*; (*with handle*)
panier *m*; **basketball** *n* basket-ball *m*

Basle [bɑːl] *n* Bâle

Basque [bæsk] *adj* basque ▷ *n* Basque *m/f*;
the ~ Country le Pays basque

bass [beɪs] *n* (*Mus*) basse *f*

bastard ['bɑːstəd] *n* enfant naturel(le),

bâtard(e); (*infl*) salaud *m* (!)

bat [bæt] *n* chauve-souris *f*; (*for baseball etc*)
batte *f*; (*BRIT: for table tennis*) raquette *f* ▷ *vt*:
he didn't ~ an eyelid il n'a pas sourcillé or
bronché

batch [bætʃ] *n* (*of bread*) fournée *f*; (*of papers*)
liasse *f*; (*of applicants, letters*) paquet *m*

bath (*pl* **~s**) [bɑːθ, bɑːðz] *n* bain *m*; (*bathtub*)
baignoire *f* ▷ *vt* baigner, donner un bain à; **to
have a ~** prendre un bain; *see also* **baths**

bathe [beɪð] *vi* se baigner ▷ *vt* baigner; (*wound
etc*) laver

bathing ['beɪðɪŋ] *n* baignade *f*; **bathing
costume** (*us* **bathing suit**) *n* maillot *m* (de
bain)

bath: **bathrobe** *n* peignoir *m* de bain;
bathroom *n* salle *f* de bains; **baths** [bɑːðz]
npl (*BRIT: also:* **swimming baths**) piscine *f*;
bath towel *n* serviette *f* de bain; **bathtub** *n*
baignoire *f*

baton ['bætən] *n* bâton *m*; (*Mus*) baguette *f*;
(*club*) matraque *f*

batter ['bætə'] *vt* battre ▷ *n* pâte *f* à frire;
battered *adj* (*hat, pan*) cabossé(e); **battered
wife/child** épouse/enfant maltraité(e) or
martyr(e)

battery ['bætərɪ] *n* (*for torch, radio*) pile *f*; (*Aut,
Mil*) batterie *f*; **battery farming** *n* élevage *m*
en batterie

battle ['bætl] *n* bataille *f*, combat *m* ▷ *vi* se
battre, lutter; **battlefield** *n* champ *m* de
bataille

bay [beɪ] *n* (*of sea*) baie *f*; (*BRIT: for parking*)
place *f* de stationnement; (: *for loading*) aire
f de chargement; **B~ of Biscay** golfe *m* de
Gascogne; **to hold sb at ~** tenir qn à distance
or en échec

bay leaf *n* laurier *m*

bazaar [bə'zɑː'] *n* (*shop, market*) bazar *m*; (*sale*)
vente *f* de charité

BBC *n abbr* (= British Broadcasting Corporation)
*office de la radiodiffusion et télévision
britannique*

B.C. *adv abbr* (= before Christ) av. J.-C.

 KEYWORD

be [biː] (*pt* **was, were**, *pp* **been**) *aux vb* **1** (*with
present participle: forming continuous tenses*):
what are you doing? que faites-vous?;
they're coming tomorrow ils viennent
demain; **I've been waiting for you for 2
hours** je t'attends depuis 2 heures
2 (*with pp: forming passives*) être; **to be killed**
être tué(e); **the box had been opened** la
boîte avait été ouverte; **he was nowhere to
be seen** on ne le voyait nulle part
3 (*in tag questions*): **it was fun, wasn't it?**
c'était drôle, n'est-ce pas?; **he's good-**

b

looking, isn't he? il est beau, n'est-ce pas?; **she's back, is she?** elle est rentrée, n'est-ce pas or alors?

4 (+to +infinitive): **the house is to be sold** (necessity) la maison doit être vendue; (future) la maison va être vendue; **he's not to open it** il ne doit pas l'ouvrir

▷ vb + complement **1** (gen) être; **I'm English** je suis anglais(e); **I'm tired** je suis fatigué(e); **I'm hot/cold** j'ai chaud/froid; **he's a doctor** il est médecin; **be careful/good/quiet!** faites attention/soyez sages/taisez-vous!; **2 and 2 are 4** 2 et 2 font 4

2 (of health) aller; **how are you?** comment allez-vous?; **I'm better now** je vais mieux maintenant; **he's very ill** il est très malade **3** (of age) avoir; **how old are you?** quel âge avez-vous?; **I'm sixteen (years old)** j'ai seize ans

4 (cost) coûter; **how much was the meal?** combien a coûté le repas?; **that'll be £5, please** ça fera 5 livres, s'il vous plaît; **this shirt is £17** cette chemise coûte 17 livres

▷ vi **1** (exist, occur etc) être, exister; **the prettiest girl that ever was** la fille la plus jolie qui ait jamais existé; **is there a God?** y a-t-il un dieu?; **be that as it may** quoi qu'il en soit; **so be it** soit

2 (referring to place) être, se trouver; **I won't be here tomorrow** je ne serai pas là demain **3** (referring to movement): **where have you been?** où êtes-vous allé(s)?

▷ impers vb **1** (referring to time) être; **it's 5 o'clock** il est 5 heures; **it's the 28th of April** c'est le 28 avril

2 (referring to distance): **it's 10 km to the village** le village est à 10 km

3 (referring to the weather) faire; **it's too hot/cold** il fait trop chaud/froid; **it's windy today** il y a du vent aujourd'hui

4 (emphatic): **it's me/the postman** c'est moi/le facteur; **it was Maria who paid the bill** c'est Maria qui a payé la note

beach [biːtʃ] n plage f ▷ vt échouer
beacon ['biːkən] n (lighthouse) fanal m; (marker) balise f
bead [biːd] n perle f; (of dew, sweat) goutte f; **beads** npl (necklace) collier m
beak [biːk] n bec m
beam [biːm] n (Archit) poutre f; (of light) rayon m ▷ vi rayonner
bean [biːn] n haricot m; (of coffee) grain m; **beansprouts** npl pousses fpl or germes mpl de soja
bear [bɛəʳ] n ours m ▷ vb (pt **bore**, pp **borne**) ▷ vt porter; (endure) supporter, rapporter ▷ vi: **to ~ right/left** obliquer à droite/gauche, se diriger vers la droite/gauche

beard [bɪəd] n barbe f
bearer ['bɛərəʳ] n porteur m; (of passport etc) titulaire m/f
bearing ['bɛərɪŋ] n maintien m, allure f; (connection) rapport m; (Tech): **(ball) bearings** npl roulement m (à billes)
beast [biːst] n bête f; (inf: person) brute f
beat [biːt] n battement m; (Mus) temps m, mesure f; (of policeman) ronde f ▷ vt, vi (pt ~, pp ~en) battre; **off the ~en track** hors des chemins or sentiers battus; **to ~ it** (inf) ficher le camp; **beat up** vt (inf: person) tabasser; **beating** n raclée f
beautiful ['bjuːtɪful] adj beau (belle); **beautifully** adv admirablement
beauty ['bjuːtɪ] n beauté f; **beauty parlour** (us **beauty parlor**) [-'pɑːləʳ] n institut m de beauté; **beauty salon** n institut m de beauté; **beauty spot** n (on skin) grain m de beauté; (BRIT Tourism) site naturel (d'une grande beauté)
beaver ['biːvəʳ] n castor m
became [bɪ'keɪm] pt of **become**
because [bɪ'kɔz] conj parce que; **~ of** prep à cause de
beckon ['bɛkən] vt (also: **~ to**) faire signe (de venir) à
become [bɪ'kʌm] vi devenir; **to ~ fat/thin** grossir/maigrir; **to ~ angry** se mettre en colère
bed [bɛd] n lit m; (of flowers) parterre m; (of coal, clay) couche f; (of sea, lake) fond m; **to go to ~** aller se coucher; **bed and breakfast** n (terms) chambre et petit déjeuner; (place) ≈ chambre f d'hôte; voir encadré; **bedclothes** npl couvertures fpl et draps mpl; **bedding** n literie f; **bed linen** n draps mpl de lit (et taies fpl d'oreillers), literie f; **bedroom** n chambre f (à coucher); **bedside** n: **at sb's bedside** au chevet de qn; **bedside lamp** n lampe f de chevet; **bedside table** n table f de chevet; **bedsit(ter)** n (BRIT) chambre meublée, studio m; **bedspread** n couvre-lit m, dessus-de-lit m; **bedtime** n: **it's bedtime** c'est l'heure de se coucher

BED AND BREAKFAST

Un **bed and breakfast** est une petite pension dans une maison particulière ou une ferme où l'on peut louer une chambre avec petit déjeuner compris pour un prix modique par rapport à ce que l'on paierait dans un hôtel. Ces établissements sont communément appelés "B & B", et sont signalés par une pancarte dans le jardin ou au-dessus de la porte.

bee [biː] n abeille f

beech [biːtʃ] n hêtre m

beef [biːf] n bœuf m; **roast ~** rosbif m; **beefburger** n hamburger m; **Beefeater** n hallebardier m (de la tour de Londres)

been [biːn] pp of **be**

beer [bɪə^r] n bière f; **beer garden** n (BRIT) jardin m d'un pub (où l'on peut emmener ses consommations)

beet [biːt] n (vegetable) betterave f; (US: also: **red ~**) betterave (potagère)

beetle [ˈbiːtl] n scarabée m, coléoptère m

beetroot [ˈbiːtruːt] n (BRIT) betterave f

before [bɪˈfɔː^r] prep (of time) avant; (of space) devant ▷ conj avant que + sub; avant de ▷ adv avant; **~ going** avant de partir; **~ she goes** avant qu'elle (ne) parte; **the week ~** la semaine précédente or d'avant; **I've never seen it ~** c'est la première fois que je le vois; **beforehand** adv au préalable, à l'avance

beg [bɛg] vi mendier ▷ vt mendier; (forgiveness, mercy etc) demander; (entreat) supplier; **to ~ sb to do sth** supplier qn de faire qch; see also **pardon**

began [bɪˈgæn] pt of **begin**

beggar [ˈbɛgə^r] n mendiant(e)

begin [bɪˈgɪn] (pt **began**, pp **begun**) vt, vi commencer; **to ~ doing** or **to do sth** commencer à faire qch; **beginner** n débutant(e); **beginning** n commencement m, début m

begun [bɪˈgʌn] pp of **begin**

behalf [bɪˈhɑːf] n: **on ~ of**, (US) **in ~ of** (representing) de la part de; (for benefit of) pour le compte de; **on my/his ~** de ma/sa part

behave [bɪˈheɪv] vi se conduire, se comporter; (well: also: **~ o.s.**) se conduire bien or comme il faut; **behaviour** (US **behavior**) n comportement m, conduite f

behind [bɪˈhaɪnd] prep derrière; (time) en retard sur; (supporting): **to be ~ sb** soutenir qn ▷ adv derrière; en retard ▷ n derrière m; **~ the scenes** dans les coulisses; **to be ~ (schedule) with sth** être en retard dans qch

beige [beɪʒ] adj beige

Beijing [ˈbeɪˈdʒɪŋ] n Pékin

being [ˈbiːɪŋ] n être m; **to come into ~** prendre naissance

belated [bɪˈleɪtɪd] adj tardif(-ive)

belch [bɛltʃ] vi avoir un renvoi, roter ▷ vt (also: **~ out**: smoke etc) vomir, cracher

Belgian [ˈbɛldʒən] adj belge, de Belgique ▷ n Belge m/f

Belgium [ˈbɛldʒəm] n Belgique f

belief [bɪˈliːf] n (opinion) conviction f; (trust, faith) foi f

believe [bɪˈliːv] vt, vi croire, estimer; **to ~ in** (God) croire en; (ghosts, method) croire à; **believer** n (in idea, activity) partisan(e); (Rel) croyant(e)

bell [bɛl] n cloche f; (small) clochette f, grelot m; (on door) sonnette f; (electric) sonnerie f

bellboy [ˈbɛlbɔɪ] (US **bellhop** [ˈbɛlhɔp]) n groom m, chasseur m

bellow [ˈbɛləʊ] vi (bull) meugler; (person) brailler

bell pepper n (esp US) poivron m

belly [ˈbɛlɪ] n ventre m; **belly button** (inf) n nombril m

belong [bɪˈlɔŋ] vi: **to ~** appartenir à; (club etc) faire partie de; **this book ~s here** ce livre va ici, la place de ce livre est ici; **belongings** npl affaires fpl, possessions fpl

beloved [bɪˈlʌvɪd] adj (bien-)aimé(e), chéri(e)

below [bɪˈləʊ] prep sous, au-dessous de ▷ adv en dessous; en contre-bas; **see ~** voir plus bas or plus loin or ci-dessous

belt [bɛlt] n ceinture f; (Tech) courroie f ▷ vt (thrash) donner une raclée à; **beltway** n (US Aut) route f de ceinture; (: motorway) périphérique m

bemused [bɪˈmjuːzd] adj médusé(e)

bench [bentʃ] n banc m; (in workshop) établi m; **the B~** (Law: judges) la magistrature, la Cour

bend [bend] vb (pt, pp **bent**) ▷ vt courber; (leg, arm) plier ▷ vi se courber ▷ n (BRIT: in road) virage m, tournant m; (in pipe, river) coude m; **bend down** vi se baisser; **bend over** vi se pencher

beneath [bɪˈniːθ] prep sous, au-dessous de; (unworthy of) indigne de ▷ adv dessous, au-dessous, en bas

beneficial [bɛnɪˈfɪʃəl] adj: **~ (to)** salutaire (pour), bénéfique (à)

benefit [ˈbɛnɪfɪt] n avantage m, profit m; (allowance of money) allocation f ▷ vt faire du bien à, profiter à ▷ vi: **he'll ~ from it** cela lui fera du bien, il y gagnera or s'en trouvera bien

Benelux [ˈbɛnɪlʌks] n Bénélux m

benign [bɪˈnaɪn] adj (person, smile) bienveillant(e), affable; (Med) bénin(-igne)

bent [bent] pt, pp of **bend** ▷ n inclination f, penchant m ▷ adj: **to be ~ on** être résolu(e) à

bereaved [bɪˈriːvd] n: **the ~** la famille du disparu

beret [ˈbɛreɪ] n béret m

Berlin [bəːˈlɪn] n Berlin

Bermuda [bəːˈmjuːdə] n Bermudes fpl

Bern [bəːn] n Berne

berry [ˈbɛrɪ] n baie f

berth [bəːθ] n (bed) couchette f; (for ship) poste m d'amarrage, mouillage m ▷ vi (in harbour) venir à quai; (at anchor) mouiller

beside [bɪˈsaɪd] prep à côté de; (compared with) par rapport à; **that's ~ the point** ça n'a rien à voir; **to be ~ o.s. (with anger)** être hors de soi; **besides** adv en outre, de plus ▷ prep en plus de; (except) excepté

best [bɛst] adj meilleur(e) ▷ adv le mieux; **the ~ part of** (quantity) le plus clair de, la plus grande partie de; **at ~** au mieux; **to make the ~ of sth** s'accommoder de qch (du mieux que l'on peut); **to do one's ~** faire de son mieux; **to the ~ of my knowledge** pour autant que je sache; **to the ~ of my ability** du mieux que je pourrai; **best-before date** n date f de limite d'utilisation or de consommation; **best man** (irreg) n garçon m d'honneur; **bestseller** n best-seller m, succès m de librairie

bet [bɛt] n pari m ▷ vt, vi (pt, pp ~ or ~ted) parier; **to ~ sb sth** parier qch à qn

betray [bɪ'treɪ] vt trahir

better ['bɛtə'] adj meilleur(e) ▷ adv mieux ▷ vt améliorer ▷ n: **to get the ~ of** triompher de, l'emporter sur; **you had ~ do it** vous feriez mieux de le faire; **he thought ~ of it** il s'est ravisé; **to get ~** (Med) aller mieux; (improve) s'améliorer

betting ['bɛtɪŋ] n paris mpl; **betting shop** n (BRIT) bureau m de paris

between [bɪ'twiːn] prep entre ▷ adv au milieu, dans l'intervalle

beverage ['bɛvərɪdʒ] n boisson f (gén sans alcool)

beware [bɪ'wɛə'] vi: **to ~ (of)** prendre garde (à); **"~ of the dog"** (attention) chien méchant"

bewildered [bɪ'wɪldəd] adj dérouté(e), ahuri(e)

beyond [bɪ'jɔnd] prep (in space, time) au-delà de; (exceeding) au-dessus de ▷ adv au-delà; **~ doubt** hors de doute; **~ repair** irréparable

bias ['baɪəs] n (prejudice) préjugé m, parti pris; (preference) prévention f; **bias(s)ed** adj partial(e), montrant un parti pris

bib [bɪb] n bavoir m

Bible ['baɪbl] n Bible f

bicarbonate of soda [baɪ'kɑːbənɪt-] n bicarbonate m de soude

biceps ['baɪsɛps] n biceps m

bicycle ['baɪsɪkl] n bicyclette f; **bicycle pump** n pompe f à vélo

bid [bɪd] n offre f; (at auction) enchère f; (attempt) tentative f ▷ vb (pt ~ or **bade**, pp ~ or ~den) ▷ vi faire une enchère or offre ▷ vt faire une enchère or offre de; **to ~ sb good day** souhaiter le bonjour à qn; **bidder** n: **the highest bidder** le plus offrant

bidet ['biːdeɪ] n bidet m

big [bɪg] adj (in height: person, building, tree) grand(e); (in bulk, amount: person, parcel, book) gros(se); **bigheaded** adj prétentieux(-euse);

big toe n gros orteil

● **BIG APPLE**
●
● Si l'on sait que "The Big Apple" désigne la
● ville de New York ("apple" est en réalité un
● terme d'argot signifiant "grande ville"), on
● connaît moins les surnoms donnés aux
● autres grandes villes américaines. Chicago
● est surnommée "Windy City" à cause
● des rafales soufflant du lac Michigan, La
● Nouvelle-Orléans doit son sobriquet de
● "Big Easy" à son style de vie décontracté, et
● l'industrie automobile a donné à Detroit
● son surnom de "Motown".

bike [baɪk] n vélo m; **bike lane** n piste f cyclable

bikini [bɪ'kiːnɪ] n bikini m

bilateral [baɪ'lætərl] adj bilatéral(e)

bilingual [baɪ'lɪŋgwəl] adj bilingue

bill [bɪl] n note f, facture f; (in restaurant) addition f, note f; (Pol) projet m de loi; (us: banknote) billet m (de banque); (notice) affiche f; (of bird) bec m; **put it on my ~** mettez-le sur mon compte; **"post no ~s"** "défense d'afficher"; **to fit** or **fill the ~** (fig) faire l'affaire; **billboard** (us) n panneau m d'affichage; **billfold** ['bɪlfəʊld] n (us) portefeuille m

billiards ['bɪljədz] n (jeu m de) billard m

billion ['bɪljən] n (BRIT) billion m (million de millions); (us) milliard m

bin [bɪn] n boîte f; (BRIT: also: **dust~**, **litter~**) poubelle f; (for coal) coffre m

bind (pt, pp **bound**) [baɪnd, baʊnd] vt attacher; (book) relier; (oblige) obliger, contraindre ▷ n (inf: nuisance) scie f

binge [bɪndʒ] n (inf): **to go on a ~** faire la bringue

bingo ['bɪŋgəʊ] n sorte de jeu de loto pratiqué dans des établissements publics

binoculars [bɪ'nɔkjʊləz] npl jumelles fpl

bio... [baɪə'] prefix: **biochemistry** n biochimie f; **biodegradable** ['baɪəʊdɪ'greɪdə bl] adj biodégradable; **biography** [baɪ'ɔgrə fɪ] n biographie f; **biological** adj biologique; **biology** [baɪ'ɔlədʒɪ] n biologie f; **biometric** [baɪə'mɛtrɪk] adj biométrique

birch [bəːtʃ] n bouleau m

bird [bəːd] n oiseau m; (BRIT inf: girl) nana f; **bird flu** n grippe f aviaire; **bird of prey** n oiseau m de proie; **birdwatching** n ornithologie f (d'amateur)

Biro® ['baɪərəʊ] n stylo m à bille

birth [bəːθ] n naissance f; **to give ~ to** donner naissance à, mettre au monde; (subj: animal) mettre bas; **birth certificate** n acte m de naissance; **birth control** n (policy) limitation f des naissances; (methods) méthode(s) contraceptive(s); **birthday** n anniversaire m ▷ cpd (cake, card etc) d'anniversaire; **birthmark** n envie f, tache f de vin; **birthplace** n lieu m de naissance

biscuit ['bɪskɪt] n (BRIT) biscuit m; (US) petit pain au lait

bishop ['bɪʃəp] n évêque m; (Chess) fou m

bistro ['bi:strəu] n petit restaurant m, bistrot m

bit [bɪt] pt of **bite** ▷ n morceau m; (Comput) bit m, élément m binaire; (of tool) mèche f; (of horse) mors m; **a ~ of** un peu de; **a ~ mad/dangerous** un peu fou/risqué; **~ by ~** petit à petit

bitch [bɪtʃ] n (dog) chienne f; (inf!) salope f(!), garce f

bite [baɪt] vt, vi (pt **bit**, pp **bitten**) mordre; (insect) piquer ▷ n morsure f; (insect bite) piqûre f; (mouthful) bouchée f; **let's have a ~ (to eat)** mangeons un morceau; **to ~ one's nails** se ronger les ongles

bitten ['bɪtn] pp of **bite**

bitter ['bɪtə'] adj amer(-ère); (criticism) cinglant(e); (icy: weather, wind) glacial(e) ▷ n (BRIT: beer) bière f (à forte teneur en houblon)

bizarre [bɪ'zɑ:'] adj bizarre

black [blæk] adj noir(e) ▷ n (colour) noir m; (person): **B~** noir(e) ▷ vt (BRIT Industry) boycotter; **to give sb a ~ eye** pocher l'œil à qn, faire un œil au beurre noir à qn; **to be in the ~** (in credit) avoir un compte créditeur; **~ and blue** (bruised) couvert(e) de bleus; **black out** vi (faint) s'évanouir; **blackberry** n mûre f; **blackbird** n merle m; **blackboard** n tableau noir; **black coffee** n café noir; **blackcurrant** n cassis m; **black ice** n verglas m; **blackmail** n chantage m ▷ vt faire chanter, soumettre au chantage; **black market** n marché noir; **blackout** n panne f d'électricité; (in wartime) black-out m; (TV) interruption f d'émission; (fainting) syncope f; **black pepper** n poivre noir; **black pudding** n boudin (noir); **Black Sea** n: **the Black Sea** la mer Noire

bladder ['blædə'] n vessie f

blade [bleɪd] n lame f; (of propeller) pale f; **a ~ of grass** un brin d'herbe

blame [bleɪm] n faute f, blâme m ▷ vt: **to ~ sb/sth for sth** attribuer à qn/qch la responsabilité de qch; reprocher qch à qn/qch; **I'm not to ~** ce n'est pas ma faute

bland [blænd] adj (taste, food) doux (douce), fade

blank [blæŋk] adj blanc (blanche); (look) sans expression, dénué(e) d'expression ▷ n espace m vide, blanc m; (cartridge) cartouche f à blanc; **his mind was a ~** il avait la tête vide

blanket ['blæŋkɪt] n couverture f; (of snow, cloud) couche f

blast [blɑ:st] n explosion f; (shock wave) souffle m; (of air, steam) bouffée f ▷ vt faire sauter or exploser

blatant ['bleɪtənt] adj flagrant(e), criant(e)

blaze [bleɪz] n (fire) incendie m; (fig) flamboiement m ▷ vi (fire) flamber; (fig) flamboyer, resplendir ▷ vt: **to ~ a trail** (fig) montrer la voie; **in a ~ of publicity** à grand renfort de publicité

blazer ['bleɪzə'] n blazer m

bleach [bli:tʃ] n (also: **household ~**) eau f de Javel ▷ vt (linen) blanchir; **bleachers** npl (US Sport) gradins mpl (en plein soleil)

bleak [bli:k] adj morne, désolé(e); (weather) triste, maussade; (smile) lugubre; (prospect, future) morose

bled [bled] pt, pp of **bleed**

bleed (pt, pp **bled**) [bli:d, bled] vt saigner; (brakes, radiator) purger ▷ vi saigner; **my nose is ~ing** je saigne du nez

blemish ['blemɪʃ] n défaut m; (on reputation) tache f

blend [blend] n mélange m ▷ vt mélanger ▷ vi (colours etc: also: **~ in**) se mélanger, se fondre, s'allier; **blender** n (Culin) mixeur m

bless (pt, pp **~ed** or **blest**) [bles, blest] vt bénir; **~ you!** (after sneeze) à tes souhaits!; **blessing** n bénédiction f; (godsend) bienfait m

blew [blu:] pt of **blow**

blight [blaɪt] vt (hopes etc) anéantir, briser

blind [blaɪnd] adj aveugle ▷ n (for window) store m ▷ vt aveugler; **the blind** npl les aveugles mpl; **blind alley** n impasse f; **blindfold** n bandeau m ▷ adj, adv les yeux bandés ▷ vt bander les yeux à

blink [blɪŋk] vi cligner des yeux; (light) clignoter

bliss [blɪs] n félicité f, bonheur m sans mélange

blister ['blɪstə'] n (on skin) ampoule f, cloque f; (on paintwork) boursouflure f ▷ vi (paint) se boursoufler, se cloquer

blizzard ['blɪzəd] n blizzard m, tempête f de neige

bloated ['bləutɪd] adj (face) bouffi(e); (stomach, person) gonflé(e)

blob [blɔb] n (drop) goutte f; (stain, spot) tache f

block [blɔk] n bloc m; (in pipes) obstruction f; (toy) cube m; (of buildings) pâté m (de maisons) ▷ vt bloquer; (fig) faire obstacle à; **the sink is ~ed** l'évier est bouché; **~ of flats** (BRIT) immeuble (locatif); **mental ~** blocage m; **block up** vt boucher; **blockade** [blɔ'keɪd] n blocus m ▷ vt faire le blocus de; **blockage** n obstruction f; **blockbuster** n (film, book) grand succès; **block capitals** npl majuscules fpl d'imprimerie; **block letters** npl majuscules fpl

blog [blɔg] n blog m, blogue m

bloke [bləuk] n (BRIT inf) type m

blond(e) [blɔnd] adj, n blond(e)

blood [blʌd] n sang m; **blood donor** n

donneur(-euse) de sang; **blood group** n groupe sanguin; **blood poisoning** n empoisonnement m du sang; **blood pressure** n tension (artérielle); **bloodshed** n effusion f de sang, carnage m; **bloodshot** adj: **bloodshot eyes** yeux injectés de sang; **bloodstream** n sang m, système sanguin; **blood test** analyse f de sang; **blood transfusion** n transfusion f de sang; **blood type** n groupe sanguin; **blood vessel** n vaisseau sanguin; **bloody** adj sanglant(e); (BRIT infl): **this bloody ...** ce foutu ..., ce putain de ... (!) ▷ adv: **bloody strong/good** (BRIT: infl) vachement or sacrément fort/bon

bloom [blu:m] n fleur f ▷ vi être en fleur

blossom ['blɒsəm] n fleur(s) f(pl) ▷ vi être en fleurs; (fig) s'épanouir

blot [blɒt] n tache f ▷ vt tacher; (ink) sécher

blouse [blauz] n (feminine garment) chemisier m, corsage m

blow [bləu] n coup m ▷ vb (pt **blew**, pp **~n**) ▷ vi souffler ▷ vt (instrument) jouer de; (fuse) faire sauter; **to ~ one's nose** se moucher; **blow away** vi s'envoler ▷ vt chasser, faire s'envoler; **blow out** vi (fire, flame) s'éteindre; (tyre) éclater; (fuse) sauter; **blow up** vi exploser, sauter ▷ vt faire sauter; (tyre) gonfler; (Phot) agrandir; **blow-dry** n (hairstyle) brushing m

blown [bləun] pp of **blow**

blue [blu:] adj bleu(e); (depressed) triste; **~ film/joke** film m/histoire f pornographique; **out of the ~** (fig) à l'improviste, sans qu'on s'y attende; **bluebell** n jacinthe f des bois; **blueberry** n myrtille f, airelle f; **blue cheese** n (fromage) bleu m; **blues** npl (Mus) **the blues** le blues; **to have the blues** (inf: feeling) avoir le cafard; **bluetit** n mésange bleue

bluff [blʌf] vi bluffer ▷ n bluff m; **to call sb's ~** mettre qn au défi d'exécuter ses menaces

blunder ['blʌndər] n gaffe f, bévue f ▷ vi faire une gaffe or une bévue

blunt [blʌnt] adj (knife) émoussé(e), peu tranchant(e); (pencil) mal taillé(e); (person) brusque, ne mâchant pas ses mots

blur [blə:r] n (shape): **to become a ~** devenir flou ▷ vt brouiller, rendre flou(e); **blurred** adj flou(e)

blush [blʌʃ] vi rougir ▷ n rougeur f; **blusher** n rouge m à joues

board [bɔ:d] n (wooden) planche f; (on wall) panneau m; (for chess etc) plateau m; (cardboard) carton m; (committee) conseil m, comité m; (in firm) conseil d'administration; (Naut, Aviat): **on ~** à bord ▷ vt (ship) monter à bord de; (train) monter dans; **full ~** (BRIT) pension complète; **half ~** (BRIT) demi-pension f; **~ and lodging** n chambre f avec pension; **to go by the ~** (hopes, principles) être abandonné(e); **board game** n jeu m de

société; **boarding card** n (Aviat, Naut) carte f d'embarquement; **boarding pass** n (BRIT) = **boarding card**; **boarding school** n internat m, pensionnat m; **board room** n salle f du conseil d'administration

boast [bəust] vi: **to ~ (about** or **of)** se vanter (de)

boat [bəut] n bateau m; (small) canot m; barque f

bob [bɒb] vi (boat, cork on water: also: **~ up and down**) danser, se balancer

bobby pin ['bɒbɪ-] n (US) pince f à cheveux

body ['bɒdɪ] n corps m; (of car) carrosserie f; (fig: society) organe m, organisme m; **body-building** n body-building m, culturisme m; **bodyguard** n garde m du corps; **bodywork** n carrosserie f

bog [bɒg] n tourbière f ▷ vt: **to get ~ged down (in)** (fig) s'enliser (dans)

bogus ['bəugəs] adj bidon inv; fantôme

boil [bɔɪl] vt (faire) bouillir ▷ n (Med) furoncle m; **to come to the** or (US) **a ~** bouillir; **boil down** vi (fig): **to ~ down to** se réduire or ramener à; **boil over** vi déborder; **boiled egg** n œuf m à la coque; **boiled potatoes** n pommes fpl à l'anglaise or à l'eau; **boiler** n chaudière f; **boiling** ['bɔɪlɪŋ] adj: **I'm boiling (hot)** (inf) je crève de chaud; **boiling point** n point m d'ébullition

bold [bəuld] adj hardi(e), audacieux(-euse); (pej) effronté(e); (outline, colour) franc (franche), tranché(e), marqué(e)

bollard ['bɒləd] n (BRIT Aut) borne lumineuse or de signalisation

bolt [bəult] n verrou m; (with nut) boulon m ▷ adv: **~ upright** droit(e) comme un piquet ▷ vt (door) verrouiller; (food) engloutir ▷ vi se sauver, filer (comme une flèche); (horse) s'emballer

bomb [bɒm] n bombe f ▷ vt bombarder; **bombard** [bɒm'bɑ:d] vt bombarder; **bomber** n (Aviat) bombardier m; (terrorist) poseur m de bombes; **bomb scare** n alerte f à la bombe

bond [bɒnd] n lien m; (binding promise) engagement m, obligation f; (Finance) obligation; **bonds** npl (chains) chaînes fpl; **in ~** (of goods) en entrepôt

bone [bəun] n os m; (of fish) arête f ▷ vt désosser; ôter les arêtes de

bonfire ['bɒnfaɪər] n feu m (de joie); (for rubbish) feu

bonnet ['bɒnɪt] n bonnet m; (BRIT: of car) capot m

bonus ['bəunəs] n (money) prime f; (advantage) avantage m

boo [bu:] excl hou!, peuh! ▷ vt huer

book [buk] n livre m; (of stamps, tickets etc) carnet m; (Comm): **books** npl comptes mpl, comptabilité f ▷ vt (ticket) prendre; (seat, room) réserver; (football player) prendre le nom de, donner un carton à; **I ~ed a table in the name of ...** j'ai réservé une table au nom de ...; **book in** vi (BRIT: at hotel) prendre sa chambre; **book up** vt réserver; **the hotel is ~ed up** l'hôtel est complet; **bookcase** n bibliothèque f (meuble); **booking** n (BRIT) réservation f; **I confirmed my booking by fax/e-mail** j'ai confirmé ma réservation par fax/e-mail; **booking office** n (BRIT) bureau m de location; **book-keeping** n comptabilité f; **booklet** n brochure f; **bookmaker** n bookmaker m; **bookmark** n (for book) marque-page m; (Comput) signet m; **bookseller** n libraire m/f; **bookshelf** n (single) étagère f (à livres); (bookcase) bibliothèque f; **bookshop, bookstore** n librairie f

boom [bu:m] n (noise) grondement m; (in prices, population) forte augmentation; (busy period) boom m, vague f de prospérité ▷ vi gronder; prospérer

boost [bu:st] n stimulant m, remontant m ▷ vt stimuler

boot [bu:t] n botte f; (for hiking) chaussure f (de marche); (ankle boot) bottine f; (BRIT: of car) coffre m; (Comput) lancer, mettre en route; **to ~** (in addition) par-dessus le marché, en plus

booth [bu:ð] n (at fair) baraque (foraine); (of telephone centre) cabine f; (also: **voting ~**) isoloir m

booze [bu:z] (inf) n boissons fpl alcooliques, alcool m

border ['bɔ:dəʳ] n bordure f; bord m; (of a country) frontière f; **borderline** n (fig) ligne f de démarcation

bore [bɔ:ʳ] pt of **bear** ▷ vt (person) ennuyer, raser; (hole) percer; (well, tunnel) creuser ▷ n (person) raseur(-euse); (boring thing) barbe f; (of gun) calibre m; **bored** adj: **to be bored** s'ennuyer; **boredom** n ennui m

boring ['bɔ:rɪŋ] adj ennuyeux(-euse)

born [bɔ:n] adj: **to be ~** naître; **I was ~ in 1960** je suis né en 1960

borne [bɔ:n] pp of **bear**

borough ['bʌrə] n municipalité f

borrow ['bɔrəʊ] vt: **to ~ sth (from sb)** emprunter qch (à qn)

Bosnia(-Herzegovina) ['bɔːsnɪə(hɜːzə'gəʊviːnə)] n Bosnie-Herzégovine f; **Bosnian** ['bɔznɪən] adj bosniaque, bosnien(ne) ▷ n Bosniaque m/f, Bosnien(ne)

bosom ['buzəm] n poitrine f; (fig) sein m

boss [bɔs] n patron(ne) ▷ vt (also: **~ about**, **~ around**) mener à la baguette; **bossy** adj autoritaire

both [bəʊθ] adj les deux, l'un(e) et l'autre ▷ pron: **~ (of them)** les deux, tous (toutes) (les) deux, l'un(e) et l'autre; **~ of us went, we ~ went** nous y sommes allés tous les deux ▷ adv: **~ A and B** A et B

bother ['bɔðəʳ] vt (worry) tracasser; (needle, bait) importuner, ennuyer; (disturb) déranger ▷ vi (also: **~ o.s.**) se tracasser, se faire du souci ▷ n (trouble) ennuis mpl; **to ~ doing** prendre la peine de faire; **don't ~** ce n'est pas la peine; **it's no ~** aucun problème

bottle ['bɔtl] n bouteille f; (baby's) biberon m; (of perfume, medicine) flacon m ▷ vt mettre en bouteille(s); **bottle bank** n conteneur m (de bouteilles); **bottle-opener** n ouvre-bouteille m

bottom ['bɔtəm] n (of container, sea etc) fond m; (buttocks) derrière m; (of page, list) bas m; (of mountain, tree, hill) pied m ▷ adj (shelf, step) du bas

bought [bɔːt] pt, pp of **buy**

boulder ['bəʊldəʳ] n gros rocher (gén lisse, arrondi)

bounce [baʊns] vi (ball) rebondir; (cheque) être refusé (étant sans provision) ▷ vt faire rebondir ▷ n (rebound) rebond m; **bouncer** n (inf: at dance, club) videur m

bound [baʊnd] pt, pp of **bind** ▷ n (gen pl) limite f; (leap) bond m ▷ vi (leap) bondir ▷ vt (limit) borner ▷ adj: **to be ~ to do sth** (obliged) être obligé(e) or avoir obligation de faire qch; **he's ~ to fail** (likely) il est sûr d'échouer, son échec est inévitable or assuré; **~ by** (law, regulation) engagé(e) par; **~ for** à destination de; **out of ~s** dont l'accès est interdit

boundary ['baʊndrɪ] n frontière f

bouquet ['bukeɪ] n bouquet m

bourbon ['buəbən] n (US: also: **~ whiskey**) bourbon m

bout [baʊt] n période f; (of malaria etc) accès m, crise f, attaque f; (Boxing etc) combat m, match m

boutique [buːˈtiːk] n boutique f

bow¹ [bəʊ] n nœud m; (weapon) arc m; (Mus) archet m

bow² [baʊ] n (with body) révérence f, inclination f (du buste or corps); (Naut: also: **~s**) proue f ▷ vi faire une révérence, s'incliner

bowels [baʊəlz] npl intestins mpl; (fig) entrailles fpl

bowl [bəʊl] n (for eating) bol m; (for washing) cuvette f; (ball) boule f ▷ vi (Cricket) lancer (la balle); **bowler** n (Cricket) lanceur m (de la balle); (BRIT: also: **bowler hat**) (chapeau m) melon m; **bowling** n (game) jeu m de boules, jeu de quilles; **bowling alley** n bowling m; **bowling green** n terrain m de boules (gazonné et carré); **bowls** n (jeu m de) boules fpl

bow tie [bəʊ-] n nœud m papillon

box [bɔks] n boîte f; (also: **cardboard ~**) carton m; (Theat) loge f ▷ vt mettre en boîte ▷ vi boxer, faire de la boxe; **boxer** n ['bɔksəʳ] (person) boxeur m; **boxer shorts** npl caleçon m;

boxing ['bɔksɪŋ] n (sport) boxe f; **Boxing Day** n (BRIT) le lendemain de Noël; voir encadré; **boxing gloves** npl gants mpl de boxe; **boxing ring** n ring m; **box junction** n (BRIT Aut) zone f (de carrefour) d'accès réglementé; **box office** n bureau m de location

boy [bɔɪ] n garçon m; **boy band** n boys band m
boycott ['bɔɪkɔt] n boycottage m ▷ vt boycotter
boyfriend ['bɔɪfrɛnd] n (petit) ami
bra [brɑː] n soutien-gorge m
brace [breɪs] n (support) attache f, agrafe f; (BRIT: also: ~s: on teeth) appareil m (dentaire); (tool) vilebrequin m ▷ vt (support) consolider, soutenir; **braces** npl (BRIT: for trousers) bretelles fpl; **to ~ o.s.** (fig) se préparer mentalement
bracelet ['breɪslɪt] n bracelet m
bracket ['brækɪt] n (Tech) tasseau m, support m; (group) classe f, tranche f; (also: **brace ~**) accolade f; (also: **round ~**) parenthèse f; (also: **square ~**) crochet m ▷ vt mettre entre parenthèses; **in ~s** entre parenthèses or crochets
brag [bræg] vi se vanter
braid [breɪd] n (trimming) galon m; (of hair) tresse f, natte f
brain [breɪn] n cerveau m; **brains** npl (intellect, food) cervelle f
braise [breɪz] vt braiser
brake [breɪk] n frein m ▷ vt, vi freiner; **brake light** n feu m de stop
bran [bræn] n son m
branch [brɑːntʃ] n branche f; (Comm) succursale f; (: of bank) agence f; **branch off** vi (road) bifurquer; **branch out** vi diversifier ses activités
brand [brænd] n marque (commerciale) ▷ vt (cattle) marquer (au fer rouge); **brand name** n nom m de marque; **brand-new** adj tout(e) neuf (neuve), flambant neuf (neuve)
brandy ['brændɪ] n cognac m
brash [bræʃ] adj effronté(e)
brass [brɑːs] n cuivre m (jaune), laiton m; **the ~** (Mus) les cuivres; **brass band** n fanfare f
brat [bræt] n (pej) mioche m/f, môme m/f
brave [breɪv] adj courageux(-euse), brave ▷ vt braver, affronter; **bravery** n bravoure f, courage m
brawl [brɔːl] n rixe f, bagarre f

Brazil [brə'zɪl] n Brésil m; **Brazilian** adj brésilien(ne) ▷ n Brésilien(ne)
breach [briːtʃ] vt ouvrir une brèche dans ▷ n (gap) brèche f; (breaking): **~ of contract** rupture f de contrat; **~ of the peace** attentat m à l'ordre public
bread [brɛd] n pain m; **breadbin** n (BRIT) boîte f or huche f à pain; **breadbox** n (US) boîte f or huche f à pain; **breadcrumbs** npl miettes fpl de pain; (Culin) chapelure f, panure f
breadth [brɛtθ] n largeur f
break [breɪk] (pt **broke**, pp **broken**) vt casser, briser; (promise) rompre; (law) violer ▷ vi se casser, se briser; (weather) tourner; (storm) éclater; (day) se lever ▷ n (gap) brèche f; (fracture) cassure f; (rest) interruption f, arrêt m; (: short) pause f; (: at school) récréation f; (chance) chance f, occasion f favorable; **to ~ one's leg** etc se casser la jambe etc; **to ~ a record** battre un record; **to ~ the news to sb** annoncer la nouvelle à qn; **break down** vt (door etc) enfoncer; (figures, data) décomposer, analyser ▷ vi s'effondrer; (Med) faire une dépression (nerveuse); (Aut) tomber en panne; **my car has broken down** ma voiture est en panne; **break in** vt (horse etc) dresser ▷ vi (burglar) entrer par effraction; (interrupt) interrompre; **break into** vt fus (house) s'introduire or pénétrer par effraction dans; **break off** vi (speaker) s'interrompre; (branch) se rompre ▷ vt (talks, engagement) rompre; **break out** vi éclater, se déclarer; (prisoner) s'évader; **to ~ out in spots** se couvrir de boutons; **break up** vi (partnership) cesser, prendre fin; (marriage) se briser; (crowd, meeting) se séparer; (ship) se disloquer; (Scol: pupils) être en vacances; (line) couper; **the line's** or **you're ~ing up** la coupe ▷ vt fracasser, casser; (fight etc) interrompre, faire cesser; (marriage) désunir; **breakdown** n (Aut) panne f; (in communications, marriage) rupture f; (Med: also: **nervous breakdown**) dépression (nerveuse); (of figures) ventilation f, répartition f; **breakdown truck** (US **breakdown van**) n dépanneuse f
breakfast ['brɛkfəst] n petit déjeuner m; **what time is ~?** le petit déjeuner est à quelle heure?
break: **break-in** n cambriolage m; **breakthrough** n percée f
breast [brɛst] n (of woman) sein m; (chest) poitrine f; (of chicken, turkey) blanc m; **breast-feed** vt, vi (irreg: like **feed**) allaiter; **breast-stroke** n brasse f
breath [brɛθ] n haleine f, souffle m; **to take a deep ~** respirer à fond; **out of ~** à bout de souffle, essoufflé(e)
Breathalyser® ['brɛθəlaɪzəʳ] (BRIT) n alcootest m

breathe [bri:ð] vt, vi respirer; **breathe in**
vi inspirer ▷ vt aspirer; **breathe out** vt, vi
expirer; **breathing** n respiration f

breath n essoufflé(e);
haletant(e); **breathtaking** adj stupéfiant(e),
à vous couper le souffle; **breath test** n
alcootest m

bred [bred] pt, pp of **breed**

breed [bri:d] (pt, pp **bred**) vt élever, faire
l'élevage de ▷ vi se reproduire ▷ n race f,
variété f

breeze [bri:z] n brise f

breezy ['bri:zɪ] adj (day, weather)
venteux(-euse); (manner) désinvolte; (person)
jovial(e)

brew [bru:] vt (tea) faire infuser; (beer) brasser
▷ vi (fig) se préparer, couver; **brewery** n
brasserie f (fabrique)

bribe [braɪb] n pot-de-vin m ▷ vt acheter;
soudoyer; **bribery** n corruption f

bric-a-brac ['brɪkəbræk] n bric-à-brac m

brick [brɪk] n brique f; **bricklayer** n
maçon m

bride [braɪd] n mariée f, épouse f; **bridegroom**
n marié m, époux m; **bridesmaid** n demoiselle
f d'honneur

bridge [brɪdʒ] n pont m; (Naut) passerelle f
(de commandement); (of nose) arête f; (Cards,
Dentistry) bridge m ▷ vt (gap) combler

bridle ['braɪdl] n bride f

brief [bri:f] adj bref (brève) ▷ n (Law)
dossier m, cause f; (gen) tâche f ▷ vt mettre
au courant; **briefs** npl slip m; **briefcase** n
serviette f, porte-documents m inv; **briefing** n
instructions fpl; (Press) briefing m; **briefly** adv
brièvement

brigadier [brɪgə'dɪəʳ] n brigadier général

bright [braɪt] adj brillant(e); (room, weather)
clair(e); (person: clever) intelligent(e), doué(e);
(: cheerful) gai(e); (idea) génial(e); (colour) vif
(vive)

brilliant ['brɪljənt] adj brillant(e); (light,
sunshine) éclatant(e); (inf: great) super

brim [brɪm] n bord m

brine [braɪn] n (Culin) saumure f

bring (pt, pp **brought**) [brɪŋ, brɔːt] vt (thing)
apporter; (person) amener; **bring about**
vt provoquer, entraîner; **bring back** vt
rapporter; (person) ramener; **bring down**
vt (lower) abaisser; (shoot down) abattre;
(government) faire s'effondrer; **bring in** vt
(person) faire entrer; (object) rentrer; (Pol:
legislation) introduire; (produce: income)
rapporter; **bring on** vt (illness, attack)
provoquer; (player, substitute) amener;
bring out vt sortir; (meaning) faire ressortir,
mettre en relief; **bring up** vt élever; (carry
up) monter; (question) soulever; (food: vomit)
vomir, rendre

brink [brɪŋk] n bord m

brisk [brɪsk] adj vif (vive); (abrupt) brusque;
(trade etc) actif(-ive)

bristle ['brɪsl] n poil m ▷ vi se hérisser

Brit [brɪt] n abbr (inf: = British person)
Britannique m/f

Britain ['brɪtən] n (also: **Great ~**) la Grande-
Bretagne

British ['brɪtɪʃ] adj britannique ▷ npl: **the ~**
les Britanniques mpl; **British Isles** npl: **the
British Isles** les îles fpl Britanniques

Briton ['brɪtən] n Britannique m/f

Brittany ['brɪtənɪ] n Bretagne f

brittle ['brɪtl] adj cassant(e), fragile

B road n (BRIT) ≈ route départementale

broad [brɔːd] adj large; (distinction) général(e);
(accent) prononcé(e); **in ~ daylight** en plein
jour; **broadband** n transmission f à haut
débit; **broad bean** n fève f; **broadcast** n
émission f ▷ vb (pt, pp **broadcast**) ▷ vt (Radio)
radiodiffuser; (TV) téléviser ▷ vi émettre;
broaden vt élargir; **to broaden one's mind**
élargir ses horizons ▷ vi s'élargir; **broadly** adv
en gros, généralement; **broad-minded** adj
large d'esprit

broccoli ['brɔkəlɪ] n brocoli m

brochure ['brəʊʃjʊəʳ] n prospectus m,
dépliant m

broil [brɔɪl] (us) vt rôtir

broiler ['brɔɪləʳ] n (fowl) poulet m (à rôtir); (us:
grill) gril m

broke [brəʊk] pt of **break** ▷ adj (inf) fauché(e)

broken ['brəʊkn] pp of **break** ▷ adj (stick, leg
etc) cassé(e); (machine: also: **~ down**) fichu(e);
in ~ French/English dans un français/anglais
approximatif or hésitant

broker ['brəʊkəʳ] n courtier m

bronchitis [brɔŋ'kaɪtɪs] n bronchite f

bronze [brɔnz] n bronze m

brooch [brəʊtʃ] n broche f

brood [bru:d] n couvée f ▷ vi (person) méditer
(sombrement), ruminer

broom [brum] n balai m; (Bot) genêt m

Bros. abbr (Comm: = brothers) Frères

broth [brɔθ] n bouillon m de viande et de
légumes

brothel ['brɔθl] n maison close, bordel m

brother ['brʌðəʳ] n frère m; **brother-in-law** n
beau-frère m

brought [brɔːt] pt, pp of **bring**

brow [brau] n front m; (eyebrow) sourcil m; (of
hill) sommet m

brown [braun] adj brun(e), marron inv; (hair)
châtain inv; (tanned) bronzé(e) ▷ n (colour)
brun m, marron m ▷ vt brunir; (Culin) faire
dorer, faire roussir; **brown bread** n pain m bis

Brownie ['braunɪ] n jeannette f éclaireuse
(cadette)

brown rice n riz m complet

brown sugar n cassonade f
browse [brauz] vi (in shop) regarder (sans acheter); **to ~ through a book** feuilleter un livre; **browser** n (Comput) navigateur m
bruise [bru:z] n bleu m, ecchymose f, contusion f ▷ vt contusionner, meurtrir
brunette [bru:'nɛt] n (femme) brune
brush [brʌʃ] n brosse f; (for painting) pinceau m; (for shaving) blaireau m; (quarrel) accrochage m, prise f de bec ▷ vt brosser; (also: ~ past, ~ against) effleurer, frôler
Brussels ['brʌslz] n Bruxelles
Brussels sprout [-spraut] n chou m de Bruxelles
brutal ['bru:tl] adj brutal(e)
B.Sc. n abbr = **Bachelor of Science**
BSE n abbr (= bovine spongiform encephalopathy) ESB f, BSE f
bubble ['bʌbl] n bulle f ▷ vi bouillonner, faire des bulles; (sparkle, fig) pétiller; **bubble bath** n bain moussant; **bubble gum** n chewing-gum m; **bubblejet printer** ['bʌbldʒɛt-] n imprimante f à bulle d'encre
buck [bʌk] n mâle m (d'un lapin, lièvre, daim etc); (us inf) dollar m ▷ vi ruer, lancer une ruade; **to pass the ~ (to sb)** se décharger de la responsabilité (sur qn)
bucket ['bʌkɪt] n seau m
buckle ['bʌkl] n boucle f ▷ vt (belt etc) boucler, attacher ▷ vi (warp) tordre, gauchir; (: wheel) se voiler
bud [bʌd] n bourgeon m; (of flower) bouton m ▷ vi bourgeonner; (flower) éclore
Buddhism ['budɪzəm] n bouddhisme m
Buddhist ['budɪst] adj bouddhiste ▷ n Bouddhiste m/f
buddy ['bʌdɪ] n (us) copain m
budge [bʌdʒ] vt faire bouger ▷ vi bouger
budgerigar ['bʌdʒərɪgɑː'] n perruche f
budget ['bʌdʒɪt] n budget m ▷ vi: **to ~ for sth** inscrire qch au budget
budgie ['bʌdʒɪ] n = **budgerigar**
buff [bʌf] adj (couleur f) chamois m ▷ n (inf: enthusiast) mordu(e)
buffalo (pl ~ or ~es) ['bʌfələu] n (BRIT) buffle m; (us) bison m
buffer ['bʌfə'] n tampon m; (Comput) mémoire f tampon
buffet n ['bufei] (food BRIT: bar) buffet m ▷ vt ['bʌfɪt] secouer, ébranler; **buffet car** n (BRIT Rail) voiture-bar f
bug [bʌg] n (bedbug etc) punaise f; (esp us: any insect) insecte m, bestiole f; (fig: germ) virus m, microbe m; (spy device) dispositif m d'écoute (électronique), micro clandestin; (Comput: of program) erreur f ▷ vt (room) poser des micros dans; (inf: annoy) embêter
buggy ['bʌgɪ] n poussette f
build [bɪld] n (of person) carrure f, charpente

f ▷ vt (pt, pp **built**) construire, bâtir; **build up** vt accumuler, amasser; (business) développer; (reputation) bâtir; **builder** n entrepreneur m; **building** n (trade) construction f; (structure) bâtiment m, construction f; (: residential, offices) immeuble m; **building site** n chantier m (de construction); **building society** n (BRIT) société f de crédit immobilier
built [bɪlt] pt, pp of **build**; **built-in** adj (cupboard) encastré(e); (device) incorporé(e); intégré(e); **built-up** adj: **built-up area** zone urbanisée
bulb [bʌlb] n (Bot) bulbe m, oignon m; (Elec) ampoule f
Bulgaria [bʌl'gɛərɪə] n Bulgarie f; **Bulgarian** adj bulgare ▷ n Bulgare m/f
bulge [bʌldʒ] n renflement m, gonflement m ▷ vi faire saillie; présenter un renflement; (pocket, file): **to be bulging with** être plein(e) à craquer de
bulimia [bə'lɪmɪə] n boulimie f
bulimic [bju:'lɪmɪk] adj, n boulimique (m/f)
bulk [bʌlk] n masse f, volume m; **in ~** (Comm) en gros, en vrac; **the ~ of** la plus grande or grosse partie de; **bulky** adj volumineux(-euse), encombrant(e)
bull [bul] n taureau m; (male elephant, whale) mâle m
bulldozer ['buldəuzə'] n bulldozer m
bullet ['bulɪt] n balle f (de fusil etc)
bulletin ['bulɪtɪn] n bulletin m, communiqué m; (also: **news ~**) (bulletin d') informations fpl; **bulletin board** n (Comput) messagerie f (électronique)
bullfight ['bulfaɪt] n corrida f, course f de taureaux; **bullfighter** n torero m; **bullfighting** n tauromachie f
bully ['bulɪ] n brute f, tyran m ▷ vt tyranniser, rudoyer
bum [bʌm] n (inf: BRIT: backside) derrière m; (: esp us: tramp) vagabond(e), traîne-savates m/f inv; (: idler) glandeur m
bumblebee ['bʌmblbi:] n bourdon m
bump [bʌmp] n (blow) coup m, choc m; (jolt) cahot m; (on road etc, on head) bosse f ▷ vt heurter, cogner; (car) emboutir; **bump into** vt fus rentrer dans, tamponner; (inf: meet) tomber sur; **bumper** n pare-chocs m inv ▷ adj: **bumper crop/harvest** récolte/moisson exceptionnelle; **bumpy** adj (road) cahoteux(-euse); **it was a bumpy flight/ride** on a été secoués dans l'avion/la voiture
bun [bʌn] n (cake) petit gâteau; (bread) petit pain au lait; (of hair) chignon m
bunch [bʌntʃ] n (of flowers) bouquet m; (of keys) trousseau m; (of bananas) régime m; (of people) groupe m; **bunches** npl (in hair) couettes fpl; **~ of grapes** grappe f de raisin
bundle ['bʌndl] n paquet m ▷ vt (also: ~ up)

faire un paquet de; (*put*): **to ~ sth/sb into** fourrer or enfourner qch/qn dans

bungalow ['bʌŋɡələu] *n* bungalow *m*

bungee jumping ['bʌndʒiːˈdʒʌmpɪŋ] *n* saut *m* à l'élastique

bunion ['bʌnjən] *n* oignon *m* (*au pied*)

bunk [bʌŋk] *n* couchette *f*; **bunk beds** *npl* lits superposés

bunker ['bʌŋkə*ʳ*] *n* (*coal store*) soute *f* à charbon; (*Mil, Golf*) bunker *m*

bunny ['bʌnɪ] *n* (*also*: **~ rabbit**) lapin *m*

buoy [bɔɪ] *n* bouée *f*; **buoyant** *adj* (*ship*) flottant(e); (*carefree*) gai(e), plein(e) d'entrain; (*Comm: market, economy*) actif(-ive)

burden ['bəːdn] *n* fardeau *m*, charge *f* ▷ *vt* charger; (*oppress*) accabler, surcharger

bureau (*pl* **~x**) ['bjuərəu, -z] *n* (*BRIT: writing desk*) bureau *m*, secrétaire *m*; (*us: chest of drawers*) commode *f*; (*office*) bureau, office *m*

bureaucracy [bjuəˈrɔkrəsɪ] *n* bureaucratie *f*

bureaucrat ['bjuərəkræt] *n* bureaucrate *m/f*, rond-de-cuir *m*

bureau de change [-dəˈʃɑʒ] (*pl* **bureaux de change**) *n* bureau *m* de change

bureaux ['bjuərəuz] *npl* of **bureau**

burger ['bəːɡə*ʳ*] *n* hamburger *m*

burglar ['bəːɡlə*ʳ*] *n* cambrioleur *m*; **burglar alarm** *n* sonnerie *f* d'alarme; **burglary** *n* cambriolage *m*

Burgundy ['bəːɡəndɪ] *n* Bourgogne *f*

burial ['berɪəl] *n* enterrement *m*

burn [bəːn] *vt, vi* (*pt, pp* **~ed** or **~t**) brûler ▷ *n* brûlure *f*; **burn down** *vt* incendier, détruire par le feu; **burn out** *vt* (*writer etc*): **to ~ o.s. out** s'user (à force de travailler); **burning** *adj* (*building, forest*) en flammes; (*issue, question*) brûlant(e); (*ambition*) dévorant(e)

Burns' Night [bəːnz-] *n* fête écossaise à la mémoire du poète Robert Burns

burnt [bəːnt] *pt, pp* of **burn**

burp [bəːp] (*inf*) *n* rot *m* ▷ *vi* roter

burrow ['bʌrəu] *n* terrier *m* ▷ *vi* (*rabbit*) creuser un terrier; (*rummage*) fouiller

burst [bəːst] (*pt, pp* **~**) *vt* faire éclater; (*river: banks etc*) rompre ▷ *vi* éclater; (*tyre*) crever ▷ *n* explosion *f*; (*also*: **~ pipe**) fuite *f* (*due à une rupture*); **a ~ of enthusiasm/energy** un accès d'enthousiasme/d'énergie; **to ~ into flames** s'enflammer soudainement; **to ~ out laughing** éclater de rire; **to ~ into tears** fondre en larmes; **to ~ open** *vi* s'ouvrir violemment or soudainement; **to be ~ing with** (*container*) être plein(e) (à craquer) de, regorger de; (*fig*) être débordant(e) de; **burst into** *vt fus* (*room etc*) faire irruption dans

bury ['berɪ] *vt* enterrer

bus (*pl* **~es**) [bʌs, 'bʌsɪz] *n* autobus *m*; **bus conductor** *n* receveur(-euse) *m/f* de bus

bush [buʃ] *n* buisson *m*; (*scrub land*) brousse *f*; **to beat about the ~** tourner autour du pot

business ['bɪznɪs] *n* (*matter, firm*) affaire *f*; (*trading*) affaires *fpl*; (*job, duty*) travail *m*; **to be away on ~** être en déplacement d'affaires; **it's none of my ~** cela ne me regarde pas, ce ne sont pas mes affaires; **he means ~** il ne plaisante pas, il est sérieux; **business class** *n* (*on plane*) classe *f* affaires; **businesslike** *adj* sérieux(-euse), efficace; **businessman** (*irreg*) *n* homme *m* d'affaires; **business trip** *n* voyage *m* d'affaires; **businesswoman** (*irreg*) *n* femme *f* d'affaires

busker ['bʌskə*ʳ*] *n* (*BRIT*) artiste ambulant(e)

bus: **bus pass** *n* carte *f* de bus; **bus shelter** *n* abribus *m*; **bus station** *n* gare routière; **bus-stop** *n* arrêt *m* d'autobus

bust [bʌst] *n* buste *m*; (*measurement*) tour *m* de poitrine ▷ *adj* (*inf: broken*) fichu(e), fini(e); **to go ~** faire faillite

bustling ['bʌslɪŋ] *adj* (*town*) très animé(e)

busy ['bɪzɪ] *adj* occupé(e); (*shop, street*) très fréquenté(e); (*us: telephone, line*) occupé ▷ *vt*: **to ~ o.s.** s'occuper; **busy signal** *n* (*us*) tonalité *f* occupé *inv*

KEYWORD

but [bʌt] *conj* mais; **I'd love to come, but I'm busy** j'aimerais venir mais je suis occupé; **he's not English but French** il n'est pas anglais mais français; **but that's far too expensive!** mais c'est bien trop cher!

▷ *prep* (*apart from, except*) sauf, excepté; **nothing but** rien d'autre que; **we've had nothing but trouble** nous n'avons eu que des ennuis; **no-one but him can do it** lui seul peut le faire; **who but a lunatic would do such a thing?** qui sinon un fou ferait une chose pareille?; **but for you/your help** sans toi/ton aide; **anything but that** tout sauf or excepté ça, tout mais pas ça

▷ *adv* (*just, only*) ne ... que; **she's but a child** elle n'est qu'une enfant; **had I but known**

si seulement j'avais su; **I can but try** je
peux toujours essayer; **all but finished**
pratiquement terminé

butcher ['butʃər] n boucher m ▷ vt massacrer;
(cattle etc for meat) tuer; **butcher's (shop)** n
boucherie f
butler ['bʌtlər] n maître m d'hôtel
butt [bʌt] n (cask) gros tonneau; (of gun) crosse
f; (of cigarette) mégot m; (BRIT fig: target) cible f
▷ vt donner un coup de tête à
butter ['bʌtər] n beurre m ▷ vt beurrer;
buttercup n bouton m d'or
butterfly ['bʌtəflaɪ] n papillon m; (Swimming:
also: ~ **stroke**) brasse f papillon
buttocks ['bʌtəks] npl fesses fpl
button ['bʌtn] n bouton m; (US: badge) pin m
▷ vt (also: ~ **up**) boutonner ▷ vi se boutonner
buy [baɪ] (pt, pp bought) vt acheter ▷ n achat
m; **to ~ sb sth/sth from sb** acheter qch à qn;
to ~ sb a drink offrir un verre or à boire à qn;
can I ~ you a drink? je vous offre un verre?;
where can I ~ some postcards? où est-ce que
je peux acheter des cartes postales?; **buy out**
vt (partner) désintéresser; **buy up** vt acheter
en bloc, rafler; **buyer** n acheteur(-euse) m/f
buzz [bʌz] n bourdonnement m; (inf: phone
call): **to give sb a ~** passer un coup de fil à
qn ▷ vi bourdonner; **buzzer** n timbre m
électrique

 KEYWORD

by [baɪ] prep **1** (referring to cause, agent) par,
de; **killed by lightning** tué par la foudre;
surrounded by a fence entouré d'une
barrière; **a painting by Picasso** un tableau
de Picasso
2 (referring to method, manner, means): **by
bus/car** en autobus/voiture; **by train** par le or
en train; **to pay by cheque** payer par chèque;
by moonlight/candlelight à la lueur de la
lune/d'une bougie; **by saving hard, he ...** à
force d'économiser, il ...
3 (via, through) par; **we came by Dover** nous
sommes venus par Douvres
4 (close to, past) à côté de; **the house by the
school** la maison à côté de l'école; **a holiday
by the sea** des vacances au bord de la mer;
she went by me elle est passée à côté de moi;
I go by the post office every day je passe
devant la poste tous les jours
5 (with time: not later than) avant; (: during):
by daylight à la lumière du jour; **by night** la
nuit, de nuit; **by 4 o'clock** avant 4 heures; **by
this time tomorrow** d'ici demain à la même
heure; **by the time I got here it was too late**
lorsque je suis arrivé il était déjà trop tard
6 (amount) à; **by the kilo/metre** au kilo/au

mètre; **paid by the hour** payé à l'heure
7 (Math: measure): **to divide/multiply by 3**
diviser/multiplier par 3; **a room 3 metres by 4**
une pièce de 3 mètres sur 4; **it's broader by a
metre** c'est plus large d'un mètre
8 (according to) d'après, selon; **it's 3 o'clock by
my watch** il est 3 heures à ma montre; **it's all
right by me** je n'ai rien contre
9: **(all) by oneself** etc tout(e) seul(e)
▷ adv **1** see **go**; **pass** etc
2: **by and by** un peu plus tard, bientôt; **by and
large** dans l'ensemble

bye(-bye) ['baɪ('baɪ)] excl au revoir!, salut!
by-election ['baɪɪlekʃən] n (BRIT) élection
(législative) partielle
bypass ['baɪpɑːs] n rocade f; (Med) pontage
m ▷ vt éviter
byte [baɪt] n (Comput) octet m

C [siː] n (Mus): **C** do m

cab [kæb] n taxi m; (of train, truck) cabine f

cabaret ['kæbəreɪ] n (show) spectacle m de cabaret

cabbage ['kæbɪdʒ] n chou m

cabin ['kæbɪn] n (house) cabane f, hutte f; (on ship) cabine f; (on plane) compartiment m; **cabin crew** n (Aviat) équipage m

cabinet ['kæbɪnɪt] n (Pol) cabinet m; (furniture) petit meuble à tiroirs et rayons; (also: **display ~**) vitrine f, petite armoire vitrée; **cabinet minister** n ministre m (membre du cabinet)

cable ['keɪbl] n câble m ⊳ vt câbler, télégraphier; **cable car** n téléphérique m; **cable television** n télévision f par câble

cactus (pl **cacti**) ['kæktəs, -taɪ] n cactus m

café ['kæfeɪ] n ≈ café(-restaurant) m (sans alcool)

cafeteria [kæfɪ'tɪərɪə] n cafétéria f

caffein(e) ['kæfiːn] n caféine f

cage [keɪdʒ] n cage f

cagoule [kə'guːl] n K-way® m

Cairo ['kaɪərəʊ] n le Caire

cake [keɪk] n gâteau m; **~ of soap** savonnette f

calcium ['kælsɪəm] n calcium m

calculate ['kælkjuleɪt] vt calculer; (estimate: chances, effect) évaluer; **calculation** [kælkju'leɪʃən] n calcul m; **calculator** n calculatrice f

calendar ['kæləndə^r] n calendrier m

calf (pl **calves**) [kɑːf, kɑːvz] n (of cow) veau m; (of other animals) petit m; (also: **~skin**) veau m, vachette f; (Anat) mollet m

calibre (us **caliber**) ['kælɪbə^r] n calibre m

call [kɔːl] vt appeler; (meeting) convoquer ⊳ vi appeler; (visit: also: **~ in**, **~ round**) passer ⊳ n (shout) appel m, cri m; (also: **telephone ~**) coup m de téléphone; **to be on ~** être de permanence; **to be ~ed** s'appeler; **can I make a ~ from here?** est-ce que je peux téléphoner d'ici?; **call back** vi (return) repasser; (Tel) rappeler ⊳ vt (Tel) rappeler; **can you ~ back later?** pouvez-vous rappeler plus tard?; **call for** vt fus (demand) demander; (fetch) passer prendre; **call in** vt (doctor, expert, police) appeler, faire venir; **call off** vt annuler; **call on** vt fus (visit) rendre visite à, passer voir; (request): **to ~ on sb to do** inviter qn à faire; **call out** vi pousser un cri or des cris; **call up** vt (Mil) appeler, mobiliser; (Tel) appeler; **callbox** n (BRIT) cabine f téléphonique; **call centre** (us **call center**) n centre m d'appels; **caller** n (Tel) personne f qui appelle; (visitor) visiteur m

callous ['kæləs] adj dur(e), insensible

calm [kɑːm] adj calme ⊳ n calme m ⊳ vt calmer, apaiser; **calm down** vi se calmer, s'apaiser ⊳ vt calmer, apaiser; **calmly** ['kɑːmlɪ] adv calmement, avec calme

Calor gas® ['kælə^r-] n (BRIT) butane m, butagaz® m

calorie ['kælərɪ] n calorie f

calves [kɑːvz] npl of **calf**

Cambodia [kæm'bəudɪə] n Cambodge m

camcorder ['kæmkɔːdə^r] n caméscope m

came [keɪm] pt of **come**

camel ['kæməl] n chameau m

camera ['kæmərə] n appareil-photo m; (Cine, TV) caméra f; **in ~** à huis clos, en privé; **cameraman** n caméraman m; **camera phone** n téléphone m avec appareil photo numérique intégré

camouflage ['kæməflɑːʒ] n camouflage m ⊳ vt camoufler

camp [kæmp] n camp m ⊳ vi camper ⊳ adj (man) efféminé(e)

campaign [kæm'peɪn] n (Mil, Pol etc) campagne f ⊳ vi (also fig) faire campagne; **campaigner** n: **campaigner for** partisan(e) de; **campaigner against** opposant(e) à

camp: **campbed** n (BRIT) lit m de camp; **camper** n campeur(-euse); (vehicle) camping-car m; **campground** (us) n (terrain m de) camping m; **camping** n camping m; **to go camping** faire du camping; **campsite** n (terrain m de) camping)

camping m

campus ['kæmpəs] n campus m

can¹ [kæn] n (of milk, oil, water) bidon m; (tin) boîte f (de conserve) ▷ vt mettre en conserve

KEYWORD

can² [kæn] (negative **cannot, can't**, conditional and pt **could**) aux vb **1** (be able to) pouvoir; **you can do it if you try** vous pouvez le faire si vous essayez; **I can't hear you** je ne t'entends pas
2 (know how to) savoir; **I can swim/play tennis/drive** je sais nager/jouer au tennis/ conduire; **can you speak French?** parlez-vous français?
3 (may) pouvoir; **can I use your phone?** puis-je me servir de votre téléphone?
4 (expressing disbelief, puzzlement etc): **it can't be true!** ce n'est pas possible!; **what CAN he want?** qu'est-ce qu'il peut bien vouloir?
5 (expressing possibility, suggestion etc): **he could be in the library** il est peut-être dans la bibliothèque; **she could have been delayed** il se peut qu'elle ait été retardée

Canada ['kænədə] n Canada m; **Canadian** [kə'neɪdɪən] adj canadien(ne) ▷ n Canadien(ne)

canal [kə'næl] n canal m

canary [kə'nɛərɪ] n canari m, serin m

cancel ['kænsəl] vt annuler; (train) supprimer; (party, appointment) décommander; (cross out) barrer, rayer; (cheque) faire opposition à; **I would like to ~ my booking** je voudrais annuler ma réservation; **cancellation** [kænsə'leɪʃən] n annulation f; suppression f

Cancer ['kænsər] n (Astrology) le Cancer

cancer ['kænsər] n cancer m

candidate ['kændɪdeɪt] n candidat(e)

candle ['kændl] n bougie f; (in church) cierge m; **candlestick** n (also: **candle holder**) bougeoir m; (bigger, ornate) chandelier m

candy ['kændɪ] n sucre candi; (US) bonbon m; **candy bar** (US) n barre f chocolatée; **candyfloss** n (BRIT) barbe f à papa

cane [keɪn] n canne f; (for baskets, chairs etc) rotin m ▷ vt (BRIT Scol) administrer des coups de bâton à

canister ['kænɪstər] n boîte f (gén en métal); (of gas) bombe f

cannabis ['kænəbɪs] n (drug) cannabis m

canned ['kænd] adj (food) en boîte, en conserve; (inf: music) enregistré(e); (BRIT inf: drunk) bourré(e); (US inf: worker) mis(e) à la porte

cannon (pl ~ or ~s) ['kænən] n (gun)

canon m

cannot ['kænɔt] = **can not**

canoe [kə'nu:] n pirogue f; (Sport) canoë m; **canoeing** n (sport) canoë m

canon ['kænən] n (clergyman) chanoine m; (standard) canon m

can-opener [-'əupnər] n ouvre-boîte m

can't [kɑ:nt] = **can not**

canteen [kæn'ti:n] n (eating place) cantine f; (BRIT: of cutlery) ménagère f

canter ['kæntər] vi aller au petit galop

canvas ['kænvəs] n toile f

canvass ['kænvəs] vi (Pol): **to ~ for** faire campagne pour ▷ vt (citizens, opinions) sonder

canyon ['kænjən] n cañon m, gorge f (profonde)

cap [kæp] n casquette f; (for swimming) bonnet m de bain; (of pen) capuchon m; (of bottle) capsule f; (BRIT: contraceptive: also: **Dutch ~**) diaphragme m ▷ vt (outdo) surpasser; (put limit on) plafonner

capability [keɪpə'bɪlɪtɪ] n aptitude f, capacité f

capable ['keɪpəbl] adj capable

capacity [kə'pæsɪtɪ] n (of container) capacité f, contenance f; (ability) aptitude f

cape [keɪp] n (garment) cape f; (Geo) cap m

caper ['keɪpər] n (Culin: gen pl) câpre f; (prank) farce f

capital ['kæpɪtl] n (also: **~ city**) capitale f; (money) capital m; (also: **~ letter**) majuscule f; **capitalism** n capitalisme m; **capitalist** adj, n capitaliste m/f; **capital punishment** n peine capitale

Capitol ['kæpɪtl] n: **the ~** le Capitole

Capricorn ['kæprɪkɔ:n] n le Capricorne

capsize [kæp'saɪz] vt faire chavirer ▷ vi chavirer

capsule ['kæpsju:l] n capsule f

captain ['kæptɪn] n capitaine m

caption ['kæpʃən] n légende f

captivity [kæp'tɪvɪtɪ] n captivité f

capture ['kæptʃər] vt (prisoner, animal) capturer; (town) prendre; (attention) capter; (Comput) saisir ▷ n capture f; (of data) saisie f de données

car [kɑ:r] n voiture f, auto f; (US Rail) wagon m, voiture

carafe [kə'ræf] n carafe f

caramel ['kærəməl] n caramel m

carat ['kærət] n carat m

caravan ['kærəvæn] n caravane f; **caravan site** n (BRIT) camping m pour caravanes

carbohydrate [kɑ:bəu'haɪdreɪt] n hydrate m de carbone; (food) féculent m

carbon ['kɑ:bən] n carbone m; **carbon dioxide** [-daɪ'ɔksaɪd] n gaz m carbonique, dioxyde m de carbone; **carbon monoxide** [-mɔ'nɔksaɪd] n oxyde m de carbone

car boot sale n voir encadré

● **CAR BOOT SALE**
●
● Type de brocante très populaire, où chacun
● vide sa cave ou son grenier. Les articles
● sont présentés dans des coffres de voitures
● et la vente a souvent lieu sur un parking
● ou dans un champ. Les brocanteurs d'un
● jour doivent s'acquitter d'une petite
● contribution pour participer à la vente.

carburettor (us **carburetor**) [kɑːbjuˈretəʳ] n carburateur m

card [kɑːd] n carte f; (material) carton m; **cardboard** n carton m; **card game** n jeu m de cartes

cardigan [ˈkɑːdɪɡən] n cardigan m

cardinal [ˈkɑːdɪnl] adj cardinal(e); (importance) capital(e) ▷ n cardinal m

cardphone [ˈkɑːdfəun] n téléphone m à carte (magnétique)

care [kɛəʳ] n soin m, attention f; (worry) souci m ▷ vi: **to ~ about** (feel interest for) se soucier de, s'intéresser à; (person: love) être attaché(e) à; **in sb's ~** à la garde de qn, confié à qn; **~ of** (on letter) chez; **to take ~ (to do)** faire attention (à faire); **to take ~ of** s'occuper de; **I don't ~** ça m'est bien égal, peu m'importe; **I couldn't ~ less** cela m'est complètement égal, je m'en fiche complètement; **care for** vt fus s'occuper de; (like) aimer

career [kəˈrɪəʳ] n carrière f ▷ vi (also: **~ along**) aller à toute allure

care: **carefree** adj sans souci, insouciant(e); **careful** adj soigneux(-euse); (cautious) prudent(e); **(be) careful!** (fais) attention!; **carefully** adv avec soin, soigneusement, prudemment; **caregiver** (us) n (professional) travailleur social; (unpaid) personne qui s'occupe d'un proche qui est malade; **careless** adj négligent(e); (heedless) insouciant(e); **carelessness** n manque m de soin, négligence f; insouciance f; **carer** [ˈkɛərəʳ] n (professional) travailleur social; (unpaid) personne qui s'occupe d'un proche qui est malade; **caretaker** n gardien(ne), concierge m/f

car-ferry [ˈkɑːfɛrɪ] n (on sea) ferry(-boat) m; (on river) bac m

cargo (pl **~es**) [ˈkɑːɡəu] n cargaison f, chargement m

car hire n (BRIT) location f de voitures

Caribbean [kærɪˈbiːən] adj, n: **the ~ (Sea)** la mer des Antilles or des Caraïbes

caring [ˈkɛərɪŋ] adj (person) bienveillant(e); (society, organization) humanitaire

carnation [kɑːˈneɪʃən] n œillet m

carnival [ˈkɑːnɪvl] n (public celebration) carnaval m; (us: funfair) fête foraine

carol [ˈkærəl] n: **(Christmas) ~** chant m de Noël

carousel [kærəˈsɛl] n (for luggage) carrousel m; (us) manège m

car park (BRIT) n parking m, parc m de stationnement

carpenter [ˈkɑːpɪntəʳ] n charpentier m; (joiner) menuisier m

carpet [ˈkɑːpɪt] n tapis m ▷ vt recouvrir (d'un tapis); **fitted ~** (BRIT) moquette f

car rental n (us) location f de voitures

carriage [ˈkærɪdʒ] n (BRIT Rail) wagon m; (horse-drawn) voiture f; (of goods) transport m; (: cost) port m; **carriageway** n (BRIT: part of road) chaussée f

carrier [ˈkærɪəʳ] n transporteur m, camionneur m; (company) entreprise f de transport; (Med) porteur(-euse); **carrier bag** n (BRIT) sac m en papier or en plastique

carrot [ˈkærət] n carotte f

carry [ˈkærɪ] vt (subj: person) porter; (: vehicle) transporter; (involve: responsibilities etc) comporter, impliquer; (Med: disease) être porteur de ▷ vi (sound) porter; **to get carried away** (fig) s'emballer, s'enthousiasmer; **carry on** vi (continue) continuer ▷ vt (conduct: business) diriger; (: conversation) entretenir; (continue: business, conversation) continuer; **to ~ on with sth/doing** continuer qch/à faire; **carry out** vt (orders) exécuter; (investigation) effectuer

cart [kɑːt] n charrette f ▷ vt (inf) transporter

carton [ˈkɑːtən] n (box) carton m; (of yogurt) pot m (en carton)

cartoon [kɑːˈtuːn] n (Press) dessin m (humoristique); (satirical) caricature f; (comic strip) bande dessinée; (Cine) dessin animé

cartridge [ˈkɑːtrɪdʒ] n (for gun, pen) cartouche f

carve [kɑːv] vt (meat: also: **~ up**) découper; (wood, stone) tailler, sculpter; **carving** n (in wood etc) sculpture f

car wash n station f de lavage (de voitures)

case [keɪs] n cas m; (Law) affaire f, procès m; (box) caisse f, boîte f; (for glasses) étui m; (BRIT: also: **suit~**) valise f; **in ~ of** en cas de; **in ~ he** au cas où il; **just in ~** à tout hasard; **in any ~** en tout cas, de toute façon

cash [kæʃ] n argent m; (Comm) (argent m) liquide m ▷ vt encaisser; **to pay (in) ~** payer (en argent) comptant or en espèces; **~ with order/on delivery** (Comm) payable or paiement à la commande/livraison; **I haven't got any ~** je n'ai pas de liquide; **cashback** n (discount) remise f; (at supermarket etc) retrait m (à la caisse); **cash card** n carte f de retrait; **cash desk** n (BRIT) caisse f; **cash dispenser** n distributeur m automatique de billets

cashew [kæˈʃuː] n (also: **~ nut**) noix f de cajou

cashier [kæˈʃɪəʳ] n caissier(-ère)

cashmere [ˈkæʃmɪəʳ] n cachemire m

cash point n distributeur m automatique de billets

cash register n caisse enregistreuse

casino [kəˈsiːnəu] n casino m

casket [ˈkɑːskɪt] n coffret m; (US: coffin) cercueil m

casserole [ˈkæsərəul] n (pot) cocotte f; (food) ragoût m (en cocotte)

cassette [kæˈset] n cassette f; **cassette player** n lecteur m de cassettes

cast [kɑːst] (vb: pt, pp ~) vt (throw) jeter; (shadow: lit) projeter; (: fig) jeter; (glance) jeter ▷ n (Theat) distribution f; (also: plaster ~) plâtre m; **to ~ sb as Hamlet** attribuer à qn le rôle d'Hamlet; **to ~ one's vote** voter, exprimer son suffrage; **to ~ doubt on** jeter un doute sur; **cast off** vi (Naut) larguer les amarres; (Knitting) arrêter les mailles

castanets [kæstəˈnets] npl castagnettes fpl

caster sugar [ˈkɑːstə-] n (BRIT) sucre m semoule

cast-iron [ˈkɑːstaɪən] adj (lit) de or en fonte; (fig: will) de fer; (alibi) en béton

castle [ˈkɑːsl] n château m; (fortress) château-fort m; (Chess) tour f

casual [ˈkæʒjul] adj (by chance) de hasard, fait(e) au hasard, fortuit(e); (irregular: work etc) temporaire; (unconcerned) désinvolte; **~ wear** vêtements mpl sport inv

casualty [ˈkæʒjultɪ] n accidenté(e), blessé(e); (dead) victime f, mort(e); (BRIT: Med: department) urgences fpl

cat [kæt] n chat m

Catalan [ˈkætəlæn] adj catalan(e)

catalogue (US **catalog**) [ˈkætəlɔg] n catalogue m ▷ vt cataloguer

catalytic converter [kætəˈlɪtɪkkən'vəːtəʳ] n pot m catalytique

cataract [ˈkætərækt] n (also Med) cataracte f

catarrh [kəˈtɑːʳ] n rhume m chronique, catarrhe f

catastrophe [kəˈtæstrəfɪ] n catastrophe f

catch [kætʃ] (pt, pp **caught**) vt attraper; (person: by surprise) prendre, surprendre; (understand) saisir; (get entangled) accrocher ▷ vi (fire) prendre; (get entangled) s'accrocher ▷ n (fish etc) prise f; (hidden problem) attrape f; (Tech) loquet m; cliquet m; **to ~ sb's attention** or **eye** attirer l'attention de qn; **to ~ fire** prendre feu; **to ~ sight of** apercevoir; **catch up** vi (with work) se rattraper, combler son retard ▷ vt (also: **~ up with**) rattraper; **catching** [ˈkætʃɪŋ] adj (Med) contagieux(-euse)

category [ˈkætɪgərɪ] n catégorie f

cater [ˈkeɪtəʳ] vi: **to ~ for** (BRIT: needs) satisfaire, pourvoir à; (: readers, consumers) s'adresser à; pourvoir aux besoins de; (Comm: parties etc) préparer des repas pour

caterpillar [ˈkætəpɪləʳ] n chenille f

cathedral [kəˈθiːdrəl] n cathédrale f

Catholic [ˈkæθəlɪk] (Rel) adj catholique ▷ n catholique m/f

Catseye® [ˈkætsaɪ] n (BRIT Aut) (clou m à) catadioptre m

cattle [ˈkætl] npl bétail m, bestiaux mpl

catwalk [ˈkætwɔːk] n passerelle f; (for models) podium m (de défilé de mode)

caught [kɔːt] pt, pp of **catch**

cauliflower [ˈkɔlɪflauəʳ] n chou-fleur m

cause [kɔːz] n cause f ▷ vt causer

caution [ˈkɔːʃən] n prudence f; (warning) avertissement m ▷ vt avertir, donner un avertissement à; **cautious** adj prudent(e)

cave [keɪv] n caverne f, grotte f; **cave in** vi (roof etc) s'effondrer

caviar(e) [ˈkævɪɑːʳ] n caviar m

cavity [ˈkævɪtɪ] n cavité f; (Med) carie f

cc abbr (= cubic centimetre) cm³; (on letter etc) = **carbon copy**

CCTV n abbr = **closed-circuit television**

CD n abbr (= compact disc) CD m; **CD burner** n graveur m de CD; **CD player** n platine f laser; **CD-ROM** [siːdiːˈrɔm] n abbr (= compact disc read-only memory) CD-ROM m inv; **CD writer** n graveur m de CD

cease [siːs] vt, vi cesser; **ceasefire** n cessez-le-feu m

cedar [ˈsiːdəʳ] n cèdre m

ceilidh [ˈkeɪlɪ] n bal m folklorique écossais or irlandais

ceiling [ˈsiːlɪŋ] n (also fig) plafond m

celebrate [ˈselɪbreɪt] vt, vi célébrer; **celebration** [selɪˈbreɪʃən] n célébration f

celebrity [sɪˈlebrɪtɪ] n célébrité f

celery [ˈselərɪ] n céleri m (en branches)

cell [sel] n (gen) cellule f; (Elec) élément m (de pile)

cellar [ˈseləʳ] n cave f

cello [ˈtʃeləu] n violoncelle m

Cellophane® [ˈseləfeɪn] n cellophane® f

cellphone [ˈselfəun] n téléphone m cellulaire

Celsius [ˈselsɪəs] adj Celsius inv

Celtic [ˈkeltɪk, ˈseltɪk] adj celte, celtique

cement [səˈment] n ciment m

cemetery [ˈsemɪtrɪ] n cimetière m

censor [ˈsensəʳ] n censeur m ▷ vt censurer; **censorship** n censure f

census [ˈsensəs] n recensement m

cent [sent] n (unit of dollar, euro) cent m (= un centième du dollar, de l'euro); see also **per**

centenary [senˈtiːnərɪ] (US **centennial**) [senˈtenɪəl] n centenaire m

center [ˈsentəʳ] (US) = **centre**

centi... [sentɪ] prefix: **centigrade** adj centigrade; **centimetre** (US **centimeter**) n centimètre m; **centipede** ['sɛntɪpiːd] n millepattes m inv

central ['sɛntrəl] adj central(e); **Central America** n Amérique centrale; **central heating** n chauffage central; **central reservation** n (BRIT Aut) terre-plein central

centre (US **center**) ['sɛntə'] n centre m ▷ vt centrer; **centre-forward** n (Sport) avantcentre m; **centre-half** n (Sport) demi-centre m

century ['sɛntjʊrɪ] n siècle m; **in the twentieth ~** au vingtième siècle

CEO n abbr (US) = **chief executive officer**

ceramic [sɪ'ræmɪk] adj céramique

cereal ['siːrɪəl] n céréale f

ceremony ['sɛrɪmənɪ] n cérémonie f; **to stand on ~** faire des façons

certain ['səːtən] adj certain(e); **to make ~ of** s'assurer de; **for ~** certainement, sûrement; **certainly** adv certainement; **certainty** n certitude f

certificate [sə'tɪfɪkɪt] n certificat m

certify ['səːtɪfaɪ] vt certifier; (award diploma to) conférer un diplôme etc à; (declare insane) déclarer malade mental(e)

cf. abbr (= compare) cf., voir

CFC n abbr (= chlorofluorocarbon) CFC m

chain [tʃeɪn] n (gen) chaîne f ▷ vt (also: ~ **up**) enchaîner, attacher (avec une chaîne); **chainsmoke** vi fumer cigarette sur cigarette

chair [tʃɛə'] n chaise f; (armchair) fauteuil m; (of university) chaire f; (of meeting) présidence f ▷ vt (meeting) présider; **chairlift** n télésiège m; **chairman** n président m; **chairperson** n président(e); **chairwoman** n présidente f

chalet ['ʃæleɪ] n chalet m

chalk [tʃɔːk] n craie f; **chalkboard** (US) n tableau noir

challenge ['tʃælɪndʒ] n défi m ▷ vt défier; (statement, right) mettre en question, contester; **to ~ sb to do** mettre qn au défi de faire; **challenging** adj (task, career) qui représente un défi or une gageure; (tone, look) de défi, provocateur(-trice)

chamber ['tʃeɪmbə'] n chambre f; (BRIT Law: gen pl) cabinet m; **~ of commerce** chambre de commerce; **chambermaid** n femme f de chambre

champagne [ʃæm'peɪn] n champagne m

champion ['tʃæmpɪən] n (also of cause) champion(ne); **championship** n championnat m

chance [tʃɑːns] n (luck) hasard m; (opportunity) occasion f, possibilité f; (hope, likelihood) chance f; (risk) risque m ▷ vt (risk) risquer ▷ adj fortuit(e), de hasard; **to take a ~** prendre un risque; **by ~** par hasard; **to ~ it** risquer le coup, essayer

chancellor ['tʃɑːnsələ'] n chancelier m; **Chancellor of the Exchequer** [-ɪks'tʃekə']

(BRIT) n chancelier m de l'Échiquier

chandelier [ʃændə'lɪə'] n lustre m

change [tʃeɪndʒ] vt (alter, replace: Comm: money) changer; (switch, substitute: hands, trains, clothes, one's name etc) changer de ▷ vi (gen) changer; (change clothes) se changer; (be transformed) **to ~ into** se changer or transformer en ▷ n changement m; (money) monnaie f; **to ~ gear** (Aut) changer de vitesse; **to ~ one's mind** changer d'avis; **a ~ of clothes** des vêtements de rechange; **for a ~** pour changer; **do you have ~ for £10?** vous avez la monnaie de 10 livres?; **where can I ~ some money?** où est-ce que je peux changer de l'argent?; **keep the ~!** gardez la monnaie!; **change over** vi (swap) échanger; (change: drivers etc) changer; (change sides: players etc) changer de côté; **to ~ over from sth to sth** passer de qch à qch; **changeable** adj (weather) variable; **change machine** n distributeur m de monnaie; **changing room** n (BRIT: in shop) salon m d'essayage; (: Sport) vestiaire m

channel ['tʃænl] n (TV) chaîne f; (waveband, groove, fig: medium) canal m; (of river, sea) chenal m ▷ vt canaliser; **the (English) C~** la Manche; **Channel Islands** npl: **the Channel Islands** les îles fpl Anglo-Normandes; **Channel Tunnel** n: **the Channel Tunnel** le tunnel sous la Manche

chant [tʃɑːnt] n chant m; (Rel) psalmodie f ▷ vt chanter, scander

chaos ['keɪɔs] n chaos m

chaotic [keɪ'ɔtɪk] adj chaotique

chap [tʃæp] n (BRIT inf: man) type m

chapel ['tʃæpl] n chapelle f

chapped [tʃæpt] adj (skin, lips) gercé(e)

chapter ['tʃæptə'] n chapitre m

character ['kærɪktə'] n caractère m; (in novel, film) personnage m; (eccentric person) numéro m, phénomène m; **characteristic** ['kærɪktə'rɪstɪk] adj, n caractéristique (f); **characterize** ['kærɪktəraɪz] vt caractériser

charcoal ['tʃɑːkəʊl] n charbon m de bois; (Art) charbon

charge [tʃɑːdʒ] n (accusation) accusation f; (Law) inculpation f; (cost) prix (demandé) ▷ vt (gun, battery, Mil: enemy) charger; (customer, sum) faire payer ▷ vi foncer; **charges** npl (costs) frais mpl; (BRIT Tel): **to reverse the ~s** téléphoner en PCV; **to take ~ of** se charger de; **to be in ~ of** être responsable de, s'occuper de; **to ~ sb (with)** (Law) inculper qn (de); **charge card** n carte f de client (émise par un grand magasin); **charger** n (also: **battery charger**) chargeur m

charismatic [kærɪz'mætɪk] adj charismatique

charity ['tʃærɪtɪ] n charité f; (organization) institution f charitable or de bienfaisance, œuvre f (de charité); **charity shop** n (BRIT) boutique vendant des articles d'occasion au profit d'une organisation caritative

charm [tʃɑːm] n charme m; (on bracelet) breloque f ▷ vt charmer, enchanter; **charming** adj charmant(e)

chart [tʃɑːt] n tableau m, diagramme m; graphique m; (map) carte marine ▷ vt dresser or établir la carte de; (sales, progress) établir la courbe de; **charts** npl (Mus) hit-parade m; **to be in the ~s** (record, pop group) figurer au hit-parade

charter ['tʃɑːtəʳ] vt (plane) affréter ▷ n (document) charte f; **chartered accountant** n (BRIT) expert-comptable m; **charter flight** n charter m

chase [tʃeɪs] vt poursuivre, pourchasser; (also: ~ **away**) chasser ▷ n poursuite f, chasse f

chat [tʃæt] vi (also: **have a ~**) bavarder, causer; (on Internet) chatter ▷ n conversation f; **chat up** vt (BRIT inf: girl) baratiner; **chat room** n (Internet) forum m de discussion; **chat show** n (BRIT) talk-show m

chatter ['tʃætəʳ] vi (person) bavarder, papoter ▷ n bavardage m, papotage m; **my teeth are ~ing** je claque des dents

chauffeur ['ʃəufəʳ] n chauffeur m (de maître)

chauvinist ['ʃəuvɪnɪst] n (also: **male ~**) phallocrate m, macho m; (nationalist) chauvin(e)

cheap [tʃiːp] adj bon marché inv, pas cher (chère); (reduced: ticket) à prix réduit; (: fare) réduit(e); (joke) facile, d'un goût douteux; (poor quality) à bon marché, de qualité médiocre ▷ adv à bon marché, pour pas cher; **can you recommend a ~ hotel/restaurant, please?** pourriez-vous m'indiquer un hôtel/restaurant bon marché?; **cheap day return** n billet m d'aller et retour réduit (valable pour la journée); **cheaply** adv à bon marché, à bon compte

cheat [tʃiːt] vi tricher; (in exam) copier ▷ vt tromper, duper; (rob): **to ~ sb out of sth** escroquer qch à qn ▷ n tricheur(-euse) m/f; escroc m; **cheat on** vt fus tromper

Chechnya [tʃɪtʃˈnjaː] n Tchétchénie f

check [tʃɛk] vt vérifier; (passport, ticket) contrôler; (halt) enrayer; (restrain) maîtriser ▷ vi (official etc) se renseigner ▷ n vérification f; contrôle m; (curb) frein m; (BRIT: bill) addition f; (US) = **cheque**; (pattern: gen pl) carreaux mpl; **to ~ with sb** demander à qn; **check in** vi (in hotel) remplir sa fiche (d'hôtel); (at airport) se présenter à l'enregistrement ▷ vt (luggage) (faire) enregistrer; **check off** vt (tick off) cocher; **check out** vi (in hotel) régler sa note ▷ vt (investigate: story) vérifier; **check up** vi: **to ~ up (on sth)** vérifier (qch); **to ~ up on sb** se renseigner sur le compte de qn; **checkbook** (US) = **chequebook**; **checked** adj

(pattern, cloth) à carreaux; **checkers** n (US) jeu m de dames; **check-in** n (also: **check-in desk**: at airport) enregistrement m; **checking account** n (US) compte courant; **checklist** n liste f de contrôle; **checkmate** n échec et mat m; **checkout** n (in supermarket) caisse f; **checkpoint** n contrôle m; **checkroom** (US) n consigne f; **checkup** n (Med) examen médical, check-up m

cheddar ['tʃedəʳ] n (also: **~ cheese**) cheddar m

cheek [tʃiːk] n joue f; (impudence) toupet m, culot m; **what a ~!** quel toupet!; **cheekbone** n pommette f; **cheeky** adj effronté(e), culotté(e)

cheer [tʃɪəʳ] vt acclamer, applaudir; (gladden) réjouir, réconforter ▷ vi applaudir ▷ n (gen pl) acclamations fpl, applaudissements mpl; bravos mpl, hourras mpl; **~s!** à la vôtre!; **cheer up** vi se dérider, reprendre courage ▷ vt remonter le moral à or de, dérider, égayer; **cheerful** adj gai(e), joyeux(-euse)

cheerio [tʃɪərɪˈəu] excl (BRIT) salut!, au revoir!

cheerleader ['tʃɪəliːdəʳ] n membre d'un groupe de majorettes qui chantent et dansent pour soutenir leur équipe pendant les matchs de football américain

cheese [tʃiːz] n fromage m; **cheeseburger** n cheeseburger m; **cheesecake** n tarte f au fromage

chef [ʃef] n chef (cuisinier)

chemical ['kemɪkl] adj chimique ▷ n produit m chimique

chemist ['kemɪst] n (BRIT: pharmacist) pharmacien(ne); (scientist) chimiste m/f; **chemistry** n chimie f; **chemist's (shop)** n (BRIT) pharmacie f

cheque (US **check**) [tʃek] n chèque m; **chequebook** (US **checkbook**) n chéquier m, carnet m de chèques; **cheque card** n (BRIT) carte f (d'identité) bancaire

cherry ['tʃerɪ] n cerise f; (also: **~ tree**) cerisier m

chess [tʃes] n échecs mpl

chest [tʃest] n poitrine f; (box) coffre m, caisse f

chestnut ['tʃesnʌt] n châtaigne f; (also: **~ tree**) châtaignier m

chest of drawers n commode f

chew [tʃuː] vt mâcher; **chewing gum** n chewing-gum m

chic [ʃiːk] adj chic inv, élégant(e)

chick [tʃɪk] n poussin m; (inf) pépée f

chicken ['tʃɪkɪn] n poulet m; (inf: coward) poule mouillée; **chicken out** vi (inf) se dégonfler; **chickenpox** n varicelle f

chickpea ['tʃɪkpiː] n pois m chiche

chief [tʃiːf] n chef m ▷ adj principal(e); **chief executive** (US **chief executive officer**) n directeur(-trice) général(e); **chiefly** adv principalement, surtout

child (pl **~ren**) [tʃaɪld, 'tʃɪldrən] n enfant

m/f; **child abuse** *n* maltraitance *f* d'enfants; (*sexual*) abus *mpl* sexuels sur des enfants; **child benefit** *n* (BRIT) ≈ allocations familiales; **childbirth** *n* accouchement *m*; **child-care** *n* (*for working parents*) garde *f* des enfants (*pour les parents qui travaillent*); **childhood** *n* enfance *f*; **childish** *adj* puéril(e), enfantin(e); **child minder** *n* (BRIT) garde *f* d'enfants; **children** ['tʃɪldrən] *npl of* **child**

Chile ['tʃɪlɪ] *n* Chili *m*

chill [tʃɪl] *n* (*of water*) froid *m*; (*of air*) fraîcheur *f*; (*Med*) refroidissement *m*, coup *m* de froid ▷ *vt* (*person*) faire frissonner; (*Culin*) mettre au frais, rafraîchir; **chill out** *vi* (*inf: esp us*) se relaxer

chil(l)i ['tʃɪlɪ] *n* piment *m* (rouge)

chilly ['tʃɪlɪ] *adj* froid(e), glacé(e); (*sensitive to cold*) frileux(-euse)

chimney ['tʃɪmnɪ] *n* cheminée *f*

chimpanzee [tʃɪmpæn'ziː] *n* chimpanzé *m*

chin [tʃɪn] *n* menton *m*

China ['tʃaɪnə] *n* Chine *f*

china ['tʃaɪnə] *n* (*material*) porcelaine *f*; (*crockery*) (vaisselle *f* en) porcelaine

Chinese [tʃaɪ'niːz] *adj* chinois(e) ▷ *n* (*pl inv*) Chinois(e); (*Ling*) chinois *m*

chip [tʃɪp] *n* (*gen pl*: Culin: BRIT) frite *f* (; (: us: also: **potato ~**) chip *m*; (*of wood*) copeau *m*; (*of glass, stone*) éclat *m*; (*also*: **micro~**) puce *f*; (*in gambling*) fiche *f* ▷ *vt* ébrécher; **chip shop** *n* (BRIT) friterie *f*

○ **CHIP SHOP**

○
○ Un **chip shop**, que l'on appelle également
○ un "fish-and-chip shop", est un magasin
○ où l'on vend des plats à emporter. Les
○ **chip shops** sont d'ailleurs à l'origine des
○ "takeaways". On y achète en particulier
○ du poisson frit et des frites, mais on y
○ trouve également des plats traditionnels
○ britanniques ("steak pies", saucisses, etc).
○ Tous les plats étaient à l'origine emballés
○ dans du papier journal. Dans certains
○ de ces magasins, on peut s'asseoir pour
○ consommer sur place.

---

chiropodist [kɪ'rɔpədɪst] *n* (BRIT) pédicure *m/f*

chisel ['tʃɪzl] *n* ciseau *m*

chives [tʃaɪvz] *npl* ciboulette *f*, civette *f*

chlorine ['klɔːriːn] *n* chlore *m*

choc-ice ['tʃɔkaɪs] *n* (BRIT) esquimau® *m*

chocolate ['tʃɔklɪt] *n* chocolat *m*

choice [tʃɔɪs] *n* choix *m* ▷ *adj* de choix

choir ['kwaɪəʳ] *n* chœur *m*, chorale *f*

choke [tʃəuk] *vi* étouffer ▷ *vt* étrangler; étouffer; (*block*) boucher, obstruer ▷ *n* (*Aut*) starter *m*

cholesterol [kə'lɛstərɔl] *n* cholestérol *m*

choose (*pt* **chose**, *pp* **chosen**) [tʃuːz, tʃəuz, 'tʃəuzn] *vt* choisir; **to ~ to do** décider de faire, juger bon de faire

chop [tʃɔp] *vt* (*wood*) couper (à la hache); (*Culin: also*: **~ up**) couper (fin), émincer, hacher (en morceaux) ▷ *n* (*Culin*) côtelette *f*; **chop down** *vt* (*tree*) abattre; **chop off** *vt* trancher; **chopsticks** ['tʃɔpstɪks] *npl* baguettes *fpl*

chord [kɔːd] *n* (*Mus*) accord *m*

chore [tʃɔːʳ] *n* travail *m* de routine; **household ~s** travaux *mpl* du ménage

chorus ['kɔːrəs] *n* chœur *m*; (*repeated part of song, also fig*) refrain *m*

chose [tʃəuz] *pt of* **choose**

chosen ['tʃəuzn] *pp of* **choose**

Christ [kraɪst] *n* Christ *m*

christen ['krɪsn] *vt* baptiser; **christening** *n* baptême *m*

Christian ['krɪstɪən] *adj, n* chrétien(ne); **Christianity** [krɪstɪ'ænɪtɪ] *n* christianisme *m*; **Christian name** *n* prénom *m*

Christmas ['krɪsməs] *n* Noël *m or f*; **happy or merry ~!** joyeux Noël!; **Christmas card** *n* carte *f* de Noël; **Christmas carol** *n* chant *m* de Noël; **Christmas Day** *n* le jour de Noël; **Christmas Eve** *n* la veille de Noël; la nuit de Noël; **Christmas pudding** *n* (*esp* BRIT) Christmas pudding; **Christmas tree** *n* arbre *m* de Noël

chrome [krəum] *n* chrome *m*

chronic ['krɔnɪk] *adj* chronique

chrysanthemum [krɪ'sænθəməm] *n* chrysanthème *m*

chubby ['tʃʌbɪ] *adj* potelé(e), rondelet(te)

chuck [tʃʌk] *vt* (*inf*) lancer, jeter; (BRIT: *also*: **~ up**: *job*) lâcher; **chuck out** *vt* (*inf: person*) flanquer dehors *or* à la porte; (: *rubbish etc*) jeter

chuckle ['tʃʌkl] *vi* glousser

chum [tʃʌm] *n* copain (copine)

chunk [tʃʌŋk] *n* gros morceau

church [tʃəːtʃ] *n* église *f*; **churchyard** *n* cimetière *m*

churn [tʃəːn] *n* (*for butter*) baratte *f*; (*also*: **milk ~**) (grand) bidon à lait

chute [ʃuːt] *n* goulotte *f*; (*also*: **rubbish ~**) vide-ordures *m inv*; (BRIT: *children's slide*) toboggan *m*

chutney ['tʃʌtnɪ] *n* chutney *m*

CIA *n abbr* (= *Central Intelligence Agency*) CIA *f*

CID *n abbr* (= *Criminal Investigation Department*) ≈ P.J. *f*

cider ['saɪdəʳ] *n* cidre *m*

cigar [sɪ'gɑːʳ] *n* cigare *m*

cigarette [sɪgə'rɛt] *n* cigarette *f*; **cigarette lighter** *n* briquet *m*

cinema ['sɪnəmə] *n* cinéma *m*

cinnamon ['sɪnəmən] *n* cannelle *f*

circle ['səːkl] *n* cercle *m*; (*in cinema*) balcon *m* ▷ *vi* faire *or* décrire des cercles ▷ *vt* (*surround*) entourer, encercler; (*move round*) faire le tour

circuit ['sɜːkɪt] n circuit m; (lap) tour m

circular ['sɜːkjʊləʳ] adj circulaire ▷ n circulaire f; (as advertisement) prospectus m

circulate ['sɜːkjuleɪt] vi circuler ▷ vt faire circuler; **circulation** [sɜːkjuˈleɪʃən] n circulation f; (of newspaper) tirage m

circumstances ['sɜːkəmstənsɪz] npl circonstances fpl; (financial condition) moyens mpl, situation financière

circus ['sɜːkəs] n cirque m

cite [saɪt] vt citer

citizen ['sɪtɪzn] n (Pol) citoyen(ne); (resident): **the ~s of this town** les habitants de cette ville; **citizenship** n citoyenneté f; (BRIT: Scol) ≈ éducation f civique

citrus fruits ['sɪtrəs-] npl agrumes mpl

city ['sɪtɪ] n (grande) ville f; **the C~** la Cité de Londres (centre des affaires); **city centre** n centre ville m; **city technology college** n (BRIT) établissement m d'enseignement technologique (situé dans un quartier défavorisé)

civic ['sɪvɪk] adj civique; (authorities) municipal(e)

civil ['sɪvɪl] adj civil(e); (polite) poli(e), civil(e); **civilian** [sɪˈvɪlɪən] adj, n civil(e)

civilization [sɪvɪlaɪˈzeɪʃən] n civilisation f

civilized ['sɪvɪlaɪzd] adj civilisé(e); (fig) où règnent les bonnes manières

civil: **civil law** n code civil; (study) droit civil; **civil rights** npl droits mpl civiques; **civil servant** n fonctionnaire m/f; **Civil Service** n fonction publique, administration f; **civil war** n guerre civile

CJD n abbr (= Creutzfeldt-Jakob disease) MCJ f

claim [kleɪm] vt (rights etc) revendiquer; (compensation) réclamer; (assert) déclarer, prétendre ▷ vi (for insurance) faire une déclaration de sinistre ▷ n revendication f; prétention f; (right) droit m; **(insurance) ~** demande f d'indemnisation, déclaration f de sinistre; **claim form** n (gen) formulaire m de demande

clam [klæm] n palourde f

clamp [klæmp] n crampon m; (on workbench) valet m; (on car) sabot m de Denver ▷ vt attacher; (car) mettre un sabot à; **clamp down on** vt fus sévir contre, prendre des mesures draconiennes à l'égard de

clan [klæn] n clan m

clap [klæp] vi applaudir

claret ['klærət] n (vin m de) bordeaux m (rouge)

clarify ['klærɪfaɪ] vt clarifier

clarinet [klærɪˈnɛt] n clarinette f

clarity ['klærɪtɪ] n clarté f

clash [klæʃ] n (sound) choc m, fracas m; (with police) affrontement m; (fig) conflit m ▷ vi se heurter; être or entrer en conflit; (colours) jurer; (dates, events) tomber en même temps

clasp [klɑːsp] n (of necklace, bag) fermoir m ▷ vt serrer, étreindre

class [klɑːs] n (gen) classe f; (group, category) catégorie f ▷ vt classer, classifier

classic ['klæsɪk] adj classique ▷ n (author, work) classique m; **classical** adj classique

classification [klæsɪfɪˈkeɪʃən] n classification f

classify ['klæsɪfaɪ] vt classifier, classer

classmate ['klɑːsmeɪt] n camarade m/f de classe

classroom ['klɑːsrum] n (salle f de) classe f; **classroom assistant** n assistant(-e) d'éducation

classy ['klɑːsɪ] (inf) adj classe (inf)

clatter ['klætəʳ] n cliquetis m ▷ vi cliqueter

clause [klɔːz] n clause f; (Ling) proposition f

claustrophobic [klɔːstrəˈfəubɪk] adj (person) claustrophobe; (place) où l'on se sent claustrophobe

claw [klɔː] n griffe f; (of bird of prey) serre f; (of lobster) pince f

clay [kleɪ] n argile f

clean [kliːn] adj propre; (clear, smooth) net(te); (record, reputation) sans tache; (joke, story) correct(e) ▷ vt nettoyer; **clean up** vt nettoyer; (fig) remettre de l'ordre dans; **cleaner** n (person) nettoyeur(-euse), femme f de ménage; (product) détachant m; **cleaner's** n (also: **dry cleaner's**) teinturier m; **cleaning** n nettoyage m

cleanser ['klɛnzəʳ] n (for face) démaquillant m

clear [klɪəʳ] adj clair(e); (glass, plastic) transparent(e); (road, way) libre, dégagé(e); (profit, majority) net(te); (conscience) tranquille; (skin) frais (fraîche); (sky) dégagé(e) ▷ vt (road) dégager, déblayer; (table) débarrasser; (room etc: of people) faire évacuer; (cheque) compenser; (Law: suspect) innocenter; (obstacle) franchir or sauter sans heurter ▷ vi (weather) s'éclaircir; (fog) se dissiper ▷ adv: **~ of** à distance de, à l'écart de; **to ~ the table** débarrasser la table, desservir; **clear away** vt (things, clothes etc) enlever; **to ~ away the dishes** débarrasser la table; **clear up** vt ranger, mettre en ordre; (mystery) éclaircir, résoudre; **clearance** n (removal) déblayage m; (permission) autorisation f; **clear-cut** adj précis(e), nettement défini(e); **clearing** n (in forest) clairière f; **clearly** adv clairement; (obviously) de toute évidence; **clearway** n (BRIT) route f à stationnement interdit

clench [klɛntʃ] vt serrer

clergy ['klɜːdʒɪ] n clergé m

clerk [klɑːk, US klɜːrk] n (BRIT) employé(e) de bureau; (US: salesman/woman) vendeur(-euse)

clever ['klɛvəʳ] adj (intelligent) intelligent(e); (skilful) habile, adroit(e); (device, arrangement)

ingénieux(-euse), astucieux(-euse)
cliché ['kli:feɪ] n cliché m
click [klɪk] n (Comput) cliquer ▷ vt: **to ~ one's
tongue** faire claquer sa langue; **to ~ one's
heels** claquer des talons; **to ~ on an icon**
cliquer sur une icône
client ['klaɪənt] n client(e)
cliff [klɪf] n falaise f
climate ['klaɪmɪt] n climat m; **climate
change** n changement m climatique
climax ['klaɪmæks] n apogée m, point
culminant; (sexual) orgasme m
climb [klaɪm] vi grimper, monter; (plane)
prendre de l'altitude ▷ vt (stairs) monter;
(mountain) escalader; (tree) grimper à ▷ n
montée f, escalade f; **to ~ over a wall**
passer par dessus un mur; **climb down**
vi (re)descendre; (BRIT fig) rabattre de ses
prétentions; **climber** n (also: **rock climber**)
grimpeur(-euse), varappeur(-euse); (plant)
plante grimpante; **climbing** n (also: **rock
climbing**) escalade f, varappe f
clinch [klɪntʃ] vt (deal) conclure, sceller
cling (pt, pp clung) [klɪŋ, klʌŋ] vi: **to ~ (to)**
se cramponner (à), s'accrocher (à); (clothes)
coller (à)
Clingfilm® ['klɪŋfɪlm] n film m alimentaire
clinic ['klɪnɪk] n clinique f; centre médical
clip [klɪp] n (for hair) barrette f; (also: **paper ~**)
trombone m; (TV, Cinema) clip m ▷ vt (also: **~
together**) papers) attacher; (hair, nails) couper;
(hedge) tailler; **clipping** n (from newspaper)
coupure f de journal
cloak [kləuk] n grande cape ▷ vt (fig) masquer,
cacher; **cloakroom** n (for coats etc) vestiaire m;
(BRIT: W.C.) toilettes fpl
clock [klɔk] n (large) horloge f; (small) pendule
f; **clock in or on** (BRIT) vi (with card) pointer
(en arrivant); (start work) commencer à
travailler; **clock off or out** (BRIT) vi (with
card) pointer (en partant); (leave work) quitter
le travail; **clockwise** adv dans le sens des
aiguilles d'une montre; **clockwork** n rouages
mpl, mécanisme m; (of clock) mouvement m
(d'horlogerie) ▷ adj (toy, train) mécanique
clog [klɔg] n sabot m ▷ vt boucher, encrasser
▷ vi (also: **~ up**) se boucher, s'encrasser
clone [kləun] n clone m ▷ vt cloner
close¹ [kləus] adj (near): **~ (to)** près (de),
proche (de); (contact, link, watch) étroit(e);
(examination) attentif(-ive), minutieux(-euse);
(contest) très serré(e); (weather) lourd(e),
étouffant(e) ▷ adv près, à proximité; **~ to** prep
près de; **~ by**, **~ at hand** adj, adv tout(e) près; **a
~ friend** un ami intime; **to have a ~ shave** (fig)
l'échapper belle
close² [kləuz] vt fermer ▷ vi (shop etc) fermer;
(lid, door etc) se fermer; (end) se terminer, se
conclure ▷ n (end) conclusion f; **what time**

do you ~? à quelle heure fermez-vous?; **close
down** vi fermer (définitivement); **closed** adj
(shop etc) fermé(e)
closely ['kləuslɪ] adv (examine, watch) de près
closet ['klɔzɪt] n (cupboard) placard m, réduit m
close-up ['kləusʌp] n gros plan
closing time n heure f de fermeture
closure ['kləuʒə'] n fermeture f
clot [klɔt] n (of blood, milk) caillot m; (inf: person)
ballot m ▷ vi (: external bleeding) se coaguler
cloth [klɔθ] n (material) tissu m, étoffe f; (BRIT:
also: **tea ~**) torchon m; lavette f; (also: **table~**)
nappe f
clothes [kləuðz] npl vêtements mpl,
habits mpl; **clothes line** n corde f (à linge);
clothes peg (US **clothes pin**) n pince f à linge
clothing ['kləuðɪŋ] n = **clothes**
cloud [klaud] n nuage m; **cloud over** vi
se couvrir; (fig) s'assombrir; **cloudy** adj
nuageux(-euse), couvert(e); (liquid) trouble
clove [kləuv] n clou m de girofle; **a ~ of garlic**
une gousse d'ail
clown [klaun] n clown m ▷ vi (also: **~ about**, **~
around**) faire le clown
club [klʌb] n (society) club m; (weapon) massue f,
matraque f; (also: **golf ~**) club ▷ vt matraquer
▷ vi: **to ~ together** s'associer; **clubs** npl (Cards)
trèfle m; **club class** n (Aviat) classe f club
clue [klu:] n indice m; (in crosswords) définition
f; **I haven't a ~** je n'en ai pas la moindre idée
clump [klʌmp] n: **~ of trees** bouquet m
d'arbres
clumsy ['klʌmzɪ] adj (person) gauche,
maladroit(e); (object) malcommode, peu
maniable
clung [klʌŋ] pt, pp of **cling**
cluster ['klʌstə'] n (petit) groupe; (of flowers)
grappe f ▷ vi se rassembler
clutch [klʌtʃ] n (Aut) embrayage m; (grasp):
~es étreinte f, prise f ▷ vt (grasp) agripper; (hold
tightly) serrer fort; (hold on to) se cramponner à
cm abbr (= centimetre)
Co. abbr = **company, county**
c/o abbr (= care of), aux bons soins de
coach [kəutʃ] n (bus) autocar m; (horse-drawn)
diligence f; (of train) voiture f, wagon m;
(Sport: trainer) entraîneur(-euse); (school:
tutor) répétiteur(-trice) ▷ vt (Sport) entraîner;
(student) donner des leçons particulières à;
coach station (BRIT) n gare routière; **coach
trip** n excursion f en car
coal [kəul] n charbon m
coalition [kəuə'lɪʃən] n coalition f
coarse [kɔ:s] adj grossier(-ère), rude; (vulgar)
vulgaire
coast [kəust] n côte f ▷ vi (car, cycle) descendre
en roue libre; **coastal** adj côtier(-ère);
coastguard n garde-côte m; **coastline** n
côte f, littoral m

coat [kəut] n manteau m; (of animal) pelage m, poil m; (of paint) couche f ▷ vt couvrir, enduire; **coat hanger** n cintre m; **coating** n couche f, enduit m

coax [kəuks] vt persuader par des cajoleries

cob [kɔb] n see **corn**

cobbled ['kɔbld] adj pavé(e)

cobweb ['kɔbwɛb] n toile f d'araignée

cocaine [kə'keın] n cocaïne f

cock [kɔk] n (rooster) coq m; (male bird) mâle m ▷ vt (gun) armer; **cockerel** n jeune coq m

cockney ['kɔknı] n cockney m/f (habitant des quartiers populaires de l'East End de Londres), ≈ faubourien(ne)

cockpit ['kɔkpıt] n (in aircraft) poste m de pilotage, cockpit m

cockroach ['kɔkrəutʃ] n cafard m, cancrelat m

cocktail ['kɔkteıl] n cocktail m

cocoa ['kəukəu] n cacao m

coconut ['kəukənʌt] n noix f de coco

C.O.D. abbr = **cash on delivery**

cod [kɔd] n morue fraîche, cabillaud m

code [kəud] n code m; (Tel: area code) indicatif m

coeducational ['kəuɛdju'keıʃənl] adj mixte

coffee ['kɔfı] n café m; **coffee bar** n (BRIT) café m; **coffee bean** n grain m de café; **coffee break** n pause-café f; **coffee maker** n cafetière f; **coffeepot** n cafetière f; **coffee shop** n café m; **coffee table** n (petite) table basse

coffin ['kɔfın] n cercueil m

cog [kɔg] n (wheel) roue dentée; (tooth) dent f (d'engrenage)

cognac ['kɔnjæk] n cognac m

coherent [kəu'hıərənt] adj cohérent(e)

coil [kɔıl] n rouleau m, bobine f; (contraceptive) stérilet m ▷ vt enrouler

coin [kɔın] n pièce f (de monnaie) ▷ vt (word) inventer

coincide [kəuın'saıd] vi coïncider; **coincidence** [kəu'ınsıdəns] n coïncidence f

Coke® [kəuk] n coca m

coke [kəuk] n (coal) coke m

colander ['kɔləndə'] n passoire f (à légumes)

cold [kəuld] adj froid(e) ▷ n froid m; (Med) rhume m; **it's ~** il fait froid; **to be ~** (person) avoir froid; **to catch a ~** s'enrhumer, attraper un rhume; **in ~ blood** de sang-froid; **cold cuts** (us) npl viandes froides; **cold sore** n bouton m de fièvre

coleslaw ['kəulslɔ:] n sorte de salade de chou cru

colic ['kɔlık] n colique(s) f(pl)

collaborate [kə'læbəreıt] vi collaborer

collapse [kə'læps] vi s'effondrer, s'écrouler; (Med) avoir un malaise ▷ n effondrement m, écroulement m; (of government) chute f

collar ['kɔlə'] n (of coat, shirt) col m; (for dog) collier m; **collarbone** n clavicule f

colleague ['kɔli:g] n collègue m/f

collect [kə'lɛkt] vt rassembler; (pick up) ramasser; (as a hobby) collectionner; (BRIT: call for) (passer) prendre; (mail) faire la levée de, ramasser; (money owed) encaisser; (donations, subscriptions) recueillir ▷ vi (people) se rassembler; (dust, dirt) s'amasser; **to call ~** (us Tel) téléphoner en PCV; **collection** [kə'lɛkʃən] n collection f; (of mail) levée f; (for money) collecte f, quête f; **collective** [kə'lɛktıv] adj collectif(-ive); **collector** n collectionneur m

college ['kɔlıdʒ] n collège m; (of technology, agriculture etc) institut m

collide [kə'laıd] vi: **to ~ (with)** entrer en collision (avec)

collision [kə'lıʒən] n collision f, heurt m

cologne [kə'ləun] n (also: **eau de ~**) eau f de cologne

colon ['kəulən] n (sign) deux-points mpl; (Med) côlon m

colonel ['kə:nl] n colonel m

colonial [kə'ləunıəl] adj colonial(e)

colony ['kɔlənı] n colonie f

colour etc (us **color** etc) ['kʌlə'] n couleur f ▷ vt colorer; (dye) teindre; (paint) peindre; (with crayons) colorier; (news) fausser, exagérer ▷ vi (blush) rougir; **I'd like a different ~** je le voudrais dans un autre coloris; **colour in** vt colorier; **colour-blind** adj daltonien(ne); **coloured** adj coloré(e); (photo) en couleur; **colour film** n (for camera) pellicule f (en) couleur; **colourful** adj coloré(e), vif (vive); (personality) pittoresque, haut(e) en couleurs; **colouring** n colorant m; (complexion) teint m; **colour television** n télévision f (en) couleur

column ['kɔləm] n colonne f; (fashion column, sports column etc) rubrique f

coma ['kəumə] n coma m

comb [kəum] n peigne m ▷ vt (hair) peigner; (area) ratisser, passer au peigne fin

combat ['kɔmbæt] n combat m ▷ vt combattre, lutter contre

combination [kɔmbı'neıʃən] n (gen) combinaison f

combine vb [kəm'baın] ▷ vt combiner ▷ vi s'associer; (Chem) se combiner ▷ n ['kɔmbaın] (Econ) trust m; **to ~ sth with sth** (one quality with another) joindre ou allier qch à qch

come [pt **came**, pp ~] [kʌm, keım] vi
1 (movement towards) venir; **to ~ running** arriver en courant; **he's ~ here to work** il est venu ici pour travailler; **~ with me** suivez-moi
2 (arrive) arriver; **to ~ home** rentrer (chez soi or à la maison); **we've just ~ from Paris** nous arrivons de Paris
3 (reach): **to ~ to** (decision etc) parvenir à, arriver à; **the bill came to £40** la note s'est élevée à 40 livres
4 (occur): **an idea came to me** il m'est venu

une idée

5 (be, become): **to ~ loose/undone** se défaire/desserrer; **I've ~ to like him** j'ai fini par bien l'aimer; **come across** vt fus rencontrer par hasard, tomber sur; **come along** vi (BRIT: pupil, work) faire des progrès, avancer; **come back** vi revenir; **come down** vi descendre; (prices) baisser; (buildings) s'écrouler; (: be demolished) être démoli(e); **come from** vt fus (source) venir de; (place) venir de, être originaire de; **come in** vi entrer; (train) arriver; (fashion) entrer en vogue; (on deal etc) participer; **come off** vi (button) se détacher; (attempt) réussir; **come on** vi (lights, electricity) s'allumer; (central heating) se mettre en marche; (pupil, work, project) faire des progrès, avancer; **~ on!** viens!; allons!, allez!; **come out** vi sortir; (sun) se montrer; (book) paraître; (stain) s'enlever; (strike) cesser le travail, se mettre en grève; **come round** vi (after faint, operation) revenir à soi, reprendre connaissance; **come to** vi revenir à soi; **come up** vi monter; (sun) se lever; (problem) se poser; (event) survenir; (in conversation) être soulevé; **come up with** vt fus (money) fournir; **he came up with an idea** il a eu une idée, il a proposé quelque chose

comeback ['kʌmbæk] n (Theat etc) rentrée f

comedian [kə'miːdɪən] n (comic) comique m; (Theat) comédien m

comedy ['kɒmɪdɪ] n comédie f; (humour) comique m

comet ['kɒmɪt] n comète f

comfort ['kʌmfət] n confort m, bien-être m; (solace) consolation f, réconfort m ▷ vt consoler, réconforter; **comfortable** adj confortable; (person) à l'aise; (financially) aisé(e); (patient) dont l'état est stationnaire; **comfort station** n (US) toilettes fpl

comic ['kɒmɪk] adj (also: ~al) comique ▷ n (person) comique m; (BRIT: magazine: for children) magazine m de bandes dessinées or de BD; (: for adults) illustré m; **comic book** (US) n (for children) magazine m de bandes dessinées or de BD; (for adults) illustré m; **comic strip** n bande dessinée

comma ['kɒmə] n virgule f

command [kə'mɑːnd] n ordre m, commandement m; (Mil: authority) commandement m; (mastery) maîtrise f ▷ vt (troops) commander; **to ~ sb to do** donner l'ordre or commander à qn de faire; **commander** n (Mil) commandant m

commemorate [kə'mɛməreɪt] vt commémorer

commence [kə'mɛns] vt, vi commencer; **commencement** (US) n (University) remise f des diplômes

commend [kə'mɛnd] vt louer; (recommend) recommander

comment ['kɒmɛnt] n commentaire m ▷ vi: **to ~ on** faire des remarques sur; **"no ~"** je n'ai rien à déclarer"; **commentary** ['kɒməntərɪ] n commentaire m; (Sport) reportage m (en direct); **commentator** ['kɒməntertər] n commentateur m; (Sport) reporter m

commerce ['kɒmɜːs] n commerce m

commercial [kə'mɜːʃəl] adj commercial(e) ▷ n (Radio, TV) annonce f publicitaire, spot m (publicitaire); **commercial break** n (Radio, TV) spot m (publicitaire)

commission [kə'mɪʃən] n (committee, fee) commission f ▷ vt (work of art) commander, charger un artiste de l'exécution de; **out of ~** (machine) hors service; **commissioner** n (Police) préfet m (de police)

commit [kə'mɪt] vt (act) commettre; (resources) consacrer; (to sb's care) confier (à); **to ~ o.s. (to do)** s'engager (à faire); **to ~ suicide** se suicider; **commitment** n engagement m; (obligation) responsabilité(s) (fpl)

committee [kə'mɪtɪ] n comité m; commission f

commodity [kə'mɒdɪtɪ] n produit m, marchandise f, article m

common ['kɒmən] adj (gen) commun(e); (usual) courant(e) ▷ n terrain communal; **commonly** adv communément, généralement; couramment; **commonplace** adj banal(e), ordinaire; **Commons** npl (BRIT Pol): **the (House of) Commons** la chambre des Communes; **common sense** n bon sens; **Commonwealth** n: **the Commonwealth** le Commonwealth

communal ['kɒmjuːnl] adj (life) communautaire; (for common use) commun(e)

commune n ['kɒmjuːn] (group) communauté f ▷ vi [kə'mjuːn]: **to ~ with** (nature) communier avec

communicate [kə'mjuːnɪkeɪt] vt communiquer, transmettre ▷ vi: **to ~ (with)** communiquer (avec)

communication [kəmjuːnɪ'keɪʃən] n communication f

communion [kə'mjuːnɪən] n (also: **Holy C~**) communion f

communism ['kɒmjunɪzəm] n communisme m; **communist** adj, n communiste m/f

community [kə'mjuːnɪtɪ] n communauté f; **community centre** (US **community center**) n foyer socio-éducatif, centre m de loisirs; **community service** n ≈ travail m d'intérêt général, TIG m

commute [kə'mjuːt] vi faire le trajet journalier (de son domicile à un lieu de travail assez éloigné) ▷ vt (Law) commuer; **commuter** n banlieusard(e) (qui fait un trajet journalier pour se rendre à son travail)

compact adj [kəm'pækt] compact(e) ▷ n ['kɔmpækt] (also: **powder ~**) poudrier m; **compact disc** n disque compact; **compact disc player** n lecteur m de disques compacts

companion [kəm'pænjən] n compagnon (compagne)

company ['kʌmpənɪ] n compagnie f; **to keep sb ~** tenir compagnie à qn; **company car** n voiture f de fonction; **company director** n administrateur(-trice)

comparable ['kɔmpərəbl] adj comparable

comparative [kəm'pærətɪv] adj (study) comparatif(-ive); (relative) relatif(-ive); **comparatively** adv (relatively) relativement

compare [kəm'pɛə'] vt: **to ~ sth/sb with** or **to** comparer qch/qn avec or à ▷ vi: **to ~ (with)** se comparer (à); être comparable (à); **comparison** [kəm'pærɪsn] n comparaison f

compartment [kəm'pɑ:tmənt] n (also Rail) compartiment m; **a non-smoking ~** un compartiment non-fumeurs

compass ['kʌmpəs] n boussole f; **compasses** npl (Math) compas m

compassion [kəm'pæʃən] n compassion f, humanité f

compatible [kəm'pætɪbl] adj compatible

compel [kəm'pɛl] vt contraindre, obliger; **compelling** adj (fig: argument) irrésistible

compensate ['kɔmpənseɪt] vt indemniser, dédommager ▷ vi: **to ~ for** compenser; **compensation** [kɔmpən'seɪʃən] n compensation f; (money) dédommagement m, indemnité f

compete [kəm'pi:t] vi (take part) concourir; (vie): **to ~ (with)** rivaliser (avec), faire concurrence (à)

competent ['kɔmpɪtənt] adj compétent(e), capable

competition [kɔmpɪ'tɪʃən] n (contest) compétition f, concours m; (Econ) concurrence f

competitive [kəm'pɛtɪtɪv] adj (Econ) concurrentiel(le); (sports) de compétition; (person) qui a l'esprit de compétition

competitor [kəm'pɛtɪtər] n concurrent(e)

complacent [kəm'pleɪsnt] adj (trop) content(e) de soi

complain [kəm'pleɪn] vi: **to ~ (about)** se plaindre (de); (in shop etc) réclamer (au sujet de); **complaint** n plainte f; (in shop etc) réclamation f; (Med) affection f

complement ['kɔmplɪmənt] n complément m; (esp of ship's crew etc) effectif complet ▷ vt (enhance) compléter; **complementary** [kɔmplɪ'mɛntərɪ] adj complémentaire

complete [kəm'pli:t] adj complet(-ète); (finished) achevé(e) ▷ vt achever, parachever; (set, group) compléter; (a form) remplir; **completely** adv complètement; **completion** [kəm'pli:ʃən] n achèvement m; (of contract) exécution f

complex ['kɔmplɛks] adj complexe ▷ n (Psych, buildings etc) complexe m

complexion [kəm'plɛkʃən] n (of face) teint m

compliance [kəm'plaɪəns] n (submission) docilité f; (agreement): **~ with** le fait de se conformer à; **in ~ with** en conformité avec, conformément à

complicate ['kɔmplɪkeɪt] vt compliquer; **complicated** adj compliqué(e); **complication** [kɔmplɪ'keɪʃən] n complication f

compliment n ['kɔmplɪmənt] compliment m ▷ vt ['kɔmplɪmənt] complimenter; **complimentary** [kɔmplɪ'mɛntərɪ] adj flatteur(-euse); (free) à titre gracieux

comply [kəm'plaɪ] vi: **to ~ with** se soumettre à, se conformer à

component [kəm'pəunənt] adj composant(e), constituant(e) ▷ n composant m, élément m

compose [kəm'pəuz] vt composer; (form): **to be ~d of** se composer de; **to ~ o.s.** se calmer, se maîtriser; **composer** n (Mus) compositeur m; **composition** [kɔmpə'zɪʃən] n composition f

composure [kəm'pəuʒər] n calme m, maîtrise f de soi

compound ['kɔmpaund] n (Chem, Ling) composé m; (enclosure) enclos m, enceinte f ▷ adj composé(e); (fracture) compliqué(e)

comprehension [kɔmprɪ'hɛnʃən] n compréhension f

comprehensive [kɔmprɪ'hɛnsɪv] adj (très) complet(-ète); **~ policy** (Insurance) assurance f tous risques; **comprehensive (school)** n (BRIT) école secondaire non sélective avec libre circulation d'une section à l'autre, ≈ CES m

> Be careful not to translate *comprehensive* by the French word *compréhensif*.

compress vt [kəm'prɛs] comprimer; (text, information) condenser ▷ n ['kɔmprɛs] (Med) compresse f

comprise [kəm'praɪz] vt (also: **be ~d of**) comprendre; (constitute) constituer, représenter

compromise ['kɔmprəmaɪz] n compromis m ▷ vt compromettre ▷ vi transiger, accepter un compromis

compulsive [kəm'pʌlsɪv] adj (Psych) compulsif(-ive); (book, film etc) captivant(e)

compulsory [kəm'pʌlsərɪ] adj obligatoire

computer [kəm'pju:tər] n ordinateur m; **computer game** n jeu m vidéo; **computer-generated** adj de synthèse; **computerize** vt (data) traiter par ordinateur; (system, office) informatiser; **computer programmer**

n programmeur(-euse); **computer programming** *n* programmation *f*; **computer science** *n* informatique *f*; **computer studies** *npl* informatique *f*; **computing** [kəm'pju:tɪŋ] *n* informatique *f*

con [kɔn] *vt* duper; (*cheat*) escroquer ⊳ *n* escroquerie *f*

conceal [kən'si:l] *vt* cacher, dissimuler

concede [kən'si:d] *vt* concéder ⊳ *vi* céder

conceited [kən'si:tɪd] *adj* vaniteux(-euse), suffisant(e)

conceive [kən'si:v] *vt, vi* concevoir

concentrate ['kɔnsəntreɪt] *vi* se concentrer ⊳ *vt* concentrer

concentration [kɔnsən'treɪʃən] *n* concentration *f*

concept ['kɔnsɛpt] *n* concept *m*

concern [kən'sə:n] *n* affaire *f*; (*Comm*) entreprise *f*, firme *f*; (*anxiety*) inquiétude *f*, souci *m* ⊳ *vt* (*worry*) inquiéter; (*involve*) concerner; (*relate to*) se rapporter à; **to be ~ed (about)** s'inquiéter (de), être inquiet(-ète) (au sujet de); **concerning** *prep* en ce qui concerne, à propos de

concert ['kɔnsət] *n* concert *m*; **concert hall** *n* salle *f* de concert

concerto [kən'tʃə:təu] *n* concerto *m*

concession [kən'sɛʃən] *n* (*compromise*) concession *f*; (*reduced price*) réduction *f*; **tax ~** dégrèvement fiscal; **"~s"** tarif réduit

concise [kən'saɪs] *adj* concis(e)

conclude [kən'klu:d] *vt* conclure; **conclusion** [kən'klu:ʒən] *n* conclusion *f*

concrete ['kɔnkri:t] *n* béton *m* ⊳ *adj* concret(-ète); (*Constr*) en béton

concussion [kən'kʌʃən] *n* (*Med*) commotion (cérébrale)

condemn [kən'dɛm] *vt* condamner

condensation [kɔndɛn'seɪʃən] *n* condensation *f*

condense [kən'dɛns] *vi* se condenser ⊳ *vt* condenser

condition [kən'dɪʃən] *n* condition *f*; (*disease*) maladie *f* ⊳ *vt* déterminer, conditionner; **on ~ that** à condition que + *sub*, à condition de; **conditional** [kən'dɪʃənl] *adj* conditionnel(le); **conditioner** *n* (*for hair*) baume démêlant; (*for fabrics*) assouplissant *m*

condo ['kɔndəu] *n* (*us inf*) = **condominium**

condom ['kɔndəm] *n* préservatif *m*

condominium [kɔndə'mɪnɪəm] *n* (*us: building*) immeuble *m* (en copropriété); (*: rooms*) appartement *m* (dans un immeuble en copropriété)

condone [kən'dəun] *vt* fermer les yeux sur, approuver (tacitement)

conduct *n* ['kɔndʌkt] conduite *f* ⊳ *vt* [kə n'dʌkt] conduire; (*manage*) mener, diriger; (*Mus*) diriger; **to ~ o.s.** se conduire, se

comporter; **conducted tour** (*BRIT*) *n* voyage organisé; (*of building*) visite guidée; **conductor** *n* (*of orchestra*) chef *m* d'orchestre; (*on bus*) receveur *m*; (*us: on train*) chef *m* de train; (*Elec*) conducteur *m*

cone [kəun] *n* cône *m*; (*for ice-cream*) cornet *m*; (*Bot*) pomme *f* de pin, cône

confectionery [kən'fɛkʃənrɪ] *n* (*sweets*) confiserie *f*

confer [kən'fə:'] *vt*: **to ~ sth on** conférer qch à ⊳ *vi* conférer, s'entretenir

conference ['kɔnfərns] *n* conférence *f*

confess [kən'fɛs] *vt* confesser, avouer ⊳ *vi* (*admit sth*) avouer; (*Rel*) se confesser; **confession** [kən'fɛʃən] *n* confession *f*

confide [kən'faɪd] *vi*: **to ~ in** s'ouvrir à, se confier à

confidence ['kɔnfɪdns] *n* confiance *f*; (*also:* **self-~**) assurance *f*, confiance en soi; (*secret*) confidence *f*; **in ~** (*speak, write*) en confidence, confidentiellement; **confident** *adj* (*self-assured*) sûr(e) de soi; (*sure*) sûr; **confidential** [kɔnfɪ'dɛnʃəl] *adj* confidentiel(le)

confine [kən'faɪn] *vt* limiter, borner; (*shut up*) confiner, enfermer; **confined** *adj* (*space*) restreint(e), réduit(e)

confirm [kən'fə:m] *vt* (*report, Rel*) confirmer; (*appointment*) ratifier; **confirmation** [kɔnfə'meɪʃən] *n* confirmation *f*; ratification *f*

confiscate ['kɔnfɪskeɪt] *vt* confisquer

conflict *n* ['kɔnflɪkt] conflit *m*, lutte *f* ⊳ *vi* [kə n'flɪkt] (*opinions*) s'opposer, se heurter

conform [kən'fɔ:m] *vi*: **to ~ (to)** se conformer (à)

confront [kən'frʌnt] *vt* (*two people*) confronter; (*enemy, danger*) affronter, faire face à; (*problem*) faire face à; **confrontation** [kɔnfrən'teɪʃən] *n* confrontation *f*

confuse [kən'fju:z] *vt* (*person*) troubler; (*situation*) embrouiller; (*one thing with another*) confondre; **confused** *adj* (*person*) dérouté(e), désorienté(e); (*situation*) embrouillé(e); **confusing** *adj* peu clair(e), déroutant(e); **confusion** [kən'fju:ʒən] *n* confusion *f*

congestion [kən'dʒɛstʃən] *n* (*Med*) congestion *f*; (*fig: traffic*) encombrement *m*

congratulate [kən'grætjuleɪt] *vt*: **to ~ sb (on)** féliciter qn (de); **congratulations** [kə ngrætju'leɪʃənz] *npl*: **congratulations (on)** félicitations *fpl* (pour) ⊳ *excl*: **congratulations!** (toutes mes) félicitations!

congregation [kɔngrɪ'geɪʃən] *n* assemblée *f* (des fidèles)

congress ['kɔngrɛs] *n* congrès *m*; (*Pol*): **C~** Congrès *m*; **congressman** *n* membre *m* du Congrès; **congresswoman** *n* membre *m* du Congrès

conifer ['kɔnɪfə'] *n* conifère *m*

conjugate ['kɔndʒugeɪt] *vt* conjuguer

conjugation [kɔndʒə'geɪʃən] n conjugaison f

conjunction [kən'dʒʌŋkʃən] n conjonction f; **in ~ with** (conjointement) avec

conjure ['kʌndʒə'] vi faire des tours de passe-passe

connect [kə'nɛkt] vt joindre, relier; (Elec) connecter; (Tel: caller) mettre en connexion; (: subscriber) brancher; (fig) établir un rapport entre, faire un rapprochement entre ▷ vi (train): **to ~ with** assurer la correspondance avec; **to be ~ed with** avoir un rapport avec; (have dealings with) avoir des rapports avec, être en relation avec; **connecting flight** n (vol m de) correspondance f; **connection** [kə'nɛkʃən] n relation f, lien m; (Elec) connexion f; (Tel) communication f; (train etc) correspondance f

conquer ['kɔŋkə'] vt conquérir; (feelings) vaincre, surmonter

conquest ['kɔŋkwɛst] n conquête f

cons [kɔnz] npl see **convenience**; **pro**

conscience ['kɔnʃəns] n conscience f

conscientious [kɔnʃɪ'ɛnʃəs] adj consciencieux(-euse)

conscious ['kɔnʃəs] adj conscient(e); (deliberate: insult, error) délibéré(e); **consciousness** n conscience f; (Med) connaissance f

consecutive [kən'sɛkjutɪv] adj consécutif(-ive); **on three ~ occasions** trois fois de suite

consensus [kən'sɛnsəs] n consensus m

consent [kən'sɛnt] n consentement m ▷ vi: **to ~ (to)** consentir (à)

consequence ['kɔnsɪkwəns] n suites fpl, conséquence f; (significance) importance f

consequently ['kɔnsɪkwəntlɪ] adv par conséquent, donc

conservation [kɔnsə'veɪʃən] n préservation f, protection f; (also: **nature ~**) défense f de l'environnement

conservative [kən'sə:vətɪv] adj conservateur(-trice); (cautious) prudent(e); **Conservative** adj, n (BRIT Pol) conservateur(-trice)

conservatory [kən'sə:vətrɪ] n (room) jardin m d'hiver; (Mus) conservatoire m

consider [kən'sɪdə'] vt (study) considérer, réfléchir à; (take into account) penser à, prendre en considération; (regard, judge) considérer, estimer; **to ~ doing sth** envisager de faire qch; **considerable** adj considérable; **considerably** adv nettement; **considerate** adj prévenant(e), plein(e) d'égards; **consideration** [kənsɪdə'reɪʃən] n considération f; (reward) rétribution f, rémunération f; **considering** prep; **considering (that)** étant donné (que)

consignment [kən'saɪnmənt] n arrivage m, envoi m

consist [kən'sɪst] vi: **to ~ of** consister en, se composer de

consistency [kən'sɪstənsɪ] n (thickness) consistance f; (fig) cohérence f

consistent [kən'sɪstənt] adj logique, cohérent(e)

consolation [kɔnsə'leɪʃən] n consolation f

console[1] [kən'səul] vt consoler

console[2] ['kɔnsəul] n console f

consonant ['kɔnsənənt] n consonne f

conspicuous [kən'spɪkjuəs] adj voyant(e), qui attire l'attention

conspiracy [kən'spɪrəsɪ] n conspiration f, complot m

constable ['kʌnstəbl] n (BRIT) ≈ agent m de police, gendarme m; **chief ~** ≈ préfet m de police

constant ['kɔnstənt] adj constant(e); incessant(e); **constantly** adv constamment, sans cesse

constipated ['kɔnstɪpeɪtɪd] adj constipé(e); **constipation** [kɔnstɪ'peɪʃən] n constipation f

constituency [kən'stɪtjuənsɪ] n (Pol: area) circonscription électorale; (: electors) électorat m

constitute ['kɔnstɪtjuːt] vt constituer

constitution [kɔnstɪ'tjuːʃən] n constitution f

constraint [kən'streɪnt] n contrainte f

construct [kən'strʌkt] vt construire; **construction** [kən'strʌkʃən] n construction f; **constructive** adj constructif(-ive)

consul ['kɔnsl] n consul m; **consulate** ['kɔnsjulɪt] n consulat m

consult [kən'sʌlt] vt consulter; **consultant** n (Med) médecin consultant; (other specialist) consultant m, (expert-)conseil m; **consultation** [kɔnsəl'teɪʃən] n consultation f; **consulting room** n (BRIT) cabinet m de consultation

consume [kən'sjuːm] vt consommer; (subj: flames, hatred, desire) consumer; **consumer** n consommateur(-trice)

consumption [kən'sʌmpʃən] n consommation f

cont. abbr (= continued) suite

contact ['kɔntækt] n contact m; (person) connaissance f, relation f ▷ vt se mettre en contact or en rapport avec; **contact lenses** npl verres mpl de contact

contagious [kən'teɪdʒəs] adj contagieux(-euse)

contain [kən'teɪn] vt contenir; **to ~ o.s.** se contenir, se maîtriser; **container** n récipient m; (for shipping etc) conteneur m

contaminate [kən'tæmɪneɪt] vt contaminer

cont'd abbr (= continued) suite

contemplate ['kɔntəmpleɪt] vt contempler; (consider) envisager

contemporary [kən'tɛmpərərɪ] adj
contemporain(e); (design, wallpaper) moderne
▷ n contemporain(e)

contempt [kən'tɛmpt] n mépris m, dédain
m; **~ of court** (Law) outrage m à l'autorité de
la justice

contend [kən'tɛnd] vt: **to ~ that** soutenir
or prétendre que ▷ vi: **to ~ with** (compete)
rivaliser avec; (struggle) lutter avec

content [kən'tɛnt] adj content(e), satisfait(e)
▷ vt contenter, satisfaire ▷ n ['kɔntɛnt]
contenu m; (of fat, moisture) teneur f; **contents**
npl (of container etc) contenu m; **(table
of) ~s** table f des matières; **contented** adj
content(e), satisfait(e)

contest n ['kɔntɛst] combat m, lutte f;
(competition) concours m ▷ vt [kən'tɛst]
contester, discuter; (compete for) disputer;
(Law) attaquer; **contestant** [kən'tɛstənt] n
concurrent(e); (in fight) adversaire m/f

context ['kɔntɛkst] n contexte m

continent ['kɔntɪnənt] n continent m; **the
C~** (BRIT) l'Europe continentale; **continental**
[kɔntɪ'nɛntl] adj continental(e); **continental
breakfast** n café (or thé) complet;
continental quilt n (BRIT) couette f

continual [kən'tɪnjuəl] adj continuel(le);
continually adv continuellement, sans cesse

continue [kən'tɪnjuː] vi continuer ▷ vt
continuer; (start again) reprendre

continuity [kɔntɪ'njuːɪtɪ] n continuité f; (TV
etc) enchaînement m

continuous [kən'tɪnjuəs] adj continu(e),
permanent(e); (Ling) progressif(-ive);
continuous assessment (BRIT) n contrôle
continu; **continuously** adv (repeatedly)
continuellement; (uninterruptedly) sans
interruption

contour ['kɔntuəʳ] n contour m, profil m; (also:
~ line) courbe f de niveau

contraception [kɔntrə'sɛpʃən] n
contraception f

contraceptive [kɔntrə'sɛptɪv] adj
contraceptif(-ive), anticonceptionnel(le) ▷ n
contraceptif m

contract n ['kɔntrækt] contrat m ▷ vb [kə
n'trækt] ▷ vi (become smaller) se contracter,
se resserrer ▷ vt contracter; (Comm): **to ~ to
do sth** s'engager (par contrat) à faire qch;
contractor n entrepreneur m

contradict [kɔntrə'dɪkt] vt contredire;
contradiction [kɔntrə'dɪkʃən] n
contradiction f

contrary[1] ['kɔntrərɪ] adj contraire,
opposé(e) ▷ n contraire m; **on the ~** au
contraire; **unless you hear to the ~** sauf avis
contraire

contrary[2] [kən'trɛərɪ] adj (perverse)
contrariant(e), entêté(e)

contrast n ['kɔntrɑːst] contraste m ▷ vt [kə
n'trɑːst] mettre en contraste, contraster; **in ~
to** or **with** contrairement à, par
opposition à

contribute [kən'trɪbjuːt] vi contribuer ▷ vt:
to ~ £10/an article to donner 10 livres/un
article à; **to ~ to** (gen) contribuer à; (newspaper)
collaborer à; (discussion) prendre part à;
contribution [kɔntrɪ'bjuːʃən] n contribution
f; (BRIT: for social security) cotisation f; (to
publication) article m; **contributor** n (to
newspaper) collaborateur(-trice); (of money,
goods) donateur(-trice)

control [kən'trəul] vt (process, machinery)
commander; (temper) maîtriser; (disease)
enrayer ▷ n maîtrise f; (power) autorité f;
controls npl (of machine etc) commandes fpl;
(on radio) boutons mpl de réglage; **to be in ~
of** être maître de, maîtriser; (in charge of) être
responsable de; **everything is under ~** j'ai (or
il a etc) la situation en main; **the car went out
of ~** j'ai (or il a etc) perdu le contrôle du véhicule;
control tower n (Aviat) tour f de contrôle

controversial [kɔntrə'vəːʃl] adj discutable,
controversé(e)

controversy ['kɔntrəvəːsɪ] n controverse f,
polémique f

convenience [kən'viːnɪəns] n commodité f;
at your ~ quand or comme cela vous convient;
all modern ~s, all mod cons (BRIT) avec tout
le confort moderne, tout confort

convenient [kən'viːnɪənt] adj commode

convent ['kɔnvənt] n couvent m

convention [kən'vɛnʃən] n convention
f; (custom) usage m; **conventional** adj
conventionnel(le)

conversation [kɔnvə'seɪʃən] n conversation f

conversely [kɔn'vəːslɪ] adv inversement,
réciproquement

conversion [kən'vəːʃən] n conversion f; (BRIT:
of house) transformation f, aménagement m;
(Rugby) transformation f

convert vt [kən'vəːt] (Rel, Comm) convertir;
(alter) transformer; (house) aménager ▷ n
['kɔnvəːt] converti(e); **convertible** adj
convertible ▷ n (voiture f) décapotable f

convey [kən'veɪ] vt transporter; (thanks)
transmettre; (idea) communiquer; **conveyor
belt** n convoyeur m tapis roulant

convict vt [kən'vɪkt] déclarer (or reconnaître)
coupable ▷ n ['kɔnvɪkt] forçat m,
convict m; **conviction** [kən'vɪkʃən] n (Law)
condamnation f; (belief) conviction f

convince [kən'vɪns] vt convaincre, persuader;
convinced adj: **convinced of/that**
convaincu(e) de/que; **convincing** adj
persuasif(-ive), convaincant(e)

convoy ['kɔnvɔɪ] n convoi m

cook [kuk] vt (faire) cuire ▷ vi cuire; (person)

faire la cuisine ▷ n cuisinier(-ière); **cookbook**
n livre m de cuisine; **cooker** n cuisinière f;
cookery n cuisine f; **cookery book** n
(BRIT) = **cookbook**; **cookie** n (US) biscuit
m, petit gâteau sec; **cooking** n cuisine f
cool [kuːl] adj frais (fraîche); (not afraid) calme;
(unfriendly) froid(e); (inf: trendy) cool inv (inf); (:
great) super inv (inf) ▷ vt, vi rafraîchir, refroidir;
cool down vi refroidir; (fig: person, situation) se
calmer; **cool off** vi (become calmer) se
calmer; (lose enthusiasm) perdre son enthousiasme
cop [kɔp] n (inf) flic m
cope [kəup] vi s'en sortir, tenir le coup;
to ~ with (problem) faire face à
copper ['kɔpə'] n cuivre m;
(BRIT: inf: policeman) flic m
copy ['kɔpɪ] n copie f; (book etc) exemplaire
m ▷ vt copier; (imitate) imiter; **copyright**
n droit m d'auteur, copyright m
coral ['kɔrəl] n corail m
cord [kɔːd] n corde f; (fabric) velours côtelé;
(Elec) cordon m (d'alimentation), fil m
(électrique); **cords** npl (trousers) pantalon
m de velours côtelé; **cordless** adj sans fil
corduroy ['kɔːdərɔɪ] n velours côtelé
core [kɔː'] n (of fruit) trognon m, cœur
m; (fig: of problem etc) cœur ▷ vt
enlever le trognon or le cœur de
coriander [kɔrɪ'ændə'] n coriandre f
cork [kɔːk] n (material) liège m; (of bottle)
bouchon m; **corkscrew** n tire-bouchon m
corn [kɔːn] n (BRIT: wheat) blé m; (US:
maize) maïs m; (on foot) cor m; **~ on the
cob** (Culin) épi m de maïs au naturel
corned beef ['kɔːnd-] n corned-beef m
corner ['kɔːnə'] n coin m; (in road) tournant
m, virage m; (Football) corner m ▷ vt (trap:
prey) acculer; (fig) coincer; (Comm: market)
accaparer ▷ vi prendre un virage; **corner
shop** (BRIT) n magasin m du coin
cornflakes ['kɔːnfleɪks] npl cornflakes mpl
cornflour ['kɔːnflauə'] n (BRIT)
farine f de maïs, maïzena® f
cornstarch ['kɔːnstɑːtʃ] n (US)
farine f de maïs, maïzena® f
Cornwall ['kɔːnwəl] n Cornouailles f
coronary ['kɔrənəri] n: **~
(thrombosis)** infarctus m (du
myocarde), thrombose f coronaire
coronation [kɔrə'neɪʃən] n couronnement m
coroner ['kɔrənə'] n coroner m, officier de police
judiciaire chargé de déterminer les causes d'un décès
corporal ['kɔːpərl] n caporal m, brigadier m
▷ adj: **~ punishment** châtiment corporel
corporate ['kɔːpərɪt] adj (action, ownership)
en commun; (Comm) de la société
corporation [kɔːpə'reɪʃən] n (of
town) municipalité f, conseil
municipal; (Comm) société f

corps [kɔː', pl kɔːz] n corps m; **the diplomatic
~** le corps diplomatique; **the press ~** la presse
corpse [kɔːps] n cadavre m
correct [kə'rɛkt] adj (accurate) correct(e),
exact(e); (proper) correct, convenable ▷ vt
corriger; **correction** [kə'rɛkʃən] n correction f
correspond [kɔrɪs'pɔnd] vi correspondre;
to ~ to sth (be equivalent to) correspondre à
qch; **correspondence** n correspondance f;
correspondent n correspondant(e);
corresponding adj correspondant(e)
corridor ['kɔrɪdɔː'] n couloir m, corridor m
corrode [kə'rəud] vt corroder,
ronger ▷ vi se corroder
corrupt [kə'rʌpt] adj corrompu(e);
(Comput) altéré(e) ▷ vt corrompre;
(Comput) altérer; **corruption** n corruption
f; (Comput) altération f (de données)
Corsica ['kɔːsɪkə] n Corse f
cosmetic [kɔz'mɛtɪk] n produit m de
beauté, cosmétique m ▷ adj (fig: reforms)
symbolique, superficiel(le); **cosmetic
surgery** n chirurgie f esthétique
cosmopolitan [kɔzmə'pɔlɪtn]
adj cosmopolite
cost [kɔst] n coût m ▷ vb (pt, pp ~) ▷ vi
coûter ▷ vt établir or calculer le prix de
revient de; **costs** npl (Comm) frais mpl;
(Law) dépens mpl; **how much does it ~?**
combien ça coûte?; **to ~ sb time/effort**
demander du temps/un effort à qn; **it ~ him
his life/job** ça lui a coûté la vie/son emploi;
at all ~s coûte que coûte, à tout prix
co-star ['kəustɑː'] n partenaire m/f
costly ['kɔstlɪ] adj coûteux(-euse)
cost of living n coût m de la vie
costume ['kɔstjuːm] n costume m; (BRIT:
also: **swimming ~**) maillot m (de bain)
cosy (US **cozy**) ['kəuzɪ] adj (room,
bed) douillet(te); **to be ~** (person)
être bien (au chaud)
cot [kɔt] n (BRIT: child's) lit m d'enfant,
petit lit; (US: campbed) lit de camp
cottage ['kɔtɪdʒ] n petite maison (à
la campagne), cottage m; **cottage
cheese** n fromage blanc (maigre)
cotton ['kɔtn] n coton m; (thread) fil
m (de coton); **cotton on** vi (inf): **to ~
on (to sth)** piger (qch); **cotton bud**
(BRIT) n coton-tige ® m; **cotton candy**
(US) n barbe f à papa; **cotton wool** n
(BRIT) ouate f, coton m hydrophile
couch [kautʃ] n canapé m; divan m
cough [kɔf] vi tousser ▷ n toux f; **I've
got a ~** j'ai la toux; **cough mixture,
cough syrup** n sirop m pour la toux
could [kud] pt of **can²**; **couldn't** = **could not**
council ['kaunsl] n conseil m; **city** or
town ~ conseil municipal; **council**

estate n (BRIT) (quartier m or zone f de) logements loués à/par la municipalité; **council house** n (BRIT) maison f (à loyer modéré) louée par la municipalité; **councillor** (US **councilor**) n conseiller(-ère); **council tax** n (BRIT) impôts locaux

counsel ['kaunsl] n (lawyer) avocat(e) ▷ vt: **to ~ (sb to do sth)** conseiller (à qn de faire qch); **counselling** (US **counseling**) n (Psych) aide psychosociale; **counsellor** (US **counselor**) n conseiller(-ère); (US Law) avocat m

count [kaunt] vt, vi compter ▷ n compte m; (nobleman) comte m; **count in** vt (inf): **to ~ sb in on sth** inclure qn dans qch; **count on** vt fus compter sur; **countdown** n compte m à rebours

counter ['kauntə'] n comptoir m; (in post office, bank) guichet m; (in game) jeton m ▷ vt aller à l'encontre de, opposer ▷ adv: **~ to** à l'encontre de; contrairement à; **counterclockwise** (US) adv en sens inverse des aiguilles d'une montre

counterfeit ['kauntəfɪt] n faux m, contrefaçon f ▷ vt contrefaire ▷ adj faux (fausse)

counterpart ['kauntəpɑ:t] n (of person) homologue m/f

countess ['kauntɪs] n comtesse f

countless ['kauntlɪs] adj innombrable

country ['kʌntrɪ] n pays m; (native land) patrie f; (as opposed to town) campagne f; (region) région f, pays; **country and western (music)** n musique f country; **country house** n manoir m, (petit) château; **countryside** n campagne f

county ['kauntɪ] n comté m

coup [ku:, pl ku:z] n (achievement) beau coup; (also: **~ d'état**) coup d'État

couple ['kʌpl] n couple m; **a ~ of** (two) deux; (a few) deux ou trois

coupon ['ku:pɔn] n (voucher) bon m de réduction; (detachable form) coupon m détachable, coupon-réponse m

courage ['kʌrɪdʒ] n courage m; **courageous** [kə'reɪdʒəs] adj courageux(-euse)

courgette [kuə'ʒet] n (BRIT) courgette f

courier ['kurɪə'] n messager m, courrier m; (for tourists) accompagnateur(-trice)

course [kɔ:s] n cours m; (of ship) route f; (for golf) terrain m; (part of meal) plat m; **of ~** adv bien sûr; **(no,) of ~ not!** bien sûr que non!, évidemment que non!; **~ of treatment** (Med) traitement m

court [kɔ:t] n cour f; (Law) cour, tribunal m; (Tennis) court m ▷ vt (woman) courtiser, faire la cour à; **to take to ~** actionner or poursuivre en justice

courtesy ['kə:təsɪ] n courtoisie f, politesse f; **(by) ~ of** avec l'aimable autorisation de;

courtesy bus, courtesy coach n navette gratuite

court: **court-house** ['kɔ:thaus] n (US) palais m de justice; **courtroom** ['kɔ:trum] n salle f de tribunal; **courtyard** ['kɔ:tjɑ:d] n cour f

cousin ['kʌzn] n cousin(e); **first ~** cousin(e) germain(e)

cover ['kʌvə'] vt couvrir; (Press: report on) faire un reportage sur; (feelings, mistake) cacher; (include) englober; (discuss) traiter ▷ n (of book, Comm) couverture f; (of pan) couvercle m; (over furniture) housse f; (shelter) abri m; **covers** npl (on bed) couvertures; **to take ~** se mettre à l'abri; **under ~** à l'abri; **under ~ of darkness** à la faveur de la nuit; **under separate ~** (Comm) sous pli séparé; **cover up** vi: **to ~ up for sb** (fig) couvrir qn; **coverage** n (in media) reportage m; **cover charge** n couvert m (supplément à payer); **cover-up** n tentative f pour étouffer une affaire

cow [kau] n vache f ▷ vt effrayer, intimider

coward ['kauəd] n lâche m/f; **cowardly** adj lâche

cowboy ['kaubɔɪ] n cow-boy m

cozy ['kəuzɪ] adj (US) = **cosy**

crab [kræb] n crabe m

crack [kræk] n (split) fente f, fissure f; (in cup, bone) fêlure f; (in wall) lézarde f; (noise) craquement m, coup (sec); (Drugs) crack m ▷ vt fendre, fissurer; fêler; lézarder; (whip) faire claquer; (nut) casser; (problem) résoudre; (code) déchiffrer ▷ cpd (athlete) de première classe, d'élite; **crack down on** vt fus (crime) sévir contre, réprimer; **cracked** adj (cup, bone) fêlé(e); (broken) cassé(e); (wall) lézardé(e); (surface) craquelé(e); (inf) toqué(e), timbré(e); **cracker** n (also: **Christmas cracker**) pétard m; (biscuit) biscuit (salé), craquelin m

crackle ['krækl] vi crépiter, grésiller

cradle ['kreɪdl] n berceau m

craft [krɑ:ft] n métier m (artisanal); (cunning) ruse f, astuce f; (boat: pl inv) embarcation f, barque f; (plane: pl inv) appareil m; **craftsman** (irreg) n artisan m, ouvrier (qualifié); **craftsmanship** n métier m, habileté f

cram [kræm] vt (fill): **to ~ sth with** bourrer qch de; (put): **to ~ sth into** fourrer qch dans ▷ vi (for exams) bachoter

cramp [kræmp] n crampe f; **I've got ~ in my leg** j'ai une crampe à la jambe; **cramped** adj à l'étroit, très serré(e)

cranberry ['krænbərɪ] n canneberge f

crane [kreɪn] n grue f

crap [kræp] n (infl: nonsense) conneries fpl (!); (: excrement) merde f (!)

crash [kræʃ] n (noise) fracas m; (of car, plane) collision f; (of business) faillite f ▷ vt (plane) écraser ▷ vi (plane) s'écraser; (two cars) se percuter, s'emboutir; (business) s'effondrer;

to ~ into se jeter or se fracasser contre; **crash course** n cours intensif; **crash helmet** n casque (protecteur)

crate [kreɪt] n cageot m; (for bottles) caisse f

crave [kreɪv] vt, vi: **to ~ (for)** avoir une envie irrésistible de

crawl [krɔːl] vi ramper; (vehicle) avancer au pas ▷ n (Swimming) crawl m

crayfish ['kreɪfɪʃ] n (pl inv: freshwater) écrevisse f; (saltwater) langoustine f

crayon ['kreɪən] n crayon m (de couleur)

craze [kreɪz] n engouement m

crazy ['kreɪzɪ] adj fou (folle); **to be ~ about sb/sth** (inf) être fou de qn/qch

creak [kriːk] vi (hinge) grincer; (floor, shoes) craquer

cream [kriːm] n crème f ▷ adj (colour) crème inv; **cream cheese** n fromage m à la crème, fromage blanc; **creamy** adj crémeux (-euse)

crease [kriːs] n pli m ▷ vt froisser, chiffonner ▷ vi se froisser, se chiffonner

create [kriː'eɪt] vt créer; **creation** [kriː'eɪʃən] n création f; **creative** adj créatif (-ive); **creator** n créateur (-trice)

creature ['kriːtʃə'] n créature f

crèche [krɛʃ] n garderie f, crèche f

credentials [krɪ'dɛnʃlz] npl (references) références fpl; (identity papers) pièce f d'identité

credibility [krɛdɪ'bɪlɪtɪ] n crédibilité f

credible ['krɛdɪbl] adj digne de foi, crédible

credit ['krɛdɪt] n crédit m; (recognition) honneur m; (Scol) unité f de valeur ▷ vt (Comm) créditer; (believe: also: **give ~ to**) ajouter foi à, croire; **credits** npl (Cine) générique m; **to be in ~** (person, bank account) être créditeur (-trice); **to ~ sb with** (fig) prêter or attribuer à qn; **credit card** n carte f de crédit; **do you take credit cards?** acceptez-vous les cartes de crédit?

creek [kriːk] n (inlet) crique f, anse f; (us: stream) ruisseau m, petit cours d'eau

creep (pt, pp crept) [kriːp, krɛpt] vi ramper

cremate [krɪ'meɪt] vt incinérer

crematorium (pl crematoria) [krɛmə'tɔːrɪə m, -'tɔːrɪə] n four m crématoire

crept [krɛpt] pt, pp of **creep**

crescent ['krɛsnt] n croissant m; (street) rue f (en arc de cercle)

cress [krɛs] n cresson m

crest [krɛst] n crête f; (of coat of arms) timbre m

crew [kruː] n équipage m; (Cine) équipe f (de tournage); **crew-neck** n col ras

crib [krɪb] n lit m d'enfant; (for baby) berceau m ▷ vt (inf) copier

cricket ['krɪkɪt] n (insect) grillon m, cri-cri m inv; (game) cricket m; **cricketer** n joueur m de cricket

crime [kraɪm] n crime m; **criminal** ['krɪmɪnl] adj, n criminel(le)

crimson ['krɪmzn] adj cramoisi(e)

cringe [krɪndʒ] vi avoir un mouvement de recul

cripple ['krɪpl] n boiteux (-euse), infirme m/f ▷ vt (person) estropier, paralyser; (ship, plane) immobiliser; (production, exports) paralyser

crisis (pl crises) ['kraɪsɪs, -siːz] n crise f

crisp [krɪsp] adj croquant(e); (weather) vif (vive); (manner etc) brusque; **crisps** (BRIT) npl (pommes fpl) chips fpl; **crispy** adj croustillant(e)

criterion (pl criteria) [kraɪ'tɪərɪən, -'tɪərɪə] n critère m

critic ['krɪtɪk] n critique m/f; **critical** adj critique; **criticism** ['krɪtɪsɪzəm] n critique f; **criticize** ['krɪtɪsaɪz] vt critiquer

Croat ['krəuæt] adj, n = **Croatian**

Croatia [krəu'eɪʃə] n Croatie f; **Croatian** adj croate ▷ n Croate m/f; (Ling) croate m

crockery ['krɔkərɪ] n vaisselle f

crocodile ['krɔkədaɪl] n crocodile m

crocus ['krəukəs] n crocus m

croissant ['krwasã] n croissant m

crook [kruk] n escroc m; (of shepherd) houlette f; **crooked** ['krukɪd] adj courbé(e), tordu(e); (action) malhonnête

crop [krɔp] n (produce) culture f; (amount produced) récolte f; (riding crop) cravache f ▷ vt (hair) tondre; **crop up** vi surgir, se présenter, survenir

cross [krɔs] n croix f; (Biol) croisement m ▷ vt (street etc) traverser; (arms, legs, Biol) croiser; (cheque) barrer ▷ adj en colère, fâché(e); **cross off** or **out** vt barrer, rayer; **cross over** vi traverser; **cross-Channel ferry** ['krɔs'tʃænl-] n ferry m qui fait la traversée de la Manche; **crosscountry (race)** n cross (-country) m; **crossing** n (sea passage) traversée f; (also: **pedestrian crossing**) passage clouté; **how long does the crossing take?** combien de temps dure la traversée?; **crossing guard** (us) n contractuel qui fait traverser la rue aux enfants; **crossroads** n carrefour m; **crosswalk** n (us) passage clouté; **crossword** n mots mpl croisés

crotch [krɔtʃ] n (of garment) entrejambe m; (Anat) entrecuisse m

crouch [krautʃ] vi s'accroupir; (hide) se tapir; (before springing) se ramasser

crouton ['kruːtɔn] n croûton m

crow [krəu] n (bird) corneille f; (of cock) chant m du coq, cocorico m ▷ vi (cock) chanter

crowd [kraud] n foule f ▷ vt bourrer, remplir ▷ vi affluer, s'attrouper, s'entasser; **crowded** adj bondé(e), plein(e)

crown [kraun] n couronne f; (of head) sommet m de la tête; (of hill) sommet m ▷ vt (also tooth) couronner; **crown jewels** npl joyaux mpl de la Couronne

crucial ['kruːʃl] adj crucial(e), décisif (-ive)

crucifix ['kruːsɪfɪks] n crucifix m

crude [kruːd] adj (materials) brut(e); non raffiné(e); (basic) rudimentaire, sommaire; (vulgar) cru(e), grossier(-ière); **crude (oil)** n (pétrole) brut m

cruel ['kruəl] adj cruel(le); **cruelty** n cruauté f

cruise [kruːz] n croisière f ▷ vi (ship) croiser; (car) rouler; (aircraft) voler

crumb [krʌm] n miette f

crumble ['krʌmbl] vt émietter ▷ vi (plaster etc) s'effriter; (land, earth) s'ébouler; (building) s'écrouler, crouler; (fig) s'effondrer

crumpet ['krʌmpɪt] n petite crêpe (épaisse)

crumple ['krʌmpl] vt froisser, friper

crunch [krʌntʃ] vt croquer; (underfoot) faire craquer, écraser; faire crisser ▷ n (fig) instant m or moment m critique, moment de vérité; **crunchy** adj croquant(e), croustillant(e)

crush [krʌʃ] n (crowd) foule f, cohue f; (love): **to have a ~ on sb** avoir le béguin pour qn; (drink): **lemon ~** citron pressé ▷ vt écraser; (crumple) froisser; (grind, break up: garlic, ice) piler; (: grapes) presser; (hopes) anéantir

crust [krʌst] n croûte f; **crusty** adj croustillant(e); (inf: person) revêche, bourru(e)

crutch [krʌtʃ] n béquille f; (also: **crotch**) entrejambe m

cry [kraɪ] vi pleurer; (shout: also: ~ **out**) crier ▷ n cri m; **cry out** vi (call out, shout) pousser un cri ▷ vt crier

crystal ['krɪstl] n cristal m

cub [kʌb] n petit m (d'un animal); (also: ~ **scout**) louveteau m

Cuba ['kjuːbə] n Cuba m

cube [kjuːb] n cube m ▷ vt (Math) élever au cube

cubicle ['kjuːbɪkl] n (in hospital) box m; (at pool) cabine f

cuckoo ['kuku:] n coucou m

cucumber ['kjuːkʌmbə'] n concombre m

cuddle ['kʌdl] vt câliner, caresser ▷ vi se blottir l'un contre l'autre

cue [kjuː] n queue f de billard; (Theat etc) signal m

cuff [kʌf] n (BRIT: of shirt, coat etc) poignet m, manchette f; (US: on trousers) revers m; (blow) gifle f; **off the ~** adv à l'improviste; **cufflinks** n boutons m de manchette

cuisine [kwɪ'ziːn] n cuisine f

cul-de-sac ['kʌldəsæk] n cul-de-sac m, impasse f

cull [kʌl] vt sélectionner ▷ n (of animals) abattage sélectif

culminate ['kʌlmɪneɪt] vi: **to ~ in** finir or se terminer par; (lead to) mener à

culprit ['kʌlprɪt] n coupable m/f

cult [kʌlt] n culte m

cultivate ['kʌltɪveɪt] vt cultiver

cultural ['kʌltʃərəl] adj culturel(le)

culture ['kʌltʃə'] n culture f

cumin ['kʌmɪn] n (spice) cumin m

cunning ['kʌnɪŋ] n ruse f, astuce f ▷ adj rusé(e), malin(-igne); (clever: device, idea) astucieux(-euse)

cup [kʌp] n tasse f; (prize, event) coupe f; (of bra) bonnet m

cupboard ['kʌbəd] n placard m

cup final n (BRIT Football) finale f de la coupe

curator [kjuə'reɪtə'] n conservateur m (d'un musée etc)

curb [kə:b] vt refréner, mettre un frein à ▷ n (fig) frein m; (US) bord m du trottoir

curdle ['kə:dl] vi (se) cailler

cure [kjuə'] vt guérir; (Culin: salt) saler; (: smoke) fumer; (: dry) sécher ▷ n remède m

curfew ['kə:fjuː] n couvre-feu m

curiosity [kjuərɪ'ɔsɪtɪ] n curiosité f

curious ['kjuərɪəs] adj curieux(-euse); **I'm ~ about him** il m'intrigue

curl [kə:l] n boucle f (de cheveux) ▷ vt, vi boucler; (tightly) friser; **curl up** vi s'enrouler; (person) se pelotonner; **curler** n bigoudi m, rouleau m; **curly** adj bouclé(e); (tightly curled) frisé(e)

currant ['kʌrnt] n raisin m de Corinthe, raisin sec; (fruit) groseille f

currency ['kʌrnsɪ] n monnaie f; **to gain ~** (fig) s'accréditer

current ['kʌrnt] n courant m ▷ adj (common) courant(e); (tendency, price, event) actuel(le); **current account** n (BRIT) compte courant; **current affairs** npl (questions fpl d')actualité f; **currently** adv actuellement

curriculum (pl **~s** or **curricula**) [kə'rɪkjulə m, -lə] n programme m d'études; **curriculum vitae** [-'viːtaɪ] n curriculum vitae (CV) m

curry ['kʌrɪ] n curry m ▷ vt: **to ~ favour with** chercher à gagner la faveur or à s'attirer les bonnes grâces de; **curry powder** n poudre f de curry

curse [kə:s] vi jurer, blasphémer ▷ vt maudire ▷ n (spell) malédiction f; (problem, scourge) fléau m; (swearword) juron m

cursor ['kə:sə'] n (Comput) curseur m

curt [kə:t] adj brusque, sec(-sèche)

curtain ['kə:tn] n rideau m

curve [kə:v] n courbe f; (in the road) tournant m, virage m ▷ vi se courber; (road) faire une courbe; **curved** adj courbe

cushion ['kuʃən] n coussin m ▷ vt (fall, shock) amortir

custard ['kʌstəd] n (for pouring) crème anglaise

custody ['kʌstədɪ] n (of child) garde f; (for offenders): **to take sb into ~** placer qn en détention préventive

custom ['kʌstəm] n coutume f, usage m; (Comm) clientèle f

customer ['kʌstəmə'] n client(e)

customized ['kʌstəmaɪzd] adj personnalisé(e); (car etc) construit(e) sur commande

customs ['kʌstəmz] npl douane f; **customs officer** n douanier m

cut [kʌt] vb (pt, pp ~) ▷ vt couper; (meat) découper; (reduce) réduire ▷ vi couper ▷ n (gen) coupure f; (of clothes) coupe f; (in salary etc) réduction f; (of meat) morceau m; **to ~ a tooth** percer une dent; **to ~ one's finger** se couper le doigt; **to get one's hair ~** se faire couper les cheveux; **I've ~ myself** je me suis coupé; **cut back** vt (plants) tailler; (production, expenditure) réduire; **cut down** vt (tree) abattre; (reduce) réduire; **cut off** vt couper; (fig) isoler; **cut out** vt (picture etc) découper; (remove) supprimer; **cut up** vt découper; **cutback** n réduction f

cute [kju:t] adj mignon(ne), adorable

cutlery ['kʌtlərɪ] n couverts mpl

cutlet ['kʌtlɪt] n côtelette f

cut-price ['kʌt'praɪs] (us **cut-rate** ['kʌt'reɪt]) adj au rabais, à prix réduit

cutting ['kʌtɪŋ] adj (fig) cinglant(e) ▷ n (BRIT: from newspaper) coupure f (de journal); (from plant) bouture f

CV n abbr = **curriculum vitae**

cwt abbr = **hundredweight(s)**

cyberspace ['saɪbəspeɪs] n cyberespace m

cycle ['saɪkl] n cycle m; (bicycle) bicyclette f, vélo m ▷ vi faire de la bicyclette; **cycle hire** n location f de vélos; **cycle lane, cycle path** n piste f cyclable; **cycling** n cyclisme m; **cyclist** n cycliste m/f

cyclone ['saɪkləun] n cyclone m

cylinder ['sɪlɪndə'] n cylindre m

cymbals ['sɪmblz] npl cymbales fpl

cynical ['sɪnɪkl] adj cynique

Cypriot ['sɪprɪət] adj cypriote, chypriote ▷ n Cypriote m/f, Chypriote m/f

Cyprus ['saɪprəs] n Chypre f

cyst [sɪst] n kyste m; **cystitis** [sɪs'taɪtɪs] n cystite f

czar [zɑ:'] n tsar m

Czech [tʃɛk] adj tchèque ▷ n Tchèque m/f; (Ling) tchèque m; **Czech Republic** n: **the Czech Republic** la République tchèque

d

D [di:] n (Mus): **D** ré m

dab [dæb] vt (eyes, wound) tamponner; (paint, cream) appliquer (par petites touches or rapidement)

dad, daddy [dæd, 'dædɪ] n papa m

daffodil ['dæfədɪl] n jonquille f

daft [dɑ:ft] adj (inf) idiot(e), stupide

dagger ['dægə'] n poignard m

daily ['deɪlɪ] adj quotidien(ne), journalier(-ière) ▷ adv tous les jours

dairy ['dɛərɪ] n (shop) crèmerie f, laiterie f; (on farm) laiterie; **dairy produce** n produits laitiers

daisy ['deɪzɪ] n pâquerette f

dam [dæm] n (wall) barrage m; (water) réservoir m, lac m de retenue ▷ vt endiguer

damage ['dæmɪdʒ] n dégâts mpl, dommages mpl; (fig) tort m ▷ vt endommager, abîmer; (fig) faire du tort à; **damages** npl (Law) dommages-intérêts mpl

damn [dæm] vt condamner; (curse) maudire ▷ n (inf): **I don't give a ~** je m'en fous ▷ adj (inf: also: **~ed**): **this ~ ...** ce sacré or foutu ...; **~ (it)!** zut!

damp [dæmp] adj humide ▷ n humidité f ▷ vt (also: **~en**: cloth, rag) humecter; (: enthusiasm etc) refroidir

dance [dɑ:ns] n danse f; (ball) bal m ▷ vi danser; **dance floor** n piste f de danse; **dancer** n danseur(-euse); **dancing** n danse f

dandelion ['dændɪlaɪən] n pissenlit m
dandruff ['dændrəf] n pellicules fpl
D & T n abbr (BRIT: Scol) = **design and technology**
Dane [deɪn] n Danois(e)
danger ['deɪndʒər] n danger m; ~! (on sign) danger!; **in** ~ en danger; **he was in** ~ **of falling** il risquait de tomber; **dangerous** adj dangereux(-euse)
dangle ['dæŋgl] vt balancer ▷ vi pendre, se balancer
Danish ['deɪnɪʃ] adj danois(e) ▷ n (Ling) danois m
dare [dɛər] vt: **to** ~ **sb to do** défier qn or mettre qn au défi de faire ▷ vi: **to** ~ **(to) do sth** oser faire qch; **I** ~ **say he'll turn up** il est probable qu'il viendra; **daring** adj hardi(e), audacieux(-euse) ▷ n audace f, hardiesse f
dark [dɑːk] adj (night, room) obscur(e), sombre; (colour, complexion) foncé(e), sombre ▷ n: **in the** ~ dans le noir; **to be in the** ~ **about** (fig) ignorer tout de; **after** ~ après la tombée de la nuit; **darken** vt obscurcir, assombrir ▷ vi s'obscurcir, s'assombrir; **darkness** n obscurité f; **darkroom** n chambre noire
darling ['dɑːlɪŋ] adj, n chéri(e)
dart [dɑːt] n fléchette f; (in sewing) pince f ▷ vi: **to** ~ **towards** se précipiter or s'élancer vers; **dartboard** n cible f (de jeu de fléchettes); **darts** n jeu m de fléchettes
dash [dæʃ] n (sign) tiret m; (small quantity) goutte f, larme f (throw) jeter or lancer violemment; (hopes) anéantir ▷ vi: **to** ~ **towards** se précipiter or se ruer vers
dashboard ['dæʃbɔːd] n (Aut) tableau m de bord
data ['deɪtə] npl données fpl; **database** n base f de données; **data processing** n traitement m (électronique) de l'information
date [deɪt] n date f; (with sb) rendez-vous m; (fruit) datte f ▷ vt dater; (person) sortir avec; ~ **of birth** date de naissance; **to** ~ adv à ce jour; **out of** ~ périmé(e); **up to** ~ à la page, mis(e) à jour, moderne; **dated** adj démodé(e)
daughter ['dɔːtər] n fille f; **daughter-in-law** n belle-fille f, bru f
daunting ['dɔːntɪŋ] adj décourageant(e), intimidant(e)
dawn [dɔːn] n aube f, aurore f ▷ vi (day) se lever, poindre; **it** ~**ed on him that ...** il lui vint à l'esprit que ...
day [deɪ] n jour m; (as duration) journée f; (period of time, age) époque f, temps m; **the** ~ **before** la veille, le jour précédent; **the** ~ **after, the following** ~ le lendemain, le jour suivant; **the** ~ **before yesterday** avant-hier; **the** ~ **after tomorrow** après-demain; **by** ~ de jour; **day-care centre** ['deɪkɛə–] n (for elderly etc) centre m d'accueil de jour; (for children) garderie f;

daydream vi rêver (tout éveillé); **daylight** n (lumière f du) jour m; **day return** n (BRIT) billet m d'aller-retour (valable pour la journée); **daytime** n jour m, journée f; **day-to-day** adj (routine, expenses) journalier(-ière); **day trip** n excursion f (d'une journée)
dazed [deɪzd] adj abruti(e)
dazzle ['dæzl] vt éblouir, aveugler; **dazzling** adj (light) aveuglant(e), éblouissant(e); (fig) éblouissant(e)
DC abbr (Elec) = **direct current**
dead [dɛd] adj mort(e); (numb) engourdi(e), insensible; (battery) à plat ▷ adv (completely) absolument, complètement; (exactly) juste; **he was shot** ~ il a été tué d'un coup de revolver; ~ **tired** éreinté(e), complètement fourbu(e); **to stop** ~ s'arrêter pile or net; **the line is** ~ (Tel) la ligne est coupée; **dead end** n impasse f; **deadline** n date for heure f limite; **deadly** adj mortel(le); (weapon) meurtrier(-ière); **Dead Sea** n: **the Dead Sea** la mer Morte
deaf [dɛf] adj sourd(e); **deafen** vt rendre sourd(e); **deafening** adj assourdissant(e)
deal [diːl] n affaire f, marché m ▷ vt (pt, pp ~t) (blow) porter; (cards) donner, distribuer; **a great** ~ **of** beaucoup de; **deal with** vt fus (handle) s'occuper or se charger de; (be about: book etc) traiter de; **dealer** n (Comm) marchand m; (Cards) donneur m; **dealings** npl (in goods, shares) opérations fpl, transactions fpl; (relations) relations fpl, rapports mpl
dealt [dɛlt] pt, pp of **deal**
dean [diːn] n (Rel, BRIT Scol) doyen m; (US Scol) conseiller principal (conseillère principale) d'éducation
dear [dɪər] adj cher (chère); (expensive) cher, coûteux(-euse) ▷ n: **my** ~ mon cher (ma chère) ▷ excl: ~ **me!** mon Dieu!; **D~ Sir/Madam** (in letter) Monsieur/Madame; **D~ Mr/Mrs X** Cher Monsieur X (Chère Madame X); **dearly** adv (love) tendrement; (pay) cher
death [dɛθ] n mort f; (Admin) décès m; **death penalty** n peine f de mort; **death sentence** n condamnation f à mort
debate [dɪˈbeɪt] n discussion f, débat m ▷ vt discuter, débattre
debit ['dɛbɪt] n débit m ▷ vt: **to** ~ **a sum to sb** or **to sb's account** porter une somme au débit de qn, débiter qn d'une somme; **debit card** n carte f de paiement
debris ['dɛbriː] n débris mpl, décombres mpl
debt [dɛt] n dette f; **to be in** ~ avoir des dettes, être endetté(e)
debut ['deɪbjuː] n début(s) m(pl)
Dec. abbr (= December) déc
decade ['dɛkeɪd] n décennie f, décade f
decaffeinated [dɪˈkæfɪneɪtɪd] adj décaféiné(e)
decay [dɪˈkeɪ] n (of building) délabrement m;

(also: **tooth ~**) carie f (dentaire) ▷ vi (rot) se décomposer, pourrir; (: teeth) se carier

deceased [dɪ'si:st] n: **the ~** le (la) défunt(e)

deceit [dɪ'si:t] n tromperie f, supercherie f; **deceive** [dɪ'si:v] vt tromper

December [dɪ'sɛmbə'] n décembre m

decency ['di:sənsɪ] n décence f

decent ['di:sənt] adj (proper) décent(e), convenable

deception [dɪ'sɛpʃən] n tromperie f

deceptive [dɪ'sɛptɪv] adj trompeur(-euse)

decide [dɪ'saɪd] vt (subj: person) décider; (question, argument) trancher, régler ▷ vi se décider, décider; **to ~ to do/that** décider de faire/que; **to ~ on** décider, se décider pour

decimal ['dɛsɪməl] adj décimal(e) ▷ n décimale f

decision [dɪ'sɪʒən] n décision f

decisive [dɪ'saɪsɪv] adj décisif(-ive); (manner, person) décidé(e), catégorique

deck [dɛk] n (Naut) pont m; (of cards) jeu m; (record deck) platine f; (of bus): **top ~** impériale f; **deckchair** n chaise longue

declaration [dɛklə'reɪʃən] n déclaration f

declare [dɪ'klɛə'] vt déclarer

decline [dɪ'klaɪn] n (decay) déclin m; (lessening) baisse f ▷ vt refuser, décliner ▷ vi décliner; (business) baisser

decorate ['dɛkəreɪt] vt (adorn, give a medal to) décorer; (paint and paper) peindre et tapisser; **decoration** [dɛkə'reɪʃən] n (medal etc, adornment) décoration f; **decorator** n peintre m en bâtiment

decrease n ['di:kri:s] diminution f ▷ vt, vi [di:'kri:s] diminuer

decree [dɪ'kri:] n (Pol, Rel) décret m; (Law) arrêt m, jugement m

dedicate ['dɛdɪkeɪt] vt consacrer; (book etc) dédier; **dedicated** adj (person) dévoué(e); (Comput) spécialisé(e), dédié(e); **dedicated word processor** station f de traitement de texte; **dedication** [dɛdɪ'keɪʃən] n (devotion) dévouement m; (in book) dédicace f

deduce [dɪ'dju:s] vt déduire, conclure

deduct [dɪ'dʌkt] vt: **to ~ sth (from)** déduire qch (de), retrancher qch (de); **deduction** [dɪ'dʌkʃən] n (deducting, deducing) déduction f; (from wage etc) prélèvement m, retenue f

deed [di:d] n action f, acte m; (Law) acte notarié, contrat m

deem [di:m] vt (formal) juger, estimer

deep [di:p] adj profond(e); (voice) grave ▷ adv: **spectators stood 20 ~** il y avait 20 rangs de spectateurs; **4 metres ~** de 4 mètres de profondeur; **how ~ is the water?** l'eau à quelle profondeur?; **deep-fry** vt faire frire (dans une friteuse); **deeply** adv profondément; (regret, interested) vivement

deer [dɪə'] n (pl inv) (red) ~ cerf m; (fallow) ~

daim m; **(roe) ~** chevreuil m

default [dɪ'fɔːlt] n (Comput: also: **~ value**) valeur f par défaut; **by ~** (Law) par défaut, par contumace; (Sport) par forfait

defeat [dɪ'fi:t] n défaite f ▷ vt (team, opponents) battre

defect n ['di:fɛkt] défaut m ▷ vi [dɪ'fɛkt]: **to ~ to the enemy/the West** passer à l'ennemi/l'Ouest; **defective** [dɪ'fɛktɪv] adj défectueux(-euse)

defence (us **defense**) [dɪ'fɛns] n défense f

defend [dɪ'fɛnd] vt défendre; **defendant** n défendeur(-deresse); (in criminal case) accusé(e), prévenu(e); **defender** n défenseur m

defense [dɪ'fɛns] (us) = **defence**

defensive [dɪ'fɛnsɪv] adj défensif(-ive) ▷ n: **on the ~** sur la défensive

defer [dɪ'fə'] vt (postpone) différer, ajourner

defiance [dɪ'faɪəns] n défi m; **in ~ of** au mépris de; **defiant** [dɪ'faɪənt] adj provocant(e), de défi; (person) rebelle, intraitable

deficiency [dɪ'fɪʃənsɪ] n (lack) insuffisance f; (: Med) carence f; (flaw) faiblesse f; **deficient** [dɪ'fɪʃənt] adj (inadequate) insuffisant(e); **to be deficient in** manquer de

deficit ['dɛfɪsɪt] n déficit m

define [dɪ'faɪn] vt définir

definite ['dɛfɪnɪt] adj (fixed) défini(e), (bien) déterminé(e); (clear, obvious) net(te), manifeste; (certain) sûr(e); **he was ~ about it** il a été catégorique; **definitely** adv sans aucun doute

definition [dɛfɪ'nɪʃən] n définition f; (clearness) netteté f

deflate [di:'fleɪt] vt dégonfler

deflect [dɪ'flɛkt] vt détourner, faire dévier

defraud [dɪ'frɔːd] vt: **to ~ sb of sth** escroquer qch à qn

defrost [di:'frɔst] vt (fridge) dégivrer; (frozen food) décongeler

defuse [di:'fju:z] vt désamorcer

defy [dɪ'faɪ] vt défier; (efforts etc) résister à; **it defies description** cela défie toute description

degree [dɪ'gri:] n degré m; (Scol) diplôme m (universitaire); **a (first) ~ in maths** (BRIT) une licence en maths; **by ~s** (gradually) par degrés; **to some ~** jusqu'à un certain point, dans une certaine mesure

dehydrated [di:haɪ'dreɪtɪd] adj déshydraté(e); (milk, eggs) en poudre

de-icer ['di:'aɪsə'] n dégivreur m

delay [dɪ'leɪ] vt retarder; (payment) différer ▷ vi s'attarder ▷ n délai m, retard m; **to be ~ed** être en retard

delegate n ['dɛlɪgɪt] délégué(e) ▷ vt ['dɛlɪgeɪt] déléguer

delete [dɪ'li:t] vt rayer, supprimer; (Comput)

effacer

deli ['dɛlɪ] n épicerie fine

deliberate adj [dɪ'lɪbərɪt] (intentional) délibéré(e); (slow) mesuré(e) ▷ vi [dɪ'lɪbəreɪt] délibérer, réfléchir; **deliberately** adv (on purpose) exprès, délibérément

delicacy ['dɛlɪkəsɪ] n délicatesse f; (choice food) mets fin or délicat, friandise f

delicate ['dɛlɪkɪt] adj délicat(e)

delicatessen [dɛlɪkə'tɛsn] n épicerie fine

delicious [dɪ'lɪʃəs] adj délicieux(-euse)

delight [dɪ'laɪt] n (grande) joie, grand plaisir ▷ vt enchanter; **she's a ~ to work with** c'est un plaisir de travailler avec elle; **to take ~ in** prendre grand plaisir à; **delighted** adj: **delighted (at or with sth)** ravi(e) (de qch); **to be delighted to do sth/that** être enchanté(e) or ravi(e) de faire qch/que; **delightful** adj (person) adorable; (meal, evening) merveilleux(-euse)

delinquent [dɪ'lɪŋkwənt] adj, n délinquant(e)

deliver [dɪ'lɪvə⁺] vt (mail) distribuer; (goods) livrer; (message) remettre; (speech) prononcer; (Med: baby) mettre au monde; **delivery** n (of mail) distribution f; (of goods) livraison f; (of speaker) élocution f; (Med) accouchement m; **to take delivery of** prendre livraison de

delusion [dɪ'luːʒən] n illusion f

de luxe [də'lʌks] adj de luxe

delve [dɛlv] vi: **to ~ into** fouiller dans

demand [dɪ'mɑːnd] vt réclamer, exiger ▷ n exigence f; (claim) revendication f; (Econ) demande f; **in ~** demandé(e), recherché(e); **on ~** sur demande; **demanding** adj (person) exigeant(e); (work) astreignant(e)

> Be careful not to translate **to demand** by the French word **demander**.

demise [dɪ'maɪz] n décès m

demo ['dɛməu] n abbr (inf) = demonstration (protest) manif f; (Comput) démonstration f

democracy [dɪ'mɔkrəsɪ] n démocratie f; **democrat** ['dɛməkræt] n démocrate m/f; **democratic** [dɛmə'krætɪk] adj démocratique

demolish [dɪ'mɔlɪʃ] vt démolir

demolition [dɛmə'lɪʃən] n démolition f

demon ['diːmən] n démon m

demonstrate ['dɛmənstreɪt] vt démontrer, prouver; (show) faire une démonstration de ▷ vi: **to ~ (for/against)** manifester (en faveur de/contre); **demonstration** [dɛmən'streɪʃən] n démonstration f; (Pol etc) manifestation f; **demonstrator** n (Pol etc) manifestant(e)

demote [dɪ'məut] vt rétrograder

den [dɛn] n (of lion) tanière f; (room) repaire m

denial [dɪ'naɪəl] n (of accusation) démenti m; (of rights, guilt, truth) dénégation f

denim ['dɛnɪm] n jean m; **denims** npl (blue-)jeans mpl

Denmark ['dɛnmɑːk] n Danemark m

denomination [dɪnɔmɪ'neɪʃən] n (money) valeur f; (Rel) confession f

denounce [dɪ'nauns] vt dénoncer

dense [dɛns] adj dense; (inf: stupid) obtus(e)

density ['dɛnsɪtɪ] n densité f; **single-/double-~ disk** (Comput) disquette f (à) simple/double densité

dent [dɛnt] n bosse f ▷ vt (also: **make a ~ in**) cabosser

dental ['dɛntl] adj dentaire; **dental floss** [-flɔs] n fil m dentaire; **dental surgery** n cabinet m de dentiste

dentist ['dɛntɪst] n dentiste m/f

dentures ['dɛntʃəz] npl dentier msg

deny [dɪ'naɪ] vt nier; (refuse) refuser

deodorant [diː'əudərənt] n déodorant m

depart [dɪ'pɑːt] vi partir; **to ~ from** (fig: differ from) s'écarter de

department [dɪ'pɑːtmənt] n (Comm) rayon m; (Scol) section f; (Pol) ministère m, département m; **department store** n grand magasin

departure [dɪ'pɑːtʃə] n départ m; (fig): **a new ~** une nouvelle voie; **departure lounge** n salle f de départ

depend [dɪ'pɛnd] vi: **to ~ (up)on** dépendre de; (rely on) compter sur; **it ~s** cela dépend; **~ing on the result ...** selon le résultat ...; **dependant** n personne f à charge; **dependent** adj: **to be dependent (on)** dépendre (de) ▷ n = **dependant**

depict [dɪ'pɪkt] vt (in picture) représenter; (in words) (dé)peindre, décrire

deport [dɪ'pɔːt] vt déporter, expulser

deposit [dɪ'pɔzɪt] n (Chem, Comm, Geo) dépôt m; (of ore, oil) gisement m; (part payment) arrhes fpl, acompte m; (on bottle etc) consigne f; (for hired goods etc) cautionnement m, garantie f ▷ vt déposer; **deposit account** n compte m sur livret

depot ['dɛpəu] n dépôt m; (us: Rail) gare f

depreciate [dɪ'priːʃɪeɪt] vi se déprécier, se dévaloriser

depress [dɪ'prɛs] vt déprimer; (press down) appuyer sur, abaisser; (wages etc) faire baisser; **depressed** adj (person) déprimé(e); (area) en déclin, touché(e) par le sous-emploi; **depressing** adj déprimant(e); **depression** [dɪ'prɛʃən] n dépression f

deprive [dɪ'praɪv] vt: **to ~ sb of** priver qn de; **deprived** adj déshérité(e)

dept. abbr (= department) dép, dépt

depth [dɛpθ] n profondeur f; **to be in the ~s of despair** être au plus profond du désespoir; **to be out of one's ~** (brit: swimmer) ne plus avoir pied; (fig) être dépassé(e), nager

deputy ['dɛpjutɪ] n (second in command) adjoint(e); (Pol) député m; (us: also: ~ sheriff) shérif adjoint ▷ adj: **~ head**

255 | **devote**

(Scol) directeur(-trice) adjoint(e), sous-directeur(-trice)

derail [dɪ'reɪl] vt: **to be ~ed** dérailler

derelict ['dɛrɪlɪkt] adj abandonné(e), à l'abandon

derive [dɪ'raɪv] vt: **to ~ sth from** tirer qch de; trouver qch dans ▷ vi: **to ~ from** provenir de, dériver de

descend [dɪ'sɛnd] vt, vi descendre; **to ~ from** descendre de, être issu(e) de; **to ~ to** s'abaisser à; **descendant** n descendant(e); **descent** n descente f; (origin) origine f

describe [dɪs'kraɪb] vt décrire; **description** [dɪs'krɪpʃən] n description f; (sort) sorte f, espèce f

desert n ['dɛzət] désert m ▷ vb [dɪ'zəːt] ▷ vt déserter, abandonner ▷ vi (Mil) déserter; **deserted** [dɪ'zəːtɪd] adj désert(e)

deserve [dɪ'zəːv] vt mériter

design [dɪ'zaɪn] n (sketch) plan m, dessin m; (layout, shape) conception f, ligne f; (pattern) dessin, motif(s) m(pl); (of dress, car) modèle m; (art) design m, stylisme m; (intention) dessein m ▷ vt dessiner; (plan) concevoir; **design and technology** n (BRIT: Scol) technologie f

designate vt ['dɛzɪgneɪt] désigner ▷ adj ['dɛzɪgnɪt] désigné(e)

designer [dɪ'zaɪnəʳ] n (Archit, Art) dessinateur(-trice); (Industry) concepteur m, designer m; (Fashion) styliste m/f

desirable [dɪ'zaɪərəbl] adj (property, location, purchase) attrayant(e)

desire [dɪ'zaɪəʳ] n désir m ▷ vt désirer, vouloir

desk [dɛsk] n (in office) bureau m; (for pupil) pupitre m; (BRIT: in shop, restaurant) caisse f; (in hotel, at airport) réception f; **desk-top publishing** ['dɛsktɔp-] n publication assistée par ordinateur, PAO f

despair [dɪs'pɛəʳ] n désespoir m ▷ vi: **to ~ of** désespérer de

despatch [dɪs'pætʃ] n, vt = **dispatch**

desperate ['dɛspərɪt] adj désespéré(e); (fugitive) prêt(e) à tout; **to be ~ for sth/to do sth** avoir désespérément besoin de qch/de faire qch; **desperately** adv désespérément; (very) terriblement, extrêmement; **desperation** [dɛspə'reɪʃən] n désespoir m; **in (sheer) desperation** en désespoir de cause

despise [dɪs'paɪz] vt mépriser

despite [dɪs'paɪt] prep malgré, en dépit de

dessert [dɪ'zəːt] n dessert m; **dessertspoon** n cuiller f à dessert

destination [dɛstɪ'neɪʃən] n destination f

destined ['dɛstɪnd] adj: **~ for London** à destination de Londres

destiny ['dɛstɪnɪ] n destinée f, destin m

destroy [dɪs'trɔɪ] vt détruire; (injured horse) abattre; (dog) faire piquer

destruction [dɪs'trʌkʃən] n destruction f

destructive [dɪs'trʌktɪv] adj destructeur(-trice)

detach [dɪ'tætʃ] vt détacher; **detached** adj (attitude) détaché(e); **detached house** n pavillon m maison(nette) (individuelle)

detail ['diːteɪl] n détail m ▷ vt raconter en détail, énumérer; **in ~** en détail; **detailed** adj détaillé(e)

detain [dɪ'teɪn] vt retenir; (in captivity) détenir

detect [dɪ'tɛkt] vt déceler, percevoir; (Med, Police) dépister; (Mil, Radar, Tech) détecter; **detection** [dɪ'tɛkʃən] n découverte f; **detective** n policier m; **private detective** détective privé; **detective story** n roman policier

detention [dɪ'tɛnʃən] n détention f; (Scol) retenue f, consigne f

deter [dɪ'təːʳ] vt dissuader

detergent [dɪ'təːdʒənt] n détersif m, détergent m

deteriorate [dɪ'tɪərɪəreɪt] vi se détériorer, se dégrader

determination [dɪtəːmɪ'neɪʃən] n détermination f

determine [dɪ'təːmɪn] vt déterminer; **to ~ to do** résoudre de faire, se déterminer à faire; **determined** adj (person) déterminé(e), décidé(e); **determined to do** bien décidé à faire

deterrent [dɪ'tɛrənt] n effet m de dissuasion; force f de dissuasion

detest [dɪ'tɛst] vt détester, avoir horreur de

detour ['diːtuəʳ] n détour m; (US Aut: diversion) déviation f

detract [dɪ'trækt] vt: **to ~ from** (quality, pleasure) diminuer; (reputation) porter atteinte à

detrimental [dɛtrɪ'mɛntl] adj: **~ to** préjudiciable or nuisible à

devastating ['dɛvəsteɪtɪŋ] adj dévastateur(-trice); (news) accablant(e)

develop [dɪ'vɛləp] vt (gen) développer; (disease) commencer à souffrir de; (resources) mettre en valeur, exploiter; (land) aménager ▷ vi se développer; (situation, disease: evolve) évoluer; (facts, symptoms: appear) se manifester, se produire; **can you ~ this film?** pouvez-vous développer cette pellicule?; **developing country** n pays m en voie de développement; **development** n développement m; (of land) exploitation f; (new fact, event) rebondissement m, fait(s) nouveau(x)

device [dɪ'vaɪs] n (apparatus) appareil m, dispositif m

devil ['dɛvl] n diable m; démon m

devious ['diːvɪəs] adj (person) sournois(e), dissimulé(e)

devise [dɪ'vaɪz] vt imaginer, concevoir

devote [dɪ'vəut] vt: **to ~ sth to** consacrer qch

à; **devoted** adj dévoué(e); **to be devoted to** être dévoué(e) or très attaché(e) à; (book etc) être consacré(e) à; **devotion** n dévouement m, attachement m; (Rel) dévotion f, piété f

devour [dɪ'vauəʳ] vt dévorer

devout [dɪ'vaut] adj pieux(-euse), dévot(e)

dew [dju:] n rosée f

diabetes [daɪə'bi:ti:z] n diabète m

diabetic [daɪə'bɛtɪk] n diabétique m/f ⊳ adj (person) diabétique

diagnose [daɪəg'nəuz] vt diagnostiquer

diagnosis (pl **diagnoses**) [daɪəg'nəusɪs, -si:z] n diagnostic m

diagonal [daɪ'ægənl] adj diagonal(e) ⊳ n diagonale f

diagram ['daɪəgræm] n diagramme m, schéma m

dial ['daɪəl] n cadran m ⊳ vt (number) faire, composer

dialect ['daɪəlɛkt] n dialecte m

dialling code ['daɪəlɪŋ-] (US **dial code**) n indicatif m (téléphonique); **what's the ~ for Paris?** quel est l'indicatif de Paris?

dialling tone ['daɪəlɪŋ-] (US **dial tone**) n tonalité f

dialogue (US **dialog**) ['daɪəlɔg] n dialogue m

diameter [daɪ'æmɪtəʳ] n diamètre m

diamond ['daɪəmənd] n diamant m; (shape) losange m; **diamonds** npl (Cards) carreau m

diaper ['daɪəpəʳ] n (US) couche f

diarrhoea (US **diarrhea**) [daɪə'ri:ə] n diarrhée f

diary ['daɪərɪ] n (daily account) journal m; (book) agenda m

dice [daɪs] n (pl inv) dé m ⊳ vt (Culin) couper en dés or en cubes

dictate [dɪk'teɪt] vt dicter; **dictation** [dɪk'teɪʃən] n dictée f

dictator [dɪk'teɪtəʳ] n dictateur m

dictionary ['dɪkʃənrɪ] n dictionnaire m

did [dɪd] pt of **do**

didn't [dɪdnt] = **did not**

die [daɪ] vi mourir; **to be dying for sth** avoir une envie folle de qch; **to be dying to do sth** mourir d'envie de faire qch; **die down** vi se calmer, s'apaiser; **die out** vi disparaître, s'éteindre

diesel ['di:zl] n (vehicle) diesel m; (also: ~ **oil**) carburant m diesel, gas-oil m

diet ['daɪət] n alimentation f; (restricted food) régime m ⊳ vi (also: **be on a ~**) suivre un régime

differ ['dɪfəʳ] vi: **to ~ from sth** (be different) être différent(e) de qch, différer de qch; **to ~ from sb over sth** ne pas être d'accord avec qn au sujet de qch; **difference** n différence f; (quarrel) différend m, désaccord m; **different** adj différent(e); **differentiate** [dɪfə'rɛnʃɪeɪt] vi: **to differentiate between**

faire une différence entre; **differently** adv différemment

difficult ['dɪfɪkəlt] adj difficile; **difficulty** n difficulté f

dig [dɪg] vt (pt, pp **dug**) (hole) creuser; (garden) bêcher ⊳ n (prod) coup m de coude; (fig: remark) coup de griffe or de patte; (Archaeology) fouille f; **to ~ one's nails into** enfoncer ses ongles dans; **dig up** vt déterrer

digest vt [daɪ'dʒɛst] digérer ⊳ n ['daɪdʒɛst] sommaire m, résumé m; **digestion** [dɪ'dʒɛstʃən] n digestion f

digit ['dɪdʒɪt] n (number) chiffre m (de o à 9); (finger) doigt m; **digital** adj (system, recording, radio) numérique; (watch) à affichage numérique or digital; **digital camera** n appareil m photo numérique; **digital TV** n télévision f numérique

dignified ['dɪgnɪfaɪd] adj digne

dignity ['dɪgnɪtɪ] n dignité f

digs [dɪgz] npl (BRIT inf) piaule f, chambre meublée

dilemma [daɪ'lɛmə] n dilemme m

dill [dɪl] n aneth m

dilute [daɪ'lu:t] vt diluer

dim [dɪm] adj (light, eyesight) faible; (memory, outline) vague, indécis(e); (room) sombre; (inf: stupid) borné(e), obtus(e) ⊳ vt (light) réduire, baisser; (US Aut) mettre en code, baisser

dime [daɪm] n (US) pièce f de 10 cents

dimension [daɪ'mɛnʃən] n dimension f

diminish [dɪ'mɪnɪʃ] vt, vi diminuer

din [dɪn] n vacarme m

dine [daɪn] vi dîner; **diner** n (person) dîneur(-euse); (US: eating place) petit restaurant

dinghy ['dɪŋgɪ] n youyou m; (inflatable) canot m pneumatique; (also: **sailing ~**) voilier m, dériveur m

dingy ['dɪndʒɪ] adj miteux(-euse), minable

dining car ['daɪnɪŋ-] n (BRIT) voiture-restaurant f, wagon-restaurant m

dining room ['daɪnɪŋ-] n salle f à manger

dining table [daɪnɪŋ-] n table f de (la) salle à manger

dinner ['dɪnəʳ] n (evening meal) dîner m; (lunch) déjeuner m; (public) banquet m; **dinner jacket** n smoking m; **dinner party** n dîner m; **dinner time** n (evening) heure f du dîner; (midday) heure du déjeuner

dinosaur ['daɪnəsɔːʳ] n dinosaure m

dip [dɪp] n (slope) déclivité f; (in sea) baignade f, bain m; (Culin) ≈ sauce f ⊳ vt tremper, plonger; (BRIT Aut: lights) mettre en code, baisser ⊳ vi plonger

diploma [dɪ'pləumə] n diplôme m

diplomacy [dɪ'pləuməsɪ] n diplomatie f

diplomat ['dɪpləmæt] n diplomate m; **diplomatic** [dɪplə'mætɪk] adj diplomatique

dipstick ['dɪpstɪk] n (BRIT Aut) jauge f de niveau d'huile

dire [daɪə^r] adj (poverty) extrême; (awful) affreux(-euse)

direct [daɪ'rɛkt] adj direct(e) ▷ vt (tell way) diriger, orienter; (letter, remark) adresser; (Cine, TV) réaliser; (Theat) mettre en scène; (order): **to ~ sb to do sth** ordonner à qn de faire qch ▷ adv directement; **can you ~ me to ...?** pouvez-vous m'indiquer le chemin de ...?; **direct debit** n (BRIT Banking) prélèvement m automatique

direction [dɪ'rɛkʃən] n direction f; **directions** npl (to a place) indications fpl; **~s for use** mode m d'emploi; **sense of ~** sens m de l'orientation

directly [dɪ'rɛktlɪ] adv (in straight line) directement, tout droit; (at once) tout de suite, immédiatement

director [dɪ'rɛktə^r] n directeur m; (Theat) metteur m en scène; (Cine, TV) réalisateur(-trice)

directory [dɪ'rɛktərɪ] n annuaire m; (Comput) répertoire m; **directory enquiries** (US **directory assistance**) n (Tel: service) renseignements mpl

dirt [də:t] n saleté f; (mud) boue f; **dirty** adj sale; (joke) cochon(ne) ▷ vt salir

disability [dɪsə'bɪlɪtɪ] n invalidité f, infirmité f

disabled [dɪs'eɪbld] adj handicapé(e); (maimed) mutilé(e)

disadvantage [dɪsəd'vɑ:ntɪdʒ] n désavantage m, inconvénient m

disagree [dɪsə'gri:] vi (differ) ne pas concorder; (be against, think otherwise): **to ~ (with)** ne pas être d'accord (avec); **disagreeable** adj désagréable; **disagreement** n désaccord m, différend m

disappear [dɪsə'pɪə^r] vi disparaître; **disappearance** n disparition f

disappoint [dɪsə'pɔɪnt] vt décevoir; **disappointed** adj déçu(e); **disappointing** adj décevant(e); **disappointment** n déception f

disapproval [dɪsə'pru:vəl] n désapprobation f

disapprove [dɪsə'pru:v] vi: **to ~ of** désapprouver

disarm [dɪs'ɑ:m] vt désarmer; **disarmament** [dɪs'ɑ:məmənt] n désarmement m

disaster [dɪ'zɑ:stə^r] n catastrophe f, désastre m; **disastrous** adj désastreux(-euse)

disbelief ['dɪsbə'li:f] n incrédulité f

disc [dɪsk] n disque m; (Comput) = **disk**

discard [dɪs'kɑ:d] vt (old things) se débarrasser de; (fig) écarter, renoncer à

discharge vt [dɪs'tʃɑ:dʒ] (duties) s'acquitter de; (waste etc) déverser; décharger; (patient) renvoyer (chez lui); (employee, soldier) congédier, licencier ▷ n [dɪstʃɑ:dʒ] (Elec, Med) émission f; (dismissal) renvoi m; licenciement m

discipline ['dɪsɪplɪn] n discipline f ▷ vt discipliner; (punish) punir

disc jockey n disque-jockey m (DJ)

disclose [dɪs'kləuz] vt révéler, divulguer

disco ['dɪskəu] n abbr discothèque f

discoloured [dɪs'kʌləd] (US **discolored**) adj décoloré(e), jauni(e)

discomfort [dɪs'kʌmfət] n malaise m, gêne f; (lack of comfort) manque m de confort

disconnect [dɪskə'nɛkt] vt (Elec, Radio) débrancher; (gas, water) couper

discontent [dɪskən'tɛnt] n mécontentement m

discontinue [dɪskən'tɪnju:] vt cesser, interrompre; **"~d"** (Comm) "fin de série"

discount n ['dɪskaunt] remise f, rabais m ▷ vt [dɪs'kaunt] (report etc) ne pas tenir compte de

discourage [dɪs'kʌrɪdʒ] vt décourager

discover [dɪs'kʌvə^r] vt découvrir; **discovery** n découverte f

discredit [dɪs'krɛdɪt] vt (idea) mettre en doute; (person) discréditer

discreet [dɪ'skri:t] adj discret(-ète)

discrepancy [dɪ'skrɛpənsɪ] n divergence f, contradiction f

discretion [dɪ'skrɛʃən] n discrétion f; **at the ~ of** à la discrétion de

discriminate [dɪ'skrɪmɪneɪt] vi: **to ~ between** établir une distinction entre, faire la différence entre; **to ~ against** pratiquer une discrimination contre; **discrimination** [dɪskrɪmɪ'neɪʃən] n discrimination f; (judgment) discernement m

discuss [dɪ'skʌs] vt discuter de; (debate) discuter; **discussion** [dɪ'skʌʃən] n discussion f

disease [dɪ'zi:z] n maladie f

disembark [dɪsɪm'bɑ:k] vt, vi débarquer

disgrace [dɪs'greɪs] n honte f; (disfavour) disgrâce f ▷ vt déshonorer, couvrir de honte; **disgraceful** adj scandaleux(-euse), honteux(-euse)

disgruntled [dɪs'grʌntld] adj mécontent(e)

disguise [dɪs'gaɪz] n déguisement m ▷ vt déguiser; **in ~** déguisé(e)

disgust [dɪs'gʌst] n dégoût m, aversion f ▷ vt dégoûter, écœurer

disgusted [dɪs'gʌstɪd] adj dégoûté(e), écœuré(e)

disgusting [dɪs'gʌstɪŋ] adj dégoûtant(e)

dish [dɪʃ] n plat m; **to do** or **wash the ~es** faire la vaisselle; **dishcloth** n (for drying) torchon m; (for washing) lavette f

dishonest [dɪs'ɔnɪst] adj malhonnête

dishtowel [dɪʃ'tauəl] n (US) torchon m (à vaisselle)

dishwasher ['dɪʃwɔʃə^r] n lave-vaisselle m

disillusion [dɪsɪ'lu:ʒən] vt désabuser, désenchanter

disinfectant [dɪsɪn'fɛktənt] n désinfectant m

disintegrate [dɪs'ɪntɪgreɪt] vi se désintégrer

disk [dɪsk] n (Comput) disquette f; **single-/double-sided ~** disquette une face/double face; **disk drive** n lecteur m de disquette; **diskette** n (Comput) disquette f

dislike [dɪsˈlaɪk] n aversion f, antipathie f ▷ vt ne pas aimer

dislocate [ˈdɪsləkeɪt] vt disloquer, déboîter

disloyal [dɪsˈlɔɪəl] adj déloyal(e)

dismal [ˈdɪzml] adj (gloomy) lugubre, maussade; (very bad) lamentable

dismantle [dɪsˈmæntl] vt démonter

dismay [dɪsˈmeɪ] n consternation f ▷ vt consterner

dismiss [dɪsˈmɪs] vt congédier, renvoyer; (idea) écarter; (Law) rejeter; **dismissal** n renvoi m

disobedient [dɪsəˈbiːdɪənt] adj désobéissant(e), indiscipliné(e)

disobey [dɪsəˈbeɪ] vt désobéir à

disorder [dɪsˈɔːdəʳ] n désordre m; (rioting) désordres mpl; (Med) troubles mpl

disorganized [dɪsˈɔːɡənaɪzd] adj désorganisé(e)

disown [dɪsˈəʊn] vt renier

dispatch [dɪsˈpætʃ] vt expédier, envoyer ▷ n envoi m, expédition f; (Mil, Press) dépêche f

dispel [dɪsˈpɛl] vt dissiper, chasser

dispense [dɪsˈpɛns] vt (medicine) préparer (et vendre); **dispense with** vt fus se passer de; **dispenser** n (device) distributeur m

disperse [dɪsˈpəːs] vt disperser ▷ vi se disperser

display [dɪsˈpleɪ] n (of goods) étalage m; affichage m; (Comput: information) visualisation f; (: device) visuel m; (of feeling) manifestation f ▷ vt montrer; (goods) mettre à l'étalage, exposer; (results, departure times) afficher; (pej) faire étalage de

displease [dɪsˈpliːz] vt mécontenter, contrarier

disposable [dɪsˈpəʊzəbl] adj (pack etc) jetable; (income) disponible

disposal [dɪsˈpəʊzl] n (of rubbish) évacuation f, destruction f; (of property etc: by selling) vente f; (: by giving away) cession f; **at one's ~** à sa disposition

dispose [dɪsˈpəʊz] vi: **to ~ of** (unwanted goods) se débarrasser de, se défaire de; (problem) expédier; **disposition** [dɪspəˈzɪʃən] n disposition f; (temperament) naturel m

disproportionate [dɪsprəˈpɔːʃənət] adj disproportionné(e)

dispute [dɪsˈpjuːt] n discussion f; (also: **industrial ~**) conflit m ▷ vt (question) contester; (matter) discuter

disqualify [dɪsˈkwɒlɪfaɪ] vt (Sport) disqualifier; **to ~ sb for sth/from doing** rendre qn inapte à qch/à faire

disregard [dɪsrɪˈɡɑːd] vt ne pas tenir compte de

disrupt [dɪsˈrʌpt] vt (plans, meeting, lesson) perturber, déranger; **disruption** [dɪsˈrʌpʃən] n perturbation f, dérangement m

dissatisfaction [dɪssætɪsˈfækʃən] n mécontentement m, insatisfaction f

dissatisfied [dɪsˈsætɪsfaɪd] adj: **~ (with)** insatisfait(e) (de)

dissect [dɪˈsɛkt] vt disséquer

dissent [dɪˈsɛnt] n dissentiment m, différence f d'opinion

dissertation [dɪsəˈteɪʃən] n (Scol) mémoire m

dissolve [dɪˈzɒlv] vt dissoudre ▷ vi se dissoudre, fondre; **to ~ in(to) tears** fondre en larmes

distance [ˈdɪstns] n distance f; **in the ~** au loin

distant [ˈdɪstnt] adj lointain(e), éloigné(e); (manner) distant(e), froid(e)

distil (us **distill**) [dɪsˈtɪl] vt distiller; **distillery** n distillerie f

distinct [dɪsˈtɪŋkt] adj distinct(e); (clear) marqué(e); **as ~ from** par opposition à; **distinction** [dɪsˈtɪŋkʃən] n distinction f; (in exam) mention f très bien; **distinctive** adj distinctif(-ive)

distinguish [dɪsˈtɪŋɡwɪʃ] vt distinguer; **to ~ o.s.** se distinguer; **distinguished** adj (eminent, refined) distingué(e)

distort [dɪsˈtɔːt] vt déformer

distract [dɪsˈtrækt] vt distraire, déranger; **distracted** adj (not concentrating) distrait(e); (worried) affolé(e); **distraction** [dɪsˈtrækʃən] n distraction f

distraught [dɪsˈtrɔːt] adj éperdu(e)

distress [dɪsˈtrɛs] n détresse f ▷ vt affliger; **distressing** adj douloureux(-euse), pénible

distribute [dɪsˈtrɪbjuːt] vt distribuer; **distribution** [dɪstrɪˈbjuːʃən] n distribution f; **distributor** n (gen: Tech) distributeur m; (Comm) concessionnaire m/f

district [ˈdɪstrɪkt] n (of country) région f; (of town) quartier m; (Admin) district m; **district attorney** n (us) ≈ procureur m de la République

distrust [dɪsˈtrʌst] n méfiance f, doute m ▷ vt se méfier de

disturb [dɪsˈtəːb] vt troubler; (inconvenience) déranger; **disturbance** n dérangement m; (political etc) troubles mpl; **disturbed** adj (worried, upset) agité(e), troublé(e); **to be emotionally disturbed** avoir des problèmes affectifs; **disturbing** adj troublant(e), inquiétant(e)

ditch [dɪtʃ] n fossé m; (for irrigation) rigole f ▷ vt (inf) abandonner; (person) plaquer

ditto [ˈdɪtəʊ] adv idem

dive [daɪv] n plongeon m; (of submarine) plongée f ▷ vi plonger; **to ~ into** (bag etc) plonger la main dans; (place) se précipiter dans; **diver** n plongeur m

diverse [daɪˈvəːs] adj divers(e)

diversion [daɪˈvəːʃən] n (BRIT Aut) déviation f; (distraction, Mil) diversion f

diversity [daɪˈvəːsɪtɪ] n diversité f, variété f

divert [daɪˈvəːt] vt (BRIT: traffic) dévier; (plane) dérouter; (train, river) détourner

divide [dɪˈvaɪd] vt diviser; (separate) séparer ▷ vi se diviser; **divided highway** (US) n route f à quatre voies

divine [dɪˈvaɪn] adj divin(e)

diving [ˈdaɪvɪŋ] n plongée (sous-marine); **diving board** n plongeoir m

division [dɪˈvɪʒən] n division f; (separation) séparation f; (Comm) service m

divorce [dɪˈvɔːs] n divorce m ▷ vt divorcer d'avec; **divorced** adj divorcé(e); **divorcee** [dɪvɔːˈsiː] n divorcé(e)

D.I.Y. adj, n abbr (BRIT) = **do-it-yourself**

dizzy [ˈdɪzɪ] adj: **I feel ~** la tête me tourne, j'ai la tête qui tourne

DJ n abbr = **disc jockey**

DNA n abbr (= deoxyribonucleic acid) ADN m

KEYWORD

do [duː] (pt **did**, pp **done**) n (inf: party etc) soirée f, fête f
▷ vb **1** (in negative constructions) non traduit; **I don't understand** je ne comprends pas
2 (to form questions) non traduit; **didn't you know?** vous ne le saviez pas?; **what do you think?** qu'en pensez-vous?
3 (for emphasis, in polite expressions): **people do make mistakes sometimes** on peut toujours se tromper; **she does seem rather late** je trouve qu'elle est bien en retard; **do sit down/help yourself** asseyez-vous/servez-vous je vous en prie; **do take care!** faites bien attention à vous!
4 (used to avoid repeating vb): **she swims better than I do** elle nage mieux que moi; **do you agree? - yes, I do/no I don't** vous êtes d'accord? - oui/non; **she lives in Glasgow - so do I** elle habite Glasgow - moi aussi; **he didn't like it and neither did we** il n'a pas aimé ça, et nous non plus; **who broke it? - I did** qui l'a cassé? - c'est moi; **he asked me to help him and I did** il m'a demandé de l'aider, et c'est ce que j'ai fait
5 (in question tags): **you like him, don't you?** vous l'aimez bien, n'est-ce pas?; **I don't know him, do I?** je ne crois pas le connaître
▷ vt **1** (gen: carry out, perform etc) faire; (visit: city, museum) faire, visiter; **what are you doing tonight?** qu'est-ce que vous faites ce soir?; **what do you do?** (job) que faites-vous dans la vie?; **what can I do for you?** que puis-je faire pour vous?; **to do the cooking/washing-up** faire la cuisine/la vaisselle; **to do one's teeth/**

hair/nails se brosser les dents/se coiffer/se faire les ongles
2 (Aut etc: distance) faire; (: speed) faire du; **we've done 200 km already** nous avons déjà fait 200 km; **the car was doing 100** la voiture faisait du 100 (à l'heure); **he can do 100 in that car** il peut faire du 100 (à l'heure) dans cette voiture-là
▷ vi **1** (act, behave) faire; **do as I do** faites comme moi
2 (get on, fare) marcher; **the firm is doing well** l'entreprise marche bien; **he's doing well/badly at school** ça marche bien/mal pour lui à l'école; **how do you do?** comment allez-vous?; (on being introduced) enchanté(e)!
3 (suit) aller; **will it do?** est-ce que ça ira?
4 (be sufficient) suffire, aller; **will £10 do?** est-ce que 10 livres suffiront?; **that'll do** ça suffit, ça ira; **that'll do!** (in annoyance) ça va or suffit comme ça!; **to make do (with)** se contenter (de)

do up vt (laces, dress) attacher; (buttons) boutonner; (zip) fermer; (renovate: room) refaire; (: house) remettre à neuf

do with vt fus (need): **I could do with a drink/some help** quelque chose à boire/un peu d'aide ne serait pas de refus; **it could do with a wash** ça ne lui ferait pas de mal d'être lavé; (be connected with): **that has nothing to do with you** cela ne vous concerne pas; **I won't have anything to do with it** je ne veux pas m'en mêler

do without vi s'en passer; **if you're late for tea then you'll do without** si vous êtes en retard pour le dîner il faudra vous en passer ▷ vt fus se passer de; **I can do without a car** je peux me passer de voiture

dock [dɔk] n dock m; (wharf) quai m; (Law) banc m des accusés ▷ vi se mettre à quai; (Space) s'arrimer; **docks** npl (Naut) docks

doctor [ˈdɔktəʳ] n médecin m, docteur m; (PhD etc) docteur ▷ vt (drink) frelater; **call a ~!** appelez un docteur or un médecin!; **Doctor of Philosophy (PhD)** n (degree) doctorat m; (person) titulaire m/f d'un doctorat

document [ˈdɔkjumənt] n document m; **documentary** [dɔkjuˈmɛntərɪ] adj, n documentaire (m); **documentation** [dɔkjumənˈteɪʃən] n documentation f

dodge [dɔdʒ] n truc m; combine f ▷ vt esquiver, éviter

dodgy [ˈdɔdʒɪ] adj (inf: uncertain) douteux(-euse); (: shady) louche

does [dʌz] vb see **do**

doesn't [ˈdʌznt] = **does not**

dog [dɔg] n chien(ne) ▷ vt (follow closely) suivre de près; (fig: memory etc) poursuivre, harceler; **doggy bag** [ˈdɔgɪ-] n petit sac pour emporter *les restes*

do-it-yourself ['du:ɪtjɔː'sɛlf] *n* bricolage *m*

dole [dəʊl] *n* (BRIT: *payment*) allocation *f* de chômage; **on the ~** au chômage

doll [dɒl] *n* poupée *f*

dollar ['dɒləʳ] *n* dollar *m*

dolphin ['dɒlfɪn] *n* dauphin *m*

dome [dəʊm] *n* dôme *m*

domestic [də'mɛstɪk] *adj* (*duty, happiness*) familial(e); (*policy, affairs, flight*) intérieur(e); (*animal*) domestique; **domestic appliance** *n* appareil ménager

dominant ['dɒmɪnənt] *adj* dominant(e)

dominate ['dɒmɪneɪt] *vt* dominer

domino ['dɒmɪnəʊ] (*pl* **~es**) *n* domino *m*; **dominoes** *n* (*game*) dominos *mpl*

donate [də'neɪt] *vt* faire don de, donner; **donation** [də'neɪʃən] *n* donation *f*, don *m*

done [dʌn] *pp* *of* **do**

donkey ['dɒŋkɪ] *n* âne *m*

donor ['dəʊnəʳ] *n* (*of blood etc*) donneur(-euse); (*to charity*) donateur(-trice); **donor card** *n* carte *f* de don d'organes

don't [dəʊnt] = **do not**

donut ['dəʊnʌt] (US) *n* = **doughnut**

doodle ['du:dl] *vi* griffonner, gribouiller

doom [du:m] *n* (*fate*) destin *m* ▷ *vt*: **to be ~ed to failure** être voué(e) à l'échec

door [dɔːʳ] *n* porte *f*; (*Rail, car*) portière *f*; **doorbell** *n* sonnette *f*; **door handle** *n* poignée *f* de porte; (*of car*) poignée de portière; **doorknob** *n* poignée *f* or bouton *m* de porte; **doorstep** *n* pas *m* de (la) porte, seuil *m*; **doorway** *n* (embrasure *f* de) porte *f*

dope [dəʊp] *n* (*inf: drug*) drogue *f*; (: *person*) andouille *f* ▷ *vt* (*horse etc*) doper

dormitory ['dɔːmɪtrɪ] *n* (BRIT) dortoir *m*; (US: *hall of residence*) résidence *f* universitaire

DOS [dɒs] *n abbr* (= *disk operating system*) DOS *m*

dosage ['dəʊsɪdʒ] *n* dose *f*; dosage *m*; (*on label*) posologie *f*

dose [dəʊs] *n* dose *f*

dot [dɒt] *n* point *m*; (*on material*) pois *m* ▷ *vt*: **~ted with** parsemé(e) de; **on the ~** à l'heure tapante; **dotcom** [dɒt'kɒm] *n* point com *m*, pointcom *m*; **dotted line** ['dɒtɪd-] *n* ligne pointillée; **to sign on the dotted line** signer à l'endroit indiqué *or* sur la ligne pointillée

double ['dʌbl] *adj* double ▷ *adv* (*twice*): **to cost ~ (sth)** coûter le double (de qch) or deux fois plus (que qch) ▷ *n* double *m*; (*Cine*) doublure *f* ▷ *vt* doubler; (*fold*) plier en deux ▷ *vi* doubler; **on the ~**, **at the ~** au pas de course; **double back** *vi* (*person*) revenir sur ses pas; **double bass** *n* contrebasse *f*; **double bed** *n* grand lit; **double-check** *vt, vi* revérifier; **double-click** *vi* (*Comput*) double-cliquer; **double-cross** *vt* doubler, trahir; **doubledecker** *n* autobus *m* à impériale; **double glazing** *n* (BRIT) double

vitrage *m*; **double room** *n* chambre *f* pour deux; **doubles** *n* (*Tennis*) double *m*; **double yellow lines** *npl* (BRIT: *Aut*) double bande jaune marquant l'interdiction de stationner

doubt [daʊt] *n* doute *m* ▷ *vt* douter de; **no ~** sans doute; **to ~ that** douter que + *sub*; **doubtful** *adj* douteux(-euse); (*person*) incertain(e); **doubtless** *adv* sans doute, sûrement

dough [dəʊ] *n* pâte *f*; **doughnut** (US **donut**) *n* beignet *m*

dove [dʌv] *n* colombe *f*

Dover ['dəʊvəʳ] *n* Douvres

down [daʊn] *n* (*fluff*) duvet *m* ▷ *adv* en bas, vers le bas; (*on the ground*) par terre ▷ *prep* en bas de; (*along*) le long de ▷ *vt* (*inf: drink*) siffler; **to walk ~ a hill** descendre une colline; **to run ~ the street** descendre la rue en courant; **~ with X!** à bas X!; **down-and-out** *n* (*tramp*) clochard(e); **downfall** *n* chute *f*, ruine *f*; **downhill** *adv*: **to go downhill** descendre; (*business*) péricliter

Downing Street ['daʊnɪŋ-] *n* (BRIT): **10 ~** résidence du Premier ministre

down: **download** *vt* (*Comput*) télécharger; **downright** *adj* (*lie etc*) effronté(e); (*refusal*) catégorique

Down's syndrome [daʊnz-] *n* trisomie *f*

down: **downstairs** *adv* (*on or to ground floor*) au rez-de-chaussée; (*on or to floor below*) à l'étage inférieur; **down-to-earth** *adj* terre à terre *inv*; **downtown** *adv* en ville; **down under** *adv* en Australie *or* Nouvelle Zélande; **downward** ['daʊnwəd] *adj, adv* vers le bas; **downwards** ['daʊnwədz] *adv* vers le bas

doz. *abbr* = **dozen**

doze [dəʊz] *vi* sommeiller

dozen ['dʌzn] *n* douzaine *f*; **a ~ books** une douzaine de livres; **~s of** des centaines de

Dr. *abbr* (= *doctor*) Dr; (*in street names*) = **drive**

drab [dræb] *adj* terne, morne

draft [drɑːft] *n* (*of letter, school work*) brouillon *m*; (*of literary work*) ébauche *f*; (*Comm*) traite *f*; (US: *call-up*) conscription *f* ▷ *vt* faire le brouillon de; (*Mil: send*) détacher; *see also* **draught**

drag [dræg] *vt* traîner; (*river*) draguer ▷ *vi* traîner ▷ *n* (*inf*) casse-pieds *m/f*; (*women's clothing*): **in ~** (en) travesti; **to ~ and drop**

(*Comput*) glisser-poser

dragon ['drægən] n dragon m

dragonfly ['drægənflaɪ] n libellule f

drain [dreɪn] n égout m; (*on resources*) saignée f ▷ vt (*land, marshes*) drainer, assécher; (*vegetables*) égoutter; (*reservoir etc*) vider ▷ vi (*water*) s'écouler; **drainage** n (*system*) système m d'égouts; (*act*) drainage m; **drainpipe** n tuyau m d'écoulement

drama ['drɑːmə] n (*art*) théâtre m, art m dramatique; (*play*) pièce f; (*event*) drame m; **dramatic** [drə'mætɪk] adj (*Theat*) dramatique; (*impressive*) spectaculaire

drank [dræŋk] pt of **drink**

drape [dreɪp] vt draper; **drapes** npl (*US*) rideaux mpl

drastic ['dræstɪk] adj (*measures*) d'urgence, énergique; (*change*) radical(e)

draught (*US* **draft**) [drɑːft] n courant m d'air; **on ~** (*beer*) à la pression; **draught beer** n bière f (à la) pression; **draughts** n (*BRIT: game*) (jeu m de) dames fpl

draw [drɔː] (*vb: pt* **drew**, *pp* **~n**) vt tirer; (*picture*) dessiner; (*attract*) attirer; (*line, circle*) tracer; (*money*) retirer; (*wages*) toucher ▷ vi (*Sport*) faire match nul ▷ n match nul; (*lottery*) loterie f; (*: picking of ticket*) tirage m au sort; **draw out** vi (*lengthen*) s'allonger ▷ vt (*money*) retirer; **draw up** vi (*stop*) s'arrêter ▷ vt (*document*) établir, dresser; (*plan*) formuler, dessiner; (*chair*) approcher; **drawback** n inconvénient m, désavantage m

drawer [drɔːʳ] n tiroir m

drawing ['drɔːɪŋ] n dessin m; **drawing pin** n (*BRIT*) punaise f; **drawing room** n salon m

drawn [drɔːn] pp of **draw**

dread [drɛd] n épouvante f, effroi m ▷ vt redouter, appréhender; **dreadful** adj épouvantable, affreux(-euse)

dream [driːm] n rêve m ▷ vt, vi (*pt, pp* **~ed** or **~t**) rêver; **dreamer** n rêveur(-euse)

dreamt [drɛmt] pt, pp of **dream**

dreary ['drɪərɪ] adj triste; monotone

drench [drɛntʃ] vt tremper

dress [drɛs] n robe f; (*clothing*) habillement m, tenue f ▷ vt habiller; (*wound*) panser ▷ vi: **to get ~ed** s'habiller; **dress up** vi s'habiller; (*in fancy dress*) se déguiser; **dress circle** n (*BRIT*) premier balcon; **dresser** n (*furniture*) vaisselier m; (*: US*) coiffeuse f, commode f; **dressing** n (*Med*) pansement m; (*Culin*) sauce f, assaisonnement m; **dressing gown** n (*BRIT*) robe f de chambre; **dressing room** n (*Theat*) loge f; (*Sport*) vestiaire m; **dressing table** n coiffeuse f; **dressmaker** n couturière f

drew [druː] pt of **draw**

dribble ['drɪbl] vi (*baby*) baver ▷ vt (*ball*) dribbler

dried [draɪd] adj (*fruit, beans*) sec (sèche); (*eggs, milk*) en poudre

drier ['draɪəʳ] n = **dryer**

drift [drɪft] n (*of current etc*) force f, direction f; (*of snow*) rafale f; coulée f; (*: on ground*) congère f; (*general meaning*) sens général ▷ vi (*boat*) aller à la dérive, dériver; (*sand, snow*) s'amonceler, s'entasser

drill [drɪl] n perceuse f; (*bit*) foret m; (*of dentist*) roulette f, fraise f; (*Mil*) exercice m ▷ vt percer; (*troops*) entraîner ▷ vi (*for oil*) faire un or des forage(s)

drink [drɪŋk] n boisson f; (*alcoholic*) verre m ▷ vt, vi (*pt* **drank**, *pp* **drunk**) boire; **to have a ~** boire quelque chose, boire un verre; **a ~ of water** un verre d'eau; **would you like a ~?** tu veux boire quelque chose?; **drink-driving** n conduite f en état d'ivresse; **drinker** n buveur(-euse); **drinking water** n eau f potable

drip [drɪp] n (*drop*) goutte f; (*Med: device*) goutte-à-goutte m inv; (*: liquid*) perfusion f ▷ vi tomber goutte à goutte; (*tap*) goutter

drive [draɪv] n promenade f or trajet m en voiture; (*also*: **~way**) allée f; (*energy*) dynamisme m, énergie f; (*push*) effort (concerté); campagne f; (*Comput: also*: **disk ~**) lecteur m de disquette f ▷ vb (*pt* **drove**, *pp* **~n**) ▷ vt conduire; (*nail*) enfoncer; (*push*) chasser, pousser; (*Tech: motor*) actionner; entraîner ▷ vi (*be at the wheel*) conduire; (*travel by car*) aller en voiture; **left-/right-hand ~** (*Aut*) conduite f à gauche/droite; **to ~ sb mad** rendre qn fou (folle); **drive out** vt (*force out*) chasser; **drive-in** adj, n (*esp US*) drive-in m

driven ['drɪvn] pp of **drive**

driver ['draɪvəʳ] n conducteur(-trice); (*of taxi, bus*) chauffeur m; **driver's license** n (*US*) permis m de conduire

driveway ['draɪvweɪ] n allée f

driving ['draɪvɪŋ] n conduite f; **driving instructor** n moniteur m d'auto-école; **driving lesson** n leçon f de conduite; **driving licence** n (*BRIT*) permis m de conduire; **driving test** n examen m du permis de conduire

drizzle ['drɪzl] n bruine f, crachin m

droop [druːp] vi (*flower*) commencer à se faner; (*shoulders, head*) tomber

drop [drɔp] n (*of liquid*) goutte f; (*fall*) baisse f; (*also*: **parachute ~**) saut m ▷ vt laisser tomber; (*voice, eyes, price*) baisser; (*passenger*) déposer ▷ vi tomber; **drop in** vi (*inf: visit*): **to ~ in (on)** faire un saut (chez), passer (chez); **drop off** vi (*sleep*) s'assoupir ▷ vt (*passenger*) déposer; **drop out** vi (*withdraw*) se retirer; (*student etc*) abandonner, décrocher

drought [draut] n sécheresse f

drove [drəuv] pt of **drive**

drown [draun] vt noyer ▷ vi se noyer

drowsy ['drauzɪ] adj somnolent(e)

drug [drʌg] n médicament m; (narcotic) drogue f ▷ vt droguer; **to be on ~s** se droguer; **drug addict** n toxicomane m/f; **drug dealer** n revendeur(-euse) de drogue; **druggist** n (US) pharmacien(ne)-droguiste; **drugstore** n (US) pharmacie-droguerie f, drugstore m

drum [drʌm] n tambour m; (for oil, petrol) bidon m; **drums** npl (Mus) batterie f; **drummer** n (joueur m de) tambour m

drunk [drʌŋk] pp of **drink** ▷ adj ivre, soûl(e) ▷ n (also: **~ard**) ivrogne m/f; **to get ~** se soûler; **drunken** adj ivre, soûl(e); (rage, stupor) ivrogne, d'ivrogne

dry [draɪ] adj sec (sèche); (day) sans pluie ▷ vt sécher; (clothes) faire sécher ▷ vi sécher; **dry off** vi, vt sécher; **dry up** vi (river, supplies) se tarir; **dry-cleaner's** n teinturerie f; **dry-cleaning** n (process) nettoyage m à sec; **dryer** n (tumble-dryer) sèche-linge m inv; (for hair) sèche-cheveux m inv

DSS n abbr (BRIT) = Department of Social Security

DTP n abbr (= desktop publishing) PAO f

dual ['djuəl] adj double; **dual carriageway** n (BRIT) route f à quatre voies

dubious ['dju:bɪəs] adj hésitant(e), incertain(e); (reputation, company) douteux(-euse)

duck [dʌk] n canard m ▷ vi se baisser vivement, baisser subitement la tête

due [dju:] adj (money, payment) dû (due); (expected) attendu(e); (fitting) qui convient ▷ adv: **~ north** droit vers le nord; **~ to** (because of) en raison de; (caused by) dû à; **the train is ~ at 8 a.m.** le train est attendu à 8 h; **she is ~ back tomorrow** elle doit rentrer demain; **he is ~ £10** on lui doit 10 livres; **to give sb his** or **her ~** être juste envers qn

duel ['djuəl] n duel m

duet [dju:'et] n duo m

dug [dʌg] pt, pp of **dig**

duke [dju:k] n duc m

dull [dʌl] adj (boring) ennuyeux(-euse); (not bright) morne, terne; (sound, pain) sourd(e); (weather, day) gris(e), maussade ▷ vt (pain, grief) atténuer; (mind, senses) engourdir

dumb [dʌm] adj (muet(te); (stupid) bête

dummy ['dʌmɪ] n (tailor's model) mannequin m; (mock-up) factice m, maquette f; (BRIT: for baby) tétine f ▷ adj faux (fausse), factice

dump [dʌmp] n (also: **rubbish ~**) décharge (publique); (inf: place) trou m ▷ vt (put down) déposer; déverser; (get rid of) se débarrasser de; (Comput) lister

dumpling ['dʌmplɪŋ] n boulette f (de pâte)

dune [dju:n] n dune f

dungarees [dʌŋgə'ri:z] npl bleu(s) m(pl); (for child, woman) salopette f

dungeon ['dʌndʒən] n cachot m

duplex ['dju:pleks] n (US: also: **~ apartment**) duplex m

duplicate n ['dju:plɪkət] double m ▷ vt ['dju:plɪkeɪt] faire un double de; (on machine) polycopier; **in ~** en deux exemplaires, en double

durable ['djuərəbl] adj durable; (clothes, metal) résistant(e), solide

duration [djuə'reɪʃən] n durée f

during ['djuərɪŋ] prep pendant, au cours de

dusk [dʌsk] n crépuscule m

dust [dʌst] n poussière f ▷ vt (furniture) essuyer, épousseter; (cake etc) **to ~ with** saupoudrer de; **dustbin** n (BRIT) poubelle f; **duster** n chiffon m; **dustman** n (BRIT: irreg) boueux m, éboueur m; **dustpan** n pelle f à poussière; **dusty** adj poussiéreux(-euse)

Dutch [dʌtʃ] adj hollandais(e), néerlandais(e) ▷ n (Ling) hollandais m, néerlandais m ▷ adv: **to go ~** or **dutch** (inf) partager les frais; **the Dutch** npl les Hollandais, les Néerlandais; **Dutchman** (irreg) n Hollandais m; **Dutchwoman** (irreg) n Hollandaise f

duty ['dju:tɪ] n devoir m; (tax) droit m, taxe f; **on ~** de service; (at night etc) de garde; **off ~** libre, pas de service or de garde; **duty-free** adj exempté(e) de douane, hors-taxe

duvet ['du:veɪ] n (BRIT) couette f

DVD n abbr (= digital versatile or video disc) DVD m; **DVD burner** n graveur m de DVD; **DVD player** n lecteur m de DVD; **DVD writer** n graveur m de DVD

dwarf (pl **dwarves**) [dwɔ:f, dwɔ:vz] n nain(e) ▷ vt écraser

dwell (pt, pp **dwelt**) [dwel, dwelt] vi demeurer; **dwell on** vt fus s'étendre sur

dwelt [dwelt] pt, pp of **dwell**

dwindle ['dwɪndl] vi diminuer, décroître

dye [daɪ] n teinture f ▷ vt teindre

dying ['daɪɪŋ] adj mourant(e), agonisant(e)

dynamic [daɪ'næmɪk] adj dynamique

dynamite ['daɪnəmaɪt] n dynamite f

dyslexia [dɪs'leksɪə] n dyslexie f

dyslexic [dɪs'leksɪk] adj, n dyslexique m/f

e

E [iː] n (Mus): **E** mi m

E111 n abbr (= form E111) formulaire m E111

each [iːtʃ] adj chaque ▷ pron chacun(e); ~ **other** l'un l'autre; **they hate ~ other** ils se détestent (mutuellement); **they have 2 books ~** ils ont 2 livres chacun; **they cost £5 ~** ils coûtent 5 livres (la) pièce

eager ['iːgər] adj (person, buyer) empressé(e); (keen: pupil, worker) enthousiaste; **to be ~ to do sth** (impatient) brûler de faire qch; (keen) désirer vivement faire qch; **to be ~ for** (event) désirer vivement; (vengeance, affection, information) être avide de

eagle ['iːgl] n aigle m

ear [ɪər] n oreille f; (of corn) épi m; **earache** n mal m aux oreilles; **eardrum** n tympan m

earl [əːl] n comte m

earlier ['əːlɪər] adj (date etc) plus rapproché(e); (edition etc) plus ancien(ne), antérieur(e) ▷ adv plus tôt

early ['əːlɪ] adv tôt, de bonne heure; (ahead of time) en avance; (near the beginning) au début ▷ adj précoce, qui se manifeste (or se fait) tôt or de bonne heure; (Christians, settlers) premier(-ière); (reply) rapide; (death) prématuré(e); (work) de jeunesse; **to have an ~ night/start** se coucher/partir tôt or de bonne heure; **in the ~** or **~ in the spring/19th century** au début or commencement du printemps/19ème siècle; **early retirement** n retraite anticipée

earmark ['ɪəmɑːk] vt: **to ~ sth for** réserver or destiner qch à

earn [əːn] vt gagner; (Comm: yield) rapporter; **to ~ one's living** gagner sa vie

earnest ['əːnɪst] adj sérieux(-euse) ▷ n: **in ~** adv sérieusement, pour de bon

earnings ['əːnɪŋz] npl salaire m; gains mpl; (of company etc) profits mpl, bénéfices mpl

ear: earphones npl écouteurs mpl; **earplugs** npl boules fpl Quiès®; (to keep out water) protège-tympans mpl; **earring** n boucle f d'oreille

earth [əːθ] n (gen, also BRIT Elec) terre f ▷ vt (BRIT Elec) relier à la terre; **earthquake** n tremblement m de terre, séisme m

ease [iːz] n facilité f, aisance f; (comfort) bien-être m ▷ vt (soothe: mind) tranquilliser; (reduce: pain, problem) atténuer; (: tension) réduire; (loosen) relâcher, détendre; (help pass): **to ~ sth in/out** faire pénétrer/sortir qch délicatement or avec douceur, faciliter la pénétration/la sortie de qch; **at ~** à l'aise; (Mil) au repos

easily ['iːzɪlɪ] adv facilement; (by far) de loin

east [iːst] n est m ▷ adj (wind) d'est; (side) est inv ▷ adv à l'est, vers l'est; **the E~** l'Orient m; (Pol) les pays mpl de l'Est; **eastbound** adj en direction de l'est; (carriageway) est inv

Easter ['iːstər] n Pâques fpl; **Easter egg** n œuf m de Pâques

eastern ['iːstən] adj de l'est, oriental(e)

Easter Sunday n le dimanche de Pâques

easy ['iːzɪ] adj facile; (manner) aisé(e) ▷ adv: **to take it** or **things ~** (rest) ne pas se fatiguer; (not worry) ne pas (trop) s'en faire; **easy-going** adj accommodant(e), facile à vivre

eat (pt **ate**, pp **~en**) [iːt, eɪt, 'iːtn] vt, vi manger; **can we have something to ~?** est-ce qu'on peut manger quelque chose?; **eat out** vi manger au restaurant

eavesdrop ['iːvzdrɔp] vi: **to ~ (on)** écouter de façon indiscrète

e-book ['iːbuk] n livre m électronique

e-business ['iːbɪznɪs] n (company) entreprise f électronique; (commerce) commerce m électronique

EC n abbr (= European Community) CE f

eccentric [ɪk'sɛntrɪk] adj, n excentrique m/f

echo, echoes ['ɛkəu] n écho m ▷ vt répéter ▷ vi résonner; faire écho

eclipse [ɪ'klɪps] n éclipse f

eco-friendly [iːkəu'frɛndlɪ] adj non nuisible à or qui ne nuit pas à l'environnement

ecological [iːkə'lɔdʒɪkəl] adj écologique

ecology [ɪ'kɔlədʒɪ] n écologie f

e-commerce [iːkɔmə:s] n commerce m électronique

economic [iːkə'nɔmɪk] adj économique; (profitable) rentable; **economical** adj

économique; (*person*) économe; **economics** n
(*Scol*) économie f politique ▷ npl (*of project etc*)
côté m or aspect m économique

economist [ɪˈkɒnəmɪst] n économiste m/f

economize [ɪˈkɒnəmaɪz] vi économiser, faire
des économies

economy [ɪˈkɒnəmɪ] n économie f; **economy
class** n (*Aviat*) classe f touriste; **economy
class syndrome** n syndrome m de la classe
économique

ecstasy [ˈɛkstəsɪ] n extase f; (*Drugs*) ecstasy m;
ecstatic [ɛksˈtætɪk] adj extatique, en extase

eczema [ˈɛksɪmə] n eczéma m

edge [ɛdʒ] n bord m; (*of knife etc*) tranchant m,
fil m ▷ vt border; **on ~** (*fig*) crispé(e), tendu(e)

edgy [ˈɛdʒɪ] adj crispé(e), tendu(e)

edible [ˈɛdɪbl] adj comestible; (*meal*)
mangeable

Edinburgh [ˈɛdɪnbərə] n Édimbourg

● **EDINBURGH FESTIVAL**
●
● Le Festival d'Édimbourg, qui se tient chaque
● année durant trois semaines au mois d'août,
● est l'un des grands festivals européens. Il
● est réputé pour son programme officiel
● mais aussi pour son festival "off" (the
● Fringe) qui propose des spectacles aussi
● bien traditionnels que résolument d'avant-
● garde. Pendant la durée du Festival se tient
● par ailleurs, sur l'esplanade du château, un
● grand spectacle de musique militaire, le
● "Military Tattoo".

edit [ˈɛdɪt] vt (*text, book*) éditer; (*report*)
préparer; (*film*) monter; (*magazine*)
diriger; (*newspaper*) être le rédacteur or
la rédactrice en chef de; **edition** [ɪˈdɪʃə
n] n édition f; **editor** n (*of newspaper*)
rédacteur(-trice), rédacteur(-trice) en chef;
(*of sb's work*) éditeur(-trice); (*also*: **film editor**)
monteur(-euse); **political/foreign editor**
rédacteur politique/au service étranger;
editorial [ɛdɪˈtɔːrɪəl] adj de la rédaction,
éditorial(e) ▷ n éditorial m

educate [ˈɛdjukeɪt] vt (*teach*) instruire; (*bring
up*) éduquer; **educated** [ˈɛdjukeɪtɪd] adj
(*person*) cultivé(e)

education [ɛdjuˈkeɪʃən] n éducation f;
(*studies*) études fpl; (*teaching*) enseignement m,
instruction f; **educational** adj pédagogique;
(*institution*) scolaire; (*game, toy*) éducatif(-ive)

eel [iːl] n anguille f

eerie [ˈɪərɪ] adj inquiétant(e), spectral(e),
surnaturel(le)

effect [ɪˈfɛkt] n effet m ▷ vt effectuer; **effects**
npl (*property*) effets, affaires fpl; **to take ~**
(*Law*) entrer en vigueur, prendre effet; (*drug*)
agir, faire son effet; **in ~** en fait; **effective** adj

efficace; (*actual*) véritable; **effectively** adv
efficacement; (*in reality*) effectivement, en fait

efficiency [ɪˈfɪʃənsɪ] n efficacité f; (*of machine,
car*) rendement m

efficient [ɪˈfɪʃənt] adj efficace; (*machine,
car*) d'un bon rendement; **efficiently** adv
efficacement

effort [ˈɛfət] n effort m; **effortless** adj sans
effort, aisé(e); (*achievement*) facile

e.g. adv abbr (= *exempli gratia*) par exemple,
p. ex.

egg [ɛg] n œuf m; **hard-boiled/soft-boiled
~** œuf dur/à la coque; **eggcup** n coquetier m;
egg plant n (*US*) aubergine f; **eggshell** n
coquille f d'œuf; **egg white** n blanc m d'œuf;
egg yolk n jaune m d'œuf

ego [ˈiːgəu] n (*self-esteem*) amour-propre m;
(*Psych*) moi m

Egypt [ˈiːdʒɪpt] n Égypte f; **Egyptian**
[ɪˈdʒɪpʃən] adj égyptien(ne) ▷ n Égyptien(ne)

Eiffel Tower [ˈaɪfəl-] n tour f Eiffel

eight [eɪt] num huit; **eighteen** num dix-huit;
eighteenth num dix-huitième; **eighth** num
huitième; **eightieth** [ˈeɪtɪɪθ] num quatre-
vingtième

eighty [ˈeɪtɪ] num quatre-vingt(s)

Eire [ˈɛərə] n République f d'Irlande

either [ˈaɪðər] adj l'un ou l'autre; (*both, each*)
chaque ▷ pron: **~ (of them)** l'un ou l'autre
▷ adv non plus ▷ conj: **~ good or bad** soit
bon soit mauvais; **on ~ side** de chaque côté;
I don't like ~ je n'aime ni l'un ni l'autre; **no, I
don't ~** moi non plus; **which bike do you
want? - ~ will do** quel vélo voulez-vous?
- n'importe lequel; **answer with ~ yes or no**
répondez par oui ou par non

eject [ɪˈdʒɛkt] vt (*tenant etc*) expulser; (*object*)
éjecter

elaborate adj [ɪˈlæbərɪt] compliqué(e),
recherché(e), minutieux(-euse) ▷ vb
[ɪˈlæbəreɪt] ▷ vt élaborer ▷ vi entrer dans les
détails

elastic [ɪˈlæstɪk] adj, n élastique (m); **elastic
band** n (*BRIT*) élastique m

elbow [ˈɛlbəu] n coude m

elder [ˈɛldər] adj aîné(e) ▷ n (*tree*) sureau m;
one's ~s ses aînés; **elderly** adj âgé(e) ▷ npl:
the elderly les personnes âgées

eldest [ˈɛldɪst] adj, n: **the ~ (child)** l'aîné(e)
(des enfants)

elect [ɪˈlɛkt] vt élire; (*choose*): **to ~ to do** choisir
de faire ▷ adj: **the president ~** le président
désigné; **election** n élection f; **electoral** adj
électoral(e); **electorate** n électorat m

electric [ɪˈlɛktrɪk] adj électrique; **electrical**
adj électrique; **electric blanket** n couverture
chauffante; **electric fire** n (*BRIT*) radiateur
m électrique; **electrician** [ɪlɛkˈtrɪʃən] n
électricien m; **electricity** [ɪlɛkˈtrɪsɪtɪ] n

électricité f; **electric shock** n choc m or décharge f électrique; **electrify** [ɪˈlɛktrɪfaɪ] vt (Rail) électrifier; (audience) électriser

electronic [ɪlɛkˈtrɒnɪk] adj électronique; **electronic mail** n courrier m électronique; **electronics** n électronique f

elegance [ˈɛlɪɡəns] n élégance f

elegant [ˈɛlɪɡənt] adj élégant(e)

element [ˈɛlɪmənt] n (gen) élément m; (of heater, kettle etc) résistance f

elementary [ɛlɪˈmɛntərɪ] adj élémentaire; (school, education) primaire; **elementary school** n (US) école f primaire

elephant [ˈɛlɪfənt] n éléphant m

elevate [ˈɛlɪveɪt] vt élever

elevator [ˈɛlɪveɪtəʳ] n (in warehouse etc) élévateur m, monte-charge m inv; (US: lift) ascenseur m

eleven [ɪˈlɛvn] num onze; **eleventh** num onzième

eligible [ˈɛlɪdʒəbl] adj éligible; (for membership) admissible; **an ~ young man** un beau parti; **to be ~ for sth** remplir les conditions requises pour qch

eliminate [ɪˈlɪmɪneɪt] vt éliminer

elm [ɛlm] n orme m

eloquent [ˈɛləkwənt] adj éloquent(e)

else [ɛls] adv: **something ~** quelque chose d'autre, autre chose; **somewhere ~** ailleurs, autre part; **everywhere ~** partout ailleurs; **everyone ~** tous les autres; **nothing ~** rien d'autre; **where ~?** à quel autre endroit; **little ~** pas grand-chose d'autre; **elsewhere** adv ailleurs, autre part

elusive [ɪˈluːsɪv] adj insaisissable

e-mail [ˈiːmeɪl] n abbr (= electronic mail) e-mail m, courriel m ▷ vt: **to ~ sb** envoyer un e-mail or un courriel à qn; **e-mail address** n adresse f e-mail

embankment [ɪmˈbæŋkmənt] n (of road, railway) remblai m, talus m; (of river) berge f, quai m; (dyke) digue f

embargo, embargoes [ɪmˈbɑːɡəʊ] n (Comm, Naut) embargo m; (prohibition) interdiction f

embark [ɪmˈbɑːk] vi embarquer ▷ vt embarquer; **to ~ on** (journey etc) commencer, entreprendre; (fig) se lancer or s'embarquer dans

embarrass [ɪmˈbærəs] vt embarrasser, gêner; **embarrassed** adj gêné(e); **embarrassing** adj gênant(e), embarrassant(e); **embarrassment** n embarras m, gêne f; (embarrassing thing, person) source f d'embarras

embassy [ˈɛmbəsɪ] n ambassade f

embrace [ɪmˈbreɪs] vt embrasser, étreindre; (include) embrasser ▷ vi s'embrasser, s'étreindre ▷ n étreinte f

embroider [ɪmˈbrɔɪdəʳ] vt broder;

embroidery n broderie f

embryo [ˈɛmbrɪəʊ] n (also fig) embryon m

emerald [ˈɛmərəld] n émeraude f

emerge [ɪˈmɜːdʒ] vi apparaître; (from room, car) surgir; (from sleep, imprisonment) sortir

emergency [ɪˈmɜːdʒənsɪ] n (crisis) cas m d'urgence; (Med) urgence f; **in an ~** en cas d'urgence; **state of ~** état m d'urgence; **emergency brake** (US) n frein m à main; **emergency exit** n sortie f de secours; **emergency landing** n atterrissage forcé; **emergency room** n (US: Med) urgences fpl; **emergency services** npl: **the emergency services** (fire, police, ambulance) les services mpl d'urgence

emigrate [ˈɛmɪɡreɪt] vi émigrer; **emigration** [ɛmɪˈɡreɪʃən] n émigration f

eminent [ˈɛmɪnənt] adj éminent(e)

emissions [ɪˈmɪʃənz] npl émissions fpl

emit [ɪˈmɪt] vt émettre

emotion [ɪˈməʊʃən] n sentiment m; **emotional** adj (person) émotif(-ive), très sensible; (needs) affectif(-ive); (scene) émouvant(e); (tone, speech) qui fait appel aux sentiments

emperor [ˈɛmpərəʳ] n empereur m

emphasis (pl **-ases**) [ˈɛmfəsɪs, -siːz] n accent m; **to lay** or **place ~ on sth** (fig) mettre l'accent sur, insister sur

emphasize [ˈɛmfəsaɪz] vt (syllable, word, point) appuyer or insister sur; (feature) souligner, accentuer

empire [ˈɛmpaɪəʳ] n empire m

employ [ɪmˈplɔɪ] vt employer; **employee** [ɪmplɔɪˈiː] n employé(e); **employer** n employeur(-euse); **employment** n emploi m; **employment agency** n agence f or bureau m de placement

empower [ɪmˈpaʊəʳ] vt: **to ~ sb to do** autoriser or habiliter qn à faire

empress [ˈɛmprɪs] n impératrice f

emptiness [ˈɛmptɪnɪs] n vide m; (of area) aspect m désertique

empty [ˈɛmptɪ] adj vide; (street, area) désert(e); (threat, promise) en l'air, vain(e) ▷ vt vider ▷ vi se vider; (liquid) s'écouler; **empty-handed** adj les mains vides

EMU n abbr (= European Monetary Union) UME f

emulsion [ɪˈmʌlʃən] n émulsion f; (also: ~ paint) peinture mate

enable [ɪˈneɪbl] vt: **to ~ sb to do** permettre à qn de faire

enamel [ɪˈnæməl] n émail m; (also: ~ paint) (peinture f) laque f

enchanting [ɪnˈtʃɑːntɪŋ] adj ravissant(e), enchanteur(-eresse)

encl. abbr (on letters etc: = enclosed) ci-joint(e); (= enclosure) PJ f

enclose [ɪnˈkləʊz] vt (land) clôturer; (space, object) entourer; (letter etc) to ~ (with) joindre (à); **please find ~d** veuillez trouver ci-joint

enclosure [ɪnˈkləʊʒəʳ] n enceinte f

encore [ɔŋˈkɔːʳ] excl, n bis (m)

encounter [ɪnˈkaʊntəʳ] n rencontre f ▷ vt rencontrer

encourage [ɪnˈkʌrɪdʒ] vt encourager; **encouragement** n encouragement m

encouraging [ɪnˈkʌrɪdʒɪŋ] adj encourageant(e)

encyclop(a)edia [ɛnsaɪkləʊˈpiːdɪə] n encyclopédie f

end [ɛnd] n fin f; (of table, street, rope etc) bout m, extrémité f ▷ vt terminer; (also: **bring to an ~, put an ~ to**) mettre fin à ▷ vi se terminer, finir; **in the ~** finalement; **on ~** (object) debout, dressé(e); **to stand on ~** (hair) se dresser sur la tête; **for hours on ~** pendant des heures (et des heures); **end up** vi: **to ~ up in** (condition) finir or se terminer par; (place) finir or aboutir à

endanger [ɪnˈdeɪndʒəʳ] vt mettre en danger; **an ~ed species** une espèce en voie de disparition

endearing [ɪnˈdɪərɪŋ] adj attachant(e)

endeavour (US **endeavor**) [ɪnˈdɛvəʳ] n effort m; (attempt) tentative f ▷ vt: **to ~ to do** tenter or s'efforcer de faire

ending [ˈɛndɪŋ] n dénouement m, conclusion f; (Ling) terminaison f

endless [ˈɛndlɪs] adj sans fin, interminable

endorse [ɪnˈdɔːs] vt (cheque) endosser; (approve) appuyer, approuver, sanctionner; **endorsement** n (approval) appui m, aval m; (BRIT: on driving licence) contravention f (portée au permis de conduire)

endurance [ɪnˈdjʊərəns] n endurance f

endure [ɪnˈdjʊəʳ] vt (bear) supporter, endurer ▷ vi (last) durer

enemy [ˈɛnəmɪ] adj, n ennemi(e)

energetic [ɛnəˈdʒɛtɪk] adj énergique; (activity) très actif(-ive), qui fait se dépenser (physiquement)

energy [ˈɛnədʒɪ] n énergie f

enforce [ɪnˈfɔːs] vt (law) appliquer, faire respecter

engaged [ɪnˈɡeɪdʒd] adj (BRIT: busy, in use) occupé(e); (betrothed) fiancé(e); **to get ~** se fiancer; **the line's ~** la ligne est occupée; **engaged tone** n (BRIT Tel) tonalité f occupé inv

engagement [ɪnˈɡeɪdʒmənt] n (undertaking) obligation f, engagement m; (appointment) rendez-vous m inv; (to marry) fiançailles fpl; **engagement ring** n bague f de fiançailles

engaging [ɪnˈɡeɪdʒɪŋ] adj engageant(e), attirant(e)

engine [ˈɛndʒɪn] n (Aut) moteur m; (Rail) locomotive f

> Be careful not to translate **engine** by the French word **engin**.

engineer [ɛndʒɪˈnɪəʳ] n ingénieur m; (BRIT: repairer) dépanneur m; (Navy, US Rail) mécanicien m; **engineering** n engineering m, ingénierie f; (of bridges, ships) génie m; (of machine) mécanique f

England [ˈɪŋɡlənd] n Angleterre f

English [ˈɪŋɡlɪʃ] adj anglais(e) ▷ n (Ling) anglais m; **the ~** npl les Anglais; **English Channel** n: **the English Channel** la Manche; **Englishman** (irreg) n Anglais m; **Englishwoman** (irreg) n Anglaise f

engrave [ɪnˈɡreɪv] vt graver

engraving [ɪnˈɡreɪvɪŋ] n gravure f

enhance [ɪnˈhɑːns] vt rehausser, mettre en valeur

enjoy [ɪnˈdʒɔɪ] vt aimer, prendre plaisir à; (have benefit of: health, fortune) jouir de; (: success) connaître; **to ~ o.s.** s'amuser; **enjoyable** adj agréable; **enjoyment** n plaisir m

enlarge [ɪnˈlɑːdʒ] vt accroître; (Phot) agrandir ▷ vi: **to ~ on** (subject) s'étendre sur; **enlargement** n (Phot) agrandissement m

enlist [ɪnˈlɪst] vt recruter; (support) s'assurer ▷ vi s'engager

enormous [ɪˈnɔːməs] adj énorme

enough [ɪˈnʌf] adj: **~ time/books** assez or suffisamment de temps/livres ▷ adv: **big ~** assez or suffisamment grand ▷ pron: **have you got ~?** (en) avez-vous assez?; **~ to eat** assez à manger; **that's ~, thanks** cela suffit or c'est assez, merci; **I've had ~ of him** j'en ai assez de lui; **he has not worked ~** il n'a pas assez or suffisamment travaillé, il n'a pas travaillé assez or suffisamment; **... which, funnily or oddly ~ ...** qui, chose curieuse

enquire [ɪnˈkwaɪəʳ] vt, vi = **inquire**

enquiry [ɪnˈkwaɪərɪ] n = **inquiry**

enrage [ɪnˈreɪdʒ] vt mettre en fureur or en rage, rendre furieux(-euse)

enrich [ɪnˈrɪtʃ] vt enrichir

enrol (US **enroll**) [ɪnˈrəʊl] vt inscrire ▷ vi s'inscrire; **enrolment** (US **enrollment**) n inscription f

en route [ɔnˈruːt] adv en route, en chemin

en suite [ˈɒnswiːt] adj: **with ~ bathroom** avec salle de bains en attenante

ensure [ɪnˈʃʊəʳ] vt assurer, garantir

entail [ɪnˈteɪl] vt entraîner, nécessiter

enter [ˈɛntəʳ] vt (room) entrer dans, pénétrer dans; (club, army) entrer à; (competition) s'inscrire à or pour; (sb for a competition) (faire) inscrire; (write down) inscrire, noter; (Comput) entrer, introduire ▷ vi entrer

enterprise [ˈɛntəpraɪz] n (company, undertaking) entreprise f; (initiative) (esprit

m d')initiative *f*; **free ~** libre entreprise;
private ~ entreprise privée; **enterprising**
adj entreprenant(e), dynamique; (*scheme*)
audacieux(-euse)

entertain [ɛntəˈteɪn] *vt* amuser, distraire;
(*invite*) recevoir (à dîner); (*idea, plan*) envisager;
entertainer *n* artiste *m/f* de variétés;
entertaining *adj* amusant(e), distrayant(e);
entertainment *n* (*amusement*) distraction
f, divertissement *m*, amusement *m*; (*show*)
spectacle *m*

enthusiasm [ɪnˈθuːzɪæzəm] *n*
enthousiasme *m*

enthusiast [ɪnˈθuːzɪæst] *n* enthousiaste
m/f; **enthusiastic** [ɪnθuːzɪˈæstɪk] *adj*
enthousiaste; **to be enthusiastic about** être
enthousiasmé(e) par

entire [ɪnˈtaɪə*] *adj* (tout) entier(-ère);
entirely *adv* entièrement, complètement

entitle [ɪnˈtaɪtl] *vt*: **to ~ sb to sth** donner droit
à qch à qn; **entitled** *adj* (*book*) intitulé(e); **to
be entitled to do** avoir le droit de faire

entrance *n* [ˈɛntrns] entrée *f* ▷ *vt* [ɪnˈtrɑː
ns] enchanter, ravir; **where's the ~?** où est
l'entrée?; **to gain ~ to** (*university etc*) être
admis à; **entrance examination** *n* examen
m d'entrée or d'admission; **entrance fee** *n* (*to
museum etc*) prix *m* d'entrée; (*to join club etc*)
droit *m* d'inscription; **entrance ramp** *n* (*us
Aut*) bretelle *f* d'accès; **entrant** *n* (*in race etc*)
participant(e), concurrent(e); (*BRIT: in exam*)
candidat(e)

entrepreneur [ˈɔntrəprəˈnəː*] *n*
entrepreneur *m*

entrust [ɪnˈtrʌst] *vt*: **to ~ sth to** confier qch à

entry [ˈɛntrɪ] *n* entrée *f*; (*in register, diary*)
inscription *f*; **"no ~"** "défense d'entrer",
"entrée interdite"; (*Aut*) "sens interdit"; **entry
phone** *n* (*BRIT*) interphone *m* (*à l'entrée d'un
immeuble*)

envelope [ˈɛnvələup] *n* enveloppe *f*

envious [ˈɛnvɪəs] *adj* envieux(-euse)

environment [ɪnˈvaɪərnmənt] *n* (*social,
moral*) milieu *m*; (*natural world*): **the ~**
l'environnement *m*; **environmental** [ɪnvaɪə
rnˈmɛntl] *adj* (*of surroundings*) du milieu;
(*issue, disaster*) écologique; **environmentally**
[ɪnvaɪərnˈmɛntlɪ] *adv*: **environmentally
sound/friendly** qui ne nuit pas à
l'environnement

envisage [ɪnˈvɪzɪdʒ] *vt* (*foresee*) prévoir

envoy [ˈɛnvɔɪ] *n* envoyé(e); (*diplomat*) ministre
m plénipotentiaire

envy [ˈɛnvɪ] *n* envie *f* ▷ *vt* envier; **to ~ sb sth**
envier qch à qn

epic [ˈɛpɪk] *n* épopée *f* ▷ *adj* épique

epidemic [ɛpɪˈdɛmɪk] *n* épidémie *f*

epilepsy [ˈɛpɪlɛpsɪ] *n* épilepsie *f*; **epileptic**
adj, n épileptique *m/f*; **epileptic fit** *n* crise *f*
d'épilepsie

episode [ˈɛpɪsəud] *n* épisode *m*

equal [ˈiːkwl] *adj* égal(e) ▷ *vt* égaler; **~ to**
(*task*) à la hauteur de; **equality** [iːˈkwɔlɪtɪ]
n égalité *f*; **equalize** *vt, vi* (*Sport*) égaliser;
equally *adv* également; (*share*) en parts
égales; (*treat*) de la même façon; (*pay*) autant;
(*just as*) tout aussi

equation [ɪˈkweɪʃən] *n* (*Math*) équation *f*

equator [ɪˈkweɪtə*] *n* équateur *m*

equip [ɪˈkwɪp] *vt* équiper; **to ~ sb/sth with**
équiper or munir qn/qch de; **equipment** *n*
équipement *m*; (*electrical etc*) appareillage *m*,
installation *f*

equivalent [ɪˈkwɪvəlnt] *adj* équivalent(e)
▷ *n* équivalent *m*; **to be ~ to** équivaloir à, être
équivalent(e) à

ER *abbr* (*BRIT*: = *Elizabeth Regina*) la reine
Élisabeth; (*US: Med*: = *emergency room*)
urgences *fpl*

era [ˈɪərə] *n* ère *f*, époque *f*

erase [ɪˈreɪz] *vt* effacer; **eraser** *n* gomme *f*

erect [ɪˈrɛkt] *adj* droit(e) ▷ *vt* construire;
(*monument*) ériger, élever; (*tent etc*) dresser;
erection [ɪˈrɛkʃən] *n* (*Physiol*) érection *f*; (*of
building*) construction *f*

ERM *n abbr* (= *Exchange Rate Mechanism*)
mécanisme *m* des taux de change

erode [ɪˈrəud] *vt* éroder; (*metal*) ronger

erosion [ɪˈrəuʒən] *n* érosion *f*

erotic [ɪˈrɔtɪk] *adj* érotique

errand [ˈɛrnd] *n* course *f*, commission *f*

erratic [ɪˈrætɪk] *adj* irrégulier(-ière),
inconstant(e)

error [ˈɛrə*] *n* erreur *f*

erupt [ɪˈrʌpt] *vi* entrer en éruption; (*fig*)
éclater; **eruption** [ɪˈrʌpʃən] *n* éruption *f*; (*of
anger, violence*) explosion *f*

escalate [ˈɛskəleɪt] *vi* s'intensifier; (*costs*)
monter en flèche

escalator [ˈɛskəleɪtə*] *n* escalier roulant

escape [ɪˈskeɪp] *n* évasion *f*, fuite *f*; (*of gas etc*)
fuite ▷ *vi* s'échapper, fuir; (*from jail*) s'évader;
(*fig*) s'en tirer; (*leak*) s'échapper ▷ *vt* échapper
à; **to ~ from** (*person*) échapper à; (*place*)
s'échapper de; (*fig*) fuir; **his name ~s me** son
nom m'échappe

escort *vt* [ɪˈskɔːt] escorter ▷ *n* [ˈɛskɔːt] (*Mil*)
escorte *f*

especially [ɪˈspɛʃlɪ] *adv* (*particularly*)
particulièrement; (*above all*) surtout

espionage [ˈɛspɪənɑːʒ] *n* espionnage *m*

essay [ˈɛseɪ] *n* (*Scol*) dissertation *f*; (*Literature*)
essai *m*

essence [ˈɛsns] *n* essence *f*; (*Culin*) extrait *m*

essential [ɪˈsɛnʃl] *adj* essentiel(le); (*basic*)
fondamental(e); **essentials** *npl* éléments
essentiels; **essentially** *adv* essentiellement

establish [ɪˈstæblɪʃ] *vt* établir; (*business*)

fonder, créer; (*one's power etc*) asseoir, affirmer;
establishment n établissement m; (*founding*)
création f; (*institution*) établissement; **the
Establishment** les pouvoirs établis; l'ordre
établi

estate [ɪ'steɪt] n (*land*) domaine m, propriété
f; (*Law*) biens mpl, succession f; (BRIT: *also*:
housing ~) lotissement m; **estate agent** n
(BRIT) agent immobilier; **estate car** n (BRIT)
break m

estimate n ['estɪmət] estimation f; (*Comm*)
devis m ▷ vb ['estɪmeɪt] ▷ vt estimer

etc abbr (= *et cetera*) etc

eternal [ɪ'təːnl] adj éternel(le)

eternity [ɪ'təːnɪtɪ] n éternité f

ethical ['eθɪkl] adj moral(e); **ethics** ['eθɪks] n
éthique f ▷ npl moralité f

Ethiopia [iːθɪ'əʊpɪə] n Éthiopie f

ethnic ['eθnɪk] adj ethnique; (*clothes, food*)
folklorique, exotique, *propre aux minorités
ethniques non-occidentales*; **ethnic minority** n
minorité f ethnique

e-ticket ['iːtɪkɪt] n billet m électronique

etiquette ['etɪket] n convenances fpl,
étiquette f

EU n abbr (= *European Union*) UE f

euro ['jʊərəʊ] n (*currency*) euro m

Europe ['jʊərəp] n Europe f; **European** [jʊə
rə'piːən] adj européen(ne) ▷ n Européen(ne);
European Community n Communauté
européenne; **European Union** n Union
européenne

Eurostar® ['jʊərəʊstɑːʳ] n Eurostar® m

evacuate [ɪ'vækjueɪt] vt évacuer

evade [ɪ'veɪd] vt échapper à; (*question etc*)
éluder; (*duties*) se dérober à

evaluate [ɪ'væljueɪt] vt évaluer

evaporate [ɪ'væpəreɪt] vi s'évaporer; (*fig:
hopes, fear*) s'envoler; (*anger*) se dissiper

eve [iːv] n: **on the ~ of** à la veille de

even ['iːvn] adj (*level, smooth*) régulier(-ière);
(*equal*) égal(e); (*number*) pair(e) ▷ adv même; ~
if même si + *indic*; ~ **though** alors même que +
cond; ~ **more** encore plus; ~ **faster** encore plus
vite; ~ **so** quand même; **not** ~ pas même; ~ **he
was there** même lui était là; ~ **on Sundays**
même le dimanche; **to get ~ with sb** prendre
sa revanche sur qn

evening ['iːvnɪŋ] n soir m; (*as duration, event*)
soirée f; **in the ~** le soir; **evening class** n
cours m du soir; **evening dress** n (*man's*)
tenue f de soirée, smoking m; (*woman's*) robe
f de soirée

event [ɪ'vent] n événement m; (*Sport*)
épreuve f; **in the ~ of** en cas de; **eventful** adj
mouvementé(e)

eventual [ɪ'ventʃuəl] adj final(e)

■ Be careful not to translate **eventual** by
the French word *éventuel*.

eventually [ɪ'ventʃuəlɪ] adv finalement

■ Be careful not to translate **eventually** by
the French word *éventuellement*.

ever ['evəʳ] adv jamais; (*at all times*) toujours;
(*in questions*): **why ~ not?** mais enfin, pourquoi
pas?; **the best ~** le meilleur qu'on ait jamais vu;
have you ~ seen it? l'as-tu déjà vu?, as-tu eu
l'occasion or t'est-il arrivé de le voir?; ~ **since**
(*as adv*) depuis; (*as conj*) depuis que; ~ **so
pretty** si joli; **evergreen** n arbre m à feuilles
persistantes

 KEYWORD

every ['evrɪ] adj **1** (*each*) chaque; **every one of
them** tous (sans exception); **every shop in
town was closed** tous les magasins en ville
étaient fermés
2 (*all possible*) tous (toutes) les; **I gave you
every assistance** j'ai fait tout mon possible
pour vous aider; **I have every confidence in
him** j'ai entièrement or pleinement confiance
en lui; **we wish you every success** nous vous
souhaitons beaucoup de succès
3 (*showing recurrence*) tous les; **every day** tous
les jours, chaque jour; **every other car** une
voiture sur deux; **every other/third day** tous
les deux/trois jours; **every now and then**
de temps en temps; **everybody = everyone;
everyday** adj (*expression*) courant(e), d'usage
courant; (*use*) courant; (*clothes, life*) de tous
les jours; (*occurrence, problem*) quotidien(ne);
everyone pron tout le monde, tous pl;
everything pron tout; **everywhere** adv
partout; **everywhere you go you meet ...** où
qu'on aille, on rencontre ...

evict [ɪ'vɪkt] vt expulser

evidence ['evɪdns] n (*proof*) preuve(s) f(pl); (*of
witness*) témoignage m; (*sign*): **to show ~ of**
donner des signes de; **to give ~** témoigner,
déposer

evident ['evɪdnt] adj évident(e); **evidently**
adv de toute évidence; (*apparently*)
apparemment

evil ['iːvl] adj mauvais(e) ▷ n mal m

evoke [ɪ'vəʊk] vt évoquer

evolution [iːvə'luːʃən] n évolution f

evolve [ɪ'vɒlv] vt élaborer ▷ vi évoluer, se
transformer

ewe [juː] n brebis f

ex [eks] n (*inf*) **my ex** mon ex

ex- [eks] prefix ex-

exact [ɪg'zækt] adj exact(e) ▷ vt: **to ~ sth
(from)** (*signature, confession*) extorquer qch
(à); (*apology*) exiger qch (de); **exactly** adv
exactement

exaggerate [ɪg'zædʒəreɪt] vt, vi exagérer;
exaggeration [ɪgzædʒə'reɪʃən] n

exagération f

exam [ɪgˈzæm] n abbr (Scol) = **examination**

examination [ɪgzæmɪˈneɪʃən] n (Scol, Med) examen m; **to take** or **sit an ~** (BRIT) passer un examen

examine [ɪgˈzæmɪn] vt (gen) examiner; (Scol, Law: person) interroger; **examiner** n examinateur(-trice)

example [ɪgˈzɑːmpl] n exemple m; **for ~** par exemple

exasperated [ɪgˈzɑːspəreɪtɪd] adj exaspéré(e)

excavate [ˈɛkskəveɪt] vt (site) fouiller, excaver; (object) mettre au jour

exceed [ɪkˈsiːd] vt dépasser; (one's powers) outrepasser; **exceedingly** adv extrêmement

excel [ɪkˈsɛl] vi exceller ▷ vt surpasser; **to ~ o.s.** se surpasser

excellence [ˈɛksələns] n excellence f

excellent [ˈɛksələnt] adj excellent(e)

except [ɪkˈsɛpt] prep (also: **~ for, ~ing**) sauf, excepté, à l'exception de ▷ vt excepter; **~ if/when** sauf si/quand; **~ that** excepté que, si ce n'est que; **exception** [ɪkˈsɛpʃən] n exception f; **to take exception to** s'offusquer de; **exceptional** [ɪkˈsɛpʃənl] adj exceptionnel(le); **exceptionally** [ɪkˈsɛpʃənəlɪ] adv exceptionnellement

excerpt [ˈɛksəpt] n extrait m

excess [ɪkˈsɛs] n excès m; **excess baggage** n excédent m de bagages; **excessive** adj excessif(-ive)

exchange [ɪksˈtʃeɪndʒ] n échange m; (also: **telephone ~**) central m ▷ vt: **to ~ (for)** échanger (contre); **could I ~ this, please?** est-ce que je peux échanger ceci, s'il vous plaît?; **exchange rate** n taux m de change

excite [ɪkˈsaɪt] vt exciter; **excited** adj (tout (toute)) excité(e); **to get excited** s'exciter; **excitement** n excitation f; **exciting** adj passionnant(e)

exclaim [ɪkˈskleɪm] vi s'exclamer; **exclamation** [ɛkskləˈmeɪʃən] n exclamation f; **exclamation mark** (us **exclamation point**) n point m d'exclamation

exclude [ɪkˈskluːd] vt exclure

excluding [ɪkˈskluːdɪŋ] prep: **~ VAT** la TVA non comprise

exclusion [ɪkˈskluːʒən] n exclusion f

exclusive [ɪkˈskluːsɪv] adj exclusif(-ive); (club, district) sélect(e); (item of news) en exclusivité; **~ of VAT** TVA non comprise; **exclusively** adv exclusivement

excruciating [ɪkˈskruːʃɪeɪtɪŋ] adj (pain) atroce, déchirant(e); (embarrassing) pénible

excursion [ɪkˈskəːʃən] n excursion f

excuse n [ɪkˈskjuːs] excuse f ▷ vt [ɪkˈskjuːz] (forgive) excuser; **to ~ sb from** (activity) dispenser qn de; **~ me!** excusez-moi!, pardon!;

now if you will **~ me, ...** maintenant, si vous (le) permettez ...

ex-directory [ˈɛksdɪˈrɛktərɪ] adj (BRIT) sur la liste rouge

execute [ˈɛksɪkjuːt] vt exécuter; **execution** [ɛksɪˈkjuːʃən] n exécution f

executive [ɪgˈzɛkjutɪv] n (person) cadre m; (managing group) bureau m; (Pol) exécutif m ▷ adj exécutif(-ive); (position, job) de cadre

exempt [ɪgˈzɛmpt] adj: **~ from** exempté(e) or dispensé(e) de ▷ vt: **to ~ sb from** exempter or dispenser qn de

exercise [ˈɛksəsaɪz] n exercice m ▷ vt exercer; (patience etc) faire preuve de; (dog) promener ▷ vi (also: **to take ~**) prendre de l'exercice; **exercise book** n cahier m

exert [ɪgˈzəːt] vt exercer, employer; **to ~ o.s.** se dépenser; **exertion** [ɪgˈzəːʃən] n effort m

exhale [ɛksˈheɪl] vt exhaler ▷ vi expirer

exhaust [ɪgˈzɔːst] n (also: **~ fumes**) gaz mpl d'échappement; (also: **~ pipe**) tuyau m d'échappement ▷ vt épuiser; **exhausted** adj épuisé(e); **exhaustion** [ɪgˈzɔːstʃən] n épuisement m; **nervous exhaustion** fatigue nerveuse

exhibit [ɪgˈzɪbɪt] n (Art) pièce f or objet m exposé(e); (Law) pièce à conviction ▷ vt (Art) exposer; (courage, skill) faire preuve de; **exhibition** [ɛksɪˈbɪʃən] n exposition f

exhilarating [ɪgˈzɪləreɪtɪŋ] adj grisant(e), stimulant(e)

exile [ˈɛksaɪl] n exil m; (person) exilé(e) ▷ vt exiler

exist [ɪgˈzɪst] vi exister; **existence** n existence f; **existing** adj actuel(le)

exit [ˈɛksɪt] n sortie f ▷ vi (Comput, Theat) sortir; **where's the ~?** où est la sortie?; **exit ramp** n (us Aut) bretelle f d'accès

exotic [ɪgˈzɔtɪk] adj exotique

expand [ɪkˈspænd] vt (area) agrandir; (quantity) accroître ▷ vi (trade, etc) se développer, s'accroître; (gas, metal) se dilater

expansion [ɪkˈspænʃən] n (territorial, economic) expansion f; (of trade, influence etc) développement m; (of production) accroissement m; (of population) croissance f; (of gas, metal) expansion, dilatation f

expect [ɪkˈspɛkt] vt (anticipate) s'attendre à, s'attendre à ce que + sub; (count on) compter sur, escompter; (require) demander, exiger; (suppose) supposer; (await: also baby) attendre ▷ vi: **to be ~ing** (pregnant woman) être enceinte; **expectation** [ɛkspɛkˈteɪʃən] n (hope) attente f, espérance(s) f(pl); (belief) attente

expedition [ɛkspəˈdɪʃən] n expédition f

expel [ɪkˈspɛl] vt chasser, expulser; (Scol) renvoyer, exclure

expenditure [ɪkˈspɛndɪtʃəʳ] n (act of spending)

dépense f; (*money spent*) dépenses fpl
expense [ɪk'spɛns] n (*high cost*) coût m;
(*spending*) dépense f, frais mpl; **expenses**
npl frais mpl; dépenses; **at the ~ of** (fig) aux
dépens de; **expense account** n (note f de)
frais mpl
expensive [ɪk'spɛnsɪv] adj cher (chère),
coûteux(-euse); **it's too ~** ça coûte trop cher
experience [ɪk'spɪərɪəns] n expérience f ▷ vt
connaître; (*feeling*) éprouver; **experienced** adj
expérimenté(e)
experiment [ɪk'spɛrɪmənt] n expérience
f ▷ vi faire une expérience; **experimental**
[ɪkspɛrɪ'mɛntl] adj expérimental(e)
expert ['ɛkspəːt] adj expert(e) ▷ n expert m;
expertise [ɛkspəː'tiːz] n (grande)
compétence
expire [ɪk'spaɪə'] vi expirer; **expiry** n
expiration f; **expiry date** n date f d'expiration;
(*on label*) à utiliser avant ...
explain [ɪk'spleɪn] vt expliquer; **explanation**
[ɛksplə'neɪʃən] n explication f
explicit [ɪk'splɪsɪt] adj explicite; (*definite*)
formel(le)
explode [ɪk'spləud] vi exploser
exploit n ['ɛksplɔɪt] exploit m ▷ vt [ɪk'splɔɪt]
exploiter; **exploitation** [ɛksplɔɪ'teɪʃən] n
exploitation f
explore [ɪk'splɔː'] vt explorer; (*possibilities*)
étudier, examiner; **explorer** n
explorateur(-trice)
explosion [ɪk'spləuʒən] n explosion f;
explosive [ɪk'spləusɪv] adj explosif(-ive) ▷ n
explosif m
export vt [ɛk'spɔːt] exporter ▷ n ['ɛkspɔːt]
exportation f ▷ cpd d'exportation; **exporter** n
exportateur m
expose [ɪk'spəuz] vt exposer; (*unmask*)
démasquer, dévoiler; **exposed** adj (*land*,
house) exposé(e); **exposure** [ɪk'spəuʒə'] n
exposition f; (*publicity*) couverture f; (*Phot*:
speed) (temps m de) pose f; (: *shot*) pose; **to die
of exposure** (*Med*) mourir de froid
express [ɪk'sprɛs] adj (*definite*) formel(le),
exprès(-esse); (BRIT: *letter etc*) exprès inv ▷ n
(*train*) rapide m ▷ vt exprimer; **expression**
[ɪk'sprɛʃən] n expression f; **expressway** n
(US) voie f express (à plusieurs files)
exquisite [ɛk'skwɪzɪt] adj exquis(e)
extend [ɪk'stɛnd] vt (*visit*, *street*) prolonger,
remettre; (*building*) agrandir; (*offer*) présenter,
offrir; (*hand*, *arm*) tendre ▷ vi (*land*) s'étendre;
extension n (*of visit*, *street*) prolongation
f; (*building*) annexe f; (*telephone*: *in offices*)
poste m; (: *in private house*) téléphone m
supplémentaire; **extension cable**, **extension
lead** n (*Elec*) rallonge f; **extensive** adj
étendu(e), vaste; (*damage*, *alterations*)
considérable; (*inquiries*) approfondi(e)

extent [ɪk'stɛnt] n étendue f; **to some ~** dans
une certaine mesure; **to the ~ of ...** au point
de ...; **to what ~?** dans quelle mesure?, jusqu'à
quel point?; **to such an ~ that ...** à tel point
que ...
exterior [ɛk'stɪərɪə'] adj extérieur(e) ▷ n
extérieur m
external [ɛk'stəːnl] adj externe
extinct [ɪk'stɪŋkt] adj (*volcano*) éteint(e);
(*species*) disparu(e); **extinction** n extinction f
extinguish [ɪk'stɪŋgwɪʃ] vt éteindre
extra ['ɛkstrə] adj supplémentaire, de plus
▷ adv (*in addition*) en plus ▷ n supplément m;
(*perk*) à-coté m; (*Cine*, *Theat*) figurant(e)
extract vt [ɪk'strækt] extraire; (*tooth*)
arracher; (*money*, *promise*) soutirer ▷ n
['ɛkstrækt] extrait m
extradite ['ɛkstrədaɪt] vt extrader
extraordinary [ɪk'strɔːdnrɪ] adj
extraordinaire
extravagance [ɪk'strævəgəns] n (*excessive
spending*) prodigalités fpl; (*thing bought*)
folie f, dépense excessive; **extravagant** adj
extravagant(e); (*in spending*: *person*) prodigue,
dépensier(-ière); (: *tastes*) dispendieux(-euse)
extreme [ɪk'striːm] adj, n extrême (m);
extremely adv extrêmement
extremist [ɪk'striːmɪst] adj, n extrémiste m/f
extrovert ['ɛkstrəvəːt] n extraverti(e)
eye [aɪ] n œil m ((yeux) pl); (*of needle*) trou
m, chas m ▷ vt examiner; **to keep an ~ on**
surveiller; **eyeball** n globe m oculaire;
eyebrow n sourcil m; **eyedrops** npl
gouttes fpl pour les yeux; **eyelash** n cil m;
eyelid n paupière f; **eyeliner** n eye-liner m;
eyeshadow n ombre f à paupières; **eyesight**
n vue f; **eye witness** n témoin m oculaire

F [ɛf] n (Mus): **F** fa m

fabric ['fæbrɪk] n tissu m

fabulous ['fæbjuləs] adj fabuleux(-euse); (inf: super) formidable, sensationnel(le)

face [feɪs] n visage m, figure f; (expression) air m; (of clock) cadran m; (of cliff) paroi f; (of mountain) face f; (of building) façade f ▷ vt faire face à; (facts etc) accepter; **~ down** (person) à plat ventre; (card) face en dessous; **to lose/save ~** perdre/sauver la face; **to pull a ~** faire une grimace; **in the ~ of** (difficulties etc) face à, devant; **on the ~ of it** à première vue; **~ to ~** face à face; **face up to** vt fus faire face à, affronter; **face cloth** n (BRIT) gant m de toilette; **face pack** n (BRIT) masque m (de beauté)

facial ['feɪʃl] adj facial(e) ▷ n soin complet du visage

facilitate [fə'sɪlɪteɪt] vt faciliter

facilities [fə'sɪlɪtɪz] npl installations fpl, équipement m; **credit ~** facilités de paiement

fact [fækt] n fait m; **in ~** en fait

faction ['fækʃən] n faction f

factor ['fæktə'] n facteur m; (of sun cream) indice m (de protection); **I'd like a ~ 15 suntan lotion** je voudrais une crème solaire d'indice 15

factory ['fæktərɪ] n usine f, fabrique f

factual ['fæktjuəl] adj basé(e) sur les faits

faculty ['fækəltɪ] n faculté f; (US: teaching staff) corps enseignant

fad [fæd] n (personal) manie f; (craze) engouement m

fade [feɪd] vi se décolorer, passer; (light, sound) s'affaiblir; (flower) se faner; **fade away** vi (sound) s'affaiblir

fag [fæg] n (BRIT inf: cigarette) clope f

Fahrenheit ['fɑːrənhaɪt] n Fahrenheit m inv

fail [feɪl] vt (exam) échouer à; (candidate) recaler; (subj: courage, memory) faire défaut à ▷ vi échouer; (eyesight, health, light: also: be **~ing**) baisser, s'affaiblir; (brakes) lâcher; **to ~ to do sth** (neglect) négliger de or ne pas faire qch; (be unable) ne pas arriver or parvenir à faire qch; **without ~** à coup sûr; sans faute; **failing** n défaut m ▷ prep faute de; **failing that** à défaut, sinon; **failure** ['feɪljə'] n échec m; (person) raté(e); (mechanical etc) défaillance f

faint [feɪnt] adj faible; (recollection) vague; (mark) à peine visible ▷ n évanouissement m ▷ vi s'évanouir; **to feel ~** défaillir; **faintest** adj: **I haven't the faintest idea** je n'en ai pas la moindre idée; **faintly** adv faiblement; (vaguely) vaguement

fair [fɛə'] adj équitable, juste; (hair) blond(e); (skin, complexion) pâle, blanc (blanche); (weather) beau (belle); (good enough) assez bon(ne); (sizeable) considérable ▷ adv: **to play ~** jouer franc jeu ▷ n foire f; (BRIT: funfair) fête (foraine); **fairground** n champ m de foire; **fair-haired** adj (person) aux cheveux clairs, blond(e); **fairly** adv (justly) équitablement; (quite) assez; **fair trade** n commerce m équitable; **fairway** n (Golf) fairway m

fairy ['fɛərɪ] n fée f; **fairy tale** n conte m de fées

faith [feɪθ] n foi f; (trust) confiance f; (sect) culte m, religion f; **faithful** adj fidèle; **faithfully** adv fidèlement; **yours faithfully** (BRIT: in letters) veuillez agréer l'expression de mes salutations les plus distinguées

fake [feɪk] n (painting etc) faux m; (person) imposteur m ▷ adj faux (fausse) ▷ vt (emotions) simuler; (painting) faire un faux de

falcon ['fɔːlkən] n faucon m

fall [fɔːl] n chute f; (decrease) baisse f; (US: autumn) automne m ▷ vi (pt fell, pp **~en**) tomber; (price, temperature, dollar) baisser; **falls** npl (waterfall) chute f d'eau, cascade f; **to ~ flat** vi (on one's face) tomber de tout son long, s'étaler; (joke) tomber à plat; (plan) échouer; **fall apart** vi (object) tomber en morceaux; **fall down** vi (person) tomber; (building) s'effondrer, s'écrouler; **fall for** vt fus (trick) se laisser prendre à; (person) tomber amoureux(-euse) de; **fall off** vi tomber; (diminish) baisser, diminuer; **fall out** vi (friends etc) se brouiller; (hair, teeth) tomber; **fall over** vi tomber (par terre); **fall through** vi (plan, project) tomber à l'eau

fallen ['fɔːlən] pp of **fall**

fallout ['fɔːlaut] n retombées (radioactives)

false [fɔːls] adj faux (fausse); **under ~ pretences** sous un faux prétexte; **false alarm** n fausse alerte; **false teeth** npl (BRIT) fausses dents, dentier m

fame [feɪm] n renommée f, renom m

familiar [fə'mɪlɪə'] adj familier(-ière); **to be ~ with sth** connaître qch; **familiarize** [fə'mɪlɪəraɪz] vt: **to familiarize o.s. with** se familiariser avec

family ['fæmɪlɪ] n famille f; **family doctor** n médecin m de famille; **family planning** n planning familial

famine ['fæmɪn] n famine f

famous ['feɪməs] adj célèbre

fan [fæn] n (folding) fantaisie f, envie f; (Elec) ventilateur m; (person) fan m, admirateur(-trice); (Sport) supporter m/f ▷ vt éventer; (fire, quarrel) attiser

fanatic [fə'nætɪk] n fanatique m/f

fan belt n courroie f de ventilateur

fan club n fan-club m

fancy ['fænsɪ] n (whim) fantaisie f, envie f; (imagination) imagination f ▷ adj (luxury) de luxe; (elaborate: jewellery, packaging) fantaisie inv ▷ vt (feel like, want) avoir envie de; (imagine) imaginer; **to take a ~ to** se prendre d'affection pour; s'enticher de; **he fancies her** elle lui plaît; **fancy dress** n déguisement m, travesti m

fan heater n (BRIT) radiateur soufflant

fantasize ['fæntəsaɪz] vi fantasmer

fantastic [fæn'tæstɪk] adj fantastique

fantasy ['fæntəsɪ] n imagination f, fantaisie f; (unreality) fantasme m

fanzine ['fænziːn] n fanzine m

FAQ n abbr (= frequently asked question) FAQ f inv, faq f inv

far [fɑː'] adj (distant) lointain(e), éloigné(e) ▷ adv loin; **the ~ side/end** l'autre côté/bout; **it's not ~ (from here)** ce n'est pas loin (d'ici); **~ away, ~ off** au loin, dans le lointain; **~ better** beaucoup mieux; **~ from** loin de; **by ~** de loin, de beaucoup; **go as ~ as the bridge** allez jusqu'au pont; **as ~ as I know** pour autant que je sache; **how ~ is it to ...?** combien y a-t-il jusqu'à ...?; **how ~ have you got with your work?** où en êtes-vous dans votre travail?

farce [fɑːs] n farce f

fare [fɛə'] n (on trains, buses) prix m du billet; (in taxi) prix de la course; (food) table f, chère f; **half ~** demi-tarif; **full ~** plein tarif

Far East n: **the ~** l'Extrême-Orient m

farewell [fɛə'wɛl] excl, n adieu m

farm [fɑːm] n ferme f ▷ vt cultiver; **farmer** n fermier(-ière); **farmhouse** n (maison f de) ferme f; **farming** n agriculture f; (of animals) élevage m; **farmyard** n cour f de ferme

far-reaching ['fɑː'riːtʃɪŋ] adj d'une grande portée

fart [fɑːt] (inf!) vi péter

farther ['fɑːðə'] adv plus loin ▷ adj plus éloigné(e), plus lointain(e)

farthest ['fɑːðɪst] superlative of **far**

fascinate ['fæsɪneɪt] vt fasciner, captiver; **fascinated** adj fasciné(e)

fascinating ['fæsɪneɪtɪŋ] adj fascinant(e)

fascination [fæsɪ'neɪʃən] n fascination f

fascist ['fæʃɪst] adj, n fasciste m/f

fashion ['fæʃən] n mode f; (manner) façon f, manière f ▷ vt façonner; **in ~** à la mode; **out of ~** démodé(e); **fashionable** adj à la mode; **fashion show** n défilé m de mannequins or de mode

fast [fɑːst] adj rapide; (clock): **to be ~** avancer; (dye, colour) grand or bon teint inv ▷ adv vite, rapidement; (stuck, held) solidement ▷ n jeûne m ▷ vi jeûner; **~ asleep** profondément endormi

fasten ['fɑːsn] vt attacher, fixer; (coat) attacher, fermer ▷ vi se fermer, s'attacher

fast food n fast food m, restauration f rapide

fat [fæt] adj gros(se) ▷ n graisse f; (on meat) gras m; (for cooking) matière grasse

fatal ['feɪtl] adj (mistake) fatal(e); (injury) mortel(le); **fatality** [fə'tælɪtɪ] n (road death etc) victime f, décès m; **fatally** adv fatalement; (injured) mortellement

fate [feɪt] n destin m; (of person) sort m

father ['fɑːðə'] n père m; **Father Christmas** n le Père Noël; **father-in-law** n beau-père m

fatigue [fə'tiːg] n fatigue f

fattening ['fætnɪŋ] adj (food) qui fait grossir

fatty ['fætɪ] adj (food) gras(se) ▷ n (inf) gros (grosse)

faucet ['fɔːsɪt] n (US) robinet m

fault [fɔːlt] n faute f; (defect) défaut m; (Geo) faille f ▷ vt trouver des défauts à, prendre en défaut; **it's my ~** c'est de ma faute; **to find ~ with** trouver à redire or à critiquer à; **at ~** fautif(-ive), coupable; **faulty** adj défectueux(-euse)

fauna ['fɔːnə] n faune f

favour etc (US **favor** etc) ['feɪvə'] n faveur f; (help) service m ▷ vt (proposition) être en faveur de; (pupil etc) favoriser; (team, horse) donner gagnant; **to do sb a ~** rendre un service à qn; **in ~ of** en faveur de; **to find ~ with sb** trouver grâce aux yeux de qn; **favourable** adj favorable; **favourite** ['feɪvrɪt] adj, n favori(te)

fawn [fɔːn] n (deer) faon m ▷ adj (also: **~-coloured**) fauve ▷ vi: **to ~ (up)on** flatter servilement

fax [fæks] n (document) télécopie f; (machine) télécopieur m ▷ vt envoyer par télécopie

FBI n abbr (US: = Federal Bureau of Investigation) FBI m

fear [fɪəʳ] n crainte f, peur f ▷ vt craindre; **for ~ of** de peur que + sub or de + infinitive; **fearful** adj craintif(-ive); (sight, noise) affreux(-euse), épouvantable; **fearless** adj intrépide

feasible ['fiːzəbl] adj faisable, réalisable

feast [fiːst] n festin m, banquet m; (Rel: also: ~ day) fête f ▷ vi festoyer

feat [fiːt] n exploit m, prouesse f

feather ['fɛðəʳ] n plume f

feature ['fiːtʃəʳ] n caractéristique f, (article) chronique f, rubrique f ▷ vt (film) avoir pour vedette(s) ▷ vi figurer (en bonne place); **features** npl (of face) traits mpl; **a (special) ~ on sth/sb** un reportage sur qch/qn; **feature film** n long métrage

Feb. abbr (= February) fév

February ['fɛbruərɪ] n février m

fed [fɛd] pt, pp of **feed**

federal ['fɛdərəl] adj fédéral(e)

federation [fɛdə'reɪʃən] n fédération f

fed up adj: **to be ~ (with)** en avoir marre or plein le dos (de)

fee [fiː] n rémunération f; (of doctor, lawyer) honoraires mpl; (of school, college etc) frais mpl de scolarité; (for examination) droits mpl

feeble ['fiːbl] adj faible; (attempt, excuse) pauvre; (joke) piteux(-euse)

feed [fiːd] n (of animal) nourriture f, pâture f, (on printer) mécanisme m d'alimentation ▷ vt (pt, pp **fed**) (person) nourrir; (BRIT: baby: breastfeed) allaiter; (: with bottle) donner le biberon à; (horse etc) donner à manger à; (machine) alimenter; (data etc): **to ~ sth into** enregistrer qch dans; **feedback** n (Elec) effet m Larsen; (from person) réactions fpl

feel [fiːl] n (sensation) sensation f; (impression) impression f ▷ vt (pt, pp **felt**) (touch) toucher; (explore) tâter, palper; (cold, pain) sentir; (grief, anger) ressentir, éprouver; (think, believe): **to ~ (that)** trouver que; **to ~ hungry/cold** avoir faim/froid; **to ~ lonely/better** se sentir seul/ mieux; **I don't ~ well** je ne me sens pas bien; **it ~s soft** c'est doux au toucher; **to ~ like** (want) avoir envie de; **feeling** n (physical) sensation f; (emotion, impression) sentiment m; **to hurt sb's feelings** froisser qn

feet [fiːt] npl of **foot**

fell [fɛl] pt of **fall** ▷ vt (tree) abattre

fellow ['fɛləu] n type m; (comrade) compagnon m; (of learned society) membre m ▷ cpd: **their ~ prisoners/students** leurs camarades prisonniers/étudiants; **fellow citizen** n concitoyen(ne); **fellow countryman** n (irreg) compatriote m; **fellow men** npl semblables mpl; **fellowship** n (society) association f; (comradeship) amitié f, camaraderie f; (Scol) sorte de bourse universitaire

felony ['fɛlənɪ] n crime m, forfait m

felt [fɛlt] pt, pp of **feel** ▷ n feutre m; **felt-tip** n (also: **felt-tip pen**) stylo-feutre m

female ['fiːmeɪl] n (Zool) femelle f; (pej: woman) bonne femme f ▷ adj (Biol) femelle; (sex, character) féminin(e); (vote etc) des femmes

feminine ['fɛmɪnɪn] adj féminin(e)

feminist ['fɛmɪnɪst] n féministe m/f

fence [fɛns] n barrière f ▷ vi faire de l'escrime; **fencing** n (sport) escrime f

fend [fɛnd] vi: **to ~ for o.s.** se débrouiller (tout seul); **fend off** vt (attack etc) parer; (questions) éluder

fender ['fɛndəʳ] n garde-feu m inv; (on boat) défense f; (US: of car) aile f

fennel ['fɛnl] n fenouil m

ferment vi [fə'mɛnt] fermenter ▷ n ['fəː- mɛnt] (fig) agitation f, effervescence f

fern [fəːn] n fougère f

ferocious [fə'rəuʃəs] adj féroce

ferret ['fɛrɪt] n furet m

ferry ['fɛrɪ] n (small) bac m; (large: also: ~boat) ferry(-boat m) m ▷ vt transporter

fertile ['fəːtaɪl] adj fertile; (Biol) fécond(e); **fertilize** ['fəːtɪlaɪz] vt fertiliser; (Biol) féconder; **fertilizer** n engrais m

festival ['fɛstɪvəl] n (Rel) fête f; (Art, Mus) festival m

festive ['fɛstɪv] adj de fête; **the ~ season** (BRIT: Christmas) la période des fêtes

fetch [fɛtʃ] vt aller chercher; (BRIT: sell for) rapporter

fête [feɪt] n fête f, kermesse f

fetus ['fiːtəs] n (US) = **foetus**

feud [fjuːd] n querelle f, dispute f

fever ['fiːvəʳ] n fièvre f; **feverish** adj fiévreux(-euse), fébrile

few [fjuː] adj (not many) peu de ▷ pron peu; **a ~** (as adj) quelques; (as pron) quelques- uns(-unes); **quite a ~ ...** adj un certain nombre de ..., pas mal de ...; **in the past ~ days** ces derniers jours; **fewer** adj moins de; **fewest** adj le moins nombreux

fiancé [fɪ'ɑ̃ːnseɪ] n fiancé m; **fiancée** n fiancée f

fiasco [fɪ'æskəu] n fiasco m

fib [fɪb] n bobard m

fibre (US **fiber**) ['faɪbəʳ] n fibre f; **fibreglass** (US **Fiberglass®**) n fibre f de verre

fickle ['fɪkl] adj inconstant(e), volage, capricieux(-euse)

fiction ['fɪkʃən] n romans mpl, littérature f romanesque; (invention) fiction f; **fictional** adj fictif(-ive)

fiddle ['fɪdl] n (Mus) violon m; (cheating) combine f, escroquerie f ▷ vt (BRIT: accounts) falsifier, maquiller; **fiddle with** vt fus tripoter

fidelity [fɪ'dɛlɪtɪ] n fidélité f

fidget ['fɪdʒɪt] vi se trémousser, remuer

field [fiːld] n champ m; (fig) domaine m, champ; (Sport: ground) terrain m; **field**

marshal n maréchal m

fierce [fɪəs] adj (look, animal) féroce, sauvage; (wind, attack, person) (très) violent(e); (fighting, enemy) acharné(e)

fifteen [fɪf'tiːn] num quinze; **fifteenth** num quinzième

fifth [fɪfθ] num cinquième

fiftieth [ˈfɪftɪɪθ] num cinquantième

fifty [ˈfɪftɪ] num cinquante; **fifty-fifty** adv moitié-moitié ▷ adj: **to have a fifty-fifty chance (of success)** avoir une chance sur deux (de réussir)

fig [fɪg] n figue f

fight [faɪt] n (between persons) bagarre f; (argument) dispute f; (Mil) combat m; (against cancer etc) lutte f ▷ vb (pt, pp **fought**) ▷ vt se battre contre; (cancer, alcoholism, emotion) combattre, lutter contre; (election) se présenter à ▷ vi se battre; (argue) se disputer; (fig): **to ~ (for/against)** lutter (pour/contre); **fight back** vi rendre les coups; (after illness) reprendre le dessus ▷ vt (tears) réprimer; **fight off** vt repousser; (disease, sleep, urge) lutter contre; **fighting** n combats mpl; (brawls) bagarres fpl

figure [ˈfɪgəʳ] n (Drawing, Geom) figure f; (number) chiffre m; (body, outline) silhouette f; (person's shape) ligne f, formes fpl; (person) personnage m ▷ vt (us: think) supposer ▷ vi (appear) figurer; (us: make sense) s'expliquer; **figure out** vt (understand) arriver à comprendre; (plan) calculer

file [faɪl] n (tool) lime f; (dossier) dossier m; (folder) dossier, chemise f; (: binder) classeur m; (Comput) fichier m; (row) file f ▷ vt (nails, wood) limer; (papers) classer; (Law: claim) faire enregistrer; déposer; **filing cabinet** n classeur m (meuble)

Filipino [fɪlɪ'piːnəu] adj philippin(e) ▷ n (person) Philippin(e)

fill [fɪl] vt remplir; (vacancy) pourvoir à ▷ n: **to eat one's ~** manger à sa faim; **to ~ with** remplir de; **fill in** vt (hole) boucher; (form) remplir; **fill out** vt (form, receipt) remplir; **fill up** vt remplir ▷ vi (Aut) faire le plein

fillet [ˈfɪlɪt] n filet m; **fillet steak** n filet m de bœuf, tournedos m

filling [ˈfɪlɪŋ] n (Culin) garniture f, farce f; (for tooth) plombage m; **filling station** n station-service f, station f d'essence

film [fɪlm] n film m; (Phot) pellicule f, film; (of powder, liquid) couche f, pellicule ▷ vt (scene) filmer ▷ vi tourner; **I'd like a 36-exposure ~** je voudrais une pellicule de 36 poses; **film star** n vedette f de cinéma

filter [ˈfɪltəʳ] n filtre m ▷ vt filtrer; **filter lane** n (BRIT Aut: at traffic lights) voie f de dégagement; (: on motorway) voie f de sortie

filth [fɪlθ] n saleté f; **filthy** adj sale,

dégoûtant(e); (language) ordurier(-ière), grossier(-ière)

fin [fɪn] n (of fish) nageoire f; (of shark) aileron m; (of diver) palme f

final [ˈfaɪnl] adj final(e), dernier(-ière); (decision, answer) définitif(-ive) ▷ n (BRIT Sport) finale f; **finals** npl (Scol) examens mpl de dernière année; (us Sport) finale f; **finale** [fɪ'nɑːlɪ] n finale m; **finalist** n (Sport) finaliste m/f; **finalize** vt mettre au point; **finally** adv (eventually) enfin, finalement; (lastly) en dernier lieu

finance [faɪ'næns] n finance f ▷ vt financer; **finances** npl finances fpl; **financial** [faɪ'nænʃəl] adj financier(-ière); **financial year** n année f budgétaire

find [faɪnd] vt (pt, pp **found**) trouver; (lost object) retrouver ▷ n trouvaille f, découverte f; **to ~ sb guilty** (Law) déclarer qn coupable; **find out** vt se renseigner sur; (truth, secret) découvrir; (person) démasquer ▷ vi: **to ~ out about** (make enquiries) se renseigner sur; (by chance) apprendre; **findings** npl (Law) conclusions fpl, verdict m; (of report) constatations fpl

fine [faɪn] adj (weather) beau (belle); (excellent) excellent(e); (thin, subtle, not coarse) fin(e); (acceptable) bien inv ▷ adv (well) très bien; (small) fin, finement ▷ n (Law) amende f; contravention f ▷ vt (Law) condamner à une amende; donner une contravention à; **he's ~** il va bien; **the weather is ~** il fait beau; **fine arts** npl beaux-arts mpl

finger [ˈfɪŋgəʳ] n doigt m ▷ vt palper, toucher; **index ~** index m; **fingernail** n ongle m (de la main); **fingerprint** n empreinte digitale; **fingertip** n bout m du doigt

finish [ˈfɪnɪʃ] n fin f; (Sport) arrivée f; (polish etc) finition f ▷ vt finir, terminer ▷ vi finir, se terminer; **to ~ doing sth** finir de faire qch; **to ~ third** arriver or terminer troisième; **when does the show ~?** quand est-ce que le spectacle se termine?; **finish off** vt finir, terminer; (kill) achever; **finish up** vi, vt finir

Finland [ˈfɪnlənd] n Finlande f; **Finn** n Finnois(e), Finlandais(e); **Finnish** adj finnois(e), finlandais(e) ▷ n (Ling) finnois m

fir [fəːʳ] n sapin m

fire [ˈfaɪəʳ] n feu m; (accidental) incendie m; (heater) radiateur m ▷ vt (discharge): **to ~ a gun** tirer un coup de feu; (fig: interest) enflammer, animer; (inf: dismiss) mettre à la porte, renvoyer ▷ vi (shoot) tirer, faire feu; **~!** au feu!; **on ~** en feu; **to set ~ to sth, set sth on ~** mettre le feu à qch; **fire alarm** n avertisseur m d'incendie; **firearm** n arme f à feu; **fire brigade** n (us **fire department**) (régiment m de sapeurs-)pompiers mpl; **fire engine** n (BRIT) pompe f à incendie; **fire**

escape n escalier m de secours; **fire exit** n issue f or sortie f de secours; **fire extinguisher** n extincteur m; **fireman** (irreg) n pompier m; **fireplace** n cheminée f; **fire station** n caserne f de pompiers; **fire truck** (us) n = **fire engine**; **firewall** n (Internet) pare-feu m; **firewood** n bois m de chauffage; **fireworks** npl (display) feu(x) m(pl) d'artifice

firm [fə:m] adj ferme ▷ n compagnie f, firme f; **firmly** adv fermement

first [fə:st] adj premier(-ière) ▷ adv (before other people) le premier, la première; (before other things) en premier, d'abord; (when listing reasons etc) en premier lieu, premièrement; (in the beginning) au début ▷ n (person: in race) premier(-ière); (BRIT Scol) mention f très bien; (Aut) première f; **the ~ of January** le premier janvier; **at ~** au commencement, au début; **~ of all** tout d'abord, pour commencer; **first aid** n premiers secours or soins; **first-aid kit** n trousse f à pharmacie; **first-class** adj (ticket etc) de première classe; (excellent) excellent(e), exceptionnel(le); (post) en tarif prioritaire; **first-hand** adj de première main; **first lady** n (us) femme f du président; **firstly** adv premièrement, en premier lieu; **first name** n prénom m; **first-rate** adj excellent(e)

fiscal ['fɪskl] adj fiscal(e); **fiscal year** n exercice financier

fish [fɪʃ] n (pl inv) poisson m ▷ vt, vi pêcher; **~ and chips** n poisson frit et frites; **fisherman** (irreg) n pêcheur m; **fish fingers** npl (BRIT) bâtonnets de poisson (congelés); **fishing** n pêche f; **to go fishing** aller à la pêche; **fishing boat** n barque f de pêche; **fishing line** n ligne f (de pêche); **fishmonger** n (BRIT) marchand m de poisson; **fishmonger's (shop)** n (BRIT) poissonnerie f; **fish sticks** npl (us) = **fish fingers**; **fishy** adj (inf) suspect(e), louche

fist [fɪst] n poing m

fit [fɪt] adj (Med, Sport) en (bonne) forme; (proper) convenable; approprié(e) ▷ vt (subj: clothes) aller à; (put in, attach) installer, poser; (equip) équiper, garnir, munir; (suit) convenir à ▷ vi (clothes) aller; (parts) s'adapter; (in space, gap) entrer, s'adapter ▷ n (Med) accès m, crise f, (of anger) accès; (of hysterics, jealousy) crise; **~ to** (ready to) en état de; **~ for** (worthy) digne de; (capable) apte à; **to keep ~** se maintenir en forme; **this dress is a tight/good ~** cette robe est un peu juste/(me) va très bien; **a ~ of coughing** une quinte de toux; **by ~s and starts** par à-coups; **fit in** vi (add up) cadrer; (integrate) s'intégrer; (to new situation) s'adapter; **fitness** n (Med) forme f physique; **fitted** adj (jacket, shirt) ajusté(e); **fitted carpet** n moquette f; **fitted kitchen** n (BRIT) cuisine équipée; **fitted sheet** n drap-housse m; **fitting** adj approprié(e) ▷ n (of

dress) essayage m; (of piece of equipment) pose f, installation f; **fitting room** n (in shop) cabine f d'essayage; **fittings** npl installations fpl

five [faɪv] num cinq; **fiver** n (inf: BRIT) billet m de cinq livres; (: us) billet de cinq dollars

fix [fɪks] vt (date, amount etc) fixer; (sort out) arranger; (mend) réparer; (make ready: meal, drink) préparer ▷ n: **to be in a ~** être dans le pétrin; **fix up** vt (meeting) arranger; **to ~ sb up with sth** faire avoir qch à qn; **fixed** adj (prices etc) fixe; **fixture** n installation f (fixe); (Sport) rencontre f (au programme)

fizzy ['fɪzɪ] adj pétillant(e), gazeux(-euse)

flag [flæg] n drapeau m; (also: **~stone**) dalle f ▷ vi faiblir, fléchir; **flag down** vt héler, faire signe (de s'arrêter) à; **flagpole** n mât m

flair [flɛəʳ] n flair m

flak [flæk] n (Mil) tir antiaérien; (inf: criticism) critiques fpl

flake [fleɪk] n (of rust, paint) écaille f; (of snow, soap powder) flocon m ▷ vi (also: **~ off**) s'écailler

flamboyant [flæm'bɔɪənt] adj flamboyant(e), éclatant(e); (person) haut(e) en couleur

flame [fleɪm] n flamme f

flamingo [flə'mɪŋɡəʊ] n flamant m (rose)

flammable ['flæməbl] adj inflammable

flan [flæn] n (BRIT) tarte f

flank [flæŋk] n flanc m ▷ vt flanquer

flannel ['flænl] n (BRIT: also: **face ~**) gant m de toilette; (fabric) flanelle f

flap [flæp] n (of pocket, envelope) rabat m ▷ vt (wings) battre (de) ▷ vi (sail, flag) claquer

flare [flɛəʳ] n (signal) signal lumineux; (Mil) fusée éclairante; (in skirt etc) évasement m; **flares** npl (trousers) pantalon m à pattes d'éléphant; **flare up** vi s'embraser; (fig: person) se mettre en colère, s'emporter; (: revolt) éclater

flash [flæʃ] n éclair m; (also: **news ~**) flash m (d'information); (Phot) flash ▷ vt (switch on) allumer (brièvement); (direct): **to ~ sth at** braquer qch sur; (send: message) câbler; (smile) lancer ▷ vi briller; jeter des éclairs; (light on ambulance etc) clignoter; **a ~ of lightning** un éclair; **in a ~** en un clin d'œil; **to ~ one's headlights** faire un appel de phares; **he ~ed by** or **past** il passa (devant nous) comme un éclair; **flashback** n flashback m, retour m en arrière; **flashbulb** n ampoule f de flash; **flashlight** n lampe f de poche

flask [flɑ:sk] n flacon m, bouteille f; (also: **vacuum ~**) bouteille f thermos®

flat [flæt] adj plat(e); (tyre) dégonflé(e), à plat; (beer) éventé(e); (battery) à plat; (denial) catégorique; (Mus) bémol inv; (: voice) faux (fausse) ▷ n (BRIT: apartment) appartement m; (Aut) crevaison f, pneu crevé; (Mus) bémol m; **~ out** (work) sans relâche; (race) à fond; **flatten**

vt (also: **flatten out**) aplatir; (crop) coucher; (house, city) raser

flatter ['flætə^r] vt flatter; **flattering** adj flatteur(-euse); (clothes) seyant(e)

flaunt [flɔ:nt] vt faire étalage de

flavour etc (us **flavor** etc) ['fleɪvə^r] n goût m, saveur f; (of ice cream etc) parfum m ▷ vt parfumer, aromatiser; **vanilla-~ed** à l'arôme de vanille, vanillé(e); **what ~s do you have?** quels parfums avez-vous?; **flavouring** n arôme m (synthétique)

flaw [flɔ:] n défaut m; **flawless** adj sans défaut

flea [fli:] n puce f; **flea market** n marché m aux puces

flee (pt, pp **fled**) [fli:, fled] vt fuir, s'enfuir de ▷ vi fuir, s'enfuir

fleece [fli:s] n (of sheep) toison f; (top) (laine f) polaire f ▷ vt (inf) voler, filouter

fleet [fli:t] n flotte f; (of lorries, cars etc) parc m; convoi m

fleeting ['fli:tɪŋ] adj fugace, fugitif(-ive); (visit) très bref (brève)

Flemish ['flemɪʃ] adj flamand(e) ▷ n (Ling) flamand m; **the ~** npl les Flamands

flesh [fleʃ] n chair f

flew [flu:] pt of **fly**

flex [fleks] n fil m or câble m électrique (souple) ▷ vt (knee) fléchir; (muscles) tendre; **flexibility** n flexibilité f; **flexible** adj flexible; (person, schedule) souple; **flexitime** (us **flextime**) n horaire m variable or à la carte

flick [flɪk] n petit coup; (with finger) chiquenaude f ▷ vt donner un petit coup à; (switch) appuyer sur; **flick through** vt fus feuilleter

flicker ['flɪkə^r] vi (light, flame) vaciller

flies [flaɪz] npl of **fly**

flight [flaɪt] n vol m; (escape) fuite f; (also: ~ **of steps**) escalier m; **flight attendant** n steward m, hôtesse f de l'air

flimsy ['flɪmzɪ] adj peu solide; (clothes) trop léger(-ère); (excuse) pauvre, mince

flinch [flɪntʃ] vi tressaillir; **to ~ from** se dérober à, reculer devant

fling [flɪŋ] vt (pt, pp **flung**) jeter, lancer

flint [flɪnt] n silex m; (in lighter) pierre f (à briquet)

flip [flɪp] vt (throw) donner une chiquenaude à; (switch) appuyer sur; (us: pancake) faire sauter; **to ~ sth over** retourner qch

flip-flops ['flɪpflɔps] npl (esp BRIT) tongs fpl

flipper ['flɪpə^r] n (of animal) nageoire f; (for swimmer) palme f

flirt [flə:t] vi flirter ▷ n flirteur(-euse)

float [fləut] n flotteur m; (in procession) char m; (sum of money) réserve f ▷ vi flotter

flock [flɔk] n (of sheep) troupeau m; (of birds) vol m; (of people) foule f

flood [flʌd] n inondation f; (of letters, refugees

etc) flot m ▷ vt inonder ▷ vi (place) être inondé; (people): **to ~ into** envahir; **flooding** n inondation f; **floodlight** n projecteur m

floor [flɔ:^r] n sol m; (storey) étage m; (of sea, valley) fond m ▷ vt (knock down) terrasser; (baffle) désorienter; **ground ~**, (us) **first ~** rez-de-chaussée m; **first ~**, (us) **second ~** premier étage; **what ~ is it on?** c'est à quel étage?; **floorboard** n planche f (du plancher); **flooring** n sol m; (wooden) plancher m; (covering) revêtement m de sol; **floor show** n spectacle m de variétés

flop [flɔp] n fiasco m ▷ vi (fail) faire fiasco; (fall) s'affaler, s'effondrer; **floppy** adj lâche, flottant(e) ▷ n (Comput: also: **floppy disk**) disquette f

flora ['flɔ:rə] n flore f

floral ['flɔ:rl] adj floral(e); (dress) à fleurs

florist ['flɔrɪst] n fleuriste m/f; **florist's (shop)** n magasin m or boutique f de fleuriste

flotation [fləu'teɪʃən] n (of shares) émission f; (of company) lancement m (en Bourse)

flour ['flauə^r] n farine f

flourish ['flʌrɪʃ] vi prospérer ▷ n (gesture) moulinet m

flow [fləu] n (of water, traffic etc) écoulement m; (tide, influx) flux m; (of blood, Elec) circulation f; (of river) courant m ▷ vi couler; (traffic) s'écouler; (robes, hair) flotter

flower ['flauə^r] n fleur f ▷ vi fleurir; **flower bed** n plate-bande f; **flowerpot** n pot m (à fleurs)

flown [fləun] pp of **fly**

fl. oz. abbr = **fluid ounce**

flu [flu:] n grippe f

fluctuate ['flʌktjueɪt] vi varier, fluctuer

fluent ['flu:ənt] adj (speech, style) coulant(e), aisé(e); **he speaks ~ French, he's ~ in French** il parle le français couramment

fluff [flʌf] n duvet m; (on jacket, carpet) peluche f; **fluffy** adj duveteux(-euse); (toy) en peluche

fluid ['flu:ɪd] n fluide m; (in diet) liquide m ▷ adj fluide; **fluid ounce** n (BRIT) = 0.028 l; 0.05 pints

fluke [flu:k] n coup m de veine

flung [flʌŋ] pt, pp of **fling**

fluorescent [fluə'resnt] adj fluorescent(e)

fluoride ['fluəraɪd] n fluor m

flurry ['flʌrɪ] n (of snow) rafale f, bourrasque f; **a ~ of activity** un affairement soudain

flush [flʌʃ] n (on face) rougeur f; (fig: of youth etc) éclat m ▷ vt nettoyer à grande eau ▷ vi rougir ▷ adj (level): **~ with** au ras de, de niveau avec; **to ~ the toilet** tirer la chasse (d'eau)

flute [flu:t] n flûte f

flutter ['flʌtə^r] n (of panic, excitement) agitation f; (of wings) battement m ▷ vi (bird) battre des ailes, voleter

fly [flaɪ] n (insect) mouche f; (on trousers: also:

flies) braguette f ▷ vb (pt **flew**, pp **flown**) ▷ vt (plane) piloter; (passengers, cargo) transporter (par avion); (distance) parcourir ▷ vi voler; (passengers) aller en avion; (escape) s'enfuir, fuir; (flag) se déployer; **fly away, fly off** vi s'envoler; **fly-drive** n formule f avion plus voiture; **flying** n (activity) aviation f; (action) vol m ▷ adj: **flying visit** visite f éclair inv; **with flying colours** haut la main; **flying saucer** n soucoupe volante; **flyover** n (BRIT: overpass) pont routier

FM abbr (Radio: = frequency modulation) FM

foal [fəʊl] n poulain m

foam [fəʊm] n écume f; (on beer) mousse f; (also: **~ rubber**) caoutchouc m mousse ▷ vi (liquid) écumer; (soapy water) mousser

focus ['fəʊkəs] n (pl **~es**) foyer m; (of interest) centre m ▷ vt (field glasses etc) mettre au point ▷ vi: **to ~ (on)** (with camera) régler la mise au point (sur); (with eyes) fixer son regard (sur); (fig: concentrate) se concentrer; **out of/in ~** (picture) flou(e)/net(te); (camera) pas au point/au point

foetus (US **fetus**) ['fiːtəs] n fœtus m

fog [fɒg] n brouillard m; **foggy** adj: **it's foggy** il y a du brouillard; **fog lamp** (US **fog light**) n (Aut) phare m anti-brouillard

foil [fɔɪl] vt déjouer, contrecarrer ▷ n feuille f de métal; (kitchen foil) papier m d'alu(minium); **to act as a ~ to** (fig) servir de repoussoir or de faire-valoir à

fold [fəʊld] n (bend, crease) pli m; (Agr) parc m à moutons; (fig) bercail m ▷ vt plier; **to ~ one's arms** croiser les bras; **fold up** vi (map etc) se plier, se replier; (business) fermer boutique ▷ vt (map etc) plier, replier; **folder** n (for papers) chemise f; (: binder) classeur m; (Comput) dossier m; **folding** adj (chair, bed) pliant(e)

foliage ['fəʊlɪdʒ] n feuillage m

folk [fəʊk] npl gens mpl ▷ cpd folklorique; **folks** npl (inf: parents) famille f, parents mpl; **folklore** ['fəʊklɔː] n folklore m; **folk music** n musique f folklorique; (contemporary) musique folk, folk m; **folk song** n chanson f folklorique; (contemporary) chanson folk inv

follow ['fɒləʊ] vt suivre ▷ vi suivre; (result) s'ensuivre; **to ~ suit** (fig) faire de même; **follow up** vt (letter, offer) donner suite à; (case) suivre; **follower** n disciple m/f, partisan(e); **following** adj suivant(e) ▷ n partisans mpl, disciples mpl; **follow-up** n suite f; (on file, case) suivi m

fond [fɒnd] adj (memory, look) tendre, affectueux(-euse); (hopes, dreams) un peu fou (folle); **to be ~ of** aimer beaucoup

food [fuːd] n nourriture f; **food mixer** n mixeur m; **food poisoning** n intoxication f alimentaire; **food processor** n robot m de cuisine; **food stamp** n (US) bon m de

nourriture (pour indigents)

fool [fuːl] n idiot(e); (Culin) mousse f de fruits ▷ vt berner, duper; **fool about, fool around** vi (pej: waste time) traînailler, glandouiller; (: behave foolishly) faire l'idiot or l'imbécile; **foolish** adj idiot(e), stupide; (rash) imprudent(e); **foolproof** adj (plan etc) infaillible

foot (pl **feet**) [fʊt, fiːt] n pied m; (of animal) patte f; (measure) pied (= 30.48 cm; 12 inches) ▷ vt (bill) payer; **on ~** à pied; **footage** n (Cine: length) ≈ métrage m; (: material) séquences fpl; **foot-and-mouth (disease)** [fʊtənd'maʊθ-] n fièvre aphteuse; **football** n (ball) ballon m (de football); (sport: BRIT) football m; (: US) football américain; **footballer** n (BRIT) = **football player**; **football match** n (BRIT) match m de foot(ball); **football player** n footballeur(-euse), joueur(-euse) de football; (US) joueur(-euse) de football américain; **footbridge** n passerelle f; **foothills** npl contreforts mpl; **foothold** n prise f (de pied); **footing** n (fig) position f; **to lose one's footing** perdre pied; **footnote** n note f (en bas de page); **footpath** n sentier m; **footprint** n trace f (de pied); **footstep** n pas m; **footwear** n chaussures fpl

○ **KEYWORD**

for [fɔːʳ] prep **1** (indicating destination, intention, purpose) pour; **the train for London** le train pour (or à destination de) Londres; **he left for Rome** il est parti pour Rome; **he went for the paper** il est allé chercher le journal; **is this for me?** c'est pour moi?; **it's time for lunch** c'est l'heure du déjeuner; **what's it for?** ça sert à quoi?; **what for?** (why) pourquoi?; (to what end) pour quoi faire?, à quoi bon?; **for sale** à vendre; **to pray for peace** prier pour la paix

2 (on behalf of, representing) pour; **the MP for Hove** le député de Hove; **to work for sb/sth** travailler pour qn/qch; **I'll ask him for you** je vais lui demander pour toi; **G for George** G comme Georges

3 (because of) pour; **for this reason** pour cette raison; **for fear of being criticized** de peur d'être critiqué

4 (with regard to) pour; **it's cold for July** il fait froid pour juillet; **a gift for languages** un don pour les langues

5 (in exchange for): **I sold it for £5** je l'ai vendu 5 livres; **to pay 50 pence for a ticket** payer un billet 50 pence

6 (in favour of) pour; **are you for or against us?** êtes-vous pour ou contre nous?; **I'm all for it** je suis tout à fait pour; **vote for X** votez pour X

7 (referring to distance) pendant, sur; **there**

are roadworks for 5 km il y a des travaux sur
or pendant 5 km; **we walked for miles** nous
avons marché pendant des kilomètres
8 (referring to time) depuis; pour; **he
was away for 2 years** il a été absent pendant
2 ans; **she will be away for a month** elle sera
absente (pendant) un mois; **it hasn't rained
for 3 weeks** ça fait 3 semaines qu'il ne pleut
pas, il ne pleut pas depuis 3 semaines; **I have
known her for years** je la connais depuis des
années; **can you do it for tomorrow?** est-ce
que tu peux le faire pour demain?
9 (with infinitive clauses): **it is not for me to
decide** ce n'est pas à moi de décider; **it would
be best for you to leave** le mieux serait que
vous partiez; **there is still time for you to
do it** vous avez encore le temps de le faire;
for this to be possible ... pour que cela soit
possible ..
10 (in spite of): **for all that** malgré cela,
néanmoins; **for all his work/efforts** malgré
tout son travail/tous ses efforts; **for all his
complaints, he's very fond of her** il a beau
se plaindre, il l'aime beaucoup
▷ conj (since, as: rather formal) car

forbid (pt **forbad(e)**, pp **~den**) [fə'bɪd, -'bæd,
-'bɪdn] vt défendre, interdire; **to ~ sb to do**
défendre or interdire à qn de faire; **forbidden**
adj défendu(e)
force [fɔːs] n force f ▷ vt forcer; (push) pousser
(de force); **to ~ o.s. to do** se forcer à faire; **in
~** (being used: rule, law, prices) en vigueur; (in
large numbers) en force; **forced** adj forcé(e);
forceful adj énergique
ford [fɔːd] n gué m
fore [fɔːʳ] n: **to the ~** en évidence; **forearm**
n avant-bras m inv; **forecast** n prévision
f; (also: **weather forecast**) prévisions fpl
météorologiques, météo f ▷ vt (irreg: like **cast**)
prévoir; **forecourt** n (of garage) devant m;
forefinger n index m; **forefront** n: **in the
forefront of** au premier rang or plan de;
foreground n premier plan; **forehead** ['fɔrɪd]
n front m
foreign ['fɔrɪn] adj étranger(-ère); (trade)
extérieur(e); (travel) à l'étranger; **foreign
currency** n devises étrangères; **foreigner** n
étranger(-ère); **foreign exchange** n (system)
change m; (money) devises fpl; **Foreign Office**
n (BRIT) ministère m des Affaires étrangères;
Foreign Secretary n (BRIT) ministre m des
Affaires étrangères
fore: **foreman** (irreg) n (in construction)
contremaître m; **foremost** adj le (la) plus en
vue, premier(-ière) ▷ adv: **first and foremost**
avant tout, tout d'abord; **forename** n
prénom m
forensic [fə'rɛnsɪk] adj: **~ medicine** médecine

légale
foresee (pt **foresaw**, pp **~n**) [fɔː'siː, -'sɔː, -'siːn]
vt prévoir; **foreseeable** adj prévisible
forest ['fɔrɪst] n forêt f; **forestry** n
sylviculture f
forever [fə'rɛvəʳ] adv pour toujours; (fig:
endlessly) continuellement
foreword ['fɔːwəːd] n avant-propos m inv
forfeit ['fɔːfɪt] vt perdre
forgave [fə'geɪv] pt of **forgive**
forge [fɔːdʒ] n forge f ▷ vt (signature)
contrefaire; (wrought iron) forger; **to ~ money**
(BRIT) fabriquer de la fausse monnaie; **forger** n
faussaire m; **forgery** n faux m, contrefaçon f
forget (pt **forgot**, pp **forgotten**) [fə'gɛt, -'gɔt,
-'gɔtn] vt, vi oublier; **I've forgotten my key/
passport** j'ai oublié ma clé/mon passeport;
forgetful adj distrait(e), étourdi(e)
forgive (pt **forgave**, pp **~n**) [fə'gɪv, -'geɪv, -
'gɪvn] vt pardonner; **to ~ sb for sth/for doing
sth** pardonner qch à qn/à qn de faire qch
forgot [fə'gɔt] pt of **forget**
forgotten [fə'gɔtn] pp of **forget**
fork [fɔːk] n (for eating) fourchette f; (for
gardening) fourche f; (of roads) bifurcation f ▷ vi
(road) bifurquer
forlorn [fə'lɔːn] adj (deserted) abandonné(e);
(hope, attempt) désespéré(e)
form [fɔːm] n forme f; (Scol) classe f;
(questionnaire) formulaire m ▷ vt former;
(habit) contracter; **to ~ part of sth** faire partie
de qch; **on top ~** en pleine forme
formal ['fɔːməl] adj (offer, receipt) en bonne
et due forme; (person) cérémonieux(-euse);
(occasion, dinner) officiel(le); (garden) à la
française; (clothes) de soirée; **formality**
[fɔː'mælɪtɪ] n formalité f
format ['fɔːmæt] n format m ▷ vt (Comput)
formater
formation [fɔː'meɪʃən] n formation f
former ['fɔːməʳ] adj ancien(ne); (before)
précédent(e); **the ~ ... the latter** le premier ...
le second, celui-là ... celui-ci; **formerly** adv
autrefois
formidable ['fɔːmɪdəbl] adj redoutable
formula ['fɔːmjulə] n formule f
fort [fɔːt] n fort m
forthcoming [fɔːθ'kʌmɪŋ] adj qui va paraître
or avoir lieu prochainement; (character)
ouvert(e), communicatif(-ive); (available)
disponible
fortieth ['fɔːtɪɪθ] num quarantième
fortify ['fɔːtɪfaɪ] vt (city) fortifier; (person)
remonter
fortnight ['fɔːtnaɪt] n (BRIT) quinzaine
f, quinze jours mpl; **fortnightly** adj
bimensuel(le) ▷ adv tous les quinze jours
fortress ['fɔːtrɪs] n forteresse f
fortunate ['fɔːtʃənɪt] adj heureux(-euse);

(*person*) chanceux(-euse); **it is ~ that** c'est une chance que, il est heureux que; **fortunately** *adv* heureusement, par bonheur

fortune ['fɔːtʃən] *n* chance *f*; (*wealth*) fortune *f*; **fortune-teller** *n* diseuse *f* de bonne aventure

forty ['fɔːtɪ] *num* quarante

forum ['fɔːrəm] *n* forum *m*, tribune *f*

forward ['fɔːwəd] *adj* (*movement, position*) en avant, vers l'avant; (*not shy*) effronté(e); (*in time*) en avance ▷ *adv* (*also:* **~s**) en avant *m* (*Sport*) avant *m* ▷ *vt* (*letter*) faire suivre; (*parcel, goods*) expédier; (*fig*) promouvoir, favoriser; **to move ~** avancer; **forwarding address** *n* adresse *f* de réexpédition

forward slash *n* barre *f* oblique

fossil ['fɔsl] *adj, n* fossile *m*

foster ['fɔstə'] *vt* (*encourage*) encourager, favoriser; (*child*) élever (*sans adopter*); **foster child** *n* enfant élevé dans une famille d'accueil

foster parent *n* parent qui élève un enfant sans l'adopter

fought [fɔːt] *pt, pp of* **fight**

foul [faul] *adj* (*weather, smell, food*) infect(e); (*language*) ordurier(-ière) ▷ *n* (*Football*) faute *f* ▷ *vt* (*dirty*) salir, encrasser; **he's got a ~ temper** il a un caractère de chien; **foul play** *n* (*Law*) acte criminel

found [faund] *pt, pp of* **find** ▷ *vt* (*establish*) fonder; **foundation** [faun'deɪʃən] *n* (*act*) fondation *f*; (*base*) fondement *m*; (*also:* **foundation cream**) fond *m* de teint; **foundations** *npl* (*of building*) fondations *fpl*

founder ['faundə'] *n* fondateur *m* ▷ *vi* couler, sombrer

fountain ['fauntɪn] *n* fontaine *f*; **fountain pen** *n* stylo *m* (à encre)

four [fɔː'] *num* quatre; **on all ~s** à quatre pattes; **four-letter word** *n* obscénité *f*, gros mot; **four-poster** *n* (*also:* **four-poster bed**) lit *m* à baldaquin; **fourteen** *num* quatorze; **fourteenth** *num* quatorzième; **fourth** *num* quatrième ▷ *n* (*Aut: also:* **fourth gear**) quatrième *f*; **four-wheel drive** *n* (*Aut: car*) voiture *f* à quatre roues motrices

fowl [faul] *n* volaille *f*

fox [fɔks] *n* renard *m* ▷ *vt* mystifier

foyer ['fɔɪeɪ] *n* (*in hotel*) vestibule *m*; (*Theat*) foyer *m*

fraction ['frækʃən] *n* fraction *f*

fracture ['fræktʃə'] *n* fracture *f* ▷ *vt* fracturer

fragile ['frædʒaɪl] *adj* fragile

fragment ['frægmənt] *n* fragment *m*

fragrance ['freɪgrəns] *n* parfum *m*

frail [freɪl] *adj* fragile, délicat(e); (*person*) frêle

frame [freɪm] *n* (*of building*) charpente *f*; (*of human, animal*) charpente, ossature *f*; (*of picture*) cadre *m*; (*of door, window*) encadrement *m*, chambranle *m*; (*of spectacles: also:* **~s**) monture *f* ▷ *vt* (*picture*) encadrer; **~ of mind**

disposition *f* d'esprit; **framework** *n* structure *f*

France [frɑːns] *n* la France

franchise ['fræntʃaɪz] *n* (*Pol*) droit *m* de vote; (*Comm*) franchise *f*

frank [fræŋk] *adj* franc (franche) ▷ *vt* (*letter*) affranchir; **frankly** *adv* franchement

frantic ['fræntɪk] *adj* (*hectic*) frénétique; (*distraught*) hors de soi

fraud [frɔːd] *n* supercherie *f*, fraude *f*, tromperie *f*; (*person*) imposteur *m*

fraught [frɔːt] *adj* (*tense: person*) très tendu(e); (*: situation*) pénible; **~ with** (*difficulties etc*) chargé(e) de, plein(e) de

fray [freɪ] *vt* effilocher ▷ *vi* s'effilocher

freak [friːk] *n* (*eccentric person*) phénomène *m*; (*unusual event*) hasard *m* extraordinaire; (*pej: fanatic*): **health food ~** fana *m/f* of obsédé(e) de l'alimentation saine ▷ *adj* (*storm*) exceptionnel(le); (*accident*) bizarre

freckle ['frɛkl] *n* tache *f* de rousseur

free [friː] *adj* libre; (*gratis*) gratuit(e) ▷ *vt* (*prisoner etc*) libérer; (*jammed object or person*) dégager; **is this seat ~?** la place est libre?; **~ (of charge)** gratuitement; **freedom** *n* liberté *f*; **Freefone®** *n* numéro vert; **free gift** *n* prime *f*; **free kick** *n* (*Sport*) coup franc; **freelance** *adj* (*journalist etc*) indépendant(e), free-lance *inv* ▷ *adv* en free-lance; **freely** *adv* librement; (*liberally*) libéralement; **Freepost®** *n* (BRIT) port payé; **free-range** *adj* (*egg*) de ferme; (*chicken*) fermier; **freeway** *n* (US) autoroute *f*; **free will** *n* libre arbitre *m*; **of one's own free will** de son plein gré

freeze [friːz] *vb* (*pt* **froze**, *pp* **frozen**) ▷ *vi* geler ▷ *vt* geler; (*food*) congeler; (*prices, salaries*) bloquer, geler ▷ *n* gel *m*; (*of prices, salaries*) blocage *m*; **freezer** *n* congélateur *m*; **freezing** *adj*: **freezing (cold)** (*room etc*) glacial(e); (*person, hands*) gelé(e), glacé(e) ▷ *n*: **3 degrees below freezing** 3 degrés au-dessous de zéro; **it's freezing** il fait un froid glacial; **freezing point** *n* point *m* de congélation

freight [freɪt] *n* (*goods*) fret *m*, cargaison *f*; (*money charged*) fret, prix *m* du transport; **freight train** *n* (US) train *m* de marchandises

French [frɛntʃ] *adj* français(e) ▷ *n* (*Ling*) français *m*; **the ~** *npl* les Français; **what's the ~ (word) for ...?** comment dit-on ... en français?; **French bean** *n* (BRIT) haricot vert; **French bread** *n* pain *m* français; **French dressing** *n* (*Culin*) vinaigrette *f*; **French fried potatoes** (US **French fries**) *npl* (pommes de terre *fpl*) frites *fpl*; **Frenchman** (*irreg*) *n* Français *m*; **French stick** *n* ≈ baguette *f*; **French window** *n* porte-fenêtre *f*; **Frenchwoman** (*irreg*) *n* Française *f*

frenzy ['frɛnzɪ] *n* frénésie *f*

frequency ['friːkwənsɪ] *n* fréquence *f*

frequent *adj* ['friːkwənt] fréquent(e) ▷ *vt*

[frɪ'kwɛnt] fréquenter; **frequently** ['freʃkwəntlɪ] adv fréquemment

fresh [freʃ] adj frais (fraîche); (new) nouveau (nouvelle); (cheeky) familier(-ière), culotté(e); **freshen** vi (wind, air) fraîchir; **freshen up** vi faire un brin de toilette; **fresher** n (BRIT University: inf) bizuth m, étudiant(e) de première année; **freshly** adv nouvellement, récemment; **freshman** (US: irreg) n = **fresher**; **freshwater** adj (fish) d'eau douce

fret [fret] vi s'agiter, se tracasser

Fri abbr (= Friday) ve

friction ['frɪkʃən] n friction f, frottement m

Friday ['fraɪdɪ] n vendredi m

fridge [frɪdʒ] n (BRIT) frigo m, frigidaire® m

fried [fraɪd] adj frit(e); **~ egg** œuf m sur le plat

friend [frɛnd] n ami(e); **friendly** adj amical(e); (kind) sympathique, gentil(le); (place) accueillant(e); (Pol: country) ami(e) ▷ n (also: **friendly match**) match amical; **friendship** n amitié f

fries [fraɪz] (esp US) npl = **French fried potatoes**

frigate ['frɪgɪt] n frégate f

fright [fraɪt] n peur f, effroi m; **to give sb a ~** faire peur à qn; **to take ~** prendre peur, s'effrayer; **frighten** vt effrayer, faire peur à; **frightened** adj: **to be frightened (of)** avoir peur (de); **frightening** adj effrayant(e); **frightful** adj affreux(-euse)

frill [frɪl] n (of dress) volant m; (of shirt) jabot m

fringe [frɪndʒ] n (BRIT: of hair) frange f; (edge: of forest etc) bordure f

Frisbee® ['frɪzbɪ] n Frisbee® m

fritter ['frɪtə'] n beignet m

frivolous ['frɪvələs] adj frivole

fro [frəʊ] see **to**

frock [frɔk] n robe f

frog [frɔg] n grenouille f; **frogman** (irreg) n homme-grenouille m

 KEYWORD

from [frɔm] prep **1** (indicating starting place, origin etc) de; **where do you come from?**, **where are you from?** d'où venez-vous?; **where has he come from?** d'où arrive-t-il?; **from London to Paris** de Londres à Paris; **to escape from sb/sth** échapper à qn/qch; **a letter/telephone call from my sister** une lettre/un appel de ma sœur; **to drink from the bottle** boire à (même) la bouteille; **tell him from me that ...** dites-lui de ma part que ...

2 (indicating time) (à partir) de; **from one o'clock to or until or till two** d'une heure à deux heures; **from January (on)** à partir de janvier

3 (indicating distance) de; **the hotel is one kilometre from the beach** l'hôtel est à un kilomètre de la plage

4 (indicating price, number etc) de; **prices range from £10 to £50** les prix varient entre 10 livres et 50 livres; **the interest rate was increased from 9% to 10%** le taux d'intérêt est passé de 9% à 10%

5 (indicating difference) de; **he can't tell red from green** il ne peut pas distinguer le rouge du vert; **to be different from sb/sth** être différent de qn/qch

6 (because of, on the basis of): **from what he says** d'après ce qu'il dit; **weak from hunger** affaibli par la faim

front [frʌnt] n (of house, dress) devant m; (of coach, train) avant m; (promenade: also: **sea ~**) bord m de mer; (Mil, Pol, Meteorology) front m; (fig: appearances) contenance f, façade f ▷ adj de devant; (seat, wheel) avant inv ▷ vi: **in ~ (of)** devant; **front door** n porte f d'entrée; (of car) portière f avant; **frontier** ['frʌntɪə'] n frontière f; **front page** n première page; **front-wheel drive** n traction f avant

frost [frɔst] n gel m, gelée f; (also: **hoar~**) givre m; **frostbite** n gelures fpl; **frosting** n (esp US: on cake) glaçage m; **frosty** adj (window) couvert(e) de givre; (weather, welcome) glacial(e)

froth [frɔθ] n mousse f; écume f

frown [fraʊn] n froncement m de sourcils ▷ vi froncer les sourcils

froze [frəʊz] pt of **freeze**

frozen ['frəʊzn] pp of **freeze** ▷ adj (food) congelé(e); (very cold: person: Comm: assets) gelé(e)

fruit [fruːt] n (pl inv) fruit m; **fruit juice** n jus m de fruit; **fruit machine** n (BRIT) machine f à sous; **fruit salad** n salade f de fruits

frustrate [frʌs'treɪt] vt frustrer; **frustrated** adj frustré(e)

fry (pt, pp fried) [fraɪ, -d] vt (faire) frire; **small ~** le menu fretin; **frying pan** n poêle f (à frire)

ft. abbr = **foot**; **feet**

fudge [fʌdʒ] n (Culin) sorte de confiserie à base de sucre, de beurre et de lait

fuel [fjʊəl] n (for heating) combustible m; (for engine) carburant m; **fuel tank** n (in vehicle) réservoir m de or à carburant

fulfil (US **fulfill**) [fʊl'fɪl] vt (function, condition) remplir; (order) exécuter; (wish, desire) satisfaire, réaliser

full [fʊl] adj plein(e); (details, hotel, bus) complet(-ète); (busy: day) chargé(e); (skirt) ample, large ▷ adv: **to know ~ well that** savoir fort bien que; **I'm ~ (up)** j'ai bien mangé; **~ employment/fare** plein emploi/tarif; **a ~ two hours** deux bonnes heures; **at ~ speed** à toute vitesse; **in ~** (reproduce, quote, pay) intégralement; (write name etc) en toutes lettres; **full-length** adj (portrait) en pied; (coat) long(ue); **full-length film** long métrage; **full moon** n pleine lune; **full-scale** adj (model) grandeur nature inv; (search, retreat) complet(-ète), total(e); **full stop** n point m; **full-time** adj, adv (work) à plein temps; **fully** adv entièrement, complètement; (at least)

fumble ['fʌmbl] vi fouiller, tâtonner; **fumble with** vt fus tripoter

fume [fjuːm] vi (rage) rager; **fumes** npl vapeurs fpl, émanations fpl, gaz mpl

fun [fʌn] n amusement m, divertissement m; **to have ~** s'amuser; **for ~** pour rire; **to make ~ of** se moquer de

function ['fʌŋkʃən] n fonction f; (reception, dinner) cérémonie f, soirée officielle ▷ vi fonctionner

fund [fʌnd] n caisse f, fonds m; (source, store) source f, mine f; **funds** npl (money) fonds mpl

fundamental [fʌndə'mentl] adj fondamental(e)

funeral ['fjuːnərəl] n enterrement m, obsèques fpl (more formal occasion); **funeral director** n entrepreneur m des pompes funèbres; **funeral parlour** [-'pɑːlə'] n (BRIT) dépôt m mortuaire

funfair ['fʌnfɛə'] n (BRIT) fête (foraine)

fungus (pl **fungi**) ['fʌŋgəs, -gaɪ] n champignon m; (mould) moisissure f

funnel ['fʌnl] n entonnoir m; (of ship) cheminée f

funny ['fʌnɪ] adj amusant(e), drôle; (strange) curieux(-euse), bizarre

fur [fəː'] n fourrure f; (BRIT: in kettle etc) (dépôt m de) tartre m; **fur coat** n manteau m de fourrure

furious ['fjuərɪəs] adj furieux(-euse); (effort) acharné(e)

furnish ['fəːnɪʃ] vt meubler; (supply) fournir; **furnishings** npl mobilier m, articles mpl d'ameublement

furniture ['fəːnɪtʃə'] n meubles mpl, mobilier m; **piece of ~** meuble m

furry ['fəːrɪ] adj (animal) à fourrure; (toy) en peluche

further ['fəːðə'] adj supplémentaire, autre; nouveau (nouvelle) ▷ adv plus loin; (more) davantage; (moreover) de plus ▷ vt faire avancer or progresser, promouvoir; **further education** n enseignement m postscolaire (recyclage, formation professionnelle); **furthermore** adv de plus, en outre

furthest ['fəːðɪst] superlative of **far**

fury ['fjuərɪ] n fureur f

fuse (US **fuze**) [fjuːz] n fusible m; (for bomb etc) amorce f, détonateur m ▷ vt, vi (metal) fondre; (BRIT: Elec): **to ~ the lights** faire sauter les fusibles or les plombs; **fuse box** n boîte f à fusibles

fusion ['fjuːʒən] n fusion f

fuss [fʌs] n (anxiety, excitement) chichis mpl, façons fpl; (commotion) tapage m; (complaining, trouble) histoire(s) f(pl); **to make a ~** faire des façons (or des histoires); **to make a ~ of sb** dorloter qn; **fussy** adj (person) tatillon(ne), difficile, chichiteux(-euse); (dress, style) tarabiscoté(e)

future ['fjuːtʃə'] adj futur(e) ▷ n avenir m; (Ling) futur m; **futures** npl (Comm) opérations fpl à terme; **in (the) ~** à l'avenir

fuze [fjuːz] n, vt, vi (US) = **fuse**

fuzzy ['fʌzɪ] adj (Phot) flou(e); (hair) crépu(e)

f

g

G [dʒiː] n (Mus): **G** sol m

g. abbr (= gram) g

gadget ['gædʒɪt] n gadget m

Gaelic ['geɪlɪk] adj, n (Ling) gaélique (m)

gag [gæg] n (on mouth) bâillon m; (joke) gag m
▷ vt (prisoner etc) bâillonner

gain [geɪn] n (improvement) gain m; (profit) gain,
profit m ▷ vt gagner ▷ vi (watch) avancer; **to
~ from/by** gagner de/à; **to ~ on sb** (catch up)
rattraper qn; **to ~ 3lbs (in weight)** prendre 3
livres; **to ~ ground** gagner du terrain

gal. abbr = **gallon**

gala ['gɑːlə] n gala m

galaxy ['gæləksɪ] n galaxie f

gale [geɪl] n coup m de vent

gall bladder ['gɔːl-] n vésicule f biliaire

gallery ['gælərɪ] n (also: **art ~**) musée m; (:
private) galerie; (: in theatre) dernier balcon

gallon ['gæln] n gallon m (BRIT = 4.543 l; US =
3.785 l)

gallop ['gæləp] n galop m ▷ vi galoper

gallstone ['gɔːlstəun] n calcul m (biliaire)

gamble ['gæmbl] n pari m, risque calculé ▷ vt,
vi jouer; **to ~ on** (fig) miser sur; **gambler** n
joueur m; **gambling** n jeu m

game [geɪm] n jeu m; (event) match m; (of
tennis, chess, cards) partie f; (Hunting) gibier m
▷ adj (willing): **to be ~ (for)** être prêt(e) (à or
pour); **big ~** gros gibier; **games** npl (Scol) sport
m; (sport event) jeux; **games console** ['geɪmz-]
n console f de jeux vidéo; **game show** n jeu
télévisé

gammon ['gæmən] n (bacon) quartier m de
lard fumé; (ham) jambon fumé or salé

gang [gæŋ] n bande f; (of workmen) équipe f

gangster ['gæŋstər] n gangster m, bandit m

gap [gæp] n trou m; (in time) intervalle m;
(difference): **~ (between)** écart m (entre)

gape [geɪp] vi (person) être or rester bouche
bée; (hole, shirt) être ouvert(e)

gap year n année que certains étudiants prennent
pour voyager ou pour travailler avant d'entrer à
l'université

garage ['gærɑːʒ] n garage m; **garage sale** n
vide-grenier m

garbage ['gɑːbɪdʒ] n (us: rubbish) ordures
fpl, détritus mpl; (inf: nonsense) âneries fpl;
garbage can n (us) poubelle f, boîte f à
ordures; **garbage collector** n (us) éboueur m

garden ['gɑːdn] n jardin m; **gardens** npl
(public) jardin public; (private) parc m; **garden
centre** (BRIT) n pépinière f, jardinerie f;
gardener n jardinier m; **gardening** n
jardinage m

garlic ['gɑːlɪk] n ail m

garment ['gɑːmənt] n vêtement m

garnish ['gɑːnɪʃ] (Culin) vt garnir ▷ n
décoration f

garrison ['gærɪsn] n garnison f

gas [gæs] n gaz m; (us: gasoline) essence f
▷ vt asphyxier; **I can smell ~** ça sent le gaz;
gas cooker n (BRIT) cuisinière f à gaz; **gas
cylinder** n bouteille f de gaz; **gas fire** n (BRIT)
radiateur m à gaz

gasket ['gæskɪt] n (Aut) joint m de culasse

gasoline ['gæsəliːn] n (us) essence f

gasp [gɑːsp] n halètement m; (of shock etc): **she
gave a small ~ of pain** la douleur lui coupa le
souffle ▷ vi haleter; (fig) avoir le souffle coupé

gas: **gas pedal** n (us) accélérateur m; **gas
station** n (us) station-service f; **gas tank** n
(us Aut) réservoir m d'essence

gate [geɪt] n (of garden) portail m; (of field, at
level crossing) barrière f; (of building, town, at
airport) porte f

gateau (pl **~x**) ['gætəu, -z] n gros gâteau à
la crème

gatecrash ['geɪtkræʃ] vt s'introduire sans
invitation dans

gateway ['geɪtweɪ] n porte f

gather ['gæðər] vt (flowers, fruit) cueillir; (pick
up) ramasser; (assemble: objects) rassembler;
(: people) réunir; (information) recueillir;
(understand) comprendre; (Sewing) froncer ▷ vi
(assemble) se rassembler; **to ~ speed** prendre
de la vitesse; **gathering** n rassemblement m

gauge [geɪdʒ] n (instrument) jauge f ▷ vt
jauger; (fig) juger de

gave [geɪv] pt of **give**

gay [geɪ] adj (homosexual) homosexuel(le); (colour) gai, vif (vive)

gaze [geɪz] n regard m fixe ▷ vi: **to ~ at** vt fixer du regard

GB abbr = **Great Britain**

GCSE n abbr (BRIT: = General Certificate of Secondary Education) examen passé à l'âge de 16 ans sanctionnant les connaissances de l'élève

gear [gɪə^r] n matériel m, équipement m; (Tech) engrenage m; (Aut) vitesse f ▷ vt (fig: adapt) adapter; **top** or (us) **high/low ~** quatrième (or cinquième)/première vitesse; **in ~** en prise; **gear up** vi: **to ~ up (to do)** se préparer (à faire); **gear box** n boîte f de vitesse; **gear lever** n levier m de vitesse; **gear shift** (us) n = **gear lever**; **gear stick** (BRIT) n = **gear lever**

geese [giːs] npl of **goose**

gel [dʒɛl] n gelée f

gem [dʒɛm] n pierre précieuse

Gemini ['dʒɛmɪnaɪ] n les Gémeaux mpl

gender ['dʒɛndə^r] n genre m; (person's sex) sexe m

gene [dʒiːn] n (Biol) gène m

general ['dʒɛnərl] n général m ▷ adj général(e); (in ~ en général; **general anaesthetic** (us **general anesthetic**) n anesthésie générale; **general election** n élection(s) législative(s); **generalize** vi généraliser; **generally** adv généralement; **general practitioner** n généraliste m/f; **general store** n épicerie f

generate ['dʒɛnəreɪt] vt engendrer; (electricity) produire

generation [dʒɛnə'reɪʃən] n génération f; (of electricity etc) production f

generator ['dʒɛnəreɪtə^r] n générateur m

generosity [dʒɛnə'rɒsɪtɪ] n générosité f

generous ['dʒɛnərəs] adj généreux(-euse); (copious) copieux(-euse)

genetic [dʒɪ'nɛtɪk] adj génétique; **~ engineering** ingénierie m génétique; **~ fingerprinting** système m d'empreinte génétique; **genetically modified** adj (food etc) génétiquement modifié(e); **genetics** n génétique f

Geneva [dʒɪ'niːvə] n Genève

genitals ['dʒɛnɪtlz] npl organes génitaux

genius ['dʒiːnɪəs] n génie m

gent [dʒɛnt] n abbr (BRIT inf) = **gentleman**

gentle ['dʒɛntl] adj doux (douce); (breeze, touch) léger(-ère)

gentleman (irreg) ['dʒɛntlmən] n monsieur m; (well-bred man) gentleman m

gently ['dʒɛntlɪ] adv doucement

gents [dʒɛnts] n W.-C. mpl (pour hommes)

genuine ['dʒɛnjuɪn] adj véritable, authentique; (person, emotion) sincère; **genuinely** adv sincèrement, vraiment

geographic(al) [dʒɪə'græfɪk(l)] adj géographique

geography [dʒɪ'ɒgrəfɪ] n géographie f

geology [dʒɪ'ɒlədʒɪ] n géologie f

geometry [dʒɪ'ɒmətrɪ] n géométrie f

geranium [dʒɪ'reɪnɪəm] n géranium m

geriatric [dʒɛrɪ'ætrɪk] adj gériatrique ▷ n patient(e) gériatrique

germ [dʒəːm] n (Med) microbe m

German ['dʒəːmən] adj allemand(e) ▷ n Allemand(e); (Ling) allemand m; **German measles** n rubéole f

Germany ['dʒəːmənɪ] n Allemagne f

gesture ['dʒɛstjə^r] n geste m

KEYWORD

get [gɛt] (pt, pp **got**, pp **gotten** (US)) vi
1 (become, be) devenir; **to get old/tired** devenir vieux/fatigué, vieillir/se fatiguer; **to get drunk** s'enivrer; **to get dirty** se salir; **to get married** se marier; **when do I get paid?** quand est-ce que je serai payé?; **it's getting late** il se fait tard
2 (go): **to get to/from** aller à/de; **to get home** rentrer chez soi; **how did you get here?** comment es-tu arrivé ici?
3 (begin) commencer or se mettre à; **to get to know sb** apprendre à connaître qn; **I'm getting to like him** je commence à l'apprécier; **let's get going** or **started** allons-y
4 (modal aux vb): **you've got to do it** il faut que vous le fassiez; **I've got to tell the police** je dois le dire à la police

▷ vt **1**: **to get sth done** (do) faire qch; (have done) faire faire qch; **to get sth/sb ready** préparer qch/qn; **to get one's hair cut** se faire couper les cheveux; **to get the car going** or **to go** (faire) démarrer la voiture; **to get sb to do sth** faire faire qch à qn
2 (obtain: money, permission, results) obtenir, avoir; (buy) acheter; (find: job, flat) trouver; (fetch: person, object) aller chercher; **to get sth for sb** procurer qch à qn; **get me Mr Jones, please** (on phone) passez-moi Mr Jones, s'il vous plaît; **can I get you a drink?** est-ce que je peux vous servir à boire?
3 (receive: present, letter) recevoir, avoir; (acquire: reputation) avoir; (prize) obtenir; **what did you get for your birthday?** qu'est-ce que tu as eu pour ton anniversaire?; **how much did you get for the painting?** combien avez-vous vendu le tableau?
4 (catch) prendre, saisir, attraper; (hit: target etc) atteindre; **to get sb by the arm/throat** prendre or saisir or attraper qn par le bras/à la gorge; **get him!** arrête-le!; **the bullet got him in the leg** il a pris la balle dans la jambe
5 (take, move): **to get sth to sb** faire parvenir qch à qn; **do you think we'll get it through**

the door? on arrivera à le faire passer par la porte?

6 (*catch, take: plane, bus etc*) prendre; **where do I get the train for Birmingham?** où prend-on le train pour Birmingham?

7 (*understand*) comprendre, saisir; (*hear*) entendre; **I've got it!** j'ai compris!; **I don't get your meaning** je ne vois or comprends pas ce que vous voulez dire; **I didn't get your name** je n'ai pas entendu votre nom

8 (*have, possess*): **to have got** avoir; **how many have you got?** vous en avez combien?

9 (*illness*) avoir; **I've got a cold** j'ai le rhume; **she got pneumonia and died** elle a fait une pneumonie et elle en est morte

get away *vi* partir, s'en aller; (*escape*) s'échapper

get away with *vt fus* (*punishment*) en être quitte pour; (*crime etc*) se faire pardonner

get back *vi* (*return*) rentrer
▷ *vt* récupérer, recouvrer; **when do we get back?** quand serons-nous de retour?

get in *vi* entrer; (*arrive home*) rentrer; (*train*) arriver

get into *vt fus* entrer dans; (*car, train etc*) monter dans; (*clothes*) mettre, enfiler, endosser; **to get into bed/a rage** se mettre au lit/en colère

get off *vi* (*from train etc*) descendre; (*depart: person, car*) s'en aller
▷ *vt* (*remove: clothes, stain*) enlever
▷ *vt fus* (*train, bus*) descendre de; **where do I get off?** où est-ce que je dois descendre?

get on *vi* (*at exam etc*) se débrouiller; (*agree*): **to get on (with)** s'entendre (avec); **how are you getting on?** comment ça va?
▷ *vt fus* monter dans; (*horse*) monter sur

get out *vi* sortir; (*of vehicle*) descendre
▷ *vt* sortir

get out of *vt fus* sortir de; (*duty etc*) échapper à, se soustraire à

get over *vt fus* (*illness*) se remettre de

get through *vi* (*Tel*) avoir la communication; **to get through to sb** atteindre qn

get up *vi* (*rise*) se lever
▷ *vt fus* monter

getaway ['gɛtəweɪ] *n* fuite *f*

Ghana ['gɑːnə] *n* Ghana *m*

ghastly ['gɑːstlɪ] *adj* atroce, horrible

ghetto ['gɛtəu] *n* ghetto *m*

ghost [gəust] *n* fantôme *m*, revenant *m*

giant ['dʒaɪənt] *n* géant(e) *f* ▷ *adj* géant(e), énorme

gift [gɪft] *n* cadeau *m*; (*donation, talent*) don *m*; **gifted** *adj* doué(e); **gift shop** (*us* **gift store**) *n* boutique *f* de cadeaux; **gift token, gift voucher** *n* chèque-cadeau *m*

gig [gɪg] *n* (*inf: concert*) concert *m*

gigabyte ['dʒɪgəbaɪt] *n* gigaoctet *m*

gigantic [dʒaɪˈgæntɪk] *adj* gigantesque

giggle ['gɪgl] *vi* pouffer, ricaner sottement

gills [gɪlz] *npl* (*of fish*) ouïes *fpl*, branchies *fpl*

gilt [gɪlt] *n* dorure *f* ▷ *adj* doré(e)

gimmick ['gɪmɪk] *n* truc *m*

gin [dʒɪn] *n* gin *m*

ginger ['dʒɪndʒə*r*] *n* gingembre *m*

gipsy ['dʒɪpsɪ] *n* = **gypsy**

giraffe [dʒɪˈrɑːf] *n* girafe *f*

girl [gəːl] *n* fille *f*, fillette *f*; (*young unmarried woman*) jeune fille; (*daughter*) fille *f*; **an English ~** une jeune Anglaise; **girl band** *n* girls band *m*; **girlfriend** *n* (*of girl*) amie *f*; (*of boy*) petite amie; **Girl Guide** *n* (*BRIT*) éclaireuse *f*; (*Roman Catholic*) guide *f*; **Girl Scout** *n* (*US*) = **Girl Guide**

gist [dʒɪst] *n* essentiel *m*

give [gɪv] *vb* (*pt* **gave**, *pp* **~n**) ▷ *vt* donner ▷ *vi* (*break*) céder; (*stretch: fabric*) se prêter; **to ~ sb sth, ~ sth to sb** donner qch à qn; (*gift*) offrir qch à qn; (*message*) transmettre qch à qn; **to ~ sb a call/kiss** appeler/embrasser qn; **to ~ a cry/sigh** pousser un cri/un soupir; **give away** *vt* donner; (*give free*) faire cadeau de; (*betray*) donner, trahir; (*disclose*) révéler; **give back** *vt* rendre; **give in** *vi* céder ▷ *vt* donner; **give out** *vt* (*food etc*) distribuer; **give up** *vi* renoncer ▷ *vt* renoncer à; **to ~ up smoking** arrêter de fumer; **to ~ o.s. up** se rendre

given ['gɪvn] *pp of* **give** ▷ *adj* (*fixed: time, amount*) donné(e), déterminé(e) ▷ *conj*: **~ the circumstances ...** étant donné les circonstances ..., vu les circonstances ...; **~ that ...** étant donné que ...

glacier ['glæsɪə*r*] *n* glacier *m*

glad [glæd] *adj* content(e); **gladly** ['glædlɪ] *adv* volontiers

glamorous ['glæmərəs] *adj* (*person*) séduisant(e); (*job*) prestigieux(-euse)

glamour (*us* **glamor**) ['glæmə*r*] *n* éclat *m*, prestige *m*

glance [glɑːns] *n* coup *m* d'œil ▷ *vi*: **to ~ at** jeter un coup d'œil à

gland [glænd] *n* glande *f*

glare [glɛə*r*] *n* (*of anger*) regard furieux; (*of light*) lumière éblouissante; (*of publicity*) feux *mpl* ▷ *vi* briller d'un éclat aveuglant; **to ~ at** lancer un regard or des regards furieux à; **glaring** *adj* (*mistake*) criant(e), qui saute aux yeux

glass [glɑːs] *n* verre *m*; **glasses** *npl* (*spectacles*) lunettes *fpl*

glaze [gleɪz] *vt* (*door*) vitrer; (*pottery*) vernir ▷ *n* vernis *m*

gleam [gliːm] *vi* luire, briller

glen [glɛn] *n* vallée *f*

glide [glaɪd] *vi* glisser; (*Aviat, bird*) planer; **glider** *n* (*Aviat*) planeur *m*

glimmer ['glɪmə*r*] *n* lueur *f*

glimpse [glɪmps] *n* vision passagère, aperçu

m ▷ vt entrevoir, apercevoir

glint [glɪnt] vi étinceler

glisten ['glɪsn] vi briller, luire

glitter ['glɪtə'] vi scintiller, briller

global ['gləubl] adj (world-wide) mondial(e); (overall) global(e); **globalization** n mondialisation f; **global warming** n réchauffement m de la planète

globe [gləub] n globe m

gloom [glu:m] n obscurité f; (sadness) tristesse f, mélancolie f; **gloomy** adj (person) morose; (place, outlook) sombre

glorious ['glɔːrɪəs] adj glorieux(-euse); (beautiful) splendide

glory ['glɔːrɪ] n gloire f, splendeur f

gloss [glɒs] n (shine) brillant m, vernis m; (also: ~ **paint**) peinture brillante ou laquée

glossary ['glɒsərɪ] n glossaire m, lexique m

glossy ['glɒsɪ] adj brillant(e), luisant(e) ▷ n (also: ~ **magazine**) revue f de luxe

glove [glʌv] n gant m; **glove compartment** n (Aut) boîte f à gants, vide-poches m inv

glow [gləu] vi rougeoyer; (face) rayonner; (eyes) briller

glucose ['glu:kəus] n glucose m

glue [glu:] n colle f ▷ vt coller

GM abbr (= genetically modified) génétiquement modifié(e)

gm abbr (= gram) g

GMO n abbr (= genetically modified organism) OGM m

GMT abbr (= Greenwich Mean Time) GMT

gnaw [nɔː] vt ronger

go [gəu] vb (pt **went**, pp **gone**) ▷ vi aller; (depart) partir, s'en aller; (work) marcher; (break) céder; (time) passer; (be sold): **to go for £10** se vendre 10 livres; (become): **to go pale/mouldy** pâlir/moisir ▷ n (pl **goes**): **to have a go (at)** essayer (de faire); **to be on the go** être en mouvement; **whose go is it?** à qui est-ce de jouer?; **he's going to do it** il va le faire, il est sur le point de le faire; **to go for a walk** aller se promener; **to go dancing/shopping** aller danser/faire les courses; **to go and see sb, to go to see sb** aller voir qn; **how did it go?** comment est-ce que ça s'est passé?; **to go round the back/by the shop** passer par derrière/devant le magasin; **... to go** (us: food) ... à emporter; **go ahead** vi (take place) avoir lieu; (get going) y aller; **go away** vi partir, s'en aller; **go back** vi rentrer; revenir; (go again) retourner; **go by** vi (years, time) passer, s'écouler ▷ vt fus s'en tenir à; (believe) en croire; **go down** vi descendre; (number, price, amount) baisser; (ship) couler; (sun) se coucher ▷ vt fus descendre; **go for** vt fus (fetch) aller chercher; (like) aimer; (attack) s'en prendre à; attaquer; **go in** vi entrer; **go into** vt fus entrer dans; (investigate) étudier, examiner; (embark on) se

lancer dans; **go off** vi partir, s'en aller; (food) se gâter; (milk) tourner; (bomb) sauter; (alarm clock) sonner; (alarm) se déclencher; (lights etc) s'éteindre; (event) se dérouler ▷ vt fus ne plus aimer; **the gun went off** le coup est parti; **go on** vi continuer; (happen) se passer; (lights) s'allumer ▷ vt fus: **to go on doing** continuer à faire; **go out** vi sortir; (fire, light) s'éteindre; (tide) descendre; **to go out with sb** sortir avec qn; **go over** vi, vt fus (check) revoir, vérifier; **go past** vt fus: **to go past sth** passer devant qch; **go round** vi (circulate: news, rumour) circuler; (revolve) tourner; (suffice) suffire (pour tout le monde); (visit): **to go round to sb's** passer chez qn; aller chez qn; (make a detour): **to go round (by)** faire un détour (par); **go through** vt fus (town etc) traverser; (search through) fouiller; (suffer) subir; (approve: price) augmenter ▷ vt fus gravir; **go with** vt fus aller avec; **go without** vt fus se passer de

go-ahead ['gəuəhɛd] adj dynamique, entreprenant(e) ▷ n feu vert

goal [gəul] n but m; **goalkeeper** n gardien m de but; **goal-post** n poteau m de but

goat [gəut] n chèvre f

gobble ['gɒbl] vt (also: ~ **down**, ~ **up**) engloutir

god [gɒd] n dieu m; **G~** Dieu; **godchild** n filleul(e); **goddaughter** n filleule f; **goddess** n déesse f; **godfather** n parrain m; **godmother** n marraine f; **godson** n filleul m

goggles ['gɒglz] npl (for skiing etc) lunettes (protectrices); (for swimming) lunettes de piscine

going ['gəuɪŋ] n (conditions) état m du terrain ▷ adj: **the ~ rate** le tarif en vigueur

gold [gəuld] n or m ▷ adj en or; (reserves) d'or; **golden** adj (made of gold) en or; (gold in colour) doré(e); **goldfish** n poisson m rouge; **goldmine** n mine f d'or; **gold-plated** adj plaqué(e) or inv

golf [gɒlf] n golf m; **golf ball** n balle f de golf; (on typewriter) boule f; **golf club** n club m de golf; (stick) club m, crosse f de golf; **golf course** n terrain m de golf; **golfer** n joueur(-euse) de golf

gone [gɒn] pp of **go**

gong [gɒŋ] n gong m

good [gud] adj bon(ne); (kind) gentil(le); (child) sage; (weather) beau (belle) ▷ n bien m; **goods** npl marchandise f, articles mpl; **~!** bon!, très bien!; **to be ~ at** être bon en; **to be ~ for** être bon pour; **it's no ~ complaining** cela ne sert à rien de se plaindre; **to make ~** (deficit) combler; (losses) compenser; **for ~** (for ever) pour de bon, une fois pour toutes; **would you be ~ enough to ...?** auriez-vous la bonté ou l'amabilité de ...?; **is this any ~?** (will it do?) est-ce que ceci fera l'affaire?, est-ce que cela peut vous rendre service?; (what's it like?)

qu'est-ce que ça vaut?; **a ~ deal (of)** beaucoup (de); **a ~ many** beaucoup (de); **~ morning/ afternoon!** bonjour!; **~ evening!** bonsoir!; **~ night!** bonsoir!; (on going to bed) bonne nuit!; **goodbye** excl au revoir!; **to say goodbye to sb** dire au revoir à qn; **Good Friday** n Vendredi saint; **good-looking** adj beau (belle), bien inv; **good-natured** adj (person) qui a un bon naturel; **goodness** n (of person) bonté f; **for goodness sake!** je vous en prie!; **goodness gracious!** mon Dieu!; **goods train** n (BRIT) train m de marchandises; **goodwill** n bonne volonté

goose (pl **geese**) [guːs, giːs] n oie f

gooseberry ['guzbəri] n groseille f à maquereau; **to play ~** (BRIT) tenir la chandelle

goose bumps, goose pimples npl chair f de poule

gorge [gɔːdʒ] n gorge f ▷ vt: **to ~ o.s. (on)** se gorger (de)

gorgeous ['gɔːdʒəs] adj splendide, superbe

gorilla [gə'rɪlə] n gorille m

gosh (inf) [gɔʃ] excl mince alors!

gospel ['gɔspl] n évangile m

gossip ['gɔsɪp] n (chat) bavardages mpl; (malicious) commérage m, cancans mpl; (person) commère f ▷ vi bavarder; cancaner, faire des commérages; **gossip column** n (Press) échos mpl

got [gɔt] pt, pp of **get**

gotten ['gɔtn] (US) pp of **get**

gourmet ['guəmeɪ] n gourmet m, gastronome m/f

govern ['gʌvən] vt gouverner; (influence) déterminer; **government** n gouvernement m; (BRIT: ministers) ministère m; **governor** n (of colony, state, bank) gouverneur m; (of school, hospital etc) administrateur(-trice); (BRIT: of prison) directeur(-trice)

gown [gaun] n robe f; (of teacher, BRIT: of judge) toge f

G.P. n abbr (Med) = **general practitioner**

grab [græb] vt saisir, empoigner ▷ vi: **to ~ at** essayer de saisir

grace [greɪs] n grâce f ▷ vt (honour) honorer; (adorn) orner; **5 days' ~** un répit de 5 jours; **graceful** adj gracieux(-euse), élégant(e); **gracious** ['greɪʃəs] adj bienveillant(e)

grade [greɪd] n (Comm: quality) qualité f; (size) calibre m; (type) catégorie f; (in hierarchy) grade m, échelon m; (Scol) note f; (US: school class) classe f; (: gradient) pente f ▷ vt classer; (by size) calibrer; **grade crossing** n (US) passage m à niveau; **grade school** n (US) école f primaire

gradient ['greɪdɪənt] n inclinaison f, pente f

gradual ['grædjuəl] adj graduel(le), progressif(-ive); **gradually** adv peu à peu, graduellement

graduate n ['grædjuɪt] diplômé(e)

d'université; (US: of high school) diplômé(e) de fin d'études ▷ vi ['grædjueɪt] obtenir un diplôme d'université (or de fin d'études); **graduation** [grædju'eɪʃən] n cérémonie f de remise des diplômes

graffiti [grə'fiːtɪ] npl graffiti mpl

graft [grɑːft] n (Agr, Med) greffe f; (bribery) corruption f ▷ vt greffer; **hard ~** (BRIT: inf) boulot acharné

grain [greɪn] n (single piece) grain m; (no pl: cereals) céréales fpl; (US: corn) blé m

gram [græm] n gramme m

grammar ['græmə'] n grammaire f; **grammar school** n (BRIT) ≈ lycée m

gramme [græm] n = **gram**

gran (inf) [græn] n (BRIT) mamie f (inf), mémé f (inf)

grand [grænd] adj magnifique, splendide; (gesture etc) noble; **grandad** (inf) n = **granddad**; **grandchild** (pl **~ren**) n petit-fils m, petite-fille f; **grandchildren** npl petits-enfants; **granddad** n (inf) papy m (inf), papi m (inf), pépé m (inf); **granddaughter** n petite-fille f; **grandfather** n grand-père m; **grandma** n (inf) = **gran**; **grandmother** n grand-mère f; **grandpa** n (inf) = **granddad**; **grandparents** npl grands-parents mpl; **grand piano** n piano m à queue; **Grand Prix** [grɑ̃'priː] n (Aut) grand prix automobile; **grandson** n petit-fils m

granite ['grænɪt] n granit m

granny ['grænɪ] n (inf) = **gran**

grant [grɑːnt] vt accorder; (a request) accéder à; (admit) concéder ▷ n (Scol) bourse f; (Admin) subside m, subvention f; **to take sth for ~ed** considérer qch comme acquis; **to take sb for ~ed** considérer qn comme faisant partie du décor

grape [greɪp] n raisin m

grapefruit ['greɪpfruːt] n pamplemousse m

graph [grɑːf] n graphique m, courbe f; **graphic** ['græfɪk] adj graphique; (vivid) vivant(e); **graphics** n (art) arts mpl graphiques; (process) graphisme m ▷ npl (drawings) illustrations fpl

grasp [grɑːsp] vt saisir ▷ n (grip) prise f; (fig) compréhension f, connaissance f

grass [grɑːs] n herbe f; (lawn) gazon m; **grasshopper** n sauterelle f

grate [greɪt] n grille f de cheminée ▷ vi grincer ▷ vt (Culin) râper

grateful ['greɪtful] adj reconnaissant(e)

grater ['greɪtə'] n râpe f

gratitude ['grætɪtjuːd] n gratitude f

grave [greɪv] n tombe f ▷ adj grave, sérieux(-euse)

gravel ['grævl] n gravier m

gravestone ['greɪvstəun] n pierre tombale

graveyard ['greɪvjɑːd] n cimetière m

gravity ['grævɪtɪ] n (Physics) gravité f;

pesanteur f; (seriousness) gravité
gravy ['greɪvɪ] n jus m (de viande), sauce f (au jus de viande)
gray [greɪ] adj (US) = **grey**
graze [greɪz] vi paître, brouter ▷ vt (touch lightly) frôler, effleurer; (scrape) écorcher ▷ n écorchure f
grease [gri:s] n (fat) graisse f; (lubricant) lubrifiant m ▷ vt graisser; lubrifier; **greasy** adj gras(se), graisseux(-euse); (hands, clothes) graisseux
great [greɪt] adj grand(e); (heat, pain etc) très fort(e), intense; (inf) formidable; **Great Britain** n Grande-Bretagne f; **great-grandfather** n arrière-grand-père m; **great-grandmother** n arrière-grand-mère f; **greatly** adv très, grandement; (with verbs) beaucoup
Greece [gri:s] n Grèce f
greed [gri:d] n (also: **~iness**) avidité f; (for food) gourmandise f; **greedy** adj avide; (for food) gourmand(e)
Greek [gri:k] adj grec (grecque) ▷ n Grec (Grecque); (Ling) grec m
green [gri:n] adj vert(e); (inexperienced) (bien) jeune, naïf(-ive); (ecological: product etc) écologique ▷ n (colour) vert m; (on golf course) green m; (stretch of grass) pelouse f; **greens** npl (vegetables) légumes verts; **green card** n (Aut) carte verte; (US: work permit) permis m de travail; **greengage** n reine-claude f; **greengrocer** n (BRIT) marchand m de fruits et légumes; **greengrocer's (shop)** n magasin m de fruits et légumes; **greenhouse** n serre f; **greenhouse effect** n: **the greenhouse effect** l'effet m de serre
Greenland ['gri:nlənd] n Groenland m
green salad n salade verte
greet [gri:t] vt accueillir; (welcome) saluer; **greeting** n salutation f; **Christmas/birthday greetings** souhaits mpl de Noël/de bon anniversaire; **greeting(s) card** n carte f de vœux
grew [gru:] pt of **grow**
grey (US **gray**) [greɪ] adj gris(e); (dismal) sombre; **grey-haired** adj aux cheveux gris; **greyhound** n lévrier m
grid [grɪd] n grille f; (Elec) réseau m; **gridlock** n (traffic jam) embouteillage m
grief [gri:f] n chagrin m, douleur f
grievance ['gri:vəns] n doléance f, grief m; (cause for complaint) grief
grieve [gri:v] vi avoir du chagrin; se désoler ▷ vt faire de la peine à, affliger; **to ~ for sb** pleurer qn
grill [grɪl] n (on cooker) gril m; (also: **mixed ~**) grillade(s) f(pl) ▷ vt (BRIT) griller; (inf: question) cuisiner
grille [grɪl] n grillage m; (Aut) calandre f
grim [grɪm] adj sinistre, lugubre; (serious, stern)

sévère
grime [graɪm] n crasse f
grin [grɪn] n large sourire m ▷ vi sourire
grind [graɪnd] vb (pt, pp **ground**) ▷ vt écraser; (coffee, pepper etc) moudre; (US: meat) hacher ▷ n (work) corvée f
grip [grɪp] n (handclasp) poigne f; (control) prise f; (handle) poignée f; (holdall) sac m de voyage ▷ vt saisir, empoigner; (viewer, reader) captiver; **to come to ~s with** se colleter avec, en venir aux prises avec; **to ~ the road** (Aut) adhérer à la route; **gripping** adj prenant(e), palpitant(e)
grit [grɪt] n gravillon m; (courage) cran m ▷ vt (road) sabler; **to ~ one's teeth** serrer les dents
grits [grɪts] npl (US) gruau m de maïs
groan [grəun] n (of pain) gémissement m ▷ vi gémir
grocer ['grəusə'] n épicier m; **groceries** npl provisions fpl; **grocer's (shop), grocery** n épicerie f
groin [grɔɪn] n aine f
groom [gru:m] n (for horses) palefrenier m; (also: **bride~**) marié m ▷ vt (horse) panser; (fig): **to ~ sb for** former qn pour
groove [gru:v] n sillon m, rainure f
grope [grəup] vi tâtonner; **to ~ for** chercher à tâtons
gross [grəus] adj grossier(-ière); (Comm) brut(e); **grossly** adv (greatly) très, grandement
grotesque [grə'tɛsk] adj grotesque
ground [graund] pt, pp of **grind** ▷ n sol m, terre f; (land) terrain m, terres fpl; (Sport) terrain; (reason: gen pl) raison f; (US: also: **~ wire**) terre f ▷ vt (plane) empêcher de décoller, retenir au sol; (US Elec) équiper d'une prise de terre; **grounds** npl (gardens etc) parc m, domaine m; (of coffee) marc m; **on the ~**, **to the ~** par terre; **to gain/lose ~** gagner/perdre du terrain; **ground floor** n (BRIT) rez-de-chaussée m; **groundsheet** n (BRIT) tapis m de sol; **groundwork** n préparation f
group [gru:p] n groupe m ▷ vt (also: **~ together**) grouper ▷ vi (also: **~ together**) se grouper
grouse [graus] n (pl inv: bird) grouse f (sorte de coq de bruyère) ▷ vi (complain) rouspéter, râler
grovel ['grɔvl] vi (fig): **to ~ (before)** ramper (devant)
grow (pt **grew**, pp **~n**) [grəu, gru:, grəun] vi (plant) pousser, croître; (person) grandir; (increase) augmenter, se développer; (become) devenir; **to ~ rich/weak** s'enrichir/s'affaiblir ▷ vt cultiver, faire pousser; (hair, beard) laisser pousser; **grow on** vt fus: **that painting is ~ing on me** je finirai par aimer ce tableau; **grow up** vi grandir
growl [graul] vi grogner
grown [grəun] pp of **grow**; **grown-up** n adulte m/f, grande personne

growth [grəʊθ] n croissance f, développement m; (what has grown) pousse f; poussée f; (Med) grosseur f, tumeur f

grub [grʌb] n larve f; (inf: food) bouffe f

grubby ['grʌbɪ] adj crasseux(-euse)

grudge [grʌdʒ] n rancune f ▷ vt: **to ~ sb sth** (in giving) donner qch à qn à contre-cœur; (resent) reprocher qch à qn; **to bear sb a ~ (for)** garder rancune or en vouloir à qn (de)

gruelling (us **grueling**) ['grʊəlɪŋ] adj exténuant(e)

gruesome ['gruːsəm] adj horrible

grumble ['grʌmbl] vi rouspéter, ronchonner

grumpy ['grʌmpɪ] adj grincheux(-euse)

grunt [grʌnt] vi grogner

guarantee [gærən'tiː] n garantie f ▷ vt garantir

guard [gɑːd] n garde f; (one man) garde m; (BRIT Rail) chef m de train; (safety device: on machine) dispositif m de sûreté; (also: **fire~**) garde-feu m inv ▷ vt garder, surveiller; (protect): **to ~ sb/sth (against** or **from)** protéger qn/qch (contre); **to be on one's ~** (fig) être sur ses gardes; **guardian** n gardien(ne); (of minor) tuteur(-trice)

guerrilla [gə'rɪlə] n guérillero m

guess [gɛs] vi deviner ▷ vt deviner; (estimate) évaluer; (us) croire, penser ▷ n supposition f, hypothèse f; **to take** or **have a ~** essayer de deviner

guest [gɛst] n invité(e); (in hotel) client(e); **guest house** n pension f; **guest room** n chambre f d'amis

guidance ['gaɪdəns] n (advice) conseils mpl

guide [gaɪd] n (person) guide m/f; (book) guide m; (also: **Girl G~**) éclaireuse f; (Roman Catholic) guide f ▷ vt guider; **is there an English-speaking ~?** est-ce que l'un des guides parle anglais?; **guidebook** n guide m; **guide dog** n chien m d'aveugle; **guided tour** n visite guidée; **what time does the guided tour start?** la visite guidée commence à quelle heure?; **guidelines** npl (advice) instructions générales, conseils mpl

guild [gɪld] n (History) corporation f; (sharing interests) cercle m, association f

guilt [gɪlt] n culpabilité f; **guilty** adj coupable

guinea pig ['gɪnɪ-] n cobaye m

guitar [gɪ'tɑː] n guitare f; **guitarist** n guitariste m/f

gulf [gʌlf] n golfe m; (abyss) gouffre m

gull [gʌl] n mouette f

gulp [gʌlp] vi avaler sa salive; (from emotion) avoir la gorge serrée, s'étrangler ▷ vt (also: **~ down**) avaler

gum [gʌm] n (Anat) gencive f; (glue) colle f; (also: **chewing-~**) chewing-gum m ▷ vt coller

gun [gʌn] n (small) revolver m, pistolet m; (rifle) fusil m, carabine f; (cannon) canon m; **gunfire** n fusillade f; **gunman** (irreg) n bandit armé; **gunpoint** n: **at gunpoint** sous la menace du pistolet (or fusil); **gunpowder** n poudre f à canon; **gunshot** n coup m de feu

gush [gʌʃ] vi jaillir; (fig) se répandre en effusions

gust [gʌst] n (of wind) rafale f

gut [gʌt] n intestin m, boyau m; **guts** npl (Anat) boyaux mpl; (inf: courage) cran m

gutter ['gʌtə'] n (of roof) gouttière f; (in street) caniveau m

guy [gaɪ] n (inf: man) type m; (also: **~rope**) corde f; (figure) effigie de Guy Fawkes

Guy Fawkes' Night [gaɪ'fɔːks-] n voir encadré

● **GUY FAWKES' NIGHT**

● **Guy Fawkes' Night**, que l'on appelle
● également "bonfire night", commémore
● l'échec du complot (le "Gunpowder Plot")
● contre James Ist et son parlement le 5
● novembre 1605. L'un des conspirateurs,
● Guy Fawkes, avait été surpris dans les
● caves du parlement alors qu'il s'apprêtait
● à y mettre le feu. Chaque année pour le 5
● novembre, les enfants préparent à l'avance
● une effigie de Guy Fawkes et ils demandent
● aux passants "un penny pour le guy" avec
● lequel ils pourront s'acheter des fusées de
● feu d'artifice. Beaucoup de gens font encore
● un feu dans leur jardin sur lequel ils brûlent
● le "guy".

gym [dʒɪm] n (also: **~nasium**) gymnase m; (also: **~nastics**) gym f; **gymnasium** n gymnase m; **gymnast** n gymnaste m/f; **gymnastics** n, npl gymnastique f; **gym shoes** npl chaussures fpl de gym(nastique)

gynaecologist (us **gynecologist**) [gaɪnɪ'kɔlədʒɪst] n gynécologue m/f

gypsy ['dʒɪpsɪ] n gitan(e), bohémien(ne)

h

haberdashery [hæbə'dæʃərɪ] n (BRIT) mercerie f

habit ['hæbɪt] n habitude f; (costume: Rel) habit m

habitat ['hæbɪtæt] n habitat m

hack [hæk] vt hacher, tailler ▷ n (pej: writer) nègre m; **hacker** n (Comput) pirate m (informatique)

had [hæd] pt, pp of **have**

haddock (pl ~ or ~s) ['hædək] n églefin m; **smoked ~** haddock m

hadn't ['hædnt] = **had not**

haemorrhage (us **hemorrhage**) ['hɛmərɪdʒ] n hémorragie f

haemorrhoids (us **hemorrhoids**) ['hɛmərɔɪdz] npl hémorroïdes fpl

haggle ['hægl] vi marchander

Hague [heɪg] n: **The ~** La Haye

hail [heɪl] n grêle f ▷ vt (call) héler; (greet) acclamer ▷ vi grêler; **hailstone** n grêlon m

hair [hɛəʳ] n cheveux mpl; (on body) poils mpl; (of animal) pelage m; (single hair: on head) cheveu m; (: on body, of animal) poil m; **to do one's ~** se coiffer; **hairband** n (elasticated) bandeau m; (plastic) serre-tête m; **hairbrush** n brosse f à cheveux; **haircut** n coupe f (de cheveux); **hairdo** n coiffure f; **hairdresser** n coiffeur(-euse); **hairdresser's** n salon m de coiffure, coiffeur m; **hair dryer** n sèche-cheveux m, séchoir m; **hair gel** n gel m pour cheveux; **hair spray** n laque f (pour les cheveux); **hairstyle** n coiffure f; **hairy** adj poilu(e), chevelu(e); (inf: frightening) effrayant(e)

hake (pl ~ or ~s) [heɪk] n colin m, merlu m

half [hɑːf] n (pl **halves**) moitié f; (of beer: also: ~ **pint**) ≈ demi m; (Rail, bus: also: ~ **fare**) demi-tarif m; (Sport: of match) mi-temps f ▷ adj demi(e) ▷ adv (à) moitié, à demi; ~ **an hour** une demi-heure; ~ **a dozen** une demi-douzaine; ~ **a pound** une demi-livre, ≈ 250 g; **two and a ~** deux et demi; **to cut sth in ~** couper qch en deux; **half board** n (BRIT: in hotel) demi-pension f; **half-brother** n demi-frère m; **half day** n demi-journée f; **half fare** n demi-tarif m; **half-hearted** adj tiède, sans enthousiasme; **half-hour** n demi-heure f; **half-price** adj à moitié prix ▷ adv (also: **at half-price**) à moitié prix; **half term** n (BRIT Scol) vacances fpl (de demi-trimestre); **half-time** n mi-temps f; **halfway** adv à mi-chemin; **halfway through sth** au milieu de qch

hall [hɔːl] n salle f; (entrance way: big) hall m; (small) entrée f; (us: corridor) couloir m; (mansion) château m, manoir m

hallmark ['hɔːlmɑːk] n poinçon m; (fig) marque f

hallo [hə'ləu] excl = **hello**

hall of residence n (BRIT) pavillon m or résidence f universitaire

Halloween, Hallowe'en ['hæləu'iːn] n veille f de la Toussaint; voir encadré

- **HALLOWEEN**
-
- Selon la tradition, **Halloween** est la nuit
- des fantômes et des sorcières. En Écosse
- et aux États-Unis surtout (et de plus en
- plus en Angleterre) les enfants, pour fêter
- **Halloween**, se déguisent ce soir-là et ils
- vont ainsi de porte en porte en demandant
- de petits cadeaux (du chocolat, une pomme
- etc).

---

hallucination [həluːsɪ'neɪʃən] n hallucination f

hallway ['hɔːlweɪ] n (entrance) vestibule m; (corridor) couloir m

halo ['heɪləu] n (of saint etc) auréole f

halt [hɔːlt] n halte f, arrêt m ▷ vt faire arrêter; (progress etc) interrompre ▷ vi faire halte, s'arrêter

halve [hɑːv] vt (apple etc) partager or diviser en deux; (reduce by half) réduire de moitié

halves [hɑːvz] npl of **half**

ham [hæm] n jambon m

hamburger ['hæmbəːgəʳ] n hamburger m

hamlet ['hæmlɪt] n hameau m

hammer ['hæməʳ] n marteau m ▷ vt (nail)

enfoncer; (fig) éreinter, démolir ▷ vi (at door) frapper à coups redoublés; **to ~ a point home to sb** faire rentrer qch dans la tête de qn

hammock ['hæmək] n hamac m

hamper ['hæmpə^r] vt gêner ▷ n panier m (d'osier)

hamster ['hæmstə^r] n hamster m

hamstring ['hæmstrɪŋ] n (Anat) tendon m du jarret

hand [hænd] n main f; (of clock) aiguille f; (handwriting) écriture f; (at cards) jeu m; (worker) ouvrier(-ière) ▷ vt passer, donner; **to give sb a ~** donner un coup de main à qn; **at ~** à portée de la main; **in ~** (situation) en main; (work) en cours; **to be on ~** (person) être disponible; (emergency services) se tenir prêt(e) (à intervenir); **to ~** (information etc) sous la main, à portée de la main; **on the one ~ ..., on the other ~** d'une part ..., d'autre part; **hand down** vt passer; (tradition, heirloom) transmettre; (us: sentence, verdict) prononcer; **hand in** vt remettre; **hand out** vt distribuer; **hand over** vt remettre; (powers etc) transmettre; **handbag** n sac m à main; **hand baggage** n = **hand luggage**; **handbook** n manuel m; **handbrake** n frein m à main; **handcuffs** npl menottes fpl; **handful** n poignée f

handicap ['hændɪkæp] n handicap m ▷ vt handicaper; **mentally/physically ~ped** handicapé(e) mentalement/physiquement

handkerchief ['hæŋkətʃɪf] n mouchoir m

handle ['hændl] n (of door etc) poignée f; (of cup etc) anse f; (of knife etc) manche m; (of saucepan) queue f; (for winding) manivelle f ▷ vt toucher, manier; (deal with) s'occuper de; (treat: people) prendre; **"~ with care"** "fragile"; **to fly off the ~** s'énerver; **handlebar(s)** n(pl) guidon m

hand: **hand luggage** n bagages mpl à main; **handmade** adj fait(e) à la main; **handout** n (money) aide f, don m; (leaflet) prospectus m; (at lecture) polycopié m; **hands-free** adj (phone) mains libres inv ▷ n (also: **hands-free kit**) kit m mains libres inv

handsome ['hænsəm] adj beau (belle); (profit) considérable

handwriting ['hændraɪtɪŋ] n écriture f

handy ['hændɪ] adj (person) adroit(e); (close at hand) sous la main; (convenient) pratique

hang (pt, pp hung) [hæŋ, hʌŋ] vt accrocher; (criminal: pt, pp **~ed**) pendre ▷ vi pendre; (hair, drapery) tomber ▷ n: **to get the ~ of (doing) sth** (inf) attraper le coup pour faire qch; **hang about, hang around** vi traîner; **hang down** vi pendre; **hang on** vi (wait) attendre; **hang out** vt (washing) étendre (dehors) ▷ vi (inf: live) habiter, percher; (: spend time) traîner; **hang round** vi = **hang around**; **hang up** vi (Tel) raccrocher ▷ vt (coat, painting etc) accrocher,

suspendre

hanger ['hæŋə^r] n cintre m, portemanteau m

hang-gliding ['hæŋglaɪdɪŋ] n vol m libre or sur aile delta

hangover ['hæŋəuvə^r] n (after drinking) gueule f de bois

hankie, hanky ['hæŋkɪ] n abbr = **handkerchief**

happen ['hæpən] vi arriver, se passer, se produire; **what's ~ing?** que se passe-t-il?; **she ~ed to be free** il s'est trouvé (or se trouvait) qu'elle était libre; **as it ~s** justement

happily ['hæpɪlɪ] adv heureusement; (cheerfully) joyeusement

happiness ['hæpɪnɪs] n bonheur m

happy ['hæpɪ] adj heureux(-euse); **~ with** (arrangements etc) satisfait(e) de; **to be ~ to do** faire volontiers; **~ birthday!** bon anniversaire!

harass ['hærəs] vt accabler, tourmenter; **harassment** n tracasseries fpl

harbour (us **harbor**) ['ha:bə^r] n port m ▷ vt héberger, abriter; (hopes, suspicions) entretenir

hard [ha:d] adj dur(e); (question, problem) difficile; (facts, evidence) concret(-ète) ▷ adv (work) dur; (think, try) sérieusement; **to look ~ at** regarder fixement; (thing) regarder de près; **no ~ feelings!** sans rancune!; **to be ~ of hearing** être dur(e) d'oreille; **to be ~ done by** être traité(e) injustement; **hardback** n livre relié; **hardboard** n Isorel® m; **hard disk** n (Comput) disque dur; **harden** vt durcir; (fig) endurcir ▷ vi (substance) durcir

hardly ['ha:dlɪ] adv (scarcely) à peine; (harshly) durement; **~ anywhere/ever** presque nulle part/jamais

hard: **hardship** n (difficulties) épreuves fpl; (deprivation) privations fpl; **hard shoulder** n (BRIT Aut) accotement stabilisé; **hard-up** adj (inf) fauché(e); **hardware** n quincaillerie f; (Comput, Mil) matériel m; **hardware shop** (us **hardware store**) n quincaillerie f; **hard-working** adj travailleur(-euse), consciencieux(-euse)

hardy ['ha:dɪ] adj robuste; (plant) résistant(e) au gel

hare [hɛə^r] n lièvre m

harm [ha:m] n mal m; (wrong) tort m ▷ vt (person) faire du mal or du tort à; (thing) endommager; **out of ~'s way** à l'abri du danger, en lieu sûr; **harmful** adj nuisible; **harmless** adj inoffensif(-ive)

harmony ['ha:mənɪ] n harmonie f

harness ['ha:nɪs] n harnais m ▷ vt (horse) harnacher; (resources) exploiter

harp [ha:p] n harpe f ▷ vi: **to ~ on about** revenir toujours sur

harsh [ha:ʃ] adj (hard) dur(e); (severe) sévère; (unpleasant: sound) discordant(e); (: light) cru(e)

harvest ['ha:vɪst] n (of corn) moisson f; (of

fruit) récolte *f*; (*of grapes*) vendange *f* ▷ *vt*
moissonner; récolter; vendanger

has [hæz] *vb see* **have**

hasn't ['hæznt] = **has not**

hassle ['hæsl] *n* (*inf: fuss*) histoire(s) *f(pl)*

haste [heɪst] *n* hâte *f*, précipitation *f*; **hasten**
['heɪsn] *vt* hâter, accélérer ▷ *vi* se hâter,
s'empresser; **hastily** *adv* à la hâte; (*leave*)
précipitamment; **hasty** *adj* (*decision, action*)
hâtif(-ive); (*departure, escape*) précipité(e)

hat [hæt] *n* chapeau *m*

hatch [hætʃ] *n* (*Naut: also:* **~way**) écoutille *f*;
(BRIT: *also:* **service ~**) passe-plats *m inv* ▷ *vi*
éclore

hatchback ['hætʃbæk] *n* (*Aut*) modèle *m* avec
hayon arrière

hate [heɪt] *vt* haïr, détester ▷ *n* haine *f*;
hatred ['heɪtrɪd] *n* haine *f*

haul [hɔːl] *vt* traîner, tirer ▷ *n* (*of fish*) prise *f*; (*of
stolen goods etc*) butin *m*

haunt [hɔːnt] *vt* (*subj: ghost, fear*) hanter; (:
person) fréquenter ▷ *n* repaire *m*; **haunted** *adj*
(*castle etc*) hanté(e); (*look*) égaré(e), hagard(e)

KEYWORD

have [hæv] (*pt, pp* **had**) *aux vb* **1** (*gen*) avoir;
être; **to have eaten/slept** avoir mangé/
dormi; **to have arrived/gone** être arrivé(e)/
allé(e); **having finished** *or* **when he had
finished, he left** quand il a eu fini, il est parti;
we'd already eaten nous avions déjà mangé
2 (*in tag questions*): **you've done it, haven't
you?** vous l'avez fait, n'est-ce pas?
3 (*in short answers and questions*): **no I
haven't!/yes we have!** mais non!/mais si!;
so I have! ah oui!, oui c'est vrai!; **I've been
there before, have you?** j'y suis déjà allé, et
vous?
▷ *modal aux vb* (*be obliged*): **to have (got) to do
sth** devoir faire qch, être obligé(e) de faire qch;
she has (got) to do it elle doit le faire, il faut
qu'elle le fasse; **you haven't to tell her** vous
n'êtes pas obligé de le lui dire; (*must not*) ne le
lui dites surtout pas; **do you have to book?** il
faut réserver?
▷ *vt* **1** (*possess*) avoir; **he has (got) blue eyes/
dark hair** il a les yeux bleus/les cheveux bruns
2 (*referring to meals etc*): **to have breakfast**
prendre le petit déjeuner; **to have dinner/
lunch** dîner/déjeuner; **to have a drink**
prendre un verre; **to have a cigarette** fumer
une cigarette
3 (*receive*) avoir, recevoir; (*obtain*) avoir;
may I have your address? puis-je avoir
votre adresse?; **you can have it for £5** vous
pouvez l'avoir pour 5 livres; **I must have it for
tomorrow** il me le faut pour demain; **to have
a baby** avoir un bébé

4 (*maintain, allow*): **I won't have it!** ça ne se
passera pas comme ça!; **we can't have that**
nous ne tolérerons pas ça
5 (*by sb else*): **to have sth done** faire faire qch;
to have one's hair cut se faire couper les
cheveux; **to have sb do sth** faire faire qch à qn
6 (*experience, suffer*) avoir: **to have a cold/flu**
avoir un rhume/la grippe; **to have an
operation** se faire opérer; **she had her bag
stolen** elle s'est fait voler son sac
7 (*+noun*): **to have a swim/walk** nager/se
promener; **to have a bath/shower** prendre
un bain/une douche; **let's have a look**
regardons; **to have a meeting** se réunir; **to
have a party** organiser une fête; **let me have
a try** laissez-moi essayer

haven ['heɪvn] *n* port *m*; (*fig*) havre *m*

haven't ['hævnt] = **have not**

havoc ['hævək] *n* ravages *mpl*

Hawaii [hə'waːiː] *n* (*îles fpl*) Hawaï *m*

hawk [hɔːk] *n* faucon *m*

hawthorn ['hɔːθɔːn] *n* aubépine *f*

hay [heɪ] *n* foin *m*; **hay fever** *n* rhume *m* des
foins; **haystack** *n* meule *f* de foin

hazard ['hæzəd] *n* (*risk*) danger *m*, risque
m ▷ *vt* risquer, hasarder; **hazardous** *adj*
hasardeux(-euse), risqué(e); **hazard warning
lights** *npl* (*Aut*) feux *mpl* de détresse

haze [heɪz] *n* brume *f*

hazel [heɪzl] *n* (*tree*) noisetier *m* ▷ *adj* (*eyes*)
noisette *inv*; **hazelnut** *n* noisette *f*

hazy ['heɪzɪ] *adj* brumeux(-euse); (*idea*) vague

he [hiː] *pron* il; **it is he who ...** c'est lui qui ...;
here he is le voici

head [hɛd] *n* tête *f*; (*leader*) chef *m*; (*of school*)
directeur(-trice); (*of secondary school*) proviseur
m ▷ *vt* (*list*) être en tête de; (*group, company*)
être à la tête de; **~s or tails** pile ou face; **~
first** la tête la première; **~ over heels in love**
follement *or* éperdument amoureux(-euse);
to ~ the ball faire une tête; **head for** *vt fus*
se diriger vers; (*disaster*) aller à; **head off** *vt*
(*threat, danger*) détourner; **headache** *n* mal
m de tête; **to have a headache** avoir mal
à la tête; **heading** *n* titre *m*; (*subject title*)
rubrique *f*; **headlamp** (BRIT) *n* = **headlight**;
headlight *n* phare *m*; **headline** *n* titre *m*;
head office *n* siège *m*, bureau *m* central;
headphones *npl* casque *m* (à écouteurs);
headquarters *npl* (*of business*) bureau *or* siège
central; (*Mil*) quartier général; **headroom**
n (*in car*) hauteur *f* de plafond; (*under bridge*)
hauteur limite; **headscarf** *n* foulard *m*;
headset *n* = **headphones**; **headteacher**
n directeur(-trice); (*of secondary school*)
proviseur *m*; **head waiter** *n* maître *m* d'hôtel

heal [hiːl] *vt, vi* guérir

health [hɛlθ] *n* santé *f*; **health care** *n* services médicaux; **health centre** n (BRIT) centre m de santé; **health food** n aliment(s) naturel(s); **Health Service** n: **the Health Service** (BRIT) ≈ la Sécurité Sociale; **healthy** adj (person) en bonne santé; (climate, food, attitude etc) sain(e)

heap [hi:p] n tas m ▷ vt (also: **~ up**) entasser, amonceler; **she ~ed her plate with cakes** elle a chargé son assiette de gâteaux; **~s (of)** (inf: lots) des tas (de)

hear (pt, pp **~d**) [hɪəʳ, hɜ:d] vt entendre; (news) apprendre ▷ vi entendre; **to ~ about** entendre parler de; (have news of) avoir des nouvelles de; **to ~ from sb** recevoir des nouvelles de qn

heard [hɜ:d] pt, pp of **hear**

hearing ['hɪərɪŋ] n (sense) ouïe f; (of witnesses) audition f, (of a case) audience f; **hearing aid** n appareil m acoustique

hearse [hɜ:s] n corbillard m

heart [hɑ:t] n cœur m; **hearts** npl (Cards) cœur; **at ~** au fond; **by ~** (learn, know) par cœur; **to lose/take ~** perdre/prendre courage; **heart attack** n crise f cardiaque; **heartbeat** n battement m de cœur; **heartbroken** adj: **to be heartbroken** avoir beaucoup de chagrin; **heartburn** n brûlures fpl d'estomac; **heart disease** n maladie f cardiaque

hearth [hɑ:θ] n foyer m, cheminée f

heartless ['hɑ:tlɪs] adj (person) sans cœur, insensible; (treatment) cruel(le)

hearty ['hɑ:tɪ] adj chaleureux(-euse); (appetite) solide; (dislike) cordial(e); (meal) copieux(-euse)

heat [hi:t] n chaleur f; (Sport: also: **qualifying ~**) éliminatoire f ▷ vt chauffer; **heat up** vi (liquid) chauffer; (room) se réchauffer ▷ vt réchauffer; **heated** adj chauffé(e); (fig) passionné(e), échauffé(e), excité(e); **heater** n appareil m de chauffage; radiateur m; (in car) chauffage m; (water heater) chauffe-eau m

heather ['hɛðəʳ] n bruyère f

heating ['hi:tɪŋ] n chauffage m

heatwave ['hi:tweɪv] n vague f de chaleur

heaven ['hɛvn] n ciel m, paradis m; (fig) paradis m; **heavenly** adj céleste, divin(e)

heavily ['hɛvɪlɪ] adv lourdement; (drink, smoke) beaucoup; (sleep, sigh) profondément

heavy ['hɛvɪ] adj lourd(e); (work, rain, user, eater) gros(se); (drinker, smoker) grand(e); (schedule, week) chargé(e)

Hebrew ['hi:bru:] adj hébraïque ▷ n (Ling) hébreu m

Hebrides ['hɛbrɪdi:z] npl: **the ~** les Hébrides fpl

hectare ['hɛktɑ:ʳ] n (BRIT) hectare m

hectic ['hɛktɪk] adj (schedule) très chargé(e); (day) mouvementé(e); (lifestyle) trépidant(e)

he'd [hi:d] = **he would**; = **he had**

hedge [hɛdʒ] n haie f ▷ vi se dérober ▷ vt: **to ~ one's bets** (fig) se couvrir

hedgehog ['hɛdʒhɔg] n hérisson m

heed [hi:d] vt (also: **take ~ of**) tenir compte de, prendre garde à

heel [hi:l] n talon m ▷ vt retalonner

hefty ['hɛftɪ] adj (person) costaud(e); (parcel) lourd(e); (piece, price) gros(se)

height [haɪt] n (of person) taille f, grandeur f; (of object) hauteur f; (of plane, mountain) altitude f; (high ground) hauteur, éminence f; (fig: of glory, fame, power) sommet m; (: of luxury, stupidity) comble m; **at the ~ of summer** au cœur de l'été; **heighten** vt hausser, surélever; (fig) augmenter

heir [ɛəʳ] n héritier m; **heiress** n héritière f

held [hɛld] pt, pp of **hold**

helicopter ['hɛlɪkɔptəʳ] n hélicoptère m

hell [hɛl] n enfer m; **oh ~!** (inf) merde!

he'll [hi:l] = **he will**; = **he shall**

hello [həˈləu] excl bonjour!; (to attract attention) hé!; (surprise) tiens!

helmet ['hɛlmɪt] n casque m

help [hɛlp] n aide f; (cleaner etc) femme f de ménage ▷ vt, vi aider; **~!** au secours!; **~ yourself** servez-vous; **can you ~ me?** pouvez-vous m'aider?; **can I ~ you?** (in shop) vous désirez?; **he can't ~ it** il n'y peut rien; **help out** vi aider ▷ vt: **to ~ sb out** aider qn; **helper** n aide m/f, assistant(e); **helpful** adj serviable, obligeant(e); (useful) utile; **helping** n portion f; **helpless** adj impuissant(e); (baby) sans défense; **helpline** n service m d'assistance téléphonique; (free) ≈ numéro vert

hem [hɛm] n ourlet m ▷ vt ourler

hemisphere ['hɛmɪsfɪəʳ] n hémisphère m

hemorrhage ['hɛmərɪdʒ] n (US) = **haemorrhage**

hemorrhoids ['hɛmərɔɪdz] npl (US) = **haemorrhoids**

hen [hɛn] n poule f; (female bird) femelle f

hence [hɛns] adv (therefore) d'où, de là; **2 years ~** d'ici 2 ans

hen night, hen party n soirée f entre filles (avant le mariage de l'une d'elles)

hepatitis [hɛpəˈtaɪtɪs] n hépatite f

her [hɜ:ʳ] pron (direct) la, l' + vowel or h mute; (indirect) lui; (stressed, after prep) elle ▷ adj son (sa), ses pl; see also **me**; **my**

herb [hɜ:b] n herbe f; **herbal** adj à base de plantes; **herbal tea** n tisane f

herd [hɜ:d] n troupeau m

here [hɪəʳ] adv ici; (time) alors ▷ excl tiens!, tenez!; **~!** (present) présent!; **~ is, ~ are** voici; **~ he/she is** le (la) voici

hereditary [hɪˈrɛdɪtrɪ] adj héréditaire

heritage ['hɛrɪtɪdʒ] n héritage m, patrimoine m

hernia ['hɜ:nɪə] n hernie f

hero (pl **~es**) ['hɪərəu] n héros m; **heroic** [hɪˈrəuɪk] adj héroïque

heroin ['hɛrəʊɪn] n héroïne f (drogue)

heroine ['hɛrəʊɪn] n héroïne f (femme)

heron ['hɛrən] n héron m

herring ['hɛrɪŋ] n hareng m

hers [hə:z] pron le (la) sien(ne), les siens (siennes); see also **mine**¹

herself [hə:'sɛlf] pron (reflexive) se; (emphatic) elle-même; (after prep) elle; see also **oneself**

he's [hi:z] = **he is**; **he has**

hesitant ['hɛzɪtənt] adj hésitant(e), indécis(e)

hesitate ['hɛzɪteɪt] vi: **to ~ (about/to do)** hésiter (sur/à faire); **hesitation** [hɛzɪ'teɪʃən] n hésitation f

heterosexual ['hɛtərəʊ'sɛksjuəl] adj, n hétérosexuel(le)

hexagon ['hɛksəgən] n hexagone m

hey [heɪ] excl hé!

heyday ['heɪdeɪ] n: **the ~ of** l'âge m d'or de, les beaux jours de

HGV n abbr = **heavy goods vehicle**

hi [haɪ] excl salut!; (to attract attention) hé!

hibernate ['haɪbəneɪt] vi hiberner

hiccough, hiccup ['hɪkʌp] vi hoqueter ▷ n: **to have (the) ~s** avoir le hoquet

hid [hɪd] pt of **hide**

hidden ['hɪdn] pp of **hide** ▷ adj: **~ agenda** intentions non déclarées

hide [haɪd] n (skin) peau f ▷ vb (pt **hid**, pp **hidden**) ▷ vt cacher ▷ vi: **to ~ (from sb)** se cacher (de qn)

hideous ['hɪdɪəs] adj hideux(-euse), atroce

hiding ['haɪdɪŋ] n (beating) correction f, volée f de coups; **to be in ~** (concealed) se tenir caché(e)

hi-fi ['haɪfaɪ] adj, n abbr (= high fidelity) hi-fi f inv

high [haɪ] adj haut(e); (speed, respect, number) grand(e); (price) élevé(e); (wind) fort(e), violent(e); (voice) aigu(ë) ▷ adv haut, en haut; **20 m ~** haut(e) de 20 m; **~ in the air** haut dans le ciel; **highchair** n (child's) chaise haute; **high-class** adj (neighbourhood, hotel) chic inv, de grand standing; **higher education** n études supérieures; **high heels** npl talons hauts, hauts talons; **high jump** n (Sport) saut m en hauteur; **highlands** ['haɪləndz] npl région montagneuse; **the Highlands** (in Scotland) les Highlands mpl; **highlight** n (fig: of event) point culminant ▷ vt (emphasize) faire ressortir, souligner; **highlights** npl (in hair) reflets mpl; **highlighter** n (pen) surligneur (lumineux); **highly** adv extrêmement, très; (unlikely) fort; (recommended, skilled, qualified) hautement; **to speak highly of** dire beaucoup de bien de; **highness** n: **His/Her Highness** son Altesse f; **high-rise** n (also: **high-rise block, high-rise building**) tour f (d'habitation); **high school** n lycée m; (US) établissement m d'enseignement supérieur; **high season** n (BRIT) haute saison; **high street** n (BRIT) grand-rue f; **high-tech**

(inf) adj de pointe; **highway** n (BRIT) route f; (US) route nationale; **Highway Code** n (BRIT) code m de la route

hijack ['haɪdʒæk] vt détourner (par la force); **hijacker** n auteur m d'un détournement d'avion, pirate m de l'air

hike [haɪk] vi faire des excursions à pied ▷ n excursion f à pied, randonnée f; **hiker** n promeneur(-euse), excursionniste m/f; **hiking** n excursions fpl à pied, randonnée f

hilarious [hɪ'lɛərɪəs] adj (behaviour, event) désopilant(e)

hill [hɪl] n colline f; (fairly high) montagne f; (on road) côte f; **hillside** n (flanc m de) coteau m; **hill walking** n randonnée f de basse montagne; **hilly** adj vallonné(e), montagneux(-euse)

him [hɪm] pron (direct) le, l' + vowel or h mute; (stressed, indirect, after prep) lui; see also **me**; **himself** pron (reflexive) se; (emphatic) lui-même; (after prep) lui; see also **oneself**

hind [haɪnd] adj de derrière

hinder ['hɪndə'] vt gêner; (delay) retarder

hindsight ['haɪndsaɪt] n: **with (the benefit of) ~** avec du recul, rétrospectivement

Hindu ['hɪndu:] n Hindou(e); **Hinduism** n (Rel) hindouisme m

hinge [hɪndʒ] n charnière f ▷ vi (fig): **to ~ on** dépendre de

hint [hɪnt] n allusion f; (advice) conseil m; (clue) indication f ▷ vt: **to ~ that** insinuer que ▷ vi: **to ~ at** faire une allusion à

hip [hɪp] n hanche f

hippie, hippy ['hɪpɪ] n hippie m/f

hippo ['hɪpəʊ] (pl **-s**) n hippopotame m

hippopotamus [hɪpə'pɔtəməs] (pl **~es** or **hippopotami**) n hippopotame m

hippy ['hɪpɪ] n = **hippie**

hire ['haɪə'] vt (BRIT: car, equipment) louer; (worker) embaucher, engager ▷ n location f; **for ~** à louer; (taxi) libre; **I'd like to ~ a car** je voudrais louer une voiture; **hire(d) car** n (BRIT) voiture f de location; **hire purchase** n (BRIT) achat m (or vente f) à tempérament or crédit

his [hɪz] pron le (la) sien(ne), les siens (siennes) ▷ adj son (sa), ses pl; see also **mine**¹; **my**

Hispanic [hɪs'pænɪk] adj (in US) hispano-américain(e) ▷ n Hispano-Américain(e)

hiss [hɪs] vi siffler

historian [hɪ'stɔ:rɪən] n historien(ne)

historic(al) [hɪ'stɔrɪk(l)] adj historique

history ['hɪstərɪ] n histoire f

hit [hɪt] vt (pt, pp **~**) frapper; (reach: target) atteindre, toucher; (collide with: car) entrer en collision avec, heurter; (fig: affect) toucher ▷ n coup m; (success) succès m; (song) tube m; (to website) visite f; (on search engine) résultat m de recherche; **to ~ it off with sb** bien s'entendre

avec qn; **hit back** vi: **to ~ back at sb** prendre
sa revanche sur qn

hitch [hɪtʃ] vt (fasten) accrocher, attacher;
(also: **~ up**) remonter d'une saccade ▷ vi
faire de l'autostop ▷ n (difficulty) anicroche
f, contretemps m; **to ~ a lift** faire du stop;
hitch-hike vi faire de l'auto-stop; **hitch-hiker**
n auto-stoppeur(-euse); **hitch-hiking** n auto-
stop m, stop m (inf)

hi-tech ['haɪtɛk] adj de pointe

hitman ['hɪtmæn] (irreg) n (inf) tueur m à
gages

HIV n abbr (= human immunodeficiency
virus) HIV m, VIH m; **~-negative/positive**
séronégatif(-ive)/positif(-ive)

hive [haɪv] n ruche f

hoard [hɔːd] n (of food) provisions fpl, réserves
fpl; (of money) trésor m ▷ vt amasser

hoarse [hɔːs] adj enroué(e)

hoax [həuks] n canular m

hob [hɔb] n plaque chauffante

hobble ['hɔbl] vi boitiller

hobby ['hɔbɪ] n passe-temps favori

hobo ['həubəu] n (us) vagabond m

hockey ['hɔkɪ] n hockey m; **hockey stick** n
crosse f de hockey

hog [hɔg] n porc (châtré) ▷ vt (fig) accaparer;
to go the whole ~ aller jusqu'au bout

Hogmanay [hɔgmə'neɪ] n réveillon m du jour
de l'An, Saint-Sylvestre f; voir encadré

○ **HOGMANAY**

○ La Saint-Sylvestre ou "New Year's Eve" se
○ nomme **Hogmanay** en Écosse. En cette
○ occasion, la famille et les amis se réunissent
○ pour entendre sonner les douze coups de
○ minuit et pour fêter le "first-footing", une
○ coutume qui veut qu'on se rende chez
○ ses amis et voisins en apportant quelque
○ chose à boire (du whisky en général) et un
○ morceau de charbon en gage de prospérité
○ pour la nouvelle année.

hoist [hɔɪst] n palan m ▷ vt hisser

hold [həuld] (pt, pp **held**) vt tenir; (contain)
contenir; (meeting) tenir; (keep back) retenir;
(believe) considérer; (possess) avoir ▷ vi
(withstand pressure) tenir (bon); (be valid)
valoir; (on telephone) attendre ▷ n prise f; (find)
influence f; (Naut) cale f; **to catch** or **get (a) ~**
of saisir; **to get ~ of** (find) trouver; **~ the line!**
(Tel) ne quittez pas!; **to ~ one's own** (fig) (bien)
se défendre; **hold back** vt retenir; (secret)
cacher; **hold on** vi tenir bon; (wait) attendre;
~ on! (Tel) ne quittez pas!; **to ~ on to sth**
(grasp) se cramponner à qch; (keep) conserver
or garder qch; **hold out** vt offrir ▷ vi (resist):
to ~ out (against) résister (devant), tenir bon

(devant); **hold up** vt (raise) lever; (support)
soutenir; (delay) retarder; (: traffic) ralentir;
(rob) braquer; **holdall** n (BRIT) fourre-tout m
inv; **holder** n (container) support m; (of ticket,
record) détenteur(-trice); (of office, title, passport
etc) titulaire m/f

hole [həul] n trou m

holiday ['hɔlədɪ] n (BRIT: vacation) vacances
fpl; (day off) jour m de congé; (public) jour férié;
to be on ~ être en vacances; **I'm here on ~** je
suis ici en vacances; **holiday camp** n (also:
holiday centre) camp m de vacances; **holiday
job** n (BRIT) boulot m (inf) de vacances;
holiday-maker n (BRIT) vacancier(-ière);
holiday resort n centre m de villégiature or
de vacances

Holland ['hɔlənd] n Hollande f

hollow ['hɔləu] adj creux(-euse); (fig) faux
(fausse) ▷ n creux m; (in land) dépression f (de
terrain), cuvette f ▷ vt: **to ~ out** creuser, évider

holly ['hɔlɪ] n houx m

Hollywood ['hɔlɪwud] n Hollywood m

holocaust ['hɔləkɔːst] n holocauste m

holy ['həulɪ] adj saint(e); (bread, water)
bénit(e); (ground) sacré(e)

home [həum] n foyer m, maison f; (country)
pays natal, patrie f; (institution) maison ▷ adj
de famille; (Econ, Pol) national(e), intérieur(e);
(Sport: team) qui reçoit; (: match, win) sur leur
(or notre) terrain ▷ adv chez soi, à la maison;
au pays natal; (right in: nail etc) à fond; **at
~** chez soi, à la maison; **to go** (or **come**) **~**
rentrer (chez soi), rentrer à la maison (or au
pays); **make yourself at ~** faites comme chez
vous; **home address** n domicile permanent;
homeland n patrie f; **homeless** adj sans
foyer, sans abri; **homely** adj (plain) simple,
sans prétention; (welcoming) accueillant(e);
home-made adj fait(e) à la maison; **home
match** n match m à domicile; **Home Office** n
(BRIT) ministère m de l'Intérieur; **home owner**
n propriétaire occupant; **home page** n
(Comput) page f d'accueil; **Home Secretary** n
(BRIT) ministre m de l'Intérieur; **homesick** adj:
to be homesick avoir le mal du pays; (missing
one's family) s'ennuyer de sa famille; **home
town** n ville natale; **homework** n devoirs mpl

homicide ['hɔmɪsaɪd] n (us) homicide m

homoeopathic (us **homeopathic**) [hə
umɪə'pæθɪk] adj (medicine) homéopathique;
(doctor) homéopathe

homoeopathy (us **homeopathy**) [hə
umɪ'ɔpəθɪ] n homéopathie f

homosexual [hɔməu'sɛksjuəl] adj, n
homosexuel(le)

honest ['ɔnɪst] adj honnête; (sincere) franc
(franche); **honestly** adv honnêtement;
franchement; **honesty** n honnêteté f

honey ['hʌnɪ] n miel m; **honeymoon** n

lune f de miel, voyage m de noces; **we're on honeymoon** nous sommes en voyage de noces; **honeysuckle** n chèvrefeuille m

Hong Kong ['hɒŋ'kɒŋ] n Hong Kong

honorary ['ɒnərərɪ] adj honoraire; (duty, title) honorifique; **~ degree** diplôme m honoris causa

honour (us **honor**) ['ɒnəʳ] vt honorer ▷ n honneur m; **to graduate with ~s** obtenir sa licence avec mention; **honourable** (us **honorable**) adj honorable; **honours degree** n (Scol) = licence f avec mention

hood [hud] n capuchon m; (of cooker) hotte f; (BRIT Aut) capote f; (us Aut) capot m; **hoodie** ['hudɪ] n (top) sweat m à capuche

hoof (pl **~s** or **hooves**) [hu:f, hu:vz] n sabot m

hook [huk] n crochet m; (on dress) agrafe f; (for fishing) hameçon m ▷ vt accrocher; **off the ~** (Tel) décroché

hooligan ['hu:lɪɡən] n voyou m

hoop [hu:p] n cerceau m

hooray [hu:'reɪ] excl = **hurray**

hoot [hu:t] vi (BRIT: Aut) klaxonner; (siren) mugir; (owl) hululer

Hoover® ['hu:vəʳ] n (BRIT) aspirateur m ▷ vt: **to hoover** (room) passer l'aspirateur dans; (carpet) passer l'aspirateur sur

hooves [hu:vz] npl of **hoof**

hop [hɒp] vi sauter; (on one foot) sauter à cloche-pied; (bird) sautiller

hope [həup] vt, vi espérer ▷ n espoir m; **I ~ so** je l'espère; **I ~ not** j'espère que non; **hopeful** adj (person) plein(e) d'espoir; (situation) prometteur(-euse), encourageant(e); **hopefully** adv (expectantly) avec espoir, avec optimisme; (one hopes) avec un peu de chance; **hopeless** adj désespéré(e); (useless) nul(le)

hops [hɒps] npl houblon m

horizon [hə'raɪzn] n horizon m; **horizontal** [hɒrɪ'zɒntl] adj horizontal(e)

hormone ['hɔ:məun] n hormone f

horn [hɔ:n] n corne f; (Mus) cor m; (Aut) klaxon m

horoscope ['hɒrəskəup] n horoscope m

horrendous [hə'rɛndəs] adj horrible, affreux(-euse)

horrible ['hɒrɪbl] adj horrible, affreux(-euse)

horrid ['hɒrɪd] adj (person) détestable; (weather, place, smell) épouvantable

horrific [hɒ'rɪfɪk] adj horrible

horrifying ['hɒrɪfaɪɪŋ] adj horrifiant(e)

horror ['hɒrəʳ] n horreur f; **horror film** n film m d'épouvante

hors d'œuvre [ɔ:'də:vrə] n hors d'œuvre m

horse [hɔ:s] n cheval m; **horseback: on horseback** n, adv à cheval; **horse chestnut** n (nut) marron m (d'Inde); (tree) marronnier m (d'Inde); **horsepower** n puissance f (en chevaux); (unit) cheval-vapeur m (CV); **horse-**

racing n courses fpl de chevaux; **horseradish** n raifort m; **horse riding** n (BRIT) équitation f

hose [həuz] n (also: **~pipe**) tuyau m; (also: **garden ~**) tuyau d'arrosage; **hosepipe** n tuyau m; (in garden) tuyau d'arrosage

hospital ['hɒspɪtl] n hôpital m; **in ~** à l'hôpital; **where's the nearest ~?** où est l'hôpital le plus proche?

hospitality [hɒspɪ'tælɪtɪ] n hospitalité f

host [həust] n hôte m; (TV, Radio) présentateur(-trice), animateur(-trice); (large number): **a ~ of** une foule de; (Rel) hostie f

hostage ['hɒstɪdʒ] n otage m

hostel ['hɒstl] n foyer m; (also: **youth ~**) auberge f de jeunesse

hostess ['həustɪs] n hôtesse f; (BRIT: also: **air ~**) hôtesse de l'air; (TV, Radio) animatrice f

hostile ['hɒstaɪl] adj hostile

hostility [hɒ'stɪlɪtɪ] n hostilité f

hot [hɒt] adj chaud(e); (as opposed to only warm) très chaud; (spicy) fort(e); (fig: contest) acharné(e); (topic) brûlant(e); (temper) violent(e), passionné(e); **to be ~** (person) avoir chaud; (thing) être (très) chaud; (weather) faire chaud; **hot dog** n hot-dog m

hotel [həu'tɛl] n hôtel m

hot-water bottle [hɒt'wɔ:tə-] n bouillotte f

hound [haund] vt poursuivre avec acharnement ▷ n chien courant

hour ['auəʳ] n heure f; **hourly** adj toutes les heures; (rate) horaire

house n [haus] maison f; (Pol) chambre f; (Theat) salle f, auditoire m ▷ vt [hauz] (person) loger, héberger; **on the ~** (fig) aux frais de la maison; **household** n (Admin etc) ménage m; (people) famille f, maisonnée f; **householder** n propriétaire m/f; (head of house) chef m de famille; **housekeeper** n gouvernante f; **housekeeping** n (work) ménage m; **housewife** (irreg) n ménagère f; femme f au foyer; **house wine** n cuvée f maison or du patron; **housework** n (travaux mpl du) ménage m

housing ['hauzɪŋ] n logement m; **housing development** (BRIT **housing estate**) n (blocks of flats) cité f; (houses) lotissement m

hover ['hɒvəʳ] vi planer; **hovercraft** n aéroglisseur m, hovercraft m

how [hau] adv comment; **~ are you?** comment allez-vous?; **~ do you do?** bonjour; (on being introduced) enchanté(e); **~ long have you been here?** depuis combien de temps êtes-vous là?; **~ lovely/awful!** que or comme c'est joli/affreux!; **~ much time/many people?** combien de temps/gens?; **~ much does it cost?** ça coûte combien?; **~ old are you?** quel âge avez-vous?; **~ tall is he?** combien mesure-t-il?; **~ is school?** ça va à l'école?; **~ was the film?** comment était le film?

h

however [hau'ɛvə'] *conj* pourtant, cependant ▷ *adv*: **~ I do it** de quelque manière que je m'y prenne; **~ cold it is** même s'il fait très froid; **~ did you do it?** comment y êtes-vous donc arrivé?

howl [haul] *n* hurlement *m* ▷ *vi* hurler; (*wind*) mugir

H.P. *n abbr* (*BRIT*) = **hire purchase**

h.p. *abbr* (*Aut*) = **horsepower**

HQ *n abbr* (= *headquarters*) QG *m*

hr(s) *abbr* (= *hour(s)*) h

HTML *n abbr* (= *hypertext markup language*) HTML *m*

hubcap [hʌbkæp] *n* (*Aut*) enjoliveur *m*

huddle ['hʌdl] *vi*: **to ~ together** se blottir les uns contre les autres

huff [hʌf] *n*: **in a ~** fâché(e)

hug [hʌg] *vt* serrer dans ses bras; (*shore, kerb*) serrer ▷ *n*: **to give sb a ~** serrer qn dans ses bras

huge [hju:dʒ] *adj* énorme, immense

hull [hʌl] *n* (*of ship*) coque *f*

hum [hʌm] *vt* (*tune*) fredonner ▷ *vi* fredonner; (*insect*) bourdonner; (*plane, tool*) vrombir

human ['hju:mən] *adj* humain(e) ▷ *n* (*also*: **~ being**) être humain

humane [hju:'meɪn] *adj* humain(e), humanitaire

humanitarian [hju:mænɪ'tɛərɪən] *adj* humanitaire

humanity [hju:'mænɪtɪ] *n* humanité *f*

human rights *npl* droits *mpl* de l'homme

humble ['hʌmbl] *adj* humble, modeste

humid ['hju:mɪd] *adj* humide; **humidity** [hju:'mɪdɪtɪ] *n* humidité *f*

humiliate [hju:'mɪlɪeɪt] *vt* humilier

humiliating [hju:'mɪlɪeɪtɪŋ] *adj* humiliant(e)

humiliation [hju:mɪlɪ'eɪʃən] *n* humiliation *f*

hummus ['huməs] *n* houm(m)ous *m*

humorous ['hju:mərəs] *adj* humoristique

humour (*us* **humor**) ['hju:mə'] *n* humour *m*; (*mood*) humeur *f* ▷ *vt* (*person*) faire plaisir à; se prêter aux caprices de

hump [hʌmp] *n* bosse *f*

hunch [hʌntʃ] *n* (*premonition*) intuition *f*

hundred ['hʌndrəd] *num* cent; **~s of** des centaines de; **hundredth** [-ɪdθ] *num* centième

hung [hʌŋ] *pt, pp of* **hang**

Hungarian [hʌŋ'gɛərɪən] *adj* hongrois(e) ▷ *n* Hongrois(e); (*Ling*) hongrois *m*

Hungary ['hʌŋgərɪ] *n* Hongrie *f*

hunger ['hʌŋgə'] *n* faim *f* ▷ *vi*: **to ~ for** avoir faim de, désirer ardemment

hungry ['hʌŋgrɪ] *adj* affamé(e); **to be ~** avoir faim; **~ for** (*fig*) avide de

hunt [hʌnt] *vt* (*seek*) chercher; (*Sport*) chasser ▷ *vi* (*search*): **to ~ for** chercher (partout); (*Sport*) chasser ▷ *n* (*Sport*) chasse *f*; **hunter** *n* chasseur *m*; **hunting** *n* chasse *f*

hurdle ['hə:dl] *n* (*Sport*) haie *f*; (*fig*) obstacle *m*

hurl [hə:l] *vt* lancer (avec violence); (*abuse, insults*) lancer

hurrah, hurray [hu'rɑ:, hu'reɪ] *excl* hourra!

hurricane ['hʌrɪkən] *n* ouragan *m*

hurry ['hʌrɪ] *n* hâte *f*, précipitation *f* ▷ *vi* se presser, se dépêcher ▷ *vt* (*person*) faire presser, faire se dépêcher; (*work*) presser; **to be in a ~** être pressé(e); **to do sth in a ~** faire qch en vitesse; **hurry up** se dépêcher

hurt [hə:t] (*pt, pp* **~**) *vt* (*cause pain to*) faire mal à; (*injure, fig*) blesser ▷ *vi* faire mal ▷ *adj* blessé(e); **my arm ~s** j'ai mal au bras; **to ~ o.s.** se faire mal

husband ['hʌzbənd] *n* mari *m*

hush [hʌʃ] *n* calme *m*, silence *m* ▷ *vt* faire taire; **~!** chut!

husky ['hʌskɪ] *adj* (*voice*) rauque ▷ *n* chien *m* esquimau *or* de traîneau

hut [hʌt] *n* hutte *f*; (*shed*) cabane *f*

hyacinth ['haɪəsɪnθ] *n* jacinthe *f*

hydrangea [haɪ'dreɪndʒə] *n* hortensia *m*

hydrofoil ['haɪdrəfɔɪl] *n* hydrofoil *m*

hydrogen ['haɪdrədʒən] *n* hydrogène *m*

hygiene ['haɪdʒi:n] *n* hygiène *f*; **hygienic** [haɪ'dʒi:nɪk] *adj* hygiénique

hymn [hɪm] *n* hymne *m*; cantique *m*

hype [haɪp] *n* (*inf*) matraquage *m* publicitaire *or* médiatique

hypermarket ['haɪpəmɑ:kɪt] (*BRIT*) *n* hypermarché *m*

hyphen ['haɪfn] *n* trait *m* d'union

hypnotize ['hɪpnətaɪz] *vt* hypnotiser

hypocrite ['hɪpəkrɪt] *n* hypocrite *m/f*

hypocritical [hɪpə'krɪtɪkl] *adj* hypocrite

hypothesis (*pl* **hypotheses**) [haɪ'pɒθɪsɪs, -si:z] *n* hypothèse *f*

hysterical [hɪ'stɛrɪkl] *adj* hystérique; (*funny*) hilarant(e)

hysterics [hɪ'stɛrɪks] *npl*: **to be in/have ~** (*anger, panic*) avoir une crise de nerfs; (*laughter*) attraper un fou rire

I [aɪ] *pron* je; (*before vowel*) j'; (*stressed*) moi

ice [aɪs] *n* glace *f*; (*on road*) verglas *m* ▷ *vt* (*cake*) glacer ▷ *vi* (*also*: **~ over**) geler; (*also*: **~ up**) se givrer; **iceberg** *n* iceberg *m*; **ice cream** *n* glace *f*; **ice cube** *n* glaçon *m*; **ice hockey** *n* hockey *m* sur glace

Iceland ['aɪslənd] *n* Islande *f*; **Icelander** *n* Islandais(e); **Icelandic** [aɪs'lændɪk] *adj* islandais(e) ▷ *n* (*Ling*) islandais *m*

ice: **ice lolly** *n* (BRIT) esquimau *m*; **ice rink** *n* patinoire *f*; **ice skating** *n* patinage *m* (sur glace)

icing ['aɪsɪŋ] *n* (*Culin*) glaçage *m*; **icing sugar** *n* (BRIT) sucre *m* glace

icon ['aɪkɔn] *n* icône *f*

ICT *n abbr* (BRIT: Scol: = information and communications technology) TIC *fpl*

icy ['aɪsɪ] *adj* glacé(e); (*road*) verglacé(e); (*weather, temperature*) glacial(e)

I'd [aɪd] = **I would**; **I had**

ID card *n* carte *f* d'identité

idea [aɪ'dɪə] *n* idée *f*

ideal [aɪ'dɪəl] *n* idéal *m* ▷ *adj* idéal(e); **ideally** [aɪ'dɪəlɪ] *adv* (*preferably*) dans l'idéal; (*perfectly*): **he is ideally suited to the job** il est parfait pour ce poste

identical [aɪ'dɛntɪkl] *adj* identique

identification [aɪdɛntɪfɪ'keɪʃən] *n* identification *f*; **means of ~** pièce *f* d'identité

identify [aɪ'dɛntɪfaɪ] *vt* identifier

identity [aɪ'dɛntɪtɪ] *n* identité *f*; **identity card** *n* carte *f* d'identité; **identity theft** *n* usurpation *f* d'identité

ideology [aɪdɪ'ɔlədʒɪ] *n* idéologie *f*

idiom ['ɪdɪəm] *n* (*phrase*) expression *f* idiomatique; (*style*) style *m*

idiot ['ɪdɪət] *n* idiot(e), imbécile *m/f*

idle ['aɪdl] *adj* (*doing nothing*) sans occupation, désœuvré(e); (*lazy*) oisif(-ive), paresseux(-euse); (*unemployed*) au chômage; (*machinery*) au repos; (*question, pleasures*) vain(e), futile ▷ *vi* (*engine*) tourner au ralenti

idol ['aɪdl] *n* idole *f*

idyllic [ɪ'dɪlɪk] *adj* idyllique

i.e. *abbr* (= *id est: that is*) c. à d., c'est-à-dire

if [ɪf] *conj* si; **if necessary** si nécessaire, le cas échéant; **if so** si c'est le cas; **if not** sinon; **if only I could!** si seulement je pouvais!; *see also* **as**; **even**

ignite [ɪg'naɪt] *vt* mettre le feu à, enflammer ▷ *vi* s'enflammer

ignition [ɪg'nɪʃən] *n* (*Aut*) allumage *m*; **to switch on/off the ~** mettre/couper le contact

ignorance ['ɪgnərəns] *n* ignorance *f*

ignorant ['ɪgnərənt] *adj* ignorant(e); **to be ~ of** (*subject*) ne rien connaître en; (*events*) ne pas être au courant de

ignore [ɪg'nɔːʳ] *vt* ne tenir aucun compte de; (*mistake*) ne pas relever; (*person: pretend to not see*) faire semblant de ne pas reconnaître; (: *pay no attention to*) ignorer

ill [ɪl] *adj* (*sick*) malade; (*bad*) mauvais(e) ▷ *n* mal *m* ▷ *adv*: **to speak/think ~ of sb** dire/penser du mal de qn; **to be taken ~** tomber malade

I'll [aɪl] = **I will**; **I shall**

illegal [ɪ'liːgl] *adj* illégal(e)

illegible [ɪ'lɛdʒɪbl] *adj* illisible

illegitimate [ɪlɪ'dʒɪtɪmət] *adj* illégitime

ill health *n* mauvaise santé

illiterate [ɪ'lɪtərət] *adj* illettré(e)

illness ['ɪlnɪs] *n* maladie *f*

illuminate [ɪ'luːmɪneɪt] *vt* (*room, street*) éclairer; (*for special effect*) illuminer

illusion [ɪ'luːʒən] *n* illusion *f*

illustrate ['ɪləstreɪt] *vt* illustrer

illustration [ɪlə'streɪʃən] *n* illustration *f*

I'm [aɪm] = **I am**

image ['ɪmɪdʒ] *n* image *f*; (*public face*) image de marque

imaginary [ɪ'mædʒɪnərɪ] *adj* imaginaire

imagination [ɪmædʒɪ'neɪʃən] *n* imagination *f*

imaginative [ɪ'mædʒɪnətɪv] *adj* imaginatif(-ive); (*person*) plein(e) d'imagination

imagine [ɪ'mædʒɪn] *vt* s'imaginer; (*suppose*) imaginer, supposer

imbalance [ɪm'bæləns] n déséquilibre m
imitate ['ɪmɪteɪt] vt imiter; **imitation** [ɪmɪ'teɪʃən] n imitation f
immaculate [ɪ'mækjulət] adj impeccable; (Rel) immaculé(e)
immature [ɪmə'tjuər] adj (fruit) qui n'est pas mûr(e); (person) qui manque de maturité
immediate [ɪ'miːdɪət] adj immédiat(e); **immediately** adv (at once) immédiatement; **immediately next to** juste à côté de
immense [ɪ'mɛns] adj immense, énorme; **immensely** adv (+adj) extrêmement; (+vb) énormément
immerse [ɪ'məːs] vt immerger, plonger; **to be ~d in** (fig) être plongé dans
immigrant ['ɪmɪɡrənt] n immigrant(e); (already established) immigré(e); **immigration** [ɪmɪ'ɡreɪʃən] n immigration f
imminent ['ɪmɪnənt] adj imminent(e)
immoral [ɪ'mɔrl] adj immoral(e)
immortal [ɪ'mɔːtl] adj, n immortel(le)
immune [ɪ'mjuːn] adj: **~ (to)** immunisé(e) (contre); **immune system** n système m immunitaire
immunize ['ɪmjunaɪz] vt immuniser
impact ['ɪmpækt] n choc m, impact m; (fig) impact
impair [ɪm'pɛər] vt détériorer, diminuer
impartial [ɪm'pɑːʃl] adj impartial(e)
impatience [ɪm'peɪʃəns] n impatience f
impatient [ɪm'peɪʃənt] adj impatient(e); **to get or grow ~** s'impatienter
impeccable [ɪm'pɛkəbl] adj impeccable, parfait(e)
impending [ɪm'pɛndɪŋ] adj imminent(e)
imperative [ɪm'pɛrətɪv] adj (need) urgent(e), pressant(e); (tone) impérieux(-euse) ▷ n (Ling) impératif m
imperfect [ɪm'pəːfɪkt] adj imparfait(e); (goods etc) défectueux(-euse) ▷ n (Ling: also: **~ tense**) imparfait m
imperial [ɪm'pɪərɪəl] adj impérial(e); (BRIT: measure) légal(e)
impersonal [ɪm'pəːsənl] adj impersonnel(le)
impersonate [ɪm'pəːsəneɪt] vt se faire passer pour; (Theat) imiter
impetus ['ɪmpətəs] n impulsion f; (of runner) élan m
implant [ɪm'plɑːnt] vt (Med) implanter; (fig: idea, principle) inculquer
implement n ['ɪmplɪmənt] outil m, instrument m; (for cooking) ustensile m ▷ vt ['ɪmplɪment] exécuter
implicate ['ɪmplɪkeɪt] vt impliquer, compromettre
implication [ɪmplɪ'keɪʃən] n implication f; **by ~** indirectement
implicit [ɪm'plɪsɪt] adj implicite; (complete) absolu(e), sans réserve

imply [ɪm'plaɪ] vt (hint) suggérer, laisser entendre; (mean) indiquer, supposer
impolite [ɪmpə'laɪt] adj impoli(e)
import vt [ɪm'pɔːt] importer ▷ n ['ɪmpɔːt] (Comm) importation f; (meaning) portée f, signification f
importance [ɪm'pɔːtns] n importance f
important [ɪm'pɔːtnt] adj important(e); **it's not ~** c'est sans importance, ce n'est pas important
importer [ɪm'pɔːtər] n importateur(-trice)
impose [ɪm'pəuz] vt imposer ▷ vi: **to ~ on sb** abuser de la gentillesse de qn; **imposing** adj imposant(e), impressionnant(e)
impossible [ɪm'pɔsɪbl] adj impossible
impotent ['ɪmpətnt] adj impuissant(e)
impoverished [ɪm'pɔvərɪʃt] adj pauvre, appauvri(e)
impractical [ɪm'præktɪkl] adj pas pratique; (person) qui manque d'esprit pratique
impress [ɪm'prɛs] vt impressionner, faire impression sur; (mark) imprimer, marquer; **to ~ sth on sb** faire bien comprendre qch à qn
impression [ɪm'prɛʃən] n impression f; (of stamp, seal) empreinte f; (imitation) imitation f; **to be under the ~ that** avoir l'impression que
impressive [ɪm'prɛsɪv] adj impressionnant(e)
imprison [ɪm'prɪzn] vt emprisonner, mettre en prison; **imprisonment** n emprisonnement m; (period): **to sentence sb to 10 years' imprisonment** condamner qn à 10 ans de prison
improbable [ɪm'prɔbəbl] adj improbable; (excuse) peu plausible
improper [ɪm'prɔpər] adj (unsuitable) déplacé(e), de mauvais goût; (indecent) indécent(e); (dishonest) malhonnête
improve [ɪm'pruːv] vt améliorer ▷ vi s'améliorer; (pupil etc) faire des progrès; **improvement** n amélioration f; (of pupil etc) progrès m
improvise ['ɪmprəvaɪz] vt, vi improviser
impulse ['ɪmpʌls] n impulsion f; **on ~** impulsivement, sur un coup de tête; **impulsive** [ɪm'pʌlsɪv] adj impulsif(-ive)

○ KEYWORD

in [ɪn] prep 1 (indicating place, position) dans; **in the house/the fridge** dans la maison/le frigo; **in the garden** dans le or au jardin; **in town** en ville; **in the country** à la campagne; **in school** à l'école; **in here/there** ici/là
2 (with place names: of town, region, country): **in London** à Londres; **in England** en Angleterre; **in Japan** au Japon; **in the United States** aux États-Unis
3 (indicating time: during): **in spring** au printemps; **in summer** en été; **in May/2005**

en mai/2005; **in the afternoon** (dans) l'après-midi; **at 4 o'clock in the afternoon** à 4 heures de l'après-midi

4 (*indicating time: in the space of*) en; (: *future*) dans; **I did it in 3 hours/days** je l'ai fait en 3 heures/jours; **I'll see you in 2 weeks** *or* **in 2 weeks' time** je te verrai dans 2 semaines

5 (*indicating manner etc*) à; **in a loud/soft voice** à voix haute/basse; **in pencil** au crayon; **in writing** par écrit; **in French** en français; **the boy in the blue shirt** le garçon à *or* avec la chemise bleue

6 (*indicating circumstances*): **in the sun** au soleil; **in the shade** à l'ombre; **in the rain** sous la pluie; **a change in policy** un changement de politique

7 (*indicating mood, state*): **in tears** en larmes; **in anger** sous le coup de la colère; **in despair** au désespoir; **in good condition** en bon état; **to live in luxury** vivre dans le luxe

8 (*with ratios, numbers*): **1 in 10 households, 1 household in 10** 1 ménage sur 10; **20 pence in the pound** 20 pence par livre sterling; **they lined up in twos** ils se mirent en rangs (deux) par deux; **in hundreds** par centaines

9 (*referring to people, works*) chez; **the disease is common in children** c'est une maladie courante chez les enfants; **in (the works of) Dickens** chez Dickens, dans (l'œuvre de) Dickens

10 (*indicating profession etc*) dans; **to be in teaching** être dans l'enseignement

11 (*after superlative*) de; **the best pupil in the class** le meilleur élève de la classe

12 (*with present participle*): **in saying this** en disant ceci

▷ *adv*: **to be in** (*person: at home, work*) être là; (*train, ship, plane*) être arrivé(e); (*in fashion*) être à la mode; **to ask sb in** inviter qn à entrer; **to run/limp** *etc* **in** entrer en courant/boitant *etc* ▷ *n*: **the ins and outs (of)** (*of proposal, situation etc*) les tenants et aboutissants (de)

inability [ɪnə'bɪlɪtɪ] *n* incapacité *f*; **~ to pay** incapacité de payer

inaccurate [ɪn'ækjurət] *adj* inexact(e); (*person*) qui manque de précision

inadequate [ɪn'ædɪkwət] *adj* insuffisant(e), inadéquat(e)

inadvertently [ɪnəd'vɜːtntlɪ] *adv* par mégarde

inappropriate [ɪnə'prəuprɪət] *adj* inopportun(e), mal à propos; (*word, expression*) impropre

inaugurate [ɪ'nɔːgjureɪt] *vt* inaugurer; (*president, official*) investir de ses fonctions

Inc. *abbr* = **incorporated**

incapable [ɪn'keɪpəbl] *adj*: **~ (of)** incapable (de)

incense *n* ['ɪnsɛns] encens *m* ▷ *vt* [ɪn'sɛns] (*anger*) mettre en colère

incentive [ɪn'sɛntɪv] *n* encouragement *m*, raison *f* de se donner de la peine

inch [ɪntʃ] *n* pouce *m* (=25 mm; 12 *in a foot*); **within an ~ of** à deux doigts de; **he wouldn't give an ~** (*fig*) il n'a pas voulu céder d'un pouce

incidence ['ɪnsɪdns] *n* (*of crime, disease*) fréquence *f*

incident ['ɪnsɪdnt] *n* incident *m*

incidentally [ɪnsɪ'dɛntəlɪ] *adv* (*by the way*) à propos

inclination [ɪnklɪ'neɪʃən] *n* inclination *f*; (*desire*) envie *f*

incline *n* ['ɪnklaɪn] pente *f*, plan incliné ▷ *vb* [ɪn'klaɪn] ▷ *vt* incliner ▷ *vi* (*surface*) s'incliner; **to be ~d to do** (*have a tendency to do*) avoir tendance à faire

include [ɪn'kluːd] *vt* inclure, comprendre; **service is/is not ~d** le service est compris/n'est pas compris; **including** *prep* y compris; **inclusion** *n* inclusion *f*; **inclusive** *adj* inclus(e), compris(e); **inclusive of tax** taxes comprises

income ['ɪnkʌm] *n* revenu *m*; (*from property etc*) rentes *fpl*; **income support** *n* (*BRIT*) ≈ revenu *m* minimum d'insertion, RMI *m*; **income tax** *n* impôt *m* sur le revenu

incoming ['ɪnkʌmɪŋ] *adj* (*passengers, mail*) à l'arrivée; (*government, tenant*) nouveau (nouvelle)

incompatible [ɪnkəm'pætɪbl] *adj* incompatible

incompetence [ɪn'kɔmpɪtns] *n* incompétence *f*, incapacité *f*

incompetent [ɪn'kɔmpɪtnt] *adj* incompétent(e), incapable

incomplete [ɪnkəm'pliːt] *adj* incomplet(-ète)

inconsistent [ɪnkən'sɪstnt] *adj* qui manque de constance; (*work*) irrégulier(-ière); (*statement*) peu cohérent(e); **~ with** en contradiction avec

inconvenience [ɪnkən'viːnjəns] *n* inconvénient *m*; (*trouble*) dérangement *m* ▷ *vt* déranger

inconvenient [ɪnkən'viːnjənt] *adj* malcommode; (*time, place*) mal choisi(e), qui ne convient pas; (*visitor*) importun(e)

incorporate [ɪn'kɔːpəreɪt] *vt* incorporer; (*contain*) contenir

incorrect [ɪnkə'rɛkt] *adj* incorrect(e); (*opinion, statement*) inexact(e)

increase *n* ['ɪnkriːs] augmentation *f* ▷ *vi, vt* [ɪn'kriːs] augmenter; **increasingly** *adv* de plus en plus

incredible [ɪn'krɛdɪbl] *adj* incroyable; **incredibly** *adv* incroyablement

incur [ɪn'kɜː] *vt* (*expenses*) encourir; (*anger, risk*) s'exposer à; (*debt*) contracter; (*loss*) subir

indecent [ɪnˈdiːsnt] adj indécent(e), inconvenant(e)

indeed [ɪnˈdiːd] adv (confirming, agreeing) en effet, effectivement; (for emphasis) vraiment; (furthermore) d'ailleurs; **yes ~!** certainement!

indefinitely [ɪnˈdɛfɪnɪtlɪ] adv (wait) indéfiniment

independence [ɪndɪˈpɛndns] n indépendance f; **Independence Day** n (US) fête de l'Indépendance américaine; voir encadré

● **INDEPENDENCE DAY**
●
● L'**Independence Day** est la fête nationale
● aux États-Unis, le 4 juillet. Il commémore
● l'adoption de la déclaration d'Indépendance,
● en 1776, écrite par Thomas Jefferson et
● proclamant la séparation des 13 colonies
● américaines de la Grande-Bretagne.

independent [ɪndɪˈpɛndnt] adj indépendant(e); (radio) libre; **independent school** n (BRIT) école privée

index [ˈɪndɛks] n (pl ~es) (in book) index m; (: in library etc) catalogue m (pl **indices**) (ratio, sign) indice m

India [ˈɪndɪə] n Inde f; **Indian** adj indien(ne) ▷ n indien(ne); **(American) Indian** Indien(ne) (d'Amérique)

indicate [ˈɪndɪkeɪt] vt indiquer ▷ vi (BRIT Aut): **to ~ left/right** mettre son clignotant à gauche/à droite; **indication** [ɪndɪˈkeɪʃən] n indication f, signe m; **indicative** [ɪnˈdɪkətɪv] adj: **to be indicative of sth** être symptomatique de qch ▷ n (Ling) indicatif m; **indicator** n (sign) indicateur m; (Aut) clignotant m

indices [ˈɪndɪsiːz] npl of **index**

indict [ɪnˈdaɪt] vt accuser; **indictment** n accusation f

indifference [ɪnˈdɪfrəns] n indifférence f

indifferent [ɪnˈdɪfrənt] adj indifférent(e); (poor) médiocre, quelconque

indigenous [ɪnˈdɪdʒɪnəs] adj indigène

indigestion [ɪndɪˈdʒɛstʃən] n indigestion f, mauvaise digestion

indignant [ɪnˈdɪɡnənt] adj: **~ (at sth/with sb)** indigné(e) (de qch/contre qn)

indirect [ɪndɪˈrɛkt] adj indirect(e)

indispensable [ɪndɪˈspɛnsəbl] adj indispensable

individual [ɪndɪˈvɪdjuəl] n individu m ▷ adj individuel(le); (characteristic) particulier(-ière), original(e); **individually** adv individuellement

Indonesia [ɪndəˈniːzɪə] n Indonésie f

indoor [ˈɪndɔːʳ] adj d'intérieur; (plant) d'appartement; (swimming pool) couvert(e); (sport, games) pratiqué(e) en salle; **indoors** [ɪnˈdɔːz] adv à l'intérieur

induce [ɪnˈdjuːs] vt (persuade) persuader; (bring about) provoquer; (labour) déclencher

indulge [ɪnˈdʌldʒ] vt (whim) céder à, satisfaire; (child) gâter ▷ vi: **to ~ in sth** (luxury) s'offrir qch, se permettre qch; (fantasies etc) se livrer à qch; **indulgent** adj indulgent(e)

industrial [ɪnˈdʌstrɪəl] adj industriel(le); (injury) du travail; (dispute) ouvrier(-ière); **industrial estate** n (BRIT) zone industrielle; **industrialist** n industriel m; **industrial park** n (US) zone industrielle

industry [ˈɪndəstrɪ] n industrie f; (diligence) zèle m, application f

inefficient [ɪnɪˈfɪʃənt] adj inefficace

inequality [ɪnɪˈkwɔlɪtɪ] n inégalité f

inevitable [ɪnˈɛvɪtəbl] adj inévitable; **inevitably** adv inévitablement, fatalement

inexpensive [ɪnɪkˈspɛnsɪv] adj bon marché inv

inexperienced [ɪnɪkˈspɪərɪənst] adj inexpérimenté(e)

inexplicable [ɪnɪkˈsplɪkəbl] adj inexplicable

infamous [ˈɪnfəməs] adj infâme, abominable

infant [ˈɪnfənt] n (baby) nourrisson m; (young child) petit(e) enfant

infantry [ˈɪnfəntrɪ] n infanterie f

infant school n (BRIT) classes fpl préparatoires (entre 5 et 7 ans)

infect [ɪnˈfɛkt] vt (wound) infecter; (person, blood) contaminer; **infection** [ɪnˈfɛkʃən] n infection f; (contagion) contagion f; **infectious** [ɪnˈfɛkʃəs] adj infectieux(-euse); (also fig) contagieux(-euse)

infer [ɪnˈfəːʳ] vt: **to ~ (from)** conclure (de), déduire (de)

inferior [ɪnˈfɪərɪəʳ] adj inférieur(e); (goods) de qualité inférieure ▷ n inférieur(e); (in rank) subalterne m/f

infertile [ɪnˈfəːtaɪl] adj stérile

infertility [ɪnfəːˈtɪlɪtɪ] n infertilité f, stérilité f

infested [ɪnˈfɛstɪd] adj: **~ (with)** infesté(e) (de)

infinite [ˈɪnfɪnɪt] adj infini(e); (time, money) illimité(e); **infinitely** adv infiniment

infirmary [ɪnˈfəːmərɪ] n hôpital m; (in school, factory) infirmerie f

inflamed [ɪnˈfleɪmd] adj enflammé(e)

inflammation [ɪnfləˈmeɪʃən] n inflammation f

inflatable [ɪnˈfleɪtəbl] adj gonflable

inflate [ɪnˈfleɪt] vt (tyre, balloon) gonfler; (fig: exaggerate) grossir; (: increase) gonfler; **inflation** [ɪnˈfleɪʃən] n (Econ) inflation f

inflexible [ɪnˈflɛksɪbl] adj inflexible, rigide

inflict [ɪnˈflɪkt] vt: **to ~ on** infliger à

influence [ˈɪnfluəns] n influence f ▷ vt influencer; **under the ~ of alcohol** en état d'ébriété; **influential** [ɪnfluˈɛnʃl] adj influent(e)

influenza [ɪnfluˈɛnzə] n grippe f

influx ['ɪnflʌks] n afflux m

info (inf) ['ɪnfəu] n (= information) renseignements mpl

inform [ɪn'fɔːm] vt: **to ~ sb (of)** informer or avertir qn (de) ▷ vi: **to ~ on sb** dénoncer qn, informer contre qn

informal [ɪn'fɔːml] adj (person, manner, party) simple; (visit, discussion) dénué(e) de formalités; (announcement, invitation) non officiel(le); (colloquial) familier(-ère)

information [ɪnfə'meɪʃən] n information(s) f(pl); renseignements mpl; (knowledge) connaissances fpl; **a piece of ~** un renseignement; **information office** n bureau m de renseignements; **information technology** n informatique f

informative [ɪn'fɔːmətɪv] adj instructif(-ive)

infra-red [ɪnfrə'rɛd] adj infrarouge

infrastructure ['ɪnfrəstrʌktʃər] n infrastructure f

infrequent [ɪn'friːkwənt] adj peu fréquent(e), rare

infuriate [ɪn'fjuərɪeɪt] vt mettre en fureur

infuriating [ɪn'fjuərɪeɪtɪŋ] adj exaspérant(e)

ingenious [ɪn'dʒiːnjəs] adj ingénieux(-euse)

ingredient [ɪn'griːdɪənt] n ingrédient m; (fig) élément m

inhabit [ɪn'hæbɪt] vt habiter; **inhabitant** n habitant n

inhale [ɪn'heɪl] vt inhaler; (perfume) respirer; (smoke) avaler ▷ vi (breathe in) aspirer; (in smoking) avaler la fumée; **inhaler** n inhalateur m

inherent [ɪn'hɪərənt] adj: **~ (in or to)** inhérent(e) (à)

inherit [ɪn'hɛrɪt] vt hériter (de); **inheritance** n héritage m

inhibit [ɪn'hɪbɪt] vt (Psych) inhiber; (growth) freiner; **inhibition** [ɪnhɪ'bɪʃən] n inhibition f

initial [ɪ'nɪʃl] adj initial(e) ▷ n initiale f ▷ vt parafer; **initials** npl initiales fpl; (as signature) parafe m; **initially** adv initialement, au début

initiate [ɪ'nɪʃɪeɪt] vt (start) entreprendre; amorcer; (enterprise) lancer; (person) initier; **to ~ proceedings against sb** (Law) intenter une action à qn, engager des poursuites contre qn

initiative [ɪ'nɪʃətɪv] n initiative f

inject [ɪn'dʒɛkt] vt injecter; (person): **to ~ sb with sth** faire une piqûre de qch à qn; **injection** [ɪn'dʒɛkʃən] n injection f, piqûre f

injure ['ɪndʒər] vt blesser; (damage: reputation etc) compromettre; **to ~ o.s.** se blesser; **injured** adj (person, leg etc) blessé(e); **injury** n blessure f; (wrong) tort m

injustice [ɪn'dʒʌstɪs] n injustice f

ink [ɪŋk] n encre f; **ink-jet printer** ['ɪŋkdʒɛt-] n imprimante f à jet d'encre

inland adj ['ɪnlənd] intérieur(e) ▷ adv [ɪn'lænd] à l'intérieur, dans les terres; **Inland**

Revenue n (BRIT) fisc m

in-laws ['ɪnlɔːz] npl beaux-parents mpl; belle famille

inmate ['ɪnmeɪt] n (in prison) détenu(e); (in asylum) interné(e)

inn [ɪn] n auberge f

inner ['ɪnər] adj intérieur(e); **inner-city** adj (schools, problems) de quartiers déshérités

inning ['ɪnɪŋ] n (US: Baseball) tour m de batte; **innings** npl (Cricket) tour de batte

innocence ['ɪnəsns] n innocence f

innocent ['ɪnəsnt] adj innocent(e)

innovation [ɪnəu'veɪʃən] n innovation f

innovative ['ɪnəu'veɪtɪv] adj novateur(-trice); (product) innovant(e)

in-patient ['ɪnpeɪʃənt] n malade hospitalisé(e)

input ['ɪnput] n (contribution) contribution f; (resources) ressources fpl; (Comput) entrée f (de données); (: data) données fpl ▷ vt (Comput) introduire, entrer

inquest ['ɪnkwɛst] n enquête (criminelle); (coroner's) enquête judiciaire

inquire [ɪn'kwaɪər] vi demander ▷ vt demander; **to ~ about** s'informer de, se renseigner sur; **to ~ when/where/whether** demander quand/où/si; **inquiry** n demande f de renseignements; (Law) enquête f, investigation f; **"inquiries"** renseignements"

ins. abbr = **inches**

insane [ɪn'seɪn] adj fou (folle); (Med) aliéné(e)

insanity [ɪn'sænɪtɪ] n folie f; (Med) aliénation (mentale)

insect ['ɪnsɛkt] n insecte m; **insect repellent** n crème f anti-insectes

insecure [ɪnsɪ'kjuər] adj (person) anxieux(-euse); (job) précaire; (building etc) peu sûr(e)

insecurity [ɪnsɪ'kjuərɪtɪ] n insécurité f

insensitive [ɪn'sɛnsɪtɪv] adj insensible

insert vt [ɪn'səːt] insérer ▷ n ['ɪnsəːt] insertion f

inside ['ɪn'saɪd] n intérieur m ▷ adj intérieur(e) ▷ adv à l'intérieur, dedans ▷ prep à l'intérieur de; (of time): **~ 10 minutes** en moins de 10 minutes; **to go ~** rentrer; **inside lane** n (Aut: in Britain) voie f de gauche; (: in US, Europe) voie f de droite; **inside out** adv à l'envers; (know) à fond; **to turn sth inside out** retourner qch

insight ['ɪnsaɪt] n perspicacité f; (glimpse, idea) aperçu m

insignificant [ɪnsɪg'nɪfɪknt] adj insignifiant(e)

insincere [ɪnsɪn'sɪər] adj hypocrite

insist [ɪn'sɪst] vi insister; **to ~ on doing** insister pour faire; **to ~ on sth** exiger qch; **to ~ that** insister pour que + sub; (claim) maintenir or soutenir que; **insistent** adj insistant(e), pressant(e); (noise, action) ininterrompu(e)

insomnia [ɪnˈsɒmnɪə] n insomnie f
inspect [ɪnˈspɛkt] vt inspecter; (BRIT: ticket) contrôler; **inspection** [ɪnˈspɛkʃən] n inspection f; (BRIT: of tickets) contrôle m; **inspector** n inspecteur(-trice); (BRIT: on buses, trains) contrôleur(-euse)
inspiration [ɪnspəˈreɪʃən] n inspiration f; **inspire** [ɪnˈspaɪər] vt inspirer; **inspiring** adj inspirant(e)
instability [ɪnstəˈbɪlɪtɪ] n instabilité f
install (US **instal**) [ɪnˈstɔːl] vt installer; **installation** [ɪnstəˈleɪʃən] n installation f
instalment (US **installment**) [ɪnˈstɔːlmənt] n (payment) acompte m, versement partiel; (of TV serial etc) épisode m; **in ~s** (pay) à tempérament; (receive) en plusieurs fois
instance [ˈɪnstəns] n exemple m; **for ~** par exemple; **in the first ~** tout d'abord, en premier lieu
instant [ˈɪnstənt] n instant m ▷ adj immédiat(e), urgent(e); (coffee, food) instantané(e), en poudre; **instantly** adv immédiatement, tout de suite; **instant messaging** n messagerie f instantanée
instead [ɪnˈstɛd] adv au lieu de cela; **~ of** au lieu de; **~ of sb** à la place de qn
instinct [ˈɪnstɪŋkt] n instinct m; **instinctive** adj instinctif(-ive)
institute [ˈɪnstɪtjuːt] n institut m ▷ vt instituer, établir; (inquiry) ouvrir; (proceedings) entamer
institution [ɪnstɪˈtjuːʃən] n institution f; (school) établissement m (scolaire); (for care) établissement (psychiatrique etc)
instruct [ɪnˈstrʌkt] vt: **to ~ sb in sth** enseigner qch à qn; **to ~ sb to do sth** charger qn or ordonner à qn de faire; **instruction** [ɪnˈstrʌkʃən] n instruction f; **instructions** npl (orders) directives fpl; **instructions for use** mode m d'emploi; **instructor** n professeur m; (for skiing, driving) moniteur m
instrument [ˈɪnstrumənt] n instrument m; **instrumental** [ɪnstruˈmɛntl] adj (Mus) instrumental(e); **to be instrumental in sth/ in doing sth** contribuer à qch/à faire qch
insufficient [ɪnsəˈfɪʃənt] adj insuffisant(e)
insulate [ˈɪnsjuleɪt] vt isoler; (against sound) insonoriser; **insulation** [ɪnsjuˈleɪʃən] n isolation f; (against sound) insonorisation f
insulin [ˈɪnsjulɪn] n insuline f
insult n [ˈɪnsʌlt] insulte f, affront m ▷ vt [ɪnˈsʌlt] insulter, faire un affront à; **insulting** adj insultant(e), injurieux(-euse)
insurance [ɪnˈʃuərəns] n assurance f; **fire/life ~** assurance-incendie/-vie; **insurance company** n compagnie f or société f d'assurances; **insurance policy** n police f d'assurance
insure [ɪnˈʃuər] vt assurer; **to ~ (o.s.) against**

(fig) parer à
intact [ɪnˈtækt] adj intact(e)
intake [ˈɪnteɪk] n (Tech) admission f; (consumption) consommation f; (BRIT Scol): **an ~ of 200 a year** 200 admissions par an
integral [ˈɪntɪɡrəl] adj (whole) intégral(e); (part) intégrant(e)
integrate [ˈɪntɪɡreɪt] vt intégrer ▷ vi s'intégrer
integrity [ɪnˈtɛɡrɪtɪ] n intégrité f
intellect [ˈɪntəlɛkt] n intelligence f; **intellectual** [ɪntəˈlɛktjuəl] adj, n intellectuel(le)
intelligence [ɪnˈtɛlɪdʒəns] n intelligence f; (Mil etc) informations fpl, renseignements mpl
intelligent [ɪnˈtɛlɪdʒənt] adj intelligent(e)
intend [ɪnˈtɛnd] vt (gift etc): **to ~ sth for** destiner qch à; **to ~ to do** avoir l'intention de faire
intense [ɪnˈtɛns] adj intense; (person) véhément(e)
intensify [ɪnˈtɛnsɪfaɪ] vt intensifier
intensity [ɪnˈtɛnsɪtɪ] n intensité f
intensive [ɪnˈtɛnsɪv] adj intensif(-ive); **intensive care** n: **to be in intensive care** être en réanimation; **intensive care unit** n service m de réanimation
intent [ɪnˈtɛnt] n intention f ▷ adj attentif(-ive), absorbé(e); **to all ~s and purposes** en fait, pratiquement; **to be ~ on doing sth** être (bien) décidé à faire qch
intention [ɪnˈtɛnʃən] n intention f; **intentional** adj intentionnel(le), délibéré(e)
interact [ɪntərˈækt] vi avoir une action réciproque; (people) communiquer; **interaction** [ɪntərˈækʃən] n interaction f; **interactive** adj (Comput) interactif, conversationnel(le)
intercept [ɪntəˈsɛpt] vt intercepter; (person) arrêter au passage
interchange n [ˈɪntətʃeɪndʒ] (exchange) échange m; (on motorway) échangeur m
intercourse [ˈɪntəkɔːs] n: **sexual ~** rapports sexuels
interest [ˈɪntrɪst] n intérêt m; (Comm: stake, share) participation f, intérêts mpl ▷ vt intéresser; **interested** adj intéressé(e); **to be interested in sth** s'intéresser à qch; **I'm interested in going** ça m'intéresse d'y aller; **interesting** adj intéressant(e); **interest rate** n taux m d'intérêt
interface [ˈɪntəfeɪs] n (Comput) interface f
interfere [ɪntəˈfɪər] vi: **to ~ in** (quarrel) s'immiscer dans; (other people's business) se mêler de; **to ~ with** (object) tripoter, toucher à; (plans) contrecarrer; (duty) être en conflit avec; **interference** n (gen) ingérence f; (Radio, TV) parasites mpl
interim [ˈɪntərɪm] adj provisoire; (post)

intérimaire ▷ n: **in the ~** dans l'intérim
interior [ɪnˈtɪərɪəʳ] n intérieur m ▷ adj intérieur(e); (minister, department) de l'intérieur; **interior design** n architecture f d'intérieur
intermediate [ɪntəˈmiːdɪət] adj intermédiaire; (Scol: course, level) moyen(ne)
intermission [ɪntəˈmɪʃən] n pause f; (Theat, Cine) entracte m
intern vt [ɪnˈtəːn] interner ▷ n ['ɪntəːn] (us) interne m/f
internal [ɪnˈtəːnl] adj interne; (dispute, reform etc) intérieur(e); **Internal Revenue Service** n (us) fisc m
international [ɪntəˈnæʃənl] adj international(e) ▷ n (BRIT Sport) international m
Internet [ɪntəˈnet] n: **the ~** l'Internet m; **Internet café** n cybercafé m; **Internet Service Provider** n fournisseur m d'accès à Internet; **Internet user** n internaute m/f
interpret [ɪnˈtəːprɪt] vt interpréter ▷ vi servir d'interprète; **interpretation** [ɪntəːprɪˈteɪʃən] n interprétation f; **interpreter** n interprète m/f; **could you act as an interpreter for us?** pourriez-vous nous servir d'interprète?
interrogate [ɪnˈtɛrəʊdʒeɪt] vt interroger; (suspect etc) soumettre à un interrogatoire; **interrogation** [ɪntɛrəʊˈgeɪʃən] n interrogation f; (by police) interrogatoire m
interrogative [ɪntəˈrɔgətɪv] adj interrogateur(-trice) ▷ n (Ling) interrogatif m
interrupt [ɪntəˈrʌpt] vt, vi interrompre; **interruption** [ɪntəˈrʌpʃən] n interruption f
intersection [ɪntəˈsekʃən] n (of roads) croisement m
interstate ['ɪntəsteɪt] (us) n autoroute f (qui relie plusieurs États)
interval ['ɪntəvl] n intervalle m; (BRIT: Theat) entracte m; (: Sport) mi-temps f; **at ~s** par intervalles
intervene [ɪntəˈviːn] vi (time) s'écouler (entre-temps); (event) survenir; (person) intervenir
interview ['ɪntəvjuː] n (Radio, TV etc) interview f; (for job) entrevue f ▷ vt interviewer; avoir une entrevue avec; **interviewer** n (Radio, TV etc) interviewer m
intimate adj ['ɪntɪmət] intime; (friendship) profond(e); (knowledge) approfondi(e) ▷ vt ['ɪntɪmeɪt] suggérer, laisser entendre; (announce) faire savoir
intimidate [ɪnˈtɪmɪdeɪt] vt intimider; **intimidating** [ɪnˈtɪmɪdeɪtɪŋ] adj intimidant(e)
into ['ɪntu] prep dans; **~ pieces/French** en morceaux/français
intolerant [ɪnˈtɔlərnt] adj: **~ (of)** intolérant(e) (de)
intranet [ɪnˈtrənet] n intranet m

intransitive [ɪnˈtrænsɪtɪv] adj intransitif(-ive)
intricate ['ɪntrɪkət] adj complexe, compliqué(e)
intrigue [ɪnˈtriːg] n intrigue f ▷ vt intriguer; **intriguing** adj fascinant(e)
introduce [ɪntrəˈdjuːs] vt introduire; (TV show etc) présenter; **to ~ sb (to sb)** présenter qn (à qn); **to ~ sb to** (pastime, technique) initier qn à; **introduction** [ɪntrəˈdʌkʃən] n introduction f; (of person) présentation f; (to new experience) initiation f; **introductory** [ɪntrəˈdʌktərɪ] adj préliminaire, introductif(-ive)
intrude [ɪnˈtruːd] vi (person) être importun(e); **to ~ on** or **into** (conversation etc) s'immiscer dans; **intruder** n intrus(e)
intuition [ɪntjuːˈɪʃən] n intuition f
inundate ['ɪnʌndeɪt] vt: **to ~ with** inonder de
invade [ɪnˈveɪd] vt envahir
invalid n ['ɪnvəlɪd] malade m/f; (with disability) invalide m/f ▷ adj [ɪnˈvælɪd] (not valid) invalide, non valide
invaluable [ɪnˈvæljuəbl] adj inestimable, inappréciable
invariably [ɪnˈvɛərɪəblɪ] adv invariablement; **she is ~ late** elle est toujours en retard
invasion [ɪnˈveɪʒən] n invasion f
invent [ɪnˈvent] vt inventer; **invention** [ɪnˈvenʃən] n invention f; **inventor** n inventeur(-trice)
inventory ['ɪnvəntrɪ] n inventaire m
inverted commas [ɪnˈvəːtɪd-] npl (BRIT) guillemets mpl
invest [ɪnˈvest] vt investir ▷ vi: **to ~ in** placer de l'argent or investir dans; (fig: acquire) s'offrir, faire l'acquisition de
investigate [ɪnˈvestɪgeɪt] vt étudier, examiner; (crime) faire une enquête sur; **investigation** [ɪnvestɪˈgeɪʃən] n (of crime) enquête f, investigation f
investigator [ɪnˈvestɪgeɪtəʳ] n investigateur(-trice); **private ~** détective privé
investment [ɪnˈvestmənt] n investissement m, placement m
investor [ɪnˈvestəʳ] n épargnant(e); (shareholder) actionnaire m/f
invisible [ɪnˈvɪzɪbl] adj invisible
invitation [ɪnvɪˈteɪʃən] n invitation f
invite [ɪnˈvaɪt] vt inviter; (opinions etc) demander; **inviting** adj engageant(e), attrayant(e)
invoice ['ɪnvɔɪs] n facture f ▷ vt facturer
involve [ɪnˈvɔlv] vt (entail) impliquer; (concern) concerner; (require) nécessiter; **to ~ sb in** (theft etc) impliquer qn dans; (activity, meeting) faire participer qn à; **involved** adj (complicated) complexe; **to be involved in** (take part) participer à; **involvement** n (personal role) rôle m; (participation) participation f; (enthusiasm)

enthousiasme *m*

inward ['ɪnwəd] *adj* (*movement*) vers l'intérieur; (*thought, feeling*) profond(e), intime ▷ *adv* = **inwards**; **inwards** *adv* vers l'intérieur

IQ *n abbr* (= *intelligence quotient*) Q.I. *m*

IRA *n abbr* (= *Irish Republican Army*) IRA *f*

Iran [ɪˈrɑːn] *n* Iran *m*; **Iranian** [ɪˈreɪnɪən] *adj* iranien(ne) ▷ *n* Iranien(ne)

Iraq [ɪˈrɑːk] *n* Irak *m*; **Iraqi** *adj* irakien(ne) ▷ *n* Irakien(ne)

Ireland ['aɪələnd] *n* Irlande *f*

iris, irises ['aɪrɪs, -ɪz] *n* iris *m*

Irish ['aɪrɪʃ] *adj* irlandais(e) ▷ *npl*: **the ~** les Irlandais; **Irishman** (*irreg*) *n* Irlandais *m*; **Irishwoman** (*irreg*) *n* Irlandaise *f*

iron ['aɪən] *n* fer *m*; (*for clothes*) fer *m* à repasser ▷ *adj* de or en fer ▷ *vt* (*clothes*) repasser

ironic(al) [aɪˈrɔnɪk(l)] *adj* ironique; **ironically** *adv* ironiquement

ironing ['aɪənɪŋ] *n* (*activity*) repassage *m*; (*clothes: ironed*) linge repassé; (: *to be ironed*) linge à repasser; **ironing board** *n* planche *f* à repasser

irony ['aɪrənɪ] *n* ironie *f*

irrational [ɪˈræʃənl] *adj* irrationnel(le); (*person*) qui n'est pas rationnel

irregular [ɪˈrɛgjulər] *adj* irrégulier(-ière); (*surface*) inégal(e); (*action, event*) peu orthodoxe

irrelevant [ɪˈrɛləvənt] *adj* sans rapport, hors de propos

irresistible [ɪrɪˈzɪstɪbl] *adj* irrésistible

irresponsible [ɪrɪˈspɔnsɪbl] *adj* (*act*) irréfléchi(e); (*person*) qui n'a pas le sens des responsabilités

irrigation [ɪrɪˈgeɪʃən] *n* irrigation *f*

irritable ['ɪrɪtəbl] *adj* irritable

irritate ['ɪrɪteɪt] *vt* irriter; **irritating** *adj* irritant(e); **irritation** [ɪrɪˈteɪʃən] *n* irritation *f*

IRS *n abbr* (US) = **Internal Revenue Service**

is [ɪz] *vb see* **be**

ISDN *n abbr* (= *Integrated Services Digital Network*) RNIS *m*

Islam ['ɪzlɑːm] *n* Islam *m*; **Islamic** [ɪzˈlɑːmɪk] *adj* islamique

island ['aɪlənd] *n* île *f*; (*also*: **traffic ~**) refuge *m* (pour piétons); **islander** *n* habitant(e) d'une île, insulaire *m/f*

isle [aɪl] *n* île *f*

isn't ['ɪznt] = **is not**

isolated ['aɪsəleɪtɪd] *adj* isolé(e)

isolation [aɪsəˈleɪʃən] *n* isolement *m*

ISP *n abbr* = **Internet Service Provider**

Israel ['ɪzreɪl] *n* Israël *m*; **Israeli** [ɪzˈreɪlɪ] *adj* israélien(ne) ▷ *n* Israélien(ne)

issue ['ɪʃuː] *n* question *f*, problème *m*; (*of banknotes*) émission *f*; (*of newspaper*) numéro *m*; (*of book*) publication *f*, parution *f* ▷ *vt* (*rations, equipment*) distribuer; (*orders*) donner;

(*statement*) publier, faire; (*certificate, passport*) délivrer; (*banknotes, cheques, stamps*) émettre, mettre en circulation; **at ~** en jeu, en cause; **to take ~ with sb (over sth)** exprimer son désaccord avec qn (sur qch)

IT *n abbr* = **information technology**

 KEYWORD

it [ɪt] *pron* **1** (*specific: subject*) il (elle); (: *direct object*) le (la, l'); (: *indirect object*) lui; **it's on the table** c'est or il (or elle) est sur la table; **I can't find it** je n'arrive pas à le trouver; **give it to me** donne-le-moi

2 (*after prep*): **about/from/of it** en; **I spoke to him about it** je lui en ai parlé; **what did you learn from it?** qu'est-ce que vous en avez retiré?; **I'm proud of it** j'en suis fier; **in/to it** y; **put the book in it** mettez-y le livre; **he agreed to it** il y a consenti; **did you go to it?** (*party, concert etc*) est-ce que vous y êtes allé(s)?

3 (*impersonal*) il; ce, cela, ça; **it's raining** il pleut; **it's Friday tomorrow** demain, c'est vendredi *or* nous sommes, vendredi; **it's 6 o'clock** il est 6 heures; **how far is it? — it's 10 miles** c'est loin? — c'est à 10 miles; **who is it? — it's me** qui est-ce? — c'est moi

Italian [ɪˈtæljən] *adj* italien(ne) ▷ *n* Italien(ne); (*Ling*) italien *m*

italics [ɪˈtælɪks] *npl* italique *m*

Italy ['ɪtəlɪ] *n* Italie *f*

itch [ɪtʃ] *n* démangeaison *f* ▷ *vi* (*person*) éprouver des démangeaisons; (*part of body*) démanger; **I'm ~ing to do** l'envie me démange de faire; **itchy** *adj*: **my back is itchy** j'ai le dos qui me démange

it'd ['ɪtd] = **it would**; **it had**

item ['aɪtəm] *n* (*gen*) article *m*; (*on agenda*) question *f*, point *m*; (*also*: **news ~**) nouvelle *f*

itinerary [aɪˈtɪnərərɪ] *n* itinéraire *m*

it'll ['ɪtl] = **it will**; **it shall**

its [ɪts] *adj* son (sa), ses *pl*

it's [ɪts] = **it is**; **it has**

itself [ɪtˈsɛlf] *pron* (*reflexive*) se; (*emphatic*) lui-même (elle-même)

ITV *n abbr* (BRIT: = *Independent Television*) chaîne de télévision commerciale

I've [aɪv] = **I have**

ivory ['aɪvərɪ] *n* ivoire *m*

ivy ['aɪvɪ] *n* lierre *m*

J

jab [dʒæb] vt: **to ~ sth into** enfoncer or planter qch dans ▷ n (Med: inf) piqûre f

jack [dʒæk] n (Aut) cric m; (Cards) valet m

jacket ['dʒækɪt] n veste f, veston m; (of book) couverture f, jaquette f; **jacket potato** n pomme f de terre en robe des champs

jackpot ['dʒækpɔt] n gros lot

Jacuzzi® [dʒə'ku:zɪ] n jacuzzi® m

jagged ['dʒægɪd] adj dentelé(e)

jail [dʒeɪl] n prison f ▷ vt emprisonner, mettre en prison; **jail sentence** n peine f de prison

jam [dʒæm] n confiture f; (also: **traffic ~**) embouteillage m ▷ vt (passage etc) encombrer, obstruer; (mechanism, drawer etc) bloquer, coincer; (Radio) brouiller ▷ vi (mechanism, sliding part) se coincer, se bloquer; (gun) s'enrayer; **to be in a ~** (inf) être dans le pétrin; **to ~ sth into** (stuff) entasser or comprimer qch dans; (thrust) enfoncer qch dans

Jamaica [dʒə'meɪkə] n Jamaïque f

jammed [dʒæmd] adj (window etc) coincé(e)

Jan abbr (= January) janv

janitor ['dʒænɪtər] n (caretaker) concierge m

January ['dʒænjuərɪ] n janvier m

Japan [dʒə'pæn] n Japon m; **Japanese** [dʒæpə'ni:z] adj japonais(e) ▷ n (pl inv) Japonais(e); (Ling) japonais m

jar [dʒɑ:ʳ] n (stone, earthenware) pot m; (glass) bocal m ▷ vi (sound) produire un son grinçant or discordant; (colours etc) détonner, jurer

jargon ['dʒɑ:gən] n jargon m

javelin ['dʒævlɪn] n javelot m

jaw [dʒɔ:] n mâchoire f

jazz [dʒæz] n jazz m

jealous ['dʒɛləs] adj jaloux(-ouse); **jealousy** n jalousie f

jeans [dʒi:nz] npl jean m

Jello® ['dʒɛləu] (us) n gelée f

jelly ['dʒɛlɪ] n (dessert) gelée f; (us: jam) confiture f; **jellyfish** n méduse f

jeopardize ['dʒɛpədaɪz] vt mettre en danger or péril

jerk [dʒə:k] n secousse f, saccade f; (of muscle) spasme m; (inf) pauvre type m ▷ vt (shake) donner une secousse à; (pull) tirer brusquement ▷ vi (vehicles) cahoter

jersey ['dʒə:zɪ] n tricot m; (fabric) jersey m

Jesus ['dʒi:zəs] n Jésus

jet [dʒɛt] n (of gas, liquid) jet m; (Aviat) avion m à réaction, jet m; **jet lag** n décalage m horaire; **jet-ski** vi faire du jet-ski or scooter des mers

jetty ['dʒɛtɪ] n jetée f, digue f

Jew [dʒu:] n Juif m

jewel ['dʒu:əl] n bijou m, joyau m; (in watch) rubis m; **jeweller** (us **jeweler**) n bijoutier(-ière), joaillier m; **jeweller's (shop)** (us **jewelry store**) n bijouterie f, joaillerie f; **jewellery** (us **jewelry**) n bijoux mpl

Jewish ['dʒu:ɪʃ] adj juif (juive)

jigsaw ['dʒɪgsɔ:] n (also: **~ puzzle**) puzzle m

job [dʒɔb] n (chore, task) travail m, tâche f; (employment) emploi m, poste m, place f; **it's a good ~ that …** c'est heureux or c'est une chance que … + sub; **just the ~!** (c'est) juste or exactement ce qu'il faut!; **job centre** (BRIT) n ≈ ANPE f, ≈ Agence nationale pour l'emploi; **jobless** adj sans travail, au chômage

jockey ['dʒɔkɪ] n jockey m ▷ vi: **to ~ for position** manœuvrer pour être bien placé

jog [dʒɔg] vt secouer ▷ vi (Sport) faire du jogging; **to ~ sb's memory** rafraîchir la mémoire de qn; **jogging** n jogging m

join [dʒɔɪn] vt (put together) unir, assembler; (become member of) s'inscrire à; (meet) rejoindre, retrouver; (queue) se joindre à ▷ vi (roads, rivers) se rejoindre, se rencontrer ▷ n raccord m; **join in** vi se mettre de la partie ▷ vt fus se mêler à; **join up** vi (meet) se rejoindre; (Mil) s'engager

joiner ['dʒɔɪnəʳ] (BRIT) n menuisier m

joint [dʒɔɪnt] n (Tech) jointure f; joint m; (Anat) articulation f, jointure f; (BRIT Culin) rôti m; (inf: place) boîte f; (of cannabis) joint m ▷ adj commun(e); (committee) mixte, paritaire; (winner) ex aequo; **joint account** n compte joint; **jointly** adv ensemble, en commun

joke [dʒəuk] n plaisanterie f; (also: **practical ~**) farce f ▷ vi plaisanter; **to play a ~ on** jouer un tour à, faire une farce à; **joker** n (Cards) joker m

jolly ['dʒɔlɪ] adj gai(e), enjoué(e); (enjoyable)

amusant(e), plaisant(e) ▷ adv (BRIT inf) rudement, drôlement

jolt [dʒəʊlt] n cahot m, secousse f; (shock) choc m ▷ vt cahoter, secouer

Jordan [ˈdʒɔːdən] n (country) Jordanie f

journal [ˈdʒəːnl] n journal m; **journalism** n journalisme m; **journalist** n journaliste m/f

journey [ˈdʒəːnɪ] n voyage m; (distance covered) trajet m; **the ~ takes two hours** le trajet dure deux heures; **how was your ~?** votre voyage s'est bien passé?

joy [dʒɔɪ] n joie f; **joyrider** n voleur(-euse) de voiture (qui fait une virée dans le véhicule volé); **joy stick** n (Aviat) manche m à balai; (Comput) manche m à balai, manette f (de jeu)

Jr abbr = **junior**

judge [dʒʌdʒ] n juge m ▷ vt juger; (estimate: weight, size etc) apprécier; (consider) estimer

judo [ˈdʒuːdəʊ] n judo m

jug [dʒʌg] n pot m, cruche f

juggle [ˈdʒʌgl] vi jongler; **juggler** n jongleur m

juice [dʒuːs] n jus m; **juicy** adj juteux(-euse)

Jul abbr (= July) juil

July [dʒuːˈlaɪ] n juillet m

jumble [ˈdʒʌmbl] n fouillis m ▷ vt (also: **~ up**, **~ together**) mélanger, brouiller; **jumble sale** n (BRIT) vente f de charité

● **JUMBLE SALE**
●
● Les **jumble sales** ont lieu dans les églises,
● salles des fêtes ou halls d'écoles, et l'on
● y vend des articles de toutes sortes, en
● général bon marché et surtout d'occasion,
● pour collecter des fonds pour une œuvre
● de charité, une école (par exemple, pour
● acheter un ordinateur), ou encore une
● église (pour réparer un toit etc).

jumbo [ˈdʒʌmbəʊ] adj (also: **~ jet**) (avion) gros porteur (à réaction)

jump [dʒʌmp] vi sauter, bondir; (with fear etc) sursauter; (increase) monter en flèche ▷ vt sauter, franchir ▷ n saut m, bond m; (with fear etc) sursaut m; (fence) obstacle m; **to ~ the queue** (BRIT) passer avant son tour

jumper [ˈdʒʌmpəʳ] n (BRIT: pullover) pull-over m; (US: pinafore dress) robe-chasuble f

jump leads (US **jumper cables**) npl câbles mpl de démarrage

Jun. abbr = **June**; **junior**

junction [ˈdʒʌŋkʃən] n (BRIT: of roads) carrefour m; (of rails) embranchement m

June [dʒuːn] n juin m

jungle [ˈdʒʌŋgl] n jungle f

junior [ˈdʒuːnɪəʳ] adj, n: **he's ~ to me (by 2 years)**, **he's my ~ (by 2 years)** il est mon cadet (de 2 ans), il est plus jeune que moi (de 2 ans); **he's ~ to me** (seniority) il est en

dessous de moi (dans la hiérarchie), j'ai plus d'ancienneté que lui; **junior high school** n (US) ≈ collège m d'enseignement secondaire; see also **high school**; **junior school** n (BRIT) école f primaire, cours moyen

junk [dʒʌŋk] n (rubbish) camelote f; (cheap goods) bric-à-brac m inv; **junk food** n snacks vite prêts (sans valeur nutritive)

junkie [ˈdʒʌŋkɪ] n (inf) junkie m, drogué(e)

junk mail n prospectus mpl; (Comput) messages mpl publicitaires

Jupiter [ˈdʒuːpɪtəʳ] n (planet) Jupiter f

jurisdiction [dʒuərɪsˈdɪkʃən] n juridiction f; **it falls** or **comes within/outside our ~** cela est/n'est pas de notre compétence or ressort

jury [ˈdʒuərɪ] n jury m

just [dʒʌst] adj juste ▷ adv: **he's ~ done it/left** il vient de le faire/partir; **~ right/two o'clock** exactement or juste ce qu'il faut/deux heures; **we were ~ going** nous partions; **I was ~ about to phone** j'allais téléphoner; **~ as he was leaving** au moment or à l'instant précis où il partait; **~ before/enough/here** juste avant/assez/là; **it's ~ me/a mistake** ce n'est que moi/(rien) qu'une erreur; **~ missed/caught** manqué/attrapé de justesse; **~ listen to this!** écoutez un peu ça!; **she's ~ as clever as you** elle est tout aussi intelligente que vous; **it's ~ as well that you ...** heureusement que vous ...; **~ a minute!**, **~ one moment!** un instant (s'il vous plaît)!

justice [ˈdʒʌstɪs] n justice f; (US: judge) juge m de la Cour suprême

justification [dʒʌstɪfɪˈkeɪʃən] n justification f

justify [ˈdʒʌstɪfaɪ] vt justifier

jut [dʒʌt] vi (also: **~ out**) dépasser, faire saillie

juvenile [ˈdʒuːvənaɪl] adj juvénile; (court, books) pour enfants ▷ n adolescent(e)

K, k [keɪ] *abbr* (= *one thousand*) K; (= *kilobyte*) Ko

kangaroo [kæŋgə'ruː] *n* kangourou *m*

karaoke [kɑːrəˈəʊkɪ] *n* karaoké *m*

karate [kəˈrɑːtɪ] *n* karaté *m*

kebab [kəˈbæb] *n* kébab *m*

keel [kiːl] *n* quille *f*; **on an even ~** (*fig*) à flot

keen [kiːn] *adj* (*eager*) plein(e) d'enthousiasme; (*interest, desire, competition*) vif (vive); (*eye, intelligence*) pénétrant(e); (*edge*) effilé(e); **to be ~ to do** *or* **on doing sth** désirer vivement faire qch, tenir beaucoup à faire qch; **to be ~ on sth/sb** aimer beaucoup qch/qn

keep [kiːp] (*pt, pp* **kept**) *vt* (*retain, preserve*) garder; (*hold back*) retenir; (*shop, accounts, promise, diary*) tenir; (*support*) entretenir; (*chickens, bees, pigs etc*) élever ▷ *vi* (*food*) se conserver; (*remain: in a certain state or place*) rester ▷ *n* (*of castle*) donjon *m*; (*food etc*): **enough for his ~** assez pour (assurer) sa subsistance; **to ~ doing sth** (*continue*) continuer à faire qch; (*repeatedly*) ne pas arrêter de faire qch; **to ~ sb from doing/sth from happening** empêcher qn de faire or que qn (ne) fasse/que qch (n')arrive; **to ~ sb happy/a place tidy** faire que qn soit content/qu'un endroit reste propre; **to ~ sth to o.s.** garder qch pour soi, tenir qch secret; **to ~ sth from sb** cacher qch à qn; **to ~ time** (*clock*) être à l'heure, ne pas retarder; **for ~s** (*inf*) pour de bon, pour toujours; **keep away** *vt*: **to ~ sth/sb away**

from sb tenir qch/qn éloigné de qn ▷ *vi*: **to ~ away (from)** ne pas s'approcher (de); **keep back** *vt* (*crowds, tears, money*) retenir; (*conceal: information*): **to ~ sth back from sb** cacher qch à qn ▷ *vi* rester en arrière; **keep off** *vt* (*dog, person*) éloigner ▷ *vi*: **if the rain ~s off** s'il ne pleut pas; **~ your hands off!** pas touche! (*inf*); **"~ off the grass"** "pelouse interdite"; **keep on** *vi* continuer; **to ~ on doing** continuer à faire; **don't ~ on about it!** arrête (d'en parler)!; **keep out** *vt* empêcher d'entrer ▷ *vi* (*stay out*) rester en dehors; **"~ out"** "défense d'entrer"; **keep up** *vi* (*fig: in comprehension*) suivre ▷ *vt* continuer, maintenir; **to ~ up with sb** (*in work etc*) se maintenir au même niveau que qn; (*in race etc*) aller aussi vite que qn; **keeper** *n* gardien(ne); **keep-fit** *n* gymnastique *f* (d'entretien); **keeping** *n* (*care*) garde *f*; **in keeping with** en harmonie avec

kennel ['kɛnl] *n* niche *f*; **kennels** *npl* (*for boarding*) chenil *m*

Kenya ['kɛnjə] *n* Kenya *m*

kept [kɛpt] *pt, pp of* **keep**

kerb [kəːb] *n* (BRIT) bordure *f* du trottoir

kerosene ['kɛrəsiːn] *n* kérosène *m*

ketchup ['kɛtʃəp] *n* ketchup *m*

kettle ['kɛtl] *n* bouilloire *f*

key [kiː] *n* (*gen, Mus*) clé *f*; (*of piano, typewriter*) touche *f*; (*on map*) légende *f* ▷ *adj* (*factor, role, area*) clé *inv* ▷ *vt* (*also: ~ **in**: *text*) saisir; **can I have my ~?** je peux avoir ma clé?; **a ~ issue** un problème fondamental; **keyboard** *n* clavier *m*; **keyhole** *n* trou *m* de la serrure; **keyring** *n* porte-clés *m*

kg *abbr* (= *kilogram*) K

khaki ['kɑːkɪ] *adj, n* kaki *m*

kick [kɪk] *vt* donner un coup de pied à ▷ *vi* (*horse*) ruer ▷ *n* coup *m* de pied; (*inf: thrill*): **he does it for ~s** il le fait parce que ça l'excite, il le fait pour le plaisir; **to ~ the habit** (*inf*) arrêter; **kick off** *vi* (*Sport*) donner le coup d'envoi; **kick-off** *n* (*Sport*) coup *m* d'envoi

kid [kɪd] *n* (*inf: child*) gamin(e), gosse *m/f*; (*animal, leather*) chevreau *m* ▷ *vi* (*inf*) plaisanter, blaguer

kidnap ['kɪdnæp] *vt* enlever, kidnapper; **kidnapping** *n* enlèvement *m*

kidney ['kɪdnɪ] *n* (*Anat*) rein *m*; (*Culin*) rognon *m*; **kidney bean** *n* haricot *m* rouge

kill [kɪl] *vt* tuer ▷ *n* mise *f* à mort; **to ~ time** tuer le temps; **killer** *n* tueur(-euse); (*murderer*) meurtrier(-ière); **killing** *n* meurtre *m*; (*of group of people*) tuerie *f*, massacre *m*; (*inf*): **to make a killing** se remplir les poches, réussir un beau coup

kiln [kɪln] *n* four *m*

kilo ['kiːləu] *n* kilo *m*; **kilobyte** *n* (*Comput*) kilo-octet *m*; **kilogram(me)** *n* kilogramme *m*; **kilometre** (*us* **kilometer**) ['kɪləmiːtəʳ] *n* kilomètre *m*; **kilowatt** *n* kilowatt *m*

kilt [kɪlt] *n* kilt *m*

kin [kɪn] *n see* next-of-kin

kind [kaɪnd] *adj* gentil(le), aimable ▷ *n* sorte *f*, espèce *f*; (*species*) genre *m*; **to be two of a ~** se ressembler; **in ~** (*Comm*) en nature; **~ of** (*inf: rather*) plutôt; **a ~ of** une sorte de; **what ~ of ...?** quelle sorte de ...?

kindergarten ['kɪndəgɑːtn] *n* jardin *m* d'enfants

kindly ['kaɪndlɪ] *adj* bienveillant(e), plein(e) de gentillesse ▷ *adv* avec bonté; **will you ~ ...** auriez-vous la bonté *or* l'obligeance de ...

kindness ['kaɪndnɪs] *n* (*quality*) bonté *f*, gentillesse *f*

king [kɪŋ] *n* roi *m*; **kingdom** *n* royaume *m*; **kingfisher** *n* martin-pêcheur *m*; **king-size(d) bed** *n* grand lit (*de 1,95 m de large*)

kiosk ['kiːɔsk] *n* kiosque *m*; (*BRIT: also*: **telephone ~**) cabine *f* (téléphonique)

kipper ['kɪpər] *n* hareng fumé et salé

kiss [kɪs] *n* baiser *m* ▷ *vt* embrasser; **to ~ (each other)** s'embrasser; **kiss of life** *n* (*BRIT*) bouche à bouche *m*

kit [kɪt] *n* équipement *m*, matériel *m*; (*set of tools etc*) trousse *f*; (*for assembly*) kit *m*

kitchen ['kɪtʃɪn] *n* cuisine *f*

kite [kaɪt] *n* (*toy*) cerf-volant *m*

kitten ['kɪtn] *n* petit chat, chaton *m*

kitty ['kɪtɪ] *n* (*money*) cagnotte *f*

kiwi ['kiːwiː] *n* (*also*: **~ fruit**) kiwi *m*

km *abbr* (= *kilometre*) km

km/h *abbr* (= *kilometres per hour*) km/h

knack [næk] *n*: **to have the ~ (of doing)** avoir le coup (pour faire)

knee [niː] *n* genou *m*; **kneecap** *n* rotule *f*

kneel (*pt, pp* **knelt**) [niːl, nɛlt] *vi* (*also*: **~ down**) s'agenouiller

knelt [nɛlt] *pt, pp of* **kneel**

knew [njuː] *pt of* **know**

knickers ['nɪkəz] *npl* (*BRIT*) culotte *f* (de femme)

knife [naɪf] *n* (*pl* **knives**) couteau *m* ▷ *vt* poignarder, frapper d'un coup de couteau

knight [naɪt] *n* chevalier *m*; (*Chess*) cavalier *m*

knit [nɪt] *vt* tricoter ▷ *vi* tricoter; (*broken bones*) se ressouder; **to ~ one's brows** froncer les sourcils; **knitting** *n* tricot *m*; **knitting needle** *n* aiguille *f* à tricoter; **knitwear** *n* tricots *mpl*, lainages *mpl*

knives [naɪvz] *npl of* **knife**

knob [nɔb] *n* bouton *m*; (*BRIT*): **a ~ of butter** une noix de beurre

knock [nɔk] *vt* frapper; (*bump into*) heurter; (*fig: col*) dénigrer ▷ *vi* (*at door etc*): **to ~ at/on** frapper à/sur ▷ *n* coup *m*; **knock down** *vt* renverser; (*price*) réduire; **knock off** *vi* (*inf: finish*) s'arrêter (de travailler) ▷ *vt* (*vase, object*) faire tomber; (*inf: steal*) piquer; (*fig: from price*

etc): **to ~ off £10** faire une remise de 10 livres; **knock out** *vt* assommer; (*Boxing*) mettre k.-o.; (*in competition*) éliminer; **knock over** *vt* (*object*) faire tomber; (*pedestrian*) renverser; **knockout** *n* (*Boxing*) knock-out *m*, K.-O. *m*; **knockout competition** (*BRIT*) compétition *f* avec épreuves éliminatoires

knot [nɔt] *n* (*gen*) nœud *m* ▷ *vt* nouer

know [nəu] *vt* (*pt* **knew**, *pp* **~n**) savoir; (*person, place*) connaître; **to ~ that** savoir que; **to ~ how to do** savoir faire; **to ~ how to swim** savoir nager; **to ~ about/of sth** (*event*) être au courant de qch; (*subject*) connaître qch; **I don't ~ je** ne sais pas; **do you ~ where I can ...?** savez-vous où je peux ...?; **know-all** *n* (*BRIT pej*) je-sais-tout *m/f*; **know-how** *n* savoir-faire *m*, technique *f*, compétence *f*; **knowing** *adj* (*look etc*) entendu(e); **knowingly** *adv* (*on purpose*) sciemment; (*smile, look*) d'un air entendu; **know-it-all** *n* (*US*) = **know-all**

knowledge ['nɔlɪdʒ] *n* connaissance *f*; (*learning*) connaissances, savoir *m*; **without my ~** à mon insu; **knowledgeable** *adj* bien informé(e)

known [nəun] *pp of* **know** ▷ *adj* (*thief, facts*) notoire; (*expert*) célèbre

knuckle ['nʌkl] *n* articulation *f* (des phalanges), jointure *f*

koala [kəu'ɑːlə] *n* (*also*: **~ bear**) koala *m*

Koran [kɔ'rɑːn] *n* Coran *m*

Korea [kə'rɪə] *n* Corée *f*; **Korean** *adj* coréen(ne) ▷ *n* Coréen(ne)

kosher ['kəuʃər] *adj* kascher *inv*

Kosovar, Kosovan ['kɔsəvɑːr, 'kɔsəvən] *adj* kosovar(e)

Kosovo ['kɔsəvəu] *n* Kosovo *m*

Kuwait [ku'weɪt] *n* Koweït *m*

L

L *abbr* (BRIT Aut: = *learner*) signale un conducteur débutant

l. *abbr* (= *litre*) l

lab [læb] *n abbr* (= *laboratory*) labo *m*

label ['leɪbl] *n* étiquette *f*; (*brand: of record*) marque *f* ▷ *vt* étiqueter

labor *etc* ['leɪbər] (US) = **labour** *etc*

laboratory [lə'bɔrətəri] *n* laboratoire *m*

Labor Day *n* (US, CANADA) fête *f* du travail (*le premier lundi de septembre*)

> ● **LABOR DAY**
> ●
> ● La fête du Travail aux États-Unis et au
> ● Canada est fixée au premier lundi de
> ● septembre. Instituée par le Congrès en
> ● 1894 après avoir été réclamée par les
> ● mouvements ouvriers pendant douze
> ● ans, elle a perdu une grande partie de son
> ● caractère politique pour devenir un jour
> ● férié assez ordinaire et l'occasion de partir
> ● pour un long week-end avant la rentrée
> ● des classes.

labor union *n* (US) syndicat *m*

Labour ['leɪbər] *n* (BRIT Pol: *also*: **the ~ Party**) le parti travailliste, les travaillistes *mpl*

labour (US **labor**) ['leɪbər] *n* (*work*) travail *m*; (*workforce*) main-d'œuvre *f* ▷ *vi*: **to ~ (at)** travailler dur (à), peiner (sur) ▷ *vt*: **to ~ a point**

insister sur un point; **in ~** (Med) en travail; **labourer** *n* manœuvre *m*; **farm labourer** ouvrier *m* agricole

lace [leɪs] *n* dentelle *f*; (*of shoe etc*) lacet *m* ▷ *vt* (*shoe: also*: **~ up**) lacer

lack [læk] *n* manque *m* ▷ *vt* manquer de; **through** *or* **for ~ of** faute de, par manque de; **to be ~ing** manquer, faire défaut; **to be ~ing in** manquer de

lacquer ['lækər] *n* laque *f*

lacy ['leɪsɪ] *adj* (*of lace*) en dentelle; (*like lace*) comme de la dentelle

lad [læd] *n* garçon *m*, gars *m*

ladder ['lædər] *n* échelle *f*; (BRIT: *in tights*) maille filée ▷ *vt, vi* (BRIT: *tights*) filer

ladle ['leɪdl] *n* louche *f*

lady ['leɪdɪ] *n* dame *f*; **"ladies and gentlemen ..."** "Mesdames (et) Messieurs ..."; **young ~** jeune fille *f*; (*married*) jeune femme *f*; **the ladies' (room)** les toilettes *fpl* des dames; **ladybird** (US **ladybug**) *n* coccinelle *f*

lag [læg] *n* retard *m* ▷ *vi* (*also*: **~ behind**) rester en arrière, traîner; (*fig*) rester à la traîne ▷ *vt* (*pipes*) calorifuger

lager ['lɑːgər] *n* bière blonde

lagoon [lə'guːn] *n* lagune *f*

laid [leɪd] *pt, pp of* **lay**; **laid back** *adj* (*inf*) relaxe, décontracté(e)

lain [leɪn] *pp of* **lie**

lake [leɪk] *n* lac *m*

lamb [læm] *n* agneau *m*

lame [leɪm] *adj* (*also fig*) boiteux(-euse)

lament [lə'mɛnt] *n* lamentation *f* ▷ *vt* pleurer, se lamenter sur

lamp [læmp] *n* lampe *f*; **lamppost** *n* (BRIT) réverbère *m*; **lampshade** *n* abat-jour *m inv*

land [lænd] *n* (*as opposed to sea*) terre *f* (*ferme*); (*country*) pays *m*; (*soil*) terre; (*piece of land*) terrain *m*; (*estate*) terre(s), domaine(s) *m*(*pl*) ▷ *vi* (*from ship*) débarquer; (*Aviat*) atterrir; (*fig: fall*) (re)tomber ▷ *vt* (*passengers, goods*) débarquer; (*obtain*) décrocher; **to ~ sb with sth** (*inf*) coller qch à qn; **landing** *n* (*from ship*) débarquement *m*; (*Aviat*) atterrissage *m*; (*of staircase*) palier *m*; **landing card** *n* carte *f* de débarquement; **landlady** *n* propriétaire *f*, logeuse *f*; (*of pub*) patronne *f*; **landlord** *n* propriétaire *m*, logeur *m*; (*of pub etc*) patron *m*; **landmark** *n* (*point m de*) repère *m*; **to be a landmark** (*fig*) faire date *or* époque; **landowner** *n* propriétaire foncier *or* terrien; **landscape** *n* paysage *m*; **landslide** *n* (*Geo*) glissement *m* (*de terrain*); (*fig: Pol*) raz-de-marée (*électoral*)

lane [leɪn] *n* (*in country*) chemin *m*; (Aut: *of road*) voie *f*; (: *line of traffic*) file *f*; (*in race*) couloir *m*

language ['læŋgwɪdʒ] *n* langue *f*; (*way one speaks*) langage *m*; **what ~s do you speak?** quelles langues parlez-vous?; **bad ~**

grossièretés *fpl*, langage grossier; **language laboratory** *n* laboratoire *m* de langues; **language school** *n* école *f* de langue

lantern ['læntn] *n* lanterne *f*

lap [læp] *n* (*of track*) tour *m* (de piste); (*of body*): **in** *or* **on one's ~** sur les genoux ▷ *vt* (*also*: **~ up**) laper ▷ *vi* (*waves*) clapoter

lapel [lə'pɛl] *n* revers *m*

lapse [læps] *n* défaillance *f*; (*in behaviour*) écart *m* (de conduite) ▷ *vi* (*Law*) cesser d'être en vigueur; (*contract*) expirer; **to ~ into bad habits** prendre de mauvaises habitudes; **~ of time** laps *m* de temps, intervalle *m*

laptop (computer) ['læptɔp-] *n* portable *m*

lard [lɑːd] *n* saindoux *m*

larder ['lɑːdə'] *n* garde-manger *m inv*

large [lɑːdʒ] *adj* grand(e); (*person, animal*) gros (grosse); **at ~** (*free*) en liberté; (*generally*) en général; pour la plupart; *see also* **by**; **largely** *adv* en grande partie; (*principally*) surtout; **large-scale** *adj* (*map, drawing etc*) à grande échelle; (*fig*) important(e)

lark [lɑːk] *n* (*bird*) alouette *f*; (*joke*) blague *f*, farce *f*

laryngitis [lærɪn'dʒaɪtɪs] *n* laryngite *f*

lasagne [lə'zænjə] *n* lasagne *f*

laser ['leɪzə'] *n* laser *m*; **laser printer** *n* imprimante *f* laser

lash [læʃ] *n* coup *m* de fouet; (*also*: **eye~**) cil *m* ▷ *vt* fouetter; (*tie*) attacher; **lash out** *vi*: **to ~ out (at** *or* **against sb/sth)** attaquer violemment (qn/qch)

lass [læs] (*BRIT*) *n* (jeune) fille *f*

last [lɑːst] *adj* dernier(-ière) ▷ *adv* en dernier; (*most recently*) la dernière fois; (*finally*) finalement ▷ *vi* durer; **~ week** la semaine dernière; **~ night** (*evening*) hier soir; (*night*) la nuit dernière; **at ~** enfin; **~ but one** avant-dernier(-ière); **lastly** *adv* en dernier lieu, pour finir; **last-minute** *adj* de dernière minute

latch [lætʃ] *n* loquet *m*; **latch onto** *vt fus* (*cling to: person, group*) s'accrocher à; (*idea*) se mettre en tête

late [leɪt] *adj* (*not on time*) en retard; (*far on in day etc*) tardif(-ive); (*: edition, delivery*) dernier(-ière); (*dead*) défunt(e) ▷ *adv* tard; (*behind time, schedule*) en retard; **to be 10 minutes ~** avoir 10 minutes de retard; **sorry I'm ~** désolé d'être en retard; **it's too ~** il est trop tard; **of ~** dernièrement; **in ~ May** vers la fin (du mois) de mai, fin mai; **the ~ Mr X** feu M. X; **latecomer** *n* retardataire *m/f*; **lately** *adv* récemment; **later** *adj* (*date etc*) ultérieur(e); (*version etc*) plus récent(e) ▷ *adv* plus tard; **latest** ['leɪtɪst] *adj* tout(e) dernier(-ière); **at the latest** au plus tard

lather ['lɑːðə'] *n* mousse *f* (de savon) ▷ *vt* savonner

Latin ['lætɪn] *n* latin *m* ▷ *adj* latin(e); **Latin America** *n* Amérique latine; **Latin American** *adj* latino-américain(e), d'Amérique latine ▷ *n* Latino-Américain(e)

latitude ['lætɪtjuːd] *n* (*also fig*) latitude *f*

latter ['lætə'] *adj* deuxième, dernier(-ière) ▷ *n*: **the ~** ce dernier, celui-ci

laugh [lɑːf] *n* rire *m* ▷ *vi* rire; **(to do sth) for a ~** (faire qch) pour rire; **laugh at** *vt fus* se moquer de; (*joke*) rire de; **laughter** *n* rire *m*; (*of several people*) rires *mpl*

launch [lɔːntʃ] *n* lancement *m*; (*also*: **motor ~**) vedette *f* ▷ *vt* (*ship, rocket, plan*) lancer; **launch into** *vt fus* se lancer dans

launder ['lɔːndə'] *vt* laver; (*fig: money*) blanchir

Launderette® [lɔːn'drɛt] (*BRIT*) (*US* **Laundromat®** ['lɔːndrəmæt]) *n* laverie *f* (automatique)

laundry ['lɔːndrɪ] *n* (*clothes*) linge *m*; (*business*) blanchisserie *f*; (*room*) buanderie *f*; **to do the ~** faire la lessive

lava ['lɑːvə] *n* lave *f*

lavatory ['lævətərɪ] *n* toilettes *fpl*

lavender ['lævəndə'] *n* lavande *f*

lavish ['lævɪʃ] *adj* (*amount*) copieux(-euse); (*person: giving freely*): **~ with** prodigue de ▷ *vt*: **to ~ sth on sb** prodiguer qch à qn; (*money*) dépenser qch sans compter pour qn

law [lɔː] *n* loi *f*; (*science*) droit *m*; **lawful** *adj* légal(e), permis(e); **lawless** *adj* (*action*) illégal(e); (*place*) sans loi

lawn [lɔːn] *n* pelouse *f*; **lawnmower** *n* tondeuse *f* à gazon

lawsuit ['lɔːsuːt] *n* procès *m*

lawyer ['lɔːjə'] *n* (*consultant, with company*) juriste *m*; (*for sales, wills etc*) ≈ notaire *m*; (*partner, in court*) ≈ avocat *m*

lax [læks] *adj* relâché(e)

laxative ['læksətɪv] *n* laxatif *m*

lay [leɪ] *pt of* **lie** ▷ *adj* (*not expert*) profane ▷ *vt* (*pt, pp* **laid**) poser, mettre; (*eggs*) pondre; (*trap*) tendre; (*plans*) élaborer; **to ~ the table** mettre la table; **lay down** *vt* poser; (*rules etc*) établir; **to ~ down the law** (*fig*) faire la loi; **lay off** *vt* (*workers*) licencier; (*provide: meal etc*) fournir; **lay out** *vt* (*design*) dessiner, concevoir; (*display*) disposer; (*spend*) dépenser; **lay-by** *n* (*BRIT*) aire *f* de stationnement (sur le bas-côté)

layer ['leɪə'] *n* couche *f*

layman ['leɪmən] (*irreg*) *n* (*Rel*) laïque *m*; (*non-expert*) profane *m*

layout ['leɪaut] *n* disposition *f*, plan *m*, agencement *m*; (*Press*) mise *f* en page

lazy ['leɪzɪ] *adj* paresseux(-euse)

lb. *abbr* (*weight*) = **pound**

lead[1] [liːd] *n* (*front position*) tête *f*; (*distance, time ahead*) avance *f*; (*clue*) piste *f*; (*Elec*) fil *m*; (*for dog*) laisse *f*; (*Theat*) rôle principal ▷ *vb* (*pt, pp* **led**) ▷ *vt* (*guide*) mener, conduire; (*be leader of*) être à la tête de ▷ vi (Sport) mener, être en tête; **to ~ to** (road, pipe) mener à, conduire à; (result in) conduire à; aboutir à; **to be in the ~** (Sport: in race) mener, être en tête; (: in match) mener (à la marque); **to ~ sb to do sth** amener qn à faire qch; **to ~ the way** montrer le chemin; **lead up to** vt conduire à; (in conversation) en venir à

lead² [lɛd] n (metal) plomb m; (in pencil) mine f

leader ['liːdə'] n (of team) chef m; (of party etc) dirigeant(e), leader m; (Sport: in league) leader; (: in race) coureur m de tête; **leadership** n (position) direction f; **under the leadership of ...** sous la direction de ...; **qualities of leadership** qualités fpl de chef or de meneur

lead-free ['lɛdfriː] adj sans plomb

leading ['liːdɪŋ] adj de premier plan; (main) principal(e); (in race) de tête

lead singer [liːd-] n (in pop group) (chanteur m) vedette f

leaf (pl **leaves**) [liːf, liːvz] n feuille f; (of table) rallonge f; **to turn over a new ~** (fig) changer de conduite or d'existence; **leaf through** vt (book) feuilleter

leaflet ['liːflɪt] n prospectus m, brochure f; (Pol, Rel) tract m

league [liːɡ] n ligue f; (Football) championnat m; **to be in ~ with** avoir partie liée avec, être de mèche avec

leak [liːk] n (out: also fig) fuite f ▷ vi (pipe, liquid etc) fuir; (shoes) prendre l'eau; (ship) faire eau ▷ vt (liquid) répandre; (information) divulguer

lean [liːn] adj maigre ▷ vb (pt, pp **~ed** or **~t**) ▷ vt: **to ~ sth on** appuyer qch sur ▷ vi (slope) pencher; (rest): **to ~ against** s'appuyer contre; être appuyé(e) contre; **to ~ on** s'appuyer sur; **lean forward** vi se pencher en avant; **lean over** vi se pencher; **leaning** n: **leaning (towards)** penchant m (pour)

leant [lɛnt] pt, pp of **lean**

leap [liːp] n bond m, saut m ▷ vi (pt, pp **~ed** or **~t**) bondir, sauter

leapt [lɛpt] pt, pp of **leap**

leap year n année f bissextile

learn (pt, pp **~ed** or **~t**) [ləːn, -t] vt, vi apprendre; **to ~ (how) to do sth** apprendre à faire qch; **to ~ about sth** (Scol) étudier qch; (hear, read) apprendre qch; **learner** n débutant(e); (BRIT: also: **learner driver**) (conducteur(-trice)) débutant(e); **learning** n savoir m

learnt [ləːnt] pp of **learn**

lease [liːs] n bail m ▷ vt louer à bail

leash [liːʃ] n laisse f

least [liːst] adj: **the ~** (+ noun) le (la) plus petit(e), le (la) moindre; (smallest amount of) le moins de ▷ pron: **(the) ~** le moins ▷ adv (+ verb) le moins; (+ adj): **the ~** le (la) moins; **the ~ money** le moins d'argent; **the ~ expensive** le

(la) moins cher (chère); **the ~ possible effort** le moins d'effort possible; **at ~** au moins; (or rather) du moins; **you could at ~ have written** tu aurais pu écrire; **not in the ~** pas le moins du monde

leather ['lɛðə'] n cuir m

leave [liːv] (vb: pt, pp **left**) vt laisser; (go away from) quitter; (forget) oublier ▷ vi partir, s'en aller ▷ n (time off) congé m; (Mil, also: consent) permission f; **what time does the train/bus ~?** le train/le bus part à quelle heure?; **to ~ sth to sb** (money etc) laisser qch à qn; **to be left** rester; **there's some milk left over** il reste du lait; **~ it to me!** laissez-moi faire!, je m'en occupe!; **on ~** en permission; **leave behind** vt (also fig) laisser; (forget) laisser, oublier; **leave out** vt oublier, omettre

leaves [liːvz] npl of **leaf**

Lebanon ['lɛbənən] n Liban m

lecture ['lɛktʃə'] n conférence f; (Scol) cours (magistral) ▷ vi donner des cours; enseigner ▷ vt (scold) sermonner, réprimander; **to give a ~ (on)** faire une conférence (sur), faire un cours (sur); **lecture hall** n amphithéâtre m; **lecturer** n (speaker) conférencier(-ière); (BRIT: at university) professeur m (d'université), prof m/f de fac (inf); **lecture theatre** n = **lecture hall**

> Be careful not to translate *lecture* by the French word *lecture*.

led [lɛd] pt, pp of **lead¹**

ledge [lɛdʒ] n (of window, on wall) rebord m; (of mountain) saillie f, corniche f

leek [liːk] n poireau m

left [lɛft] pt, pp of **leave** ▷ adj gauche ▷ adv à gauche ▷ n gauche f; **there are two ~** il en reste deux; **on the ~, to the ~** à gauche; **the L~** (Pol) la gauche; **left-hand** adj: **the left-hand side** la gauche; **left-hand drive** n (BRIT: vehicle) véhicule m avec la conduite à gauche; **left-handed** adj gaucher(-ère); (scissors etc) pour gauchers; **left-luggage locker** n (BRIT) (casier m à) consigne f automatique; **left-luggage (office)** n (BRIT) consigne f; **left-overs** npl restes mpl; **left-wing** adj (Pol) de gauche

leg [lɛɡ] n jambe f; (of animal) patte f; (of furniture) pied m; (Culin: of chicken) cuisse f; (of journey) étape f; **lst/2nd ~** (Sport) match m aller/retour; **~ of lamb** (Culin) gigot m d'agneau

legacy ['lɛɡəsɪ] n (also fig) héritage m, legs m

legal ['liːɡl] adj (permitted by law) légal(e); (relating to law) juridique; **legal holiday** (US) n jour férié; **legalize** vt légaliser; **legally** adv légalement

legend ['lɛdʒənd] n légende f; **legendary** ['lɛdʒəndərɪ] adj légendaire

leggings ['lɛɡɪŋz] npl caleçon m

legible ['ledʒəbl] adj lisible

legislation [ledʒɪs'leɪʃən] n législation f

legislative ['ledʒɪslətɪv] adj législatif(-ive)

legitimate [lɪ'dʒɪtɪmət] adj légitime

leisure ['leʒəʳ] n (free time) temps libre, loisirs mpl; **at ~** (tout) à loisir; **at your ~** (later) à tête reposée; **leisure centre** n (BRIT) centre m de loisirs; **leisurely** adj tranquille, fait(e) sans se presser

lemon ['lemən] n citron m; **lemonade** n (fizzy) limonade f; **lemon tea** n thé m au citron

lend (pt, pp **lent**) [lend, lent] vt: **to ~ sth (to sb)** prêter qch (à qn); **could you ~ me some money?** pourriez-vous me prêter de l'argent?

length [leŋθ] n longueur f; (section: of road, pipe etc) morceau m, bout m; **~ of time** durée f; **it is 2 metres in ~** cela fait 2 mètres de long; **at ~** (at last) enfin, à la fin; (lengthily) longuement; **lengthen** vt allonger, prolonger ▷ vi s'allonger; **lengthways** adv dans le sens de la longueur, en long; **lengthy** adj (très) long (longue)

lens [lenz] n lentille f; (of spectacles) verre m; (of camera) objectif m

Lent [lent] n carême m

lent [lent] pt, pp of **lend**

lentil ['lentl] n lentille f

Leo ['li:əu] n le Lion

leopard ['lepəd] n léopard m

leotard ['li:əta:d] n justaucorps m

leprosy ['leprəsi] n lèpre f

lesbian ['lezbiən] n lesbienne f ▷ adj lesbien(ne)

less [les] adj moins de ▷ pron, adv moins ▷ prep: **~ tax/10% discount** avant impôt/moins 10% de remise; **~ than that/you** moins que cela/vous; **~ than half** moins de la moitié; **~ than ever** moins que jamais; **~ and ~** de moins en moins; **the ~ he works ...** moins il travaille ...; **lessen** vi diminuer, s'amoindrir, s'atténuer ▷ vt diminuer, réduire, atténuer; **lesser** ['lesəʳ] adj moindre; **to a lesser extent** or **degree** à un degré moindre

lesson ['lesn] n leçon f; **to teach sb a ~** (fig) donner une bonne leçon à qn

let (pt, pp **~**) [let] vt laisser; (BRIT: lease) louer; **to ~ sb do sth** laisser qn faire qch; **to ~ sb know sth** faire savoir qch à qn, prévenir qn de qch; **to ~ go** lâcher prise; **to ~ go of sth, to ~ sth go** lâcher qch; **~'s go** allons-y; **~ him come** qu'il vienne; **"to ~"** (BRIT) "à louer"; **let down** vt (lower) baisser; (BRIT: tyre) dégonfler; (disappoint) décevoir; **let in** vt laisser entrer; (visitor etc) faire entrer; **let off** vt (allow to leave) laisser partir; (not punish) ne pas punir; (firework etc) faire partir; (bomb) faire exploser; **let out** vt laisser sortir; (scream) laisser échapper; (BRIT: rent out) louer

lethal ['li:θl] adj mortel(le), fatal(e); (weapon)

meurtrier(-ère)

letter ['letəʳ] n lettre f; **letterbox** n (BRIT) boîte f aux or à lettres

lettuce ['letɪs] n laitue f, salade f

leukaemia (US **leukemia**) [lu:'ki:mɪə] n leucémie f

level ['levl] adj (flat) plat(e), plan(e), uni(e); (horizontal) horizontal(e) ▷ n niveau m ▷ vt niveler, aplanir; **"A" ~s** npl (BRIT) ≈ baccalauréat m; **to be ~ with** être au même niveau que; **to draw ~ with** (runner, car) arriver à la hauteur de, rattraper; **on the ~** (fig: honest) régulier(-ière); **level crossing** n (BRIT) passage m à niveau

lever ['li:vəʳ] n levier m; **leverage** n (influence): **leverage (on** or **with)** prise f (sur)

levy ['levi] n taxe f, impôt m ▷ vt (tax) lever; (fine) infliger

liability [laɪə'bɪlətɪ] n responsabilité f; (handicap) handicap m

liable ['laɪəbl] adj (subject): **~ to** sujet(te) à, passible de; (responsible): **~ (for)** responsable (de); (likely): **~ to do** susceptible de faire

liaise [li:'eɪz] vi: **to ~ with** assurer la liaison avec

liar ['laɪəʳ] n menteur(-euse)

libel ['laɪbl] n diffamation f; (document) écrit m diffamatoire ▷ vt diffamer

liberal ['lɪbərl] adj libéral(e); (generous): **~ with** prodigue de, généreux(-euse) avec ▷ n: **L~** (Pol) libéral(e); **Liberal Democrat** n (BRIT) libéral(e)-démocrate

liberate ['lɪbəreɪt] vt libérer

liberation [lɪbə'reɪʃən] n libération f

liberty ['lɪbətɪ] n liberté f; **to be at ~** (criminal) être en liberté; **at ~ to do** libre de faire; **to take the ~ of** prendre la liberté de, se permettre de

Libra ['li:brə] n la Balance

librarian [laɪ'brɛərɪən] n bibliothécaire m/f

library ['laɪbrərɪ] n bibliothèque f

> Be careful not to translate **library** by the French word **librairie**.

Libya ['lɪbɪə] n Libye f

lice [laɪs] npl of **louse**

licence (US **license**) ['laɪsns] n autorisation f, permis m; (Comm) licence f; (Radio, TV) redevance f; (also: **driving ~**, US: also: **driver's license**) permis m (de conduire)

license ['laɪsns] n (US) = **licence** ▷ vt donner une patente à, autoriser; **licensed** adj (for alcohol) patenté(e) pour la vente des spiritueux, qui a une patente de débit de boissons; (car) muni(e) de la vignette; **license plate** n (US Aut) plaque f minéralogique; **licensing hours** (BRIT) npl heures fpl d'ouvertures (des pubs)

lick [lɪk] vt lécher; (inf: defeat) écraser, flanquer une piquette or raclée à; **to ~ one's lips** (fig) se frotter les mains

lid [lɪd] n couvercle m; (eyelid) paupière f

lie [laɪ] n mensonge m ▷ vi (pt, pp **~d**) (tell lies) mentir; (pt **lay**, pp **lain**) (rest) être étendu(e) or allongé(e) or couché(e); (object: be situated) se trouver, être; **to ~ low** (fig) se cacher, rester caché(e); **to tell ~s** mentir; **lie about, lie around** vi (things) traîner; (BRIT: person) traînasser, flemmarder; **lie down** vi se coucher, s'étendre

Liechtenstein ['lɪktənstaɪn] n Liechtenstein m

lie-in ['laɪɪn] n (BRIT): **to have a ~** faire la grasse matinée

lieutenant [lefˈtɛnənt, US luːˈtɛnənt] n lieutenant m

life (pl **lives**) [laɪf, laɪvz] n vie f; **to come to ~** (fig) s'animer; **life assurance** n (BRIT) = **life insurance**; **lifeboat** n canot m or chaloupe f de sauvetage; **lifeguard** n surveillant m de baignade; **life insurance** n assurance-vie f; **life jacket** n gilet m or ceinture f de sauvetage; **lifelike** adj qui semble vrai(e) or vivant(e), ressemblant(e); (painting) réaliste; **life preserver** n (US) gilet m or ceinture f de sauvetage; **life sentence** n condamnation f à vie or à perpétuité; **lifestyle** n style m de vie; **lifetime** n: **in his lifetime** de son vivant

lift [lɪft] vt soulever, lever; (end) supprimer, lever ▷ vi (fog) se lever ▷ n (BRIT: elevator) ascenseur m; **to give sb a ~** (BRIT) emmener or prendre qn en voiture; **can you give me a ~ to the station?** pouvez-vous m'emmener à la gare?; **lift up** vt soulever; **lift-off** n décollage m

light [laɪt] n lumière f; (lamp) lampe f; (Aut: rear light) feu m; (: headlamp) phare m; (for cigarette etc) **have you got a ~?** avez-vous du feu? ▷ vt (pt, pp **~ed** or **lit**) (candle, cigarette, fire) allumer; (room) éclairer ▷ adj (room, colour) clair(e); (not heavy, also fig) léger(-ère); (not strenuous) peu fatigant(e); **lights** npl (traffic lights) feux mpl; **to come to ~** être dévoilé(e) or découvert(e); **in the ~ of** à la lumière de; étant donné; **light up** vi s'allumer; (face) s'éclairer; (smoke) allumer une cigarette or une pipe etc ▷ vt (illuminate) éclairer, illuminer; **light bulb** n ampoule f; **lighten** vt (light up) éclairer; (make lighter) éclaircir; (make less heavy) alléger; **lighter** n (also: **cigarette lighter**) briquet m; **light-hearted** adj gai(e), joyeux(-euse), enjoué(e); **lighthouse** n phare m; **lighting** n éclairage m; (in theatre) éclairages; **lightly** adv légèrement; **to get off lightly** s'en tirer à bon compte

lightning ['laɪtnɪŋ] n foudre f; (flash) éclair m

lightweight ['laɪtweɪt] adj (suit) léger(-ère) ▷ n (Boxing) poids léger

like [laɪk] vt aimer (bien) ▷ prep comme ▷ adj semblable, pareil(le) ▷ n: **the ~** (pej) (d')autres du même genre or acabit; **his ~s and dislikes** ses goûts mpl or préférences fpl; **I would ~, I'd ~** je voudrais, j'aimerais; **would you ~ a coffee?** voulez-vous du café?; **to be/look ~ sb/sth** ressembler à qn/qch; **what's he ~?** comment est-il?; **what does it look ~?** de quoi est-ce que ça a l'air?; **what does it taste ~?** quel goût est-ce que ça a?; **that's just ~ him** c'est bien de lui, ça lui ressemble; **do it ~ this** fais-le comme ceci; **it's nothing ~ ...** ce n'est pas du tout comme ...; **likeable** adj sympathique, agréable

likelihood ['laɪklɪhud] n probabilité f

likely ['laɪklɪ] adj (result, outcome) probable; (excuse) plausible; **he's ~ to leave** il va sûrement partir, il risque fort de partir; **not ~!** (inf) pas de danger!

likewise ['laɪkwaɪz] adv de même, pareillement

liking ['laɪkɪŋ] n (for person) affection f; (for thing) penchant m, goût m; **to be to sb's ~** être au goût de qn, plaire à qn

lilac ['laɪlək] n lilas m

Lilo® ['laɪləu] n matelas m pneumatique

lily ['lɪlɪ] n lis m; **~ of the valley** muguet m

limb [lɪm] n membre m

limbo ['lɪmbəu] n: **to be in ~** (fig) être tombé(e) dans l'oubli

lime [laɪm] n (tree) tilleul m; (fruit) citron vert, lime f; (Geo) chaux f

limelight ['laɪmlaɪt] n: **in the ~** (fig) en vedette, au premier plan

limestone ['laɪmstəun] n pierre f à chaux; (Geo) calcaire m

limit ['lɪmɪt] n limite f ▷ vt limiter; **limited** adj limité(e), restreint(e); **to be limited to** se limiter à, ne concerner que

limousine ['lɪməziːn] n limousine f

limp [lɪmp] n: **to have a ~** boiter ▷ vi boiter ▷ adj mou (molle)

line [laɪn] n (gen) ligne f; (stroke) trait m; (wrinkle) ride f; (rope) corde f; (wire) fil m; (of poem) vers m; (row, series) rangée f; (of people) file f, queue f; (railway track) voie f; (Comm: series of goods) article(s) m(pl), ligne de produits; (work) métier m ▷ vt: **to ~ (with)** (clothes) doubler (de); (box) garnir or tapisser (de); (subj: trees, crowd) border; **to stand in ~** (US) faire la queue; **in his ~ of business** dans sa partie, dans son rayon; **to be in ~ for sth** (fig) être en lice pour qch; **in ~ with** en accord avec, en conformité avec; **in a ~** aligné(e); **line up** vi s'aligner, se mettre en rang(s); (in queue) faire la queue ▷ vt aligner; (event) prévoir; (find) trouver; **to have sb/sth ~d up** avoir qn/qch en vue or de prévu(e)

linear ['lɪnɪəʳ] adj linéaire

linen ['lɪnɪn] n linge m (de corps or de maison); (cloth) lin m

liner ['laɪnəʳ] n (ship) paquebot m de ligne; (for

bin) sac-poubelle m

line-up ['laɪnʌp] n (us: queue) file f; (also: **police ~**) parade f d'identification; (Sport) (composition f de l') équipe f

linger ['lɪŋgəʳ] vi s'attarder; traîner; (smell, tradition) persister

lingerie ['lænʒəriː] n lingerie f

linguist ['lɪŋgwɪst] n linguiste m/f; **to be a good ~** être doué(e) pour les langues; **linguistic** adj linguistique

lining ['laɪnɪŋ] n doublure f; (of brakes) garniture f

link [lɪŋk] n (connection) lien m, rapport m; (Internet) lien; (of a chain) maillon m ▷ vt relier, lier, unir; **links** npl (Golf) (terrain m de) golf m; **link up** vt relier ▷ vi (people) se rejoindre; (companies etc) s'associer

lion ['laɪən] n lion m; **lioness** n lionne f

lip [lɪp] n lèvre f; (of cup etc) rebord m; **lipread** vi lire sur les lèvres; **lip salve** [-sælv] n pommade f pour les lèvres, pommade rosat; **lipstick** n rouge m à lèvres

liqueur [lɪˈkjuəʳ] n liqueur f

liquid ['lɪkwɪd] n liquide m ▷ adj liquide; **liquidizer** ['lɪkwɪdaɪzəʳ] n (BRIT Culin) mixer m

liquor ['lɪkəʳ] n spiritueux m, alcool m; **liquor store** (us) n magasin m de vins et spiritueux

Lisbon ['lɪzbən] n Lisbonne

lisp [lɪsp] n zézaiement m ▷ vi zézayer

list [lɪst] n liste f ▷ vt (write down) inscrire; (make list of) faire la liste de; (enumerate) énumérer

listen ['lɪsn] vi écouter; **to ~ to** écouter; **listener** n auditeur(-trice)

lit [lɪt] pt, pp of **light**

liter ['liːtəʳ] n (us) = **litre**

literacy ['lɪtərəsɪ] n degré m d'alphabétisation, fait m de savoir lire et écrire

literal ['lɪtərl] adj littéral(e); **literally** adv littéralement; (really) réellement

literary ['lɪtərərɪ] adj littéraire

literate ['lɪtərət] adj qui sait lire et écrire; (educated) instruit(e)

literature ['lɪtrɪtʃəʳ] n littérature f; (brochures etc) copie f publicitaire, prospectus mpl

litre (us **liter**) ['liːtəʳ] n litre m

litter ['lɪtəʳ] n (rubbish) détritus mpl; (dirtier) ordures fpl; (young animals) portée f; **litter bin** n (BRIT) poubelle f; **littered** adj: **littered with** (scattered) jonché(e) de

little ['lɪtl] adj (small) petit(e); (not much): **~ milk** peu de lait ▷ adv peu; **a ~** un peu (de); **a ~ milk** un peu de lait; **a ~ bit** un peu; **as ~ as possible** le moins possible; **~ by ~** petit à petit, peu à peu; **little finger** n auriculaire m, petit doigt

live¹ [laɪv] adj (animal) vivant(e), en vie; (wire) sous tension; (broadcast) (transmis(e) en direct; (unexploded) non explosé(e)

live² [lɪv] vi vivre; (reside) vivre, habiter; **to ~ in London** habiter (à) Londres; **where do you ~?** où habitez-vous?; **live together** vivre ensemble, cohabiter; **live up to** vt fus se montrer à la hauteur de

livelihood ['laɪvlɪhud] n moyens mpl d'existence

lively ['laɪvlɪ] adj vif (vive), plein(e) d'entrain; (place, book) vivant(e)

liven up ['laɪvn-] vt (room etc) égayer; (discussion, evening) animer ▷ vi s'animer

liver ['lɪvəʳ] n foie m

lives [laɪvz] npl of **life**

livestock ['laɪvstɔk] n cheptel m, bétail m

living ['lɪvɪŋ] adj vivant(e), en vie ▷ n: **to earn** or **make a ~** gagner sa vie; **living room** n salle f de séjour

lizard ['lɪzəd] n lézard m

load [ləud] n (weight) poids m; (thing carried) chargement m, charge f; (Elec, Tech) charge ▷ vt (also: **~ up**): **to ~ (with)** (lorry, ship) charger (de); (gun, camera) charger (avec); (Comput) charger; **a ~ of**, **~s of** (fig) un or des tas de, des masses de; **to talk a ~ of rubbish** (inf) dire des bêtises; **loaded** adj (dice) pipé(e); (question) insidieux(-euse); (inf: rich) bourré(e) de fric

loaf (pl **loaves**) [ləuf, ləuvz] n pain m, miche f ▷ vi (also: **~ about**, **~ around**) fainéanter, traîner

loan [ləun] n prêt m ▷ vt prêter; **on ~** prêté(e), en prêt

loathe [ləuð] vt détester, avoir en horreur

loaves [ləuvz] npl of **loaf**

lobby ['lɔbɪ] n hall m, entrée f; (Pol) groupe m de pression, lobby m ▷ vt faire pression sur

lobster ['lɔbstəʳ] n homard m

local ['ləukl] adj local(e) ▷ n (BRIT: pub) pub m or café m du coin; **the locals** npl les gens mpl du pays or du coin; **local anaesthetic** n anesthésie locale; **local authority** n collectivité locale, municipalité f; **local government** n administration locale or municipale; **locally** ['ləukəlɪ] adv localement; dans les environs or la région

locate [ləuˈkeɪt] vt (find) trouver, repérer; (situate) situer; **to be ~d in** être situé à or en

location [ləuˈkeɪʃən] n emplacement m; **on ~** (Cine) en extérieur

> Be careful not to translate **location** by the French word **location**.

loch [lɔx] n lac m, loch m

lock [lɔk] n (of door, box) serrure f; (of canal) écluse f; (of hair) mèche f, boucle f ▷ vt (with key) fermer à clé ▷ vi (door etc) fermer à clé; (wheels) se bloquer; **lock in** vt enfermer; **lock out** vt enfermer dehors; (on purpose) mettre à la porte; **lock up** vt (person) enfermer; (house) fermer à clé ▷ vi tout fermer (à clé)

locker ['lɔkəʳ] n casier m; (in station) consigne

ƒautomatique; **locker-room** (us) n (Sport) vestiaire m

locksmith ['lɒksmɪθ] n serrurier m

locomotive [ləukə'məutɪv] n locomotive ƒ

locum ['ləukəm] n (Med) suppléant(e) de médecin etc

lodge [lɒdʒ] n pavillon m (de gardien); (also: **hunting ~**) pavillon de chasse ▷ vi (person): **to ~ with** être logé(e) chez, être en pension chez; (bullet) se loger ▷ vt (appeal etc) présenter; déposer; **to ~ a complaint** porter plainte; **lodger** n locataire m/ƒ; (with room and meals) pensionnaire m/ƒ

lodging ['lɒdʒɪŋ] n logement m

loft [lɒft] n grenier m; (apartment) grenier aménagé (en appartement) (gén dans ancien entrepôt ou fabrique)

log [lɒg] n (of wood) bûche ƒ; (Naut) livre m or journal m de bord; (of car) ≈ carte grise ▷ vt enregistrer; **log in, log on** vi (Comput) ouvrir une session, entrer dans le système; **log off, log out** vi (Comput) clore une session, sortir du système

logic ['lɒdʒɪk] n logique ƒ; **logical** adj logique

logo ['ləugəu] n logo m

Loire [lwaː] n: **the (River) ~** la Loire

lollipop ['lɒlɪpɒp] n sucette ƒ; **lollipop man/ lady** (BRIT: irreg) n contractuel qui fait traverser la rue aux enfants

lolly ['lɒlɪ] n (inf: ice) esquimau m; (: lollipop) sucette ƒ

London ['lʌndən] n Londres; **Londoner** n Londonien(ne)

lone [ləun] adj solitaire

loneliness ['ləunlınıs] n solitude ƒ, isolement m

lonely ['ləunlı] adj seul(e); (childhood etc) solitaire; (place) solitaire, isolé(e)

long [lɒŋ] adj long (longue) ▷ adv longtemps ▷ vi: **to ~ for sth/to do sth** avoir très envie de qch/de faire qch, attendre qch avec impatience/attendre avec impatience de faire qch; **how ~ is this river/course?** quelle est la longueur de ce fleuve/la durée de ce cours?; **6 metres ~** (long) de 6 mètres; **6 months ~** qui dure 6 mois, de 6 mois; **all night ~** toute la nuit; **he no ~er comes** il ne vient plus; **I can't stand it any ~er** je ne peux plus le supporter; **~ before** longtemps avant; **before ~** (+ future) avant peu, dans peu de temps; (+ past) peu de temps après; **don't be ~!** fais vite!, dépêche-toi!; **I shan't be ~** je n'en ai pas pour longtemps; **as ~ as** enfin; **so or as ~ as** à condition que + sub; **long-distance** adj (race) de fond; (call) interurbain(e); **long-haul** adj (flight) long-courrier; **longing** n désir m, envie ƒ; (nostalgia) nostalgie ƒ ▷ adj plein(e) d'envie or de nostalgie

longitude ['lɒŋgɪtjuːd] n longitude ƒ

long: **long jump** n saut m en longueur; **long-life** adj (batteries etc) longue durée inv; (milk) longue conservation; **long-sighted** adj (BRIT) presbyte; (fig) prévoyant(e); **long-standing** adj de longue date; **long-term** adj à long terme

loo [luː] n (BRIT inf) w.-c mpl, petit coin

look [luk] vi regarder; (seem) sembler, paraître, avoir l'air; (building etc): **to ~ south/on to the sea** donner au sud/sur la mer ▷ n regard m; (appearance) air m, allure ƒ, aspect m; **looks** npl (good looks) physique m, beauté ƒ; **to ~ like** ressembler à; **to have a ~** regarder; **to have a ~ at sth** jeter un coup d'œil à qch; **~ (here)!** (annoyance) écoutez!; **look after** vt ƒus s'occuper de; (luggage etc: watch over) garder, surveiller; **look around** vi regarder autour de soi; **look at** vt ƒus regarder; (problem etc) examiner; **look back** vi: **to ~ back at sth/sb** se retourner pour regarder qch/qn; **to ~ back on** (event, period) évoquer, repenser à; **look down** vt ƒus (fig) regarder de haut, dédaigner; **look for** vt ƒus chercher; **we're ~ing for a hotel/restaurant** nous cherchons un hôtel/restaurant; **look forward to** vt ƒus attendre avec impatience; **~ing forward to hearing from you** (in letter) dans l'attente de vous lire; **look into** vt ƒus (matter, possibility) examiner, étudier; **look out** vi (beware): **to ~ out (for)** prendre garde (à), faire attention (à); **~ out!** attention!; **look out for** vt ƒus (seek) être à la recherche de; (try to spot) guetter; **look round** vt ƒus (house, shop) faire le tour de ▷ vi (turn) regarder derrière soi, se retourner; **look through** vt ƒus (papers, book) examiner; (: briefly) parcourir; **look up** vi lever les yeux; (improve) s'améliorer ▷ vt (word) chercher; **look up to** vt ƒus avoir du respect pour; **lookout** n (tower etc) poste m de guet; (person) guetteur m; **to be on the lookout (for)** guetter

loom [luːm] vi (also: **~ up**) surgir; (event) paraître imminent(e); (threaten) menacer

loony ['luːnı] adj, n (inf) timbré(e), cinglé(e) m/ƒ

loop [luːp] n boucle ƒ ▷ vt: **to ~ sth round sth** passer qch autour de qch; **loophole** n (fig) porte ƒ de sortie; échappatoire ƒ

loose [luːs] adj (knot, screw) desserré(e); (clothes) vague, ample, lâche; (hair) dénoué(e), épars(e); (not firmly fixed) pas solide; (morals, discipline) relâché(e); (translation) approximatif(-ive) ▷ n: **to be on the ~** être en liberté; **~ connection** (Elec) mauvais contact; **to be at a ~ end** or (us) **at ~ ends** (fig) ne pas trop savoir quoi faire; **loosely** adv sans serrer; (imprecisely) approximativement; **loosen** vt desserrer, relâcher; défaire

loot [luːt] n butin m ▷ vt piller

lop-sided ['lɔp'saɪdɪd] adj de travers, asymétrique

lord [lɔ:d] n seigneur m; **L~ Smith** lord Smith; **the L~** (Rel) le Seigneur; **my L~** (to noble) Monsieur le comte/le baron; (to judge) Monsieur le juge; (to bishop) Monseigneur; **good L~!** mon Dieu!; **Lords** npl (BRIT: Pol): **the (House of) Lords** (BRIT) la Chambre des Lords

lorry ['lɔrɪ] n (BRIT) camion m; **lorry driver** n (BRIT) camionneur m, routier m

lose (pt, pp **lost**) [lu:z, lɔst] vt perdre ▷ vi perdre; **I've lost my wallet/passport** j'ai perdu mon portefeuille/passeport; **to ~ (time)** (clock) retarder; **lose out** vi être perdant(e); **loser** n perdant(e)

loss [lɔs] n perte f; **to make a ~** enregistrer une perte; **to be at a ~** être perplexe or embarrassé(e)

lost [lɔst] pt, pp of **lose** ▷ adj perdu(e); **to get ~** vi se perdre; **I'm ~** je me suis perdu; **~ and found property** n (US) objets trouvés; **~ and found** n (US) (bureau m des) objets trouvés; **lost property** n (BRIT) objets trouvés; **lost property office** or **department** (bureau m des) objets trouvés

lot [lɔt] n (at auctions, set) lot m; (destiny) sort m, destinée f; **the ~** (everything) le tout; (everyone) tous mpl, toutes fpl; **a ~** beaucoup; **a ~ of** beaucoup de; **~s of** tas de; **to draw ~s (for sth)** tirer (qch) au sort

lotion ['ləuʃən] n lotion f

lottery ['lɔtərɪ] n loterie f

loud [laud] adj bruyant(e), sonore; (voice) fort(e); (condemnation etc) vigoureux(-euse); (gaudy) voyant(e), tapageur(-euse) ▷ adv (speak etc) fort; **out ~** tout haut; **loudly** adv fort, bruyamment; **loudspeaker** n haut-parleur m

lounge [laundʒ] n salon m; (of airport) salle f; (BRIT: also: **~ bar**) (salle de) café m or bar m ▷ vi (also: **~ about** or **around**) se prélasser, paresser

louse (pl **lice**) [laus, laɪs] n pou m

lousy ['lauzɪ] (inf) adj (bad quality) infect(e), moche; **I feel ~** je suis mal fichu(e)

love [lʌv] n amour m ▷ vt aimer; (caringly, kindly) aimer beaucoup; **I ~ chocolate** j'adore le chocolat; **to ~ to do** aimer beaucoup or adorer faire; **"15 ~"** (Tennis) "15 à rien or zéro"; **to be/fall in ~ with** être/tomber amoureux(-euse) de; **to make ~** faire l'amour; **~ from Anne, ~, Anne** affectueusement, Anne; **I ~ you** je t'aime; **love affair** n liaison (amoureuse); **love life** n vie sentimentale

lovely ['lʌvlɪ] adj (pretty) ravissant(e); (friend, wife) charmant(e); (holiday, surprise) très agréable, merveilleux(-euse)

lover ['lʌvər] n amant m; (person in love) amoureux(-euse); (amateur): **a ~ of** un(e) ami(e) de, un(e) amoureux(-euse) de

loving ['lʌvɪŋ] adj affectueux(-euse), tendre, aimant(e)

low [ləu] adj bas (basse); (quality) mauvais(e), inférieur(e) ▷ adv bas ▷ n (Meteorology) dépression f; **to feel ~** se sentir déprimé(e); **he's very ~** (ill) il est bien bas or très affaibli; **to turn (down) ~** vt baisser; **to be ~ on** (supplies etc) être à court de; **to reach a new** or **an all-time ~** tomber au niveau le plus bas; **low-alcohol** adj à faible teneur en alcool, peu alcoolisé(e); **low-calorie** adj hypocalorique

lower ['ləuər] adj inférieur(e) ▷ vt baisser; (resistance) diminuer; **to ~ o.s. to** s'abaisser à

low-fat ['ləu'fæt] adj maigre

loyal ['lɔɪəl] adj loyal(e), fidèle; **loyalty** n loyauté f, fidélité f; **loyalty card** n carte f de fidélité

L.P. n abbr = **long-playing record**

L-plates ['ɛlpleɪts] npl (BRIT) plaques fpl (obligatoires) d'apprenti conducteur

Lt abbr (= lieutenant) Lt.

Ltd abbr (Comm: company: = limited) ≈ S.A.

luck [lʌk] n chance f; **bad ~** malchance f, malheur m; **good ~!** bonne chance!; **bad** or **hard** or **tough ~!** pas de chance!; **luckily** adv heureusement, par bonheur; **lucky** adj (person) qui a de la chance; (coincidence) heureux(-euse); (number etc) qui porte bonheur

lucrative ['lu:krətɪv] adj lucratif(-ive), rentable, qui rapporte

ludicrous ['lu:dɪkrəs] adj ridicule, absurde

luggage ['lʌgɪdʒ] n bagages mpl; **our ~ hasn't arrived** nos bagages ne sont pas arrivés; **could you send someone to collect our ~?** pourriez-vous envoyer quelqu'un chercher nos bagages?; **luggage rack** n (in train) porte-bagages m inv; (: on car) galerie f

lukewarm ['lu:kwɔ:m] adj tiède

lull [lʌl] n accalmie f; (in conversation) pause f ▷ vt: **to ~ sb to sleep** bercer qn pour qu'il s'endorme; **to be ~ed into a false sense of security** s'endormir dans une fausse sécurité

lullaby ['lʌləbaɪ] n berceuse f

lumber ['lʌmbər] n (wood) bois m de charpente; (junk) bric-à-brac m inv ▷ vt (BRIT inf): **to ~ sb with sth/sb** coller or refiler qch/qn à qn

luminous ['lu:mɪnəs] adj lumineux(-euse)

lump [lʌmp] n morceau m; (in sauce) grumeau m; (swelling) grosseur f ▷ vt (also: **~ together**) réunir, mettre en tas; **lump sum** n somme globale or forfaitaire; **lumpy** adj (sauce) qui a des grumeaux; (bed) défoncé(e), peu confortable

lunatic ['lu:nətɪk] n fou (folle), dément(e) ▷ adj fou (folle), dément(e)

lunch [lʌntʃ] n déjeuner m ▷ vi déjeuner; **lunch break, lunch hour** n pause f de midi, heure f du déjeuner; **lunchtime** n: **it's**

lunchtime c'est l'heure du déjeuner
lung [lʌŋ] n poumon m
lure [luəʳ] n (attraction) attrait m, charme m; (in hunting) appât m, leurre m ▷ vt attirer or persuader par la ruse
lurk [lə:k] vi se tapir, se cacher
lush [lʌʃ] adj luxuriant(e)
lust [lʌst] n (sexual) désir (sexuel); (Rel) luxure f; (fig): ~ **for** soif f de
Luxembourg ['lʌksəmbə:g] n Luxembourg m
luxurious [lʌg'zjuəriəs] adj luxueux(-euse)
luxury ['lʌkʃəri] n luxe m ▷ cpd de luxe
Lycra® ['laıkrə] n Lycra® m
lying ['laıŋ] n mensonge(s) m(pl) ▷ adj (statement, story) mensonger(-ère), faux (fausse); (person) menteur(-euse)
Lyons ['ljɔ̃] n Lyon
lyrics ['lırıks] npl (of song) paroles fpl

m

m. abbr (= metre) m; (= million) M; (= mile) mi
M.A. n abbr (Scol) = **Master of Arts**
ma [mɑ:] (inf) n maman f
mac [mæk] n (BRIT) imper(méable m) m
macaroni [mækə'rəuni] n macaronis mpl
Macedonia [mæsı'dəuniə] n Macédoine f; **Macedonian** [mæsı'dəuniən] adj macédonien(ne) ▷ n Macédonien(ne); (Ling) macédonien m
machine [mə'ʃi:n] n machine f ▷ vt (dress etc) coudre à la machine; (Tech) usiner; **machine gun** n mitrailleuse f; **machinery** n machinerie f, machines fpl; (fig) mécanisme(s) m(pl); **machine washable** adj (garment) lavable en machine
macho ['mætʃəu] adj macho inv
mackerel ['mækrl] n (pl inv) maquereau m
mackintosh ['mækıntɔʃ] n (BRIT) imperméable m
mad [mæd] adj fou (folle); (foolish) insensé(e); (angry) furieux(-euse); **to be ~ (keen) about** or **on sth** (inf) être follement passionné de qch, être fou de qch
Madagascar [mædə'gæskəʳ] n Madagascar m
madam ['mædəm] n madame f
mad cow disease n maladie f des vaches folles
made [meıd] pt, pp of **make**; **made-to-measure** adj (BRIT) fait(e) sur mesure;

made-up ['meɪdʌp] adj (story) inventé(e), fabriqué(e)

madly ['mædlɪ] adv follement; **~ in love** éperdument amoureux(-euse)

madman ['mædmən] (irreg) n fou m, aliéné m

madness ['mædnɪs] n folie f

Madrid [mə'drɪd] n Madrid

Mafia ['mæfɪə] n maf(f)ia f

mag [mæg] n abbr (BRIT inf: = magazine) magazine m

magazine [mægə'ziːn] n (Press) magazine m, revue f; (Radio, TV) magazine m

maggot ['mægət] n ver m, asticot m

magic ['mædʒɪk] n magie f ▷ adj magique; **magical** adj magique; (experience, evening) merveilleux(-euse); **magician** [mə'dʒɪʃən] n magicien(ne)

magistrate ['mædʒɪstreɪt] n magistrat m; juge m

magnet ['mægnɪt] n aimant m; **magnetic** [mæg'netɪk] adj magnétique

magnificent [mæg'nɪfɪsnt] adj superbe, magnifique; (splendid: robe, building) somptueux(-euse), magnifique

magnify ['mægnɪfaɪ] vt grossir; (sound) amplifier; **magnifying glass** n loupe f

magpie ['mægpaɪ] n pie f

mahogany [mə'hɔgənɪ] n acajou m

maid [meɪd] n bonne f; (in hotel) femme f de chambre; **old ~** (pej) vieille fille

maiden name n nom m de jeune fille

mail [meɪl] n poste f; (letters) courrier m ▷ vt envoyer (par la poste); **by ~** par la poste; **mailbox** n (US: also Comput) boîte f aux lettres; **mailing list** n liste f d'adresses; **mailman** (irreg) n (US) facteur m; **mail-order** n vente f or achat m par correspondance

main [meɪn] adj principal(e) ▷ n (pipe) conduite principale, canalisation f; **the ~s** (Elec) le secteur; **the ~ thing** l'essentiel m; **in the ~** dans l'ensemble; **main course** n (Culin) plat m de résistance; **mainland** n continent m; **mainly** adv principalement, surtout; **main road** n grand axe, route nationale; **mainstream** n (fig) courant principal; **main street** n rue f principale

maintain [meɪn'teɪn] vt entretenir; (continue) maintenir, préserver; (affirm) soutenir; **maintenance** ['meɪntənəns] n entretien m; (Law: alimony) pension f alimentaire

maisonette [meɪzə'nɛt] n (BRIT) appartement m en duplex

maize [meɪz] n (BRIT) maïs m

majesty ['mædʒɪstɪ] n majesté f; (title): **Your M~** Votre Majesté

major ['meɪdʒə'] n (Mil) commandant m ▷ adj (important) important(e); (most important) principal(e); (Mus) majeur(e) ▷ vi (US Scol): **to ~ (in)** se spécialiser (en)

Majorca [mə'jɔːkə] n Majorque f

majority [mə'dʒɔrɪtɪ] n majorité f

make [meɪk] vt (pt, pp **made**) faire; (manufacture) faire, fabriquer; (earn) gagner; (decision) prendre; (friend) se faire; (speech) faire, prononcer; (cause to be): **to ~ sb sad** etc rendre qn triste etc; (force): **to ~ sb do sth** obliger qn à faire qch, faire faire qch à qn; (equal): **2 and 2 ~ 4** 2 et 2 font 4 ▷ n (manufacture) fabrication f; (brand) marque f; **to ~ a fool of sb** (ridicule) ridiculiser qn; (trick) avoir or duper qn; **to ~ a profit** faire un or des bénéfice(s); **to ~ a loss** essuyer une perte; **to ~ it** (in time etc) y arriver; (succeed) réussir; **what time do you ~ it?** quelle heure avez-vous?; **I ~ it £249** d'après mes calculs ça fait 249 livres; **to be made of** être en; **to ~ do with** se contenter de; se débrouiller avec; **make off** vi filer; **make out** vt (write out: cheque) faire; (decipher) déchiffrer; (understand) comprendre; (see) distinguer; (claim, imply) prétendre, vouloir faire croire; **make up** vt (invent) inventer, imaginer; (constitute) constituer; (parcel, bed) faire ▷ vi se réconcilier; (with cosmetics) se maquiller, se farder; **to be made up of** se composer de; **make up for** vt fus compenser; (lost time) rattraper; **makeover** ['meɪkəʊvə'] n (by beautician) soins mpl de maquillage; (change of image) changement m d'image; **maker** n fabricant m; (of film, programme) réalisateur(-trice); **makeshift** adj provisoire, improvisé(e); **make-up** n maquillage m

making ['meɪkɪŋ] n (fig): **in the ~** en formation or gestation; **to have the ~s of** (actor, athlete) avoir l'étoffe de

malaria [mə'lɛərɪə] n malaria f, paludisme m

Malaysia [mə'leɪzɪə] n Malaisie f

male [meɪl] n (Biol, Elec) mâle m ▷ adj (sex, attitude) masculin(e); (animal) mâle; (child etc) du sexe masculin

malicious [mə'lɪʃəs] adj méchant(e), malveillant(e)

> Be careful not to translate **malicious** by the French word **malicieux**.

malignant [mə'lɪgnənt] adj (Med) malin(-igne)

mall [mɔːl] n (also: **shopping ~**) centre commercial

mallet ['mælɪt] n maillet m

malnutrition [mælnjuː'trɪʃən] n malnutrition f

malpractice [mæl'præktɪs] n faute professionnelle; négligence f

malt [mɔːlt] n malt m ▷ cpd (whisky) pur malt

Malta ['mɔːltə] n Malte f; **Maltese** [mɔːl'tiːz] adj maltais(e) ▷ n (pl inv) Maltais(e)

mammal ['mæml] n mammifère m

mammoth ['mæməθ] n mammouth m ▷ adj géant(e), monstre

man (pl **men**) [mæn, mɛn] n homme m;
(Sport) joueur m; (Chess) pièce f ▷ vt (Naut:
ship) garnir d'hommes; (machine) assurer le
fonctionnement de; (Mil: gun) servir; (: post)
être de service à; **an old ~** un vieillard; **~ and
wife** mari et femme
manage ['mænɪdʒ] vi se débrouiller; (succeed)
y arriver, réussir ▷ vt (business) gérer; (team,
operation) diriger; (control: ship) manier,
manœuvrer; (: person) savoir s'y prendre avec;
to ~ to do se débrouiller pour faire; (succeed)
réussir à faire; **manageable** adj maniable;
(task etc) faisable; (number) raisonnable;
management n (running) administration f,
direction f; (people in charge: of business, firm)
dirigeants mpl, cadres mpl; (: of hotel, shop,
theatre) direction; **manager** n (of business)
directeur m; (of institution etc) administrateur
m; (of department, unit) responsable m/f, chef
m; (of hotel etc) gérant m; (Sport) manager
m; (of artist) impresario m; **manageress** n
directrice f; (of hotel etc) gérante f; **managerial**
[mænɪ'dʒɪərɪəl] adj directorial(e); (skills)
de cadre, de gestion; **managing director** n
directeur général
mandarin ['mændərɪn] n (also: ~ **orange**)
mandarine f
mandate ['mændeɪt] n mandat m
mandatory ['mændətərɪ] adj obligatoire
mane [meɪn] n crinière f
maneuver [mə'nuːvəʳ] (US) = manoeuvre
mangetout ['mɒnʒ'tuː] n mange-tout m inv
mango (pl **~es**) ['mæŋɡəu] n mangue f
man: mankind [mæn'kaɪnd] n humanité f,
genre humain; **manly** adj viril(e); (fibre)
synthétique; **man-made**
adj artificiel(le); (fibre) synthétique
mania ['meɪnɪə] n manie f; **maniac**
['meɪnɪæk] n maniaque m/f; (fig) fou (folle)
manic ['mænɪk] adj maniaque
manicure ['mænɪkjuəʳ] n manucure f
manifest ['mænɪfɛst] vt manifester ▷ adj
manifeste, évident(e)
manifesto [mænɪ'fɛstəu] n (Pol) manifeste m
manipulate [mə'nɪpjuleɪt] vt manipuler;
(system, situation) exploiter
man: mankind [mæn'kaɪnd] n humanité f,
genre humain; **manly** adj viril(e); **man-made**
adj artificiel(le); (fibre) synthétique
manner ['mænəʳ] n manière f, façon f;
(behaviour) attitude f, comportement m;
manners npl: (**good**) **~s** (bonnes) manières;
bad ~s mauvaises manières; **all ~ of** toutes
sortes de
manoeuvre (US **maneuver**) [mə'nuːvəʳ]
vt (move) manœuvrer; (manipulate: person)
manipuler; (: situation) exploiter ▷ n
manœuvre f
manpower ['mænpauəʳ] n main-d'œuvre f
mansion ['mænʃən] n château m, manoir m
manslaughter ['mænslɔːtəʳ] n homicide m
involontaire
mantelpiece ['mæntlpiːs] n cheminée f
manual ['mænjuəl] adj manuel(le) ▷ n
manuel m
manufacture [mænju'fæktʃəʳ] vt fabriquer
▷ n fabrication f; **manufacturer** n fabricant m
manure [mə'njuəʳ] n fumier m; (artificial)
engrais m
manuscript ['mænjuskrɪpt] n manuscrit m
many ['mɛnɪ] adj beaucoup de, de
nombreux(-euses) ▷ pron beaucoup, un grand
nombre; **a great ~** un grand nombre (de); **~ a ...**
bien des ..., plus d'un(e) ...
map [mæp] n carte f; (of town) plan m; **can
you show it to me on the ~?** pouvez-vous me
l'indiquer sur la carte?; **map out** vt tracer; (fig:
task) planifier
maple ['meɪpl] n érable m
Mar abbr = **March**
mar [mɑːʳ] vt gâcher, gâter
marathon ['mærəθɒn] n marathon m
marble ['mɑːbl] n marbre m; (toy) bille f
March [mɑːtʃ] n mars m
march [mɑːtʃ] vi marcher au pas;
(demonstrators) défiler ▷ n marche f;
(demonstration) manifestation f
mare [mɛəʳ] n jument f
margarine [mɑːdʒə'riːn] n margarine f
margin ['mɑːdʒɪn] n marge f; **marginal**
adj marginal(e); **marginal seat** (Pol) siège
disputé; **marginally** adv très légèrement,
sensiblement
marigold ['mærɪɡəuld] n souci m
marijuana [mærɪ'wɑːnə] n marijuana f
marina [mə'riːnə] n marina f
marinade n [mærɪ'neɪd] marinade f
marinate ['mærɪneɪt] vt (faire) mariner
marine [mə'riːn] adj marin(e) ▷ n fusilier
marin; (US) marine m
marital ['mærɪtl] adj matrimonial(e); **marital
status** n situation f de famille
maritime ['mærɪtaɪm] adj maritime
marjoram ['mɑːdʒərəm] n marjolaine f
mark [mɑːk] n marque f; (of skid etc) trace
f; (BRIT Scol) note f; (oven temperature): **(gas)
~ 4** thermostat m 4 ▷ vt (also Sport: player)
marquer; (stain) tacher; (BRIT Scol) corriger,
noter; **to ~ time** marquer le pas; **marked** adj
(obvious) marqué(e), net(te); **marker** n (sign)
jalon m; (bookmark) signet m
market ['mɑːkɪt] n marché m ▷ vt (Comm)
commercialiser; **marketing** n marketing m;
marketplace n place f du marché; (Comm)
marché m; **market research** n étude f de
marché
marmalade ['mɑːməleɪd] n confiture f
d'oranges
maroon [mə'ruːn] vt: **to be ~ed** être
abandonné(e); (fig) être bloqué(e) ▷ adj

m

(colour) bordeaux *inv*

marquee [maː'kiː] *n* chapiteau *m*

marriage ['mærɪdʒ] *n* mariage *m*; **marriage certificate** *n* extrait *m* d'acte de mariage

married ['mærɪd] *adj* marié(e); *(life, love)* conjugal(e)

marrow ['mærəu] *n (of bone)* moelle *f*; *(vegetable)* courge *f*

marry ['mærɪ] *vt* épouser, se marier avec; *(subj: father, priest etc)* marier ▷ *vi (also:* **get married)** se marier

Mars [maːz] *n (planet)* Mars *f*

Marseilles [maː'seɪ] *n* Marseille

marsh [maːʃ] *n* marais *m*, marécage *m*

marshal ['maːʃl] *n* maréchal *m*; *(us: fire, police)* ≈ capitaine *m*; *(for demonstration, meeting)* membre *m* du service d'ordre ▷ *vt* rassembler

martyr ['maːtəʳ] *n* martyr(e)

marvel ['maːvl] *n* merveille *f* ▷ *vi:* **to ~ (at)** s'émerveiller (de); **marvellous** *(us* **marvelous)** *adj* merveilleux(-euse)

Marxism ['maːksɪzəm] *n* marxisme *m*

Marxist ['maːksɪst] *adj, n* marxiste *(m/f)*

marzipan ['maːzɪpæn] *n* pâte *f* d'amandes

mascara [mæs'kaːrə] *n* mascara *m*

mascot ['mæskət] *n* mascotte *f*

masculine ['mæskjulɪn] *adj* masculin(e) ▷ *n* masculin *m*

mash [mæʃ] *vt (Culin)* faire une purée de; **mashed potato(es)** *n(pl)* purée *f* de pommes de terre

mask [maːsk] *n* masque *m* ▷ *vt* masquer

mason ['meɪsn] *n (also:* **stone~)** maçon *m*; *(also:* **free~)** franc-maçon *m*; **masonry** *n* maçonnerie *f*

mass [mæs] *n* multitude *f*, masse *f*; *(Physics)* masse; *(Rel)* messe *f* ▷ *cpd (communication)* de masse; *(unemployment)* massif(-ive) ▷ *vi* se masser; **masses** *npl:* **the ~es** les masses; **~es of** *(inf)* des tas de

massacre ['mæsəkəʳ] *n* massacre *m*

massage ['mæsɑːʒ] *n* massage *m* ▷ *vt* masser

massive ['mæsɪv] *adj* énorme, massif(-ive)

mass media *npl* mass-media *mpl*

mass-produce ['mæsprə'djuːs] *vt* fabriquer en série

mast [maːst] *n* mât *m*; *(Radio, TV)* pylône *m*

master ['maːstəʳ] *n* maître *m*; *(in secondary school)* professeur *m*; *(in primary school)* instituteur *m*; *(title for boys):* **M~ X** Monsieur X ▷ *vt* maîtriser; *(learn)* apprendre à fond; **M~ of Arts/Science (MA/MSc)** *n* ≈ titulaire *m/f* d'une maîtrise (en lettres/science); **M~ of Arts/Science degree (MA/MSc)** *n* ≈ maîtrise *f*; **mastermind** *n* esprit supérieur ▷ *vt* diriger, être le cerveau de; **masterpiece** *n* chef-d'œuvre *m*

masturbate ['mæstəbeɪt] *vi* se masturber

mat [mæt] *n* petit tapis; *(also:* **door~)**

paillasson *m*; *(also:* **table~)** set *m* de table ▷ *adj* = **matt**

match [mætʃ] *n* allumette *f*; *(game)* match *m*, partie *f*; *(fig)* égal(e) ▷ *vt (also:* **~ up)** assortir; *(go well with)* aller bien avec, s'assortir à; *(equal)* égaler, valoir ▷ *vi* être assorti(e); **to be a good ~** être bien assorti(e); **matchbox** *n* boîte *f* d'allumettes; **matching** *adj* assorti(e)

mate [meɪt] *n (inf)* copain (copine); *(animal)* partenaire *m/f*, mâle (femelle); *(in merchant navy)* second *m* ▷ *vi* s'accoupler

material [mə'tɪərɪəl] *n (substance)* matière *f*, matériau *m*; *(cloth)* tissu *m*, étoffe *f*; *(information, data)* données *fpl* ▷ *adj* matériel(le); *(relevant: evidence)* pertinent(e); **materials** *npl (equipment)* matériaux *mpl*

materialize [mə'tɪərɪəlaɪz] *vi* se matérialiser, se réaliser

maternal [mə'təːnl] *adj* maternel(le)

maternity [mə'təːnɪtɪ] *n* maternité *f*; **maternity hospital** *n* maternité *f*; **maternity leave** *n* congé *m* de maternité

math [mæθ] *n (us:* = **mathematics)** maths *fpl*

mathematical [mæθə'mætɪkl] *adj* mathématique

mathematician [mæθəmə'tɪʃən] *n* mathématicien(ne)

mathematics [mæθə'mætɪks] *n* mathématiques *fpl*

maths [mæθs] *n abbr (BRIT:* = **mathematics)** maths *fpl*

matinée ['mætɪneɪ] *n* matinée *f*

matron ['meɪtrən] *n (in hospital)* infirmière-chef *f*; *(in school)* infirmière *f*

matt [mæt] *adj* mat(e)

matter ['mætəʳ] *n* question *f*; *(Physics)* matière *f*, substance *f*; *(Med: pus)* pus *m* ▷ *vi* importer; **matters** *npl (affairs, situation)* la situation; **it doesn't ~** cela n'a pas d'importance; *(I don't mind)* cela ne fait rien; **what's the ~?** qu'est-ce qu'il y a?, qu'est-ce qui ne va pas?; **no ~ what** quoi qu'il arrive; **as a ~ of course** tout naturellement; **as a ~ of fact** en fait; **reading ~** *(BRIT)* de quoi lire, de la lecture

mattress ['mætrɪs] *n* matelas *m*

mature [mə'tjuəʳ] *adj* mûr(e); *(cheese)* fait(e); *(wine)* arrivé(e) à maturité ▷ *vi* mûrir; *(cheese, wine)* se faire; **mature student** *n* étudiant(e) plus âgé(e) que la moyenne; **maturity** *n* maturité *f*

maul [mɔːl] *vt* lacérer

mauve [məuv] *adj* mauve

max *abbr* = **maximum**

maximize ['mæksɪmaɪz] *vt (profits etc, chances)* maximiser

maximum ['mæksɪməm] *(pl* **maxima)** *adj* maximum ▷ *n* maximum *m*

May [meɪ] *n* mai *m*

may [meɪ] *(conditional* **might)** *vi (indicating*

possibility): **he ~ come** il se peut qu'il vienne; (*be allowed to*): **~ I smoke?** puis-je fumer?; (*wishes*): **~ God bless you!** (que) Dieu vous bénisse!; **you ~ as well go** vous feriez aussi bien d'y aller

maybe ['meɪbi:] *adv* peut-être; **~ he'll ...** peut-être qu'il ...

May Day *n* le Premier mai

mayhem ['meɪhɛm] *n* grabuge *m*

mayonnaise [meɪə'neɪz] *n* mayonnaise *f*

mayor [mɛə'] *n* maire *m*; **mayoress** *n* (*female mayor*) maire *m*; (*wife of mayor*) épouse *f* du maire

maze [meɪz] *n* labyrinthe *m*, dédale *m*

MD *n abbr* (*Comm*) = **managing director**

me [mi:] *pron* me, m' + *vowel or h mute*; (*stressed, after prep*) moi; **it's me** c'est moi; **he heard me** il m'a entendu; **give me a book** donnez-moi un livre; **it's for me** c'est pour moi

meadow ['mɛdəu] *n* prairie *f*, pré *m*

meagre (*us* **meager**) ['mi:gə'] *adj* maigre

meal [mi:l] *n* repas *m*; (*flour*) farine *f*; **mealtime** *n* heure *f* du repas

mean [mi:n] *adj* (*with money*) avare, radin(e), (*unkind*) mesquin(e), méchant(e); (*shabby*) misérable; (*average*) moyen(ne) ▷ *vt* (*pt, pp* **~t**) (*signify*) signifier, vouloir dire; (*refer to*) faire allusion à, parler de; (*intend*): **to ~ to do** avoir l'intention de faire ▷ *n* moyenne *f*; **means** *npl* (*way, money*) moyens *mpl*; **by ~s of** (*instrument*) au moyen de; **by all ~s** je vous en prie; **to be ~t for** être destiné(e) à; **do you ~ it?** vous êtes sérieux?; **what do you ~?** que voulez-vous dire?

meaning ['mi:nɪŋ] *n* signification *f*, sens *m*; **meaningful** *adj* significatif(-ive); (*relationship*) valable; **meaningless** *adj* dénué(e) de sens

meant [mɛnt] *pt, pp of* **mean**

meantime ['mi:ntaɪm] *adv* (*also*: **in the ~**) pendant ce temps

meanwhile ['mi:nwaɪl] *adv* = **meantime**

measles ['mi:zlz] *n* rougeole *f*

measure ['mɛʒə'] *vt, vi* mesurer ▷ *n* mesure *f*; (*ruler*) règle (graduée)

measurements ['mɛʒəməntz] *npl* mesures *fpl*; **chest/hip ~** tour *m* de poitrine/hanches

meat [mi:t] *n* viande *f*; **I don't eat ~** je ne mange pas de viande; **cold ~s** (*brit*) viandes froides; **meatball** *n* boulette *f* de viande

Mecca ['mɛkə] *n* la Mecque

mechanic [mɪ'kænɪk] *n* mécanicien *m*; **can you send a ~?** pouvez-vous nous envoyer un mécanicien?; **mechanical** *adj* mécanique

mechanism ['mɛkənɪzəm] *n* mécanisme *m*

medal ['mɛdl] *n* médaille *f*; **medallist** (*us* **medalist**) *n* (*Sport*) médaillé(e)

meddle ['mɛdl] *vi*: **to ~ in** se mêler de, s'occuper de; **to ~ with** toucher à

media ['mi:dɪə] *npl* media *mpl* ▷ *npl of* **medium**

mediaeval [mɛdɪ'i:vl] *adj* = **medieval**

mediate ['mi:dɪeɪt] *vi* servir d'intermédiaire

medical ['mɛdɪkl] *adj* médical(e) ▷ *n* (*also*: **~ examination**) visite médicale; (*private*) examen médical; **medical certificate** *n* certificat médical

medicated ['mɛdɪkeɪtɪd] *adj* traitant(e), médicamenteux(-euse)

medication [mɛdɪ'keɪʃən] *n* (*drugs etc*) médication *f*

medicine ['mɛdsɪn] *n* médecine *f*; (*drug*) médicament *m*

medieval [mɛdɪ'i:vl] *adj* médiéval(e)

mediocre [mi:dɪ'əukə'] *adj* médiocre

meditate ['mɛdɪteɪt] *vi*: **to ~ (on)** méditer (sur)

meditation [mɛdɪ'teɪʃən] *n* méditation *f*

Mediterranean [mɛdɪtə'reɪnɪən] *adj* méditerranéen(ne); **the ~ (Sea)** la (mer) Méditerranée

medium ['mi:dɪəm] *adj* moyen(ne) ▷ *n* (*pl* **media**: *means*) moyen *m*; (*pl* **~s**: *person*) médium *m*; **the happy ~** le juste milieu; **medium-sized** *adj* de taille moyenne; **medium wave** *n* (*Radio*) ondes moyennes, petites ondes

meek [mi:k] *adj* doux (douce), humble

meet (*pt, pp* **met**) [mi:t, mɛt] *vt* rencontrer; (*by arrangement*) retrouver, rejoindre; (*for the first time*) faire la connaissance de; (*go and fetch*) **I'll ~ you at the station** j'irai te chercher à la gare; (*opponent, danger, problem*) faire face à; (*requirements*) satisfaire à, répondre à ▷ *vi* (*friends*) se rencontrer; se retrouver; (*in session*) se réunir; (*join: lines, roads*) se joindre; **nice ~ing you** ravi d'avoir fait votre connaissance; **meet up** *vi*: **to ~ up with sb** rencontrer qn; **meet with** *vt fus* (*difficulty*) rencontrer; **to ~ with success** être couronné(e) de succès; **meeting** *n* (*of group of people*) réunion *f*; (*between individuals*) rendez-vous *m*; **she's at** *or* **in a meeting** (*Comm*) elle est en réunion; **meeting place** *n* lieu *m* de (la) réunion; (*for appointment*) lieu de rendez-vous

megabyte ['mɛgəbaɪt] *n* (*Comput*) méga-octet *m*

megaphone ['mɛgəfəun] *n* porte-voix *m inv*

megapixel ['mɛgəpɪksl] *n* mégapixel *m*

melancholy ['mɛlənkəlɪ] *n* mélancolie *f* ▷ *adj* mélancolique

melody ['mɛlədɪ] *n* mélodie *f*

melon ['mɛlən] *n* melon *m*

melt [mɛlt] *vi* fondre ▷ *vt* faire fondre

member ['mɛmbə'] *n* membre *m*; **Member of Congress** (*us*) *n* membre *m* du Congrès, ≈ député *m*; **Member of Parliament (MP)** *n* (*brit*) député *m*; **Member of the European Parliament (MEP)** *n* Eurodéputé *m*;

m

Member of the House of Representatives (MHR) n (us) membre m de la Chambre des représentants; **Member of the Scottish Parliament (MSP)** n (BRIT) député m au Parlement écossais; **membership** n (becoming a member) adhésion f; admission f; (the members) membres mpl, adhérents mpl; **membership card** n carte f de membre

memento [məˈmɛntəu] n souvenir m

memo [ˈmɛməu] n note f (de service)

memorable [ˈmɛmərəbl] adj mémorable

memorandum (pl **memoranda**) [mɛməˈrændəm, -də] n note f (de service)

memorial [mɪˈmɔːrɪəl] n mémorial m ▷ adj commémoratif(-ive)

memorize [ˈmɛməraɪz] vt apprendre or retenir par cœur

memory [ˈmɛmərɪ] n (also Comput) mémoire f; (recollection) souvenir m; **in ~ of** à la mémoire de; **memory card** n (for digital camera) carte f mémoire

men [mɛn] npl of **man**

menace [ˈmɛnɪs] n menace f; (inf: nuisance) peste f, plaie f ▷ vt menacer

mend [mɛnd] vt réparer; (darn) raccommoder, repriser ▷ n: **on the ~** en voie de guérison; **to ~ one's ways** s'amender

meningitis [mɛnɪnˈdʒaɪtɪs] n méningite f

menopause [ˈmɛnəupɔːz] n ménopause f

men's room (us) n: **the men's room** les toilettes fpl pour hommes

menstruation [mɛnstruˈeɪʃən] n menstruation f

menswear [ˈmɛnzwɛəʳ] n vêtements mpl d'hommes

mental [ˈmɛntl] adj mental(e); **mental hospital** n hôpital m psychiatrique; **mentality** [mɛnˈtælɪtɪ] n mentalité f; **mentally** adv: **to be mentally handicapped** être handicapé(e) mental(e); **the mentally ill** les malades mentaux

menthol [ˈmɛnθɔl] n menthol m

mention [ˈmɛnʃən] n mention f ▷ vt mentionner, faire mention de; **don't ~ it!** je vous en prie, il n'y a pas de quoi!

menu [ˈmɛnjuː] n (set menu, Comput) menu m; (list of dishes) carte f; **could we see the ~?** est-ce qu'on peut voir la carte?

MEP n abbr = **Member of the European Parliament**

mercenary [ˈməːsɪnərɪ] adj (person) intéressé(e), mercenaire ▷ n mercenaire m

merchandise [ˈməːtʃəndaɪz] n marchandises fpl

merchant [ˈməːtʃənt] n négociant m, marchand m; **merchant bank** n (BRIT) banque f d'affaires; **merchant navy** (us **merchant marine**) n marine marchande

merciless [ˈməːsɪlɪs] adj impitoyable, sans pitié

mercury [ˈməːkjurɪ] n mercure m

mercy [ˈməːsɪ] n pitié f, merci f; (Rel) miséricorde f; **at the ~ of** à la merci de

mere [mɪəʳ] adj simple; (chance) pur(e); **a ~ two hours** seulement deux heures; **merely** adv simplement, purement

merge [məːdʒ] vt unir; (Comput) fusionner, interclasser ▷ vi (colours, shapes, sounds) se mêler; (roads) se joindre; (Comm) fusionner; **merger** n (Comm) fusion f

meringue [məˈræŋ] n meringue f

merit [ˈmɛrɪt] n mérite m, valeur f ▷ vt mériter

mermaid [ˈməːmeɪd] n sirène f

merry [ˈmɛrɪ] adj gai(e); **M~ Christmas!** joyeux Noël!; **merry-go-round** n manège m

mesh [mɛʃ] n mailles fpl

mess [mɛs] n désordre m, fouillis m, pagaille f; (muddle: of life) gâchis m; (: of economy) pagaille f; (dirt) saleté f; (Mil) mess m, cantine f; **to be (in) a ~** être en désordre; **to be/get o.s. in a ~** (fig) être/se mettre dans le pétrin; **mess about** or **around** (inf) vi perdre son temps; **mess up** vt (dirty) salir; (spoil) gâcher; **mess with** (inf) vt fus (challenge, confront) se frotter à; (interfere with) toucher à

message [ˈmɛsɪdʒ] n message m; **can I leave a ~?** est-ce que je peux laisser un message?; **are there any ~s for me?** est-ce que j'ai des messages?

messenger [ˈmɛsɪndʒəʳ] n messager m

Messrs, Messrs. [ˈmɛsəz] abbr (on letters: = messieurs) MM

messy [ˈmɛsɪ] adj (dirty) sale; (untidy) en désordre

met [mɛt] pt, pp of **meet**

metabolism [mɛˈtæbəlɪzəm] n métabolisme m

metal [ˈmɛtl] n métal m ▷ cpd en métal; **metallic** [mɛˈtælɪk] adj métallique

metaphor [ˈmɛtəfəʳ] n métaphore f

meteor [ˈmiːtɪəʳ] n météore m; **meteorite** [ˈmiːtɪəraɪt] n météorite m or f

meteorology [miːtɪəˈrɔlədʒɪ] n météorologie f

meter [ˈmiːtəʳ] n (instrument) compteur m; (also: **parking ~**) parc(o)mètre m; (us: unit) = **metre** ▷ vt (us Post) affranchir à la machine

method [ˈmɛθəd] n méthode f; **methodical** [mɪˈθɔdɪkl] adj méthodique

methylated spirit [ˈmɛθɪleɪtɪd-] n (BRIT: also: **meths**) alcool m à brûler

meticulous [mɛˈtɪkjuləs] adj méticuleux(-euse)

metre (us **meter**) [ˈmiːtəʳ] n mètre m

metric [ˈmɛtrɪk] adj métrique

metro [ˈmɛtrəu] n métro m

metropolitan [mɛtrəˈpɔlɪtən] adj métropolitain(e); **the M~ Police** (BRIT) la police londonienne

Mexican ['mɛksɪkən] *adj* mexicain(e) ▷ *n* Mexicain(e)

Mexico ['mɛksɪkəʊ] *n* Mexique *m*

mg *abbr* (= *milligram*) mg

mice [maɪs] *npl of* **mouse**

micro... [maɪkrəʊ] *prefix*: **microchip** *n* (*Elec*) puce *f*; **microphone** *n* microphone *m*; **microscope** *n* microscope *m*; **microwave** *n* (*also*: **microwave oven**) four *m* à micro-ondes

mid [mɪd] *adj*: **~ May** la mi-mai; **~ afternoon** le milieu de l'après-midi; **in ~ air** en plein ciel; **he's in his ~ thirties** il a dans les trente-cinq ans; **midday** *n* midi *m*

middle ['mɪdl] *n* milieu *m*; (*waist*) ceinture *f*, taille *f* ▷ *adj* du milieu; (*average*) moyen(ne); **in the ~ of the night** au milieu de la nuit; **middle-aged** *adj* d'un certain âge, ni vieux ni jeune; **Middle Ages** *npl*: **the Middle Ages** le moyen âge; **middle-class** *adj* bourgeois(e); **middle class(es)** *n(pl)*: **the middle class(es)** ≈ les classes moyennes; **Middle East** *n*: **the Middle East** le Proche-Orient, le Moyen-Orient; **middle name** *n* second prénom; **middle school** *n* (*US*) école pour les enfants de 12 à 14 ans, ≈ collège *m*; (*BRIT*) école pour les enfants de 8 à 14 ans

midge [mɪdʒ] *n* moucheron *m*

midget ['mɪdʒɪt] *n* nain(e)

midnight ['mɪdnaɪt] *n* minuit *m*

midst [mɪdst] *n*: **in the ~ of** au milieu de

midsummer [mɪd'sʌmə^r] *n* milieu *m* de l'été

midway [mɪd'weɪ] *adj, adv*: **~ (between)** à mi-chemin (entre); **~ through ...** au milieu de ..., en plein(e) ...

midweek [mɪd'wiːk] *adv* au milieu de la semaine, en pleine semaine

midwife (*pl* **midwives**) ['mɪdwaɪf, -vz] *n* sage-femme *f*

midwinter [mɪd'wɪntə^r] *n* milieu *m* de l'hiver

might [maɪt] *vb see* **may** ▷ *n* puissance *f*, force *f*; **mighty** *adj* puissant(e)

migraine ['miːgreɪn] *n* migraine *f*

migrant ['maɪgrənt] *n* (*bird, animal*) migrateur *m*; (*person*) migrant(e) ▷ *adj* migrateur(-trice); migrant(e); (*worker*) saisonnier(-ière)

migrate [maɪ'greɪt] *vi* migrer

migration [maɪ'greɪʃən] *n* migration *f*

mike [maɪk] *n abbr* (= *microphone*) micro *m*

mild [maɪld] *adj* doux (douce); (*reproach, infection*) léger(-ère); (*illness*) bénin(-igne); (*interest*) modéré(e); (*taste*) peu relevé(e); **mildly** ['maɪldlɪ] *adv* doucement; légèrement; **to put it mildly** (*inf*) c'est le moins qu'on puisse dire

mile [maɪl] *n* mil(l)e *m* (= *1609 m*); **mileage** *n* distance *f* en milles, ≈ kilométrage *m*; **mileometer** [maɪ'lɔmɪtə^r] *n* compteur *m* kilométrique; **milestone** *n* borne *f*; (*fig*)

jalon *m*

military ['mɪlɪtərɪ] *adj* militaire

militia [mɪ'lɪʃə] *n* milice *f*

milk [mɪlk] *n* lait *m* ▷ *vt* (*cow*) traire; (*fig: person*) dépouiller, plumer; (: *situation*) exploiter à fond; **milk chocolate** *n* chocolat *m* au lait; **milkman** (*irreg*) *n* laitier *m*; **milky** *adj* (*drink*) au lait; (*colour*) laiteux(-euse)

mill [mɪl] *n* moulin *m*; (*factory*) usine *f*, fabrique *f*; (*spinning mill*) filature *f*; (*flour mill*) minoterie *f* ▷ *vt* moudre, broyer ▷ *vi* (*also*: **~ about**) grouiller

millennium (*pl* **~s** *or* **millennia**) [mɪ'lɛnɪəm, -'lɛnɪə] *n* millénaire *m*

milli... ['mɪlɪ] *prefix* milli...; **milligram(me)** *n* milligramme *m*; **millilitre** (*US* **milliliter**) ['mɪlɪliːtə^r] *n* millilitre *m*; **millimetre** (*US* **millimeter**) *n* millimètre *m*

million ['mɪljən] *n* million *m*; **a ~ pounds** un million de livres sterling; **millionaire** [mɪljə'nɛə^r] *n* millionnaire *m*; **millionth** [-θ] *num* millionième

milometer [maɪ'lɔmɪtə^r] *n* = **mileometer**

mime [maɪm] *n* mime *m* ▷ *vt, vi* mimer

mimic ['mɪmɪk] *n* imitateur(-trice) ▷ *vt, vi* imiter, contrefaire

min. *abbr* (= *minute(s)*) mn.; (= *minimum*) min.

mince [mɪns] *vt* hacher ▷ *n* (*BRIT Culin*) viande hachée, hachis *m*; **mincemeat** *n* hachis *de fruits secs utilisés en pâtisserie*; (*US*) viande hachée, hachis *m*; **mince pie** *n* sorte de tarte aux fruits secs

mind [maɪnd] *n* esprit *m* ▷ *vt* (*attend to, look after*) s'occuper de; (*be careful*) faire attention à; (*object to*): **I don't ~ the noise** je ne crains pas le bruit, le bruit ne me dérange pas; **it is on my ~** cela me préoccupe; **to change one's ~** changer d'avis; **to my ~** à mon avis, selon moi; **to bear sth in ~** tenir compte de qch; **to have sb/sth in ~** avoir qn/qch en tête; **to make up one's ~** se décider; **do you ~ if ...?** est-ce que cela vous gêne si ...?; **I don't ~** cela ne me dérange pas; (*don't care*) ça m'est égal; **~ you, ...** remarquez, ...; **never ~** peu importe, ça ne fait rien; (*don't worry*) ne vous en faites pas; **"~ the step"** "attention à la marche"; **mindless** *adj* irréfléchi(e); (*violence, crime*) insensé(e); (*boring: job*) idiot(e)

mine¹ [maɪn] *pron* le (la) mien(ne), les miens (miennes); **a friend of ~** un de mes amis, un ami à moi; **this book is ~** ce livre est à moi

mine² [maɪn] *n* mine *f* ▷ *vt* (*coal*) extraire; (*ship, beach*) miner; **minefield** *n* champ *m* de mines; **miner** *n* mineur *m*

mineral ['mɪnərəl] *adj* minéral(e) ▷ *n* minéral *m*; **mineral water** *n* eau minérale

mingle ['mɪŋgl] *vi*: **to ~ with** se mêler à

miniature ['mɪnətʃə^r] *adj* (en) miniature ▷ *n* miniature *f*

minibar ['mɪnɪbaːʳ] n minibar m

minibus ['mɪnɪbʌs] n minibus m

minicab ['mɪnɪkæb] n (BRIT) taxi m
indépendant

minimal ['mɪnɪml] adj minimal(e)

minimize ['mɪnɪmaɪz] vt (reduce) réduire au
minimum; (play down) minimiser

minimum ['mɪnɪməm] n (pl minima)
minimum m ▷ adj minimum

mining ['maɪnɪŋ] n exploitation minière

miniskirt ['mɪnɪskəːt] n mini-jupe f

minister ['mɪnɪstəʳ] n (BRIT Pol) ministre m;
(Rel) pasteur m

ministry ['mɪnɪstrɪ] n (BRIT Pol) ministère m;
(Rel): **to go into the ~** devenir pasteur

minor ['maɪnəʳ] adj petit(e), de peu
d'importance; (Mus, poet, problem) mineur(e)
▷ n (Law) mineur(e)

minority [maɪ'nɒrɪtɪ] n minorité f

mint [mɪnt] n (plant) menthe f; (sweet) bonbon
m à la menthe ▷ vt (coins) battre; **the (Royal)
M~, the (US) M~** ≈ l'hôtel m de la Monnaie; **in ~
condition** à l'état de neuf

minus ['maɪnəs] n (also: **~ sign**) signe m moins
▷ prep moins; **12 ~ 6 equals 6** 12 moins 6 égal 6;
~ 24°C moins 24°C

minute¹ n ['mɪnɪt] minute f; **minutes** npl (of
meeting) procès-verbal m, compte rendu; **wait
a ~!** (attendez) un instant!; **at the last ~** à la
dernière minute

minute² adj [maɪ'njuːt] minuscule; (detailed)
minutieux(-euse); **in ~ detail** par le menu

miracle ['mɪrəkl] n miracle m

miraculous [mɪ'rækjuləs] adj
miraculeux(-euse)

mirage ['mɪrɑːʒ] n mirage m

mirror ['mɪrəʳ] n miroir m, glace f; (in car)
rétroviseur m

misbehave [mɪsbɪ'heɪv] vi mal se conduire

misc. abbr = **miscellaneous**

miscarriage ['mɪskærɪdʒ] n (Med) fausse
couche; **~ of justice** erreur f judiciaire

miscellaneous [mɪsɪ'leɪnɪəs] adj (items,
expenses) divers(es); (selection) varié(e)

mischief ['mɪstʃɪf] n (naughtiness) sottises
fpl; (playfulness) espièglerie f; (harm) mal m,
dommage m; (maliciousness) méchanceté f;
mischievous ['mɪstʃɪvəs] adj (playful,
naughty) coquin(e), espiègle

misconception ['mɪskən'sɛpʃən] n idée
fausse

misconduct [mɪs'kɒndʌkt] n inconduite f;
professional ~ faute professionnelle

miser ['maɪzəʳ] n avare m/f

miserable ['mɪzərəbl] adj (person, expression)
malheureux(-euse); (conditions) misérable;
(weather) maussade; (offer, donation) minable;
(failure) pitoyable

misery ['mɪzərɪ] n (unhappiness) tristesse f;
(pain) souffrances fpl; (wretchedness) misère f

misfortune [mɪs'fɔːtʃən] n malchance f,
malheur m

misgiving [mɪs'gɪvɪŋ] n (apprehension)
craintes fpl; **to have ~s about sth** avoir des
doutes quant à qch

misguided [mɪs'gaɪdɪd] adj malavisé(e)

mishap ['mɪshæp] n mésaventure f

misinterpret [mɪsɪn'təːprɪt] vt mal
interpréter

misjudge [mɪs'dʒʌdʒ] vt méjuger, se
méprendre sur le compte de

mislay [mɪs'leɪ] vt (irreg: like **lay**) égarer

mislead [mɪs'liːd] vt (irreg: like **lead**) induire
en erreur; **misleading** adj trompeur(-euse)

misplace [mɪs'pleɪs] vt égarer; **to be ~d** (trust
etc) être mal placé(e)

misprint ['mɪsprɪnt] n faute f d'impression

misrepresent [mɪsrɛprɪ'zɛnt] vt présenter
sous un faux jour

Miss [mɪs] n Mademoiselle

miss [mɪs] vt (fail to get, attend, see) manquer,
rater; (regret the absence of): **I ~ him/it** il/cela
me manque ▷ vi manquer ▷ n (shot) coup
manqué; **we ~ed our train** nous avons raté
notre train; **you can't ~ it** vous ne pouvez
pas vous tromper; **miss out** vt (BRIT) oublier;
miss out on vt fus (fun, party) rater, manquer;
(chance, bargain) laisser passer

missile ['mɪsaɪl] n (Aviat) missile m; (object
thrown) projectile m

missing ['mɪsɪŋ] adj manquant(e); (after
escape, disaster: person) disparu(e); **to go
~** disparaître; **~ in action** (Mil) porté(e)
disparu(e)

mission ['mɪʃən] n mission f; **on a ~ to sb**
en mission auprès de qn; **missionary** n
missionnaire m/f

misspell ['mɪs'spɛl] vt (irreg: like **spell**) mal
orthographier

mist [mɪst] n brume f ▷ vi (also: **~ over, ~ up**)
devenir brumeux(-euse); (BRIT: windows)
s'embuer

mistake [mɪs'teɪk] n erreur f, faute f ▷ vt
(irreg: like **take**) (meaning) mal comprendre;
(intentions) se méprendre sur; **to ~ for** prendre
pour; **by ~** par erreur, par inadvertance; **to
make a ~** (in writing) faire une faute; (in
calculating etc) faire une erreur; **there must be
some ~** il doit y avoir une erreur, se tromper;
mistaken pp of **mistake** ▷ adj (idea etc)
erroné(e); **to be mistaken** faire erreur, se
tromper

mister ['mɪstəʳ] n (inf) Monsieur m; see **Mr**

mistletoe ['mɪsltəu] n gui m

mistook [mɪs'tuk] pt of **mistake**

mistress ['mɪstrɪs] n maîtresse f; (BRIT: in
primary school) institutrice f; (: in secondary
school) professeur m

mistrust [mɪs'trʌst] vt se méfier de

misty ['mɪstɪ] adj brumeux(-euse); (glasses, window) embué(e)

misunderstand [mɪsʌndə'stænd] vt, vi (irreg: like **stand**) mal comprendre; **misunderstanding** n méprise f, malentendu m; **there's been a misunderstanding** il y a eu un malentendu

misunderstood [mɪsʌndə'stud] pt, pp of **misunderstand** ▷ adj (person) incompris(e)

misuse n [mɪs'ju:s] mauvais emploi; (of power) abus m ▷ vt [mɪs'ju:z] mal employer; abuser de

mitt(en) ['mɪt(n)] n moufle f; (fingerless) mitaine f

mix [mɪks] vt mélanger; (sauce, drink etc) préparer ▷ vi se mélanger; (socialize): **he doesn't ~ well** il est peu sociable ▷ n mélange m; **to ~ sth with sth** mélanger qch à qch; **cake ~** préparation f pour gâteau; **mix up** vt mélanger; (confuse) confondre; **to be ~ed up in sth** être mêlé(e) à qch or impliqué(e) dans qch; **mixed** adj (feelings, reactions) contradictoire; (school, marriage) mixte; **mixed grill** n (BRIT) assortiment de grillades; **mixed salad** n salade f de crudités; **mixed-up** adj (person) désorienté(e), embrouillé(e); **mixer** n (for food) batteur m, mixeur m; (drink) boisson gazeuse (servant à couper un alcool); (person): **he is a good mixer** il est très sociable; **mixture** n assortiment m, mélange m; (Med) préparation f; **mix-up** n: **there was a mix-up** il y a eu confusion

ml abbr (= millilitre(s)) ml

mm abbr (= millimetre) mm

moan [məun] n gémissement m ▷ vi gémir; (inf: complain): **to ~ (about)** se plaindre (de)

moat [məut] n fossé m, douves fpl

mob [mɔb] n foule f; (disorderly) cohue f ▷ vt assaillir

mobile ['məubaɪl] adj mobile ▷ n (Art) mobile m; **mobile home** n caravane f; **mobile phone** n téléphone portatif

mobility [məu'bɪlɪtɪ] n mobilité f

mobilize ['məubɪlaɪz] vt, vi mobiliser

mock [mɔk] vt ridiculiser; (laugh at) se moquer de ▷ adj faux (fausse); **mocks** npl (BRIT: Scol) examens blancs; **mockery** n moquerie f, raillerie f

mod cons ['mɔd'kɔnz] npl abbr (BRIT) = **modern conveniences**; see **convenience**

mode [məud] n mode m; (of transport) moyen m

model ['mɔdl] n modèle m; (person: for fashion) mannequin m; (: for artist) modèle ▷ vt (with clay etc) modeler ▷ vi travailler comme mannequin ▷ adj (railway: toy) modèle réduit inv; (child, factory) modèle; **to ~ clothes** présenter des vêtements; **to ~ o.s. on** imiter

modem ['məudɛm] n modem m

moderate adj ['mɔdərət] modéré(e); (amount, change) peu important(e) ▷ vi se modérer, se calmer ▷ vt modérer; **moderation** [mɔdə'reɪʃən] n modération f, mesure f; **in ~** à dose raisonnable, pris(e) or pratiqué(e) modérément

modern ['mɔdən] adj moderne; **modernize** vt moderniser; **modern languages** npl langues vivantes

modest ['mɔdɪst] adj modeste; **modesty** n modestie f

modification [mɔdɪfɪ'keɪʃən] n modification f

modify ['mɔdɪfaɪ] vt modifier

module ['mɔdju:l] n module m

mohair ['məuhɛər] n mohair m

Mohammed [mə'hæmɛd] n Mahomet m

moist [mɔɪst] adj humide, moite; **moisture** ['mɔɪstʃər] n humidité f; (on glass) buée f; **moisturizer** ['mɔɪstʃəraɪzər] n crème hydratante

mold etc [məuld] (US) = **mould** etc

mole [məul] n (animal, spy) taupe f; (spot) grain m de beauté

molecule ['mɔlɪkju:l] n molécule f

molest [məu'lɛst] vt (assault sexually) attenter à la pudeur de

molten ['məultən] adj fondu(e); (rock) en fusion

mom [mɔm] n (US) = **mum**

moment ['məumənt] n moment m, instant m; **at the ~** en ce moment; **momentarily** ['məuməntrɪlɪ] adv momentanément; (US: soon) bientôt; **momentary** adj momentané(e), passager(-ère); **momentous** [məu'mɛntəs] adj important(e), capital(e)

momentum [məu'mɛntəm] n élan m, vitesse acquise; (fig) dynamique f; **to gather ~** prendre de la vitesse; (fig) gagner du terrain

mommy ['mɔmɪ] n (US: mother) maman f

Mon abbr (= Monday) l.

Monaco ['mɔnəkəu] n Monaco f

monarch ['mɔnək] n monarque m; **monarchy** n monarchie f

monastery ['mɔnəstərɪ] n monastère m

Monday ['mʌndɪ] n lundi m

monetary ['mʌnɪtərɪ] adj monétaire

money ['mʌnɪ] n argent m; **to make ~** (person) gagner de l'argent; (business) rapporter; **money belt** n ceinture-portefeuille f; **money order** n mandat m

mongrel ['mʌŋgrəl] n (dog) bâtard m

monitor ['mɔnɪtər] n (TV, Comput) écran m, moniteur m ▷ vt contrôler; (foreign station) être à l'écoute de; (progress) suivre de près

monk [mʌŋk] n moine m

monkey ['mʌŋkɪ] n singe m

monologue ['mɔnəlɔg] n monologue m

m

monopoly [mə'nɔpəlɪ] n monopole m
monosodium glutamate [mɔnə'səʊdɪəm 'gluːtəmeɪt] n glutamate m de sodium
monotonous [mə'nɔtənəs] adj monotone
monsoon [mɔn'suːn] n mousson f
monster ['mɔnstəʳ] n monstre m
month [mʌnθ] n mois m; **monthly** adj mensuel(le) ▷ adv mensuellement
Montreal [mɔntrɪ'ɔːl] n Montréal
monument ['mɔnjumənt] n monument m
mood [muːd] n humeur f, disposition f; **to be in a good/bad ~** être de bonne/mauvaise humeur; **moody** adj (variable) d'humeur changeante, lunatique; (sullen) morose, maussade
moon [muːn] n lune f; **moonlight** n clair m de lune
moor [muəʳ] n lande f ▷ vt (ship) amarrer ▷ vi mouiller
moose [muːs] n (pl inv) élan m
mop [mɔp] n balai m à laver; (for dishes) lavette f à vaisselle ▷ vt éponger, essuyer; **~ of hair** tignasse f; **mop up** vt éponger
mope [məʊp] vi avoir le cafard, se morfondre
moped ['məʊpɛd] n cyclomoteur m
moral ['mɔrl] adj moral(e) ▷ n morale f; **morals** npl moralité f
morale [mɔ'rɑːl] n moral m
morality [mə'rælɪtɪ] n moralité f
morbid ['mɔːbɪd] adj morbide

 KEYWORD

more [mɔːʳ] adj **1** (greater in number etc) plus (de), davantage (de); **more people/work (than)** plus de gens/de travail (que) **2** (additional) encore (de); **do you want (some) more tea?** voulez-vous encore du thé?; **is there any more wine?** reste-t-il du vin?; **I have no** or **I don't have any more money** je n'ai plus d'argent; **it'll take a few more weeks** ça prendra encore quelques semaines
▷ pron plus, davantage; **more than 10** plus de 10; **it cost more than we expected** cela a coûté plus que prévu; **I want more** j'en veux plus or davantage; **is there any more?** est-ce qu'il en reste?; **there's no more** il n'y en a plus; **a little more** un peu plus; **many/much more** beaucoup plus, bien davantage
▷ adv plus; **more dangerous/easily (than)** plus dangereux/facilement (que); **more and more expensive** de plus en plus cher; **more or less** plus ou moins; **more than ever** plus que jamais; **once more** encore une fois, une fois de plus

moreover [mɔː'rəʊvəʳ] adv de plus
morgue [mɔːg] n morgue f

morning ['mɔːnɪŋ] n matin m; (as duration) matinée f ▷ cpd matinal(e); (paper) du matin; **in the ~** le matin; **7 o'clock in the ~** 7 heures du matin; **morning sickness** n nausées matinales
Moroccan [mə'rɔkən] adj marocain(e) ▷ n Marocain(e)
Morocco [mə'rɔkəʊ] n Maroc m
moron ['mɔːrɔn] n idiot(e), minus m/f
morphine ['mɔːfiːn] n morphine f
morris dancing ['mɔrɪs-] n (BRIT) danses folkloriques anglaises

MORRIS DANCING

Le **Morris dancing** est une danse folklorique anglaise traditionnellement réservée aux hommes. Habillés tout en blanc et portant des clochettes, ils exécutent différentes figures avec des mouchoirs et de longs bâtons. Cette danse est très populaire dans les fêtes de village.

Morse [mɔːs] n (also: **~ code**) morse m
mortal ['mɔːtl] adj, n mortel(le)
mortar ['mɔːtəʳ] n mortier m
mortgage ['mɔːgɪdʒ] n hypothèque f; (loan) prêt m (or crédit m) hypothécaire ▷ vt hypothéquer
mortician [mɔː'tɪʃən] n (US) entrepreneur m de pompes funèbres
mortified ['mɔːtɪfaɪd] adj mort(e) de honte
mortuary ['mɔːtjuərɪ] n morgue f
mosaic [məʊ'zeɪɪk] n mosaïque f
Moscow ['mɔskəʊ] n Moscou
Moslem ['mɔzləm] adj, n = **Muslim**
mosque [mɔsk] n mosquée f
mosquito (pl **~es**) [mɔs'kiːtəʊ] n moustique m
moss [mɔs] n mousse f
most [məʊst] adj (majority of) la plupart de; (greatest amount of) le plus de ▷ pron la plupart ▷ adv le plus; (very) très, extrêmement; **the ~ le plus; ~ fish** la plupart des poissons; **the ~ beautiful woman in the world** la plus belle femme du monde; **~ of** (with plural) la plupart de; (with singular) la plus grande partie de; **~ of them** la plupart d'entre eux; **~ of the time** la plupart du temps; **I saw ~** (a lot but not all) j'en ai vu la plupart; (more than anyone else) c'est moi qui en ai vu le plus; **at the (very) ~** au plus; **to make the ~ of** profiter au maximum de; **mostly** adv (chiefly) surtout, principalement; (usually) généralement
MOT n abbr (BRIT) = Ministry of Transport; **the ~ (test)** visite technique (annuelle) obligatoire des véhicules à moteur
motel [məʊ'tɛl] n motel m
moth [mɔθ] n papillon m de nuit; (in clothes)

mite f

mother ['mʌðəʳ] n mère f ▷ vt (pamper, protect) dorloter; **motherhood** n maternité f; **mother-in-law** n belle-mère f; **mother-of-pearl** n nacre f; **Mother's Day** n fête f des Mères; **mother-to-be** n future maman; **mother tongue** n langue maternelle

motif [məu'ti:f] n motif m

motion ['məuʃən] n mouvement m; (gesture) geste m; (at meeting) motion f ▷ vt, vi: **to ~ (to) sb to do** faire signe à qn de faire; **motionless** adj immobile, sans mouvement; **motion picture** n film m

motivate ['məutiveit] vt motiver

motivation [məuti'veiʃən] n motivation f

motive ['məutiv] n motif m, mobile m

motor ['məutəʳ] n moteur m; (BRIT inf: vehicle) auto f; **motorbike** n moto f; **motorboat** n bateau m à moteur; **motorcar** n (BRIT) automobile f; **motorcycle** n moto f; **motorcyclist** n motocycliste m/f; **motoring** (BRIT) n tourisme m automobile; **motorist** n automobiliste m/f; **motor racing** n (BRIT) course f automobile; **motorway** n (BRIT) autoroute f

motto (pl **~es**) ['mɔtəu] n devise f

mould (US **mold**) [məuld] n moule m; (mildew) moisissure f ▷ vt mouler, modeler; (fig) façonner; **mouldy** adj moisi(e); (smell) de moisi

mound [maund] n monticule m, tertre m

mount [maunt] n (hill) mont m, montagne f; (horse) monture f; (for picture) carton m de montage ▷ vt monter; (horse) monter à; (bike) monter sur; (picture) monter sur carton ▷ vi (inflation, tension) augmenter; **mount up** vi s'élever, monter; (bills, problems, savings) s'accumuler

mountain ['mauntin] n montagne f ▷ cpd de (la) montagne; **mountain bike** n VTT m, vélo m tout terrain; **mountaineer** n alpiniste m/f; **mountaineering** n alpinisme m; **mountainous** adj montagneux(-euse); **mountain range** n chaîne f de montagnes

mourn [mɔ:n] vt pleurer ▷ vi: **to ~ for sb** pleurer qn; **to ~ for sth** se lamenter sur qch; **mourner** n parent(e) or ami(e) du défunt; personne f en deuil or venue rendre hommage au défunt; **mourning** n deuil m; **in mourning** en deuil

mouse (pl **mice**) [maus, mais] n (also Comput) souris f; **mouse mat** n (Comput) tapis m de souris

moussaka [mu'sa:kə] n moussaka f

mousse [mu:s] n mousse f

moustache (US **mustache**) [məs'ta:ʃ] n moustache(s) f(pl)

mouth [mauθ, pl -ðz] n bouche f; (of dog, cat) gueule f; (of river) embouchure f; (of hole, cave) ouverture f; **mouthful** n bouchée f; **mouth organ** n harmonica m; **mouthpiece** n (of musical instrument) bec m, embouchure f; (spokesperson) porte-parole m inv; **mouthwash** n eau f dentifrice

move [mu:v] n (movement) mouvement m; (in game) coup m; (: turn to play) tour m; (change of house) déménagement m; (change of job) changement m d'emploi ▷ vt déplacer, bouger; (emotionally) émouvoir; (Pol: resolution etc) proposer ▷ vi (gen) bouger, remuer; (traffic) circuler; (also: ~ house) déménager; (in game) jouer; **can you ~ your car, please?** pouvez-vous déplacer votre voiture, s'il vous plaît?; **to ~ sb to do sth** pousser or inciter qn à faire qch; **to get a ~ on** se dépêcher, se remuer; **move back** vi revenir, retourner; **move in** vi (to a house) emménager; (police, soldiers) intervenir; **move off** vi s'éloigner, s'en aller; **move on** vi se remettre en route; **move out** vi (of house) déménager; **move over** vi se pousser, se déplacer; **move up** vi avancer; (employee) avoir de l'avancement; (pupil) passer dans la classe supérieure; **movement** n mouvement m

movie ['mu:vi] n film m; **movies** npl: **the ~s** le cinéma; **movie theater** (US) n cinéma m

moving ['mu:viŋ] adj en mouvement; (touching) émouvant(e)

mow (pt **~ed**, pp **~ed** or **~n**) [məu, -d, -n] vt faucher; (lawn) tondre; **mower** n (also: **lawnmower**) tondeuse f à gazon

Mozambique [məuzəm'bi:k] n Mozambique m

MP n abbr (BRIT) = **Member of Parliament**

MP3 n mp3 m; **MP3 player** n lecteur m mp3

mpg n abbr = miles per gallon (30 mpg = 9,4 l. aux 100 km)

m.p.h. abbr = miles per hour (60 mph = 96 km/h)

Mr (US **Mr.**) ['mistəʳ] n: **Mr X** Monsieur X, M. X

Mrs (US **Mrs.**) ['misiz] n: **~ X** Madame X, Mme X

Ms (US **Ms.**) [miz] n (Miss or Mrs): **Ms X** Madame X, Mme X

MSP n abbr (= Member of the Scottish Parliament) député m au Parlement écossais

Mt abbr (Geo: = mount) Mt

much [mʌtʃ] adj beaucoup de ▷ adv, n or pron beaucoup; **we don't have ~ time** nous n'avons pas beaucoup de temps; **how ~ is it?** combien est-ce que ça coûte?; **it's not ~** ce n'est pas beaucoup; **too ~** trop (de); **so ~** tant (de); **I like it very/so ~** j'aime beaucoup/tellement ça; **as ~ as** autant de; **that's ~ better** c'est beaucoup mieux

muck [mʌk] n (mud) boue f; (dirt) ordures fpl; **muck up** vt (inf: ruin) gâcher, esquinter; (: dirty) salir; (: exam, interview) se planter à; **mucky** adj (dirty) boueux(-euse), sale

mucus ['mju:kəs] n mucus m

mud [mʌd] n boue f

m

muddle ['mʌdl] n (mess) pagaille f, fouillis m; (mix-up) confusion f ▷ vt (also: ~ **up**) brouiller, embrouiller; **to get in a ~** (while explaining etc) s'embrouiller

muddy ['mʌdɪ] adj boueux(-euse)

mudguard ['mʌdɡɑːd] n garde-boue m inv

muesli ['mjuːzlɪ] n muesli m

muffin ['mʌfɪn] n (roll) petit pain rond et plat; (cake) petit gâteau au chocolat ou aux fruits

muffled ['mʌfld] adj étouffé(e), voilé(e)

muffler ['mʌflər] n (scarf) cache-nez m inv; (us Aut) silencieux m

mug [mʌɡ] n (cup) tasse f (sans soucoupe); (: for beer) chope f; (inf: face) bouille f; (: fool) poire f ▷ vt (assault) agresser; **mugger** ['mʌɡər] n agresseur m; **mugging** n agression f

muggy ['mʌɡɪ] adj lourd(e), moite

mule [mjuːl] n mule f

multicoloured (us **multicolored**) ['mʌltɪkʌləd] adj multicolore

multimedia ['mʌltɪ'miːdɪə] adj multimédia inv

multinational [mʌltɪ'næʃənl] n multinationale f ▷ adj multinational(e)

multiple ['mʌltɪpl] adj multiple ▷ n multiple m; **multiple choice (test)** n QCM m, questionnaire m à choix multiple; **multiple sclerosis** [-sklɪ'rəusɪs] n sclérose f en plaques

multiplex (cinema) ['mʌltɪpleks-] n (cinéma m) multisalles m

multiplication [mʌltɪplɪ'keɪʃən] n multiplication f

multiply ['mʌltɪplaɪ] vt multiplier ▷ vi se multiplier

multistorey ['mʌltɪ'stɔːrɪ] adj (BRIT: building) à étages, (: car park) à étages or niveaux multiples

mum [mʌm] n (BRIT) maman f ▷ adj: **to keep ~** ne pas souffler mot

mumble ['mʌmbl] vt, vi marmotter, marmonner

mummy ['mʌmɪ] n (BRIT: mother) maman f; (embalmed) momie f

mumps [mʌmps] n oreillons mpl

munch [mʌntʃ] vt, vi mâcher

municipal [mjuː'nɪsɪpl] adj municipal(e)

mural ['mjuərl] n peinture murale

murder ['məːdər] n meurtre m, assassinat m ▷ vt assassiner; **murderer** n meurtrier m, assassin m

murky ['məːkɪ] adj sombre, ténébreux(-euse); (water) trouble

murmur ['məːmər] n murmure m ▷ vt, vi murmurer

muscle ['mʌsl] n muscle m; (fig) force f; **muscular** ['mʌskjulər] adj musculaire; (person, arm) musclé(e)

museum [mjuː'zɪəm] n musée m

mushroom ['mʌʃrum] n champignon m ▷ vi

(fig) pousser comme un (or des) champignon(s)

music ['mjuːzɪk] n musique f; **musical** adj musical(e); (person) musicien(ne) ▷ n (show) comédie musicale; **musical instrument** n instrument m de musique; **musician** [mjuː'zɪʃən] n musicien(ne)

Muslim ['mʌzlɪm] adj, n musulman(e)

muslin ['mʌzlɪn] n mousseline f

mussel ['mʌsl] n moule f

must [mʌst] aux vb (obligation): **I ~ do it** je dois le faire, il faut que je le fasse; (probability): **he ~ be there by now** il doit y être maintenant, il y est probablement maintenant; (suggestion, invitation): **you ~ come and see me** il faut que vous veniez me voir ▷ n nécessité f, impératif m; **it's a ~** c'est indispensable; **I ~ have made a mistake** j'ai dû me tromper

mustache ['mʌstæʃ] n (us) = moustache

mustard ['mʌstəd] n moutarde f

mustn't ['mʌsnt] = must not

mute [mjuːt] adj, n muet(te)

mutilate ['mjuːtɪleɪt] vt mutiler

mutiny ['mjuːtɪnɪ] n mutinerie f ▷ vi se mutiner

mutter ['mʌtər] vt, vi marmonner, marmotter

mutton ['mʌtn] n mouton m

mutual ['mjuːtʃuəl] adj mutuel(le), réciproque; (benefit, interest) commun(e)

muzzle ['mʌzl] n museau m; (protective device) muselière f; (of gun) gueule f ▷ vt museler

my [maɪ] adj mon (ma), mes pl; **my house/car/gloves** ma maison/ma voiture/mes gants; **I've washed my hair/cut my finger** je me suis lavé les cheveux/coupé le doigt; **is this my pen or yours?** c'est mon stylo ou c'est le vôtre?

myself [maɪ'self] pron (reflexive) me; (emphatic) moi-même; (after prep) moi; see also **oneself**

mysterious [mɪs'tɪərɪəs] adj mystérieux(-euse)

mystery ['mɪstərɪ] n mystère m

mystical ['mɪstɪkl] adj mystique

mystify ['mɪstɪfaɪ] vt (deliberately) mystifier; (puzzle) ébahir

myth [mɪθ] n mythe m; **mythology** [mɪ'θɔlədʒɪ] n mythologie f

n

n/a *abbr* (= *not applicable*) n.a.

nag [næg] *vt* (*scold*) être toujours après, reprendre sans arrêt

nail [neɪl] *n* (*human*) ongle *m*; (*metal*) clou *m* ▷ *vt* clouer; **to ~ sth to sth** clouer qch à qch; **to ~ sb down to a date/price** contraindre qn à accepter *or* donner une date/un prix; **nailbrush** *n* brosse *f* à ongles; **nailfile** *n* lime *f* à ongles; **nail polish** *n* vernis *m* à ongles; **nail polish remover** *n* dissolvant *m*; **nail scissors** *npl* ciseaux *mpl* à ongles; **nail varnish** *n* (BRIT) = **nail polish**

naïve [naɪˈiːv] *adj* naïf(-ïve)

naked [ˈneɪkɪd] *adj* nu(e)

name [neɪm] *n* nom *m*; (*reputation*) réputation *f* ▷ *vt* nommer; (*identify: accomplice etc*) citer; (*price, date*) fixer, donner; **by ~** par son nom; **in the ~ of** au nom de; **what's your ~?** comment vous appelez-vous?, quel est votre nom?; **namely** *adv* à savoir

nanny [ˈnænɪ] *n* bonne *f* d'enfants

nap [næp] *n* (*sleep*) (petit) somme

napkin [ˈnæpkɪn] *n* serviette *f* (de table)

nappy [ˈnæpɪ] *n* (BRIT) couche *f*

narcotics [nɑːˈkɔtɪkz] *npl* (*illegal drugs*) stupéfiants *mpl*

narrative [ˈnærətɪv] *n* récit *m* ▷ *adj* narratif(-ive)

narrator [nəˈreɪtəʳ] *n* narrateur(-trice)

narrow [ˈnærəu] *adj* étroit(e); (*fig*) restreint(e), limité(e) ▷ *vi* (*road*) devenir plus étroit, se rétrécir; (*gap, difference*) se réduire; **to have a ~ escape** l'échapper belle; **narrow down** *vt* restreindre; **narrowly** *adv*: **he narrowly missed injury/the tree** il a failli se blesser/rentrer dans l'arbre; **he only narrowly missed the target** il a manqué la cible de peu *or* de justesse; **narrow-minded** *adj* à l'esprit étroit, borné(e); (*attitude*) borné(e)

nasal [ˈneɪzl] *adj* nasal(e)

nasty [ˈnɑːstɪ] *adj* (*person: malicious*) méchant(e); (: *rude*) très désagréable; (*smell*) dégoûtant(e); (*wound, situation*) mauvais(e), vilain(e)

nation [ˈneɪʃən] *n* nation *f*

national [ˈnæʃənl] *adj* national(e) ▷ *n* (*abroad*) ressortissant(e); (*when home*) national(e); **national anthem** *n* hymne national; **national dress** *n* costume national; **National Health Service** *n* (BRIT) *service national de santé*, ≈ Sécurité Sociale; **National Insurance** *n* (BRIT) ≈ Sécurité Sociale; **nationalist** *adj*, *n* nationaliste *m/f*; **nationality** [næʃəˈnælɪtɪ] *n* nationalité *f*; **nationalize** *vt* nationaliser; **national park** *n* parc national; **National Trust** *n* (BRIT) ≈ Caisse *f* nationale des monuments historiques et des sites

⬤ **NATIONAL TRUST**

⬤
⬤ Le **National Trust** est un organisme
⬤ indépendant, à but non lucratif, dont
⬤ la mission est de protéger et de mettre
⬤ en valeur les monuments et les sites
⬤ britanniques en raison de leur intérêt
⬤ historique ou de leur beauté naturelle.

nationwide [ˈneɪʃənwaɪd] *adj* s'étendant à l'ensemble du pays; (*problem*) à l'échelle du pays entier

native [ˈneɪtɪv] *n* habitant(e) du pays, autochtone *m/f* ▷ *adj* du pays, indigène; (*country*) natal(e); (*language*) maternel(le); (*ability*) inné(e); **Native American** *n* Indien(ne) d'Amérique ▷ *adj* amérindien(ne); **native speaker** *n* locuteur natif

NATO [ˈneɪtəu] *n abbr* (= *North Atlantic Treaty Organization*) OTAN *f*

natural [ˈnætʃrəl] *adj* naturel(le); **natural gas** *n* gaz naturel; **natural history** *n* histoire naturelle; **naturally** *adv* naturellement; **natural resources** *npl* ressources naturelles

nature [ˈneɪtʃəʳ] *n* nature *f*; **by ~** par tempérament, de nature; **nature reserve** *n* (BRIT) réserve naturelle

naughty [ˈnɔːtɪ] *adj* (*child*) vilain(e), pas sage

nausea [ˈnɔːsɪə] *n* nausée *f*

naval [ˈneɪvl] *adj* naval(e)

navel ['neɪvl] n nombril m

navigate ['nævɪgeɪt] vt (steer) diriger, piloter ▷ vi naviguer; (Aut) indiquer la route à suivre; **navigation** [nævɪ'geɪʃən] n navigation f

navy ['neɪvɪ] n marine f

navy-blue ['neɪvɪ'bluː] adj bleu marine inv

Nazi ['nɑːtsɪ] n Nazi(e)

NB abbr (= nota bene) NB

near [nɪəʳ] adj proche ▷ adv près ▷ prep (also: **~ to**) près de ▷ vt approcher de; **in the ~ future** dans un proche avenir; **nearby** [nɪə'baɪ] adj proche ▷ adv tout près, à proximité; **nearly** adv presque; **I nearly fell** j'ai failli tomber; **it's not nearly big enough** ce n'est vraiment pas assez grand, c'est loin d'être assez grand; **near-sighted** adj myope

neat [niːt] adj (person, work) soigné(e); (room etc) bien tenu(e) or rangé(e); (solution, plan) habile; (spirits) pur(e); **neatly** adv avec soin or ordre; (skilfully) habilement

necessarily ['nesɪsrɪlɪ] adv nécessairement; **not ~** pas nécessairement or forcément

necessary ['nesɪsrɪ] adj nécessaire; **if ~** si besoin est, le cas échéant

necessity [nɪ'sesɪtɪ] n nécessité f; chose nécessaire or essentielle

neck [nek] n cou m; (of horse, garment) encolure f; (of bottle) goulot m; **~ and ~** à égalité; **necklace** ['neklɪs] n collier m; **necktie** ['nektaɪ] n (esp us) cravate f

nectarine ['nektərɪn] n brugnon m, nectarine f

need [niːd] n besoin m ▷ vt avoir besoin de; **to ~ to do** devoir faire; avoir besoin de faire; **you don't ~ to go** vous n'avez pas besoin or vous n'êtes pas obligé de partir; **a signature is ~ed** il faut une signature; **there's no ~ to do ....** il n'y a pas lieu de faire ..., il n'est pas nécessaire de faire ...

needle ['niːdl] n aiguille f ▷ vt (inf) asticoter, tourmenter

needless ['niːdlɪs] adj inutile; **~ to say, ...** inutile de dire que ...

needlework ['niːdlwɜːk] n (activity) travaux mpl d'aiguille; (object) ouvrage m

needn't ['niːdnt] = **need not**

needy ['niːdɪ] adj nécessiteux(-euse)

negative ['negətɪv] n (Phot, Elec) négatif m; (Ling) terme m de négation ▷ adj négatif(-ive)

neglect [nɪ'glekt] vt négliger; (garden) ne pas entretenir; (duty) manquer à ▷ n (of person, duty, garden) le fait de négliger; (state of) ~ abandon m; **to ~ to do sth** négliger or omettre de faire qch; **to ~ one's appearance** se négliger

negotiate [nɪ'gəʊʃɪeɪt] vi négocier ▷ vt négocier; (obstacle) franchir, négocier; **to ~ with sb for sth** négocier avec qn en vue d'obtenir qch

negotiation [nɪgəʊʃɪ'eɪʃən] n négociation f, pourparlers mpl

negotiator [nɪ'gəʊʃɪeɪtəʳ] n négociateur(-trice)

neighbour (us **neighbor** etc) ['neɪbəʳ] n voisin(e); **neighbourhood** n (place) quartier m; (people) voisinage m; **neighbouring** adj voisin(e), avoisinant(e)

neither ['naɪðəʳ] adj, pron aucun(e) (des deux), ni l'un(e) ni l'autre ▷ conj: **~ do I** moi non plus ▷ adv: **~ good nor bad** ni bon ni mauvais; **~ of them** ni l'un ni l'autre

neon ['niːɔn] n néon m

Nepal [nɪ'pɔːl] n Népal m

nephew ['nevjuː] n neveu m

nerve [nɜːv] n nerf m; (bravery) sang-froid m, courage m; (cheek) aplomb m, toupet m; **nerves** npl (nervousness) nervosité f; **he gets on my ~s** il m'énerve

nervous ['nɜːvəs] adj nerveux(-euse); (anxious) inquiet(-ète), plein(e) d'appréhension; (timid) intimidé(e); **nervous breakdown** n dépression nerveuse

nest [nest] n nid m ▷ vi (se) nicher, faire son nid

Net [net] n (Comput): **the ~** (Internet) le Net

net [net] n filet m; (fabric) tulle f ▷ adj net(te) ▷ vt (fish etc) prendre au filet; **netball** n netball m

Netherlands ['neðələndz] npl: **the ~** les Pays-Bas mpl

nett [net] adj = **net**

nettle ['netl] n ortie f

network ['netwɜːk] n réseau m

neurotic [njuə'rɔtɪk] adj névrosé(e)

neuter ['njuːtəʳ] adj neutre ▷ vt (cat etc) châtrer, couper

neutral ['njuːtrəl] adj neutre ▷ n (Aut) point mort

never ['nevəʳ] adv (ne ...) jamais; **I ~ went** je n'y suis pas allé; **I've ~ been to Spain** je ne suis jamais allé en Espagne; **~ again** plus jamais; **~ in my life** jamais de ma vie; see also **mind**; **never-ending** adj interminable; **nevertheless** [nevəðə'les] adv néanmoins, malgré tout

new [njuː] adj nouveau (nouvelle); (brand new) neuf (neuve); **New Age** n New Age m; **newborn** adj nouveau-né(e); **newcomer** ['njuːkʌməʳ] n nouveau venu (nouvelle venue); **newly** adv nouvellement, récemment

news [njuːz] n nouvelle(s) f(pl); (Radio, TV) informations fpl, actualités fpl; **a piece of ~** une nouvelle; **news agency** n agence f de presse; **newsagent** n (BRIT) marchand m de journaux; **newscaster** n (Radio, TV) présentateur(-trice); **news dealer** n (us) marchand m de journaux; **newsletter** n bulletin m; **newspaper** n journal m;

newsreader n = **newscaster**
newt [njuːt] n triton m
New Year n Nouvel An; **Happy ~!** Bonne
Année!; **New Year's Day** n le jour de l'An; **New
Year's Eve** n la Saint-Sylvestre
New York [-'jɔːk] n New York
New Zealand [-'ziːlənd] n Nouvelle-
Zélande f; **New Zealander** n Néo-
Zélandais(e)
next [nɛkst] adj (in time) prochain(e); (seat,
room) voisin(e), d'à côté; (meeting, bus stop)
suivant(e) ▷ adv la fois suivante; la prochaine
fois; (afterwards) ensuite; **~ to** prep à côté
de; **~ to nothing** presque rien; **~ time** adv la
prochaine fois; **the ~ day** le lendemain, le jour
suivant or d'après; **~ year** l'année prochaine; **~
please!** (at doctor's etc) au suivant!; **the week
after ~** dans deux semaines; **next door** adv à
côté ▷ adj (neighbour) d'à côté; **next-of-kin** n
parent m le plus proche
NHS n abbr (BRIT) = **National Health Service**
nibble ['nɪbl] vt grignoter
nice [naɪs] adj (holiday, trip, taste) agréable; (flat,
picture) joli(e); (person) gentil(le); (distinction,
point) subtil(e); **nicely** adv agréablement;
joliment; gentiment; subtilement
niche [niːʃ] n (Archit) niche f
nick [nɪk] n (indentation) encoche f; (wound)
entaille f; (BRIT inf) **in good ~** en bon état ▷ vt
(cut): **to ~ o.s.** se couper; (inf: steal) faucher,
piquer; **in the ~ of time** juste à temps
nickel ['nɪkl] n nickel m; (us) pièce f de 5 cents
nickname ['nɪkneɪm] n surnom m ▷ vt
surnommer
nicotine ['nɪkətiːn] n nicotine f
niece [niːs] n nièce f
Nigeria [naɪ'dʒɪərɪə] n Nigéria m or f
night [naɪt] n nuit f; (evening) soir m; **at ~** la
nuit; **by ~** de nuit; **last ~** (evening) hier soir;
(night-time) la nuit dernière; **night club** n
boîte f de nuit; **nightdress** n chemise f de nuit;
nightie ['naɪtɪ] n chemise f de nuit; **nightlife**
n vie f nocturne; **nightly** adj (news) du soir; (by
night) nocturne ▷ adv (every evening) tous les
soirs; (every night) toutes les nuits; **nightmare**
n cauchemar m; **night school** n cours mpl
du soir; **night shift** n équipe f de nuit; **night-
time** n nuit f
nil [nɪl] n (BRIT Sport) zéro m
nine [naɪn] num neuf; **nineteen** num dix-neuf;
nineteenth [naɪn'tiːnθ] num dix-neuvième;
ninetieth ['naɪntɪɪθ] num quatre-vingt-
dixième; **ninety** num quatre-vingt-dix
ninth [naɪnθ] num neuvième
nip [nɪp] vt pincer ▷ vi (BRIT inf): **to ~
out/down/up** sortir/descendre/monter
en vitesse
nipple ['nɪpl] n (Anat) mamelon m, bout m
du sein

nitrogen ['naɪtrədʒən] n azote m

 KEYWORD

no [nəu] (pl **noes**) adv (opposite of "yes") non;
are you coming? — no (I'm not) est-ce que
vous venez? — non; **would you like some
more? — no thank you** vous en voulez
encore? — non merci
▷ adj (not any) (ne ...) pas de, (ne ...) aucun(e);
I have no money/books je n'ai pas d'argent/
de livres; **no student would have done it**
aucun étudiant ne l'aurait fait; **"no smoking"**
"défense de fumer"; **"no dogs"** "les chiens ne
sont pas admis"
▷ n non m

nobility [nəu'bɪlɪtɪ] n noblesse f
noble ['nəubl] adj noble
nobody ['nəubədɪ] pron (ne ...) personne
nod [nɔd] vi faire un signe de (la) tête (affirmatif
ou amical); (sleep) somnoler ▷ vt: **to ~ one's
head** faire un signe de (la) tête; (in agreement)
faire signe que oui ▷ n signe m de (la) tête; **nod
off** vi s'assoupir
noise [nɔɪz] n bruit m; **I can't sleep for the ~**
je n'arrive pas à dormir à cause du bruit; **noisy**
adj bruyant(e)
nominal ['nɔmɪnl] adj (rent, fee) symbolique;
(value) nominal(e)
nominate ['nɔmɪneɪt] vt (propose) proposer;
(appoint) nommer; **nomination** [nɔmɪ'neɪʃə
n] n nomination f; **nominee** [nɔmɪ'niː] n
candidat agréé; personne nommée
none [nʌn] pron aucun(e); **~ of you** aucun
d'entre vous, personne parmi vous; **I have ~
left** je n'en ai plus; **he's ~ the worse for it** il ne
s'en porte pas plus mal
nonetheless ['nʌnðə'lɛs] adv néanmoins
non-fiction [nɔn'fɪkʃən] n littérature f non-
romanesque
nonsense ['nɔnsəns] n absurdités fpl, idioties
fpl; **~!** ne dites pas d'idioties!
non: non-smoker n non-fumeur m; **non-
smoking** adj non-fumeur; **non-stick** adj qui
n'attache pas
noodles ['nuːdlz] npl nouilles fpl
noon [nuːn] n midi m
no-one ['nəuwʌn] pron = **nobody**
nor [nɔːʳ] conj = **neither** ▷ adv see **neither**
norm [nɔːm] n norme f
normal ['nɔːml] adj normal(e); **normally** adv
normalement
Normandy ['nɔːməndɪ] n Normandie f
north [nɔːθ] n nord m ▷ adj nord inv; (wind)
du nord ▷ adv au or vers le nord; **North
Africa** n Afrique f du Nord; **North African** adj
nord-africain(e), d'Afrique du Nord ▷ n Nord-
Africain(e); **North America** n Amérique f du

n

Nord; **North American** n Nord-Américain(e)
▷ adj nord-américain(e), d'Amérique du
Nord; **northbound** ['nɔ:θbaund] adj (traffic)
en direction du nord; (carriageway) nord inv;
north-east n nord-est m; **northeastern** adj
(du) nord-est inv; **northern** ['nɔ:ðən] adj du
nord, septentrional(e); **Northern Ireland**
n Irlande f du Nord; **North Korea** n Corée
f du Nord; **North Pole** n: **the North Pole** le
pôle Nord; **North Sea** n: **the North Sea** la
mer du Nord; **north-west** n nord-ouest m;
northwestern ['nɔ:θ'westən] adj (du) nord-
ouest inv

Norway ['nɔ:weɪ] n Norvège f; **Norwegian**
[nɔ:'wi:dʒən] adj norvégien(ne) ▷ n
Norvégien(ne); (Ling) norvégien m

nose [nəuz] n nez m; (of dog, cat) museau
m; (fig) flair m; **nose about, nose around**
vi fouiner or fureter (partout); **nosebleed**
n saignement m de nez; **nosey** adj (inf)
curieux(-euse)

nostalgia [nɔs'tældʒɪə] n nostalgie f

nostalgic [nɔs'tældʒɪk] adj nostalgique

nostril ['nɔstrɪl] n narine f; (of horse) naseau m

nosy ['nəuzɪ] (inf) adj = **nosey**

not [nɔt] adv (ne ...) pas; **he is ~** or **isn't here** il
n'est pas ici; **you must ~** or **mustn't do that**
tu ne dois pas faire ça; **I hope ~** j'espère que
non; **~ at all** pas du tout; (after thanks) de rien;
it's too late, isn't it? c'est trop tard, n'est-ce
pas?; **~ yet/now** pas encore/maintenant; see
also **only**

notable ['nəutəbl] adj notable; **notably**
adv (particularly) en particulier; (markedly)
spécialement

notch [nɔtʃ] n encoche f

note [nəut] n note f; (letter) mot m; (banknote)
billet m ▷ vt (also: **~ down**) noter; (notice)
constater; **notebook** n carnet m; (for
shorthand etc) bloc-notes m; **noted** ['nəutɪd]
adj réputé(e); **notepad** n bloc-notes m;
notepaper n papier m à lettres

nothing ['nʌθɪŋ] n rien m; **he does ~** il ne fait
rien; **~ new** rien de nouveau; **for ~** (free) pour
rien, gratuitement; (in vain) pour rien; **~ at all**
rien du tout; **~ much** pas grand-chose

notice ['nəutɪs] n (announcement, warning) avis
m ▷ vt remarquer, s'apercevoir de; **advance
~** préavis m; **at short ~** dans un délai très
court; **until further ~** jusqu'à nouvel ordre; **to
give ~, hand in one's ~** (employee) donner sa
démission, démissionner; **to take ~ of** prêter
attention à; **to bring sth to sb's ~** porter qch à
la connaissance de qn; **noticeable** adj visible

notice board n (BRIT) panneau m d'affichage

notify ['nəutɪfaɪ] vt: **to ~ sb of sth** avertir qn
de qch

notion ['nəuʃən] n idée f; (concept) notion f;
notions npl (US: haberdashery) mercerie f

notorious [nəu'tɔ:rɪəs] adj notoire (souvent
en mal)

notwithstanding [nɔtwɪθ'stændɪŋ] adv
néanmoins ▷ prep en dépit de

nought [nɔ:t] n zéro m

noun [naun] n nom m

nourish ['nʌrɪʃ] vt nourrir; **nourishment** n
nourriture f

Nov. abbr (= November) nov

novel ['nɔvl] n roman m ▷ adj nouveau
(nouvelle), original(e); **novelist** n
romancier m; **novelty** n nouveauté f

November [nəu'vɛmbəʳ] n novembre m

novice ['nɔvɪs] n novice m/f

now [nau] adv maintenant (que); **right ~** tout de suite;
by ~ à l'heure qu'il est; **just ~**: **that's the
fashion just ~** c'est la mode en ce moment
or maintenant; **~ and then, ~ and again**
de temps en temps; **from ~ on** dorénavant;
nowadays ['nauədeɪz] adv de nos jours

nowhere ['nəuwɛəʳ] adv (ne ...) nulle part

nozzle ['nɔzl] n (of hose) jet m, lance f; (of
vacuum cleaner) suceur m

nr abbr (BRIT) = **near**

nuclear ['nju:klɪəʳ] adj nucléaire

nucleus (pl **nuclei**) ['nju:klɪəs, 'nju:klɪaɪ] n
noyau m

nude [nju:d] adj nu(e) ▷ n (Art) nu m; **in the ~**
(tout(e)) nu(e)

nudge [nʌdʒ] vt donner un (petit) coup de
coude à

nudist ['nju:dɪst] n nudiste m/f

nudity ['nju:dɪtɪ] n nudité f

nuisance ['nju:sns] n: **it's a ~** c'est (très)
ennuyeux or gênant; **he's a ~** il est assommant
or casse-pieds; **what a ~!** quelle barbe!

numb [nʌm] adj engourdi(e); (with fear)
paralysé(e)

number ['nʌmbəʳ] n nombre m; (numeral)
chiffre m; (of house, car, telephone, newspaper)
numéro m ▷ vt numéroter; (amount to)
compter; **a ~ of** un certain nombre de; **they
were seven in ~** ils étaient (au nombre
de) sept; **to be ~ed among** compter
parmi; **number plate** n (BRIT Aut) plaque f
minéralogique or d'immatriculation; **Number
Ten** n (BRIT: 10 Downing Street) résidence du
Premier ministre

numerical [nju:'mɛrɪkl] adj numérique

numerous ['nju:mərəs] adj nombreux(-euse)

nun [nʌn] n religieuse f, sœur f

nurse [nə:s] n infirmière f; (also: **~maid**) bonne
f d'enfants ▷ vt (patient, cold) soigner

nursery ['nə:sərɪ] n (room) nursery f;
(institution) crèche f, garderie f; (for plants)
pépinière f; **nursery rhyme** n comptine f,
chansonnette f pour enfants; **nursery school**
n école maternelle; **nursery slope** n (BRIT Ski)

piste *f* pour débutants

nursing ['nəːsɪŋ] *n* (*profession*) profession *f*
d'infirmière; (*care*) soins *mpl*; **nursing home**
n clinique *f*; (*for convalescence*) maison *f* de
convalescence *or* de repos; (*for old people*)
maison de retraite

nurture ['nəːtʃəʳ] *vt* élever

nut [nʌt] *n* (*of metal*) écrou *m*; (*fruit: walnut*)
noix *f*; (: *hazelnut*) noisette *f*; (: *peanut*)
cacahuète *f* (*terme générique en anglais*)

nutmeg ['nʌtmɛg] *n* (noix *f*) muscade *f*

nutrient ['njuːtrɪənt] *n* substance nutritive

nutrition [njuːˈtrɪʃən] *n* nutrition *f*,
alimentation *f*

nutritious [njuːˈtrɪʃəs] *adj* nutritif(-ive),
nourrissant(e)

nuts [nʌts] (*inf*) *adj* dingue

NVQ *n abbr* (*BRIT*) = **National Vocational
Qualification**

nylon ['naɪlɔn] *n* nylon *m* ▷ *adj* de *or* en nylon

oak [əuk] *n* chêne *m* ▷ *cpd* de *or* en (bois de)
chêne

O.A.P. *n abbr* (*BRIT*) = **old age pensioner**

oar [ɔːʳ] *n* aviron *m*, rame *f*

oasis (*pl* **oases**) [əuˈeɪsɪs, əuˈeɪsiːz] *n* oasis *f*

oath [əuθ] *n* serment *m*; (*swear word*) juron
m; **on** (*BRIT*) *or* **under ~** sous serment;
assermenté(e)

oatmeal ['əutmiːl] *n* flocons *mpl* d'avoine

oats [əuts] *n* avoine *f*

obedience [əˈbiːdɪəns] *n* obéissance *f*

obedient [əˈbiːdɪənt] *adj* obéissant(e)

obese [əuˈbiːs] *adj* obèse

obesity [əuˈbiːsɪtɪ] *n* obésité *f*

obey [əˈbeɪ] *vt* obéir à; (*instructions, regulations*)
se conformer à ▷ *vi* obéir

obituary [əˈbɪtjuərɪ] *n* nécrologie *f*

object *n* ['ɔbdʒɪkt] objet *m*; (*purpose*) but *m*,
objet; (*Ling*) complément *m* d'objet ▷ *vi* [ə
bˈdʒɛkt]: **to ~ to** (*attitude*) désapprouver;
(*proposal*) protester contre, élever une
objection contre; **I ~!** je proteste!; **he ~ed
that ...** il a fait valoir *or* a objecté que ...;
money is no ~ l'argent n'est pas un problème;
objection [əbˈdʒɛkʃən] *n* objection *f*; **if you
have no objection** si vous n'y voyez pas
d'inconvénient; **objective** *n* objectif *m* ▷ *adj*
objectif(-ive)

obligation [ɔblɪˈgeɪʃən] *n* obligation *f*, devoir
m; (*debt*) dette *f* (de reconnaissance)

obligatory [əˈblɪɡətərɪ] adj obligatoire

oblige [əˈblaɪdʒ] vt (force): **to ~ sb to do** obliger or forcer qn à faire; (do a favour) rendre service à, obliger; **to be ~d to sb for sth** être obligé(e) à qn de qch

oblique [əˈbliːk] adj oblique; (allusion) indirect(e)

obliterate [əˈblɪtəreɪt] vt effacer

oblivious [əˈblɪvɪəs] adj: **~ of** oublieux(-euse) de

oblong [ˈɔblɔŋ] adj oblong(ue) ▷ n rectangle m

obnoxious [əbˈnɔkʃəs] adj odieux(-euse); (smell) nauséabond(e)

oboe [ˈəʊbəʊ] n hautbois m

obscene [əbˈsiːn] adj obscène

obscure [əbˈskjuəʳ] adj obscur(e) ▷ vt obscurcir; (hide: sun) cacher

observant [əbˈzəːvnt] adj observateur(-trice)

observation [ɔbzəˈveɪʃən] n observation f; (by police etc) surveillance f

observatory [əbˈzəːvətrɪ] n observatoire m

observe [əbˈzəːv] vt observer; (remark) faire observer or remarquer; **observer** n observateur(-trice)

obsess [əbˈsɛs] vt obséder; **obsession** [əbˈsɛʃən] n obsession f; **obsessive** adj obsédant(e)

obsolete [ˈɔbsəliːt] adj dépassé(e), périmé(e)

obstacle [ˈɔbstəkl] n obstacle m

obstinate [ˈɔbstɪnɪt] adj obstiné(e); (pain, cold) persistant(e)

obstruct [əbˈstrʌkt] vt (block) boucher, obstruer; (hinder) entraver; **obstruction** [əbˈstrʌkʃən] n obstruction f; (to plan, progress) obstacle m

obtain [əbˈteɪn] vt obtenir

obvious [ˈɔbvɪəs] adj évident(e), manifeste; **obviously** adv manifestement; (of course): **obviously!** bien sûr!; **obviously not!** évidemment pas!, bien sûr que non!

occasion [əˈkeɪʒən] n occasion f; (event) événement m; **on occasion** en temps; (worker, spending) occasionnel(le); **occasionally** adv de temps en temps, quelquefois

occult [ɔˈkʌlt] adj occulte ▷ n: **the ~** le surnaturel

occupant [ˈɔkjupənt] n occupant m

occupation [ɔkjuˈpeɪʃən] n occupation f; (job) métier m, profession f

occupy [ˈɔkjupaɪ] vt occuper; **to ~ o.s. with** or **by doing** s'occuper à faire

occur [əˈkəːʳ] vi se produire; (difficulty, opportunity) se présenter; (phenomenon, error) se rencontrer; **to ~ to sb** venir à l'esprit de qn; **occurrence** [əˈkʌrəns] n (existence) présence f, existence f; (event) cas m, fait m

ocean [ˈəʊʃən] n océan m

o'clock [əˈklɔk] adv: **it is 5 o'clock** il est 5 heures

Oct. abbr (= October) oct

October [ɔkˈtəʊbəʳ] n octobre m

octopus [ˈɔktəpəs] n pieuvre f

odd [ɔd] adj (strange) bizarre, curieux(-euse); (number) impair(e); (not of a set) dépareillé(e); **60-~** 60 et quelques; **at ~ times** de temps en temps; **the ~ one out** l'exception f; **oddly** adv bizarrement, curieusement; **odds** npl (in betting) cote f; **it makes no odds** cela n'a pas d'importance; **odds and ends** de petites choses; **at odds** en désaccord

odometer [ɔˈdɔmɪtəʳ] n (us) odomètre m

odour (us **odor**) [ˈəʊdəʳ] n odeur f

 KEYWORD

of [ɔv, əv] prep **1** (gen) de; **a friend of ours** un de nos amis; **a boy of 10** un garçon de 10 ans; **that was kind of you** c'était gentil de votre part

2 (expressing quantity, amount, dates etc) de; **a kilo of flour** un kilo de farine; **how much of this do you need?** combien vous en faut-il?; **there were three of them** (people) ils étaient 3; (objects) il y en avait 3; **three of us went** 3 d'entre nous y sont allé(e)s; **the 5th of July** le 5 juillet; **a quarter of 4** (us) 4 heures moins le quart

3 (from, out of) en, de; **a statue of marble** une statue de or en marbre; **made of wood** (fait) en bois

off [ɔf] adj, adv (engine) coupé(e); (light, TV) éteint(e); (tap) fermé(e); (BRIT: food) mauvais(e), avancé(e); (: milk) tourné(e); (absent) absent(e); (cancelled) annulé(e); (removed): **the lid was ~** le couvercle était retiré or n'était pas mis; (away): **to run/drive ~** partir en courant/en voiture ▷ prep de; **to be ~** (to leave) partir, s'en aller; **to be ~ sick** être absent pour cause de maladie; **a day ~** un jour de congé; **to have an ~ day** n'être pas en forme; **he had his coat ~** il avait enlevé son manteau; **10% ~** (Comm) 10% de rabais; **5 km ~ (the road)** à 5 km (de la route); **~ the coast** au large de la côte; **it's a long way ~** c'est loin (d'ici); **I'm ~ meat** je ne mange plus de viande; je n'aime plus la viande; **on the ~ chance** à tout hasard; **~ and on, on and ~** de temps à autre

offence (us **offense**) [əˈfɛns] n (crime) délit m, infraction f; **to take ~ at** se vexer de, s'offenser de

offend [əˈfɛnd] vt (person) offenser, blesser; **offender** n délinquant(e); (against regulations) contrevenant(e)

offense [əˈfɛns] n (us) = **offence**

offensive [əˈfɛnsɪv] *adj* offensant(e), choquant(e); (*smell etc*) très déplaisant(e); (*weapon*) offensif(-ive) ▷ *n* (*Mil*) offensive *f*

offer [ˈɔfəʳ] *n* offre *f*, proposition *f* ▷ *vt* offrir, proposer; **"on ~"** (*Comm*) "en promotion"

offhand [ɔfˈhænd] *adj* désinvolte ▷ *adv* spontanément

office [ˈɔfɪs] *n* (*place*) bureau *m*; (*position*) charge *f*, fonction *f*; **doctor's ~** (*US*) cabinet (médical); **to take ~** entrer en fonctions; **office block** (*US* **office building**) *n* immeuble *m* de bureaux; **office hours** *npl* heures *fpl* de bureau; (*US Med*) heures de consultation

officer [ˈɔfɪsəʳ] *n* (*Mil etc*) officier *m*; (*also*: **police ~**) agent *m* (de police); (*of organization*) membre *m* du bureau directeur

office worker *n* employé(e) de bureau

official [əˈfɪʃl] *adj* (*authorized*) officiel(le) ▷ *n* officiel *m*; (*civil servant*) fonctionnaire *m/f*; (*of railways, post office, town hall*) employé(e)

off: **off-licence** *n* (*BRIT*: *shop*) débit *m* de vins et de spiritueux; **off-line** *adj* (*Comput*) (en mode) autonome; (: *switched off*) non connecté(e); **off-peak** *adj* aux heures creuses; (*electricity, ticket*) au tarif heures creuses; **off-putting** *adj* (*BRIT*: *remark*) rébarbatif(-ive); (*person*) rebutant(e), peu engageant(e); **off-season** *adj*, *adv* hors-saison *inv*

offset [ˈɔfsɛt] *vt* (*irreg*: *like* **set**) (*counteract*) contrebalancer, compenser

offshore [ɔfˈʃɔːʳ] *adj* (*breeze*) de terre; (*island*) proche du littoral; (*fishing*) côtier(-ière)

offside [ˈɔfˈsaɪd] *adj* (*Sport*) hors jeu; (*Aut*: *in Britain*) de droite; (: *in US, Europe*) de gauche

offspring [ˈɔfsprɪŋ] *n* progéniture *f*

often [ˈɔfn] *adv* souvent; **how ~ do you go?** vous y allez tous les combien?; **every so ~** de temps en temps, de temps à autre

oh [əu] *excl* ô!, oh!, ah!

oil [ɔɪl] *n* huile *f*; (*petroleum*) pétrole *m*; (*for central heating*) mazout *m* ▷ *vt* (*machine*) graisser; **oil filter** *n* (*Aut*) filtre *m* à huile; **oil painting** *n* peinture *f* à l'huile; **oil refinery** *n* raffinerie *f* de pétrole; **oil rig** *n* derrick *m*; (*at sea*) plate-forme pétrolière; **oil slick** *n* nappe *f* de mazout; **oil tanker** *n* (*ship*) pétrolier *m*; (*truck*) camion-citerne *m*; **oil well** *n* puits *m* de pétrole; **oily** *adj* huileux(-euse); (*food*) gras(se)

ointment [ˈɔɪntmənt] *n* onguent *m*

O.K., okay [ˈəuˈkeɪ] (*inf*) *excl* d'accord! ▷ *vt* approuver, donner son accord à ▷ *adj* (*not bad*) pas mal; **is it O.K.?, are you O.K.?** ça va?

old [əuld] *adj* vieux (vieille), âgé(e); (*person*) vieux, âgé(e); (*former*) ancien(ne), vieux; **how ~ are you?** quel âge avez-vous?; **he's 10 years ~** il a 10 ans, il est âgé de 10 ans; **~er brother/sister** frère/sœur aîné(e); **old age** *n* vieillesse *f*; **old-age pension** *n* (*BRIT*) (pension *f* de) retraite *f* (de la sécurité sociale); **old-age pensioner** *n* (*BRIT*) retraité(e); **old-fashioned** *adj* démodé(e); (*person*) vieux jeu *inv*; **old people's home** *n* (*esp BRIT*) maison *f* de retraite

olive [ˈɔlɪv] *n* (*fruit*) olive *f*; (*tree*) olivier *m* ▷ *adj* (*also*: **~-green**) (vert) olive *inv*; **olive oil** *n* huile *f* d'olive

Olympic [əuˈlɪmpɪk] *adj* olympique; **the ~ Games, the ~s** les Jeux *mpl* olympiques

omelet(te) [ˈɔmlɪt] *n* omelette *f*

omen [ˈəumən] *n* présage *m*

ominous [ˈɔmɪnəs] *adj* menaçant(e), inquiétant(e); (*event*) de mauvais augure

omit [əuˈmɪt] *vt* omettre

 KEYWORD

on [ɔn] *prep* **1** (*indicating position*) sur; **on the table** sur la table; **on the wall** sur le *or* au mur; **on the left** à gauche

2 (*indicating means, method, condition etc*): **on foot** à pied; **on the train/plane** (*be*) dans le train/l'avion; (*go*) en train/avion; **on the telephone/radio/television** au téléphone/à la radio/à la télévision; **to be on drugs** se droguer; **on holiday** (*BRIT*), **on vacation** (*US*) en vacances

3 (*referring to time*): **on Friday** vendredi; **on Fridays** le vendredi; **on June 20th** le 20 juin; **a week on Friday** vendredi en huit; **on arrival** à l'arrivée; **on seeing this** en voyant cela

4 (*about, concerning*) sur, de; **a book on Balzac/physics** un livre sur Balzac/de physique

▷ *adv* **1** (*referring to dress*): **to have one's coat on** avoir (mis) son manteau; **to put one's coat on** mettre son manteau; **what's she got on?** qu'est-ce qu'elle porte?

2 (*referring to covering*): **screw the lid on tightly** vissez bien le couvercle

3 (*further, continuously*): **to walk etc on** continuer à marcher *etc*; **from that day on** depuis ce jour

▷ *adj* **1** (*in operation: machine*) en marche; (: *radio, TV, light*) allumé(e); (: *tap, gas*) ouvert(e); (: *brakes*) mis(e); **is the meeting still on?** (*not cancelled*) est-ce que la réunion a bien lieu?; (*in progress*) la réunion dure-t-elle encore?; **when is this film on?** quand passe ce film?

2 (*inf*): **that's not on!** (*not acceptable*) cela ne se fait pas!; (*not possible*) pas question!

once [wʌns] *adv* une fois; (*formerly*) autrefois ▷ *conj* une fois que + *sub*; **~ he had left/it was done** une fois qu'il fut parti/ que ce fut terminé; **at ~** tout de suite, immédiatement; (*simultaneously*) à la fois; **all at ~** *adv* tout d'un coup; **~ a week** une fois par semaine; **~ more** encore une fois; **~ and for all** une fois pour toutes; **~ upon a time there was ...** il y avait une fois ..., il était une fois ...

oncoming ['ɔnkʌmɪŋ] *adj* (*traffic*) venant en sens inverse

 KEYWORD

one [wʌn] *num* un(e); **one hundred and fifty** cent cinquante; **one by one** un(e) à *or* par un(e); **one day** un jour
▷ *adj* **1** (*sole*) seul(e), unique; **the one book which** l'unique *or* le seul livre qui; **the one man who** le seul (homme) qui
2 (*same*) même; **they came in the one car** ils sont venus dans la même voiture
▷ *pron* **1**: **this one** celui-ci (celle-ci); **that one** celui-là (celle-là); **I've already got one/a red one** j'en ai déjà un(e)/un(e) rouge; **which one do you want?** lequel voulez-vous?
2: **one another** l'un(e) l'autre; **to look at one another** se regarder
3 (*impersonal*) on; **one never knows** on ne sait jamais; **to cut one's finger** se couper le doigt; **one needs to eat** il faut manger

one-off [wʌn'ɔf] (*BRIT inf*) *n* exemplaire *m* unique

oneself [wʌn'sɛlf] *pron* se; (*after prep, also emphatic*) soi-même; **to hurt ~** se faire mal; **to keep sth for ~** garder qch pour soi; **to talk to ~** se parler à soi-même; **by ~** tout seul

one: **one-shot** [wʌn'ʃɔt] (*US*) *n* = **one-off**; **one-sided** *adj* (*argument, decision*) unilatéral(e); **one-to-one** *adj* (*relationship*) univoque; **one-way** *adj* (*street, traffic*) à sens unique

ongoing ['ɔngəʊɪŋ] *adj* en cours; (*relationship*) suivi(e)

onion ['ʌnjən] *n* oignon *m*

on-line ['ɔnlaɪn] *adj* (*Comput*) en ligne; (: *switched on*) connecté(e)

onlooker ['ɔnlʊkəʳ] *n* spectateur(-trice)

only ['əʊnlɪ] *adv* seulement ▷ *adj* seul(e), unique ▷ *conj* seulement, mais; **an ~ child** un enfant unique; **not ~ ... but also** non seulement ... mais aussi; **I ~ took one** j'en ai seulement pris un, je n'en ai pris qu'un

on-screen [ɔn'skri:n] *adj* à l'écran

onset ['ɔnsɛt] *n* début *m*; (*of winter, old age*) approche *f*

onto ['ɔntu] *prep* = **on to**

onward(s) ['ɔnwəd(z)] *adv* (*move*) en avant; **from that time ~** à partir de ce moment

oops [ups] *excl* houp!

ooze [u:z] *vi* suinter

opaque [əʊ'peɪk] *adj* opaque

open ['əʊpn] *adj* ouvert(e); (*car*) découvert(e); (*road, view*) dégagé(e); (*meeting*) public(-ique); (*admiration*) manifeste ▷ *vt* ouvrir ▷ *vi* (*flower, eyes, door, debate*) s'ouvrir; (*shop, bank, museum*)

ouvrir; (*book etc: commence*) commencer, débuter; **is it ~ to public?** est-ce ouvert au public?; **what time do you ~?** à quelle heure ouvrez-vous?; **in the ~ (air)** en plein air; **open up** *vt* ouvrir; (*blocked road*) dégager ▷ *vi* s'ouvrir; **open-air** *adj* en plein air; **opening** *n* ouverture *f*; (*opportunity*) occasion *f*; (*work*) débouché *m*; (*job*) poste vacant; **opening hours** *npl* heures *fpl* d'ouverture; **open learning** *n* enseignement universitaire à la carte, notamment par correspondance; (*distance learning*) télé-enseignement *m*; **openly** *adv* ouvertement; **open-minded** *adj* à l'esprit ouvert; **open-necked** *adj* à col ouvert; **open-plan** *adj* sans cloisons; **Open University** *n* (*BRIT*) cours universitaires par correspondance

● **OPEN UNIVERSITY**
●
● L'**Open University** a été fondée en 1969.
● L'enseignement comprend des cours
● (certaines plages horaires sont réservées
● à cet effet à la télévision et à la radio), des
● devoirs qui sont envoyés par l'étudiant à
● son directeur ou sa directrice d'études, et
● un séjour obligatoire en université d'été. Il
● faut préparer un certain nombre d'unités
● de valeur pendant une période de temps
● déterminée et obtenir la moyenne à un
● certain nombre d'entre elles pour recevoir le
● diplôme visé.

opera ['ɔpərə] *n* opéra *m*; **opera house** *n* opéra *m*; **opera singer** *n* chanteur(-euse) d'opéra

operate ['ɔpəreɪt] *vt* (*machine*) faire marcher, faire fonctionner ▷ *vi* fonctionner; **to ~ on sb (for)** (*Med*) opérer qn (de)

operating room *n* (*US: Med*) salle *f* d'opération

operating theatre *n* (*BRIT: Med*) salle *f* d'opération

operation [ɔpə'reɪʃən] *n* opération *f*; (*of machine*) fonctionnement *m*; **to have an ~ (for)** se faire opérer (de); **to be in ~** (*machine*) être en service; (*system*) être en vigueur; **operational** *adj* opérationnel(le); (*ready for use*) en état de marche

operative ['ɔpərətɪv] *adj* (*measure*) en vigueur ▷ *n* (*in factory*) ouvrier(-ière)

operator ['ɔpəreɪtəʳ] *n* (*of machine*) opérateur(-trice); (*Tel*) téléphoniste *m/f*

opinion [ə'pɪnjən] *n* opinion *f*, avis *m*; **in my ~** à mon avis; **opinion poll** *n* sondage *m* d'opinion

opponent [ə'pəʊnənt] *n* adversaire *m/f*

opportunity [ɔpə'tju:nɪtɪ] *n* occasion *f*; **to take the ~ to do** *or* **of doing** profiter de l'occasion pour faire

oppose [ə'pəʊz] vt s'opposer à; **to be ~d to sth** être opposé(e) à qch; **as ~d to** par opposition à

opposite ['ɔpəzɪt] adj opposé(e); (house etc) d'en face ▷ adv en face ▷ prep en face de ▷ n opposé m, contraire m; (of word) contraire

opposition [ɔpə'zɪʃən] n opposition f

oppress [ə'prɛs] vt opprimer

opt [ɔpt] vi: **to ~ for** opter pour; **to ~ to do** choisir de faire; **opt out** vi: **to ~ out of** choisir de ne pas participer à or de ne pas faire

optician [ɔp'tɪʃən] n opticien(ne)

optimism ['ɔptɪmɪzəm] n optimisme m

optimist ['ɔptɪmɪst] n optimiste m/f; **optimistic** [ɔptɪ'mɪstɪk] adj optimiste

optimum ['ɔptɪməm] adj optimum

option ['ɔpʃən] n choix m, option f; (Scol) matière f à option; **optional** adj facultatif(-ive)

or [ɔː] conj ou; (with negative): **he hasn't seen or heard anything** il n'a rien vu ni entendu; **or else** sinon; ou bien

oral ['ɔːrəl] adj oral(e) ▷ n oral m

orange ['ɔrɪndʒ] n (fruit) orange f ▷ adj orange inv; **orange juice** n jus m d'orange; **orange squash** n orangeade f

orbit ['ɔːbɪt] n orbite f ▷ vt graviter autour de

orchard ['ɔːtʃəd] n verger m

orchestra ['ɔːkɪstrə] n orchestre m; (us: seating) (fauteuils mpl d')orchestre

orchid ['ɔːkɪd] n orchidée f

ordeal [ɔː'diːl] n épreuve f

order ['ɔːdər] n ordre m; (Comm) commande f ▷ vt ordonner; (Comm) commander; **in ~** en ordre; (of document) en règle; **out of ~** (not in correct order) en désordre; (machine) hors service; (telephone) en dérangement; **a machine in working ~** une machine en état de marche; **in ~ to do/that** pour faire/que + sub; **could I ~ now, please?** je peux commander, s'il vous plaît?; **to be on ~** être en commande; **to ~ sb to do** ordonner à qn de faire; **order form** n bon m de commande; **orderly** n (Mil) ordonnance f; (Med) garçon m de salle ▷ adj (room) en ordre; (mind) méthodique; (person) qui a de l'ordre

ordinary ['ɔːdnrɪ] adj ordinaire, normal(e); (pej) ordinaire, quelconque; **out of the ~** exceptionnel(le)

ore [ɔːr] n minerai m

oregano [ɔrɪ'gɑːnəʊ] n origan m

organ ['ɔːgən] n organe m; (Mus) orgue m, orgues fpl; **organic** [ɔː'gænɪk] adj organique; (crops etc) biologique, naturel(le); **organism** n organisme m

organization [ɔːgənaɪ'zeɪʃən] n organisation f

organize ['ɔːgənaɪz] vt organiser; **organized** ['ɔːgənaɪzd] adj (planned) organisé(e); (efficient) bien organisé; **organizer** n organisateur(-trice)

orgasm ['ɔːgæzəm] n orgasme m

orgy ['ɔːdʒɪ] n orgie f

oriental [ɔːrɪ'ɛntl] adj oriental(e)

orientation [ɔːrɪɛn'teɪʃən] n (attitudes) tendance f; (in job) orientation f; (of building) orientation, exposition f

origin ['ɔrɪdʒɪn] n origine f

original [ə'rɪdʒɪnl] adj original(e); (earliest) originel(le) ▷ n original m; **originally** adv (at first) à l'origine

originate [ə'rɪdʒɪneɪt] vi: **to ~ from** être originaire de; (suggestion) provenir de; **to ~ in** (custom) prendre naissance dans, avoir son origine dans

Orkney ['ɔːknɪ] n (also: **the ~s, the ~ Islands**) les Orcades fpl

ornament ['ɔːnəmənt] n ornement m; (trinket) bibelot m; **ornamental** [ɔːnə'mɛntl] adj décoratif(-ive); (garden) d'agrément

ornate [ɔː'neɪt] adj très orné(e)

orphan ['ɔːfn] n orphelin(e)

orthodox ['ɔːθədɔks] adj orthodoxe

orthopaedic (us **orthopedic**) [ɔːθə'piːdɪk] adj orthopédique

osteopath ['ɔstɪəpæθ] n ostéopathe m/f

ostrich ['ɔstrɪtʃ] n autruche f

other ['ʌðər] adj autre ▷ pron: **the ~ (one)** l'autre; **~s** (other people) d'autres ▷ adv: **~ than** autrement que; à part; **the ~ day** l'autre jour; **otherwise** adv, conj autrement

Ottawa ['ɔtəwə] n Ottawa

otter ['ɔtər] n loutre f

ouch [autʃ] excl aïe!

ought (pt ~) [ɔːt] aux vb: **I ~ to do it** je devrais le faire, il faudrait que je le fasse; **this ~ to have been corrected** cela aurait dû être corrigé; **he ~ to win** (probability) il devrait gagner

ounce [auns] n once f (28.35g; 16 in a pound)

our ['auər] adj notre, nos pl; see also **my**; **ours** pron le (la) nôtre, les nôtres; see also **mine**[1]; **ourselves** pron pl (reflexive, after preposition) nous; (emphatic) nous-mêmes; see also **oneself**

oust [aust] vt évincer

out [aut] adv dehors; (published, not at home etc) sorti(e); (light, fire) éteint(e); **~ there** là-bas; **he's ~** (absent) il est sorti; **to be ~ in one's calculations** s'être trompé dans ses calculs; **to run/back** etc **~** sortir en courant/en reculant etc; **~ loud** adv à haute voix; **~ of** prep (outside) en dehors de; (because of: anger etc) par; (from among) de; **10 ~ of 10** sur 10; (without): **~ of petrol** sans essence, à court d'essence; **~ of order** (machine) en panne; (Tel: line) en dérangement; **outback** n (in Australia) intérieur m; **outbound** adj: **outbound (from/for)** en partance (de/pour); **outbreak** n (of violence) éruption f, explosion f; (of disease)

de nombreux cas; **the outbreak of war south
of the border** la guerre qui s'est déclarée au
sud de la frontière; **outburst** n explosion f,
accès m; **outcast** n exilé(e); (socially) paria m;
outcome n issue f, résultat m; **outcry** n tollé
(général); **outdated** adj démodé(e); **outdoor**
adj de or en plein air; **outdoors** adv dehors;
au grand air

outer ['autər] adj extérieur(e); **outer space** n
espace m cosmique

outfit ['autfit] n (clothes) tenue f

out: **outgoing** adj (president, tenant) sortant(e);
(character) ouvert(e), extraverti(e); **outgoings**
npl (expenses) dépenses fpl; **outhouse** n
appentis m, remise f

outing ['autiŋ] n sortie f, excursion f

out: **outlaw** n hors-la-loi m inv ▷ vt (person)
mettre hors la loi; (practice) proscrire; **outlay**
n dépenses fpl; (investment) mise f de fonds;
outlet n (for liquid etc) issue f, sortie f; (for
emotion) exutoire m; (also: **retail outlet**)
point m de vente; (us: Elec) prise f de courant;
outline n (shape) contour m; (summary)
esquisse f, grandes lignes ▷ vt (fig: theory,
plan) exposer à grands traits; **outlook**
n perspective f; (point of view) attitude f;
outnumber vt surpasser en nombre;
out-of-date adj (passport, ticket) périmé(e);
(theory, idea) dépassé(e); (custom) désuet(-ète);
(clothes) démodé(e); **out-of-doors** adv
= **outdoors**; **out-of-the-way** adj loin de
tout; **out-of-town** adj (shopping centre etc)
en périphérie; **outpatient** n malade m/f en
consultation externe; **outpost** n avant-
poste m; **output** n rendement m, production f;
(Comput) sortie f ▷ vt (Comput) sortir

outrage ['autreidʒ] n (anger) indignation
f; (violent act) atrocité f, acte m de violence;
(scandal) scandale m ▷ vt outrager;
outrageous [aut'reidʒəs] adj atroce;
(scandalous) scandaleux(-euse)

outright adv [aut'rait] complètement; (deny,
refuse) catégoriquement; (ask) carrément;
(kill) sur le coup ▷ adj ['autrait] complet(-ète);
catégorique

outset ['autset] n début m

outside [aut'said] n extérieur m ▷ adj
extérieur(e) ▷ adv (au) dehors, à l'extérieur
▷ prep hors de, à l'extérieur de; (in front of)
devant; **at the ~** (fig) au plus or maximum;
outside lane n (Aut: in Britain) voie f de droite;
(: in US, Europe) voie de gauche; **outside line**
n (Tel) ligne extérieure; **outsider** n (stranger)
étranger(-ère)

out: **outsize** adj énorme; (clothes) grande
taille inv; **outskirts** npl faubourgs mpl;
outspoken adj très franc (franche);
outstanding adj remarquable,
exceptionnel(le); (unfinished: work, business)

en suspens, en souffrance; (debt) impayé(e);
(problem) non réglé(e)

outward ['autwəd] adj (sign, appearances)
extérieur(e); (journey) (d')aller; **outwards** adv
(esp BRIT) = **outward**

outweigh [aut'wei] vt l'emporter sur

oval ['əuvl] adj, n ovale m

ovary ['əuvəri] n ovaire m

oven ['ʌvn] n four m; **oven glove** n gant m de
cuisine; **ovenproof** adj allant au four; **oven-
ready** adj prêt(e) à cuire

over ['əuvər] adv (par-)dessus ▷ adj (or adv)
(finished) fini(e), terminé(e); (too much) en
plus ▷ prep sur; par-dessus; (above) au-dessus
de; (on the other side of) de l'autre côté de;
(more than) plus de; (during) pendant; (about,
concerning): **they fell out – money/her** ils se
sont brouillés pour des questions d'argent/à
cause d'elle; **~ here** ici; **~ there** là-bas; **all
~** (everywhere) partout; **~ and ~ (again)** à
plusieurs reprises; **~ and above** en plus de; **to
ask sb ~** inviter qn (à passer); **to fall ~** tomber;
to turn sth ~ retourner qch

overall ['əuvərɔːl] adj (length) total(e); (study,
impression) d'ensemble ▷ n (BRIT) blouse f
▷ adv [əuvər'ɔːl] dans l'ensemble, en général;
overalls npl (boiler suit) bleus mpl (de travail)

overboard ['əuvəbɔːd] adv (Naut) par-dessus
bord

overcame [əuvə'keim] pt of **overcome**

overcast ['əuvəkɑːst] adj couvert(e)

overcharge [əuvə'tʃɑːdʒ] vt: **to ~ sb for sth**
faire payer qch trop cher à qn

overcoat ['əuvəkəut] n pardessus m

overcome [əuvə'kʌm] vt (irreg: like **come**)
(defeat) triompher de; (difficulty) surmonter
▷ adj (emotionally) bouleversé(e); **~ with grief**
accablé(e) de douleur

over: **overcrowded** adj bondé(e); (city,
country) surpeuplé(e); **overdo** vt (irreg:
like **do**) exagérer; (overcook) trop cuire; **to
overdo it**, **to overdo things** (work too hard)
en faire trop, se surmener; **overdone** [ə
uvə'dʌn] adj (vegetables, steak) trop cuit(e);
overdose n dose excessive; **overdraft** n
découvert m; **overdrawn** adj (account) à
découvert; **overdue** adj en retard; (bill)
impayé(e); (change) qui tarde; **overestimate**
vt surestimer

overflow vi [əuvə'fləu] déborder ▷ n ['əuvə
fləu] (also: **~ pipe**) tuyau m d'écoulement,
trop-plein m

overgrown [əuvə'grəun] adj (garden)
envahi(e) par la végétation

overhaul vt [əuvə'hɔːl] réviser ▷ n ['əuvəhɔː
l] révision f

overhead adv [əuvə'hɛd] au-dessus ▷ adj,
n ['əuvəhɛd] ▷ adj aérien(ne); (lighting)
vertical(e) ▷ n (US) = **overheads**; **overhead**

projector n rétroprojecteur m; **overheads**
npl (BRIT) frais généraux
over: **overhear** vt (irreg: like **hear**) entendre
(par hasard); **overheat** vi (engine) chauffer;
overland adj, adv par voie de terre; **overlap**
vi se chevaucher; **overleaf** adv au verso;
overload vt surcharger; **overlook** vt (have
view of) donner sur; (miss) oublier, négliger;
(forgive) fermer les yeux sur
overnight adv [əuvə'naɪt] (happen) durant
la nuit; (fig) soudain ▷ adj ['əuvənaɪt] d'une
(or de) nuit; soudain(e); **to stay ~ (with sb)**
passer la nuit (chez qn); **overnight bag** n
nécessaire m de voyage
overpass ['əuvəpɑːs] n (US: for cars) pont
autoroutier; (: for pedestrians) passerelle f,
pont m
overpower [əuvə'pauər] vt vaincre; (fig)
accabler; **overpowering** adj irrésistible; (heat,
stench) suffocant(e)
over: **overreact** [əuvəri:'ækt] vi réagir de
façon excessive; **overrule** vt (decision)
annuler; (claim) rejeter; (person) rejeter l'avis
de; **overrun** vt (irreg: like **run**) (Mil: country etc)
occuper; (time limit etc) dépasser ▷ vi dépasser
le temps imparti
overseas [əuvə'si:z] adv outre-mer; (abroad)
à l'étranger ▷ adj (trade) extérieur(e); (visitor)
étranger(-ère)
oversee [əuvə'si:] vt (irreg: like **see**) surveiller
overshadow [əuvə'ʃædəu] vt (fig) éclipser
oversight ['əuvəsaɪt] n omission f, oubli m
oversleep [əuvə'sli:p] vi (irreg: like **sleep**) se
réveiller (trop) tard
overspend [əuvə'spɛnd] vi (irreg: like **spend**)
dépenser de trop
overt [əu'və:t] adj non dissimulé(e)
overtake [əuvə'teɪk] vt (irreg: like **take**)
dépasser; (BRIT: Aut) dépasser, doubler
over: **overthrow** vt (irreg: like **throw**)
(government) renverser; **overtime** n heures fpl
supplémentaires
overtook [əuvə'tuk] pt of **overtake**
over: **overturn** vt renverser; (decision, plan)
annuler ▷ vi se retourner; **overweight**
adj (person) trop gros(se); **overwhelm** vt
(subj: emotion) accabler, submerger; (enemy,
opponent) écraser; **overwhelming** adj (victory,
defeat) écrasant(e); (desire) irrésistible
ow [au] excl aïe!
owe [əu] vt devoir; **to ~ sb sth, to ~ sth to
sb** devoir qch à qn; **how much do I ~ you?**
combien est-ce que je vous dois?; **owing to**
prep à cause de, en raison de
owl [aul] n hibou m
own [əun] vt posséder ▷ adj propre; **a room of
my ~** une chambre à moi, ma propre chambre;
to get one's ~ back prendre sa revanche; **on
one's ~** tout(e) seul(e); **own up** vi avouer;

owner n propriétaire m/f; **ownership** n
possession f
ox (pl **oxen**) [ɔks, 'ɔksn] n bœuf m
Oxbridge ['ɔksbrɪdʒ] n (BRIT) les universités
d'Oxford et de Cambridge
oxen ['ɔksən] npl of **ox**
oxygen ['ɔksɪdʒən] n oxygène m
oyster ['ɔɪstər] n huître f
oz. abbr = **ounce(s)**
ozone ['əuzəun] n ozone m; **ozone friendly**
adj qui n'attaque pas or qui préserve la couche
d'ozone; **ozone layer** n couche f d'ozone

o

p *abbr* (BRIT) = **penny; pence**

P.A. *n abbr* = **personal assistant; public address system**

p.a. *abbr* = **per annum**

pace [peɪs] *n* pas *m*; (*speed*) allure *f*; vitesse *f* ▷ *vi*: **to ~ up and down** faire les cent pas; **to keep ~ with** aller à la même vitesse que; (*events*) se tenir au courant de; **pacemaker** *n* (*Med*) stimulateur *m* cardiaque; (*Sport: also*: **pacesetter**) meneur(-euse) de train

Pacific [pə'sɪfɪk] *n*: **the ~ (Ocean)** le Pacifique, l'océan *m* Pacifique

pacifier ['pæsɪfaɪəʳ] *n* (US: *dummy*) tétine *f*

pack [pæk] *n* paquet *m*; (*of hounds*) meute *f*; (*of thieves, wolves etc*) bande *f*; (*of cards*) jeu *m*; (US: *of cigarettes*) paquet; (*back pack*) sac *m* à dos ▷ *vt* (*goods*) empaqueter, emballer; (*in suitcase etc*) emballer; (*box*) remplir; (*cram*) entasser ▷ *vi*: **to ~ (one's bags)** faire ses bagages; **pack in** (BRIT inf) ▷ *vi* (*machine*) tomber en panne ▷ *vt* (*boyfriend*) plaquer; **~ it in!** laisse tomber!; **pack off** *vt*: **to ~ sb off to** expédier qn à; **pack up** *vi* (BRIT inf: *machine*) tomber en panne; (: *person*) se tirer ▷ *vt* (*belongings*) ranger; (*goods, presents*) empaqueter, emballer

package ['pækɪdʒ] *n* paquet *m*; (*also*: **~ deal**: *agreement*) marché global; (: *purchase*) forfait *m*; (*Comput*) progiciel *m* ▷ *vt* (*goods*) conditionner; **package holiday** *n* (BRIT) vacances organisées; **package tour** *n* voyage organisé

packaging ['pækɪdʒɪŋ] *n* (*wrapping materials*) emballage *m*

packed [pækt] *adj* (*crowded*) bondé(e); **packed lunch** (BRIT) *n* repas froid

packet ['pækɪt] *n* paquet *m*

packing ['pækɪŋ] *n* emballage *m*

pact [pækt] *n* pacte *m*, traité *m*

pad [pæd] *n* bloc(-notes *m*) *m*; (*to prevent friction*) tampon *m* ▷ *vt* rembourrer; **padded** *adj* (*jacket*) matelassé(e); (*bra*) rembourré(e)

paddle ['pædl] *n* (*oar*) pagaie *f*; (US: *for table tennis*) raquette *f* de ping-pong ▷ *vi* (*with feet*) barboter, faire trempette ▷ *vt*: **to ~ a canoe** *etc* pagayer; **paddling pool** *n* petit bassin

paddock ['pædək] *n* enclos *m*; (*Racing*) paddock *m*

padlock ['pædlɔk] *n* cadenas *m*

paedophile (US **pedophile**) ['piːdəʊfaɪl] *n* pédophile *m*

page [peɪdʒ] *n* (*of book*) page *f*; (*also*: **~ boy**) groom *m*, chasseur *m*; (*at wedding*) garçon *m* d'honneur ▷ *vt* (*in hotel etc*) (faire) appeler

pager ['peɪdʒəʳ] *n* bip *m* (*inf*), Alphapage® *m*

paid [peɪd] *pt, pp of* **pay** ▷ *adj* (*work, official*) rémunéré(e); (*holiday*) payé(e); **to put ~ to** (BRIT) mettre fin à, mettre par terre

pain [peɪn] *n* douleur *f*; (*inf: nuisance*) plaie *f*; **to be in ~** souffrir, avoir mal; **to take ~s to do** se donner du mal pour faire; **painful** *adj* douloureux(-euse); (*difficult*) difficile, pénible; **painkiller** *n* calmant *m*, analgésique *m*; **painstaking** ['peɪnzteɪkɪŋ] *adj* (*person*) soigneux(-euse); (*work*) soigné(e)

paint [peɪnt] *n* peinture *f* ▷ *vt* peindre; **to ~ the door blue** peindre la porte en bleu; **paintbrush** *n* pinceau *m*; **painter** *n* peintre *m*; **painting** *n* peinture *f*; (*picture*) tableau *m*

pair [pɛəʳ] *n* (*of shoes, gloves etc*) paire *f*; (*of people*) couple *m*; **~ of scissors** (paire de) ciseaux *mpl*; **~ of trousers** pantalon *m*

pajamas [pə'dʒɑːməz] *npl* (US) pyjama(s) *m(pl)*

Pakistan [pɑːkɪ'stɑːn] *n* Pakistan *m*; **Pakistani** *adj* pakistanais(e) ▷ *n* Pakistanais(e)

pal [pæl] *n* (*inf*) copain (copine)

palace ['pæləs] *n* palais *m*

pale [peɪl] *adj* pâle; **~ blue** *adj* bleu pâle *inv*

Palestine ['pælɪstaɪn] *n* Palestine *f*; **Palestinian** [pælɪs'tɪnɪən] *adj* palestinien(ne) ▷ *n* Palestinien(ne)

palm [pɑːm] *n* (*Anat*) paume *f*; (*also*: **~ tree**) palmier *m* ▷ *vt*: **to ~ sth off on sb** (*inf*) refiler qch à qn

pamper ['pæmpəʳ] *vt* gâter, dorloter

pamphlet ['pæmflət] *n* brochure *f*

pan [pæn] *n* (*also*: **sauce~**) casserole *f*; (*also*:

frying ~) poêle f
pancake ['pænkeik] n crêpe f
panda ['pændə] n panda m
pane [pein] n carreau m (de fenêtre), vitre f
panel ['pænl] n (of wood, cloth etc) panneau m;
(Radio, TV) panel m, invités mpl; (for interview,
exams) jury m
panhandler ['pænhændlə'] n (US inf)
mendiant(e)
panic ['pænik] n panique f, affolement m ▷ vi
s'affoler, paniquer
panorama [pænə'rɑ:mə] n panorama m
pansy ['pænzi] n (Bot) pensée f
pant [pænt] vi haleter
panther ['pænθə'] n panthère f
panties ['pæntiz] npl slip m, culotte f
pantomime ['pæntəmaim] n (BRIT)
spectacle m de Noël; voir encadré

PANTOMIME

Une **pantomime** (à ne pas confondre
avec le mot tel qu'on l'utilise en français),
que l'on appelle également de façon
familière "panto", est un genre de farce où
le personnage principal est souvent un
jeune garçon et où il y a toujours une "dame",
c'est-à-dire une vieille femme jouée par
un homme, et un méchant. La plupart du
temps, l'histoire est basée sur un conte de
fées comme Cendrillon ou Le Chat botté,
et le public est encouragé à participer en
prévenant le héros d'un danger imminent.
Ce genre de spectacle, qui s'adresse
surtout aux enfants, vise également un
public d'adultes au travers des nombreuses
plaisanteries faisant allusion à des faits
d'actualité.

pants [pænts] n (BRIT: woman's) culotte f,
slip m; (: man's) slip, caleçon m; (US: trousers)
pantalon m
pantyhose ['pæntihəuz] (US) npl collant m
paper ['peipə'] n papier m; (also: **wall~**) papier
peint; (also: **news~**) journal m; (academic essay)
article m; (exam) épreuve écrite ▷ adj en or de
papier ▷ vt tapisser (de papier peint); **papers**
npl (also: **identity ~s**) papiers mpl (d'identité);
paperback n livre broché or non relié; (small)
livre m de poche; **paper bag** n sac m en papier;
paper clip n trombone m; **paper shop** n
(BRIT) marchand m de journaux; **paperwork** n
papiers mpl; (pej) paperasserie f
paprika ['pæprikə] n paprika m
par [pɑ:'] n pair m; (Golf) normale f du parcours;
on a ~ with à égalité avec, au même niveau
que
paracetamol [pærə'si:təmɔl] (BRIT) n
paracétamol m

parachute ['pærəʃu:t] n parachute m
parade [pə'reid] n défilé m ▷ vt (fig) faire
étalage de ▷ vi défiler
paradise ['pærədais] n paradis m
paradox ['pærədɔks] n paradoxe m
paraffin ['pærəfin] n (BRIT): **~ (oil)** pétrole
(lampant)
paragraph ['pærəgrɑ:f] n paragraphe m
parallel ['pærəlɛl] adj: **~ (with or to)** parallèle
(à); (fig) analogue (à) ▷ n (line) parallèle f; (fig,
Geo) parallèle m
paralysed ['pærəlaizd] adj paralysé(e)
paralysis (pl **paralyses**) [pə'rælisis, -si:z] n
paralysie f
paramedic [pærə'mɛdik] n auxiliaire m/f
médical(e)
paranoid ['pærənɔid] adj (Psych)
paranoïaque; (neurotic) paranoïde
parasite ['pærəsait] n parasite m
parcel ['pɑ:sl] n paquet m, colis m ▷ vt (also: **~
up**) empaqueter
pardon ['pɑ:dn] n pardon m; (Law) grâce f ▷ vt
pardonner à; (Law) gracier; **~!** pardon!; **~ me!**
(after burping etc) excusez-moi!; **I beg your ~!**
(I'm sorry) pardon!, je suis désolé!; **(I beg your)
~?, (US) ~ me?** (what did you say?) pardon?
parent ['pɛərənt] n (father) père m; (mother)
mère f; **parents** npl parents mpl; **parental**
[pə'rɛntl] adj parental(e), des parents
Paris ['pæris] n Paris
parish ['pæriʃ] n paroisse f; (BRIT: civil)
≈ commune f
Parisian [pə'riziən] adj parisien(ne), de Paris
▷ n Parisien(ne)
park [pɑ:k] n parc m, jardin public ▷ vt garer
▷ vi se garer; **can I ~ here?** est-ce que je peux
me garer ici?
parking ['pɑ:kiŋ] n stationnement m; **"no ~"**
"stationnement interdit"; **parking lot** n (US)
parking m, parc m de stationnement; **parking
meter** n parc(o)mètre m; **parking ticket** n
P.-V. m

> Be careful not to translate **parking** by the
> French word **parking**.

parkway ['pɑ:kwei] n (US) route f express (en
site vert ou aménagé)
parliament ['pɑ:ləmənt] n parlement m;
parliamentary [pɑ:lə'mɛntəri] adj
parlementaire
Parmesan [pɑ:mi'zæn] n (also: **~ cheese**)
Parmesan m
parole [pə'rəul] n: **on ~** en liberté
conditionnelle
parrot ['pærət] n perroquet m
parsley ['pɑ:sli] n persil m
parsnip ['pɑ:snip] n panais m
parson ['pɑ:sn] n ecclésiastique m; (Church of
England) pasteur m
part [pɑ:t] n partie f; (of machine) pièce f; (Theat

etc) rôle *m*; (*of serial*) épisode *m*; (*US: in hair*) raie *f* ▷ *adv* = **partly** ▷ *vt* séparer ▷ *vi* (*people*) se séparer; (*crowd*) s'ouvrir; **to take ~ in** participer à, prendre part à; **to take sb's ~** prendre le parti de qn, prendre parti pour qn; **for my ~** en ce qui me concerne; **for the most ~** en grande partie; dans la plupart des cas; **in ~** en partie; **to take sth in good/bad ~** prendre qch du bon/mauvais côté; **part with** *vt fus* (*person*) se séparer de; (*possessions*) se défaire de

partial ['pɑːʃəl] *adj* (*incomplete*) partiel(le); **to be ~ to** aimer, avoir un faible pour

participant [pɑːˈtɪsɪpənt] *n* (*in competition, campaign*) participant(e)

participate [pɑːˈtɪsɪpeɪt] *vi*: **to ~ (in)** participer (à), prendre part (à)

particle ['pɑːtɪkl] *n* particule *f*; (*of dust*) grain *m*

particular [pəˈtɪkjʊləʳ] *adj* (*specific*) particulier(-ière); (*special*) particulier, spécial(e); (*fussy*) difficile, exigeant(e); (*careful*) méticuleux(-euse); **in ~** en particulier, surtout; **particularly** *adv* particulièrement; (*in particular*) en particulier; **particulars** *npl* détails *mpl*; (*information*) renseignements *mpl*

parting ['pɑːtɪŋ] *n* séparation *f*; (*BRIT: in hair*) raie *f*

partition [pɑːˈtɪʃən] *n* (*Pol*) partition *f*, division *f*; (*wall*) cloison *f*

partly ['pɑːtlɪ] *adv* en partie, partiellement

partner ['pɑːtnəʳ] *n* (*Comm*) associé(e); (*Sport*) partenaire *m/f*; (*spouse*) conjoint(e); (*lover*) ami(e); (*at dance*) cavalier(-ière); **partnership** *n* association *f*

part of speech *n* (*Ling*) partie *f* du discours

partridge ['pɑːtrɪdʒ] *n* perdrix *f*

part-time ['pɑːt'taɪm] *adj*, *adv* à mi-temps, à temps partiel

party ['pɑːtɪ] *n* (*Pol*) parti *m*; (*celebration*) fête *f*; (: *formal*) réception *f*; (: *in evening*) soirée *f*; (*group*) groupe *m*; (*Law*) partie *f*

pass [pɑːs] *vt* (*time, object*) passer; (*place*) passer devant; (*friend*) croiser; (*exam*) être reçu(e) à, réussir; (*overtake*) dépasser; (*approve*) approuver, accepter ▷ *vi* passer; (*Scol*) être reçu(e) or admis(e), réussir ▷ *n* (*permit*) laissez-passer *m inv*; (*membership card*) carte *f* d'accès *or* d'abonnement; (*in mountains*) col *m*; (*Sport*) passe *f*; (*Scol*: *also*: **~ mark**) ~ à être reçu(e) (sans mention); **to ~ sb sth** passer qch à qn; **could you ~ the salt/oil, please?** pouvez-vous me passer le sel/l'huile, s'il vous plaît?; **to make a ~ at sb** (*inf*) faire des avances à qn; **pass away** *vi* mourir; **pass by** *vi* passer ▷ *vt* (*ignore*) négliger; **pass on** *vt* (*hand on*): **to ~ on (to)** transmettre (à); **pass out** *vi* s'évanouir; **pass over** *vt* (*ignore*) passer sous silence; **pass up** *vt* (*opportunity*) laisser passer; **passable** *adj*

(*road*) praticable; (*work*) acceptable

> Be careful not to translate **to pass an exam** by the French expression **passer un examen**.

passage ['pæsɪdʒ] *n* (*also*: **~way**) couloir *m*; (*gen, in book*) passage *m*; (*by boat*) traversée *f*

passenger ['pæsɪndʒəʳ] *n* passager(-ère)

passer-by [pɑːsəˈbaɪ] *n* passant(e)

passing place *n* (*Aut*) aire *f* de croisement

passion ['pæʃən] *n* passion *f*; **passionate** *adj* passionné(e); **passion fruit** *n* fruit *m* de la passion

passive ['pæsɪv] *adj* (*also Ling*) passif(-ive)

passport ['pɑːspɔːt] *n* passeport *m*; **passport control** *n* contrôle *m* des passeports; **passport office** *n* bureau *m* de délivrance des passeports

password ['pɑːswɜːd] *n* mot *m* de passe

past [pɑːst] *prep* (*in front of*) devant; (*further than*) au delà de, plus loin que; après; (*later than*) après ▷ *adv*: **to run ~** passer en courant ▷ *adj* passé(e); (*president etc*) ancien(ne) ▷ *n* passé *m*; **he's ~ forty** il a dépassé la quarantaine, il a plus de *or* passé quarante ans; **ten/quarter ~ eight** huit heures dix/un *or* et quart; **for the ~ few/3 days** depuis quelques/3 jours; ces derniers/3 derniers jours

pasta ['pæstə] *n* pâtes *fpl*

paste [peɪst] *n* pâte *f*; (*Culin: meat*) pâté *m* (à tartiner); (: *tomato*) purée *f*, concentré *m*; (*glue*) colle *f* (de pâte) ▷ *vt* coller

pastel ['pæstl] *adj* pastel *inv* ▷ *n* (*Art: pencil*) (crayon *m*) pastel *m*; (: *drawing*) (dessin *m* au) pastel; (*colour*) ton *m* pastel *inv*

pasteurized ['pæstəraɪzd] *adj* pasteurisé(e)

pastime ['pɑːstaɪm] *n* passe-temps *m inv*, distraction *f*

pastor ['pɑːstəʳ] *n* pasteur *m*

past participle [-'pɑːtɪsɪpl] *n* (*Ling*) participe passé

pastry ['peɪstrɪ] *n* pâte *f*; (*cake*) pâtisserie *f*

pasture ['pɑːstʃəʳ] *n* pâturage *m*

pasty¹ *n* ['pæstɪ] *n* petit pâté (en croûte)

pasty² ['peɪstɪ] *adj* (*complexion*) terreux(-euse)

pat [pæt] *vt* donner une petite tape à; (*dog*) caresser

patch [pætʃ] *n* (*of material*) pièce *f*; (*eye patch*) cache *m*; (*spot*) tache *f*; (*of land*) parcelle *f*; (*on tyre*) rustine *f* ▷ *vt* (*clothes*) rapiécer; **a bad ~** (*BRIT*) une période difficile; **patchy** *adj* inégal(e); (*incomplete*) fragmentaire

pâté ['pæteɪ] *n* pâté *m*, terrine *f*

patent ['peɪtnt, *US* 'pætnt] *n* brevet *m* (d'invention) ▷ *vt* faire breveter ▷ *adj* patent(e), manifeste

paternal [pəˈtɜːnl] *adj* paternel(le)

paternity leave [pəˈtɜːnɪtɪ-] *n* congé *m* de paternité

path [pɑːθ] *n* chemin *m*, sentier *m*; (*in garden*)

allée f; (of missile) trajectoire f

pathetic [pəˈθɛtɪk] adj (pitiful) pitoyable; (very bad) lamentable, minable

pathway [ˈpɑːθweɪ] n chemin m, sentier m; (in garden) allée f

patience [ˈpeɪʃns] n patience f; (BRIT: Cards) réussite f

patient [ˈpeɪʃnt] n malade m/f; (of dentist etc) patient(e) ▷ adj patient(e)

patio [ˈpætɪəu] n patio m

patriotic [pætrɪˈɒtɪk] adj patriotique; (person) patriote

patrol [pəˈtrəul] n patrouille f ▷ vt patrouiller dans; **patrol car** n voiture f de police

patron [ˈpeɪtrən] n (in shop) client(e); (of charity) patron(ne); **~ of the arts** mécène m

patronizing [ˈpætrənaɪzɪŋ] adj condescendant(e)

pattern [ˈpætən] n (Sewing) patron m; (design) motif m; **patterned** adj à motifs

pause [pɔːz] n pause f, arrêt m ▷ vi faire une pause, s'arrêter

pave [peɪv] vt paver, daller; **to ~ the way for** ouvrir la voie à

pavement [ˈpeɪvmənt] n (BRIT) trottoir m; (US) chaussée f

pavilion [pəˈvɪlɪən] n pavillon m; (Sport) stand m

paving [ˈpeɪvɪŋ] n (material) pavé m, dalle f

paw [pɔː] n patte f

pawn [pɔːn] n (Chess, also fig) pion m ▷ vt mettre en gage; **pawnbroker** n prêteur m sur gages

pay [peɪ] n salaire m; (of manual worker) paie f ▷ vb (pt, pp **paid**) ▷ vt payer ▷ vi payer; (be profitable) être rentable; **can I ~ by credit card?** est-ce que je peux payer par carte de crédit?; **to ~ attention (to)** prêter attention (à); **to ~ sb a visit** rendre visite à qn; **to ~ one's respects to sb** présenter ses respects à qn; **pay back** vt rembourser; **pay for** vt fus payer; **pay in** vt verser; **pay off** vt (debts) régler, acquitter; (person) rembourser ▷ vi (scheme, decision) se révéler payant(e); **pay out** vt (money) payer, sortir de sa poche; **pay up** vt (amount) payer; **payable** adj payable; **to make a cheque payable to sb** établir un chèque à l'ordre de qn; **pay day** n jour m de paie; **pay envelope** n (US) paie f; **payment** n paiement m; (of bill) règlement m; (of deposit, cheque) versement m; **monthly payment** mensualité f; **payout** n (from insurance) dédommagement m; (in competition) prix m; **pay packet** n (BRIT) paie f; **pay phone** n cabine f téléphonique, téléphone public; **pay raise** n (US) = **pay rise**; **pay rise** n (BRIT) augmentation f (de salaire); **payroll** n registre m du personnel; **pay slip** n (BRIT) bulletin m de paie, feuille f de paie; **pay television** n

chaînes fpl payantes

PC n abbr = **personal computer**; (BRIT) = **police constable** ▷ adj abbr = **politically correct**

p.c. abbr = **per cent**

PDA n abbr (= personal digital assistant) agenda m électronique

PE n abbr (= physical education) EPS f

pea [piː] n (petit) pois

peace [piːs] n paix f; (calm) calme m, tranquillité f; **peaceful** adj paisible, calme

peach [piːtʃ] n pêche f

peacock [ˈpiːkɔk] n paon m

peak [piːk] n (mountain) pic m, cime f; (of cap) visière f; (fig: highest level) maximum m; (: of career, fame) apogée m; **peak hours** npl heures fpl d'affluence or de pointe

peanut [ˈpiːnʌt] n arachide f, cacahuète f; **peanut butter** n beurre m de cacahuète

pear [pɛər] n poire f

pearl [pəːl] n perle f

peasant [ˈpɛznt] n paysan(ne)

peat [piːt] n tourbe f

pebble [ˈpɛbl] n galet m, caillou m

peck [pɛk] vt (also: **~ at**) donner un coup de bec à; (food) picorer ▷ n coup m de bec; (kiss) bécot m; **peckish** adj (BRIT inf): **I feel peckish** je mangerais bien quelque chose, j'ai la dent

peculiar [pɪˈkjuːlɪər] adj (odd) étrange, bizarre, curieux(-euse); (particular) particulier(-ière); **~ to** particulier à

pedal [ˈpɛdl] n pédale f ▷ vi pédaler

pedalo [ˈpɛdələu] n pédalo m

pedestal [ˈpɛdəstl] n piédestal m

pedestrian [pɪˈdɛstrɪən] n piéton m; **pedestrian crossing** n (BRIT) passage clouté; **pedestrianized** adj: **a pedestrianized street** une rue piétonne; **pedestrian precinct** (US **pedestrian zone**) n (BRIT) zone piétonne

pedigree [ˈpɛdɪɡriː] n ascendance f; (of animal) pedigree m ▷ cpd (animal) de race

pedophile [ˈpiːdəufaɪl] (US) n = **paedophile**

pee [piː] vi (inf) faire pipi, pisser

peek [piːk] vi jeter un coup d'œil (furtif)

peel [piːl] n pelure f, épluchure f; (of orange, lemon) écorce f ▷ vt peler, éplucher ▷ vi (paint etc) s'écailler; (wallpaper) se décoller; (skin) peler

peep [piːp] n (BRIT: look) coup d'œil furtif; (sound) pépiement m ▷ vi (BRIT) jeter un coup d'œil (furtif)

peer [pɪər] vi: **to ~ at** regarder attentivement, scruter ▷ n (noble) pair m; (equal) pair, égal(e)

peg [pɛɡ] n (for coat etc) patère f; (BRIT: also: **clothes ~**) pince f à linge

pelican [ˈpɛlɪkən] n pélican m; **pelican crossing** n (BRIT Aut) feu m à commande manuelle

pelt [pɛlt] vt: **to ~ sb (with)** bombarder qn (de)

▷ vi (rain) tomber à seaux; (inf: run) courir à toutes jambes ▷ n peau f

pelvis ['pelvɪs] n bassin m

pen [pen] n (for writing) stylo m; (for sheep) parc m

penalty ['penltɪ] n pénalité f; sanction f; (fine) amende f; (Sport) pénalisation f; (Football) penalty m; (Rugby) pénalité f

pence [pens] npl of **penny**

pencil ['pensl] n crayon m; **pencil in** vt noter provisoirement; **pencil case** n trousse f (d'écolier); **pencil sharpener** n taille-crayon(s) m inv

pendant ['pendnt] n pendentif m

pending ['pendɪŋ] prep en attendant ▷ adj en suspens

penetrate ['penɪtreɪt] vt pénétrer dans; (enemy territory) entrer en

penfriend ['penfrend] n (BRIT) correspondant(e)

penguin ['peŋgwɪn] n pingouin m

penicillin [penɪ'sɪlɪn] n pénicilline f

peninsula [pə'nɪnsjulə] n péninsule f

penis ['piːnɪs] n pénis m, verge f

penitentiary [penɪ'tenʃərɪ] n (US) prison f

penknife ['pennaɪf] n canif m

penniless ['penɪlɪs] adj sans le sou

penny (pl **pennies** or **pence**) ['penɪ, 'penɪz, pens] n (BRIT) penny m; (US) cent m

penpal ['penpæl] n correspondant(e)

pension ['penʃən] n (from company) retraite f; **pensioner** n (BRIT) retraité(e)

pentagon ['pentəgən] n: **the P~** (US Pol) le Pentagone

penthouse ['penthaus] n appartement m (de luxe) en attique

penultimate [pɪ'nʌltɪmət] adj pénultième, avant-dernier(-ière)

people ['piːpl] npl gens mpl; personnes fpl; (inhabitants) population f; (Pol) peuple m ▷ n (nation, race) peuple m; **several ~ came** plusieurs personnes sont venues; **~ say that ...** on dit or les gens disent que ...

pepper ['pepə'] n poivre m; (vegetable) poivron m ▷ vt (Culin) poivrer; **peppermint** n (sweet) pastille f de menthe

per [pə:'] prep par; **~ hour** (miles etc) à l'heure; (fee) (de) l'heure; **~ kilo** etc le kilo etc; **~ day/person** par jour/personne; **~ annum** per an

perceive [pə'siːv] vt percevoir; (notice) remarquer, s'apercevoir de

per cent adv pour cent

percentage [pə'sentɪdʒ] n pourcentage m

perception [pə'sepʃən] n perception f; (insight) sensibilité f

perch [pə:tʃ] n (fish) perche f; (for bird) perchoir m ▷ vi (se) percher

percussion [pə'kʌʃən] n percussion f

perennial [pə'renɪəl] n (Bot) (plante f) vivace f,

plante pluriannuelle

perfect ['pə:fɪkt] adj parfait(e) ▷ n (also: ~ tense) parfait m ▷ vt [pə'fekt] (technique, skill, work of art) parfaire; (method, plan) mettre au point; **perfection** [pə'fekʃən] n perfection f; **perfectly** ['pə:fɪktlɪ] adv parfaitement

perform [pə'fɔːm] vt (carry out) exécuter; (concert etc) jouer, donner ▷ vi (actor, musician) jouer; **performance** n représentation f, spectacle m; (of an artist) interprétation f; (Sport: of car, engine) performance f; (of company, economy) résultats mpl; **performer** n artiste m/f

perfume ['pə:fjuːm] n parfum m

perhaps [pə'hæps] adv peut-être

perimeter [pə'rɪmɪtə'] n périmètre m

period ['pɪərɪəd] n période f, (History) époque f; (Scol) cours m; (full stop) point m; (Med) règles fpl ▷ adj (costume, furniture) d'époque; **periodical** [pɪərɪ'ɔdɪkl] n périodique m; **periodically** adv périodiquement

perish ['perɪʃ] vi périr, mourir; (decay) se détériorer

perjury ['pə:dʒərɪ] n (Law: in court) faux témoignage; (breach of oath) parjure m

perk [pə:k] n (inf) avantage m, à-côté m

perm [pə:m] n (for hair) permanente f

permanent ['pə:mənənt] adj permanent(e); **permanently** adv de façon permanente; (move abroad) définitivement; (open, closed) en permanence; (tired, unhappy) constamment

permission [pə'mɪʃən] n permission f, autorisation f

permit n ['pə:mɪt] permis m

perplex [pə'pleks] vt (person) rendre perplexe

persecute ['pə:sɪkjuːt] vt persécuter

persecution [pə:sɪ'kjuːʃən] n persécution f

persevere [pə:sɪ'vɪə'] vi persévérer

Persian ['pə:ʃən] adj persan(e); **the ~ Gulf** le golfe Persique

persist [pə'sɪst] vi: **to ~ (in doing)** persister (à faire), s'obstiner (à faire); **persistent** adj persistant(e), tenace

person ['pə:sn] n personne f; **in ~** en personne; **personal** adj personnel(le); **personal assistant** n secrétaire personnel(le); **personal computer** n ordinateur individuel, PC m; **personality** [pə:sə'nælɪtɪ] n personnalité f; **personally** adv personnellement; **to take sth personally** se sentir visé(e) par qch; **personal organizer** n agenda (personnel) (style Filofax®); (electronic) agenda électronique; **personal stereo** n Walkman® m, baladeur m

personnel [pə:sə'nɛl] n personnel m

perspective [pə'spektɪv] n perspective f

perspiration [pə:spɪ'reɪʃən] n transpiration f

persuade [pə'sweɪd] vt: **to ~ sb to do sth** persuader qn de faire qch, amener or décider qn à faire qch

persuasion [pə'sweɪʒən] n persuasion f; (creed) conviction f

persuasive [pə'sweɪsɪv] adj persuasif(-ive)

perverse [pə'vəːs] adj pervers(e); (contrary) entêté(e), contrariant(e)

pervert n ['pəːvəːt] perverti(e) ▷ vt [pə'vəːt] pervertir; (words) déformer

pessimism ['pesɪmɪzəm] n pessimisme m

pessimist ['pesɪmɪst] n pessimiste m/f; **pessimistic** [pesɪ'mɪstɪk] adj pessimiste

pest [pest] n animal m (or insecte m) nuisible; (fig) fléau m

pester ['pestə'] vt importuner, harceler

pesticide ['pestɪsaɪd] n pesticide m

pet [pet] n animal familier ▷ cpd (favourite) favori(e) ▷ vt (stroke) caresser, câliner; **teacher's ~** chouchou m du professeur; **~ hate** bête noire

petal ['petl] n pétale m

petite [pə'tiːt] adj menu(e)

petition [pə'tɪʃən] n pétition f

petrified ['petrɪfaɪd] adj (fig) mort(e) de peur

petrol ['petrəl] n (BRIT) essence f; **I've run out of ~** je suis en panne d'essence

> Be careful not to translate **petrol** by the French word **pétrole**.

petroleum [pə'trəulɪəm] n pétrole m

petrol: **petrol pump** n (BRIT: in car, at garage) pompe f à essence; **petrol station** n (BRIT) station-service f; **petrol tank** n (BRIT) réservoir m d'essence

petticoat ['petɪkəut] n jupon m

petty ['petɪ] adj (mean) mesquin(e); (unimportant) insignifiant(e), sans importance

pew [pjuː] n banc m (d'église)

pewter ['pjuːtə'] n étain m

phantom ['fæntəm] n fantôme m

pharmacist ['fɑːməsɪst] n pharmacien(ne)

pharmacy ['fɑːməsɪ] n pharmacie f

phase [feɪz] n phase f, période f; **phase in** vt introduire progressivement; **phase out** vt supprimer progressivement

Ph.D. abbr = Doctor of Philosophy

pheasant ['feznt] n faisan m

phenomena [fə'nɔmɪnə] npl of **phenomenon**

phenomenal [fɪ'nɔmɪnl] adj phénoménal(e)

phenomenon (pl **phenomena**) [fə'nɔmɪnən, -nə] n phénomène m

Philippines ['fɪlɪpiːnz] npl (also: **Philippine Islands**): **the ~** les Philippines fpl

philosopher [fɪ'lɔsəfə'] n philosophe m

philosophical [fɪlə'sɔfɪkl] adj philosophique

philosophy [fɪ'lɔsəfɪ] n philosophie f

phlegm [flem] n flegme m

phobia ['fəubɪə] n phobie f

phone [fəun] n téléphone m ▷ vt téléphoner à ▷ vi téléphoner; **to be on the ~** avoir le téléphone; (be calling) être au téléphone; **phone back** vt, vi rappeler; **phone up** vt téléphoner à ▷ vi téléphoner; **phone book** n annuaire m; **phone box** (US **phone booth**) n cabine f téléphonique; **phone call** n coup m de fil or de téléphone; **phonecard** n télécarte f; **phone number** n numéro m de téléphone

phonetics [fə'netɪks] n phonétique f

phoney ['fəunɪ] adj faux (fausse), factice; (person) pas franc (franche)

photo ['fəutəu] n photo f; **photo album** n album m de photos; **photocopier** n copieur m; **photocopy** n photocopie f ▷ vt photocopier

photograph ['fəutəgræf] n photographie f ▷ vt photographier; **photographer** [fə'tɔgrə fə'] n photographe m/f; **photography** [fə'tɔgrəfɪ] n photographie f

phrase [freɪz] n expression f; (Ling) locution f ▷ vt exprimer; **phrase book** n recueil m d'expressions (pour touristes)

physical ['fɪzɪkl] adj physique; **physical education** n éducation f physique; **physically** adv physiquement

physician [fɪ'zɪʃən] n médecin m

physicist ['fɪzɪsɪst] n physicien(ne)

physics ['fɪzɪks] n physique f

physiotherapist [fɪzɪəu'θerəpɪst] n kinésithérapeute m/f

physiotherapy [fɪzɪəu'θerəpɪ] n kinésithérapie f

physique [fɪ'ziːk] n (appearance) physique m; (health etc) constitution f

pianist ['piːənɪst] n pianiste m/f

piano [pɪ'ænəu] n piano m

pick [pɪk] n (tool: also: **~-axe**) pic m, pioche f ▷ vt choisir; (gather) cueillir; (remove) prendre; (lock) forcer; **take your ~** faites votre choix; **the ~ of** le (la) meilleur(e) de; **to ~ one's nose** se mettre les doigts dans le nez; **to ~ one's teeth** se curer les dents; **to ~ a quarrel with sb** chercher noise à qn; **pick on** vt fus (person) harceler; **pick out** vt choisir; (distinguish) distinguer; **pick up** vi (improve) remonter, s'améliorer ▷ vt ramasser; (collect) passer prendre; (Aut: give lift to) prendre; (learn) apprendre; (Radio) capter; **to ~ up speed** prendre de la vitesse; **to ~ o.s. up** se relever

pickle ['pɪkl] n (also: **~s**: as condiment) pickles mpl ▷ vt conserver dans du vinaigre or dans de la saumure; **in a ~** (fig) dans le pétrin

pickpocket ['pɪkpɔkɪt] n pickpocket m

pick-up ['pɪkʌp] n (also: **~ truck**) pick-up m inv

picnic ['pɪknɪk] n pique-nique m ▷ vi pique-niquer; **picnic area** n aire f de pique-nique

picture ['pɪktʃə'] n (also TV) image f; (painting) peinture f, tableau m; (photograph) photo(graphie) f; (drawing) dessin m; (film) film m; (fig: description) description f ▷ vt (imagine) se représenter; **pictures** npl: **the ~s** (BRIT) le cinéma; **to take a ~ of sb/sth** prendre qn/qch en photo; **would you take a ~ of us, please?** pourriez-vous nous prendre en photo, s'il vous plaît?; **picture frame** n cadre m; **picture messaging** n picture messaging m, messagerie f d'images

picturesque [pɪktʃə'resk] adj pittoresque

pie [paɪ] n tourte f; (of fruit) tarte f; (of meat) pâté m en croûte

piece [piːs] n morceau m; (item): **a ~ of furniture/advice** un meuble/conseil ▷ vt: **to ~ together** rassembler; **to take to ~s** démonter

pie chart n graphique m à secteurs, camembert m

pier [pɪəʳ] n jetée f

pierce [pɪəs] vt percer, transpercer; **pierced** adj (ears) percé(e)

pig [pɪɡ] n cochon m, porc m; (pej: unkind person) mufle m; (: greedy person) goinfre m

pigeon [ˈpɪdʒən] n pigeon m

piggy bank [ˈpɪɡɪ-] n tirelire f

pigsty [ˈpɪɡstaɪ] n porcherie f

pigtail [ˈpɪɡteɪl] n natte f, tresse f

pike [paɪk] n (fish) brochet m

pilchard [ˈpɪltʃəd] n pilchard m (sorte de sardine)

pile [paɪl] n (pillar, of books) pile f; (heap) tas m; (of carpet) épaisseur f; **pile up** vi (accumulate) s'entasser, s'accumuler ▷ vt (put in heap) empiler, entasser; (accumulate) accumuler; **piles** npl hémorroïdes fpl; **pile-up** n (Aut) télescopage m, collision f en série

pilgrim [ˈpɪlɡrɪm] n pèlerin m

● **PILGRIM FATHERS**
●
● Les "Pères pèlerins" sont un groupe de
● puritains qui quittèrent l'Angleterre en 1620
● pour fuir les persécutions religieuses. Ayant
● traversé l'Atlantique à bord du "Mayflower",
● ils fondèrent New Plymouth en Nouvelle-
● Angleterre, dans ce qui est aujourd'hui le
● Massachusetts. Ces Pères pèlerins sont
● considérés comme les fondateurs des États-
● Unis, et l'on commémore chaque année, le
● jour de "Thanksgiving", la réussite de leur
● première récolte.

pilgrimage [ˈpɪlɡrɪmɪdʒ] n pèlerinage m

pill [pɪl] n pilule f; **the ~** la pilule

pillar [ˈpɪləʳ] n pilier m

pillow [ˈpɪləʊ] n oreiller m; **pillowcase, pillowslip** n taie f d'oreiller

pilot [ˈpaɪlət] n pilote m ▷ cpd (scheme etc) pilote, expérimental(e) ▷ vt piloter; **pilot light** n veilleuse f

pimple [ˈpɪmpl] n bouton m

PIN n abbr (= personal identification number) code

m confidentiel

pin [pɪn] n épingle f; (Tech) cheville f ▷ vt épingler; **~s and needles** fourmis fpl; **to ~ sb down** (fig) coincer qn; **to ~ sth on sb** (fig) mettre qch sur le dos de qn

pinafore [ˈpɪnəfɔːʳ] n tablier m

pinch [pɪntʃ] n pincement m; (of salt etc) pincée f ▷ vt pincer; (inf: steal) piquer, chiper ▷ vi (shoe) serrer; **at a ~** à la rigueur

pine [paɪn] n (also: ~ tree) pin m ▷ vi: **to ~ for** aspirer à, désirer ardemment

pineapple [ˈpaɪnæpl] n ananas m

ping [pɪŋ] n (noise) tintement m; **ping-pong®** n ping-pong® m

pink [pɪŋk] adj rose ▷ n (colour) rose m

pinpoint [ˈpɪnpɔɪnt] vt indiquer (avec précision)

pint [paɪnt] n pinte f (BRIT = 0.57 l; US = 0.47 l); (BRIT inf) ≈ demi m, ≈ pot m

pioneer [paɪə'nɪəʳ] n pionnier m

pious [ˈpaɪəs] adj pieux(-euse)

pip [pɪp] n (seed) pépin m; **pips** npl: **the ~s** (BRIT: time signal on radio) le top

pipe [paɪp] n tuyau m, conduite f; (for smoking) pipe f ▷ vt amener par tuyau; **pipeline** n (for gas) gazoduc m, pipeline m; (for oil) oléoduc m, pipeline; **piper** n (flautist) joueur(-euse) de pipeau; (of bagpipes) joueur(-euse) de cornemuse

pirate [ˈpaɪərət] n pirate m ▷ vt (CD, video, book) pirater

Pisces [ˈpaɪsiːz] n les Poissons mpl

piss [pɪs] vi (inf!) pisser (!); **pissed** (inf!) adj (BRIT: drunk) bourré(e); (US: angry) furieux(-euse)

pistol [ˈpɪstl] n pistolet m

piston [ˈpɪstən] n piston m

pit [pɪt] n trou m, fosse f; (also: **coal ~**) puits m de mine; (also: **orchestra ~**) fosse d'orchestre; (US: fruit stone) noyau m ▷ vt: **to ~ o.s. or one's wits against** se mesurer à

pitch [pɪtʃ] n (BRIT Sport) terrain m; (Mus) ton m; (fig: degree) degré m; (tar) poix f ▷ vt (throw) lancer; (tent) dresser ▷ vi (fall): **to ~ into/off** tomber dans/de; **pitch-black** adj noir(e) comme poix

pitfall [ˈpɪtfɔːl] n piège m

pith [pɪθ] n (of orange etc) intérieur m de l'écorce

pitiful [ˈpɪtɪful] adj (touching) pitoyable; (contemptible) lamentable

pity [ˈpɪtɪ] n pitié f ▷ vt plaindre; **what a ~!** quel dommage!

pizza [ˈpiːtsə] n pizza f

placard [ˈplækɑːd] n affiche f; (in march) pancarte f

place [pleɪs] n endroit m, lieu m; (proper position, job, rank, seat) place f; (home): **at/to his ~** chez lui ▷ vt (position) placer, mettre; (identify) situer; reconnaître; **to take ~** avoir lieu; **to change ~s with sb** changer de place avec qn; **out of ~** (not suitable) déplacé(e), inopportun(e); **in the first ~** d'abord, en premier; **place mat** n set m de table; (in linen etc) napperon m; **placement** n (during studies) stage m

placid ['plæsɪd] adj placide

plague [pleɪg] n (Med) peste f ▷ vt (fig) tourmenter

plaice [pleɪs] n (pl inv) carrelet m

plain [pleɪn] adj (in one colour) uni(e); (clear) clair(e), évident(e); (simple) simple; (not handsome) quelconque, ordinaire ▷ adv franchement, carrément ▷ n plaine f; **plain chocolate** n chocolat m à croquer; **plainly** adv clairement; (frankly) carrément, sans détours

plaintiff ['pleɪntɪf] n plaignant(e)

plait [plæt] n tresse f, natte f

plan [plæn] n plan m; (scheme) projet m ▷ vt (think in advance) projeter; (prepare) organiser ▷ vi faire des projets; **to ~ to do** projeter de faire

plane [pleɪn] n (Aviat) avion m; (also: ~ tree) platane m; (tool) rabot m; (Art, Math etc) plan m; (fig) niveau m, plan ▷ vt (with tool) raboter

planet ['plænɪt] n planète f

plank [plæŋk] n planche f

planning ['plænɪŋ] n planification f; **family ~** planning familial

plant [plɑːnt] n plante f; (machinery) matériel m; (factory) usine f ▷ vt planter; (bomb) déposer, poser; (microphone, evidence) cacher

plantation [plæn'teɪʃən] n plantation f

plaque [plæk] n plaque f

plaster ['plɑːstəʳ] n plâtre m; (also: ~ of Paris) plâtre à mouler; (BRIT: also: sticking ~) pansement adhésif ▷ vt plâtrer; (cover): **to ~ with** couvrir de; **plaster cast** n (Med) plâtre m; (model, statue) moule m

plastic ['plæstɪk] n plastique m ▷ adj (made of plastic) en plastique; **plastic bag** n sac m en plastique; **plastic surgery** n chirurgie f esthétique

plate [pleɪt] n (dish) assiette f; (sheet of metal, on door; Phot) plaque f; (in book) gravure f; (dental) dentier m

plateau (pl ~s or ~x) ['plætəʊ, -z] n plateau m

platform ['plætfɔːm] n (at meeting) tribune f; (stage) estrade f; (Rail) quai m; (Pol) plateforme f

platinum ['plætɪnəm] n platine m

platoon [plə'tuːn] n peloton m

platter ['plætəʳ] n plat m

plausible ['plɔːzɪbl] adj plausible; (person) convaincant(e)

play [pleɪ] n jeu m; (Theat) pièce f (de théâtre) ▷ vt (game) jouer à; (team, opponent) jouer contre; (instrument) jouer de; (part, piece of music, note) jouer; (CD etc) passer ▷ vi jouer; **to ~ safe** ne prendre aucun risque; **play back** vt repasser, réécouter; **play up** vi (cause trouble) faire des siennes; **player** n joueur(-euse); (Mus) musicien(ne); **playful** adj enjoué(e); **playground** n cour f de récréation; (in park) aire f de jeux; **playgroup** n garderie f; **playing card** n carte f à jouer; **playing field** n terrain m de sport; **playschool** n = **playgroup**; **playtime** n (Scol) récréation f; **playwright** n dramaturge m

plc abbr (BRIT: = public limited company) ≈ SARL f

plea [pliː] n (request) appel m; (Law) défense f

plead [pliːd] vt plaider; (give as excuse) invoquer ▷ vi (Law) plaider; (beg): **to ~ with sb (for sth)** implorer qn (d'accorder qch); **to ~ guilty/not guilty** plaider coupable/non coupable

pleasant ['plɛznt] adj agréable

please [pliːz] excl s'il te (or vous) plaît ▷ vt plaire à ▷ vi (think fit): **do as you ~** faites comme il vous plaira; **~ yourself!** (inf) (faites) comme vous voulez!; **pleased** adj: **pleased (with)** content(e) (de); **pleased to meet you** enchanté (de faire votre connaissance)

pleasure ['plɛʒəʳ] n plaisir m; **"it's a ~"** "je vous en prie"

pleat [pliːt] n pli m

pledge [plɛdʒ] n (promise) promesse f ▷ vt promettre

plentiful ['plɛntɪful] adj abondant(e), copieux(-euse)

plenty ['plɛntɪ] n: **~ of** beaucoup de; (sufficient) (bien) assez de

pliers ['plaɪəz] npl pinces fpl

plight [plaɪt] n situation f critique

plod [plɔd] vi avancer péniblement; (fig) peiner

plonk [plɔŋk] (inf) n (BRIT: wine) pinard m, piquette f ▷ vt: **to ~ sth down** poser brusquement qch

plot [plɔt] n complot m, conspiration f; (of story, play) intrigue f; (of land) lot m de terrain, lopin m ▷ vt (mark out) tracer point par point; (Naut) pointer; (make graph of) faire le graphique de; (conspire) comploter ▷ vi comploter

plough (US **plow**) [plaʊ] n charrue f ▷ vt (earth) labourer; **to ~ money into** investir dans; **ploughman's lunch** n (BRIT) assiette froide avec du pain, du fromage et des pickles

plow [plaʊ] (US) = **plough**

ploy [plɔɪ] n stratagème m

pluck [plʌk] vt (fruit) cueillir; (musical instrument) pincer; (bird) plumer; **to ~ one's eyebrows** s'épiler les sourcils; **to ~ up courage** prendre son courage à deux mains

plug [plʌg] n (stopper) bouchon m, bonde f; (Elec) prise f de courant; (Aut: also: spark(ing) ~) bougie f ▷ vt (hole) boucher; (inf: advertise) faire du battage pour, matraquer; **plug in** vt (Elec) brancher; **plughole** n (BRIT) trou m

P

(d'écoulement)

plum [plʌm] n (fruit) prune f

plumber ['plʌmər] n plombier m

plumbing ['plʌmɪŋ] n (trade) plomberie f; (piping) tuyauterie f

plummet ['plʌmɪt] vi (person, object) plonger; (sales, prices) dégringoler

plump [plʌmp] adj rondelet(te), dodu(e), bien en chair; **plump for** vt fus (inf: choose) se décider pour

plunge [plʌndʒ] n plongeon m; (fig) chute f ▷ vt plonger ▷ vi (fall) tomber, dégringoler; (dive) plonger; **to take the ~** se jeter à l'eau

pluperfect [pluː'pəːfɪkt] n (Ling) plus-que-parfait m

plural ['pluərl] adj pluriel(le) ▷ n pluriel m

plus [plʌs] n (also: **~ sign**) signe m plus; (advantage) atout m ▷ prep plus; **ten/twenty ~** plus de dix/vingt

ply [plaɪ] n (of wool) fil m ▷ vt (a trade) exercer ▷ vi (ship) faire la navette; **to ~ sb with drink** donner continuellement à boire à qn; **plywood** n contreplaqué m

P.M. n abbr (BRIT) = **prime minister**

p.m. adv abbr (= post meridiem) de l'après-midi

PMS n abbr (= premenstrual syndrome) syndrome prémenstruel

PMT n abbr (= premenstrual tension) syndrome prémenstruel

pneumatic drill [njuː'mætɪk-] n marteau-piqueur m

pneumonia [njuː'məunɪə] n pneumonie f

poach [pəutʃ] vt (cook) pocher; (steal) pêcher (or chasser) sans permis ▷ vi braconner; **poached** adj (egg) poché(e)

P.O. Box n abbr = **post office box**

pocket ['pɔkɪt] n poche f ▷ vt empocher; **to be (£5) out of ~** (BRIT) en être de sa poche (pour 5 livres); **pocketbook** n (US: wallet) portefeuille m; **pocket money** n argent m de poche

pod [pɔd] n cosse f

podcast n podcast m

podiatrist [pɔ'diːətrɪst] n (US) pédicure m/f

podium ['pəudɪəm] n podium m

poem ['pəuɪm] n poème m

poet ['pəuɪt] n poète m; **poetic** [pəu'etɪk] adj poétique; **poetry** n poésie f

poignant ['pɔɪnjənt] adj poignant(e)

point [pɔɪnt] n point m; (tip) pointe f; (in time) moment m; (in space) endroit m; (subject, idea) point, sujet m; (purpose) but m; (also: **decimal ~**): **2 ~ 3 (2.3)** 2 virgule 3 (2,3); (BRIT Elec: also: **power ~**) prise f (de courant) ▷ vt (show) indiquer; (gun etc): **to ~ sth at** braquer or diriger qch sur ▷ vi: **to ~ at** montrer du doigt; **points** npl (Rail) aiguillage m; **to make a ~ of doing sth** ne pas manquer de faire qch; **to get/miss the ~** comprendre/ne pas

comprendre; **to come to the ~** en venir au fait; **there's no ~ (in doing)** cela ne sert à rien (de faire), à quoi ça sert?; **to be on the ~ of doing sth** être sur le point de faire qch; **point out** vt (mention) faire remarquer, souligner; **point-blank** adv (fig) catégoriquement; (also: **at point-blank range**) à bout portant; **pointed** adj (shape) pointu(e); (remark) plein(e) de sous-entendus; **pointer** n (needle) aiguille f; (clue) indication f; (advice) tuyau m; **pointless** adj inutile, vain(e); **point of view** n point m de vue

poison ['pɔɪzn] n poison m ▷ vt empoisonner; **poisonous** adj (snake) venimeux(-euse); (substance, plant) vénéneux(-euse); (fumes) toxique

poke [pəuk] vt (jab with finger, stick etc) piquer; pousser du doigt; (put): **to ~ sth in(to)** fourrer or enfoncer qch dans; **poke about** vi fureter; **poke out** vi (stick out) sortir

poker ['pəukər] n tisonnier m; (Cards) poker m

Poland ['pəulənd] n Pologne f

polar ['pəulər] adj polaire; **polar bear** n ours blanc

Pole [pəul] n Polonais(e)

pole [pəul] n (of wood) mât m, perche f; (Elec) poteau m; (Geo) pôle m; **pole bean** n (US) haricot m (à rames); **pole vault** n saut m à la perche

police [pə'liːs] npl police f ▷ vt maintenir l'ordre dans; **police car** n voiture f de police; **police constable** n (BRIT) agent m de police; **police force** n police f, forces fpl de l'ordre; **policeman** (irreg) n agent m de police, policier m; **police officer** n agent m de police; **police station** n commissariat m de police; **policewoman** (irreg) n femme-agent f

policy ['pɔlɪsɪ] n politique f; (also: **insurance ~**) police f (d'assurance)

polio ['pəulɪəu] n polio f

Polish ['pəulɪʃ] adj polonais(e) ▷ n (Ling) polonais m

polish ['pɔlɪʃ] n (for shoes) cirage m; (for floor) cire f, encaustique f; (for nails) vernis m; (shine) éclat m, poli m; (fig: refinement) raffinement m ▷ vt (put polish on: shoes, wood) cirer; (make shiny) astiquer, faire briller; **polish off** vt (food) liquider; **polished** adj (fig) raffiné(e)

polite [pə'laɪt] adj poli(e); **politeness** n politesse f

political [pə'lɪtɪkl] adj politique; **politically** adv politiquement; **politically correct** politiquement correct(e)

politician [pɔlɪ'tɪʃən] n homme/femme politique, politicien(ne)

politics ['pɔlɪtɪks] n politique f

poll [pəul] n scrutin m, vote m; (also: **opinion ~**) sondage m (d'opinion) ▷ vt (votes) obtenir

pollen ['pɔlən] n pollen m

polling station n (BRIT) bureau m de vote

pollute [pə'lu:t] vt polluer

pollution [pə'lu:ʃən] n pollution f

polo ['pəuləu] n polo m; **polo-neck** adj à col roulé ▷ n (sweater) pull m à col roulé; **polo shirt** n polo m

polyester [pɔlɪ'estəʳ] n polyester m

polystyrene [pɔlɪ'staɪri:n] n polystyrène m

polythene ['pɔlɪθi:n] n (BRIT) polyéthylène m; **polythene bag** n sac m en plastique

pomegranate ['pɔmɪgrænɪt] n grenade f

pompous ['pɔmpəs] adj pompeux(-euse)

pond [pɔnd] n étang m; (stagnant) mare f

ponder ['pɔndəʳ] vt considérer, peser

pony ['pəunɪ] n poney m; **ponytail** n queue f de cheval; **pony trekking** n (BRIT) randonnée f équestre or à cheval

poodle ['pu:dl] n caniche m

pool [pu:l] n (of rain) flaque f; (pond) mare f; (artificial) bassin m; (also: **swimming ~**) piscine f; (sth shared) fonds commun; (billiards) poule f ▷ vt mettre en commun; **pools** npl (football) ≈ loto sportif

poor [puəʳ] adj pauvre; (mediocre) médiocre, faible, mauvais(e) ▷ npl: **the ~** les pauvres mpl; **poorly** adv (badly) mal, médiocrement ▷ adj souffrant(e), malade

pop [pɔp] n (noise) bruit sec; (Mus) musique f pop; (inf: drink) soda m; (US inf: father) papa m ▷ vt (put) fourrer, mettre (rapidement) ▷ vi éclater; (cork) sauter; **pop in** vi entrer en passant; **pop out** vi sortir; **popcorn** n pop-corn m

pope [pəup] n pape m

poplar ['pɔplər] n peuplier m

popper ['pɔpəʳ] n (BRIT) bouton-pression m

poppy ['pɔpɪ] n (wild) coquelicot m; (cultivated) pavot m

Popsicle® ['pɔpsɪkl] n (US) esquimau m (glace)

pop star n pop star f

popular ['pɔpjuləʳ] adj populaire; (fashionable) à la mode; **popularity** [pɔpju'lærɪtɪ] n popularité f

population [pɔpju'leɪʃən] n population f

pop-up adj (Comput: menu, window) pop up inv ▷ n pop up m inv, fenêtre f pop up

porcelain ['pɔ:slɪn] n porcelaine f

porch [pɔ:tʃ] n porche m; (US) véranda f

pore [pɔ:ʳ] n pore m ▷ vi: **to ~ over** s'absorber dans, être plongé(e) dans

pork [pɔ:k] n porc m; **pork chop** n côte f de porc; **pork pie** n pâté m de porc en croûte

porn [pɔ:n] adj (inf) porno ▷ n (inf) porno m; **pornographic** [pɔ:nə'græfɪk] adj pornographique; **pornography** [pɔ:'nɔgrəfɪ] n pornographie f

porridge ['pɔrɪdʒ] n porridge m

port [pɔ:t] n (harbour) port m; (Naut: left side) bâbord m; (wine) porto m; (Comput) port m, accès m; **~ of call** (port d')escale f

portable ['pɔ:təbl] adj portatif(-ive)

porter ['pɔ:təʳ] n (for luggage) porteur m; (doorkeeper) gardien(ne); portier m

portfolio [pɔ:t'fəuliəu] n portefeuille m; (of artist) portfolio m

portion ['pɔ:ʃən] n portion f, part f

portrait ['pɔ:treɪt] n portrait m

portray [pɔ:'treɪ] vt faire le portrait de; (in writing) dépeindre, représenter; (subj: actor) jouer

Portugal ['pɔ:tjugl] n Portugal m

Portuguese [pɔ:tju'gi:z] adj portugais(e) ▷ n (pl inv) Portugais(e); (Ling) portugais m

pose [pəuz] n pose f ▷ vi poser; (pretend): **to ~ as** se faire passer pour ▷ vt poser; (problem) créer

posh [pɔʃ] adj (inf) chic inv

position [pə'zɪʃən] n position f; (job, situation) situation f ▷ vt mettre en place or en position

positive ['pɔzɪtɪv] adj positif(-ive); (certain) sûr(e), certain(e); (definite) formel(le), catégorique; **positively** adv (affirmatively, enthusiastically) de façon positive; (inf: really) carrément

possess [pə'zes] vt posséder; **possession** [pə'zeʃən] n possession f; **possessions** npl (belongings) affaires fpl; **possessive** adj possessif(-ive)

possibility [pɔsɪ'bɪlɪtɪ] n possibilité f; (event) éventualité f

possible ['pɔsɪbl] adj possible; **as big as ~** aussi gros que possible; **possibly** adv (perhaps) peut-être; **I cannot possibly come** il m'est impossible de venir

post [pəust] n (BRIT: mail) poste f; (: letters, delivery) courrier m; (job, situation) poste m; (pole) poteau m ▷ vt (BRIT: send by post) poster; (: appoint): **to ~ to** affecter à; **where can I ~ these cards?** où est-ce que je peux poster ces cartes postales?; **postage** n tarifs mpl d'affranchissement; **postal** adj postal(e); **postal order** n mandat(-poste m) m; **postbox** n (BRIT) boîte f aux lettres (publique); **postcard** n carte postale; **postcode** n (BRIT) code postal

poster ['pəustəʳ] n affiche f

postgraduate ['pəust'grædjuət] n ≈ étudiant(e) de troisième cycle

postman ['pəustmən] (BRIT: irreg) n facteur m

postmark ['pəustmɑ:k] n cachet m (de la poste)

post-mortem [pəust'mɔ:təm] n autopsie f

post office n (building) poste f; (organization): **the Post Office** les postes fpl

postpone [pəs'pəun] vt remettre (à plus tard), reculer

posture ['pɔstʃəʳ] n posture f; (fig) attitude f

postwoman ['pəust'wumən] (BRIT: irreg) n factrice f

p

pot [pɒt] n (for cooking) marmite f; casserole f; (teapot) théière f; (for coffee) cafetière f; (for plants, jam) pot m; (inf: marijuana) herbe f ▷ vt (plant) mettre en pot; **to go to ~** (inf) aller à vau-l'eau

potato (pl **-es**) [pə'teɪtəʊ] n pomme f de terre; **potato peeler** n épluche-légumes m

potent ['pəʊtnt] adj puissant(e); (drink) fort(e), très alcoolisé(e); (man) viril

potential [pə'tɛnʃl] adj potentiel(le) ▷ n potentiel m

pothole ['pɒthəʊl] n (in road) nid m de poule; (BRIT: underground) gouffre m, caverne f

pot plant n plante f d'appartement

potter ['pɒtər] n potier m ▷ vi (BRIT): **to ~ around** or **about** bricoler; **pottery** n poterie f

potty ['pɒtɪ] n (child's) pot m

pouch [paʊtʃ] n (Zool) poche f; (for tobacco) blague f; (for money) bourse f

poultry ['pəʊltrɪ] n volaille f

pounce [paʊns] vi: **to ~ (on)** bondir (sur), fondre (sur)

pound [paʊnd] n livre f (weight = 453g, 16 ounces; money = 100 pence); (for dogs, cars) fourrière f ▷ vt (beat) bourrer de coups, marteler; (crush) piler, pulvériser ▷ vi (heart) battre violemment, taper; **pound sterling** n livre f sterling

pour [pɔːr] vt verser ▷ vi couler à flots; (rain) pleuvoir à verse; **to ~ sb a drink** verser or servir à boire à qn; **pour in** vi (people) affluer, se précipiter; (news, letters) arriver en masse; **pour out** vi (people) sortir en masse ▷ vt vider; (fig) déverser; (serve: a drink) verser; **pouring** adj: **pouring rain** pluie torrentielle

pout [paʊt] vi faire la moue

poverty ['pɒvətɪ] n pauvreté f, misère f

powder ['paʊdər] n poudre f ▷ vt poudrer; **powdered milk** n lait m en poudre

power ['paʊər] n (strength, nation) puissance f, force f; (ability, Pol: of party, leader) pouvoir m; (of speech, thought) faculté f; (Elec) courant m; **to be in ~** être au pouvoir; **power cut** n (BRIT) coupure f de courant; **power failure** n panne f de courant; **powerful** adj puissant(e); (performance etc) très fort(e); **powerless** adj impuissant(e); **power point** n (BRIT) prise f de courant; **power station** n centrale f électrique

p.p. abbr (= per procurationem: by proxy) p.p.

PR n abbr = **public relations**

practical ['præktɪkl] adj pratique; **practical joke** n farce f, tour m; **practically** adv (almost) pratiquement

practice ['præktɪs] n pratique f; (of profession) exercice m; (at football etc) entraînement m; (business) cabinet m ▷ vt, vi (US) = **practise**; **in ~** (in reality) en pratique; **out of ~** rouillé(e)

practise (US **practice**) ['præktɪs] vt (work

at: piano, backhand etc) s'exercer à, travailler; (train for: sport) s'entraîner à; (a sport, religion, method) pratiquer; (profession) exercer ▷ vi s'exercer, travailler; (train) s'entraîner; (lawyer, doctor) exercer; **practising** (US **practicing**) adj (Christian etc) pratiquant(e); (lawyer) en exercice

practitioner [præk'tɪʃənər] n praticien(ne)

pragmatic [præg'mætɪk] adj pragmatique

prairie ['prɛərɪ] n savane f

praise [preɪz] n éloge(s) m(pl), louange(s) f(pl) ▷ vt louer, faire l'éloge de

pram [præm] n (BRIT) landau m, voiture f d'enfant

prank [præŋk] n farce f

prawn [prɔːn] n crevette f (rose); **prawn cocktail** n cocktail m de crevettes

pray [preɪ] vi prier; **prayer** [prɛər] n prière f

preach [priːtʃ] vi prêcher; **preacher** n prédicateur m; (US: clergyman) pasteur m

precarious [prɪ'kɛərɪəs] adj précaire

precaution [prɪ'kɔːʃən] n précaution f

precede [prɪ'siːd] vt, vi précéder; **precedent** ['prɛsɪdənt] n précédent m; **preceding** [prɪ'siːdɪŋ] adj qui précède (or précédait)

precinct ['priːsɪŋkt] n (US: district) circonscription f, arrondissement m; **pedestrian ~** (BRIT) zone piétonnière; **shopping ~** (BRIT) centre commercial

precious ['prɛʃəs] adj précieux(-euse)

precise [prɪ'saɪs] adj précis(e); **precisely** adv précisément

precision [prɪ'sɪʒən] n précision f

predator ['prɛdətər] n prédateur m, rapace m

predecessor ['priːdɪsɛsər] n prédécesseur m

predicament [prɪ'dɪkəmənt] n situation f difficile

predict [prɪ'dɪkt] vt prédire; **predictable** adj prévisible; **prediction** [prɪ'dɪkʃən] n prédiction f

predominantly [prɪ'dɔmɪnəntlɪ] adv en majeure partie; (especially) surtout

preface ['prɛfəs] n préface f

prefect ['priːfɛkt] n (BRIT: in school) élève chargé de certaines fonctions de discipline

prefer [prɪ'fəːr] vt préférer; **preferable** ['prɛfrəbl] adj préférable; **preferably** ['prɛfrəblɪ] adv de préférence; **preference** ['prɛfrəns] n préférence f

prefix ['priːfɪks] n préfixe m

pregnancy ['prɛgnənsɪ] n grossesse f

pregnant ['prɛgnənt] adj enceinte adj f; (animal) pleine

prehistoric ['priːhɪs'tɔrɪk] adj préhistorique

prejudice ['prɛdʒudɪs] n préjugé m; **prejudiced** adj (person) plein(e) de préjugés; (in a matter) partial(e)

preliminary [prɪ'lɪmɪnərɪ] adj préliminaire

prelude ['prɛljuːd] n prélude m

premature ['prɛmətʃuə'] adj prématuré(e)

premier ['prɛmɪə'] adj premier(-ière), principal(e) ▷ n (Pol: Prime Minister) premier ministre; (Pol: President) chef m de l'État

premiere ['prɛmɪə'] n première f

Premier League n première division

premises ['prɛmɪsɪz] npl locaux mpl; **on the ~** sur les lieux; sur place

premium ['priːmɪəm] n prime f; **to be at a ~** (fig: housing etc) être très demandé(e), être rarissime

premonition [prɛmə'nɪʃən] n prémonition f

preoccupied [pri:'ɔkjupaɪd] adj préoccupé(e)

prepaid [pri:'peɪd] adj payé(e) d'avance

preparation [prɛpə'reɪʃən] n préparation f; **preparations** npl (for trip, war) préparatifs mpl

preparatory school n école primaire privée; (US) lycée privé

prepare [prɪ'pɛə'] vt préparer ▷ vi: **to ~ for** se préparer à

prepared [prɪ'pɛəd] adj: **~ for** préparé(e) à; **~ to** prêt(e) à

preposition [prɛpə'zɪʃən] n préposition f

prep school n = **preparatory school**

prerequisite [pri:'rɛkwɪzɪt] n condition f préalable

preschool ['pri:'sku:l] adj préscolaire; (child) d'âge préscolaire

prescribe [prɪ'skraɪb] vt prescrire

prescription [prɪ'skrɪpʃən] n (Med) ordonnance f; (: medicine) médicament m (obtenu sur ordonnance); **could you write me a ~?** pouvez-vous me faire une ordonnance?

presence ['prɛzns] n présence f; **in sb's ~** en présence de qn; **~ of mind** présence d'esprit

present ['prɛznt] adj présent(e); (current) présent, actuel(le) ▷ n cadeau m; (actuality) présent m ▷ vt ['prɪ'zɛnt] présenter; (prize, medal) remettre; (give): **to ~ sb with sth** offrir qch à qn; **at ~** en ce moment; **to give sb a ~** offrir un cadeau à qn; **presentable** [prɪ'zɛntəbl] adj présentable; **presentation** [prɛzn'teɪʃən] n présentation f; (ceremony) remise f du cadeau (or de la médaille etc); **present-day** adj contemporain(e), actuel(le); **presenter** [prɪ'zɛntə'] n (BRIT Radio, TV) présentateur(-trice); **presently** adv (soon) tout à l'heure, bientôt; (with verb in past) peu après; (at present) en ce moment; **present participle** [-'pɑ:tɪsɪpl] n participe m présent

preservation [prɛzə'veɪʃən] n préservation f, conservation f

preservative [prɪ'zə:vətɪv] n agent m de conservation

preserve [prɪ'zə:v] vt (keep safe) préserver, protéger; (maintain) conserver, garder; (food) mettre en conserve ▷ n (for game, fish) réserve f; (often pl: jam) confiture f

preside [prɪ'zaɪd] vi présider

president ['prɛzɪdənt] n président(e); **presidential** [prɛzɪ'dɛnʃl] adj présidentiel(le)

press [prɛs] n (tool, machine, newspapers) presse f; (for wine) pressoir m ▷ vt (push) appuyer sur; (squeeze) presser, serrer; (clothes: iron) repasser; (insist): **to ~ sth on sb** presser qn d'accepter qch; (urge, entreat): **to ~ sb to do** or **into doing sth** pousser qn à faire qch ▷ vi appuyer; **we are ~ed for time** le temps nous manque; **to ~ for sth** faire pression pour obtenir qch; **press conference** n conférence f de presse; **pressing** adj urgent(e), pressant(e); **press stud** n (BRIT) bouton-pression m; **press-up** n (BRIT) traction f

pressure ['prɛʃə'] n pression f; (stress) tension f; **to put ~ on sb (to do sth)** faire pression sur qn (pour qu'il fasse qch); **pressure cooker** n cocotte-minute f; **pressure group** n groupe m de pression

prestige [prɛs'ti:ʒ] n prestige m

prestigious [prɛs'tɪdʒəs] adj prestigieux(-euse)

presumably [prɪ'zju:məblɪ] adv vraisemblablement

presume [prɪ'zju:m] vt présumer, supposer

pretence (US **pretense**) [prɪ'tɛns] n (claim) prétention f; **under false ~s** sous des prétextes fallacieux

pretend [prɪ'tɛnd] vt (feign) feindre, simuler ▷ vi (feign) faire semblant

pretense [prɪ'tɛns] n (US) = **pretence**

pretentious [prɪ'tɛnʃəs] adj prétentieux(-euse)

pretext ['pri:tɛkst] n prétexte m

pretty ['prɪtɪ] adj joli(e) ▷ adv assez

prevail [prɪ'veɪl] vi (win) l'emporter, prévaloir; (be usual) avoir cours; **prevailing** adj (widespread) courant(e), répandu(e); (wind) dominant(e)

prevalent ['prɛvələnt] adj répandu(e), courant(e)

prevent [prɪ'vɛnt] vt: **to ~ (from doing)** empêcher (de faire); **prevention** [prɪ'vɛnʃən] n prévention f; **preventive** adj préventif(-ive)

preview ['pri:vju:] n (of film) avant-première f

previous ['pri:vɪəs] adj (last) précédent(e); (earlier) antérieur(e); **previously** adv précédemment, auparavant

prey [preɪ] n proie f ▷ vi: **to ~ on** s'attaquer à; **it was ~ing on his mind** ça le rongeait or minait

price [praɪs] n prix m ▷ vt (goods) fixer le prix de; **priceless** adj sans prix, inestimable; **price list** n tarif m

prick [prɪk] n (sting) piqûre f ▷ vt piquer; **to ~ up one's ears** dresser or tendre l'oreille

prickly ['prɪklɪ] adj piquant(e), épineux(-euse); (fig: person) irritable

P

pride [praɪd] n fierté f; (pej) orgueil m ▷ vt: **to ~ o.s. on** se flatter de; s'enorgueillir de

priest [priːst] n prêtre m

primarily ['praɪmərɪlɪ] adv principalement, essentiellement

primary ['praɪmərɪ] adj primaire; (first in importance) premier(-ière), primordial(e) ▷ n (us: election) (élection f) primaire f; **primary school** n (BRIT) école f primaire

prime [praɪm] adj primordial(e), fondamental(e); (excellent) excellent(e) ▷ vt (fig) mettre au courant ▷ n: **in the ~ of life** dans la fleur de l'âge; **Prime Minister** n Premier ministre

primitive ['prɪmɪtɪv] adj primitif(-ive)

primrose ['prɪmrəuz] n primevère f

prince [prɪns] n prince m

princess [prɪn'sɛs] n princesse f

principal ['prɪnsɪpl] adj principal(e) ▷ n (head teacher) directeur m, principal m; **principally** adv principalement

principle ['prɪnsɪpl] n principe m; **in ~** en principe; **on ~** par principe

print [prɪnt] n (mark) empreinte f; (letters) caractères mpl; (fabric) imprimé m; (Art) gravure f, estampe f; (Phot) épreuve f ▷ vt imprimer; (publish) publier; (write in capitals) écrire en majuscules; **out of ~** épuisé(e); **print out** vt (Comput) imprimer; **printer** n (machine) imprimante f; (person) imprimeur m; **printout** n (Comput) sortie f imprimante

prior ['praɪər] adj antérieur(e), précédent(e); (more important) prioritaire ▷ adv: **~ to doing** avant de faire

priority [praɪ'ɔrɪtɪ] n priorité f; **to have** or **take ~ over sth/sb** avoir la priorité sur qch/qn

prison ['prɪzn] n prison f ▷ cpd pénitentiaire; **prisoner** n prisonnier(-ière); **prisoner of war** n prisonnier(-ière) de guerre

pristine ['prɪstiːn] adj virginal(e)

privacy ['prɪvəsɪ] n intimité f, solitude f

private ['praɪvɪt] adj (not public) privé(e); (personal) personnel(le); (house, car, lesson) particulier(-ière); (quiet: place) tranquille ▷ n soldat m de deuxième classe; **"~"** (on envelope) "personnelle"; (on door) "privé"; **in ~** en privé; **privately** adv en privé; (within oneself) intérieurement; **private property** n propriété privée; **private school** n école privée

privatize ['praɪvətaɪz] vt privatiser

privilege ['prɪvɪlɪdʒ] n privilège m

prize [praɪz] n prix m ▷ adj (example, idiot) parfait(e); (bull, novel) primé(e) ▷ vt priser, faire grand cas de; **prize-giving** n distribution f des prix; **prizewinner** n gagnant(e)

pro [prəu] n (inf: Sport) professionnel(le) ▷ prep pro ...; **pros** npl: **the ~s and cons** le pour et le contre

probability [prɔbə'bɪlɪtɪ] n probabilité f; **in all ~** très probablement

probable ['prɔbəbl] adj probable

probably ['prɔbəblɪ] adv probablement

probation [prə'beɪʃən] n: **on ~** (employee) à l'essai; (Law) en liberté surveillée

probe [prəub] n (Med, Space) sonde f; (enquiry) enquête f, investigation f ▷ vt sonder, explorer

problem ['prɔbləm] n problème m

procedure [prə'siːdʒər] n (Admin, Law) procédure f; (method) marche f à suivre, façon f de procéder

proceed [prə'siːd] vi (go forward) avancer; (act) procéder; (continue): **to ~ (with)** continuer, poursuivre; **to ~ to do** se mettre à faire; **proceedings** npl (measures) mesures fpl; (Law: against sb) poursuites fpl; (meeting) réunion f, séance f; (records) compte rendu; actes mpl; **proceeds** ['prəusiːdz] npl produit m, recette f

process ['prəusɛs] n processus m; (method) procédé m ▷ vt traiter

procession [prə'sɛʃən] n défilé m, cortège m; **funeral ~** (on foot) cortège funèbre; (in cars) convoi m mortuaire

proclaim [prə'kleɪm] vt déclarer, proclamer

prod [prɔd] vt pousser

produce n ['prɔdjuːs] (Agr) produits mpl ▷ vt [prə'djuːs] produire; (show) présenter; (cause) provoquer, causer; (Theat) monter, mettre en scène; (TV: programme) réaliser; (: play, film) mettre en scène; (Radio: programme) réaliser; (: play) mettre en ondes; **producer** n (Theat) metteur m en scène; (Agr, Comm, Cine) producteur m; (TV: of programme) réalisateur m; (: of play, film) metteur m en scène; (Radio: of programme) réalisateur m; (: of play) metteur m en ondes

product ['prɔdʌkt] n produit m; **production** [prə'dʌkʃən] n production f; (Theat) mise f en scène; **productive** [prə'dʌktɪv] adj productif(-ive); **productivity** [prɔdʌk'tɪvɪtɪ] n productivité f

Prof. [prɔf] abbr (= professor) Prof

profession [prə'fɛʃən] n profession f; **professional** n professionnel(le) ▷ adj professionnel(le); (work) de professionnel

professor [prə'fɛsər] n professeur m (titulaire d'une chaire); (us: teacher) professeur m

profile ['prəufaɪl] n profil m

profit ['prɔfɪt] n (from trading) bénéfice m; (advantage) profit m ▷ vi: **to ~ (by or from)** profiter (de); **profitable** adj lucratif(-ive), rentable

profound [prə'faund] adj profond(e)

programme (us **program**) ['prəugræm] n (Comput: also BRIT: **program**) programme m; (Radio, TV) émission f ▷ vt programmer; **programmer** (us **programer**) n

programmeur(-euse); **programming** (US **programing**) n programmation f
progress n ['prəʊgres] progrès m(pl) ▷ vi [prə'gres] progresser, avancer; **in ~** en cours; **progressive** [prə'gresiv] adj progressif(-ive); (person) progressiste
prohibit [prə'hibit] vt interdire, défendre
project n ['prɒdʒekt] (plan) projet m, plan m; (venture) opération f, entreprise f; (Scol: research) étude f, dossier m ▷ vb [prə'dʒekt] ▷ vt projeter ▷ vi (stick out) faire saillie, s'avancer; **projection** [prə'dʒekʃən] n projection f; (overhang) saillie f; **projector** [prə'dʒektə'] n projecteur m
prolific [prə'lifik] adj prolifique
prolong [prə'lɒŋ] vt prolonger
prom [prɒm] n abbr = **promenade** (US: ball) bal m d'étudiants; **the P~s** série de concerts de musique classique; voir encadré

● **PROM**

● En Grande-Bretagne, un **promenade**
● **concert** ou **prom** est un concert de
● musique classique, ainsi appelé car, à
● l'origine, le public restait debout et se
● promenait au lieu de rester assis. De nos
● jours, une partie du public reste debout,
● mais il y a également des places assises
● (plus chères). Les **Proms** les plus connus
● sont les Proms londoniens. La dernière
● séance (the **Last Night of the Proms**) est
● un grand événement médiatique où se
● jouent des airs traditionnels et patriotiques.
● Aux États-Unis et au Canada, le **prom** ou
● **promenade** est un bal organisé par le lycée.

promenade [prɒmə'nɑːd] n (by sea) esplanade f, promenade f
prominent ['prɒminənt] adj (standing out) proéminent(e); (important) important(e)
promiscuous [prə'miskjuəs] adj (sexually) de mœurs légères
promise ['prɒmis] n promesse f ▷ vt, vi promettre; **promising** adj prometteur(-euse)
promote [prə'məʊt] vt promouvoir; (new product) lancer; **promotion** [prə'məʊʃən] n promotion f
prompt [prɒmpt] adj rapide ▷ n (Comput) message m (de guidage) ▷ vt (cause) entraîner, provoquer; (Theat) souffler (son rôle or ses répliques) à; **at 8 o'clock ~** à 8 heures précises; **to ~ sb to do** inciter or pousser qn à faire; **promptly** adv (quickly) rapidement, sans délai; (on time) ponctuellement
prone [prəʊn] adj (lying) couché(e) (face contre terre); (liable): **~ to** enclin(e) à
prong [prɒŋ] n (of fork) dent f
pronoun ['prəʊnaʊn] n pronom m

pronounce [prə'naʊns] vt prononcer; **how do you ~ it?** comment est-ce que ça se prononce?
pronunciation [prənʌnsɪ'eɪʃən] n prononciation f
proof [pruːf] n preuve f ▷ adj: **~ against** à l'épreuve de
prop [prɒp] n support m, étai m; (fig) soutien m ▷ vt (also: **~ up**) étayer, soutenir; **props** npl accessoires mpl
propaganda [prɒpə'gændə] n propagande f
propeller [prə'pelə'] n hélice f
proper ['prɒpə'] adj (suited, right) approprié(e), bon (bonne); (seemly) correct(e), convenable; (authentic) vrai(e), véritable; (referring to place): **the village ~** le village proprement dit; **properly** adv correctement, convenablement; **proper noun** n nom m propre
property ['prɒpəti] n (possessions) biens mpl; (house etc) propriété f; (land) terres fpl, domaine m
prophecy ['prɒfisi] n prophétie f
prophet ['prɒfit] n prophète m
proportion [prə'pɔːʃən] n proportion f; (share) part f; partie f; **proportions** npl (size) dimensions fpl; **proportional, proportionate** adj proportionnel(le)
proposal [prə'pəʊzl] n proposition f, offre f; (plan) projet m; (of marriage) demande f en mariage
propose [prə'pəʊz] vt proposer, suggérer ▷ vi faire sa demande en mariage; **to ~ to do** avoir l'intention de faire
proposition [prɒpə'zɪʃən] n proposition f
proprietor [prə'praɪətə'] n propriétaire m/f
prose [prəʊz] n prose f; (Scol: translation) thème m
prosecute ['prɒsikjuːt] vt poursuivre; **prosecution** [prɒsi'kjuːʃən] n poursuites fpl judiciaires; (accusing side: in criminal case) accusation f; (: in civil case) la partie plaignante; **prosecutor** n (lawyer) procureur m; (also: **public prosecutor**) ministère public; (US: plaintiff) plaignant(e)
prospect n ['prɒspekt] perspective f; (hope) espoir m, chances fpl ▷ vt, vi [prə'spekt] prospecter; **prospects** npl (for work etc) possibilités fpl d'avenir, débouchés mpl; **prospective** [prə'spektiv] adj (possible) éventuel(le); (future) futur(e)
prospectus [prə'spektəs] n prospectus m
prosper ['prɒspə'] vi prospérer; **prosperity** [prɒ'speriti] n prospérité f; **prosperous** adj prospère
prostitute ['prɒstitjuːt] n prostituée f; **male ~** prostitué m
protect [prə'tekt] vt protéger; **protection** [prə'tekʃən] n protection f; **protective** adj

P

protecteur(-trice); (clothing) de protection
protein ['prəʊti:n] n protéine f
protest n ['prəʊtest] protestation f ▷ vb
[prə'test] ▷ vi: **to ~ against/about** protester
contre/à propos de; **to ~ (that)** protester que
Protestant ['prɒtɪstənt] adj, n protestant(e)
protester, protestor [prə'testər] n (in
demonstration) manifestant f
protractor [prə'træktər] n (Geom)
rapporteur m
proud [praʊd] adj fier(-ère); (pej)
orgueilleux(-euse)
prove [pru:v] vt prouver, démontrer ▷ vi: **to ~
correct** etc s'avérer juste etc; **to ~ o.s.** montrer
ce dont on est capable
proverb ['prɒvə:b] n proverbe m
provide [prə'vaɪd] vt fournir; **to ~ sb with sth**
fournir qch à qn; **provide for** vt fus (person)
subvenir aux besoins de; (future event) prévoir;
provided conj: **provided (that)** à condition
que + sub; **providing** [prə'vaɪdɪŋ] conj à
condition que + sub
province ['prɒvɪns] n province f; (fig)
domaine m; **provincial** [prə'vɪnʃəl] adj
provincial(e)
provision [prə'vɪʒən] n (supplying) fourniture
f; approvisionnement m; (stipulation)
disposition f; **provisions** npl (food)
provisions fpl; **provisional** adj provisoire
provocative [prə'vɒkətɪv] adj
provocateur(-trice), provocant(e)
provoke [prə'vəʊk] vt provoquer
prowl [praʊl] vi (also: ~ about, ~ around)
rôder
proximity [prɒk'sɪmɪtɪ] n proximité f
proxy ['prɒksɪ] n: **by ~** par procuration
prudent ['pru:dnt] adj prudent(e)
prune [pru:n] n pruneau m ▷ vt élaguer
pry [praɪ] vi: **to ~ into** fourrer son nez dans
PS n abbr (= postscript) PS m
pseudonym ['sju:dənɪm] n pseudonyme m
PSHE n abbr (BRIT: Scol: = personal, social and
health education) cours d'éducation personnelle,
sanitaire et sociale préparant à la vie adulte
psychiatric [saɪkɪ'ætrɪk] adj psychiatrique
psychiatrist [saɪ'kaɪətrɪst] n psychiatre m/f
psychic ['saɪkɪk] adj (also: ~al)
(méta)psychique; (person) doué(e) de
télépathie ou d'un sixième sens
psychoanalysis (pl -ses) [saɪkəʊə'næləsɪs,
-si:z] n psychanalyse f
psychological [saɪkə'lɒdʒɪkl] adj
psychologique
psychologist [saɪ'kɒlədʒɪst] n psychologue
m/f
psychology [saɪ'kɒlədʒɪ] n psychologie f
psychotherapy [saɪkəʊ'θerəpɪ] n
psychothérapie f
pt abbr = pint(s); point(s)

PTO abbr (= please turn over) TSVP
pub [pʌb] n abbr (= public house) pub m
puberty ['pju:bətɪ] n puberté f
public ['pʌblɪk] adj public(-ique) ▷ n public m;
in ~ en public; **to make ~** rendre public
publication [pʌblɪ'keɪʃən] n publication f
public: **public company** n société f anonyme;
public convenience n (BRIT) toilettes fpl;
public holiday n (BRIT) jour férié; **public
house** n (BRIT) pub m
publicity [pʌb'lɪsɪtɪ] n publicité f
publicize ['pʌblɪsaɪz] vt (make known) faire
connaître, rendre public; (advertise) faire de la
publicité pour
public: **public limited company** n ≈ société
f anonyme (SA) (cotée en Bourse); **publicly** adv
publiquement, en public; **public opinion** n
opinion publique; **public relations** n or npl
relations publiques (RP); **public school** n
(BRIT) école privée; (US) école publique; **public
transport** (US **public transportation**) n
transports mpl en commun
publish ['pʌblɪʃ] vt publier; **publisher** n
éditeur m; **publishing** n (industry) édition f
pub lunch n repas m de bistrot
pudding ['pʊdɪŋ] n (BRIT: dessert) dessert m,
entremets m; (sweet dish) pudding m, gâteau m
puddle ['pʌdl] n flaque f d'eau
puff [pʌf] n bouffée f ▷ vt (also: ~ out: sails,
cheeks) gonfler ▷ vi (pant) haleter; **puff pastry**
(US **puff paste**) n pâte feuilletée
pull [pʊl] n (tug): **to give sth a ~** tirer sur
qch ▷ vt tirer; (trigger) presser; (strain: muscle,
tendon) se claquer ▷ vi tirer; **to ~ to pieces**
mettre en morceaux; **to ~ one's punches**
(also fig) ménager son adversaire; **to ~ one's
weight** y mettre du sien; **to ~ o.s. together**
se ressaisir; **to ~ sb's leg** (fig) faire marcher
qn; **pull apart** vt (break) mettre en pièces,
démantibuler; **pull away** vi (vehicle: move
off) partir; (draw back) s'éloigner; **pull back** vt
(lever etc) tirer sur; (curtains) ouvrir ▷ vi (refrain)
s'abstenir; (Mil: withdraw) se retirer; **pull down**
vt baisser, abaisser; (house) démolir; **pull in** vi
(Aut) se ranger; (Rail) entrer en gare; **pull off**
vt enlever, ôter; (deal etc) conclure; **pull out** vi
démarrer, partir; (Aut: come out of line) déboîter
▷ vt (from bag, pocket) sortir; (remove) arracher;
pull over vi (Aut) se ranger; **pull up** vi (stop)
s'arrêter ▷ vt remonter; (uproot) déraciner,
arracher
pulley ['pʊlɪ] n poulie f
pullover ['pʊləʊvər] n pull-over m, tricot m
pulp [pʌlp] n (of fruit) pulpe f; (for paper) pâte
f à papier
pulpit ['pʊlpɪt] n chaire f
pulse [pʌls] n (of blood) pouls m; (of
heart) battement m; **pulses** npl (Culin)
légumineuses fpl

puma ['pjuːmə] n puma m

pump [pʌmp] n pompe f; (shoe) escarpin m
▷ vt pomper; **pump up** vt gonfler

pumpkin ['pʌmpkɪn] n potiron m, citrouille f

pun [pʌn] n jeu m de mots, calembour m

punch [pʌntʃ] n (blow) coup m de poing; (tool)
poinçon m; (drink) punch m ▷ vt (make a hole in)
poinçonner, perforer; (hit): **to ~ sb/sth** donner
un coup de poing à qn/sur qch; **punch-up** n
(BRIT inf) bagarre f

punctual ['pʌŋktjuəl] adj ponctuel(le)

punctuation [pʌŋktju'eɪʃən] n ponctuation f

puncture ['pʌŋktʃəʳ] n (BRIT) crevaison f ▷ vt
crever

punish ['pʌnɪʃ] vt punir; **punishment** n
punition f, châtiment m

punk [pʌŋk] n (person: also: ~ rocker) punk
m/f; (music: also: ~ rock) le punk; (US inf:
hoodlum) voyou m

pup [pʌp] n chiot m

pupil ['pjuːpl] n élève m/f; (of eye) pupille f

puppet ['pʌpɪt] n marionnette f, pantin m

puppy ['pʌpɪ] n chiot m, petit chien

purchase ['pəːtʃɪs] n achat m ▷ vt acheter

pure [pjuəʳ] adj pur(e); **purely** adv purement

purify ['pjuərɪfaɪ] vt purifier, épurer

purity ['pjuərɪtɪ] n pureté f

purple ['pəːpl] adj violet(te); (face) cramoisi(e)

purpose ['pəːpəs] n intention f, but m; **on ~**
exprès

purr [pəːʳ] vi ronronner

purse [pəːs] n (BRIT: for money) porte-monnaie
m inv; (US: handbag) sac m (à main) ▷ vt serrer,
pincer

pursue [pə'sjuː] vt poursuivre

pursuit [pə'sjuːt] n poursuite f; (occupation)
occupation f, activité f

pus [pʌs] n pus m

push [puʃ] n poussée f ▷ vt pousser; (button)
appuyer sur; (fig: product) mettre en avant,
faire de la publicité pour ▷ vi pousser; **to ~
for** (better pay, conditions) réclamer; **push
in** vi s'introduire de force; **push off** vi (inf)
filer, ficher le camp; **push on** vi (continue)
continuer; **push over** vt renverser; **push
through** vi (in crowd) se frayer un chemin;
pushchair n (BRIT) poussette f; **pusher** n
(also: **drug pusher**) revendeur(-euse) (de
drogue), ravitailleur(-euse) (en drogue); **push-
up** n (US) traction f

pussy(-cat) ['pusɪ-] n (inf) minet m

put (pt, pp ~) [put] vt mettre; (place) poser,
placer; (say) dire, exprimer; (a question) poser;
(case, view) exposer, présenter; (estimate)
estimer; **put aside** vt mettre de côté; **put
away** vt (store) ranger; **put back** vt (replace)
remettre, replacer; (postpone) remettre; **put
by** vt (money) mettre de côté, économiser; **put
down** vt (parcel etc) poser, déposer; (in writing)

mettre par écrit, inscrire; (suppress: revolt etc)
réprimer, écraser; (attribute) attribuer; (animal)
abattre; (cat, dog) faire piquer; **put forward** vt
(ideas) avancer, proposer; **put in** vt (complaint)
soumettre; (time, effort) consacrer; **put off**
vt (postpone) remettre à plus tard, ajourner;
(discourage) dissuader; **put on** vt (clothes,
lipstick, CD) mettre; (light etc) allumer; (play
etc) monter; (weight) prendre; (assume: accent,
manner) prendre; (one's hand) tendre; (light etc)
éteindre; (person: inconvenience) déranger,
gêner; **put through** vt (Tel: caller) mettre en
communication; (: call) passer; (plan) faire
accepter; **put together** vt mettre ensemble;
(assemble: furniture) monter, assembler; (meal)
préparer; **put up** vt (raise) lever, relever,
remonter; (hang) accrocher; (build) construire,
ériger; (increase) augmenter; (accommodate)
loger; **put up with** vt fus supporter

putt [pʌt] n putt m; **putting green** n green m

puzzle ['pʌzl] n énigme f, mystère m; (game)
jeu m, casse-tête m; (jigsaw) puzzle m; (also:
crossword ~) mots croisés ▷ vt intriguer,
rendre perplexe ▷ vi: **to ~ over** chercher à
comprendre; **puzzled** adj perplexe; **puzzling**
adj déconcertant(e), inexplicable

pyjamas [pɪ'dʒɑːməz] npl (BRIT) pyjama m

pylon ['paɪlən] n pylône m

pyramid ['pɪrəmɪd] n pyramide f

Pyrenees [pɪrə'niːz] npl Pyrénées fpl

P

q

quack [kwæk] n (of duck) coin-coin m inv; (pej: doctor) charlatan m

quadruple [kwɔ'druːpl] vt, vi quadrupler

quail [kweɪl] n (Zool) caille f ▷ vi: **to ~ at** or **before** reculer devant

quaint [kweɪnt] adj bizarre; (old-fashioned) désuet(-ète); (picturesque) au charme vieillot, pittoresque

quake [kweɪk] vi trembler ▷ n abbr = earthquake

qualification [kwɔlɪfɪ'keɪʃən] n (often pl: degree etc) diplôme m; (training) qualification(s) f(pl); (ability) compétence(s) f(pl); (limitation) réserve f, restriction f

qualified ['kwɔlɪfaɪd] adj (trained) qualifié(e); (professionally) diplômé(e); (fit, competent) compétent(e), qualifié(e); (limited) conditionnel(le)

qualify ['kwɔlɪfaɪ] vt qualifier; (modify) atténuer, nuancer ▷ vi: **to ~ (as)** obtenir son diplôme (de); **to ~ (for)** remplir les conditions requises (pour); (Sport) se qualifier (pour)

quality ['kwɔlɪtɪ] n qualité f

qualm [kwɑːm] n doute m; scrupule m

quantify ['kwɔntɪfaɪ] vt quantifier

quantity ['kwɔntɪtɪ] n quantité f

quarantine ['kwɔrntiːn] n quarantaine f

quarrel ['kwɔrl] n querelle f, dispute f ▷ vi se disputer, se quereller

quarry ['kwɔrɪ] n (for stone) carrière f; (animal) proie f, gibier m

quart [kwɔːt] n ≈ litre m

quarter ['kwɔːtər] n quart m; (of year) trimestre m; (district) quartier m; (US, CANADA: 25 cents) (pièce f de) vingt-cinq cents mpl ▷ vt partager en quartiers or en quatre; (Mil) caserner, cantonner; **quarters** npl logement m; (Mil) quartiers mpl, cantonnement m; **a ~ of an hour** un quart d'heure; **quarter final** n quart m de finale; **quarterly** adj trimestriel(le) ▷ adv tous les trois mois

quartet(te) [kwɔː'tɛt] n quatuor m; (jazz players) quartette m

quartz [kwɔːts] n quartz m

quay [kiː] n (also: **~side**) quai m

queasy ['kwiːzɪ] adj: **to feel ~** avoir mal au cœur

Quebec [kwɪ'bɛk] n (city) Québec; (province) Québec m

queen [kwiːn] n (gen) reine f; (Cards etc) dame f

queer [kwɪər] adj étrange, curieux(-euse); (suspicious) louche ▷ n (inf: highly offensive) homosexuel m

quench [kwɛntʃ] vt: **to ~ one's thirst** se désaltérer

query ['kwɪərɪ] n question f ▷ vt (disagree with, dispute) mettre en doute, questionner

quest [kwɛst] n recherche f, quête f

question ['kwɛstʃən] n question f ▷ vt (person) interroger; (plan, idea) mettre en question or en doute; **beyond ~** sans aucun doute; **out of the ~** hors de question; **questionable** adj discutable; **question mark** n point m d'interrogation; **questionnaire** [kwɛstʃə'nɛər] n questionnaire m

queue [kjuː] (BRIT) n queue f, file f ▷ vi (also: **~ up**) faire la queue

quiche [kiːʃ] n quiche f

quick [kwɪk] adj rapide; (mind) vif (vive); (agile) agile, vif (vive) ▷ n: **cut to the ~** (fig) touché(e) au vif; **be ~!** dépêche-toi!; **quickly** adv (fast) vite, rapidement; (immediately) tout de suite

quid [kwɪd] n (pl inv: BRIT inf) livre f

quiet ['kwaɪət] adj tranquille, calme; (voice) bas(se); (ceremony, colour) discret(-ète) ▷ n tranquillité f, calme m; (silence) silence m; **quietly** adv tranquillement; (silently) silencieusement; (discreetly) discrètement

quilt [kwɪlt] n édredon m; (continental quilt) couette f

quirky ['kwɜːkɪ] adj singulier(-ère)

quit [kwɪt] (pt, pp **~** or **~ted**) vt quitter ▷ vi (give up) abandonner, renoncer; (resign) démissionner

quite [kwaɪt] adv (rather) assez, plutôt; (entirely) complètement, tout à fait; **~ a few of them** un assez grand nombre d'entre eux; **that's not ~ right** ce n'est pas tout à fait juste; **~ (so)!** exactement!

quits [kwɪts] *adj*: **~ (with)** quitte (envers); **let's call it ~** restons-en là

quiver ['kwɪvə'] *vi* trembler, frémir

quiz [kwɪz] *n (on TV)* jeu-concours *m* (télévisé); *(in magazine etc)* test *m* de connaissances ▷ *vt* interroger

quota ['kwəutə] *n* quota *m*

quotation [kwəu'teɪʃən] *n* citation *f*; *(estimate)* devis *m*; **quotation marks** *npl* guillemets *mpl*

quote [kwəut] *n* citation *f*; *(estimate)* devis *m* ▷ *vt (sentence, author)* citer; *(price)* donner, soumettre ▷ *vi*: **to ~ from** citer; **quotes** *npl (inverted commas)* guillemets *mpl*

Rabat [rə'bɑːt] *n* Rabat

rabbi ['ræbaɪ] *n* rabbin *m*

rabbit ['ræbɪt] *n* lapin *m*

rabies ['reɪbiːz] *n* rage *f*

RAC *n abbr* (BRIT: = Royal Automobile Club) ≈ ACF *m*

rac(c)oon [rə'kuːn] *n* raton *m* laveur

race [reɪs] *n (species)* race *f*; *(competition, rush)* course *f* ▷ *vt (person)* faire la course avec ▷ *vi (compete)* faire la course, courir; *(pulse)* battre très vite; **race car** *n (US)* = **racing car**; **racecourse** *n* champ *m* de courses; **racehorse** *n* cheval *m* de course; **racetrack** *n* piste *f*

racial ['reɪʃl] *adj* racial(e)

racing ['reɪsɪŋ] *n* courses *fpl*; **racing car** *n* (BRIT) voiture *f* de course; **racing driver** *n* (BRIT) pilote *m* de course

racism ['reɪsɪzəm] *n* racisme *m*; **racist** ['reɪsɪst] *adj*, *n* raciste *m/f*

rack [ræk] *n (for guns, tools)* râtelier *m*; *(for clothes)* portant *m*; *(for bottles)* casier *m*; *(also:* **luggage ~**) filet *m* à bagages; *(also:* **roof ~**) galerie *f*; *(also:* **dish ~**) égouttoir *m* ▷ *vt* tourmenter; **to ~ one's brains** se creuser la cervelle

racket ['rækɪt] *n (for tennis)* raquette *f*; *(noise)* tapage *m*, vacarme *m*; *(swindle)* escroquerie *f*

racquet ['rækɪt] *n* raquette *f*

radar ['reɪdɑː'] *n* radar *m*

radiation [ˌreɪdɪˈeɪʃən] n rayonnement m; (*radioactive*) radiation f

radiator [ˈreɪdɪeɪtəʳ] n radiateur m

radical [ˈrædɪkl] adj radical(e)

radio [ˈreɪdɪəʊ] n radio f ▷ vt (*person*) appeler par radio; **on the ~** à la radio; **radioactive** adj radioactif(-ive); **radio station** n station f de radio

radish [ˈrædɪʃ] n radis m

RAF n abbr (BRIT) = **Royal Air Force**

raffle [ˈræfl] n tombola f

raft [rɑːft] n (*craft: also*: **life ~**) radeau m; (*logs*) train m de flottage

rag [ræg] n chiffon m; (*pej: newspaper*) feuille f, torchon m; (*for charity*) attractions organisées par les étudiants au profit d'œuvres de charité; **rags** npl haillons mpl

rage [reɪdʒ] n (*fury*) rage f, fureur f ▷ vi (*person*) être fou (folle) de rage; (*storm*) faire rage, être déchaîné(e); **it's all the ~** cela fait fureur

ragged [ˈrægɪd] adj (*edge*) inégal(e), qui accroche; (*clothes*) en loques; (*appearance*) déguenillé(e)

raid [reɪd] n (*Mil*) raid m; (*criminal*) hold-up m inv; (*by police*) descente f, rafle f ▷ vt faire un raid sur or un hold-up dans or une descente dans

rail [reɪl] n (*on stair*) rampe f; (*on bridge, balcony*) balustrade f; (*of ship*) bastingage m; (*for train*) rail m; **railcard** n (BRIT) carte f de chemin de fer; **railing(s)** n(pl) grille f; **railway** (US **railroad**) n chemin m de fer; (*track*) voie f ferrée; **railway line** n (BRIT) ligne f de chemin de fer; (*track*) voie ferrée; **railway station** n (BRIT) gare f

rain [reɪn] n pluie f ▷ vi pleuvoir; **in the ~** sous la pluie; **it's ~ing** il pleut; **rainbow** n arc-en-ciel m; **raincoat** n imperméable m; **raindrop** n goutte f de pluie; **rainfall** n chute f de pluie; (*measurement*) hauteur f des précipitations; **rainforest** n forêt tropicale; **rainy** adj pluvieux(-euse)

raise [reɪz] n augmentation f ▷ vt (*lift*) lever, hausser; (*increase*) augmenter; (*morale*) remonter; (*standards*) améliorer; (*a protest, doubt*) provoquer, causer; (*a question*) soulever; (*cattle, family*) élever; (*crop*) faire pousser; (*army, funds*) rassembler; (*loan*) obtenir; **to ~ one's voice** élever la voix

raisin [ˈreɪzn] n raisin sec

rake [reɪk] n (*tool*) râteau m; (*person*) débauché m ▷ vt (*garden*) ratisser

rally [ˈrælɪ] n (*Pol etc*) meeting m, rassemblement m; (*Aut*) rallye m; (*Tennis*) échange m ▷ vt rassembler, rallier; (*support*) gagner ▷ vi (*sick person*) aller mieux; (*Stock Exchange*) reprendre

RAM [ræm] n abbr (*Comput: = random access memory*) mémoire vive

ram [ræm] n bélier m ▷ vt (*push*) enfoncer; (*crash into: vehicle*) emboutir; (: *lamppost etc*) percuter

Ramadan [ræməˈdæn] n Ramadan m

ramble [ˈræmbl] n randonnée f ▷ vi (*walk*) se promener, faire une randonnée; (*pej: also: ~ on*) discourir, pérorer; **rambler** n promeneur(-euse), randonneur(-euse); **rambling** adj (*speech*) décousu(e); (*house*) plein(e) de coins et de recoins; (*Bot*) grimpant(e)

ramp [ræmp] n (*incline*) rampe f; (*Aut*) dénivellation f; (*in garage*) pont m; **on/off ~** (US Aut) bretelle f d'accès

rampage [ræmˈpeɪdʒ] n: **to be on the ~** se déchaîner

ran [ræn] pt of **run**

ranch [rɑːntʃ] n ranch m

random [ˈrændəm] adj fait(e) or établi(e) au hasard; (*Comput, Math*) aléatoire ▷ n: **at ~** au hasard

rang [ræŋ] pt of **ring**

range [reɪndʒ] n (*of mountains*) chaîne f; (*of missile, voice*) portée f; (*of products*) choix m, gamme f; (*also*: **shooting ~**) champ m de tir; (*also*: **kitchen ~**) fourneau m (de cuisine) ▷ vt (*place*) mettre en rang, placer ▷ vi: **to ~ over** couvrir; **to ~ from ... to** aller de ... à

ranger [ˈreɪndʒəʳ] n garde m forestier

rank [ræŋk] n rang m; (*Mil*) grade m; (BRIT: *also*: **taxi ~**) station f de taxis ▷ vi: **to ~ among** compter or se classer parmi ▷ adj (*smell*) nauséabond(e); **the ~ and file** (*fig*) la masse, la base

ransom [ˈrænsəm] n rançon f; **to hold sb to ~** (*fig*) exercer un chantage sur qn

rant [rænt] vi fulminer

rap [ræp] n (*music*) rap m ▷ vt (*door*) frapper sur or à; (*table etc*) taper sur

rape [reɪp] n viol m; (*Bot*) colza m ▷ vt violer

rapid [ˈræpɪd] adj rapide; **rapidly** adv rapidement; **rapids** npl (*Geo*) rapides mpl

rapist [ˈreɪpɪst] n auteur m d'un viol

rapport [ræˈpɔːʳ] n entente f

rare [rɛəʳ] adj rare; (*Culin: steak*) saignant(e); **rarely** adv rarement

rash [ræʃ] adj imprudent(e), irréfléchi(e) ▷ n (*Med*) rougeur f, éruption f; (*of events*) série f (noire)

rasher [ˈræʃəʳ] n fine tranche (de lard)

raspberry [ˈrɑːzbərɪ] n framboise f

rat [ræt] n rat m

rate [reɪt] n (*ratio*) taux m, pourcentage m; (*speed*) vitesse f, rythme m; (*price*) tarif m ▷ vt (*price*) évaluer, estimer; (*people*) classer; **rates** npl (BRIT: *property tax*) impôts locaux; **to ~ sb/sth as** considérer qn/qch comme

rather [ˈrɑːðəʳ] adv (*somewhat*) assez, plutôt; (*to some extent*) un peu; **it's ~ expensive**

c'est assez cher; (too much) c'est un peu cher; **there's ~ a lot** il y en a beaucoup; **I would** or **I'd ~ go** j'aimerais mieux or je préférerais partir; **or ~** (more accurately) ou plutôt

rating ['reɪtɪŋ] n (assessment) évaluation f; (score) classement m; (Finance) cote f; **ratings** npl (Radio) indice(s) m(pl) d'écoute; (TV) Audimat®

ratio ['reɪʃɪəu] n proportion f; **in the ~ of 100 to 1** dans la proportion de 100 contre 1

ration ['ræʃən] n ration f ▷ vt rationner; **rations** npl (food) vivres mpl

rational ['ræʃənl] adj raisonnable, sensé(e); (solution, reasoning) logique; (Med: person) lucide

rat race n foire f d'empoigne

rattle ['rætl] n (of door, window) battement m; (of coins, chain) cliquetis m; (of train, engine) bruit m de ferraille; (for baby) hochet m ▷ vi cliqueter; (car, bus): **to ~ along** rouler en faisant un bruit de ferraille ▷ vt agiter (bruyamment); (inf: disconcert) déconcerter

rave [reɪv] vi (in anger) s'emporter; (with enthusiasm) s'extasier; (Med) délirer ▷ n (inf: party) rave f, soirée f techno

raven ['reɪvən] n grand corbeau

ravine [rə'viːn] n ravin m

raw [rɔː] adj (uncooked) cru(e); (not processed) brut(e); (sore) à vif, irrité(e); (inexperienced) inexpérimenté(e); **~ materials** matières premières

ray [reɪ] n rayon m; **~ of hope** lueur f d'espoir

razor ['reɪzər] n rasoir m; **razor blade** n lame f de rasoir

Rd abbr = **road**

RE n abbr (BRIT) = **religious education**

re [riː] prep concernant

reach [riːtʃ] n portée f, atteinte f; (of river etc) étendue f ▷ vt atteindre, arriver à; (conclusion, decision) parvenir à ▷ vi s'étendre; **out of/ within ~** (object) hors de/à portée; **reach out** vt tendre ▷ vi: **to ~ out (for)** allonger le bras (pour prendre)

react [riː'ækt] vi réagir; **reaction** [riː'ækʃən] n réaction f; **reactor** [riː'æktər] n réacteur m

read (pt, pp ~) [riːd, rɛd] vi lire ▷ vt lire; (understand) comprendre, interpréter; (study) étudier; (meter) relever; (subj: instrument etc) indiquer, marquer; **read out** vt lire à haute voix; **reader** n lecteur(-trice)

readily ['rɛdɪlɪ] adv volontiers, avec empressement; (easily) facilement

reading ['riːdɪŋ] n lecture f; (understanding) interprétation f; (on instrument) indications fpl

ready ['rɛdɪ] adj prêt(e); (willing) prêt, disposé(e); (available) disponible ▷ n: **at the ~** (Mil) prêt à faire feu; **when will my photos be ~?** quand est-ce que mes photos seront prêtes?; **to get ~** (as vi) se préparer; (as vt) préparer;

ready-cooked adj précuit(e); **ready-made** adj tout(e) faite(e)

real [rɪəl] adj (world, life) réel(le); (genuine) véritable; (proper) vrai(e) ▷ adv (US inf: very) vraiment; **real ale** n bière traditionnelle; **real estate** n biens fonciers or immobiliers; **realistic** [rɪə'lɪstɪk] adj réaliste; **reality** [riː'ælɪtɪ] n réalité f

reality TV n téléréalité f

realization [rɪəlaɪ'zeɪʃən] n (awareness) prise f de conscience; (fulfilment: also: of asset) réalisation f

realize ['rɪəlaɪz] vt (understand) se rendre compte de, prendre conscience de; (a project, Comm: asset) réaliser

really ['rɪəlɪ] adv vraiment; **~?** vraiment?, c'est vrai?

realm [rɛlm] n royaume m; (fig) domaine m

realtor ['rɪəltɔːr] n (US) agent immobilier

reappear [riːə'pɪər] vi réapparaître, reparaître

rear [rɪər] adj de derrière, arrière inv; (Aut: wheel etc) arrière ▷ n arrière m ▷ vt (cattle, family) élever ▷ vi (also: ~ up: animal) se cabrer

rearrange [riːə'reɪndʒ] vt réarranger

rear: **rear-view mirror** n (Aut) rétroviseur m; **rear-wheel drive** n (Aut) traction f arrière

reason ['riːzn] n raison f ▷ vi: **to ~ with sb** raisonner qn, faire entendre raison à qn; **it stands to ~ that** il va sans dire que; **reasonable** adj raisonnable; (not bad) acceptable; **reasonably** adv (behave) raisonnablement; (fairly) assez; **reasoning** n raisonnement m

reassurance [riːə'ʃuərəns] n (factual) assurance f, garantie f; (emotional) réconfort m

reassure [riːə'ʃuər] vt rassurer

rebate ['riːbeɪt] n (on tax etc) dégrèvement m

rebel n ['rɛbl] rebelle m/f ▷ vi [rɪ'bɛl] se rebeller, se révolter; **rebellion** [rɪ'bɛljən] n rébellion f, révolte f; **rebellious** [rɪ'bɛljəs] adj rebelle

rebuild [riː'bɪld] vt (irreg: like **build**) reconstruire

recall vt [rɪ'kɔːl] rappeler; (remember) se rappeler, se souvenir de ▷ n ['riːkɔl] rappel m; (ability to remember) mémoire f

rec'd abbr of **received**

receipt [rɪ'siːt] n (document) reçu m; (for parcel etc) accusé m de réception; (act of receiving) réception f; **receipts** npl (Comm) recettes fpl; **can I have a ~, please?** je peux avoir un reçu, s'il vous plaît?

receive [rɪ'siːv] vt recevoir; (guest) recevoir, accueillir; **receiver** n (Tel) récepteur m, combiné m; (Radio) récepteur m; (of stolen goods) receleur m; (for bankruptcies) administrateur m judiciaire

recent ['riːsnt] adj récent(e); **recently** adv récemment

reception [rɪ'sɛpʃən] n réception f; (welcome) accueil m, réception; **reception desk** n réception f; **receptionist** n réceptionniste m/f
recession [rɪ'sɛʃən] n (Econ) récession f
recharge [riː'tʃɑːdʒ] vt (battery) recharger
recipe ['rɛsɪpɪ] n recette f
recipient [rɪ'sɪpɪənt] n (of payment) bénéficiaire m/f; (of letter) destinataire m/f
recital [rɪ'saɪtl] n récital m
recite [rɪ'saɪt] vt (poem) réciter
reckless ['rɛkləs] adj (driver etc) imprudent(e); (spender etc) insouciant(e)
reckon ['rɛkən] vt (count) calculer, compter; (consider) considérer, estimer; (think): **I ~ (that)** ... je pense (que) ..., j'estime (que) ...
reclaim [rɪ'kleɪm] vt (land: from sea) assécher; (demand back) réclamer (le remboursement or la restitution de); (waste materials) récupérer
recline [rɪ'klaɪn] vi être allongé(e) or étendu(e)
recognition [rɛkəg'nɪʃən] n reconnaissance f; **transformed beyond ~** méconnaissable
recognize ['rɛkəgnaɪz] vt: **to ~ (by/as)** reconnaître (à/comme étant)
recollection [rɛkə'lɛkʃən] n souvenir m
recommend [rɛkə'mɛnd] vt recommander; **can you ~ a good restaurant?** pouvez-vous me conseiller un bon restaurant?; **recommendation** [rɛkəmɛn'deɪʃən] n recommandation f
reconcile ['rɛkənsaɪl] vt (two people) réconcilier; (two facts) concilier, accorder; **to ~ o.s.** se résigner à
reconsider [riː'kən'sɪdə] vt reconsidérer
reconstruct [riː'kən'strʌkt] vt (building) reconstruire; (crime, system) reconstituer
record n ['rɛkɔːd] rapport m, récit m; (of meeting etc) procès-verbal m; (register) registre m; (file) dossier m; (Comput) article m; (also: **police ~**) casier m judiciaire; (Mus: disc) disque m; (Sport) record m ▷ adj record inv ▷ vt [rɪ'kɔːd] (set down) noter; (Mus: song etc) enregistrer; **public ~s** archives fpl; **in ~ time** dans un temps record; **recorded delivery** n (BRIT Post): **to send sth recorded delivery** ≈ envoyer qch en recommandé; **recorder** n (Mus) flûte f à bec; **recording** n (Mus) enregistrement m; **record player** n tourne-disque m
recount [rɪ'kaunt] vt raconter
recover [rɪ'kʌvə] vt récupérer ▷ vi (from illness) se rétablir; (from shock) se remettre; **recovery** n récupération f; rétablissement m; (Econ) redressement m
recreate [riː'krɪ'eɪt] vt recréer
recreation [rɛkrɪ'eɪʃən] n (leisure) récréation f, détente f; **recreational drug** n drogue récréative; **recreational vehicle** n (US) camping-car m
recruit [rɪ'kruːt] n recrue f ▷ vt recruter; **recruitment** n recrutement m

rectangle ['rɛktæŋgl] n rectangle m; **rectangular** [rɛk'tæŋgjulə] adj rectangulaire
rectify ['rɛktɪfaɪ] vt (error) rectifier, corriger
rector ['rɛktə] n (Rel) pasteur m
recur [rɪ'kə] vi se reproduire; (idea, opportunity) se retrouver; (symptoms) réapparaître; **recurring** adj (problem) périodique, fréquent(e); (Math) périodique
recyclable [riː'saɪkləbl] adj recyclable
recycle [riː'saɪkl] vt, vi recycler
recycling [riː'saɪklɪŋ] n recyclage m
red [rɛd] n rouge m; (Pol: pej) rouge m/f ▷ adj rouge; (hair) roux (rousse); **in the ~** (account) à découvert; (business) en déficit; **Red Cross** n Croix-Rouge f; **redcurrant** n groseille f (rouge)
redeem [rɪ'diːm] vt (debt) rembourser; (sth in pawn) dégager; (fig, also Rel) racheter
red: red-haired adj roux (rousse); **redhead** n roux (rousse); **red-hot** adj chauffé(e) au rouge, brûlant(e); **red light** n: **to go through a red light** (Aut) brûler un feu rouge; **red-light district** n quartier mal famé
red meat n viande f rouge
reduce [rɪ'djuːs] vt réduire; (lower) abaisser; **"~ speed now"** (Aut) "ralentir"; **to ~ sb to tears** faire pleurer qn; **reduced** adj réduit(e); **"greatly reduced prices"** "gros rabais"; **at a reduced price** (goods) au rabais; (ticket etc) à prix réduit; **reduction** [rɪ'dʌkʃən] n réduction f; (of price) baisse f; (discount) rabais m; réduction; **is there a reduction for children/students?** y a-t-il une réduction pour les enfants/les étudiants?
redundancy [rɪ'dʌndənsɪ] n (BRIT) licenciement m, mise f au chômage
redundant [rɪ'dʌndnt] adj (BRIT: worker) licencié(e), mis(e) au chômage; (detail, object) superflu(e); **to be made ~** (worker) être licencié, être mis au chômage
reed [riːd] n (Bot) roseau m
reef [riːf] n (at sea) récif m, écueil m
reel [riːl] n bobine f; (Fishing) moulinet m; (Cine) bande f; (dance) quadrille écossais ▷ vi (sway) chanceler
ref [rɛf] n abbr (inf: = referee) arbitre m
refectory [rɪ'fɛktərɪ] n réfectoire m
refer [rɪ'fə] vt: **to ~ sb to** (inquirer, patient) adresser qn à; (reader: to text) renvoyer qn à ▷ vi: **to ~ to** (allude to) parler de, faire allusion à; (consult) se reporter à; (apply to) s'appliquer à
referee [rɛfə'riː] n arbitre m; (BRIT: for job application) répondant(e) ▷ vt arbitrer
reference ['rɛfrəns] n référence f, renvoi m; (mention) allusion f, mention f; (for job application: letter) références; lettre f de recommandation; **with ~ to** en ce qui concerne; (Comm: in letter) me référant à; **reference number** n (Comm) numéro m de

référence

refill vt [riː'fɪl] remplir à nouveau; (pen, lighter etc) recharger ▷ n ['riːfɪl] (for pen etc) recharge f

refine [rɪ'faɪn] vt (sugar, oil) raffiner; (taste) affiner; (idea, theory) peaufiner; **refined** adj (person, taste) raffiné(e); **refinery** n raffinerie f

reflect [rɪ'flɛkt] vt (light, image) réfléchir, refléter ▷ vi (think) réfléchir, méditer; **it ~s badly on him** cela le discrédite; **it ~s well on him** c'est tout à son honneur; **reflection** [rɪ'flɛkʃən] n réflexion f; (image) reflet m; **on reflection** réflexion faite

reflex ['riːflɛks] adj, n réflexe (m)

reform [rɪ'fɔːm] n réforme f ▷ vt réformer

refrain [rɪ'freɪn] vi: **to ~ from doing** s'abstenir de faire ▷ n refrain m

refresh [rɪ'frɛʃ] vt rafraîchir; (subj: food, sleep etc) redonner des forces à; **refreshing** adj (drink) rafraîchissant(e); (sleep) réparateur(-trice); **refreshments** npl rafraîchissements mpl

refrigerator [rɪ'frɪdʒəreɪtəʳ] n réfrigérateur m, frigidaire m

refuel [riː'fjʊəl] vi se ravitailler en carburant

refuge ['rɛfjuːdʒ] n refuge m; **to take ~ in** se réfugier dans; **refugee** [rɛfjuˈdʒiː] n réfugié(e)

refund n ['riːfʌnd] remboursement m ▷ vt [rɪ'fʌnd] rembourser

refurbish [riː'fəːbɪʃ] vt remettre à neuf

refusal [rɪ'fjuːzəl] n refus m; **to have first ~ on sth** avoir droit de préemption sur qch

refuse¹ ['rɛfjuːs] n ordures fpl, détritus mpl

refuse² [rɪ'fjuːz] vt, vi refuser; **to ~ to do sth** refuser de faire qch

regain [rɪ'geɪn] vt (lost ground) regagner; (strength) retrouver

regard [rɪ'gɑːd] n respect m, estime f, considération f ▷ vt considérer; **to give one's ~s to** faire ses amitiés à; **"with kindest ~s"** "bien amicalement"; **as ~s, with ~ to** en ce qui concerne; **regarding** prep en ce qui concerne; **regardless** adv quand même; **regardless of** sans se soucier de

regenerate [rɪ'dʒɛnəreɪt] vt régénérer ▷ vi se régénérer

reggae ['rɛgeɪ] n reggae m

regiment ['rɛdʒɪmənt] n régiment m

region ['riːdʒən] n région f; **in the ~ of** (fig) aux alentours de; **regional** adj régional(e)

register ['rɛdʒɪstəʳ] n registre m; (also: **electoral ~**) liste électorale ▷ vt enregistrer, inscrire; (birth) déclarer; (vehicle) immatriculer; (letter) envoyer en recommandé; (subj: instrument) marquer ▷ vi s'inscrire; (at hotel) signer le registre; (make impression) être (bien) compris(e); **registered** adj (BRIT: letter) recommandé(e)

registered trademark n marque déposée

registrar ['rɛdʒɪstrɑːʳ] n officier m de l'état civil

registration [rɛdʒɪs'treɪʃən] n (act) enregistrement m; (of student) inscription f; (BRIT Aut: also: **~ number**) numéro m d'immatriculation

registry office ['rɛdʒɪstrɪ-] n (BRIT) bureau m de l'état civil; **to get married in a ~** ≈ se marier à la mairie

regret [rɪ'grɛt] n regret m ▷ vt regretter; **regrettable** adj regrettable, fâcheux(-euse)

regular ['rɛgjuləʳ] adj régulier(-ière); (usual) habituel(le), normal(e); (soldier) de métier; (Comm: size) ordinaire ▷ n (client etc) habitué(e); **regularly** adv régulièrement

regulate ['rɛgjuleɪt] vt régler; **regulation** [rɛgjuˈleɪʃən] n (rule) règlement m; (adjustment) réglage m

rehabilitation ['riːəbɪlɪ'teɪʃən] n (of offender) réhabilitation f; (of addict) réadaptation f

rehearsal [rɪ'həːsəl] n répétition f

rehearse [rɪ'həːs] vt répéter

reign [reɪn] n règne m ▷ vi régner

reimburse [riːɪm'bəːs] vt rembourser

rein [reɪn] n (for horse) rêne f

reincarnation [riːɪnkɑːˈneɪʃən] n réincarnation f

reindeer ['reɪndɪəʳ] n (pl inv) renne m

reinforce [riːɪn'fɔːs] vt renforcer; **reinforcements** npl (Mil) renfort(s) m(pl)

reinstate [riːɪn'steɪt] vt rétablir, réintégrer

reject n ['riːdʒɛkt] (Comm) article m de rebut ▷ vt [rɪ'dʒɛkt] refuser; (idea) rejeter; **rejection** [rɪ'dʒɛkʃən] n rejet m, refus m

rejoice [rɪ'dʒɔɪs] vi: **to ~ (at or over)** se réjouir (de)

relate [rɪ'leɪt] vt (tell) raconter; (connect) établir un rapport entre ▷ vi: **to ~ to** (connect) se rapporter à; **to ~ to sb** (interact) entretenir des rapports avec qn; **related** adj apparenté(e); **related to** (subject) lié(e) à; **relating to** prep concernant

relation [rɪ'leɪʃən] n (person) parent(e); (link) rapport m, lien m; **relations** npl (relatives) famille f; **relationship** n rapport m, lien m; (personal ties) relations fpl, rapports; (also: **family relationship**) lien de parenté; (affair) liaison f

relative ['rɛlətɪv] n parent(e) ▷ adj relatif(-ive); (respective) respectif(-ive); **relatively** adv relativement

relax [rɪ'læks] vi (muscle) se relâcher; (person: unwind) se détendre ▷ vt relâcher; (mind, person) détendre; **relaxation** [riːlæk'seɪʃən] n relâchement m; (of mind) détente f; (recreation) détente, délassement m; **relaxed** adj relâché(e); détendu(e); **relaxing** adj délassant(e)

relay ['riːleɪ] n (Sport) course f de relais ▷ vt

(*message*) retransmettre, relayer

release [rɪ'liːs] *n* (*from prison, obligation*) libération *f*; (*of gas etc*) émission *f*; (*of film etc*) sortie *f*; (*new recording*) disque *m* ▷ *vt* (*prisoner*) libérer; (*book, film*) sortir; (*report, news*) rendre public, publier; (*gas etc*) émettre, dégager; (*free: from wreckage etc*) dégager; (*Tech: catch, spring etc*) déclencher; (*let go: person, animal*) relâcher; (: *hand, object*) lâcher; (: *grip, brake*) desserrer

relegate ['rɛləgeɪt] *vt* reléguer; (*BRIT Sport*): **to be ~d** descendre dans une division inférieure

relent [rɪ'lɛnt] *vi* se laisser fléchir; **relentless** *adj* implacable; (*non-stop*) continuel(le)

relevant ['rɛləvənt] *adj* (*question*) pertinent(e); (*corresponding*) approprié(e); (*fact*) significatif(-ive); (*information*) utile

reliable [rɪ'laɪəbl] *adj* (*person, firm*) sérieux(-euse), fiable; (*method, machine*) fiable; (*news, information*) sûr(e)

relic ['rɛlɪk] *n* (*Rel*) relique *f*; (*of the past*) vestige *m*

relief [rɪ'liːf] *n* (*from pain, anxiety*) soulagement *m*; (*help, supplies*) secours *m(pl)*; (*Art, Geo*) relief *m*

relieve [rɪ'liːv] *vt* (*pain, patient*) soulager; (*fear, worry*) dissiper; (*bring help*) secourir; (*take over from: gen*) relayer; (: *guard*) relever; **to ~ sb of sth** débarrasser qn de qch; **to ~ o.s.** (*euphemism*) se soulager, faire ses besoins; **relieved** *adj* soulagé(e)

religion [rɪ'lɪdʒən] *n* religion *f*

religious [rɪ'lɪdʒəs] *adj* religieux(-euse); (*book*) de piété; **religious education** *n* instruction religieuse

relish ['rɛlɪʃ] *n* (*Culin*) condiment *m*; (*enjoyment*) délectation *f* ▷ *vt* (*food etc*) savourer; **to ~ doing** se délecter à faire

relocate [riːləʊ'keɪt] *vt* (*business*) transférer ▷ *vi* se transférer, s'installer *or* s'établir ailleurs

reluctance [rɪ'lʌktəns] *n* répugnance *f*

reluctant [rɪ'lʌktənt] *adj* peu disposé(e), qui hésite; **reluctantly** *adv* à contrecœur, sans enthousiasme

rely on [rɪ'laɪ-] *vt fus* (*be dependent on*) dépendre de; (*trust*) compter sur

remain [rɪ'meɪn] *vi* rester; **remainder** *n* reste *m*; (*Comm*) fin *f* de série; **remaining** *adj* qui reste; **remains** *npl* restes *mpl*

remand [rɪ'mɑːnd] *n*: **on ~** en détention préventive ▷ *vt*: **to be ~ed in custody** être placé(e) en détention préventive

remark [rɪ'mɑːk] *n* remarque *f*, observation *f* ▷ *vt* (*faire*) remarquer, dire; **remarkable** *adj* remarquable

remarry [riː'mærɪ] *vi* se remarier

remedy ['rɛmədɪ] *n*: **~ (for)** remède *m* (contre *or* à) ▷ *vt* remédier à

remember [rɪ'mɛmbər] *vt* se rappeler, se

souvenir de; (*send greetings*): **~ me to him** saluez-le de ma part; **Remembrance Day** [rɪ'mɛmbrəns-] *n* (*BRIT*) ≈ (le jour de) l'Armistice *m*, ≈ le 11 novembre

● REMEMBRANCE DAY

● **Remembrance Day** ou **Remembrance Sunday** est le dimanche le plus proche du 11 novembre, jour où la Première Guerre mondiale a officiellement pris fin. Il rend hommage aux victimes des deux guerres mondiales. À cette occasion, on observe deux minutes de silence à 11h, heure de la signature de l'armistice avec l'Allemagne en 1918; certaines membres de la famille royale et du gouvernement déposent des gerbes de coquelicots au cénotaphe de Whitehall, et des couronnes sont placées sur les monuments aux morts dans toute la Grande-Bretagne; par ailleurs, les gens portent des coquelicots artificiels fabriqués et vendus par des membres de la légion britannique blessés au combat, au profit des blessés de guerre et de leur famille.

remind [rɪ'maɪnd] *vt*: **to ~ sb of sth** rappeler qch à qn; **to ~ sb to do** faire penser à qn à faire, rappeler à qn qu'il doit faire; **reminder** *n* (*Comm: letter*) rappel *m*; (*note etc*) pense-bête *m*; (*souvenir*) souvenir *m*

reminiscent [rɛmɪ'nɪsnt] *adj*: **~ of** qui rappelle, qui fait penser à

remnant ['rɛmnənt] *n* reste *m*, restant *m*; (*of cloth*) coupon *m*

remorse [rɪ'mɔːs] *n* remords *m*

remote [rɪ'məʊt] *adj* éloigné(e), lointain(e); (*person*) distant(e); (*possibility*) vague; **remote control** *n* télécommande *f*; **remotely** *adv* au loin; (*slightly*) très vaguement

removal [rɪ'muːvəl] *n* (*taking away*) enlèvement *m*; suppression *f*; (*BRIT: from house*) déménagement *m*; (*from office: dismissal*) renvoi *m*; (*of stain*) nettoyage *m*; (*Med*) ablation *f*; **removal man** (*irreg*) *n* (*BRIT*) déménageur *m*; **removal van** *n* (*BRIT*) camion *m* de déménagement

remove [rɪ'muːv] *vt* enlever, retirer; (*employee*) renvoyer; (*stain*) faire partir; (*abuse*) supprimer; (*doubt*) chasser

Renaissance [rɪ'neɪsɑ̃s] *n*: **the ~** la Renaissance

rename [riː'neɪm] *vt* rebaptiser

render ['rɛndər] *vt* rendre

rendezvous ['rɒndɪvuː] *n* rendez-vous *m inv*

renew [rɪ'njuː] *vt* renouveler; (*negotiations*) reprendre; (*acquaintance*) renouer

renovate ['rɛnəveɪt] *vt* rénover; (*work of art*) restaurer

renowned [rɪ'naund] adj renommé(e)

rent [rɛnt] pt, pp of **rend** ▷ n loyer m ▷ vt louer; **rental** n (for television, car) (prix m de) location f

reorganize [riː'ɔːɡənaɪz] vt réorganiser

rep [rɛp] n abbr (Comm) = **representative**

repair [rɪ'pɛəʳ] n réparation f ▷ vt réparer; **in good/bad ~ed** en bon/mauvais état; **where can I get this ~ed?** où est-ce que je peux faire réparer ceci?; **repair kit** n trousse f de réparations

repay [riː'peɪ] vt (irreg: like **pay**) (money, creditor) rembourser; (sb's efforts) récompenser; **repayment** n remboursement m

repeat [rɪ'piːt] n (Radio, TV) reprise f ▷ vt répéter; (promise, attack, also Comm: order) renouveler; (Scol: a class) redoubler ▷ vi répéter; **can you ~ that, please?** pouvez-vous répéter, s'il vous plaît?; **repeatedly** adv souvent, à plusieurs reprises; **repeat prescription** n (BRIT): **I'd like a repeat prescription** je voudrais renouveler mon ordonnance

repellent [rɪ'pɛlənt] adj repoussant(e) ▷ n: **insect ~** insectifuge m

repercussions [riːpə'kʌʃənz] npl répercussions fpl

repetition [rɛpɪ'tɪʃən] n répétition f

repetitive [rɪ'pɛtɪtɪv] adj (movement, work) répétitif(-ive); (speech) plein(e) de redites

replace [rɪ'pleɪs] vt (put back) remettre, replacer; (take the place of) remplacer; **replacement** n (substitution) remplacement m; (person) remplaçant(e)

replay ['riːpleɪ] n (of match) match rejoué; (of tape, film) répétition f

replica ['rɛplɪkə] n réplique f, copie exacte

reply [rɪ'plaɪ] n réponse f ▷ vi répondre

report [rɪ'pɔːt] n rapport m; (Press etc) reportage m; (BRIT: also: **school ~**) bulletin m (scolaire); (of gun) détonation f ▷ vt rapporter, faire un compte rendu de; (Press etc) faire un reportage sur; (notify: accident) signaler; (: culprit) dénoncer ▷ vi (make a report) faire un rapport; **I'd like to ~ a theft** je voudrais signaler un vol; (present o.s.): **to ~ (to sb)** se présenter (chez qn); **report card** n (US, SCOTTISH) bulletin m (scolaire); **reportedly** adv: **she is reportedly living in Spain** elle habiterait en Espagne; **he reportedly told them to ...** il leur aurait dit de ...; **reporter** n reporter m

represent [rɛprɪ'zɛnt] vt représenter; (view, belief) présenter, expliquer; (describe): **to ~ sth as** présenter or décrire qch comme; **representation** [rɛprɪzɛn'teɪʃən] n représentation f; **representative** n représentant(e); (US Pol) député m ▷ adj représentatif(-ive), caractéristique

repress [rɪ'prɛs] vt réprimer; **repression** [rɪ'prɛʃən] n répression f

reprimand ['rɛprɪmɑːnd] n réprimande f ▷ vt réprimander

reproduce [riːprə'djuːs] vt reproduire ▷ vi se reproduire; **reproduction** [riːprə'dʌkʃən] n reproduction f

reptile ['rɛptaɪl] n reptile m

republic [rɪ'pʌblɪk] n république f; **republican** adj, n républicain(e)

reputable ['rɛpjutəbl] adj de bonne réputation; (occupation) honorable

reputation [rɛpju'teɪʃən] n réputation f

request [rɪ'kwɛst] n demande f; (formal) requête f ▷ vt: **to ~ (of or from sb)** demander (à qn); **request stop** n (BRIT: for bus) arrêt facultatif

require [rɪ'kwaɪəʳ] vt (need: subj: person) avoir besoin de; (: thing, situation) nécessiter, demander; (want) exiger; (order): **to ~ sb to do sth/sth of sb** exiger que qn fasse qch/qch de qn; **requirement** n (need) exigence f; besoin m; (condition) condition f (requise)

resat [riː'sæt] pt, pp of **resit**

rescue ['rɛskjuː] n (from accident) sauvetage m; (help) secours mpl ▷ vt sauver

research [rɪ'sɜːtʃ] n recherche(s) f(pl) ▷ vt faire des recherches sur

resemblance [rɪ'zɛmbləns] n ressemblance f

resemble [rɪ'zɛmbl] vt ressembler à

resent [rɪ'zɛnt] vt être contrarié e par; **resentful** adj irrité(e), plein(e) de ressentiment; **resentment** n ressentiment m

reservation [rɛzə'veɪʃən] n (booking) réservation f; **to make a ~ (in an hotel/a restaurant/on a plane)** réserver or retenir une chambre/une table/une place; **reservation desk** n (US: in hotel) réception f

reserve [rɪ'zɜːv] n réserve f; (Sport) remplaçant(e) ▷ vt (seats etc) réserver, retenir; **reserved** adj réservé(e)

reservoir ['rɛzəvwɑːʳ] n réservoir m

reshuffle [riː'ʃʌfl] n: **Cabinet ~** (Pol) remaniement ministériel

residence ['rɛzɪdəns] n résidence f; **residence permit** n (BRIT) permis m de séjour

resident ['rɛzɪdənt] n (of country) résident(e); (of area, house) habitant(e); (in hotel) pensionnaire ▷ adj résidant(e); **residential** [rɛzɪ'dɛnʃəl] adj de résidence; (area) résidentiel(le); (course) avec hébergement sur place

residue ['rɛzɪdjuː] n reste m; (Chem, Physics) résidu m

resign [rɪ'zaɪn] vt (one's post) se démettre de ▷ vi démissionner; **to ~ o.s. to (endure)** se résigner à; **resignation** [rɛzɪɡ'neɪʃən] n (from post) démission f; (state of mind) résignation f

resin ['rɛzɪn] n résine f

resist [rɪˈzɪst] vt résister à; **resistance** n
résistance f

resit (BRIT) vt [riːˈsɪt] (pt, pp **resat**) (exam)
repasser ▷ n [ˈriːsɪt] deuxième session f (d'un
examen)

resolution [rezəˈluːʃən] n résolution f

resolve [rɪˈzɒlv] n résolution f ▷ vt (decide): **to
~ to do** résoudre or décider de faire; (problem)
résoudre

resort [rɪˈzɔːt] n (seaside town) station f
balnéaire; (for skiing) station de ski; (recourse)
recours m ▷ vi: **to ~ to** avoir recours à; **in the
last ~** en dernier ressort

resource [rɪˈsɔːs] n ressource f; **resourceful**
adj ingénieux(-euse), débrouillard(e)

respect [rɪsˈpɛkt] n respect m ▷ vt respecter;
respectable adj respectable; (quite
good: result etc) honorable; **respectful**
adj respectueux(-euse); **respective**
adj respectif(-ive); **respectively** adv
respectivement

respite [ˈrɛspaɪt] n répit m

respond [rɪsˈpɒnd] vi répondre; (react) réagir;
response [rɪsˈpɒns] n réponse f; (reaction)
réaction f

responsibility [rɪspɒnsɪˈbɪlɪti] n
responsabilité f

responsible [rɪsˈpɒnsɪbl] adj (liable): **~ (for)**
responsable (de); (person) digne de confiance;
(job) qui comporte des responsabilités;
responsibly adv avec sérieux

responsive [rɪsˈpɒnsɪv] adj (student, audience)
réceptif(-ive); (brakes, steering) sensible

rest [rɛst] n repos m; (stop) arrêt m, pause f;
(Mus) silence m; (support) support m, appui m;
(remainder) reste m, restant m ▷ vi se reposer;
(be supported): **to ~ on** appuyer or reposer sur
▷ vt (lean): **to ~ sth on/against** appuyer qch
sur/contre; **the ~ of them** les autres

restaurant [ˈrɛstərɔŋ] n restaurant m;
restaurant car n (BRIT Rail) wagon-
restaurant m

restless [ˈrɛstlɪs] adj agité(e)

restoration [rɛstəˈreɪʃən] n (of building)
restauration f; (of stolen goods) restitution f

restore [rɪsˈtɔːʳ] vt (building) restaurer; (sth
stolen) restituer; (peace, health) rétablir; **to ~ to**
(former state) ramener à

restrain [rɪsˈtreɪn] vt (feeling) contenir;
(person): **to ~ (from doing)** retenir (de
faire); **restraint** n (restriction) contrainte f;
(moderation) retenue f; (of style) sobriété f

restrict [rɪsˈtrɪkt] vt restreindre, limiter;
restriction [rɪsˈtrɪkʃən] n restriction f,
limitation f

rest room n (US) toilettes fpl

restructure [riːˈstrʌktʃəʳ] vt restructurer

result [rɪˈzʌlt] n résultat m ▷ vi: **to ~ in** aboutir
à, se terminer par; **as a ~ of** à la suite de

resume [rɪˈzjuːm] vt (work, journey) reprendre
▷ vi (work etc) reprendre

résumé [ˈreɪzjuːmeɪ] n (summary) résumé m;
(US: curriculum vitae) curriculum vitae m inv

resuscitate [rɪˈsʌsɪteɪt] vt (Med) réanimer

retail [ˈriːteɪl] adj de or au détail ▷ adv au
détail; **retailer** n détaillant(e)

retain [rɪˈteɪn] vt (keep) garder, conserver

retaliation [rɪtælɪˈeɪʃən] n représailles fpl,
vengeance f

retarded [rɪˈtɑːdɪd] adj retardé(e)

retire [rɪˈtaɪəʳ] vi (give up work) prendre sa
retraite; (withdraw) se retirer, partir; (go to
bed) (aller) se coucher; **retired** adj (person)
retraité(e); **retirement** n retraite f

retort [rɪˈtɔːt] vi riposter

retreat [rɪˈtriːt] n retraite f ▷ vi battre en
retraite

retrieve [rɪˈtriːv] vt (sth lost) récupérer;
(situation, honour) sauver; (error, loss) réparer;
(Comput) rechercher

retrospect [ˈrɛtrəspɛkt] n: **in ~**
rétrospectivement, après coup;
retrospective [rɛtrəˈspɛktɪv] adj
rétrospectif(-ive); (law) rétroactif(-ive) ▷ n
(Art) rétrospective f

return [rɪˈtəːn] n (going or coming back) retour
m; (of sth stolen etc) restitution f; (Finance:
from land, shares) rapport m ▷ cpd (journey) de
retour; (BRIT: ticket) aller et retour; (match)
retour ▷ vi (person etc: come back) revenir;
(: go back) retourner ▷ vt rendre; (bring back)
rapporter; (send back) renvoyer; (put back)
remettre; (Pol: candidate) élire; **returns**
npl (Comm) recettes fpl; (Finance) bénéfices
mpl; **many happy ~s (of the day)!** bon
anniversaire!; **by ~ (of post)** par retour (du
courrier); **in ~ (for)** en échange (de); **a ~
(ticket) for …** un billet aller et retour pour …;
return ticket n (esp BRIT) billet m aller-retour

reunion [riːˈjuːnɪən] n réunion f

reunite [riːjuːˈnaɪt] vt réunir

revamp [riːˈvæmp] vt (house) retaper; (firm)
réorganiser

reveal [rɪˈviːl] vt (make known) révéler; (display)
laisser voir; **revealing** adj révélateur(-trice);
(dress) au décolleté généreux or suggestif

revel [ˈrɛvl] vi: **to ~ in sth/in doing** se délecter
de qch/à faire

revelation [rɛvəˈleɪʃən] n révélation f

revenge [rɪˈvɛndʒ] n vengeance f; (in game
etc) revanche f ▷ vt venger; **to take ~ (on)** se
venger (sur)

revenue [ˈrɛvənjuː] n revenu m

Reverend [ˈrɛvərənd] adj (in titles): **the ~
John Smith** (Anglican) le révérend John Smith;
(Catholic) l'abbé (John) Smith; (Protestant) le
pasteur (John) Smith

reversal [rɪˈvəːsl] n (of opinion) revirement

m; (of order) renversement m; (of direction) changement m

reverse [rɪ'vəːs] n contraire m, opposé m; (back) dos m, envers m; (of paper) verso m; (of coin) revers m; (Aut: also: ~ **gear**) marche f arrière ▷ adj (order, direction) opposé(e), inverse ▷ vt (order, position) changer, inverser; (direction, policy) changer complètement de; (decision) annuler; (roles) renverser ▷ vi (BRIT Aut) faire marche arrière; **reverse-charge call** n (BRIT Tel) communication f en PCV; **reversing lights** npl (BRIT Aut) feux mpl de marche arrière or de recul

revert [rɪ'vəːt] vi: **to ~ to** revenir à, retourner à

review [rɪ'vjuː] n revue f; (of book, film) critique f; (of situation, policy) examen m, bilan m; (us: examination) examen ▷ vt passer en revue; faire la critique de; examiner

revise [rɪ'vaɪz] vt réviser, modifier; (manuscript) revoir, corriger ▷ vi (study) réviser; **revision** [rɪ'vɪʒən] n révision f

revival [rɪ'vaɪvəl] n reprise f; (recovery) rétablissement m; (of faith) renouveau m

revive [rɪ'vaɪv] vt (person) ranimer; (economy) relancer; (hope, courage) raviver, faire renaître; (play, fashion) reprendre ▷ vi (person) reprendre connaissance; (: from ill health) se rétablir; (hope etc) renaître; (activity) reprendre

revolt [rɪ'vəʊlt] n révolte f ▷ vi se révolter, se rebeller ▷ vt révolter, dégoûter; **revolting** adj dégoûtant(e)

revolution [rɛvə'luːʃən] n révolution f; (of wheel etc) tour m, révolution; **revolutionary** adj, n révolutionnaire (m/f)

revolve [rɪ'vɔlv] vi tourner

revolver [rɪ'vɔlvəʳ] n revolver m

reward [rɪ'wɔːd] n récompense f ▷ vt: **to ~ (for)** récompenser (de); **rewarding** adj (fig) qui (en) vaut la peine, gratifiant(e)

rewind [riː'waɪnd] vt (irreg: like wind) (tape) réembobiner

rewritable [riː'raɪtəbl] adj (CD, DVD) réinscriptible

rewrite [riː'raɪt] (pt rewrote, pp rewritten) vt récrire

rheumatism ['ruːmətɪzəm] n rhumatisme m

Rhine [raɪn] n: **the (River) ~** le Rhin

rhinoceros [raɪ'nɔsərəs] n rhinocéros m

Rhône [rəʊn] n: **the (River) ~** le Rhône

rhubarb ['ruːbɑːb] n rhubarbe f

rhyme [raɪm] n rime f; (verse) vers mpl

rhythm ['rɪðm] n rythme m

rib [rɪb] n (Anat) côte f

ribbon ['rɪbən] n ruban m; **in ~s** (torn) en lambeaux

rice [raɪs] n riz m; **rice pudding** n riz m au lait

rich [rɪtʃ] adj riche; (gift, clothes) somptueux(-euse); **to be ~ in sth** être riche en qch

rid [rɪd] (pt, pp ~) vt: **to ~ sb of** débarrasser qn de; **to get ~ of** se débarrasser de

riddle ['rɪdl] n (puzzle) énigme f ▷ vt: **to be ~d with** être criblé(e) de; (fig) être en proie à

ride [raɪd] n promenade f, tour m; (distance covered) trajet m ▷ vb (pt rode, pp ridden) ▷ vi (as sport) monter (à cheval), faire du cheval; (go somewhere: on horse, bicycle) aller (à cheval or bicyclette etc); (travel: on bicycle, motor cycle, bus) rouler ▷ vt (a horse) monter; (distance) parcourir, faire; **to ~ a horse/bicycle** monter à cheval/à bicyclette; **to take sb for a ~** (fig) faire marcher qn; (cheat) rouler qn; **rider** n cavalier(-ière); (in race) jockey m; (on bicycle) cycliste m/f; (on motorcycle) motocycliste m/f

ridge [rɪdʒ] n (of hill) faîte m; (of roof, mountain) arête f; (on object) strie f

ridicule ['rɪdɪkjuːl] n ridicule m; dérision f ▷ vt ridiculiser, tourner en dérision; **ridiculous** [rɪ'dɪkjuləs] adj ridicule

riding ['raɪdɪŋ] n équitation f; **riding school** n manège m, école f d'équitation

rife [raɪf] adj répandu(e); **~ with** abondant(e) en

rifle ['raɪfl] n fusil m (à canon rayé) ▷ vt vider, dévaliser

rift [rɪft] n fente f, fissure f; (fig: disagreement) désaccord m

rig [rɪg] n (also: **oil ~**: on land) derrick m; (: at sea) plate-forme pétrolière ▷ vt (election etc) truquer

right [raɪt] adj (true) juste, exact(e); (correct) bon (bonne); (suitable) approprié(e), convenable; (just) juste, équitable; (morally good) bien inv; (not left) droit(e) ▷ n (moral good) bien m; (title, claim) droit m; (not left) droite f ▷ adv (answer) correctement; (treat) bien, comme il faut; (not on the left) à droite ▷ vt redresser ▷ excl bon!; **do you have the ~ time?** avez-vous l'heure juste or exacte?; **to be ~** (person) avoir raison; (answer) être juste or correct(e); **by ~s** en toute justice; **on the ~** à droite; **to be in the ~** avoir raison; **~ in the middle** en plein milieu; **~ away** immédiatement; **right angle** n (Math) angle droit; **rightful** adj (heir) légitime; **right-hand** adj: **the right-hand side** la droite; **right-hand drive** n (BRIT) conduite f à droite; (vehicle) véhicule m avec la conduite à droite; **right-handed** adj (person) droitier(-ière); **rightly** adv bien, correctement; (with reason) à juste titre; **right of way** n (on path etc) droit m de passage; (Aut) priorité f; **right-wing** adj (Pol) de droite

rigid ['rɪdʒɪd] adj rigide; (principle, control) strict(e)

rigorous ['rɪgərəs] adj rigoureux(-euse)

rim [rɪm] n bord m; (of spectacles) monture f; (of

r

wheel) jante f

rind [raɪnd] n (*of bacon*) couenne f; (*of lemon etc*) écorce f, zeste m; (*of cheese*) croûte f

ring [rɪŋ] n anneau m; (*on finger*) bague f; (*also:* **wedding ~**) alliance f; (*of people, objects*) cercle m; (*of spies*) réseau m; (*of smoke etc*) rond m; (*arena*) piste f, arène f; (*for boxing*) ring m; (*sound of bell*) sonnerie f ⊳ vb (*pt* **rang**, *pp* **rung**) ⊳ vi (*telephone, bell*) sonner; (*person: by telephone*) téléphoner; (*ears*) bourdonner; (*also:* **~ out**: *voice, words*) retentir ⊳ vt (BRIT Tel: *also:* **~ up**) téléphoner à, appeler; **to ~ the bell** sonner; **to give sb a ~** (Tel) passer un coup de téléphone or de fil à qn; **ring back** vt, vi (BRIT Tel) rappeler; **ring off** vi (BRIT Tel) raccrocher; **ring up** (BRIT) ⊳ vt (Tel) téléphoner à, appeler; **ringing tone** n (BRIT Tel) tonalité f d'appel; **ringleader** n (*of gang*) chef m, meneur m; **ring road** n (BRIT) rocade f; (*motorway*) périphérique m; **ringtone** n (*on mobile*) sonnerie f (*de téléphone portable*)

rink [rɪŋk] n (*also:* **ice ~**) patinoire f

rinse [rɪns] n rinçage m ⊳ vt rincer

riot ['raɪət] n émeute f, bagarres fpl ⊳ vi (*demonstrators*) manifester avec violence; (*population*) se soulever, se révolter; **to run ~** se déchaîner

rip [rɪp] n déchirure f ⊳ vt déchirer ⊳ vi se déchirer; **rip off** vt (*inf: cheat*) arnaquer; **rip up** vt déchirer

ripe [raɪp] adj (*fruit*) mûr(e); (*cheese*) fait(e)

rip-off ['rɪpɔf] n (*inf*): **it's a ~!** c'est du vol manifeste!, c'est de l'arnaque!

ripple ['rɪpl] n ride f, ondulation f; (*of applause, laughter*) cascade f ⊳ vi se rider, onduler

rise [raɪz] n (*slope*) côte f, pente f; (*hill*) élévation f; (*increase: in wages:* BRIT) augmentation f; (*: in prices, temperature*) hausse f, augmentation f; (*fig: to power etc*) ascension f ⊳ vi (*pt* **rose**, *pp* **~n**) s'élever, monter; (*prices, numbers*) augmenter, monter; (*waters, river*) monter; (*sun, wind, person: from chair, bed*) se lever; (*also:* **~ up**: *tower, building*) s'élever; (*: rebel*) se révolter; se rebeller; (*in rank*) s'élever; **to give ~ to** donner lieu à; **to ~ to the occasion** se montrer à la hauteur; **risen** ['rɪzn] pp of **rise**; **rising** adj (*increasing: number, prices*) en hausse; (*tide*) montant(e); (*sun, moon*) levant(e)

risk [rɪsk] n risque m ⊳ vt risquer; **to take** or **run the ~ of doing** courir le risque de faire; **at ~** en danger; **at one's own ~** à ses risques et périls; **risky** adj risqué(e)

rite [raɪt] n rite m; **the last ~s** les derniers sacrements

ritual ['rɪtjuəl] adj rituel(le) ⊳ n rituel m

rival ['raɪvl] n rival(e); (*in business*) concurrent(e) ⊳ adj rival(e); qui fait concurrence ⊳ vt (*match*) égaler; **rivalry** n rivalité f; (*in business*) concurrence f

river ['rɪvə'] n rivière f; (*major: also fig*) fleuve m ⊳ cpd (*port, traffic*) fluvial(e); **up/down ~** en amont/aval; **riverbank** n rive f, berge f

rivet ['rɪvɪt] n rivet m ⊳ vt (*fig*) river, fixer

Riviera [rɪvɪ'eərə] n: **the (French) ~** la Côte d'Azur

road [rəud] n route f; (*in town*) rue f; (*fig*) chemin, voie f ⊳ cpd (*accident*) de la route; **major/minor ~** route principale or à priorité/voie secondaire; **which ~ do I take for ...?** quelle route dois-je prendre pour aller à...?; **roadblock** n barrage routier; **road map** n carte routière; **road rage** n comportement très agressif de certains usagers de la route; **road safety** n sécurité routière; **roadside** n bord m de la route, bas-côté m; **roadsign** n panneau m de signalisation; **road tax** n (BRIT Aut) taxe f sur les automobiles; **roadworks** npl travaux mpl (de réfection des routes)

roam [rəum] vi errer, vagabonder

roar [rɔː'] n rugissement m; (*of crowd*) hurlements mpl; (*of vehicle, thunder, storm*) grondement m ⊳ vi rugir; hurler; gronder; **to ~ with laughter** rire à gorge déployée; **to do a ~ing trade** faire des affaires en or

roast [rəust] n rôti m ⊳ vt (*meat*) (faire) rôtir; (*coffee*) griller, torréfier; **roast beef** n rôti m de bœuf, rosbif m

rob [rɔb] vt (*person*) voler; (*bank*) dévaliser; **to ~ sb of sth** voler or dérober qch à qn; (*fig: deprive*) priver qn de qch; **robber** n bandit m, voleur m; **robbery** n vol m

robe [rəub] n (*for ceremony etc*) robe f; (*also:* **bath~**) peignoir m; (*us: rug*) couverture f ⊳ vt revêtir (d'une robe)

robin ['rɔbɪn] n rouge-gorge m

robot ['rəubɔt] n robot m

robust [rəu'bʌst] adj robuste; (*material, appetite*) solide

rock [rɔk] n (*substance*) roche f, roc m; (*boulder*) rocher m, roche; (*us: small stone*) caillou m; (BRIT: *sweet*) ≈ sucre m d'orge ⊳ vt (*swing gently: cradle*) balancer; (*: child*) bercer; (*shake*) ébranler, secouer ⊳ vi se balancer, être ébranlé(e) or secoué(e); **on the ~s** (*drink*) avec des glaçons; (*marriage etc*) en train de craquer; **rock and roll** n rock (and roll) m, rock'n'roll m; **rock climbing** n varappe f

rocket ['rɔkɪt] n fusée f; (Mil) fusée, roquette f; (Culin) roquette

rocking chair ['rɔkɪŋ-] n fauteuil m à bascule

rocky ['rɔkɪ] adj (*hill*) rocheux(-euse); (*path*) rocailleux(-euse)

rod [rɔd] n (*metallic*) tringle f; (Tech) tige f; (*wooden*) baguette f; (*also:* **fishing ~**) canne f à pêche

rode [rəud] pt of **ride**

rodent ['rəudnt] n rongeur m

rogue [rəug] n coquin(e)

role [rəul] n rôle m; **role-model** n modèle m
à émuler
roll [rəul] n rouleau m; (of banknotes) liasse
f; (also: **bread ~**) petit pain; (register) liste f;
(sound: of drums etc) roulement m ▷ vt rouler;
(also: **~ up**: string) enrouler; (also: **~ out**:
pastry) étendre au rouleau, abaisser ▷ vi
rouler; **roll over** vi se retourner; **roll up**
vi (inf: arrive) arriver, s'amener ▷ vt (carpet,
cloth, map) rouler; (sleeves) retrousser; **roller**
n rouleau m; (wheel) roulette f; (for road)
rouleau compresseur; (for hair) bigoudi m;
roller coaster n montagnes fpl russes; **roller
skates** npl patins mpl à roulettes; **roller-
skating** n patin m à roulettes; **to go roller-
skating** faire du patin à roulettes; **rolling pin**
n rouleau m à pâtisserie
ROM [rɔm] n abbr (Comput: = read-only memory)
mémoire morte, ROM f
Roman ['rəumən] adj romain(e) ▷ n
Romain(e); **Roman Catholic** adj, n
catholique (m/f)
romance [rə'mæns] n (love affair) idylle f;
(charm) poésie f; (novel) roman m à l'eau de rose
Romania etc [rəu'meɪnɪə] = **Rumania** etc
Roman numeral n chiffre romain
romantic [rə'mæntɪk] adj romantique; (novel,
attachment) sentimental(e)
Rome [rəum] n Rome
roof [ru:f] n toit m; (of tunnel, cave) plafond m
▷ vt couvrir (d'un toit); **the ~ of the mouth** la
voûte du palais; **roof rack** n (Aut) galerie f
rook [ruk] n (bird) freux m; (Chess) tour f
room [ru:m] n (in house) pièce f; (also: **bed~**)
chambre f (à coucher); (in school etc) salle
f; (space) place f; **roommate** n camarade
m/f de chambre; **room service** n service
m des chambres (dans un hôtel); **roomy** adj
spacieux(-euse); (garment) ample
rooster ['ru:stə'] n coq m
root [ru:t] n (Bot, Math) racine f; (fig: of problem)
origine f, fond m ▷ vi (plant) s'enraciner
rope [rəup] n corde f; (Naut) cordage m ▷ vt
(tie up or together) attacher; (climbers: also: **~
together**) encorder; (area: also: **~ off**) interdire
l'accès de; (: divide off) séparer; **to know the ~s**
(fig) être au courant, connaître les ficelles
rose [rəuz] pt of **rise** ▷ n rose f; (also: **~bush**)
rosier m
rosé ['rəuzeɪ] n rosé m
rosemary ['rəuzmərɪ] n romarin m
rosy ['rəuzɪ] adj rose; **a ~ future** un bel avenir
rot [rɔt] n (decay) pourriture f; (fig: pej: nonsense)
idioties fpl, balivernes fpl ▷ vt, vi pourrir
rota ['rəutə] n liste f, tableau m de service
rotate [rəu'teɪt] vt (revolve) faire tourner;
(change round: crops) alterner; (: jobs) faire à
tour de rôle ▷ vi (revolve) tourner
rotten ['rɔtn] adj (decayed) pourri(e);

(dishonest) corrompu(e); (inf: bad) mauvais(e),
moche; **to feel ~** (ill) être mal fichu(e)
rough [rʌf] adj (cloth, skin) rêche,
rugueux(-euse); (terrain) accidenté(e); (path)
rocailleux(-euse); (voice) rauque, rude;
(person, manner: coarse) rude, fruste; (: violent)
brutal(e); (district, weather) mauvais(e); (sea)
houleux(-euse); (plan) ébauché(e); (guess)
approximatif(-ive) ▷ n (Golf) rough m ▷ vt: **to
~ it** vivre à la dure; **to sleep ~** (BRIT) coucher
à la dure; **roughly** adv (handle) rudement,
brutalement; (speak) avec brusquerie; (make)
grossièrement; (approximately) à peu près, en
gros
roulette [ru:'let] n roulette f
round [raund] adj rond(e) ▷ n rond m, cercle
m; (BRIT: of toast) tranche f; (duty: of policeman,
milkman etc) tournée f; (: of doctor) visites fpl;
(game: of cards, in competition) partie f; (Boxing)
round m; (of talks) série f ▷ vt (corner) tourner
▷ prep autour de ▷ adv: **right ~, all ~** tout
autour; **~ of ammunition** cartouche f; **~ of
applause** applaudissements mpl; **~ of drinks**
tournée f; **~ of sandwiches** (BRIT) sandwich
m; **the long way ~** (par) le chemin le plus long;
all (the) year ~ toute l'année; **it's just ~ the
corner** (fig) c'est tout près; **to go ~ to sb's
(house)** aller chez qn; **to go ~ the back** passez
par derrière; **enough to go ~** assez pour tout
le monde; **she arrived ~ (about) noon** (BRIT)
elle est arrivée vers midi; **~ the clock** 24 heures
sur 24; **round off** vt (speech etc) terminer;
round up vt rassembler; (criminals) effectuer
une rafle de; (prices) arrondir (au chiffre
supérieur); **roundabout** n (BRIT Aut) rond-
point m (à sens giratoire); (at fair) manège
m (de chevaux de bois) ▷ adj (route, means)
détourné(e); **round trip** n (voyage m) aller et
retour m; **roundup** n rassemblement m; (of
criminals) rafle f
rouse [rauz] vt (wake up) réveiller; (stir
up) susciter, provoquer; (interest) éveiller;
(suspicions) susciter, éveiller
route [ru:t] n itinéraire m; (of bus) parcours m;
(of trade, shipping) route f
routine [ru:'ti:n] adj (work) ordinaire,
courant(e); (procedure) d'usage ▷ n (habits)
habitudes fpl; (pej) train-train m; (Theat)
numéro m
row¹ [rəu] n (line) rangée f; (of people, seats,
Knitting) rang m; (behind one another: of cars,
people) file f ▷ vi (in boat) ramer; (as sport) faire
de l'aviron ▷ vt (boat) faire aller à la rame or à
l'aviron; **in a ~** (fig) d'affilée
row² [rau] n (noise) vacarme m; (dispute)
dispute f, querelle f; (scolding) réprimande f,
savon m ▷ vi (also: **to have a ~**) se disputer, se
quereller
rowboat ['rəubəut] n (US) canot m (à rames)

rowing ['rəʊɪŋ] n canotage m; (as sport) aviron m; **rowing boat** n (BRIT) canot m (à rames)

royal ['rɔɪəl] adj royal(e); **royalty** n (royal persons) (membres mpl de la) famille royale; (payment: to author) droits mpl d'auteur; (: to inventor) royalties fpl

rpm abbr (= revolutions per minute) t/mn (= tours/minute)

R.S.V.P. abbr (= répondez s'il vous plaît) RSVP

Rt. Hon. abbr (BRIT: = Right Honourable) titre donné aux députés de la Chambre des communes

rub [rʌb] n: **to give sth a ~** donner un coup de chiffon or de torchon à qch ▷ vt frotter; (person) frictionner; (hands) se frotter; **to ~ sb up** (BRIT) or **to ~ sb** (US) **the wrong way** prendre qn à rebrousse-poil; **rub in** vt (ointment) faire pénétrer; **rub off** vi partir; **rub out** vt effacer

rubber ['rʌbə'] n caoutchouc m; (BRIT: eraser) gomme f (à effacer); **rubber band** n élastique m; **rubber gloves** npl gants mpl en caoutchouc

rubbish ['rʌbɪʃ] n (from household) ordures fpl; (fig: pej) choses fpl sans valeur; camelote f; (nonsense) bêtises fpl, idioties fpl; **rubbish bin** n (BRIT) boîte f à ordures, poubelle f; **rubbish dump** n (BRIT: in town) décharge publique, dépotoir m

rubble ['rʌbl] n décombres mpl; (smaller) gravats mpl; (Constr) blocage m

ruby ['ru:bɪ] n rubis m

rucksack ['rʌksæk] n sac m à dos

rudder ['rʌdə'] n gouvernail m

rude [ru:d] adj (impolite: person) impoli(e); (: word, manners) grossier(-ière); (shocking) indécent(e), inconvenant(e)

ruffle ['rʌfl] vt (hair) ébouriffer; (clothes) chiffonner; (fig: person): **to get ~d** s'énerver

rug [rʌg] n petit tapis; (BRIT: blanket) couverture f

rugby ['rʌgbɪ] n (also: ~ **football**) rugby m

rugged ['rʌgɪd] adj (landscape) accidenté(e); (features, character) rude

ruin ['ru:ɪn] n ruine f ▷ vt ruiner; (spoil: clothes) abîmer; (: event) gâcher; **ruins** npl (of building) ruine(s)

rule [ru:l] n règle f; (regulation) règlement m; (government) autorité f, gouvernement m ▷ vt (country) gouverner; (person) dominer; (decide) décider ▷ vi commander; (Law): **as a ~** normalement, en règle générale; **rule out** vt exclure; **ruler** n (sovereign) souverain(e); (leader) chef m (d'État); (for measuring) règle f; **ruling** adj (party) au pouvoir; (class) dirigeant(e) ▷ n (Law) décision f

rum [rʌm] n rhum m

Rumania [ru:'meɪnɪə] n Roumanie f; **Rumanian** adj roumain(e) ▷ n Roumain(e); (Ling) roumain m

rumble ['rʌmbl] n grondement m; (of stomach, pipe) gargouillement m ▷ vi gronder; (stomach, pipe) gargouiller

rumour (US **rumor**) ['ru:mə'] n rumeur f, bruit m (qui court) ▷ vt: **it is ~ed that** le bruit court que

rump steak n romsteck m

run [rʌn] n (race) course f; (outing) tour m or promenade f (en voiture); (distance travelled) parcours m, trajet m; (series) suite f, série f; (Theat) série de représentations; (Ski) piste f; (Cricket, Baseball) point m; (in tights, stockings) maille filée, échelle f ▷ vb (pt ran, pp ~) ▷ vt (business) diriger; (competition, course) organiser; (hotel, house) tenir; (race) participer à; (Comput: program) exécuter; (to pass: hand, finger): **to ~ sth over** promener or passer qch sur; (water, bath) faire couler; (Press: feature) publier ▷ vi courir; (pass: road etc) passer; (work: machine, factory) marcher; (bus, train) circuler; (continue: play) se jouer, être à l'affiche; (: contract) être valide or en vigueur; (flow: river, bath, nose) couler; (colours, washing) déteindre; (in election) être candidat, se présenter; **at a ~** au pas de course; **to go for a ~** aller courir or faire un peu de course à pied; (in car) faire un tour or une promenade (en voiture); **there was a ~ on** (meat, tickets) les gens se sont rués sur; **in the long ~** à la longue; **on the ~** en fuite; **I'll ~ you to the station** je vais vous emmener or conduire à la gare; **to ~ a risk** courir un risque; **run after** vt fus (to catch up) courir après; (chase) poursuivre; **run away** vi s'enfuir; **run down** vi (Aut: knock over) renverser; (BRIT: reduce: production) réduire progressivement; (: factory/shop) réduire progressivement la production/l'activité de; (criticize) critiquer, dénigrer; **to be ~ down** (tired) être fatigué(e) or à plat; **run into** vt fus (meet: person) rencontrer par hasard; (: trouble) se heurter à; (collide with) heurter; **run off** vi s'enfuir ▷ vt (water) laisser s'écouler; (copies) tirer; **run out** vi (person) sortir en courant; (liquid) couler; (lease) expirer; (money) être épuisé(e); **run out of** vt fus se trouver à court de; **run over** vt (Aut) écraser ▷ vt fus (revise) revoir, reprendre; **run through** vt fus (recap) reprendre, revoir; (play) répéter; **run up** vi: **to ~ up against** (difficulties) se heurter à; **runaway** adj (horse) emballé(e); (truck) fou (folle); (person) fugitif(-ive); (child) fugueur(-euse)

rung [rʌŋ] pp of **ring** ▷ n (of ladder) barreau m

runner ['rʌnə'] n (in race: person) coureur(-euse); (: horse) partant m; (on sledge) patin m; (for drawer etc) coulisseau m; **runner bean** n (BRIT) haricot m (à rames); **runner-up** n second(e)

running ['rʌnɪŋ] n (in race etc) course f; (of

business, organization) direction *f*, gestion *f*
▷ *adj* (*water*) courant(e); (*commentary*) suivi(e);
6 days ~ 6 jours de suite; **to be in/out of the ~**
for sth être/ne pas être sur les rangs pour qch
runny ['rʌnɪ] *adj* qui coule
run-up ['rʌnʌp] *n* (*BRIT*): **~ to sth** période *f*
précédant qch
runway ['rʌnweɪ] *n* (*Aviat*) piste *f* (d'envol *or*
d'atterrissage)
rupture ['rʌptʃəʳ] *n* (*Med*) hernie *f*
rural ['ruərl] *adj* rural(e)
rush [rʌʃ] *n* (*of crowd, Comm: sudden demand*)
ruée *f*; (*hurry*) hâte *f*; (*of anger, joy*) accès
m; (*current*) flot *m*; (*Bot*) jonc *m* ▷ *vt* (*hurry*)
transporter *or* envoyer d'urgence ▷ *vi* se
précipiter; **to ~ sth off** (*do quickly*) faire qch à
la hâte; **rush hour** *n* heures *fpl* de pointe *or*
d'affluence
Russia ['rʌʃə] *n* Russie *f*; **Russian** *adj* russe ▷ *n*
Russe *m/f*; (*Ling*) russe *m*
rust [rʌst] *n* rouille *f* ▷ *vi* rouiller
rusty ['rʌstɪ] *adj* rouillé(e)
ruthless ['ruːθlɪs] *adj* sans pitié, impitoyable
RV *n abbr* (*US*) = **recreational vehicle**
rye [raɪ] *n* seigle *m*

S

Sabbath ['sæbəθ] *n* (*Jewish*) sabbat *m*;
(*Christian*) dimanche *m*
sabotage ['sæbətɑːʒ] *n* sabotage *m* ▷ *vt*
saboter
saccharin(e) ['sækərɪn] *n* saccharine *f*
sachet ['sæʃeɪ] *n* sachet *m*
sack [sæk] *n* (*bag*) sac *m* ▷ *vt* (*dismiss*) renvoyer,
mettre à la porte; (*plunder*) piller, mettre à sac;
to get the ~ être renvoyé(e) *or* mis(e) à la porte
sacred ['seɪkrɪd] *adj* sacré(e)
sacrifice ['sækrɪfaɪs] *n* sacrifice *m* ▷ *vt*
sacrifier
sad [sæd] *adj* (*unhappy*) triste; (*deplorable*)
triste, fâcheux(-euse); (*inf: pathetic: thing*)
triste, lamentable; (: *person*) minable
saddle ['sædl] *n* selle *f* ▷ *vt* (*horse*) seller; **to be**
~d with sth (*inf*) avoir qch sur les bras
sadistic [sə'dɪstɪk] *adj* sadique
sadly ['sædlɪ] *adv* tristement; (*unfortunately*)
malheureusement; (*seriously*) fort
sadness ['sædnɪs] *n* tristesse *f*
s.a.e. *n abbr* (*BRIT*: = *stamped addressed*
envelope) enveloppe affranchie pour la réponse
safari [sə'fɑːrɪ] *n* safari *m*
safe [seɪf] *adj* (*out of danger*) hors de danger,
en sécurité; (*not dangerous*) sans danger;
(*cautious*) prudent(e); (*sure: bet etc*) assuré(e)
▷ *n* coffre-fort *m*; **could you put this in**
the ~, please? pourriez-vous mettre ceci
dans le coffre-fort?; **~ and sound** sain(e) et

sauf (sauve); **(just) to be on the ~ side** pour plus de sûreté, par précaution; **safely** adv (assume, say) sans risque d'erreur; (drive, arrive) sans accident; **safe sex** n rapports sexuels protégés

safety ['seɪftɪ] n sécurité f; **safety belt** n ceinture f de sécurité; **safety pin** n épingle f de sûreté or de nourrice

saffron ['sæfrən] n safran m

sag [sæg] vi s'affaisser, fléchir; (hem, breasts) pendre

sage [seɪdʒ] n (herb) sauge f; (person) sage m

Sagittarius [sædʒɪ'teərɪəs] n le Sagittaire

Sahara [sə'hɑːrə] n: **the ~ (Desert)** le (désert du) Sahara m

said [sed] pt, pp of **say**

sail [seɪl] n (on boat) voile f; (trip): **to go for a ~** faire un tour en bateau ▷ vt (boat) manœuvrer, piloter ▷ vi (travel: ship) avancer, naviguer; (set off) partir, prendre la mer; (Sport) faire de la voile; **they ~ed into Le Havre** ils sont entrés dans le port du Havre; **sailboat** n (US) bateau m à voiles, voilier m; **sailing** (Sport) voile f; **to go sailing** faire de la voile; **sailing boat** n bateau m à voiles, voilier m; **sailor** n marin m, matelot m

saint [seɪnt] n saint(e)

sake [seɪk] n: **for the ~ of** (out of concern for) pour l'amour de), dans l'intérêt de; (out of consideration for) par égard pour

salad ['sæləd] n salade f; **salad cream** n (BRIT) (sorte f de) mayonnaise f; **salad dressing** n vinaigrette f

salami [sə'lɑːmɪ] n salami m

salary ['sælərɪ] n salaire m, traitement m

sale [seɪl] n vente f; (at reduced prices) soldes mpl; **sales** npl (total amount sold) chiffre m de ventes; **"for ~"** "à vendre"; **on ~** en vente; **sales assistant** (US **sales clerk**) n vendeur(-euse); **salesman** (irreg) n (in shop) vendeur m; **salesperson** (irreg) n (in shop) vendeur(-euse); **sales rep** n (Comm) représentant(e) m/f; **saleswoman** (irreg) n (in shop) vendeuse f

saline ['seɪlaɪn] adj salin(e)

saliva [sə'laɪvə] n salive f

salmon ['sæmən] n (pl inv) saumon m

salon ['sælɔn] n salon m

saloon [sə'luːn] n (US) bar m; (BRIT Aut) berline f; (ship's lounge) salon m

salt [sɔːlt] n sel m ▷ vt saler; **saltwater** adj (fish etc) (d'eau) de mer; **salty** adj salé(e)

salute [sə'luːt] n salut m; (of guns) salve f ▷ vt saluer

salvage ['sælvɪdʒ] n (saving) sauvetage m; (things saved) biens sauvés or récupérés ▷ vt sauver, récupérer

Salvation Army [sæl'veɪʃən-] n Armée f du Salut

same [seɪm] adj même ▷ pron: **the ~** le (la) même, les mêmes; **the ~ book as** le même livre que; **at the ~ time** en même temps; (yet) néanmoins; **all** or **just the ~** tout de même, quand même; **to do the ~** faire de même, en faire autant; **to do the ~ as sb** faire comme qn; **and the ~ to you!** et à vous de même!; (after insult) toi-même!

sample ['sɑːmpl] n échantillon m; (Med) prélèvement m ▷ vt (food, wine) goûter

sanction ['sæŋkʃən] n approbation f, sanction f ▷ vt cautionner, sanctionner; **sanctions** npl (Pol) sanctions

sanctuary ['sæŋktjuərɪ] n (holy place) sanctuaire m; (refuge) asile m; (for wildlife) réserve f

sand [sænd] n sable m ▷ vt (also: ~ **down**: wood etc) poncer

sandal ['sændl] n sandale f

sand: **sandbox** n (US: for children) tas m de sable; **sandcastle** n château m de sable; **sand dune** n dune f de sable; **sandpaper** n papier m de verre; **sandpit** n (BRIT: for children) tas m de sable; **sands** npl plage f (de sable); **sandstone** ['sændstəun] n grès m

sandwich ['sændwɪtʃ] n sandwich m ▷ vt (also: ~ **in**) intercaler; **~ed between** pris en sandwich entre; **cheese/ham ~** sandwich au fromage/jambon

sandy ['sændɪ] adj sablonneux(-euse); (colour) sable inv, blond roux inv

sane [seɪn] adj (person) sain(e) d'esprit; (outlook) sensé(e), sain(e)

sang [sæŋ] pt of **sing**

sanitary towel (US **sanitary napkin**) ['sænɪtərɪ-] n serviette f hygiénique

sanity ['sænɪtɪ] n santé mentale; (common sense) bon sens

sank [sæŋk] pt of **sink**

Santa Claus [sæntə'klɔːz] n le Père Noël

sap [sæp] n (of plants) sève f ▷ vt (strength) saper, miner

sapphire ['sæfaɪə'] n saphir m

sarcasm ['sɑːkæzm] n sarcasme m, raillerie f

sarcastic [sɑː'kæstɪk] adj sarcastique

sardine [sɑː'diːn] n sardine f

SASE n abbr (US: = self-addressed stamped envelope) enveloppe affranchie pour la réponse

sat [sæt] pt, pp of **sit**

Sat. abbr (= Saturday) sa

satchel ['sætʃl] n cartable m

satellite ['sætəlaɪt] n satellite m; **satellite dish** n antenne f parabolique; **satellite television** n télévision f par satellite

satin ['sætɪn] n satin m ▷ adj en or de satin, satiné(e)

satire ['sætaɪə'] n satire f

satisfaction [sætɪs'fækʃən] n satisfaction f

satisfactory [sætɪs'fæktərɪ] adj satisfaisant(e)

satisfied ['sætɪsfaɪd] adj satisfait(e); **to be ~ with sth** être satisfait de qch

satisfy ['sætɪsfaɪ] vt satisfaire, contenter; (convince) convaincre, persuader

Saturday ['sætədɪ] n samedi m

sauce [sɔːs] n sauce f; **saucepan** n casserole f

saucer ['sɔːsəʳ] n soucoupe f

Saudi Arabia ['saudɪ-] n Arabie f Saoudite

sauna ['sɔːnə] n sauna m

sausage ['sɔsɪdʒ] n saucisse f; (salami etc) saucisson m; **sausage roll** n friand m

sautéed ['səuteɪd] adj sauté(e)

savage ['sævɪdʒ] adj (cruel, fierce) brutal(e), féroce; (primitive) primitif(-ive), sauvage ▷ n sauvage m/f ▷ vt attaquer férocement

save [seɪv] vt (person, belongings) sauver; (money) mettre de côté, économiser; (time) (faire) gagner; (keep) garder; (Comput) sauvegarder; (Sport: stop) arrêter; (avoid: trouble) éviter ▷ vi (also: ~ up) mettre de l'argent de côté ▷ n (Sport) arrêt m (du ballon) ▷ prep sauf, à l'exception de

savings ['seɪvɪŋz] npl économies fpl; **savings account** n compte m d'épargne; **savings and loan association** (us) n ≈ société f de crédit immobilier

savoury (us **savory**) ['seɪvərɪ] adj savoureux(-euse); (dish: not sweet) salé(e)

saw [sɔː] pt of **see** ▷ n (tool) scie f ▷ vt (pt **~ed**, pp **~ed** or **~n**) scier; **sawdust** n sciure f

sawn [sɔːn] pp of **saw**

saxophone ['sæksəfəun] n saxophone m

say [seɪ] n: **to have one's ~** dire ce qu'on a à dire ▷ vt (pt, pp **said**) dire; **to have a ~** avoir voix au chapitre; **could you ~ that again?** pourriez-vous répéter ce que vous venez de dire?; **to ~ yes/no** dire oui/non; **my watch ~s 3 o'clock** ma montre dit 3 heures, il est 3 heures à ma montre; **that is to ~** c'est-à-dire, cela va sans dire, cela va de soi; **saying** n dicton m, proverbe m

scab [skæb] n croûte f; (pej) jaune m

scaffolding ['skæfəldɪŋ] n échafaudage m

scald [skɔːld] n brûlure f ▷ vt ébouillanter

scale [skeɪl] n (of fish) écaille f; (Mus) gamme f; (of ruler, thermometer etc) graduation f, échelle (graduée); (of salaries, fees etc) barème m; (of map, also size, extent) échelle ▷ vt (mountain) escalader; **scales** npl balance f; (larger) bascule f; (also: **bathroom ~s**) pèse-personne m inv; **~ of charges** tableau m des tarifs; **on a large ~** sur une grande échelle, en grand

scallion ['skæljən] n (us: salad onion) ciboule f

scallop ['skɔləp] n coquille f Saint-Jacques; (Sewing) feston m

scalp [skælp] n cuir chevelu ▷ vt scalper

scalpel ['skælpl] n scalpel m

scam [skæm] n (inf) arnaque f

scampi ['skæmpɪ] npl langoustines (frites),

scampi mpl

scan [skæn] vt (examine) scruter, examiner; (glance at quickly) parcourir; (TV, Radar) balayer ▷ n (Med) scanographie f

scandal ['skændl] n scandale m; (gossip) ragots mpl

Scandinavia [skændɪ'neɪvɪə] n Scandinavie f; **Scandinavian** adj scandinave ▷ n Scandinave m/f

scanner ['skænəʳ] n (Radar, Med) scanner m, scanographe m; (Comput) scanner, numériseur m

scapegoat ['skeɪpgəut] n bouc m émissaire

scar [skɑːʳ] n cicatrice f ▷ vt laisser une cicatrice or une marque à

scarce [skeəs] adj rare, peu abondant(e); **to make o.s. ~** (inf) se sauver; **scarcely** adv à peine, presque pas

scare [skeəʳ] n peur f, panique f ▷ vt effrayer, faire peur à; **to ~ sb stiff** faire une peur bleue à qn; **bomb ~** alerte f à la bombe; **scarecrow** n épouvantail m; **scared** adj: **to be scared** avoir peur

scarf (pl **scarves**) [skɑːf, skɑːvz] n (long) écharpe f; (square) foulard m

scarlet ['skɑːlɪt] adj écarlate

scarves [skɑːvz] npl of **scarf**

scary ['skeərɪ] adj (inf) effrayant(e); (film) qui fait peur

scatter ['skætəʳ] vt éparpiller, répandre; (crowd) disperser ▷ vi se disperser

scenario [sɪ'nɑːrɪəu] n scénario m

scene [siːn] n (Theat, fig etc) scène f; (of crime, accident) lieu(x) m(pl), endroit m; (sight, view) spectacle m, vue f; **scenery** n (Theat) décor(s) m(pl); (landscape) paysage m; **scenic** adj offrant de beaux paysages or panoramas

scent [sɛnt] n parfum m, odeur f; (fig: track) piste f

sceptical (us **skeptical**) ['skeptɪkl] adj sceptique

schedule ['ʃedjuːl, us 'skedjuːl] n programme m, plan m; (of trains) horaire m; (of prices etc) barème m, tarif m ▷ vt prévoir; **on ~** à l'heure (prévue); à la date prévue; **to be ahead of/behind ~** avoir de l'avance/du retard; **scheduled flight** n vol régulier

scheme [skiːm] n plan m, projet m; (plot) complot m, combine f; (arrangement) arrangement m, classification f; (pension scheme etc) régime m ▷ vt, vi comploter, manigancer

schizophrenic [skɪtsə'frenɪk] adj schizophrène

scholar ['skɔləʳ] n érudit(e); (pupil) boursier(-ère); **scholarship** n érudition f; (grant) bourse f (d'études)

school [skuːl] n (gen) école f; (secondary school) collège m, lycée m; (in university) faculté f;

(*US: university*) université f ▷ *cpd* scolaire;
schoolbook n livre m scolaire or de classe;
schoolboy n écolier m; (*at secondary school*)
collégien m, lycéen m; **schoolchildren** npl
écoliers mpl; (*at secondary school*) collégiens
mpl, lycéens mpl; **schoolgirl** n écolière f; (*at
secondary school*) collégienne f, lycéenne f;
schooling n instruction f, études fpl;
schoolteacher n (*primary*) instituteur(-trice);
(*secondary*) professeur m

science ['saɪəns] n science f; **science fiction**
n science-fiction f; **scientific** [saɪən'tɪfɪk]
adj scientifique; **scientist** n scientifique m/f;
(*eminent*) savant m

sci-fi ['saɪfaɪ] n abbr (inf: = science fiction) SF f

scissors ['sɪzəz] npl ciseaux mpl; **a pair of ~**
une paire de ciseaux

scold [skəʊld] vt gronder

scone [skɒn] n sorte de petit pain rond au lait

scoop [sku:p] n pelle f (à main); (*for ice cream*)
boule f à glace; (*Press*) reportage exclusif or à
sensation

scooter ['sku:tə'] n (*motor cycle*) scooter m;
(*toy*) trottinette f

scope [skəʊp] n (*capacity: of plan, undertaking*)
portée f, envergure f; (: *of person*) compétence f,
capacités fpl; (*opportunity*) possibilités fpl

scorching ['skɔ:tʃɪŋ] adj torride, brûlant(e)

score [skɔ:'] n score m, décompte m des points;
(*Mus*) partition f ▷ vt (*goal, point*) marquer;
(*success*) remporter; (*cut: leather, wood, card*)
entailler, inciser ▷ vi marquer des points;
(*Football*) marquer un but; (*keep score*) compter
les points; **on that ~** sur ce chapitre, à cet
égard; **a ~ of** (*twenty*) vingt; **~s of** (*fig*) des tas
de; **to ~ 6 out of 10** obtenir 6 sur 10; **score
out** vt rayer, barrer, biffer; **scoreboard** n
tableau m; **scorer** n (*Football*) auteur m du but;
buteur m; (*keeping score*) marqueur m

scorn [skɔ:n] n mépris m, dédain m

Scorpio ['skɔ:pɪəʊ] n le Scorpion

scorpion ['skɔ:pɪən] n scorpion m

Scot [skɒt] n Écossais(e)

Scotch [skɒtʃ] n whisky m, scotch m

Scotch tape® (*US*) n scotch® m, ruban
adhésif

Scotland ['skɒtlənd] n Écosse f

Scots [skɒts] adj écossais(e); **Scotsman**
(*irreg*) n Écossais m; **Scotswoman** (*irreg*) n
Écossaise f; **Scottish** ['skɒtɪʃ] adj écossais(e);
Scottish Parliament n Parlement écossais

scout [skaʊt] n (*Mil*) éclaireur m; (*also:* **boy ~**)
scout m; **girl ~** (*US*) guide f

scowl [skaʊl] vi se renfrogner, avoir l'air
maussade; **to ~ at** regarder de travers

scramble ['skræmbl] n (*rush*) bousculade f,
ruée f ▷ vi grimper/descendre tant bien que
mal; **to ~ for** se bousculer or se disputer pour
(avoir); **to go scrambling** (*Sport*) faire du trial;

scrambled eggs npl œufs brouillés

scrap [skræp] n bout m, morceau m; (*fight*)
bagarre f; (*also:* **~ iron**) ferraille f ▷ vt jeter,
mettre au rebut; (*fig*) abandonner, laisser
tomber ▷ vi se bagarrer; **scraps** npl (*waste*)
déchets mpl; **scrapbook** n album m

scrape [skreɪp] vt, vi gratter, racler ▷ n: **to get
into a ~** s'attirer des ennuis; **scrape through**
vi (*exam etc*) réussir de justesse

scrap paper n papier m brouillon

scratch [skrætʃ] n égratignure f, rayure f; (*on
paint*) éraflure f; (*from claw*) coup m de griffe
▷ vt (*rub*) (se) gratter; (*paint etc*) érafler; (*with
claw, nail*) griffer ▷ vi (se) gratter; **to start
from ~** partir de zéro; **to be up to ~** être à la
hauteur; **scratch card** n carte f à gratter

scream [skri:m] n cri perçant, hurlement m
▷ vi crier, hurler

screen [skri:n] n écran m; (*in room*) paravent
m; (*fig*) écran, rideau m ▷ vt masquer, cacher;
(*from the wind etc*) abriter, protéger; (*film*)
projeter; (*candidates etc*) filtrer; **screening** n
(*of film*) projection f; (*Med*) test m (or tests) de
dépistage; **screenplay** n scénario m; **screen
saver** n (*Comput*) économiseur m d'écran

screw [skru:] n vis f ▷ vt (*also:* **~ in**) visser;
screw up vt (*paper etc*) froisser; **to ~ up
one's eyes** se plisser les yeux; **screwdriver** n
tournevis m

scribble ['skrɪbl] n gribouillage m ▷ vt
gribouiller, griffonner

script [skrɪpt] n (*Cine etc*) scénario m, texte m;
(*writing*) (écriture f) script m

scroll [skrəʊl] n rouleau m ▷ vt (*Comput*) faire
défiler (sur l'écran)

scrub [skrʌb] n (*land*) broussailles fpl ▷ vt
(*floor*) nettoyer à la brosse; (*pan*) récurer;
(*washing*) frotter

scruffy ['skrʌfɪ] adj débraillé(e)

scrum(mage) ['skrʌm(ɪdʒ)] n mêlée f

scrutiny ['skru:tɪnɪ] n examen minutieux

scuba diving ['sku:bə-] n plongée sous-
marine (autonome)

sculptor ['skʌlptə'] n sculpteur m

sculpture ['skʌlptʃə'] n sculpture f

scum [skʌm] n écume f, mousse f; (*pej: people*)
rebut m, lie f

scurry ['skʌrɪ] vi filer à toute allure; **to ~ off**
détaler, se sauver

sea [si:] n mer f ▷ *cpd* marin(e), de (la) mer,
maritime; **by** or **beside the ~** (*holiday, town*) au
bord de la mer; **by ~** par mer, en bateau; **out to
~ au large**; (**out**) **at ~** en mer; **to be all at ~** (*fig*)
nager complètement; **seafood** n fruits mpl
de mer; **sea front** n bord m de mer; **seagull**
n mouette f

seal [si:l] n (*animal*) phoque m; (*stamp*) sceau
m, cachet m ▷ vt sceller; (*envelope*) coller; (:
with seal) cacheter; **seal off** vt (*forbid entry to*)

interdire l'accès de
sea level n niveau m de la mer
seam [siːm] n couture f; (of coal) veine f, filon m
search [səːtʃ] n (for person, thing, Comput)
recherche(s) f(pl); (of drawer, pockets) fouille f;
(Law: at sb's home) perquisition f ▷ vt
(examine) examiner minutieusement; scruter
▷ vi: **to ~ for** chercher; **in ~ of** à la recherche
de; **search engine** n (Comput) moteur m de
recherche; **search party** n expédition f de
secours
sea: **seashore** n rivage m, plage f, bord m de
(la) mer; **seasick** adj: **to be seasick** avoir le
mal de mer; **seaside** n bord m de mer; **seaside
resort** n station f balnéaire
season ['siːzn] n saison f ▷ vt assaisonner,
relever; **to be in/out of ~** être/ne pas être
de saison; **seasonal** adj saisonnier(-ière);
seasoning n assaisonnement m; **season
ticket** n carte f d'abonnement
seat [siːt] n siège m; (in bus, train: place) place
f; (buttocks) postérieur m; (of trousers) fond m
▷ vt faire asseoir, placer; (have room for) avoir
des places assises pour, pouvoir accueillir;
I'd like to book two ~s je voudrais réserver
deux places; **to be ~ed** être assis; **seat belt**
n ceinture f de sécurité; **seating** n sièges fpl,
places assises
sea: **sea water** n eau f de mer; **seaweed** n
algues fpl
sec. abbr (= second) sec
secluded [sɪ'kluːdɪd] adj retiré(e), à l'écart
second ['sɛkənd] num deuxième, second(e)
▷ adv (in race etc) en seconde position ▷ n
(unit of time) seconde f; (Aut: also: **~ gear**)
seconde; (Comm: imperfect) article m de second
choix; (BRIT Scol) ≈ licence f avec mention ▷ vt
(motion) appuyer; **seconds** npl (inf: food) rab m
(inf); **secondary** adj secondaire; **secondary
school** n collège m; lycée m; **second-class** adj
de deuxième classe; (Rail) de seconde (classe);
(Post) au tarif réduit; (pej) de qualité inférieure
▷ adv (Rail) en seconde; (Post) au tarif réduit;
secondhand adj d'occasion; (information) de
seconde main; **secondly** adv deuxièmement;
second-rate adj de deuxième ordre, de
qualité inférieure; **second thoughts** npl:
to have second thoughts changer d'avis;
on second thoughts or **thought** (us) à la
réflexion
secrecy ['siːkrəsɪ] n secret m
secret ['siːkrɪt] adj secret(-ète) ▷ n secret m;
in ~ adv en secret, secrètement, en cachette
secretary ['sɛkrətrɪ] n secrétaire m/f; **S~ of
State (for)** (Brit Pol) ministre m (de)
secretive ['siːkrətɪv] adj réservé(e); (pej)
cachottier(-ière), dissimulé(e)
secret service n services secrets
sect [sɛkt] n secte f

section ['sɛkʃən] n section f; (Comm) rayon m;
(of document) section, article m, paragraphe m;
(cut) coupe f
sector ['sɛktə^r] n secteur m
secular ['sɛkjulə^r] adj laïque
secure [sɪ'kjuə^r] adj (free from anxiety) sans
inquiétude, sécurisé(e); (firmly fixed) solide,
bien attaché(e) (or fermé(e) etc); (in safe place)
en lieu sûr, en sûreté ▷ vt (fix) fixer, attacher;
(get) obtenir, se procurer
security [sɪ'kjuərɪtɪ] n sécurité f, mesures
fpl de sécurité; (for loan) caution f, garantie
f; **securities** npl (Stock Exchange) valeurs fpl,
titres mpl; **security guard** n garde chargé de
la sécurité; (transporting money) convoyeur m
de fonds
sedan [sə'dæn] n (us Aut) berline f
sedate [sɪ'deɪt] adj calme; posé(e) ▷ vt donner
des sédatifs à
sedative ['sɛdɪtɪv] n calmant m, sédatif m
seduce [sɪ'djuːs] vt séduire; **seductive**
[sɪ'dʌktɪv] adj séduisant(e); (smile)
séducteur(-trice); (fig: offer) alléchant(e)
see [siː] vb (pt **saw**, pp **~n**) ▷ vt (gen) voir;
(accompany): **to ~ sb to the door** reconduire
or raccompagner qn jusqu'à la porte ▷ vi
voir; **to ~ that** (ensure) veiller à ce que + sub,
faire en sorte que + sub, s'assurer que; **~ you
soon/later/tomorrow!** à bientôt/plus
tard/demain!; **see off** vt accompagner (à la
gare or à l'aéroport etc); **see out** vt (take to
door) raccompagner à la porte; **see through** vt
mener à bonne fin ▷ vt fus voir clair dans; **see
to** vt fus s'occuper de, se charger de
seed [siːd] n graine f; (fig) germe m; (Tennis etc)
tête f de série; **to go to ~** (plant) monter en
graine; (fig) se laisser aller
seeing ['siːɪŋ] conj: **~ (that)** vu que, étant
donné que
seek (pt, pp **sought**) [siːk, sɔːt] vt chercher,
rechercher
seem [siːm] vi sembler, paraître; **there ~s to
be ...** il semble qu'il y a ..., on dirait qu'il y a ...;
seemingly adv apparemment
seen [siːn] pp of **see**
seesaw ['siːsɔː] n (jeu m de) bascule f
segment ['sɛgmənt] n segment m; (of orange)
quartier m
segregate ['sɛgrɪgeɪt] vt séparer, isoler
Seine [seɪn] n: **the (River) ~** la Seine
seize [siːz] vt (grasp) saisir, attraper; (take
possession of) s'emparer de; (opportunity) saisir
seizure ['siːʒə^r] n (Med) crise f, attaque f; (of
power) prise f
seldom ['sɛldəm] adv rarement
select [sɪ'lɛkt] adj choisi(e), d'élite; (hotel,
restaurant, club) chic inv, sélect inv ▷ vt
sélectionner, choisir; **selection** n sélection f,
choix m; **selective** adj sélectif(-ive); (school) à

s

recrutement sélectif

self [sɛlf] n (pl **selves**): **the ~** le moi inv ▷ prefix auto-; **self-assured** adj sûr(e) de soi, plein(e) d'assurance; **self-catering** adj (BRIT: flat) avec cuisine, où l'on peut faire sa cuisine; (: holiday) en appartement (or chalet etc) loué; **self-centred** (US **self-centered**) adj égocentrique; **self-confidence** n confiance f en soi; **self-confident** adj sûr(e) de soi, plein(e) d'assurance; **self-conscious** adj timide, qui manque d'assurance; **self-contained** adj (BRIT: flat) avec entrée particulière, indépendant(e); **self-control** n maîtrise f de soi; **self-defence** (US **self-defense**) n autodéfense f; (Law) légitime défense f; **self-drive** adj (BRIT): **self-drive car** voiture f de location; **self-employed** adj qui travaille à son compte; **self-esteem** n amour-propre m; **self-indulgent** adj qui ne se refuse rien; **self-interest** n intérêt personnel; **selfish** adj égoïste; **self-pity** n apitoiement m sur soi-même; **self-raising** [sɛlfˈreɪzɪŋ] (US **self-rising** [sɛlfˈraɪzɪŋ]) adj: **self-raising flour** farine f pour gâteaux (avec levure incorporée); **self-respect** n respect m de soi, amour-propre m; **self-service** adj, n libre-service (m), self-service (m)

sell (pt, pp **sold**) [sɛl, səuld] vt vendre ▷ vi se vendre; **to ~ at** or **for 10 euros** se vendre 10 euros; **sell off** vt liquider; **sell out** vi: **to ~ out (of sth)** (use up stock) vendre tout son stock (de qch); **sell-by date** n date f limite de vente; **seller** n vendeur(-euse), marchand(e)

Sellotape® [ˈsɛləuteɪp] n (BRIT) scotch® m

selves [sɛlvz] npl of **self**

semester [sɪˈmɛstəʳ] n (esp US) semestre m

semi... [ˈsɛmɪ] prefix semi-, demi-; à demi, à moitié; **semicircle** n demi-cercle m; **semidetached (house)** n (BRIT) maison jumelée or jumelle; **semi-final** n demi-finale f

seminar [ˈsɛmɪnɑːʳ] n séminaire m

semi-skimmed [ˈsɛmɪˈskɪmd] adj demi-écrémé(e)

senate [ˈsɛnɪt] n sénat m; (US): **the S~** le Sénat; **senator** n sénateur m

send (pt, pp **sent**) [sɛnd, sɛnt] vt envoyer; **send back** vt renvoyer; **send for** vt fus (by post) se faire envoyer, commander par correspondance; **send in** vt (report, application, resignation) remettre; **send off** vt (goods) envoyer, expédier; (BRIT Sport: player) expulser or renvoyer du terrain; **send on** vt (BRIT: letter) faire suivre; (luggage etc: in advance) (faire) expédier à l'avance; **send out** vt (invitation) envoyer (par la poste); (emit: light, heat, signal) émettre; **send up** vt (person, price) faire monter; (BRIT: parody) mettre en boîte, parodier; **sender** n expéditeur(-trice); **send-off** n: **a good send-off** des adieux chaleureux

senile [ˈsiːnaɪl] adj sénile

senior [ˈsiːnɪəʳ] adj (high-ranking) de haut niveau; (of higher rank): **to be ~ to sb** être le supérieur de qn; **senior citizen** n personne f du troisième âge; **senior high school** n (US) ≈ lycée m

sensation [sɛnˈseɪʃən] n sensation f; **sensational** adj qui fait sensation; (marvellous) sensationnel(le)

sense [sɛns] n sens m; (feeling) sentiment m; (meaning) sens, signification f; (wisdom) bon sens ▷ vt sentir, pressentir; **it makes ~** c'est logique; **senseless** adj insensé(e), stupide; (unconscious) sans connaissance; **sense of humour** (US **sense of humor**) n sens m de l'humour

sensible [ˈsɛnsɪbl] adj sensé(e), raisonnable; (shoes etc) pratique

> Be careful not to translate **sensible** by the French word **sensible**.

sensitive [ˈsɛnsɪtɪv] adj: **~ (to)** sensible (à)

sensual [ˈsɛnsjuəl] adj sensuel(le)

sensuous [ˈsɛnsjuəs] adj voluptueux(-euse), sensuel(le)

sent [sɛnt] pt, pp of **send**

sentence [ˈsɛntns] n (Ling) phrase f; (Law: judgment) condamnation f, sentence f; (: punishment) peine f ▷ vt: **to ~ sb to death/to 5 years** condamner qn à mort/à 5 ans

sentiment [ˈsɛntɪmənt] n sentiment m; (opinion) opinion f, avis m; **sentimental** [sɛntɪˈmɛntl] adj sentimental(e)

Sep. abbr (= September) septembre

separate adj [ˈsɛprɪt] séparé(e); (organization) indépendant(e); (day, occasion, issue) différent(e) ▷ vb [ˈsɛpəreɪt] ▷ vt séparer; (distinguish) distinguer ▷ vi se séparer; **separately** adv séparément; **separates** npl (clothes) coordonnés mpl; **separation** [sɛpəˈreɪʃən] n séparation f

September [sɛpˈtɛmbəʳ] n septembre m

septic [ˈsɛptɪk] adj (wound) infecté(e); **septic tank** n fosse f septique

sequel [ˈsiːkwl] n conséquence f; séquelles fpl; (of story) suite f

sequence [ˈsiːkwəns] n ordre m, suite f; (in film) séquence f; (dance) numéro m

sequin [ˈsiːkwɪn] n paillette f

Serb [səːb] adj, n = **Serbian**

Serbia [ˈsəːbɪə] n Serbie f

Serbian [ˈsəːbɪən] adj serbe ▷ n Serbe m/f; (Ling) serbe m

sergeant [ˈsɑːdʒənt] n sergent m; (Police) brigadier m

serial [ˈsɪərɪəl] n feuilleton m; **serial killer** n meurtrier m tuant en série; **serial number** n numéro m de série

series [ˈsɪəriːz] n série f; (Publishing) collection f

serious [ˈsɪərɪəs] adj sérieux(-euse); (accident

etc) grave; **seriously** *adv* sérieusement; (*hurt*) gravement

sermon ['sə:mən] *n* sermon *m*

servant ['sə:vənt] *n* domestique *m/f*; (*fig*) serviteur (servante)

serve [sə:v] *vt* (*employer etc*) servir, être au service de; (*purpose*) servir à; (*customer, food, meal*) servir; (*subj: train*) desservir; (*apprenticeship*) faire, accomplir; (*prison term*) faire; purger ▷ *vi* (*Tennis*) servir; (*be useful*): **to ~ as/for/to do** servir de/à/à faire ▷ *n* (*Tennis*) service *m*; **it ~s him right** c'est bien fait pour lui; **server** *n* (*Comput*) serveur *m*

service ['sə:vɪs] *n* (*gen*) service *m*; (*Aut*) révision *f*; (*Rel*) office *m* ▷ *vt* (*car etc*) réviser; **services** *npl* (*Econ: tertiary sector*) secteur *m* tertiaire, secteur des services; (*BRIT: on motorway*) station-service *f*; (*Mil*): **the S~s** *npl* les forces armées; **to be of ~ to sb, to do sb a ~** rendre service à qn; **~ included/not included** service compris/non compris; **service area** *n* (*on motorway*) aire *f* de services; **service charge** *n* (*BRIT*) service *m*; **serviceman** (*irreg*) *n* militaire *m*; **service station** *n* station-service *f*

serviette [sə:vɪ'ɛt] *n* (*BRIT*) serviette *f* (de table)

session ['sɛʃən] *n* (*sitting*) séance *f*; **to be in ~** siéger, être en session *or* en séance

set [sɛt] *n* série *f*, assortiment *m*; (*of tools etc*) jeu *m*; (*Radio, TV*) poste *m*; (*Tennis*) set *m*; (*group of people*) cercle *m*, milieu *m*; (*Cine*) plateau *m*; (*Theat: stage*) scène *f*; (*: scenery*) décor *m*; (*Math*) ensemble *m*; (*Hairdressing*) mise *f* en plis ▷ *adj* (*fixed*) fixe, déterminé(e); (*ready*) prêt(e) ▷ *vb* (*pt, pp* **~**) ▷ *vt* (*place*) mettre, poser, placer; (*fix, establish*) fixer; (*: record*) établir; (*assign: task, homework*) donner; (*exam*) composer; (*adjust*) régler; (*decide: rules etc*) fixer, choisir ▷ *vi* (*sun*) se coucher; (*jam, jelly, concrete*) prendre; (*bone*) se ressouder; **to be ~ on doing** être résolu(e) à faire; **to ~ to music** mettre en musique; **to ~ on fire** mettre le feu à; **to ~ free** libérer; **to ~ sth going** déclencher qch; **to ~ sail** partir, prendre la mer; **set aside** *vt* mettre de côté; (*time*) garder; **set down** *vt* (*subj: bus, train*) déposer; **set in** *vi* (*infection, bad weather*) s'installer; (*complications*) survenir, surgir; **set off** *vi* se mettre en route, partir ▷ *vt* (*bomb*) faire exploser; (*cause to start*) déclencher; (*show up well*) mettre en valeur, faire valoir; **set out** *vi*: **to ~ out (from)** partir (de) ▷ *vt* (*arrange*) disposer; (*state*) présenter, exposer; **to ~ out to do** entreprendre de faire; avoir pour but *or* intention de faire; **set up** *vt* (*organization*) fonder, créer; **setback** *n* (*hitch*) revers *m*, contretemps *m*; **set menu** *n* menu *m*

settee [sɛ'ti:] *n* canapé *m*

setting ['sɛtɪŋ] *n* cadre *m*; (*of jewel*) monture *f*; (*position: of controls*) réglage *m*

settle ['sɛtl] *vt* (*argument, matter, account*) régler; (*problem*) résoudre; (*Med: calm*) calmer ▷ *vi* (*bird, dust etc*) se poser; **to ~ for sth** accepter qch, se contenter de qch; **to ~ on sth** opter *or* se décider pour qch; **settle down** *vi* (*get comfortable*) s'installer; (*become calmer*) se calmer; se ranger; (*live quietly*) se fixer; **settle in** *vi* s'installer; **settle up** *vi*: **to ~ up with sb** régler (ce que l'on doit à) qn; **settlement** *n* (*payment*) règlement *m*; (*agreement*) accord *m*; (*village etc*) village *m*, hameau *m*

setup ['sɛtʌp] *n* (*arrangement*) manière *f* dont les choses sont organisées; (*situation*) situation *f*, allure *f* des choses

seven ['sɛvn] *num* sept; **seventeen** *num* dix-sept; **seventeenth** [sɛvn'ti:nθ] *num* dix-septième; **seventh** *num* septième; **seventieth** ['sɛvntɪɪθ] *num* soixante-dixième; **seventy** *num* soixante-dix

sever ['sɛvə'] *vt* couper, trancher; (*relations*) rompre

several ['sɛvərl] *adj, pron* plusieurs *pl*; **~ of us** plusieurs d'entre nous

severe [sɪ'vɪə'] *adj* (*stern*) sévère, strict(e); (*serious*) grave, sérieux(-euse); (*plain*) sévère, austère

sew (*pt* **~ed**, *pp* **~n**) [səu, səud, səun] *vt, vi* coudre

sewage ['su:ɪdʒ] *n* vidange(s) *f(pl)*

sewer ['su:ə'] *n* égout *m*

sewing ['səuɪŋ] *n* couture *f*; (*item(s)*) ouvrage *m*; **sewing machine** *n* machine *f* à coudre

sewn [səun] *pp of* **sew**

sex [sɛks] *n* sexe *m*; **to have ~ with** avoir des rapports (sexuels) avec; **sexism** ['sɛksɪzə m] *n* sexisme *m*; **sexist** *adj* sexiste; **sexual** ['sɛksjuəl] *adj* sexuel(le); **sexual intercourse** *n* rapports sexuels; **sexuality** [sɛksju'ælɪtɪ] *n* sexualité *f*; **sexy** *adj* sexy *inv*

shabby ['ʃæbɪ] *adj* miteux(-euse); (*behaviour*) mesquin(e), méprisable

shack [ʃæk] *n* cabane *f*, hutte *f*

shade [ʃeɪd] *n* ombre *f*; (*for lamp*) abat-jour *m inv*; (*of colour*) nuance *f*, ton *m*; (*us: window shade*) store *m*; (*small quantity*): **a ~ of** un soupçon de ▷ *vt* abriter du soleil, ombrager; **shades** *npl* (*us: sunglasses*) lunettes *fpl* de soleil; **in the ~** à l'ombre; **a ~ smaller** un tout petit peu plus petit

shadow ['ʃædəu] *n* ombre *f* ▷ *vt* (*follow*) filer; **shadow cabinet** *n* (*BRIT Pol*) cabinet parallèle formé par le parti qui n'est pas au pouvoir

shady ['ʃeɪdɪ] *adj* ombragé(e); (*fig: dishonest*) louche, véreux(-euse)

shaft [ʃɑ:ft] *n* (*of arrow, spear*) hampe *f*; (*Aut, Tech*) arbre *m*; (*of mine*) puits *m*; (*of lift*) cage *f*; (*of light*) rayon *m*, trait *m*

S

shake [ʃeɪk] vb (pt **shook**, pp **~n**) ▷ vt secouer; (bottle, cocktail) agiter; (house, confidence) ébranler ▷ vi trembler; **to ~ one's head** (in refusal etc) dire ou faire non de la tête; (in dismay) secouer la tête; **to ~ hands with sb** serrer la main à qn; **shake off** vt secouer; (pursuer) se débarrasser de; **shake up** vt secouer; **shaky** adj (hand, voice) tremblant(e); (building) branlant(e), peu solide

shall [ʃæl] aux vb: **I ~ go** j'irai; **~ I open the door?** j'ouvre la porte?; **I'll get the coffee, ~ I?** je vais chercher le café, d'accord?

shallow ['ʃæləu] adj peu profond(e); (fig) superficiel(le), qui manque de profondeur

sham [ʃæm] n frime f

shambles ['ʃæmblz] n confusion f, pagaïe f, fouillis m

shame [ʃeɪm] n honte f ▷ vt faire honte à; **it is a ~ (that/to do)** c'est dommage (que + sub/de faire); **what a ~!** quel dommage!; **shameful** adj honteux(-euse), scandaleux(-euse); **shameless** adj éhonté(e), effronté(e)

shampoo [ʃæm'puː] n shampooing m ▷ vt faire un shampooing à

shandy ['ʃændɪ] n bière panachée

shan't [ʃɑːnt] = **shall not**

shape [ʃeɪp] n forme f ▷ vt façonner, modeler; (sb's ideas, character) former; (sb's life) déterminer ▷ vi (also: **~ up**: events) prendre tournure; (: person) faire des progrès, s'en sortir; **to take ~** prendre forme ou tournure

share [ʃɛəʳ] n part f; (Comm) action f ▷ vt partager; (have in common) avoir en commun; **to ~ out (among** or **between)** partager (entre); **shareholder** n (BRIT) actionnaire m/f

shark [ʃɑːk] n requin m

sharp [ʃɑːp] adj (razor, knife) tranchant(e), bien aiguisé(e); (point, voice) aigu(ë); (nose, chin) pointu(e); (outline, increase) net(te); (cold, pain) vif (vive); (taste) piquant(e), âcre; (Mus) dièse; (person: quick-witted) vif (vive), éveillé(e); (: unscrupulous) malhonnête ▷ n (Mus) dièse m ▷ adv: **at 2 o'clock ~** à 2 heures pile ou tapantes; **sharpen** vt aiguiser; (pencil) tailler; (fig) aviver; **sharpener** n (also: **pencil sharpener**) taille-crayon(s) m inv; **sharply** adv (turn, stop) brusquement; (stand out) nettement; (criticize, retort) sèchement, vertement

shatter ['ʃætəʳ] vt briser; (fig: upset) bouleverser; (: ruin) briser, ruiner ▷ vi voler en éclats, se briser; **shattered** adj (overwhelmed, grief-stricken) bouleversé(e); (inf: exhausted) éreinté(e)

shave [ʃeɪv] vt raser ▷ vi se raser ▷ n: **to have a ~** se raser; **shaver** n (also: **electric shaver**) rasoir m électrique

shaving cream n crème f à raser

shaving foam n mousse f à raser

shavings ['ʃeɪvɪŋz] npl (of wood etc) copeaux mpl

shawl [ʃɔːl] n châle m

she [ʃiː] pron elle

sheath [ʃiːθ] n gaine f, fourreau m, étui m; (contraceptive) préservatif m

shed [ʃɛd] n remise f, resserre f ▷ vt (pt, pp **~**) (leaves, fur etc) perdre; (tears) verser, répandre; (workers) congédier

she'd [ʃiːd] = **she had**; **she would**

sheep [ʃiːp] n (pl inv) mouton m; **sheepdog** n chien m de berger; **sheepskin** n peau f de mouton

sheer [ʃɪəʳ] adj (utter) pur(e), pur et simple; (steep) à pic, abrupt(e); (almost transparent) extrêmement fin(e) ▷ adv à pic, abruptement

sheet [ʃiːt] n (on bed) drap m; (of paper) feuille f; (of glass, metal etc) feuille, plaque f

sheik(h) [ʃeɪk] n cheik m

shelf (pl **shelves**) [ʃɛlf, ʃɛlvz] n étagère f, rayon m

shell [ʃɛl] n (on beach) coquillage m; (of egg, nut etc) coquille f; (explosive) obus m; (of building) carcasse f ▷ vt (peas) écosser; (Mil) bombarder (d'obus)

she'll [ʃiːl] = **she will**; **she shall**

shellfish ['ʃɛlfɪʃ] n (pl inv: crab etc) crustacé m; (: scallop etc) coquillage m ▷ npl (as food) fruits mpl de mer

shelter ['ʃɛltəʳ] n abri m, refuge m ▷ vt abriter, protéger; (give lodging to) donner asile à ▷ vi s'abriter, se mettre à l'abri; **sheltered** adj (life) retiré(e), à l'abri des soucis; (spot) abrité(e)

shelves ['ʃɛlvz] npl of **shelf**

shelving ['ʃɛlvɪŋ] n (shelves) rayonnage(s) m(pl)

shepherd ['ʃɛpəd] n berger m ▷ vt (guide) guider, escorter; **shepherd's pie** n ≈ hachis m Parmentier

sheriff ['ʃɛrɪf] (US) n shérif m

sherry ['ʃɛrɪ] n xérès m, sherry m

she's [ʃiːz] = **she is**; **she has**

Shetland ['ʃɛtlənd] n (also: **the ~s, the ~ Isles** or **Islands**) les îles fpl Shetland

shield [ʃiːld] n bouclier m; (protection) écran m de protection ▷ vt: **to ~ (from)** protéger (de ou contre)

shift [ʃɪft] n (change) changement m; (work period) période f de travail; (of workers) équipe f, poste m ▷ vt déplacer, changer de place; (remove) enlever ▷ vi changer de place, bouger

shin [ʃɪn] n tibia m

shine [ʃaɪn] n éclat m, brillant m ▷ vb (pt, pp **shone**) ▷ vi briller ▷ vt (torch): **to ~ on** braquer sur; (polish: pt, pp **~d**) faire briller ou reluire

shingles ['ʃɪŋglz] n (Med) zona m

shiny ['ʃaɪnɪ] adj brillant(e)

ship [ʃɪp] n bateau m; (large) navire m ▷ vt transporter (par mer); (send) expédier (par mer); **shipment** n cargaison f; **shipping**

n (ships) navires mpl; (traffic) navigation f; (the industry) industrie navale; (transport) transport m; **shipwreck** n épave f, (event) naufrage m ▷ vt: **to be shipwrecked** faire naufrage; **shipyard** n chantier naval

shirt [ʃəːt] n chemise f, (woman's) chemisier m; **in ~ sleeves** en bras de chemise

shit [ʃɪt] excl (inf!) merde (!)

shiver ['ʃɪvər] n frisson m ▷ vi frissonner

shock [ʃɔk] n choc m; (Elec) secousse f, décharge f, (Med) commotion f, choc ▷ vt (scandalize) choquer, scandaliser; (upset) bouleverser; **shocking** adj (outrageous) choquant(e), scandaleux(-euse); (awful) épouvantable

shoe [ʃuː] n chaussure f, soulier m; (also: **horse~**) fer m à cheval ▷ vt (pt, pp **shod**) (horse) ferrer; **shoelace** n lacet m (de soulier); **shoe polish** n cirage m; **shoeshop** n magasin m de chaussures

shone [ʃɔn] pt, pp of **shine**

shook [ʃʊk] pt of **shake**

shoot [ʃuːt] n (on branch, seedling) pousse f ▷ vb (pt, pp **shot**) ▷ vt (game: hunt) chasser; (: aim at) tirer; (: kill) abattre; (person) blesser/tuer d'un coup de fusil (or de revolver); (execute) fusiller; (arrow) tirer; (gun) tirer un coup de; (Cine) tourner ▷ vi (with gun, bow): **to ~ (at)** tirer (sur); (Football) shooter, tirer; **shoot down** vt (plane) abattre; **shoot up** vi (fig: prices etc) monter en flèche; **shooting** n (shots) coups mpl de feu; (attack) fusillade f, (murder) homicide m (à l'aide d'une arme à feu); (Hunting) chasse f

shop [ʃɔp] n magasin m; (workshop) atelier m ▷ vi (also: **go ~ping**) faire ses courses or ses achats; **shop assistant** n (BRIT) vendeur(-euse); **shopkeeper** n marchand(e), commerçant(e); **shoplifting** n vol m à l'étalage; **shopping** n (goods) achats mpl, provisions fpl; **shopping bag** n sac m (à provisions); **shopping centre** (us **shopping center**) n centre commercial; **shopping mall** n centre commercial; **shopping trolley** n (BRIT) Caddie® m; **shop window** n vitrine f

shore [ʃɔːr] n (of sea, lake) rivage m, rive f ▷ vt: **to ~ (up)** étayer; **on ~** à terre

short [ʃɔːt] adj (not long) court(e); (soon finished) court, bref (brève); (person, step) petit(e); (curt) brusque, sec (sèche); (insufficient) insuffisant(e) ▷ n (also: **~ film**) court métrage; (Elec) court-circuit m; **to be ~ of sth** être à court de or manquer de qch; **in ~** bref; en bref; **~ of doing** à moins de faire; **everything ~ of** tout sauf; **it is ~ for** c'est l'abréviation or le diminutif de; **to cut ~** (speech, visit) abréger, écourter; **to fall ~ of** ne pas être à la hauteur de; **to run ~ of** arriver à court de, venir à manquer de; **to stop ~** s'arrêter net;

to stop ~ of ne pas aller jusqu'à; **shortage** n manque m, pénurie f, **shortbread** n ≈ sablé m; **shortcoming** n défaut m; **short(crust) pastry** n (BRIT) pâte brisée; **shortcut** n raccourci m; **shorten** vt raccourcir; (text, visit) abréger; **shortfall** n déficit m; **shorthand** n (BRIT) sténo(graphie) f; **shortlist** n (BRIT: for job) liste f des candidats sélectionnés; **short-lived** adj de courte durée; **shortly** adv bientôt, sous peu; **shorts** npl: **(a pair of) shorts** un short; **short-sighted** adj (BRIT) myope; (fig) qui manque de clairvoyance; **short-sleeved** adj à manches courtes; **short story** n nouvelle f, **short-tempered** adj qui s'emporte facilement; **short-term** adj (effect) à court terme

shot [ʃɔt] pt, pp of **shoot** ▷ n coup m (de feu); (try) coup, essai m; (injection) piqûre f, (Phot) photo f, **to be a good/poor ~** (person) tirer bien/mal; **like a ~** comme une flèche; (very readily) sans hésiter; **shotgun** n fusil m de chasse

should [ʃʊd] aux vb: **I ~ go now** je devrais partir maintenant; **he ~ be there now** il devrait être arrivé maintenant; **I ~ go if I were you** si j'étais vous j'irais; **I ~ like to** j'aimerais bien, volontiers

shoulder ['ʃəʊldər] n épaule f ▷ vt (fig) endosser, se charger de; **shoulder blade** n omoplate f

shouldn't ['ʃʊdnt] = **should not**

shout [ʃaʊt] n cri m ▷ vt crier ▷ vi crier, pousser des cris

shove [ʃʌv] vt pousser; (inf: put): **to ~ sth in** fourrer or ficher qch dans ▷ n poussée f

shovel ['ʃʌvl] n pelle f ▷ vt pelleter, enlever (or enfourner) à la pelle

show [ʃəʊ] n (of emotion) manifestation f, démonstration f, (semblance) semblant m, apparence f, (exhibition) exposition f, salon m; (Theat, TV) spectacle m; (Cine) séance f ▷ vb (pt **~ed**, pp **~n**) ▷ vt montrer; (film) passer; (courage etc) faire preuve de, manifester; (exhibit) exposer ▷ vi se voir, être visible; **can you ~ me where it is, please?** pouvez-vous me montrer où c'est?; **to be on ~** être exposé(e); **it's just for ~** c'est juste pour l'effet; **show in** vt faire entrer; **show off** vi (pej) crâner ▷ vt (display) faire valoir; (pej) faire étalage de; **show out** vt reconduire à la porte; **show up** vi (stand out) ressortir; (inf: turn up) se montrer ▷ vt (unmask) démasquer, dénoncer; (flaw) faire ressortir; **show business** n le monde du spectacle

shower ['ʃaʊər] n (for washing) douche f, (rain) averse f, (of stones etc) pluie f, grêle f, (us: party) réunion organisée pour la remise de cadeaux ▷ vi prendre une douche, se doucher ▷ vt: **to ~ sb with** (gifts etc) combler qn de; **to have** or **take a ~** prendre une douche, se doucher; **shower**

cap n bonnet m de douche; **shower gel** n gel m douche

showing ['ʃəʊɪŋ] n (of film) projection f

show jumping [-dʒʌmpɪŋ] n concours m hippique

shown [ʃəʊn] pp of **show**

show: **show-off** n (inf: person) crâneur(-euse), m'as-tu-vu(e); **showroom** n magasin m or salle f d'exposition

shrank [ʃræŋk] pt of **shrink**

shred [ʃred] n (gen pl) lambeau m, petit morceau; (fig: of truth, evidence) parcelle f ▷ vt mettre en lambeaux, déchirer; (documents) détruire; (Culin: grate) râper; (: lettuce etc) couper en lanières

shrewd [ʃruːd] adj astucieux(-euse), perspicace; (business person) habile

shriek [ʃriːk] n cri perçant or aigu, hurlement m ▷ vt, vi hurler, crier

shrimp [ʃrɪmp] n crevette grise

shrine [ʃraɪn] n (place) lieu m de pèlerinage

shrink (pt **shrank**, pp **shrunk**) [ʃrɪŋk, ʃræŋk, ʃrʌŋk] vi rétrécir; (fig) diminuer; (also: ~ **away**) reculer ▷ vt (wool) (faire) rétrécir ▷ n (inf: pej) psychanalyste m/f; **to ~ from** (doing) **sth** reculer devant (la pensée de faire) qch

shrivel ['ʃrɪvl] (also: ~ **up**) vt ratatiner, flétrir ▷ vi se ratatiner, se flétrir

shroud [ʃraʊd] n linceul m ▷ vt: **~ed in mystery** enveloppé(e) de mystère

Shrove Tuesday ['ʃrəʊv-] n (le) Mardi gras

shrub [ʃrʌb] n arbuste m

shrug [ʃrʌg] n haussement m d'épaules ▷ vt, vi: **to ~ (one's shoulders)** hausser les épaules; **shrug off** vt faire fi de

shrunk [ʃrʌŋk] pp of **shrink**

shudder ['ʃʌdə'] n frisson m, frémissement m ▷ vi frissonner, frémir

shuffle ['ʃʌfl] vt (cards) battre; **to ~ (one's feet)** traîner les pieds

shun [ʃʌn] vt éviter, fuir

shut (pt, pp ~) [ʃʌt] vt fermer ▷ vi (se) fermer; **shut down** vt fermer définitivement ▷ vi fermer définitivement; **shut up** vi (inf: keep quiet) se taire ▷ vt (close) fermer; (silence) faire taire; **shutter** n volet m; (Phot) obturateur m

shuttle ['ʃʌtl] n navette f; (also: ~ **service** (service m de) navette f; **shuttlecock** n volant m (de badminton)

shy [ʃaɪ] adj timide

siblings ['sɪblɪŋz] npl (formal) frères et sœurs mpl (de mêmes parents)

Sicily ['sɪsɪlɪ] n Sicile f

sick [sɪk] adj (ill) malade; (BRIT: vomiting): **to be ~** vomir; (humour) noir(e), macabre; **to feel ~** avoir envie de vomir, avoir mal au cœur; **to be ~ of** (fig) en avoir assez de; **sickening** adj (fig) écœurant(e), révoltant(e), répugnant(e); **sick leave** n congé m de maladie; **sickly** adj

maladif(-ive), souffreteux(-euse); (causing nausea) écœurant(e); **sickness** n maladie f; (vomiting) vomissement(s) m(pl)

side [saɪd] n côté m; (of lake, road) bord m; (of mountain) versant m; (fig: aspect) côté, aspect m; (team: Sport) équipe f; (TV: channel) chaîne f ▷ adj (door, entrance) latéral(e) ▷ vi: **to ~ with sb** prendre le parti de qn, se ranger du côté de qn; **by the ~ of** au bord de; **~ by ~** côte à côte; **to rock from ~ to ~** se balancer; **to take ~s (with)** prendre parti (pour); **sideboard** n buffet m; **sideboards** (BRIT), **sideburns** npl (whiskers) pattes fpl; **side effect** n effet m secondaire; **sidelight** n (Aut) veilleuse f; **sideline** n (Sport) (ligne f de) touche f; (fig) activité f secondaire; **side order** n garniture f; **side road** n petite route, route transversale; **side street** n rue transversale; **sidetrack** vt (fig) faire dévier de son sujet; **sidewalk** n (us) trottoir m; **sideways** adv de côté

siege [siːdʒ] n siège m

sieve [sɪv] n tamis m, passoire f ▷ vt tamiser, passer (au tamis)

sift [sɪft] vt passer au tamis or au crible; (fig) passer au crible

sigh [saɪ] n soupir m ▷ vi soupirer, pousser un soupir

sight [saɪt] n (faculty) vue f; (spectacle) spectacle m; (on gun) mire f ▷ vt apercevoir; **in ~** visible; (fig) en vue; **out of ~** hors de vue; **sightseeing** n tourisme m; **to go sightseeing** faire du tourisme

sign [saɪn] n (gen) signe m; (with hand etc) signe, geste m; (notice) panneau m, écriteau m; (also: **road~**) panneau de signalisation ▷ vt signer; **where do I ~?** où dois-je signer?; **sign for** vt fus (item) signer le reçu pour; **sign in** vi signer le registre (en arrivant); **sign on** vi (BRIT: as unemployed) s'inscrire au chômage; (enrol) s'inscrire ▷ vt (employee) embaucher; **sign over** vt: **to ~ sth over to sb** céder qch par écrit à qn; **sign up** vi (Mil) s'engager; (for course) s'inscrire

signal ['sɪgnl] n signal m ▷ vi (Aut) mettre son clignotant ▷ vt (person) faire signe à; (message) communiquer par signaux

signature ['sɪgnətʃə'] n signature f

significance [sɪgˈnɪfɪkəns] n signification f; importance f

significant [sɪgˈnɪfɪkənt] adj significatif(-ive); (important) important(e), considérable

signify ['sɪgnɪfaɪ] vt signifier

sign language n langage m par signes

signpost ['saɪnpəʊst] n poteau indicateur

Sikh [siːk] adj, n Sikh m/f

silence ['saɪləns] n silence m ▷ vt faire taire, réduire au silence

silent ['saɪlnt] adj silencieux(-euse); (film) muet(te); **to keep** or **remain ~** garder le silence, ne rien dire

silhouette [sɪluːˈɛt] n silhouette f

silicon chip [ˈsɪlɪkən-] n puce f électronique

silk [sɪlk] n soie f ▷ cpd de or en soie

silly [ˈsɪlɪ] adj stupide, sot(te), bête

silver [ˈsɪlvər] n argent m; (money) monnaie f (en pièces d'argent); (also: **~ware**) argenterie f ▷ adj (made of silver) d'argent, en argent; (in colour) argenté(e); **silver-plated** adj plaqué(e) argent

similar [ˈsɪmɪlər] adj: **~ (to)** semblable (à); **similarity** [sɪmɪˈlærɪtɪ] n ressemblance f, similarité f; **similarly** adv de la même façon, de même

simmer [ˈsɪmər] vi cuire à feu doux, mijoter

simple [ˈsɪmpl] adj simple; **simplicity** [sɪmˈplɪsɪtɪ] n simplicité f; **simplify** [ˈsɪmplɪfaɪ] vt simplifier; **simply** adv simplement; (without fuss) avec simplicité; (absolutely) absolument

simulate [ˈsɪmjuleɪt] vt simuler, feindre

simultaneous [sɪməlˈteɪnɪəs] adj simultané(e); **simultaneously** adv simultanément

sin [sɪn] n péché m ▷ vi pécher

since [sɪns] adv, prep depuis ▷ conj (time) depuis que; (because) puisque, étant donné que, comme; **~ then, ever ~** depuis ce moment-là

sincere [sɪnˈsɪər] adj sincère; **sincerely** adv sincèrement; **Yours sincerely** (at end of letter) veuillez agréer, Monsieur (or Madame) l'expression de mes sentiments distingués or les meilleurs

sing (pt **sang**, pp **sung**) [sɪŋ, sæŋ, sʌŋ] vt, vi chanter

Singapore [sɪŋɡəˈpɔːʳ] n Singapour m

singer [ˈsɪŋəʳ] n chanteur(-euse)

singing [ˈsɪŋɪŋ] n (of person, bird) chant m

single [ˈsɪŋɡl] adj seul(e), unique; (unmarried) célibataire; (not double) simple ▷ n (BRIT: also: **~ ticket**) aller m (simple); (record) 45 tours m; **singles** npl (Tennis) simple m; **every ~ day** chaque jour sans exception; **single out** vt choisir; (distinguish) distinguer; **single bed** n lit m d'une personne or à une place; **single file** n: **in single file** en file indienne; **single-handed** adv tout(e) seul(e), sans (aucune) aide; **single-minded** adj résolu(e), tenace; **single parent** n parent unique (or célibataire); **single-parent family** famille monoparentale; **single room** n chambre f à un lit or pour une personne

singular [ˈsɪŋɡjʊləʳ] adj singulier(-ière); (odd) singulier, étrange; (outstanding) remarquable; (Ling) (au) singulier, du singulier ▷ n (Ling) singulier m

sinister [ˈsɪnɪstəʳ] adj sinistre

sink [sɪŋk] n évier m; (washbasin) lavabo

m ▷ vb (pt **sank**, pp **sunk**) ▷ vt (ship) (faire) couler, faire sombrer; (foundations) creuser ▷ vi couler, sombrer; (ground etc) s'affaisser; **to ~ into sth** (chair) s'enfoncer dans qch; **sink in** vi (explanation) rentrer (inf), être compris

sinus [ˈsaɪnəs] n (Anat) sinus m inv

sip [sɪp] n petite gorgée ▷ vt boire à petites gorgées

sir [səʳ] n monsieur m; **S~ John Smith** sir John Smith; **yes ~** oui Monsieur

siren [ˈsaɪərən] n sirène f

sirloin [ˈsəːlɔɪn] n (also: **~ steak**) aloyau m

sister [ˈsɪstəʳ] n sœur f; (nun) religieuse f, (bonne) sœur; (BRIT: nurse) infirmière f en chef; **sister-in-law** n belle-sœur f

sit (pt, pp **sat**) [sɪt, sæt] vi s'asseoir; (be sitting) être assis(e); (assembly) être en séance, siéger; (for painter) poser ▷ vt (exam) passer, se présenter à; **sit back** vi (in seat) bien s'installer, se carrer; **sit down** vi s'asseoir; **sit on** vt fus (jury, committee) faire partie de; **sit up** vi s'asseoir; (straight) se redresser; (not go to bed) rester debout, ne pas se coucher

sitcom [ˈsɪtkɔm] n abbr (TV: = situation comedy) sitcom f, comédie f de situation

site [saɪt] n emplacement m, site m; (also: **building ~**) chantier m ▷ vt placer

sitting [ˈsɪtɪŋ] n (of assembly etc) séance f; (in canteen) service m; **sitting room** n salon m

situated [ˈsɪtjueɪtɪd] adj situé(e)

situation [sɪtjuˈeɪʃən] n situation f; **"~s vacant/wanted"** (BRIT) "offres/demandes d'emploi"

six [sɪks] num six; **sixteen** num seize; **sixteenth** [sɪksˈtiːnθ] num seizième; **sixth** [sɪksθ] num sixième; **sixth form** n (BRIT) ≈ classes fpl de première et de terminale; **sixth-form college** n lycée n'ayant que des classes de première et de terminale; **sixtieth** [ˈsɪkstɪɪθ] num soixantième; **sixty** num soixante

size [saɪz] n dimensions fpl; (of person) taille f; (of clothing) taille f; (of shoes) pointure f; (of problem) ampleur f; (glue) colle f; **sizeable** adj assez grand(e); (amount, problem, majority) assez important(e)

sizzle [ˈsɪzl] vi grésiller

skate [skeɪt] n patin m; (fish: pl inv) raie f ▷ vi patiner; **skateboard** n skateboard m, planche f à roulettes; **skateboarding** n skateboard m; **skater** n patineur(-euse); **skating** n patinage m; **skating rink** n patinoire f

skeleton [ˈskɛlɪtn] n squelette m; (outline) schéma m

skeptical [ˈskɛptɪkl] (US) = **sceptical**

sketch [skɛtʃ] n (drawing) croquis m, esquisse f; (outline plan) aperçu m; (Theat) sketch m, saynète f ▷ vt esquisser, faire un croquis or une esquisse de; (plan etc) esquisser

skewer [ˈskjuːəʳ] n brochette f

ski [ski:] *n* ski *m* ▷ *vi* skier, faire du ski; **ski boot** *n* chaussure *f* de ski

skid [skɪd] *n* dérapage *m* ▷ *vi* déraper

ski: skier *n* skieur(-euse); **skiing** *n* ski *m*; **to go skiing** (aller) faire du ski

skilful (*US* **skillful**) ['skɪlful] *adj* habile, adroit(e)

ski lift *n* remonte-pente *m inv*

skill [skɪl] *n* (*ability*) habileté *f*, adresse *f*, talent *m*; (*requiring training*) compétences *fpl*; **skilled** *adj* habile, adroit(e); (*worker*) qualifié(e)

skim [skɪm] *vt* (*soup*) écumer; (*glide over*) raser, effleurer ▷ *vi*: **to ~ through** (*fig*) parcourir; **skimmed milk** (*US* **skim milk**) *n* lait écrémé

skin [skɪn] *n* peau *f* ▷ *vt* (*fruit etc*) éplucher; (*animal*) écorcher; **skinhead** *n* skinhead *m*; **skinny** *adj* maigre, maigrichon(ne)

skip [skɪp] *n* petit bond *or* saut; (*BRIT: container*) benne *f* ▷ *vi* gambader, sautiller; (*with rope*) sauter à la corde ▷ *vt* (*pass over*) sauter

ski: ski pass *n* forfait-skieur(s) *m*; **ski pole** *n* bâton *m* de ski

skipper ['skɪpə^r] *n* (*Naut, Sport*) capitaine *m*; (*in race*) skipper *m*

skipping rope ['skɪpɪŋ-] (*US* **skip rope**) *n* (*BRIT*) corde *f* à sauter

skirt [skɜːt] *n* jupe *f* ▷ *vt* longer, contourner

skirting board ['skɜːtɪŋ-] *n* (*BRIT*) plinthe *f*

ski slope *n* piste *f* de ski

ski suit *n* combinaison *f* de ski

skull [skʌl] *n* crâne *m*

skunk [skʌŋk] *n* mouffette *f*

sky [skaɪ] *n* ciel *m*; **skyscraper** *n* gratte-ciel *m inv*

slab [slæb] *n* (*of stone*) dalle *f*; (*of meat, cheese*) tranche épaisse

slack [slæk] *adj* (*loose*) lâche, desserré(e); (*slow*) stagnant(e); (*careless*) négligent(e), peu sérieux(-euse) *or* consciencieux(-euse); **slacks** *npl* pantalon *m*

slain [sleɪn] *pp of* **slay**

slam [slæm] *vt* (*door*) (faire) claquer; (*throw*) jeter violemment, flanquer; (*inf: criticize*) éreinter, démolir ▷ *vi* claquer

slander ['slɑːndə^r] *n* calomnie *f*; (*Law*) diffamation *f*

slang [slæŋ] *n* argot *m*

slant [slɑːnt] *n* inclinaison *f*; (*fig*) angle *m*, point *m* de vue

slap [slæp] *n* claque *f*, gifle *f*; (*on the back*) tape *f* ▷ *vt* donner une claque *or* une gifle (*or* une tape) à; **to ~ on** (*paint*) appliquer rapidement ▷ *adv* (*directly*) tout droit, en plein

slash [slæʃ] *vt* entailler, taillader; (*fig: prices*) casser

slate [sleɪt] *n* ardoise *f* ▷ *vt* (*fig: criticize*) éreinter, démolir

slaughter ['slɔːtə^r] *n* carnage *m*, massacre *m*; (*of animals*) abattage *m* ▷ *vt* (*animal*)

abattre; (*people*) massacrer; **slaughterhouse** *n* abattoir *m*

Slav [slɑːv] *adj* slave

slave [sleɪv] *n* esclave *m/f* ▷ *vi* (*also:* **~ away**) trimer, travailler comme un forçat; **slavery** *n* esclavage *m*

slay (*pt* **slew**, *pp* **slain**) [sleɪ, sluː, sleɪn] *vt* (*literary*) tuer

sleazy ['sliːzɪ] *adj* miteux(-euse), minable

sled [slɛd] (*US*) = **sledge**

sledge [slɛdʒ] *n* luge *f*

sleek [sliːk] *adj* (*hair, fur*) brillant(e), luisant(e); (*car, boat*) aux lignes pures *or* élégantes

sleep [sliːp] *n* sommeil *m* ▷ *vi* (*pt, pp* **slept**) dormir; **to go to ~** s'endormir; **sleep in** *vi* (*oversleep*) se réveiller trop tard; (*on purpose*) faire la grasse matinée; **sleep together** *vi* (*have sex*) coucher ensemble; **sleeper** *n* (*person*) dormeur(-euse); (*BRIT Rail: on track*) traverse *f*; (: *train*) train-couchettes *m*; (: *berth*) couchette *f*; **sleeping bag** *n* sac *m* de couchage; **sleeping car** *n* wagon-lits *m*, voiture-lits *f*; **sleeping pill** *n* somnifère *m*; **sleepover** *n* nuit *f* chez un copain *or* une copine; **we're having a sleepover at Jo's** nous allons passer la nuit chez Jo; **sleepwalk** *vi* marcher en dormant; **sleepy** *adj* (*fig*) endormi(e)

sleet [sliːt] *n* neige fondue

sleeve [sliːv] *n* manche *f*; (*of record*) pochette *f*; **sleeveless** *adj* (*garment*) sans manches

sleigh [sleɪ] *n* traîneau *m*

slender ['slɛndə^r] *adj* svelte, mince; (*fig*) faible, ténu(e)

slept [slɛpt] *pt, pp of* **sleep**

slew [sluː] *pt of* **slay**

slice [slaɪs] *n* tranche *f*; (*round*) rondelle *f*; (*utensil*) spatule *f*; (*also:* **fish ~**) pelle *f* à poisson ▷ *vt* couper en tranches (*or* en rondelles)

slick [slɪk] *adj* (*skilful*) bien ficelé(e); (*salesperson*) qui a du bagout ▷ *n* (*also:* **oil ~**) nappe *f* de pétrole, marée noire

slide [slaɪd] *n* (*in playground*) toboggan *m*; (*Phot*) diapositive *f*; (*BRIT: also:* **hair ~**) barrette *f*; (*in prices*) chute *f*, baisse *f* ▷ *vb* (*pt, pp* **slid**) ▷ *vt* (faire) glisser ▷ *vi* glisser; **sliding** *adj* (*door*) coulissant(e)

slight [slaɪt] *adj* (*slim*) mince, menu(e); (*frail*) frêle; (*trivial*) faible, insignifiant(e); (*small*) petit(e), léger(-ère) *before n* ▷ *n* offense *f*, affront *m* ▷ *vt* (*offend*) blesser, offenser; **not in the ~est** pas le moins du monde, pas du tout; **slightly** *adv* légèrement, un peu

slim [slɪm] *adj* mince ▷ *vi* maigrir; (*diet*) suivre un régime amaigrissant; **slimming** *n* amaigrissement *m* ▷ *adj* (*diet, pills*) amaigrissant(e), pour maigrir; (*food*) qui ne fait pas grossir

slimy ['slaɪmɪ] *adj* visqueux(-euse), gluant(e)

sling [slɪŋ] n (Med) écharpe f; (for baby) porte-bébé m; (weapon) fronde f, lance-pierre m ▷ vt (pt, pp **slung**) lancer, jeter

slip [slɪp] n faux pas; (mistake) erreur f, bévue f; (underskirt) combinaison f; (of paper) petite feuille, fiche f ▷ vt (slide) glisser ▷ vi (slide) glisser; (move smoothly): **to ~ into/out of** se glisser or se faufiler dans/hors de; (decline) baisser; **to ~ sth on/off** enfiler/enlever qch; **to give sb the ~** fausser compagnie à qn; **a ~ of the tongue** un lapsus; **slip up** vi faire une erreur, gaffer

slipped disc [slɪpt-] n déplacement m de vertèbre

slipper ['slɪpə'] n pantoufle f

slippery ['slɪpərɪ] adj glissant(e)

slip road n (BRIT: to motorway) bretelle f d'accès

slit [slɪt] n fente f; (cut) incision f ▷ vt (pt, pp **~**) fendre; couper, inciser

slog [slɔg] n (BRIT: effort) gros effort; (: work) tâche fastidieuse ▷ vi travailler très dur

slogan ['sləugən] n slogan m

slope [sləup] n pente f, côte f; (side of mountain) versant m; (slant) inclinaison f ▷ vi: **to ~ down** être or descendre en pente; **to ~ up** monter; **sloping** adj en pente, incliné(e); (handwriting) penché(e)

sloppy ['slɔpɪ] adj (work) peu soigné(e), bâclé(e); (appearance) négligé(e), débraillé(e)

slot [slɔt] n fente f ▷ vt: **to ~ sth into** encastrer or insérer qch dans; **slot machine** n (BRIT: vending machine) distributeur m (automatique), machine f à sous; (for gambling) appareil m or machine à sous

Slovakia [sləuˈvækɪə] n Slovaquie f

Slovene [ˈsləuviːn] adj slovène ▷ n Slovène m/f; (Ling) slovène m

Slovenia [sləuˈviːnɪə] n Slovénie f; **Slovenian** adj, n = **Slovene**

slow [sləu] adj lent(e); (watch): **to be ~** retarder ▷ adv lentement ▷ vt, vi ralentir; **"~"** (road sign) "ralentir"; **slow down** vi ralentir; **slowly** adv lentement; **slow motion** n: **in slow motion** au ralenti

slug [slʌg] n limace f; (bullet) balle f; **sluggish** adj (person) mou (molle), lent(e); (stream, engine, trading) lent(e)

slum [slʌm] n (house) taudis m; **slums** npl (area) quartiers mpl pauvres

slump [slʌmp] n baisse soudaine, effondrement m; (Econ) crise f ▷ vi s'effondrer, s'affaisser

slung [slʌŋ] pt, pp of **sling**

slur [sləː'] n (smear): **~ (on)** atteinte f (à); insinuation f (contre) ▷ vt mal articuler

slush [slʌʃ] n neige fondue

sly [slaɪ] adj (person) rusé(e); (smile, expression, remark) sournois(e)

smack [smæk] n (slap) tape f; (on face) gifle f ▷ vt donner une tape à; (on face) gifler; (on bottom) donner la fessée à ▷ vi: **to ~ of** avoir des relents de, sentir

small [smɔːl] adj petit(e); **small ads** npl (BRIT) petites annonces; **small change** n petite or menue monnaie

smart [smɑːt] adj élégant(e), chic inv; (clever) intelligent(e); (quick) vif (vive), prompt(e) ▷ vi faire mal, brûler; **smartcard** n carte f à puce

smash [smæʃ] n (also: **~-up**) collision f, accident m; (Mus) succès foudroyant ▷ vt casser, briser, fracasser; (opponent) écraser; (Sport: record) pulvériser ▷ vi se briser, se fracasser; s'écraser; **smashing** adj (inf) formidable

smear [smɪə'] n (stain) tache f; (mark) trace f; (Med) frottis m ▷ vt enduire; (make dirty) salir; **smear test** n (BRIT Med) frottis m

smell [smɛl] n odeur f; (sense) odorat m ▷ vb (pt, pp **smelt** or **~ed**) ▷ vt sentir ▷ vi (pej) sentir mauvais; **smelly** adj qui sent mauvais, malodorant(e)

smelt [smɛlt] pt, pp of **smell**

smile [smaɪl] n sourire m ▷ vi sourire

smirk [sməːk] n petit sourire suffisant or affecté

smog [smɔg] n brouillard mêlé de fumée

smoke [sməuk] n fumée f ▷ vt, vi fumer; **do you mind if I ~?** ça ne vous dérange pas que je fume?; **smoke alarm** n détecteur m de fumée; **smoked** adj (bacon, glass) fumé(e); **smoker** n (person) fumeur(-euse); (Rail) wagon m fumeurs; **smoking** n: **"no smoking"** (sign) "défense de fumer"; **smoky** adj enfumé(e); (taste) fumé(e)

smooth [smuːð] adj lisse; (sauce) onctueux(-euse); (flavour, whisky) moelleux(-euse); (movement) régulier(-ière), sans à-coups or heurts; (flight) sans secousses; (pej: person) doucereux(-euse), mielleux(-euse) ▷ vt (also: **~ out**) lisser, défroisser; (creases, difficulties) faire disparaître

smother ['smʌðə'] vt étouffer

SMS n abbr (= short message service) SMS m; **SMS message** n message m SMS

smudge [smʌdʒ] n tache f, bavure f ▷ vt salir, maculer

smug [smʌg] adj suffisant(e), content(e) de soi

smuggle ['smʌgl] vt passer en contrebande or en fraude; **smuggling** n contrebande f

snack [snæk] n casse-croûte m inv; **snack bar** n snack(-bar) m

snag [snæg] n inconvénient m, difficulté f

snail [sneɪl] n escargot m

snake [sneɪk] n serpent m

snap [snæp] n (sound) claquement m, bruit sec; (photograph) photo f, instantané m ▷ adj

subit(e), fait(e) sans réfléchir ▷ vt (*fingers*)
faire claquer; (*break*) casser net ▷ vi se casser
net *or* avec un bruit sec; (*speak sharply*) parler
d'un ton brusque; **to ~ open/shut** s'ouvrir/se
refermer brusquement; **snap at** vt fus (*subj:
dog*) essayer de mordre; **snap up** vt sauter sur,
saisir; **snapshot** n photo f, instantané m

snarl [snɑːl] vi gronder

snatch [snætʃ] n (*small amount*) ▷ vt saisir
(*d'un geste vif*); (*steal*) voler; **to ~ some sleep**
arriver à dormir un peu

sneak [sniːk] (*us: pt* **snuck**) vi: **to ~ in/out**
entrer/sortir furtivement *or* à la dérobée ▷ n
(*inf: pej: informer*) faux jeton; **to ~ up on sb**
s'approcher de qn sans faire de bruit; **sneakers**
npl tennis mpl, baskets fpl

sneer [snɪə'] vi ricaner; **to ~ at sb/sth** se
moquer de qn/qch avec mépris

sneeze [sniːz] vi éternuer

sniff [snɪf] vi renifler ▷ vt renifler, flairer; (*glue,
drug*) sniffer, respirer

snigger [ˈsnɪgə'] vi ricaner

snip [snɪp] n (*cut*) entaille f, (BRIT: *inf: bargain*)
(bonne) occasion *or* affaire ▷ vt couper

sniper [ˈsnaɪpə'] n (*marksman*) tireur
embusqué

snob [snɔb] n snob m/f

snooker [ˈsnuːkə'] n sorte de jeu de billard

snoop [snuːp] vi: **to ~ about** fureter

snooze [snuːz] n petit somme ▷ vi faire un
petit somme

snore [snɔː'] vi ronfler ▷ n ronflement m

snorkel [ˈsnɔːkl] n (*of swimmer*) tuba m

snort [snɔːt] n grognement m ▷ vi grogner;
(*horse*) renâcler

snow [snəu] n neige f ▷ vi neiger; **snowball**
n boule f de neige; **snowdrift** n congère f;
snowman (*irreg*) n bonhomme m de neige;
snowplow (US **snowplow**) n chasse-
neige m inv; **snowstorm** n tempête f de neige

snub [snʌb] vt repousser, snober ▷ n
rebuffade f

snug [snʌg] adj douillet(te), confortable;
(*person*) bien au chaud

O KEYWORD

so [səu] adv **1** (*thus, likewise*) ainsi, de cette
façon; **if so** si oui; **so do** *or* **have I** moi aussi;
it's 5 o'clock - so it is! il est 5 heures - en effet!
or c'est vrai!; **I hope/think so** je l'espère/le
crois; **so far** jusqu'ici, jusqu'à maintenant; (*in
past*) jusque-là

2 (*in comparisons etc: to such a degree*) si,
tellement; **so big (that)** si *or* tellement grand
(que); **she's not so clever as her brother** elle
n'est pas aussi intelligente que son frère
3: **so much** adj, adv tant (de); **I've got so
much work** j'ai tant de travail; **I love you so**
much je vous aime tant; **so many** tant (de)
4 (*phrases*): **10 or so** à peu près *or* environ 10;
so long! (*inf: goodbye*) au revoir!, à un de ces
jours!; **so (what)?** (*inf*) (bon) et alors?, et après?
▷ conj **1** (*expressing purpose*): **so as to do** pour
faire, afin de faire; **so (that)** pour que *or* afin
que + sub
2 (*expressing result*) donc, par conséquent; **so
that** si bien que, de (telle) sorte que; **so that's
the reason!** c'est donc (pour) ça!; **so you
see, I could have gone** alors tu vois, j'aurais
pu y aller

soak [səuk] vt faire *or* laisser tremper; (*drench*)
tremper ▷ vi tremper; **soak up** vt absorber;
soaking adj (*also:* **soaking wet**) trempé(e)

so-and-so [ˈsəuənsəu] n (*somebody*) un(e)
tel(le)

soap [səup] n savon m; **soap opera** n
feuilleton télévisé (*quotidienneté réaliste
ou embellie*); **soap powder** n lessive f,
détergent m

soar [sɔː'] vi monter (en flèche), s'élancer;
(*building*) s'élancer

sob [sɔb] n sanglot m ▷ vi sangloter

sober [ˈsəubə'] adj qui n'est pas (*or* plus) ivre;
(*serious*) sérieux(-euse), sensé(e); (*colour, style*)
sobre, discret(-ète); **sober up** vi se dégriser

so-called [ˈsəuˈkɔːld] adj soi-disant inv

soccer [ˈsɔkə'] n football m

sociable [ˈsəuʃəbl] adj sociable

social [ˈsəuʃl] adj social(e); (*sociable*) sociable
▷ n (petite) fête; **socialism** n socialisme m;
socialist adj, n socialiste (m/f); **socialize** vi:
to socialize with (*meet often*) fréquenter;
(*get to know*) lier connaissance *or* parler
avec; **social life** n vie sociale; **socially** adv
socialement, en société; **social security** n
aide sociale; **social services** npl services
sociaux; **social work** n assistance sociale;
social worker n assistant(e) sociale(e)

society [səˈsaɪətɪ] n société f; (*club*) société,
association f; (*also:* **high ~**) (haute) société,
grand monde

sociology [səusɪˈɔlədʒɪ] n sociologie f

sock [sɔk] n chaussette f

socket [ˈsɔkɪt] n cavité f; (Elec: *also:* **wall ~**)
prise f de courant

soda [ˈsəudə] n (Chem) soude f; (*also:* **~ water**)
eau f de Seltz; (US: *also:* **~ pop**) soda m

sodium [ˈsəudɪəm] n sodium m

sofa [ˈsəufə] n sofa m, canapé m; **sofa bed** n
canapé-lit m

soft [sɔft] adj (*not rough*) doux (douce); (*not
hard*) doux, mou (molle); (*not loud*) doux,
léger(-ère); (*kind*) doux, gentil(le); **soft drink**
n boisson non alcoolisée; **soft drugs** npl
drogues douces; **soften** [ˈsɔfn] vt (r)amollir;
(*fig*) adoucir ▷ vi se ramollir; (*fig*) s'adoucir;

softly adv doucement; (touch) légèrement; (kiss) tendrement; **software** n (Comput) logiciel m, software m

soggy ['sɒgɪ] adj (clothes) trempé(e); (ground) détrempé(e)

soil [sɔɪl] n (earth) sol m, terre f ▷ vt salir; (fig) souiller

solar ['səʊlə'] adj solaire; **solar power** n énergie f solaire; **solar system** n système m solaire

sold [səʊld] pt, pp of **sell**

soldier ['səʊldʒə'] n soldat m, militaire m

sold out adj (Comm) épuisé(e)

sole [səʊl] n (of foot) plante f; (of shoe) semelle f, (fish: pl inv) sole f ▷ adj seul(e), unique; **solely** adv seulement, uniquement

solemn ['sɒləm] adj solennel(le); (person) sérieux(-euse), grave

solicitor [sə'lɪsɪtə'] n (BRIT: for wills etc) ≈ notaire m; (: in court) ≈ avocat m

solid ['sɒlɪd] adj (not liquid) solide; (not hollow: mass) compact(e); (: metal, rock, wood) massif(-ive) ▷ n solide m

solitary ['sɒlɪtərɪ] adj solitaire

solitude ['sɒlɪtjuːd] n solitude f

solo ['səʊləʊ] n solo m ▷ adv (fly) en solitaire; **soloist** n soliste m/f

soluble ['sɒljubl] adj soluble

solution [sə'luːʃən] n solution f

solve [sɒlv] vt résoudre

solvent ['sɒlvənt] adj (Comm) solvable ▷ n (Chem) (dis)solvant m

sombre (US **somber**) ['sɒmbə'] adj sombre, morne

KEYWORD

some [sʌm] adj **1** (a certain amount or number of): **some tea/water/ice cream** du thé/de l'eau/de la glace; **some children/apples** des enfants/pommes; **I've got some money but not much** j'ai de l'argent mais pas beaucoup **2** (certain: in contrasts): **some people say that ...** il y a des gens qui disent que ...; **some films were excellent, but most were mediocre** certains films étaient excellents, mais la plupart étaient médiocres

3 (unspecified): **some woman was asking for you** il y avait une dame qui vous demandait; **he was asking for some book (or other)** il demandait un livre quelconque; **some day** un de ces jours; **some day next week** un jour la semaine prochaine

▷ pron **1** (a certain number) quelques-un(e)s, certain(e)s; **I've got some** (books etc) j'en ai (quelques-uns); **some (of them) have been sold** certains ont été vendus

2 (a certain amount) un peu; **I've got some** (money, milk) j'en ai (un peu); **would you like**

some? est-ce que vous en voulez?, en voulez-vous?; **could I have some of that cheese?** pourrais-je avoir un peu de ce fromage?; **I've read some of the book** j'ai lu une partie du livre

▷ adv: **some 10 people** quelque 10 personnes, 10 personnes environ; **somebody** ['sʌmbə dɪ] pron = **someone**; **somehow** adv d'une façon ou d'une autre; (for some reason) pour une raison ou une autre; **someone** pron quelqu'un; **someplace** adv (US) = **somewhere**; **something** pron quelque chose m; **something interesting** quelque chose d'intéressant; **something to do** quelque chose à faire; **sometime** adv (in future) un de ces jours, un jour ou l'autre; (in past): **sometime last month** au cours du mois dernier; **sometimes** adv quelquefois, parfois; **somewhat** adv quelque peu, un peu; **somewhere** adv quelque part; **somewhere else** ailleurs, autre part

son [sʌn] n fils m

song [sɒŋ] n chanson f; (of bird) chant m

son-in-law ['sʌnɪnlɔː] n gendre m, beau-fils m

soon [suːn] adv bientôt; (early) tôt; ~ **afterwards** peu après; see also **as**; **sooner** adv (time) plus tôt; (preference): **I would sooner do that** j'aimerais autant or je préférerais faire ça; **sooner or later** tôt ou tard

soothe [suːð] vt calmer, apaiser

sophisticated [sə'fɪstɪkeɪtɪd] adj raffiné(e), sophistiqué(e); (machinery) hautement perfectionné(e), très complexe

sophomore ['sɒfəmɔː'] n (US) étudiant(e) de seconde année

soprano [sə'prɑːnəʊ] n (singer) soprano m/f

sorbet ['sɔːbeɪ] n sorbet m

sordid ['sɔːdɪd] adj sordide

sore [sɔː'] adj (painful) douloureux(-euse), sensible ▷ n plaie f

sorrow ['sɒrəʊ] n peine f, chagrin m

sorry ['sɒrɪ] adj désolé(e); (condition, excuse, tale) triste, déplorable; ~**I** pardon!, excusez-moi!; ~**?** pardon?; **to feel ~ for sb** plaindre qn

sort [sɔːt] n genre m, espèce f, sorte f; (make: of coffee, car etc) marque f ▷ vt (also: ~ **out**: select which to keep) trier; (classify) classer; (tidy) ranger; **sort out** vt (problem) résoudre, régler

SOS n SOS m

so-so ['səʊsəʊ] adv comme ci comme ça

sought [sɔːt] pt, pp of **seek**

soul [səʊl] n âme f

sound [saʊnd] adj (healthy) en bonne santé, sain(e); (safe, not damaged) solide, en bon état; (reliable, not superficial) sérieux(-euse), solide; (sensible) sensé(e) ▷ adv: ~ **asleep** profondément endormi(e) ▷ n (noise, volume) son m; (louder) bruit m; (Geo) détroit m, bras

m de mer ▷ *vt* (*alarm*) sonner,
retentir; (*fig: seem*) sembler (être); **to ~ like**
ressembler à; **sound bite** *n* phrase toute faite
(*pour être citée dans les médias*); **soundtrack** *n*
(*of film*) bande *f* sonore

soup [suːp] *n* soupe *f*, potage *m*

sour ['sauəʳ] *adj* aigre; **it's ~ grapes** c'est du
dépit

source [sɔːs] *n* source *f*

south [sauθ] *n* sud *m* ▷ *adj* sud *inv*; (*wind*)
du sud ▷ *adv* au sud, vers le sud; **South
Africa** *n* Afrique *f* du Sud; **South African**
adj sud-africain(e) ▷ *n* Sud-Africain(e);
South America *n* Amérique *f* du Sud; **South
American** *adj* sud-américain(e) ▷ *n* Sud-
Américain(e); **southbound** *adj* en direction
du sud; (*carriageway*) sud *inv*; **south-east** *n*
sud-est *m*; **southeastern** [sauθˈiːstən] *adj*
du *or* au sud-est; **southern** ['sʌðən] *adj* (du)
sud; méridional(e); **South Korea** *n* Corée *f* du
Sud; **South of France** *n*: **the South of France**
le Sud de la France, le Midi; **South Pole** *n*
Pôle *m* Sud; **southward(s)** *adv* vers le sud;
south-west *n* sud-ouest *m*; **southwestern**
[sauθˈwestən] *adj* du *or* au sud-ouest

souvenir [suːvəˈnɪəʳ] *n* souvenir *m* (*objet*)

sovereign ['sɔvrɪn] *adj*, *n* souverain(e)

sow¹ [səu] (*pt* **~ed**, *pp* **~n**) *vt* semer

sow² *n* [sau] truie *f*

soya ['sɔɪə] (*us* **soy** [sɔɪ]) *n*: **~ bean** graine *f* de
soja; **~ sauce** sauce *f* au soja

spa [spɑː] *n* (*town*) station thermale; (*us:
also*: **health ~**) établissement *m* de cure de
rajeunissement

space [speɪs] *n* (*gen*) espace *m*; (*room*) place
f, espace; (*length of time*) laps *m* de temps
▷ *cpd* spatial(e) ▷ *vt* (*also*: **~ out**) espacer;
spacecraft *n* engin *or* vaisseau spatial;
spaceship *n* = **spacecraft**

spacious ['speɪʃəs] *adj* spacieux(-euse),
grand(e)

spade [speɪd] *n* (*tool*) bêche *f*, pelle *f*; (*child's*)
pelle; **spades** *npl* (*Cards*) pique *m*

spaghetti [spəˈgɛtɪ] *n* spaghetti *mpl*

Spain [speɪn] *n* Espagne *f*

spam [spæm] *n* (*Comput*) spam *m*

span [spæn] *n* (*of bird, plane*) envergure *f*; (*of
arch*) portée *f*; (*in time*) espace *m* de temps,
durée *f* ▷ *vt* enjamber, franchir; (*fig*) couvrir,
embrasser

Spaniard ['spænjəd] *n* Espagnol(e)

Spanish ['spænɪʃ] *adj* espagnol(e), d'Espagne
▷ *n* (*Ling*) espagnol *m*; **the Spanish** *npl* les
Espagnols

spank [spæŋk] *vt* donner une fessée à

spanner ['spænəʳ] *n* (*BRIT*) clé *f* (de
mécanicien)

spare [spɛəʳ] *adj* de réserve, de rechange;
(*surplus*) de *or* en trop, de reste ▷ *n* (*part*) pièce

f de rechange, pièce détachée ▷ *vt* (*do without*)
se passer de; (*afford to give*) donner, accorder,
passer; (*not hurt*) épargner; **to ~** (*surplus*)
en surplus, de trop; **spare part** *n* pièce *f* de
rechange, pièce détachée; **spare room** *n*
chambre *f* d'ami; **spare time** *n* moments *mpl*
de loisir; **spare tyre** (*us* **spare tire**) *n* (*Aut*)
pneu *m* de rechange; **spare wheel** *n* (*Aut*)
roue *f* de secours

spark [spɑːk] *n* étincelle *f*; **spark(ing) plug**
n bougie *f*

sparkle ['spɑːkl] *n* scintillement *m*,
étincellement *m*, éclat *m* ▷ *vi* étinceler,
scintiller

sparkling ['spɑːklɪŋ] *adj* (*wine*)
mousseux(-euse), pétillant(e); (*water*)
pétillant(e), gazeux(-euse)

sparrow ['spærəu] *n* moineau *m*

sparse [spɑːs] *adj* clairsemé(e)

spasm ['spæzəm] *n* (*Med*) spasme *m*

spat [spæt] *pt*, *pp* of **spit**

spate [speɪt] *n* (*fig*): **~ of** avalanche *f or* torrent
m de

spatula ['spætjulə] *n* spatule *f*

speak (*pt* **spoke**, *pp* **spoken**) [spiːk, spəuk,
'spəukn] *vt* (*language*) parler; (*truth*) dire ▷ *vi*
parler; (*make a speech*) prendre la parole; **to ~
to sb/of** *or* **about sth** parler à qn/de qch; **I
don't ~ French** je ne parle pas français; **do
you ~ English?** parlez-vous anglais?; **can I ~
to ...?** est-ce que je peux parler à ...?; **speaker** *n*
(*in public*) orateur *m*; (*also*: **loudspeaker**) haut-
parleur *m*; (*for stereo etc*) baffle *m*, enceinte
f; (*Pol*): **the Speaker** (*BRIT*) le président de la
Chambre des communes *or* des représentants; (*us*)
le président de la Chambre

spear [spɪəʳ] *n* lance *f* ▷ *vt* transpercer

special ['spɛʃl] *adj* spécial(e); **special
delivery** *n* (*Post*): **by special delivery** en
express; **special effects** *npl* (*Cine*) effets
spéciaux; **specialist** *n* spécialiste *m/f*;
speciality [spɛʃɪˈælɪtɪ] *n* (*BRIT*) spécialité *f*;
specialize *vi*: **to specialize (in)** se spécialiser
(dans); **specially** *adv* spécialement,
particulièrement; **special needs** *npl* (*BRIT*)
difficultés *fpl* d'apprentissage scolaire; **special
offer** *n* (*Comm*) réclame *f*; **special school**
n (*BRIT*) établissement *m* d'enseignement
spécialisé; **specialty** *n* (*us*) = **speciality**

species ['spiːʃiːz] *n* (*pl inv*) espèce *f*

specific [spəˈsɪfɪk] *adj* (*not vague*) précis(e),
explicite; (*particular*) particulier(-ière);
specifically *adv* explicitement, précisément;
(*intend, ask, design*) expressément,
spécialement

specify ['spɛsɪfaɪ] *vt* spécifier, préciser

specimen ['spɛsɪmən] *n* spécimen *m*,
échantillon *m*; (*Med: of blood*) prélèvement *m*; (:
of urine) échantillon *m*

speck [spɛk] n petite tache, petit point; (particle) grain m

spectacle ['spɛktəkl] n spectacle m; **spectacles** npl (BRIT) lunettes fpl; **spectacular** [spɛk'tækjulər] adj spectaculaire

spectator [spɛk'teɪtər] n spectateur(-trice)

spectrum (pl **spectra**) ['spɛktrəm, -rə] n spectre m; (fig) gamme f

speculate ['spɛkjuleɪt] vi spéculer; (try to guess): **to ~ about** s'interroger sur

sped [spɛd] pt, pp of **speed**

speech [spiːtʃ] n (faculty) parole f; (talk) discours m, allocution f; (manner of speaking) façon f de parler, langage m; (enunciation) élocution f; **speechless** adj muet(te)

speed [spiːd] n vitesse f; (promptness) rapidité f ▷ vi (pt, pp **sped**): (Aut: exceed speed limit) faire un excès de vitesse; **at full** or **top ~** à toute vitesse or allure; **speed up** (pt, pp **~ed up**) vi aller plus vite, accélérer vt accélérer; **speedboat** n vedette f, hors-bord m inv; **speeding** n (Aut) excès m de vitesse; **speed limit** n limitation f de vitesse, vitesse maximale permise; **speedometer** [spɪ'dɔmɪtər] n compteur m (de vitesse); **speedy** adj rapide, prompt(e)

spell [spɛl] n (also: **magic ~**) sortilège m, charme m; (period of time) (courte) période ▷ vt (pt, pp **spelt** or **~ed**) (in writing) écrire, orthographier; (aloud) épeler; (fig) signifier; **to cast a ~ on sb** jeter un sort à qn; **he can't ~** il fait des fautes d'orthographe; **spell out** vt (explain): **to ~ sth out for sb** expliquer qch clairement à qn; **spellchecker** ['spɛltʃɛkər] n (Comput) correcteur m or vérificateur m orthographique; **spelling** n orthographe f

spelt [spɛlt] pt, pp of **spell**

spend (pt, pp **spent**) [spɛnd, spɛnt] vt (money) dépenser; (time, life) passer; (devote) consacrer; **spending** n: **government spending** les dépenses publiques

spent [spɛnt] pt, pp of **spend** ▷ adj (cartridge, bullets) vide

sperm [spəːm] n spermatozoïde m; (semen) sperme m

sphere [sfɪər] n sphère f; (fig) sphère, domaine m

spice [spaɪs] n épice f ▷ vt épicer

spicy ['spaɪsɪ] adj épicé(e), relevé(e); (fig) piquant(e)

spider ['spaɪdər] n araignée f

spike [spaɪk] n pointe f; (Bot) épi m

spill (pt, pp **spilt** or **~ed**) [spɪl, -t, -d] vt renverser; répandre ▷ vi se répandre; **spill over** vi déborder

spin [spɪn] n (revolution of wheel) tour m; (Aviat) (chute f en) vrille f; (trip in car) petit tour, balade f; (on ball) effet m ▷ vb (pt, pp **spun**) ▷ vt (wool etc) filer; (wheel) faire tourner ▷ vi (turn)

tourner, tournoyer

spinach ['spɪnɪtʃ] n épinards mpl

spinal ['spaɪnl] adj vertébral(e), spinal(e)

spinal cord n moelle épinière

spin doctor n (inf) personne employée pour présenter un parti politique sous un jour favorable

spin-dryer [spɪn'draɪər] n (BRIT) essoreuse f

spine [spaɪn] n colonne vertébrale; (thorn) épine f, piquant m

spiral ['spaɪərl] n spirale f ▷ vi (fig: prices etc) monter en flèche

spire ['spaɪər] n flèche f, aiguille f

spirit ['spɪrɪt] n (soul) esprit m, âme f; (ghost) esprit, revenant m; (mood) esprit, état m d'esprit; (courage) courage m, énergie f; **spirits** npl (drink) spiritueux mpl, alcool m; **in good ~s** de bonne humeur

spiritual ['spɪrɪtjuəl] adj spirituel(le); (religious) religieux(-euse)

spit [spɪt] n (for roasting) broche f; (spittle) crachat m; (saliva) salive f ▷ vi (pt, pp **spat**) cracher; (sound) crépiter; (rain) crachiner

spite [spaɪt] n rancune f, dépit m ▷ vt contrarier, vexer; **in ~ of** en dépit de, malgré; **spiteful** adj malveillant(e), rancunier(-ière)

splash [splæʃ] n (sound) plouf m; (of colour) tache f ▷ vt éclabousser ▷ vi (also: **~ about**) barboter, patauger; **splash out** vi (BRIT) faire une folie

splendid ['splɛndɪd] adj splendide, superbe, magnifique

splinter ['splɪntər] n (wood) écharde f; (metal) éclat m ▷ vi (wood) se fendre; (glass) se briser

split [splɪt] n fente f, déchirure f; (fig: Pol) scission f ▷ vb (pt, pp **~**) ▷ vt fendre, déchirer; (party) diviser; (work, profits) partager, répartir ▷ vi (break) se fendre, se briser; (divide) se diviser; **split up** vi (couple) se séparer, rompre; (meeting) se disperser

spoil (pt, pp **~ed** or **~t**) [spɔɪl, -d, -t] vt (damage) abîmer; (mar) gâcher; (child) gâter

spoilt [spɔɪlt] pt, pp of **spoil** ▷ adj (child) gâté(e); (ballot paper) nul(le)

spoke [spəuk] pt of **speak** ▷ n rayon m

spoken ['spəukn] pp of **speak**

spokesman ['spəuksmən] (irreg) n porte-parole m inv

spokesperson ['spəukspə:sn] n porte-parole m inv

spokeswoman ['spəukswumən] (irreg) n porte-parole m inv

sponge [spʌndʒ] n éponge f; (Culin: also: **~ cake**) ≈ biscuit m de Savoie ▷ vt éponger ▷ vi: **to ~ off** or **on** vivre aux crochets de; **sponge bag** n (BRIT) trousse f de toilette

sponsor ['spɔnsər] n (Radio, TV, Sport) sponsor m; (for application) parrain m, marraine f; (BRIT: for fund-raising event) donateur(-trice) ▷ vt sponsoriser, parrainer, faire un don à;

S

sponsorship n sponsoring m, parrainage m; dons mpl

spontaneous [spɔn'teɪnɪəs] adj spontané(e)

spooky ['spuːkɪ] adj (inf) qui donne la chair de poule

spoon [spuːn] n cuiller f; **spoonful** n cuillerée f

sport [spɔːt] n sport m; (person) chic type m/chic fille f ▷ vt (wear) arborer; **sport jacket** n (US) = **sports jacket**; **sports car** n voiture f de sport; **sports centre** (BRIT) n centre sportif; **sports jacket** n (BRIT) veste f de sport; **sportsman** (irreg) n sportif m; **sports utility vehicle** n véhicule m de loisirs (de type SUV); **sportswear** n vêtements mpl de sport; **sportswoman** (irreg) n sportive f; **sporty** adj sportif(-ive)

spot [spɔt] n tache f; (dot: on pattern) pois m; (pimple) bouton m; (place) endroit m, coin m; (small amount): **a ~ of** un peu de ▷ vt (notice) apercevoir, repérer; **on the ~** sur place, sur les lieux; (immediately) sur le champ; **spotless** adj immaculé(e); **spotlight** n projecteur m; (Aut) phare m auxiliaire

spouse [spauz] n époux (épouse)

sprain [spreɪn] n entorse f, foulure f ▷ vt: **to ~ one's ankle** se fouler or se tordre la cheville

sprang [spræŋ] pt of **spring**

sprawl [sprɔːl] vi s'étaler

spray [spreɪ] n jet m (en fines gouttelettes); (from sea) embruns mpl; (aerosol) vaporisateur m, bombe f; (for garden) pulvérisateur m; (of flowers) petit bouquet ▷ vt vaporiser, pulvériser; (crops) traiter

spread [spred] n (distribution) répartition f; (Culin) pâte f à tartiner; (inf: meal) festin m ▷ vb (pt, pp ~) ▷ vt (paste, contents) étendre, étaler; (rumour, disease) répandre, propager; (wealth) répartir ▷ vi s'étendre; se répandre; se propager; (stain) s'étaler; **spread out** vi (people) se disperser; **spreadsheet** n (Comput) tableur m

spree [spriː] n: **to go on a ~** faire la fête

spring [sprɪŋ] n (season) printemps m; (leap) bond m, saut m; (coiled metal) ressort m; (of water) source f ▷ vb (pt **sprang**, pp **sprung**) ▷ vi bondir, sauter; **spring up** vi (problem) se présenter, surgir; (plant, buildings) surgir de terre; **spring onion** n (BRIT) ciboule f, cive f

sprinkle ['sprɪŋkl] vt: **to ~ water etc on, ~ with water etc** asperger d'eau etc; **to ~ sugar etc on, ~ with sugar etc** saupoudrer de sucre etc

sprint [sprɪnt] n sprint m ▷ vi courir à toute vitesse; (Sport) sprinter

sprung [sprʌŋ] pp of **spring**

spun [spʌn] pt, pp of **spin**

spur [spəː] n éperon m; (fig) aiguillon m ▷ vt (also: ~ **on**) éperonner; aiguillonner; **on the ~ of the moment** sous l'impulsion du moment

spurt [spəːt] n jet m; (of blood) jaillissement m; (of energy) regain m, sursaut m ▷ vi jaillir, gicler

spy [spaɪ] n espion(ne) ▷ vi: **to ~ on** espionner, épier ▷ vt (see) apercevoir

sq. abbr = **square**

squabble ['skwɔbl] vi se chamailler

squad [skwɔd] n (Mil, Police) escouade f, groupe m; (Football) contingent m

squadron ['skwɔdrn] n (Mil) escadron m; (Aviat, Naut) escadrille f

squander ['skwɔndəʳ] vt gaspiller, dilapider

square [skwɛəʳ] n carré m; (in town) place f ▷ adj carré(e) ▷ vt (arrange) régler; arranger; (Math) élever au carré; (reconcile) concilier; **all ~** quitte; à égalité; **a ~ meal** un repas convenable; **2 metres ~** (de) 2 mètres sur 2; **1 ~ metre** 1 mètre carré; **square root** n racine carrée

squash [skwɔʃ] n (BRIT: drink): **lemon/orange ~** citronnade f/orangeade f; (Sport) squash m; (US: vegetable) courge f ▷ vt écraser

squat [skwɔt] adj petit(e) et épais(se), ramassé(e) ▷ vi (also: ~ **down**) s'accroupir; **squatter** n squatter m

squeak [skwiːk] vi (hinge, wheel) grincer; (mouse) pousser un petit cri

squeal [skwiːl] vi pousser un or des cri(s) aigu(s) or perçant(s); (brakes) grincer

squeeze [skwiːz] n pression f ▷ vt presser; (hand, arm) serrer

squid [skwɪd] n calmar m

squint [skwɪnt] vi loucher

squirm [skwəːm] vi se tortiller

squirrel ['skwɪrəl] n écureuil m

squirt [skwəːt] vi jaillir, gicler ▷ vt faire gicler

Sr abbr = **senior**

Sri Lanka [srɪ'læŋkə] n Sri Lanka m

St abbr = **saint**; **street**

stab [stæb] n (with knife etc) coup m (de couteau etc); (of pain) lancée f; (inf: try): **to have a ~ at (doing) sth** s'essayer à (faire) qch ▷ vt poignarder

stability [stə'bɪlɪtɪ] n stabilité f

stable ['steɪbl] n écurie f ▷ adj stable

stack [stæk] n tas m, pile f ▷ vt empiler, entasser

stadium ['steɪdɪəm] n stade m

staff [stɑːf] n (work force) personnel m; (BRIT Scol: also: **teaching ~**) professeurs mpl, enseignants mpl, personnel enseignant ▷ vt pourvoir en personnel

stag [stæg] n cerf m

stage [steɪdʒ] n scène f; (platform) estrade f; (point) étape f, stade m; (profession): **the ~** le théâtre ▷ vt (play) monter, mettre en scène; (demonstration) organiser; **in ~s** par étapes, par degrés

▌ Be careful not to translate stage by the French word stage.

stagger ['stægə'] vi chanceler, tituber ▷ vt (person: amaze) stupéfier; (hours, holidays) étaler, échelonner; **staggering** adj (amazing) stupéfiant(e), renversant(e)

stagnant ['stægnənt] adj stagnant(e)

stag night, stag party n enterrement m de vie de garçon

stain [steɪn] n tache f; (colouring) colorant m ▷ vt tacher; (wood) teindre; **stained glass** n (decorative) verre coloré; (in church) vitraux mpl; **stainless steel** n inox m, acier m inoxydable

staircase ['stɛəkeɪs] n = **stairway**

stairs [stɛəz] npl escalier m

stairway ['stɛəweɪ] n escalier m

stake [steɪk] n pieu m, poteau m; (Comm: interest) intérêts mpl; (Betting) enjeu m ▷ vt risquer, jouer; (also: ~ **out**: area) marquer, délimiter; **to be at** ~ être en jeu

stale [steɪl] adj (bread) rassis(e); (food) pas frais (fraîche); (beer) éventé(e); (smell) de renfermé; (air) confiné(e)

stalk [stɔ:k] n tige f ▷ vt traquer

stall [stɔ:l] n (BRIT: in street, market etc) éventaire m, étal m; (in stable) stalle f ▷ vt (Aut) caler; (fig: delay) retarder ▷ vi (Aut) caler; (fig) essayer de gagner du temps; **stalls** npl (BRIT: in cinema, theatre) orchestre m

stamina ['stæmɪnə] n vigueur f, endurance f

stammer ['stæmə'] n bégaiement m ▷ vi bégayer

stamp [stæmp] n timbre m; (also: **rubber ~**) tampon m; (mark, also fig) empreinte f; (on document) cachet m ▷ vi (also: ~ **one's foot**) taper du pied ▷ vt (letter) timbrer; (with rubber stamp) tamponner; **stamp out** vt (fire) piétiner; (crime) éradiquer; (opposition) éliminer; **stamped addressed envelope** n (BRIT) enveloppe affranchie pour la réponse

stampede [stæm'pi:d] n ruée f; (of cattle) débandade f

stance [stæns] n position f

stand [stænd] n (position) position f; (for taxis) station f (de taxis); (Comm) étalage m, stand m; (Sport: also: ~**s**) tribune f; (also: **music ~**) pupitre m ▷ vb (pt, pp **stood**) ▷ vi être or se tenir (debout); (rise) se lever, se mettre debout; (be placed) se trouver; (remain: offer etc) rester valable ▷ vt (place) mettre, poser; (tolerate, withstand) supporter; (treat, invite) offrir, payer; **to make a ~** prendre position; **to ~ for parliament** (BRIT) se présenter aux élections (comme candidat à la députation); **I can't ~ him** je ne peux pas le voir; **stand back** vi (move back) reculer, s'écarter; **stand by** vi (be ready) se tenir prêt(e) ▷ vt fus (opinion) s'en tenir à; (person) ne pas abandonner, soutenir; **stand down** vi (withdraw) se retirer; **stand for** vt fus (signify) représenter, signifier; (tolerate) supporter, tolérer; **stand in for**

vt fus remplacer; **stand out** vi (be prominent) ressortir; **stand up** vi (rise) se lever, se mettre debout; **stand up for** vt fus défendre; **stand up to** vt fus tenir tête à, résister à

standard ['stændəd] n (norm) norme f, étalon m; (level) niveau m (voulu); (criterion) critère m; (flag) étendard m ▷ adj (size etc) ordinaire, normal(e); (model, feature) standard inv; (practice) courant(e); (text) de base; **standards** npl (morals) morale f, principes mpl; **standard of living** n niveau m de vie

stand-by ticket n (Aviat) billet m stand-by

standing ['stændɪŋ] adj debout inv; (permanent) permanent(e) ▷ n réputation f, rang m, standing m; **of many years'** ~ qui dure or existe depuis longtemps; **standing order** n (BRIT: at bank) virement m automatique, prélèvement m bancaire

stand: **standpoint** n point m de vue; **standstill** n: **at a standstill** à l'arrêt; (fig) au point mort; **to come to a standstill** s'immobiliser, s'arrêter

stank [stæŋk] pt of **stink**

staple ['steɪpl] n (for papers) agrafe f ▷ adj (food, crop, industry etc) de base principal(e) ▷ vt agrafer

star [stɑ:'] n étoile f; (celebrity) vedette f ▷ vt (Cine) avoir pour vedette; **stars** npl: **the ~s** (Astrology) l'horoscope m

starboard ['stɑ:bəd] n tribord m

starch [stɑ:tʃ] n amidon m; (in food) fécule f

stardom ['stɑ:dəm] n célébrité f

stare [stɛə'] n regard m fixe ▷ vi: **to ~ at** regarder fixement

stark [stɑ:k] adj (bleak) désolé(e), morne ▷ adv: ~ **naked** complètement nu(e)

start [stɑ:t] n commencement m, début m; (of race) départ m; (sudden movement) sursaut m; (advantage) avance f, avantage m ▷ vt commencer; (cause: fight) déclencher; (rumour) donner naissance à; (fashion) lancer; (found: business, newspaper) lancer, créer; (engine) mettre en marche ▷ vi (begin) commencer; (begin journey) partir, se mettre en route; (jump) sursauter; **when does the film ~?** à quelle heure est-ce que le film commence?; **to ~ doing** or **to do sth** se mettre à faire qch; **start off** vi (begin) commencer; (leave) partir; **start out** vi (begin) commencer; (set out) partir; **start up** vi commencer; (car) démarrer ▷ vt (fight) déclencher; (business) créer; (car) mettre en marche; **starter** n (Aut) démarreur m; (Sport: official) starter m; (BRIT Culin) entrée f; **starting point** n point m de départ

startle ['stɑ:tl] vt faire sursauter; donner un choc à; **startling** adj surprenant(e), saisissant(e)

starvation [stɑ:'veɪʃən] n faim f, famine f

starve [stɑ:v] vi mourir de faim ▷ vt laisser

mourir de faim

state [steɪt] n état m; (Pol) État ▷ vt (declare) déclarer, affirmer; (specify) indiquer, spécifier; **States** npl: **the S~s** les États-Unis; **to be in a ~** être dans tous ses états; **stately home** n manoir m or château m (ouvert au public); **statement** n déclaration f; (Law) déposition f; **state school** n école publique; **statesman** (irreg) n homme m d'État

static ['stætɪk] n (Radio) parasites mpl; (also: **~ electricity**) électricité f statique ▷ adj statique

station ['steɪʃən] n gare f; (also: **police ~**) poste m or commissariat m (de police) ▷ vt placer, poster

stationary ['steɪʃnəri] adj à l'arrêt, immobile

stationer's (shop) n (BRIT) papeterie f

stationery ['steɪʃnəri] n papier m à lettres, petit matériel de bureau

station wagon n (US) break m

statistic [stə'tɪstɪk] n statistique f; **statistics** n (science) statistique f

statue ['stætjuː] n statue f

stature ['stætʃə'] n stature f; (fig) envergure f

status ['steɪtəs] n position f, situation f; (prestige) prestige m; (Admin, official position) statut m; **status quo** [-'kwəu] n: **the status quo** le statu quo

statutory ['stætjutrɪ] adj statutaire, prévu(e) par un article de loi

staunch [stɔːntʃ] adj sûr(e), loyal(e)

stay [steɪ] n (period of time) séjour m ▷ vi rester; (reside) loger; (spend some time) séjourner; **to ~ put** ne pas bouger; **to ~ the night** passer la nuit; **stay away** vi (from person, building) ne pas s'approcher; (from event) ne pas venir; **stay behind** vi rester en arrière; **stay in** vi (at home) rester à la maison; **stay on** vi rester; **stay out** vi (of house) ne pas rentrer; (strikers) rester en grève; **stay up** vi (at night) ne pas se coucher

steadily ['stɛdɪlɪ] adv (regularly) progressivement; (firmly) fermement; (walk) d'un pas ferme; (fixedly: look) sans détourner les yeux

steady ['stɛdɪ] adj stable, solide, ferme; (regular) constant(e), régulier(-ière); (person) calme, pondéré(e) ▷ vt assurer, stabiliser; (nerves) calmer; **a ~ boyfriend** un petit ami

steak [steɪk] n (meat) bifteck m, steak m; (fish, pork) tranche f

steal (pt **stole**, pp **stolen**) [stiːl, stəul, 'stəuln] vt, vi voler; (move) se faufiler, se déplacer furtivement; **my wallet has been stolen** on m'a volé mon portefeuille

steam [stiːm] n vapeur f ▷ vt (Culin) cuire à la vapeur ▷ vi fumer; **steam up** vi (window) se couvrir de buée; **to get ~ed up about sth** (fig: inf) s'exciter à propos de qch; **steamy** adj humide; (window) embué(e); (sexy) torride

steel [stiːl] n acier m ▷ cpd d'acier

steep [stiːp] adj raide, escarpé(e); (price) très élevé(e), excessif(-ive) ▷ vt (faire) tremper

steeple ['stiːpl] n clocher m

steer [stɪə'] vt diriger; (boat) gouverner; (lead: person) guider, conduire ▷ vi tenir le gouvernail; **steering** n (Aut) conduite f; **steering wheel** n volant m

stem [stɛm] n (of plant) tige f; (of glass) pied m ▷ vt contenir, endiguer; (attack, spread of disease) juguler

step [stɛp] n pas m; (stair) marche f; (action) mesure f, disposition f ▷ vi: **to ~ forward/back** faire un pas en avant/arrière, avancer/reculer; **steps** npl (BRIT) = **stepladder**; **to be in/out of ~ (with)** (fig) aller dans le sens (de)/être déphasé(e) (par rapport à); **step down** vi (fig) se retirer, se désister; **step in** vi (fig) intervenir; **step up** vt (production, sales) augmenter; (campaign, efforts) intensifier; **stepbrother** n demi-frère m; **stepchild** (pl **~ren**) n beau-fils m, belle-fille f; **stepdaughter** n belle-fille f; **stepfather** n beau-père m; **stepladder** n (BRIT) escabeau m; **stepmother** n belle-mère f; **stepsister** n demi-sœur f; **stepson** n beau-fils m

stereo ['stɛrɪəu] n (sound) stéréo f; (hi-fi) chaîne f stéréo ▷ adj (also: **~phonic**) stéréo(phonique)

stereotype ['stɪərɪətaɪp] n stéréotype m ▷ vt stéréotyper

sterile ['stɛraɪl] adj stérile; **sterilize** ['stɛrɪlaɪz] vt stériliser

sterling ['stəːlɪŋ] adj (silver) de bon aloi, fin(e) ▷ n (currency) livre f sterling inv

stern [stəːn] adj sévère ▷ n (Naut) arrière m, poupe f

steroid ['stɪərɔɪd] n stéroïde m

stew [stjuː] n ragoût m ▷ vt, vi cuire à la casserole

steward ['stjuːəd] n (Aviat, Naut, Rail) steward m; **stewardess** n hôtesse f

stick [stɪk] n bâton m; (for walking) canne f; (of chalk etc) morceau m ▷ vb (pt, pp **stuck**) ▷ vt (glue) coller; (thrust): **to ~ sth into** piquer or planter or enfoncer qch dans; (inf: put) mettre, fourrer; (: tolerate) supporter ▷ vi (adhere) tenir, coller; (remain) rester; (get jammed: door, lift) se bloquer; **stick out** vi dépasser, sortir; **stick up** vi dépasser, sortir; **stick up for** vt fus défendre; **sticker** n auto-collant m; **sticking plaster** n sparadrap m, pansement adhésif; **stick insect** n phasme m; **stick shift** n (US Aut) levier m de vitesses

sticky ['stɪkɪ] adj poisseux(-euse); (label) adhésif(-ive); (fig: situation) délicat(e)

stiff [stɪf] adj (gen) raide, rigide; (door, brush) dur(e); (difficult) difficile, ardu(e); (cold) froid(e),

distant(e); (*strong, high*) fort(e), élevé(e) ▷ *adv*: **to be bored/scared/frozen ~** s'ennuyer à mourir/être mort(e) de peur/froid

stifling ['staɪflɪŋ] *adj* (*heat*) suffocant(e)

stigma ['stɪgmə] *n* stigmate *m*

stiletto [stɪ'letəu] *n* (*BRIT: also:* **~ heel**) talon *m* aiguille

still [stɪl] *adj* immobile ▷ *adv* (*up to this time*) encore, toujours; (*even*) encore; (*nonetheless*) quand même, tout de même

stimulate ['stɪmjuleɪt] *vt* stimuler

stimulus (*pl* **stimuli**) ['stɪmjuləs, 'stɪmjulaɪ] *n* stimulant *m*; (*Biol, Psych*) stimulus *m*

sting [stɪŋ] *n* piqûre *f*; (*organ*) dard *m* ▷ *vt, vi* (*pt, pp* **stung**) piquer

stink [stɪŋk] *n* puanteur *f* ▷ *vi* (*pt* **stank**, *pp* **stunk**) puer, empester

stir [stəːr] *n* agitation *f*, sensation *f* ▷ *vt* remuer ▷ *vi* remuer, bouger; **stir up** *vt* (*trouble*) fomenter, provoquer; **stir-fry** *vt* faire sauter ▷ *n*: **vegetable stir-fry** légumes sautés à la poêle

stitch [stɪtʃ] *n* (*Sewing*) point *m*; (*Knitting*) maille *f*; (*Med*) point de suture; (*pain*) point de côté ▷ *vt* coudre, piquer; (*Med*) suturer

stock [stɔk] *n* réserve *f*, provision *f*; (*Comm*) stock *m*; (*Agr*) cheptel *m*, bétail *m*; (*Culin*) bouillon *m*; (*Finance*) valeurs *fpl*, titres *mpl*; (*descent, origin*) souche *f* ▷ *adj* (*fig: reply etc*) classique ▷ *vt* (*have in stock*) avoir, vendre; **in ~** en stock, en magasin; **out of ~** épuisé(e); **to take ~** (*fig*) faire le point; **~s and shares** valeurs (mobilières), titres; **stockbroker** ['stɔkbrəukər] *n* agent *m* de change; **stock cube** *n* (*BRIT Culin*) bouillon-cube *m*; **stock exchange** *n* Bourse *f* (des valeurs); **stockholder** ['stɔkhəuldər] *n* (*US*) actionnaire *m/f*

stocking ['stɔkɪŋ] *n* bas *m*

stock market *n* Bourse *f*, marché financier

stole [stəul] *pt of* **steal** ▷ *n* étole *f*

stolen ['stəuln] *pp of* **steal**

stomach ['stʌmək] *n* estomac *m*; (*abdomen*) ventre *m* ▷ *vt* supporter, digérer; **stomachache** *n* mal à l'estomac *or* au ventre

stone [stəun] *n* pierre *f*; (*pebble*) caillou *m*, galet *m*; (*in fruit*) noyau *m*; (*Med*) calcul *m*; (*BRIT: weight*) = 6.348 kg; 14 pounds ▷ *cpd* de *or* en pierre ▷ *vt* (*person*) lancer des pierres sur, lapider; (*fruit*) dénoyauter

stood [stud] *pt, pp of* **stand**

stool [stuːl] *n* tabouret *m*

stoop [stuːp] *vi* (*also*: **have a ~**) être voûté(e); (*also*: **~ down**: *bend*) se baisser, se courber

stop [stɔp] *n* arrêt *m*; (*in punctuation*) point *m* ▷ *vt* arrêter; (*break off*) interrompre; (*also*: **put a ~ to**) mettre fin à; (*prevent*) empêcher ▷ *vi* s'arrêter; (*rain, noise etc*) cesser, s'arrêter; **to ~**

doing sth cesser *or* arrêter de faire qch; **to ~ sb (from) doing sth** empêcher qn de faire qch; **~ it!** arrête!; **stop by** *vi* s'arrêter (au passage); **stop off** *vi* faire une courte halte; **stopover** *n* halte *f*; (*Aviat*) escale *f*; **stoppage** *n* (*strike*) arrêt *m* de travail; (*obstruction*) obstruction *f*

storage ['stɔːrɪdʒ] *n* emmagasinage *m*

store [stɔːr] *n* (*stock*) provision *f*, réserve *f*; (*depot*) entrepôt *m*; (*BRIT: large shop*) grand magasin; (*US: shop*) magasin *m* ▷ *vt* emmagasiner; (*information*) enregistrer; **stores** *npl* (*food*) provisions; **who knows what is in ~ for us?** qui sait ce que l'avenir nous réserve *or* ce qui nous attend?; **storekeeper** *n* (*US*) commerçant(e)

storey (*US* **story**) ['stɔːrɪ] *n* étage *m*

storm [stɔːm] *n* tempête *f*; (*thunderstorm*) orage *m* ▷ *vi* (*fig*) fulminer ▷ *vt* prendre d'assaut; **stormy** *adj* orageux(-euse)

story ['stɔːrɪ] *n* histoire *f*; (*Press: article*) article *m*; (*US*) = **storey**

stout [staut] *adj* (*strong*) solide; (*fat*) gros(se), corpulent(e) ▷ *n* bière brune

stove [stəuv] *n* (*for cooking*) fourneau *m*; (: *small*) réchaud *m*; (*for heating*) poêle *m*

straight [streɪt] *adj* droit(e); (*hair*) raide; (*frank*) honnête, franc (franche); (*simple*) simple ▷ *adv* (*tout*) droit; (*drink*) sec, sans eau; **to put** *or* **get ~** mettre en ordre, mettre de l'ordre dans; (*fig*) mettre au clair; **~ away**, **~ off** (*at once*) tout de suite; **straighten** *vt* ajuster; (*bed*) arranger; **straighten out** *vt* (*fig*) débrouiller; **straighten up** *vi* (*stand up*) se redresser; **straightforward** *adj* simple; (*frank*) honnête, direct(e)

strain [streɪn] *n* (*Tech*) tension *f*; pression *f*; (*physical*) effort *m*; (*mental*) tension (nerveuse); (*Med*) entorse *f*; (*breed: of plant*) variété *f*; (: *of animals*) race *f* ▷ *vt* (*fig: resources etc*) mettre à rude épreuve, grever; (*hurt: back etc*) se faire mal à; (*vegetables*) égoutter; **strains** *npl* (*Mus*) accords *mpl*, accents *mpl*; **strained** *adj* (*muscle*) froissé(e); (*laugh etc*) forcé(e), contraint(e); (*relations*) tendu(e); **strainer** *n* passoire *f*

strait [streɪt] *n* (*Geo*) détroit *m*; **straits** *npl*: **to be in dire ~s** (*fig*) avoir de sérieux ennuis

strand [strænd] *n* (*of thread*) fil *m*, brin *m*; (*of rope*) toron *m*; (*of hair*) mèche *f* ▷ *vt* (*boat*) échouer; **stranded** *adj* en rade, en plan

strange [streɪndʒ] *adj* (*not known*) inconnu(e); (*odd*) étrange, bizarre; **strangely** *adv* étrangement, bizarrement; *see also* **enough**; **stranger** *n* (*unknown*) inconnu(e); (*from somewhere else*) étranger(-ère)

strangle ['stræŋgl] *vt* étrangler

strap [stræp] *n* lanière *f*, courroie *f*, sangle *f*; (*of slip, dress*) bretelle *f*

strategic [strə'tiːdʒɪk] *adj* stratégique

strategy ['strætɪdʒɪ] n stratégie f

straw [strɔ:] n paille f; **that's the last ~!** ça c'est le comble!

strawberry ['strɔ:bərɪ] n fraise f

stray [streɪ] adj (animal) perdu(e), errant(e); (scattered) isolé(e) ▷ vi s'égarer; **~ bullet** balle perdue

streak [stri:k] n bande f, filet m; (in hair) raie f ▷ vt zébrer, strier

stream [stri:m] n (brook) ruisseau m; (current) courant m, flot m; (of people) défilé ininterrompu, flot ▷ vt (Scol) répartir par niveau ▷ vi ruisseler; **to ~ in/out** entrer/sortir à flots

street [stri:t] n rue f; **streetcar** n (US) tramway m; **street light** n réverbère m; **street map, street plan** n plan m des rues

strength [strεŋθ] n force f; (of girder, knot etc) solidité f; **strengthen** vt renforcer; (muscle) fortifier; (building, Econ) consolider

strenuous ['strεnjuəs] adj vigoureux(-euse), énergique; (tiring) ardu(e), fatigant(e)

stress [strεs] n (force, pressure) pression f; (mental strain) tension (nerveuse), stress m; (accent) accent m; (emphasis) insistance f ▷ vt insister sur, souligner; (syllable) accentuer; **stressed** adj (tense) stressé(e); (syllable) accentué(e); **stressful** adj stressant(e)

stretch [strεtʃ] n (of sand etc) étendue f ▷ vi s'étirer; (extend): **to ~ to** or **as far as** s'étendre jusqu'à ▷ vt tendre, étirer; (fig) pousser (au maximum); **at a ~** d'affilée; **stretch out** vi s'étendre ▷ vt (arm etc) allonger, tendre; (to spread) étendre

stretcher ['strεtʃəʳ] n brancard m, civière f

strict [strɪkt] adj strict(e); **strictly** adv strictement

stride [straɪd] n grand pas, enjambée f ▷ vi (pt **strode**, pp **stridden**) marcher à grands pas

strike [straɪk] n grève f; (of oil etc) découverte f; (attack) raid m ▷ vb (pt, pp **struck**) ▷ vt frapper; (oil etc) trouver, découvrir; (make: agreement, deal) conclure ▷ vi faire grève; (attack) attaquer; (clock) sonner; **to go on** or **come out on ~** se mettre en grève, faire grève; **to ~ a match** frotter une allumette; **striker** n gréviste m/f; (Sport) buteur m; **striking** adj frappant(e), saisissant(e); (attractive) éblouissant(e)

string [strɪŋ] n ficelle f, fil m; (row: of beads) rang m; (Mus) corde f ▷ vt (pt, pp **strung**): **to ~ out** échelonner; **to ~ together** enchaîner; **the strings** npl (Mus) les instruments mpl à cordes; **to pull ~s** (fig) faire jouer le piston

strip [strɪp] n bande f; (Sport) tenue f ▷ vt (undress) déshabiller; (paint) décaper; (fig) dégarnir, dépouiller; (also: **~ down**: machine) démonter ▷ vi se déshabiller; **strip off** vt (paint etc) décaper ▷ vi (person) se déshabiller

stripe [straɪp] n raie f, rayure f; (Mil) galon m; **striped** adj rayé(e), à rayures

stripper ['strɪpəʳ] n strip-teaseuse f

strip-search ['strɪpsə:tʃ] vt: **to ~ sb** fouiller qn (en le faisant se déshabiller)

strive (pt **strove**, pp **~n**) [straɪv, strəuv, 'strɪvn] vi: **to ~ to do/for sth** s'efforcer de faire/d'obtenir qch

strode [strəud] pt of **stride**

stroke [strəuk] n coup m; (Med) attaque f; (Swimming: style) (sorte f de) nage f ▷ vt caresser; **at a ~** d'un (seul) coup

stroll [strəul] n petite promenade ▷ vi flâner, se promener nonchalamment; **stroller** n (us: for child) poussette f

strong [strɔŋ] adj (gen) fort(e); (healthy) vigoureux(-euse), solide; (heart, nerves) solide; **they are 50 ~** ils sont au nombre de 50; **stronghold** n forteresse f, fort m; (fig) bastion m; **strongly** adv fortement, avec force; vigoureusement; solidement

strove [strəuv] pt of **strive**

struck [strʌk] pt, pp of **strike**

structure ['strʌktʃəʳ] n structure f; (building) construction f

struggle ['strʌgl] n lutte f ▷ vi lutter, se battre

strung [strʌŋ] pt, pp of **string**

stub [stʌb] n (of cigarette) bout m, mégot m; (of ticket etc) talon m ▷ vt: **to ~ one's toe (on sth)** se heurter le doigt de pied (contre qch); **stub out** vt écraser

stubble ['stʌbl] n chaume m; (on chin) barbe f de plusieurs jours

stubborn ['stʌbən] adj têtu(e), obstiné(e), opiniâtre

stuck [stʌk] pt, pp of **stick** ▷ adj (jammed) bloqué(e), coincé(e)

stud [stʌd] n (on boots etc) clou m; (collar stud) bouton m de col; (earring) petite boucle d'oreille; (of horses: also: **~ farm**) écurie f, haras m; (also: **~ horse**) étalon m ▷ vt (fig): **~ded with** parsemé(e) or criblé(e) de

student ['stju:dənt] n étudiant(e) ▷ adj (life) estudiantin(e), étudiant(e), d'étudiant; (residence, restaurant) universitaire; (loan, movement) étudiant; **student driver** n (us) (conducteur(-trice)) débutant(e); **students' union** n (BRIT: association) ≈ union f des étudiants; (: building) ≈ foyer m des étudiants

studio ['stju:dɪəu] n studio m, atelier m; (TV etc) studio; **studio flat** (us **studio apartment**) n studio m

study ['stʌdɪ] n étude f; (room) bureau m ▷ vt étudier; (examine) examiner ▷ vi étudier, faire ses études

stuff [stʌf] n (gen) chose(s) f(pl), truc m; (belongings) affaires fpl, trucs; (substance) substance f ▷ vt rembourrer; (Culin) farcir; (inf: push) fourrer; **stuffing** n bourre f, rembourrage m; (Culin) farce f; **stuffy** adj (room) mal ventilé(e) or aéré(e); (ideas) vieux jeu inv

stumble ['stʌmbl] vi trébucher; **to ~ across** or **on** (fig) tomber sur

stump [stʌmp] n souche f; (of limb) moignon m ▷ vt: **to be ~ed** sécher, ne pas savoir que répondre

stun [stʌn] vt (blow) étourdir; (news) abasourdir, stupéfier

stung [stʌŋ] pt, pp of **sting**

stunk [stʌŋk] pp of **stink**

stunned [stʌnd] adj assommé(e); (fig) sidéré(e)

stunning ['stʌnɪŋ] adj (beautiful) étourdissant(e); (news etc) stupéfiant(e)

stunt [stʌnt] n (in film) cascade f, acrobatie f; (publicity) truc m publicitaire ▷ vt retarder, arrêter

stupid ['stjuːpɪd] adj stupide, bête; **stupidity** [stjuːˈpɪdɪtɪ] n stupidité f, bêtise f

sturdy ['stəːdɪ] adj (person, plant) robuste, vigoureux(-euse); (object) solide

stutter ['stʌtər] n bégaiement m ▷ vi bégayer

style [staɪl] n style m; (distinction) allure f, cachet m, style; (design) modèle m; **stylish** adj élégant(e), chic inv; **stylist** n (hair stylist) coiffeur(-euse)

sub... [sʌb] prefix sub..., sous-; **subconscious** adj subconscient(e)

subdued [səbˈdjuːd] adj (light) tamisé(e); (person) qui a perdu de son entrain

subject n ['sʌbdʒɪkt] sujet m; (Scol) matière f ▷ vt [səbˈdʒɛkt]: **to ~** soumettre à; **to be ~ to** (law) être soumis(e) à; **subjective** [səbˈdʒɛktɪv] adj subjectif(-ive); **subject matter** n (content) contenu m

subjunctive [səbˈdʒʌŋktɪv] n subjonctif m

submarine [sʌbməˈriːn] n sous-marin m

submission [səbˈmɪʃən] n soumission f

submit [səbˈmɪt] vt soumettre ▷ vi se soumettre

subordinate [səˈbɔːdɪnət] adj (junior) subalterne; (Grammar) subordonné(e) ▷ n subordonné(e)

subscribe [səbˈskraɪb] vi cotiser; **to ~ to** (opinion, fund) souscrire à; (newspaper) s'abonner à; être abonné(e) à

subscription [səbˈskrɪpʃən] n (to magazine etc) abonnement m

subsequent ['sʌbsɪkwənt] adj ultérieur(e), suivant(e); **subsequently** adv par la suite

subside [səbˈsaɪd] vi (land) s'affaisser; (flood) baisser; (wind, feelings) tomber

subsidiary [səbˈsɪdɪərɪ] adj subsidiaire, accessoire; (Brit Scol: subject) complémentaire ▷ n filiale f

subsidize ['sʌbsɪdaɪz] vt subventionner

subsidy ['sʌbsɪdɪ] n subvention f

substance ['sʌbstəns] n substance f

substantial [səbˈstænʃl] adj substantiel(le); (fig) important(e)

substitute ['sʌbstɪtjuːt] n (person) remplaçant(e); (thing) succédané m ▷ vt: **to ~ sth/sb for** substituer qch/qn à, remplacer par qch/qn; **substitution** n substitution f

subtitles ['sʌbtaɪtlz] npl (Cine) sous-titres mpl

subtle ['sʌtl] adj subtil(e)

subtract [səbˈtrækt] vt soustraire, retrancher

suburb ['sʌbəːb] n faubourg m; **the ~s** la banlieue; **suburban** [səˈbəːbən] adj de banlieue, suburbain(e)

subway ['sʌbweɪ] n (Brit: underpass) passage souterrain; (us: railway) métro m

succeed [səkˈsiːd] vi réussir ▷ vt succéder à; **to ~ in doing** réussir à faire

success [səkˈsɛs] n succès m; réussite f; **successful** adj (business) prospère, qui réussit; (attempt) couronné(e) de succès; **to be successful (in doing)** réussir (à faire); **successfully** adv avec succès

succession [səkˈsɛʃən] n succession f

successive [səkˈsɛsɪv] adj successif(-ive)

successor [səkˈsɛsər] n successeur m

succumb [səˈkʌm] vi succomber

such [sʌtʃ] adj tel (telle); (of that kind): **~ a book** un livre de ce genre or pareil, un tel livre; (so much): **~ courage** un tel courage ▷ adv si; **~ a long trip** un si long voyage; **~ a lot of** tellement or tant de; **~ as** (like) tel (telle) que, comme; **as ~** adv en tant que tel (telle), à proprement parler; **such-and-such** adj tel ou tel (telle ou telle)

suck [sʌk] vt sucer; (breast, bottle) téter

Sudan [suˈdɑːn] n Soudan m

sudden ['sʌdn] adj soudain(e), subit(e); **all of a ~** soudain, tout à coup; **suddenly** adv brusquement, tout à coup, soudain

sue [suː] vt poursuivre en justice, intenter un procès à

suede [sweɪd] n daim m, cuir suédé

suffer ['sʌfər] vt souffrir, subir; (bear) tolérer, supporter, subir ▷ vi souffrir; **to ~ from** (illness) souffrir de, avoir; **suffering** n souffrance(s) f(pl)

suffice [səˈfaɪs] vi suffire

sufficient [səˈfɪʃnt] adj suffisant(e)

suffocate ['sʌfəkeɪt] vi suffoquer; étouffer

sugar ['ʃʊgər] n sucre m ▷ vt sucrer

suggest [səˈdʒɛst] vt suggérer, proposer; (indicate) sembler indiquer; **suggestion** [səˈdʒɛstʃən] n suggestion f

suicide ['suɪsaɪd] n suicide m; **~ bombing** attentat m suicide; see also **commit**; **suicide bomber** n kamikaze m/f

suit [suːt] n (man's) costume m, complet m; (woman's) tailleur m, ensemble m; (Cards) couleur f; (lawsuit) procès m ▷ vt (subj: clothes, *hairstyle*) aller à; (*be convenient for*) convenir à; (*adapt*): **to ~ sth to** adapter or approprier qch à; **well ~ed** (*couple*) faits l'un pour l'autre, très bien assortis; **suitable** *adj* qui convient; approprié(e), adéquat(e); **suitcase** *n* valise *f*

suite [swi:t] *n* (*of rooms, also Mus*) suite *f*; (*furniture*): **bedroom/dining room ~** (ensemble *m* de) chambre *f* à coucher/salle *f* à manger; **a three-piece ~** un salon (canapé et deux fauteuils)

sulfur ['sʌlfə'] (*US*) *n* = **sulphur**

sulk [sʌlk] *vi* bouder

sulphur (*US* **sulfur**) ['sʌlfə'] *n* soufre *m*

sultana [sʌl'tɑːnə] *n* (*fruit*) raisin (sec) de Smyrne

sum [sʌm] *n* somme *f*; (*Scol etc*) calcul *m*; **sum up** *vt* résumer ▷ *vi* résumer

summarize ['sʌməraɪz] *vt* résumer

summary ['sʌmərɪ] *n* résumé *m*

summer ['sʌmə'] *n* été *m* ▷ *cpd* d'été, estival(e); **in (the) ~** en été, pendant l'été; **summer holidays** *npl* grandes vacances; **summertime** *n* (*season*) été *m*

summit ['sʌmɪt] *n* sommet *m*; (*also:* **~ conference**) (conférence *f* au) sommet *m*

summon ['sʌmən] *vt* appeler, convoquer; **to ~ a witness** citer or assigner un témoin

Sun. *abbr* (= *Sunday*) dim

sun [sʌn] *n* soleil *m*; **sunbathe** *vi* prendre un bain de soleil; **sunbed** *n* lit pliant; (*with sun lamp*) lit à ultra-violets; **sunblock** *n* écran *m* total; **sunburn** *n* coup *m* de soleil; **sunburned, sunburnt** *adj* bronzé(e), hâlé(e); (*painfully*) brûlé(e) par le soleil

Sunday ['sʌndɪ] *n* dimanche *m*

sunflower ['sʌnflaʊə'] *n* tournesol *m*

sung [sʌŋ] *pp of* **sing**

sunglasses ['sʌnglɑːsɪz] *npl* lunettes *fpl* de soleil

sunk [sʌŋk] *pp of* **sink**

sun: **sunlight** *n* (lumière *f* du) soleil *m*; **sun lounger** *n* chaise longue; **sunny** *adj* ensoleillé(e); **it is sunny** il fait (du) soleil, il y a du soleil; **sunrise** *n* lever *m* du soleil; **sun roof** *n* (*Aut*) toit ouvrant; **sunscreen** *n* crème *f* solaire; **sunset** *n* coucher *m* du soleil; **sunshade** *n* (*over table*) parasol *m*; **sunshine** *n* (lumière *f* du) soleil *m*; **sunstroke** *n* insolation *f*, coup *m* de soleil; **suntan** *n* bronzage *m*; **suntan lotion** *n* lotion *f* or lait *m* solaire; **suntan oil** *n* huile *f* solaire

super ['su:pə'] *adj* (*inf*) formidable

superb [su:'pə:b] *adj* superbe, magnifique

superficial [su:pə'fɪʃəl] *adj* superficiel(le)

superintendent [su:pərɪn'tendənt] *n* directeur(-trice); (*Police*) ≈ commissaire *m*

superior [su'pɪərɪə'] *adj* supérieur(e); (*smug*) condescendant(e), méprisant(e) ▷ *n* supérieur(e)

superlative [su'pə:lətɪv] *n* (*Ling*) superlatif *m*

supermarket ['su:pəmɑːkɪt] *n* supermarché *m*

supernatural [su:pə'nætʃərəl] *adj* surnaturel(le) ▷ *n*: **the ~** le surnaturel

superpower ['su:pəpauə'] *n* (*Pol*) superpuissance *f*

superstition [su:pə'stɪʃən] *n* superstition *f*

superstitious [su:pə'stɪʃəs] *adj* superstitieux(-euse)

superstore ['su:pəstɔ:'] *n* (*BRIT*) hypermarché *m*, grande surface

supervise ['su:pəvaɪz] *vt* (*children etc*) surveiller; (*organization, work*) diriger; **supervision** [su:pə'vɪʒən] *n* surveillance *f*; (*monitoring*) contrôle *m*; (*management*) direction *f*; **supervisor** *n* surveillant(e); (*in shop*) chef *m* de rayon

supper ['sʌpə'] *n* dîner *m*; (*late*) souper *m*

supple ['sʌpl] *adj* souple

supplement *n* ['sʌplɪmənt] supplément *m* ▷ *vt* [sʌplɪ'mɛnt] ajouter à, compléter

supplier [sə'plaɪə'] *n* fournisseur *m*

supply [sə'plaɪ] *vt* (*provide*) fournir; (*equip*): **to ~ (with)** approvisionner or ravitailler (en); fournir (en) ▷ *n* provision *f*, réserve *f*; (*supplying*) approvisionnement *m*; **supplies** *npl* (*food*) vivres *mpl*; (*Mil*) subsistances *fpl*

support [sə'pɔ:t] *n* (*moral, financial etc*) soutien *m*, appui *m*; (*Tech*) support *m*, soutien ▷ *vt* soutenir, supporter; (*financially*) subvenir aux besoins de; (*uphold*) être pour, être partisan de, appuyer; (*Sport: team*) être pour; **supporter** *n* (*Pol etc*) partisan(e); (*Sport*) supporter *m*

suppose [sə'pəuz] *vt, vi* supposer; imaginer; **to be ~d to do/be** être censé(e) faire/être; **supposedly** [sə'pəuzɪdlɪ] *adv* soi-disant; **supposing** *conj* si, à supposer que + *sub*

suppress [sə'prɛs] *vt* (*revolt, feeling*) réprimer; (*information*) faire disparaître; (*scandal, yawn*) étouffer

supreme [su'pri:m] *adj* suprême

surcharge ['sə:tʃɑːdʒ] *n* surcharge *f*

sure [ʃuə'] *adj* (*gen*) sûr(e); (*definite, convinced*) sûr, certain(e); **~!** (*of course*) bien sûr!; **~ enough** effectivement; **to make ~ of sth/ that** s'assurer de qch/que, vérifier qch/que; **surely** *adv* sûrement; certainement

surf [sə:f] *n* (*waves*) ressac *m* ▷ *vt*: **to ~ the Net** surfer sur Internet, surfer sur le net

surface ['sə:fɪs] *n* surface *f* ▷ *vt* (*road*) poser un revêtement sur ▷ *vi* remonter à la surface; (*fig*) faire surface; **by ~ mail** par voie de terre; (*by sea*) par voie maritime

surfboard ['sə:fbɔːd] *n* planche *f* de surf

surfer ['sə:fə'] *n* (*in sea*) surfeur(-euse); **web** or **net ~** internaute *m/f*

surfing ['sə:fɪŋ] *n* surf *m*

surge [sə:dʒ] *n* (*of emotion*) vague *f* ▷ *vi* déferler

surgeon ['sə:dʒən] n chirurgien m
surgery ['sə:dʒərɪ] n chirurgie f; (BRIT: room) cabinet m (de consultation); (also: ~ hours) heures fpl de consultation
surname ['sə:neɪm] n nom m de famille
surpass [sə:'pɑ:s] vt surpasser, dépasser
surplus ['sə:pləs] n surplus m, excédent m ▷ adj en surplus, de trop; (Comm) excédentaire
surprise [sə'praɪz] n (gen) surprise f; (astonishment) étonnement m ▷ vt surprendre, étonner; **surprised** adj (look, smile) surpris(e), étonné(e); **to be surprised** être surpris; **surprising** adj surprenant(e), étonnant(e); **surprisingly** adv (easy, helpful) étonnamment, étrangement; **(somewhat) surprisingly, he agreed** curieusement, il a accepté
surrender [sə'rɛndər] n reddition f, capitulation f ▷ vi se rendre, capituler
surround [sə'raʊnd] vt entourer; (Mil etc) encercler; **surrounding** adj environnant(e); **surroundings** npl environs mpl, alentours mpl
surveillance [sə:'veɪləns] n surveillance f
survey n ['sə:veɪ] enquête f, étude f; (in house buying etc) inspection f, (rapport m d')expertise f; (of land) levé m ▷ vt [sə:'veɪ] (situation) passer en revue; (examine carefully) inspecter; (building) expertiser; (land) faire le levé de; (look at) embrasser du regard; **surveyor** n (of building) expert m; (of land) (arpenteur m) géomètre m
survival [sə'vaɪvl] n survie f
survive [sə'vaɪv] vi survivre; (custom etc) subsister ▷ vt (accident etc) survivre à, réchapper de; (person) survivre à; **survivor** n survivant(e)
suspect adj, n ['sʌspɛkt] suspect(e) ▷ vt [sə s'pɛkt] soupçonner, suspecter
suspend [səs'pɛnd] vt suspendre; **suspended sentence** n (Law) condamnation f avec sursis; **suspenders** npl (BRIT) jarretelles fpl; (US) bretelles fpl
suspense [səs'pɛns] n attente f, incertitude f; (in film etc) suspense m; **to keep sb in ~** tenir qn en suspens, laisser qn dans l'incertitude
suspension [səs'pɛnʃən] n (gen, Aut) suspension f; (of driving licence) retrait m provisoire; **suspension bridge** n pont suspendu
suspicion [səs'pɪʃən] n soupçon(s) m(pl); **suspicious** adj (suspecting) soupçonneux(-euse), méfiant(e); (causing suspicion) suspect(e)
sustain [səs'teɪn] vt soutenir; (subj: food) nourrir, donner des forces à; (damage) subir; (injury) recevoir
SUV n abbr (esp US: = sports utility vehicle) SUV m, véhicule m de loisirs

swallow ['swɔləʊ] n (bird) hirondelle f ▷ vt avaler; (fig: story) gober
swam [swæm] pt of **swim**
swamp [swɔmp] n marais m, marécage m ▷ vt submerger
swan [swɔn] n cygne m
swap [swɔp] n échange m, troc m ▷ vt: **to ~ (for)** échanger (contre), troquer (contre)
swarm [swɔ:m] n essaim m ▷ vi (bees) essaimer; (people) grouiller; **to be ~ing with** grouiller de
sway [sweɪ] vi se balancer, osciller ▷ vt (influence) influencer
swear [swɛər] (pt **swore**, pp **sworn**) vt, vi jurer; **swear in** vt assermenter; **swearword** n gros mot, juron m
sweat [swɛt] n sueur f, transpiration f ▷ vi suer
sweater ['swɛtər] n tricot m, pull m
sweatshirt ['swɛtʃə:t] n sweat-shirt m
sweaty ['swɛtɪ] adj en sueur, moite or mouillé(e) de sueur
Swede [swi:d] n Suédois(e)
swede [swi:d] n (BRIT) rutabaga m
Sweden ['swi:dn] n Suède f; **Swedish** ['swi:dɪʃ] adj suédois(e) ▷ n (Ling) suédois m
sweep [swi:p] n (curve) grande courbe; (also: **chimney ~**) ramoneur m ▷ vb (pt, pp **swept**) ▷ vt balayer; (subj: current) emporter
sweet [swi:t] n (BRIT: pudding) dessert m; (candy) bonbon m ▷ adj doux (douce); (not savoury) sucré(e); (kind) gentil(le); (baby) mignon(ne); **sweetcorn** n maïs doux; **sweetener** ['swi:tnər] n (Culin) édulcorant m; **sweetheart** n amoureux(-euse); **sweetshop** n (BRIT) confiserie f
swell [swɛl] n (of sea) houle f ▷ adj (US: inf: excellent) chouette ▷ vb (pt ~**ed**, pp **swollen** or ~**ed**) ▷ vt (increase) grossir, augmenter ▷ vi (increase) grossir, augmenter; (sound) s'enfler; (Med: also: ~ **up**) enfler; **swelling** n (Med) enflure f; (: lump) grosseur f
swept [swɛpt] pt, pp of **sweep**
swerve [swə:v] vi (to avoid obstacle) faire une embardée or un écart; (off the road) dévier
swift [swɪft] n (bird) martinet m ▷ adj rapide, prompt(e)
swim [swɪm] n: **to go for a ~** aller nager or se baigner ▷ vb (pt **swam**, pp **swum**) ▷ vi nager; (Sport) faire de la natation; (fig: head, room) tourner ▷ vt traverser (à la nage); **to ~ a length** nager une longueur; **swimmer** n nageur(-euse); **swimming** n nage f, natation f; **swimming costume** n (BRIT) maillot m (de bain); **swimming pool** n piscine f; **swimming trunks** npl maillot m de bain; **swimsuit** n maillot m (de bain)
swing [swɪŋ] n (in playground) balançoire f;

(*movement*) balancement *m*, oscillations *fpl*;
(*change in opinion etc*) revirement *m* ▷ *vb* (*pt,
pp* **swung**) ▷ *vt* balancer, faire osciller; (*also:*
~ round) tourner, faire virer ▷ *vi* se balancer,
osciller; (*also:* **~ round**) virer, tourner; **to be in
full ~** battre son plein

swipe card [swaɪp-] *n* carte *f* magnétique

swirl [swə:l] *vi* tourbillonner, tournoyer

Swiss [swɪs] *adj* suisse ▷ *n* (*pl inv*) Suisse(-esse)

switch [swɪtʃ] *n* (*for light, radio etc*) bouton *m*;
(*change*) changement *m*, revirement *m* ▷ *vt*
(*change*) changer; **switch off** *vt* éteindre;
(*engine, machine*) arrêter; **could you ~ off
the light?** pouvez-vous éteindre la lumière?;
switch on *vt* allumer; (*engine, machine*)
mettre en marche; **switchboard** *n* (*Tel*)
standard *m*

Switzerland ['swɪtsələnd] *n* Suisse *f*

swivel ['swɪvl] *vi* (*also:* **~ round**) pivoter,
tourner

swollen ['swəulən] *pp of* **swell**

swoop [swu:p] *n* (*by police etc*) rafle *f*, descente
f ▷ *vi* (*bird: also:* **~ down**) descendre en piqué,
piquer

swop [swɒp] *n, vt* = **swap**

sword [sɔ:d] *n* épée *f*; **swordfish** *n* espadon *m*

swore [swɔ:ʳ] *pt of* **swear**

sworn [swɔ:n] *pp of* **swear** ▷ *adj* (*statement,
evidence*) donné(e) sous serment; (*enemy*)
juré(e)

swum [swʌm] *pp of* **swim**

swung [swʌŋ] *pt, pp of* **swing**

syllable ['sɪləbl] *n* syllabe *f*

syllabus ['sɪləbəs] *n* programme *m*

symbol ['sɪmbl] *n* symbole *m*; **symbolic(al)**
[sɪm'bɒlɪk(l)] *adj* symbolique

symmetrical [sɪ'mɛtrɪkl] *adj* symétrique

symmetry ['sɪmɪtrɪ] *n* symétrie *f*

sympathetic [sɪmpə'θɛtɪk] *adj* (*showing
pity*) compatissant(e); (*understanding*)
bienveillant(e), compréhensif(-ive); **~
towards** bien disposé(e) envers

> Be careful not to translate **sympathetic**
> by the French word **sympathique**.

sympathize ['sɪmpəθaɪz] *vi:* **to ~ with sb**
plaindre qn; (*in grief*) s'associer à la douleur de
qn; **to ~ with sth** comprendre qch

sympathy ['sɪmpəθɪ] *n* (*pity*) compassion *f*

symphony ['sɪmfənɪ] *n* symphonie *f*

symptom ['sɪmptəm] *n* symptôme *m*;
indice *m*

synagogue ['sɪnəgɔg] *n* synagogue *f*

syndicate ['sɪndɪkɪt] *n* syndicat *m*,
coopérative *f*; (*Press*) agence *f* de presse

syndrome ['sɪndrəum] *n* syndrome *m*

synonym ['sɪnənɪm] *n* synonyme *m*

synthetic [sɪn'θɛtɪk] *adj* synthétique

Syria ['sɪrɪə] *n* Syrie *f*

syringe [sɪ'rɪndʒ] *n* seringue *f*

syrup ['sɪrəp] *n* sirop *m*; (BRIT: *also:* **golden ~**)
mélasse raffinée

system ['sɪstəm] *n* système *m*; (*Anat*)
organisme *m*; **systematic** [sɪstə'mætɪk] *adj*
systématique; méthodique; **systems analyst**
n analyste-programmeur *m/f*

ta [tɑ:] *excl* (BRIT inf) merci!

tab [tæb] *n* (label) étiquette *f*; (on drinks can etc) languette *f*; **to keep ~s on** (fig) surveiller

table ['teɪbl] *n* table *f* ▷ *vt* (BRIT: motion etc) présenter; **a ~ for 4, please** une table pour 4, s'il vous plaît; **to lay** *or* **set the ~** mettre le couvert *or* la table; **tablecloth** *n* nappe *f*; **table d'hôte** [tɑ:bl'dəut] *adj* (meal) à prix fixe; **table lamp** *n* lampe décorative *or* de table; **tablemat** *n* (for plate) napperon *m*, set *m*; (for hot dish) dessous-de-plat *m inv*; **tablespoon** *n* cuiller *f* de service; (also: **tablespoonful**: as measurement) cuillerée *f* à soupe

tablet ['tæblɪt] *n* (Med) comprimé *m*; (of stone) plaque *f*

table tennis *n* ping-pong *m*, tennis *m* de table

tabloid ['tæblɔɪd] *n* (newspaper) quotidien *m* populaire

taboo [tə'bu:] *adj, n* tabou (*m*)

tack [tæk] *n* (nail) petit clou; (fig) direction *f* ▷ *vt* (nail) clouer; (sew) bâtir ▷ *vi* (Naut) tirer un *or* des bord(s); **to ~ sth on to (the end of) sth** (of letter, book) rajouter qch à la fin de qch

tackle ['tækl] *n* matériel *m*, équipement *m*; (for lifting) appareil *m* de levage; (Football, Rugby) plaquage *m* ▷ *vt* (difficulty, animal, burglar) s'attaquer à; (person: challenge) s'expliquer avec; (Football, Rugby) plaquer

tacky ['tækɪ] *adj* collant(e); (paint) pas sec (sèche); (pej: poor-quality) minable; (: showing bad taste) ringard(e)

tact [tækt] *n* tact *m*; **tactful** *adj* plein(e) de tact

tactics ['tæktɪks] *npl* tactique *f*

tactless ['tæktlɪs] *adj* qui manque de tact

tadpole ['tædpəul] *n* têtard *m*

taffy ['tæfɪ] *n* (us) (bonbon *m* au) caramel *m*

tag [tæg] *n* étiquette *f*

tail [teɪl] *n* queue *f*; (of shirt) pan *m* ▷ *vt* (follow) suivre, filer; **tails** *npl* (suit) habit *m*; see also **head**

tailor ['teɪlə*r*] *n* tailleur *m* (artisan)

Taiwan ['taɪ'wɑ:n] *n* Taïwan (no article); **Taiwanese** [taɪwə'ni:z] *adj* taïwanais(e) ▷ *n inv* Taïwanais(e)

take [teɪk] *vb* (pt **took**, pp **~n**) ▷ *vt* prendre; (gain: prize) remporter; (require: effort, courage) demander; (tolerate) accepter, supporter; (hold: passengers etc) contenir; (accompany) emmener, accompagner; (bring, carry) apporter, emporter; (exam) passer, se présenter à; **to ~ sth from** (drawer etc) prendre qch dans; (person) prendre qch à; **I ~ it that** je suppose que; **to be ~n ill** tomber malade; **it won't ~ long** ça ne prendra pas longtemps; **I was quite ~n with her/it** elle/cela m'a beaucoup plu; **take after** *vt fus* ressembler à; **take apart** *vt* démonter; **take away** *vt* (carry off) emporter; (remove) enlever; (subtract) soustraire; **take back** *vt* (return) rendre, rapporter; (one's words) retirer; **take down** *vt* (building) démolir; (letter etc) prendre, écrire; **take in** *vt* (deceive) tromper, rouler; (understand) comprendre, saisir; (include) couvrir, inclure; (lodger) prendre; (dress, waistband) reprendre; **take off** *vi* (Aviat) décoller ▷ *vt* (remove) enlever; **take on** *vt* (work) accepter, se charger de; (employee) prendre, embaucher; (opponent) accepter de se battre contre; **take out** *vt* sortir; (remove) enlever; (invite) sortir avec; **to ~ sth out of** (out of drawer etc) prendre qch dans; **to ~ sb out to a restaurant** emmener qn au restaurant; **take over** *vt* (business) reprendre ▷ *vi*: **to ~ over from sb** prendre la relève de qn; **take up** *vt* (one's story) reprendre; (dress) raccourcir; (occupy: time, space) prendre, occuper; (engage in: hobby etc) se mettre à; (accept: offer, challenge) accepter; **takeaway** (BRIT) *adj* (food) à emporter ▷ *n* (shop, restaurant) ≈ magasin *m* qui vend des plats à emporter; **taken** *pp of* **take**; **is this seat taken?** la place est prise?; **takeoff** *n* (Aviat) décollage *m*; **takeout** *adj, n* (us) = **takeaway**; **takeover** *n* (Comm) rachat *m*; **takings** *npl* (Comm) recette *f*

talc [tælk] *n* (also: **~um powder**) talc *m*

tale [teɪl] *n* (story) conte *m*, histoire *f*; (account) récit *m*; **to tell ~s** (fig) rapporter

talent ['tælnt] *n* talent *m*, don *m*; **talented** *adj* doué(e), plein(e) de talent

talk [tɔːk] n (a speech) causerie f, exposé m; (conversation) discussion f; (interview) entretien m; (gossip) racontars mpl (pej) ▷ vi parler; (chatter) bavarder; **talks** npl (Pol etc) entretiens mpl; **to ~ about** parler de; **to ~ sb out of/into doing** persuader qn de ne pas faire/de faire; **to ~ shop** parler métier or affaires; **talk over** vt discuter (de); **talk show** n (TV, Radio) émission-débat f

tall [tɔːl] adj (person) grand(e); (building, tree) haut(e); **to be 6 feet ~** ≈ mesurer 1 mètre 80

tambourine [tæmbəˈriːn] n tambourin m

tame [teɪm] adj apprivoisé(e); (fig: story, style) insipide

tamper [ˈtæmpər] vi: **to ~ with** toucher à (en cachette ou sans permission)

tampon [ˈtæmpən] n tampon m hygiénique or périodique

tan [tæn] n (also: **sun~**) bronzage m ▷ vt, vi bronzer, brunir ▷ adj (colour) marron clair inv

tandem [ˈtændəm] n tandem m

tangerine [tændʒəˈriːn] n mandarine f

tangle [ˈtæŋgl] n enchevêtrement m; **to get in(to) a ~** s'emmêler

tank [tæŋk] n réservoir m; (for fish) aquarium m; (Mil) char m d'assaut, tank m

tanker [ˈtæŋkər] n (ship) pétrolier m, tanker m; (truck) camion-citerne m

tanned [tænd] adj bronzé(e)

tantrum [ˈtæntrəm] n accès m de colère

Tanzania [tænzəˈnɪə] n Tanzanie f

tap [tæp] n (on sink etc) robinet m; (gentle blow) petite tape ▷ vt frapper or taper légèrement; (resources) exploiter, utiliser; (telephone) mettre sur écoute; **on ~** a ~ (fig: resources) disponible; **tap dancing** n claquettes fpl

tape [teɪp] n (for tying) ruban m; (also: **magnetic ~**) bande f (magnétique); (cassette) cassette f; (sticky) Scotch® m ▷ vt (record) enregistrer (au magnétoscope or sur cassette); (stick) coller avec du Scotch®; **tape measure** n mètre m à ruban; **tape recorder** n magnétophone m

tapestry [ˈtæpɪstrɪ] n tapisserie f

tar [tɑː] n goudron m

target [ˈtɑːgɪt] n cible f; (fig: objective) objectif m

tariff [ˈtærɪf] n (Comm) tarif m; (taxes) tarif douanier

tarmac [ˈtɑːmæk] n (BRIT: on road) macadam m; (Aviat) aire f d'envol

tarpaulin [tɑːˈpɔːlɪn] n bâche goudronnée

tarragon [ˈtærəgən] n estragon m

tart [tɑːt] n (Culin) tarte f; (BRIT inf. pej: prostitute) poule f ▷ adj (flavour) âpre, aigrelet(te)

tartan [ˈtɑːtn] n tartan m ▷ adj écossais(e)

tartar(e) sauce n sauce f tartare

task [tɑːsk] n tâche f; **to take to ~** prendre à partie

taste [teɪst] n goût m; (fig: glimpse, idea) idée f, aperçu m ▷ vt goûter ▷ vi: **to ~ of** (fish etc) avoir le or un goût de; **you can ~ the garlic (in it)** on sent bien l'ail; **to have a ~ of sth** goûter (à) qch; **can I have a ~?** je peux goûter?; **to be in good/bad** or **poor ~** être de bon/mauvais goût; **tasteful** adj de bon goût; **tasteless** adj (food) insipide; (remark) de mauvais goût; **tasty** adj savoureux(-euse), délicieux(-euse)

tatters [ˈtætəz] npl: **in ~** (also: **tattered**) en lambeaux

tattoo [təˈtuː] n tatouage m; (spectacle) parade f militaire ▷ vt tatouer

taught [tɔːt] pt, pp of **teach**

taunt [tɔːnt] n raillerie f ▷ vt railler

Taurus [ˈtɔːrəs] n le Taureau

taut [tɔːt] adj tendu(e)

tax [tæks] n (on goods etc) taxe f; (on income) impôts mpl, contributions fpl ▷ vt taxer; imposer; (fig: patience etc) mettre à l'épreuve; **tax disc** n (BRIT Aut) vignette f (automobile); **tax-free** adj exempt(e) d'impôts

taxi [ˈtæksɪ] n taxi m ▷ vi (Aviat) rouler (lentement) au sol; **can you call me a ~, please?** pouvez-vous m'appeler un taxi, s'il vous plaît?; **taxi driver** n chauffeur m de taxi; **taxi rank** (BRIT), **taxi stand** n station f de taxis

tax payer [-peɪər] n contribuable m/f

tax return n déclaration f d'impôts or de revenus

TB n abbr = **tuberculosis**

tea [tiː] n thé m; (BRIT: snack: for children) goûter m; **high ~** (BRIT) collation combinant goûter et dîner; **tea bag** n sachet m de thé; **tea break** n (BRIT) pause-thé f

teach (pt, pp **taught**) [tiːtʃ, tɔːt] vt: **to ~ sb sth**, **to ~ sth to sb** apprendre qch à qn; (in school etc) enseigner qch à qn ▷ vi enseigner; **teacher** n (in secondary school) professeur m; (in primary school) instituteur(-trice); **teaching** n enseignement m

tea: **tea cloth** n (BRIT) torchon m; **teacup** n tasse f à thé

tea leaves npl feuilles fpl de thé

team [tiːm] n équipe f; (of animals) attelage m; **team up** vi: **to ~ up (with)** faire équipe (avec)

teapot [ˈtiːpɔt] n théière f

tear¹ [tɪər] n larme f; **in ~s** en larmes

tear² n [tɛər] déchirure f ▷ vb (pt **tore**, pp **torn**) ▷ vt déchirer ▷ vi se déchirer; **tear apart** vt (also fig) déchirer; **tear down** vt (building, statue) démolir; (poster, flag) arracher; **tear off** vt (sheet of paper etc) arracher; (one's clothes) enlever à toute vitesse; **tear up** vt (sheet of paper etc) déchirer, mettre en morceaux or pièces

tearful ['tɪəful] *adj* larmoyant(e)

tear gas ['tɪə-] *n* gaz *m* lacrymogène

tearoom ['tiːruːm] *n* salon *m* de thé

tease [tiːz] *vt* taquiner; (*unkindly*) tourmenter

tea: **teaspoon** *n* petite cuiller; (*also*: **teaspoonful**: *as measurement*) ≈ cuillerée f à café; **teatime** *n* l'heure f du thé; **tea towel** *n* (*BRIT*) torchon *m* (à vaisselle)

technical ['tɛknɪkl] *adj* technique

technician [tɛk'nɪʃən] *n* technicien(ne)

technique [tɛk'niːk] *n* technique f

technology [tɛk'nɔlədʒɪ] *n* technologie f

teddy (bear) ['tɛdɪ-] *n* ours *m* (en peluche)

tedious ['tiːdɪəs] *adj* fastidieux(-euse)

tee [tiː] *n* (*Golf*) tee *m*

teen [tiːn] *adj* = **teenage** ▷ *n* (*US*) = **teenager**

teenage ['tiːneɪdʒ] *adj* (*fashions etc*) pour jeunes, pour adolescents; (*child*) qui est adolescent(e); **teenager** *n* adolescent(e)

teens [tiːnz] *npl*: **to be in one's ~** être adolescent(e)

teeth [tiːθ] *npl of* **tooth**

teetotal ['tiː'təutl] *adj* (*person*) qui ne boit jamais d'alcool

telecommunications ['tɛlɪkəmjuːnɪ'keɪʃənz] *n* télécommunications *fpl*

telegram ['tɛlɪgræm] *n* télégramme *m*

telegraph pole ['tɛlɪgrɑːf-] *n* poteau *m* télégraphique

telephone ['tɛlɪfəun] *n* téléphone *m* ▷ *vt* (*person*) téléphoner à; (*message*) téléphoner; **to be on the ~** (*be speaking*) être au téléphone; **telephone book** *n* = **telephone directory**; **telephone booth** (*BRIT*), **telephone box** *n* cabine f téléphonique; **telephone call** *n* appel *m* téléphonique; **telephone directory** *n* annuaire *m* (du téléphone); **telephone number** *n* numéro *m* de téléphone

telesales ['tɛlɪseɪlz] *npl* télévente f

telescope ['tɛlɪskəup] *n* télescope *m*

televise ['tɛlɪvaɪz] *vt* téléviser

television ['tɛlɪvɪʒən] *n* télévision f; **on ~** à la télévision; **television programme** *n* émission f de télévision

tell (*pt, pp* **told**) [tɛl, təuld] *vt* dire; (*relate*: *story*) raconter; (*distinguish*): **to ~ sth from** distinguer qch de ▷ *vi* (*talk*): **to ~ of** parler de; (*have effect*) se faire sentir, se voir; **to ~ sb to do** dire à qn de faire; **to ~ the time** (*know how to*) savoir lire l'heure; **tell off** *vt* réprimander, gronder; **teller** *n* (*in bank*) caissier(-ière)

telly ['tɛlɪ] *n abbr* (*BRIT inf*: = *television*) télé f

temp [tɛmp] *n* (*BRIT* = *temporary worker*) intérimaire *m/f* ▷ *vi* travailler comme intérimaire

temper ['tɛmpə*] *n* (*nature*) caractère *m*; (*mood*) humeur f; (*fit of anger*) colère f ▷ *vt* (*moderate*) tempérer, adoucir; **to be in a ~** être

en colère; **to lose one's ~** se mettre en colère

temperament ['tɛmprəmənt] *n* (*nature*) tempérament *m*; **temperamental** [tɛmprə'mɛntl] *adj* capricieux(-euse)

temperature ['tɛmprətʃə*] *n* température f; **to have** *or* **run a ~** avoir de la fièvre

temple ['tɛmpl] *n* (*building*) temple *m*; (*Anat*) tempe f

temporary ['tɛmpərərɪ] *adj* temporaire, provisoire; (*job, worker*) temporaire

tempt [tɛmpt] *vt* tenter; **to ~ sb into doing** induire qn à faire; **temptation** *n* tentation f; **tempting** *adj* tentant(e); (*food*) appétissant(e)

ten [tɛn] *num* dix

tenant ['tɛnənt] *n* locataire *m/f*

tend [tɛnd] *vt* s'occuper de ▷ *vi*: **to ~ to do** avoir tendance à faire; **tendency** ['tɛndənsɪ] *n* tendance f

tender ['tɛndə*] *adj* tendre; (*delicate*) délicat(e); (*sore*) sensible ▷ *n* (*Comm*: *offer*) soumission f; (*money*): **legal ~** cours légal ▷ *vt* offrir

tendon ['tɛndən] *n* tendon *m*

tenner ['tɛnə*] *n* (*BRIT inf*) billet *m* de dix livres

tennis ['tɛnɪs] *n* tennis *m*; **tennis ball** *n* balle f de tennis; **tennis court** *n* (court *m* de) tennis *m*; **tennis match** *n* match *m* de tennis; **tennis player** *n* joueur(-euse) de tennis; **tennis racket** *n* raquette f de tennis

tenor ['tɛnə*] *n* (*Mus*) ténor *m*

tenpin bowling ['tɛnpɪn-] *n* (*BRIT*) bowling *m* (à 10 quilles)

tense [tɛns] *adj* tendu(e) ▷ *n* (*Ling*) temps *m*

tension ['tɛnʃən] *n* tension f

tent [tɛnt] *n* tente f

tentative ['tɛntətɪv] *adj* timide, hésitant(e); (*conclusion*) provisoire

tenth [tɛnθ] *num* dixième

tent: **tent peg** *n* piquet *m* de tente; **tent pole** *n* montant *m* de tente

tepid ['tɛpɪd] *adj* tiède

term [təːm] *n* terme *m*; (*Scol*) trimestre *m* ▷ *vt* appeler; **terms** *npl* (*conditions*) conditions *fpl*; (*Comm*) tarif *m*; **in the short/long ~** à court/long terme; **to come to ~s with** (*problem*) faire face à; **to be on good ~s with** bien s'entendre avec, être en bons termes avec

terminal ['təːmɪnl] *adj* (*disease*) dans sa phase terminale; (*patient*) incurable ▷ *n* (*Elec*) borne f; (*for oil, ore etc, also Comput*) terminal *m*; (*also*: **air ~**) aérogare f; (*BRIT*: *also*: **coach ~**) gare routière

terminate ['təːmɪneɪt] *vt* mettre fin à; (*pregnancy*) interrompre

termini ['təːmɪnaɪ] *npl of* **terminus**

terminology [təːmɪ'nɔlədʒɪ] *n* terminologie f

terminus (*pl* **termini**) ['təːmɪnəs, 'təːmɪnaɪ] *n* terminus *m inv*

t

terrace ['terəs] n terrasse f; (BRIT: row of
houses) rangée f de maisons (attenantes les unes
aux autres); **the ~s** (BRIT Sport) les gradins mpl; **terraced** adj (garden) en terrasses; (in a row:
house, cottage etc) attenant(e) aux maisons
voisines

terrain [te'reɪn] n terrain m (sol)

terrestrial [tɪ'restrɪəl] adj terrestre

terrible ['terɪbl] adj terrible, atroce; (weather,
work) affreux(-euse), épouvantable; **terribly**
adv terriblement; (very badly) affreusement
mal

terrier ['terɪə'] n terrier m (chien)

terrific [tə'rɪfɪk] adj (very great) fantastique,
incroyable, terrible; (wonderful) formidable,
sensationnel(le)

terrified ['terɪfaɪd] adj terrifié(e); **to be ~ of
sth** avoir très peur de qch

terrify ['terɪfaɪ] vt terrifier; **terrifying** adj
terrifiant(e)

territorial [terɪ'tɔ:rɪəl] adj territorial(e)

territory ['terɪtərɪ] n territoire m

terror ['terə'] n terreur f; **terrorism** n
terrorisme m; **terrorist** n terroriste m/f; **terrorist attack** n attentat m terroriste

test [test] n (trial, check) essai m; (: of courage
etc) épreuve f; (Med) examen m; (Chem) analyse
f; (Scol) interrogation f de contrôle; (also:
driving ~) (examen du) permis m de conduire
▷ vt essayer; mettre à l'épreuve; examiner;
analyser; faire subir une interrogation (de
contrôle) à

testicle ['testɪkl] n testicule m

testify ['testɪfaɪ] vi (Law) témoigner, déposer; **to ~ to sth** (Law) attester qch

testimony ['testɪmənɪ] n (Law) témoignage
m, déposition f

test: **test match** n (Cricket, Rugby) match
international; **test tube** n éprouvette f

tetanus ['tetənəs] n tétanos m

text [tekst] n texte m; (on mobile phone) texto m,
SMS m inv ▷ vt (inf) envoyer un texto ou SMS à; **textbook** n manuel m

textile ['tekstaɪl] n textile m

text message n texto m, SMS m inv

text messaging [-'mesɪdʒɪŋ] n messagerie
textuelle

texture ['tekstʃə'] n texture f; (of skin, paper
etc) grain m

Thai [taɪ] adj thaïlandais(e) ▷ n
Thaïlandais(e)

Thailand ['taɪlænd] n Thaïlande f

Thames [temz] n: **the (River) ~** la Tamise

than [ðæn, ðən] conj que; (with numerals): **more ~ 10/once** plus de
10/d'une fois; **I have more/less ~ you** j'en ai
plus/moins que toi; **she has more apples ~
pears** elle a plus de pommes que de poires; **it
is better to phone ~ to write** il vaut mieux

téléphoner (plutôt) qu'écrire; **she is older ~
you think** elle est plus âgée que tu le crois

thank [θæŋk] vt remercier, dire merci à; **thanks** npl remerciements mpl ▷ excl merci!; **~ you (very much)** merci (beaucoup); **~ God** Dieu merci; **~s to** prep grâce à; **thankfully** adv (fortunately) heureusement; **Thanksgiving (Day)** n jour m d'action de
grâce; voir encadré

● **THANKSGIVING (DAY)**
●
●
● **Thanksgiving (Day)** est un jour de
● congé aux États-Unis, le quatrième jeudi
● du mois de novembre, commémorant
● la bonne récolte que les Pèlerins venus
● de Grande-Bretagne ont eue en 1621;
● traditionnellement, c'était un jour où l'on
● remerciait Dieu et où l'on organisait un
● grand festin. Une fête semblable, mais qui
● n'a aucun rapport avec les Pères Pèlerins, a
● lieu au Canada le deuxième lundi d'octobre.

○ **KEYWORD**

that [ðæt] adj (demonstrative: pl **those**) ce, cet
+ vowel or h mute, cette f; **that man/woman/
book** cet homme/cette femme/ce livre; (not
this) cet homme-là/cette femme-là/ce livre-
là; **that one** celui-là (celle-là)
▷ pron **1** (demonstrative: pl **those**) ce; (not this
one) cela, ça; (that one) celui (celle); **who's
that?** qui est-ce?; **what's that?** qu'est-ce que
c'est?; **is that you?** c'est toi?; **I prefer this to
that** je préfère ceci à cela ou ça; **that's what
he said** c'est ou voilà ce qu'il a dit; **will you eat
all that?** est-ce que tu vas manger tout ça?; **that is (to say)** c'est-à-dire, à savoir
2 (relative: subject) qui; (: object) que;
(: after prep) lequel (laquelle), lesquels
(lesquelles) pl; **the book that I read** le livre
que j'ai lu; **the books that are in the library**
les livres qui sont dans la bibliothèque; **all
that I have** tout ce que j'ai; **the box that I
put it in** la boîte dans laquelle je l'ai mis; **the
people that I spoke to** les gens auxquels ou à
qui j'ai parlé
3 (relative: of time) où; **the day that he came**
le jour où il est venu
▷ conj que; **he thought that I was ill** il pensait
que j'étais malade
▷ adv (demonstrative): **I don't like it that
much** ça ne me plaît pas tant que ça; **I didn't
know it was that bad** je ne savais pas que
c'était si ou aussi mauvais; **it's about that
high** c'est à peu près de cette hauteur

thatched [θætʃt] adj (roof) de chaume; **~
cottage** chaumière f

thaw [θɔː] n dégel m ▷ vi (ice) fondre; (food) dégeler ▷ vt (food) (faire) dégeler

 KEYWORD

the [ði:, ðə] def art **1** (gen) le, la f, l' + vowel or h mute, les pl (NB: à + le(s) = **au(x)**; de + le = **du**; de + les = **des**): **the boy/girl/ink** le garçon/la fille/l'encre; **the children** les enfants; **the history of the world** l'histoire du monde; **give it to the postman** donne-le au facteur; **to play the piano/flute** jouer du piano/de la flûte
2 (+ adj to form n) le, la f, l' + vowel or h mute, les pl; **the rich and the poor** les riches et les pauvres; **to attempt the impossible** tenter l'impossible
3 (in titles): **Elizabeth the First** Elisabeth première; **Peter the Great** Pierre le Grand
4 (in comparisons): **the more he works, the more he earns** plus il travaille, plus il gagne de l'argent

theatre (us **theater**) ['θɪətər] n théâtre m; (Med: also: **operating ~**) salle f d'opération
theft [θeft] n vol m (larcin)
their [ðeər] adj leur, leurs pl; see also **my; theirs** pron le (la) leur, les leurs; see also **mine¹**
them [ðɛm, ðəm] pron (direct) les; (indirect) leur; (stressed, after prep) eux (elles); **give me a few of ~** donnez m'en quelques uns (or quelques unes); see also **me**
theme [θi:m] n thème m; **theme park** n parc m à thème
themselves [ðəm'sɛlvz] pl pron (reflexive) se; (emphatic, after prep) eux-mêmes (elles-mêmes); **between ~** entre eux (elles); see also **oneself**
then [ðɛn] adv (at that time) alors, à ce moment-là; (next) puis, ensuite; (and also) et puis ▷ conj (therefore) alors, dans ce cas ▷ adj: **the ~ president** le président d'alors or de l'époque; **by ~** (past) à ce moment-là; (future) d'ici là; **from ~ on** dès lors; **until ~** jusqu'à ce moment-là, jusque-là
theology [θɪ'ɔlədʒɪ] n théologie f
theory ['θɪərɪ] n théorie f
therapist ['θerəpɪst] n thérapeute m/f
therapy ['θerəpɪ] n thérapie f

 KEYWORD

there [ðeər] adv **1**: **there is, there are** il y a; **there are 3 of them** (people, things) il y en a 3; **there is no-one here/no bread left** il n'y a personne/il n'y a plus de pain; **there has been an accident** il y a eu un accident
2 (referring to place) là, là-bas; **it's there** c'est là(-bas); **in/on/up/down there** là-dedans/là-dessus/là-haut/en bas; **he went there on**

Friday il y est allé vendredi; **I want that book there** je veux ce livre-là; **there he is!** le voilà!
3: **there, there** (esp to child) allons, allons!

there: **thereabouts** adv (place) par là, près de là; (amount) environ, à peu près; **thereafter** adv par la suite; **thereby** adv ainsi; **therefore** adv donc, par conséquent
there's ['ðeəz] = **there is**; **there has**
thermal ['θə:ml] adj thermique; **~ underwear** sous-vêtements mpl en Thermolactyl®
thermometer [θə'mɔmɪtər] n thermomètre m
thermostat ['θə:məustæt] n thermostat m
these [ði:z] pl pron ceux-ci (celles-ci) ▷ pl adj ces; (not those): **~ books** ces livres-ci
thesis (pl **theses**) ['θi:sɪs, 'θi:si:z] n thèse f
they [ðeɪ] pl pron ils (elles); (stressed) eux (elles); **~ say that ...** (it is said that) on dit que ...; **they'd** = **they had**; **they would**; **they'll** = **they shall**; **they will**; **they're** = **they are**; **they've** = **they have**
thick [θɪk] adj épais(se); (stupid) bête, borné(e) ▷ n: **in the ~ of** au beau milieu de, en plein cœur de; **it's 20 cm ~** ça a 20 cm d'épaisseur; **thicken** vi s'épaissir ▷ vt (sauce etc) épaissir; **thickness** n épaisseur f
thief (pl **thieves**) [θi:f, θi:vz] n voleur(-euse)
thigh [θaɪ] n cuisse f
thin [θɪn] adj mince; (skinny) maigre; (soup) peu épais(se); (hair, crowd) clairsemé(e) ▷ vt (also: **~ down**: sauce, paint) délayer
thing [θɪŋ] n chose f; (object) objet m; (contraption) truc m; **things** npl (belongings) affaires fpl; **the ~ is ...** c'est que ...; **the best ~ would be to** le mieux serait de; **how are ~s?** comment ça va?; **to have a ~ about** (be obsessed by) être obsédé(e) par; (hate) détester; **poor ~!** le (or la) pauvre!
think (pt, pp **thought**) [θɪŋk, θɔ:t] vi penser, réfléchir ▷ vt penser, croire; (imagine) s'imaginer; **what did you ~ of them?** qu'avez-vous pensé d'eux?; **to ~ about sth/sb** penser à qch/qn; **I'll ~ about it** je vais y réfléchir; **to ~ of doing** avoir l'idée de faire; **I ~ so/not** je crois or pense que oui/non; **to ~ well of** avoir une haute opinion de; **think over** vt bien réfléchir à; **think up** vt inventer, trouver
third [θə:d] num troisième ▷ n (fraction) tiers m; (Aut) troisième (vitesse) f; (BRIT Scol: degree) ≈ licence f avec mention passable; **thirdly** adv troisièmement; **third party insurance** n (BRIT) assurance f au tiers; **Third World** n: **the Third World** le Tiers-Monde
thirst [θə:st] n soif f; **thirsty** adj qui a soif, assoiffé(e); (work) qui donne soif; **to be thirsty** avoir soif
thirteen [θə:'ti:n] num treize; **thirteenth** [-'ti:nθ] num treizième

t

thirtieth ['θəːtɪɪθ] num trentième

thirty ['θəːtɪ] num trente

 KEYWORD

this [ðɪs] adj (demonstrative: pl **these**) ce, cet
+ vowel or h mute, cette f; **this man/woman/
book** cet homme/cette femme/ce livre; (not
that) cet homme-ci/cette femme-ci/ce livre-
ci; **this one** celui-ci (celle-ci)
▷ pron (demonstrative: pl **these**) ce; (not that
one) celui-ci (celle-ci), ceci; **who's this?** qui
est-ce?; **what's this?** qu'est-ce que c'est?; **I
prefer this to that** je préfère ceci à cela; **this
is where I live** c'est ici que j'habite; **this is
what he said** voici ce qu'il a dit; **this is Mr
Brown** (in introductions) je vous présente Mr
Brown; (in photo) c'est Mr Brown; (on telephone)
ici Mr Brown
▷ adv (demonstrative): **it was about this big**
c'était à peu près de cette grandeur or grand
comme ça; **I didn't know it was this bad** je
ne savais pas que c'était si or aussi mauvais

thistle ['θɪsl] n chardon m

thorn [θɔːn] n épine f

thorough ['θʌrə] adj (search)
minutieux(-euse); (knowledge,
research) approfondi(e); (work, person)
consciencieux(-euse); (cleaning) à fond;
thoroughly adv (search) minutieusement;
(study) en profondeur; (clean) à fond; (very)
tout à fait

those [ðəuz] pl pron ceux-là (celles-là) ▷ pl adj
ces; (not these): **~ books** ces livres-là

though [ðəu] conj bien que + sub, quoique +
sub ▷ adv pourtant

thought [θɔːt] pt, pp of **think** ▷ n pensée
f; (idea) idée f; (opinion) avis m; **thoughtful**
adj (deep in thought) pensif(-ive); (serious)
réfléchi(e); (considerate) prévenant(e);
thoughtless adj qui manque de
considération

thousand ['θauzənd] num mille; **one ~**
mille; **two ~** deux mille; **~s of** des milliers de;
thousandth num millième

thrash [θræʃ] vt rouer de coups; (as
punishment) donner une correction à; (inf:
defeat) battre à plate(s) couture(s)

thread [θrɛd] n fil m; (of screw) pas m, filetage
m ▷ vt (needle) enfiler

threat [θrɛt] n menace f; **threaten** vi (storm)
menacer ▷ vt: **to threaten sb with sth/to do**
menacer qn de qch/de faire; **threatening** adj
menaçant(e)

three [θriː] num trois; **three-dimensional** adj
à trois dimensions; **three-piece suite** n salon
m (canapé et deux fauteuils); **three-quarters**
npl trois-quarts mpl; **three-quarters full** aux

trois-quarts plein

threshold ['θrɛʃhəuld] n seuil m

threw [θruː] pt of **throw**

thrill [θrɪl] n (excitement) émotion f, sensation
forte; (shudder) frisson m ▷ vt (audience)
électriser; **thrilled** adj: **thrilled (with)** ravi(e)
de; **thriller** n film m (or roman m or pièce
f) à suspense; **thrilling** adj (book, play etc)
saisissant(e); (news, discovery) excitant(e)

thriving ['θraɪvɪŋ] adj (business, community)
prospère

throat [θrəut] n gorge f; **to have a sore ~**
avoir mal à la gorge

throb [θrɔb] vi (heart) palpiter; (engine) vibrer;
my head is ~bing j'ai des élancements dans
la tête

throne [θrəun] n trône m

through [θruː] prep à travers; (time) pendant,
durant; (by means of) par, par l'intermédiaire
de; (owing to) à cause de ▷ adj (ticket, train,
passage) direct(e) ▷ adv à travers; **(from)
Monday ~ Friday** (us) de lundi à vendredi;
to put sb ~ to sb (Tel) passer qn à qn; **to
be ~** (BRIT: Tel) avoir la communication; (esp
us: have finished) avoir fini; **"no ~ traffic"**
(us) "passage interdit"; **"no ~ road"** (BRIT)
"impasse"; **throughout** prep (place) partout
dans; (time) durant tout(e) le (la) ▷ adv partout

throw [θrəu] n jet m; (Sport) lancer m ▷ vt (pt
threw, pp **~n**) lancer, jeter; (Sport) lancer;
(rider) désarçonner; (fig) déconcertancer; **to ~
a party** donner une réception; **throw away**
vt jeter; (money) gaspiller; **throw in** vt (Sport:
ball) remettre en jeu; (include) ajouter; **throw
off** vt se débarrasser de; **throw out** vt jeter;
(reject) rejeter; (person) mettre à la porte;
throw up vi vomir

thru [θruː] (us) = **through**

thrush [θrʌʃ] n (Zool) grive f

thrust [θrʌst] vt (pt, pp **~**) pousser
brusquement; (push in) enfoncer

thud [θʌd] n bruit sourd

thug [θʌg] n voyou m

thumb [θʌm] n (Anat) pouce m ▷ vt: **to ~ a
lift** faire de l'auto-stop, arrêter une voiture;
thumbtack n (us) punaise f (clou)

thump [θʌmp] n grand coup; (sound) bruit
sourd ▷ vt cogner sur ▷ vi cogner, frapper

thunder ['θʌndə'] n tonnerre m ▷ vi
tonner; (train etc): **to ~ past** passer dans
un grondement or un bruit de tonnerre;
thunderstorm n orage m

Thur(s) abbr (= Thursday) jeu

Thursday ['θəːzdɪ] n jeudi m

thus [ðʌs] adv ainsi

thwart [θwɔːt] vt contrecarrer

thyme [taɪm] n thym m

Tibet [tɪ'bɛt] n Tibet m

tick [tɪk] n (sound: of clock) tic-tac m; (mark)

coche f; (Zool) tique f; (BRIT inf): **in a ~** dans un instant ▷ vi faire tic-tac ▷ vt (item on list) cocher; **tick off** vt (item on list) cocher; (person) réprimander, attraper

ticket ['tɪkɪt] n billet m; (for bus, tube) ticket m; (in shop: on goods) étiquette f; (for library) carte f; (also: **parking ~**) contravention f, p.-v. m; **ticket barrier** n (BRIT: Rail) portillon m automatique; **ticket collector** n contrôleur(-euse); **ticket inspector** n contrôleur(-euse); **ticket machine** n billetterie f automatique; **ticket office** n guichet m, bureau m de vente des billets

tickle ['tɪkl] vi chatouiller ▷ vt chatouiller; **ticklish** adj (person) chatouilleux(-euse); (problem) épineux(-euse)

tide [taɪd] n marée f; (fig: of events) cours m

tidy ['taɪdɪ] adj (room) bien rangé(e); (dress, work) net (nette), soigné(e); (person) ordonné(e), qui a de l'ordre ▷ vt (also: **~ up**) ranger

tie [taɪ] n (string etc) cordon m; (BRIT: also: **neck~**) cravate f; (fig: link) lien m; (Sport: draw) égalité f de points; match nul ▷ vt (parcel) attacher; (ribbon) nouer ▷ vi (Sport) faire match nul; finir à égalité de points; **to ~ sth in a bow** faire un nœud à qch; **to ~ a knot in sth** faire un nœud à qch; **tie down** vt (fig): **to ~ sb down to** contraindre qn à accepter; **to feel ~d down** (by relationship) se sentir coincé(e); **tie up** vt (parcel) ficeler; (dog, boat) attacher; (prisoner) ligoter; (arrangements) conclure; **to be ~d up** (busy) être pris(e) or occupé(e)

tier [tɪə^r] n gradin m; (of cake) étage m

tiger ['taɪgə^r] n tigre m

tight [taɪt] adj (rope) tendu(e), raide; (clothes) étroit(e), très juste; (budget, programme, bend) serré(e); (control) strict(e), sévère; (inf: drunk) ivre, rond(e) ▷ adv (squeeze) très fort; (shut) à bloc, hermétiquement; **hold ~!** accrochez-vous bien!; **tighten** vt (rope) tendre; (screw) resserrer; (control) renforcer ▷ vi se tendre; se resserrer; **tightly** adv (grasp) bien, très fort; **tights** npl (BRIT) collant m

tile [taɪl] n (on roof) tuile f; (on wall or floor) carreau m

till [tɪl] n caisse (enregistreuse) ▷ prep, conj = **until**

tilt [tɪlt] vt pencher, incliner ▷ vi pencher, être incliné(e)

timber ['tɪmbə^r] n (material) bois m de construction

time [taɪm] n temps m; (epoch: often pl) époque f, temps; (by clock) heure f; (moment) moment m; (occasion, also Math) fois f; (Mus) mesure f ▷ vt (race) chronométrer; (programme) minuter; (visit) fixer; (remark etc) choisir le moment de; **a long ~** un long moment, longtemps; **four at a ~** quatre à la fois; **for the ~ being** pour le moment; **from ~ to ~** de temps en temps; **at ~s** parfois; **in ~** (soon enough) à temps; (after some time) avec le temps, à la longue; (Mus) en mesure; **in a week's ~** dans une semaine; **in no ~** en un rien de temps; **any ~** n'importe quand; **on ~** à l'heure; **5 ~s 5** 5 fois 5; **what ~ is it?** quelle heure est-il?; **what ~ is the museum/shop open?** à quelle heure ouvre le musée/magasin?; **to have a good ~** bien s'amuser; **time limit** n limite f de temps, délai m; **timely** adj opportun(e); **timer** n (in kitchen) compte-minutes m inv; (Tech) minuteur m; **time-share** n maison f/ appartement m en multipropriété; **timetable** n (Rail) (indicateur m) horaire m; (Scol) emploi m du temps; **time zone** n fuseau m horaire

timid ['tɪmɪd] adj timide; (easily scared) peureux(-euse)

timing ['taɪmɪŋ] n (Sport) chronométrage m; **the ~ of his resignation** le moment choisi pour sa démission

tin [tɪn] n étain m; (also: **~ plate**) fer-blanc m; (BRIT: can) boîte f (de conserve); (: for baking) moule m (à gâteau); (for storage) boîte f; **tinfoil** n papier m d'étain or d'aluminium

tingle ['tɪŋgl] vi picoter; (person) avoir des picotements

tinker ['tɪŋkə^r]; **tinker with** vt fus bricoler, rafistoler

tinned [tɪnd] adj (BRIT: food) en boîte, en conserve

tin opener [-'əupnə^r] n (BRIT) ouvre-boîte(s) m

tinsel ['tɪnsl] n guirlandes fpl de Noël (argentées)

tint [tɪnt] n teinte f; (for hair) shampooing colorant; **tinted** adj (hair) teint(e); (spectacles, glass) teinté(e)

tiny ['taɪnɪ] adj minuscule

tip [tɪp] n (end) bout m; (gratuity) pourboire m; (BRIT: for rubbish) décharge f; (advice) tuyau m ▷ vt (waiter) donner un pourboire à; (tilt) incliner; (overturn: also: **~ over**) renverser; (empty: also: **~ out**) déverser; **how much should I ~?** combien de pourboire est-ce qu'il faut laisser?; **tip off** vt prévenir, avertir

tiptoe ['tɪptəu] n: **on ~** sur la pointe des pieds

tire ['taɪə^r] n (US) = **tyre** ▷ vt fatiguer ▷ vi se fatiguer; **tired** adj fatigué(e); **to be tired of** en avoir assez de, être las (lasse) de; **tire pressure** (US) = **tyre pressure**; **tiring** adj fatigant(e)

tissue ['tɪʃu:] n tissu m; (paper handkerchief) mouchoir m en papier, kleenex® m; **tissue paper** n papier m de soie

tit [tɪt] n (bird) mésange f; **to give ~ for tat** rendre coup pour coup

title ['taɪtl] n titre m

T-junction ['ti:'dʒʌŋkʃən] n croisement m en T

TM *n abbr* = **trademark**

 KEYWORD

to [tuː, tə] *prep* **1** (*direction*) à; (*towards*) vers; envers; **to go to France/Portugal/London/school** aller en France/au Portugal/à Londres/à l'école; **to go to Claude's/the doctor's** aller chez Claude/le docteur; **the road to Edinburgh** la route d'Édimbourg

2 (*as far as*) (jusqu')à; **to count to 10** compter jusqu'à 10; **from 40 to 50 people** de 40 à 50 personnes

3 (*with expressions of time*): **a quarter to 5** 5 heures moins le quart; **it's twenty to 3** il est 3 heures moins vingt

4 (*for, of*) de; **the key to the front door** la clé de la porte d'entrée; **a letter to his wife** une lettre (adressée) à sa femme

5 (*expressing indirect object*) à; **to give sth to sb** donner qch à qn; **to talk to sb** parler à qn; **to be a danger to sb** être dangereux(-euse) pour qn

6 (*in relation to*) à; **3 goals to 2** 3 (buts) à 2; **30 miles to the gallon** ≈ 9,4 litres aux cent (km)

7 (*purpose, result*): **to come to sb's aid** venir au secours de qn, porter secours à qn; **to sentence sb to death** condamner qn à mort; **to my surprise** à ma grande surprise

▷ *with vb* **1** (*simple infinitive*): **to go/eat** aller/manger

2 (*following another vb*): **to want/try/start to do** vouloir/essayer de/commencer à faire

3 (*with vb omitted*): **I don't want to** je ne veux pas

4 (*purpose, result*) pour; **I did it to help you** je l'ai fait pour vous aider

5 (*equivalent to relative clause*): **I have things to do** j'ai des choses à faire; **the main thing is to try** l'important est d'essayer

6 (*after adjective etc*): **ready to go** prêt(e) à partir; **too old/young to ...** trop vieux/jeune pour ...

▷ *adv*: **push/pull the door to** tirez/poussez la porte

toad [təud] *n* crapaud *m*; **toadstool** *n* champignon (vénéneux)

toast [təust] *n* (*Culin*) pain grillé, toast *m*; (*drink, speech*) toast *m* ▷ *vt* (*Culin*) faire griller; (*drink to*) porter un toast à; **toaster** *n* grille-pain *m inv*

tobacco [tə'bækəu] *n* tabac *m*

toboggan [tə'bɔgən] *n* toboggan *m*; (*child's*) luge *f*

today [tə'deɪ] *adv, n* (*also fig*) aujourd'hui (*m*)

toddler ['tɔdlər] *n* enfant *m/f* qui commence à marcher, bambin *m*

toe [təu] *n* doigt *m* de pied, orteil *m*; (*of shoe*)

bout *m* ▷ *vt*: **to ~ the line** (*fig*) obéir, se conformer; **toenail** *n* ongle *m* de l'orteil

toffee ['tɔfɪ] *n* caramel *m*

together [tə'gɛðər] *adv* ensemble; (*at same time*) en même temps; **~ with** *prep* avec

toilet ['tɔɪlət] *n* (*BRIT: lavatory*) toilettes *fpl*, cabinets *mpl*; **to go to the ~** aller aux toilettes; **where's the ~?** où sont les toilettes?; **toilet bag** *n* (*BRIT*) nécessaire *m* de toilette; **toilet paper** *n* papier *m* hygiénique; **toiletries** *npl* articles *mpl* de toilette; **toilet roll** *n* rouleau *m* de papier hygiénique

token ['təukən] *n* (*sign*) marque *f*, témoignage *m*; (*metal disc*) jeton *m* ▷ *adj* (*fee, strike*) symbolique; **book/record ~** (*BRIT*) chèque-livre/-disque *m*

Tokyo ['təukjəu] *n* Tokyo

told [təuld] *pt, pp of* **tell**

tolerant ['tɔlərnt] *adj*: **~ (of)** tolérant(e) (à l'égard de)

tolerate ['tɔləreɪt] *vt* supporter

toll [təul] *n* (*tax, charge*) péage *m* ▷ *vi* (*bell*) sonner; **the accident ~ on the roads** le nombre des victimes de la route; **toll call** *n* (*US Tel*) appel *m* (à) longue distance; **toll-free** *adj* (*US*) gratuit(e) ▷ *adv* gratuitement

tomato [tə'mɑːtəu] (*pl* **~es**) *n* tomate *f*; **tomato sauce** *n* sauce *f* tomate

tomb [tuːm] *n* tombe *f*; **tombstone** *n* pierre tombale

tomorrow [tə'mɔrəu] *adv, n* (*also fig*) demain (*m*); **the day after ~** après-demain; **a week ~** demain en huit; **~ morning** demain matin

ton [tʌn] *n* tonne *f* (*BRIT*: = 1016 kg; *US* = 907 kg; *metric* = 1000 kg); **~s of** (*inf*) des tas de

tone [təun] *n* ton *m*; (*of radio, BRIT Tel*) tonalité *f* ▷ *vi* (*also*: **~ in**) s'harmoniser; **tone down** *vt* (*colour, criticism*) adoucir

tongs [tɔŋz] *npl* pinces *fpl*; (*for coal*) pincettes *fpl*; (*for hair*) fer *m* à friser

tongue [tʌŋ] *n* langue *f*; **~ in cheek** *adv* ironiquement

tonic ['tɔnɪk] *n* (*Med*) tonique *m*; (*also*: **~ water**) Schweppes® *m*

tonight [tə'naɪt] *adv, n* cette nuit; (*this evening*) ce soir

tonne [tʌn] *n* (*BRIT: metric ton*) tonne *f*

tonsil ['tɔnsl] *n* amygdale *f*; **tonsillitis** [tɔnsɪ'laɪtɪs] *n*: **to have tonsillitis** avoir une angine *or* une amygdalite

too [tuː] *adv* (*excessively*) trop; (*also*) aussi; **~ much** (*as adv*) trop; (*as adj*) trop de; **~ many** *adj* trop de

took [tuk] *pt of* **take**

tool [tuːl] *n* outil *m*; **tool box** *n* boîte *f* à outils; **tool kit** *n* trousse *f* à outils

tooth (*pl* **teeth**) [tuːθ, tiːθ] *n* (*Anat, Tech*) dent *f*; **to brush one's teeth** se laver les dents; **toothache** *n* mal *m* de dents; **to have**

toothache avoir mal aux dents; **toothbrush** n brosse f à dents; **toothpaste** n (pâte f) dentifrice m; **toothpick** n cure-dent m

top [tɔp] n (of mountain, head) sommet m; (of page, ladder) haut m; (of box, cupboard, table) dessus m; (lid: of box, jar) couvercle m; (: of bottle) bouchon m; (toy) toupie f; (Dress: blouse etc) haut; (: of pyjamas) veste f ▷ adj du haut; (in rank) premier(-ière); (best) meilleur(e) ▷ vt (exceed) dépasser; (be first in) être en tête de; **from ~ to bottom** de fond en comble; **on ~ of** sur; (in addition to) en plus de; **over the ~** (inf: behaviour etc) qui dépasse les limites; **top up** (us **top off**) vt (bottle) remplir; (salary) compléter; **to ~ up one's mobile (phone)** recharger son compte; **top floor** n dernier étage; **top hat** n haut-de-forme m

topic ['tɔpɪk] n sujet m, thème m; **topical** adj d'actualité

topless ['tɔplɪs] adj (bather etc) aux seins nus

topping ['tɔpɪŋ] n (Culin) couche de crème, fromage etc qui recouvre un plat

topple ['tɔpl] vt renverser, faire tomber ▷ vi basculer; tomber

top-up ['tɔpʌp] n (for mobile phone) recharge f, minutes fpl; **top-up card** n (for mobile phone) recharge f

torch [tɔːtʃ] n torche f; (BRIT: electric) lampe f de poche

tore [tɔːˈ] pt of **tear²**

torment n ['tɔːment] tourment m ▷ vt [tɔːˈment] tourmenter; (fig: annoy) agacer

torn [tɔːn] pp of **tear²**

tornado [tɔːˈneɪdəu] (pl ~es) n tornade f

torpedo [tɔːˈpiːdəu] (pl ~es) n torpille f

torrent ['tɔrnt] n torrent m; **torrential** [tɔˈrenʃl] adj torrentiel(le)

tortoise ['tɔːtəs] n tortue f

torture ['tɔːtʃəˈ] n torture f ▷ vt torturer

Tory ['tɔːrɪ] adj, n (BRIT Pol) tory m/f, conservateur(-trice)

toss [tɔs] vt lancer, jeter; (BRIT: pancake) faire sauter; (head) rejeter en arrière ▷ vi: **to ~ up for sth** (BRIT) jouer qch à pile ou face; **to ~ a coin** jouer à pile ou face; **to ~ and turn** (in bed) se tourner et se retourner

total ['təutl] adj total(e) ▷ n total m ▷ vt (add up) faire le total de, additionner; (amount to) s'élever à

totalitarian [təutælɪˈtɛərɪən] adj totalitaire

totally ['təutəlɪ] adv totalement

touch [tʌtʃ] n contact m, toucher m; (sense, skill: of pianist etc) toucher ▷ vt (gen) toucher; (tamper with) toucher à; **a ~ of** (fig) un petit peu de; une touche de; **to get in ~ with** prendre contact avec; **to lose ~** (friends) se perdre de vue; **touch down** vi (Aviat) atterrir; (on sea) amerrir; **touchdown** n (Aviat) atterrissage m; (on sea) amerrissage m; (us Football) essai m;

touched adj (moved) touché(e); **touching** adj touchant(e), attendrissant(e); **touchline** n (Sport) (ligne f de) touche f; **touch-sensitive** adj (keypad) à effleurement; (screen) tactile

tough [tʌf] adj dur(e); (resistant) résistant(e), solide; (meat) dur, coriace; (firm) inflexible; (task, problem, situation) difficile

tour ['tuəˈ] n voyage m; (also: **package ~**) voyage organisé; (of town, museum) tour m, visite f; (by band) tournée f ▷ vt visiter; **tour guide** n (person) guide m/f

tourism ['tuərɪzm] n tourisme m

tourist ['tuərɪst] n touriste m/f ▷ cpd touristique; **tourist office** n syndicat m d'initiative

tournament ['tuənəmənt] n tournoi m

tour operator n (BRIT) organisateur m de voyages, tour-opérateur m

tow [təu] vt remorquer; (caravan, trailer) tracter; **"on ~"**, (us) **"in ~"** (Aut) "véhicule en remorque"; **tow away** vt (subj: police) emmener à la fourrière; (: breakdown service) remorquer

toward(s) [təˈwɔːd(z)] prep vers; (of attitude) envers, à l'égard de; (of purpose) pour

towel ['tauəl] n serviette f (de toilette); **towelling** n (fabric) tissu-éponge m

tower ['tauəˈ] n tour f; **tower block** n (BRIT) tour f (d'habitation)

town [taun] n ville f; **to go to ~** aller en ville; (fig) y mettre le paquet; **town centre** n (BRIT) centre m de la ville, centre-ville m; **town hall** n ≈ mairie f

tow truck n (us) dépanneuse f

toxic ['tɔksɪk] adj toxique

toy [tɔɪ] n jouet m; **toy with** vt fus jouer avec; (idea) caresser; **toyshop** n magasin m de jouets

trace [treɪs] n trace f ▷ vt (draw) tracer, dessiner; (follow) suivre la trace de; (locate) retrouver

tracing paper ['treɪsɪŋ-] n papier-calque m

track [træk] n (mark) trace f; (path: gen) chemin m, piste f; (: of bullet etc) trajectoire f; (: of suspect, animal) piste; (Rail) voie ferrée, rails mpl; (on tape, Comput, Sport) piste; (on CD) piste f; (on record) plage f ▷ vt suivre la trace or la piste de; **to keep ~ of** suivre; **track down** vt (prey) trouver et capturer; (sth lost) finir par retrouver; **tracksuit** n survêtement m

tractor ['træktəˈ] n tracteur m

trade [treɪd] n commerce m; (skill, job) métier m ▷ vi faire du commerce ▷ vt (exchange): **to ~ sth (for sth)** échanger qch (contre qch); **to ~ with/in** faire du commerce avec/le commerce de; **trade in** vt (old car etc) faire reprendre; **trademark** n marque f de fabrique; **trader** n commerçant(e), négociant(e); **tradesman** (irreg) n (shopkeeper) commerçant m; **trade**

union n syndicat m

trading ['treɪdɪŋ] n affaires fpl, commerce m

tradition [trə'dɪʃən] n tradition f; **traditional** adj traditionnel(le)

traffic ['træfɪk] n trafic m; (cars) circulation f ▷ vi: **to ~ in** (pej: liquor, drugs) faire le trafic de; **traffic circle** n (us) rond-point m; **traffic island** n refuge m (pour piétons); **traffic jam** n embouteillage m; **traffic lights** npl feux mpl (de signalisation); **traffic warden** n contractuel(le)

tragedy ['trædʒədɪ] n tragédie f

tragic ['trædʒɪk] adj tragique

trail [treɪl] n (tracks) trace f, piste f; (path) chemin m, piste f; (of smoke etc) traînée f ▷ vt (drag) traîner, tirer; (follow) suivre ▷ vi traîner; (in game, contest) être en retard; **trailer** n (Aut) remorque f; (us) caravane f; (Cine) bande-annonce f

train [treɪn] n train m; (in underground) rame f; (of dress) traîne f; (BRIT: series): **~ of events** série f d'événements ▷ vt (apprentice, doctor etc) former; (Sport) entraîner; (dog) dresser; (memory) exercer; (point: gun etc): **to ~ sth on** braquer qch sur ▷ vi recevoir sa formation; (Sport) s'entraîner; **one's ~ of thought** le fil de sa pensée; **what time does the ~ from Paris get in?** à quelle heure arrive le train de Paris?; **is this the ~ for ...?** c'est bien le train pour...?; **trainee** [treɪ'ni:] n stagiaire m/f; (in trade) apprenti(e); **trainer** n (Sport) entraîneur(-euse); (of dogs etc) dresseur(-euse); **trainers** npl (shoes) chaussures fpl de sport; **training** n formation f; (Sport) entraînement m; (of dog etc) dressage m; **in training** (Sport) à l'entraînement; (fit) en forme; **training course** n cours m de formation professionnelle; **training shoes** npl chaussures fpl de sport

trait [treɪt] n trait m (de caractère)

traitor ['treɪtə'] n traître m

tram [træm] n (BRIT: also: **~car**) tram(way) m

tramp [træmp] n (person) vagabond(e), clochard(e); (inf: pej: woman): **to be a ~** être coureuse

trample ['træmpl] vt: **to ~ (underfoot)** piétiner

trampoline ['træmpəliːn] n trampoline m

tranquil ['træŋkwɪl] adj tranquille; **tranquillizer** (us **tranquilizer**) n (Med) tranquillisant m

transaction [træn'zækʃən] n transaction f

transatlantic ['trænzət'læntɪk] adj transatlantique

transcript ['trænskrɪpt] n transcription f (texte)

transfer n ['trænsfə'] (gen, also Sport) transfert m; (Pol: of power) passation f; (of money) virement m; (picture, design) décalcomanie f; (: stick-on) autocollant m ▷ vt [træns'fə:'] transférer; passer; virer; **to ~ the charges** (BRIT Tel) téléphoner en P.C.V.

transform [træns'fɔ:m] vt transformer; **transformation** n transformation f

transfusion [træns'fju:ʒən] n transfusion f

transit ['trænzɪt] n: **in ~** en transit

transition [træn'zɪʃən] n transition f

transitive ['trænzɪtɪv] adj (Ling) transitif(-ive)

translate [trænz'leɪt] vt: **to ~ (from/into)** traduire (du/en); **can you ~ this for me?** pouvez-vous me traduire ceci?; **translation** [trænz'leɪʃən] n traduction f; (Scol: as opposed to prose) version f; **translator** n traducteur(-trice)

transmission [trænz'mɪʃən] n transmission f

transmit [trænz'mɪt] vt transmettre; (Radio, TV) émettre; **transmitter** n émetteur m

transparent [træns'pærnt] adj transparent(e)

transplant n ['trænsplɑ:nt] (Med) transplantation f

transport n ['trænspɔ:t] transport m ▷ vt [træns'pɔ:t] transporter; **transportation** [trænspɔ:'teɪʃən] n (moyen m de) transport m

transvestite [trænz'vestaɪt] n travesti(e)

trap [træp] n (snare, trick) piège m; (carriage) cabriolet m ▷ vt prendre au piège; (confine) coincer

trash [træʃ] n (pej: goods) camelote f; (: nonsense) sottises fpl; (us: rubbish) ordures fpl; **trash can** n (us) poubelle f

trauma ['trɔ:mə] n traumatisme m; **traumatic** [trɔ:'mætɪk] adj traumatisant(e)

travel ['trævl] n voyage(s) m(pl) ▷ vi voyager; (news, sound) se propager ▷ vt (distance) parcourir; **travel agency** n agence f de voyages; **travel agent** n agent m de voyages; **travel insurance** n assurance-voyage f; **traveller** (us **traveler**) n voyageur(-euse); **traveller's cheque** (us **traveler's check**) n chèque m de voyage; **travelling** (us **traveling**) n voyage(s) m(pl); **travel-sick** adj: **to get travel-sick** avoir le mal de la route (or de mer or de l'air); **travel sickness** n mal m de la route (or de mer or de l'air)

tray [treɪ] n (for carrying) plateau m; (on desk) corbeille f

treacherous ['tretʃərəs] adj traître(sse); (ground, tide) dont il faut se méfier

treacle ['tri:kl] n mélasse f

tread [tred] n (step) pas m; (sound) bruit m de pas; (of tyre) chape f, bande f de roulement ▷ vi (pt trod, pp trodden) marcher; **tread on** vt fus marcher sur

treasure ['treʒə'] n trésor m ▷ vt (value) tenir beaucoup à; **treasurer** n trésorier(-ière)

treasury ['treʒərɪ] n: **the T~**, (us) **the T~ Department** ≈ le ministère des Finances

treat [tri:t] n petit cadeau, petite surprise ▷ vt traiter; **to ~ sb to sth** offrir qch à qn; **treatment** n traitement m

treaty ['tri:tɪ] n traité m

treble ['trɛbl] adj triple ▷ vt, vi tripler

tree [tri:] n arbre m

trek [trɛk] n (long walk) randonnée f; (tiring walk) longue marche, trotte f

tremble ['trɛmbl] vi trembler

tremendous [trɪ'mɛndəs] adj (enormous) énorme; (excellent) formidable, fantastique

trench [trɛntʃ] n tranchée f

trend [trɛnd] n (tendency) tendance f; (of events) cours m; (fashion) mode f; **trendy** adj (idea, person) dans le vent; (clothes) dernier cri inv

trespass ['trɛspəs] vi: **to ~ on** s'introduire sans permission dans; **"no ~ing"** "propriété privée", "défense d'entrer"

trial ['traɪəl] n (Law) procès m, jugement m; (test: of machine etc) essai m; **trials** npl (unpleasant experiences) épreuves fpl; **trial period** n période f d'essai

triangle ['traɪæŋgl] n (Math, Mus) triangle m

triangular [traɪ'æŋgjulə'] adj triangulaire

tribe [traɪb] n tribu f

tribunal [traɪ'bju:nl] n tribunal m

tribute ['trɪbju:t] n tribut m, hommage m; **to pay ~ to** rendre hommage à

trick [trɪk] n (magic) tour m; (joke, prank) tour, farce f; (skill, knack) astuce f; (Cards) levée f ▷ vt attraper, rouler; **to play a ~ on sb** jouer un tour à qn; **that should do the ~** (fam) ça devrait faire l'affaire

trickle ['trɪkl] n (of water etc) filet m ▷ vi couler en un filet or goutte à goutte

tricky ['trɪkɪ] adj difficile, délicat(e)

tricycle ['traɪsɪkl] n tricycle m

trifle ['traɪfl] n bagatelle f; (Culin) ≈ diplomate m ▷ adv: **a ~ long** un peu long

trigger ['trɪgə'] n (of gun) gâchette f

trim [trɪm] adj (house, garden) bien tenu(e); (figure) svelte ▷ n (haircut etc) légère coupe; (on car) garnitures fpl ▷ vt (cut) couper légèrement; (decorate): **to ~ (with)** décorer (de); (Naut: a sail) gréer

trio ['tri:əu] n trio m

trip [trɪp] n voyage m; (excursion) excursion f; (stumble) faux pas ▷ vi faire un faux pas, trébucher; **trip up** vi trébucher ▷ vt faire un croc-en-jambe à

triple ['trɪpl] adj triple

triplets ['trɪplɪts] npl triplés(-ées)

tripod ['traɪpɔd] n trépied m

triumph ['traɪʌmf] n triomphe m ▷ vi: **to ~ (over)** triompher (de); **triumphant** [traɪ'ʌmfənt] adj triomphant(e)

trivial ['trɪvɪəl] adj insignifiant(e); (commonplace) banal(e)

trod [trɔd] pt of **tread**

trodden ['trɔdn] pp of **tread**

trolley ['trɔlɪ] n chariot m

trombone [trɔm'bəun] n trombone m

troop [tru:p] n bande f, groupe m; **troops** npl (Mil) troupes fpl; (: men) hommes mpl, soldats mpl

trophy ['trəufɪ] n trophée m

tropical ['trɔpɪkl] adj tropical(e)

trot [trɔt] n trot m ▷ vi trotter; **on the ~** (BRIT: fig) d'affilée

trouble ['trʌbl] n difficulté(s) f(pl), problème(s) m(pl); (worry) ennuis mpl, soucis mpl; (bother, effort) peine f; (Pol) conflit(s) m(pl), troubles mpl; (Med): **stomach** etc ~ troubles gastriques etc ▷ vt (disturb) déranger, gêner; (worry) inquiéter ▷ vi: **to ~ to do** prendre la peine de faire; **troubles** npl (Pol etc) troubles; (personal) ennuis, soucis; **to be in ~** avoir des ennuis; (ship, climber etc) être en difficulté; **to have ~ doing sth** avoir du mal à faire qch; **it's no ~!** je vous en prie!; **the ~ is ...** le problème, c'est que ...; **what's the ~?** qu'est-ce qui ne va pas?; **troubled** adj (person) inquiet(-ète); (times, life) agité(e); **troublemaker** n élément perturbateur, fauteur m de troubles; **troublesome** adj (child) fatigant(e), difficile; (cough) gênant(e)

trough [trɔf] n (also: **drinking ~**) abreuvoir m; (also: **feeding ~**) auge f; (depression) creux m

trousers ['trauzəz] npl pantalon m; **short ~** (BRIT) culottes courtes

trout [traut] n (pl inv) truite f

trowel ['trauəl] n truelle f; (garden tool) déplantoir m

truant ['truənt] n: **to play ~** (BRIT) faire l'école buissonnière

truce [tru:s] n trêve f

truck [trʌk] n camion m; (Rail) wagon m à plate-forme; **truck driver** n camionneur m

true [tru:] adj vrai(e); (accurate) exact(e); (genuine) vrai, véritable; (faithful) fidèle; **to come ~** se réaliser

truly ['tru:lɪ] adv vraiment, réellement; (truthfully) sans mentir; **yours ~** (in letter) je vous prie d'agréer, Monsieur (or Madame etc), l'expression de mes sentiments respectueux

trumpet ['trʌmpɪt] n trompette f

trunk [trʌŋk] n (of tree, person) tronc m; (of elephant) trompe f; (case) malle f; (US Aut) coffre m; **trunks** npl (also: **swimming ~s**) maillot m or slip m de bain

trust [trʌst] n confiance f; (responsibility): **to place sth in sb's ~** confier la responsabilité de qch à qn; (Law) fidéicommis m ▷ vt (rely on) avoir confiance en; (entrust): **to ~ sth to sb** confier qch à qn; (hope): **to ~ (that)** espérer (que); **to take sth on ~** accepter qch les yeux fermés; **trusted** adj en qui l'on a confiance;

t

trustworthy adj digne de confiance
truth [truː:θ, (pl) truː:ðz] n vérité f; **truthful** adj (person) qui dit la vérité; (answer) sincère
try [traɪ] n essai m, tentative f; (Rugby) essai ▷ vt (attempt) essayer, tenter; (test: sth new: also: ~ **out**) essayer, tester; (Law: person) juger; (strain) éprouver ▷ vi essayer; **to ~ to do** essayer de faire; (seek) chercher à faire; **try on** vt (clothes) essayer; **trying** adj pénible
T-shirt ['tiː:ʃəːt] n tee-shirt m
tub [tʌb] n cuve f; (for washing clothes) baquet m; (bath) baignoire f
tube [tjuː:b] n tube m; (BRIT: underground) métro m; (for tyre) chambre f à air
tuberculosis [tjubəːkjuːˈləusɪs] n tuberculose f
tube station n (BRIT) station f de métro
tuck [tʌk] vt (put) mettre; **tuck away** vt cacher, ranger; (money) mettre de côté; (building): **to be ~ed away** être caché(e); **tuck in** vt (fall) rentrer; (child) border ▷ vi (eat) manger de bon appétit; attaquer le repas; **tuck shop** n (BRIT Scol) boutique f à provisions
Tue(s) abbr (= Tuesday) ma
Tuesday ['tjuː:zdɪ] n mardi m
tug [tʌg] n (ship) remorqueur m ▷ vt tirer (sur)
tuition [tjuːˈɪʃən] n (BRIT: lessons) leçons fpl; (: private) cours particuliers; (US: fees) frais mpl de scolarité
tulip ['tjuː:lɪp] n tulipe f
tumble ['tʌmbl] n (fall) chute f, culbute f ▷ vi tomber, dégringoler; **to ~ to sth** (inf) réaliser qch; **tumble dryer** n (BRIT) séchoir m (à linge) à air chaud
tumbler ['tʌmblə'] n verre (droit), gobelet m
tummy ['tʌmɪ] n (inf) ventre m
tumour (US **tumor**) ['tjuː:mə'] n tumeur f
tuna ['tjuː:nə] n (pl inv also: ~ **fish**) thon m
tune [tjuː:n] n (melody) air m ▷ vt (Mus) accorder; (Radio, TV, Aut) régler, mettre au point; **to be in/out of ~** (instrument) être accordé/désaccordé; (singer) chanter juste/faux; **tune in** vi (Radio, TV): **to ~ in (to)** se mettre à l'écoute (de); **tune up** vi (musician) accorder son instrument
tunic ['tjuː:nɪk] n tunique f
Tunis ['tjuː:nɪs] n Tunis
Tunisia [tjuːˈnɪzɪə] n Tunisie f
Tunisian [tjuːˈnɪzɪən] adj tunisien(ne) ▷ n Tunisien(ne)
tunnel ['tʌnl] n tunnel m; (in mine) galerie f ▷ vi creuser un tunnel (or une galerie)
turbulence ['təːbjuːləns] n (Aviat) turbulence f
turf [təːf] n gazon m; (clod) motte f (de gazon) ▷ vt gazonner
Turk [təːk] n Turc (Turque)
Turkey ['təːkɪ] n Turquie f
turkey ['təːkɪ] n dindon m, dinde f
Turkish ['təːkɪʃ] adj turc (turque) ▷ n (Ling)

turc m
turmoil ['təːmɔɪl] n trouble m, bouleversement m
turn [təːn] n tour m; (in road) tournant m; (tendency: of mind, events) tournure f; (performance) numéro m; (Med) crise f, attaque f ▷ vt tourner; (collar, steak) retourner; (change): **to ~ sth into** changer qch en; (age) atteindre ▷ vi (object, wind, milk) tourner; (person: look back) se (re)tourner; (reverse direction) faire demi-tour; (become) devenir; **to ~ into** se changer en, se transformer en; **a good ~** un service; **it gave me quite a ~** ça m'a fait un coup; **"no left ~"** (Aut) "défense de tourner à gauche"; **~ left/right at the next junction** tournez à gauche/droite au prochain carrefour; **it's your ~** c'est (à) votre tour; **in ~** à son tour; à tour de rôle; **to take ~s** se relayer; **turn around** vi (person) se retourner ▷ vt (object) tourner; **turn away** vi se détourner, tourner la tête ▷ vt (reject: person) renvoyer; (: business) refuser; **turn back** vi revenir, faire demi-tour; **turn down** vt (refuse) rejeter, refuser; (reduce) baisser; (fold) rabattre; **turn in** vi (inf: go to bed) aller se coucher ▷ vt (fold) rentrer; **turn off** vi (from road) tourner ▷ vt (light, radio etc) éteindre; (tap) fermer; (engine) arrêter; **I can't ~ the heating off** je n'arrive pas à éteindre le chauffage; **turn on** vt (light, radio etc) allumer; (tap) ouvrir; (engine) mettre en marche; **I can't ~ the heating on** je n'arrive pas à allumer le chauffage; **turn out** vt (light, gas) éteindre; (produce) produire ▷ vi (voters, troops) se présenter; **to ~ out to be ...** s'avérer ..., se révéler ...; **turn over** vi (person) se retourner ▷ vt (object) retourner; (page) tourner; **turn round** vi faire demi-tour; (rotate) tourner; **turn to** vt fus: **to ~ to sb** s'adresser à qn; **turn up** vi (person) arriver, se pointer (inf); (lost object) être retrouvé(e) ▷ vt (collar) remonter; (radio, heater) mettre plus fort; **turning** n (in road) tournant m; **turning point** n (fig) tournant m, moment décisif
turnip ['təːnɪp] n navet m
turn: **turnout** n (of voters) taux m de participation; **turnover** n (Comm: amount of money) chiffre m d'affaires; (: of goods) roulement m; (of staff) renouvellement m, changement m; **turnstile** n tourniquet m (d'entrée); **turn-up** n (BRIT: on trousers) revers m
turquoise ['təːkwɔɪz] n (stone) turquoise f ▷ adj turquoise inv
turtle ['təːtl] n tortue marine; **turtleneck (sweater)** n pullover m à col montant
tusk [tʌsk] n défense f (d'éléphant)
tutor ['tjuː:tə'] n (BRIT Scol: in college) directeur(-trice) d'études; (private teacher) précepteur(-trice); **tutorial** [tjuːˈtɔːrɪəl] n (Scol) (séance f de) travaux mpl pratiques

tuxedo [tʌkˈsiːdəu] n (US) smoking m
TV [tiːˈviː] n abbr (= television) télé f, TV f
tweed [twiːd] n tweed m
tweezers [ˈtwiːzəz] npl pince f à épiler
twelfth [twɛlfθ] num douzième
twelve [twɛlv] num douze; **at ~ (o'clock)** à midi; (midnight) à minuit
twentieth [ˈtwɛntɪɪθ] num vingtième
twenty [ˈtwɛntɪ] num vingt
twice [twaɪs] adv deux fois; **~ as much** deux fois plus
twig [twɪg] n brindille f ▷ vt, vi (inf) piger
twilight [ˈtwaɪlaɪt] n crépuscule m
twin [twɪn] adj, n jumeau(-elle) ▷ vt jumeler; **twin(-bedded) room** n chambre f à deux lits; **twin beds** npl lits mpl jumeaux
twinkle [ˈtwɪŋkl] vi scintiller; (eyes) pétiller
twist [twɪst] n torsion f, tour m; (in wire, flex) tortillon m; (bend: in road) tournant m; (in story) coup m de théâtre ▷ vt tordre; (weave) entortiller; (roll around) enrouler; (fig) déformer ▷ vi (road, river) serpenter; **to ~ one's ankle/wrist** (Med) se tordre la cheville/le poignet
twit [twɪt] n (inf) crétin(e)
twitch [twɪtʃ] n (pull) coup sec, saccade f; (nervous) tic m ▷ vi se convulser; avoir un tic
two [tuː] num deux; **to put ~ and ~ together** (fig) faire le rapprochement
type [taɪp] n (category) genre m, espèce f; (model) modèle m; (example) type m; (Typ) type, caractère m ▷ vt (letter etc) taper (à la machine); **typewriter** n machine f à écrire
typhoid [ˈtaɪfɔɪd] n typhoïde f
typhoon [taɪˈfuːn] n typhon m
typical [ˈtɪpɪkl] adj typique, caractéristique; **typically** adv (as usual) comme d'habitude; (characteristically) typiquement
typing [ˈtaɪpɪŋ] n dactylo(graphie) f
typist [ˈtaɪpɪst] n dactylo m/f
tyre (US **tire**) [ˈtaɪə*] n pneu m; **I've got a flat ~** j'ai un pneu crevé; **tyre pressure** n (BRIT) pression f (de gonflage)

UFO [ˈjuːfəu] n abbr (= unidentified flying object) ovni m
Uganda [juːˈgændə] n Ouganda m
ugly [ˈʌglɪ] adj laid(e), vilain(e); (fig) répugnant(e)
UHT adj abbr = **ultra-heat treated**; **~ milk** lait m UHT or longue conservation
UK n abbr = **United Kingdom**
ulcer [ˈʌlsə*] n ulcère m; **mouth ~** aphte f
ultimate [ˈʌltɪmət] adj ultime, final(e); (authority) suprême; **ultimately** adv (at last) en fin de compte; (fundamentally) finalement; (eventually) par la suite
ultimatum (pl **~s** or **ultimata**) [ʌltɪˈmeɪtəm, -tə] n ultimatum m
ultrasound [ˈʌltrəsaund] n (Med) ultrason m
ultraviolet [ˈʌltrəˈvaɪələt] adj ultraviolet(te)
umbrella [ʌmˈbrɛlə] n parapluie m; (for sun) parasol m
umpire [ˈʌmpaɪə*] n arbitre m; (Tennis) juge m de chaise
UN n abbr = **United Nations**
unable [ʌnˈeɪbl] adj: **to be ~ to** ne (pas) pouvoir, être dans l'impossibilité de; (not capable) être incapable de
unacceptable [ʌnəkˈsɛptəbl] adj (behaviour) inadmissible; (price, proposal) inacceptable
unanimous [juːˈnænɪməs] adj unanime
unarmed [ʌnˈɑːmd] adj (person) non armé(e); (combat) sans armes

u

unattended [ʌnə'tɛndɪd] adj (car, child, luggage) sans surveillance

unattractive [ʌnə'træktɪv] adj peu attrayant(e); (character) peu sympathique

unavailable [ʌnə'veɪləbl] adj (article, room, book) (qui n'est) pas disponible; (person) (qui n'est) pas libre

unavoidable [ʌnə'vɔɪdəbl] adj inévitable

unaware [ʌnə'wɛər] adj: **to be ~ of** ignorer, ne pas savoir, être inconscient(e) de; **unawares** adv à l'improviste, au dépourvu

unbearable [ʌn'bɛərəbl] adj insupportable

unbeatable [ʌn'biːtəbl] adj imbattable

unbelievable [ʌnbɪ'liːvəbl] adj incroyable

unborn [ʌn'bɔːn] adj à naître

unbutton [ʌn'bʌtn] vt déboutonner

uncalled-for [ʌn'kɔːldfɔːr] adj déplacé(e), injustifié(e)

uncanny [ʌn'kænɪ] adj étrange, troublant(e)

uncertain [ʌn'səːtn] adj incertain(e); (hesitant) hésitant(e); **uncertainty** n incertitude f, doutes mpl

unchanged [ʌn'tʃeɪndʒd] adj inchangé(e)

uncle ['ʌŋkl] n oncle m

unclear [ʌn'klɪər] adj (qui n'est) pas clair(e) or évident(e); **I'm still ~ about what I'm supposed to do** je ne sais pas encore exactement ce que je dois faire

uncomfortable [ʌn'kʌmfətəbl] adj inconfortable, peu confortable; (uneasy) mal à l'aise, gêné(e); (situation) désagréable

uncommon [ʌn'kɔmən] adj rare, singulier(-ière), peu commun(e)

unconditional [ʌnkən'dɪʃənl] adj sans conditions

unconscious [ʌn'kɔnʃəs] adj sans connaissance, évanoui(e); (unaware): **~ (of)** inconscient(e) (de) ▷ n: **the ~** l'inconscient m

uncontrollable [ʌnkən'trəuləbl] adj (child, dog) indiscipliné(e); (temper, laughter) irrépressible

unconventional [ʌnkən'vɛnʃənl] adj peu conventionnel(le)

uncover [ʌn'kʌvər] vt découvrir

undecided [ʌndɪ'saɪdɪd] adj indécis(e), irrésolu(e)

undeniable [ʌndɪ'naɪəbl] adj indéniable, incontestable

under ['ʌndər] prep sous; (less than) (de) moins de; au-dessous de; (according to) selon, en vertu de ▷ adv au-dessous; en dessous; **~ there** là-dessous; **~ the circumstances** étant donné les circonstances; **~ repair** en (cours de) réparation; **undercover** adj secret(-ète), clandestin(e); **underdone** adj (Culin) saignant(e); (: pej) pas assez cuit(e); **underestimate** vt sous-estimer, mésestimer; **undergo** vt (irreg: like **go**) subir; (treatment) suivre; **undergraduate** n étudiant(e) (qui prépare la licence); **underground** adj souterrain(e); (fig) clandestin(e) ▷ n (BRIT: railway) métro m; (Pol) clandestinité f; **undergrowth** n broussailles fpl, sous-bois m; **underline** vt souligner; **undermine** vt saper, miner; **underneath** [ʌndə'niːθ] adv (en) dessous ▷ prep sous, au-dessous de; **underpants** npl caleçon m, slip m; **underpass** n (BRIT: for pedestrians) passage souterrain; (: for cars) passage inférieur; **underprivileged** adj défavorisé(e); **underscore** vt souligner; **undershirt** n (US) tricot m de corps; **underskirt** n (BRIT) jupon m

understand [ʌndə'stænd] vt, vi (irreg: like **stand**) comprendre; **I don't ~** je ne comprends pas; **understandable** adj compréhensible; **understanding** adj compréhensif(-ive) ▷ n compréhension f; (agreement) accord m

understatement ['ʌndəsteɪtmənt] n: **that's an ~** c'est (bien) peu dire, le terme est faible

understood [ʌndə'stud] pt, pp of **understand** ▷ adj entendu(e); (implied) sous-entendu(e)

undertake [ʌndə'teɪk] vt (irreg: like **take**) (job, task) entreprendre; (duty) se charger de; **to ~ to do sth** s'engager à faire qch

undertaker ['ʌndəteɪkər] n (BRIT) entrepreneur m des pompes funèbres, croque-mort m

undertaking ['ʌndəteɪkɪŋ] n entreprise f; (promise) promesse f

under: underwater adv sous l'eau ▷ adj sous-marin(e); **underway** adj: **to be underway** (meeting, investigation) être en cours; **underwear** n sous-vêtements mpl; (women's only) dessous mpl; **underwent** pt of **undergo**; **underworld** n (of crime) milieu m, pègre f

undesirable [ʌndɪ'zaɪərəbl] adj peu souhaitable; (person, effect) indésirable

undisputed ['ʌndɪs'pjuːtɪd] adj incontesté(e)

undo [ʌn'duː] vt (irreg: like **do**) défaire

undone [ʌn'dʌn] pp of **undo** ▷ adj: **to come ~** se défaire

undoubtedly [ʌn'dautɪdlɪ] adv sans aucun doute

undress [ʌn'drɛs] vi se déshabiller

unearth [ʌn'əːθ] vt déterrer; (fig) dénicher

uneasy [ʌn'iːzɪ] adj mal à l'aise, gêné(e); (worried) inquiet(-ète); (feeling) désagréable; (peace, truce) fragile

unemployed [ʌnɪm'plɔɪd] adj sans travail, au chômage ▷ n: **the ~** les chômeurs mpl

unemployment [ʌnɪm'plɔɪmənt] n chômage m; **unemployment benefit** (US **unemployment compensation**) n allocation f de chômage

unequal [ʌn'iːkwəl] adj inégal(e)

uneven [ʌn'iːvn] adj inégal(e); (quality, work)

irrégulier(-ière)

unexpected [ʌnɪk'spɛktɪd] adj inattendu(e), imprévu(e); **unexpectedly** adv (succeed) contre toute attente; (arrive) à l'improviste

unfair [ʌn'fɛər] adj: **~ (to)** injuste (envers)

unfaithful [ʌn'feɪθful] adj infidèle

unfamiliar [ʌnfə'mɪliər] adj étrange, inconnu(e); **to be ~ with sth** mal connaître qch

unfashionable [ʌn'fæʃnəbl] adj (clothes) démodé(e); (place) peu chic inv

unfasten [ʌn'fɑːsn] vt défaire; (belt, necklace) détacher; (open) ouvrir

unfavourable (us **unfavorable**) [ʌn'feɪvrəbl] adj défavorable

unfinished [ʌn'fɪnɪʃt] adj inachevé(e)

unfit [ʌn'fɪt] adj (physically: ill) en mauvaise santé; (: out of condition) pas en forme; (incompetent): **~ (for)** impropre (à); (work, service) inapte (à)

unfold [ʌn'fəuld] vt déplier ▷ vi se dérouler

unforgettable [ʌnfə'gɛtəbl] adj inoubliable

unfortunate [ʌn'fɔːtʃnət] adj malheureux(-euse); (event, remark) malencontreux(-euse); **unfortunately** adv malheureusement

unfriendly [ʌn'frɛndlɪ] adj peu aimable, froid(e)

unfurnished [ʌn'fəːnɪʃt] adj non meublé(e)

unhappiness [ʌn'hæpɪnɪs] n tristesse f, peine f

unhappy [ʌn'hæpɪ] adj triste, malheureux(-euse); (unfortunate: remark etc) malheureux(-euse); (not pleased): **~ with** mécontent(e) de, peu satisfait(e) de

unhealthy [ʌn'hɛlθɪ] adj (gen) malsain(e); (person) maladif(-ive)

unheard-of [ʌn'həːdɔv] adj inouï(e), sans précédent

unhelpful [ʌn'hɛlpful] adj (person) peu serviable; (advice) peu utile

unhurt [ʌn'həːt] adj indemne, sain(e) et sauf (sauve)

unidentified [ʌnaɪ'dɛntɪfaɪd] adj non identifié(e); see also **UFO**

uniform ['juːnɪfɔːm] n uniforme m ▷ adj uniforme

unify ['juːnɪfaɪ] vt unifier

unimportant [ʌnɪm'pɔːtənt] adj sans importance

uninhabited [ʌnɪn'hæbɪtɪd] adj inhabité(e)

unintentional [ʌnɪn'tɛnʃənəl] adj involontaire

union ['juːnjən] n union f; (also: **trade ~**) syndicat m ▷ cpd du syndicat, syndical(e); **Union Jack** n drapeau du Royaume-Uni

unique [juː'niːk] adj unique

unisex ['juːnɪsɛks] adj unisexe

unit ['juːnɪt] n unité f; (section: of furniture etc)

élément m, bloc m; (team, squad) groupe m, service m; **kitchen ~** élément de cuisine

unite [juː'naɪt] vt unir ▷ vi s'unir; **united** adj uni(e); (country, party) unifié(e); (efforts) conjugué(e); **United Kingdom** n Royaume-Uni m (R.U.); **United Nations (Organization)** n (Organisation f des) Nations unies (ONU); **United States (of America)** n États-Unis mpl

unity ['juːnɪtɪ] n unité f

universal [juːnɪ'vəːsl] adj universel(le)

universe ['juːnɪvəːs] n univers m

university [juːnɪ'vəːsɪtɪ] n université f ▷ cpd (student, professor) d'université; (education, year, degree) universitaire

unjust [ʌn'dʒʌst] adj injuste

unkind [ʌn'kaɪnd] adj peu gentil(le), méchant(e)

unknown [ʌn'nəun] adj inconnu(e)

unlawful [ʌn'lɔːful] adj illégal(e)

unleaded [ʌn'lɛdɪd] n (also: **~ petrol**) essence f sans plomb

unleash [ʌn'liːʃ] vt (fig) déchaîner, déclencher

unless [ʌn'lɛs] conj: **~ he leaves** à moins qu'il (ne) parte; **~ otherwise stated** sauf indication contraire

unlike [ʌn'laɪk] adj dissemblable, différent(e) ▷ prep à la différence de, contrairement à

unlikely [ʌn'laɪklɪ] adj (result, event) improbable; (explanation) invraisemblable

unlimited [ʌn'lɪmɪtɪd] adj illimité(e)

unlisted ['ʌn'lɪstɪd] adj (us Tel) sur la liste rouge

unload [ʌn'ləud] vt décharger

unlock [ʌn'lɔk] vt ouvrir

unlucky [ʌn'lʌkɪ] adj (person) malchanceux(-euse); (object, number) qui porte malheur; **to be ~** (person) ne pas avoir de chance

unmarried [ʌn'mærɪd] adj célibataire

unmistak(e)able [ʌnmɪs'teɪkəbl] adj indubitable; qu'on ne peut pas ne pas reconnaître

unnatural [ʌn'nætʃrəl] adj non naturel(le); (perversion) contre nature

unnecessary [ʌn'nɛsəsərɪ] adj inutile, superflu(e)

UNO ['juːnəu] n abbr = **United Nations Organization**

unofficial [ʌnə'fɪʃl] adj (news) officieux(-euse), non officiel(le); (strike) ≈ sauvage

unpack [ʌn'pæk] vi défaire sa valise ▷ vt (suitcase) défaire; (belongings) déballer

unpaid [ʌn'peɪd] adj (bill) impayé(e); (holiday) non-payé(e), sans salaire; (work) non rétribué(e)

unpleasant [ʌn'plɛznt] adj déplaisant(e), désagréable

unplug [ʌn'plʌg] vt débrancher

unpopular [ʌn'pɔpjulər] adj impopulaire

unprecedented [ʌnˈprɛsɪdəntɪd] *adj* sans précédent

unpredictable [ʌnprɪˈdɪktəbl] *adj* imprévisible

unprotected [ˈʌnprəˈtɛktɪd] *adj* (*sex*) non protégé(e)

unqualified [ʌnˈkwɔlɪfaɪd] *adj* (*teacher*) non diplômé(e), sans titres; (*success*) sans réserve, total(e); (*disaster*) total(e)

unravel [ʌnˈrævl] *vt* démêler

unreal [ʌnˈrɪəl] *adj* irréel(le); (*extraordinary*) incroyable

unrealistic [ˈʌnrɪəˈlɪstɪk] *adj* (*idea*) irréaliste; (*estimate*) peu réaliste

unreasonable [ʌnˈriːznəbl] *adj* qui n'est pas raisonnable

unrelated [ʌnrɪˈleɪtɪd] *adj* sans rapport; (*people*) sans lien de parenté

unreliable [ʌnrɪˈlaɪəbl] *adj* sur qui (*or* quoi) on ne peut pas compter, peu fiable

unrest [ʌnˈrɛst] *n* agitation *f*, troubles *mpl*

unroll [ʌnˈrəʊl] *vt* dérouler

unruly [ʌnˈruːlɪ] *adj* indiscipliné(e)

unsafe [ʌnˈseɪf] *adj* (*in danger*) en danger; (*journey, car*) dangereux(-euse)

unsatisfactory [ˈʌnsætɪsˈfæktərɪ] *adj* peu satisfaisant(e)

unscrew [ʌnˈskruː] *vt* dévisser

unsettled [ʌnˈsɛtld] *adj* (*restless*) perturbé(e); (*unpredictable*) instable; incertain(e); (*not finalized*) non résolu(e)

unsettling [ʌnˈsɛtlɪŋ] *adj* qui a un effet perturbateur

unsightly [ʌnˈsaɪtlɪ] *adj* disgracieux(-euse), laid(e)

unskilled [ʌnˈskɪld] *adj*: **~ worker** manœuvre *m*

unspoiled [ˈʌnˈspɔɪld], **unspoilt** [ˈʌnˈspɔɪlt] *adj* (*place*) non dégradé(e)

unstable [ʌnˈsteɪbl] *adj* instable

unsteady [ʌnˈstɛdɪ] *adj* mal assuré(e), chancelant(e), instable

unsuccessful [ʌnsəkˈsɛsful] *adj* (*attempt*) infructueux(-euse); (*writer, proposal*) qui n'a pas de succès; **to be ~** (*in attempting sth*) ne pas réussir; ne pas avoir de succès; (*application*) ne pas être retenu(e)

unsuitable [ʌnˈsuːtəbl] *adj* qui ne convient pas, peu approprié(e); (*time*) inopportun(e)

unsure [ʌnˈʃʊəʳ] *adj* pas sûr(e); **to be ~ of o.s.** ne pas être sûr de soi, manquer de confiance en soi

untidy [ʌnˈtaɪdɪ] *adj* (*room*) en désordre; (*appearance, person*) débraillé(e); (*person: in character*) sans ordre, désordonné(e); (*work*) peu soigné(e)

untie [ʌnˈtaɪ] *vt* (*knot, parcel*) défaire; (*prisoner, dog*) détacher

until [ənˈtɪl] *prep* jusqu'à; (*after negative*)

avant ▷ *conj* jusqu'à ce que + *sub*; (*in past, after negative*) avant que + *sub*; **~ he comes** jusqu'à ce qu'il vienne, jusqu'à son arrivée; **~ now** jusqu'à présent, jusqu'ici; **~ then** jusque-là

untrue [ʌnˈtruː] *adj* (*statement*) faux (fausse)

unused[1] [ʌnˈjuːzd] *adj* (*new*) neuf (neuve)

unused[2] [ʌnˈjuːst] *adj*: **to be ~ to sth/to doing sth** ne pas avoir l'habitude de qch/de faire qch

unusual [ʌnˈjuːʒʊəl] *adj* insolite, exceptionnel(le), rare; **unusually** *adv* exceptionnellement, particulièrement

unveil [ʌnˈveɪl] *vt* dévoiler

unwanted [ʌnˈwɒntɪd] *adj* (*child, pregnancy*) non désiré(e); (*clothes etc*) à donner

unwell [ʌnˈwɛl] *adj* souffrant(e); **to feel ~** ne pas se sentir bien

unwilling [ʌnˈwɪlɪŋ] *adj*: **to be ~ to do** ne pas vouloir faire

unwind [ʌnˈwaɪnd] *vb* (*irreg: like* **wind**) ▷ *vt* dérouler ▷ *vi* (*relax*) se détendre

unwise [ʌnˈwaɪz] *adj* imprudent(e), peu judicieux(-euse)

unwittingly [ʌnˈwɪtɪŋlɪ] *adv* involontairement

unwrap [ʌnˈræp] *vt* défaire; ouvrir

unzip [ʌnˈzɪp] *vt* ouvrir (la fermeture éclair de); (*Comput*) dézipper

 KEYWORD

up [ʌp] *prep*: **he went up the stairs/the hill** il a monté l'escalier/la colline; **the cat was up a tree** le chat était dans un arbre; **they live further up the street** ils habitent plus haut dans la rue; **go up that road and turn left** remontez la rue et tournez à gauche

▷ *adv* **1** en haut; en l'air; (*upwards, higher*): **up in the sky/the mountains** (là-haut) dans le ciel/les montagnes; **put it a bit higher up** mettez-le un peu plus haut; **to stand up** (*get up*) se lever, se mettre debout; (*be standing*) être debout; **up there** là-haut; **up above** au-dessus

2: **to be up** (*out of bed*) être levé(e); (*prices*) avoir augmenté *or* monté; (*finished*): **when the year was up** à la fin de l'année

3: **up to** (*as far as*) jusqu'à; **up to now** jusqu'à présent

4: **to be up to** (*depending on*): **it's up to you** c'est à vous de décider; (*equal to*): **he's not up to it** (*job, task etc*) il n'en est pas capable; (*inf: be doing*): **what is he up to?** qu'est-ce qu'il peut bien faire?

▷ *n*: **ups and downs** hauts et bas *mpl*

up-and-coming [ʌpəndˈkʌmɪŋ] *adj* plein(e) d'avenir *or* de promesses

upbringing [ˈʌpbrɪŋɪŋ] *n* éducation *f*

update [ʌp'deɪt] vt mettre à jour

upfront [ʌp'frʌnt] adj (open) franc (franche)
▷ adv (pay) d'avance; **to be ~ about sth** ne rien
cacher de qch

upgrade [ʌp'greɪd] vt (person) promouvoir;
(job) revaloriser; (property, equipment)
moderniser

upheaval [ʌp'hiːvl] n bouleversement m; (in
room) branle-bas m; (event) crise f

uphill [ʌp'hɪl] adj qui monte; (fig: task) difficile,
pénible ▷ adv (face, look) en amont, vers
l'amont; **to go ~** monter

upholstery [ʌp'həʊlstərɪ] n rembourrage
m; (cover) tissu m d'ameublement; (of car)
garniture f

upmarket [ʌp'mɑːkɪt] adj (product) haut de
gamme inv; (area) chic inv

upon [ə'pɒn] prep sur

upper [ʌpə'] adj supérieur(e); du dessus ▷ n (of
shoe) empeigne f; **upper-class** adj de la haute
société, aristocratique; (district) élégant(e),
huppé(e); (accent, attitude) caractéristique des
classes supérieures

upright [ʌpraɪt] adj droit(e); (fig) droit,
honnête

uprising [ʌpraɪzɪŋ] n soulèvement m,
insurrection f

uproar [ʌprɔː'] n tumulte m, vacarme m;
(protests) protestations fpl

upset n [ʌpset] dérangement m ▷ vt (irreg:
like **set** [ʌp'set]) (glass etc) renverser; (plan)
déranger; (person: offend) contrarier; (: grieve)
faire de la peine à; bouleverser ▷ adj [ʌp'set]
contrarié(e); peiné(e); **to have a stomach ~**
(BRIT) avoir une indigestion

upside down [ʌpsaɪd-] adv à l'envers; **to
turn sth ~** (fig: place) mettre sens dessus
dessous

upstairs [ʌp'stɛəz] adv en haut ▷ adj (room) du
dessus, d'en haut ▷ n: **the ~** l'étage m

up-to-date [ʌptə'deɪt] adj moderne;
(information) très récent(e)

uptown [ʌptaʊn] (US) adv (live) dans les
quartiers chics; (go) vers les quartiers chics
▷ adj des quartiers chics

upward [ʌpwəd] adj ascendant(e); vers le
haut; **upward(s)** adv vers le haut; (more than):
upward(s) of plus de

uranium [juə'reɪnɪəm] n uranium m

Uranus [juə'reɪnəs] n Uranus f

urban [ə:bən] adj urbain(e)

urge [ə:dʒ] n besoin (impératif), envie
(pressante) ▷ vt (person): **to ~ sb to do**
exhorter qn à faire, pousser qn à faire,
recommander vivement à qn de faire

urgency [ə:dʒənsɪ] n urgence f; (of tone)
insistance f

urgent [ə:dʒənt] adj urgent(e); (plea, tone)
pressant(e)

urinal [juərɪnl] n (BRIT: place) urinoir m

urinate [juərɪneɪt] vi uriner

urine [juərɪn] n urine f

URL abbr (= uniform resource locator) URL f

US n abbr = **United States**

us [ʌs] pron nous; see also **me**

USA n abbr = **United States of America**

use n [juːs] emploi m, utilisation f; (usefulness)
utilité f ▷ vt [juːz] se servir de, utiliser,
employer; **in ~** en usage; **out of ~** hors d'usage;
to be of ~ servir, être utile; **it's no ~** ça ne
sert à rien; **to have the ~ of** avoir l'usage de;
she ~d to do it elle le faisait (autrefois), elle
avait coutume de le faire; **to be ~d to** avoir
l'habitude de, être habitué(e) à; **use up** vt
finir, épuiser; (food) consommer; **used** [juːzd] adj (car) d'occasion; **useful** adj utile;
useless adj inutile; (inf: person) nul(le); **user** n
utilisateur(-trice), usager m; **user-friendly** adj
convivial(e), facile d'emploi

usual [juːʒuəl] adj habituel(le); **as ~** comme
d'habitude; **usually** adv d'habitude,
d'ordinaire

utensil [juːtɛnsl] n ustensile m; **kitchen ~s**
batterie f de cuisine

utility [juːtɪlɪtɪ] n utilité f; (also: **public ~**)
service public

utilize [juːtɪlaɪz] vt utiliser; (make good use of)
exploiter

utmost [ʌtməʊst] adj extrême, le (la) plus
grand(e) ▷ n: **to do one's ~** faire tout son
possible

utter [ʌtə'] adj total(e), complet(-ète) ▷ vt
prononcer, proférer; (sounds) émettre; **utterly**
adv complètement, totalement

U-turn [juːtə:n] n demi-tour m; (fig) volte-
face f inv

u

v. *abbr* = **verse** (= *vide*) v.; (= *versus*) c.; (= *volt*) V

vacancy ['veɪkənsɪ] *n* (BRIT: *job*) poste vacant; (*room*) chambre f disponible; **"no vacancies"** "complet"

vacant ['veɪkənt] *adj* (*post*) vacant(e); (*seat etc*) libre, disponible; (*expression*) distrait(e)

vacate [və'keɪt] *vt* quitter

vacation [və'keɪʃən] *n* (*esp us*) vacances *fpl*; **on ~** en vacances; **vacationer** (*us* **vacationist**) *n* vacancier(-ière)

vaccination [væksɪ'neɪʃən] *n* vaccination f

vaccine ['væksiːn] *n* vaccin m

vacuum ['vækjum] *n* vide m; **vacuum cleaner** *n* aspirateur m

vagina [və'dʒaɪnə] *n* vagin m

vague [veɪɡ] *adj* vague, imprécis(e); (*blurred: photo, memory*) flou(e)

vain [veɪn] *adj* (*useless*) vain(e); (*conceited*) vaniteux(-euse); **in ~** en vain

Valentine's Day ['væləntaɪnz-] *n* Saint-Valentin f

valid ['vælɪd] *adj* (*document*) valide, valable; (*excuse*) valable

valley ['vælɪ] *n* vallée f

valuable ['væljuəbl] *adj* (*jewel*) de grande valeur; (*time, help*) précieux(-euse); **valuables** *npl* objets *mpl* de valeur

value ['væljuː] *n* valeur f ▷ *vt* (*fix price*) évaluer, expertiser; (*appreciate*) apprécier; **values** *npl* (*principles*) valeurs *fpl*

valve [vælv] *n* (*in machine*) soupape f; (*on tyre*) valve f; (*Med*) valve, valvule f

vampire ['væmpaɪər] *n* vampire m

van [væn] *n* (*Aut*) camionnette f

vandal ['vændl] *n* vandale m/f; **vandalism** *n* vandalisme m; **vandalize** *vt* saccager

vanilla [və'nɪlə] *n* vanille f

vanish ['vænɪʃ] *vi* disparaître

vanity ['vænɪtɪ] *n* vanité f

vapour (*us* **vapor**) ['veɪpər] *n* vapeur f; (*on window*) buée f

variable ['vɛərɪəbl] *adj* variable; (*mood*) changeant(e)

variant ['vɛərɪənt] *n* variante f

variation [vɛərɪ'eɪʃən] *n* variation f; (*in opinion*) changement m

varied ['vɛərɪd] *adj* varié(e), divers(e)

variety [və'raɪətɪ] *n* variété f; (*quantity*) nombre m, quantité f

various ['vɛərɪəs] *adj* divers(e), différent(e); (*several*) divers, plusieurs

varnish ['vɑːnɪʃ] *n* vernis m ▷ *vt* vernir

vary ['vɛərɪ] *vt, vi* varier, changer

vase [vɑːz] *n* vase m

Vaseline® ['væsɪliːn] *n* vaseline f

vast [vɑːst] *adj* vaste, immense; (*amount, success*) énorme

VAT [væt] *n abbr* (BRIT: = *value added tax*) TVA f

vault [vɔːlt] *n* (*of roof*) voûte f; (*tomb*) caveau m; (*in bank*) salle f des coffres; chambre forte ▷ *vt* (*also: ~* **over**) sauter (d'un bond)

VCR *n abbr* = **video cassette recorder**

VDU *n abbr* = **visual display unit**

veal [viːl] *n* veau m

veer [vɪər] *vi* tourner; (*car, ship*) virer

vegan ['viːɡən] *n* végétalien(ne)

vegetable ['vɛdʒtəbl] *n* légume m ▷ *adj* végétal(e)

vegetarian [vɛdʒɪ'tɛərɪən] *adj, n* végétarien(ne); **do you have any ~ dishes?** avez-vous des plats végétariens?

vegetation [vɛdʒɪ'teɪʃən] *n* végétation f

vehicle ['viːɪkl] *n* véhicule m

veil [veɪl] *n* voile m

vein [veɪn] *n* veine f; (*on leaf*) nervure f

Velcro® ['vɛlkrəʊ] *n* velcro® m

velvet ['vɛlvɪt] *n* velours m

vending machine ['vɛndɪŋ-] *n* distributeur m automatique

vendor ['vɛndər] *n* vendeur(-euse); **street ~** marchand ambulant

Venetian blind [vɪ'niːʃən-] *n* store vénitien

vengeance ['vɛndʒəns] *n* vengeance f; **with a ~** (*fig*) vraiment, pour de bon

venison ['vɛnɪsn] *n* venaison f

venom ['vɛnəm] *n* venin m

vent [vɛnt] *n* conduit m d'aération; (*in dress, jacket*) fente f ▷ *vt* (*fig: one's feelings*) donner libre cours à

ventilation [vɛntɪˈleɪʃən] n ventilation f, aération f

venture [ˈvɛntʃəʳ] n entreprise f ▷ vt risquer, hasarder ▷ vi s'aventurer, se risquer; **a business ~** une entreprise commerciale

venue [ˈvɛnjuː] n lieu m

Venus [ˈviːnəs] n (planet) Vénus f

verb [vəːb] n verbe m; **verbal** adj verbal(e)

verdict [ˈvəːdɪkt] n verdict m

verge [vəːdʒ] n bord m; **"soft ~s"** (BRIT) "accotements non stabilisés"; **on the ~ of doing** sur le point de faire

verify [ˈvɛrɪfaɪ] vt vérifier

versatile [ˈvəːsətaɪl] adj polyvalent(e)

verse [vəːs] n vers mpl; (stanza) strophe f; (in Bible) verset m

version [ˈvəːʃən] n version f

versus [ˈvəːsəs] prep contre

vertical [ˈvəːtɪkl] adj vertical(e)

very [ˈvɛrɪ] adv très ▷ adj: **the ~ book which** le livre même que; **the ~ last** le tout dernier; **at the ~ least** au moins; **~ much** beaucoup

vessel [ˈvɛsl] n (Anat, Naut) vaisseau m; (container) récipient m; see also **blood**

vest [vɛst] n (BRIT: underwear) tricot m de corps; (US: waistcoat) gilet m

vet [vɛt] n abbr (BRIT = veterinary surgeon) vétérinaire m/f; (US: = veteran) ancien(ne) combattant(e) ▷ vt examiner minutieusement

veteran [ˈvɛtərn] n vétéran m; (also: **war ~**) ancien combattant

veterinary surgeon [ˈvɛtrɪnərɪ-] (BRIT) (US **veterinarian** [vɛtrɪˈnɛərɪən]) n vétérinaire m/f

veto [ˈviːtəu] n (pl **~es**) veto m ▷ vt opposer son veto à

via [ˈvaɪə] prep par, via

viable [ˈvaɪəbl] adj viable

vibrate [vaɪˈbreɪt] vi: **to ~ (with)** vibrer (de)

vibration [vaɪˈbreɪʃən] n vibration f

vicar [ˈvɪkəʳ] n pasteur m (de l'Église anglicane)

vice [vaɪs] n (evil) vice m; (Tech) étau m; **vice-chairman** n vice-président(e)

vice versa [ˈvaɪsɪˈvəːsə] adv vice versa

vicinity [vɪˈsɪnɪtɪ] n environs mpl, alentours mpl

vicious [ˈvɪʃəs] adj (remark) cruel(le), méchant(e); (blow) brutal(e); (dog) méchant(e), dangereux(-euse); **a ~ circle** un cercle vicieux

victim [ˈvɪktɪm] n victime f

victor [ˈvɪktəʳ] n vainqueur m

Victorian [vɪkˈtɔːrɪən] adj victorien(ne)

victorious [vɪkˈtɔːrɪəs] adj victorieux(-euse)

victory [ˈvɪktərɪ] n victoire f

video [ˈvɪdɪəu] n (video film) vidéo f; (also: ~ **cassette**) vidéocassette f; (also: ~ **cassette recorder**) magnétoscope m ▷ vt (with recorder) enregistrer; (with camera) filmer;

video camera n caméra f vidéo inv; **video (cassette) recorder** n magnétoscope m; **video game** n jeu m vidéo inv; **video shop** n vidéoclub m; **video tape** n bande f vidéo inv; (cassette) vidéocassette f

vie [vaɪ] vi: **to ~ with** lutter avec, rivaliser avec

Vienna [vɪˈɛnə] n Vienne

Vietnam, Viet Nam [ˈvjɛtˈnæm] n Viêt-nam or Vietnam m; **Vietnamese** [vjɛtnəˈmiːz] adj vietnamien(ne) ▷ n (pl inv) Vietnamien(ne)

view [vjuː] n vue f; (opinion) avis m, vue ▷ vt voir, regarder; (situation) considérer; (house) visiter; **on ~** (in museum etc) exposé(e); **in full ~ of sb** sous les yeux de qn; **in my ~** à mon avis; **in ~ of the fact that** étant donné que; **viewer** n (TV) téléspectateur(-trice); **viewpoint** n point m de vue

vigilant [ˈvɪdʒɪlənt] adj vigilant(e)

vigorous [ˈvɪgərəs] adj vigoureux(-euse)

vile [vaɪl] adj (action) vil(e); (smell, food) abominable; (temper) massacrant(e)

villa [ˈvɪlə] n villa f

village [ˈvɪlɪdʒ] n village m; **villager** n villageois(e)

villain [ˈvɪlən] n (scoundrel) scélérat m; (BRIT: criminal) bandit m; (in novel etc) traître m

vinaigrette [vɪneɪˈgrɛt] n vinaigrette f

vine [vaɪn] n vigne f

vinegar [ˈvɪnɪgəʳ] n vinaigre m

vineyard [ˈvɪnjɑːd] n vignoble m

vintage [ˈvɪntɪdʒ] n (year) année f, millésime m ▷ cpd (car) d'époque; (wine) de grand cru

vinyl [ˈvaɪnl] n vinyle m

viola [vɪˈəulə] n alto m

violate [ˈvaɪəleɪt] vt violer

violation [vaɪəˈleɪʃən] n violation f; **in ~ of** (rule, law) en infraction à, en violation de

violence [ˈvaɪələns] n violence f

violent [ˈvaɪələnt] adj violent(e)

violet [ˈvaɪələt] adj (colour) violet(te) ▷ n (plant) violette f

violin [vaɪəˈlɪn] n violon m

VIP n abbr (= very important person) VIP m

virgin [ˈvəːdʒɪn] n vierge f

Virgo [ˈvəːgəu] n la Vierge

virtual [ˈvəːtjuəl] adj (Comput, Physics) virtuel(le); (in effect): **it's a ~ impossibility** c'est quasiment impossible; **virtually** adv (almost) pratiquement; **virtual reality** n (Comput) réalité virtuelle

virtue [ˈvəːtjuː] n vertu f; (advantage) mérite m, avantage m; **by ~ of** en vertu or raison de

virus [ˈvaɪərəs] n (Med, Comput) virus m

visa [ˈviːzə] n visa m

vise [vaɪs] n (US Tech) = **vice**

visibility [vɪzɪˈbɪlɪtɪ] n visibilité f

visible [ˈvɪzəbl] adj visible

vision [ˈvɪʒən] n (sight) vue f, vision f; (foresight, in dream) vision

visit ['vɪzɪt] *n* visite *f*; *(stay)* séjour *m* ▷ *vt* *(person: US: also:* **~ with**) rendre visite à; *(place)* visiter; **visiting hours** *npl* heures *fpl* de visite; **visitor** *n* visiteur(-euse); *(to one's house)* invité(e); **visitor centre** *(US* **visitor center)** *n* hall *m* or centre *m* d'accueil

visual ['vɪzjuəl] *adj* visuel(le); **visualize** *vt* se représenter

vital ['vaɪtl] *adj* vital(e); **of ~ importance (to sb/sth)** d'une importance capitale (pour qn/qch)

vitality [vaɪ'tælɪtɪ] *n* vitalité *f*

vitamin ['vɪtəmɪn] *n* vitamine *f*

vivid ['vɪvɪd] *adj (account)* frappant(e), vivant(e); *(light, imagination)* vif (vive)

V-neck ['viːnɛk] *n* décolleté *m* en V

vocabulary [vəu'kæbjuləri] *n* vocabulaire *m*

vocal ['vəukl] *adj* vocal(e); *(articulate)* qui n'hésite pas à s'exprimer, qui sait faire entendre ses opinions

vocational [vəu'keɪʃənl] *adj* professionnel(le)

vodka ['vɔdkə] *n* vodka *f*

vogue [vəug] *n*: **to be in ~** être en vogue or à la mode

voice [vɔɪs] *n* voix *f* ▷ *vt (opinion)* exprimer, formuler; **voice mail** *n (system)* messagerie *f* vocale; *(device)* boîte *f* vocale

void [vɔɪd] *n* vide *m* ▷ *adj (invalid)* nul(le); *(empty)*: **~ of** vide de, dépourvu(e) de

volatile ['vɔlətaɪl] *adj* volatil(e); *(fig: person)* versatile; *(: situation)* explosif(-ive)

volcano *(pl* **~es)** [vɔl'keɪnəu] *n* volcan *m*

volleyball ['vɔlibɔːl] *n* volley(-ball) *m*

volt [vəult] *n* volt *m*; **voltage** *n* tension *f*, voltage *m*

volume ['vɔljuːm] *n* volume *m*; *(of tank)* capacité *f*

voluntarily ['vɔləntrɪlɪ] *adv* volontairement

voluntary ['vɔləntəri] *adj* volontaire; *(unpaid)* bénévole

volunteer [vɔlən'tɪər] *n* volontaire *m/f* ▷ *vt (information)* donner spontanément ▷ *vi (Mil)* s'engager comme volontaire; **to ~ to do** se proposer pour faire

vomit ['vɔmɪt] *n* vomissure *f* ▷ *vt, vi* vomir

vote [vəut] *n* vote *m*, suffrage *m*; *(votes cast)* voix *f*, vote; *(franchise)* droit *m* de vote ▷ *vt (chairman)* élire; *(propose)*: **to ~ that** proposer que + *sub* ▷ *vi* voter; **~ of thanks** discours *m* de remerciement; **voter** *n* électeur(-trice); **voting** *n* scrutin *m*, vote *m*

voucher ['vautʃər] *n (for meal, petrol, gift)* bon *m*

vow [vau] *n* vœu *m*, serment *m* ▷ *vi* jurer

vowel ['vauəl] *n* voyelle *f*

voyage ['vɔɪɪdʒ] *n* voyage *m* par mer, traversée *f*

vulgar ['vʌlgər] *adj* vulgaire

vulnerable ['vʌlnərəbl] *adj* vulnérable

vulture ['vʌltʃər] *n* vautour *m*

waddle ['wɔdl] *vi* se dandiner

wade [weɪd] *vi*: **to ~ through** marcher dans, patauger dans; *(fig: book)* venir à bout de

wafer ['weɪfər] *n (Culin)* gaufrette *f*

waffle ['wɔfl] *n (Culin)* gaufre *f* ▷ *vi* parler pour ne rien dire; faire du remplissage

wag [wæg] *vt* agiter, remuer ▷ *vi* remuer

wage [weɪdʒ] *n (also:* **~s)** salaire *m*, paye *f* ▷ *vt*: **to ~ war** faire la guerre

wag(g)on ['wægən] *n (horse-drawn)* chariot *m*; *(BRIT Rail)* wagon *m* (de marchandises)

wail [weɪl] *n* gémissement *m*; *(of siren)* hurlement *m* ▷ *vi* gémir; *(siren)* hurler

waist [weɪst] *n* taille *f*, ceinture *f*; **waistcoat** *n (BRIT)* gilet *m*

wait [weɪt] *n* attente *f* ▷ *vi* attendre; **to ~ for sb/sth** attendre qn/qch; **to keep sb ~ing** faire attendre qn; **~ for me, please** attendez-moi, s'il vous plaît; **I can't ~ to ...** *(fig)* je meurs d'envie de ...; **to lie in ~ for** guetter; **wait on** *vt fus* servir; **waiter** *n* garçon *m* (de café), serveur *m*; **waiting list** *n* liste *f* d'attente; **waiting room** *n* salle *f* d'attente; **waitress** ['weɪtrɪs] *n* serveuse *f*

waive [weɪv] *vt* renoncer à, abandonner

wake [weɪk] *vb (pt* **woke** *or* **~d**, *pp* **woken** *or* **~d)** ▷ *vt (also:* **~ up)** réveiller ▷ *vi (also:* **~ up)** se réveiller ▷ *n (for dead person)* veillée *f* mortuaire; *(Naut)* sillage *m*

Wales [weɪlz] *n* pays *m* de Galles; **the Prince**

of ~ le prince de Galles

walk [wɔːk] n promenade f; (short) petit tour; (gait) démarche f; (path) chemin m; (in park etc) allée f ▷ vi marcher; (for pleasure, exercise) se promener ▷ vt (distance) faire à pied; (dog) promener; **10 minutes' ~ from** à 10 minutes de marche de; **to go for a ~** se promener; faire un tour; **from all ~s of life** de toutes conditions sociales; **walk out** vi (go out) sortir; (as protest) partir (en signe de protestation); (strike) se mettre en grève; **to ~ out on sb** quitter qn; **walker** n (person) marcheur(-euse); **walkie-talkie** ['wɔːkɪ'tɔːkɪ] n talkie-walkie m; **walking** n marche f à pied; **walking shoes** npl chaussures fpl de marche; **walking stick** n canne f; **Walkman®** n Walkman® m; **walkway** n promenade f, cheminement piéton

wall [wɔːl] n mur m; (of tunnel, cave) paroi f

wallet ['wɔlɪt] n portefeuille m; **I can't find my ~** je ne retrouve plus mon portefeuille

wallpaper ['wɔːlpeɪpə'] n papier peint ▷ vt tapisser

walnut ['wɔːlnʌt] n noix f; (tree, wood) noyer m

walrus (pl ~ or ~**es**) ['wɔːlrəs] n morse m

waltz [wɔːlts] n valse f ▷ vi valser

wand [wɔnd] n (also: **magic ~**) baguette f (magique)

wander ['wɔndə'] vi (person) errer, aller sans but; (thoughts) vagabonder ▷ vt errer dans

want [wɔnt] vt vouloir; (need) avoir besoin de ▷ n: **for ~ of** par manque de, faute de; **to ~ to do** vouloir faire; **to ~ sb to do** vouloir que qn fasse; **wanted** adj (criminal) recherché(e) par la police; **"cook wanted"** "on recherche un cuisinier"

war [wɔː'] n guerre f; **to make ~ (on)** faire la guerre (à)

ward [wɔːd] n (in hospital) salle f; (Pol) section électorale; (Law: child: also: **~ of court**) pupille m/f

warden ['wɔːdn] n (BRIT: of institution) directeur(-trice); (of park, game reserve) gardien(ne); (BRIT: also: **traffic ~**) contractuel(le)

wardrobe ['wɔːdrəub] n (cupboard) armoire f; (clothes) garde-robe f

warehouse ['wɛəhaus] n entrepôt m

warfare ['wɔːfɛə'] n guerre f

warhead ['wɔːhed] n (Mil) ogive f

warm [wɔːm] adj chaud(e); (person, thanks, welcome, applause) chaleureux(-euse); **it's ~** il fait chaud; **I'm ~** j'ai chaud; **warm up** vi (person, room) se réchauffer; (athlete, discussion) s'échauffer ▷ vt (food) (faire) réchauffer; (water) (faire) chauffer; (engine) faire chauffer; **warmly** adv (dress) chaudement; (thank, welcome) chaleureusement; **warmth** n chaleur f

warn [wɔːn] vt avertir, prévenir; **to ~ sb (not) to do** conseiller à qn de (ne pas) faire; **warning** n avertissement m; (notice) avis m; **warning light** n avertisseur lumineux

warrant ['wɔrnt] n (guarantee) garantie f; (Law: to arrest) mandat m d'arrêt; (: to search) mandat de perquisition ▷ vt (justify, merit) justifier

warranty ['wɔrəntɪ] n garantie f

warrior ['wɔrɪə'] n guerrier(-ière)

Warsaw ['wɔːsɔː] n Varsovie

warship ['wɔːʃɪp] n navire m de guerre

wart [wɔːt] n verrue f

wartime ['wɔːtaɪm] n: **in ~** en temps de guerre

wary ['wɛərɪ] adj prudent(e)

was [wɔz] pt of **be**

wash [wɔʃ] vt laver ▷ vi se laver; (sea): **to ~ over/against sth** inonder/baigner qch ▷ n (clothes) lessive f; (washing programme) lavage m; (of ship) sillage m; **to have a ~** se laver, faire sa toilette; **wash up** vi (BRIT) faire la vaisselle; (us: have a wash) se débarbouiller; **washbasin** n lavabo m; **wash cloth** n (us) gant m de toilette; **washer** n (Tech) rondelle f, joint m; **washing** n (BRIT: linen etc: dirty) linge m; (: clean) lessive f; **washing line** n (BRIT) corde f à linge; **washing machine** n machine f à laver; **washing powder** n (BRIT) lessive f (en poudre)

Washington ['wɔʃɪŋtən] n Washington m

wash: **washing-up** n (BRIT) vaisselle f; **washing-up liquid** n (BRIT) produit m pour la vaisselle; **washroom** n (us) toilettes fpl

wasn't ['wɔznt] = **was not**

wasp [wɔsp] n guêpe f

waste [weist] n gaspillage m; (of time) perte f; (rubbish) déchets mpl; (also: **household ~**) ordures fpl ▷ adj (land, ground: in city) à l'abandon; (leftover): **~ material** déchets ▷ vt gaspiller; (time, opportunity) perdre; **waste ground** n (BRIT) terrain m vague; **wastepaper basket** n corbeille f à papier

watch [wɔtʃ] n montre f; (act of watching) surveillance f; (guard: Mil) sentinelle f; (: Naut) homme m de quart; (Naut: spell of duty) quart m ▷ vt (look at) observer; (: match, programme) regarder; (spy on, guard) surveiller; (be careful of) faire attention à ▷ vi regarder; (keep guard) monter la garde; **to keep ~** faire le guet; **watch out** vi faire attention; **watchdog** n chien m de garde; (fig) gardien(ne); **watch strap** n bracelet m de montre

water ['wɔːtə'] n eau f ▷ vt (plant, garden) arroser ▷ vi (eyes) larmoyer; **in British ~s** dans les eaux territoriales Britanniques; **to make sb's mouth ~** mettre l'eau à la bouche de qn; **water down** vt (milk etc) couper avec de l'eau; (fig: story) édulcorer; **watercolour** (us **watercolor**) n aquarelle f; **watercress** n cresson m (de fontaine); **waterfall** n

w

chute f d'eau; **watering can** n arrosoir m; **watermelon** n pastèque f; **waterproof** adj imperméable; **water-skiing** n ski m nautique

watt [wɔt] n watt m

wave [weɪv] n vague f; (of hand) geste m, signe m; (Radio) onde f; (in hair) ondulation f; (fig: of enthusiasm, strikes etc) vague ▷ vi faire signe de la main; (flag) flotter au vent; (grass) ondoyer ▷ vt (handkerchief) agiter; (stick) brandir; **wavelength** n longueur f d'ondes

waver ['weɪvəʳ] vi vaciller; (voice) trembler; (person) hésiter

wavy ['weɪvɪ] adj (hair, surface) ondulé(e); (line) onduleux(-euse)

wax [wæks] n cire f; (for skis) fart m ▷ vt cirer; (car) lustrer; (skis) farter ▷ vi (moon) croître

way [weɪ] n chemin m, voie f; (distance) distance f; (direction) chemin, direction f; (manner) façon f, manière f; (habit) habitude f, façon; **which ~? — this ~/that ~** par où or de quel côté? — par ici/par là; **to lose one's ~** perdre son chemin; **on the ~ (to)** en route (pour); **to be on one's ~** être en route; **to be in the ~** bloquer le passage; (fig) gêner; **it's a long ~ a~** c'est loin d'ici; **to go out of one's ~ to do** (fig) se donner beaucoup de mal pour faire; **to be under ~** (work, project) être en cours; **in a ~** dans un sens; **by the ~** à propos; **"~ in"** (BRIT) "entrée"; **"~ out"** (BRIT) "sortie"; **the ~ back** le chemin du retour; **"give ~"** (BRIT Aut) "cédez la priorité"; **no ~!** (inf) pas question!

W.C. n abbr (BRIT: = water closet) w.-c. mpl, waters mpl

we [wiː] pl pron nous

weak [wiːk] adj faible; (health) fragile; (beam etc) peu solide; (tea, coffee) léger(-ère); **weaken** vi faiblir ▷ vt affaiblir; **weakness** n faiblesse f; (fault) point m faible

wealth [welθ] n (money, resources) richesse(s) f(pl); (of details) profusion f; **wealthy** adj riche

weapon ['wepən] n arme f; **~s of mass destruction** armes fpl de destruction massive

wear [weəʳ] n (use) usage m; (deterioration through use) usure f ▷ vb (pt **wore**, pp **worn**) ▷ vt (clothes) porter; (put on) mettre; (damage: through use) user ▷ vi (last) faire de l'usage; (rub etc through) s'user; **sports/baby~** vêtements mpl de sport/pour bébés; **evening ~** tenue f de soirée; **wear off** vi disparaître; **wear out** vt user; (person, strength) épuiser

weary ['wɪərɪ] adj (tired) épuisé(e); (dispirited) las (lasse); abattu(e) ▷ vi: **to ~ of** se lasser de

weasel ['wiːzl] n (Zool) belette f

weather ['weðəʳ] n temps m ▷ vt (storm: lit, fig) essuyer; (crisis) survivre à; **under the ~** (fig: ill) mal fichu(e); **weather forecast** n prévisions fpl météorologiques, météo f

weave (pt **wove**, pp **woven**) [wiːv, wəuv, 'wəuvn] vt (cloth) tisser; (basket) tresser

web [web] n (of spider) toile f; (on duck's foot) palmure f; (fig) tissu m; (Comput): **the (World-Wide) W~** le Web; **web page** n (Comput) page f Web; **website** n (Comput) site m web

wed [wed] (pt, pp **~ded**) vt épouser ▷ vi se marier

Wed abbr (= Wednesday) me

we'd [wiːd] = **we had**; **we would**

wedding ['wedɪŋ] n mariage m; **wedding anniversary** n anniversaire m de mariage; **silver/golden wedding anniversary** noces fpl d'argent/d'or; **wedding day** n jour m du mariage; **wedding dress** n robe f de mariée; **wedding ring** n alliance f

wedge [wedʒ] n (of wood etc) coin m; (under door etc) cale f; (of cake) part f ▷ vt (fix) caler; (push) enfoncer, coincer

Wednesday ['wednzdɪ] n mercredi m

wee [wiː] adj (SCOTTISH) petit(e); tout(e) petit(e)

weed [wiːd] n mauvaise herbe ▷ vt désherber; **weedkiller** n désherbant m

week [wiːk] n semaine f; **a ~ today/on Tuesday** aujourd'hui/mardi en huit; **weekday** n jour m de semaine; (Comm) jour ouvrable; **weekend** n week-end m; **weekly** adv une fois par semaine, chaque semaine ▷ adj, n hebdomadaire m

weep [wiːp] (pt, pp **wept**) vi (person) pleurer

weigh [weɪ] vt, vi peser; **to ~ anchor** lever l'ancre; **weigh up** vt examiner

weight [weɪt] n poids m; **to put on/ lose ~** grossir/maigrir; **weightlifting** n haltérophilie f

weir [wɪəʳ] n barrage m

weird [wɪəd] adj bizarre; (eerie) surnaturel(le)

welcome ['welkəm] adj bienvenu(e) ▷ n accueil m ▷ vt accueillir; (also: **bid ~**) souhaiter la bienvenue à; (be glad of) se réjouir de; **you're ~!** (after thanks) de rien, il n'y a pas de quoi

weld [weld] vt souder

welfare ['welfeəʳ] n (wellbeing) bien-être m; (social aid) assistance sociale; **welfare state** n État-providence m

well [wel] n puits m ▷ adv bien ▷ adj: **to be ~** aller bien ▷ excl eh bien!; (relief also) bon!; (resignation) enfin!; **~ done!** bravo!; **get ~ soon!** remets-toi vite!; **to do ~** bien réussir; (business) prospérer; **as ~** (in addition) aussi, également; **as ~ as** aussi bien que or de; en plus de

we'll [wiːl] = **we will**; **we shall**

well: **well-behaved** adj sage, obéissant(e); **well-built** adj (person) bien bâti(e); **well-dressed** adj bien habillé(e), bien vêtu(e)

well-groomed [-'gruːmd] adj très soigné(e)

wellies ['welɪz] (inf) npl (BRIT) = **wellingtons**

wellingtons ['welɪŋtənz] npl (also: **wellington boots**) bottes fpl en caoutchouc

well: **well-known** adj (person) bien connu(e); **well-off** adj aisé(e), assez riche; **well-paid** [wɛl'peɪd] adj bien payé(e)

Welsh [wɛlʃ] adj gallois(e) ▷ n (Ling) gallois m; **the Welsh** npl (people) les Gallois; **Welshman** (irreg) n Gallois m; **Welshwoman** (irreg) n Galloise f

went [wɛnt] pt of **go**

wept [wɛpt] pt, pp of **weep**

were [wəːʳ] pt of **be**

we're [wɪəʳ] = **we are**

weren't [wəːnt] = **were not**

west [wɛst] n ouest m ▷ adj (wind) d'ouest; (side) ouest inv ▷ adv à or vers l'ouest; **the W~** l'Occident m, l'Ouest m; **westbound** ['wɛstbaund] adj en direction de l'ouest; (carriageway) ouest inv; **western** adj occidental(e), de or à l'ouest ▷ n (Cine) western m; **West Indian** adj antillais(e) ▷ n Antillais(e)

West Indies [-'ɪndɪz] npl Antilles fpl

wet [wɛt] adj mouillé(e); (damp) humide; (soaked: also: **~ through**) trempé(e); (rainy) pluvieux(-euse); **to get ~** se mouiller; "**~ paint**" "attention peinture fraîche"; **wetsuit** n combinaison f de plongée

we've [wiːv] = **we have**

whack [wæk] vt donner un grand coup à

whale [weɪl] n (Zool) baleine f

wharf (pl **wharves**) [wɔːf, wɔːvz] n quai m

○ **KEYWORD**

what [wɔt] adj 1 (in questions) quel(le); **what size is he?** quelle taille fait-il?; **what colour is it?** de quelle couleur est-ce?; **what books do you need?** quels livres vous faut-il?
2 (in exclamations): **what a mess!** quel désordre!; **what a fool I am!** que je suis bête!
▷ pron 1 (interrogative) que; de/à/en etc quoi; **what are you doing?** que faites-vous?, qu'est-ce que vous faites?; **what is happening?** qu'est-ce qui se passe?, que se passe-t-il?; **what are you talking about?** de quoi parlez-vous?; **what are you thinking about?** à quoi pensez-vous?; **what is it called?** comment est-ce que ça s'appelle?; **what about me?** et moi?; **what about doing ...?** et si on faisait ...?
2 (relative: subject) ce qui; (: direct object) ce que; (: indirect object) ce à quoi, ce dont; **I saw what you did/was on the table** j'ai vu ce que vous avez fait/ce qui était sur la table; **tell me what you remember** dites-moi ce dont vous vous souvenez; **what I want is a cup of tea** ce que je veux, c'est une tasse de thé
▷ excl (disbelieving) quoi!, comment!

whatever [wɔt'ɛvəʳ] adj: **take ~ book you prefer** prenez le livre que vous préférez, peu importe lequel; **~ book you take** quel que soit le livre que vous preniez ▷ pron: **do ~ is necessary** faites (tout) ce qui est nécessaire; **~ happens** quoi qu'il arrive; **no reason ~** or **whatsoever** pas la moindre raison; **nothing ~** or **whatsoever** rien du tout

whatsoever [wɔtsəu'ɛvəʳ] adj see **whatever**

wheat [wiːt] n blé m, froment m

wheel [wiːl] n roue f; (Aut: also: **steering ~**) volant m; (Naut) gouvernail m ▷ vt (pram etc) pousser, rouler ▷ vi (birds) tournoyer; (also: **~ round**: person) se retourner, faire volte-face; **wheelbarrow** n brouette f; **wheelchair** n fauteuil roulant; **wheel clamp** n (Aut) sabot m (de Denver)

wheeze [wiːz] vi respirer bruyamment

○ **KEYWORD**

when [wɛn] adv quand; **when did he go?** quand est-ce qu'il est parti?
▷ conj 1 (at, during, after the time that) quand, lorsque; **she was reading when I came in** elle lisait quand or lorsque je suis entré
2 (on, at which): **on the day when I met him** le jour où je l'ai rencontré
3 (whereas) alors que; **I thought I was wrong when in fact I was right** j'ai cru que j'avais tort alors qu'en fait j'avais raison

whenever [wɛn'ɛvəʳ] adv quand donc ▷ conj quand; (every time that) chaque fois que

where [wɛəʳ] adv, conj où; **this is ~** c'est là que; **whereabouts** adv où donc ▷ n: **nobody knows his whereabouts** personne ne sait où il se trouve; **whereas** conj alors que; **whereby** adv (formal) par lequel (or laquelle etc); **wherever** adv où donc ▷ conj où que + sub; **sit wherever you like** asseyez-vous (là) où vous voulez

whether ['wɛðəʳ] conj si; **I don't know ~ to accept or not** je ne sais pas si je dois accepter ou non; **it's doubtful ~** il est peu probable que + sub; **~ you go or not** que vous y alliez ou non

○ **KEYWORD**

which [wɪtʃ] adj 1 (interrogative: direct, indirect) quel(le); **which picture do you want?** quel tableau voulez-vous?; **which one?** lequel (laquelle)?
2: **in which case** auquel cas; **we got there at 8pm, by which time the cinema was full** quand nous sommes arrivés à 20h, le cinéma était complet
▷ pron 1 (interrogative) lequel (laquelle), lesquels (lesquelles) pl; **I don't mind which** peu importe lequel; **which (of these) are yours?** lesquels sont à vous?; **tell me which**

w

you want dites-moi lesquels or ceux que vous voulez

2 (*relative: subject*) qui; (: *object*) que; sur/vers *etc* lequel (laquelle) (NB: *à* + lequel = **auquel**; *de* + lequel = **duquel**); **the apple which you ate/which is on the table** la pomme que vous avez mangée/qui est sur la table; **the chair on which you are sitting** la chaise sur laquelle vous êtes assis; **the book of which you spoke** le livre dont vous avez parlé; **he said he knew, which is true/I was afraid of** il a dit qu'il le savait, ce qui est vrai/ce que je craignais; **after which** après quoi

whichever [wɪtʃˈɛvəʳ] *adj*: **take ~ book you prefer** prenez le livre que vous préférez, peu importe lequel; **~ book you take** quel que soit le livre que vous preniez

while [waɪl] *n* moment *m* ▷ *conj* pendant que; (*as long as*) tant que; (*as, whereas*) alors que; (*though*) bien que + *sub*, quoique + *sub*; **for a ~** pendant quelque temps; **in a ~** dans un moment

whilst [waɪlst] *conj* = **while**

whim [wɪm] *n* caprice *m*

whine [waɪn] *n* gémissement *m*; (*of engine, siren*) plainte stridente ▷ *vi* gémir, geindre, pleurnicher; (*dog, engine, siren*) gémir

whip [wɪp] *n* fouet *m*; (*for riding*) cravache *f*; (*Pol: person*) chef *m* de file (*assurant la discipline dans son groupe parlementaire*) ▷ *vt* fouetter; (*snatch*) enlever (or sortir) brusquement; **whipped cream** *n* crème fouettée

whirl [wəːl] *vi* tourbillonner; (*dancers*) tournoyer ▷ *vt* faire tourbillonner; faire tournoyer

whisk [wɪsk] *n* (*Culin*) fouet *m* ▷ *vt* (*eggs*) fouetter, battre; **to ~ sb away** or **off** emmener qn rapidement

whiskers [ˈwɪskəz] *npl* (*of animal*) moustaches *fpl*; (*of man*) favoris *mpl*

whisky (*IRISH, US* **whiskey**) [ˈwɪskɪ] *n* whisky *m*

whisper [ˈwɪspəʳ] *n* chuchotement *m* ▷ *vt, vi* chuchoter

whistle [ˈwɪsl] *n* (*sound*) sifflement *m*; (*object*) sifflet *m* ▷ *vi* siffler ▷ *vt* siffler, siffloter

white [waɪt] *adj* blanc (blanche); (*with fear*) blême ▷ *n* blanc *m*; (*person*) blanc (blanche); **White House** *n* (*US*): **the White House** la Maison-Blanche; **whitewash** *n* (*paint*) lait *m* de chaux ▷ *vt* blanchir à la chaux; (*fig*) blanchir

whiting [ˈwaɪtɪŋ] *n* (*pl inv*: *fish*) merlan *m*

Whitsun [ˈwɪtsn] *n* la Pentecôte

whittle [ˈwɪtl] *vt*: **to ~ away, to ~ down** (*costs*) réduire, rogner

whizz [wɪz] *vi* aller (or passer) à toute vitesse

who [huː] *pron* qui

whoever [huːˈɛvəʳ] *pron*: **~ finds it** celui (celle) qui le trouve (, qui que ce soit) le trouve; **ask ~ you like** demandez à qui vous voulez; **~ he marries** qui que ce soit or quelle que soit la personne qu'il épouse; **~ told you that?** qui a bien pu vous dire ça?, qui donc vous a dit ça?

whole [həul] *adj* (*complete*) entier(-ière), tout(e); (*not broken*) intact(e), complet(-ète) ▷ *n* (*all*): **the ~ of** la totalité de, tout(e) le (la); (*entire unit*) tout *m*; **the ~ of the town** la ville tout entière; **on the ~, as a ~** dans l'ensemble; **wholefood(s)** *n(pl)* aliments complets; **wholeheartedly** [həulˈhɑːtɪdlɪ] *adv* sans réserve; **to agree wholeheartedly** être entièrement d'accord; **wholemeal** *adj* (*BRIT: flour, bread*) complet(-ète); **wholesale** *n* (*vente f en*) gros *m* ▷ *adj* (*price*) de gros; (*destruction*) systématique; **wholewheat** *adj* = **wholemeal**; **wholly** *adv* entièrement, tout à fait

 KEYWORD

whom [huːm] *pron* **1** (*interrogative*) qui; **whom did you see?** qui avez-vous vu?; **to whom did you give it?** à qui l'avez-vous donné?

2 (*relative*) que; à/de *etc* qui; **the man whom I saw/to whom I spoke** l'homme que j'ai vu/à qui j'ai parlé

whore [hɔːʳ] *n* (*inf: pej*) putain *f*

 KEYWORD

whose [huːz] *adj* **1** (*possessive: interrogative*): **whose book is this?, whose is this book?** à qui est ce livre?; **whose pencil have you taken?** à qui est le crayon que vous avez pris?, c'est le crayon de qui que vous avez pris?; **whose daughter are you?** de qui êtes-vous la fille?

2 (*possessive: relative*): **the man whose son you rescued** l'homme dont or de qui vous avez sauvé le fils; **the girl whose sister you were speaking to** la fille à la sœur de qui or de laquelle vous parliez; **the woman whose car was stolen** la femme dont la voiture a été volée

▷ *pron* à qui; **whose is this?** à qui est ceci?; **I know whose it is** je sais à qui c'est

KEYWORD

why [waɪ] *adv* pourquoi; **why not?** pourquoi pas?

▷ *conj*: **I wonder why he said that** je me demande pourquoi il a dit ça; **that's not why**

I'm here ce n'est pas pour ça que je suis là; **the reason why** la raison pour laquelle ▷ *excl* eh bien!, tiens!; **why, it's you!** tiens, c'est vous!; **why, that's impossible!** voyons, c'est impossible!

wicked ['wɪkɪd] *adj* méchant(e); (*mischievous: grin, look*) espiègle, malicieux(-euse); (*crime*) pervers(e); (*inf: very good*) génial(e) (*inf*)

wicket ['wɪkɪt] *n* (*Cricket: stumps*) guichet *m*; (*: grass area*) espace compris entre les deux guichets

wide [waɪd] *adj* large; (*area, knowledge*) vaste, très étendu(e); (*choice*) grand(e) ▷ *adv*: **to open ~** ouvrir tout grand; **to shoot ~** tirer à côté; **it is 3 metres ~** cela fait 3 mètres de large; **widely** *adv* (*different*) radicalement; (*spaced*) sur une grande étendue; (*believed*) généralement; (*travel*) beaucoup; **widen** *vt* élargir ▷ *vi* s'élargir; **wide open** *adj* grand(e) ouvert(e); **widespread** *adj* (*belief etc*) très répandu(e)

widow ['wɪdəu] *n* veuve *f*; **widower** *n* veuf *m*

width [wɪdθ] *n* largeur *f*

wield [wiːld] *vt* (*sword*) manier; (*power*) exercer

wife (*pl* **wives**) [waɪf, waɪvz] *n* femme *f*, épouse *f*

wig [wɪg] *n* perruque *f*

wild [waɪld] *adj* sauvage; (*sea*) déchaîné(e); (*idea, life*) fou (folle); (*behaviour*) déchaîné(e), extravagant(e); (*inf: angry*) hors de soi, furieux(-euse) ▷ *n*: **the ~** la nature; **wilderness** ['wɪldənɪs] *n* désert *m*, région *f* sauvage; **wildlife** *n* faune *f* (et flore *f*); **wildly** *adv* (*behave*) de manière déchaînée; (*applaud*) frénétiquement; (*hit, guess*) au hasard; (*happy*) follement

 KEYWORD

will [wɪl] *aux vb* **1** (*forming future tense*): **I will finish it tomorrow** je le finirai demain; **I will have finished it by tomorrow** je l'aurai fini d'ici demain; **will you do it? - yes I will/no I won't** le ferez-vous? - oui/non

2 (*in conjectures, predictions*): **he will** *or* **he'll be there by now** il doit être arrivé à l'heure qu'il est; **that will be the postman** ça doit être le facteur

3 (*in commands, requests, offers*): **will you be quiet!** voulez-vous bien vous taire!; **will you help me?** est-ce que vous pouvez m'aider?; **will you have a cup of tea?** voulez-vous une tasse de thé?; **I won't put up with it!** je ne le tolérerai pas!

▷ *vt* (*pt, pp* **willed**): **to will sb to do** souhaiter ardemment que qn fasse; **he willed himself to go on** par un suprême effort de volonté, il

continua ▷ *n* volonté *f*; (*document*) testament *m*; **against one's will** à contre-cœur

willing ['wɪlɪŋ] *adj* de bonne volonté, serviable; **he's ~ to do it** il est disposé à le faire, il veut bien le faire; **willingly** *adv* volontiers

willow ['wɪləu] *n* saule *m*

willpower ['wɪl'pauəʳ] *n* volonté *f*

wilt [wɪlt] *vi* dépérir

win [wɪn] *n* (*in sports etc*) victoire *f* ▷ *vb* (*pt, pp* **won**) ▷ *vt* (*battle, money*) gagner; (*prize, contract*) remporter; (*popularity*) acquérir ▷ *vi* gagner; **win over** *vt* convaincre

wince [wɪns] *vi* tressaillir

wind¹ [wɪnd] *n* (*also Med*) vent *m*; (*breath*) souffle *m* ▷ *vt* (*take breath away*) couper le souffle à; **the ~(s)** (*Mus*) les instruments *mpl* à vent

wind² (*pt, pp* **wound**) [waɪnd, waund] *vt* enrouler; (*wrap*) envelopper; (*clock, toy*) remonter ▷ *vi* (*road, river*) serpenter; **wind down** *vt* (*car window*) baisser; (*fig: production, business*) réduire progressivement; **wind up** *vt* (*clock*) remonter; (*debate*) terminer, clôturer

windfall ['wɪndfɔːl] *n* coup *m* de chance

winding ['waɪndɪŋ] *adj* (*road*) sinueux(-euse); (*staircase*) tournant(e)

windmill ['wɪndmɪl] *n* moulin *m* à vent

window ['wɪndəu] *n* fenêtre *f*; (*in car, train: also:* **~pane**) vitre *f*; (*in shop etc*) vitrine *f*; **window box** *n* jardinière *f*; **window cleaner** *n* (*person*) laveur(-euse) de vitres; **window pane** *n* vitre *f*, carreau *m*; **window seat** *n* (*in vehicle*) place *f* côté fenêtre; **windowsill** *n* (*inside*) appui *m* de la fenêtre; (*outside*) rebord *m* de la fenêtre

windscreen ['wɪndskriːn] *n* pare-brise *m inv*; **windscreen wiper** *n* essuie-glace *m inv*

windshield ['wɪndʃiːld] (*us*) *n* = **windscreen**

windsurfing ['wɪndsəːfɪŋ] *n* planche *f* à voile

windy ['wɪndɪ] *adj* (*day*) de vent, venteux(-euse); (*place, weather*) venteux; **it's ~** il y a du vent

wine [waɪn] *n* vin *m*; **wine bar** *n* bar *m* à vin; **wine glass** *n* verre *m* à vin; **wine list** *n* carte *f* des vins; **wine tasting** *n* dégustation *f* (de vins)

wing [wɪŋ] *n* aile *f*; **wings** *npl* (*Theat*) coulisses *fpl*; **wing mirror** *n* (*BRIT*) rétroviseur latéral

wink [wɪŋk] *n* clin *m* d'œil ▷ *vi* faire un clin d'œil; (*blink*) cligner des yeux

winner ['wɪnəʳ] *n* gagnant(e)

winning ['wɪnɪŋ] *adj* (*team*) gagnant(e); (*goal*) décisif(-ive); (*charming*) charmeur(-euse)

winter ['wɪntəʳ] *n* hiver *m* ▷ *vi* hiverner; **in ~** en hiver; **winter sports** *npl* sports *mpl* d'hiver; **wintertime** *n* hiver *m*

wipe [waɪp] *n*: **to give sth a ~** donner un coup de torchon/de chiffon/d'éponge à qch ▷ *vt* essuyer; (*erase: tape*) effacer; **to ~ one's nose** se moucher; **wipe out** *vt* (*debt*) éteindre, amortir; (*memory*) effacer; (*destroy*) anéantir; **wipe up** *vt* essuyer

wire [waɪəʳ] *n* fil *m* (de fer); (*Elec*) fil électrique; (*Tel*) télégramme *m* ▷ *vt* (*house*) faire l'installation électrique de; (*also: ~ up*) brancher; (*person: send telegram to*) télégraphier à

wiring ['waɪərɪŋ] *n* (*Elec*) installation *f* électrique

wisdom ['wɪzdəm] *n* sagesse *f*; (*of action*) prudence *f*; **wisdom tooth** *n* dent *f* de sagesse

wise [waɪz] *adj* sage, prudent(e); (*remark*) judicieux(-euse)

wish [wɪʃ] *n* (*desire*) désir *m*; (*specific desire*) souhait *m*, vœu *m* ▷ *vt* souhaiter, désirer, vouloir; **best ~es** (*on birthday etc*) meilleurs vœux; **with best ~es** (*in letter*) bien amicalement; **to ~ sb goodbye** dire au revoir à qn; **he ~ed me well** il m'a souhaité bonne chance; **to ~ to do/sb to do** désirer *or* vouloir faire/que qn fasse; **to ~ for** souhaiter

wistful ['wɪstful] *adj* mélancolique

wit [wɪt] *n* (*also: ~s: intelligence*) intelligence *f*, esprit *m*; (*presence of mind*) présence *f* d'esprit; (*wittiness*) esprit; (*person*) homme/femme d'esprit

witch [wɪtʃ] *n* sorcière *f*

KEYWORD

with [wɪð, wɪθ] *prep* **1** (*in the company of*) avec; (*at the home of*) chez; **we stayed with friends** nous avons logé chez des amis; **I'll be with you in a minute** je suis à vous dans un instant **2** (*descriptive*): **a room with a view** une chambre avec vue; **the man with the grey hat/blue eyes** l'homme au chapeau gris/aux yeux bleus **3** (*indicating manner, means, cause*): **with tears in her eyes** les larmes aux yeux; **to walk with a stick** marcher avec une canne; **red with anger** rouge de colère; **to shake with fear** trembler de peur; **to fill sth with water** remplir qch d'eau **4** (*in phrases*): **I'm with you** (*I understand*) je vous suis; **to be with it** (*inf: up-to-date*) être dans le vent

withdraw [wɪθ'drɔː] *vt* (*irreg: like* **draw**) retirer ▷ *vi* se retirer; **withdrawal** *n* retrait *m*; (*Med*) état *m* de manque; **withdrawn** *pp of* **withdraw** ▷ *adj* (*person*) renfermé(e)

withdrew [wɪθ'druː] *pt of* **withdraw**

wither ['wɪðəʳ] *vi* se faner

withhold [wɪθ'həuld] *vt* (*irreg: like* **hold**) (*money*) retenir; (*decision*) remettre; (*permission*): **to ~ (from)** (*permission*) refuser (à); (*information*): **to ~ (from)** cacher (à)

within [wɪð'ɪn] *prep* à l'intérieur de ▷ *adv* à l'intérieur; **~ his reach** à sa portée; **~ sight of** en vue de; **~ a mile of** à moins d'un mille de; **~ the week** avant la fin de la semaine

without [wɪð'aut] *prep* sans; **~ a coat** sans manteau; **~ speaking** sans parler; **to go** *or* **do ~ sth** se passer de qch

withstand [wɪθ'stænd] *vt* (*irreg: like* **stand**) résister à

witness ['wɪtnɪs] *n* (*person*) témoin *m* ▷ *vt* (*event*) être témoin de; (*document*) attester l'authenticité de; **to bear ~ to sth** témoigner de qch

witty ['wɪtɪ] *adj* spirituel(le), plein(e) d'esprit

wives [waɪvz] *npl of* **wife**

wizard ['wɪzəd] *n* magicien *m*

wk *abbr* = **week**

wobble ['wɔbl] *vi* trembler de; (*chair*) branler

woe [wəu] *n* malheur *m*

woke [wəuk] *pt of* **wake**

woken ['wəukn] *pp of* **wake**

wolf (*pl* **wolves**) [wulf, wulvz] *n* loup *m*

woman (*pl* **women**) ['wumən, 'wɪmɪn] *n* femme *f* ▷ *cpd*: **~ doctor** femme *f* médecin; **~ teacher** professeur *m* femme

womb [wuːm] *n* (*Anat*) utérus *m*

women ['wɪmɪn] *npl of* **woman**

won [wʌn] *pt, pp of* **win**

wonder ['wʌndəʳ] *n* merveille *f*, miracle *m*; (*feeling*) émerveillement *m* ▷ *vi*: **to ~ whether/why** se demander si/pourquoi; **to ~ at** (*surprise*) s'étonner de; (*admiration*) s'émerveiller de; **to ~ about** songer à; **it's no ~ that** il n'est pas étonnant que + *sub*; **wonderful** *adj* merveilleux(-euse)

won't [wəunt] = **will not**

wood [wud] *n* (*timber, forest*) bois *m*; **wooden** *adj* en bois; (*fig: actor*) raide; (: *performance*) qui manque de naturel; **woodwind** *n*: **the woodwind** (*Mus*) les bois *mpl*; **woodwork** *n* menuiserie *f*

wool [wul] *n* laine *f*; **to pull the ~ over sb's eyes** (*fig*) en faire accroire à qn; **woollen** (*us* **woolen**) *adj* de *or* en laine; **woolly** (*us* **wooly**) *adj* laineux(-euse); (*fig: ideas*) confus(e)

word [wəːd] *n* mot *m*; (*spoken*) parole *f*; (*promise*) parole; (*news*) nouvelles *fpl* ▷ *vt* rédiger, formuler; **in other ~s** en d'autres termes; **to have a ~ with sb** toucher un mot à qn; **to break/keep one's ~** manquer à sa parole/tenir (sa) parole; **wording** *n* termes *mpl*, langage *m*; (*of document*) libellé *m*; **word processing** *n* traitement *m* de texte; **word processor** *n* machine *f* de traitement de texte

wore [wɔːʳ] *pt of* **wear**

work [wəːk] *n* travail *m*; (*Art, Literature*)

œuvre f ▷ vi travailler; (*mechanism*) marcher, fonctionner; (*plan etc*) marcher; (*medicine*) agir ▷ vt (*clay, wood etc*) travailler; (*mine etc*) exploiter; (*machine*) faire marcher *or* fonctionner; (*miracles etc*) faire; **works** n (BRIT: *factory*) usine f; **how does this ~?** comment est-ce que ça marche?; **the TV isn't ~ing** la télévision est en panne *or* ne marche pas; **to be out of ~** être au chômage *or* sans emploi; **to ~ loose** se défaire, se desserrer; **work out** vi (*plans etc*) marcher; (*Sport*) s'entraîner ▷ vt (*problem*) résoudre; (*plan*) élaborer; **it ~s out at £100** ça fait 100 livres; **worker** n travailleur(-euse), ouvrier(-ière); **work experience** n stage m; **workforce** n main-d'œuvre f; **working class** n classe ouvrière ▷ adj: **working-class** ouvrier(-ière), de la classe ouvrière; **working week** n semaine f de travail; **workman** (*irreg*) n ouvrier m; **work of art** n œuvre f d'art; **workout** n (*Sport*) séance f d'entraînement; **work permit** n permis m de travail; **workplace** n lieu m de travail; **worksheet** n (*Scol*) feuille f d'exercices; **workshop** n atelier m; **work station** n poste m de travail; **work surface** n plan m de travail; **worktop** n plan m de travail

world [wəːld] n monde m ▷ cpd (*champion*) du monde; (*power, war*) mondial(e); **to think the ~ of sb** (*fig*) ne jurer que par qn; **World Cup** n: **the World Cup** (*Football*) la Coupe du monde; **world-wide** adj universel(le); **World-Wide Web** n: **the World-Wide Web** le Web

worm [wəːm] n (*also: **earth~***) ver m

worn [wɔːn] pp of **wear** ▷ adj usé(e); **worn-out** adj (*object*) complètement usé(e); (*person*) épuisé(e)

worried ['wʌrɪd] adj inquiet(-ète); **to be ~ about sth** être inquiet au sujet de qch

worry ['wʌrɪ] n souci m ▷ vt inquiéter ▷ vi s'inquiéter, se faire du souci; **worrying** adj inquiétant(e)

worse [wəːs] adj pire, plus mauvais(e) ▷ adv plus mal ▷ n pire m; **to get ~** (*condition, situation*) empirer, se dégrader; **a change for the ~** une détérioration; **worsen** vt, vi empirer; **worse off** adj moins à l'aise financièrement; (*fig*): **you'll be worse off this way** ça ira moins bien de cette façon

worship ['wəːʃɪp] n culte m ▷ vt (*God*) rendre un culte à; (*person*) adorer

worst [wəːst] adj le (la) pire, le (la) plus mauvais(e) ▷ adv le plus mal ▷ n pire m; **at ~** au pis aller

worth [wəːθ] n valeur f ▷ adj: **to be ~** valoir; **it's ~ it** cela en vaut la peine, ça vaut la peine; **it is ~ one's while (to do)** ça vaut le coup (*inf*) (de faire); **worthless** adj qui ne vaut rien; **worthwhile** adj (*activity*) qui en vaut la peine; (*cause*) louable

worthy ['wəːðɪ] adj (*person*) digne; (*motive*) louable; **~ of** digne de

 KEYWORD

would [wud] aux vb **1** (*conditional tense*): **if you asked him he would do it** si vous le lui demandiez, il le ferait; **if you had asked him he would have done it** si vous le lui aviez demandé, il l'aurait fait

2 (*in offers, invitations, requests*): **would you like a biscuit?** voulez-vous un biscuit?; **would you close the door please?** voulez-vous fermer la porte, s'il vous plaît?

3 (*in indirect speech*): **I said I would do it** j'ai dit que je le ferais

4 (*emphatic*): **it WOULD have to snow today!** naturellement il neige aujourd'hui! *or* il fallait qu'il neige aujourd'hui!

5 (*insistence*): **she wouldn't do it** elle n'a pas voulu *or* elle a refusé de le faire

6 (*conjecture*): **it would have been midnight** il devait être minuit; **it would seem so** on dirait bien

7 (*indicating habit*): **he would go there on Mondays** il y allait le lundi

wouldn't ['wudnt] = **would not**

wound[1] [wuːnd] n blessure f ▷ vt blesser

wound[2] [waund] pt, pp of **wind**

wove [wəuv] pt of **weave**

woven ['wəuvn] pp of **weave**

wrap [ræp] vt (*also: ~ **up***) envelopper; (*parcel*) emballer; (*wind*) enrouler; **wrapper** n (*on chocolate etc*) papier m; (BRIT: *of book*) couverture f; **wrapping** n (*of sweet, chocolate*) papier m; (*of parcel*) emballage m; **wrapping paper** n papier m d'emballage; (*for gift*) papier cadeau

wreath [riːθ, pl riːðz] n couronne f

wreck [rɛk] n (*sea disaster*) naufrage m; (*ship*) épave f; (*vehicle*) véhicule accidenté; (*pej: person*) loque (humaine) ▷ vt démolir; (*fig*) briser, ruiner; **wreckage** n débris mpl; (*of building*) décombres mpl; (*of ship*) naufrage m

wren [rɛn] n (*Zool*) troglodyte m

wrench [rɛntʃ] n (*Tech*) clé f (à écrous); (*tug*) violent mouvement de torsion; (*fig*) déchirement m ▷ vt tirer violemment sur, tordre; **to ~ sth from** arracher qch (violemment) à *or* de

wrestle ['rɛsl] vi: **to ~ (with sb)** lutter (avec qn); **wrestler** n lutteur(-euse); **wrestling** n lutte f; (*also: **all-in wrestling**: BRIT*) catch m

wretched ['rɛtʃɪd] adj misérable

wriggle ['rɪɡl] vi (*also: ~ **about***) se tortiller

wring (*pt, pp* **wrung**) [rɪŋ, rʌŋ] vt tordre; (*wet clothes*) essorer; (*fig*): **to ~ sth out of** arracher qch à

wrinkle ['rɪŋkl] *n* (*on skin*) ride *f*; (*on paper etc*) pli *m* ▷ *vt* rider, plisser ▷ *vi* se plisser

wrist [rɪst] *n* poignet *m*

write (*pt* **wrote**, *pp* **written**) [raɪt, rəut, 'rɪtn] *vt, vi* écrire; (*prescription*) rédiger; **write down** *vt* noter; (*put in writing*) mettre par écrit; **write off** *vt* (*debt*) passer aux profits et pertes; (*project*) mettre une croix sur; (*smash up: car etc*) démolir complètement; **write out** *vt* écrire; (*copy*) recopier; **write-off** *n* perte totale; **the car is a write-off** la voiture est bonne pour la casse; **writer** *n* auteur *m*, écrivain *m*

writing ['raɪtɪŋ] *n* écriture *f*; (*of author*) œuvres *fpl*; **in ~** par écrit; **writing paper** *n* papier *m* à lettres

written ['rɪtn] *pp of* **write**

wrong [rɔŋ] *adj* (*incorrect*) faux (fausse); (*incorrectiy chosen: number, road etc*) mauvais(e); (*not suitable*) qui ne convient pas; (*wicked*) mal; (*unfair*) injuste ▷ *adv* mal ▷ *n* tort *m* ▷ *vt* faire du tort à, léser; **you are ~ to do it** tu as tort de le faire; **you are ~ about that, you've got it ~** tu te trompes; **what's ~?** qu'est-ce qui ne va pas?; **what's ~ with the car?** qu'est-ce qu'elle a, la voiture?; **to go ~** (*person*) se tromper; (*plan*) mal tourner; (*machine*) se détraquer; **I took a ~ turning** je me suis trompé de route; **wrongly** *adv* à tort; (*answer, do, count*) mal, incorrectement; **wrong number** *n* (*Tel*): **you have the wrong number** vous vous êtes trompé de numéro

wrote [rəut] *pt of* **write**

wrung [rʌŋ] *pt, pp of* **wring**

WWW *n abbr* = **World-Wide Web**; **the ~** le Web

XL *abbr* (= *extra large*) XL

Xmas ['ɛksməs] *n abbr* = **Christmas**

X-ray ['ɛksreɪ] *n* (*ray*) rayon *m* X; (*photograph*) radio(graphie) *f* ▷ *vt* radiographier

xylophone ['zaɪləfəun] *n* xylophone *m*

yacht [jɒt] n voilier m; (motor, luxury yacht) yacht m; **yachting** n yachting m, navigation f de plaisance

yard [jɑːd] n (of house etc) cour f; (us: garden) jardin m; (measure) yard m (= 914 mm; 3 feet); **yard sale** n (us) brocante f (dans son propre jardin)

yarn [jɑːn] n fil m; (tale) longue histoire

yawn [jɔːn] n bâillement m ▷ vi bâiller

yd. abbr = **yard(s)**

yeah [jɛə] adv (inf) ouais

year [jɪəʳ] n an m, année f; (Scol etc) année; **to be 8 ~s old** avoir 8 ans; **an eight-~-old child** un enfant de huit ans; **yearly** adj annuel(le) ▷ adv annuellement; **twice yearly** deux fois par an

yearn [jəːn] vi: **to ~ for sth/to do** aspirer à qch/à faire

yeast [jiːst] n levure f

yell [jɛl] n hurlement m, cri m ▷ vi hurler

yellow ['jɛləu] adj, n jaune (m); **Yellow Pages®** npl (Tel) pages fpl jaunes

yes [jɛs] adv oui; (answering negative question) si ▷ n oui m; **to say ~ (to)** dire oui (à)

yesterday ['jɛstədɪ] adv, n hier (m); **~ morning/evening** hier matin/soir; **all day ~** toute la journée d'hier

yet [jɛt] adv encore; (in questions) déjà ▷ conj pourtant, néanmoins; **it is not finished ~** ce n'est pas encore fini or toujours pas fini; **have**

you eaten ~? vous avez déjà mangé?; **the best ~** le meilleur jusqu'ici or jusque-là; **as ~** jusqu'ici, encore

yew [juː] n if m

Yiddish ['jɪdɪʃ] n yiddish m

yield [jiːld] n production f, rendement m; (Finance) rapport m ▷ vt produire, rendre, rapporter; (surrender) céder ▷ vi céder; (us Aut) céder la priorité

yob(bo) ['jɔb(əu)] n (BRIT inf) loubar(d) m

yoga ['jəugə] n yoga m

yog(h)ourt n = **yog(h)urt**

yog(h)urt ['jɔgət] n yaourt m

yolk [jəuk] n jaune m (d'œuf)

 KEYWORD

you [juː] pron **1** (subject) tu; (polite form) vous; (plural) vous; **you are very kind** vous êtes très gentil; **you French enjoy your food** vous autres Français, vous aimez bien manger; **you and I will go** toi et moi or vous et moi, nous irons; **there you are!** vous voilà!
2 (object: direct, indirect) te, t' + vowel; vous; **I know you** je te or vous connais; **I gave it to you** je te l'ai donné, je vous l'ai donné
3 (stressed) toi; vous; **I told YOU to do it** c'est à toi or vous que j'ai dit de le faire
4 (after prep, in comparisons) toi; vous; **it's for you** c'est pour toi or vous; **she's younger than you** elle est plus jeune que toi or vous
5 (impersonal: one) on; **fresh air does you good** l'air frais fait du bien; **you never know** on ne sait jamais; **you can't do that!** ça ne se fait pas!

you'd [juːd] = **you had**; **you would**

you'll [juːl] = **you will**; **you shall**

young [jʌŋ] adj jeune ▷ npl (of animal) petits mpl; (people): **the ~** les jeunes, la jeunesse; **my ~er brother** mon frère cadet; **youngster** n jeune m/f; (child) enfant m/f

your [jɔːʳ] adj ton (ta), tes pl; (polite form, pl) votre, vos pl; see also **my**

you're [juəʳ] = **you are**

yours [jɔːz] pron le (la) tien(ne), les tiens (tiennes); (polite form, pl) le (la) vôtre, les vôtres; **is it ~?** c'est à toi (or à vous)?; **a friend of ~** un(e) de tes (or de vos) amis; see also **faithfully**; **mine¹**; **sincerely**

yourself [jɔː'sɛlf] pron (reflexive) te; (: polite form) vous; (after prep) toi; vous; (emphatic) toi-même; vous-même; see also **oneself**; **yourselves** pl pron vous; (emphatic) vous-mêmes; see also **oneself**

youth [juːθ] n jeunesse f; (young man) (pl ~s) jeune homme m; **youth club** n centre m de jeunes; **youthful** adj jeune; (enthusiasm etc) juvénile; **youth hostel** n auberge f de

y

jeunesse

you've [juːv] = **you have**

Yugoslav [ˈjuːgəslɑːv] *adj* yougoslave ▷ *n*
Yougoslave *m/f*

Yugoslavia [juːgəuˈslɑːvɪə] *n* (*Hist*)
Yougoslavie *f*

Z

zeal [ziːl] *n* (*revolutionary etc*) ferveur *f*;
(*keenness*) ardeur *f*, zèle *m*

zebra [ˈziːbrə] *n* zèbre *m*; **zebra crossing** *n*
(BRIT) passage clouté *or* pour piétons

zero [ˈzɪərəu] *n* zéro *m*

zest [zɛst] *n* entrain *m*, élan *m*; (*of lemon etc*)
zeste *m*

zigzag [ˈzɪgzæg] *n* zigzag *m* ▷ *vi* zigzaguer,
faire des zigzags

Zimbabwe [zɪmˈbɑːbwɪ] *n* Zimbabwe *m*

zinc [zɪŋk] *n* zinc *m*

zip [zɪp] *n* (*also:* **~ fastener**) fermeture *f* éclair®
or à glissière ▷ *vt* (*file*) zipper; (*also:* **~ up**)
fermer (avec une fermeture éclair®); **zip code**
n (US) code postal; **zip file** *n* (*Comput*) fichier *m*
zip *inv*; **zipper** *n* (US) = **zip**

zit [zɪt] (*inf*) *n* bouton *m*

zodiac [ˈzəudɪæk] *n* zodiaque *m*

zone [zəun] *n* zone *f*

zoo [zuː] *n* zoo *m*

zoology [zuːˈɔlədʒɪ] *n* zoologie *f*

zoom [zuːm] *vi*: **to ~ past** passer en trombe;
zoom lens *n* zoom *m*

zucchini [zuːˈkiːnɪ] *n(pl)* (US) courgette(s) *f(pl)*